Format for Bank Reconciliation:

Cash balance according to bank statement		$XXX
Add: Additions by company not on bank statement	$XXX	
Bank errors	XXX	XXX
		$XXX
Deduct: Deductions by company not on bank statement	$XXX	
Bank errors	XXX	XXX
Adjusted balance		$XXX
Cash balance according to company's records		$XXX
Add: Additions by bank not recorded by company	$XXX	
Company errors	XXX	XXX
		$XXX
Deduct: Deductions by bank not recorded by company	$XXX	
Company errors	XXX	XXX
Adjusted balance		$XXX

Inventory Costing Methods:

- First-in, First-out (FIFO)
- Last-in, First-out (LIFO)
- Average Cost

Interest Computations:

Interest = Face Amount (or Principal) × Rate × Time

Methods of Determining Annual Depreciation:

Straight-Line: $\frac{\text{Cost} - \text{Estimated Residual Value}}{\text{Estimated Life}}$

Double-Declining-Balance: Rate* × Book Value at Beginning of Period

*Rate is commonly twice the straight-line rate (1 ÷ Estimated Life).

Adjustments to Net Income (Loss) Using the Indirect Method:

	Increase (Decrease)
Net income (loss)	$ XXX
Adjustments to reconcile net income to net cash flow from operating activities:	
Depreciation of fixed assets	XXX
Amortization of intangible assets	XXX
Losses on disposal of assets	XXX
Gains on disposal of assets	(XXX)
Changes in current operating assets and liabilities:	
Increases in noncash current operating assets	(XXX)
Decreases in noncash current operating assets	XXX
Increases in current operating liabilities	XXX
Decreases in current operating liabilities	(XXX)
Net cash flow from operating activities	$ XXX or $(XXX)

Contribution Margin Ratio = $\frac{\text{Sales} - \text{Variable Costs}}{\text{Sales}}$

Break-Even Sales (Units) = $\frac{\text{Fixed Costs}}{\text{Unit Contribution Margin}}$

Sales (Units) = $\frac{\text{Fixed Costs} + \text{Target Profit}}{\text{Unit Contribution Margin}}$

Margin of Safety = $\frac{\text{Sales} - \text{Sales at Break-Even Point}}{\text{Sales}}$

Operating Leverage = $\frac{\text{Contribution Margin}}{\text{Income from Operations}}$

Variances:

$$\text{Direct Materials Price Variance} = \left(\text{Actual Price} - \text{Standard Price}\right) \times \text{Actual Quantity}$$

$$\text{Direct Materials Quantity Variance} = \left(\text{Actual Quantity} - \text{Standard Quantity}\right) \times \text{Standard Price}$$

$$\text{Direct Labor Rate Variance} = \left(\text{Actual Rate per Hour} - \text{Standard Rate per Hour}\right) \times \text{Actual Hours}$$

$$\text{Direct Labor Time Variance} = \left(\text{Actual Direct Labor Hours} - \text{Standard Direct Labor Hours}\right) \times \text{Standard Rate per Hour}$$

$$\text{Variable Factory Overhead Controllable Variance} = \text{Actual Variable Factory Overhead} - \text{Budgeted Variable Factory Overhead}$$

$$\text{Fixed Factory Overhead Volume Variance} = \left(\text{Standard Hours for 100\% of Normal Capacity} - \text{Standard Hours for Actual Units Produced}\right) \times \text{Fixed Factory Overhead Rate}$$

Rate of Return on Investment (ROI) = $\frac{\text{Income from Operations}}{\text{Invested Assets}}$

Alternative ROI Computation:

$$\text{ROI} = \frac{\text{Income from Operations}}{\text{Sales}} \times \frac{\text{Sales}}{\text{Invested Assets}}$$

Capital Investment Analysis Methods:

Methods That Ignore Present Values:

- Average Rate of Return Method
- Cash Payback Method

Methods That Use Present Values:

- Net Present Value Method
- Internal Rate of Return Method

Average Rate of Return = $\frac{\text{Estimated Average Annual Income}}{\text{Average Investment}}$

Present Value Index = $\frac{\text{Total Present Value of Net Cash Flow}}{\text{Amount to Be Invested}}$

Present Value Factor for an Annuity of $1 = $\frac{\text{Amount to Be Invested}}{\text{Equal Annual Net Cash Flows}}$

Managerial Accounting

13e

Carl S. Warren
Professor Emeritus of Accounting
University of Georgia, Athens

James M. Reeve
Professor Emeritus of Accounting
University of Tennessee, Knoxville

Jonathan E. Duchac
Professor of Accounting
Wake Forest University

Australia • Brazil • Japan • Korea • Mexico • Singapore • Spain • United Kingdom • United States

Managerial Accounting, 13e

Carl S. Warren
James M. Reeve
Jonathan E. Duchac

Vice President, General Manager, Science, Math, and Quantitative Business: Balraj Kalsi

Product Director: Mike Schenk

Sr. Product Manager: Matt Filimonov

Product Development Manager: Krista Kellman

Sr. Marketing Manager: Robin LeFevre

Sr. Marketing Coordinator: Eileen Corcoran

Managing Content Developer (Media): Scott Fidler

Content Developer (Media): Jessica Robbe

Software Development Manager: Phil Bower

Digital Content Designer: Peggy Hussey

Sr. Content Project Manager: Tim Bailey

Production Service: Cenveo Publisher Services

Manufacturing Planner: Doug Wilke

Sr. Art Director: Stacy Jenkins Shirley

Cover and Internal Designer: Red Hangar Design

Cover Image: © Design Pics Inc/Alamy

Intellectual Property:
Analyst: Christina Ciaramella
Project Manager: Betsy Hathaway

Library of Congress Control Number: 2014954727

ISBN-13: 978-1-285-86880-6
ISBN-10: 1-285-86880-3

Cengage Learning
20 Channel Center Street
Boston, MA 02210
USA

Cengage Learning is a leading provider of customized learning solutions with office locations around the globe, including Singapore, the United Kingdom, Australia, Mexico, Brazil, and Japan. Locate your local office at: **www.cengage.com/global**

Cengage Learning products are represented in Canada by Nelson Education, Ltd.

To learn more about Cengage Learning Solutions, visit **www.cengage.com**

Purchase any of our products at your local college store or at our preferred online store **www.cengagebrain.com**

Printed in the United States of America
Print Number: 02 Print Year: 2015

Warren/Reeve/Duchac Managerial Accounting & CengageNOWv2

An Integrated Learning System to Keep Students on Track and Progressing!

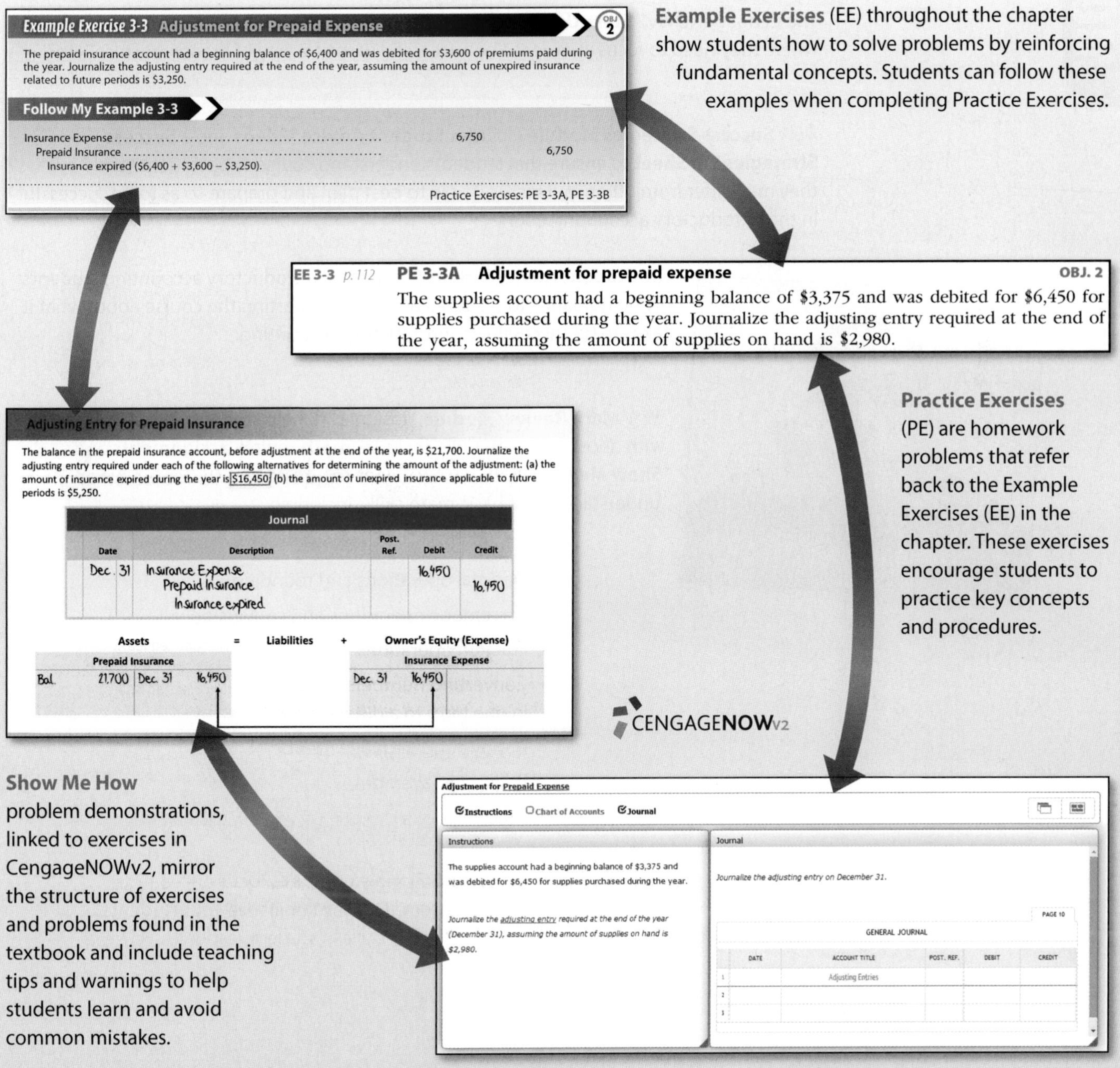

Example Exercise 3-3 Adjustment for Prepaid Expense
OBJ 2
The prepaid insurance account had a beginning balance of $6,400 and was debited for $3,600 of premiums paid during the year. Journalize the adjusting entry required at the end of the year, assuming the amount of unexpired insurance related to future periods is $3,250.
Follow My Example 3-3
Insurance Expense 6,750
Prepaid Insurance 6,750
Insurance expired ($6,400 + $3,600 − $3,250).
Practice Exercises: PE 3-3A, PE 3-3B
EE 3-3 p. 112
PE 3-3A Adjustment for prepaid expense
OBJ. 2
The supplies account had a beginning balance of $3,375 and was debited for $6,450 for supplies purchased during the year. Journalize the adjusting entry required at the end of the year, assuming the amount of supplies on hand is $2,980.
Adjusting Entry for Prepaid Insurance
The balance in the prepaid insurance account, before adjustment at the end of the year, is $21,700. Journalize the adjusting entry required under each of the following alternatives for determining the amount of the adjustment: (a) the amount of insurance expired during the year is $16,450; (b) the amount of unexpired insurance applicable to future periods is $5,250.
Journal
Date
Description
Post. Ref.
Debit
Credit
Dec. 31
Insurance Expense
Prepaid Insurance
Insurance expired
16,450
16,450
Assets = Liabilities + Owner's Equity (Expense)
Prepaid Insurance
Bal. 21,700 Dec. 31 16,450
Insurance Expense
Dec. 31 16,450
CENGAGENOWv2
Adjustment for Prepaid Expense
Instructions
Chart of Accounts
Journal
Instructions
The supplies account had a beginning balance of $3,375 and was debited for $6,450 for supplies purchased during the year.
Journalize the adjusting entry required at the end of the year (December 31), assuming the amount of supplies on hand is $2,980.
Journal
Journalize the adjusting entry on December 31.
PAGE 10
GENERAL JOURNAL
DATE
ACCOUNT TITLE
POST. REF.
DEBIT
CREDIT
Adjusting Entries

Example Exercises (EE) throughout the chapter show students how to solve problems by reinforcing fundamental concepts. Students can follow these examples when completing Practice Exercises.

Practice Exercises (PE) are homework problems that refer back to the Example Exercises (EE) in the chapter. These exercises encourage students to practice key concepts and procedures.

Show Me How problem demonstrations, linked to exercises in CengageNOWv2, mirror the structure of exercises and problems found in the textbook and include teaching tips and warnings to help students learn and avoid common mistakes.

Practice Exercises are assignable in CengageNOWv2, which allows students to access helpful resources such as Check My Work and Show Me How problem demonstrations.

MOTIVATION

Set Course Expectations and Guide Students to Success!

Motivate students by reshaping their misconceptions about the introductory accounting course. Students are often surprised by both the approach to learning accounting and the necessary amount of time they need to spend outside of class working through homework assignments.

CengageNOWv2 Start-Up Center NEW!

The CengageNOWv2 **Start-Up Center** will help students identify what they need to do and where they need to focus in order to be successful with a variety of brand new resources.

NEW **Success Strategies Module** includes **Student Advice Videos** and a **Success Strategies Tip Sheet** to ensure that students understand course expectations (and how they may differ from other courses) and how to best plan and prepare so as to be successful in the introductory accounting course.

The **Student Advice Videos** feature real introductory accounting students giving guidance to students who are just starting the course about what it takes to be successful in introductory accounting.

NEW **Math Review Module**, designed to help students get up to speed with necessary math skills, includes **math review assignments** and **Show Me How** math review videos to ensure that students have an understanding of basic math skills, including:

- Whole number operations
- Decimal operations and rounding
- Percentage operations and conversion
- Fraction operations
- Converting numbers expressed in one form to a different form
- Positive and negative numbers
- Ratios and averages

NEW **How to Use CengageNOWv2 Module** allows students to focus on learning accounting, not on a particular software system. Quickly familiarize your students with CengageNOWv2 and direct them to all of its built-in student resources.

Expose Students to Concepts Before Class Begins!

With all the outside obligations accounting students have, finding time to read the textbook before class can be a struggle. Point students to the key concepts they need to know before they attend class.

Video: Animated Activities

Animated Activities are engaging animated scenarios that visually guide students through selected core topics in introductory accounting. Each activity uses a realistic company example to illustrate how the concepts relate to the everyday activities of a business. These activities include multiple-choice questions that gauge student understanding of the overarching chapter concepts.

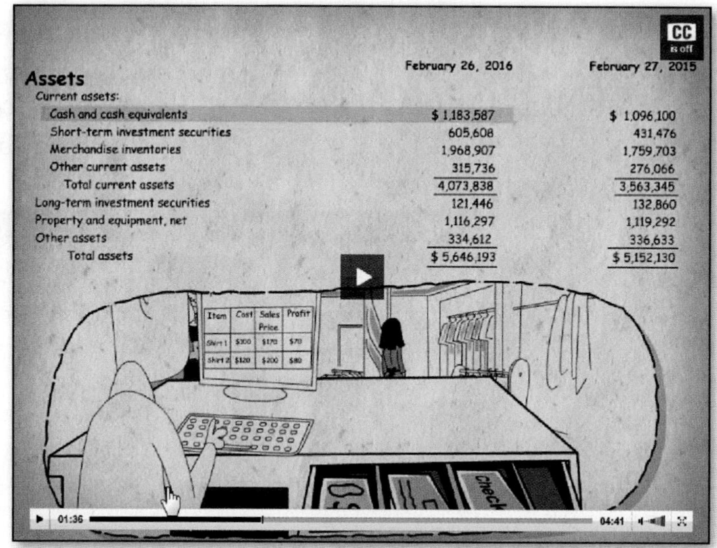

Animated Activities are assignable/gradable in CengageNOWv2 and available for self-study and review.

Prepaid Insurance

- The debit balance of $2,400 in NetSolutions' prepaid insurance account represents the December 1 prepayment of insurance for 12 months.

Dec.	31	Insurance Expense	55	200	
		Prepaid Insurance	15		200
		Insurance expired ($2,400 ÷ 12).			

Accounting Equation Impact

Assets = Liabilities + Owner's Equity (Expense)

Prepaid Insurance 15			
Bal.	2,400	Dec. 31	200
Adj. Bal.	2,200		

decrease

increase

Insurance Expense 55			
Dec. 31	200		

Tell Me More lecture activities for every Learning Objective are assignable/gradable in CengageNOWv2 and available for self-study and review.

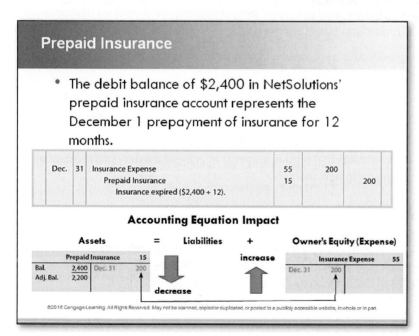

Video: Tell Me More NEW!

Tell Me More lecture activities explain the core concepts of the chapter through an engaging auditory and visual presentation that is ideal for all class formats—flipped model, online, hybrid, face-to-face.

Expose Students to Concepts Before Class Begins!

Students don't want to waste time going over concepts that they have already mastered. With the NEW Adaptive Study Plan, they can focus on learning new topics and fully understanding difficult concepts.

Adaptive Study Plan NEW!

The Adaptive Study Plan in CengageNOWv2 is an assignable/gradable study center that adapts to each student's unique needs and provides a remediation pathway to keep students progressing.

The Adaptive Study Plan is assignable/gradable in CengageNOWv2 and available for self-study and review.

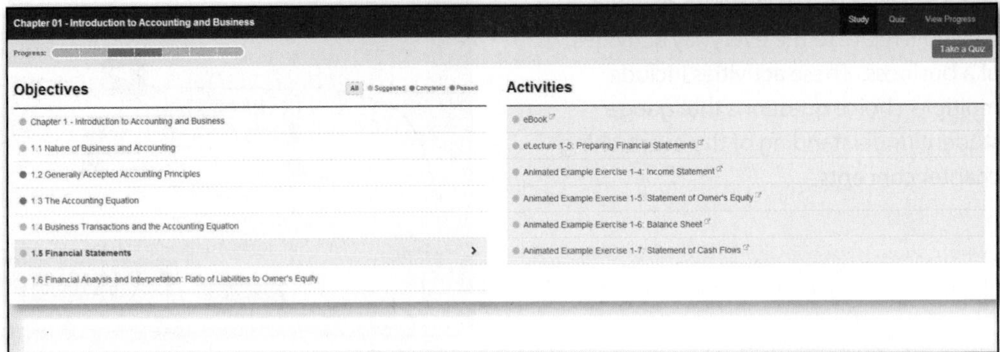

How does it work?

Step 1: Students take a chapter-level quiz consisting of randomized questions that cover both conceptual and procedural aspects of the chapter.

Step 2: Feedback is provided for each answer option explaining why the answer is right or wrong.

Step 3: Based on the quiz results, students are provided a remediation path that includes media assets and algorithmic practice problems to help them improve their understanding of the course material.

Instructors may use prerequisites that require students to achieve mastery in the Adaptive Study Plan before moving on to new material.

> *The new Adaptive Study Plan offers the benefit of customization coupled with remediation.*
>
> ***– Jennifer Schneider, professor at University of North Georgia***

Make Content Relatable!

Show students how the material they are learning matters in real life and help them connect accounting concepts to the world around them.

Experience Managerial Accounting Videos are assignable/gradable in CengageNOWv2 and available for self-study and review.

Video: Experience Managerial Accounting

Experience Managerial Accounting Videos, available in CengageNOWv2, show students how progressive companies such as Cold Stone Creamery, Second City, and Hard Rock Café incorporate managerial accounting to fuel better business performance.

Service Focus 

Service Focus features highlight the differences between manufacturing companies and service companies and illustrate how managerial accounting concepts apply to service companies such as The Walt Disney Company and Sierra Nevada.

Service Focus

PROFIT, LOSS, AND BREAK-EVEN IN MAJOR LEAGUE BASEBALL

Major League Baseball is a tough game and a tough business. Ticket prices (unit selling price), player salaries (variable costs), stadium fees (fixed costs), and attendance (volume) converge to make it difficult for teams to make a profit, or at least break even. So, which major league baseball team was the most profitable in 2013? Well, it wasn't the World Champion Boston Red Sox. Nor was it the star-studded New York Yankees. Then, it had to be the recently turned around Los Angeles Angels, right? Not even close. It was actually the worst team in baseball—the Houston Astros.

Just how profitable were the Astros? They earned $99 million in 2013, which was more than the combined 2013 profits of the six most recent World Series champions. How could the team with the worst record in baseball since 2005 have one of the most profitable years in baseball history? By paying careful attention to costs and volume. Between 2011 and 2013, the Astros cut their player payroll from $56 million to less than $13 million. That's right, all of the players on the Houston Astros baseball team combined, made less in 2013 than Alex Rodriguez (New York Yankees), Cliff Lee (Philadelphia Phillies), Prince Fielder (Detroit Tigers), and Tim Lincecum (San Francisco Giants) made individually. While attendance at Astros games has dropped by around 20% since 2011, the cost reductions from reduced player salaries have far outpaced the drop in attendance, making the 2013 Astros the most profitable team in baseball history. While no one likes losing baseball games, the Houston Astros have shown that focusing on the relationship between cost and volume can yield a hefty profit, even when they aren't winning.

Source: D. Alexander, "2013 Houston Astros: Baseball's Worst Team Is The Most Profitable In History," *Forbes*, August 26, 2013.

APPLICATION

Close the Gap Between Homework and Exam Performance!

Many students perform well on homework but struggle when it comes to exams. Now, with the new Blank Sheet of Paper Experience, students must problem-solve on their own, just as they would if taking a test on a blank sheet of paper.

> *Good tool to make students understand concepts without overly relying on technology's help.*
> **– Ramesh Narasimhan, professor at Montclair State University**

> *I like it because it appears to bridge the gap between the homework and my exam.*
> **– Lawrence Chui, professor at University of St. Thomas**

> *This will minimize students' complaints about how the exam looks different from the homework format.*
> **– Rama Ramamurthy, professor at Georgetown University**

Blank Sheet of Paper Experience

A less-leading Blank Sheet of Paper Experience discourages overreliance on the system.

- The use of drop down menus and Smart Entry (type-ahead) has been eliminated.
- Students must refer to the Chart of Accounts and decide for themselves what account is impacted.
- The number of accounts in each transactions is not given away.
- Whether the account should be debited or credited is not given away.
- Transactions may be entered in any order (as long as the entries are correct).
- Check My Work feedback only reports on what students have actually attempted, which prevents students from "guessing" their way through the assignment.

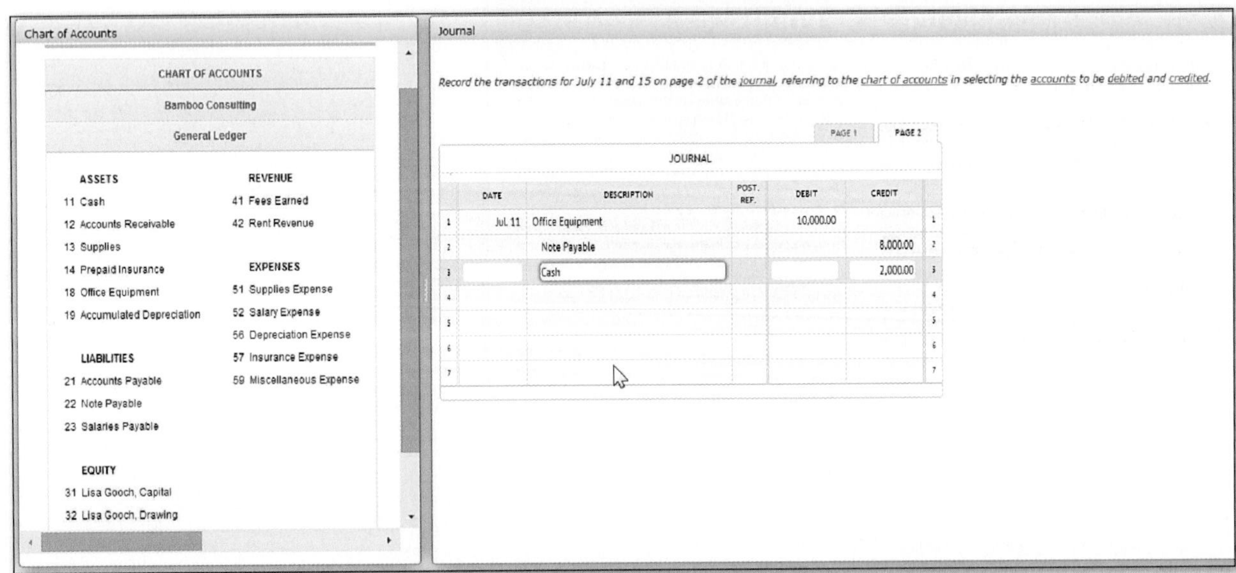

Check it out! Visit **cnowv2demo.cengage.com** for an interactive demo.

Help Students Make Connections and See the Big Picture!

Homework software should not get in the way of learning. One of the biggest complaints students have about online homework is the scrolling, which prevents students from seeing the big picture and understanding the accounting system. The new Multi-Panel View addresses this issue and enhances student learning.

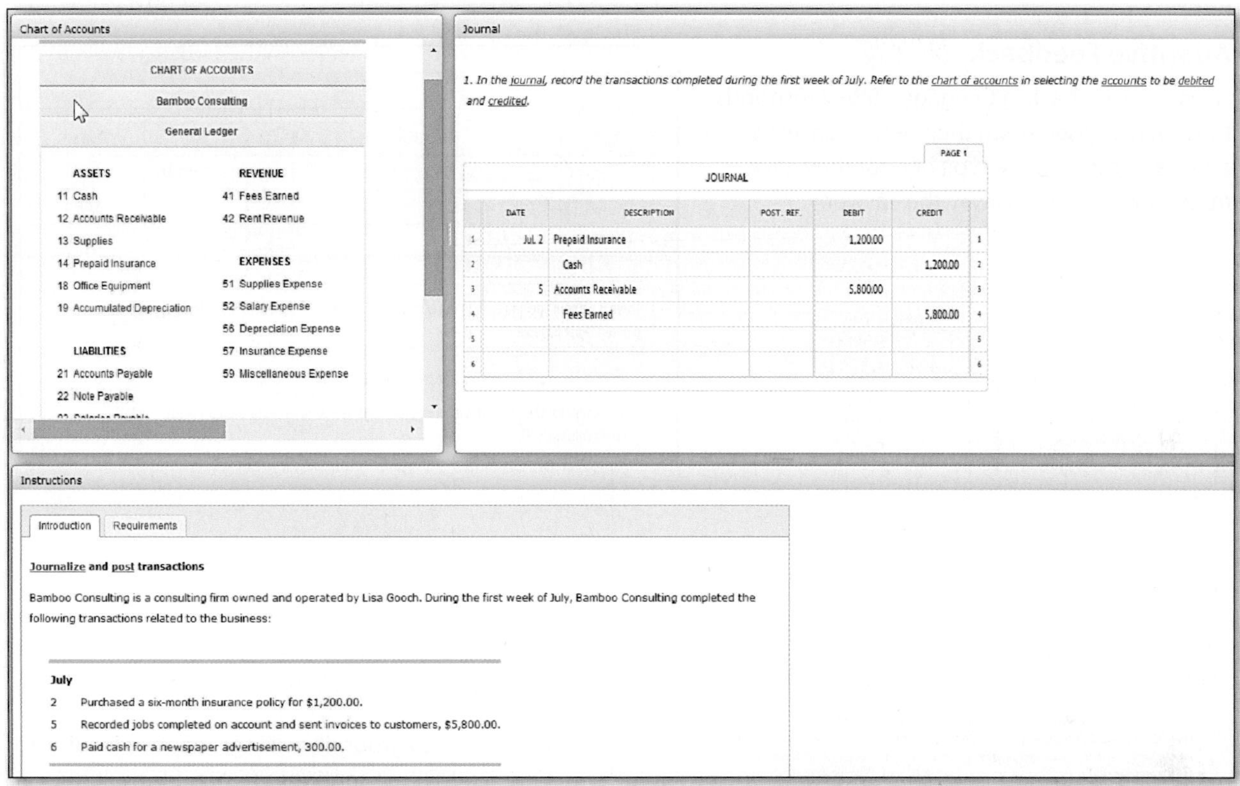

Multi-Panel View *NEW!*

The NEW Multi-Panel View in CengageNOWv2 enables students to see all the elements of a problem on one screen.

- Students make connections and see the tasks as connected components in the accounting process.
- Dramatically reduced scrolling eliminates student frustration.

With the ability to move and resize journals, ledgers, forms, and financial statements, it is easier to navigate the problem and understand the accounting system.

This is just a lot better and less confusing than scrolling up and down. . . . Having it like that would make it much easier —not so much scrolling and it wouldn't be so confusing.

– Tyler Mason, student at Northern Essex Community College

Multi-Panel View makes it much easier for students to see how each piece of the accounting cycle impacts the other pieces. Having it all in one view reduces student frustration and gives them a clearer picture of the complete accounting cycle.

– Kristen Quinn, professor at Northern Essex Community College

APPLICATION

Close the Gap Between Homework and Exam Performance!

Students often complete homework at odd times. And when they use CengageNOWv2, they get help right when they need it.

Adaptive Feedback 

Adaptive Feedback in CengageNOWv2 responds to students based upon their unique answers and alerts them to the type of error they have made without giving away the answer.

PAGE 1 | PAGE 2

JOURNAL — Score: 33/138

	DATE	DESCRIPTION	POST. REF.	DEBIT	CREDIT	
1	Jul. 11	Office Equipment		10,000.00		1
2		Cash			8,000.00	2
3		Note Payaable			2,000.00	3
4						4
5						5
6						6
7						7
8						8
9						9

There is a minor spelling error in the account title. You will be graded as if you had entered "Note Payable."

Line

- The amount for this account is incorrect, although you've entered the amount in the correct column. [-2]

PAGE 1 | PAGE 2

JOURNAL — Score: 33/138

	DATE	DESCRIPTION	POST. REF.	DEBIT	CREDIT	
1	Jul. 11	Office Equipment		10,000.00		1
2		Cash			8,000.00	2
3		Note Payaable			2,000.00	3
4						4
5						5
6						6
7						7
8						8
9						9
10						10
11						11

Points: 0.24 / 1

Feedback

▾ Check My Work

Identify which accounts are affected in each transaction. Keep in mind that every transaction involves at least two accounts. Determine whether the account increases or decreases and record each increase or decrease following the rules of debit and credit. Use the Posting Reference column to enter the corresponding account number from the general ledger account. Remember total debits should equal total credits in your entries.

Learning Objective 1
Learning Objective 2
Learning Objective 3

I like the adaptive feedback. It will reduce a number of errors that cause students to give up.

– Kevin Jones, professor at Drexel University

Excellent! Often learning from feedback is more powerful than learning from the instructor, text, etc.

– Lisa Brown, professor at Indiana Institute of Technology

In addition to groundbreaking, adaptive feedback, CengageNOWv2 continues to provide multiple layers of guidance to keep students on track and progressing.

- **Check My Work Feedback** provides general guidance and hints as students work through homework assignments.
- *NEW* **Check My Work Feedback** in CengageNOWv2 now only reports on what students have actually attempted, which prevents them from "guessing" their way through assignments.
- **Explanations** are available after the assignment has been submitted and provide a detailed description of how to arrive at the solution.

Check it out! Visit **cnowv2demo.cengage.com** for an interactive demo.

Help Students Make Connections and See the Big Picture!

The best way to learn accounting is through practice, but students often get stuck when attempting homework assignments on their own.

Video: Show Me How *NEW!*

Created for the most frequently assigned end-of-chapter items, hundreds of NEW Show Me How problem demonstration videos provide a step-by-step model of a similar problem. Embedded tips and warnings help students avoid common mistakes and pitfalls.

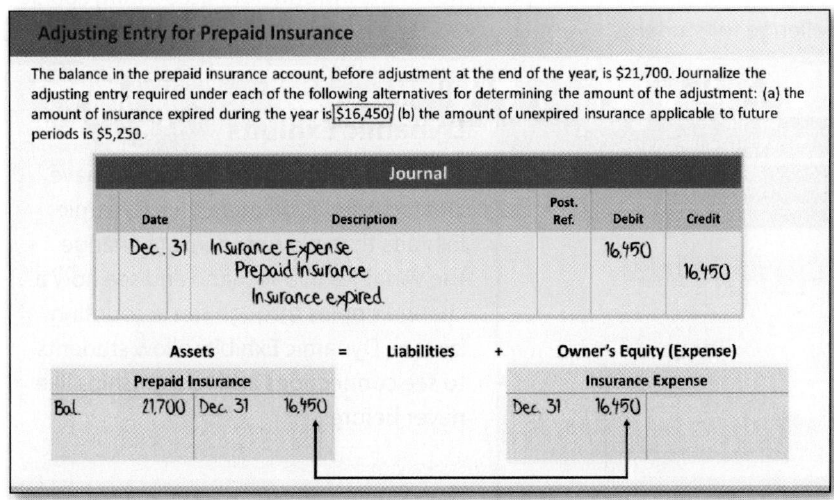

Adjusting Entry for Prepaid Insurance

The balance in the prepaid insurance account, before adjustment at the end of the year, is $21,700. Journalize the adjusting entry required under each of the following alternatives for determining the amount of the adjustment: (a) the amount of insurance expired during the year is $16,450; (b) the amount of unexpired insurance applicable to future periods is $5,250.

Journal

Date	Description	Post. Ref.	Debit	Credit
Dec. 31	Insurance Expense		16,450	
	Prepaid Insurance			16,450
	Insurance expired			

Assets = Liabilities + Owner's Equity (Expense)

Prepaid Insurance			
Bal.	21,700	Dec. 31	16,450

Insurance Expense			
Dec. 31	16,450		

Identified by an icon in the text margins, Show Me How videos are linked to assignments in CengageNOWv2 and available for self-study and review.

Blueprint Problems

Blueprint Problems are teaching problems that walk students through a single accounting topic. These problems cover the primary learning objectives and are designed to help students understand foundational content and the associated building blocks versus memorizing the formulas or journal entries.

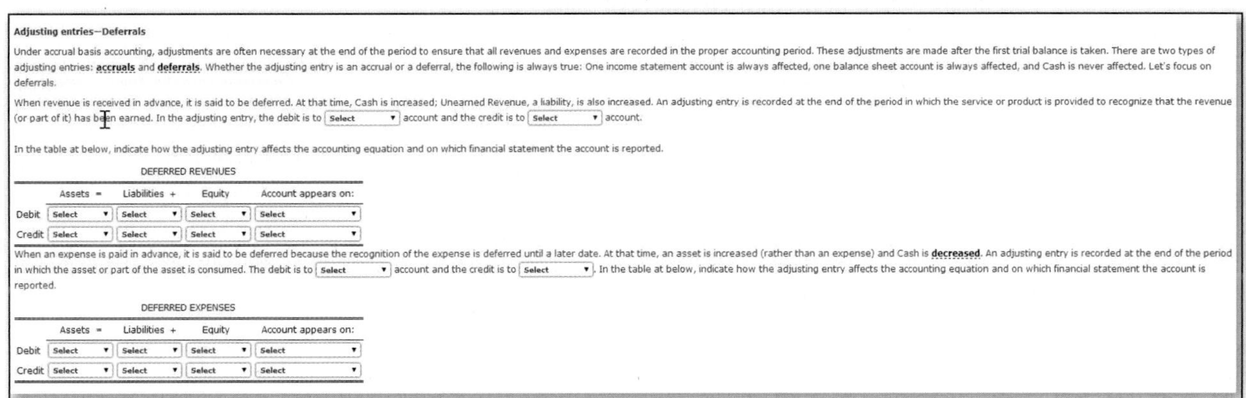

Adjusting entries—Deferrals

Under accrual basis accounting, adjustments are often necessary at the end of the period to ensure that all revenues and expenses are recorded in the proper accounting period. These adjustments are made after the first trial balance is taken. There are two types of adjusting entries: **accruals** and **deferrals**. Whether the adjusting entry is an accrual or a deferral, the following is always true: One income statement account is always affected, one balance sheet account is always affected, and Cash is never affected. Let's focus on deferrals.

When revenue is received in advance, it is said to be deferred. At that time, Cash is increased; Unearned Revenue, a liability, is also increased. An adjusting entry is recorded at the end of the period in which the service or product is provided to recognize that the revenue (or part of it) has been earned. In the adjusting entry, the debit is to [Select] account and the credit is to [Select] account.

In the table at below, indicate how the adjusting entry affects the accounting equation and on which financial statement the account is reported.

DEFERRED REVENUES

	Assets =	Liabilities +	Equity	Account appears on:
Debit	Select	Select	Select	Select
Credit	Select	Select	Select	Select

When an expense is paid in advance, it is said to be deferred because the recognition of the expense is deferred until a later date. At that time, an asset is increased (rather than an expense) and Cash is **decreased**. An adjusting entry is recorded at the end of the period in which the asset or part of the asset is consumed. The debit is to [Select] account and the credit is to [Select]. In the table at below, indicate how the adjusting entry affects the accounting equation and on which financial statement the account is reported.

DEFERRED EXPENSES

	Assets =	Liabilities +	Equity	Account appears on:
Debit	Select	Select	Select	Select
Credit	Select	Select	Select	Select

Blueprint Problems are assignable/ gradable in CengageNOWv2.

APPLICATION

Help Students Go Beyond Memorization to True Understanding!

Students often struggle to understand how concepts relate to one another. For most students, an introductory accounting course is their first exposure to both *business transactions* and the *accounting system*. While these concepts are already difficult to master individually, their combination and interdependency in the introductory accounting course often pose a challenge for students.

Dynamic Exhibits NEW!

To overcome this gap, the authors have created a series of interactive Dynamic Exhibits that allow students to change the variables in a scenario and see how a change ripples through the accounting system. Dynamic Exhibits allow students to see connections and relationships like never before!

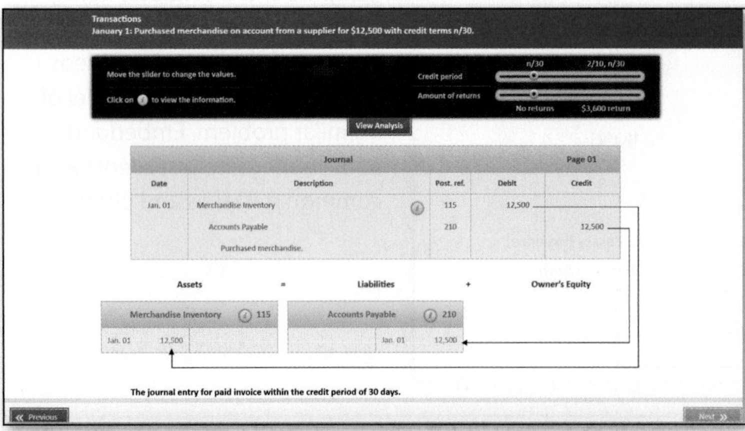

Identified by an icon in the text, Dynamic Exhibits are embedded within the MindTap eReader in CengageNOWv2. They are assignable/gradable in CengageNOWv2 and available for self-study and review.

Blueprint Connections

Blueprint Connections are scenario-based teaching problems that solidify concepts and demonstrate their interrelationships, as well as promote critical thinking. Blueprint Connections combine multiple topics, allowing students to explore a larger concept more fully, and strengthen analytical skills.

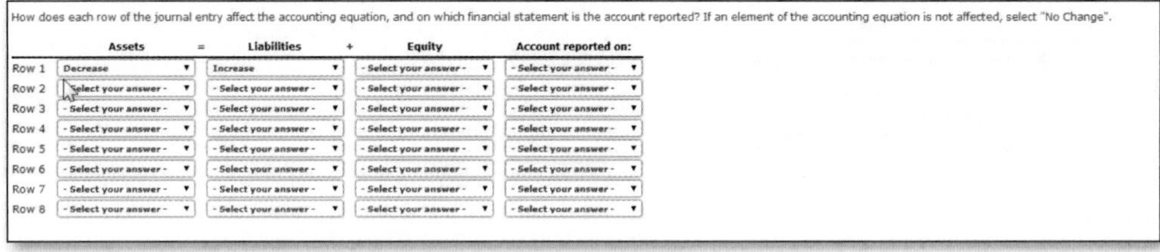

Blueprint Connections are assignable/gradable in CengageNOWv2.

Help Students Build Critical Thinking Skills!

Students often resort to memorization as a way to pass the course, but such surface learning does little to develop the critical thinking skills and deep understanding that are necessary for success in future business courses.

Activation Exercises

To overcome these challenges, the authors have created Activation Exercises to provide a learning system that focuses on developing a better understanding of:

- Key terms and definitions
- Economics of business transactions
- How transactions are recorded in the accounting system
- How transactions are ultimately reflected in the financial statements

These "what if" exercises help students understand relationships using interactive tools.

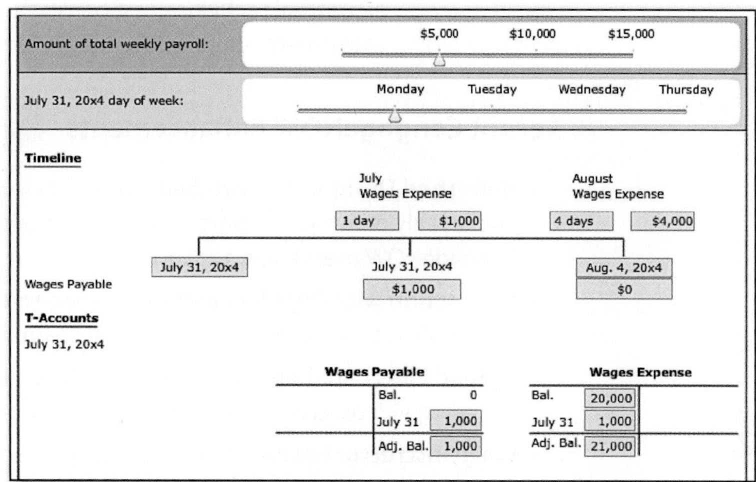

The Activation Exercises are assignable/gradable in CengageNOWv2.

> *These exercises are interactive and actually allow students to experiment with the data, visually viewing the impact when data is altered. The exercises show not only how a transaction looks in the journal and ledger accounts, but also the impact it ultimately has on financial statements. Finally, students are challenged to analyze the overall impact of a transaction by answering questions related to the topic. This is an excellent learning tool.*
>
> ***– Rita Mintz, professor at Calhoun Community College***

The Activation Exercises structure builds the critical thinking skills that are necessary for students to succeed in both introductory accounting and future accounting courses. Reviewers have enthusiastically praised the authors' online activities and indicated that they would be both ideal for pre-class activities and after-class assignments.

Financial Statement Analysis and Interpretation

The Financial Statement Analysis and Interpretation sections, at the end of financial accounting chapters, help students understand key ratios and how stakeholders interpret financial reports. These sections encourage students to go deeper into the material to analyze accounting information and improve critical thinking skills.

MASTERY

Online Solutions

CengageNOWv2 is a powerful course management and online homework resource that provides control and customization to optimize the student learning experience. Included are many proven resources including algorithmic activities, test bank, course management tools, reporting and assessment options, and much more.

Recent CengageNOW Enhancements NEW!

- **Refreshed Design:** This refreshed look will help you and your students focus easily and quickly on what is important, while maintaining the same functionality that CengageNOW users know and love.
- **Integration with Popular Learning Management Systems:** Single login, deep linking, and grade return! (Check with your local Learning Consultant for more details!)
- **Upload Files Capability:** You can now upload files in CengageNOW for student use—including videos, Excel files, Word files, and more.
- **Email Instructor Feature**: Students can now send you a screenshot of the question they are working on directly through CengageNOW and ask specific questions about where they are stuck.
- **Better Date Management**: When modifying assignment due dates for a whole course, the system will now automatically adjust due dates based on a new start date, making it easier to reuse a course from one term to the next and adjust for snow days.
- **Streamlined Assignment Creation Process:** A simplified and streamlined Assignment Creation process allows instructors to quickly set up and manage assignments from a single page!
- **New Report Options:** New reporting options allow you to get better reports on your students' progress.
- **New Student Registration Process:** When you create a course, a URL will be generated that will automatically take students right into the instructor's course without them having to enter the course key!

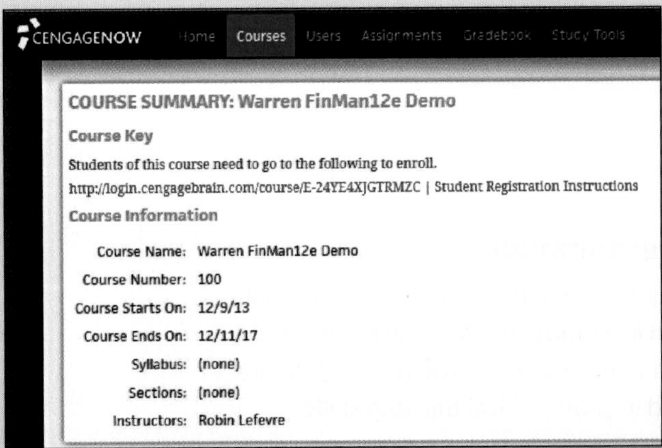

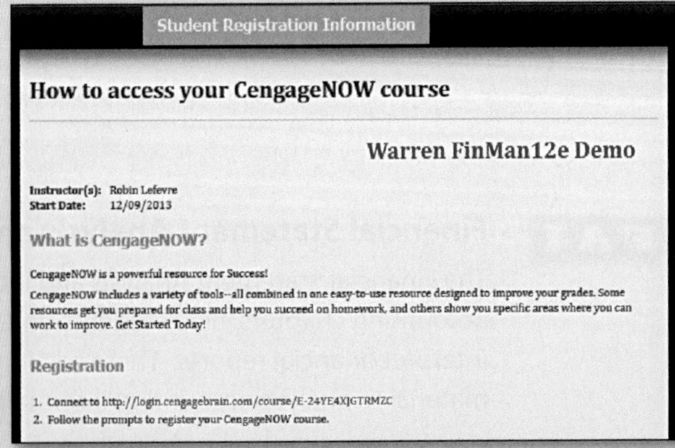

MindTap eReader

The MindTap eReader for Warren/Reeve/Duchac's *Financial and Managerial Accounting* is the most robust digital reading experience available. Hallmark features include:

- Fully optimized for the iPad.
- Note taking, highlighting, and more.
- Embedded digital media such as Dynamic Exhibits.

The MindTap eReader also features ReadSpeaker®, an online text-to-speech application that vocalizes, or "speech-enables," online educational content. This feature is ideally suited for both instructors and learners who would like to listen to content instead of (or in addition to) reading it.

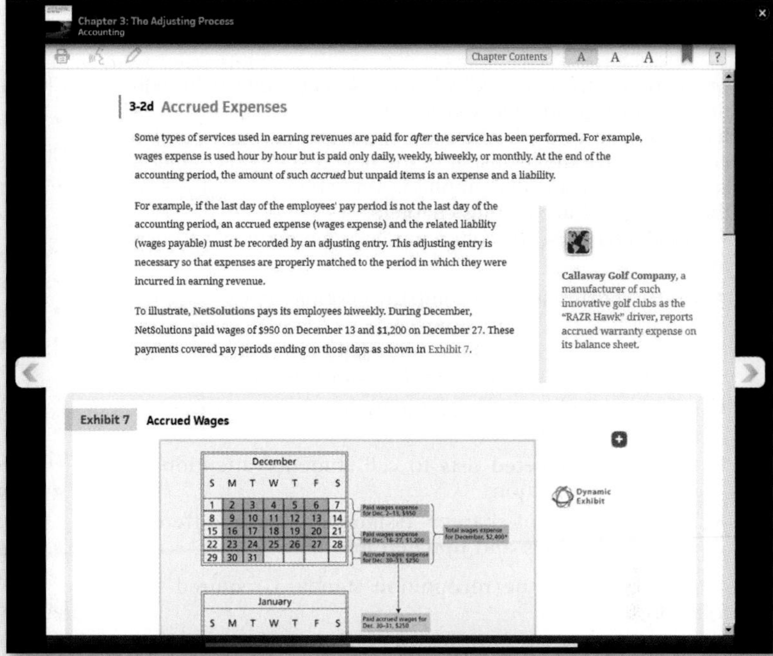

New to This Edition

In addition to the many new digital assets created for this edition of *Managerial Accounting*, the textbook content itself has also been revised. The most significant changes for this edition involve the inclusion of the new revenue recognition standard and a greater emphasis on service companies in the managerial accounting chapters.

In all chapters, the following improvements have been made:

- Updated dates and real company information for currency
- Added headers and sub-headers to help students navigate through the chapter and easily reference sections when completing homework assignments
- Set unlabeled graphics as numbered exhibits for easier student reference
- Used more bulleted lists to call students' attention to specific information
- Refreshed end-of-chapter assignments with different numerical values and updated information

The new revenue recognition standard required the following changes:

- Revised the definitions of revenue and revenue recognition in Chapters 1–3, including the glossary. These revisions are consistent with the new revenue recognition standard, **Revenue from Contracts with Customers (Topic 606)**, FASB, May 2014.
- Revised Chapter 5, *Accounting for Merchandising Businesses*, to be consistent with the preceding standard. These revisions include using the net method for all purchase and sales discounts. In addition, the accounting for customer returns and allowances, including cash refunds, has been updated. As a result, sales discounts and sales return and allowances accounts are no longer used.
- Added new Appendix D, *Revenue Recognition*, which describes and illustrates the new Five-Step process for recognizing revenue. The illustration includes the accounting for a bundled product with different performance obligations.

Chapter 1

- New exhibit with income statements for merchandising and manufacturing businesses

Chapter 2

- New Service Focus on job order costing in a law firm

Chapter 4

- New chapter opener on Ford Motor Company

Chapter 5

- New exhibit explaining the difference between absorption costing and variable costing

Chapter 6

- New chapter opener on Hendrick Motorsport
- New Service Focus on film budgeting
- Updated two learning objectives to reflect the differences between operating and financial budgets
- New Exhibit 7 on the master budget for a manufacturing company

Chapter 7

- New Business Connection on standard costing for breweries
- New Service Focus on standard costing in the restaurant industry

Chapter 8

- New Service Focus on Charles Schwab

Chapter 10

- New chapter opener on Vail Resorts, Inc.
- New Service Focus on network business models

Chapter 11

- New exhibit explaining allocation of factory overhead costs

Chapter 12

- New exhibit explaining costs of controlling quality
- Updated "just-in-time inventory" description to reflect more current "lean inventory" description

Chapter 13

- New chapter opener on The Coca-Cola Company
- Significantly streamlined learning objective 5
- New Business Connection on cash and investments in the pharmaceutical industry

Chapter 14

- New chapter opener on National Beverage Co.
- Updated Exhibit 1 to more clearly detail specific examples of sources and uses of cash

Instructor Resources

Solutions Manual

Author-written and carefully verified multiple times to ensure accuracy and consistency with the text, the Solutions Manual contains answers to the Discussion Questions, Practice Exercises, Exercises, Problems (Series A and Series B), Cases, and Continuing Problems that appear in the text. These solutions help you easily plan, assign, and efficiently grade assignments.

Test Bank *NEW!*

NEW for this edition, Test Bank content is now delivered in an online platform. Cengage Learning Testing Powered by Cognero is a flexible, online system that allows you to:

- Author, edit, and manage test bank content from multiple Cengage Learning solutions
- Create multiple test versions in an instant
- Deliver tests from your LMS, your classroom, or wherever you want

Also *NEW* for this edition, more than 50 new Test Bank questions have been added (in addition to revising numeric values for approximately 20% of the existing questions).

Companion Web Site

This robust companion Web site provides immediate access to a rich array of teaching and learning resources–including the Instructor's Manual, PowerPoint slides, and Excel Template Solutions. Easily download the instructor resources you need from the password-protected, instructor-only section of the site.

Instructor's Manual Discover new ways to engage your students by utilizing the Instructor's Manual ideas for class discussion, group learning activities, writing exercises, and Internet activities. Moreover, simplify class preparation by reviewing a brief summary of each chapter, a detailed chapter synopsis (*NEW* for this edition), teaching tips regarding a suggested approach to the material, questions students frequently ask in the classroom, lecture aids, and demonstration problems in the Instructor's Manual. Transparency Masters and Handouts (with solutions) are also included. Quickly identify the assignments that best align with your course with the assignment preparation grid that includes information about learning objective coverage, difficulty level and Bloom's taxonomy categorization, time estimates, and accrediting standard alignment for business programs, AICPA, ACBSP, and IMA.

PowerPoint Slides Bring your lectures to life with slides designed to clarify difficult concepts for your students. The lecture PowerPoints include key terms and definitions, equations, examples, exhibits, and all Example Exercises (with solutions) from the textbook.

- *NEW* for this edition, descriptions for all graphics in the PowerPoints have been added to enhance PowerPoint usability for students with disabilities.
- Two separate PowerPoint decks that include just the Example Exercises (and solutions) and just the Exhibits from the textbook are ideal for instructors that create their own PowerPoint decks and just want to refresh them.

Excel Template Solutions Excel Templates are provided for selected long or complicated end-of-chapter exercises and problems to assist the student as they set up and work the problem. Certain cells are coded to display a red asterisk when an incorrect answer is entered, which helps students stay on track. Selected problems that can be solved using these templates are designated by an icon in the textbook and are listed in the assignment preparation grid in the Instructor's Manual. The Excel Template Solutions provide answers to these templates.

Practice Set Solutions Establish a fundamental understanding of accounting with Practice Sets, which require students to complete one month of transactions for a fictional company. Brief descriptions of each practice set are provided in the table of contents. The Practice Set Solutions provide answers to these practice sets.

Student Resources

Study Guide

Now available free in CengageNOWv2, the Study Guide allows students to easily assess what they know with a "Do You Know" checklist covering the key points in each chapter. To further test their comprehension, students can work through Practice Exercises, which include a "strategy" hint and solution so they can continue to practice applying key accounting concepts.

Working Papers

Now available free in CengageNOWv2, students will find the tools they need to help work through end-of-chapter assignments with these working papers. The preformatted templates provide a starting point by giving students a basic structure for problems and journal entries. Working Papers are also available in a printed format as a bundle option.

Practice Sets

GeneralLEDGER

For more in-depth application of accounting practices, instructors may use Practice Sets for long-term assignments. Each Practice Set requires students to complete one month of transactions for a fictional company. Practice Sets can be solved manually or with the Cengage Learning General Ledger software.

Web Site

Designed specifically for your students' accounting needs, this Web site features student PowerPoint slides, Excel Templates, learning games, and flashcards.

- **PowerPoint Slides:** Students can easily take notes or review difficult concepts with the student version of this edition's PowerPoint slides.
- **Excel Templates:** These Excel Templates help students stay on track. If students enter an incorrect answer in certain cells, a red asterisk will appear to let them know something is wrong. Problems that can be solved using these templates are designated by an icon.
- **Crossword Puzzles:** Students can focus on learning the key terms and definitions for each chapter in a different way by completing these crossword puzzles.
- **Flashcards:** Students can prepare with these flashcards, which cover the key terms and definitions they need to know for each chapter.

Acknowledgements

The many enhancements to this edition of *Managerial Accounting* are the direct result of one-on-one interviews, surveys, reviews, WebExes, and focus groups with over 300 instructors and students at institutions across the country over the past two years. We would like to take this opportunity to thank those who helped us better understand the challenges of the managerial accounting course and provided valuable feedback on our content and digital assets.

Instructors:

Aaron Pennington, York College of Pennsylvania
Adam Myers, Texas A&M University
Aileen Huang, Santa Monica College
Ajay Maindiratta, New York University
Alex Gialanella, Manhattanville College
Andrea Murowski, Brookdale Community College
Angelo Luciano, Columbia College, Chicago
Ann Gervais, Springfield Technical Comm College
Ann Gregory, South Plains College
Anna Boulware, St. Charles Community College
Anne Marie Anderson, Raritan Valley Community College
April Poe, University of the Incarnate Word
Barbara Kren, Marquette University
Bea Chiang, The College of New Jersey
Becky Hancock, El Paso Community College
Brenda McVey, Green River Community College
Bruce England, Massasoit Community College
Bruce L. Darling, University of Oregon
Bruce Leung, City College of San Francisco
Carol Dickerson, Chaffey College
Carol Graham, The University of San Francisco
Cassandra H. Catlett, Carson Newman University
Cecile Roberti, Community College of Rhode Island
Charles J.F. Leflar, University of Arkansas
Charles Lewis, Houston Community College
Chris Kinney, Mount Wachusett Community College
Chris McNamara, Finger Lakes Community College
Christopher Ashley, Everest College
Christopher Demaline, Central Arizona College
Cindy Bleasdal, Hilbert College
Colleen Chung, Miami Dade College
Cynthia Bolt, The Citadel
Cynthia J. Miller, University of Kentucky
Cynthia Johnson, University of Arkansas at Little Rock
Darlene Schnuck, Waukesha County Technical College
Dave Alldredge, Salt Lake Community College
David Centers, Grand Valley State University
David E. Laurel, South Texas College
Dawn Lopez, Johnson & Wales University
Dawn Peters, Southwestern Illinois College
Dawn W. Stevens, Northwest Mississippi Community College
Debbie Adkins, Remington College Online
Debbie Luna, El Paso Community College
Debbie Rose, Northeast Wisconsin Technical College
Debora Constable, Georgia Perimeter College
Denise Teixeira, Chemeketa Community College
Don Curfman, McHenry County College
Dori Danko, Grand Valley State University
Dorothy Davis, University of Louisiana, Monroe
Edwin Pagan, Passaic County Community College
Elizabeth Ammann, Lindenwood University
Emmanuel Danso, Palm Beach State College
Ercan Sinmaz, Houston Community College
Eric Blazer, Millersville University
Erik Lindquist, Lansing Community College
Esther S. Bunn, Stephen F Austin State University
Felicia R. Baldwin, Richard J. Daley College
Gary Bower, Community College of Rhode Island
Geoffrey D. Bartlett, Drake University
Gerald Smith, University of Northern Iowa
Glenn (Mel) McQueary, Houston Community College
Gloria Grayless, Sam Houston State University
Greg Lauer, North Iowa Area Community College
Gregory Brookins, Santa Monica College
Harold Little, Western Kentucky University
Jacqueline Burke, Hofstra University
James Lock, Northern Virginia Community College
James M. Emig, Villanova University
James Webb, University of the Pacific
Jamie O'Brien, South Dakota State University
Jan Barton, Emory University
Jana Hosmer, Blue Ridge Community College
Janice Akeo, Butler Community College
Jeanette Milius, Iowa Western Community College
Jeff Varblow, College of Lake County
Jeffrey T. Kunz, Carroll University
Jennifer LeSure, Ivy Tech Community College
Jennifer Mack, Lindenwood University
Jennifer Schneider, University of North Georgia
Jennifer Spring Sneed, Arkansas State University-Newport
Jenny Resnick, Santa Monica College
Jill Mitchell, Northern Virginia Community College
Jim Shelton, Harding University
Joel Strong, St. Cloud State University
Johh G. Ahmad, Northern Virginia Community College
John Babich, Kankakee Community College
John Nader, Davenport University
John Seilo, Irvine Valley College
John Verani, White Mountains Community College

Johnna Murray, University of Missouri-St. Louis
Joseph M. Nicassio, Westmoreland County Community College
Judith A. Toland, Bucks County Community College
Judith Zander, Grossmont College
Judy Patrick, Minnesota State Community and Technical College
Judy Smith, Parkland College
Julia M. Camp, Providence College
Julie Dawson, Carthage College
Julie Miller Millmann, Chippewa Valley Technical College
Karen C. Elsom, Fayetteville Technical Community College
Katherine Sue Hewitrt, Klamath Community College
Katy Long, Hill College
Keith Hallmark, Calhoun Community College
Kevin McNelis, New Mexico State University
Kimberly Franklin, St. Louis Community College
Kirk Canzano, Long Beach City College
Kristen Quinn, Northern Essex Community College
La Vonda Ramey, Schoolcraft College
Lana Tuss, Chemeketa Community College
Larry G. Stephens, Austin Community College
Lawrence A. Roman, Cuyahoga Community College
Lawrence Chui, University of St. Thomas
Leah Arrington, Northwest Mississippi Community College
Leah Russell, Holyoke Community College
Lee Smart, Southwest Tennessee Community College
Len Heritage, Tacoma Community College
Leonard Cronin, University Center Rochester
Linda Christiansen, Indiana University Southeast
Linda H. Tarrago, Hillsborough Community College
Linda Miller, Northeast Community College
Linda Muren, Cuyahoga Community College
Linda Tarrago, Hillsborough Community College
Lisa Busto, William Rainey Harper College
Lisa Novak, Mott Community College
Lori A. Grady, Bucks County Community College
Lori Johnson, Minnesota State University Moorhead
Louann Hofheins Cummings, The University of Findlay
Lucile Faurel, University of California Irvine
Lynn Almond, Virginia Tech
Lynn K. Saubert, Radford University
Lynn Krausse, Bakersfield College
Machiavelli W. Chao, University of California, Irvine
Magan Calhoun, Austin Peay State University
Marcela Raphael, Chippewa Valley Technical College
Marci Butterfield, University of Utah
Marianne James, California State University, Los Angeles
Marie Saunders, Dakota County Technical College
Marilyn Stansbury, Calvin College
Marina Grau, Houston Community College
Martin Hart, Manchester Comm College
Mary Zenner, College of Lake County
Meg Costello Lambert, Oakland Community College
Merrily Hoffman, San Jacinto College
Michael G. Schaefer, Blinn College
Michael Goeken, Northwest Vista College
Michael Gurevitz, Montgomery College
Michael J. Gallagher, DeSales University
Michael Lawrence, Mt. Hood Community College
Michael P. Dole, Marquette University
Michael P. Prockton, Finger Lakes Community College
Michele Martinez, Hillsborough Community College
Michelle Moshier, University at Albany
Ming Lu, Santa Monica College
Mon Sellers, Lone Star College-North Harris
Nancy Emerson, North Dakota State University
Nancy L. Snow, University of Toledo
Nino Gonzalez, El Paso Community College
Noel McKeon, Florida State College at Jacksonville
Odessa Jordan, Calhoun Community College
Pam Meyer, University of Louisiana at Lafayette
Pamela Knight, Columbus Technical College
Patricia Doherty, Boston University School of Management
Patricia Walczak, Lansing Community College
Patricia Worsham, Norco College
Patrick Rogan, Cosumnes River College
Perry Sellers, Lone Star College System
Rachel Pernia, Essex County College
Rebecca Grava Davis, East Mississippi Community College
Rebecca Hancock, El Paso Community College
Richard Lau, California State University, Los Angeles
Richard Mandau, Piedmont Technical College
Rick Andrews, Sinclair Community College
Rick Rinetti, Los Angeles City College
Rita Mintz, Calhoun Community College
Robert A. Pacheco, Massasoit Community College
Robert Almon, South Texas College
Robert E. (Reb) Beatty, Anne Arundel Community College
Robert Foster, Los Angeles Pierce College
Robert Urell, Irvine Valley College
Robin D'Agati, Palm Beach State College
Ron O'Brien, Fayetteville Technical Community College
Roy Carson, Anne Arundel Community College
Ryan Smith, Columbia College
Sandra Cohen, Columbia College Chicago
Sara Barritt, Northeast Community College
Saturnino (Nino) Gonzalez, El Paso Community College
Shani N. Robinson, Sam Houston State University
Sharif Soussi, Charter Oak State College
Sharon Agee, Rollins College
Sheila Ammons, Austin Community College
Sheila Guillot, Lamar State College-Port Arthur
Sol. Ahiarah, SUNY Buffalo State
Stacy Kline, Drexel University
Stani Kantcheva, Cincinnati State Technical and Community College
Steven J. LaFave, Augsburg College
Sue Cunningham, Rowan Cabarrus Community College
Suneel Maheshwari, Marshall University
Susan Cordes, Johnson County Community College

Suzanne Laudadio, Durham Technical Community College
Sy Pearlman, California State University, Long Beach
Tara Laken, Joliet Junior College
Taylor Klett, Sam Houston State University
Teresa Thompson, Chaffey Community College
Terri Walsh, Seminole State College
Thane Butt, Champlain College
Thomas Branton, Alvin Community College
Tim Green, North Georgia Technical College
Timothy Griffin, Hillsborough Community College
Timothy J. Moran, Aurora University
Timothy Swenson, Sullivan University
Tony Cioffi, Lorain County Community College
W. Jeff Knight, Flagler College
Wanda Wong, Chabot College

Students:

Allison Seaman, University of Findlay
Amber Bostick, Joliet Junior College
Amelia Lupis, Community College of Rhode Island
Andrew Buckley, Community College of Rhode Island
Andrew Mancini, Valparaiso University
Anita Jordan, Henry Ford Community College
Billie Ma, Middlesex County College
Blair Ericksen, The University of Findlay
Bonnie Eme, Ivy Tech Community College
Bradley "The Snowman" Koepke, Valparaiso University
Briana E Garrity, Community College of Rhode Island
Brittany Smothers, Ivy Tech Community College
Carly Butler, Sinclair Community College
Carmen Macvicar, Henry Ford Community College
Cassie Skal, University of Findlay
Charlene Resch, Ivy Tech Community College
Cheila Soares, Community College of Rhode Island
Christopher W. Gregory, Fayetteville Technical Community College
Colby Zachary, Austin Community College
Courtney Murphy, Sinclair Community College
Daniel Hart, Ivy Tech Community College
David Camargo, Fayetteville Technical Community College
Debborah Gideon, Ivy Tech Community College
Diana Contreras, Joliet Junior College
Dolores Velasquez, Ivy Tech Community College
Eleticia Feliciano, Henry Ford Community College
Eli Coulton, Sinclair Community College
Emilie Ferdelman, Sinclair Community College
Geoffrey Hlavach, Joliet Junior College
Jayme Thornley, Community College of Rhode Island
Jessie Laberge, Community College of Rhode Island
Joel Mondragon, Austin Community College
Jonathan Balsavich, Joliet Junior College
Jose Nieto, Austin Community College
J. Stoll, The University of Findlay
Karolina Tovpenec, The University of Findlay
Kathryn Shaw, Ivy Tech Community College
Kaylene Slayton, The University of Findlay
Kevin McMaster, Community College of Rhode island
Khadija Brikate, Erie Community College
Kimberlee Serrano, Middlesex County College
Kimberly Arruda, Community College of Rhode Island
Krista Jalette, Community College of Rhode Island
Leslie Bryant, Henry Ford Community College
Luke Fleming, Ivy Tech Community College
Malorie Masek, Valparaiso University
Marah Jammal, Henry Ford Community College
Marshall Miller, Valparaiso University
Matthew Vizzaccaro, Henry Ford Community College
Mayra Vargas, Austin Community College
Meghan Traster, Ivy Tech Community College
M. Lallier, Community College of Rhode Island
Michael L. Bardey, Sinclair Community College
Min Dou, Valparaiso University
Nicholas Johnson, Ivy Tech Community College
Nick L., Holyoke Community College
Nicholas Oliveira, Community College of Rhode island
Rachel Brown, Sinclair Community College
Ramona Hawkins, Ivy Tech Community College
Ryan Dvorak, Joliet Junior College
Ryan Truschke, Grand Valley State University
S.J. Cross, Ivy Tech Community College
Scott Nicol, Joliet Junior College
Sean Bingham, The University of Findlay
Sheila Diodonet, Holyoke Community College
Stephanie Theresa Plante, Community College of Rhode Island
Tasha Finley, Ivy Tech Community College
Trang Thi Vu, The University of Findlay
Tyler Philbin, Community College of Rhode Island
William Carter, The University of Findlay

About the Authors

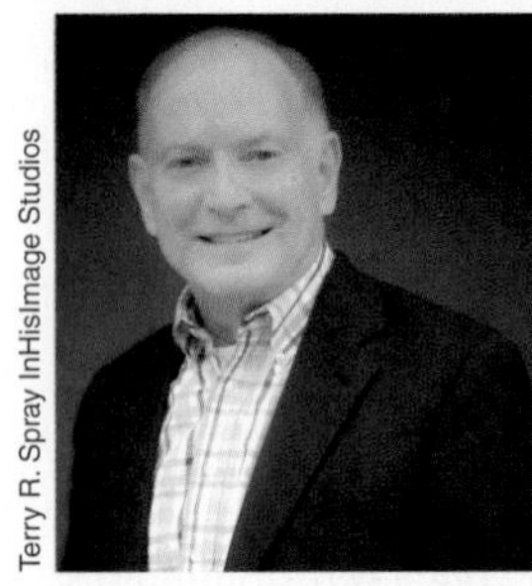
Terry R. Spray InHisImage Studios

Carl S. Warren

Dr. Carl S. Warren is Professor Emeritus of Accounting at the University of Georgia, Athens. Dr. Warren has taught classes at the University of Georgia, University of Iowa, Michigan State University, and University of Chicago. Professor Warren focused his teaching efforts on principles of accounting and auditing. He received his Ph.D. from Michigan State University and his B.B.A. and M.A. from the University of Iowa. During his career, Dr. Warren published numerous articles in professional journals, including *The Accounting Review, Journal of Accounting Research, Journal of Accountancy, The CPA Journal,* and *Auditing: A Journal of Practice & Theory*. Dr. Warren has served on numerous committees of the American Accounting Association, the American Institute of Certified Public Accountants, and the Institute of Internal Auditors. He has also consulted with numerous companies and public accounting firms. Professor Warren is an avid handball player and has played in the World Handball Championships in Portland, Oregon, and Dublin, Ireland. He enjoys backpacking and recently took an eleven-day, ten-night trip in the Thorofare area of Yellowstone National Park. He has rafted the Grand Canyon and backpacked rim-to-rim. Professor Warren also enjoys fly fishing, skiing, golfing, and motorcycling.

Charles J. Garvey III / Garvey Photography

James M. Reeve

Dr. James M. Reeve is Professor Emeritus of Accounting and Information Management at the University of Tennessee. Professor Reeve taught on the accounting faculty for 25 years, after graduating with his Ph.D. from Oklahoma State University. His teaching efforts focused on undergraduate accounting principles and graduate education in the Master of Accountancy and Senior Executive MBA programs. Beyond this, Professor Reeve is also very active in the Supply Chain Certification program, which is a major executive education and research effort of the College. His research interests are varied and include work in managerial accounting, supply chain management, lean manufacturing, and information management. He has published over 40 articles in academic and professional journals, including the *Journal of Cost Management, Journal of Management Accounting Research, Accounting Review, Management Accounting Quarterly, Supply Chain Management Review,* and *Accounting Horizons*. He has consulted or provided training around the world for a wide variety of organizations, including Boeing, Procter & Gamble, Norfolk Southern, Hershey Foods, Coca-Cola, and Sony. When not writing books, Professor Reeve plays golf and is involved in faith-based activities.

© Ken Bennett

Jonathan Duchac

Dr. Jonathan Duchac is the Merrill Lynch and Co. Professor of Accounting and Director of International Programs at Wake Forest University. He holds a joint appointment at the Vienna University of Business and Economics in Vienna, Austria. Dr. Duchac currently teaches introductory and advanced courses in financial accounting and has received a number of awards during his career, including the Wake Forest University Outstanding Graduate Professor Award, the T.B. Rose Award for Instructional Innovation, and the University of Georgia Outstanding Teaching Assistant Award. In addition to his teaching responsibilities, Dr. Duchac has served as Accounting Advisor to Merrill Lynch Equity Research, where he worked with research analysts in reviewing and evaluating the financial reporting practices of public companies. He has testified before the U.S. House of Representatives, the Financial Accounting Standards Board, and the Securities and Exchange Commission and has worked with a number of major public companies on financial reporting and accounting policy issues. In addition to his professional interests, Dr. Duchac has served on the Board of Directors of The Special Children's School of Winston-Salem, a private, nonprofit developmental day school serving children with special needs. Dr. Duchac is an avid long-distance runner, mountain biker, and snow skier. His recent events include the Grandfather Mountain Marathon, the Black Mountain Marathon, the Shut-In Ridge Trail run, and NO MAAM (Nocturnal Overnight Mountain Bike Assault on Mount Mitchell).

Brief Contents

Contents

What Successful Students Are Saying

In a recent survey of students who took managerial accounting courses, students stated that, in order to be successful in these courses, students should (in order of importance):

- Complete assigned homework
- Attend class and pay attention during the lecture
- Study
- Ask for help or get a tutor
- Complete ungraded practice assignments or review exercises

- ❑ Did you read the chapter from the required textbook prior to attending class?
- ❑ Did you attend class?
- ❑ Did you take notes during class?
- ❑ Did you ask questions of the professor either during or after class when you did not understand a concept being taught?
- ❑ Did you complete all assigned homework?
- ❑ Did you complete ungraded practice assignments or review exercises to better learn and understand accounting concepts?
- ❑ Did you obtain an explanation from the professor for incorrect answers?
- ❑ Did you utilize additional resources provided such as demonstration videos & tutorials?

Successful students spent an average of 4 hours per week outside of class time studying, including completing assigned homework.

You just need to put in the effort. If you work through the homework problems and show up to class, you will do well.

—Brandy J. Gibson, Business Administration Major Ivy Tech Community College

Do not put off homework – it is more important than you know – and when in need – ASK FOR HELP!!

—Sally Cross, Accounting Major Ivy Tech Community College

You need to attend every class and pay attention. Take good notes and do all the homework.

—Melinda Lallier, Accounting Major Community College of Rhode Island

Come to class every day – if you miss a class, you miss a lot of notes and example problems. Homework is vital and so is studying for tests – you need to learn the different formulas and equations.

—Shannon Green, General Business Major Community College of Rhode Island

Anyone can succeed at learning & understanding accounting concepts!

<u>How?</u> Preparation, time management, & practice!

Managerial Accounting

13e

Managerial Accounting Concepts and Principles

Washburn Guitars

Paul Stanley, guitarist for the legendary rock band **KISS**, has entertained millions of fans playing his guitar. His guitar was built by quality craftsmen at **Washburn Guitars** in Chicago. Washburn Guitars is well-known in the music industry and has been in business for more than 120 years.

Staying in business for 120 years requires a thorough understanding of how to manufacture high-quality guitars. In addition, it requires knowledge of how to account for the costs of making guitars. For example, Washburn needs cost information to answer the following questions:

- How much should be charged for its guitars?
- How many guitars does it have to sell in a year to cover its costs and earn a profit?
- How many employees should the company have working on each stage of the manufacturing process?
- How would purchasing automated equipment affect the costs of its guitars?

This chapter introduces managerial accounting concepts that are useful in addressing these questions.

This chapter begins by describing managerial accounting and its relationship to financial accounting. Following this overview, the management process is described along with the role of managerial accounting in this process. Finally, characteristics of managerial accounting reports, managerial accounting terms, and uses of managerial accounting information are described and illustrated.

Learning Objectives

After studying this chapter, you should be able to: | Example Exercises

OBJ 1 **Describe managerial accounting and the role of managerial accounting in a business.**
Managerial Accounting
Differences Between Managerial and Financial Accounting
The Management Accountant in the Organization
Managerial Accounting in the Management Process — **EE 1-1**

OBJ 2 **Describe and illustrate the following costs: direct and indirect costs; direct materials, direct labor, and factory overhead costs; and product and period costs.**
Manufacturing Operations: Costs and Terminology
Direct and Indirect Costs
Manufacturing Costs — **EE 1-2, 3, 4**

OBJ 3 **Describe and illustrate the following statements for a manufacturing business: balance sheet, statement of cost of goods manufactured, and income statement.**
Financial Statements for a Manufacturing Business
Balance Sheet for a Manufacturing Business
Income Statement for a Manufacturing Business — **EE 1-5**

OBJ 4 **Describe the uses of managerial accounting information.**
Uses of Managerial Accounting

At a Glance 1 Page 18

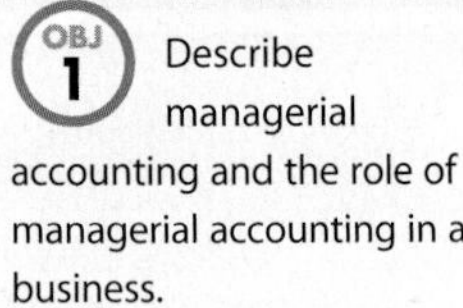

OBJ 1 Describe managerial accounting and the role of managerial accounting in a business.

Managerial Accounting

Managers make numerous decisions during the day-to-day operations of a business and in planning for the future. Managerial accounting provides much of the information used for these decisions.

Some examples of managerial accounting information along with the chapter in which it is described and illustrated follow:

- Classifying manufacturing and other costs and reporting them in the financial statements (Chapter 1)
- Determining the cost of manufacturing a product or providing a service (Chapters 2 and 3)
- Estimating the behavior of costs for various levels of activity and assessing cost-volume-profit relationships (Chapter 4)
- Evaluating operating performance using cost behavior relationships (Chapter 5)
- Planning for the future by preparing budgets (Chapter 6)
- Evaluating manufacturing costs by comparing actual with expected results (Chapter 7)
- Evaluating decentralized operations by comparing actual and budgeted costs as well as computing various measures of profitability (Chapter 8)
- Evaluating special decision-making situations by comparing differential revenues and costs, and allocating product costs using activity-based costing (Chapter 9)
- Evaluating alternative proposals for long-term investments in fixed assets (Chapter 10)
- Evaluating the impact of cost allocation on pricing products and services (Chapter 11)
- Planning operations using just-in-time concepts (Chapter 12)

Differences Between Managerial and Financial Accounting

Accounting information is often divided into two types: financial and managerial. Exhibit 1 shows the relationship between financial accounting and managerial accounting.

EXHIBIT 1 **Financial Accounting and Managerial Accounting**

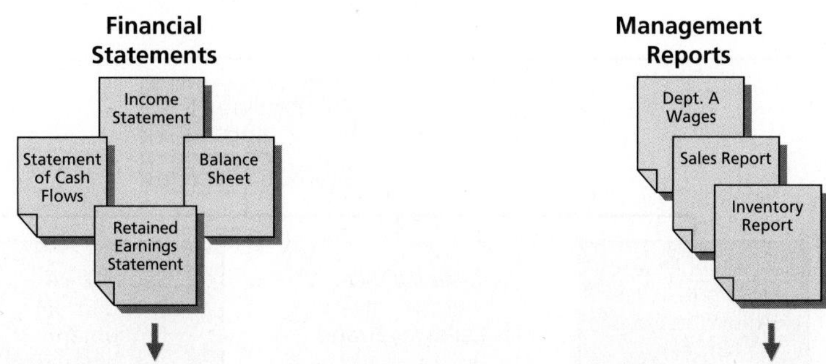

	Financial Statements	Management Reports
Users of Information	External users and company management	Management
Nature of Information	Objective	Objective and subjective
Guidelines for Preparation	Prepared according to GAAP	Prepared according to management needs
Timeliness of Reporting	Prepared at fixed intervals	Prepared at fixed intervals and on an as-needed basis
Focus of Reporting	Company as a whole	Company as a whole or segment

Financial accounting information is reported at fixed intervals (monthly, quarterly, yearly) in general-purpose financial statements. These financial statements—the income statement, retained earnings statement, balance sheet, and statement of cash flows—are prepared according to generally accepted accounting principles (GAAP). These statements are used by external users such as the following:

- Shareholders
- Creditors
- Government agencies
- The general public

Managers of a company also use general-purpose financial statements. For example, in planning future operations, managers often begin by evaluating the current income statement and statement of cash flows.

Managerial accounting information is designed to meet the specific needs of a company's management. This information includes the following:

- Historical data, which provide *objective measures* of past operations
- Estimated data, which provide *subjective estimates* about future decisions

Management uses both types of information in directing daily operations, planning future operations, and developing business strategies.

Unlike the financial statements prepared in financial accounting, managerial accounting reports do *not* always have to be:

- Prepared according to generally accepted accounting principles (GAAP). This is because *only* the company's management uses the information. Also, in many cases, GAAP are not relevant to the specific decision-making needs of management.
- Prepared at fixed intervals (monthly, quarterly, yearly). Although some management reports are prepared at fixed intervals, most reports are prepared as management needs the information.
- Prepared for the business as a whole. Most management reports are prepared for products, projects, sales territories, or other segments of the company.

The Management Accountant in the Organization

In most companies, departments or similar organizational units are assigned responsibilities for specific functions or activities. The operating structure of a company can be shown in an *organization chart*.

Exhibit 2 is a partial organization chart for **Callaway Golf Company**, the manufacturer and distributor of golf clubs, clothing, and other products.

EXHIBIT 2

Partial Organization Chart for Callaway Golf Company

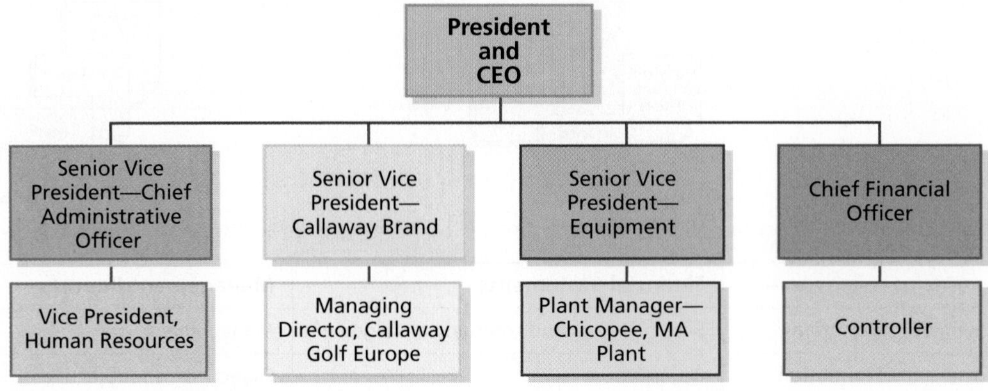

The departments in a company can be viewed as having either of the following:

- Line responsibilities
- Staff responsibilities

A **line department** is directly involved in providing goods or services to the customers of the company. For Callaway Golf (shown in Exhibit 2), the following occupy line positions:

- Senior Vice President—Equipment
- Plant Manager—Chicopee, MA Plant
- Senior Vice President—Callaway Brand
- Managing Director, Callaway Golf Europe

Individuals in these positions are responsible for manufacturing and selling Callaway's products.

The terms *line* and *staff* may be applied to service organizations. For example, the line positions in a hospital would be the nurses, doctors, and other caregivers. Staff positions would include admissions and records.

A **staff department** provides services, assistance, and advice to the departments with line or other staff responsibilities. A staff department has no direct authority over a line department. For Callaway Golf (Exhibit 2), the following are staff positions:

- Senior VP—Chief Administrative Officer
- Vice President, Human Resources
- Chief Financial Officer
- Controller

In most companies, the **controller** is the chief management accountant. The controller's staff consists of a variety of other accountants who are responsible for specialized accounting functions such as the following:

- Systems and procedures
- General accounting
- Budgets and budget analysis
- Special reports and analysis
- Taxes
- Cost accounting

Experience in managerial accounting is often an excellent training ground for senior management positions. This is not surprising because accounting touches all phases of a company's operations.

Managerial Accounting in the Management Process

As a staff department, managerial accounting supports management and the management process. The **management process** has the following five basic phases, as shown in Exhibit 3:

- Planning
- Directing
- Controlling
- Improving
- Decision making

As Exhibit 3 illustrates, the five phases interact with one another.

EXHIBIT 3

The Management Process

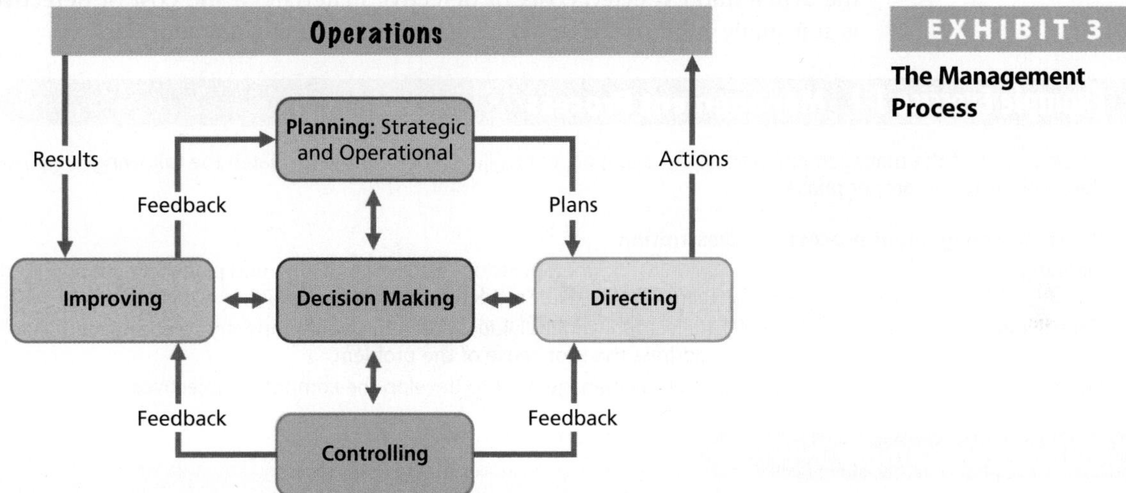

Planning Management uses **planning** in developing the company's **objectives (goals)** and translating these objectives into courses of action. For example, a company may set an objective to increase market share by 15% by introducing three new products. The actions to achieve this objective might be as follows:

- Increase the advertising budget
- Open a new sales territory
- Increase the research and development budget

Planning may be classified as follows:

- **Strategic planning**, which is developing long-term actions to achieve the company's objectives. These long-term actions are called **strategies**, which often involve periods of 5 to 10 years.
- **Operational planning**, which develops short-term actions for managing the day-to-day operations of the company.

Directing The process by which managers run day-to-day operations is called **directing**. An example of directing is a production supervisor's efforts to keep the production line moving without interruption (downtime). A credit manager's development of guidelines for assessing the ability of potential customers to pay their bills is also an example of directing.

Controlling Monitoring operating results and comparing actual results with the expected results is **controlling**. This **feedback** allows management to isolate areas for further investigation and possible remedial action. It may also lead to revising future plans. This philosophy of controlling by comparing actual and expected results is called **management by exception**.

Improving Feedback is also used by managers to support continuous process improvement. **Continuous process improvement** is the philosophy of continually improving employees, business processes, and products. The objective of continuous improvement is to eliminate the *source* of problems in a process. In this way, the right products (services) are delivered in the right quantities at the right time.

Decision Making Inherent in each of the preceding management processes is **decision making**. In managing a company, management must continually decide among alternative actions. For example, in directing operations, managers must decide on an operating structure, training procedures, and staffing of day-to-day operations.

Managerial accounting supports managers in all phases of the management process. For example, accounting reports comparing actual and expected operating results help managers plan and improve current operations. Such a report might compare the actual and expected costs of defective materials. If the cost of defective materials is unusually high, management might decide to change suppliers.

Example Exercise 1-1 Management Process (OBJ 1)

Three phases of the management process are planning, controlling, and improving. Match the following descriptions to the proper phase:

Phase of management process	Description
Planning	a. Monitoring the operating results of implemented plans and comparing the actual results with expected results.
Controlling	b. Rejects solving individual problems with temporary solutions that fail to address the root cause of the problem.
Improving	c. Used by management to develop the company's objectives.

Follow My Example 1-1

Planning (c), Controlling (a), and Improving (b).

Practice Exercises: PE 1-1A, PE 1-1B

Integrity, Objectivity, and Ethics in Business

ENVIRONMENTAL MANAGERIAL ACCOUNTING

Throughout the last decade, environmental issues have become an increasingly important part of the business environment for most companies. Companies and managers must now consider the environmental impact of their business decisions in the same way that they would consider other operational issues. To help managers make sound business decisions, the emerging field of environmental management accounting focuses on calculating the environmental-related costs of business decisions. Environmental managerial accountants evaluate a variety of issues such as the volume and level of emissions, the estimated costs of different levels of emissions, and the impact that environmental costs have on product cost. Managers use these results to consider clearly the environmental effects of their business decisions.

OBJ 2 Describe and illustrate the following costs: direct and indirect costs; direct materials, direct labor, and factory overhead costs; and product and period costs.

Manufacturing Operations: Costs and Terminology

The operations of a business can be classified as service, merchandising, or manufacturing. The accounting for service and merchandising businesses has been described and illustrated in earlier chapters. For this reason, the remaining chapters of this text focus primarily on manufacturing businesses. Most of the managerial accounting concepts discussed, however, also apply to service and merchandising businesses.

As a basis for illustration of manufacturing operations, a guitar manufacturer, **Legend Guitars**, is used. Exhibit 4 is an overview of Legend's guitar manufacturing operations.

EXHIBIT 4 **Guitar-Making Operations of Legend Guitars**

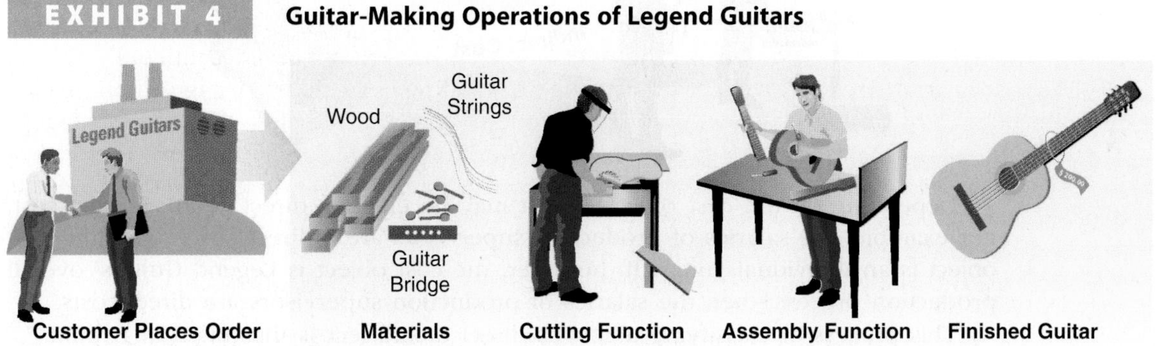

Legend's guitar-making process begins when a customer places an order for a guitar. Once the order is accepted, the manufacturing process begins by obtaining the necessary materials. An employee then cuts the body and neck of the guitar out of raw lumber. Once the wood is cut, the body and neck of the guitar are assembled. When the assembly is complete, the guitar is painted and finished.

Direct and Indirect Costs

A **cost** is a payment of cash or the commitment to pay cash in the future for the purpose of generating revenues. For example, cash (or credit) used to purchase equipment is the cost of the equipment. If equipment is purchased by exchanging assets other than cash, the current market value of the assets given up is the cost of the equipment purchased.

In managerial accounting, costs are classified according to the decision-making needs of management. For example, costs are often classified by their relationship to a segment of operations, called a **cost object**. A cost object may be a product, a sales territory, a department, or an activity, such as research and development. Costs identified with cost objects are either direct costs or indirect costs.

Direct costs are identified with and can be traced to a cost object. For example, as shown in Exhibit 5, the cost of wood (materials) used by **Legend Guitars** in manufacturing a guitar is a direct cost of the guitar.

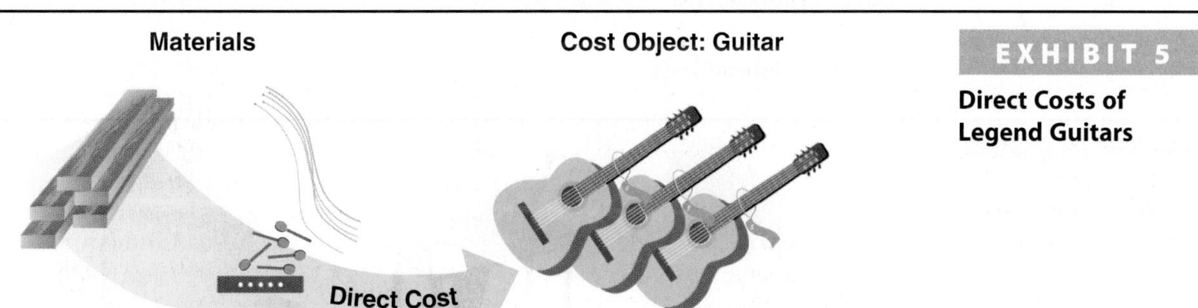

EXHIBIT 5

Direct Costs of Legend Guitars

Indirect costs cannot be identified with or traced to a cost object. For example, as shown in Exhibit 6, the salaries of the **Legend Guitars** production supervisors are indirect costs of producing a guitar. Although the production supervisors contribute to the production of a guitar, their salaries cannot be identified with or traced to any individual guitar.

EXHIBIT 6

Indirect Costs of Legend Guitars

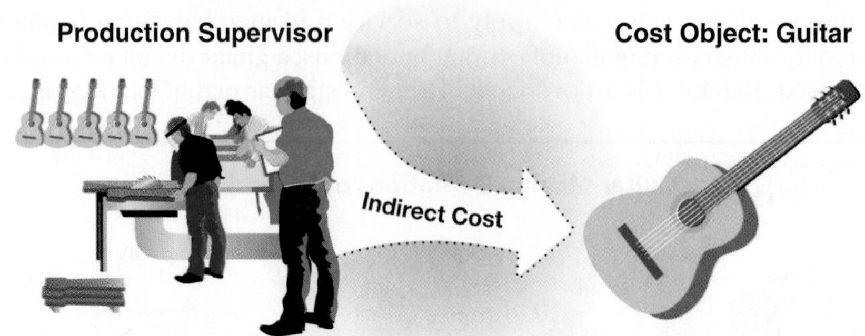

Depending on the cost object, a cost may be either a direct or an indirect cost. For example, the salaries of production supervisors are indirect costs when the cost object is an individual guitar. If, however, the cost object is Legend Guitars' overall production process, then the salaries of production supervisors are direct costs.

This process of classifying a cost as direct or indirect is illustrated in Exhibit 7.

EXHIBIT 7

Classifying Direct and Indirect Costs

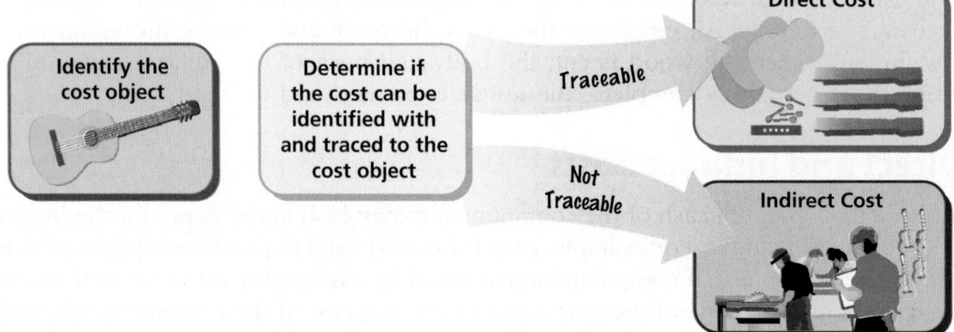

Manufacturing Costs

The cost of a manufactured product includes the cost of materials used in making the product. In addition, the cost of a manufactured product includes the cost of converting the materials into a finished product. For example, **Legend Guitars** uses employees and machines to convert wood (and other supplies) into finished guitars. Thus, as shown in Exhibit 8, the cost of a finished guitar (the cost object) includes the following:

- Direct materials cost
- Direct labor cost
- Factory overhead cost

EXHIBIT 8

Manufacturing Costs of Legend Guitars

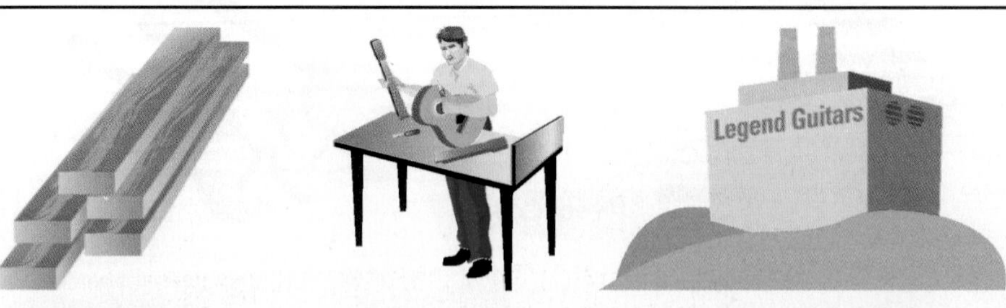

Direct Materials Cost Manufactured products begin with raw materials that are converted into finished products. The cost of any material that is an integral part of the finished product is classified as a **direct materials cost**. For **Legend Guitars**, direct materials cost includes the cost of the wood used in producing each guitar. Other examples of direct materials costs include the cost of electronic components for a television, silicon wafers for microcomputer chips, and tires for an automobile.

To be classified as a direct materials cost, the cost must be *both* of the following:

- An integral part of the finished product
- A significant portion of the total cost of the product

For Legend, the cost of the guitar strings is not a direct materials cost. This is because the cost of guitar strings is an insignificant part of the total cost of each guitar. Instead, the cost of guitar strings is classified as a factory overhead cost, which is discussed later.

Direct Labor Cost Most manufacturing processes use employees to convert materials into finished products. The cost of employee wages that is an integral part of the finished product is classified as **direct labor cost**. For **Legend Guitars**, direct labor cost includes the wages of the employees who cut each guitar out of raw lumber and assemble it. Other examples of direct labor costs include mechanics' wages for repairing an automobile, machine operators' wages for manufacturing tools, and assemblers' wages for assembling a laptop computer.

Like a direct materials cost, a direct labor cost must meet *both* of the following criteria:

- An integral part of the finished product
- A significant portion of the total cost of the product

For Legend, the wages of the janitors who clean the factory are not a direct labor cost. This is because janitorial costs are not an integral part or a significant cost of each guitar. Instead, janitorial costs are classified as a factory overhead cost, which is discussed next.

Factory Overhead Cost Costs other than direct materials and direct labor that are incurred in the manufacturing process are combined and classified as **factory overhead cost**. Factory overhead is sometimes called **manufacturing overhead** or **factory burden**.

All factory overhead costs are indirect costs of the product. Some factory overhead costs include the following:

- Heating and lighting the factory
- Repairing and maintaining factory equipment
- Property taxes on factory buildings and land
- Insurance on factory buildings
- Depreciation on factory plant and equipment

Factory overhead cost also includes materials and labor costs that do not enter directly into the finished product. Examples include the cost of oil used to lubricate machinery and the wages of janitorial and supervisory employees. Also, if the costs of direct materials or direct labor are not a significant portion of the total product cost, these costs may be classified as factory overhead costs.

As manufacturing processes have become more automated, direct labor costs have become so small that in some situations they are included as part of factory overhead.

For **Legend Guitars**, the costs of guitar strings and janitorial wages are factory overhead costs. Additional factory overhead costs of making guitars are as follows:

- Sandpaper
- Buffing compound
- Glue
- Power (electricity) to run the machines
- Depreciation of the machines and building
- Salaries of production supervisors

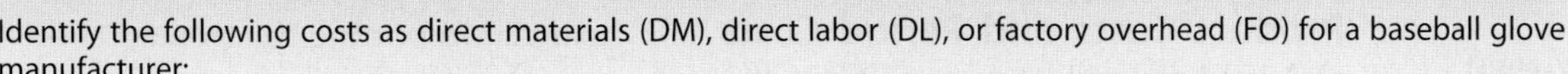

Identify the following costs as direct materials (DM), direct labor (DL), or factory overhead (FO) for a baseball glove manufacturer:

a. Leather used to make a baseball glove
b. Coolants for machines that sew baseball gloves
c. Wages of assembly line employees
d. Ink used to print a player's autograph on a baseball glove

(Continued)

Follow My Example 1-2

a. DM
b. FO
c. DL
d. FO

Practice Exercises: PE 1-2A, PE 1-2B

Prime Costs and Conversion Costs Direct materials, direct labor, and factory overhead costs may be grouped together for analysis and reporting. Two such common groupings are as follows:

- **Prime costs**, which consist of direct materials and direct labor costs
- **Conversion costs**, which consist of direct labor and factory overhead costs

Conversion costs are the costs of converting the materials into a finished product. Direct labor is both a prime cost and a conversion cost, as shown in Exhibit 9.

EXHIBIT 9

Prime Costs and Conversion Costs

Prime Costs

Direct Materials

Direct Labor

Factory Overhead

Conversion Costs

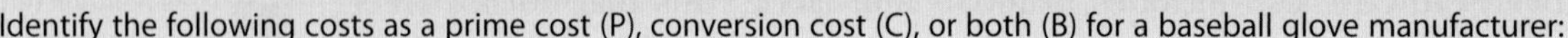

Example Exercise 1-3 Prime and Conversion Costs OBJ 2

Identify the following costs as a prime cost (P), conversion cost (C), or both (B) for a baseball glove manufacturer:

a. Leather used to make a baseball glove
b. Coolants for machines that sew baseball gloves
c. Wages of assembly line employees
d. Ink used to print a player's autograph on a baseball glove

Follow My Example 1-3

a. P
b. C
c. B
d. C

Practice Exercises: PE 1-3A, PE 1-3B

Note:
Product costs consist of direct materials, direct labor, and factory overhead costs.

Product Costs and Period Costs For financial reporting purposes, costs are classified as product costs or period costs.

- **Product costs** consist of manufacturing costs: direct materials, direct labor, and factory overhead.
- **Period costs** consist of selling and administrative expenses. *Selling expenses* are incurred in marketing the product and delivering the product to customers. *Administrative*

expenses are incurred in managing the company and are not directly related to the manufacturing or selling functions.

Examples of product costs and period costs for **Legend Guitars** are presented in Exhibit 10.

EXHIBIT 10 **Examples of Product Costs and Period Costs—Legend Guitars**

Product (Manufacturing) Costs

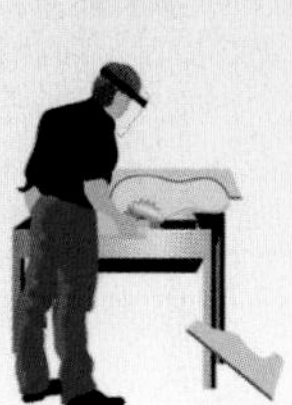

Direct Materials Cost
- Wood used in neck and body

Direct Labor Cost
- Wages of saw operator
- Wages of employees who assemble the guitar

Factory Overhead
- Guitar strings
- Wages of janitor
- Power to run the machines
- Depreciation expense—factory building
- Sandpaper and buffing materials
- Glue used in assembly of the guitar
- Salary of production supervisors

Period (Nonmanufacturing) Costs

Selling Expenses
- Advertising expenses
- Sales salaries expenses
- Commissions expenses

Administrative Expenses
- Office salaries expense
- Office supplies expense
- Depreciation expense—office building and equipment

To facilitate control, selling and administrative expenses may be reported by level of responsibility. For example, selling expenses may be reported by products, salespersons, departments, divisions, or territories. Likewise, administrative expenses may be reported by areas such as human resources, computer services, legal, accounting, or finance.

The impact on the financial statements of product and period costs is summarized in Exhibit 11. As product costs are incurred, they are recorded and reported on the balance sheet as *inventory*. When the inventory is sold, the cost of the manufactured product sold is reported as *cost of goods sold* on the income statement. Period costs are reported as *expenses* on the income statement in the period in which they are incurred and, thus, never appear on the balance sheet.

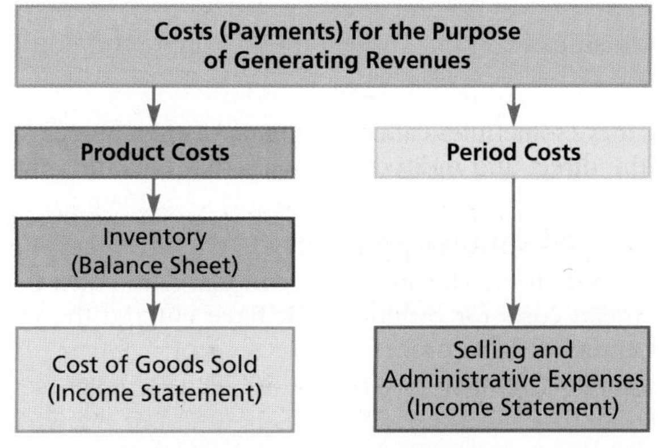

EXHIBIT 11

Product Costs, Period Costs, and the Financial Statements

Example Exercise 1-4 Product and Period Costs 

Identify the following costs as a product cost or a period cost for a baseball glove manufacturer:

a. Leather used to make a baseball glove
b. Cost of endorsement from a professional baseball player
c. Office supplies used at the company headquarters
d. Ink used to print a player's autograph on the baseball glove

Follow My Example 1-4

a. Product cost
b. Period cost
c. Period cost
d. Product cost

Practice Exercises: PE 1-4A, PE 1-4B

Business  **Connection**

OVERHEAD COSTS

Defense contractors such as **General Dynamics**, **Boeing**, and **Lockheed Martin** sell products such as airplanes, ships, and military equipment to the U.S. Department of Defense. Building large products such as these requires a significant investment in facilities and tools, all of which are classified as factory overhead costs. As a result, factory overhead costs are a much larger portion of the cost of goods sold for defense contractors than it is in other industries. For example, a U.S. General Accounting Office study of six defense contractors found that overhead costs were almost one-third of the price of the final product. This is more than three times greater than the factory overhead costs for a laptop computer, which are typically about 10% of the price of the final product.

 Describe and illustrate the following statements for a manufacturing business: balance sheet, statement of cost of goods manufactured, and income statement.

Financial Statements for a Manufacturing Business

The retained earnings and cash flow statements for a manufacturing business are similar to those illustrated in earlier chapters for service and merchandising businesses. However, the balance sheet and income statement for a manufacturing business are more complex. This is because a manufacturer makes the products that it sells and, thus, must record and report product costs. The reporting of product costs primarily affects the balance sheet and the income statement.

Balance Sheet for a Manufacturing Business

A manufacturing business reports three types of inventory on its balance sheet as follows:

- **Materials inventory** (sometimes called raw materials inventory). This inventory consists of the costs of the direct and indirect materials that have not entered the manufacturing process.

  Examples for **Legend Guitars**: Wood, guitar strings, glue, sandpaper
- **Work in process inventory.** This inventory consists of the direct materials, direct labor, and factory overhead costs for products that have entered the manufacturing process, but are not yet completed (in process).

  Example for Legend: Unfinished (partially assembled) guitars

- **Finished goods inventory.** This inventory consists of completed (or finished) products that have not been sold.

  Example for Legend: Unsold guitars

Exhibit 12 illustrates the reporting of inventory on the balance sheet for a merchandising and a manufacturing business. MusicLand Stores, Inc., a retailer of musical instruments, reports only Merchandise Inventory. In contrast, **Legend Guitars**, a manufacturer of guitars, reports Finished Goods, Work in Process, and Materials inventories. In both balance sheets, inventory is reported in the Current Assets section.

EXHIBIT 12

Balance Sheet Presentation of Inventory in Manufacturing and Merchandising Companies

MusicLand Stores, Inc.
Balance Sheet
December 31, 2016

Current assets:	
Cash	$ 25,000
Accounts receivable (net)	85,000
Merchandise inventory	142,000
Supplies	10,000
Total current assets	$ 262,000

Legend Guitars
Balance Sheet
December 31, 2016

Current assets:		
Cash		$ 21,000
Accounts receivable (net)		120,000
Inventories:		
Finished goods	$62,500	
Work in process	24,000	
Materials	35,000	121,500
Supplies		2,000
Total current assets		$ 264,500

Income Statement for a Manufacturing Business

The income statements for merchandising and manufacturing businesses differ primarily in the reporting of the cost of merchandise (goods) *available for sale* and *sold* during the period. These differences are shown in Exhibit 13.

EXHIBIT 13

Income Statements for Merchandising and Manufacturing Businesses

Merchandising Business

Income Statement		
Sales		$XXX
Beginning merchandise inventory	$XXX	
Plus net purchases	XXX	
Merchandise available for sale	$XXX	
Less ending merchandise inventory	XXX	
Cost of merchandise sold		XXX
Gross profit		$XXX

Manufacturing Business

Income Statement		
Sales		$XXX
Beginning finished goods inventory	$XXX	
Plus cost of goods manufactured	XXX	
Cost of finished goods available for sale	$XXX	
Less ending finished goods inventory	XXX	
Cost of goods sold		XXX
Gross profit		$XXX

A merchandising business purchases merchandise ready for resale to customers. The total cost of the **merchandise available for sale** during the period is determined as follows:

Beginning Merchandise Inventory + Net Purchases = Merchandise Available for Sale

The **cost of merchandise sold** is determined as follows:

Cost of Merchandise Available for Sale − Ending Merchandise Inventory = Cost of Merchandise Sold

A manufacturer makes the products it sells, using direct materials, direct labor, and factory overhead. The total cost of making products that are available for sale during the period is called the **cost of goods manufactured.**

The **cost of finished goods available for sale** is determined as follows:

Beginning Finished Goods Inventory + Cost of Goods Manufactured During the Period = Cost of Finished Goods Available for Sale

The **cost of goods sold** is determined as follows:

Cost of Finished Goods Available for Sale − Ending Finished Goods Inventory = Cost of Goods Sold

Cost of goods manufactured is required to determine the *cost of goods sold* and, thus, to prepare the income statement. The cost of goods manufactured is often determined by preparing a **statement of cost of goods manufactured.**[1] This statement summarizes the cost of goods manufactured during the period, as follows:

Statement of Cost of Goods Manufactured

Beginning work in process inventory			$XXX
Direct materials:			
Beginning materials inventory	$XXX		
Purchases	XXX		
Cost of materials available for use	$XXX		
Less ending materials inventory	XXX		
Cost of direct materials used		$XXX	
Direct labor		XXX	
Factory overhead		XXX	
Total manufacturing costs incurred			XXX
Total manufacturing costs			$XXX
Less ending work in process inventory			XXX
Cost of goods manufactured			$XXX

To illustrate, the following data for **Legend Guitars** are used:

	Jan. 1, 2016	Dec. 31, 2016
Inventories:		
Materials	$ 65,000	$ 35,000
Work in process	30,000	24,000
Finished goods	60,000	62,500
Total inventories	$155,000	$121,500
Manufacturing costs incurred during 2016:		
Materials purchased		$100,000
Direct labor		110,000
Factory overhead:		
Indirect labor	$ 24,000	
Depreciation on factory equipment	10,000	
Factory supplies and utility costs	10,000	44,000
Total		$254,000
Sales		$366,000
Selling expenses		20,000
Administrative expenses		15,000

[1] Chapters 2 and 3 describe and illustrate the use of job order and process cost systems. As will be discussed, these systems do not require a statement of cost of goods manufactured.

The statement of cost of goods manufactured is prepared using the following three steps:

- Step 1. Determine the *cost of materials used.*
- Step 2. Determine the *total manufacturing costs incurred.*
- Step 3. Determine the *cost of goods manufactured.*

Exhibit 14 summarizes how manufacturing costs flow to the income statement and balance sheet of a manufacturing business.

EXHIBIT 14

Flow of Manufacturing Costs

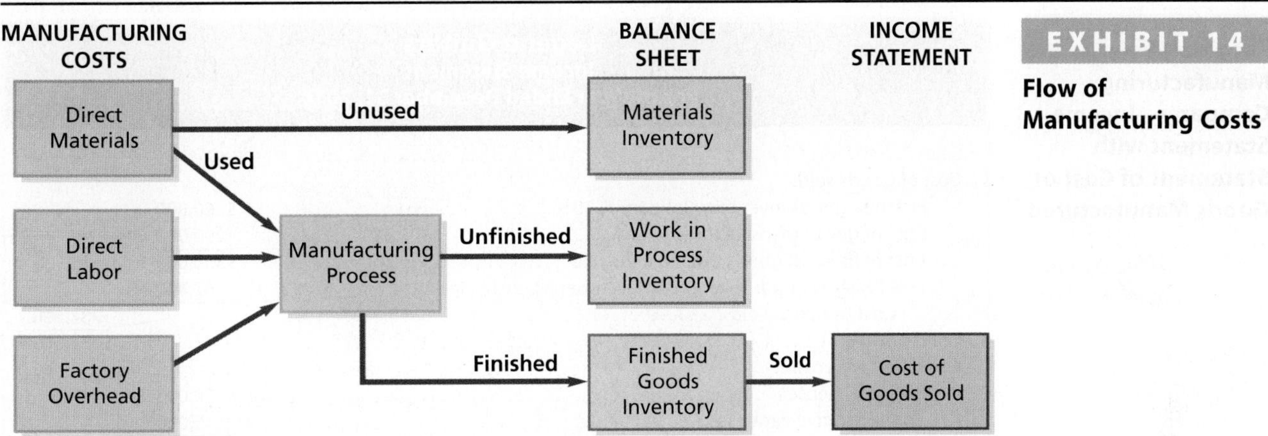

Using the data for **Legend Guitars**, the steps for determining the cost of materials used, total manufacturing costs incurred, and cost of goods manufactured are computed as follows:

Step 1. The *cost of materials used* in production is determined as follows:

Materials inventory, January 1, 2016	$ 65,000
Add materials purchased	100,000
Cost of materials available for use	$ 165,000
Less materials inventory, December 31, 2016	35,000
Cost of direct materials used	$ 130,000

The January 1, 2016 (beginning), materials inventory of $65,000 is added to the cost of materials purchased of $100,000 to yield the $165,000 total cost of materials that are available for use during 2016. Deducting the December 31, 2016 (ending), materials inventory of $35,000 yields the $130,000 cost of direct materials used in production.

Step 2. The *total manufacturing costs incurred* is determined as follows:

Direct materials used in production (Step 1)	$ 130,000
Direct labor	110,000
Factory overhead	44,000
Total manufacturing costs incurred	$284,000

The total manufacturing costs incurred in 2016 of $284,000 are determined by adding the direct materials used in production (Step 1), the direct labor cost, and the factory overhead costs.

Step 3. The *cost of goods manufactured* is determined as follows:

Work in process inventory, January 1, 2016	$ 30,000
Total manufacturing costs incurred (Step 2)	284,000
Total manufacturing costs	$ 314,000
Less work in process inventory, December 31, 2016	24,000
Cost of goods manufactured	$290,000

The cost of goods manufactured of $290,000 is determined by adding the total manufacturing costs incurred (Step 2) to the January 1, 2016 (beginning), work in process inventory of $30,000. This yields total manufacturing costs of $314,000. The December 31, 2016 (ending), work in process inventory of $24,000 is then deducted to determine the cost of goods manufactured of $290,000.

The income statement and statement of cost of goods manufactured for **Legend Guitars** are shown in Exhibit 15.

EXHIBIT 15

Manufacturing Company—Income Statement with Statement of Cost of Goods Manufactured

Legend Guitars
Income Statement
For the Year Ended December 31, 2016

Sales		$366,000
Cost of goods sold:		
Finished goods inventory, January 1, 2016	$ 60,000	
Cost of goods manufactured	290,000	
Cost of finished goods available for sale	$350,000	
Less finished goods inventory, December 31, 2016	62,500	
Cost of goods sold		287,500
Gross profit		$ 78,500
Operating expenses:		
Selling expenses	$ 20,000	
Administrative expenses	15,000	
Total operating expenses		35,000
Net income		$ 43,500

Legend Guitars
Statement of Cost of Goods Manufactured
For the Year Ended December 31, 2016

Work in process inventory, January 1, 2016			$ 30,000
Direct materials:			
Materials inventory, January 1, 2016	$ 65,000		
Purchases	100,000		
Cost of materials available for use	$165,000		
Less materials inventory, December 31, 2016	35,000		
Cost of direct materials used		$130,000	
Direct labor		110,000	
Factory overhead:			
Indirect labor	$ 24,000		
Depreciation on factory equipment	10,000		
Factory supplies and utility costs	10,000		
Total factory overhead		44,000	
Total manufacturing costs incurred			284,000
Total manufacturing costs			$314,000
Less work in process inventory, December 31, 2016			24,000
Cost of goods manufactured			$290,000

Example Exercise 1-5 Cost of Goods Sold, Cost of Goods Manufactured

OBJ 3

Gauntlet Company has the following information for January:

Cost of direct materials used in production	$25,000
Direct labor	35,000
Factory overhead	20,000
Work in process inventory, January 1	30,000
Work in process inventory, January 31	25,000
Finished goods inventory, January 1	15,000
Finished goods inventory, January 31	12,000

For January, determine (a) the cost of goods manufactured and (b) the cost of goods sold.

Follow My Example 1-5

a.	Work in process inventory, January 1		$ 30,000
	Cost of direct materials used in production	$ 25,000	
	Direct labor	35,000	
	Factory overhead	20,000	
	Total manufacturing costs incurred during January		80,000
	Total manufacturing costs		$110,000
	Less work in process inventory, January 31		25,000
	Cost of goods manufactured		$ 85,000
b.	Finished goods inventory, January 1	$ 15,000	
	Cost of goods manufactured	85,000	
	Cost of finished goods available for sale	$100,000	
	Less finished goods inventory, January 31	12,000	
	Cost of goods sold	$ 88,000	

Practice Exercises: PE 1-5A, PE 1-5B

Uses of Managerial Accounting

OBJ 4 Describe the uses of managerial accounting information.

As mentioned earlier, managerial accounting provides information and reports for managers to use in operating a business. Some examples of how managerial accounting could be used by **Legend Guitars** include the following:

- The cost of manufacturing each guitar could be used to determine its selling price.
- Comparing the costs of guitars over time can be used to monitor and control the cost of direct materials, direct labor, and factory overhead.
- Performance reports could be used to identify any large amounts of scrap or employee downtime. For example, large amounts of unusable wood (scrap) after the cutting process should be investigated to determine the underlying cause. Such scrap may be caused by saws that have not been properly maintained.
- A report could analyze the potential efficiencies and dollar savings of purchasing a new computerized saw to speed up the production process.
- A report could analyze how many guitars need to be sold to cover operating costs and expenses. Such information could be used to set monthly selling targets and bonuses for sales personnel.

As the prior examples illustrate, managerial accounting information can be used for a variety of purposes. In the remaining chapters of this text, we examine these and other areas of managerial accounting.

Service  Focus

MANAGERIAL ACCOUNTING IN THE SERVICE INDUSTRY

All businesses can benefit from managerial accounting, whether they manufacture a product or provide a service. Service businesses such as professional service firms, restaurants, maintenance companies, and airlines need managerial accounting information to direct daily operations, plan future operations, and develop business strategies.

For example, **The Walt Disney Company** relies heavily on managerial accounting to manage its operations. Disney uses budgets and financial forecasts to plan costs and allocate resources between its various business units. Based on these budgets and financial forecasts, Disney directs its operations by determining how to staff its theme parks and off cycle its theme park rides for maintenance. Operations are controlled by a variety of qualitative and quantitative metrics that provide feedback on the efficiency and quality of the customer experience. To ensure the best guest experience, Disney Theme Parks manages operations in small business units to maximize management ownership and responsibility. The results of Disney's deployment and use of managerial accounting have been impressive. The Walt Disney Company is typically ranked number 1 in *Fortune*'s listing of the 10 most admired companies for quality.

At a Glance 1

OBJ 1 **Describe managerial accounting and the role of managerial accounting in a business.**

Key Points Managerial accounting is a staff function that supports the management process by providing reports to aid management in planning, directing, controlling, improving, and decision making. This differs from financial accounting, which provides information to users outside of the organization. Managerial accounting reports are designed to meet the specific needs of management and aid management in planning long-term strategies and running the day-to-day operations.

Learning Outcomes	Example Exercises	Practice Exercises
• Describe the differences between financial accounting and managerial accounting.		
• Describe the role of the management accountant in the organization.		
• Describe the role of managerial accounting in the management process.	EE1-1	PE1-1A, 1-1B

Describe and illustrate the following costs: direct and indirect costs; direct materials, direct labor, and factory overhead costs; and product and period costs.

Key Points Manufacturing companies use machinery and labor to convert materials into a finished product. A direct cost can be directly traced to a finished product, while an indirect cost cannot. The cost of a finished product is made up of three components: direct materials, direct labor, and factory overhead.

These three manufacturing costs can be categorized into prime costs (direct materials and direct labor) or conversion costs (direct labor and factory overhead). Product costs consist of the elements of manufacturing cost—direct materials, direct labor, and factory overhead—while period costs consist of selling and administrative expenses.

Learning Outcomes	Example Exercises	Practice Exercises
• Describe a cost object.		
• Classify a cost as a direct or an indirect cost for a cost object.		
• Describe direct materials cost.	**EE1-2**	**PE1-2A, 1-2B**
• Describe direct labor cost.	**EE1-2**	**PE1-2A, 1-2B**
• Describe factory overhead cost.	**EE1-2**	**PE1-2A, 1-2B**
• Describe prime costs and conversion costs.	**EE1-3**	**PE1-3A, 1-3B**
• Describe product costs and period costs.	**EE1-4**	**PE1-4A, 1-4B**

Describe and illustrate the following statements for a manufacturing business: balance sheet, statement of cost of goods manufactured, and income statement.

Key Points The financial statements of manufacturing companies differ from those of merchandising companies. Manufacturing company balance sheets report three types of inventory: materials, work in process, and finished goods. The income statement of manufacturing companies reports the cost of goods sold, which is the total manufacturing cost of the goods sold. The income statement is supported by the statement of cost of goods manufactured, which provides the details of the cost of goods manufactured during the period.

Learning Outcomes	Example Exercises	Practice Exercises
• Describe materials inventory.		
• Describe work in process inventory.		
• Describe finished goods inventory.		
• Describe the differences between merchandising and manufacturing company balance sheets.		
• Prepare a statement of cost of goods manufactured.	**EE1-5**	**PE1-5A, 1-5B**
• Prepare an income statement for a manufacturing company.	**EE1-5**	**PE1-5A, 1-5B**

Describe the uses of managerial accounting information.

Key Points Managers need information to guide their decision making. Managerial accounting provides a variety of information and reports that help managers run the operations of their business.

Learning Outcome	Example Exercises	Practice Exercises
• Describe examples of how managerial accounting aids managers in decision making.		

Key Terms

continuous process improvement (6)
controller (4)
controlling (5)
conversion costs (10)
cost (7)
cost object (7)
cost of finished goods available for sale (14)
cost of goods manufactured (14)
cost of goods sold (14)
cost of merchandise sold (14)
decision making (6)
direct costs (7)
direct labor cost (9)
direct materials cost (8)
directing (5)
factory burden (9)
factory overhead cost (9)
feedback (5)
financial accounting (3)
finished goods inventory (13)
indirect costs (7)
line department (4)
management by exception (5)
management process (5)
managerial accounting (3)
manufacturing overhead (9)
materials inventory (12)
merchandise available for sale (14)
objectives (goals) (5)
operational planning (5)
period costs (10)
planning (5)
prime costs (10)
product costs (10)
staff department (4)
statement of cost of goods manufactured (14)
strategic planning (5)
strategies (5)
work in process inventory (12)

Illustrative Problem

The following is a list of costs that were incurred in producing this textbook:

a. Insurance on the factory building and equipment

b. Salary of the vice president of finance

c. Hourly wages of printing press operators during production

d. Straight-line depreciation on the printing presses used to manufacture the text

e. Electricity used to run the presses during the printing of the text

f. Sales commissions paid to textbook representatives for each text sold

g. Paper on which the text is printed

h. Book covers used to bind the pages

i. Straight-line depreciation on an office building

j. Salaries of staff used to develop artwork for the text

k. Glue used to bind pages to cover

Instructions

With respect to the manufacture and sale of this text, classify each cost as either a product cost or a period cost. Indicate whether each product cost is a direct materials cost, a direct labor cost, or a factory overhead cost. Indicate whether each period cost is a selling expense or an administrative expense.

Solution

	Product Cost			Period Cost	
Cost	**Direct Materials Cost**	**Direct Labor Cost**	**Factory Overhead Cost**	**Selling Expense**	**Administrative Expense**
a.			X		
b.					X
c.		X			
d.			X		
e.			X		
f.				X	
g.	X				
h.	X				
i.					X
j.			X		
k.			X		

Discussion Questions

1. What are the major differences between managerial accounting and financial accounting?
2. a. Differentiate between a department with line responsibility and a department with staff responsibility.
   b. In an organization that has a Sales Department and a Personnel Department, among others, which of the two departments has (1) line responsibility and (2) staff responsibility?
3. What manufacturing cost term is used to describe the cost of materials that are an integral part of the manufactured end product?
4. Distinguish between prime costs and conversion costs.
5. What is the difference between a product cost and a period cost?
6. Name the three inventory accounts for a manufacturing business, and describe what each balance represents at the end of an accounting period.
7. In what order should the three inventories of a manufacturing business be presented on the balance sheet?
8. What are the three categories of manufacturing costs included in the cost of finished goods and the cost of work in process?
9. For a manufacturer, what is the description of the account that is comparable to a merchandising business's cost of merchandise sold?
10. How does the Cost of Goods Sold section of the income statement differ between merchandising and manufacturing companies?

Practice Exercises

EE 1-1 *p. 6* **PE 1-1A Management process** **OBJ. 1**

Three phases of the management process are controlling, planning, and decision making. Match the following descriptions to the proper phase:

Phase of management process	Description
Controlling	a. Monitoring the operating results of implemented plans and comparing the actual results with expected results
Planning	b. Inherent in planning, directing, controlling, and improving
Decision making	c. Long-range courses of action

EE 1-1 *p. 6*

PE 1-1B Management process — OBJ. 1

Three phases of the management process are planning, directing, and controlling. Match the following descriptions to the proper phase:

Phase of management process	Description
Planning	a. Developing long-range courses of action to achieve goals.
Directing	b. Isolating significant departures from plans for further investigation and possible remedial action. It may lead to a revision of future plans.
Controlling	c. Process by which managers, given their assigned levels of responsibilities, run day-to-day operations.

EE 1-2 *p. 9*

PE 1-2A Direct materials, direct labor, and factory overhead — OBJ. 2

Identify the following costs as direct materials (DM), direct labor (DL), or factory overhead (FO) for an automobile manufacturer:

a. Wages of employees that operate painting equipment
b. Wages of the plant supervisor
c. Steel
d. Oil used for assembly line machinery

SHOW ME HOW

EE 1-2 *p. 9*

PE 1-2B Direct materials, direct labor, and factory overhead — OBJ. 2

Identify the following costs as direct materials (DM), direct labor (DL), or factory overhead (FO) for a magazine publisher:

a. Staples used to bind magazines
b. Wages of printing machine employees
c. Maintenance on printing machines
d. Paper used in the magazine

SHOW ME HOW

EE 1-3 *p. 10*

PE 1-3A Prime and conversion costs — OBJ. 2

Identify the following costs as a prime cost (P), conversion cost (C), or both (B) for an automobile manufacturer:

a. Wages of employees that operate painting equipment
b. Wages of the plant manager
c. Steel
d. Oil used for assembly line machinery

EE 1-3 *p. 10*

PE 1-3B Prime and conversion costs — OBJ. 2

Identify the following costs as a prime cost (P), conversion cost (C), or both (B) for a magazine publisher:

a. Paper used for the magazine
b. Wages of printing machine employees
c. Glue used to bind magazine
d. Maintenance on printing machines

EE 1-4 *p. 12*

PE 1-4A Product and period costs — OBJ. 2

Identify the following costs as a product cost or a period cost for an automobile manufacturer:

a. Steel
b. Wages of employees that operate painting equipment
c. Rent on office building
d. Sales staff salaries

EE 1-4 *p. 12*

SHOW ME HOW

PE 1-4B Product and period costs **OBJ. 2**

Identify the following costs as a product cost or a period cost for a magazine publisher:

a. Sales salaries
b. Paper used for the magazine
c. Maintenance on printing machines
d. Depreciation expense—corporate headquarters

EE 1-5 *p. 17*

SHOW ME HOW

PE 1-5A Cost of goods sold, cost of goods manufactured **OBJ. 3**

Timbuk 3 Company has the following information for March:

Cost of direct materials used in production	$21,000
Direct labor	54,250
Factory overhead	35,000
Work in process inventory, March 1	87,500
Work in process inventory, March 31	92,750
Finished goods inventory, March 1	36,750
Finished goods inventory, March 31	42,000

For March, determine (a) the cost of goods manufactured and (b) the cost of goods sold.

EE 1-5 *p. 17*

SHOW ME HOW

PE 1-5B Cost of goods sold, cost of goods manufactured **OBJ. 3**

Ebony Company has the following information for July:

Cost of direct materials used in production	$67,200
Direct labor	88,000
Factory overhead	44,800
Work in process inventory, July 1	32,800
Work in process inventory, July 31	29,600
Finished goods inventory, July 1	37,600
Finished goods inventory, July 31	27,200

For July, determine (a) the cost of goods manufactured and (b) the cost of goods sold.

Exercises

EX 1-1 Classifying costs as materials, labor, or factory overhead **OBJ. 2**

Indicate whether each of the following costs of an automobile manufacturer would be classified as direct materials cost, direct labor cost, or factory overhead cost:

a. Depreciation of robotic assembly line equipment
b. V8 automobile engine
c. Steering wheel
d. Wheels
e. Painting safety masks for employees working in the paint room
f. Salary of test driver
g. Glass used in the vehicle's windshield
h. Wages of assembly line worker

EX 1-2 Classifying costs as materials, labor, or factory overhead **OBJ. 2**

Indicate whether the following costs of **Procter & Gamble**, a maker of consumer products, would be classified as direct materials cost, direct labor cost, or factory overhead cost:

a. Plant manager salary for the Iowa City, Iowa, plant
b. Maintenance supplies
c. Salary of process engineers
d. Wages paid to Packaging Department employees in the Bear River City, Utah, paper products plant
e. Scents and fragrances used in making soaps and detergents
f. Wages of production line employees at the Pineville, Louisiana, soap and detergent plant
g. Depreciation on assembly line in the Mehoopany, Pennsylvania, paper products plant
h. Packaging materials
i. Resins for body wash products
j. Depreciation on the Auburn, Maine, manufacturing plant

EX 1-3 Classifying costs as factory overhead **OBJ. 2**

Which of the following items are properly classified as part of factory overhead for **Ford Motor Company**, a maker of heavy automobiles and trucks?

a. Plant manager's salary at Buffalo, New York, stamping plant, which manufactures auto and truck subassemblies
b. Depreciation on Flat Rock, Michigan, assembly plant
c. Dividends paid to shareholders
d. Machine lubricant used to maintain the assembly line at the Louisville, Kentucky, assembly plant
e. Leather to be used on vehicles that have leather interiors
f. Depreciation on mechanical robots used on the assembly line
g. Consultant fees for a study of production line efficiency
h. Dealership sales incentives
i. Vice president of human resources's salary
j. Property taxes on the Detriot, Michigan, headquarters building

EX 1-4 Classifying costs as product or period costs **OBJ. 2**

For apparel manufacturer **Abercrombie & Fitch, Inc.**, classify each of the following costs as either a product cost or a period cost:

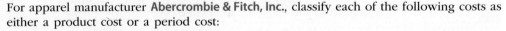

a. Research and development costs
b. Depreciation on sewing machines
c. Fabric used during production
d. Depreciation on office equipment
e. Advertising expenses
f. Repairs and maintenance costs for sewing machines
g. Salary of production quality control supervisor
h. Utility costs for office building
i. Sales commissions
j. Salaries of distribution center personnel
k. Wages of sewing machine operators
l. Factory janitorial supplies
m. Chief financial officer's salary
n. Travel costs of media relations employees
o. Factory supervisors' salaries
p. Oil used to lubricate sewing machines
q. Property taxes on factory building and equipment

EX 1-5 Concepts and terminology OBJ. 1, 2

From the choices presented in parentheses, choose the appropriate term for completing each of the following sentences:

a. Advertising costs are usually viewed as (period, product) costs.

b. Feedback is often used to (improve, direct) operations.

c. Payments of cash or the commitment to pay cash in the future for the purpose of generating revenues are (costs, expenses).

d. A product, sales territory, department, or activity to which costs are traced is called a (direct cost, cost object).

e. The balance sheet of a manufacturer would include an account for (cost of goods sold, work in process inventory).

f. Factory overhead costs combined with direct labor costs are called (prime, conversion) costs.

g. The implementation of automatic, robotic factory equipment normally (increases, decreases) the direct labor component of product costs.

EX 1-6 Concepts and terminology OBJ. 1, 2

From the choices presented in parentheses, choose the appropriate term for completing each of the following sentences:

a. The phase of the management process that uses process information to eliminate the source of problems in a process so that the process delivers the correct product in the correct quantities is called (directing, improving).

b. Direct labor costs combined with factory overhead costs are called (prime, conversion) costs.

c. The salaries of sales people are normally considered a (period, product) cost.

d. The plant manager's salary would be considered (direct, indirect) to the product.

e. Long-term plans are called (strategic, operational) plans.

f. Materials for use in production are called (supplies, materials inventory).

g. An example of factory overhead is (electricity used to run assembly line, CEO salary).

EX 1-7 Classifying costs in a service company OBJ. 2

A partial list of the costs for Wisconsin and Minnesota Railroad, a short hauler of freight, follows. Classify each cost as either indirect or direct. For purposes of classifying each cost, use the train as the cost object.

a. Cost to lease (rent) railroad cars

b. Cost of track and bed (ballast) replacement

c. Diesel fuel costs

d. Cost to lease (rent) train locomotives

e. Depreciation of terminal facilities

f. Maintenance costs of right of way, bridges, and buildings

g. Salaries of dispatching and communications personnel

h. Headquarters information technology support staff salaries

i. Safety training costs

j. Wages of train engineers

k. Wages of switch and classification yard personnel

l. Costs of accident cleanup

EX 1-8 Classifying costs **OBJ. 2, 3**

The following report was prepared for evaluating the performance of the plant manager of Marching Ants Inc. Evaluate and correct this report.

Marching Ants Inc.
Manufacturing Costs
For the Quarter Ended June 30, 2016

Materials used in production (including $56,200 of indirect materials)	$ 607,500
Direct labor (including $84,400 maintenance salaries)	562,500
Factory overhead:	
Supervisor salaries	517,500
Heat, light, and power	140,650
Sales salaries	348,750
Promotional expenses	315,000
Insurance and property taxes—plant	151,900
Insurance and property taxes—corporate offices	219,400
Depreciation—plant and equipment	123,750
Depreciation—corporate offices	90,000
Total	$3,076,950

EX 1-9 Financial statements of a manufacturing firm **OBJ. 3**

✔ a. Net income, $129,230

SHOW ME HOW

The following events took place for Video Wave Manufacturing Company during January 2016, the first month of its operations as a producer of digital video monitors:

a. Purchased $133,200 of materials.
b. Used $94,080 of direct materials in production.
c. Incurred $180,320 of direct labor wages.
d. Incurred $211,680 of factory overhead.
e. Transferred $425,320 of work in process to finished goods.
f. Sold goods with a cost of $365,000.
g. Earned revenues of $652,000.
h. Incurred $86,520 of selling expense.
i. Incurred $71,250 of administrative expense.

Using the information given, complete the following:

a. Prepare the January 2016 income statement for Video Wave Manufacturing Company.
b. Determine the inventory balances at the end of the first month of operations.

EX 1-10 Manufacturing company balance sheet **OBJ. 3**

SHOW ME HOW

Partial balance sheet data for Flat Top Company at December 31, 2016, are as follows:

Finished goods inventory	$ 40,250	Supplies	$ 71,300
Prepaid insurance	27,500	Materials inventory	87,500
Accounts receivable	105,000	Cash	112,000
Work in process inventory	157,500		

Prepare the Current Assets section of Flat Top Company's balance sheet at December 31, 2016.

EX 1-11 Cost of direct materials used in production for a manufacturing company **OBJ. 3**

SHOW ME HOW

Rextacular Manufacturing Company reported the following materials data for the month ending June 30, 2016:

Materials purchased	$828,000
Materials inventory, June 1	279,000
Materials inventory, June 30	252,000

Determine the cost of direct materials used in production by Rextacular during the month ended June 30, 2016.

✔ e. $9,800

SHOW ME HOW

EX 1-12 Cost of goods manufactured for a manufacturing company OBJ. 3

Two items are omitted from each of the following three lists of cost of goods manufactured statement data. Determine the amounts of the missing items, identifying them by letter.

Work in process inventory, August 1	$ 22,400	$ 50,400	(e)
Total manufacturing costs incurred during August	156,800	(c)	58,800
Total manufacturing costs	(a)	$294,000	$68,600
Work in process inventory, August 31	33,600	67,200	(f)
Cost of goods manufactured	(b)	(d)	$60,200

SHOW ME HOW

EX 1-13 Cost of goods manufactured for a manufacturing company OBJ. 3

The following information is available for Ethtridge Manufacturing Company for the month ending January 31, 2016:

Cost of direct materials used in production	$390,000
Direct labor	336,000
Work in process inventory, January 1	162,000
Work in process inventory, January 31	170,400
Total factory overhead	234,000

Determine Ethtridge's cost of goods manufactured for the month ended January 31, 2016.

✔ d. $198,800

EX 1-14 Income statement for a manufacturing company OBJ. 3

Two items are omitted from each of the following three lists of cost of goods sold data from a manufacturing company income statement. Determine the amounts of the missing items, identifying them by letter.

Finished goods inventory, June 1	$ 61,600	$ 46,200	(e)
Cost of goods manufactured	329,000	(c)	484,800
Cost of finished goods available for sale	(a)	$260,400	$540,000
Finished goods inventory, June 30	72,800	61,600	(f)
Cost of goods sold	(b)	(d)	$513,600

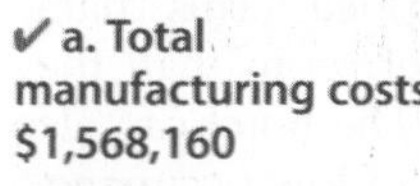

✔ a. Total manufacturing costs, $1,568,160

SHOW ME HOW

EX 1-15 Statement of cost of goods manufactured for a manufacturing company OBJ. 3

Cost data for Mix-A-Lot Manufacturing Company for the month ended March 31, 2016, are as follows:

Inventories	**March 1**	**March 31**
Materials	$315,000	$277,200
Work in process	214,200	239,400
Finished goods	163,800	189,000

Direct labor	$567,000
Materials purchased during May	604,800
Factory overhead incurred during May:	
Indirect labor	60,480
Machinery depreciation	36,000
Heat, light, and power	12,600
Supplies	10,080
Property taxes	8,820
Miscellaneous costs	16,380

a. Prepare a cost of goods manufactured statement for March 2016.

b. Determine the cost of goods sold for March 2016.

EX 1-16 Cost of goods sold, profit margin, and net income for a manufacturing company OBJ. 3

✔ **a. Cost of goods sold, $457,450**

SHOW ME HOW

The following information is available for Crouching Alligator Manufacturing Company for the month ending October 31, 2016:

Cost of goods manufactured	$450,000
Selling expenses	144,500
Administrative expenses	75,900
Sales	911,250
Finished goods inventory, July 1	101,250
Finished goods inventory, July 31	93,800

For the month ended October 31, 2016, determine Crouching Alligator's (a) cost of goods sold, (b) gross profit, and (c) net income.

EX 1-17 Cost flow relationships OBJ. 3

✔ **a. $330,000**

SHOW ME HOW

The following information is available for the first month of operations of Bahadir Company, a manufacturer of mechanical pencils:

Sales	$792,000
Gross profit	462,000
Cost of goods manufactured	396,000
Indirect labor	171,600
Factory depreciation	26,400
Materials purchased	244,200
Total manufacturing costs for the period	455,400
Materials inventory, ending	33,000

Using the information given, determine the following missing amounts:

a. Cost of goods sold
b. Finished goods inventory at the end of the month
c. Direct materials cost
d. Direct labor cost
e. Work in process inventory at the end of the month

EX 1-18 Uses of managerial accounting in a service company

Priceline.com allows customers to bid on hotel rooms by "naming their price." This "name your price" process allows customers to obtain a better rate on a hotel room than they might be able to obtain by reserving their room directly from the hotel. The hotel can also benefit from this transaction by filling empty hotel rooms during periods of low occupancy.

Natalie Mooney bids $85 for a night's stay at the Hotel Monaco in Seattle on Saturday August 10. The Hotel Monaco is not fully booked that evening and would likely accept any reasonable bids. How might the Hotel Monaco use managerial accounting information to decide whether or not to accept Natalie's bid?

Problems: Series A

PR 1-1A Classifying costs OBJ. 2

The following is a list of costs that were incurred in the production and sale of large commercial airplanes:

a. Salary of chief compliance officer of company
b. Power used by painting equipment
c. Instrument panel installed in the airplane cockpit
d. Annual bonus paid to the chief operating officer of the company
e. Turbo-charged airplane engine
f. Interior trim material used throughout the airplane cabin

g. Cost of normal scrap from production of airplane body
h. Hourly wages of employees that assemble the airplane
i. Salary of the marketing department personnel
j. Cost of paving the headquarters employee parking lot
k. Cost of electrical wiring throughout the airplane
l. Cost of electronic guidance system installed in the airplane cockpit
m. Salary of plant manager
n. Cost of miniature replicas of the airplane used to promote and market the airplane
o. Human resources department costs for the year
p. Metal used for producing the airplane body
q. Annual fee to a celebrity to promote the aircraft
r. Hydraulic pumps used in the airplane's flight control system
s. Yearly cost of the maintenance contract for robotic equipment
t. Prebuilt leather seats installed in the first-class cabin
u. Depreciation on factory equipment
v. Special advertising campaign in *Aviation World* magazine
w. Oil to lubricate factory equipment
x. Masks for use by painters in painting the airplane body
y. Decals for cockpit door, the cost of which is immaterial to the cost of the final product
z. Salary of chief financial officer

Instructions

Classify each cost as either a product cost or a period cost. Indicate whether each product cost is a direct materials cost, a direct labor cost, or a factory overhead cost. Indicate whether each period cost is a selling expense or an administrative expense. Use the following tabular headings for your answer, placing an "X" in the appropriate column:

	Product Costs			Period Costs	
Cost	**Direct Materials Cost**	**Direct Labor Cost**	**Factory Overhead Cost**	**Selling Expense**	**Administrative Expense**

PR 1-2A Classifying costs

OBJ. 2

The following is a list of costs incurred by several businesses:

a. Cost of fabric used by clothing manufacturer
b. Maintenance and repair costs for factory equipment
c. Rent for a warehouse used to store work in process and finished products
d. Wages of production quality control personnel
e. Oil lubricants for factory plant and equipment
f. Depreciation of robot used to assemble a product
g. Travel costs of marketing executives to annual sales meeting
h. Depreciation of copying machines used by the Marketing Department
i. Fees charged by collection agency on past-due customer accounts
j. Electricity used to operate factory machinery
k. Maintenance costs for factory equipment
l. Pens, paper, and other supplies used by the Accounting Department in preparing various managerial reports
m. Charitable contribution to United Fund
n. Depreciation of microcomputers used in the factory to coordinate and monitor the production schedules
o. Fees paid to lawn service for office grounds upkeep

(Continued)

p. Cost of sewing machine needles used by a shirt manufacturer
q. Cost of plastic for a telephone being manufactured
r. Telephone charges by president's office
s. Cost of 30-second television commercial
t. Surgeon's fee for heart bypass surgery
u. Depreciation of tools used in production
v. Wages of a machine operator on the production line
w. Salary of the vice president of manufacturing operations
x. Factory janitorial supplies

Instructions

Classify each of the preceding costs as a product cost or period cost. Indicate whether each product cost is a direct materials cost, a direct labor cost, or a factory overhead cost. Indicate whether each period cost is a selling expense or an administrative expense. Use the following tabular headings for preparing your answer, placing an "X" in the appropriate column:

	Product Costs			Period Costs	
Cost	Direct Materials Cost	Direct Labor Cost	Factory Overhead Cost	Selling Expense	Administrative Expense

PR 1-3A Cost classifications for a service company

OBJ. 2

A partial list of Foothills Medical Center's costs follows:

a. Cost of patient meals
b. Nurses' salaries
c. Depreciation of X-ray equipment
d. Utility costs of the hospital
e. Salary of intensive care personnel
f. Cost of X-ray test
g. Operating room supplies used on patients (catheters, sutures, etc.)
h. Salary of the nutritionist
i. General maintenance of the hospital
j. Cost of new heart wing
k. Cost of drugs used for patients
l. Cost of advertising hospital services on television
m. Cost of improvements on the employee parking lot
n. Cost of intravenous solutions used for patients
o. Training costs for nurses
p. Cost of laundry services for operating room personnel
q. Doctor's fee
r. Overtime incurred in the Patient Records Department due to a computer failure
s. Cost of blood tests
t. Cost of maintaining the staff and visitors' cafeteria
u. Depreciation on patient rooms

Instructions

1. What would be Foothills Medical Center's most logical definition for the final cost object?
2. Identify whether each of the costs is to be classified as direct or indirect. For purposes of classifying each cost as direct or indirect, use the patient as the cost object.

PR 1-4A Manufacturing income statement, statement of cost of goods manufactured OBJ. 2, 3

✔ 1. b. Volt, $516,000

Several items are omitted from the income statement and cost of goods manufactured statement data for two different companies for the month of December 2016:

	Prius Company	Volt Company
Materials inventory, December 1	$ 280,280	$ 177,000
Materials inventory, December 31	(a)	180,000
Materials purchased	712,800	342,000
Cost of direct materials used in production	752,400	(a)
Direct labor	1,058,400	(b)
Factory overhead	327,600	180,000
Total manufacturing costs incurred during December	(b)	1,035,000
Total manufacturing costs	2,678,400	1,477,500
Work in process inventory, December 1	540,000	442,500
Work in process inventory, December 31	453,600	(c)
Cost of goods manufactured	(c)	1,024,500
Finished goods inventory, December 1	475,200	204,000
Finished goods inventory, December 31	496,800	(d)
Sales	4,140,000	1,675,500
Cost of goods sold	(d)	1,051,500
Gross profit	(e)	(e)
Operating expenses	540,000	(f)
Net income	(f)	384,000

Instructions

1. Determine the amounts of the missing items, identifying them by letter.
2. Prepare Volt Company's statement of cost of goods manufactured for December.
3. Prepare Volt Company's income statement for December.

PR 1-5A Statement of cost of goods manufactured and income statement for a manufacturing company OBJ. 2, 3

✔ 1. Cost of goods manufactured, $1,516,570

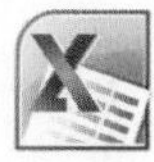

SHOW ME HOW

The following information is available for The NewQuest Corporation for 2016:

Inventories	January 1	December 31
Materials	$351,000	$436,800
Work in process	631,800	592,800
Finished goods	608,400	576,000

Advertising expense	$ 296,400
Depreciation expense—office equipment	42,120
Depreciation expense—factory equipment	56,160
Direct labor	670,800
Heat, light, and power—factory	22,460
Indirect labor	78,750
Materials purchased	659,800
Office salaries expense	185,000
Property taxes—factory	18,500
Property taxes—office building	32,400
Rent expense—factory	32,000
Sales	3,010,000
Sales salaries expense	420,000
Supplies—factory	15,400
Miscellaneous costs—factory	9,500

Instructions

1. Prepare the 2016 statement of cost of goods manufactured.
2. Prepare the 2016 income statement.

Problems: Series B

PR 1-1B Classifying costs **OBJ. 2**

The following is a list of costs that were incurred in the production and sale of lawn mowers:

a. Premiums on insurance policy for factory buildings
b. Tires for lawn mowers
c. Filter for spray gun used to paint the lawn mowers
d. Paint used to coat the lawn mowers, the cost of which is immaterial to the cost of the final product
e. Plastic for outside housing of lawn mowers
f. Salary of factory supervisor
g. Hourly wages of operators of robotic machinery used in production
h. Engine oil used in mower engines prior to shipment
i. Salary of vice president of marketing
j. Property taxes on the factory building and equipment
k. Cost of advertising in a national magazine
l. Gasoline engines used for lawn mowers
m. Electricity used to run the robotic machinery
n. Straight-line depreciation on the robotic machinery used to manufacture the lawn mowers
o. Salary of quality control supervisor who inspects each lawn mower before it is shipped
p. Attorney fees for drafting a new lease for headquarters offices
q. Payroll taxes on hourly assembly line employees
r. Telephone charges for company controller's office
s. Steering wheels for lawn mowers
t. Factory cafeteria cashier's wages
u. Cash paid to outside firm for janitorial services for factory
v. Maintenance costs for new robotic factory equipment, based on hours of usage
w. Cost of boxes used in packaging lawn mowers
x. License fees for use of patent for lawn mower blade, based on the number of lawn mowers produced
y. Steel used in producing the lawn mowers
z. Commissions paid to sales representatives, based on the number of lawn mowers sold

Instructions

Classify each cost as either a product cost or a period cost. Indicate whether each product cost is a direct materials cost, a direct labor cost, or a factory overhead cost. Indicate whether each period cost is a selling expense or an administrative expense. Use the following tabular headings for your answer, placing an "X" in the appropriate column:

	Product Costs			Period Costs	
Cost	Direct Materials Cost	Direct Labor Cost	Factory Overhead Cost	Selling Expense	Administrative Expense

PR 1-2B Classifying costs

OBJ. 2

The following is a list of costs incurred by several businesses:

a. Salary of quality control supervisor
b. Packing supplies for products sold. These supplies are a very small portion of the total cost of the product.
c. Factory operating supplies
d. Depreciation of factory equipment
e. Hourly wages of warehouse laborers
f. Wages of company controller's secretary
g. Maintenance and repair costs for factory equipment
h. Paper used by commercial printer
i. Entertainment expenses for sales representatives
j. Protective glasses for factory machine operators
k. Sales commissions
l. Cost of hogs for meat processor
m. Cost of telephone operators for a toll-free hotline to help customers operate products
n. Hard drives for a microcomputer manufacturer
o. Lumber used by furniture manufacturer
p. Wages of a machine operator on the production line
q. First-aid supplies for factory workers
r. Tires for an automobile manufacturer
s. Paper used by Computer Department in processing various managerial reports
t. Seed for grain farmer
u. Health insurance premiums paid for factory workers
v. Costs of operating a research laboratory
w. Costs for television advertisement
x. Executive bonus for vice president of marketing

Instructions

Classify each of the preceding costs as a product cost or period cost. Indicate whether each product cost is a direct materials cost, a direct labor cost, or a factory overhead cost. Indicate whether each period cost is a selling expense or an administrative expense. Use the following tabular headings for preparing your answer. Place an "X" in the appropriate column.

	Product Costs			Period Costs	
Cost	Direct Materials Cost	Direct Labor Cost	Factory Overhead Cost	Selling Expense	Administrative Expense

PR 1-3B Cost classifications for a service company

OBJ. 2

A partial list of The Grand Hotel's costs follows:

a. Cost to mail a customer survey
b. Wages of convention setup employees
c. Pay-per-view movie rental costs (in rooms)
d. Cost of food
e. Cost of room mini-bar supplies
f. Training for hotel restaurant servers
g. Cost to paint lobby

(Continued)

h. Cost of laundering towels and bedding
i. Champagne for guests
j. Salary of the hotel manager
k. Depreciation of the hotel
l. Cost of valet parking
m. Wages of bellhops
n. Cost to replace lobby furniture
o. Cost of advertising in local newspaper
p. Wages of desk clerks
q. Wages of maids
r. Cost of new carpeting
s. Guest room telephone costs for long-distance calls
t. Cost of soaps and shampoos for rooms
u. Utility cost
v. Wages of kitchen employees
w. General maintenance supplies

Instructions

1. What would be The Grand Hotel's most logical definition for the final cost object?
2. Identify whether each of the costs is to be classified as direct or indirect. For purposes of classifying each cost as direct or indirect, use the hotel guest as the cost object.

PR 1-4B Manufacturing income statement, statement of cost of goods manufactured **OBJ. 2, 3**

✓1. c. On Company, $800,800

Several items are omitted from the income statement and cost of goods manufactured statement data for two different companies for the month of December 2016:

	On Company	Off Company
Materials inventory, December 1	$ 65,800	$ 195,300
Materials inventory, December 31	(a)	91,140
Materials purchased	282,800	(a)
Cost of direct materials used in production	317,800	(b)
Direct labor	387,800	577,220
Factory overhead	148,400	256,060
Total manufacturing costs incurred in December	(b)	1,519,000
Total manufacturing costs	973,000	1,727,320
Work in process inventory, December 1	119,000	208,320
Work in process inventory, December 31	172,200	(c)
Cost of goods manufactured	(c)	1,532,020
Finished goods inventory, December 1	224,000	269,080
Finished goods inventory, December 31	197,400	(d)
Sales	1,127,000	1,944,320
Cost of goods sold	(d)	1,545,040
Gross profit	(e)	(e)
Operating expenses	117,600	(f)
Net income	(f)	164,920

Instructions

1. Determine the amounts of the missing items, identifying them by letter.
2. Prepare On Company's statement of cost of goods manufactured for December.
3. Prepare On Company's income statement for December.

PR 1-5B Statement of cost of goods manufactured and income statement for a manufacturing company OBJ. 2, 3

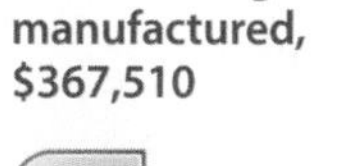
✔1. Cost of goods manufactured, $367,510

SHOW ME HOW

The following information is available for Shanika Company for 2016:

Inventories	January 1	December 31
Materials	$ 77,350	$ 95,550
Work in process	109,200	96,200
Finished goods	113,750	100,100

Advertising expense	$ 68,250
Depreciation expense—office equipment	22,750
Depreciation expense—factory equipment	14,560
Direct labor	186,550
Heat, light, and power—factory	5,850
Indirect labor	23,660
Materials purchased	123,500
Office salaries expense	77,350
Property taxes—factory	4,095
Property taxes—headquarters building	13,650
Rent expense—factory	6,825
Sales	864,500
Sales salaries expense	136,500
Supplies—factory	3,250
Miscellaneous costs—factory	4,420

Instructions

1. Prepare the 2016 statement of cost of goods manufactured.
2. Prepare the 2016 income statement.

Cases & Projects

CP 1-1 Ethics and professional conduct in business

H. Jeckel Manufacturing Company allows employees to purchase, at cost, manufacturing materials, such as metal and lumber, for personal use. To purchase materials for personal use, an employee must complete a materials requisition form, which must then be approved by the employee's immediate supervisor. Fred Rubble, an assistant cost accountant, charges the employee an amount based on H. Jeckel's net purchase cost.

Fred Rubble is in the process of replacing a deck on his home and has requisitioned lumber for personal use, which has been approved in accordance with company policy. In computing the cost of the lumber, Fred reviewed all the purchase invoices for the past year. He then used the lowest price to compute the amount due the company for the lumber.

Discuss whether Fred behaved in an ethical manner.

CP 1-2 Financial versus managerial accounting

The following statement was made by the vice president of finance of The Muppet Company: "The managers of a company should use the same information as the shareholders of the firm. When managers use the same information in guiding their internal operations as shareholders use in evaluating their investments, the managers will be aligned with the stockholders' profit objectives."

Respond to the vice president's statement.

CP 1-3 Managerial accounting in the management process

For each of the following managers, describe how managerial accounting could be used to satisfy strategic or operational objectives:

1. The vice president of the Information Systems Division of a bank.
2. A hospital administrator.
3. The chief executive officer of a food company. The food company is divided into three divisions: Nonalcoholic Beverages, Snack Foods, and Fast Food Restaurants.
4. The manager of the local campus copy shop.

CP 1-4 Classifying costs

Geek Chic Company provides computer repair services for the community. Obie Won's computer was not working, and he called Geek Chic for a home repair visit. Geek Chic Company's technician arrived at 2:00 P.M. to begin work. By 4:00 P.M. the problem was diagnosed as a failed circuit board. Unfortunately, the technician did not have a new circuit board in the truck because the technician's previous customer had the same problem, and a board was used on that visit. Replacement boards were available back at Geek Chic Company's shop. Therefore, the technician drove back to the shop to retrieve a replacement board. From 4:00 to 5:00 P.M., Geek Chic Company's technician drove the round trip to retrieve the replacement board from the shop.

At 5:00 P.M. the technician was back on the job at Obie's home. The replacement procedure is somewhat complex because a variety of tests must be performed once the board is installed. The job was completed at 6:00 P.M.

Obie's repair bill showed the following:

Circuit board	$100
Labor charges	300
Total	$400

Obie was surprised at the size of the bill and asked for some greater detail supporting the calculations. Geek Chic Company responded with the following explanations:

Cost of materials:	
Purchase price of circuit board	$ 80
Markup on purchase price to cover storage and handling	20
Total materials charge	$100

The labor charge per hour is detailed as follows:

2:00–3:00 P.M.	$ 70
3:00–4:00 P.M.	60
4:00–5:00 P.M.	80
5:00–6:00 P.M.	90
Total labor charge	$300

Further explanations in the differences in the hourly rates are as follows:

First hour:	
Base labor rate	$42
Fringe benefits	10
Overhead (other than storage and handling)	8
Total base labor rate	$60
Additional charge for first hour of any job to cover the cost of vehicle depreciation, fuel, and employee time in transit. A 30-minute transit time is assumed.	10
	$70

Third hour:	
Base labor rate	$60
The trip back to the shop includes vehicle depreciation and fuel; therefore, a charge was added to the hourly rate to cover these costs. The round trip took an hour	20
	$80
Fourth hour:	
Base labor rate	$60
Overtime premium for time worked in excess of an eight-hour day (starting at 5:00 P.M.) is equal to 1.5 times the base rate	30
	$90

1. If you were in Obie's position, how would you respond to the bill? Are there parts of the bill that appear incorrect to you? If so, what argument would you employ to convince Geek Chic Company that the bill is too high?
2. Use the headings that follow to construct a table. Fill in the table by first listing the costs identified in the activity in the left-hand column. For each cost, place a check mark in the appropriate column identifying the correct cost classification. Assume that each service call is a job.

Cost	Direct Materials	Direct Labor	Overhead

CP 1-5 Using managerial accounting information

The following situations describe decision scenarios that could use managerial accounting information:

1. The manager of High Times Restaurant wishes to determine the price to charge for various lunch plates.
2. By evaluating the cost of leftover materials, the plant manager of a precision tool facility wishes to determine how effectively the plant is being run.
3. The division controller of West Coast Supplies needs to determine the cost of products left in inventory.
4. The manager of the Maintenance Department of a large manufacturing company wishes to plan next year's anticipated expenditures.

For each situation, discuss how managerial accounting information could be used.

CP 1-6 Classifying costs

Group Project

With a group of students, visit a local copy and graphics shop or a pizza restaurant. As you observe the operation, consider the costs associated with running the business. As a group, identify as many costs as you can and classify them according to the following table headings:

Cost	Direct Materials	Direct Labor	Overhead	Selling Expenses

NEIL LUPIN/REDFERNS/GETTY IMAGES

CHAPTER 2

Job Order Costing

Paul Stanley's Guitar

As we discussed in Chapter 1, Paul Stanley of the legendary rock band **KISS** uses a custom-made guitar built by **Washburn Guitars**. In fact, Paul Stanley designed his guitar in partnership with Washburn Guitars, as have other rock stars like Dan Donnegan of the rock band **Disturbed**. Washburn's guitars are precision instruments that require high-quality materials and careful craftsmanship. As a result, amateurs and professionals are willing to pay between $1,100 and $10,000 for a PS (Paul Stanley) Series guitar. In order for Washburn to stay in business, the purchase price of the guitar must be greater than the cost of producing the guitar. So, how does Washburn determine the cost of producing a guitar?

Costs associated with creating a guitar include materials such as wood and strings, the wages of employees who build the guitar, and factory overhead. To determine the purchase price of Paul Stanley's guitar, Washburn identifies and records the costs that go into the guitar during each step of the manufacturing process. As the guitar moves through the production process, the costs of direct materials, direct labor, and factory overhead are recorded. When the guitar is complete, the costs that have been recorded are added up to determine the cost of Paul Stanley's unique guitar. The company then prices the guitar to achieve a level of profit greater than the cost of the guitar. This chapter introduces the principles of accounting systems that accumulate costs in the same manner as they were for Paul Stanley's guitar.

Learning Objectives

After studying this chapter, you should be able to: *Example Exercises*

OBJ 1 Describe cost accounting systems used by manufacturing businesses.
Cost Accounting Systems Overview

OBJ 2 Describe and illustrate a job order cost accounting system.
Job Order Cost Systems for Manufacturing Businesses

Materials	EE 2-1
Factory Labor	EE 2-2
Factory Overhead	EE 2-3, 2-4
Work in Process	EE 2-5
Finished Goods	
Sales and Cost of Goods Sold	EE 2-6
Period Costs	
Summary of Cost Flows for Legend Guitars	

OBJ 3 Describe the use of job order cost information for decision making.
Job Order Costing for Decision Making

OBJ 4 Describe the flow of costs for a service business that uses a job order cost accounting system.
Job Order Cost Systems for Professional Service Businesses

At a Glance 2 Page 56

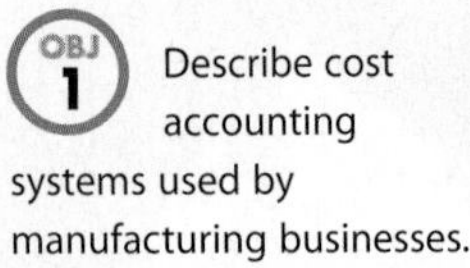
OBJ 1
Describe cost accounting systems used by manufacturing businesses.

Cost Accounting Systems Overview

Cost accounting systems measure, record, and report product costs. Managers use product costs for setting product prices, controlling operations, and developing financial statements.

The two main types of cost accounting systems for manufacturing operations are:

- Job order cost systems
- Process cost systems

Warner Bros. and other movie studios use job order cost systems to accumulate movie production and distribution costs. Costs such as actor salaries, production costs, movie print costs, and marketing costs are accumulated in a job account for a particular movie.

A **job order cost system** provides product costs for each quantity of product that is manufactured. Each quantity of product that is manufactured is called a *job*. Job order cost systems are often used by companies that manufacture custom products for customers or batches of similar products. Manufacturers that use a job order cost system are sometimes called *job shops*. An example of a job shop would be an apparel manufacturer, such as **Levi Strauss & Co.**, or a guitar manufacturer, such as **Washburn Guitars**.

A **process cost system** provides product costs for each manufacturing department or process. Process cost systems are often used by companies that manufacture units of a product that are indistinguishable from each other and are manufactured using a continuous production process. Examples would be oil refineries, paper producers, chemical processors, and food processors.

Job order and process cost systems are widely used. A company may use a job order cost system for some of its products and a process cost system for other products.

The process cost system is illustrated in Chapter 3. The job order cost system is illustrated in this chapter. As a basis for illustration, **Legend Guitars**, a manufacturer of guitars, is used. Exhibit 1 provides a summary of Legend Guitars' manufacturing operations, which were described in Chapter 1.

EXHIBIT 1

Summary of Legend Guitars' Manufacturing Operations

Manufacturing Operations	
Cutting	Employees cut the body and neck of the guitar out of wood.
Assembling	Employees assemble and finish the guitars.
Product Costs	
Direct materials	The cost of material that is an integral part of and a significant portion of the total cost of the final product. The cost of wood used in the neck and body of the guitars.
Direct labor	The cost of employee wages that are an integral part of and a significant portion of the total cost of the final product. Employee wages for cutting and assembling.
Factory overhead	Costs other than direct materials and direct labor that are incurred in the manufacturing process. The cost of guitar strings, glue, sandpaper, buffing compound, paint, salaries of production supervisors, janitorial salaries, and factory utilities.
Inventories	
Materials	Includes the cost of direct and indirect materials used to produce the guitars. Direct materials include the cost of wood used in the neck and body of the guitars. Indirect materials include guitar strings, glue, sandpaper, buffing compound, varnish, and paint.
Work in process	Includes the product costs of units that have entered the manufacturing process but have not been completed. For example, the product costs of guitars for which the neck and body have been cut but not yet assembled.
Finished goods	Includes the cost of completed (or finished) products that have not been sold. The product costs assigned to completed guitars that have not yet been sold.

Job Order Cost Systems for Manufacturing Businesses

OBJ 2 Describe and illustrate a job order cost accounting system.

A job order cost system records and summarizes manufacturing costs by jobs. The flow of manufacturing costs in a job order system is illustrated in Exhibit 2.

EXHIBIT 2 **Flow of Manufacturing Costs**

- Direct Labor
- Factory Overhead

Materials Storeroom

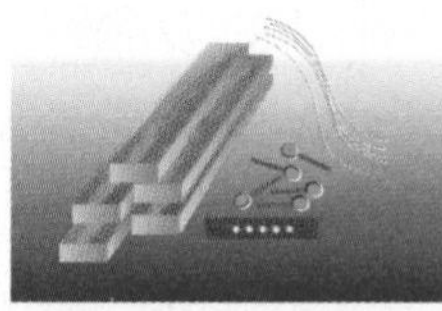

Production Process

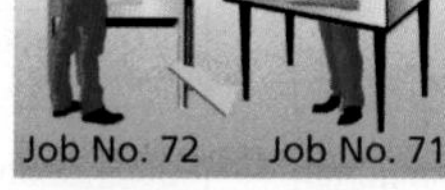

Job No. 72 Job No. 71

Warehouse

Job No. 70 Job No. 69

Music Store

Materials Inventory → Work in Process → Finished Goods → Cost of Goods Sold

Exhibit 2 indicates that although the materials for Jobs 71 and 72 have been added, both jobs are still in the production process. Thus, Jobs 71 and 72 are part of *Work in Process Inventory*. In contrast, Exhibit 2 indicates that Jobs 69 and 70 have been completed. Thus, Jobs 69 and 70 are part of *Finished Goods Inventory*. Exhibit 2 also indicates that when finished guitars are sold to music stores, their costs become part of *Cost of Goods Sold*.

In a job order cost accounting system, perpetual inventory controlling accounts and subsidiary ledgers are maintained for materials, work in process, and finished goods inventories as shown in Exhibit 3.

EXHIBIT 3 **Inventory Ledger Accounts**

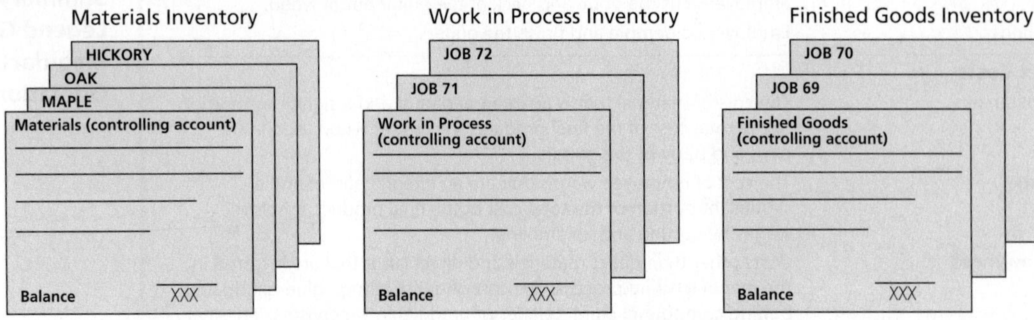

Materials

The materials account in the general ledger is a controlling account. A separate account for each type of material is maintained in a subsidiary **materials ledger**.

Exhibit 4 shows **Legend Guitars**' materials ledger account for maple. Increases (debits) and decreases (credits) to the account are as follows:

- Increases (debits) are based on *receiving reports* such as Receiving Report No. 196 for $10,500, which is supported by the supplier's invoice.
- Decreases (credits) are based on *materials requisitions* such as Requisition No. 672 for $2,000 for Job 71 and Requisition No. 704 for $11,000 for Job 72.

EXHIBIT 4

Materials Information and Cost Flows

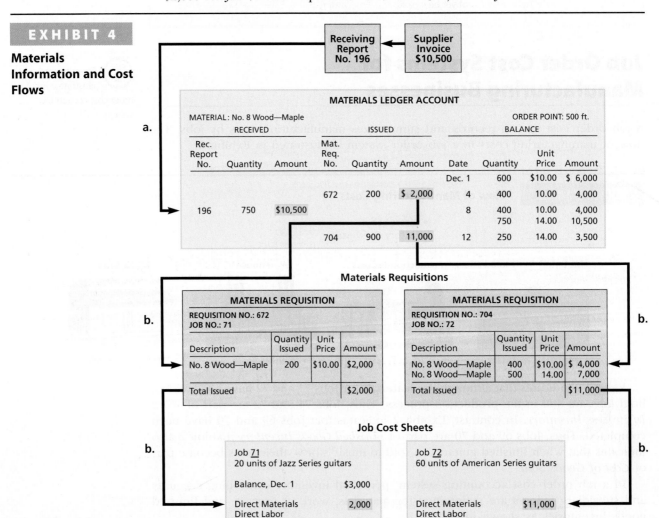

Receiving Report No. 196 ← Supplier Invoice $10,500

a.

MATERIALS LEDGER ACCOUNT

MATERIAL: No. 8 Wood—Maple ORDER POINT: 500 ft.

RECEIVED			ISSUED			BALANCE			
Rec. Report No.	Quantity	Amount	Mat. Req. No.	Quantity	Amount	Date	Quantity	Unit Price	Amount
						Dec. 1	600	$10.00	$ 6,000
			672	200	$ 2,000	4	400	10.00	4,000
196	750	$10,500				8	400	10.00	4,000
							750	14.00	10,500
			704	900	11,000	12	250	14.00	3,500

Materials Requisitions

b.

MATERIALS REQUISITION

REQUISITION NO.: 672
JOB NO.: 71

Description	Quantity Issued	Unit Price	Amount
No. 8 Wood—Maple	200	$10.00	$2,000
Total Issued			$2,000

MATERIALS REQUISITION

REQUISITION NO.: 704
JOB NO.: 72

Description	Quantity Issued	Unit Price	Amount
No. 8 Wood—Maple	400	$10.00	$ 4,000
No. 8 Wood—Maple	500	14.00	7,000
Total Issued			$11,000

b.

Job Cost Sheets

b.

Job 71
20 units of Jazz Series guitars

Balance, Dec. 1	$3,000
Direct Materials	2,000
Direct Labor	
Factory Overhead	

Job 72
60 units of American Series guitars

Direct Materials	$11,000
Direct Labor	
Factory Overhead	

b.

A **receiving report** is prepared when materials that have been ordered are received and inspected. The quantity received and the condition of the materials are entered on the receiving report. When the supplier's invoice is received, it is compared to the receiving report. If there are no discrepancies, a journal entry is made to record the purchase. The journal entry to record the supplier's invoice related to Receiving Report No. 196 in Exhibit 4 is as follows:

a.	Materials		10,500	
	Accounts Payable			10,500
	Materials purchased during December.			

The storeroom releases materials for use in manufacturing when a **materials requisition** is received. Examples of materials requisitions are shown in Exhibit 4.

The materials requisitions for each job serve as the basis for recording materials used. For direct materials, the quantities and amounts from the materials requisitions are posted to job cost sheets. **Job cost sheets**, which are also illustrated in Exhibit 4, make up the work in process subsidiary ledger.

Exhibit 4 shows the posting of $2,000 of direct materials to Job 71 and $11,000 of direct materials to Job 72.[1] Job 71 is an order for 20 units of Jazz Series guitars, while Job 72 is an order for 60 units of American Series guitars.

A summary of the materials requisitions is used as a basis for the journal entry recording the materials used for the month. For direct materials, this entry increases (debits) Work in Process and decreases (credits) Materials as follows:

b.	Work in Process		13,000	
	Materials			13,000
	Materials requisitioned to jobs ($2,000 + $11,000).			

Many companies use computerized information processes to record the use of materials. In such cases, storeroom employees electronically record the release of materials, which automatically updates the materials ledger and job cost sheets.

Integrity, Objectivity, and Ethics in Business

PHONY INVOICE SCAMS

A popular method for defrauding a company is to issue a phony invoice. The scam begins by initially contacting the target firm to discover details of key business contacts, business operations, and products. The swindler then uses this information to create a fictitious invoice. The invoice will include names, figures, and other details to give it the appearance of legitimacy. This type of scam can be avoided if invoices are matched with receiving documents prior to issuing a check.

[1] To simplify, Exhibit 4 and this chapter use the first-in, first-out cost flow method.

Example Exercise 2-1 Issuance of Materials

OBJ 2

On March 5, Hatch Company purchased 400 units of raw materials at $14 per unit. On March 10, raw materials were requisitioned for production as follows: 200 units for Job 101 at $12 per unit and 300 units for Job 102 at $14 per unit. Journalize the entry on March 5 to record the purchase and on March 10 to record the requisition from the materials storeroom.

Follow My Example 2-1

Mar. 5	Materials	5,600	
	Accounts Payable		5,600
	$5,600 = 400 × $14		
10	Work in Process	6,600*	
	Materials		6,600

*Job 101	$2,400 = 200 × $12
Job 102	4,200 = 300 × $14
Total	$6,600

Practice Exercises: PE 2-1A, PE 2-1B

Factory Labor

When employees report for work, they may use *electronic badges, clock cards,* or *in-and-out cards* to clock in. When employees work on an individual job, they use **time tickets** to record the amount of time they have worked on a specific job. Exhibit 5 illustrates time tickets for Jobs 71 and 72 at **Legend Guitars**.

EXHIBIT 5

Labor Information and Cost Flows

Dynamic Exhibit

Job 71 Time Tickets

TIME TICKET

No. 4521
Employee Name D. McInnis
Date Dec. 13, 2016
Work Description: Cutting
Job No. 71

Start Time	Finish Time	Hours Worked	Hourly Rate	Cost
8:00 A.M.	12:00 P.M.	4	$10.00	$40.00
1:00 P.M.	3:00 P.M.	2	10.00	20.00
Total Cost				$60.00

Approved by T.D.

Job 72 Time Tickets

TIME TICKET

No. 6311
Employee Name S. Andrews
Date Dec. 26, 2016
Work Description: Assembling
Job No. 72

Start Time	Finish Time	Hours Worked	Hourly Rate	Cost
9:00 A.M.	12:00 P.M.	3	$15.00	$45.00
1:00 P.M.	6:00 P.M.	5	15.00	75.00
Total Cost				$120.00

Approved by A.M.

December Job 71 Hours	350
December Job 71 Labor Costs:	$3,500

December Job 72 Hours	500
December Job 72 Labor Costs:	$7,500

Job Cost Sheets

c.

Job 71
20 units of Jazz Series guitars

Balance	$3,000
Direct Materials	2,000
Direct Labor	3,500
Factory Overhead	

c.

Job 72
60 units of American Series guitars

Direct Materials	$11,000
Direct Labor	7,500
Factory Overhead	

Exhibit 5 shows that on December 13, 2016, D. McInnis spent six hours working on Job 71 at an hourly rate of $10 for a cost of $60 (6 hrs. × $10). Exhibit 5 also indicates that a total of 350 hours was spent by employees on Job 71 during December for a total cost of $3,500. This total direct labor cost of $3,500 is posted to the job cost sheet for Job 71, as shown in Exhibit 5.

Likewise, Exhibit 5 shows that on December 26, 2016, S. Andrews spent eight hours on Job 72 at an hourly rate of $15 for a cost of $120 (8 hrs. × $15). A total of 500 hours was spent by employees on Job 72 during December for a total cost of $7,500. This total direct labor cost of $7,500 is posted to the job cost sheet for Job 72, as shown in Exhibit 5.

A summary of the time tickets is used as the basis for the journal entry recording direct labor for the month. This entry increases (debits) Work in Process and increases (credits) Wages Payable, as follows:

	c.	Work in Process		11,000	
		Wages Payable			11,000
		Factory labor used in production of jobs ($3,500 + $7,500).			

As with direct materials, many businesses use computerized information processing to record direct labor. In such cases, employees may log their time directly into computer terminals at their workstations. In other cases, employees may be issued magnetic cards, much like credit cards, to log in and out of work assignments.

Example Exercise 2-2 Direct Labor Costs

OBJ 2

During March, Hatch Company accumulated 800 hours of direct labor costs on Job 101 and 600 hours on Job 102. The total direct labor was incurred at a rate of $16 per direct labor hour for Job 101 and $12 per direct labor hour for Job 102. Journalize the entry to record the flow of labor costs into production during March.

Follow My Example 2-2

	Debit	Credit
Work in Process	20,000*	
Wages Payable		20,000

*Job 101	$12,800	= 800 hrs. × $16
Job 102	7,200	= 600 hrs. × $12
Total	$20,000	

Practice Exercises: PE 2-2A, PE 2-2B

Business  Connection

BMW'S FACTORY LABOR EXPERIMENT

In 2007, managers at **Bavarian Motorworks (BMW)** began to worry about the increasing age of their workforce. The average age of manufacturing plant workers was expected to increase from 39 to 47 by 2017. To plan for this change, BMW conducted an experiment by altering the age makeup of workers on one of the company's production lines to match the average age anticipated in 2017. In addition, the company made 70 changes to the production line to reduce the chance of error and physical strain. The changes resulted in a 7% improvement in productivity and a 2% decrease in employee absences from work. The company now uses the line as a model of quality and productivity for the rest of the company.

Source: C. Loch, F. Sting, N. Bauer, and H. Mauermann, "How BMW Is Defusing the Demographic Time Bomb," *Harvard Business Review*, March 2010.

Factory Overhead

Factory overhead includes all manufacturing costs except direct materials and direct labor. Factory overhead costs come from a variety of sources, including the following:

- *Indirect materials* comes from a summary of materials requisitions.
- *Indirect labor* comes from the salaries of production supervisors and the wages of other employees such as janitors.
- *Factory power* comes from utility bills.
- *Factory depreciation* comes from Accounting Department computations of depreciation.

To illustrate the recording of factory overhead, assume that **Legend Guitars** incurred $4,600 of overhead during December, which included $500 of indirect materials, $2,000 of indirect labor, $900 of utilities, and $1,200 of factory depreciation. The $500 of indirect materials consisted of $200 of glue and $300 of sandpaper. The entry to record the factory overhead is as follows:

d.	Factory Overhead		4,600	
	Materials			500
	Wages Payable			2,000
	Utilities Payable			900
	Accumulated Depreciation			1,200
	Factory overhead incurred in production.			

Example Exercise 2-3 Factory Overhead Costs

OBJ 2

During March, Hatch Company incurred factory overhead costs as follows: indirect materials, $800; indirect labor, $3,400; utilities cost, $1,600; and factory depreciation, $2,500. Journalize the entry to record the factory overhead incurred during March.

Follow My Example 2-3

Factory Overhead	8,300	
Materials		800
Wages Payable		3,400
Utilities Payable		1,600
Accumulated Depreciation—Factory		2,500

Practice Exercises: PE 2-3A, PE 2-3B

Allocating Factory Overhead Factory overhead is different from direct labor and direct materials in that it is *indirectly* related to the jobs. That is, factory overhead costs cannot be identified with or traced to specific jobs. For this reason, factory overhead costs are allocated to jobs. The process by which factory overhead or other costs are assigned to a cost object, such as a job, is called **cost allocation**.

The factory overhead costs are *allocated* to jobs using a common measure related to each job. This measure is called an **activity base**, *allocation base*, or *activity driver*. The activity base used to allocate overhead should reflect the consumption or use of factory overhead costs. Three common activity bases used to allocate factory overhead costs are direct labor hours, direct labor cost, and machine hours.

Predetermined Factory Overhead Rate Factory overhead costs are normally allocated or *applied* to jobs using a **predetermined factory overhead rate**. The predetermined factory overhead rate is computed as follows:

$$\text{Predetermined Factory Overhead Rate} = \frac{\text{Estimated Total Factory Overhead Costs}}{\text{Estimated Activity Base}}$$

To illustrate, assume that **Legend Guitars** estimates the total factory overhead cost as $50,000 for the year and the activity base as 10,000 direct labor hours. The predetermined factory overhead rate of $5 per direct labor hour is computed as follows:

$$\text{Predetermined Factory Overhead Rate} = \frac{\$50{,}000}{10{,}000 \text{ direct labor hours}} = \$5 \text{ per direct labor hour}$$

As illustrated, the predetermined overhead rate is computed using *estimated* amounts at the beginning of the period. This is because managers need timely information on the product costs of each job. If a company waited until all overhead costs were known at the end of the period, the allocated factory overhead would be accurate, but not timely. Only through timely reporting can managers adjust manufacturing methods or product pricing.

Many companies are using a method for accumulating and allocating factory overhead costs. This method, called **activity-based costing**, uses a different overhead rate for each type of factory overhead activity, such as inspecting, moving, and machining. Activity-based costing is discussed and illustrated in Chapter 11.

Applying Factory Overhead to Work in Process **Legend Guitars** applies factory overhead using a rate of $5 per direct labor hour. The factory overhead applied to each job is recorded in the job cost sheets, as shown in Exhibit 6.

EXHIBIT 6

Applying Factory Overhead to Jobs

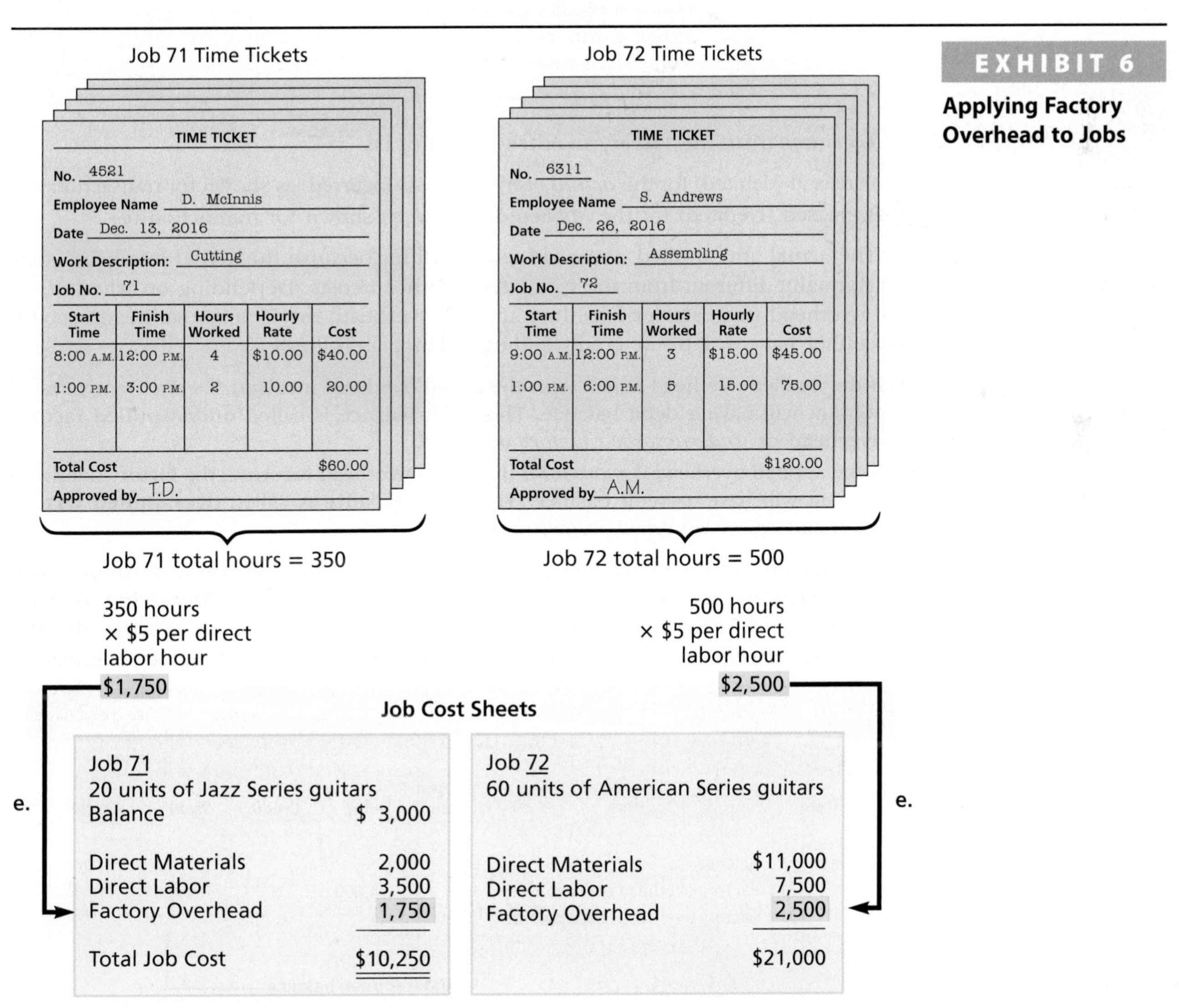

Exhibit 6 shows that 850 direct labor hours were used in Legend Guitars' December operations. Based on the time tickets, 350 hours can be traced to Job 71, and 500 hours can be traced to Job 72.

Using a factory overhead rate of $5 per direct labor hour, $4,250 of factory overhead is applied as follows:

	Direct Labor Hours	Factory Overhead Rate	Factory Overhead Applied
Job 71	350	$5	$1,750 (350 hrs. × $5)
Job 72	500	$5	2,500 (500 hrs. × $5)
Total	850		$4,250

As shown in Exhibit 6, the applied overhead is posted to each job cost sheet. Factory overhead of $1,750 is posted to Job 71, which results in a total product cost on December 31, 2016, of $10,250. Factory overhead of $2,500 is posted to Job 72, which results in a total product cost on December 31, 2016, of $21,000.

The journal entry to apply factory overhead increases (debits) Work in Process and credits Factory Overhead. This journal entry to apply overhead to Jobs 71 and 72 is as follows:

			Debit	Credit
	e.	Work in Process	4,250	
		Factory Overhead		4,250
		Factory overhead applied to jobs according to the predetermined overhead rate (850 hrs. × $5).		

To summarize, the factory overhead account is:

- Increased (debited) for the *actual overhead* costs incurred, as shown for transaction (d).
- Decreased (credited) for the *applied overhead*, as shown for transaction (e).

The actual and applied overhead usually differ because the actual overhead costs are normally different from the estimated overhead costs. Depending on whether actual overhead is greater or less than applied overhead, the factory overhead account will either have a debit or credit ending balance as follows:

- If the applied overhead is *less than* the actual overhead incurred, the factory overhead account will have a debit balance. This debit balance is called **underapplied factory overhead** or *underabsorbed factory overhead*.
- If the applied overhead is *more than* the actual overhead incurred, the factory overhead account will have a credit balance. This credit balance is called **overapplied factory overhead** or *overabsorbed factory overhead*.

The factory overhead account for Legend Guitars, which follows, illustrates both underapplied and overapplied factory overhead. Specifically, the December 1, 2016, credit balance of $200 represents overapplied factory overhead. In contrast, the December 31, 2016, debit balance of $150 represents underapplied factory overhead.

Account *Factory Overhead* — *Account No.*

Date		Item	Post. Ref.	Debit	Credit	Balance Debit	Balance Credit
2016 Dec.	1	Balance					200
	31	Factory overhead cost incurred		4,600		4,400	
	31	Factory overhead cost applied			4,250	150	

Underapplied balance (150)
Overapplied balance (200)

If the balance of factory overhead (either underapplied or overapplied) becomes large, the balance and related overhead rate should be investigated. For example, a large balance could be caused by changes in manufacturing methods. In this case, the factory overhead rate should be revised.

Example Exercise 2-4 Applying Factory Overhead

OBJ 2

Hatch Company estimates that total factory overhead costs will be $100,000 for the year. Direct labor hours are estimated to be 25,000. For Hatch Company, (a) determine the predetermined factory overhead rate using direct labor hours as the activity base, (b) determine the amount of factory overhead applied to Jobs 101 and 102 in March, using the data on direct labor hours from Example Exercise 2-2, and (c) prepare the journal entry to apply factory overhead to both jobs in March according to the predetermined overhead rate.

Follow My Example 2-4

a. $4.00 per direct labor hour = $100,000 ÷ 25,000 direct labor hours

b. Job 101	$3,200	= 800 hours × $4.00 per hour
Job 102	2,400	= 600 hours × $4.00 per hour
Total	$5,600	

c. Work in Process	5,600	
Factory Overhead		5,600

Practice Exercises: PE 2-4A, PE 2-4B

Disposal of Factory Overhead Balance During the year, the balance in the factory overhead account is carried forward and reported as a deferred debit or credit on the monthly (interim) balance sheets. However, any balance in the factory overhead account should not be carried over to the next year. This is because any such balance applies only to operations of the current year.

If the estimates for computing the predetermined overhead rate are reasonably accurate, the ending balance of Factory Overhead should be relatively small. For this reason, the balance of Factory Overhead at the end of the year is disposed of by transferring it to the cost of goods sold account as follows:[2]

- If there is an ending debit balance (underapplied overhead) in the factory overhead account, it is disposed of by the entry that follows:

		Cost of Goods Sold		XXX	
		Factory Overhead			XXX
		Transfer of underapplied overhead to cost of goods sold.			

- If there is an ending credit balance (overapplied overhead) in the factory overhead account, it is disposed of by the entry that follows:

		Factory Overhead		XXX	
		Cost of Goods Sold			XXX
		Transfer of overapplied overhead to cost of goods sold.			

[2] An ending balance in the factory overhead account may also be allocated among the work in process, finished goods, and cost of goods sold accounts. This brings these accounts into agreement with the actual costs incurred. This approach is rarely used and is only required for large ending balances in the factory overhead account. For this reason, it will not be used in this text.

To illustrate, the journal entry to dispose of **Legend Guitars**' December 31, 2016, underapplied overhead balance of $150 is as follows:

	f.	Cost of Goods Sold		150	
		Factory Overhead			150
		Closed underapplied factory overhead to cost of goods sold.			

Work in Process

During the period, Work in Process is increased (debited) for the following:

- Direct materials cost
- Direct labor cost
- Applied factory overhead cost

To illustrate, the work in process account for **Legend Guitars** is shown in Exhibit 7. The balance of Work in Process on December 1, 2016 (beginning balance), was $3,000. As shown in Exhibit 7, this balance relates to Job 71, which was the only job in process on this date. During December, Work in Process was debited for the following:

- Direct materials cost of $13,000 [transaction (b)], based on materials requisitions.
- Direct labor cost of $11,000 [transaction (c)], based on time tickets.
- Applied factory overhead of $4,250 [transaction (e)], based on the predetermined overhead rate of $5 per direct labor hour.

The preceding Work in Process debits are supported by the detail postings to job cost sheets for Jobs 71 and 72, as shown in Exhibit 7.

EXHIBIT 7

Job Cost Sheets and the Work in Process Controlling Account

Job Cost Sheets

Job 71	
20 units of Jazz Series guitars	
Balance	$ 3,000
Direct Materials	2,000
Direct Labor	3,500
Factory Overhead	1,750
Total Job Cost	$10,250
Unit Cost	$512.50

Job 72	
60 units of American Series guitars	
Direct Materials	$11,000
Direct Labor	7,500
Factory Overhead	2,500
Total Job Cost	$21,000

g.

Account *Work in Process* — *Account No.*

Date		Item	Post. Ref.	Debit	Credit	Balance Debit	Balance Credit
2016 Dec.	1	Balance				3,000	
	31	Direct materials		13,000		16,000	
	31	Direct labor		11,000		27,000	
	31	Factory overhead		4,250		31,250	
	31	Jobs completed—Job 71			10,250	21,000	

During December, Job 71 was completed. Upon completion, the product costs (direct materials, direct labor, factory overhead) are totaled. This total is divided by the number of units produced to determine the cost per unit. Thus, the 20 Jazz Series guitars produced as Job 71 cost $512.50 ($10,250 ÷ 20) per guitar.

After completion, Job 71 is transferred from Work in Process to Finished Goods by the following entry:

	g.	Finished Goods	10,250	
		Work in Process		10,250
		Job 71 completed in December.		

Job 72 was started in December but was not completed by December 31, 2016. Thus, Job 72 is still part of work in process on December 31, 2016. As shown in Exhibit 7, the balance of the job cost sheet for Job 72 ($21,000) is also the December 31, 2016, balance of Work in Process.

Example Exercise 2-5 Job Costs

OBJ 2

At the end of March, Hatch Company had completed Jobs 101 and 102. Job 101 is for 500 units, and Job 102 is for 1,000 units. Using the data from Example Exercises 2-1, 2-2, and 2-4, determine (a) the balance on the job cost sheets for Jobs 101 and 102 at the end of March and (b) the cost per unit for Jobs 101 and 102 at the end of March.

Follow My Example 2-5

a.

	Job 101	Job 102
Direct materials	$ 2,400	$ 4,200
Direct labor	12,800	7,200
Factory overhead	3,200	2,400
Total costs	$18,400	$13,800

b. Job 101 $36.80 = $18,400 ÷ 500 units
Job 102 $13.80 = $13,800 ÷ 1,000 units

Practice Exercises: PE 2-5A, PE 2-5B

Finished Goods

The finished goods account is a controlling account for the subsidiary **finished goods ledger** or *stock ledger*. Each account in the finished goods ledger contains cost data for the units manufactured, units sold, and units on hand.

Exhibit 8 illustrates the finished goods ledger account for **Legend Guitars'** Jazz Series guitars.

EXHIBIT 8

Finished Goods Ledger Account

ITEM: *Jazz Series guitars*

Manufactured			Shipped			Balance			
Job Order No.	Quantity	Amount	Ship Order No.	Quantity	Amount	Date	Quantity	Amount	Unit Cost
						Dec. 1	40	$20,000	$500.00
			643	40	$20,000	9	—	—	—
71	20	$10,250				31	20	10,250	512.50

Exhibit 8 indicates that there were 40 Jazz Series guitars on hand on December 1, 2016. During the month, 20 additional Jazz guitars were completed and transferred to Finished Goods from the completion of Job 71. In addition, the beginning inventory of 40 Jazz guitars was sold during the month.

Sales and Cost of Goods Sold

During December, **Legend Guitars** sold 40 Jazz Series guitars for $850 each, generating total sales of $34,000 ($850 × 40 guitars). Exhibit 8 indicates that the cost of these guitars was $500 per guitar or a total cost of $20,000 ($500 × 40 guitars). The entries to record the sale and related cost of goods sold are as follows:

	h.	Accounts Receivable		34,000	
		Sales			34,000
		Revenue received from guitars sold on account.			

	i.	Cost of Goods Sold		20,000	
		Finished Goods			20,000
		Cost of 40 Jazz Series guitars sold.			

In a job order cost accounting system, the preparation of a statement of cost of goods manufactured, which was discussed in Chapter 1, is not necessary. This is because job order costing uses the perpetual inventory system and, thus, the cost of goods sold can be directly determined from the finished goods ledger as illustrated in Exhibit 8.

Example Exercise 2-6 Cost of Goods Sold

OBJ 2

Nejedly Company completed 80,000 units during the year at a cost of $680,000. The beginning finished goods inventory was 10,000 units at $80,000. Determine the cost of goods sold for 60,000 units, assuming a FIFO cost flow.

Follow My Example 2-6

$505,000 = $80,000 + (50,000 × $8.50*)
*Cost per unit of goods produced during the year = $8.50 = $680,000 ÷ 80,000 units

Practice Exercises: PE 2-6A, PE 2-6B

Period Costs

Period costs are used in generating revenue during the current period but are not involved in the manufacturing process. As discussed in Chapter 1, *period costs* are recorded as expenses of the current period as either selling or administrative expenses.

Selling expenses are incurred in marketing the product and delivering sold products to customers. Administrative expenses are incurred in managing the company but are not related to the manufacturing or selling functions. During December, **Legend Guitars** recorded the following selling and administrative expenses:

	j.	Sales Salaries Expense		2,000	
		Office Salaries Expense		1,500	
		Salaries Payable			3,500
		Recorded December period costs.			

Summary of Cost Flows for Legend Guitars

Exhibit 9 shows the cost flows through the manufacturing accounts of **Legend Guitars** for December.

EXHIBIT 9 Flow of Manufacturing Costs for Legend Guitars

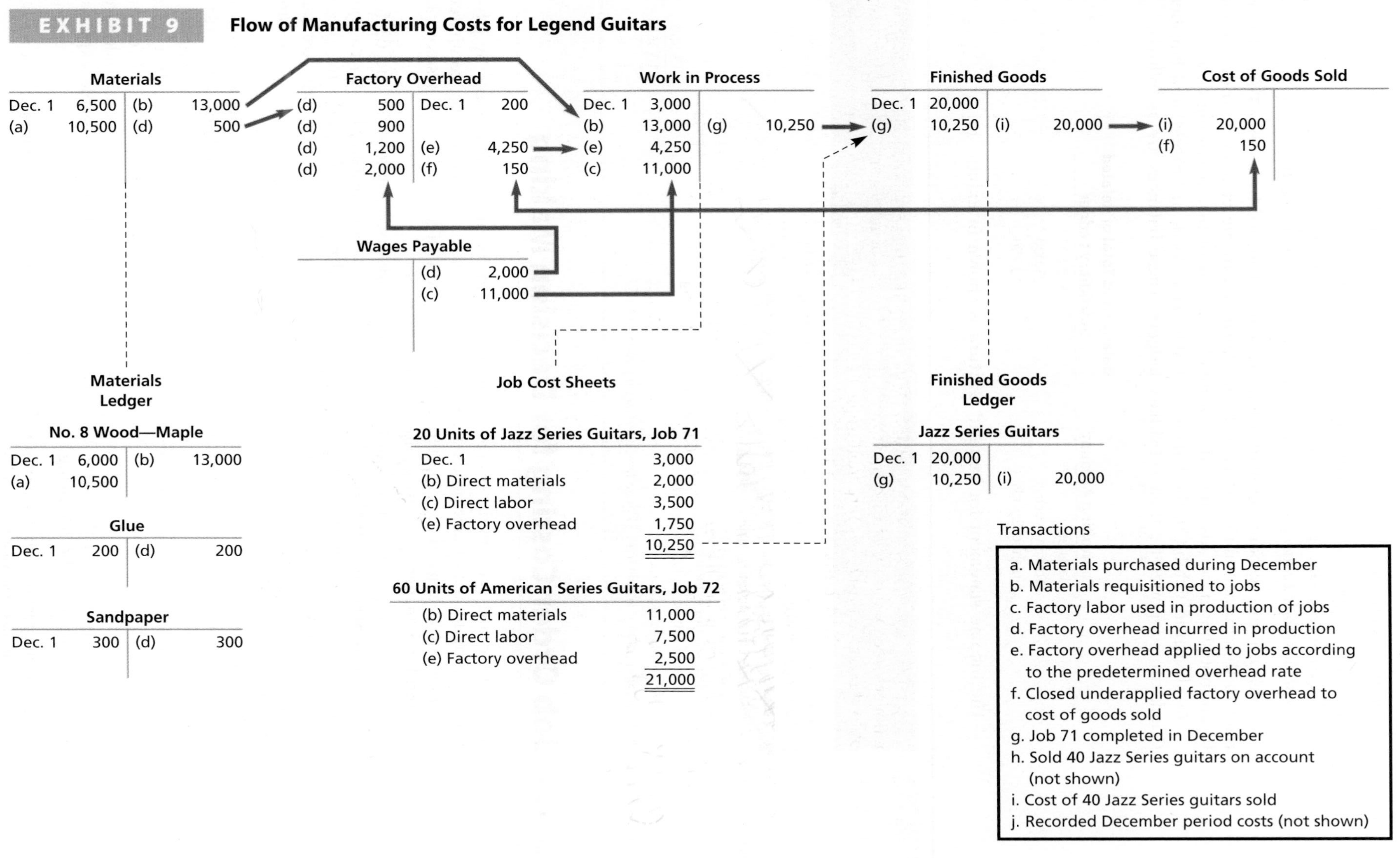

Transactions

a. Materials purchased during December
b. Materials requisitioned to jobs
c. Factory labor used in production of jobs
d. Factory overhead incurred in production
e. Factory overhead applied to jobs according to the predetermined overhead rate
f. Closed underapplied factory overhead to cost of goods sold
g. Job 71 completed in December
h. Sold 40 Jazz Series guitars on account (not shown)
i. Cost of 40 Jazz Series guitars sold
j. Recorded December period costs (not shown)

In addition, summary details of the following subsidiary ledgers are shown:

- *Materials Ledger*—the subsidiary ledger for Materials.
- *Job Cost Sheets*—the subsidiary ledger for Work in Process.
- *Finished Goods Ledger*—the subsidiary ledger for Finished Goods.

Entries in the accounts shown in Exhibit 9 are identified by letters. These letters refer to the journal entries described and illustrated in the chapter. Entries (h) and (j) are not shown because they do not involve a flow of manufacturing costs.

As shown in Exhibit 9, the balances of Materials, Work in Process, and Finished Goods are supported by their subsidiary ledgers. These balances are as follows:

Controlling Account	Balance and Total of Related Subsidiary Ledger
Materials	$ 3,500
Work in Process	21,000
Finished Goods	10,250

The income statement for **Legend Guitars** is shown in Exhibit 10.

EXHIBIT 10

Income Statement of Legend Guitars

Legend Guitars Income Statement For the Month Ended December 31, 2016		
Sales		$34,000
Cost of goods sold		20,150*
Gross profit		$13,850
Selling and administrative expenses:		
Sales salaries expense	$2,000	
Office salaries expense	1,500	
Total selling and administrative expenses		3,500
Income from operations		$10,350

*$20,150 = ($500 × 40 guitars) + $150 underapplied factory overhead

OBJ 3 Describe the use of job order cost information for decision making.

Job Order Costing for Decision Making

A job order cost accounting system accumulates and records product costs by jobs. The resulting total and unit product costs can be compared to similar jobs, compared over time, or compared to expected costs. In this way, a job order cost system can be used by managers for cost evaluation and control.

To illustrate, Exhibit 11 shows the direct materials used for Jobs 54 and 63 for **Legend Guitars**. The wood used in manufacturing guitars is measured in board feet. Because Jobs 54 and 63 produced the same type and number of guitars, the direct materials cost per unit should be about the same. However, the materials cost per guitar for Job 54 is $100, while for Job 63 it is $125. Thus, the materials costs are significantly more for Job 63.

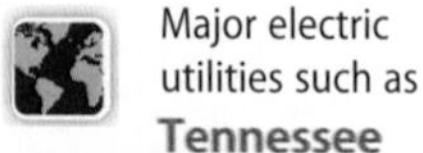

Major electric utilities such as **Tennessee Valley Authority**, **Consolidated Edison Inc.**, and **Pacific Gas and Electric Company** use job order accounting to control the costs associated with major repairs and overhauls that occur during maintenance shutdowns.

The job cost sheets shown in Exhibit 11 can be analyzed for possible reasons for the increased materials cost for Job 63. Because the materials price did not change ($10 per board foot), the increased materials cost must be related to wood consumption.

Comparing wood consumed for Jobs 54 and 63 shows that 400 board feet were used in Job 54 to produce 40 guitars. In contrast, Job 63 used 500 board feet to produce the same number of guitars. Thus, an investigation should be undertaken to determine the cause of the extra 100 board feet used for Job 63. Possible explanations could include the following:

- A new employee, who was not properly trained, cut the wood for Job 63. As a result, there was excess waste and scrap.

EXHIBIT 11

Comparing Data from Job Cost Sheets

Job 54
Item: 40 Jazz Series guitars

	Materials Quantity (board feet)	Materials Price	Materials Amount
Direct materials:			
No. 8 Wood—Maple	400	$10.00	$4,000
Direct materials per guitar			$ 100*

*$4,000 ÷ 40

Job 63
Item: 40 Jazz Series guitars

	Materials Quantity (board feet)	Materials Price	Materials Amount
Direct materials:			
No. 8 Wood—Maple	500	$10.00	$5,000
Direct materials per guitar			$ 125*

*$5,000 ÷ 40

- The wood used for Job 63 was purchased from a new supplier. The wood was of poor quality, which created excessive waste and scrap.
- The cutting tools needed repair and were not properly maintained. As a result, the wood was miscut, which created excessive waste and scrap.
- The instructions attached to the job were incorrect. The wood was cut according to the instructions. The incorrect instructions were discovered later in assembly. As a result, the wood had to be recut and the initial cuttings scrapped.

Job Order Cost Systems for Professional Service Businesses

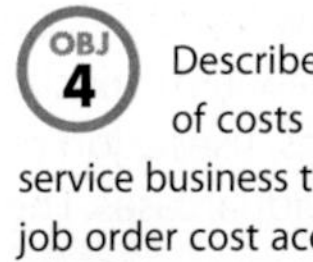

OBJ 4 Describe the flow of costs for a service business that uses a job order cost accounting system.

A job order cost accounting system may be used for a professional service business. For example, an advertising agency, an attorney, and a physician each provide services to individual customers, clients, or patients. In such cases, the customer, client, or patient can be viewed as a job for which costs are accumulated and reported.

The primary product costs for a service business are direct labor and overhead costs. Any materials or supplies used in rendering services are normally insignificant. As a result, materials and supply costs are included as part of the overhead cost.

Like a manufacturing business, direct labor and overhead costs of rendering services to clients are accumulated in a work in process account. Work in Process is supported by a cost ledger with a job cost sheet for each client.

When a job is completed and the client is billed, the costs are transferred to a cost of services account. Cost of Services is similar to the cost of merchandise sold account for a merchandising business or the cost of goods sold account for a manufacturing business. A finished goods account and related finished goods ledger are not necessary. This is because the revenues for the services are recorded only after the services are provided.

In practice, other considerations unique to service businesses may need to be considered. For example, a service business may bill clients on a weekly or monthly basis rather than when a job is completed. In such cases, a portion of the costs related to each billing is transferred from the work in process account to the cost of services account. A service business may also bill clients for services in advance, which would be accounted for as deferred revenue until the services are completed.

The flow of costs through a service business using a job order cost accounting system is shown in Exhibit 12.

EXHIBIT 12 Flow of Costs Through a Service Business

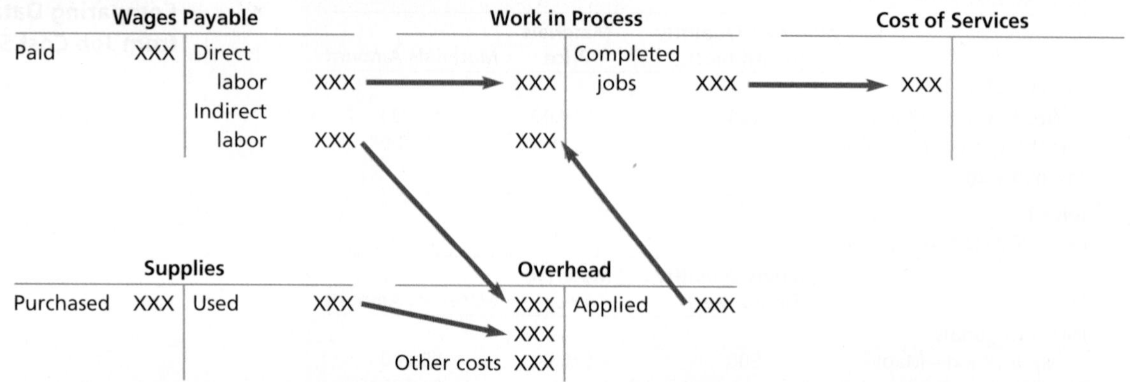

Service  Focus

JOB ORDER COSTING IN A LAW FIRM

Law firms typically use job order costing to track the costs of individual legal cases or client engagements. The costs of each job are accumulated in a job cost sheet, just as in a manufacturing firm. However, because a law firm is a service firm, there are no direct materials costs. The primary cost comes from the direct labor of the professional staff.

Law firms like, **Constangy, Brooks, and Smith**, a national law firm specializing in employment law and labor relations, uses a job order costing system to track the cost of individual cases. The direct labor costs of the professional staff are determined by multiplying the time that each attorney spends on an individual case by the attorney's hourly billing rate. Billing rates vary depending on the rank of the attorney doing the work. In addition, any costs that can be directly attributed to a specific engagement are added to the engagement's job cost sheet. For example, if a case requires the legal team to travel to another city to interview witnesses, the cost of that travel is added to the job cost sheet for that specific client. Indirect costs, such as support staff, office supplies, and office rent, are accumulated as overhead costs and allocated to individual jobs using an activity base, such as professional service hours.

At a Glance 2

Describe cost accounting systems used by manufacturing businesses.

Key Points A cost accounting system accumulates product costs. The two primary cost accounting systems are the job order and the process cost systems. Job order cost systems accumulate costs for each quantity of product that passes through the factory. Process cost systems accumulate costs for each department or process within the factory.

Learning Outcomes	Example Exercises	Practice Exercises
• Describe a cost accounting system.		
• Describe a job order cost system.		
• Describe a process cost system.		

Describe and illustrate a job order cost accounting system.

Key Points A job order cost system accumulates costs for each quantity of product, or "job," that passes through the factory. Direct materials, direct labor, and factory overhead are accumulated on the job cost sheet, which is the subsidiary cost ledger for each job. Direct materials and direct labor are assigned to individual jobs, based on the quantity used. Factory overhead costs are assigned to each job, based on an activity base that reflects the use of factory overhead costs.

Learning Outcomes	Example Exercises	Practice Exercises
• Describe the flow of materials and how materials costs are assigned.		
• Prepare the journal entry to record materials used in production.	**EE2-1**	**PE2-1A, 2-1B**
• Describe how factory labor hours are recorded and how labor costs are assigned.		
• Prepare the journal entry to record factory labor used in production.	**EE2-2**	**PE2-2A, 2-2B**
• Describe and illustrate how factory overhead costs are accumulated and assigned.	**EE2-3** **EE2-4**	**PE2-3A, 2-3B** **PE2-4A, 2-4B**
• Compute the predetermined overhead rate.	**EE2-4**	**PE2-4A, 2-4B**
• Describe and illustrate how to dispose of the balance in the factory overhead account.		
• Describe and illustrate how costs are accumulated for work in process and finished goods inventories.	**EE2-5**	**PE2-5A, 2-5B**
• Describe how costs are assigned to the cost of goods sold.	**EE2-6**	**PE2-6A, 2-6B**
• Describe and illustrate the flow of costs.		

Describe the use of job order cost information for decision making.

Key Points Job order cost systems can be used to evaluate cost performance. Unit costs can be compared over time to determine if product costs are staying within expected ranges.

Learning Outcome	Example Exercises	Practice Exercises
• Describe and illustrate how job cost sheets can be used to investigate possible reasons for increased product costs.		

Describe the flow of costs for a service business that uses a job order cost accounting system.

Key Points Job order cost accounting systems can be used by service businesses to plan and control operations. Because the product is a service, the focus is on direct labor and overhead costs. The costs of providing a service are accumulated in a work in process account and transferred to a cost of services account upon completion.

Learning Outcome	Example Exercises	Practice Exercises
• Describe how service businesses use a job order cost system.		

Key Terms

activity base (46)
activity-based costing (47)
cost accounting systems (40)
cost allocation (46)
finished goods ledger (51)
job cost sheets (43)
job order cost system (40)
materials ledger (42)
materials requisition (43)
overapplied factory overhead (48)
predetermined factory overhead rate (46)
process cost system (40)
receiving report (43)
time tickets (44)
underapplied factory overhead (48)

Illustrative Problem

Wildwing Entertainment Inc. is a manufacturer that uses a job order cost system. The following data summarize the operations related to production for March, the first month of operations:

a. Materials purchased on account, $15,500.

b. Materials requisitioned and labor used:

	Materials	Factory Labor
Job No. 100	$2,650	$1,770
Job No. 101	1,240	650
Job No. 102	980	420
Job No. 103	3,420	1,900
Job No. 104	1,000	500
Job No. 105	2,100	1,760
For general factory use	450	650

c. Factory overhead costs incurred on account, $2,700.

d. Depreciation of machinery, $1,750.

e. Factory overhead is applied at a rate of 70% of direct labor cost.

f. Jobs completed: Nos. 100, 101, 102, 104.

g. Jobs 100, 101, and 102 were shipped, and customers were billed for $8,100, $3,800, and $3,500, respectively.

Instructions

1. Journalize the entries to record these transactions.
2. Determine the account balances for Work in Process and Finished Goods.
3. Prepare a schedule of unfinished jobs to support the balance in the work in process account.
4. Prepare a schedule of completed jobs on hand to support the balance in the finished goods account.

Solution

1\. a. Materials 15,500
Accounts Payable 15,500

	Debit	Credit
1. a. Materials	15,500	
Accounts Payable		15,500
b. Work in Process	11,390	
Materials		11,390
Work in Process	7,000	
Wages Payable		7,000
Factory Overhead	1,100	
Materials		450
Wages Payable		650
c. Factory Overhead	2,700	
Accounts Payable		2,700
d. Factory Overhead	1,750	
Accumulated Depreciation—Machinery		1,750
e. Work in Process	4,900	
Factory Overhead (70% of $7,000)		4,900
f. Finished Goods	11,548	
Work in Process		11,548

Computation of the cost of jobs finished:

Job	Direct Materials	Direct Labor	Factory Overhead	Total
Job No. 100	$2,650	$1,770	$1,239	$ 5,659
Job No. 101	1,240	650	455	2,345
Job No. 102	980	420	294	1,694
Job No. 104	1,000	500	350	1,850
				$11,548

	Debit	Credit
g. Accounts Receivable	15,400	
Sales		15,400
Cost of Goods Sold	9,698	
Finished Goods		9,698

Cost of jobs sold computation:

Job No. 100	$5,659
Job No. 101	2,345
Job No. 102	1,694
	$9,698

2\. Work in Process: $11,742 ($11,390 + $7,000 + $4,900 – $11,548)

Finished Goods: $1,850 ($11,548 – $9,698)

3\. **Schedule of Unfinished Jobs**

Job	Direct Materials	Direct Labor	Factory Overhead	Total
Job No. 103	$3,420	$1,900	$1,330	$ 6,650
Job No. 105	2,100	1,760	1,232	5,092
Balance of Work in Process, March 31				$11,742

4\. **Schedule of Completed Jobs**

Job No. 104:	
Direct materials	$1,000
Direct labor	500
Factory overhead	350
Balance of Finished Goods, March 31	$1,850

Discussion Questions

1. a. Name two principal types of cost accounting systems.
   b. Which system provides for a separate record of each particular quantity of product that passes through the factory?
   c. Which system accumulates the costs for each department or process within the factory?
2. What kind of firm would use a job order cost system?
3. Which account is used in the job order cost system to accumulate direct materials, direct labor, and factory overhead applied to production costs for individual jobs?
4. What document is the source for (a) debiting the accounts in the materials ledger and (b) crediting the accounts in the materials ledger?
5. What is a job cost sheet?
6. What is the difference between a clock card and time ticket?
7. Discuss how the predetermined factory overhead rate can be used in job order cost accounting to assist management in pricing jobs.
8. a. How is a predetermined factory overhead rate calculated?
   b. Name three common bases used in calculating the rate.
9. a. What is (1) overapplied factory overhead and (2) underapplied factory overhead?
   b. If the factory overhead account has a debit balance, was factory overhead underapplied or overapplied?
   c. If the factory overhead account has a credit balance at the end of the first month of the fiscal year, where will the amount of this balance be reported on the interim balance sheet?
10. Describe how a job order cost system can be used for professional service businesses.

Practice Exercises

EE 2-1 p. 44

PE 2-1A Issuance of materials **OBJ. 2**

On April 6, Almerinda Company purchased on account 60,000 units of raw materials at $12 per unit. On April 21, raw materials were requisitioned for production as follows: 25,000 units for Job 50 at $10 per unit and 27,000 units for Job 51 at $12 per unit. Journalize the entry on April 6 to record the purchase and on April 21 to record the requisition from the materials storeroom.

EE 2-1 p. 44

PE 2-1B Issuance of materials **OBJ. 2**

On August 4, Rothchild Company purchased on account 12,000 units of raw materials at $14 per unit. On August 24, raw materials were requisitioned for production as follows: 5,000 units for Job 40 at $8 per unit and 6,200 units for Job 42 at $14 per unit. Journalize the entry on August 4 to record the purchase and on August 24 to record the requisition from the materials storeroom.

EE 2-2 *p. 45* **PE 2-2A Direct labor costs** **OBJ. 2**

During April, Almerinda Company accumulated 20,000 hours of direct labor costs on Job 50 and 24,000 hours on Job 51. The total direct labor was incurred at a rate of $20.00 per direct labor hour for Job 50 and $22.00 per direct labor hour for Job 51. Journalize the entry to record the flow of labor costs into production during April.

EE 2-2 *p. 45* **PE 2-2B Direct labor costs** **OBJ. 2**

During August, Rothchild Company accumulated 3,500 hours of direct labor costs on Job 40 and 4,200 hours on Job 42. The total direct labor was incurred at a rate of $25.00 per direct labor hour for Job 40 and $23.50 per direct labor hour for Job 42. Journalize the entry to record the flow of labor costs into production during August.

EE 2-3 *p. 46* **PE 2-3A Factory overhead costs** **OBJ. 2**

During April, Almerinda Company incurred factory overhead costs as follows: indirect materials, $42,000; indirect labor, $90,000; utilities cost, $16,000; and factory depreciation, $54,000. Journalize the entry to record the factory overhead incurred during April.

EE 2-3 *p. 46* **PE 2-3B Factory overhead costs** **OBJ. 2**

During August, Rothchild Company incurred factory overhead costs as follows: indirect materials, $17,500; indirect labor, $22,000; utilities cost, $9,600; and factory depreciation, $17,500. Journalize the entry to record the factory overhead incurred during August.

EE 2-4 *p. 49* **PE 2-4A Applying factory overhead** **OBJ. 2**

Almerinda Company estimates that total factory overhead costs will be $1,750,000 for the year. Direct labor hours are estimated to be 500,000. For Almerinda Company, (a) determine the predetermined factory overhead rate using direct labor hours as the activity base, (b) determine the amount of factory overhead applied to Jobs 50 and 51 in April using the data on direct labor hours from Practice Exercise 2-2A, and (c) prepare the journal entry to apply factory overhead to both jobs in April according to the predetermined overhead rate.

EE 2-4 *p. 49* **PE 2-4B Applying factory overhead** **OBJ. 2**

Rothchild Company estimates that total factory overhead costs will be $810,000 for the year. Direct labor hours are estimated to be 90,000. For Rothchild Company, (a) determine the predetermined factory overhead rate using direct labor hours as the activity base, (b) determine the amount of factory overhead applied to Jobs 40 and 42 in August using the data on direct labor hours from Practice Exercise 2-2B, and (c) prepare the journal entry to apply factory overhead to both jobs in August according to the predetermined overhead rate.

EE 2-5 *p. 51* **PE 2-5A Job costs** **OBJ. 2**

At the end of April, Almerinda Company had completed Jobs 50 and 51. Job 50 is for 23,040 units, and Job 51 is for 26,000 units. Using the data from Practice Exercises 2-1A, 2-2A, and 2-4A, determine (a) the balance on the job cost sheets for Jobs 50 and 51 at the end of April and (b) the cost per unit for Jobs 50 and 51 at the end of April.

EE 2-5 *p. 51* **PE 2-5B Job costs** **OBJ. 2**

At the end of August, Rothchild Company had completed Jobs 40 and 42. Job 40 is for 10,000 units, and Job 42 is for 11,000 units. Using the data from Practice Exercises 2-1B, 2-2B, and 2-4B, determine (a) the balance on the job cost sheets for Jobs 40 and 42 at the end of August and (b) the cost per unit for Jobs 40 and 42 at the end of August.

EE 2-6 *p. 52*

SHOW ME HOW

PE 2-6A Cost of goods sold

OBJ. 2

Hosmer Company completed 312,000 units during the year at a cost of $7,800,000. The beginning finished goods inventory was 22,000 units at $440,000. Determine the cost of goods sold for 325,000 units, assuming a FIFO cost flow.

EE 2-6 *p. 52*

SHOW ME HOW

PE 2-6B Cost of goods sold

OBJ. 2

Skeleton Company completed 200,000 units during the year at a cost of $3,000,000. The beginning finished goods inventory was 25,000 units at $310,000. Determine the cost of goods sold for 210,000 units, assuming a FIFO cost flow.

Exercises

EX 2-1 Transactions in a job order cost system

OBJ. 2

Five selected transactions for the current month are indicated by letters in the following T accounts in a job order cost accounting system:

Materials	
	(a)

Work in Process	
(a)	(d)
(b)	
(c)	

Wages Payable	
	(b)

Finished Goods	
(d)	(e)

Factory Overhead	
(a)	(c)
(b)	

Cost of Goods Sold	
(e)	

Describe each of the five transactions.

EX 2-2 Cost flow relationships

OBJ. 2

✔ b. $1,005,200

SHOW ME HOW

The following information is available for the first month of operations of Kellman Inc., a manufacturer of art and craft items:

Sales	$3,600,000
Gross profit	650,000
Indirect labor	216,000
Indirect materials	120,000
Other factory overhead	45,000
Materials purchased	1,224,000
Total manufacturing costs for the period	2,640,000
Materials inventory, end of period	98,800

Using this information, determine the following missing amounts:

a. Cost of goods sold
b. Direct materials cost
c. Direct labor cost

EX 2-3 Cost of materials issuances under the FIFO method

OBJ. 2

✔ b. $2,280

An incomplete subsidiary ledger of materials inventory for May is as follows:

RECEIVED			ISSUED			BALANCE			
Receiving Report Number	Quantity	Unit Price	Materials Requisition Number	Quantity	Amount	Date	Quantity	Unit Price	Amount
						May 1	285	$30.00	$8,550
40	130	$32.00				May 4	____	____	____
			91	365		May 10	____	____	____
44	110	38.00				May 21	____	____	____
			97	100		May 27	____	____	____

a. Complete the materials issuances and balances for the materials subsidiary ledger under FIFO.

b. Determine the materials inventory balance at the end of May.

c. Journalize the summary entry to transfer materials to work in process.

d. Explain how the materials ledger might be used as an aid in maintaining inventory quantities on hand.

EX 2-4 Entry for issuing materials

OBJ. 2

SHOW ME HOW

Materials issued for the current month are as follows:

Requisition No.	Material	Job No.	Amount
201	Aluminum	500	$88,700
202	Plastic	503	27,600
203	Rubber	504	3,650
204	Glue	Indirect	2,250
205	Steel	510	38,750

Journalize the entry to record the issuance of materials.

EX 2-5 Entries for materials

OBJ. 2

✔ c. fabric, $90,100

SHOW ME HOW

Eclectic Ergonomics Company manufactures designer furniture. Eclectic Ergonomics uses a job order cost system. Balances on April 1 from the materials ledger are as follows:

Fabric	$ 67,500
Polyester filling	20,200
Lumber	150,000
Glue	6,550

The materials purchased during April are summarized from the receiving reports as follows:

Fabric	$338,400
Polyester filling	470,400
Lumber	902,400
Glue	32,400

Materials were requisitioned to individual jobs as follows:

	Fabric	Polyester Filling	Lumber	Glue	Total
Job 81	$127,400	$160,800	$401,200		$ 689,400
Job 82	97,200	145,200	375,000		617,400
Job 83	91,200	118,400	210,000		419,600
Factory overhead—indirect materials				$34,800	34,800
Total	$315,800	$424,400	$986,200	$34,800	$1,761,200

(Continued)

The glue is not a significant cost, so it is treated as indirect materials (factory overhead).

a. Journalize the entry to record the purchase of materials in April.

b. Journalize the entry to record the requisition of materials in April.

c. Determine the April 30 balances that would be shown in the materials ledger accounts.

EX 2-6 Entry for factory labor costs

OBJ. 2

SHOW ME HOW

A summary of the time tickets for the current month follows:

Job No.	Amount	Job No.	Amount
100	$ 3,860	Indirect	$ 6,340
101	4,300	111	7,120
104	24,500	115	7,400
108	18,600	117	32,000

Journalize the entry to record the factory labor costs.

EX 2-7 Entry for factory labor costs

OBJ. 2

The weekly time tickets indicate the following distribution of labor hours for three direct labor employees:

	Hours			
	Job 301	Job 302	Job 303	Process Improvement
Tom Couro	10	15	13	2
David Clancy	12	12	14	2
Jose Cano	11	13	15	1

The direct labor rate earned per hour by the three employees is as follows:

Tom Couro	$32
David Clancy	36
Jose Cano	28

The process improvement category includes training, quality improvement, and other indirect tasks.

a. Journalize the entry to record the factory labor costs for the week.

b. Assume that Jobs 301 and 302 were completed but not sold during the week and that Job 303 remained incomplete at the end of the week. How would the direct labor costs for all three jobs be reflected on the financial statements at the end of the week?

EX 2-8 Entries for direct labor and factory overhead

OBJ. 2

SHOW ME HOW

Dash Industries Inc. manufactures recreational vehicles. Dash uses a job order cost system. The time tickets from April jobs are summarized as follows:

Job 201	$5,250
Job 202	6,100
Job 203	4,280
Job 204	5,620
Factory supervision	2,785

Factory overhead is applied to jobs on the basis of a predetermined overhead rate of $25 per direct labor hour. The direct labor rate is $50 per hour.

a. Journalize the entry to record the factory labor costs.

b. Journalize the entry to apply factory overhead to production for April.

✔ b. $36 per direct labor hour

SHOW ME HOW

EX 2-9 Factory overhead rates, entries, and account balance OBJ. 2

Tiny Biggs Company operates two factories. The company applies factory overhead to jobs on the basis of machine hours in Factory 1 and on the basis of direct labor hours in Factory 2. Estimated factory overhead costs, direct labor hours, and machine hours are as follows:

	Factory 1	Factory 2
Estimated factory overhead cost for fiscal year beginning September 1	$1,456,000	$954,000
Estimated direct labor hours for year		26,500
Estimated machine hours for year	52,000	
Actual factory overhead costs for September	$117,600	$102,350
Actual direct labor hours for September		2,795
Actual machine hours for September	4,250	

a. Determine the factory overhead rate for Factory 1.

b. Determine the factory overhead rate for Factory 2.

c. Journalize the entries to apply factory overhead to production in each factory for September.

d. Determine the balances of the factory overhead accounts for each factory as of September 30, and indicate whether the amounts represent overapplied or underapplied factory overhead.

SHOW ME HOW

EX 2-10 Predetermined factory overhead rate OBJ. 2

Spring Street Engine Shop uses a job order cost system to determine the cost of performing engine repair work. Estimated costs and expenses for the coming period are as follows:

Engine parts	$ 875,000
Shop direct labor	660,000
Shop and repair equipment depreciation	44,500
Shop supervisor salaries	138,000
Shop property taxes	27,500
Shop supplies	10,000
Advertising expense	22,100
Administrative office salaries	73,500
Administrative office depreciation expense	8,600
Total costs and expenses	$1,859,200

The average shop direct labor rate is $30 per hour.
Determine the predetermined shop overhead rate per direct labor hour.

✔ a. $290 per hour

SHOW ME HOW

EX 2-11 Predetermined factory overhead rate OBJ. 2

Poehling Medical Center has a single operating room that is used by local physicians to perform surgical procedures. The cost of using the operating room is accumulated by each patient procedure and includes the direct materials costs (drugs and medical devices), physician surgical time, and operating room overhead. On January 1 of the current year, the annual operating room overhead is estimated to be:

Disposable supplies	$299,600
Depreciation expense	75,000
Utilities	32,000
Nurse salaries	278,500
Technician wages	126,900
Total operating room overhead	$812,000

(Continued)

The overhead costs will be assigned to procedures, based on the number of surgical room hours. Poehling Medical Center expects to use the operating room an average of eight hours per day, seven days per week. In addition, the operating room will be shut down two weeks per year for general repairs.

a. Determine the predetermined operating room overhead rate for the year.

b. Bill Harris had a five-hour procedure on January 22. How much operating room overhead would be charged to his procedure, using the rate determined in part (a)?

c. During January, the operating room was used 240 hours. The actual overhead costs incurred for January were $67,250. Determine the overhead under- or overapplied for the period.

EX 2-12 Entry for jobs completed; cost of unfinished jobs **OBJ. 2**

✔ b. $95,200

SHOW ME HOW

The following account appears in the ledger prior to recognizing the jobs completed in August:

Work in Process	
Balance, August 1	$ 60,000
Direct materials	325,000
Direct labor	462,000
Factory overhead	210,000

Jobs finished during August are summarized as follows:

Job 210	$197,800	Job 224	$ 160,000
Job 216	240,000	Job 230	364,000

a. Journalize the entry to record the jobs completed.

b. Determine the cost of the unfinished jobs at August 31.

EX 2-13 Entries for factory costs and jobs completed **OBJ. 2**

✔ d. $73,750

Old School Publishing Inc. began printing operations on January 1. Jobs 301 and 302 were completed during the month, and all costs applicable to them were recorded on the related cost sheets. Jobs 303 and 304 are still in process at the end of the month, and all applicable costs except factory overhead have been recorded on the related cost sheets. In addition to the materials and labor charged directly to the jobs, $8,000 of indirect materials and $12,400 of indirect labor were used during the month. The cost sheets for the four jobs entering production during the month are as follows, in summary form:

Job 301		Job 302	
Direct materials	$10,000	Direct materials	$20,000
Direct labor	8,000	Direct labor	17,000
Factory overhead	6,000	Factory overhead	12,750
Total	$24,000	Total	$49,750

Job 303		Job 304	
Direct materials	$24,000	Direct materials	$14,000
Direct labor	18,000	Direct labor	12,000
Factory overhead	—	Factory overhead	—

Journalize the summary entry to record each of the following operations for January (one entry for each operation):

a. Direct and indirect materials used.

b. Direct and indirect labor used.

c. Factory overhead applied to all four jobs (a single overhead rate is used based on direct labor cost).

d. Completion of Jobs 301 and 302.

EX 2-14 Financial statements of a manufacturing firm **OBJ. 2**

✔ a. Income from operations, $170,000

The following events took place for Chi-Lite Inc. during June 2016, the first month of operations as a producer of road bikes:

- Purchased $400,000 of materials.
- Used $343,750 of direct materials in production.
- Incurred $295,000 of direct labor wages.
- Applied factory overhead at a rate of 75% of direct labor cost.
- Transferred $815,000 of work in process to finished goods.
- Sold goods with a cost of $789,000.
- Sold goods for $1,400,000.
- Incurred $316,000 of selling expenses.
- Incurred $125,000 of administrative expenses.

a. Prepare the June income statement for Chi-Lite. Assume that Chi-Lite uses the perpetual inventory method.

b. Determine the inventory balances at the end of the first month of operations.

EX 2-15 Decision making with job order costs **OBJ. 3**

Alvarez Manufacturing Inc. is a job shop. The management of Alvarez Manufacturing Inc. uses the cost information from the job sheets to assess cost performance. Information on the total cost, product type, and quantity of items produced is as follows:

Date	Job No.	Product	Quantity	Amount
Jan. 2	1	TT	520	$16,120
Jan. 15	22	SS	1,610	20,125
Feb. 3	30	SS	1,420	25,560
Mar. 7	41	TT	670	15,075
Mar. 24	49	SLK	2,210	22,100
May 19	58	SLK	2,550	31,875
June 12	65	TT	620	10,540
Aug. 18	78	SLK	3,110	48,205
Sept. 2	82	SS	1,210	16,940
Nov. 14	92	TT	750	8,250
Dec. 12	98	SLK	2,700	52,650

a. Develop a graph for *each* product (three graphs), with Job Number (in date order) on the horizontal axis and Unit Cost on the vertical axis. Use this information to determine Alvarez Manufacturing Inc.'s cost performance over time for the three products.

b. What additional information would you require in order to investigate Alvarez Manufacturing Inc.'s cost performance more precisely?

EX 2-16 Decision making with job order costs **OBJ. 3**

Raneri Trophies Inc. uses a job order cost system for determining the cost to manufacture award products (plaques and trophies). Among the company's products is an engraved plaque that is awarded to participants who complete a training program at a local business. The company sells the plaques to the local business for $80 each.

Each plaque has a brass plate engraved with the name of the participant. Engraving requires approximately 30 minutes per name. Improperly engraved names must be redone. The plate is screwed to a walnut backboard. This assembly takes approximately 15 minutes per unit. Improper assembly must be redone using a new walnut backboard.

(*Continued*)

During the first half of the year, Raneri had two separate plaque orders. The job cost sheets for the two separate jobs indicated the following information:

Job 101	**May 4**		
	Cost per Unit	**Units**	**Job Cost**
Direct materials:			
Wood	$20/unit	40 units	$ 800
Brass	15/unit	40 units	600
Engraving labor	20/hr.	20 hrs.	400
Assembly labor	30/hr.	10 hrs.	300
Factory overhead	10/hr.	30 hrs.	300
			$2,400
Plaques shipped			÷ 40
Cost per plaque			$ 60

Job 105	**June 10**		
	Cost per Unit	**Units**	**Job Cost**
Direct materials:			
Wood	$20/unit	34 units	$ 680
Brass	15/unit	34 units	510
Engraving labor	20/hr.	17 hrs.	340
Assembly labor	30/hr.	8.5 hrs.	255
Factory overhead	10/hr.	25.5 hrs.	255
			$2,040
Plaques shipped			÷ 30
Cost per plaque			$ 68

a. Why did the cost per plaque increase from $60 to $68?

b. What improvements would you recommend for Raneri Trophies Inc.?

EX 2-17 Job order cost accounting for a service company **OBJ. 4**

✔ **b. Underapplied, $5,530**

The law firm of Furlan and Benson accumulates costs associated with individual cases, using a job order cost system. The following transactions occurred during July:

July 3. Charged 175 hours of professional (lawyer) time to the Obsidian Co. breech of contract suit to prepare for the trial, at a rate of $150 per hour.

10. Reimbursed travel costs to employees for depositions related to the Obsidian case, $12,500.

14. Charged 260 hours of professional time for the Obsidian trial at a rate of $185 per hour.

18. Received invoice from consultants Wadsley and Harden for $30,000 for expert testimony related to the Obsidian trial.

27. Applied office overhead at a rate of $62 per professional hour charged to the Obsidian case.

31. Paid administrative and support salaries of $28,500 for the month.

31. Used office supplies for the month, $4,000.

31. Paid professional salaries of $74,350 for the month.

31. Billed Obsidian $172,500 for successful defense of the case.

a. Provide the journal entries for each of these transactions.

b. How much office overhead is over- or underapplied?

c. Determine the gross profit on the Obsidian case, assuming that over- or underapplied office overhead is closed monthly to cost of services.

✔ d. Dr. Cost of Services, $2,827,750

EX 2-18 Job order cost accounting for a service company

OBJ. 4

The Fly Company provides advertising services for clients across the nation. The Fly Company is presently working on four projects, each for a different client. The Fly Company accumulates costs for each account (client) on the basis of both direct costs and allocated indirect costs. The direct costs include the charged time of professional personnel and media purchases (air time and ad space). Overhead is allocated to each project as a percentage of media purchases. The predetermined overhead rate is 65% of media purchases.

On August 1, the four advertising projects had the following accumulated costs:

	August 1 Balances
Vault Bank	$270,000
Take Off Airlines	80,000
Sleepy Tired Hotels	210,000
Tastee Beverages	115,000
Total	$675,000

During August, The Fly Company incurred the following direct labor and media purchase costs related to preparing advertising for each of the four accounts:

	Direct Labor	Media Purchases
Vault Bank	$ 190,000	$ 710,000
Take Off Airlines	85,000	625,000
Sleepy Tired Hotels	372,000	455,000
Tastee Beverages	421,000	340,000
Total	$1,068,000	$2,130,000

At the end of August, both the Vault Bank and Take Off Airlines campaigns were completed. The costs of completed campaigns are debited to the cost of services account.

Journalize the summary entry to record each of the following for the month:

a. Direct labor costs
b. Media purchases
c. Overhead applied
d. Completion of Vault Bank and Take Off Airlines campaigns

Problems: Series A

PR 2-1A Entries for costs in a job order cost system

OBJ. 2

General Ledger

SHOW ME HOW

DiSalvio Co. uses a job order cost system. The following data summarize the operations related to production for May:

a. Materials purchased on account, $634,000.
b. Materials requisitioned, $646,200, of which $74,500 was for general factory use.
c. Factory labor used, $660,200, of which $91,200 was indirect.
d. Other costs incurred on account for factory overhead, $147,500; selling expenses, $234,000; and administrative expenses, $146,400.
e. Prepaid expenses expired for factory overhead were $29,200; for selling expenses, $26,800; and for administrative expenses, $18,000.
f. Depreciation of office building was $84,600; of office equipment, $43,340; and of factory equipment, $32,000.
g. Factory overhead costs applied to jobs, $362,000.
h. Jobs completed, $1,002,000.
i. Cost of goods sold, $890,000.

Instructions

Journalize the entries to record the summarized operations.

✔ 3. Work in Process balance, $27,288

General Ledger

PR 2-2A Entries and schedules for unfinished jobs and completed jobs

OBJ. 2

Tybee Industries Inc. uses a job order cost system. The following data summarize the operations related to production for January 2016, the first month of operations:

a. Materials purchased on account, $29,800.

b. Materials requisitioned and factory labor used:

Job	Materials	Factory Labor
301	$ 2,960	$2,775
302	3,620	3,750
303	2,400	1,875
304	8,100	6,860
305	5,100	5,250
306	3,750	3,340
For general factory use	1,080	4,100

c. Factory overhead costs incurred on account, $5,500.

d. Depreciation of machinery and equipment, $1,980.

e. The factory overhead rate is $54 per machine hour. Machine hours used:

Job	Machine Hours
301	25
302	36
303	30
304	72
305	40
306	25
Total	228

f. Jobs completed: 301, 302, 303 and 305.

g. Jobs were shipped and customers were billed as follows: Job 301, $8,250; Job 302, $11,200; Job 303, $15,000.

Instructions

1. Journalize the entries to record the summarized operations.
2. Post the appropriate entries to T accounts for Work in Process and Finished Goods, using the identifying letters as transaction codes. Insert memo account balances as of the end of the month.
3. Prepare a schedule of unfinished jobs to support the balance in the work in process account.
4. Prepare a schedule of completed jobs on hand to support the balance in the finished goods account.

PR 2-3A Job order cost sheet

OBJ. 2, 3

Remnant Carpet Company sells and installs commercial carpeting for office buildings. Remnant Carpet Company uses a job order cost system. When a prospective customer asks for a price quote on a job, the estimated cost data are inserted on an unnumbered job cost sheet. If the offer is accepted, a number is assigned to the job, and the costs incurred are recorded in the usual manner on the job cost sheet. After the job is completed, reasons for the variances between the estimated and actual costs are noted on the sheet. The data are then available to management in evaluating the efficiency of operations and in preparing quotes on future jobs. On October 1, 2016, Remnant Carpet Company gave Jackson Consulting an estimate of $9,450 to carpet the consulting firm's newly leased office. The estimate was based on the following data:

Estimated direct materials:	
200 meters at $35 per meter	$7,000
Estimated direct labor:	
16 hours at $20 per hour	320
Estimated factory overhead (75% of direct labor cost)	240
Total estimated costs	$7,560
Markup (25% of production costs)	1,890
Total estimate	$9,450

On October 3, Jackson Consulting signed a purchase contract, and the delivery and installation was completed on October 10.

The related materials requisitions and time tickets are summarized as follows:

Materials Requisition No.	Description	Amount
112	140 meters at $35	$4,900
114	68 meters at $35	2,380

Time Ticket No.	Description	Amount
H10	10 hours at $20	$200
H11	10 hours at $20	200

Instructions

1. Complete that portion of the job order cost sheet that would be prepared when the estimate is given to the customer.
2. Record the costs incurred, and prepare a job order cost sheet. Comment on the reasons for the variances between actual costs and estimated costs. For this purpose, assume that the additional meters of material used in the job were spoiled, the factory overhead rate has proven to be satisfactory, and an inexperienced employee performed the work.

PR 2-4A Analyzing manufacturing cost accounts — OBJ. 2

✔ G. $751,870

Fire Rock Company manufactures designer paddle boards in a wide variety of sizes and styles. The following incomplete ledger accounts refer to transactions that are summarized for June:

Materials

June 1	Balance	82,500	June 30	Requisitions	(A)
30	Purchases	330,000			

Work in Process

June 1	Balance	(B)	June 30	Completed jobs	(F)
30	Materials	(C)			
30	Direct labor	(D)			
30	Factory overhead applied	(E)			

Finished Goods

June 1	Balance	0	June 30	Cost of goods sold	(G)
30	Completed jobs	(F)			

Wages Payable

			June 30	Wages incurred	330,000

Factory Overhead

June 1	Balance	33,000	June 30	Factory overhead applied	(E)
30	Indirect labor	(H)			
30	Indirect materials	44,000			
30	Other overhead	237,500			

(Continued)

In addition, the following information is available:

a. Materials and direct labor were applied to six jobs in June:

Job No.	Style	Quantity	Direct Materials	Direct Labor
201	T100	550	$ 55,000	$ 41,250
202	T200	1,100	93,500	71,500
203	T400	550	38,500	22,000
204	S200	660	82,500	69,300
205	T300	480	60,000	48,000
206	S100	380	22,000	12,400
	Total	3,720	$351,500	$264,450

b. Factory overhead is applied to each job at a rate of 140% of direct labor cost.

c. The June 1 Work in Process balance consisted of two jobs, as follows:

Job No.	Style	Work in Process, June 1
Job 201	T100	$16,500
Job 202	T200	44,000
Total		$60,500

d. Customer jobs completed and units sold in June were as follows:

Job No.	Style	Completed in June	Units Sold in June
201	T100	X	440
202	T200	X	880
203	T400		0
204	S200	X	570
205	T300	X	420
206	S100		0

Instructions

1. Determine the missing amounts associated with each letter. Provide supporting calculations by completing a table with the following headings:

Job No.	Quantity	June 1 Work in Process	Direct Materials	Direct Labor	Factory Overhead	Total Cost	Unit Cost	Units Sold	Cost of Goods Sold

2. Determine the June 30 balances for each of the inventory accounts and factory overhead.

PR 2-5A Flow of costs and income statement **OBJ. 2**

✔ 1. Income from operations, $432,000

Ginocera Inc. is a designer, manufacturer, and distributor of low-cost, high-quality stainless steel kitchen knives. A new kitchen knife series called the Kitchen Ninja was released for production in early 2016. In January, the company spent $600,000 to develop a late-night advertising infomercial for the new product. During 2016, the company spent $1,400,000 promoting the product through these infomercials, and $800,000 in legal costs. The knives were ready for manufacture on January 1, 2016.

Ginocera uses a job order cost system to accumulate costs associated with the kitchen knife. The unit direct materials cost for the knife is:

Hardened steel blanks (used for knife shaft and blade)	$4.00
Wood (for handle)	1.50
Packaging	0.50

The production process is straightforward. First, the hardened steel blanks, which are purchased directly from a raw material supplier, are stamped into a single piece of metal that includes both the blade and the shaft. The stamping machine requires one hour per 250 knives.

After the knife shafts are stamped, they are brought to an assembly area where an employee attaches the handle to the shaft and packs the knife into a decorative box. The direct labor cost is $0.50 per unit.

The knives are sold to stores. Each store is given promotional materials, such as posters and aisle displays. Promotional materials cost $60 per store. In addition, shipping costs average $0.20 per knife.

Total completed production was 1,200,000 units during the year. Other information is as follows:

Number of customers (stores)	60,000
Number of knives sold	1,120,000
Wholesale price (to store) per knife	$16

Factory overhead cost is applied to jobs at the rate of $800 per stamping machine hour after the knife blanks are stamped. There were an additional 25,000 stamped knives, handles, and cases waiting to be assembled on December 31, 2016.

Instructions

1. Prepare an annual income statement for the Kitchen Ninja knife series, including supporting calculations, from the information provided.
2. Determine the balances in the work in process and finished goods inventories for the Kitchen Ninja knife series on December 31, 2016.

Problems: Series B

PR 2-1B Entries for costs in a job order cost system — OBJ. 2

General Ledger

SHOW ME HOW

Royal Technology Company uses a job order cost system. The following data summarize the operations related to production for March:

a. Materials purchased on account, $770,000.
b. Materials requisitioned, $680,000, of which $75,800 was for general factory use.
c. Factory labor used, $756,000, of which $182,000 was indirect.
d. Other costs incurred on account for factory overhead, $245,000; selling expenses, $171,500; and administrative expenses, $110,600.
e. Prepaid expenses expired for factory overhead were $24,500; for selling expenses, $28,420; and for administrative expenses, $16,660.
f. Depreciation of factory equipment was $49,500; of office equipment, $61,800; and of office building, $14,900.
g. Factory overhead costs applied to jobs, $568,500.
h. Jobs completed, $1,500,000.
i. Cost of goods sold, $1,375,000.

Instruction

Journalize the entries to record the summarized operations.

PR 2-2B Entries and schedules for unfinished jobs and completed jobs — OBJ. 2

✔ 3. Work in Process balance, $127,880

General Ledger

Hildreth Company uses a job order cost system. The following data summarize the operations related to production for April 2016, the first month of operations:

a. Materials purchased on account, $147,000.
b. Materials requisitioned and factory labor used:

Job No.	Materials	Factory Labor
101	$19,320	$19,500
102	23,100	28,140
103	13,440	14,000
104	38,200	36,500
105	18,050	15,540
106	18,000	18,700
For general factory use	9,000	20,160

(Continued)

c. Factory overhead costs incurred on account, $6,000.

d. Depreciation of machinery and equipment, $4,100.

e. The factory overhead rate is $40 per machine hour. Machine hours used:

Job	Machine Hours
101	154
102	160
103	126
104	238
105	160
106	174
Total	1,012

f. Jobs completed: 101, 102, 103, and 105.

g. Jobs were shipped and customers were billed as follows: Job 101, $62,900; Job 102, $80,700; Job 105, $45,500.

Instructions

1. Journalize the entries to record the summarized operations.
2. Post the appropriate entries to T accounts for Work in Process and Finished Goods, using the identifying letters as transaction codes. Insert memo account balances as of the end of the month.
3. Prepare a schedule of unfinished jobs to support the balance in the work in process account.
4. Prepare a schedule of completed jobs on hand to support the balance in the finished goods account.

PR 2-3B Job order cost sheet **OBJ. 2, 3**

Stretch and Trim Carpet Company sells and installs commercial carpeting for office buildings. Stretch and Trim Carpet Company uses a job order cost system. When a prospective customer asks for a price quote on a job, the estimated cost data are inserted on an unnumbered job cost sheet. If the offer is accepted, a number is assigned to the job, and the costs incurred are recorded in the usual manner on the job cost sheet. After the job is completed, reasons for the variances between the estimated and actual costs are noted on the sheet. The data are then available to management in evaluating the efficiency of operations and in preparing quotes on future jobs. On May 9, Stretch and Trim gave Lunden Consulting an estimate of $18,044 to carpet the consulting firm's newly leased office. The estimate was based on the following data:

Estimated direct materials:	
400 meters at $32 per meter	$12,800
Estimated direct labor:	
30 hours at $20 per hour	600
Estimated factory overhead (80% of direct labor cost)	480
Total estimated costs	$13,880
Markup (30% of production costs)	4,164
Total estimate	$18,044

On May 10, Lunden Consulting signed a purchase contract, and the carpet was delivered and installed on May 15.

The related materials requisitions and time tickets are summarized as follows:

Materials Requisition No.	Description	Amount
132	360 meters at $32	$11,520
134	50 meters at $32	1,600

Time Ticket No.	Description	Amount
H9	18 hours at $19	$342
H12	18 hours at $19	342

Instructions

1. Complete that portion of the job order cost sheet that would be prepared when the estimate is given to the customer. (Round factory overhead applied to the nearest dollar.)
2. Record the costs incurred, and prepare a job order cost sheet. Comment on the reasons for the variances between actual costs and estimated costs. For this purpose, assume that the additional meters of material used in the job were spoiled, the factory overhead rate has proven to be satisfactory, and an inexperienced employee performed the work.

✔ G. $700,284

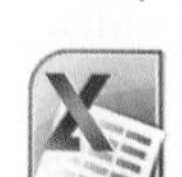

PR 2-4B Analyzing manufacturing cost accounts

OBJ. 2

Clapton Company manufactures custom guitars in a wide variety of styles. The following incomplete ledger accounts refer to transactions that are summarized for May:

Materials

May	1	Balance	105,600	May 31	Requisitions	(A)
	31	Purchases	500,000			

Work in Process

May	1	Balance	(B)	May 31	Completed jobs	(F)
	31	Materials	(C)			
	31	Direct labor	(D)			
	31	Factory overhead applied	(E)			

Finished Goods

May	1	Balance	0	May 31	Cost of goods sold	(G)
	31	Completed jobs	(F)			

Wages Payable

				May 31	Wages incurred	396,000

Factory Overhead

May	1	Balance	26,400	May 31	Factory overhead applied	(E)
	31	Indirect labor	(H)			
	31	Indirect materials	15,400			
	31	Other overhead	122,500			

In addition, the following information is available:

a. Materials and direct labor were applied to six jobs in May:

Job No.	Style	Quantity	Direct Materials	Direct Labor
101	AF1	330	$ 82,500	$ 59,400
102	AF3	380	105,400	72,600
103	AF2	500	132,000	110,000
104	VY1	400	66,000	39,600
105	VY2	660	118,800	66,000
106	AF4	330	66,000	30,800
	Total	2,600	$570,700	$378,400

b. Factory overhead is applied to each job at a rate of 50% of direct labor cost.

c. The May 1 Work in Process balance consisted of two jobs, as follows:

Job No.	Style	Work in Process, May 1
Job 101	AF1	$26,400
Job 102	AF3	46,000
Total		$72,400

(Continued)

d. Customer jobs completed and units sold in May were as follows:

Job No.	Style	Completed in May	Units Sold in May
101	AF1	X	264
102	AF3	X	360
103	AF2		0
104	VY1	X	384
105	VY2	X	530
106	AF4		0

Instructions

1. Determine the missing amounts associated with each letter. Provide supporting calculations by completing a table with the following headings:

Job No.	Quantity	May 1 Work in Process	Direct Materials	Direct Labor	Factory Overhead	Total Cost	Unit Cost	Units Sold	Cost of Goods Sold

2. Determine the May 31 balances for each of the inventory accounts and factory overhead.

PR 2-5B Flow of costs and income statement

OBJ. 2

✔ 1. Income from operations, $656,000

Technology Accessories Inc. is a designer, manufacturer, and distributor of accessories for consumer electronic products. Early in 2016, the company began production of a leather cover for tablet computers, called the iLeather. The cover is made of stitched leather with a velvet interior and fits snuggly around most tablet computers. In January, $750,000 was spent on developing marketing and advertising materials. For the first six months of 2016, the company spent $1,400,000 promoting the iLeather. The product was ready for manufacture on January 21, 2016.

Technology Accessories Inc. uses a job order cost system to accumulate costs for the iLeather. Direct materials unit costs for the iLeather are as follows:

Leather	$10.00
Velvet	5.00
Packaging	0.40
Total	$15.40

The actual production process for the iLeather is fairly straightforward. First, leather is brought to a cutting and stitching machine. The machine cuts the leather and stitches an exterior edge into the product. The machine requires one hour per 125 iLeathers.

After the iLeather is cut and stitched, it is brought to assembly, where assembly personnel affix the velvet interior and pack the iLeather for shipping. The direct labor cost for this work is $0.50 per unit.

The completed packages are then sold to retail outlets through a sales force. The sales force is compensated by a 20% commission on the wholesale price for all sales.

Total completed production was 500,000 units during the year. Other information is as follows:

Number of iLeather units sold in 2016	460,000
Wholesale price per unit	$40

Factory overhead cost is applied to jobs at the rate of $1,250 per machine hour. There were an additional 22,000 cut and stitched iLeathers waiting to be assembled on December 31, 2016.

Instructions

1. Prepare an annual income statement for the iLeather product, including supporting calculations, from the information provided.
2. Determine the balances in the finished goods and work in process inventories for the iLeather product on December 31, 2016.

Cases & Projects

CP 2-1 Managerial analysis

The controller of the plant of Minsky Company prepared a graph of the unit costs from the job cost reports for Product One. The graph appeared as follows:

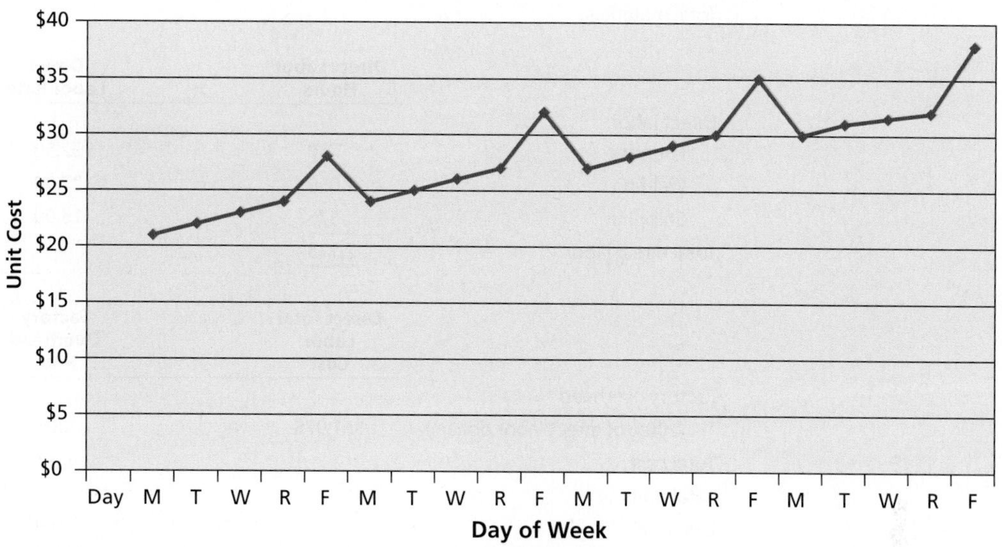

How would you interpret this information? What further information would you request?

CP 2-2 Job order decision making and rate deficiencies

RIRA Company makes attachments, such as backhoes and grader and bulldozer blades, for construction equipment. The company uses a job order cost system. Management is concerned about cost performance and evaluates the job cost sheets to learn more about the cost effectiveness of the operations. To facilitate a comparison, the cost sheet for Job 206 (50 backhoe buckets completed in October) was compared with Job 228, which was for 75 backhoe buckets completed in December. The two job cost sheets follow:

Job 206

Item: 50 backhoe buckets

Materials:	Direct Materials Quantity	×	Direct Materials Price	=	Amount
Steel (tons)	105		$1,200		$126,000
Steel components (pieces)	630		7		4,410
Total materials					$130,410

Direct labor:	Direct Labor Hours	×	Direct Labor Rate	=	Amount
Foundry	400		$22.50		$ 9,000
Welding	550		27.00		14,850
Shipping	180		18.00		3,240
Total direct labor	1,130				$ 27,090

	Direct Total Labor Cost	×	Factory Overhead Rate	=	Amount
Factory overhead					
(200% of direct labor dollars)	$27,090	×	200%		$ 54,180
Total cost					$ 211,680
Total units					÷ 50
Unit cost (rounded)					$4,233.60

(*Continued*)

Job 228

Item: 75 backhoe buckets

	Direct Materials Quantity	×	**Direct Materials Price**	=	**Amount**
Materials:					
Steel (tons)	195		$1,100		$214,500
Steel components (pieces)	945		7		6,615
Total materials					$221,115
	Direct Labor Hours	×	**Direct Labor Rate**	=	**Amount**
Direct labor:					
Foundry	750		$22.50		$ 16,875
Welding	1,050		27.00		28,350
Shipping	375		18.00		6,750
Total direct labor	2,175				$ 51,975
	Direct Total Labor Cost	×	**Factory Overhead Rate**	=	**Amount**
Factory overhead					
(200% of direct labor dollars)	$51,975	×	200%		$ 103,950
Total cost					$ 377,040
Total units					÷ 75
Unit cost					$5,027.20

Management is concerned with the increase in unit costs over the months from October to December. To understand what has occurred, management interviewed the purchasing manager and quality manager.

Purchasing Manager: Prices have been holding steady for our raw materials during the first half of the year. I found a new supplier for our bulk steel that was willing to offer a better price than we received in the past. I saw these lower steel prices and jumped at them, knowing that a reduction in steel prices would have a very favorable impact on our costs.

Quality Manager: Something happened around mid-year. All of a sudden, we were experiencing problems with respect to the quality of our steel. As a result, we've been having all sorts of problems on the shop floor in our foundry and welding operation.

1. Analyze the two job cost sheets, and identify why the unit costs have changed for the backhoe buckets. Complete the following schedule to help you in your analysis:

Item	Input Quantity per Unit—Job 206	Input Quantity per Unit—Job 228
Steel		
Foundry labor		
Welding labor		

2. How would you interpret what has happened in light of your analysis and the interviews?

CP 2-3 Factory overhead rate

Salvo Inc., a specialized equipment manufacturer, uses a job order costing system. The overhead is allocated to jobs on the basis of direct labor hours. The overhead rate is now $1,500 per direct labor hour. The design engineer thinks that this is illogical. The design engineer has stated the following:

Our accounting system doesn't make any sense to me. It tells me that every labor hour carries an additional burden of $1,500. This means that direct labor makes up only 6% of our total product cost, yet it drives all our costs. In addition, these rates give my design engineers incentives to "design out" direct labor by using machine technology. Yet, over the past years as we have had less and less direct labor, the overhead rate keeps going up and up. I won't be surprised if next year the rate is $2,000 per direct labor hour. I'm also concerned because small errors in our estimates of the direct labor content can have a large impact on our estimated costs. Just a 30-minute error in our estimate of assembly time is worth $750. Small mistakes in our direct labor time estimates really swing our bids around. I think this puts us at a disadvantage when we are going after business.

1. What is the engineer's concern about the overhead rate going "up and up"?
2. What did the engineer mean about the large overhead rate being a disadvantage when placing bids and seeking new business?
3. What do you think is a possible solution?

CP 2-4 Recording manufacturing costs

Todd Lay just began working as a cost accountant for Enteron Industries Inc., which manufactures gift items. Todd is preparing to record summary journal entries for the month. Todd begins by recording the factory wages as follows:

Wages Expense	60,000	
Wages Payable		60,000

Then the factory depreciation:

Depreciation Expense—Factory Machinery	20,000	
Accumulated Depreciation—Factory Machinery		20,000

Todd's supervisor, Jeff Fastow, walks by and notices the entries. The following conversation takes place:

Jeff: That's a very unusual way to record our factory wages and depreciation for the month.

Todd: What do you mean? This is exactly the way we were taught to record wages and depreciation in school. You know, debit an expense and credit Cash or payables, or in the case of depreciation, credit Accumulated Depreciation.

Jeff: Well, it's not the credits I'm concerned about. It's the debits—I don't think you've recorded the debits correctly. I wouldn't mind if you were recording the administrative wages or office equipment depreciation this way, but I've got real questions about recording factory wages and factory machinery depreciation this way.

Todd: Now I'm really confused. You mean this is correct for administrative costs, but not for factory costs? Well, what am I supposed to do—and why?

1. Play the role of Jeff and answer Todd's questions.
2. Why would Jeff accept the journal entries if they were for administrative costs?

CP 2-5 Predetermined overhead rates

As an assistant cost accountant for Mississippi Industries, you have been assigned to review the activity base for the predetermined factory overhead rate. The president, Tony Favre, has expressed concern that the over- or underapplied overhead has fluctuated excessively over the years.

An analysis of the company's operations and use of the current overhead rate (direct labor cost) has narrowed the possible alternative overhead bases to direct labor cost and machine hours. For the past five years, the following data have been gathered:

	2016	2015	2014	2013	2012
Actual overhead	$ 790,000	$ 870,000	$ 935,000	$ 845,000	$ 760,000
Applied overhead	777,000	882,000	924,000	840,000	777,000
(Over-) underapplied overhead	$ 13,000	$ (12,000)	$ 11,000	$ 5,000	$ (17,000)
Direct labor cost	$3,885,000	$4,410,000	$4,620,000	$4,200,000	$3,885,000
Machine hours	93,000	104,000	111,000	100,400	91,600

1. Calculate a predetermined factory overhead rate for each alternative base, assuming that rates would have been determined by relating the total amount of factory overhead for the past five years to the base.
2. For each of the past five years, determine the over- or underapplied overhead, based on the two predetermined overhead rates developed in part (1).
3. Which predetermined overhead rate would you recommend? Discuss the basis for your recommendation.

CHAPTER 3

Process Cost Systems

Dreyer's Ice Cream

In making ice cream, an electric ice cream maker is used to mix ingredients, which include milk, cream, sugar, and flavoring. After the ingredients are added, the mixer is packed with ice and salt to cool the ingredients, and it is then turned on.

After mixing for half of the required time, would you have ice cream? Of course not, because the ice cream needs to mix longer to freeze. Now, assume that you ask the question:

What costs have I incurred so far in making ice cream?

The answer to this question requires knowing the cost of the ingredients and electricity. The ingredients are added at the beginning; thus, all the ingredient costs have been incurred. Because the mixing is only half complete, only 50% of the electricity cost has been incurred. Therefore, the answer to the preceding question is:

All the materials costs and half the electricity costs have been incurred.

These same cost concepts apply to larger ice cream processes like those of **Dreyer's Ice Cream** (a subsidiary of **Nestlé**), manufacturer of Dreyer's® and Edy's® ice cream. Dreyer's mixes ingredients in 3,000-gallon vats in much the same way you would with an electric ice cream maker. Dreyer's also records the costs of the ingredients, labor, and factory overhead used in making ice cream. These costs are used by managers for decisions such as setting prices and improving operations.

This chapter describes and illustrates process cost systems that are used by manufacturers such as Dreyer's. In addition, the use of cost of production reports in decision making is described. Finally, lean manufacturing is discussed.

Learning Objectives

After studying this chapter, you should be able to: | *Example Exercises*

OBJ	Objectives	Example Exercises
1	**Describe process cost systems.**	
	Process Cost Systems	
	Comparing Job Order and Process Cost Systems	EE 3-1
	Cost Flows for a Process Manufacturer	
2	**Prepare a cost of production report.**	
	Cost of Production Report	
	Step 1: Determine the Units to Be Assigned Costs	EE 3-2
	Step 2: Compute Equivalent Units of Production	EE 3-3, 3-4
	Step 3: Determine the Cost per Equivalent Unit	EE 3-5
	Step 4: Allocate Costs to Units Transferred Out and Partially Completed Units	EE 3-6
	Preparing the Cost of Production Report	
3	**Journalize entries for transactions using a process cost system.**	
	Journal Entries for a Process Cost System	EE 3-7
4	**Describe and illustrate the use of cost of production reports for decision making.**	
	Using the Cost of Production Report for Decision Making	
	Frozen Delight	
	Holland Beverage Company	EE 3-8
	Yield	
5	**Compare lean manufacturing with traditional manufacturing processing.**	
	Lean Manufacturing	
	Traditional Production Process	
	Lean Manufacturing	

At a Glance 3 Page 107

Describe process cost systems.

Process Cost Systems

A **process manufacturer** produces products that are indistinguishable from each other using a continuous production process. For example, an oil refinery processes crude oil through a series of steps to produce a barrel of gasoline. One barrel of gasoline, the product, cannot be distinguished from another barrel. Other examples of process manufacturers include paper producers, chemical processors, aluminum smelters, and food processors.

Integrity, Objectivity, and Ethics in Business

ON BEING GREEN

Process manufacturing often involves significant energy and material resources, which can be harmful to the environment. Thus, many process manufacturing companies, such as chemical, electronic, and metal processors, must address environmental issues. Companies, such as **DuPont**, **Intel**, **Apple**, and **Alcoa**, are at the forefront of providing environmental solutions for their products and processes.

For example, Apple provides free recycling programs for Macs®, iPhones®, and iPads®. Apple recovers more than 90% by weight of the original product in reusable components, glass, and plastic. You can even receive a free gift card for voluntarily recycling an older Apple product.

Source: Apple Web site.

The cost accounting system used by process manufacturers is called the **process cost system.** A process cost system records product costs for each manufacturing department or process.

In contrast, a job order manufacturer produces custom products for customers or batches of similar products. For example, a custom printer produces wedding invitations, graduation announcements, or other special print items that are tailored to the specifications of each customer. Each item manufactured is unique to itself. Other examples of job order manufacturers include furniture manufacturers, shipbuilders, and home builders.

As described and illustrated in Chapter 2, the cost accounting system used by job order manufacturers is called the *job order cost system.* A job order cost system records product cost for each job, using job cost sheets.

Some examples of process and job order companies and their products are shown in Exhibit 1.

EXHIBIT 1

Examples of Process Cost and Job Order Companies

Process Manufacturing Companies		Job Order Companies	
Company	**Product**	**Company**	**Product**
Pepsi	soft drinks	Walt Disney	movies
Alcoa	aluminum	Nike, Inc.	athletic shoes
Intel	computer chip	Nicklaus Design	golf courses
Apple	iPhone	Heritage Log Homes	log homes
Hershey Foods	chocolate bars	DDB Advertising Agency	advertising

Comparing Job Order and Process Cost Systems

Process and job order cost systems are similar in that each system:

- Records and summarizes product costs.
- Classifies product costs as direct materials, direct labor, and factory overhead.
- Allocates factory overhead costs to products.
- Uses perpetual inventory system for materials, work in process, and finished goods.
- Provides useful product cost information for decision making.

Process and job costing systems are different in several ways. As a basis for illustrating these differences, the cost systems for **Frozen Delight** and **Legend Guitars** are used.

Exhibit 2 illustrates the process cost system for Frozen Delight, an ice cream manufacturer. As a basis for comparison, Exhibit 2 also illustrates the job order cost system for Legend Guitars, a custom guitar manufacturer. Legend Guitars was described and illustrated in Chapters 1 and 2.

Exhibit 2 indicates that Frozen Delight manufactures ice cream, using two departments:

- The Mixing Department mixes the ingredients, using large vats.
- The Packaging Department puts the ice cream into cartons for shipping to customers.

Because each gallon of ice cream is similar, product costs are recorded in each department's work in process account. As shown in Exhibit 2, Frozen Delight accumulates (records) the cost of making ice cream in *work in process accounts* for the Mixing and Packaging departments. The product costs of making a gallon of ice cream include:

- *Direct materials costs,* which include milk, cream, sugar, and packing cartons. All materials costs are added at the beginning of the process for both the Mixing Department and the Packaging Department.

EXHIBIT 2 **Process Cost and Job Order Cost Systems**

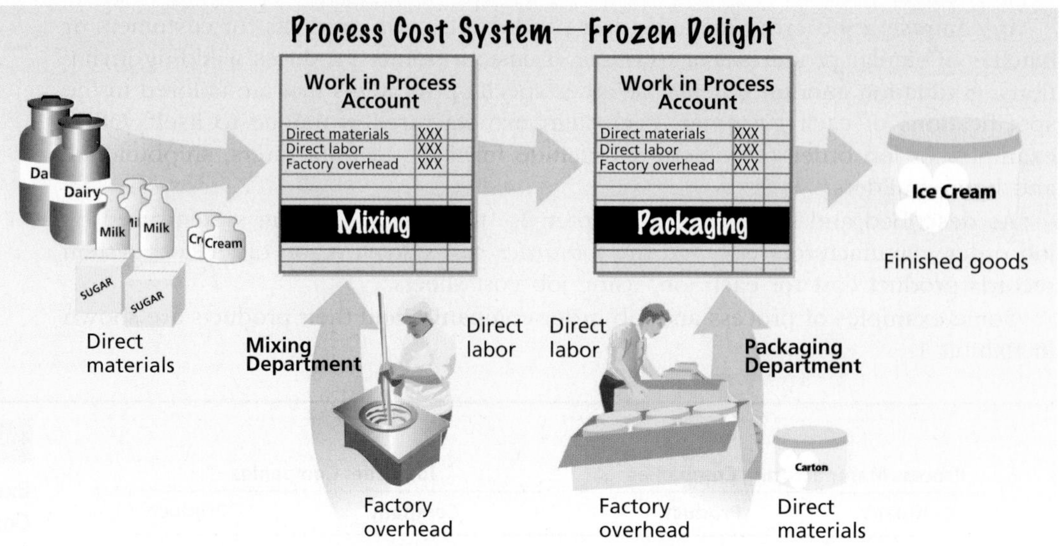

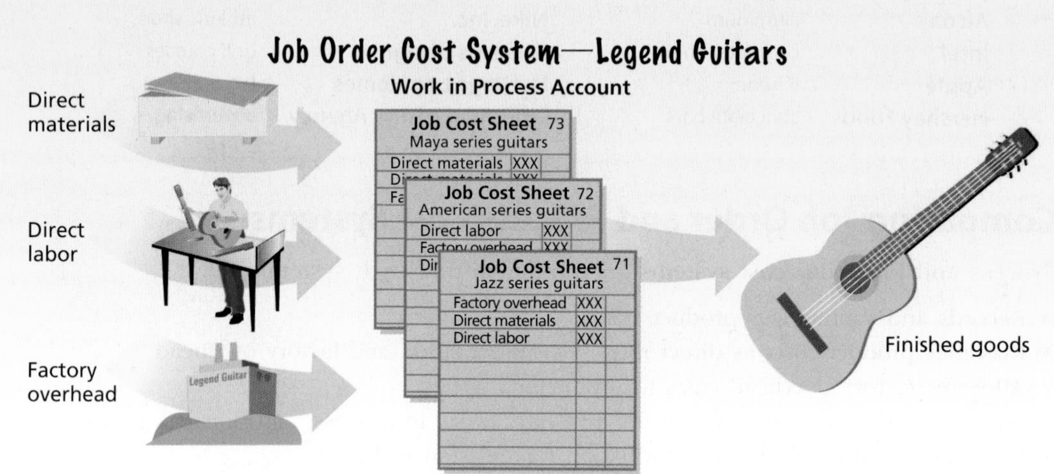

- *Direct labor costs*, which are incurred by employees in each department who run the equipment and load and unload product.
- *Factory overhead costs,* which include the utility costs (power) and depreciation on the equipment.

When the Mixing Department completes the mixing process, its product costs are transferred to the Packaging Department. When the Packaging Department completes its process, the product costs are transferred to Finished Goods. In this way, the cost of the product (a gallon of ice cream) accumulates across the entire production process.

In contrast, Exhibit 2 shows that Legend Guitars accumulates (records) product costs by jobs, using a job cost sheet for each type of guitar. Thus, Legend Guitars uses just one work in process account. As each job is completed, its product costs are transferred to Finished Goods.

In a job order cost system, the work in process at the end of the period is the sum of the job cost sheets for partially completed jobs. In a process cost system, the work in process at the end of the period is the sum of the costs remaining in each department account at the end of the period.

Example Exercise 3-1 Job Order versus Process Costing

Which of the following industries would normally use job order costing systems, and which would normally use process costing systems?

Home construction	Computer chips
Beverages	Cookies
Military aircraft	Video game design and production

Follow My Example 3-1

Home construction	Job order
Beverages	Process
Military aircraft	Job order
Computer chips	Process
Cookies	Process
Video game design and production	Job order

Practice Exercises: PE 3-1A, PE 3-1B

Cost Flows for a Process Manufacturer

Exhibit 3 illustrates the *physical flow* of materials for **Frozen Delight**. Ice cream is made in a manufacturing plant in much the same way you would make it at home, except on a larger scale.

EXHIBIT 3 **Physical Flows for a Process Manufacturer**

Materials | Mixing Department | Packaging Department | Finished Goods Inventory

Dairy | Milk | Cream | SUGAR | Freezer

In the Mixing Department, direct materials in the form of milk, cream, and sugar are placed into a vat. An employee fills each vat, sets the cooling temperature, and sets the mix speed. The vat is cooled as the direct materials are being mixed by agitators (paddles). Factory overhead includes equipment depreciation and indirect materials.

In the Packaging Department, the ice cream is received from the Mixing Department in a form ready for packaging. The Packaging Department uses direct labor and factory overhead to package the ice cream into one-gallon containers. The ice cream is then transferred to finished goods, where it is frozen and stored in refrigerators prior to shipment to customers.

The *cost flows* in a process cost accounting system are similar to the *physical flow* of materials illustrated in Exhibit 3. The cost flows for **Frozen Delight** are illustrated in Exhibit 4 as follows:

Materials costs can be as high as 70% of the total product costs for many process manufacturers.

a. The cost of materials purchased is recorded in the materials account.

b. The cost of direct materials used by the Mixing and Packaging departments is recorded in the work in process accounts for each department.

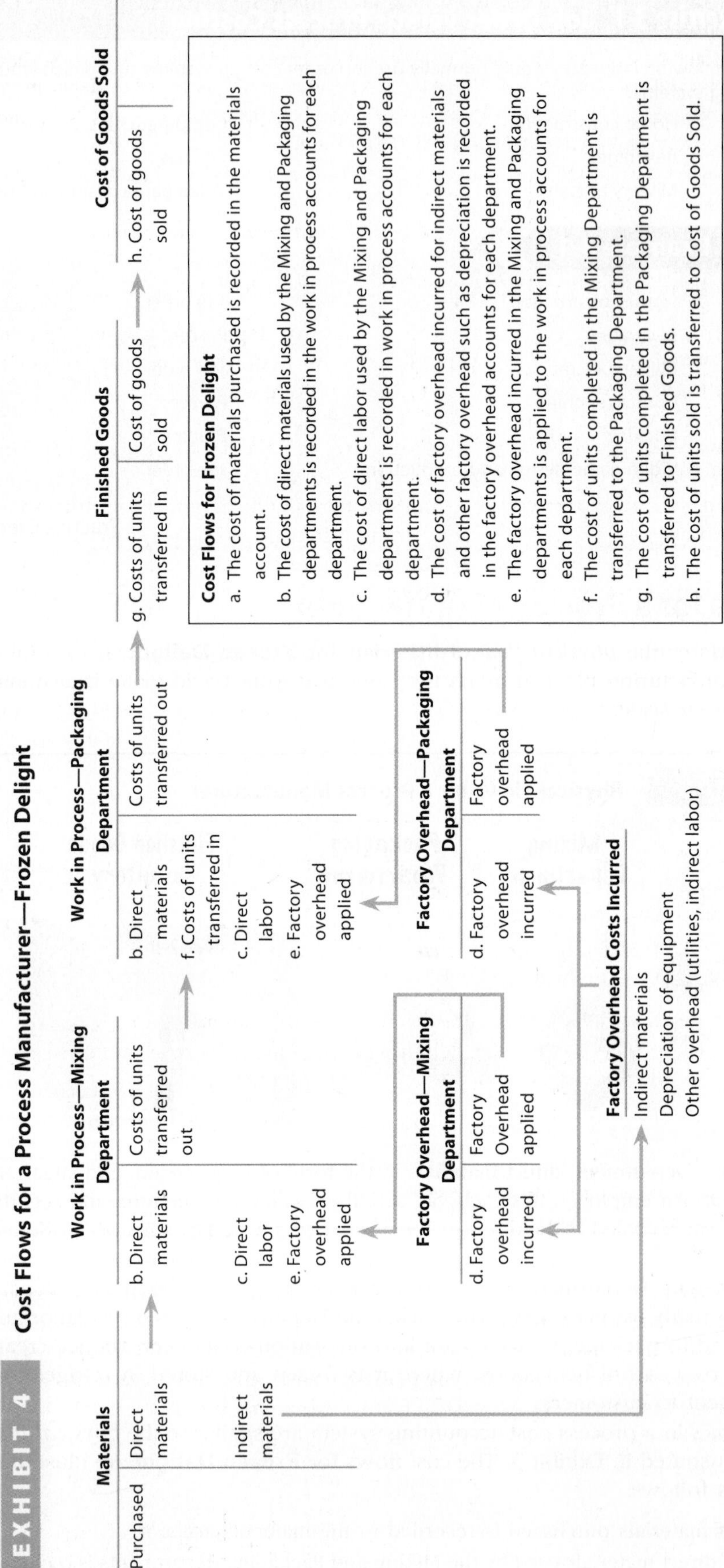
EXHIBIT 4
Cost Flows for a Process Manufacturer—Frozen Delight
Materials
a. Purchased
Direct materials
Indirect materials
Work in Process—Mixing Department
b. Direct materials
c. Direct labor
e. Factory overhead applied
Costs of units transferred out
Work in Process—Packaging Department
b. Direct materials
f. Costs of units transferred in
c. Direct labor
e. Factory overhead applied
Costs of units transferred out
Finished Goods
g. Costs of units transferred In
Cost of goods sold
Cost of Goods Sold
h. Cost of goods sold
Factory Overhead—Mixing Department
d. Factory overhead incurred
Factory Overhead applied
Factory Overhead—Packaging Department
d. Factory overhead incurred
Factory overhead applied
Factory Overhead Costs Incurred
Indirect materials
Depreciation of equipment
Other overhead (utilities, indirect labor)
Cost Flows for Frozen Delight
a. The cost of materials purchased is recorded in the materials account.
b. The cost of direct materials used by the Mixing and Packaging departments is recorded in the work in process accounts for each department.
c. The cost of direct labor used by the Mixing and Packaging departments is recorded in work in process accounts for each department.
d. The cost of factory overhead incurred for indirect materials and other factory overhead such as depreciation is recorded in the factory overhead accounts for each department.
e. The factory overhead incurred in the Mixing and Packaging departments is applied to the work in process accounts for each department.
f. The cost of units completed in the Mixing Department is transferred to the Packaging Department.
g. The cost of units completed in the Packaging Department is transferred to Finished Goods.
h. The cost of units sold is transferred to Cost of Goods Sold.

c. The cost of direct labor used by the Mixing and Packaging departments is recorded in work in process accounts for each department.
d. The cost of factory overhead incurred for indirect materials and other factory overhead such as depreciation is recorded in the factory overhead accounts for each department.
e. The factory overhead incurred in the Mixing and Packaging departments is applied to the work in process accounts for each department.
f. The cost of units completed in the Mixing Department is transferred to the Packaging Department.
g. The cost of units completed in the Packaging Department is transferred to Finished Goods.
h. The cost of units sold is transferred to Cost of Goods Sold.

As shown in Exhibit 4, the Mixing and Packaging departments have separate factory overhead accounts. The factory overhead costs incurred for indirect materials, depreciation, and other overhead are debited to each department's factory overhead account. The overhead is applied to work in process by debiting each department's work in process account and crediting the department's factory overhead account.

Exhibit 4 illustrates how the Mixing and Packaging departments have separate work in process accounts. Each work in process account is debited for direct materials, direct labor, and applied factory overhead. In addition, the work in process account for the Packaging Department is debited for the cost of the units transferred in from the Mixing Department. Each work in process account is credited for the cost of the units transferred to the next department.

Lastly, Exhibit 4 shows that the finished goods account is debited for the cost of the units transferred from the Packaging Department. The finished goods account is credited for the cost of the units sold, which is debited to the cost of goods sold account.

Cost of Production Report

Prepare a cost of production report.

In a process cost system, the cost of units transferred out of each processing department must be determined along with the cost of any partially completed units remaining in the department. The report that summarizes these costs is a cost of production report.

The **cost of production report** summarizes the production and cost data for a department as follows:

- The units the department is accountable for and the disposition of those units.
- The product costs incurred by the department and the allocation of those costs between completed (transferred out) and partially completed units.

A cost of production report is prepared using the following four steps:

- Step 1. Determine the units to be assigned costs.
- Step 2. Compute equivalent units of production.
- Step 3. Determine the cost per equivalent unit.
- Step 4. Allocate costs to units transferred out and partially completed units.

Preparing a cost of production report requires making a cost flow assumption. Like merchandise inventory, costs can be assumed to flow through the manufacturing process, using the first-in, first-out (FIFO), last in, first-out (LIFO), or average cost methods. Because the **first-in, first-out (FIFO) method** is often the same as the physical flow of units, the FIFO method is used in this chapter.[1]

[1] The average cost method is illustrated in an appendix to this chapter.

To illustrate, a cost of production report for the Mixing Department of **Frozen Delight** for July 2016 is prepared. The July data for the Mixing Department are as follows:

Inventory in process, July 1, 5,000 gallons:		
Direct materials cost, for 5,000 gallons	$5,000	
Conversion costs, for 5,000 gallons, 70% completed	1,225	
Total inventory in process, July 1		$ 6,225
Direct materials cost for July, 60,000 gallons		66,000
Direct labor cost for July		10,500
Factory overhead applied for July		7,275
Total production costs to account for		$90,000
Gallons transferred to Packaging in July (includes units in process on July 1), 62,000 gallons		?
Inventory in process, July 31, 3,000 gallons, 25% completed as to conversion costs		?

By preparing a cost of production report, the cost of the gallons transferred to the Packaging Department in July and the ending work in process inventory in the Mixing Department are determined. These amounts are indicated by question marks (?).

Step 1: Determine the Units to Be Assigned Costs

The first step is to determine the units to be assigned costs. A unit can be any measure of completed production, such as tons, gallons, pounds, barrels, or cases. For **Frozen Delight**, a unit is a gallon of ice cream.

The Mixing Department is accountable for 65,000 gallons of direct materials during July, computed as follows:

Total units (gallons) charged to production:	
In process, July 1	5,000 gallons
Received from materials storage	60,000
Total units (gallons) accounted for	65,000 gallons

For July, the following three groups of units (gallons) are assigned costs:

- Group 1. Units (gallons) in beginning work in process inventory on July 1.
- Group 2. Units (gallons) started and completed during July.
- Group 3. Units (gallons) in ending work in process inventory on July 31.

Exhibit 5 illustrates these groups of units (gallons) in the Mixing Department for July. The 5,000 gallons of beginning inventory were completed and transferred to the Packaging Department. During July, 60,000 gallons of material were started (entered into mixing). Of the 60,000 gallons started in July, 3,000 gallons were incomplete on July 31. Thus, 57,000 gallons (60,000 – 3,000) were started and completed in July.

The total units (gallons) to be assigned costs for July are summarized as follows:

Group 1	Inventory in process, July 1, completed in July	5,000 gallons
Group 2	Started and completed in July	57,000
	Transferred out to the Packaging Department in July	62,000 gallons
Group 3	Inventory in process, July 31	3,000
	Total units (gallons) to be assigned costs	65,000 gallons

The total gallons to be assigned costs (65,000) equal the total gallons accounted for (65,000) by the Mixing Department.

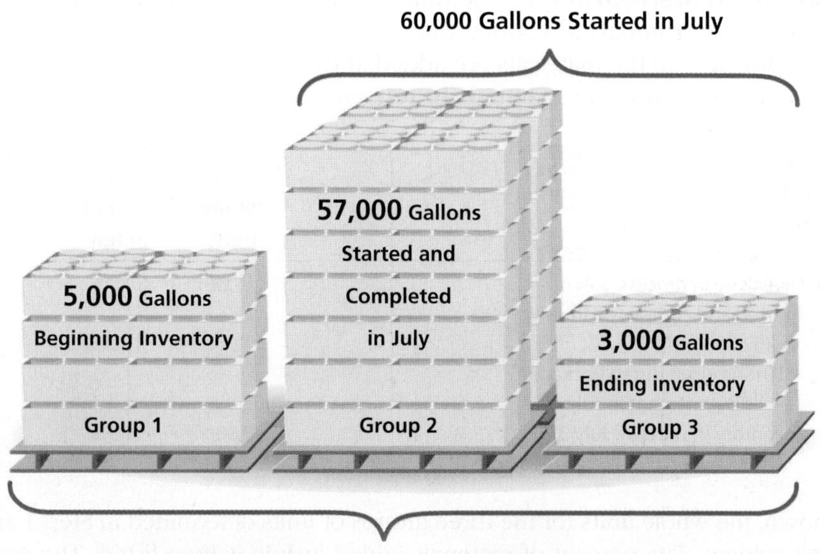

EXHIBIT 5

July Units to Be Costed—Mixing Department

Example Exercise 3-2 Units to Be Assigned Costs

OBJ 2

Rocky Springs Beverage Company has two departments, Blending and Bottling. The Bottling Department received 57,000 liters from the Blending Department. During the period, the Bottling Department completed 58,000 liters, including 4,000 liters of work in process at the beginning of the period. The ending work in process was 3,000 liters. How many liters were started and completed during the period?

Follow My Example 3-2

54,000 liters started and completed (58,000 completed – 4,000 beginning work in process), or (57,000 started – 3,000 ending work in process)

Practice Exercises: PE 3-2A, PE 3-2B

Step 2: Compute Equivalent Units of Production

Whole units are the number of units in production during a period, whether completed or not. **Equivalent units of production** are the portion of whole units that are complete with respect to materials or conversion (direct labor and factory overhead) costs.

To illustrate, assume that a 1,000-gallon batch (vat) of ice cream at **Frozen Delight** is only 40% complete in the mixing process on May 31. Thus, the batch is only 40% complete as to conversion costs such as power. In this case, the whole units and equivalent units of production are as follows:

	Whole Units	Equivalent Units
Materials costs	1,000 gallons	1,000 gallons
Conversion costs	1,000 gallons	400 gallons (1,000 × 40%)

Because the materials costs are all added at the beginning of the process, the materials costs are 100% complete for the 1,000-gallon batch of ice cream. Thus, the whole units and equivalent units for materials costs are 1,000 gallons. However, because the batch is only 40% complete as to conversion costs, the equivalent units for conversion costs are 400 gallons.

Equivalent units for materials and conversion costs are usually determined separately as shown earlier. This is because materials and conversion costs normally enter production at different times and rates. In contrast, direct labor and factory overhead normally enter production at the same time and rate. For this reason, direct labor and factory overhead are combined as conversion costs in computing equivalent units.

Materials Equivalent Units To compute equivalent units for materials, it is necessary to know how materials are added during the manufacturing process. In the case of **Frozen Delight**, all the materials are added at the beginning of the mixing process. Thus, the equivalent units for materials in July are computed as follows:

		Total Whole Units	Percent Materials Added in July	Equivalent Units for Direct Materials
Group 1	Inventory in process, July 1	5,000	0%	0
Group 2	Started and completed in July (62,000 − 5,000)	57,000	100%	57,000
	Transferred out to Packaging Department in July	62,000	—	57,000
Group 3	Inventory in process, July 31	3,000	100%	3,000
	Total gallons to be assigned cost	65,000		60,000

As shown, the whole units for the three groups of units determined in Step 1 are listed in the first column. The percent of materials added in July is then listed. The equivalent units are determined by multiplying the whole units by the percent of materials added.

To illustrate, the July 1 inventory (Group 1) has 5,000 gallons of whole units, which are complete as to materials. That is, all the direct materials for the 5,000 gallons in process on July 1 were added in June. Thus, the percent of materials added in July is zero, and the equivalent units added in July are zero.

The 57,000 gallons started and completed in July (Group 2) are 100% complete as to materials. Thus, the equivalent units for the gallons started and completed in July are 57,000 (57,000 × 100%) gallons. The 3,000 gallons in process on July 31 (Group 3) are also 100% complete as to materials because all materials are added at the beginning of the process. Therefore, the equivalent units for the inventory in process on July 31 are 3,000 (3,000 × 100%) gallons.

The equivalent units for direct materials for **Frozen Delight** are summarized in Exhibit 6.

EXHIBIT 6 **Direct Materials Equivalent Units**

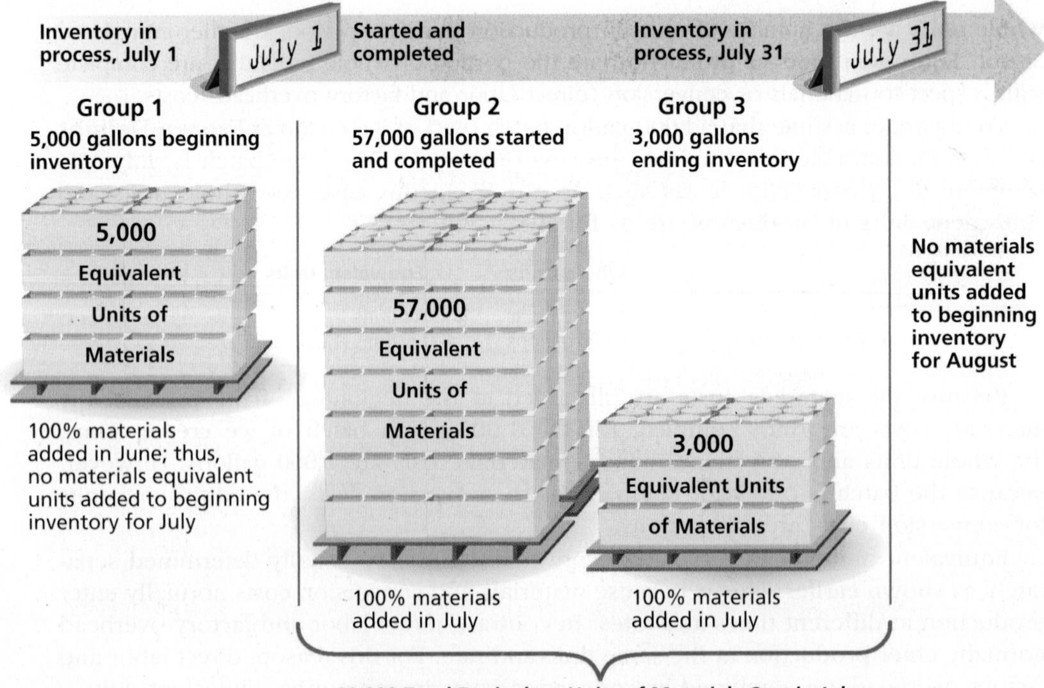

Example Exercise 3-3 Equivalent Units of Materials Cost

OBJ 2

The Bottling Department of Rocky Springs Beverage Company had 4,000 liters in the beginning work in process inventory (30% complete). During the period, 58,000 liters were completed. The ending work in process inventory was 3,000 liters (60% complete). What are the total equivalent units for direct materials if materials are added at the beginning of the process?

Follow My Example 3-3

Total equivalent units for direct materials are 57,000, computed as follows:

	Total Whole Units	Percent Materials Added in Period	Equivalent Units for Direct Materials
Inventory in process, beginning of period	4,000	0%	0
Started and completed during the period	54,000*	100%	54,000
Transferred out of Bottling (completed)	58,000	—	54,000
Inventory in process, end of period	3,000	100%	3,000
Total units to be assigned costs	61,000		57,000

*(58,000 – 4,000)

Practice Exercises: PE 3-3A, PE 3-3B

Conversion Equivalent Units To compute equivalent units for conversion costs, it is necessary to know how direct labor and factory overhead enter the manufacturing process. Direct labor, utilities, and equipment depreciation are often incurred uniformly during processing. For this reason, it is assumed that **Frozen Delight** incurs conversion costs evenly throughout its manufacturing process. Thus, the equivalent units for conversion costs in July are computed as follows:

		Total Whole Units	Percent Conversion Completed in July	Equivalent Units for Conversion
Group 1	Inventory in process, July 1 (70% completed)	5,000	30%	1,500
Group 2	Started and completed in July (62,000 − 5,000)	57,000	100%	57,000
	Transferred out to Packaging Department in July	62,000	—	58,500
Group 3	Inventory in process, July 31 (25% completed)	3,000	25%	750
	Total gallons to be assigned cost	65,000		59,250

As shown, the whole units for the three groups of units determined in Step 1 are listed in the first column. The percent of conversion costs added in July is then listed. The equivalent units are determined by multiplying the whole units by the percent of conversion costs added.

To illustrate, the July 1 inventory has 5,000 gallons of whole units (Group 1), which are 70% complete as to conversion costs. During July, the remaining 30% (100% – 70%) of conversion costs was added. Therefore, the equivalent units of conversion costs added in July are 1,500 (5,000 × 30%) gallons.

The 57,000 gallons started and completed in July (Group 2) are 100% complete as to conversion costs. Thus, the equivalent units of conversion costs for the gallons started and completed in July are 57,000 (57,000 × 100%) gallons.

The 3,000 gallons in process on July 31 (Group 3) are 25% complete as to conversion costs. Hence, the equivalent units for the inventory in process on July 31 are 750 (3,000 × 25%) gallons.

The equivalent units for conversion costs for **Frozen Delight** are summarized in Exhibit 7.

EXHIBIT 7 Conversion Equivalent Units

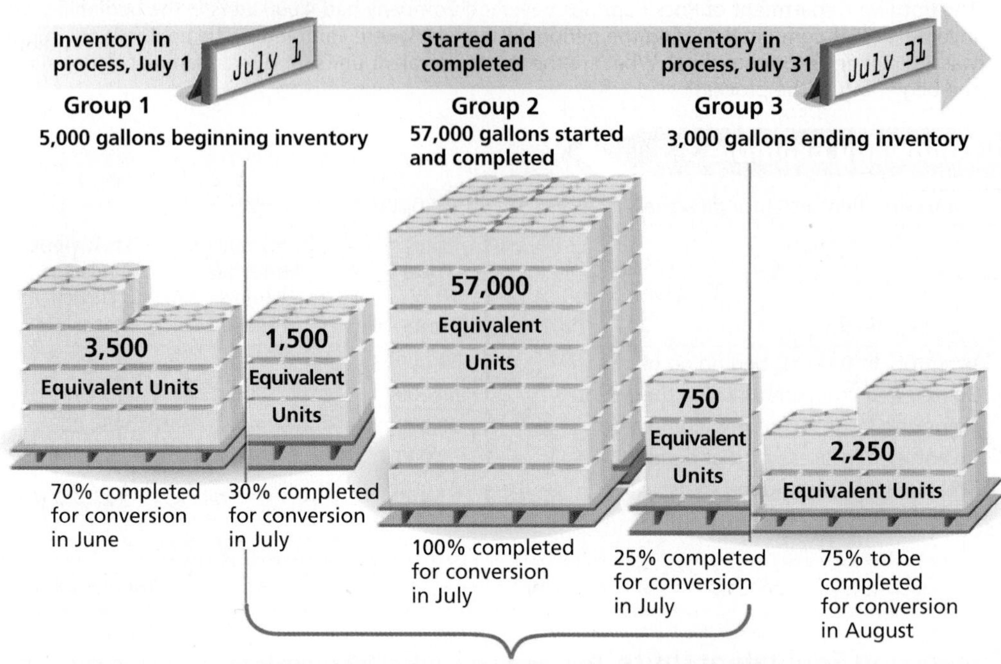

Example Exercise 3-4 Equivalent Units of Conversion Costs

OBJ 2

The Bottling Department of Rocky Springs Beverage Company had 4,000 liters in the beginning work in process inventory (30% complete). During the period, 58,000 liters were completed. The ending work in process inventory was 3,000 liters (60% complete). What are the total equivalent units for conversion costs?

Follow My Example 3-4

	Total Whole Units	Percent Conversion Completed in Period	Equivalent Units for Conversion
Inventory in process, beginning of period	4,000	70%	2,800
Started and completed during the period	54,000*	100%	54,000
Transferred out of Bottling (completed)	58,000	—	56,800
Inventory in process, end of period	3,000	60%	1,800
Total units to be assigned costs	61,000		58,600

*(58,000 − 4,000)

Practice Exercises: PE 3-4A, PE 3-4B

Step 3: Determine the Cost per Equivalent Unit

The next step in preparing the cost of production report is to compute the cost per equivalent unit for direct materials and conversion costs. The **cost per equivalent unit** for direct materials and conversion costs is computed as follows:

$$\text{Direct Materials Cost per Equivalent Unit} = \frac{\text{Total Direct Materials Cost for the Period}}{\text{Total Equivalent Units of Direct Materials}}$$

$$\text{Conversion Cost per Equivalent Unit} = \frac{\text{Total Conversion Costs for the Period}}{\text{Total Equivalent Units of Conversion Costs}}$$

The July direct materials and conversion cost equivalent units for **Frozen Delight**'s Mixing Department from Step 2 are as follows:

		Equivalent Units	
		Direct Materials	**Conversion**
Group 1	Inventory in process, July 1	0	1,500
Group 2	Started and completed in July (62,000 – 5,000)	57,000	57,000
	Transferred out to Packaging Department in July	57,000	58,500
Group 3	Inventory in process, July 31	3,000	750
	Total gallons to be assigned cost	60,000	59,250

The direct materials and conversion costs incurred by Frozen Delight in July are as follows:

Direct materials		$66,000
Conversion costs:		
Direct labor	$10,500	
Factory overhead	7,275	17,775
Total product costs incurred in July		$83,775

The direct materials and conversion costs per equivalent unit are $1.10 and $0.30 per gallon, computed as follows:

$$\text{Direct Materials Cost per Equivalent Unit} = \frac{\text{Total Direct Materials Cost for the Period}}{\text{Total Equivalent Units of Direct Materials}}$$

$$\text{Direct Materials Cost per Equivalent Unit} = \frac{\$66{,}000}{60{,}000 \text{ gallons}} = \$1.10 \text{ per gallon}$$

$$\text{Conversion Cost per Equivalent Unit} = \frac{\text{Total Conversion Costs for the Period}}{\text{Total Equivalent Units of Conversion Costs}}$$

$$\text{Conversion Cost per Equivalent Unit} = \frac{\$17{,}775}{59{,}250 \text{ gallons}} = \$0.30 \text{ per gallon}$$

The preceding costs per equivalent unit are used in Step 4 to allocate the direct materials and conversion costs to the completed and partially completed units.

Example Exercise 3-5 Cost per Equivalent Unit

OBJ 2

The cost of direct materials transferred into the Bottling Department of Rocky Springs Beverage Company is $22,800. The conversion cost for the period in the Bottling Department is $8,790. The total equivalent units for direct materials and conversion are 57,000 liters and 58,600 liters, respectively. Determine the direct materials and conversion costs per equivalent unit.

Follow My Example 3-5

$$\text{Direct Materials Cost per Equivalent Unit} = \frac{\$22{,}800}{57{,}000 \text{ liters}} = \$0.40 \text{ per liter}$$

$$\text{Conversion Cost per Equivalent Unit} = \frac{\$8{,}790}{58{,}600 \text{ liters}} = \$0.15 \text{ per liter}$$

Practice Exercises: PE 3-5A, PE 3-5B

Step 4: Allocate Costs to Units Transferred Out and Partially Completed Units

Product costs must be allocated to the units transferred out and the partially completed units on hand at the end of the period. The product costs are allocated using the costs per equivalent unit for materials and conversion costs that were computed in Step 3.

The total production costs to be assigned for **Frozen Delight** in July are $90,000, computed as follows:

Inventory in process, July 1, 5,000 gallons:	
Direct materials cost, for 5,000 gallons	$ 5,000
Conversion costs, for 5,000 gallons, 70% completed	1,225
Total inventory in process, July 1	$ 6,225
Direct materials cost for July, 60,000 gallons	66,000
Direct labor cost for July	10,500
Factory overhead applied for July	7,275
Total production costs to account for	$90,000

The units to be assigned these costs follow. The costs to be assigned these units are indicated by question marks (?).

		Units	Total Cost
Group 1	Inventory in process, July 1, completed in July	5,000 gallons	?
Group 2	Started and completed in July	57,000	?
	Transferred out to the Packaging Department in July	62,000 gallons	?
Group 3	Inventory in process, July 31	3,000	?
	Total	65,000 gallons	$90,000

Group 1: Inventory in Process on July 1 The 5,000 gallons of inventory in process on July 1 (Group 1) were completed and transferred out to the Packaging Department in July. The cost of these units of $6,675 is determined as follows:

	Direct Materials Costs	Conversion Costs	Total Costs
Inventory in process, July 1 balance			$6,225
Equivalent units for completing the July 1 in-process inventory	0	1,500	
Cost per equivalent unit	× $1.10	× $0.30	
Cost of completed July 1 in-process inventory	0	$450	450
Cost of July 1 in-process inventory transferred to Packaging Department			$6,675

As shown, $6,225 of the cost of the July 1 in-process inventory of 5,000 gallons was carried over from June. This cost plus the cost of completing the 5,000 gallons in July was transferred to the Packaging Department during July. The cost of completing the 5,000 gallons during July is $450. The $450 represents the conversion costs necessary to complete the remaining 30% of the processing. There were no direct materials costs added in July because all the materials costs had been added in June. Thus, the cost of the 5,000 gallons in process on July 1 (Group 1) transferred to the Packaging Department is $6,675.

Group 2: Started and Completed The 57,000 units started and completed in July (Group 2) incurred all (100%) of their direct materials and conversion costs in July. Thus, the cost of the 57,000 gallons started and completed is $79,800, computed by multiplying 57,000 gallons by the costs per equivalent unit for materials and conversion costs as follows:

	Direct Materials Costs	Conversion Costs	Total Costs
Units started and completed in July	57,000 gallons	57,000 gallons	
Cost per equivalent unit	× $1.10	× $0.30	
Cost of the units started and completed in July	$62,700	$17,100	$79,800

The total cost of $86,475 transferred to the Packaging Department in July is the sum of the beginning inventory cost and the costs of the units started and completed in July, computed as follows:

Group 1	Cost of July 1 in-process inventory	$ 6,675
Group 2	Cost of the units started and completed in July	79,800
	Total costs transferred to Packaging Department in July	$86,475

Group 3: Inventory in Process on July 31 The 3,000 gallons in process on July 31 (Group 3) incurred all their direct materials costs and 25% of their conversion costs in July. The cost of these partially completed units of $3,525 is computed as follows:

	Direct Materials Costs	Conversion Costs	Total Costs
Equivalent units in ending inventory	3,000 gallons	750 gallons	
Cost per equivalent unit	× $1.10	× $0.30	
Cost of July 31 in-process inventory	$3,300	$225	$3,525

The 3,000 gallons in process on July 31 received all (100%) of their materials in July. Therefore, the direct materials cost incurred in July is $3,300 (3,000 × $1.10). The conversion costs of $225 represent the cost of the 750 (3,000 × 25%) equivalent gallons multiplied by the cost of $0.30 per equivalent unit for conversion costs. The sum of the direct materials cost ($3,300) and the conversion costs ($225) equals the total cost of the July 31 work in process inventory of $3,525 ($3,300 + $225).

To summarize, the total manufacturing costs for Frozen Delight in July were assigned as follows. In doing so, the question marks (?) for the costs to be assigned to units in Groups 1, 2, and 3 have been answered.

		Units	Total Cost
Group 1	Inventory in process, July 1, completed in July	5,000 gallons	$ 6,675
Group 2	Started and completed in July	57,000	79,800
	Transferred out to the Packaging Department in July	62,000 gallons	$86,475
Group 3	Inventory in process, July 31	3,000	3,525
	Total	65,000 gallons	$90,000

Example Exercise 3-6 Cost of Units Transferred Out and Ending Work in Process

OBJ 2

The costs per equivalent unit of direct materials and conversion in the Bottling Department of Rocky Springs Beverage Company are $0.40 and $0.15, respectively. The equivalent units to be assigned costs are as follows:

	Equivalent Units	
	Direct Materials	Conversion
Inventory in process, beginning of period	0	2,800
Started and completed during the period	54,000	54,000
Transferred out of Bottling (completed)	54,000	56,800
Inventory in process, end of period	3,000	1,800
Total units to be assigned costs	57,000	58,600

The beginning work in process inventory had a cost of $1,860. Determine the cost of units transferred out and the ending work in process inventory.

Follow My Example 3-6

	Direct Materials Costs		Conversion Costs	Total Costs
Inventory in process, beginning of period				$ 1,860
Inventory in process, beginning of period	0	+	2,800 × $0.15	420
Started and completed during the period	54,000 × $0.40	+	54,000 × $0.15	29,700
Transferred out of Bottling (completed)				$31,980
Inventory in process, end of period	3,000 × $0.40	+	1,800 × $0.15	1,470
Total costs assigned by the Bottling Department				$33,450
Completed and transferred out of production	$31,980			
Inventory in process, ending	$ 1,470			

Practice Exercises: PE 3-6A, PE 3-6B

Preparing the Cost of Production Report

A cost of production report is prepared for each processing department at periodic intervals. The report summarizes the following production quantity and cost data:

- The units for which the department is accountable and the disposition of those units
- The production costs incurred by the department and the allocation of those costs between completed (transferred out) and partially completed units

Using Steps 1–4, the July cost of production report for **Frozen Delight**'s Mixing Department is shown in Exhibit 8. During July, the Mixing Department was accountable for 65,000 units (gallons). Of these units, 62,000 units were completed and transferred to the Packaging Department. The remaining 3,000 units are partially completed and are part of the in-process inventory as of July 31.

The Mixing Department was responsible for $90,000 of production costs during July. The cost of goods transferred to the Packaging Department in July was $86,475. The remaining cost of $3,525 is part of the in-process inventory as of July 31.

EXHIBIT 8 **Cost of Production Report for Frozen Delight's Mixing Department—FIFO**

	A	B	C	D	E	
1		Frozen Delight				
2		Cost of Production Report—Mixing Department				
3		For the Month Ended July 31, 2016				Step 1
4						Step 2
5		Whole Units	Equivalent Units			
6	UNITS		Direct Materials	Conversion		
7	Units charged to production:					
8	Inventory in process, July 1	5,000				
9	Received from materials storeroom	60,000				
10	Total units accounted for by the Mixing Department	65,000				
11						
12	Units to be assigned costs:					
13	Inventory in process, July 1 (70% completed)	5,000	0	1,500		
14	Started and completed in July	57,000	57,000	57,000		
15	Transferred to Packaging Department in July	62,000	57,000	58,500		
16	Inventory in process, July 31 (25% completed)	3,000	3,000	750		
17	Total units to be assigned costs	65,000	60,000	59,250		
18						
19			Costs			
20	COSTS		Direct Materials	Conversion	Total	
21						
22	Costs per equivalent unit:					
23	Total costs for July in Mixing Department		$ 66,000	$ 17,775		
24	Total equivalent units (from Step 2)		÷60,000	÷59,250		
25	Cost per equivalent unit		$ 1.10	$ 0.30		
26						Step 3
27	Costs assigned to production:					
28	Inventory in process, July 1				$ 6,225	
29	Costs incurred in July				83,775[a]	
30	Total costs accounted for by the Mixing Department				$90,000	
31						
32						
33	Cost allocated to completed and partially					
34	completed units:					
35	Inventory in process, July 1—balance				$ 6,225	
36	To complete inventory in process, July 1		$ 0 +	$ 450[b] =	450	
37	Cost of completed July 1 work in process				$ 6,675	Step 4
38	Started and completed in July		62,700[c] +	17,100[d] =	79,800	
39	Transferred to Packaging Department in July				$86,475	
40	Inventory in process, July 31		$ 3,300[e] +	$ 225[f] =	3,525	
41	Total costs assigned by the Mixing Department				$90,000	
42						

[a]$66,000 + $10,500 + $7,275 = $83,775 [b]1,500 units × $0.30 = $450 [c]57,000 units × $1.10 = $62,700 [d]57,000 units × $0.30 = $17,100
[e]3,000 units × $1.10 = $3,300 [f]750 units × $0.30 = $225

Journal Entries for a Process Cost System

OBJ 3 Journalize entries for transactions using a process cost system.

The journal entries to record the cost flows and transactions for a process cost system are illustrated in this section. As a basis for illustration, the July transactions for **Frozen Delight** are used. To simplify, the entries are shown in summary form, even though many of the transactions would be recorded daily.

a. Purchased materials, including milk, cream, sugar, packaging, and indirect materials on account, $88,000.

	Account	Debit	Credit
a.	Materials	88,000	
	Accounts Payable		88,000

b. The Mixing Department requisitioned milk, cream, and sugar, $66,000. This is the total amount from the original July data. Packaging materials of $8,000 were requisitioned by the Packaging Department. Indirect materials for the Mixing and Packaging departments were $4,125 and $3,000, respectively.

	Account	Debit	Credit
b.	Work in Process—Mixing	66,000	
	Work in Process—Packaging	8,000	
	Factory Overhead—Mixing	4,125	
	Factory Overhead—Packaging	3,000	
	Materials		81,125

c. Incurred direct labor in the Mixing and Packaging departments of $10,500 and $12,000, respectively.

	Account	Debit	Credit
c.	Work in Process—Mixing	10,500	
	Work in Process—Packaging	12,000	
	Wages Payable		22,500

d. Recognized equipment depreciation for the Mixing and Packaging departments of $3,350 and $1,000, respectively.

	Account	Debit	Credit
d.	Factory Overhead—Mixing	3,350	
	Factory Overhead—Packaging	1,000	
	Accumulated Depreciation—Equipment		4,350

e. Applied factory overhead to Mixing and Packaging departments of $7,275 and $3,500, respectively.

	Account	Debit	Credit
e.	Work in Process—Mixing	7,275	
	Work in Process—Packaging	3,500	
	Factory Overhead—Mixing		7,275
	Factory Overhead—Packaging		3,500

f. Transferred costs of $86,475 from the Mixing Department to the Packaging Department per the cost of production report in Exhibit 8.

	Account	Debit	Credit
f.	Work in Process—Packaging	86,475	
	Work in Process—Mixing		86,475

g. Transferred goods of $106,000 out of the Packaging Department to Finished Goods according to the Packaging Department cost of production report (not illustrated).

g.	Finished Goods—Ice Cream		106,000	
	Work in Process—Packaging			106,000

h. Recorded the cost of goods sold out of the finished goods inventory of $107,000.

h.	Cost of Goods Sold		107,000	
	Finished Goods—Ice Cream			107,000

Exhibit 9 shows the flow of costs for each transaction. The highlighted amounts in Exhibit 9 were determined from assigning the costs in the Mixing Department. These amounts were computed and are shown at the bottom of the cost of production report for the Mixing Department in Exhibit 8. Likewise, the amount transferred out of the Packaging Department to Finished Goods would have also been determined from a cost of production report for the Packaging Department.

EXHIBIT 9 **Frozen Delight's Cost Flows**

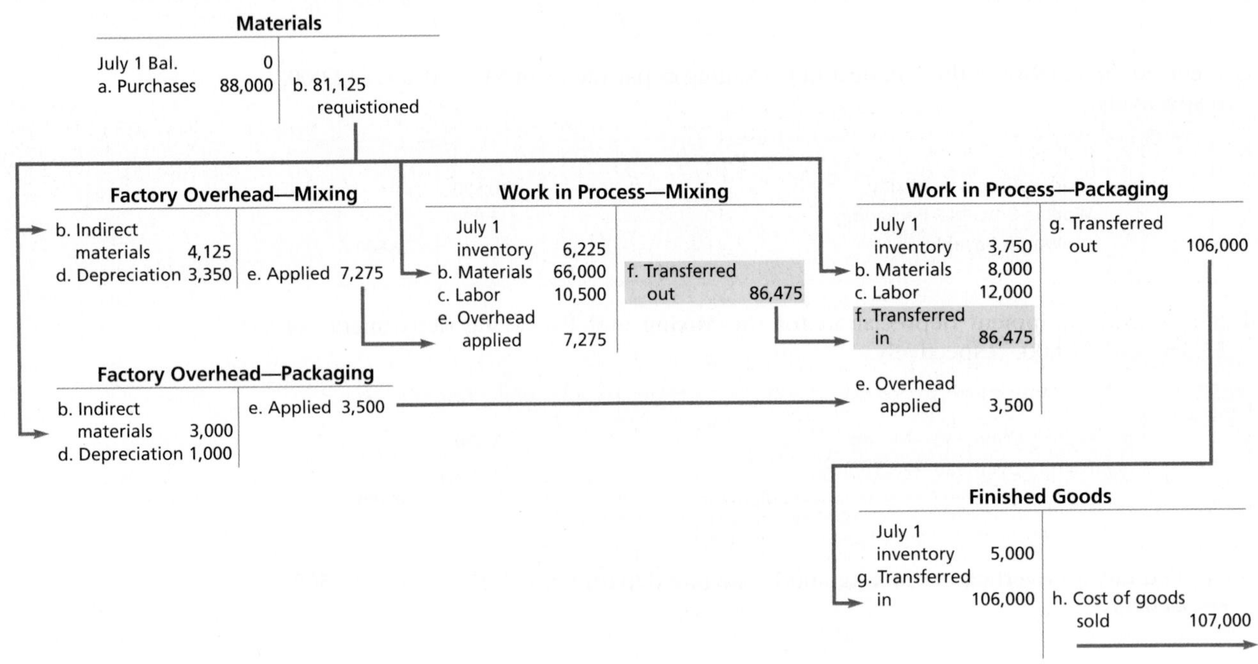

The ending inventories for Frozen Delight are reported on the July 31 balance sheet as follows:

Materials	$ 6,875
Work in Process—Mixing Department	3,525
Work in Process—Packaging Department	7,725
Finished Goods	4,000
Total inventories	$22,125

The $3,525 balance of Work in Process—Mixing Department is the amount determined from the bottom of the cost of production report in Exhibit 8.

Example Exercise 3-7 Process Cost Journal Entries

The cost of materials transferred into the Bottling Department of Rocky Springs Beverage Company is $22,800, including $20,000 from the Blending Department and $2,800 from the materials storeroom. The conversion cost for the period in the Bottling Department is $8,790 ($3,790 factory overhead applied and $5,000 direct labor). The total cost transferred to Finished Goods for the period was $31,980. The Bottling Department had a beginning inventory of $1,860.

a. Journalize (1) the cost of transferred-in materials, (2) conversion costs, and (3) the costs transferred out to Finished Goods.
b. Determine the balance of Work in Process—Bottling at the end of the period.

Follow My Example 3-7

a.	1. Work in Process—Bottling	22,800	
	Work in Process—Blending		20,000
	Materials		2,800
	2. Work in Process—Bottling	8,790	
	Factory Overhead—Bottling		3,790
	Wages Payable		5,000
	3. Finished Goods	31,980	
	Work in Process—Bottling		31,980

b. $1,470 ($1,860 + $22,800 + $8,790 − $31,980)

Practice Exercises: PE 3-7A, PE 3-7B

Service  Focus

COSTING THE POWER STACK

Process costing can also be used in service businesses where the nature of the service is uniform across all units. Examples include electricity generation, wastewater treatment, and natural gas transmission. To illustrate, in generating electricity, the unit of production is called a *megawatt hour*, where each megawatt hour is the same across all sources of generation.

Unlike product manufacturing, service companies often do not have inventory. For example, in generating electricity, the electricity cannot be stored. Thus, electric companies such as **Duke Energy Corporation** match the production of electricity to the demand in real time. Electric companies use what is called the *power stack* to match power supply to demand by arranging generating facilities in order of cost per megawatt hour. The least cost per megawatt hour facilities satisfy initial demand at the bottom of the stack, while the highest cost per megawatt hour power sources are placed at top of the stack to satisfy peak loads, as illustrated in the following graph:

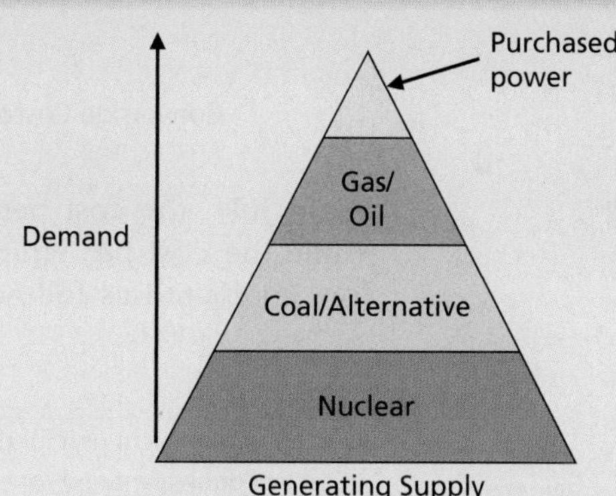

The cost per megawatt hour is determined using process costing by accumulating the conversion costs such as equipment depreciation, labor, and maintenance plus the cost of fuel for each facility. These costs are divided by the megawatt hours generated. Because there are no inventories, the additional complexity of equivalent units is avoided. The resulting cost per megawatt hour by facility is used to develop the power stack.

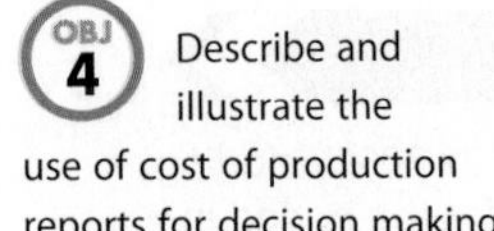
Describe and illustrate the use of cost of production reports for decision making.

Using the Cost of Production Report for Decision Making

The cost of production report is often used by managers for decisions involving the control and improvement of operations. To illustrate, cost of production reports for **Frozen Delight** and **Holland Beverage Company** are used. Finally, the computation and use of yield are discussed.

Frozen Delight

The cost of production report for the Mixing Department is shown in Exhibit 8. The cost per equivalent unit for June can be determined from the beginning inventory. The original Frozen Delight data indicate that the July 1 inventory in process of $6,225 consists of the following costs:

Direct materials cost, 5,000 gallons	$5,000
Conversion costs, 5,000 gallons, 70% completed	1,225
Total inventory in process, July 1	$6,225

Using the preceding data, the June costs per equivalent unit of materials and conversion costs can be determined as follows:

$$\text{Direct Materials Cost per Equivalent Unit} = \frac{\text{Total Direct Materials Cost for the Period}}{\text{Total Equivalent Units of Direct Materials}}$$

$$\text{Direct Materials Cost per Equivalent Unit} = \frac{\$5{,}000}{5{,}000 \text{ gallons}} = \$1.00 \text{ per gallon}$$

$$\text{Conversion Cost per Equivalent Unit} = \frac{\text{Total Conversion Costs for the Period}}{\text{Total Equivalent Units of Conversion Costs}}$$

$$\text{Conversion Cost per Equivalent Unit} = \frac{\$1{,}225}{(5{,}000 \times 70\%) \text{ gallons}} = \$0.35 \text{ per gallon}$$

In July, the cost per equivalent unit of materials increased by $0.10 per gallon, while the cost per equivalent unit for conversion costs decreased by $0.05 per gallon, computed as follows:

	July*	June	Increase (Decrease)
Cost per equivalent unit for direct materials	$1.10	$1.00	$0.10
Cost per equivalent unit for conversion costs	0.30	0.35	(0.05)

*From Exhibit 8

Frozen Delight's management could use the preceding analysis as a basis for investigating the increase in the direct materials cost per equivalent unit and the decrease in the conversion cost per equivalent unit.

Holland Beverage Company

A cost of production report may be prepared showing more cost categories beyond just direct materials and conversion costs. This greater detail can help managers isolate problems and seek opportunities for improvement.

To illustrate, the Blending Department of Holland Beverage Company prepared cost of production reports for April and May. To simplify, assume that the Blending Department had no beginning or ending work in process inventory in either month. That is, all units started were completed in each month. The cost of production reports showing multiple cost categories for April and May in the Blending Department are as follows:

	A	B	C
1	Cost of Production Reports		
2	Holland Beverage Company—Blending Department		
3	For the Months Ended April 30 and May 31, 2016		
4		April	May
5	Direct materials	$ 20,000	$ 40,600
6	Direct labor	15,000	29,400
7	Energy	8,000	20,000
8	Repairs	4,000	8,000
9	Tank cleaning	3,000	8,000
10	Total	$ 50,000	$106,000
11	Units completed	÷100,000	÷200,000
12	Cost per unit	$ 0.50	$ 0.53
13			

The May results indicate that total unit costs have increased from $0.50 to $0.53, or 6% in May. To determine the possible causes for this increase, the cost of production report is restated in per-unit terms by dividing the costs by the number of units completed, as follows:

	A	B	C	D
1	Blending Department			
2	Per-Unit Expense Comparisons			
3		April	May	% Change
4	Direct materials	$0.200	$0.203	1.50%
5	Direct labor	0.150	0.147	−2.00%
6	Energy	0.080	0.100	25.00%
7	Repairs	0.040	0.040	0.00%
8	Tank cleaning	0.030	0.040	33.33%
9	Total	$0.500	$0.530	6.00%
10				

Both energy and tank cleaning per-unit costs have increased significantly in May. These increases should be further investigated. For example, the increase in energy may be due to the machines losing fuel efficiency. This could lead management to repair the machines. The tank cleaning costs could be investigated in a similar fashion.

Yield

In addition to unit costs, managers of process manufacturers are also concerned about yield. The **yield** is computed as follows:

$$\text{Yield} = \frac{\text{Quantity of Material Output}}{\text{Quantity of Material Input}}$$

To illustrate, assume that 1,000 pounds of sugar enter the Packaging Department, and 980 pounds of sugar were packed. The yield is 98%, computed as follows:

$$\text{Yield} = \frac{\text{Quantity of Material Output}}{\text{Quantity of Material Input}} = \frac{\text{980 pounds}}{\text{1,000 pounds}} = 98\%$$

Thus, two percent (100% – 98%) or 20 pounds of sugar were lost or spilled during the packing process. Managers can investigate significant changes in yield over time or significant differences in yield from industry standards.

Example Exercise 3-8 Using Process Costs for Decision Making

The cost of energy consumed in producing good units in the Bottling Department of Rocky Springs Beverage Company was $4,200 and $3,700 for March and April, respectively. The number of equivalent units produced in March and April was 70,000 liters and 74,000 liters, respectively. Evaluate the change in the cost of energy between the two months.

Follow My Example 3-8

$$\text{Energy cost per liter, March} = \frac{\$4{,}200}{70{,}000 \text{ liters}} = \$0.06$$

$$\text{Energy cost per liter, April} = \frac{\$3{,}700}{74{,}000 \text{ liters}} = \$0.05$$

The cost of energy has improved by 1 cent per liter between March and April.

Practice Exercises: PE 3-8A, PE 3-8B

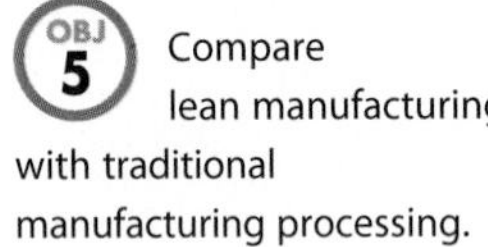

Compare lean manufacturing with traditional manufacturing processing.

Lean Manufacturing

The objective of most manufacturers is to produce products with high quality, low cost, and instant availability. In attempting to achieve this objective, many manufacturers have implemented lean manufacturing (or just-in-time processing). **Lean manufacturing** is a management approach that produces products with high quality, low cost, fast response, and immediate availabililty. Lean manufacturing obtains efficiencies and flexibility by reorganizing the traditional production process.

Traditional Production Process

A traditional manufacturing process for a furniture manufacturer is shown in Exhibit 10. The product (chair) moves through seven processes. In each process, workers are assigned a specific job, which is performed repeatedly as unfinished products are received from the preceding department. The product moves from process to process as each function or step is completed.

EXHIBIT 10 **Traditional Production Line**

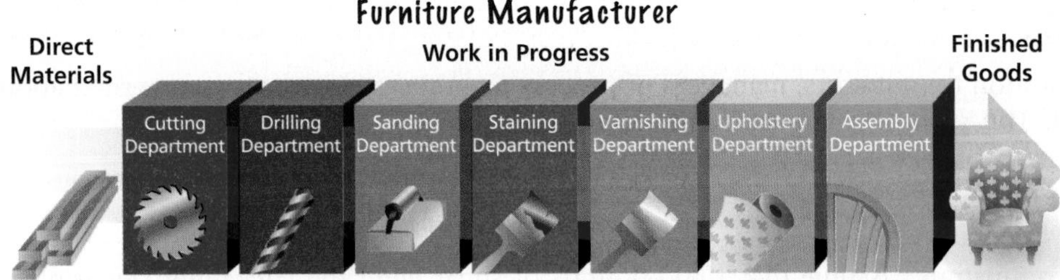

For the furniture maker in Exhibit 10, the product (chair) moves through the following processes:

1. In the Cutting Department, the wood is cut to design specifications.
2. In the Drilling Department, the wood is drilled to design specifications.
3. In the Sanding Department, the wood is sanded.
4. In the Staining Department, the wood is stained.
5. In the Varnishing Department, varnish and other protective coatings are applied.

6. In the Upholstery Department, fabric and other materials are added.
7. In the Assembly Department, the product (chair) is assembled.

In the traditional production process, supervisors enter materials into manufacturing so as to keep all the manufacturing departments (processes) operating. Some departments, however, may process materials more rapidly than others. In addition, if one department stops because of machine breakdowns, for example, the preceding departments usually continue production in order to avoid idle time. In such cases, a buildup of work in process inventories results in some departments.

Lean Manufacturing

In lean manufacturing, processing functions are combined into work centers, sometimes called **manufacturing cells**. For example, the seven departments illustrated in Exhibit 10 might be reorganized into the following three work centers:

1. Work Center 1 performs the cutting, drilling, and sanding functions.
2. Work Center 2 performs the staining and varnishing functions.
3. Work Center 3 performs the upholstery and assembly functions.

The preceding lean manufacturing process is illustrated in Exhibit 11.

EXHIBIT 11 **Lean Production Line**

In traditional manufacturing, a worker typically performs only one function. However, in lean manufacturing, work centers complete several functions. Thus, workers are often cross-trained to perform more than one function. Research has indicated that workers who perform several functions identify better with the end product. This creates pride in the product and improves quality and productivity.

The activities supporting the manufacturing process are called *service activities*. For example, repair and maintenance of manufacturing equipment are service activities. In lean manufacturing, service activities may be assigned to individual work centers, rather than to centralized service departments. For example, each work center may be assigned responsibility for the repair and maintenance of its machinery and equipment. This creates an environment in which workers gain a better understanding of the production process and their machinery. In turn, workers tend to take better care of the machinery, which decreases repairs and maintenance costs, reduces machine downtime, and improves product quality.

In lean manufacturing, the product is often placed on a movable carrier that is centrally located in the work center. After the workers in a work center have completed their activities with the product, the entire carrier and any additional materials are moved just in time to satisfy the demand or need of the next work center. In this sense, the product is said to be "pulled through." Each work center is connected to other work centers through information contained on a Kanban, which is a Japanese term for cards.

In summary, the primary objective of lean manufacturing is to increase the speed and quality, while reducing the cost of operations. This is achieved by eliminating waste and simplifying the production process. Lean manufacturing, including lean accounting and activity analysis, are further described and illustrated in Chapter 12.

Before **Caterpillar** implemented JIT, a transmission traveled 10 miles through the factory and required 1,000 pieces of paper to support the manufacturing process. After implementing JIT, a transmission travels only 200 feet and requires only 10 pieces of paper.

Business Connection

RADICAL IMPROVEMENT: JUST IN TIME FOR PULASKI'S CUSTOMERS

Pulaski Furniture Corporation embraced lean manufacturing principles and revolutionized its business. The company wanted to "be easier to do business with" by offering its customers smaller shipments more frequently. It was able to accomplish this by taking the following steps:

- Mapping processes to properly align labor, machines, and materials
- Eliminating 100 feet of conveyor line
- Moving machines into manufacturing cells
- Reducing manufacturing run sizes by simplifying the product design
- Making every product more frequently in order to reduce the customer's waiting time for a product

As a result of these lean manufacturing changes, the company significantly improved its inventory position while simultaneously improving its shipping times to the customer. Its lumber inventory was reduced by 25%, finished goods inventory was reduced by 40%, and work in process inventory was reduced by 50%. At the same time, customers' shipment waiting times were shortened from months to weeks.

Source: Jeff Linville, "Pulaski's Passion for Lean Plumps up Dealer Service," *Furniture Today*, June 2006.

APPENDIX

Average Cost Method

A cost flow assumption must be used as product costs flow through manufacturing processes. In this chapter, the first-in, first-out cost flow method was used for the Mixing Department of Frozen Delight. In this appendix, the average cost flow method is illustrated for **S&W Ice Cream Company (S&W)**.

Determining Costs Using the Average Cost Method

S&W's operations are similar to those of Frozen Delight. Like Frozen Delight, S&W mixes direct materials (milk, cream, sugar) in refrigerated vats and has two manufacturing departments, Mixing and Packaging.

The manufacturing data for the Mixing Department for July 2016 are as follows:

Inventory in process, July 1, 5,000 gallons (70% completed)	$ 6,200
Direct materials cost incurred in July, 60,000 gallons	66,000
Direct labor cost incurred in July	10,500
Factory overhead applied in July	6,405
Total production costs to account for	$89,105
Cost of goods transferred to Packaging in July (includes units in process on July 1), 62,000 gallons	?
Cost of work in process inventory, July 31, 3,000 gallons, 25% completed as to conversion costs	?

Using the average cost method, the objective is to allocate the total costs of production of $89,105 to the following:

- The 62,000 gallons completed and transferred to the Packaging Department
- The 3,000 gallons in the July 31 (ending) work in process inventory

The preceding costs show two question marks. These amounts are determined by preparing a cost of production report, using the following four steps:

- Step 1. Determine the units to be assigned costs.
- Step 2. Compute equivalent units of production.
- Step 3. Determine the cost per equivalent unit.
- Step 4. Allocate costs to transferred out and partially completed units.

Under the average cost method, all production costs (materials and conversion costs) are combined together for determining equivalent units and cost per equivalent unit.

Step 1: Determine the Units to Be Assigned Costs The first step is to determine the units to be assigned costs. A unit can be any measure of completed production, such as tons, gallons, pounds, barrels, or cases. For **S&W**, a unit is a gallon of ice cream.

S&W's Mixing Department had 65,000 gallons of direct materials to account for during July, as shown here.

Total gallons to account for:	
Inventory in process, July 1	5,000 gallons
Received from materials storeroom	60,000
Total units to account for by the Packaging Department	65,000 gallons

There are two groups of units to be assigned costs for the period.

Group 1	Units completed and transferred out
Group 2	Units in the July 31 (ending) work in process inventory

During July, the Mixing Department completed and transferred 62,000 gallons to the Packaging Department. Of the 60,000 gallons started in July, 57,000 (60,000 − 3,000) gallons were completed and transferred to the Packaging Department. Thus, the ending work in process inventory consists of 3,000 gallons.

The total units (gallons) to be assigned costs for S&W can be summarized as follows:

Group 1	Units transferred out to the Packaging Department in July	62,000 gallons
Group 2	Inventory in process, July 31	3,000
	Total gallons to be assigned costs	65,000 gallons

The total units (gallons) to be assigned costs (65,000 gallons) equal the total units to account for (65,000 gallons).

Step 2: Compute Equivalent Units of Production **S&W** has 3,000 gallons of whole units in the work in process inventory for the Mixing Department on July 31. Because these units are 25% complete, the number of equivalent units in process in the Mixing Department on July 31 is 750 gallons (3,000 gallons × 25%). Because the units transferred to the Packaging Department have been completed, the whole units (62,000 gallons) transferred are the same as the equivalent units transferred.

The total equivalent units of production for the Mixing Department are determined by adding the equivalent units in the ending work in process inventory to the units transferred and completed during the period, computed as follows:

Equivalent units completed and transferred to the Packaging Department during July	62,000 gallons
Equivalent units in ending work in process, July 31	750
Total equivalent units	62,750 gallons

Step 3: Determine the Cost per Equivalent Unit Because materials and conversion costs are combined under the average cost method, the cost per equivalent unit is determined by dividing the total production costs by the total equivalent units of production as follows:

$$\text{Cost per Equivalent Unit} = \frac{\text{Total Production Costs}}{\text{Total Equivalent Units}}$$

$$\text{Cost per Equivalent Unit} = \frac{\text{Total Production Costs}}{\text{Total Equivalent Units}} = \frac{\$89{,}105}{62{,}750 \text{ gallons}} = \$1.42$$

The cost per equivalent unit is used in Step 4 to allocate the production costs to the completed and partially completed units.

Step 4: Allocate Costs to Transferred Out and Partially Completed Units

The cost of transferred and partially completed units is determined by multiplying the cost per equivalent unit times the equivalent units of production. For **S&W**'s Mixing Department, these costs are determined as follows:

Group 1	Transferred out to the Packaging Department (62,000 gallons × $1.42)	$88,040
Group 2	Inventory in process, July 31 (3,000 gallons × 25% × $1.42).................	1,065
	Total production costs assigned	$89,105

The Cost of Production Report

The July cost of production report for **S&W**'s Mixing Department is shown in Exhibit 12. This cost of production report summarizes the following:

- The units for which the department is accountable and the disposition of those units
- The production costs incurred by the department and the allocation of those costs between completed and partially completed units

EXHIBIT 12 **Cost of Production Report for S&W's Mixing Department—Average Cost**

	A	B	C
1	**S&W Ice Cream Company**		
2	**Cost of Production Report—Mixing Department**		
3	**For the Month Ended July 31, 2016**		
4	**UNITS**		
5		Whole Units	Equivalent Units
6			of Production
7	Units to account for during production:		
8	Inventory in process, July 1	5,000	
9	Received from materials storeroom	60,000	
10	Total units accounted for by the Mixing Department	65,000	
11			
12	Units to be assigned costs:		
13	Transferred to Packaging Department in July	62,000	62,000
14	Inventory in process, July 31 (25% completed)	3,000	750
15	Total units to be assigned costs	65,000	62,750
16			
17	**COSTS**		**Costs**
18			
19	Cost per equivalent unit:		
20	Total production costs for July in Mixing Department		$89,105
21	Total equivalent units (from Step 2)		÷62,750
22	Cost per equivalent unit		$ 1.42
23			
24	Costs assigned to production:		
25	Inventory in process, July 1		$ 6,200
26	Direct materials, direct labor, and factory overhead incurred in July		82,905
27	Total costs accounted for by the Mixing Department		$89,105
28			
29			
30	Costs allocated to completed and partially completed units:		
31	Transferred to Packaging Department in July (62,000 gallons × $1.42)		$88,040
32	Inventory in process, July 31 (3,000 gallons × 25% × $1.42)		1,065
33	Total costs assigned by the Mixing Department		$89,105
34			

Step 1 (Whole Units, rows 4–15); Step 2 (Equivalent Units of Production, rows 4–15); Step 3 (rows 19–27); Step 4 (rows 30–33)

At a Glance 3

Describe process cost systems.

Key Points The process cost system is best suited for industries that mass produce identical units of a product. Costs are charged to processing departments, rather than to jobs as with the job order cost system. These costs are transferred from one department to the next until production is completed.

Learning Outcomes	Example Exercises	Practice Exercises
• Identify the characteristics of a process manufacturer.		
• Compare and contrast the job order cost system with the process cost system.	EE3-1	PE3-1A, 3-1B
• Describe the physical and cost flows of a process manufacturer.		

Prepare a cost of production report.

Key Points Manufacturing costs must be allocated between the units that have been completed and those that remain within the department. This allocation is accomplished by allocating costs using equivalent units of production.

Learning Outcomes	Example Exercises	Practice Exercises
• Determine the whole units charged to production and to be assigned costs.	EE3-2	PE3-2A, 3-2B
• Compute the equivalent units with respect to materials.	EE3-3	PE3-3A, 3-3B
• Compute the equivalent units with respect to conversion.	EE3-4	PE3-4A, 3-4B
• Compute the costs per equivalent unit.	EE3-5	PE3-5A, 3-5B
• Allocate the costs to beginning inventory, units started and completed, and ending inventory.	EE3-6	PE3-6A, 3-6B
• Prepare a cost of production report.		

Journalize entries for transactions using a process cost system.

Key Points Prepare the summary journal entries for materials, labor, applied factory overhead, and transferred costs incurred in production.

Learning Outcomes	Example Exercises	Practice Exercises
• Prepare journal entries for process costing transactions.	EE3-7	PE3-7A, 3-7B
• Summarize cost flows in T account form.		
• Compute the ending inventory balances.		

Describe and illustrate the use of cost of production reports for decision making.

Key Points The cost of production report provides information for controlling and improving operations. The report(s) can provide details of a department for a single period, or over a period of time.

Yield measures the quantity of output of production relative to the inputs.

Learning Outcomes	Example Exercises	Practice Exercises
• Prepare and evaluate a report showing the change in costs per unit by cost category for comparative periods. • Compute and interpret yield.	EE3-8	PE3-8A, 3-8B

Compare lean manufacturing with traditional manufacturing processing.

Key Points The lean manufacturing philosophy focuses on reducing time, cost, and poor quality within the process.

Learning Outcome

- Identify the characteristics of lean manufacturing.

Key Terms

cost of production report (87)
cost per equivalent unit (92)
equivalent units of production (89)
first-in, first-out (FIFO) method (87)
lean manufacturing (102)
manufacturing cells (103)
process cost system (83)
process manufacturer (82)
whole units (89)
yield (101)

Illustrative Problem

Southern Aggregate Company manufactures concrete by a series of four processes. All materials are introduced in Crushing. From Crushing, the materials pass through Sifting, Baking, and Mixing, emerging as finished concrete. All inventories are costed by the first-in, first-out method.

The balances in the accounts Work in Process—Mixing and Finished Goods were as follows on May 1, 2016:

Inventory in Process—Mixing (2,000 units, 1/4 completed)	$13,700
Finished Goods (1,800 units at $8.00 a unit)	14,400

The following costs were charged to Work in Process—Mixing during May:

Direct materials transferred from Baking: 15,200 units at $6.50 a unit	$98,800
Direct labor	17,200
Factory overhead	11,780

During May, 16,000 units of concrete were completed, and 15,800 units were sold. Inventories on May 31 were as follows:

Inventory in Process—Mixing: 1,200 units, 1/2 completed
Finished Goods: 2,000 units

Instructions

1. Prepare a cost of production report for the Mixing Department.
2. Determine the cost of goods sold (indicate number of units and unit costs).
3. Determine the finished goods inventory, May 31, 2016.

Solution

1.

	A	B	C	D	E
1	**Southern Aggregate Company**				
2	**Cost of Production Report—Mixing Department**				
3	**For the Month Ended May 31, 2016**				
4			Equivalent Units		
5	**UNITS**	Whole Units	Direct Materials	Conversion	
6	Units charged to production:				
7	Inventory in process, May 1	2,000			
8	Received from Baking	15,200			
9	Total units accounted for by the Mixing Department	17,200			
10					
11	Units to be assigned costs:				
12	Inventory in process, May 1 (25% completed)	2,000	0	1,500	
13	Started and completed in May	14,000	14,000	14,000	
14	Transferred to finished goods in May	16,000	14,000	15,500	
15	Inventory in process, May 31 (50% completed)	1,200	1,200	600	
16	Total units to be assigned costs	17,200	15,200	16,100	
17					
18				**Costs**	
19	**COSTS**		Direct Materials	Conversion	Total
20	Unit costs:				
21	Total costs for May in Mixing		$ 98,800	$ 28,980	
22	Total equivalent units (row 16)		÷15,200	÷16,100	
23	Cost per equivalent unit		$ 6.50	$ 1.80	
24					
25	Costs assigned to production:				
26	Inventory in process, May 1				$ 13,700
27	Costs incurred in May				127,780
28	Total costs accounted for by the Mixing Department				$141,480
29					
30	Cost allocated to completed and partially				
31	completed units:				
32	Inventory in process, May 1—balance				$ 13,700
33	To complete inventory in process, May 1		$ 0	$ 2,700[a]	2,700
34	Cost of completed May 1 work in process				$ 16,400
35	Started and completed in May		91,000[b]	25,200[c]	116,200
36	Transferred to finished goods in May				$132,600
37	Inventory in process, May 31		7,800[d]	1,080[e]	8,880
38	Total costs assigned by the Mixing Department				$141,480
39					

[a]1,500 × $1.80 = $2,700 [b]14,000 × $6.50 = $91,000 [c]14,000 × $1.80 = $25,200 [d]1,200 × $6.50 = $7,800 [e]600 × $1.80 = $1,080

2. Cost of goods sold:

1,800 units at $8.00	$ 14,400	(from finished goods beginning inventory)
2,000 units at $8.20*	16,400	(from inventory in process beginning inventory)
12,000 units at $8.30**	99,600	(from May production started and completed)
15,800 units	$130,400	

*($13,700 + $2,700) ÷ 2,000
**$116,200 ÷ 14,000

3. Finished goods inventory, May 31:

2,000 units at $8.30 $16,600

Discussion Questions

1. Which type of cost system, process or job order, would be best suited for each of the following: (a) TV assembler, (b) building contractor, (c) automobile repair shop, (d) paper manufacturer, (e) custom jewelry manufacturer? Give reasons for your answers.
2. In job order cost accounting, the three elements of manufacturing cost are charged directly to job orders. Why is it not necessary to charge manufacturing costs in process cost accounting to job orders?
3. In a job order cost system, direct labor and factory overhead applied are debited to individual jobs. How are these items treated in a process cost system and why?
4. Why is the cost per equivalent unit often determined separately for direct materials and conversion costs?
5. What is the purpose for determining the cost per equivalent unit?
6. Rameriz Company is a process manufacturer with two production departments, Blending and Filling. All direct materials are introduced in Blending from the materials store area. What is included in the cost transferred to Filling?
7. What is the most important purpose of the cost of production report?
8. How are cost of production reports used for controlling and improving operations?
9. How is "yield" determined for a process manufacturer?
10. How does lean manufacturing differ from the conventional manufacturing process?

Practice Exercises

EE 3-1 *p. 85*

SHOW ME HOW

PE 3-1A Job order versus process costing **OBJ. 1**

Which of the following industries would typically use job order costing, and which would typically use process costing?

Dentist	Movie studio
Gasoline refining	Paper manufacturing
Flour mill	Custom printing

EE 3-1 *p. 85*

SHOW ME HOW

PE 3-1B Job order versus process costing **OBJ. 1**

Which of the following industries would typically use job order costing, and which would typically use process costing?

Steel manufactuirng	Computer chip manufacturing
Business consulting	Candy making
Web designer	Designer clothes manufacturing

EE 3-2 *p. 89*

SHOW ME HOW

PE 3-2A Units to be assigned costs **OBJ. 2**

Lilac Skin Care Company consists of two departments, Blending and Filling. The Filling Department received 45,000 ounces from the Blending Department. During the period, the Filling Department completed 42,800 ounces, including 4,000 ounces of work in process at the beginning of the period. The ending work in process inventory was 6,200 ounces. How many ounces were started and completed during the period?

EE 3-2 *p. 89*

SHOW ME HOW

PE 3-2B Units to be assigned costs **OBJ. 2**

Keystone Steel Company has two departments, Casting and Rolling. In the Rolling Department, ingots from the Casting Department are rolled into steel sheet. The Rolling Department received 8,500 tons from the Casting Department. During the period, the Rolling Department completed 7,900 tons, including 400 tons of work in process at the beginning of the period. The ending work in process inventory was 1,000 tons. How many tons were started and completed during the period?

EE 3-3 *p. 91*

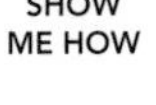
SHOW ME HOW

PE 3-3A Equivalent units of materials cost **OBJ. 2**

The Filling Department of Lilac Skin Care Company had 4,000 ounces in beginning work in process inventory (70% complete). During the period, 42,800 ounces were completed. The ending work in process inventory was 6,200 ounces (40% complete). What are the total equivalent units for direct materials if materials are added at the beginning of the process?

EE 3-3 *p. 91*

SHOW ME HOW

PE 3-3B Equivalent units of materials cost **OBJ. 2**

The Rolling Department of Keystone Steel Company had 400 tons in beginning work in process inventory (20% complete). During the period, 7,900 tons were completed. The ending work in process inventory was 1,000 tons (30% complete). What are the total equivalent units for direct materials if materials are added at the beginning of the process?

EE 3-4 *p. 92*

SHOW ME HOW

PE 3-4A Equivalent units of conversion costs **OBJ. 2**

The Filling Department of Lilac Skin Care had 4,000 ounces in beginning work in process inventory (70% complete). During the period, 42,800 ounces were completed. The ending work in process inventory was 6,200 ounces (40% complete). What are the total equivalent units for conversion costs?

EE 3-4 p. 92

PE 3-4B Equivalent units of conversion costs **OBJ. 2**

SHOW ME HOW

The Rolling Department of Keystone Steel Company had 400 tons in beginning work in process inventory (20% complete). During the period, 7,900 tons were completed. The ending work in process inventory was 1,000 tons (30% complete). What are the total equivalent units for conversion costs?

EE 3-5 p. 93

PE 3-5A Cost per equivalent unit **OBJ. 2**

SHOW ME HOW

The cost of direct materials transferred into the Filling Department of Lilac Skin Care Company is $20,250. The conversion cost for the period in the Filling Department is $6,372. The total equivalent units for direct materials and conversion are 45,000 ounces and 42,480 ounces, respectively. Determine the direct materials and conversion costs per equivalent unit.

EE 3-5 p. 93

PE 3-5B Cost per equivalent unit **OBJ. 2**

SHOW ME HOW

The cost of direct materials transferred into the Rolling Department of Keystone Steel Company is $510,000. The conversion cost for the period in the Rolling Department is $81,200. The total equivalent units for direct materials and conversion are 8,500 tons and 8,120 tons, respectively. Determine the direct materials and conversion costs per equivalent unit.

EE 3-6 p. 95

PE 3-6A Cost of units transferred out and ending work in process **OBJ. 2**

SHOW ME HOW

The costs per equivalent unit of direct materials and conversion in the Filling Department of Lilac Skin Care Company are $0.45 and $0.15, respectively. The equivalent units to be assigned costs are as follows:

	Equivalent Units	
	Direct Materials	**Conversion**
Inventory in process, beginning of period	0	1,200
Started and completed during the period	38,800	38,800
Transferred out of Filling (completed)	38,800	40,000
Inventory in process, end of period	6,200	2,480
Total units to be assigned costs	45,000	42,480

The beginning work in process inventory had a cost of $25,000. Determine the cost of completed and transferred-out production and the ending work in process inventory.

EE 3-6 p. 95

PE 3-6B Cost of units transferred out and ending work in process **OBJ. 2**

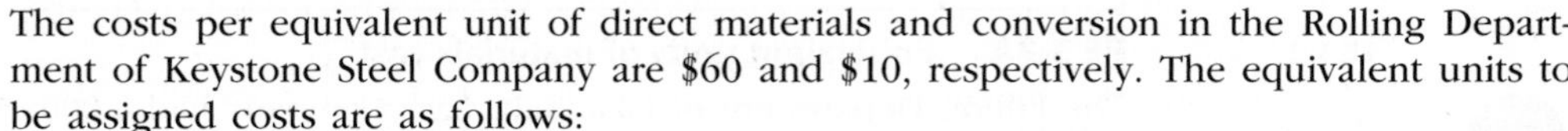
SHOW ME HOW

The costs per equivalent unit of direct materials and conversion in the Rolling Department of Keystone Steel Company are $60 and $10, respectively. The equivalent units to be assigned costs are as follows:

	Equivalent Units	
	Direct Materials	**Conversion**
Inventory in process, beginning of period	0	320
Started and completed during the period	7,500	7,500
Transferred out of Rolling (completed)	7,500	7,820
Inventory in process, end of period	1,000	300
Total units to be assigned costs	8,500	8,120

The beginning work in process inventory had a cost of $25,000. Determine the cost of completed and transferred-out production and the ending work in process inventory.

EE 3-7 p. 99

PE 3-7A Process cost journal entries **OBJ. 3**

SHOW ME HOW

The cost of materials transferred into the Filling Department of Lilac Skin Care Company is $20,250, including $6,000 from the Blending Department and $14,250 from the materials storeroom. The conversion cost for the period in the Filling Department is $6,372

($1,600 factory overhead applied and $4,772 direct labor). The total cost transferred to Finished Goods for the period was $25,660. The Filling Department had a beginning inventory of $2,200.

a. Journalize (1) the cost of transferred-in materials, (2) conversion costs, and (3) the costs transferred out to Finished Goods.

b. Determine the balance of Work in Process—Filling at the end of the period.

EE 3-7 *p. 99*

SHOW ME HOW

PE 3-7B Process cost journal entries **OBJ. 3**

The cost of materials transferred into the Rolling Department of Keystone Steel Company is $510,000 from the Casting Department. The conversion cost for the period in the Rolling Department is $81,200 ($54,700 factory overhead applied and $26,500 direct labor). The total cost transferred to Finished Goods for the period was $553,200. The Rolling Department had a beginning inventory of $25,000.

a. Journalize (1) the cost of transferred-in materials, (2) conversion costs, and (3) the costs transferred out to Finished Goods.

b. Determine the balance of Work in Process—Rolling at the end of the period.

EE 3-8 *p. 102*

SHOW ME HOW

PE 3-8A Using process costs for decision making **OBJ. 4**

The costs of energy consumed in producing good units in the Baking Department of Pan Company were $14,875 and $14,615 for June and July, respectively. The number of equivalent units produced in June and July was 42,500 pounds and 39,500 pounds, respectively. Evaluate the change in the cost of energy between the two months.

EE 3-8 *p. 102*

SHOW ME HOW

PE 3-8B Using process costs for decision making **OBJ. 4**

The costs of materials consumed in producing good units in the Forming Department of Thomas Company were $76,000 and $77,350 for September and October, respectively. The number of equivalent units produced in September and October was 800 tons and 850 tons, respectively. Evaluate the change in the cost of materials between the two months.

Exercises

EX 3-1 Entries for materials cost flows in a process cost system **OBJ. 1, 3**

The Hershey Foods Company manufactures chocolate confectionery products. The three largest raw materials are cocoa, sugar, and dehydrated milk. These raw materials first go into the Blending Department. The blended product is then sent to the Molding Department, where the bars of candy are formed. The candy is then sent to the Packing Department, where the bars are wrapped and boxed. The boxed candy is then sent to the distribution center, where it is eventually sold to food brokers and retailers.

Show the accounts debited and credited for each of the following business events:

a. Materials used by the Blending Department

b. Transfer of blended product to the Molding Department

c. Transfer of chocolate to the Packing Department

d. Transfer of boxed chocolate to the distribution center

e. Sale of boxed chocolate

EX 3-2 Flowchart of accounts related to service and processing departments **OBJ. 1**

Alcoa Inc. is the world's largest producer of aluminum products. One product that Alcoa manufactures is aluminum sheet products for the aerospace industry. The entire output of the Smelting Department is transferred to the Rolling Department. Part of the fully processed goods from the Rolling Department are sold as rolled sheet, and the remainder of the goods are transferred to the Converting Department for further processing into sheared sheet.

(Continued)

Prepare a chart of the flow of costs from the processing department accounts into the finished goods accounts and then into the cost of goods sold account. The relevant accounts are as follows:

Cost of Goods Sold	Finished Goods—Rolled Sheet
Materials	Finished Goods—Sheared Sheet
Factory Overhead—Smelting Department	Work in Process—Smelting Department
Factory Overhead—Rolling Department	Work in Process—Rolling Department
Factory Overhead—Converting Department	Work in Process—Converting Department

EX 3-3 Entries for flow of factory costs for process cost system **OBJ. 1, 3**

SHOW ME HOW

Domino Foods, Inc., manufactures a sugar product by a continuous process, involving three production departments—Refining, Sifting, and Packing. Assume that records indicate that direct materials, direct labor, and applied factory overhead for the first department, Refining, were $372,000, $143,000, and $98,400, respectively. Also, work in process in the Refining Department at the beginning of the period totaled $29,400, and work in process at the end of the period totaled $28,700.

Journalize the entries to record (a) the flow of costs into the Refining Department during the period for (1) direct materials, (2) direct labor, and (3) factory overhead, and (b) the transfer of production costs to the second department, Sifting.

EX 3-4 Factory overhead rate, entry for applying factory overhead, and factory overhead account balance **OBJ. 1, 3**

✔ a. 140%

SHOW ME HOW

The chief cost accountant for Fizzy Fruit Beverage Co. estimated that total factory overhead cost for the Blending Department for the coming fiscal year beginning April 1 would be $147,000, and total direct labor costs would be $105,000. During April, the actual direct labor cost totaled $12,000, and factory overhead cost incurred totaled $17,050.

a. What is the predetermined factory overhead rate based on direct labor cost?

b. Journalize the entry to apply factory overhead to production for April.

c. What is the April 30 balance of the account Factory Overhead—Blending Department?

d. Does the balance in part (c) represent over- or underapplied factory overhead?

EX 3-5 Equivalent units of production **OBJ. 2**

✔ Direct materials, 14,050 units

SHOW ME HOW

The Converting Department of Soft Touch Towel and Tissue Company had 790 units in work in process at the beginning of the period, which were 60% complete. During the period, 13,700 units were completed and transferred to the Packing Department. There were 1,140 units in process at the end of the period, which were 25% complete. Direct materials are placed into the process at the beginning of production. Determine the number of equivalent units of production with respect to direct materials and conversion costs.

EX 3-6 Equivalent units of production **OBJ. 2**

✔ a. Conversion, 96,720 units

SHOW ME HOW

Units of production data for the two departments of Pacific Cable and Wire Company for November of the current fiscal year are as follows:

	Drawing Department	Winding Department
Work in process, November 1	5,000 units, 40% completed	3,200 units, 80% completed
Completed and transferred to next processing department during November	95,000 units	95,100 units
Work in process, November 30	6,200 units, 60% completed	3,100 units, 15% completed

If all direct materials are placed in process at the beginning of production, determine the direct materials and conversion equivalent units of production for November for (a) the Drawing Department and (b) the Winding Department.

EX 3-7 Equivalent units of production OBJ. 2

✔ b. Conversion, 201,800

SHOW ME HOW

The following information concerns production in the Baking Department for August. All direct materials are placed in process at the beginning of production.

ACCOUNT *Work in Process—Baking Department* ACCOUNT NO.

Date		Item	Debit	Credit	Balance Debit	Balance Credit
Aug.	1	Bal., 5,000 units, ⅖ completed			8,000	
	31	Direct materials, 204,000 units	306,000		314,000	
	31	Direct labor	35,500		349,500	
	31	Factory overhead	29,076		378,576	
	31	Goods finished, 196,000 units		356,580	21,996	
	31	Bal. ? units, ⅗ completed			21,996	

a. Determine the number of units in work in process inventory at the end of the month.

b. Determine the equivalent units of production for direct materials and conversion costs in August.

EX 3-8 Costs per equivalent unit OBJ. 2, 4

✔ a. 2. Conversion cost per equivalent unit, $0.32

SHOW ME HOW

a. Based upon the data in Exercise 3-7, determine the following:

1. Direct materials cost per equivalent unit.
2. Conversion cost per equivalent unit.
3. Cost of the beginning work in process completed during August.
4. Cost of units started and completed during August.
5. Cost of the ending work in process.

b. Assuming that the direct materials cost is the same for July and August, did the conversion cost per equivalent unit increase, decrease, or remain the same in August?

EX 3-9 Equivalent units of production OBJ. 2

Kellogg Company manufactures cold cereal products, such as *Frosted Flakes*. Assume that the inventory in process on March 1 for the Packing Department included 1,200 pounds of cereal in the packing machine hopper (enough for 800 24-oz. boxes), and 800 empty 24-oz. boxes held in the package carousel of the packing machine. During March, 65,400 boxes of 24-oz. cereal were packaged. Conversion costs are incurred when a box is filled with cereal. On March 31, the packing machine hopper held 900 pounds of cereal, and the package carousel held 600 empty 24-oz. (1½-pound) boxes. Assume that once a box is filled with cereal, it is immediately transferred to the finished goods warehouse.

Determine the equivalent units of production for cereal, boxes, and conversion costs for March. An equivalent unit is defined as "pounds" for cereal and "24-oz. boxes" for boxes and conversion costs.

EX 3-10 Costs per equivalent unit OBJ. 2

✔ c. $2.40

SHOW ME HOW

Georgia Products Inc. completed and transferred 89,000 particle board units of production from the Pressing Department. There was no beginning inventory in process in the department. The ending in-process inventory was 2,400 units, which were ⅗ complete as to conversion cost. All materials are added at the beginning of the process. Direct materials cost incurred was $219,360, direct labor cost incurred was 28,100, and factory overhead applied was $12,598.

Determine the following for the Pressing Department:

a. Total conversion cost

b. Conversion cost per equivalent unit

c. Direct materials cost per equivalent unit

EX 3-11 Equivalent units of production and related costs **OBJ. 2**

✔ a. 1,000 units

SHOW ME HOW

The charges to Work in Process—Assembly Department for a period, together with information concerning production, are as follows. All direct materials are placed in process at the beginning of production.

Work in Process—Assembly Department

Bal., 1,600 units, 35% completed	17,440	To Finished Goods, 29,600 units	?
Direct materials, 29,000 units @ $9.50	275,500		
Direct labor	84,600		
Factory overhead	39,258		
Bal. ? units, 45% completed	?		

Determine the following:

a. The number of units in work in process inventory at the end of the period
b. Equivalent units of production for direct materials and conversion
c. Costs per equivalent unit for direct materials and conversion
d. Cost of the units started and completed during the period

EX 3-12 Cost of units completed and in process **OBJ. 2, 4**

✔ a. 1. $21,808

a. Based on the data in Exercise 3-11, determine the following:
   1. Cost of beginning work in process inventory completed this period
   2. Cost of units transferred to finished goods during the period
   3. Cost of ending work in process inventory
   4. Cost per unit of the completed beginning work in process inventory, rounded to the nearest cent

b. Did the production costs change from the preceding period? Explain.

c. Assuming that the direct materials cost per unit did not change from the preceding period, did the conversion costs per equivalent unit increase, decrease, or remain the same for the current period?

EX 3-13 Errors in equivalent unit computation **OBJ. 2**

Napco Refining Company processes gasoline. On June 1 of the current year, 6,400 units were 3/5 completed in the Blending Department. During June, 55,000 units entered the Blending Department from the Refining Department. During June, the units in process at the beginning of the month were completed. Of the 55,000 units entering the department, all were completed except 5,200 units that were 1/5 completed. The equivalent units for conversion costs for June for the Blending Department were computed as follows:

Equivalent units of production in June:	
To process units in inventory on June 1: 6,400 × 3/5	3,840
To process units started and completed in June: 55,000 – 6,400	48,600
To process units in inventory on June 30: 5,200 × 1/5	1,040
Equivalent units of production	53,480

List the errors in the computation of equivalent units for conversion costs for the Blending Department for June.

EX 3-14 Cost per equivalent unit **OBJ. 2**

✔ a. 12,400 units

SHOW ME HOW

The following information concerns production in the Forging Department for November. All direct materials are placed into the process at the beginning of production, and conversion costs are incurred evenly throughout the process. The beginning inventory consists of $9,000 of direct materials.

ACCOUNT *Work in Process—Forging Department* ACCOUNT NO.

Date		Item	Debit	Credit	Balance	
					Debit	Credit
Nov.	1	Bal., 900 units, 60% completed			10,566	
	30	Direct materials, 12,900 units	123,840		134,406	
	30	Direct labor	21,650		156,056	
	30	Factory overhead	16,870		172,926	
	30	Goods transferred, ? units		?	?	
	30	Bal., 1,400 units, 70% completed			?	

a. Determine the number of units transferred to the next department.
b. Determine the costs per equivalent unit of direct materials and conversion.
c. Determine the cost of units started and completed in November.

✔ a. $11,646

EX 3-15 Costs per equivalent unit and production costs **OBJ. 2, 4**

Based on the data in Exercise 3-14, determine the following:

a. Cost of beginning work in process inventory completed in November
b. Cost of units transferred to the next department during November
c. Cost of ending work in process inventory on November 30
d. Costs per equivalent unit of direct materials and conversion included in the November 1 beginning work in process
e. The November increase or decrease in costs per equivalent unit for direct materials and conversion from the previous month

✔ a. 4. $2,092

EX 3-16 Cost of production report **OBJ. 2, 4**

The debits to Work in Process—Roasting Department for Morning Brew Coffee Company for August 2016, together with information concerning production, are as follows:

Work in process, August 1, 700 pounds, 20% completed		$ 3,479*
*Direct materials (700 × $4.70)	$3,290	
Conversion (700 × 20% × $1.35)	189	
	$3,479	
Coffee beans added during August, 14,300 pounds		65,780
Conversion costs during August		21,942
Work in process, August 31, 400 pounds, 42% completed		?
Goods finished during August, 14,600 pounds		?

All direct materials are placed in process at the beginning of production.

a. Prepare a cost of production report, presenting the following computations:
   1. Direct materials and conversion equivalent units of production for August
   2. Direct materials and conversion costs per equivalent unit for August
   3. Cost of goods finished during August
   4. Cost of work in process at August 31, 2016
b. Compute and evaluate the change in cost per equivalent unit for direct materials and conversion from the previous month (July).

EX 3-17 Cost of production report OBJ. 2, 4

✔ Conversion cost per equivalent unit, $5.10

The Cutting Department of Karachi Carpet Company provides the following data for January 2016. Assume that all materials are added at the beginning of the process.

Work in process, January 1, 1,400 units, 75% completed		$ 22,960*
*Direct materials (1,400 × $12.65)	$17,710	
Conversion (1,400 × 75% × $5.00)	5,250	
	$22,960	
Materials added during January from Weaving Department, 58,000 units		$742,400
Direct labor for January		134,550
Factory overhead for January		151,611
Goods finished during January (includes goods in process, January 1), 56,200 units		—
Work in process, January 31, 3,200 units, 30% completed		—

a. Prepare a cost of production report for the Cutting Department.

b. Compute and evaluate the change in the costs per equivalent unit for direct materials and conversion from the previous month (December).

EX 3-18 Cost of production and journal entries OBJ. 1, 2, 3, 4

✔ b. $29,760

AccuBlade Castings Inc. casts blades for turbine engines. Within the Casting Department, alloy is first melted in a crucible, then poured into molds to produce the castings. On May 1, there were 230 pounds of alloy in process, which were 60% complete as to conversion. The Work in Process balance for these 230 pounds was $32,844, determined as follows:

Direct materials (230 × $132)	$30,360
Conversion (230 × 60% × $18)	2,484
	$32,844

During May, the Casting Department was charged $350,000 for 2,500 pounds of alloy and $19,840 for direct labor. Factory overhead is applied to the department at a rate of 150% of direct labor. The department transferred out 2,530 pounds of finished castings to the Machining Department. The May 31 inventory in process was 44% complete as to conversion.

a. Prepare the following May journal entries for the Casting Department:
   1. The materials charged to production
   2. The conversion costs charged to production
   3. The completed production transferred to the Machining Department

b. Determine the Work in Process—Casting Department May 31 balance.

c. Compute and evaluate the change in the costs per equivalent unit for direct materials and conversion from the previous month (April).

EX 3-19 Cost of production and journal entries OBJ. 1, 2, 3

✔ b. $14,319

Lighthouse Paper Company manufactures newsprint. The product is manufactured in two departments, Papermaking and Converting. Pulp is first placed into a vessel at the beginning of papermaking production. The following information concerns production in the Papermaking Department for March:

ACCOUNT *Work in Process—Papermaking Department* ACCOUNT NO.

Date		Item	Debit	Credit	Balance Debit	Balance Credit
Mar.	1	Bal., 2,600 units, 35% completed			9,139	
	31	Direct materials, 105,000 units	330,750		339,889	
	31	Direct labor	40,560		380,449	
	31	Factory overhead	54,795		435,244	
	31	Goods transferred, 103,900 units		?	?	
	31	Bal., 3,700 units, 80% completed			?	

a. Prepare the following March journal entries for the Papermaking Department:
   1. The materials charged to production.
   2. The conversion costs charged to production.
   3. The completed production transferred to the Converting Department.

b. Determine the Work in Process—Papermaking Department March 31 balance.

EX 3-20 Process costing for a service company

OBJ. 4

Madison Electric Company uses a fossil fuel (coal) plant for generating electricity. The facility can generate 900 megawatts (million watts) per hour. The plant operates 600 hours during March. Electricity is used as it is generated; thus, there are no inventories at the beginning or end of the period. The March conversion and fuel costs are as follows:

Conversion costs	$40,500,000
Fuel	10,800,000
Total	$51,300,000

Madison also has a wind farm that can generate 100 megawatts per hour. The wind farm receives sufficient wind to run 300 hours for March. The March conversion costs for the wind farm (mostly depreciation) are as follows:

Conversion costs	$2,700,000

a. Determine the cost per megawatt hour (MWh) for the fossil fuel plant and the wind farm to identify the lowest cost facility in March.

b. Why are equivalent units of production not needed in determining the cost per megawatt hour (MWh) for generating electricity?

c. What advantage does the fossil fuel plant have over the wind farm?

EX 3-21 Decision making

OBJ. 4

Mystic Bottling Company bottles popular beverages in the Bottling Department. The beverages are produced by blending concentrate with water and sugar. The concentrate is purchased from a concentrate producer. The concentrate producer sets higher prices for the more popular concentrate flavors. A simplified Bottling Department cost of production report separating the cost of bottling the four flavors follows:

	A	B	C	D	E
1		Orange	Cola	Lemon-Lime	Root Beer
2	Concentrate	$ 4,625	$129,000	$ 105,000	$ 7,600
3	Water	1,250	30,000	25,000	2,000
4	Sugar	3,000	72,000	60,000	4,800
5	Bottles	5,500	132,000	110,000	8,800
6	Flavor changeover	3,000	4,800	4,000	10,000
7	Conversion cost	1,750	24,000	20,000	2,800
8	Total cost transferred to finished goods	$19,125	$391,800	$324,000	$36,000
9	Number of cases	2,500	60,000	50,000	4,000
10					

Beginning and ending work in process inventories are negligible, so they are omitted from the cost of production report. The flavor changeover cost represents the cost of cleaning the bottling machines between production runs of different flavors.

Prepare a memo to the production manager, analyzing this comparative cost information. In your memo, provide recommendations for further action, along with supporting schedules showing the total cost per case and cost per case by cost element.

EX 3-22 Decision making **OBJ. 4**

Pix Paper Inc. produces photographic paper for printing digital images. One of the processes for this operation is a coating (solvent spreading) operation, where chemicals are coated onto paper stock. There has been some concern about the cost performance of this operation. As a result, you have begun an investigation. You first discover that all materials and conversion prices have been stable for the last six months. Thus, increases in prices for inputs are not an explanation for increasing costs. However, you have discovered three possible problems from some of the operating personnel whose quotes follow:

Operator 1: "I've been keeping an eye on my operating room instruments. I feel as though our energy consumption is becoming less efficient."

Operator 2: "Every time the coating machine goes down, we produce waste on shutdown and subsequent startup. It seems like during the last half year we have had more unscheduled machine shutdowns than in the past. Thus, I feel as though our yields must be dropping."

Operator 3: "My sense is that our coating costs are going up. It seems to me like we are spreading a thicker coating than we should. Perhaps the coating machine needs to be recalibrated."

The Coating Department had no beginning or ending inventories for any month during the study period. The following data from the cost of production report are made available:

	A	B	C	D	E	F	G
1		January	February	March	April	May	June
2	Paper stock	$67,200	$63,840	$60,480	$64,512	$57,120	$53,760
3	Coating	$11,520	$11,856	$12,960	$15,667	$16,320	$18,432
4	Conversion cost (incl. energy)	$38,400	$36,480	$34,560	$36,864	$32,640	$30,720
5	Pounds input to the process	100,000	95,000	90,000	96,000	85,000	80,000
6	Pounds transferred out	96,000	91,200	86,400	92,160	81,600	76,800
7							

a. Prepare a table showing the paper cost per output pound, coating cost per output pound, conversion cost per output pound, and yield (pounds transferred out/pounds input) for each month.

b. Interpret your table results.

EX 3-23 Lean manufacturing **OBJ. 5**

The following are some quotes provided by a number of managers at Hawkeye Machining Company regarding the company's planned move toward a lean manufacturing system:

Director of Sales: I'm afraid we'll miss some sales if we don't keep a large stock of items on hand just in case demand increases. It only makes sense to me to keep large inventories in order to assure product availability for our customers.

Director of Purchasing: I'm very concerned about moving to a lean system for materials. What would happen if one of our suppliers were unable to make a shipment? A supplier could fall behind in production or have a quality problem. Without some safety stock in our materials, our whole plant would shut down.

Director of Manufacturing: If we go to lean manufacturing, I think our factory output will drop. We need in-process inventory in order to "smooth out" the inevitable problems that occur during manufacturing. For example, if a machine that is used to process a product breaks down, it would starve the next machine if I don't have in-process inventory between the two machines. If I have in-process inventory, then I can keep the next operation busy while I fix the broken machine. Thus, the in-process inventories give me a safety valve that I can use to keep things running when things go wrong.

How would you respond to these managers?

Appendix

EX 3-24 Equivalent units of production: average cost method

✔ a. 17,000

The Converting Department of Tender Soft Tissue Company uses the average cost method and had 1,900 units in work in process that were 60% complete at the beginning of the period. During the period, 15,800 units were completed and transferred to the Packing Department. There were 1,200 units in process that were 30% complete at the end of the period.

a. Determine the number of whole units to be accounted for and to be assigned costs for the period.

b. Determine the number of equivalent units of production for the period.

Appendix
EX 3-25 Equivalent units of production: average cost method

✔ a. 12,100 units to be accounted for

Units of production data for the two departments of Atlantic Cable and Wire Company for July of the current fiscal year are as follows:

	Drawing Department	Winding Department
Work in process, July 1	500 units, 50% completed	350 units, 30% completed
Completed and transferred to next processing department during July	11,400 units	10,950 units
Work in process, July 31	700 units, 55% completed	800 units, 25% completed

Each department uses the average cost method.

a. Determine the number of whole units to be accounted for and to be assigned costs and the equivalent units of production for the Drawing Department.

b. Determine the number of whole units to be accounted for and to be assigned costs and the equivalent units of production for the Winding Department.

Appendix
EX 3-26 Equivalent units of production: average cost method

✔ a. 3,100

The following information concerns production in the Finishing Department for May. The Finishing Department uses the average cost method.

ACCOUNT *Work in Process—Finishing Department* ACCOUNT NO.

Date		Item	Debit	Credit	Balance	
					Debit	Credit
May	1	Bal., 4,200 units, 70% completed			36,500	
	31	Direct materials, 23,600 units	125,800		162,300	
	31	Direct labor	75,400		237,700	
	31	Factory overhead	82,675		320,375	
	31	Goods transferred, 24,700 units		308,750	11,625	
	31	Bal., ? units, 30% completed			11,625	

a. Determine the number of units in work in process inventory at the end of the month.

b. Determine the number of whole units to be accounted for and to be assigned costs and the equivalent units of production for May.

Appendix
EX 3-27 Equivalent units of production and related costs

✔ b. 8,820 units

The charges to Work in Process—Baking Department for a period as well as information concerning production are as follows. The Baking Department uses the average cost method, and all direct materials are placed in process during production.

Work in Process—Baking Department

Bal., 900 units, 40% completed	2,466	To Finished Goods, 8,100 units	?
Direct materials, 8,400 units	34,500		
Direct labor	16,200		
Factory overhead	8,574		
Bal., 1,200 units, 60% completed	?		

Determine the following:

a. The number of whole units to be accounted for and to be assigned costs

b. The number of equivalent units of production

c. The cost per equivalent unit

d. The cost of units transferred to Finished Goods

e. The cost of units in ending Work in Process

Appendix
EX 3-28 Cost per equivalent unit: average cost method

✔ a. $26.00

The following information concerns production in the Forging Department for June. The Forging Department uses the average cost method.

ACCOUNT *Work in Process—Forging Department* ACCOUNT NO.

Date		Item	Debit	Credit	Balance Debit	Balance Credit
June	1	Bal., 500 units, 40% completed			5,000	
	30	Direct materials, 3,700 units	49,200		54,200	
	30	Direct labor	25,200		79,400	
	30	Factory overhead	25,120		104,520	
	30	Goods transferred, 3,600 units		?	?	
	30	Bal., 600 units, 70% completed			?	

a. Determine the cost per equivalent unit.

b. Determine cost of units transferred to Finished Goods.

c. Determine the cost of units in ending Work in Process.

Appendix
EX 3-29 Cost of production report: average cost method

✔ Cost per equivalent unit, $3.60

The increases to Work in Process—Roasting Department for Highlands Coffee Company for May 2016 as well as information concerning production are as follows:

Work in process, May 1, 1,150 pounds, 40% completed	$ 1,700
Coffee beans added during May, 10,900 pounds	28,600
Conversion costs during May	12,504
Work in process, May 31, 800 pounds, 80% completed	—
Goods finished during May, 11,250 pounds	—

Prepare a cost of production report, using the average cost method.

Appendix
EX 3-30 Cost of production report: average cost method

✔ Cost per equivalent unit, $9.00

Prepare a cost of production report for the Cutting Department of Dalton Carpet Company for January 2016. Use the average cost method with the following data:

Work in process, January 1, 3,400 units, 75% completed	$ 23,000
Materials added during January from Weaving Department, 64,000 units	366,200
Direct labor for January	105,100
Factory overhead for January	80,710
Goods finished during January (includes goods in process, January 1), 63,500 units	—
Work in process, January 31, 3,900 units, 10% completed	—

Problems: Series A

PR 3-1A Entries for process cost system **OBJ. 1, 3**

✔ 2. Materials October 31 balance, $5,900

General Ledger

SHOW ME HOW

FloorMate Carpet Company manufactures carpets. Fiber is placed in process in the Spinning Department, where it is spun into yarn. The output of the Spinning Department is transferred to the Tufting Department, where carpet backing is added at the beginning of the process and the process is completed. On October 1, FloorMate Carpet Company had the following inventories:

Finished Goods	$5,600
Work in Process—Spinning Department	1,500
Work in Process—Tufting Department	2,300
Materials	4,800

Departmental accounts are maintained for factory overhead, and both have zero balances on October 1.

Manufacturing operations for October are summarized as follows:

a. Materials purchased on account	$ 84,900
b. Materials requisitioned for use:	
Fiber—Spinning Department	$ 43,600
Carpet backing—Tufting Department	34,100
Indirect materials—Spinning Department	3,200
Indirect materials—Tufting Department	2,900
c. Labor used:	
Direct labor—Spinning Department	$ 26,300
Direct labor—Tufting Department	17,900
Indirect labor—Spinning Department	12,100
Indirect labor—Tufting Department	11,700
d. Depreciation charged on fixed assets:	
Spinning Department	$ 5,300
Tufting Department	3,400
e. Expired prepaid factory insurance:	
Spinning Department	$ 1,200
Tufting Department	1,000
f. Applied factory overhead:	
Spinning Department	$ 22,000
Tufting Department	18,700
g. Production costs transferred from Spinning Department to Tufting Department	$ 88,000
h. Production costs transferred from Tufting Department to Finished Goods	$159,000
i. Cost of goods sold during the period	$160,500

Instructions

1. Journalize the entries to record the operations, identifying each entry by letter.
2. Compute the October 31 balances of the inventory accounts.
3. Compute the October 31 balances of the factory overhead accounts.

PR 3-2A Cost of production report **OBJ. 2, 4**

✔ 1. Conversion cost per equivalent unit, $0.80

Fresh Mountain Coffee Company roasts and packs coffee beans. The process begins by placing coffee beans into the Roasting Department. From the Roasting Department, coffee beans are then transferred to the Packing Department. The following is a partial work in process account of the Roasting Department at March 31, 2016:

ACCOUNT *Work in Process—Roasting Department* ACCOUNT NO.

Date		Item	Debit	Credit	Balance	
					Debit	Credit
Mar.	1	Bal., 1,500 units, 30% completed			6,150	
	31	Direct materials, 22,300 units	86,970		93,120	
	31	Direct labor	11,900		105,020	
	31	Factory overhead	5,772		110,792	
	31	Goods transferred, 21,700 units		?		
	31	Bal., ? units, 40% completed			?	

Instructions

1. Prepare a cost of production report, and identify the missing amounts for Work in Process—Roasting Department.
2. Assuming that the March 1 work in process inventory includes $5,700 of direct materials, determine the increase or decrease in the cost per equivalent unit for direct materials and conversion between February and March.

PR 3-3A Equivalent units and related costs; cost of production report; entries OBJ. 2, 3, 4

✔ 2. Transferred to Packaging Dept., $40,183

White Diamond Flour Company manufactures flour by a series of three processes, beginning with wheat grain being introduced in the Milling Department. From the Milling Department, the materials pass through the Sifting and Packaging departments, emerging as packaged refined flour.

The balance in the account Work in Process—Sifting Department was as follows on July 1, 2016:

Work in Process—Sifting Department (900 units, ⅗ completed):	
Direct materials (900 × $2.05)	$1,845
Conversion (900 × ⅗ × $0.40)	216
	$2,061

The following costs were charged to Work in Process—Sifting Department during July:

Direct materials transferred from Milling Department:	
15,700 units at $2.15 a unit	$33,755
Direct labor	4,420
Factory overhead	2,708

During July, 15,500 units of flour were completed. Work in Process—Sifting Department on July 31 was 1,100 units, ⅘ completed.

Instructions

1. Prepare a cost of production report for the Sifting Department for July.
2. Journalize the entries for costs transferred from Milling to Sifting and the costs transferred from Sifting to Packaging.
3. Determine the increase or decrease in the cost per equivalent unit from June to July for direct materials and conversion costs.
4. Discuss the uses of the cost of production report and the results of part (3).

PR 3-4A Work in process account data for two months; cost of production reports OBJ. 1, 2, 3, 4

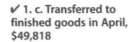

✔ 1. c. Transferred to finished goods in April, $49,818

Hearty Soup Co. uses a process cost system to record the costs of processing soup, which requires the cooking and filling processes. Materials are entered from the cooking process at the beginning of the filling process. The inventory of Work in Process—Filling on April 1 and debits to the account during April 2016 were as follows:

Bal., 800 units, 30% completed:	
Direct materials (800 × $4.30)	$ 3,440
Conversion (800 × 30% × $1.75)	420
	$ 3,860
From Cooking Department, 7,800 units	$34,320
Direct labor	8,562
Factory overhead	6,387

During April, 800 units in process on April 1 were completed, and of the 7,800 units entering the department, all were completed except 550 units that were 90% completed.

Charges to Work in Process—Filling for May were as follows:

From Cooking Department, 9,600 units	$44,160
Direct labor	12,042
Factory overhead	6,878

During May, the units in process at the beginning of the month were completed, and of the 9,600 units entering the department, all were completed except 300 units that were 35% completed.

Instructions

1. Enter the balance as of April 1, 2016, in a four-column account for Work in Process—Filling. Record the debits and the credits in the account for April. Construct a cost of production report, and present computations for determining (a) equivalent units of production for materials and conversion, (b) costs per equivalent unit, (c) cost of goods

finished, differentiating between units started in the prior period and units started and finished in April, and (d) work in process inventory.

2. Provide the same information for May by recording the May transactions in the four-column work in process account. Construct a cost of production report, and present the May computations (a through d) listed in part (1).
3. Comment on the change in costs per equivalent unit for March through May for direct materials and conversion costs.

Appendix

PR 3-5A Cost of production report: average cost method

✔ Cost per equivalent unit, $2.70

Sunrise Coffee Company roasts and packs coffee beans. The process begins in the Roasting Department. From the Roasting Department, the coffee beans are transferred to the Packing Department. The following is a partial work in process account of the Roasting Department at December 31, 2016:

ACCOUNT *Work in Process—Roasting Department* ACCOUNT NO.

Date		Item	Debit	Credit	Balance Debit	Balance Credit
Dec.	1	Bal., 10,500 units, 75% completed			21,000	
	31	Direct materials, 210,400 units	246,800		267,800	
	31	Direct labor	135,700		403,500	
	31	Factory overhead	168,630		572,130	
	31	Goods transferred, 208,900 units		?	?	
	31	Bal., ? units, 25% completed			?	

Instructions

Prepare a cost of production report, using the average cost method, and identify the missing amounts for Work in Process—Roasting Department.

Problems: Series B

PR 3-1B Entries for process cost system

OBJ. 1, 3

✔ 2. Materials July 31 balance, $11,390

Preston & Grover Soap Company manufactures powdered detergent. Phosphate is placed in process in the Making Department, where it is turned into granulars. The output of Making is transferred to the Packing Department, where packaging is added at the beginning of the process. On July 1, Preston & Grover Soap Company had the following inventories:

Finished Goods	$13,500
Work in Process—Making	6,790
Work in Process—Packing	7,350
Materials	5,100

Departmental accounts are maintained for factory overhead, which both have zero balances on July 1.

Manufacturing operations for July are summarized as follows:

a. Materials purchased on account	$149,800
b. Materials requisitioned for use:	
Phosphate—Making Department	$105,700
Packaging—Packing Department	31,300
Indirect materials—Making Department	4,980
Indirect materials—Packing Department	1,530

(Continued)

c. Labor used:

Direct labor—Making Department	$ 32,400
Direct labor—Packing Department	40,900
Indirect labor—Making Department	15,400
Indirect labor—Packing Department	18,300

d. Depreciation charged on fixed assets:

Making Department	$ 10,700
Packing Department	7,900

e. Expired prepaid factory insurance:

Making Department	$ 2,000
Packing Department	1,500

f. Applied factory overhead:

Making Department	$ 32,570
Packing Department	30,050

g. Production costs transferred from Making Department to Packing Department $166,790

h. Production costs transferred from Packing Department to Finished Goods.......... $263,400

i. Cost of goods sold during the period $265,200

Instructions

1. Journalize the entries to record the operations, identifying each entry by letter.
2. Compute the July 31 balances of the inventory accounts.
3. Compute the July 31 balances of the factory overhead accounts.

PR 3-2B Cost of production report **OBJ. 2, 4**

✔ **1. Conversion cost per equivalent unit, $6.00**

Bavarian Chocolate Company processes chocolate into candy bars. The process begins by placing direct materials (raw chocolate, milk, and sugar) into the Blending Department. All materials are placed into production at the beginning of the blending process. After blending, the milk chocolate is then transferred to the Molding Department, where the milk chocolate is formed into candy bars. The following is a partial work in process account of the Blending Department at October 31, 2016:

ACCOUNT *Work in Process—Blending Department* ACCOUNT NO.

Date		Item	Debit	Credit	Balance Debit	Balance Credit
Oct.	1	Bal., 2,300 units, 3/5 completed			46,368	
	31	Direct materials, 26,000 units	429,000		475,368	
	31	Direct labor	100,560		575,928	
	31	Factory overhead	48,480		624,408	
	31	Goods transferred, 25,700 units		?		
	31	Bal., ? units, 1/5 completed			?	

Instructions

1. Prepare a cost of production report, and identify the missing amounts for Work in Process—Blending Department.
2. Assuming that the October 1 work in process inventory includes direct materials of $38,295, determine the increase or decrease in the cost per equivalent unit for direct materials and conversion between September and October.

PR 3-3B Equivalent units and related costs; cost of production report; entries — OBJ. 2, 3, 4

✔ 2. Transferred to finished goods, $705,376

Dover Chemical Company manufactures specialty chemicals by a series of three processes, all materials being introduced in the Distilling Department. From the Distilling Department, the materials pass through the Reaction and Filling departments, emerging as finished chemicals.

The balance in the account Work in Process—Filling was as follows on January 1, 2016:

Work in Process—Filling Department	
(3,400 units, 60% completed):	
Direct materials (3,400 × $9.58)	$32,572
Conversion (3,400 × 60% × $3.90)	7,956
	$40,528

The following costs were charged to Work in Process—Filling during January:

Direct materials transferred from Reaction Department: 52,300 units at $9.50 a unit	$496,850
Direct labor	101,560
Factory overhead	95,166

During January, 53,000 units of specialty chemicals were completed. Work in Process—Filling Department on January 31 was 2,700 units, 30% completed.

Instructions

1. Prepare a cost of production report for the Filling Department for January.
2. Journalize the entries for costs transferred from Reaction to Filling and the costs transferred from Filling to Finished Goods.
3. Determine the increase or decrease in the cost per equivalent unit from December to January for direct materials and conversion costs.
4. 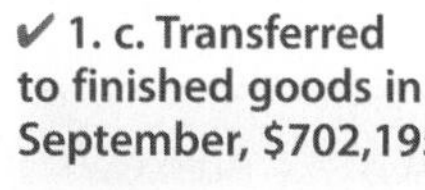 Discuss the uses of the cost of production report and the results of part (3).

PR 3-4B Work in process account data for two months; cost of production reports — OBJ. 1, 2, 3, 4

✔ 1. c. Transferred to finished goods in September, $702,195

Pittsburgh Aluminum Company uses a process cost system to record the costs of manufacturing rolled aluminum, which consists of the smelting and rolling processes. Materials are entered from smelting at the beginning of the rolling process. The inventory of Work in Process—Rolling on September 1, 2016, and debits to the account during September were as follows:

Bal., 2,600 units, ¼ completed:	
Direct materials (2,600 × $15.50)	$40,300
Conversion (2,600 × ¼ × $8.50)	5,525
	$45,825
From Smelting Department, 28,900 units	462,400
Direct labor	158,920
Factory overhead	101,402

During September, 2,600 units in process on September 1 were completed, and of the 28,900 units entering the department, all were completed except 2,900 units that were ⅘ completed.

Charges to Work in Process—Rolling for October were as follows:

From Smelting Department, 31,000 units	$511,500
Direct labor	162,850
Factory overhead	104,494

During October, the units in process at the beginning of the month were completed, and of the 31,000 units entering the department, all were completed except 2,000 units that were ⅖ completed.

(Continued)

Instructions

1. Enter the balance as of September 1, 2016, in a four-column account for Work in Process—Rolling. Record the debits and the credits in the account for September. Construct a cost of production report and present computations for determining (a) equivalent units of production for materials and conversion, (b) costs per equivalent unit, (c) cost of goods finished, differentiating between units started in the prior period and units started and finished in September, and (d) work in process inventory.
2. Provide the same information for October by recording the October transactions in the four-column work in process account. Construct a cost of production report, and present the October computations (a through d) listed in part (1).
3. Comment on the change in costs per equivalent unit for August through October for direct materials and conversion cost.

Appendix
PR 3-5B Cost of production report: average cost method

✔ **Transferred to Packaging Dept., $54,000**

Blue Ribbon Flour Company manufactures flour by a series of three processes, beginning in the Milling Department. From the Milling Department, the materials pass through the Sifting and Packaging departments, emerging as packaged refined flour.

The balance in the account Work in Process—Sifting Department was as follows on May 1, 2016:

Work in Process—Sifting Department (1,500 units, 75% completed)	$3,400

The following costs were charged to Work in Process—Sifting Department during May:

Direct materials transferred from Milling Department: 18,300 units	$32,600
Direct labor	14,560
Factory overhead	7,490

During May, 18,000 units of flour were completed and transferred to finished goods. Work in Process—Sifting Department on May 31 was 1,800 units, 75% completed.

Instructions

Prepare a cost of production report for the Sifting Department for May, using the average cost method.

Cases & Projects

CP 3-1 Ethics and professional conduct in business

Assume you are the division controller for Auntie M's Cookie Company. Auntie M has introduced a new chocolate chip cookie called Full of Chips, and it is a success. As a result, the product manager responsible for the launch of this new cookie was promoted to division vice president and became your boss. A new product manager, Bishop, has been brought in to replace the promoted manager. Bishop notices that the Full of Chips cookie uses a lot of chips, which increases the cost of the cookie. As a result, Bishop has ordered that the amount of chips used in the cookies be reduced by 10%. The manager believes that a 10% reduction in chips will not adversely affect sales but will reduce costs and, hence, improve margins. The increased margins would help Bishop meet profit targets for the period.

You are looking over some cost of production reports segmented by cookie line. You notice that there is a drop in the materials costs for Full of Chips. On further investigation, you discover why the chip costs have declined (fewer chips). Both you and Bishop report to the division vice president, who was the original product manager for Full of Chips. You are trying to decide what to do, if anything.

Discuss the options you might consider.

CP 3-2 Accounting for materials costs

In papermaking operations for companies such as **International Paper Company**, wet pulp is fed into paper machines, which press and dry pulp into a continuous sheet of paper. The paper is formed at very high speeds (60 mph). Once the paper is formed, the paper is rolled onto a reel at the back end of the paper machine. One of the characteristics of papermaking is the creation of "broke" paper. Broke is paper that fails to satisfy quality standards and is therefore rejected for final shipment to customers. Broke is recycled back to the beginning of the process by combining the recycled paper with virgin (new) pulp material. The combination of virgin pulp and recycled broke is sent to the paper machine for papermaking. Broke is fed into this recycle process continuously from all over the facility.

In this industry, it is typical to charge the papermaking operation with the cost of direct materials, which is a mixture of virgin materials and broke. Broke has a much lower cost than does virgin pulp. Therefore, the more broke in the mixture, the lower the average cost of direct materials to the department. Papermaking managers will frequently comment on the importance of broke for keeping their direct materials costs down.

a. How do you react to this accounting procedure?

b. What "hidden costs" are not considered when accounting for broke as described?

CP 3-3 Analyzing unit costs

Midstate Containers Inc. manufactures cans for the canned food industry. The operations manager of a can manufacturing operation wants to conduct a cost study investigating the relationship of tin content in the material (can stock) to the energy cost for enameling the cans. The enameling was necessary to prepare the cans for labeling. A higher percentage of tin content in the can stock increases the cost of material. The operations manager believed that a higher tin content in the can stock would reduce the amount of energy used in enameling. During the analysis period, the amount of tin content in the steel can stock was increased for every month, from April to September. The following operating reports were available from the controller:

	A	B	C	D	E	F	G
1		April	May	June	July	August	September
2	Energy	$ 14,000	$ 34,800	$ 33,000	$ 21,700	$ 28,800	$ 33,000
3	Materials	13,000	28,800	24,200	14,000	17,100	16,000
4	Total cost	$ 27,000	$ 63,600	$ 57,200	$ 35,700	$ 45,900	$ 49,000
5	Units produced	÷50,000	÷120,000	÷110,000	÷ 70,000	÷ 90,000	÷100,000
6	Cost per unit	$ 0.54	$ 0.53	$ 0.52	$ 0.51	$ 0.51	$ 0.49
7							

Differences in materials unit costs were entirely related to the amount of tin content.

Interpret this information and report to the operations manager your recommendations with respect to tin content.

CP 3-4 Decision making

Jamarcus Bradshaw, plant manager of Georgia Paper Company's papermaking mill, was looking over the cost of production reports for July and August for the Papermaking Department. The reports revealed the following:

	July	August
Pulp and chemicals	$295,600	$304,100
Conversion cost	146,000	149,600
Total cost	$441,600	$453,700
Number of tons	÷ 1,200	÷ 1,130
Cost per ton	$ 368	$ 401.50

(Continued)

Jamarcus was concerned about the increased cost per ton from the output of the department. As a result, he asked the plant controller to perform a study to help explain these results. The controller, Leann Brunswick, began the analysis by performing some interviews of key plant personnel in order to understand what the problem might be. Excerpts from an interview with Len Tyson, a paper machine operator, follow:

Len: We have two papermaking machines in the department. I have no data, but I think paper machine No. 1 is applying too much pulp and, thus, is wasting both conversion and materials resources. We haven't had repairs on paper machine No. 1 in a while. Maybe this is the problem.

Leann: How does too much pulp result in wasted resources?

Len: Well, you see, if too much pulp is applied, then we will waste pulp material. The customer will not pay for the extra weight. Thus, we just lose that amount of material. Also, when there is too much pulp, the machine must be slowed down in order to complete the drying process. This results in a waste of conversion costs.

Leann: Do you have any other suspicions?

Len: Well, as you know, we have two products—green paper and yellow paper. They are identical except for the color. The color is added to the papermaking process in the paper machine. I think that during August these two color papers have been behaving very differently. I don't have any data, but it just seems as though the amount of waste associated with the green paper has increased.

Leann: Why is this?

Len: I understand that there has been a change in specifications for the green paper, starting near the beginning of August. This change could be causing the machines to run poorly when making green paper. If this is the case, the cost per ton would increase for green paper.

Leann also asked for a database printout providing greater detail on August's operating results.

September 9 Requested by: Leann Brunswick
Papermaking Department—August detail

	A	B	C	D	E	F
1	**Production**					
2	**Run**	**Paper**		**Material**	**Conversion**	
3	**Number**	**Machine**	**Color**	**Costs**	**Costs**	**Tons**
4	1	1	Green	40,300	18,300	150
5	2	1	Yellow	41,700	21,200	140
6	3	1	Green	44,600	22,500	150
7	4	1	Yellow	36,100	18,100	120
8	5	2	Green	38,300	18,900	160
9	6	2	Yellow	33,900	15,200	140
10	7	2	Green	35,600	18,400	130
11	8	2	Yellow	33,600	17,000	140
12		Total		304,100	149,600	1,130
13						

Assuming that you're Leann Brunswick, write a memo to Jamarcus Bradshaw with a recommendation to management. You should analyze the August data to determine whether the paper machine or the paper color explains the increase in the unit cost from July. Include any supporting schedules that are appropriate.

CP 3-5 Process costing companies

Group Project

The following categories represent typical process manufacturing industries:

Beverages	Metals
Chemicals	Petroleum refining
Food	Pharmaceuticals
Forest and paper products	Soap and cosmetics

In groups of two or three, for each category identify one company (following your instructor's specific instructions) and determine the following:

1. Typical products manufactured by the selected company, including brand names
2. Typical raw materials used by the selected company
3. Types of processes used by the selected company

Use annual reports, the Internet, or library resources in doing this activity.

© CHATCHAI SOMWAT/SHUTTERSTOCK.COM

CHAPTER 4

Cost Behavior and Cost-Volume-Profit Analysis

Ford Motor Company

Making a profit isn't easy for U.S. auto manufacturers like the **Ford Motor Company.** The cost of materials, labor, equipment, and advertising make it very expensive to produce cars and trucks.

How many cars does Ford need to produce and sell to break even? The answer depends on the relationship between Ford's sales revenue and costs. Some of Ford's costs, like direct labor and materials, will change in direct proportion to the number of vehicles that are built. Other costs, such as the costs of manufacturing equipment, are fixed and do not change with the number of vehicles that are produced. Ford will break even when it generates enough sales revenue to cover both its fixed and variable costs.

During the depths of the 2009 recession, Ford renegotiated labor contracts with their employees. These renegotiations reduced the direct labor cost incurred to build each car, which lowered the number of cars that the company needed to sell to break even by 45%.

As with Ford, understanding how costs behave, and the relationship between costs, profits, and volume, is important for all businesses. This chapter discusses commonly used methods for classifying costs according to how they change and techniques for determining how many units must be sold for a company to break even. Techniques that management can use to evaluate costs in order to make sound business decisions are also discussed.

Source: J. Booton, "Moody's Upgrades Ford's Credit Rating, Returns Blue Oval Trademark," Fox Business, May 22, 2012.

Learning Objectives

After studying this chapter, you should be able to: *Example Exercises*

At a Glance 4 Page 159

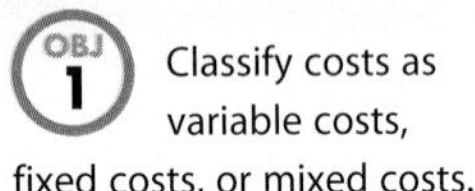

Classify costs as variable costs, fixed costs, or mixed costs.

Cost Behavior

Cost behavior is the manner in which a cost changes as a related activity changes. The behavior of costs is useful to managers for a variety of reasons. For example, knowing how costs behave allows managers to predict profits as sales and production volumes change. Knowing how costs behave is also useful for estimating costs, which affects a variety of decisions such as whether to replace a machine.

Understanding the behavior of a cost depends on the following:

- Identifying the activities that cause the cost to change. These activities are called **activity bases** (or *activity drivers*).
- Specifying the range of activity over which the changes in the cost are of interest. This range of activity is called the **relevant range**.

To illustrate, assume that a hospital is concerned about planning and controlling patient food costs. A good activity base is the number of patients who *stay* overnight in the hospital. The number of patients who are *treated* is not as good an activity base because some patients are outpatients and, thus, do not consume food. Once an activity base is identified, food costs can then be analyzed over the range of the number of patients who normally stay in the hospital (the relevant range).

Costs are normally classified as variable costs, fixed costs, or mixed costs.

Variable Costs

Variable costs are costs that vary in proportion to changes in the activity base. When the activity base is units produced, direct materials and direct labor costs are normally classified as variable costs.

To illustrate, assume that Jason Sound Inc. produces stereo systems. The parts for the stereo systems are purchased from suppliers for $10 per unit and are assembled by Jason Sound. For Model JS-12, the direct materials costs for the relevant range of 5,000 to 30,000 units of production are as follows:

Number of Units of Model JS-12 Produced	Direct Materials Cost per Unit	Total Direct Materials Cost
5,000 units	$10	$ 50,000
10,000	10	100,000
15,000	10	150,000
20,000	10	200,000
25,000	10	250,000
30,000	10	300,000

As shown, variable costs have the following characteristics:

- *Cost per unit* remains the same regardless of changes in the activity base. For Jason Sound, units produced is the activity base. For Model JS-12, the cost per unit is $10.
- *Total cost* changes in proportion to changes in the activity base. For Model JS-12, the direct materials cost for 10,000 units ($100,000) is twice the direct materials cost for 5,000 units ($50,000).

Exhibit 1 illustrates how the variable costs for direct materials for Model JS-12 behave in total and on a per-unit basis as production changes.

EXHIBIT 1 **Variable Cost Graphs**

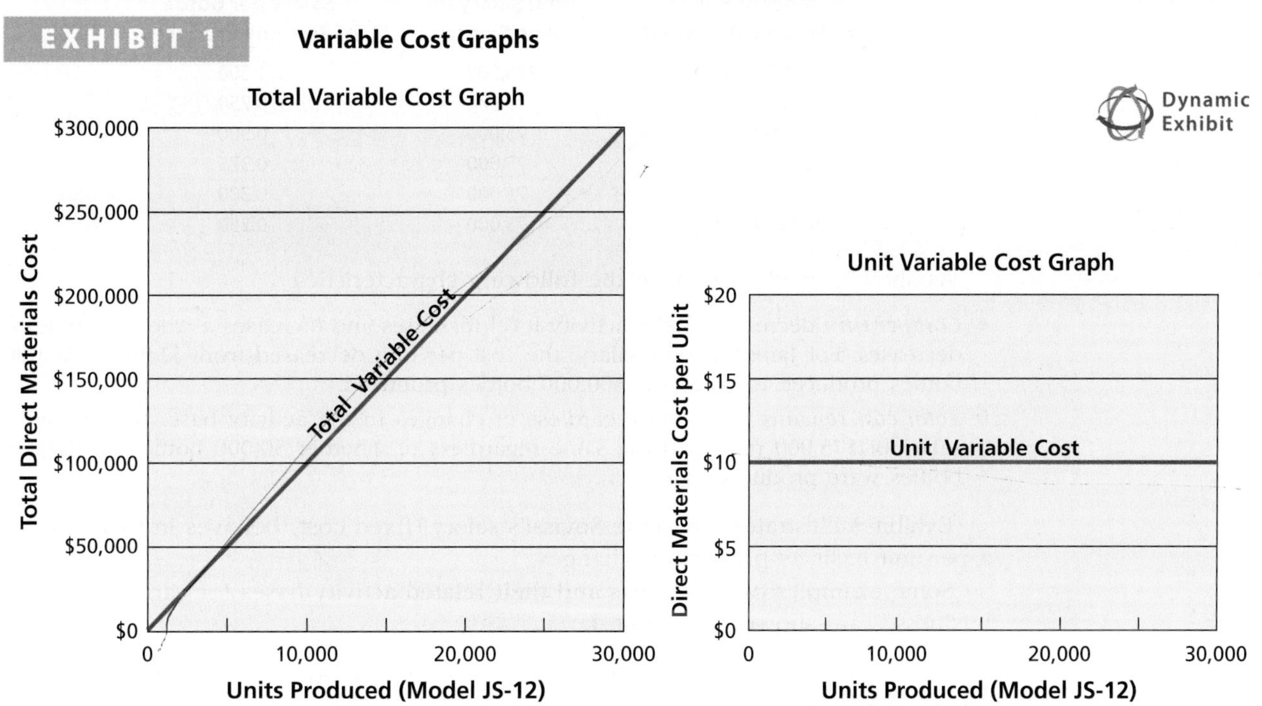

Some examples of variable costs and their related activity bases for various types of businesses are shown in Exhibit 2.

EXHIBIT 2 **Variable Costs and Their Activity Bases**

Type of Business	Cost	Activity Base
University	Instructor salaries	Number of classes
Passenger airline	Fuel	Number of miles flown
Manufacturing	Direct materials	Number of units produced
Hospital	Nurse wages	Number of patients
Hotel	Maid wages	Number of guests
Bank	Teller wages	Number of banking transactions

Fixed Costs

Fixed costs are costs that remain the same in total dollar amount as the activity base changes. When the activity base is units produced, many factory overhead costs such as straight-line depreciation are classified as fixed costs.

To illustrate, assume that Minton Inc. manufactures, bottles, and distributes perfume. The production supervisor is Jane Sovissi, who is paid a salary of $75,000 per year. For the relevant range of 50,000 to 300,000 bottles of perfume, the total fixed cost of $75,000 does not vary as production increases. As a result, the fixed cost per bottle decreases as the units produced increase. This is because the fixed cost is spread over a larger number of bottles, as follows:

Number of Bottles of Perfume Produced	Total Salary for Jane Sovissi	Salary per Bottle of Perfume Produced
50,000 bottles	$75,000	$1.500
100,000	75,000	0.750
150,000	75,000	0.500
200,000	75,000	0.375
250,000	75,000	0.300
300,000	75,000	0.250

As shown, fixed costs have the following characteristics:

- *Cost per unit* decreases as the activity level increases and increases as the activity level decreases. For Jane Sovissi's salary, the cost per unit decreased from $1.50 for 50,000 bottles produced to $0.25 for 300,000 bottles produced.
- *Total cost* remains the same regardless of changes in the activity base. Jane Sovissi's salary of $75,000 remained the same regardless of whether 50,000 bottles or 300,000 bottles were produced.

Exhibit 3 illustrates how Jane Sovissi's salary (fixed cost) behaves in total and on a per-unit basis as production changes.

Some examples of fixed costs and their related activity bases for various types of businesses are shown in Exhibit 4.

Mixed Costs

A salesperson's compensation can be a mixed cost comprised of a salary (fixed portion) plus a commission as a percent of sales (variable portion).

Mixed costs are costs that have characteristics of both a variable and a fixed cost. Mixed costs are sometimes called *semivariable* or *semifixed costs.*

To illustrate, assume that Simpson Inc. manufactures sails, using rented machinery. The rental charges are as follows:

Rental Charge = $15,000 per year + $1 for each hour used in excess of 10,000 hours

EXHIBIT 3 **Fixed Cost Graphs**

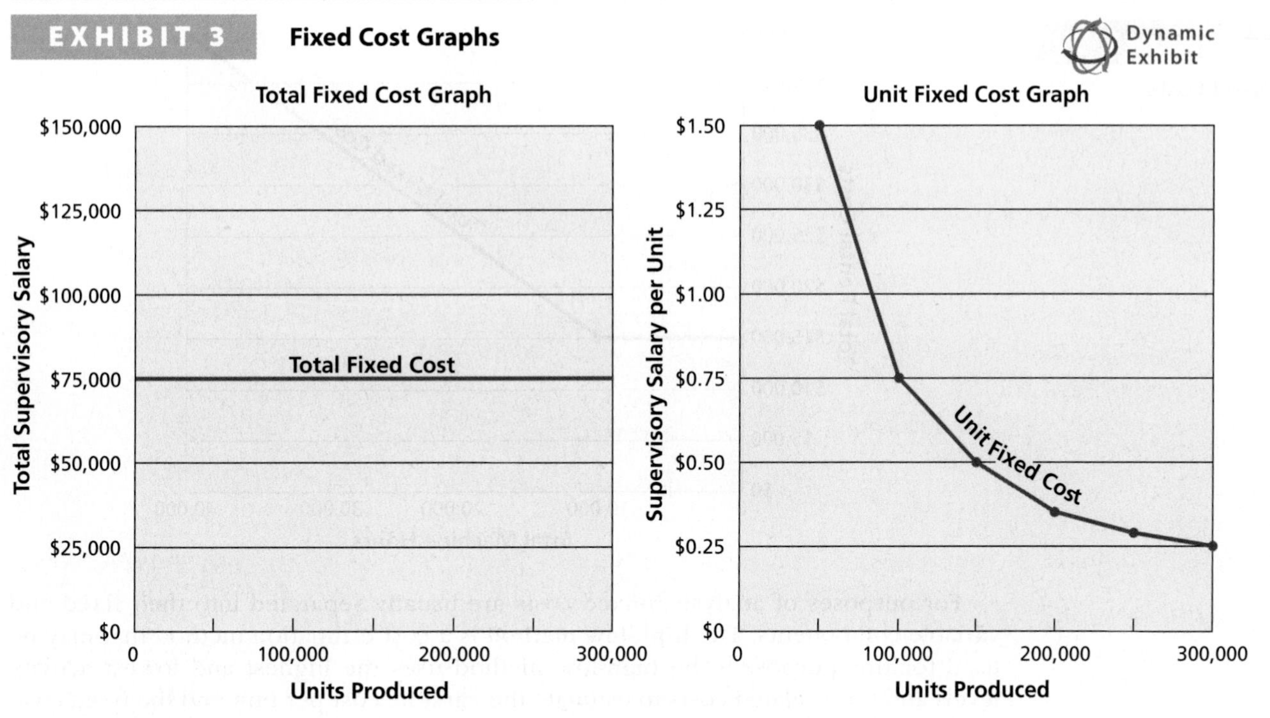

EXHIBIT 4 **Fixed Costs and Their Activity Bases**

Type of Business	Fixed Cost	Activity Base
University	Building (straight-line) depreciation	Number of students
Passenger airline	Airplane (straight-line) depreciation	Number of miles flown
Manufacturing	Plant manager salary	Number of units produced
Hospital	Property insurance	Number of patients
Hotel	Property taxes	Number of guests
Bank	Branch manager salary	Number of customer accounts

The rental charges for various hours used within the relevant range of 8,000 hours to 40,000 hours are as follows:

Hours Used	Rental Charge
8,000 hours	$15,000
12,000	$17,000 {$15,000 + [(12,000 hrs. – 10,000 hrs.) × $1]}
20,000	$25,000 {$15,000 + [(20,000 hrs. – 10,000 hrs.) × $1]}
40,000	$45,000 {$15,000 + [(40,000 hrs. – 10,000 hrs.) × $1]}

Exhibit 5 illustrates the preceding mixed cost behavior.

EXHIBIT 5

Mixed Costs

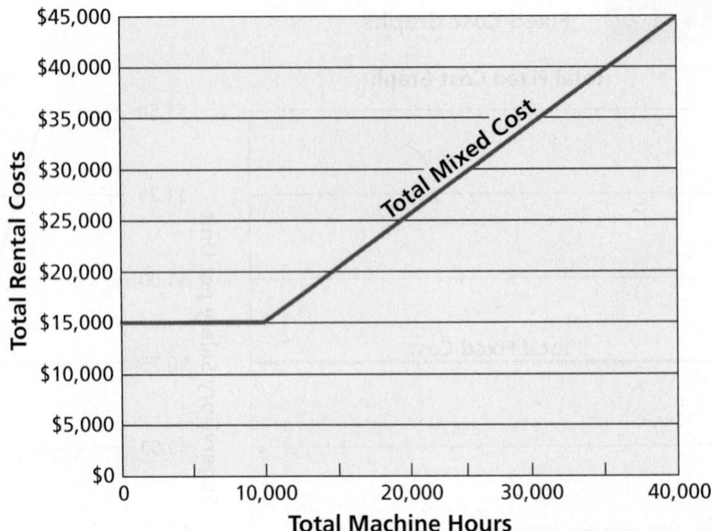

For purposes of analysis, mixed costs are usually separated into their fixed and variable components. The **high-low method** is a cost estimation method that may be used for this purpose.[1] The high-low method uses the highest and lowest activity levels and their related costs to estimate the variable cost per unit and the fixed cost.

To illustrate, assume that the Equipment Maintenance Department of Kason Inc. incurred the following costs during the past five months:

	Units Produced	Total Cost
June	1,000 units	$45,550
July	1,500	52,000
August	2,100	61,500
September	1,800	57,500
October	750	41,250

The number of units produced is the activity base, and the relevant range is the units produced between June and October. For Kason, the difference between the units produced and the total costs at the highest and lowest levels of production are as follows:

	Units Produced	Total Cost
Highest level	2,100 units	$61,500
Lowest level	750	41,250
Difference	1,350 units	$20,250

The total fixed cost does not change with changes in production. Thus, the $20,250 difference in the total cost is the change in the total variable cost. Dividing this difference of $20,250 by the difference in production is an estimate of the variable cost per unit. For Kason, this estimate is $15, computed as follows:

$$\text{Variable Cost per Unit} = \frac{\text{Difference in Total Cost}}{\text{Difference in Units Produced}}$$

$$= \frac{\$20{,}250}{1{,}350 \text{ units}} = \$15 \text{ per unit}$$

The fixed cost is estimated by subtracting the total variable costs from the total costs for the units produced, as follows:

$$\text{Fixed Cost} = \text{Total Costs} - (\text{Variable Cost per Unit} \times \text{Units Produced})$$

[1] Other methods of estimating costs, such as the scattergraph method and the least squares method, are discussed in cost accounting textbooks.

The fixed cost is the same at the highest and the lowest levels of production, as follows for Kason:

Highest level (2,100 units)

Fixed Cost = Total Costs – (Variable Cost per Unit × Units Produced)
= $61,500 – ($15 × 2,100 units)
= $61,500 – $31,500
= $30,000

Lowest level (750 units)

Fixed Cost = Total Costs – (Variable Cost per Unit × Units Produced)
= $41,250 – ($15 × 750 units)
= $41,250 – $11,250
= $30,000

Using the variable cost per unit and the fixed cost, the total equipment maintenance cost for Kason can be computed for various levels of production as follows:

Total Cost = (Variable Cost per Unit × Units Produced) + Fixed Costs
= ($15 × Units Produced) + $30,000

To illustrate, the estimated total cost of 2,000 units of production is $60,000, computed as follows:

Total Cost = ($15 × Units Produced) + $30,000
= ($15 × 2,000 units) + $30,000 = $30,000 + $30,000
= $60,000

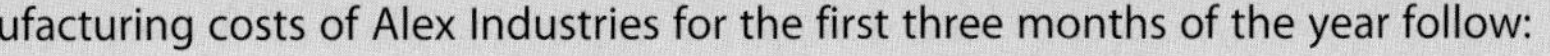

Example Exercise 4-1 High-Low Method

OBJ 1

The manufacturing costs of Alex Industries for the first three months of the year follow:

	Total Cost	Production
January	$ 80,000	1,000 units
February	125,000	2,500
March	100,000	1,800

Using the high-low method, determine (a) the variable cost per unit and (b) the total fixed cost.

Follow My Example 4-1

a. $30 per unit = ($125,000 – $80,000) ÷ (2,500 – 1,000)
b. $50,000 = $125,000 – ($30 × 2,500), or $80,000 – ($30 × 1,000)

Practice Exercises: PE 4-1A, PE 4-1B

Summary of Cost Behavior Concepts

The cost behavior of variable costs and fixed costs is summarized in Exhibit 6.

EXHIBIT 6

Variable and Fixed Cost Behavior

	Effect of Changing Activity Level	
Cost	**Total Amount**	**Per-Unit Amount**
Variable	Increases and decreases proportionately with activity level.	Remains the same regardless of activity level.
Fixed	Remains the same regardless of activity level.	Increases and decreases inversely with activity level.

Mixed costs contain a fixed cost component that is incurred even if nothing is produced. For analysis, the fixed and variable cost components of mixed costs are separated using the high-low method.

Exhibit 7 provides some examples of variable, fixed, and mixed costs for the activity base of *units produced.*

EXHIBIT 7

Variable, Fixed, and Mixed Cost

Variable Costs	Fixed Costs	Mixed Costs
• Direct materials	• Straight-line depreciation	• Quality Control Department salaries
• Direct labor	• Property taxes	• Purchasing Department salaries
• Electricity expense	• Production supervisor salaries	• Maintenance expenses
• Supplies	• Insurance expense	• Warehouse expenses

One method of reporting variable and fixed costs is called **variable costing** or *direct costing*. Under variable costing, only the variable manufacturing costs (direct materials, direct labor, and variable factory overhead) are included in the product cost. The fixed factory overhead is treated as an expense of the period in which it is incurred. Variable costing is described and illustrated in the appendix to this chapter.

Business  **Connection**

FRANCHISING

Many restaurant chains such as **McDonald's**, **Wendy's**, **Dunkin' Donuts**, and **Fatburger** operate as franchises. In a franchise, the restaurant chain (called the *franchisor*) sells the right to sell products using its trademark or brand name to a franchisee. The franchisee typically pays an initial franchise fee, which is a fixed cost. In addition, the franchisee must normally make royalty payments to the franchisor based on a percentage of sales revenues, which is a variable cost. Prior to signing a franchise agreement, most franchisees conduct a break-even analysis to determine how much sales volume their franchise must generate to earn a profit. For example, McDonald's franchises require an initial investment of more than $500,000 and typically take several years to break even.

Source: B. Beshel, *An Introduction to Franchising*, IFA Educational Foundation, 2000.

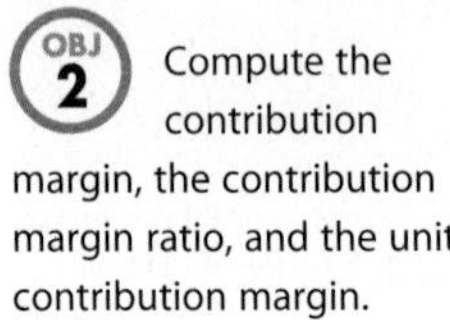

Compute the contribution margin, the contribution margin ratio, and the unit contribution margin.

Cost-Volume-Profit Relationships

Cost-volume-profit analysis is the examination of the relationships among selling prices, sales and production volume, costs, expenses, and profits. Cost-volume-profit analysis is useful for managerial decision making. Some of the ways cost-volume-profit analysis may be used include the following:

- Analyzing the effects of changes in selling prices on profits
- Analyzing the effects of changes in costs on profits
- Analyzing the effects of changes in volume on profits
- Setting selling prices
- Selecting the mix of products to sell
- Choosing among marketing strategies

Contribution Margin

Contribution margin is especially useful because it provides insight into the profit potential of a company. **Contribution margin** is the excess of sales over variable costs, computed as follows:

Contribution Margin = Sales – Variable Costs

To illustrate, assume the following data for Lambert Inc.:

Sales	50,000 units
Sales price per unit	$20 per unit
Variable cost per unit	$12 per unit
Fixed costs	$300,000

Exhibit 8 illustrates an income statement for Lambert prepared in a contribution margin format.

EXHIBIT 8

Contribution Margin Income Statement Format

Sales (50,000 units × $20)	$1,000,000
Variable costs (50,000 units × $12)	600,000
Contribution margin (50,000 units × $8)	$ 400,000
Fixed costs	300,000
Income from operations	$ 100,000

Lambert's contribution margin of $400,000 is available to cover the fixed costs of $300,000. Once the fixed costs are covered, any additional contribution margin increases income from operations.

A room night at **Hilton Hotels** has a high contribution margin. The high contribution margin per room night is necessary to cover the high fixed costs of the hotel.

Contribution Margin Ratio

Contribution margin can also be expressed as a percentage. The **contribution margin ratio**, sometimes called the *profit-volume ratio*, indicates the percentage of each sales dollar available to cover fixed costs and to provide income from operations. The contribution margin ratio is computed as follows:

$$\text{Contribution Margin Ratio} = \frac{\text{Contribution Margin}}{\text{Sales}}$$

The contribution margin ratio is 40% for Lambert Inc., computed as follows:

$$\text{Contribution Margin Ratio} = \frac{\$400,000}{\$1,000,000} = 40\%$$

The contribution margin ratio is most useful when the increase or decrease in sales volume is measured in sales *dollars*. In this case, the change in sales dollars multiplied by the contribution margin ratio equals the change in income from operations, computed as follows:

Change in Income from Operations = Change in Sales Dollars × Contribution Margin Ratio

To illustrate, if Lambert adds $80,000 in sales from the sale of an additional 4,000 units, its income from operations will increase by $32,000, computed as follows:

Change in Income from Operations = Change in Sales Dollars × Contribution Margin Ratio
Change in Income from Operations = $80,000 × 40% = $32,000

The preceding analysis is confirmed by the contribution margin income statement of Lambert that follows:

Sales (54,000 units × $20)	$1,080,000
Variable costs (54,000 units × $12)	648,000*
Contribution margin (54,000 units × $8)	$ 432,000**
Fixed costs	300,000
Income from operations	$ 132,000

*$1,080,000 × 60%
**$1,080,000 × 40%

Income from operations increased from $100,000 to $132,000 when sales increased from $1,000,000 to $1,080,000. Variable costs as a percentage of sales are equal to 100% minus the contribution margin ratio. Thus, in the preceding income statement, the variable costs are 60% (100% – 40%) of sales, or $648,000 ($1,080,000 × 60%). The total contribution margin, $432,000, can also be computed directly by multiplying the total sales by the contribution margin ratio ($1,080,000 × 40%).

In the preceding analysis, factors other than sales volume, such as variable cost per unit and sales price, are assumed to remain constant. If such factors change, their effect must also be considered.

The contribution margin ratio is also useful in developing business strategies. For example, assume that a company has a high contribution margin ratio and is producing below 100% of capacity. In this case, a large increase in income from operations can be expected from an increase in sales volume. Therefore, the company might consider implementing a special sales campaign to increase sales. In contrast, a company with a small contribution margin ratio will probably want to give more attention to reducing costs before attempting to promote sales.

Unit Contribution Margin

The unit contribution margin is also useful for analyzing the profit potential of proposed decisions. The **unit contribution margin** is computed as follows:

Unit Contribution Margin = Sales Price per Unit – Variable Cost per Unit

To illustrate, if Lambert Inc.'s unit selling price is $20 and its variable cost per unit is $12, the unit contribution margin is $8, computed as follows:

Unit Contribution Margin = Sales Price per Unit – Variable Cost per Unit
Unit Contribution Margin = $20 – $12 = $8

The unit contribution margin is most useful when the increase or decrease in sales volume is measured in sales *units* (quantities). In this case, the change in sales volume (units) multiplied by the unit contribution margin equals the change in income from operations, computed as follows:

Change in Income from Operations = Change in Sales Units × Unit Contribution Margin

To illustrate, assume that Lambert's sales could be increased by 15,000 units, from 50,000 units to 65,000 units. Lambert's income from operations would increase by $120,000 (15,000 units × $8), computed as follows:

Change in Income from Operations = Change in Sales Units × Unit Contribution Margin
Change in Income from Operations = 15,000 units × $8 = $120,000

The preceding analysis is confirmed by the contribution margin income statement of Lambert that follows, which shows that income increased to $220,000 when 65,000 units are sold. The income statement in Exhibit 8 indicates income of $100,000 when 50,000 units are sold. Thus, selling an additional 15,000 units increases income by $120,000 ($220,000 – $100,000).

Sales (65,000 units × $20)	$1,300,000
Variable costs (65,000 units × $12)	780,000
Contribution margin (65,000 units × $8)	$ 520,000
Fixed costs	300,000
Income from operations	$ 220,000

Unit contribution margin analysis is useful information for managers. For example, in the preceding illustration, Lambert could spend up to $120,000 for special advertising or other product promotions to increase sales by 15,000 units and still increase income by $100,000, the $220,000 increase in sales minus the $120,000 cost of special advertising.

Example Exercise 4-2 Contribution Margin

Molly Company sells 20,000 units at $12 per unit. Variable costs are $9 per unit, and fixed costs are $25,000. Determine the (a) contribution margin ratio, (b) unit contribution margin, and (c) income from operations.

Follow My Example 4-2

a. 25% = ($12 – $9) ÷ $12, or ($240,000 – $180,000) ÷ $240,000

b. $3 per unit = $12 – $9

c.

Sales	$240,000	(20,000 units × $12 per unit)
Variable costs	180,000	(20,000 units × $9 per unit)
Contribution margin	$ 60,000	[20,000 units × ($12 – $9)]
Fixed costs	25,000	
Income from operations	$ 35,000	

Practice Exercises: PE 4-2A, PE 4-2B

Mathematical Approach to Cost-Volume-Profit Analysis

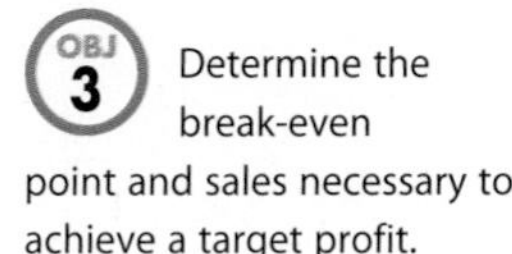

Determine the break-even point and sales necessary to achieve a target profit.

The mathematical approach to cost-volume-profit analysis uses equations to determine the following:

- Sales necessary to break even
- Sales necessary to make a target or desired profit

Break-Even Point

The **break-even point** is the level of operations at which a company's revenues and expenses are equal, as shown in Exhibit 9. At break-even, a company reports neither income nor a loss from operations.

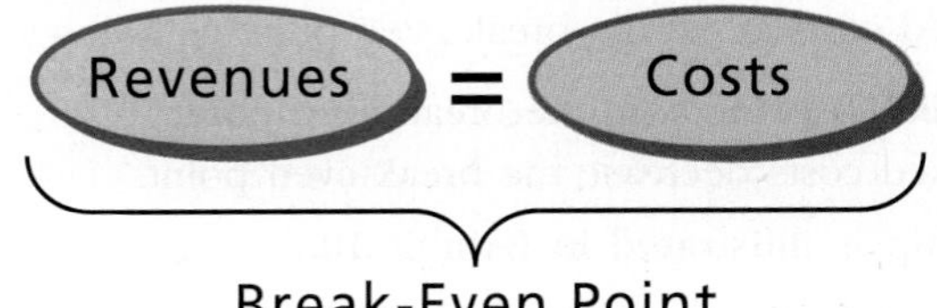

EXHIBIT 9
Break-Even Point

The break-even point in *sales units* is computed as follows:

$$\text{Break-Even Sales (units)} = \frac{\text{Fixed Costs}}{\text{Unit Contribution Margin}}$$

To illustrate, assume the following data for Baker Corporation:

Fixed costs	$90,000
Unit selling price	$25
Unit variable cost	15
Unit contribution margin	$10

The break-even point for Baker is 9,000 units, computed as follows:

$$\text{Break-Even Sales (units)} = \frac{\text{Fixed Costs}}{\text{Unit Contribution Margin}} = \frac{\$90,000}{\$10} = 9,000 \text{ units}$$

The following income statement for Baker verifies the break-even point of 9,000 units:

Sales (9,000 units × \$25)	\$225,000
Variable costs (9,000 units × \$15)	135,000
Contribution margin	\$ 90,000
Fixed costs	90,000
Income from operations	\$ 0

As shown in Baker's income statement, the break-even point is \$225,000 (9,000 units × \$25) of sales. The break-even point in *sales dollars* can be determined directly as follows:

$$\text{Break-Even Sales (dollars)} = \frac{\text{Fixed Costs}}{\text{Contribution Margin Ratio}}$$

The contribution margin ratio can be computed using the unit contribution margin and unit selling price as follows:

$$\text{Contribution Margin Ratio} = \frac{\text{Unit Contribution Margin}}{\text{Unit Selling Price}}$$

The contribution margin ratio for Baker is 40%, computed as follows:

$$\text{Contribution Margin Ratio} = \frac{\text{Unit Contribution Margin}}{\text{Unit Selling Price}} = \frac{\$10}{\$25} = 40\%$$

Thus, the break-even sales dollars for Baker of \$225,000 can be computed directly as follows:

$$\text{Break-Even Sales (dollars)} = \frac{\text{Fixed Costs}}{\text{Contribution Margin Ratio}} = \frac{\$90{,}000}{40\%} = \$225{,}000$$

The break-even point is affected by changes in the fixed costs, unit variable costs, and the unit selling price.

Effect of Changes in Fixed Costs Fixed costs do not change in total with changes in the level of activity. However, fixed costs may change because of other factors such as advertising campaigns, changes in property tax rates, or changes in factory supervisors' salaries.

Changes in fixed costs affect the break-even point as follows:

- Increases in fixed costs increase the break-even point.
- Decreases in fixed costs decrease the break-even point.

This relationship is illustrated in Exhibit 10.

EXHIBIT 10

Effect of Change in Fixed Costs on Break-Even Point

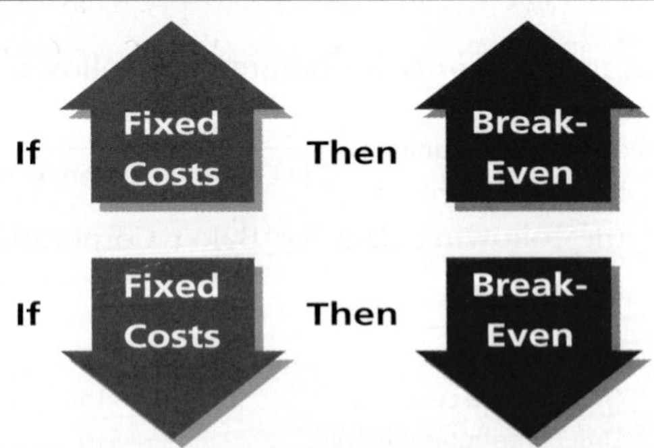

To illustrate, assume that Bishop Co. is evaluating a proposal to budget an additional \$100,000 for advertising. The data for Bishop follows:

	Current	Proposed
Unit selling price	\$90	\$90
Unit variable cost	70	70
Unit contribution margin	\$20	\$20
Fixed costs	\$600,000	\$700,000

Bishop's break-even point *before* the additional advertising expense of $100,000 is 30,000 units, computed as follows:

$$\text{Break-Even Sales (units)} = \frac{\text{Fixed Costs}}{\text{Unit Contribution Margin}} = \frac{\$600,000}{\$20} = 30,000 \text{ units}$$

Bishop's break-even point *after* the additional advertising expense of $100,000 is 35,000 units, computed as follows:

$$\text{Break-Even Sales (units)} = \frac{\text{Fixed Costs}}{\text{Unit Contribution Margin}} = \frac{\$700,000}{\$20} = 35,000 \text{ units}$$

As shown for Bishop, the $100,000 increase in advertising (fixed costs) requires an additional 5,000 units (35,000 – 30,000) of sales to break even.[2] In other words, an increase in sales of 5,000 units is required in order to generate an additional $100,000 of total contribution margin (5,000 units × $20) to cover the increased fixed costs.

Effect of Changes in Unit Variable Costs Unit variable costs do not change with changes in the level of activity. However, unit variable costs may be affected by other factors such as changes in the cost per unit of direct materials, changes in the wage rate for direct labor, or changes in the sales commission paid to salespeople.

Changes in unit variable costs affect the break-even point as follows:

- Increases in unit variable costs increase the break-even point.
- Decreases in unit variable costs decrease the break-even point.

This relationship is illustrated in Exhibit 11.

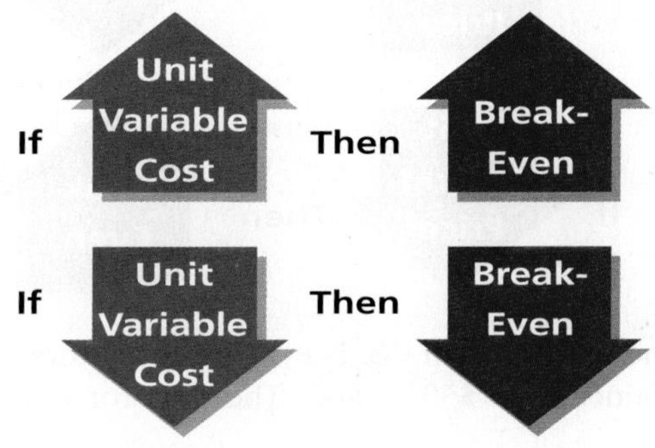

EXHIBIT 11

Effect of Change in Unit Variable Cost on Break-Even Point

To illustrate, assume that Park Co. is evaluating a proposal to pay an additional 2% commission on sales to its salespeople as an incentive to increase sales. The data for Park follows:

	Current	Proposed
Unit selling price	$250	$250
Unit variable cost	145	150*
Unit contribution margin	$105	$100
Fixed costs	$840,000	$840,000

*$150 = $145 + (2% × $250 unit selling price).

Park's break-even point *before* the additional 2% commission is 8,000 units, computed as follows:

$$\text{Break-Even Sales (units)} = \frac{\text{Fixed Costs}}{\text{Unit Contribution Margin}} = \frac{\$840,000}{\$105} = 8,000 \text{ units}$$

[2] The increase of 5,000 units can also be computed by dividing the increase in fixed costs of $100,000 by the unit contribution margin, $20, as follows: 5,000 units = $100,000 ÷ $20.

If the 2% sales commission proposal is adopted, unit variable costs will increase by $5 ($250 × 2%), from $145 to $150 per unit. This increase in unit variable costs will decrease the unit contribution margin from $105 to $100 ($250 – $150). Thus, Park's break-even point *after* the additional 2% commission is 8,400 units, computed as follows:

$$\text{Break-Even Sales (units)} = \frac{\text{Fixed Costs}}{\text{Unit Contribution Margin}} = \frac{\$840{,}000}{\$100} = 8{,}400 \text{ units}$$

As shown for Park, an additional 400 units of sales will be required in order to break even. This is because if 8,000 units are sold, the new unit contribution margin of $100 provides only $800,000 (8,000 units × $100) of contribution margin. Thus, $40,000 more contribution margin is necessary to cover the total fixed costs of $840,000. This additional $40,000 of contribution margin is provided by selling 400 more units (400 units × $100).

Effect of Changes in Unit Selling Price Changes in the unit selling price affect the unit contribution margin and, thus, the break-even point. Specifically, changes in the unit selling price affect the break-even point as follows:

- Increases in the unit selling price decrease the break-even point.
- Decreases in the unit selling price increase the break-even point.

This relationship is illustrated in Exhibit 12.

EXHIBIT 12

Effect of Change in Unit Selling Price on Break-Even Point

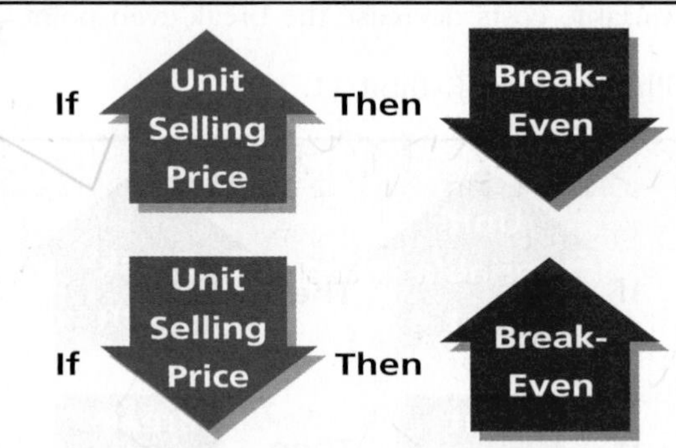

To illustrate, assume that Graham Co. is evaluating a proposal to increase the unit selling price of its product from $50 to $60. The data for Graham follows:

	Current	Proposed
Unit selling price	$50	$60
Unit variable cost	30	30
Unit contribution margin	$20	$30
Fixed costs	$600,000	$600,000

Graham's break-even point *before* the price increase is 30,000 units, computed as follows:

$$\text{Break-Even Sales (units)} = \frac{\text{Fixed Costs}}{\text{Unit Contribution Margin}} = \frac{\$600{,}000}{\$20} = 30{,}000 \text{ units}$$

The increase of $10 per unit in the selling price increases the unit contribution margin by $10. Thus, Graham's break-even point *after* the price increase is 20,000 units, computed as follows:

$$\text{Break-Even Sales (units)} = \frac{\text{Fixed Costs}}{\text{Unit Contribution Margin}} = \frac{\$600{,}000}{\$30} = 20{,}000 \text{ units}$$

As shown for Graham, the price increase of $10 increased the unit contribution margin by $10, which decreased the break-even point by 10,000 units (30,000 units – 20,000 units).

Summary of Effects of Changes on Break-Even Point The break-even point in sales changes in the same direction as changes in the variable cost per unit and fixed costs. In contrast, the break-even point in sales changes in the opposite direction as changes in the unit selling price. These changes on the break-even point in sales are summarized in Exhibit 13.

EXHIBIT 13

Effects of Changes in Selling Price and Costs on Break-Even Point.

Type of Change	Direction of Change	Effect of Change on Break-Even Sales
Fixed cost	↑	↑
	↓	↓
Unit variable cost	↑	↑
	↓	↓
Unit selling price	↑	↓
	↓	↑

Example Exercise 4-3 Break-Even Point

Nicolas Enterprises sells a product for $60 per unit. The variable cost is $35 per unit, while fixed costs are $80,000. Determine the (a) break-even point in sales units and (b) break-even point in sales units if the selling price were increased to $67 per unit.

Follow My Example 4-3

a. 3,200 units = $80,000 ÷ ($60 – $35)
b. 2,500 units = $80,000 ÷ ($67 – $35)

Practice Exercises: PE 4-3A, PE 4-3B

Business Connection

BREAKING EVEN IN THE AIRLINE INDUSTRY

Airlines have high fixed costs and operate in a very competitive industry. As a result, many airlines struggle to break even. In the late 2000s, many of the major airlines were unable to break even and filed bankruptcy. After emerging from bankruptcy, several airlines merged in an attempt to reduce their cost structure and become more competitive. As the table shows, airlines like **United Airlines, Southwest Airlines, Delta Air Lines,** and **American Airlines** still face challenges in breaking even, as a small change in ticket prices determines whether an airline is able to break even.

	United	Southwest	Delta	American
Average one-way airfare per passenger*	$269.56	$141.14	$209.60	$208.59
Average cost per passenger*	240.25	133.68	184.88	209.67

* Airfare and cost data obtained from AirlineFinancials.com

Target Profit

At the break-even point, sales and costs are exactly equal. However, the goal of most companies is to make a profit.

By modifying the break-even equation, the sales required to earn a target or desired amount of profit may be computed. For this purpose, target profit is added to the break-even equation, as follows:

$$\text{Sales (units)} = \frac{\text{Fixed Costs} + \text{Target Profit}}{\text{Unit Contribution Margin}}$$

To illustrate, assume the following data for Waltham Co.:

Fixed costs	$200,000
Target profit	100,000
Unit selling price	$75
Unit variable cost	45
Unit contribution margin	$30

The sales necessary for Waltham to earn the target profit of $100,000 would be 10,000 units, computed as follows:

$$\text{Sales (units)} = \frac{\text{Fixed Costs} + \text{Target Profit}}{\text{Unit Contribution Margin}} = \frac{\$200{,}000 + \$100{,}000}{\$30} = 10{,}000 \text{ units}$$

The following income statement for Waltham verifies this computation:

Sales (10,000 units × $75)	$750,000
Variable costs (10,000 units × $45)	450,000
Contribution margin (10,000 units × $30)	$300,000
Fixed costs	200,000
Income from operations	$100,000

As shown in the income statement for Waltham, sales of $750,000 (10,000 units × $75) are necessary to earn the target profit of $100,000. The sales of $750,000 needed to earn the target profit of $100,000 can be computed directly using the contribution margin ratio, computed as follows:

$$\text{Contribution Margin Ratio} = \frac{\text{Unit Contribution Margin}}{\text{Unit Selling Price}} = \frac{\$30}{\$75} = 40\%$$

$$\text{Sales (dollars)} = \frac{\text{Fixed Costs} + \text{Target Profit}}{\text{Contribution Margin Ratio}}$$

$$= \frac{\$200{,}000 + \$100{,}000}{40\%} = \frac{\$300{,}000}{40\%} = \$750{,}000$$

Example Exercise 4-4 Target Profit

OBJ 3

Forest Company sells a product for $140 per unit. The variable cost is $60 per unit, and fixed costs are $240,000. Determine the (a) break-even point in sales units and (b) the sales units required to achieve a target profit of $50,000.

Follow My Example 4-4

a. 3,000 units = $240,000 ÷ ($140 – $60)
b. 3,625 units = ($240,000 + $50,000) ÷ ($140 – $60)

Practice Exercises: PE 4-4A, PE 4-4B

Integrity, Objectivity, and Ethics in Business

ORPHAN DRUGS

Each year, pharmaceutical companies develop new drugs that cure a variety of physical conditions. In order to be profitable, drug companies must sell enough of a product for a reasonable price to exceed break even. Break-even points, however, create a problem for drugs, called "orphan drugs," targeted at rare diseases. These drugs are typically expensive to develop and have low sales volumes, making it impossible to achieve break even. To ensure that orphan drugs are not overlooked, Congress passed the Orphan Drug Act, which provides incentives for pharmaceutical companies to develop drugs for rare diseases that might not generate enough sales to reach break even. The program has been a great success. Since 1982, more than 200 orphan drugs have come to market, including **Jacobus Pharmaceuticals Company, Inc.**'s drug for the treatment of tuberculosis and **Novartis AG**'s drug for the treatment of Paget's disease.

Graphic Approach to Cost-Volume-Profit Analysis

OBJ 4 Using a cost-volume-profit chart and a profit-volume chart, determine the break-even point and sales necessary to achieve a target profit.

Cost-volume-profit analysis can be presented graphically as well as in equation form. Many managers prefer the graphic form because the operating profit or loss for different levels can be easily seen.

Cost-Volume-Profit (Break-Even) Chart

A **cost-volume-profit chart**, sometimes called a *break-even chart*, graphically shows sales, costs, and the related profit or loss for various levels of units sold. It assists in understanding the relationship among sales, costs, and operating profit or loss.

To illustrate, the cost-volume-profit chart in Exhibit 14 is based on the following data for Munoz Co.:

Total fixed costs	$100,000
Unit selling price	$50
Unit variable cost	30
Unit contribution margin	$20

The cost-volume-profit chart in Exhibit 14 is constructed using the following steps:

- Step 1. Volume in units of sales is indicated along the horizontal axis. The range of volume shown is the relevant range in which the company expects to operate. Dollar amounts of total sales and total costs are indicated along the vertical axis.
- Step 2. A total sales line is plotted by connecting the point at zero on the left corner of the graph to a second point on the chart. The second point is determined by multiplying the maximum number of units in the relevant range, which is found on the far right of the horizontal axis, by the unit sales price. A line is then drawn through both of these points. This is the total sales line. For Munoz, the maximum number of units in the relevant range is 10,000. The second point on the line is determined by multiplying the 10,000 units by the $50 unit selling price to get the second point for the total sales line of $500,000 (10,000 units × $50). The sales line is drawn upward to the right from zero through the $500,000 point at the end of the relevant range.
- Step 3. A total cost line is plotted by beginning with total fixed costs on the vertical axis. A second point is determined by multiplying the maximum number of units in the relevant range, which is found on the far right of the horizontal axis by the unit variable costs and adding the total fixed costs. A line is then drawn through both of these points. This is the total cost line. For Munoz, the maximum number of units in the relevant range is 10,000. The second point on the line is determined by multiplying the 10,000 units by the $30 unit variable

cost and then adding the $100,000 total fixed costs to get the second point for the total estimated costs of $400,000 [(10,000 units × $30) + $100,000]. The cost line is drawn upward to the right from $100,000 on the vertical axis through the $400,000 point at the end of the relevant range.

- Step 4. The break-even point is the intersection point of the total sales and total cost lines. A vertical dotted line drawn downward at the intersection point indicates the units of sales at the break-even point. A horizontal dotted line drawn to the left at the intersection point indicates the sales dollars and costs at the break-even point.

EXHIBIT 14

Cost-Volume-Profit Chart

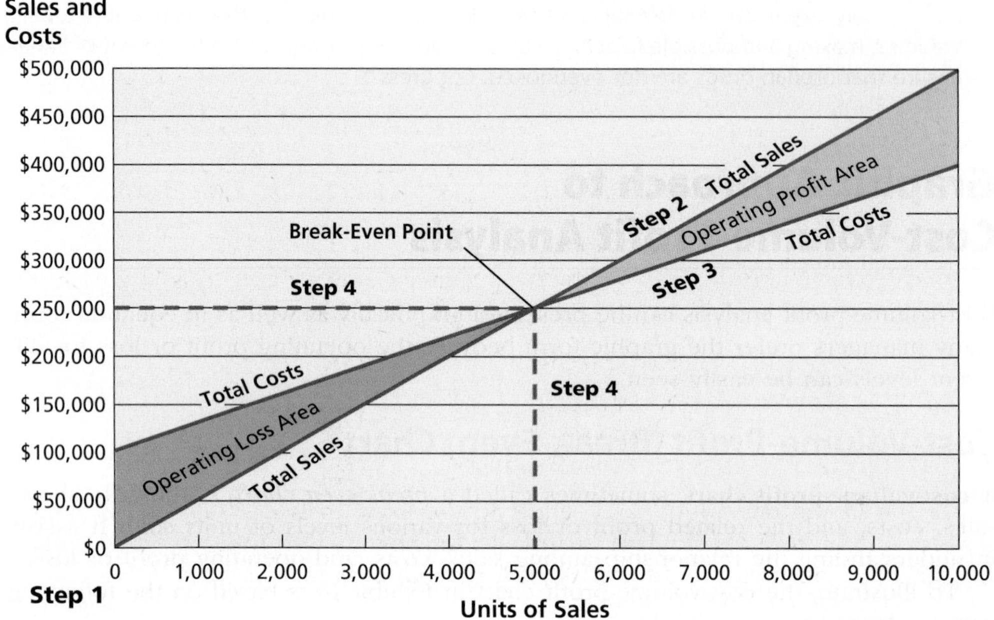

In Exhibit 14, the break-even point for Munoz is $250,000 of sales, which represents sales of 5,000 units. Operating profits will be earned when sales levels are to the right of the break-even point (*operating profit area*). Operating losses will be incurred when sales levels are to the left of the break-even point (*operating loss area*).

Changes in the unit selling price, total fixed costs, and unit variable costs can be analyzed by using a cost-volume-profit chart. Using the data in Exhibit 14, assume that Munoz is evaluating a proposal to reduce fixed costs by $20,000. In this case, the total fixed costs would be $80,000 ($100,000 – $20,000).

Under this scenario, the total sales line is not changed, but the total cost line will change. As shown in Exhibit 15, the total cost line is redrawn, starting at the $80,000 point (total fixed costs) on the vertical axis. The second point is determined by multiplying the maximum number of units in the relevant range, which is found on the far right of the horizontal axis, by the unit variable costs and adding the fixed costs. For Munoz, this is the total estimated cost for 10,000 units, which is $380,000 [(10,000 units × $30) + $80,000]. The cost line is drawn upward to the right from $80,000 on the vertical axis through the $380,000 point. The revised cost-volume-profit chart in Exhibit 15 indicates that the break-even point for Munoz decreases to $200,000 and 4,000 units of sales.

Profit-Volume Chart

Another graphic approach to cost-volume-profit analysis is the profit-volume chart. The **profit-volume chart** plots only the difference between total sales and total costs (or profits). In this way, the profit-volume chart allows managers to determine the operating profit (or loss) for various levels of units sold.

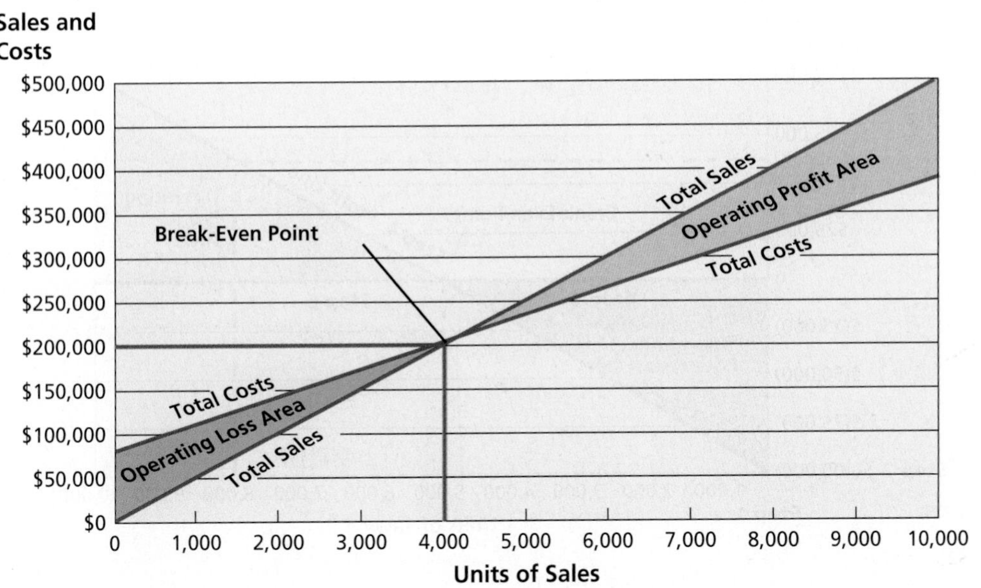

EXHIBIT 15

Revised Cost-Volume-Profit Chart

To illustrate, the profit-volume chart for Munoz Co. in Exhibit 16 is based on the same data as used in Exhibit 14. These data are as follows:

Total fixed costs	$100,000
Unit selling price	$50
Unit variable cost	30
Unit contribution margin	$20

The maximum operating loss is equal to the fixed costs of $100,000. Assuming that the maximum units that can be sold within the relevant range is 10,000 units, the maximum operating profit is $100,000, computed as follows:

Sales (10,000 units × $50)	$500,000	
Variable costs (10,000 units × $30)	300,000	
Contribution margin (10,000 units × $20)	$200,000	
Fixed costs	100,000	
Operating profit	$100,000	← Maximum profit

The profit-volume chart in Exhibit 16 is constructed using the following steps:

- Step 1. Volume in units of sales is indicated along the horizontal axis. The range of volume shown is the relevant range in which the company expects to operate. In Exhibit 16, the maximum units of sales is 10,000 units. Dollar amounts indicating operating profits and losses are shown along the vertical axis.
- Step 2. A point representing the maximum operating loss is plotted on the vertical axis at the left. This loss is equal to the total fixed costs at the zero level of sales. Thus, the maximum operating loss is equal to the fixed costs of $100,000.
- Step 3. A point representing the maximum operating profit within the relevant range is plotted on the right. Assuming that the maximum unit sales within the relevant range is 10,000 units, the maximum operating profit is $100,000.
- Step 4. A diagonal profit line is drawn connecting the maximum operating loss point with the maximum operating profit point.
- Step 5. The profit line intersects the horizontal zero operating profit line at the break-even point in units of sales. The area indicating an operating profit is identified to the right of the intersection, and the area indicating an operating loss is identified to the left of the intersection.

EXHIBIT 16

Profit-Volume Chart

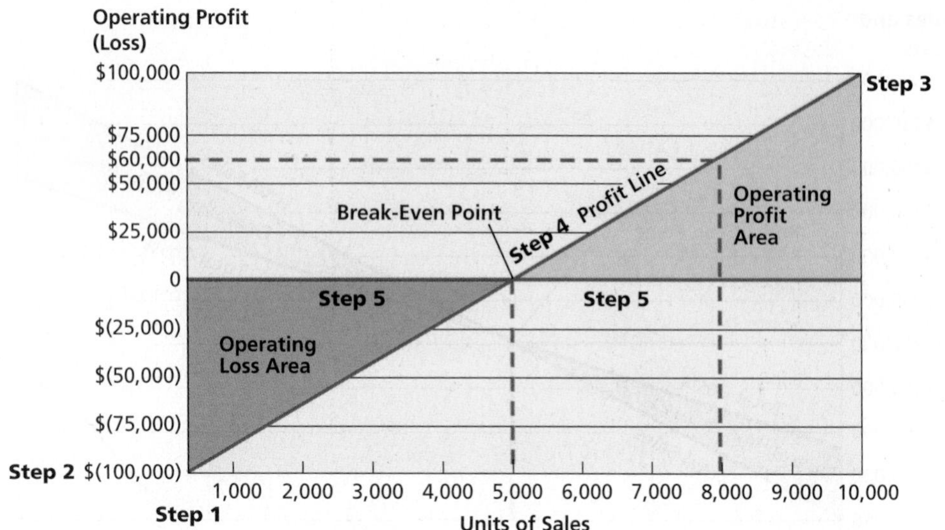

In Exhibit 16, the break-even point for Munoz is 5,000 units of sales, which is equal to total sales of $250,000 (5,000 units × $50). Operating profit will be earned when sales levels are to the right of the break-even point (*operating profit area*). Operating losses will be incurred when sales levels are to the left of the break-even point (*operating loss area*). For example, at sales of 8,000 units, an operating profit of $60,000 will be earned, as shown in Exhibit 16.

The effect of changes in the unit selling price, total fixed costs, and unit variable costs on profit can be analyzed using a profit-volume chart. Using the data in Exhibit 16, consider the effect that a $20,000 increase in fixed costs will have on profit. In this case, the total fixed costs will increase to $120,000 ($100,000 + $20,000), and the maximum operating loss will also increase to $120,000. At the maximum sales of 10,000 units, the maximum operating profit would be $80,000, computed as follows:

Sales (10,000 units × $50)	$500,000	
Variable costs (10,000 units × $30)	300,000	
Contribution margin (10,000 units × $20)	$200,000	
Fixed costs	120,000	
Operating profit	$ 80,000	← Revised maximum profit

A revised profit-volume chart is constructed by plotting the maximum operating loss and maximum operating profit points and drawing the revised profit line. The original and the revised profit-volume charts for Munoz are shown in Exhibit 17.

The revised profit-volume chart indicates that the break-even point for Munoz is 6,000 units of sales. This is equal to total sales of $300,000 (6,000 units × $50). The operating loss area of the chart has increased, while the operating profit area has decreased.

Use of Computers in Cost-Volume-Profit Analysis

With computers, the graphic approach and the mathematical approach to cost-volume-profit analysis are easy to use. Managers can vary assumptions regarding selling prices, costs, and volume and can observe the effects of each change on the break-even point and profit. Such an analysis is called a *"what if"* analysis or *sensitivity* analysis.

EXHIBIT 17

Original Profit-Volume Chart and Revised Profit-Volume Chart

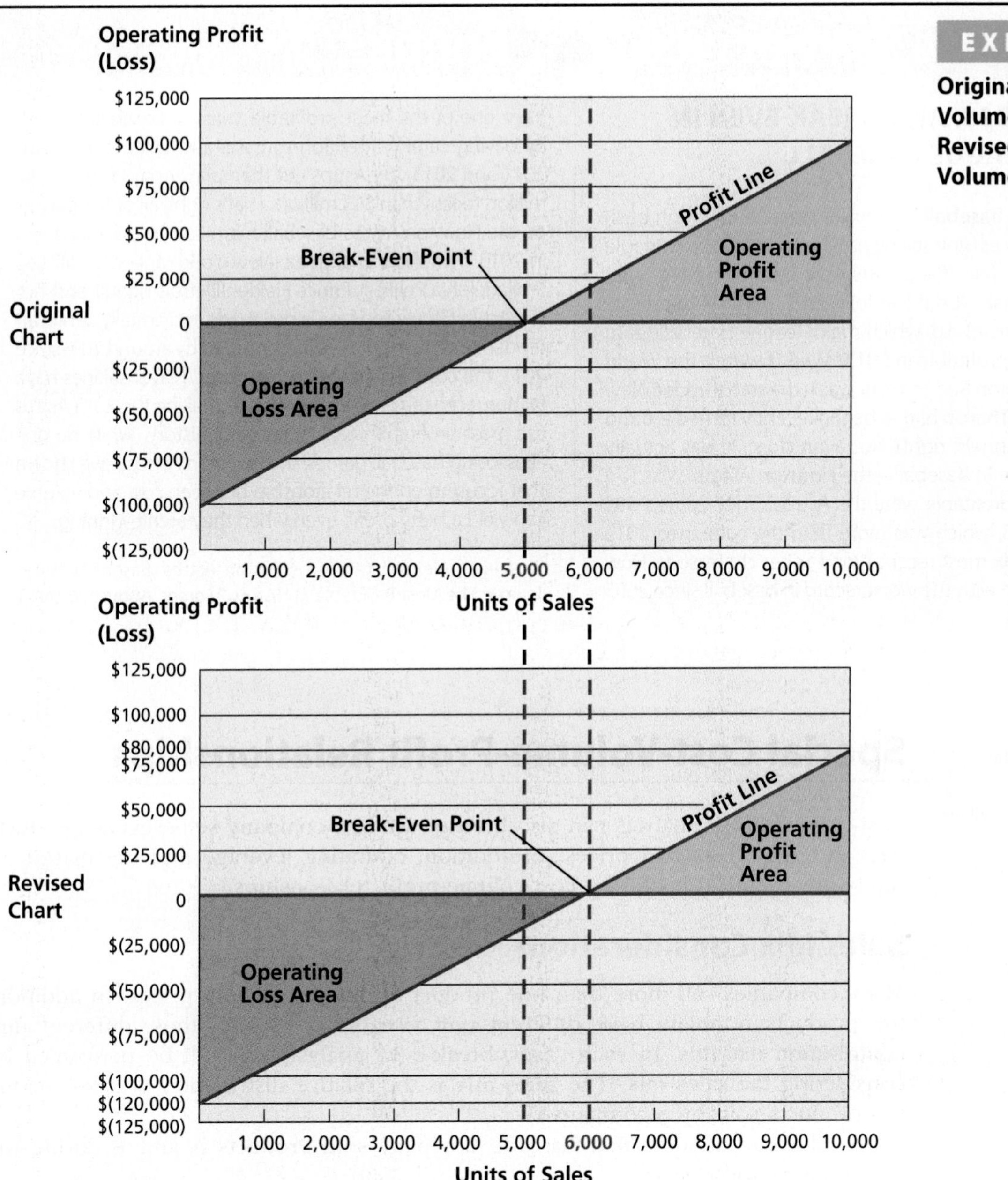

Assumptions of Cost-Volume-Profit Analysis

Cost-volume-profit analysis depends on several assumptions. The primary assumptions are as follows:

- Total sales and total costs can be represented by straight lines.
- Within the relevant range of operating activity, the efficiency of operations does not change.
- Costs can be divided into fixed and variable components.
- The sales mix is constant.
- There is no change in the inventory quantities during the period.

These assumptions simplify cost-volume-profit analysis. Because they are often valid for the relevant range of operations, cost-volume-profit analysis is useful for decision making.[3]

[3] The impact of violating these assumptions is discussed in advanced accounting texts.

Service Focus

PROFIT, LOSS, AND BREAK-EVEN IN MAJOR LEAGUE BASEBALL

Major League Baseball is a tough game and a tough business. Ticket prices (unit selling price), player salaries (variable costs), stadium fees (fixed costs), and attendance (volume) converge to make it difficult for teams to make a profit, or at least break even. So, which major league baseball team was the most profitable in 2013? Well, it wasn't the World Champion Boston Red Sox. Nor was it the star-studded New York Yankees. Then, it had to be the recently turned around Los Angeles Angels, right? Not even close. It was actually the worst team in baseball—the Houston Astros.

Just how profitable were the Astros? They earned $99 million in 2013, which was more than the combined 2013 profits of the six most recent World Series champions. How could the team with the worst record in baseball since 2005 have one of the most profitable years in baseball history? By paying careful attention to costs and volume. Between 2011 and 2013, the Astros cut their player payroll from $56 million to less than $13 million. That's right, all of the players on the Houston Astros baseball team combined, made less in 2013 than Alex Rodriguez (New York Yankees), Cliff Lee (Philadelphia Phillies), Prince Fielder (Detroit Tigers), and Tim Lincecum (San Francisco Giants) made individually. While attendance at Astros games has dropped by around 20% since 2011, the cost reductions from reduced player salaries have far outpaced the drop in attendance, making the 2013 Astros the most profitable team in baseball history. While no one likes losing baseball games, the Houston Astros have shown that focusing on the relationship between cost and volume can yield a hefty profit, even when they aren't winning.

Source: D. Alexander, "2013 Houston Astros: Baseball's Worst Team Is The Most Profitable In History," *Forbes,* August 26, 2013.

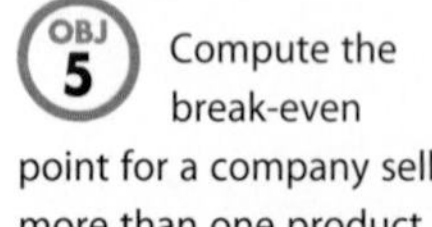

Compute the break-even point for a company selling more than one product, the operating leverage, and the margin of safety.

Special Cost-Volume-Profit Relationships

Cost-volume-profit analysis can also be used when a company sells several products with different costs and prices. In addition, operating leverage and the margin of safety are useful in analyzing cost-volume-profit relationships.

Sales Mix Considerations

Many companies sell more than one product at different selling prices. In addition, the products normally have different unit variable costs and, thus, different unit contribution margins. In such cases, break-even analysis can still be performed by considering the sales mix. The **sales mix** is the relative distribution of sales among the products sold by a company.

To illustrate, assume that Cascade Company sold Products A and B during the past year, as follows:

Total fixed costs	$200,000	
	Product A	**Product B**
Unit selling price	$90	$140
Unit variable cost	70	95
Unit contribution margin	$20	$ 45
Units sold	8,000	2,000
Sales mix	80%	20%

The sales mix for Products A and B is expressed as a percentage of total units sold. For Cascade, a total of 10,000 (8,000 + 2,000) units were sold during the year. Therefore, the sales mix is 80% (8,000 ÷ 10,000) for Product A and 20% for Product B (2,000 ÷ 10,000), as shown in Exhibit 18. The sales mix could also be expressed as the ratio 80:20.

EXHIBIT 18

Multiple Product Sales Mix

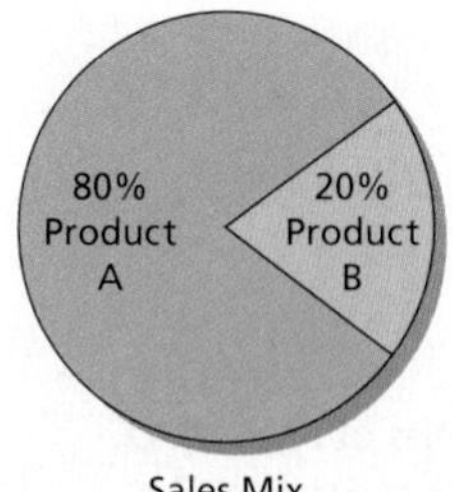

Sales Mix

For break-even analysis, it is useful to think of Products A and B as components of one overall enterprise product called E. The unit selling price of E equals the sum of the unit selling prices of each product multiplied by its sales mix percentage. Likewise, the unit variable cost and unit contribution margin of E equal the sum of the unit variable costs and unit contribution margins of each product multiplied by its sales mix percentage.

For Cascade, the unit selling price, unit variable cost, and unit contribution margin for E are computed as follows:

Product E			Product A		Product B
Unit selling price of E	$100	=	($90 × 0.8)	+	($140 × 0.2)
Unit variable cost of E	75	=	($70 × 0.8)	+	($95 × 0.2)
Unit contribution margin of E	$ 25	=	($20 × 0.8)	+	($45 × 0.2)

Cascade has total fixed costs of $200,000. The break-even point of 8,000 units of E can be determined as follows using the unit selling price, unit variable cost, and unit contribution margin of E:

$$\text{Break-Even Sales (units) for E} = \frac{\text{Fixed Costs}}{\text{Unit Contribution Margin}} = \frac{\$200{,}000}{\$25} = 8{,}000 \text{ units}$$

Because the sales mix for Products A and B is 80% and 20% respectively, the break-even quantity of A is 6,400 units (8,000 units × 80%) and B is 1,600 units (8,000 units × 20%).

The preceding break-even analysis is verified in Exhibit 19.

EXHIBIT 19

Break-Even Sales: Multiple Products

	Product A	Product B	Total
Sales:			
6,400 units × $90	$576,000		$576,000
1,600 units × $140		$224,000	224,000
Total sales	$576,000	$224,000	$800,000
Variable costs:			
6,400 units × $70	$448,000		$448,000
1,600 units × $95		$152,000	152,000
Total variable costs	$448,000	$152,000	$600,000
Contribution margin	$128,000	$ 72,000	$200,000
Fixed costs			200,000
Income from operations			$ 0

← Break-even point

The effects of changes in the sales mix on the break-even point can be determined by assuming a different sales mix. The break-even point of E can then be recomputed.

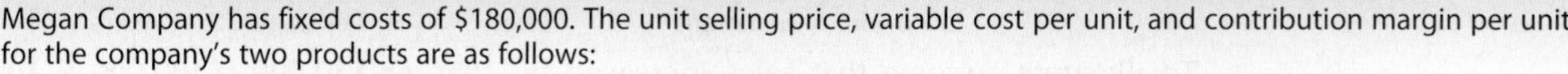

Example Exercise 4-5 Sales Mix and Break-Even Analysis

OBJ 5

Megan Company has fixed costs of $180,000. The unit selling price, variable cost per unit, and contribution margin per unit for the company's two products are as follows:

Product	Selling Price	Variable Cost per Unit	Contribution Margin per Unit
Q	$160	$100	$60
Z	100	80	20

The sales mix for products Q and Z is 75% and 25%, respectively. Determine the break-even point in units of Q and Z.

(Continued)

Follow My Example 4-5

Unit selling price of E:	[($160 × 0.75) + ($100 × 0.25)] =	$145
Unit variable cost of E:	[($100 × 0.75) + ($80 × 0.25)] =	95
Unit contribution margin of E:		$ 50

Break-Even Sales (units) for E = $180,000 ÷ $50 = 3,600 units
Break-Even Sales (units) for Q = 3,600 units of E × 75% = 2,700 units of Product Q
Break-Even Sales (units) for Z = 3,600 units of E × 25% = 900 units of Product Z

Practice Exercises: PE 4-5A, PE 4-5B

Operating Leverage

The relationship between a company's contribution margin and income from operations is measured by **operating leverage**. A company's operating leverage is computed as follows:

$$\text{Operating Leverage} = \frac{\text{Contribution Margin}}{\text{Income from Operations}}$$

The difference between contribution margin and income from operations is fixed costs. Thus, companies with high fixed costs will normally have high operating leverage. Examples of such companies include airline and automotive companies, like **Ford Motor Company**. Low operating leverage is normal for companies that are labor intensive, such as professional service companies, which have low fixed costs.

To illustrate operating leverage, assume the following data for Jones Inc. and Wilson Inc.:

	Jones Inc.	**Wilson Inc.**
Sales	$400,000	$400,000
Variable costs	300,000	300,000
Contribution margin	$100,000	$100,000
Fixed costs	80,000	50,000
Income from operations	$ 20,000	$ 50,000

As shown, Jones and Wilson have the same sales, the same variable costs, and the same contribution margin. However, Jones has larger fixed costs than Wilson and, thus, a higher operating leverage. The operating leverage for each company is computed as follows:

Jones Inc.

$$\text{Operating Leverage} = \frac{\text{Contribution Margin}}{\text{Income from Operations}} = \frac{\$100,000}{\$20,000} = 5$$

Wilson Inc.

$$\text{Operating Leverage} = \frac{\text{Contribution Margin}}{\text{Income from Operations}} = \frac{\$100,000}{\$50,000} = 2$$

Operating leverage can be used to measure the impact of changes in sales on income from operations. Using operating leverage, the effect of changes in sales on income from operations is computed as follows:

$$\begin{matrix}\text{Percent Change in} \\ \text{Income from Operations}\end{matrix} = \begin{matrix}\text{Percent Change in} \\ \text{Sales}\end{matrix} \times \begin{matrix}\text{Operating} \\ \text{Leverage}\end{matrix}$$

To illustrate, assume that sales increased by 10%, or $40,000 ($400,000 × 10%), for Jones and Wilson. The percent increase in income from operations for Jones and Wilson is computed as follows:

Jones Inc.

$$\text{Percent Change in Income from Operations} = \text{Percent Change in Sales} \times \text{Operating Leverage}$$

$$= 10\% \times 5 = 50\%$$

Wilson Inc.

$$\text{Percent Change in Income from Operations} = \text{Percent Change in Sales} \times \text{Operating Leverage}$$

$$= 10\% \times 2 = 20\%$$

As shown, Jones's income from operations increases by 50%, while Wilson's income from operations increases by only 20%. The validity of this analysis is shown in the following income statements for Jones and Wilson based on the 10% increase in sales:

	Jones Inc.	Wilson Inc.
Sales	$440,000	$440,000
Variable costs	330,000	330,000
Contribution margin	$110,000	$110,000
Fixed costs	80,000	50,000
Income from operations	$ 30,000	$ 60,000

The preceding income statements indicate that Jones's income from operations increased from $20,000 to $30,000, a 50% increase ($10,000 ÷ $20,000). In contrast, Wilson's income from operations increased from $50,000 to $60,000, a 20% increase ($10,000 ÷ $50,000).

Because even a small increase in sales will generate a large percentage increase in income from operations, Jones might consider ways to increase sales. Such actions could include special advertising or sales promotions. In contrast, Wilson might consider ways to increase operating leverage by reducing variable costs.

The impact of a change in sales on income from operations for companies with high and low operating leverage is summarized in Exhibit 20.

EXHIBIT 20

Effect of Operating Leverage on Income from Operations

Operating Leverage	Percentage Impact on Income from Operations from a Change in Sales
High	Large
Low	Small

Example Exercise 4-6 Operating Leverage

OBJ 5

Tucker Company reports the following data:

Sales	$750,000
Variable costs	500,000
Contribution margin	$250,000
Fixed costs	187,500
Income from operations	$ 62,500

Determine Tucker Company's operating leverage.

Follow My Example 4-6

$$\text{Operating Leverage} = \frac{\text{Contribution Margin}}{\text{Income from Operations}} = \frac{\$250,000}{\$62,500} = 4.0$$

Practice Exercises: PE 4-6A, PE 4-6B

Margin of Safety

The **margin of safety** indicates the possible decrease in sales that may occur before an operating loss results. Thus, if the margin of safety is low, even a small decline in sales revenue may result in an operating loss.

The margin of safety may be expressed in the following ways:

- Dollars of sales
- Units of sales
- Percent of current sales

To illustrate, assume the following data:

Sales	$250,000
Sales at the break-even point	200,000
Unit selling price	25

The margin of safety in dollars of sales is $50,000 ($250,000 – $200,000). The margin of safety in units is 2,000 units ($50,000 ÷ $25). The margin of safety expressed as a percent of current sales is 20%, computed as follows:

$$\text{Margin of Safety} = \frac{\text{Sales} - \text{Sales at Break-Even Point}}{\text{Sales}}$$

$$= \frac{\$250{,}000 - \$200{,}000}{\$250{,}000} = \frac{\$50{,}000}{\$250{,}000} = 20\%$$

Therefore, the current sales may decline $50,000, 2,000 units, or 20% before an operating loss occurs.

Example Exercise 4-7 Margin of Safety

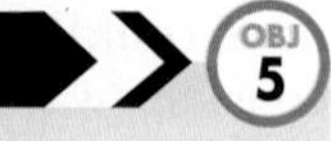

Rachel Company has sales of $400,000, and the break-even point in sales dollars is $300,000. Determine the company's margin of safety as a percent of current sales.

Follow My Example 4-7

$$\text{Margin of Safety} = \frac{\text{Sales} - \text{Sales at Break-Even Point}}{\text{Sales}} = \frac{\$400{,}000 - \$300{,}000}{\$400{,}000} = \frac{\$100{,}000}{\$400{,}000} = 25\%$$

Practice Exercises: PE 4-7A, PE 4-7B

APPENDIX

Variable Costing

The cost of manufactured products consists of direct materials, direct labor, and factory overhead. The reporting of all these costs in financial statements is called **absorption costing**. Absorption costing is required under generally accepted accounting principles for financial statements distributed to external users. However, alternative reports may be prepared for decision-making purposes by managers and other internal users. One such alternative reporting is *variable costing* or *direct costing*.

In *variable costing*, the cost of goods manufactured is composed only of variable costs. Thus, the cost of goods manufactured consists of direct materials, direct labor, and *variable* factory overhead.

In a variable costing income statement, *fixed* factory overhead costs do not become a part of the cost of goods manufactured. Instead, fixed factory overhead costs are treated as a period expense. The differences between absorption and variable cost of goods manufactured is summarized in Exhibit 21.

EXHIBIT 21

Absorption Versus Variable Cost of Goods Manufactured

Cost of Goods Manufactured	
Absorption Costing	**Variable Costing**
Direct materials	Direct materials
Direct labor	Direct labor
Variable factory overhead	Variable factory overhead
Fixed factory overhead	

The form of a variable costing income statement is as follows:

Sales		$XXX
Variable cost of goods sold		XXX
Manufacturing margin		$XXX
Variable selling and administrative expenses		XXX
Contribution margin		$XXX
Fixed costs:		
Fixed manufacturing costs	$XXX	
Fixed selling and administrative expenses	XXX	XXX
Income from operations		$XXX

Manufacturing margin is the excess of sales over variable cost of goods sold.

Manufacturing Margin = Sales – Variable Cost of Goods Sold

Variable cost of goods sold consists of direct materials, direct labor, and variable factory overhead for the units sold. *Contribution margin* is the excess of manufacturing margin over variable selling and administrative expenses.

Contribution Margin = Manufacturing Margin – Variable Selling and Administrative Expenses

Subtracting fixed costs from contribution margin yields *income from operations.*

Income from Operations = Contribution Margin – Fixed Costs

The variable costing income statement facilitates managerial decision making because manufacturing margin and contribution margin are reported directly. As illustrated in this chapter, contribution margin is used in break-even analysis and other analyses.

To illustrate the variable costing income statement, assume that Martinez Co. manufactures 15,000 units, which are sold at a price of $50. The related costs and expenses for Martinez are as follows:

	Total Cost	Number of Units	Unit Cost
Manufacturing costs:			
Variable	$375,000	15,000	$25
Fixed	150,000	15,000	10
Total	$525,000		$35
Selling and administrative expenses:			
Variable ($5 per unit sold)	$ 75,000		
Fixed	50,000		
Total	$125,000		

Exhibit 22 shows the variable costing income statement prepared for Martinez. The computations are shown in parentheses.

EXHIBIT 22

Variable Costing Income Statement

Sales (15,000 × $50)		$750,000
Variable cost of goods sold (15,000 × $25)		375,000
Manufacturing margin		$375,000
Variable selling and administrative expenses (15,000 × $5)		75,000
Contribution margin		$300,000
Fixed costs:		
Fixed manufacturing costs	$150,000	
Fixed selling and administrative expenses	50,000	200,000
Income from operations		$100,000

Exhibit 23 illustrates the absorption costing income statement prepared for Martinez. The absorption costing income statement does not distinguish between variable and fixed costs. All manufacturing costs are included in the cost of goods sold. Deducting the cost of goods sold from sales yields the *gross profit.* Deducting the selling and administrative expenses from gross profit yields the *income from operations.*

EXHIBIT 23

Absorption Costing Income Statement

Sales (15,000 × $50)	$750,000
Cost of goods sold (15,000 × $35)	525,000
Gross profit	$225,000
Selling and administrative expenses ($75,000 + $50,000)	125,000
Income from operations	$100,000

The relationship between variable and absorption costing *income from operations* is summarized in Exhibit 24.

EXHIBIT 24 **Relationship Between Variable and Absorption Costing Income**

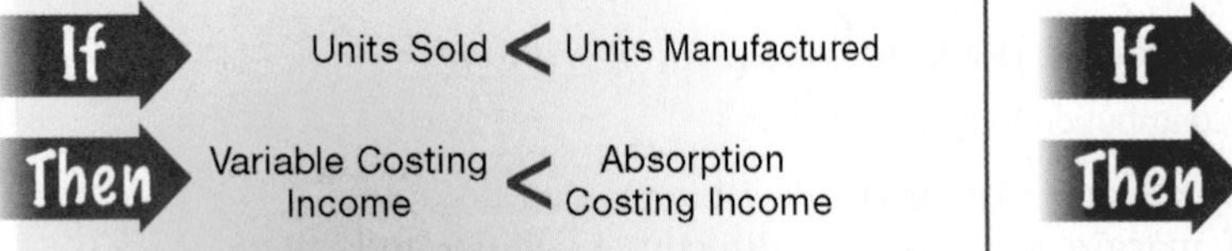

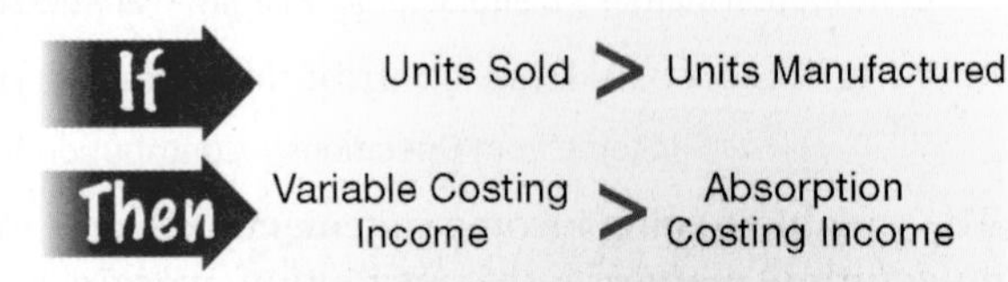

In Exhibits 22 and 23, Martinez manufactured and sold 15,000 units. Thus, the variable and absorption costing income statements reported the same income from operations of $100,000. However, assume that only 12,000 units of the 15,000 units Martinez manufactured were sold. Exhibit 25 shows the related variable and absorption costing income statements.

Exhibit 25 shows a $30,000 ($70,000 – $40,000) difference in income from operations. This difference is due to the fixed manufacturing costs. All of the $150,000 of fixed manufacturing costs is included as a period expense in the variable costing statement. However, the 3,000 units of ending inventory in the absorption costing statement include $30,000 (3,000 units × $10) of fixed manufacturing costs. By being included in inventory, this $30,000 is thus excluded from the current cost of goods sold. Thus, the absorption costing income from operations is $30,000 higher than the income from operations for variable costing.

A similar analysis could be used to illustrate that income from operations under variable costing is greater than income from operations under absorption costing when the units manufactured are less than the units sold.

Under absorption costing, increases or decreases in income from operations can result from changes in inventory levels. For example, for Martinez, a 3,000 increase in ending inventory created a $30,000 increase in income from operations under absorption

EXHIBIT 25

Units Manufactured Exceed Units Sold

Variable Costing Income Statement		
Sales (12,000 × $50)		$600,000
Variable cost of goods sold:		
Variable cost of goods manufactured (15,000 × $25)	$375,000	
Less ending inventory (3,000 × $25)	75,000	
Variable cost of goods sold		300,000
Manufacturing margin		$300,000
Variable selling and administrative expenses (12,000 × $5)		60,000
Contribution margin		$240,000
Fixed costs:		
Fixed manufacturing costs	$150,000	
Fixed selling and administrative expenses	50,000	200,000
Income from operations		$ 40,000

Absorption Costing Income Statement		
Sales (12,000 × $50)		$600,000
Cost of goods sold:		
Cost of goods manufactured (15,000 × $35)	$525,000	
Less ending inventory (3,000 × $35)	105,000	
Cost of goods sold		420,000
Gross profit		$180,000
Selling and administrative expenses [(12,000 × $5) + $50,000]		110,000
Income from operations		$ 70,000

costing. Such increases (decreases) could be misinterpreted by managers using absorption costing as operating efficiencies (inefficiencies). This is one of the reasons that variable costing is often used by managers for cost control, product pricing, and production planning. Such uses of variable costing are discussed in advanced accounting texts.

At a Glance 4

Classify costs as variable costs, fixed costs, or mixed costs.

Key Points Variable costs vary in proportion to changes in the level of activity. Fixed costs remain the same in total dollar amount as the level of activity changes. Mixed costs are comprised of both fixed and variable costs.

Learning Outcomes	Example Exercises	Practice Exercises
• Describe variable costs.		
• Describe fixed costs.		
• Describe mixed costs.		
• Separate mixed costs, using the high-low method.	EE4-1	PE4-1A, 4-1B

Compute the contribution margin, the contribution margin ratio, and the unit contribution margin.

Key Points Contribution margin is the excess of sales revenue over variable costs and can be expressed as a ratio (contribution margin ratio) or a dollar amount (unit contribution margin).

Learning Outcomes	Example Exercises	Practice Exercises
• Describe the contribution margin.		
• Compute the contribution margin ratio.	EE4-2	PE4-2A, 4-2B
• Compute the unit contribution margin.	EE4-2	PE4-2A, 4-2B

Determine the break-even point and sales necessary to achieve a target profit.

Key Points The break-even point is the point at which a business's revenues exactly equal costs. The mathematical approach to cost-volume-profit analysis uses the unit contribution margin concept and mathematical equations to determine the break-even point and the volume necessary to achieve a target profit.

Learning Outcomes	Example Exercises	Practice Exercises
• Compute the break-even point in units.	EE4-3	PE4-3A, 4-3B
• Describe how changes in fixed costs affect the break-even point.		
• Describe how changes in unit variable costs affect the break-even point.		
• Describe how a change in the unit selling price affects the break-even point.	EE4-3	PE4-3A, 4-3B
• Modify the break-even equation to compute the unit sales required to earn a target profit.	EE4-4	PE4-4A, 4-4B

Using a cost-volume-profit chart and a profit-volume chart, determine the break-even point and sales necessary to achieve a target profit.

Key Points Graphical methods can be used to determine the break-even point and the volume necessary to achieve a target profit. A cost-volume-profit chart focuses on the relationship among costs, sales, and operating profit or loss. The profit-volume chart focuses on profits rather than on revenues and costs.

Learning Outcomes	Example Exercises	Practice Exercises
• Describe how to construct a cost-volume-profit chart.		
• Determine the break-even point, using a cost-volume-profit chart.		
• Describe how to construct a profit-volume chart.		
• Determine the break-even point, using a profit-volume chart.		
• Describe factors affecting the reliability of cost-volume-profit analysis.		

Compute the break-even point for a company selling more than one product, the operating leverage, and the margin of safety.

Key Points Cost-volume-profit relationships can be used for analyzing (1) sales mix, (2) operating leverage, and (3) margin of safety.

Learning Outcomes	*Example Exercises*	*Practice Exercises*
• Compute the break-even point for a mix of products.	**EE4-5**	**PE4-5A, 4-5B**
• Compute operating leverage.	**EE4-6**	**PE4-6A, 4-6B**
• Compute the margin of safety.	**EE4-7**	**PE4-7A, 4-7B**

Key Terms

absorption costing (156)
activity bases (drivers) (132)
break-even point (141)
contribution margin (138)
contribution margin ratio (139)
cost behavior (132)
cost-volume-profit analysis (138)
cost-volume-profit chart (147)
fixed costs (134)
high-low method (136)
margin of safety (156)
mixed costs (134)
operating leverage (154)
profit-volume chart (148)
relevant range (132)
sales mix (152)
unit contribution margin (140)
variable costing (138)
variable costs (133)

Illustrative Problem

Wyatt Inc. expects to maintain the same inventories at the end of the year as at the beginning of the year. The estimated fixed costs for the year are $288,000, and the estimated variable costs per unit are $14. It is expected that 60,000 units will be sold at a price of $20 per unit. Maximum sales within the relevant range are 70,000 units.

Instructions

1. What is (a) the contribution margin ratio and (b) the unit contribution margin?
2. Determine the break-even point in units.
3. Construct a cost-volume-profit chart, indicating the break-even point.
4. Construct a profit-volume chart, indicating the break-even point.
5. What is the margin of safety?

Solution

1. a. $$\text{Contribution Margin Ratio} = \frac{\text{Sales} - \text{Variable Costs}}{\text{Sales}}$$

$$= \frac{(60{,}000 \text{ units} \times \$20) - (60{,}000 \text{ units} \times \$14)}{(60{,}000 \text{ units} \times \$20)}$$

$$= \frac{\$1,200,000 - \$840,000}{\$1,200,000} = \frac{\$360,000}{\$1,200,000}$$

= 30%

b. Unit Contribution Margin = Unit Selling Price – Unit Variable Costs
= \$20 – \$14 = \$6

2. Break-Even Sales (units) = $\frac{\text{Fixed Costs}}{\text{Unit Contribution Margin}}$

$$= \frac{\$288,000}{\$6} = 48,000 \text{ units}$$

3.

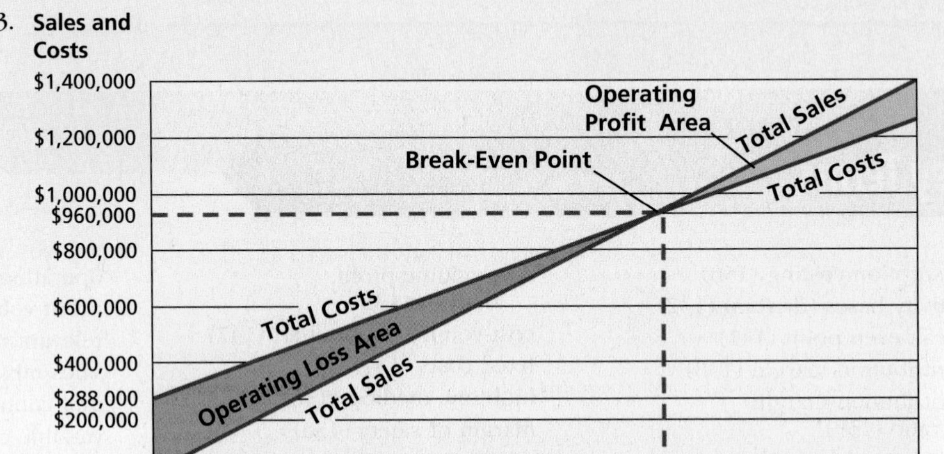

4.

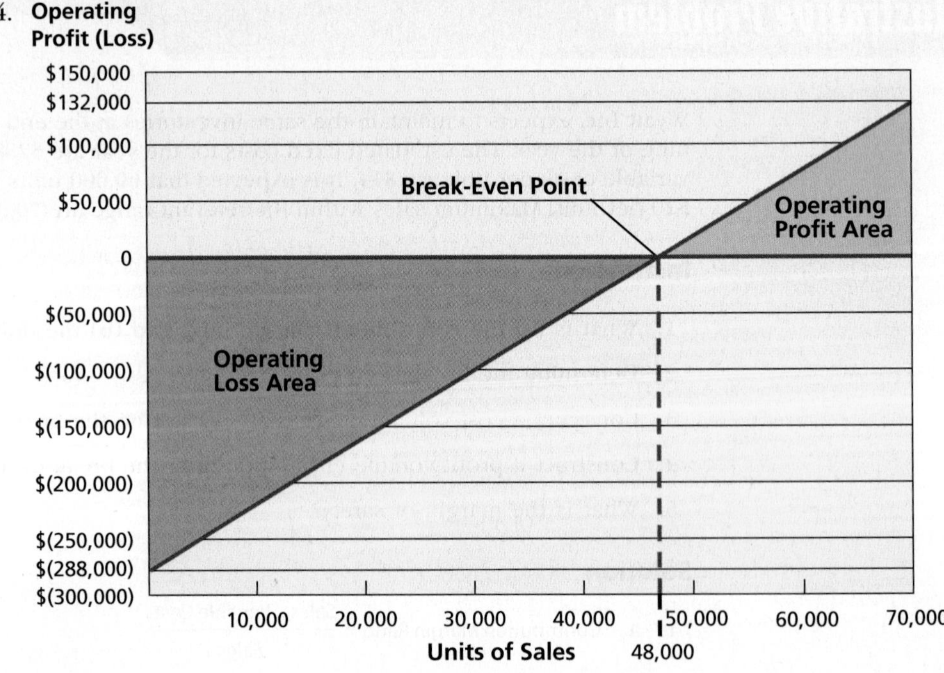

5. Margin of safety:

Expected sales (60,000 units × \$20)	\$1,200,000
Break-even point (48,000 units × \$20)	960,000
Margin of safety	\$ 240,000

or

$$\text{Margin of Safety (units)} = \frac{\text{Margin of Safety (dollars)}}{\text{Unit Selling Price}}$$

or

12,000 units (\$240,000 ÷ \$20)

or

$$\text{Margin of Safety} = \frac{\text{Sales} - \text{Sales at Break-Even Point}}{\text{Sales}}$$

$$= \frac{\$240{,}000}{\$1{,}200{,}000} = 20\%$$

Discussion Questions

1. Describe how total variable costs and unit variable costs behave with changes in the level of activity.
2. Which of the following costs would be classified as variable and which would be classified as fixed, if units produced is the activity base?
   a. Direct materials costs
   b. Electricity costs of \$0.35 per kilowatt-hour
3. Describe how total fixed costs and unit fixed costs behave with changes in the level of activity.
4. In applying the high-low method of cost estimation to mixed costs, how is the total fixed cost estimated?
5. If fixed costs increase, what would be the impact on the (a) contribution margin? (b) income from operations?
6. An examination of the accounting records of Clowney Company disclosed a high contribution margin ratio and production at a level below maximum capacity. Based on this information, suggest a likely means of improving income from operations. Explain.
7. If the unit cost of direct materials is decreased, what effect will this change have on the break-even point?
8. Both Austin Company and Hill Company had the same unit sales, total costs, and income from operations for the current fiscal year; yet, Austin Company had a lower break-even point than Hill Company. Explain the reason for this difference in break-even points.
9. How does the sales mix affect the calculation of the break-even point?
10. What does operating leverage measure, and how is it computed?

Practice Exercises

EE 4-1 p. 137

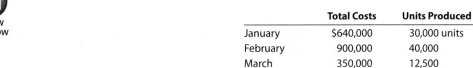

PE 4-1A High-low method **OBJ. 1**

SHOW ME HOW

The manufacturing costs of Lightfoot Industries for three months of the year follow:

	Total Costs	Units Produced
January	\$640,000	30,000 units
February	900,000	40,000
March	350,000	12,500

Using the high-low method, determine (a) the variable cost per unit and (b) the total fixed cost.

EE 4-1 p. 137

PE 4-1B High-low method

OBJ. 1

The manufacturing costs of Carrefour Enterprises for the first three months of the year follow:

	Total Costs	Units Produced
June	$300,000	2,700 units
July	440,000	5,500
August	325,000	3,500

Using the high-low method, determine (a) the variable cost per unit and (b) the total fixed cost.

EE 4-2 p. 141

PE 4-2A Contribution margin

OBJ. 2

Michigan Company sells 10,000 units at $100 per unit. Variable costs are $75 per unit, and fixed costs are $125,000. Determine (a) the contribution margin ratio, (b) the unit contribution margin, and (c) income from operations.

EE 4-2 p. 141

PE 4-2B Contribution margin

OBJ. 2

Weidner Company sells 22,000 units at $30 per unit. Variable costs are $24 per unit, and fixed costs are $40,000. Determine (a) the contribution margin ratio, (b) the unit contribution margin, and (c) income from operations.

EE 4-3 p. 145

PE 4-3A Break-even point

OBJ. 3

Santana sells a product for $115 per unit. The variable cost is $75 per unit, while fixed costs are $65,000. Determine (a) the break-even point in sales units and (b) the break-even point if the selling price were increased to $125 per unit.

EE 4-3 p. 145

PE 4-3B Break-even point

OBJ. 3

Elrod Inc. sells a product for $75 per unit. The variable cost is $45 per unit, while fixed costs are $48,000. Determine (a) the break-even point in sales units and (b) the break-even point if the selling price were increased to $95 per unit.

EE 4-4 p. 146

PE 4-4A Target profit

OBJ. 3

Versa Inc. sells a product for $100 per unit. The variable cost is $75 per unit, and fixed costs are $45,000. Determine (a) the break-even point in sales units and (b) the break-even point in sales units if the company desires a target profit of $25,000.

EE 4-4 p. 146

PE 4-4B Target profit

OBJ. 3

Scrushy Company sells a product for $150 per unit. The variable cost is $110 per unit, and fixed costs are $200,000. Determine (a) the break-even point in sales units and (b) the break-even point in sales units if the company desires a target profit of $50,000.

EE 4-5 p. 153

PE 4-5A Sales mix and break-even analysis

OBJ. 5

Wide Open Industries Inc. has fixed costs of $475,000. The unit selling price, variable cost per unit, and contribution margin per unit for the company's two products follow:

Product	Selling Price	Variable Cost per Unit	Contribution Margin per Unit
AA	$145	$105	$40
BB	110	75	35

The sales mix for products AA and BB is 60% and 40%, respectively. Determine the break-even point in units of AA and BB.

SHOW ME HOW

EE 4-5 *p. 153*

PE 4-5B Sales mix and break-even analysis

OBJ. 5

Einhorn Company has fixed costs of $105,000. The unit selling price, variable cost per unit, and contribution margin per unit for the company's two products follow:

Product	Selling Price	Variable Cost per Unit	Contribution Margin per Unit
QQ	$50	$35	$15
ZZ	60	30	30

The sales mix for products QQ and ZZ is 40% and 60%, respectively. Determine the break-even point in units of QQ and ZZ.

SHOW ME HOW

EE 4-6 *p. 155*

PE 4-6A Operating leverage

OBJ. 5

SungSam Enterprises reports the following data:

Sales	$340,000
Variable costs	180,000
Contribution margin	$160,000
Fixed costs	80,000
Income from operations	$ 80,000

Determine SungSam Enterprises's operating leverage.

SHOW ME HOW

EE 4-6 *p. 155*

PE 4-6B Operating leverage

OBJ. 5

Westminster Co. reports the following data:

Sales	$875,000
Variable costs	425,000
Contribution margin	$450,000
Fixed costs	150,000
Income from operations	$300,000

Determine Westminster Co.'s operating leverage.

SHOW ME HOW

EE 4-7 *p. 156*

PE 4-7A Margin of safety

OBJ. 5

Melton Inc. has sales of $1,750,000, and the break-even point in sales dollars is $875,000. Determine the company's margin of safety as a percent of current sales.

SHOW ME HOW

EE 4-7 *p. 156*

PE 4-7B Margin of safety

OBJ. 5

Junck Company has sales of $550,000, and the break-even point in sales dollars is $385,000. Determine the company's margin of safety as a percent of current sales.

Exercises

EX 4-1 Classify costs

OBJ. 1

Following is a list of various costs incurred in producing replacement automobile parts. With respect to the production and sale of these auto parts, classify each cost as either variable, fixed, or mixed.

1. Oil used in manufacturing equipment
2. Plastic
3. Property taxes, $165,000 per year on factory building and equipment
4. Salary of plant manager
5. Cost of labor for hourly workers
6. Packaging
7. Factory cleaning costs, $6,000 per month
8. Metal

(Continued)

9. Rent on warehouse, $10,000 per month plus $25 per square foot of storage used
10. Property insurance premiums, $3,600 per month plus $0.01 for each dollar of property over $1,200,000
11. Straight-line depreciation on the production equipment
12. Hourly wages of machine operators
13. Electricity costs, $0.20 per kilowatt-hour
14. Computer chip (purchased from a vendor)
15. Pension cost, $1.00 per employee hour on the job

EX 4-2 Identify cost graphs **OBJ. 1**

The following cost graphs illustrate various types of cost behavior:

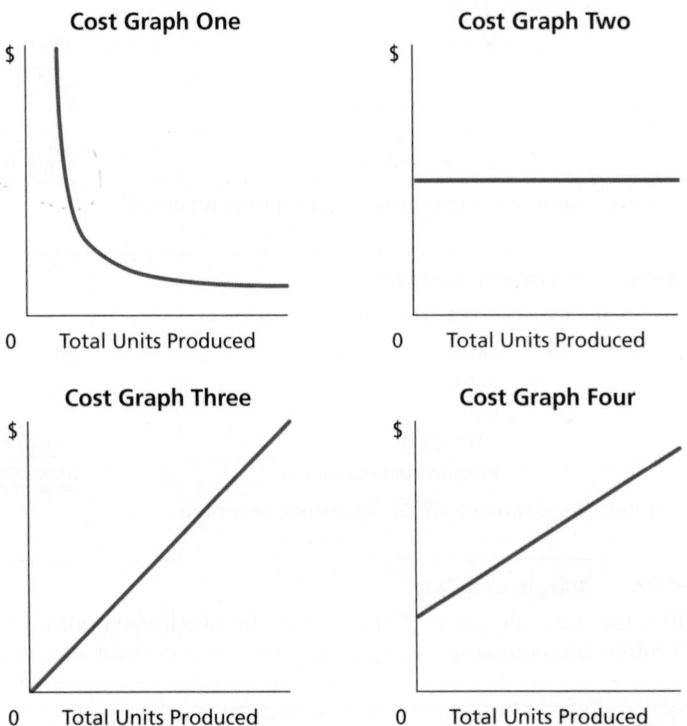

For each of the following costs, identify the cost graph that best illustrates its cost behavior as the number of units produced increases:

a. Total direct materials cost
b. Electricity costs of $1,000 per month plus $0.10 per kilowatt-hour
c. Per-unit cost of straight-line depreciation on factory equipment
d. Salary of quality control supervisor, $20,000 per month
e. Per-unit direct labor cost

EX 4-3 Identify activity bases **OBJ. 1**

For a major university, match each cost in the following table with the activity base most appropriate to it. An activity base may be used more than once or not used at all.

Cost:	Activity Base:
1. Financial aid office salaries	a. Number of enrollment applications
2. Office supplies	b. Number of students
3. Instructor salaries	c. Student credit hours
4. Housing personnel wages	d. Number of enrolled students and alumni
5. Student records office salaries	e. Number of financial aid applications
6. Admissions office salaries	f. Number of students living on campus

EX 4-4 Identify activity bases

OBJ. 1

From the following list of activity bases for an automobile dealership, select the base that would be most appropriate for each of these costs: (1) preparation costs (cleaning, oil, and gasoline costs) for each car received, (2) salespersons' commission of 5% of the sales price for each car sold, and (3) administrative costs for ordering cars.

a. Number of cars sold
b. Dollar amount of cars ordered
c. Number of cars ordered
d. Number of cars on hand
e. Number of cars received
f. Dollar amount of cars sold
g. Dollar amount of cars received
h. Dollar amount of cars on hand

EX 4-5 Identify fixed and variable costs

OBJ. 1

Intuit Inc. develops and sells software products for the personal finance market, including popular titles such as Quickbooks® and TurboTax®. Classify each of the following costs and expenses for this company as either variable or fixed to the number of units produced and sold:

a. Packaging costs
b. Sales commissions
c. Property taxes on general offices
d. Shipping expenses
e. Straight-line depreciation of computer equipment
f. President's salary
g. Salaries of software developers
h. Salaries of human resources personnel
i. Wages of telephone order assistants
j. CDs
k. Users' guides

EX 4-6 Relevant range and fixed and variable costs

OBJ. 1

✔ a. $1.25

SHOW ME HOW

Quigley Inc. manufactures memory chips for electronic toys within a relevant range of 200,000 to 600,000 memory chips per year. Within this range, the following partially completed manufacturing cost schedule has been prepared:

Components produced	200,000	400,000	600,000
Total costs:			
Total variable costs	$ 250,000	(d)	(j)
Total fixed costs	600,000	(e)	(k)
Total costs	$850,000	(f)	(l)
Cost per unit:			
Variable cost per unit	(a)	(g)	(m)
Fixed cost per unit	(b)	(h)	(n)
Total cost per unit	(c)	(i)	(o)

Complete the cost schedule, identifying each cost by the appropriate letter (a) through (o).

EX 4-7 High-low method

OBJ. 1

✔ a. $24.00 per unit

Diamond Inc. has decided to use the high-low method to estimate the total cost and the fixed and variable cost components of the total cost. The data for various levels of production are as follows:

Units Produced	Total Costs
12,000	$424,000
15,000	496,000
21,000	640,000

SHOW ME HOW

(Continued)

a. Determine the variable cost per unit and the total fixed cost.

b. Based on part (a), estimate the total cost for 17,000 units of production.

EX 4-8 High-low method for a service company **OBJ. 1**

✔ Fixed cost, $600,000

Boston Railroad decided to use the high-low method and operating data from the past six months to estimate the fixed and variable components of transportation costs. The activity base used by Boston Railroad is a measure of railroad operating activity, termed "gross-ton miles," which is the total number of tons multiplied by the miles moved.

SHOW ME HOW

	Transportation Costs	Gross-Ton Miles
January	$1,776,000	560,000
February	2,700,000	1,000,000
March	1,650,000	500,000
April	1,860,000	600,000
May	1,440,000	400,000
June	1,566,000	460,000

Determine the variable cost per gross-ton mile and the total fixed cost.

EX 4-9 Contribution margin ratio **OBJ. 2**

✔ a. 30%

SHOW ME HOW

a. Segar Company budgets sales of $3,200,000, fixed costs of $700,000, and variable costs of $2,240,000. What is the contribution margin ratio for Segar Company?

b. If the contribution margin ratio for Domino Company is 35%, sales were $2,100,000, and fixed costs were $400,000, what was the income from operations?

EX 4-10 Contribution margin and contribution margin ratio **OBJ. 2**

✔ b. 35.5%

SHOW ME HOW

For a recent year, **McDonald's** company-owned restaurants had the following sales and expenses (in millions):

Sales	$18,602.5
Food and packaging	$ 6,318.2
Payroll	4,710.3
Occupancy (rent, depreciation, etc.)	4,195.2
General, selling, and administrative expenses	2,445.2
	17,668.9
Income from operations	$ 933.6

Assume that the variable costs consist of food and packaging, payroll, and 40% of the general, selling, and administrative expenses.

a. What is McDonald's contribution margin? Round to the nearest tenth of a million (one decimal place).

b. What is McDonald's contribution margin ratio? Round to one decimal place.

c. How much would income from operations increase if same-store sales increased by $900 million for the coming year, with no change in the contribution margin ratio or fixed costs? Round your answer to the nearest tenth of a million (one decimal place).

EX 4-11 Break-even sales and sales to realize income from operations **OBJ. 3**

✔ b. 35,000 units

SHOW ME HOW

For the current year ended March 31, Benatar Company expects fixed costs of $1,250,000, a unit variable cost of $140, and a unit selling price of $100.

a. Compute the anticipated break-even sales (units).

b. Compute the sales (units) required to realize income from operations of $150,000.

EX 4-12 Break-even sales **OBJ. 3**

✔ a. 150,331,823 barrels

Anheuser-Busch InBev Companies, Inc., reported the following operating information for a recent year (in millions):

Sales	$39,758
Cost of goods sold	$16,447
Selling, general and administration	10,578
	$27,025
Income from operations	$12,733*

*Before special items

In addition, assume that Anheuser-Busch InBev sold 320 million barrels of beer during the year. Assume that variable costs were 70% of the cost of goods sold and 40% of selling, general, and administration expenses. Assume that the remaining costs are fixed. For the following year, assume that Anheuser-Busch InBev expects pricing, variable costs per barrel, and fixed costs to remain constant, except that new distribution and general office facilities are expected to increase fixed costs by $400 million.

a. Compute the break-even number of barrels for the current year. *Note:* For the selling price per barrel and variable costs per barrel, round to the nearest cent. Also, round the break-even to the nearest barrel.

b. Compute the anticipated break-even number of barrels for the following year.

EX 4-13 Break-even sales **OBJ. 3**

✔ a. 18,125 units

SHOW ME HOW

Currently, the unit selling price of a product is $160, the unit variable cost is $120, and the total fixed costs are $725,000. A proposal is being evaluated to increase the unit selling price to $170.

a. Compute the current break-even sales (units).

b. Compute the anticipated break-even sales (units), assuming that the unit selling price is increased and all costs remain constant.

EX 4-14 Break-even analysis **OBJ. 3**

The Junior League of Yadkinville, California, collected recipes from members and published a cookbook entitled *Food for Everyone*. The book will sell for $18 per copy. The chairwoman of the cookbook development committee estimated that the club needed to sell 2,000 books to break even on its $4,000 investment. What is the variable cost per unit assumed in the Junior League's analysis?

EX 4-15 Break-even analysis **OBJ. 3**

Media outlets such as **ESPN** and **Fox Sports** often have Web sites that provide in-depth coverage of news and events. Portions of these Web sites are restricted to members who pay a monthly subscription to gain access to exclusive news and commentary. These Web sites typically offer a free trial period to introduce viewers to the Web site. Assume that during a recent fiscal year, ESPN.com spent $4,200,000 on a promotional campaign for the ESPN.com Web site that offered two free months of service for new subscribers. In addition, assume the following information:

Number of months an average new customer stays with the service (including the two free months)	14 months
Revenue per month per customer subscription	$10.00
Variable cost per month per customer subscription	$5.00

Determine the number of new customer accounts needed to break even on the cost of the promotional campaign. In forming your answer, (1) treat the cost of the promotional campaign as a fixed cost, and (2) treat the revenue less variable cost per account for the subscription period as the unit contribution margin.

EX 4-16 Break-even analysis for a service company **OBJ. 3**

Sprint Nextel is one of the largest digital wireless service providers in the United States. In a recent year, it had approximately 32.5 million direct subscribers (accounts) that generated revenue of $35,345 million. Costs and expenses for the year were as follows (in millions):

Cost of revenue	$20,841
Selling, general, and administrative expenses	9,765
Depreciation	2,239

Assume that 70% of the cost of revenue and 30% of the selling, general, and administrative expenses are variable to the number of direct subscribers (accounts).

a. What is Sprint Nextel's break-even number of accounts, using the data and assumptions given? Round units (accounts) and per-account amounts to one decimal place.

b. How much revenue per account would be sufficient for Sprint Nextel to break even if the number of accounts remained constant?

EX 4-17 Cost-volume-profit chart **OBJ. 4**

✔ b. $1,500,000

For the coming year, Loudermilk Inc. anticipates fixed costs of $600,000, a unit variable cost of $75, and a unit selling price of $125. The maximum sales within the relevant range are $2,500,000.

a. Construct a cost-volume-profit chart.

b. Estimate the break-even sales (dollars) by using the cost-volume-profit chart constructed in part (a).

c. What is the main advantage of presenting the cost-volume-profit analysis in graphic form rather than equation form?

EX 4-18 Profit-volume chart **OBJ. 4**

✔ b. $400,000

Using the data for Loudermilk Inc. in Exercise 4-17, (a) determine the maximum possible operating loss, (b) compute the maximum possible operating profit, (c) construct a profit-volume chart, and (d) estimate the break-even sales (units) by using the profit-volume chart constructed in part (c).

EX 4-19 Break-even chart **OBJ. 4**

Name the following chart, and identify the items represented by the letters (a) through (f):

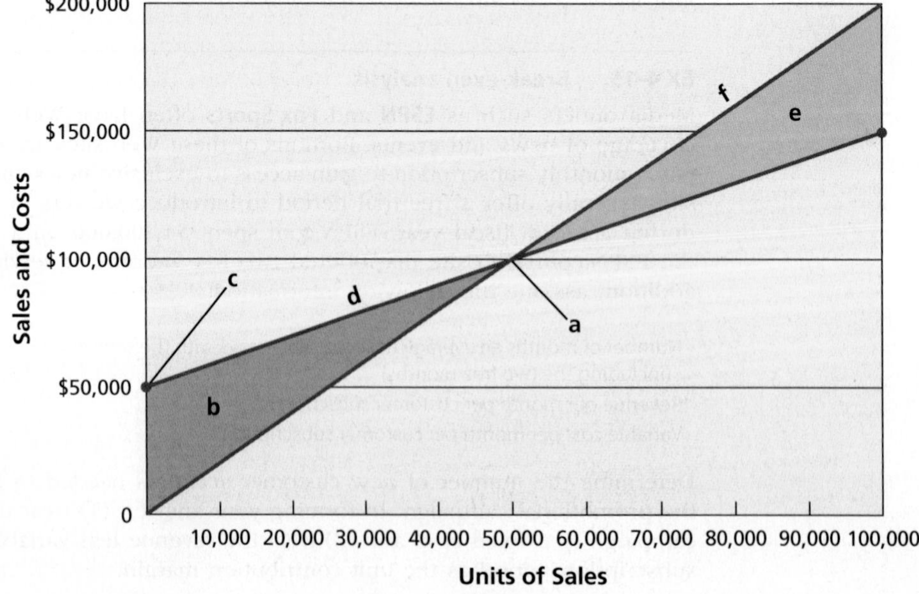

EX 4-20 Break-even chart **OBJ. 4**

Name the following chart, and identify the items represented by the letters (a) through (f):

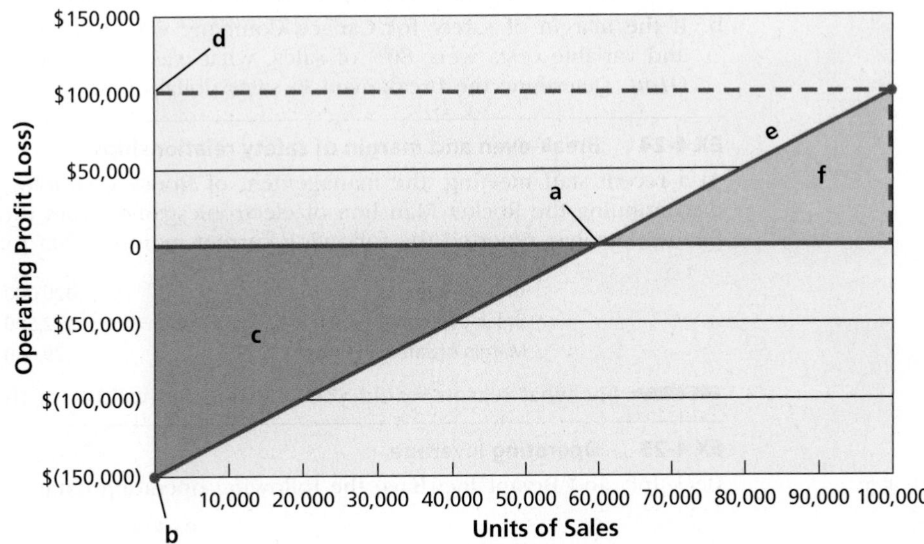

EX 4-21 Sales mix and break-even sales **OBJ. 5**

✔ a. 15,500 units

SHOW ME HOW

Dragon Sports Inc. manufactures and sells two products, baseball bats and baseball gloves. The fixed costs are $620,000, and the sales mix is 40% bats and 60% gloves. The unit selling price and the unit variable cost for each product are as follows:

Products	Unit Selling Price	Unit Variable Cost
Bats	$ 90	$50
Gloves	105	65

a. Compute the break-even sales (units) for the overall product, E.

b. How many units of each product, baseball bats and baseball gloves, would be sold at the break-even point?

EX 4-22 Break-even sales and sales mix for a service company **OBJ. 5**

✔ a. 60 seats

Zero Turbulence Airline provides air transportation services between Los Angeles, California, and Kona, Hawaii. A single Los Angeles to Kona round-trip flight has the following operating statistics:

Fuel	$7,000
Flight crew salaries	3,200
Airplane depreciation	3,480
Variable cost per passenger—business class	140
Variable cost per passenger—economy class	120
Round-trip ticket price—business class	800
Round-trip ticket price—economy class	300

It is assumed that the fuel, crew salaries, and airplane depreciation are fixed, regardless of the number of seats sold for the round-trip flight.

a. Compute the break-even number of seats sold on a single round-trip flight for the overall product, E. Assume that the overall product mix is 10% business class and 90% economy class tickets.

b. How many business class and economy class seats would be sold at the break-even point?

EX 4-23 Margin of safety

OBJ. 5

✔ a. (2) 20%

SHOW ME HOW

a. If Canace Company, with a break-even point at $960,000 of sales, has actual sales of $1,200,000, what is the margin of safety expressed (1) in dollars and (2) as a percentage of sales?

b. If the margin of safety for Canace Company was 20%, fixed costs were $1,875,000, and variable costs were 80% of sales, what was the amount of actual sales (dollars)? (*Hint:* Determine the break-even in sales dollars first.)

EX 4-24 Break-even and margin of safety relationships

OBJ. 5

At a recent staff meeting, the management of Boost Technologies Inc. was considering discontinuing the Rocket Man line of electronic games from the product line. The chief financial analyst reported the following current monthly data for the Rocket Man:

Units of sales	420,000
Break-even units	472,500
Margin of safety in units	29,400

For what reason would you question the validity of these data?

EX 4-25 Operating leverage

OBJ. 5

✔ a. Beck, 5.0

Beck Inc. and Bryant Inc. have the following operating data:

	Beck Inc.	Bryant Inc.
Sales	$1,250,000	$2,000,000
Variable costs	750,000	1,250,000
Contribution margin	$ 500,000	$ 750,000
Fixed costs	400,000	450,000
Income from operations	$ 100,000	$ 300,000

a. Compute the operating leverage for Beck Inc. and Bryant Inc.

b. How much would income from operations increase for each company if the sales of each increased by 20%?

c. Why is there a difference in the increase in income from operations for the two companies? Explain.

Appendix
EX 4-26 Items on variable costing income statement

In the following equations, based on the variable costing income statement, identify the items designated by X:

a. Sales − X = Manufacturing Margin

b. Manufacturing Margin − X = Contribution Margin

c. Contribution Margin − X = Income from Operations

Appendix
EX 4-27 Variable costing income statement

✔ a. Contribution margin, $1,934,400

On July 31, 2016, the end of the first month of operations, Rhys Company prepared the following income statement, based on the absorption costing concept:

Sales (96,000 units)		$4,440,000
Cost of goods sold:		
Cost of goods manufactured	$3,120,000	
Less ending inventory (24,000 units)	624,000	
Cost of goods sold		2,496,000
Gross profit		$1,944,000
Selling and administrative expenses		288,000
Income from operations		$1,656,000

a. Prepare a variable costing income statement, assuming that the fixed manufacturing costs were $132,000 and the variable selling and administrative expenses were $115,200.

b. Reconcile the absorption costing income from operations of $1,656,000 with the variable costing income from operations determined in (a).

Appendix
EX 4-28 Absorption costing income statement

✔ a. Gross profit, $1,435,600

On June 30, 2016, the end of the first month of operations, Tudor Manufacturing Co. prepared the following income statement, based on the variable costing concept:

Sales (420,000 units)		$7,450,000
Variable cost of goods sold:		
Variable cost of goods manufactured (500,000 units × $14 per unit)	$7,000,000	
Less ending inventory (80,000 units × $14 per unit)	1,120,000	
Variable cost of goods sold		5,880,000
Manufacturing margin		$1,570,000
Variable selling and administrative expenses		80,000
Contribution margin		$1,490,000
Fixed costs:		
Fixed manufacturing costs	$ 160,000	
Fixed selling and administrative expenses	75,000	235,000
Income from operations		$1,255,000

a. Prepare an absorption costing income statement.

b. Reconcile the variable costing income from operations of $1,255,000 with the absorption costing income from operations determined in (a).

Problems: Series A

PR 4-1A Classify costs **OBJ. 1**

Seymour Clothing Co. manufactures a variety of clothing types for distribution to several major retail chains. The following costs are incurred in the production and sale of blue jeans:

a. Shipping boxes used to ship orders
b. Consulting fee of $200,000 paid to industry specialist for marketing advice
c. Straight-line depreciation on sewing machines
d. Salesperson's salary, $10,000 plus 2% of the total sales
e. Fabric
f. Dye
g. Thread
h. Salary of designers
i. Brass buttons
j. Legal fees paid to attorneys in defense of the company in a patent infringement suit, $50,000 plus $87 per hour
k. Insurance premiums on property, plant, and equipment, $70,000 per year plus $5 per $30,000 of insured value over $8,000,000
l. Rental costs of warehouse, $5,000 per month plus $4 per square foot of storage used
m. Supplies
n. Leather for patches identifying the brand on individual pieces of apparel
o. Rent on plant equipment, $50,000 per year
p. Salary of production vice president
q. Janitorial services, $2,200 per month
r. Wages of machine operators
s. Electricity costs of $0.10 per kilowatt-hour
t. Property taxes on property, plant, and equipment

Instructions

Classify the preceding costs as either fixed, variable, or mixed. Use the following tabular headings and place an X in the appropriate column. Identify each cost by letter in the cost column.

Cost	Fixed Cost	Variable Cost	Mixed Cost

PR 4-2A Break-even sales under present and proposed conditions **OBJ. 2, 3**

✔ 2. (b) $50

SHOW ME HOW

BeeGee Company, operating at full capacity, sold 150,000 units at a price of $116 per unit during the current year. Its income statement is as follows:

Sales		$17,400,000
Cost of goods sold		6,000,000
Gross profit		$11,400,000
Expenses:		
Selling expenses	$4,000,000	
Administrative expenses	3,000,000	
Total expenses		7,000,000
Income from operations		$ 4,400,000

The division of costs between variable and fixed is as follows:

	Variable	Fixed
Cost of goods sold	80%	20%
Selling expenses	75%	25%
Administrative expenses	70%	30%

Management is considering a plant expansion program for the following year that will permit an increase of $3,625,000 in yearly sales. The expansion will increase fixed costs by $1,000,000 but will not affect the relationship between sales and variable costs.

Instructions

1. Determine the total variable costs and the total fixed costs for the current year.
2. Determine (a) the unit variable cost and (b) the unit contribution margin for the current year.
3. Compute the break-even sales (units) for the current year.
4. Compute the break-even sales (units) under the proposed program for the following year.
5. Determine the amount of sales (units) that would be necessary under the proposed program to realize the $4,400,000 of income from operations that was earned in the current year.
6. Determine the maximum income from operations possible with the expanded plant.
7. If the proposal is accepted and sales remain at the current level, what will the income or loss from operations be for the following year?
8. Based on the data given, would you recommend accepting the proposal? Explain.

PR 4-3A Break-even sales and cost-volume-profit chart **OBJ. 3, 4**

✔ 1. 12,000 units

For the coming year, Cleves Company anticipates a unit selling price of $100, a unit variable cost of $60, and fixed costs of $480,000.

Instructions

1. Compute the anticipated break-even sales (units).
2. Compute the sales (units) required to realize a target profit of $240,000.
3. Construct a cost-volume-profit chart, assuming maximum sales of 20,000 units within the relevant range.
4. Determine the probable income (loss) from operations if sales total 16,000 units.

PR 4-4A Break-even sales and cost-volume-profit chart **OBJ. 3, 4**

✔ 1. 1,000 units

Last year, Hever Inc. had sales of $500,000, based on a unit selling price of $250. The variable cost per unit was $175, and fixed costs were $75,000. The maximum sales within Hever Inc.'s relevant range are 2,500 units. Hever Inc. is considering a proposal to spend an additional $33,750 on billboard advertising during the current year in an attempt to increase sales and utilize unused capacity.

Instructions

1. Construct a cost-volume-profit chart indicating the break-even sales for last year. Verify your answer, using the break-even equation.
2. Using the cost-volume-profit chart prepared in part (1), determine (a) the income from operations for last year and (b) the maximum income from operations that could have been realized during the year. Verify your answers using the mathematical approach to cost-volume-profit analysis.

3. Construct a cost-volume-profit chart indicating the break-even sales for the current year, assuming that a noncancellable contract is signed for the additional billboard advertising. No changes are expected in the unit selling price or other costs. Verify your answer, using the break-even equation.
4. Using the cost-volume-profit chart prepared in part (3), determine (a) the income from operations if sales total 2,000 units and (b) the maximum income from operations that could be realized during the year. Verify your answers using the mathematical approach to cost-volume-profit analysis.

PR 4-5A Sales mix and break-even sales — OBJ. 5

✔ 1. 4,030 units

Data related to the expected sales of laptops and tablets for Tech Products Inc. for the current year, which is typical of recent years, are as follows:

Products	Unit Selling Price	Unit Variable Cost	Sales Mix
Laptops	$1,600	$800	40%
Tablets	850	350	60%

The estimated fixed costs for the current year are $2,498,600.

Instructions

1. Determine the estimated units of sales of the overall (total) product, E, necessary to reach the break-even point for the current year.
2. Based on the break-even sales (units) in part (1), determine the unit sales of both laptops and tablets for the current year.
3. Assume that the sales mix was 50% laptops and 50% tablets. Compare the break-even point with that in part (1). Why is it so different?

PR 4-6A Contribution margin, break-even sales, cost-volume-profit chart, margin of safety, and operating leverage — OBJ. 2, 3, 4, 5

✔ 2. 25%

Wolsey Industries Inc. expects to maintain the same inventories at the end of 2016 as at the beginning of the year. The total of all production costs for the year is therefore assumed to be equal to the cost of goods sold. With this in mind, the various department heads were asked to submit estimates of the costs for their departments during the year. A summary report of these estimates is as follows:

	Estimated Fixed Cost	Estimated Variable Cost (per unit sold)
Production costs:		
Direct materials	—	$ 46
Direct labor	—	40
Factory overhead	$200,000	20
Selling expenses:		
Sales salaries and commissions	110,000	8
Advertising	40,000	—
Travel	12,000	—
Miscellaneous selling expense	7,600	1
Administrative expenses:		
Office and officers' salaries	132,000	—
Supplies	10,000	4
Miscellaneous administrative expense	13,400	1
Total	$525,000	$120

It is expected that 21,875 units will be sold at a price of $160 a unit. Maximum sales within the relevant range are 27,000 units.

Instructions

1. Prepare an estimated income statement for 2016.
2. What is the expected contribution margin ratio?
3. Determine the break-even sales in units and dollars.
4. Construct a cost-volume-profit chart indicating the break-even sales.
5. What is the expected margin of safety in dollars and as a percentage of sales?
6. Determine the operating leverage.

Problems: Series B

PR 4-1B Classify costs

OBJ. 1

Cromwell Furniture Company manufactures sofas for distribution to several major retail chains. The following costs are incurred in the production and sale of sofas:

a. Fabric for sofa coverings
b. Wood for framing the sofas
c. Legal fees paid to attorneys in defense of the company in a patent infringement suit, $25,000 plus $160 per hour
d. Salary of production supervisor
e. Cartons used to ship sofas
f. Rent on experimental equipment, $50 for every sofa produced
g. Straight-line depreciation on factory equipment
h. Rental costs of warehouse, $30,000 per month
i. Property taxes on property, plant, and equipment
j. Insurance premiums on property, plant, and equipment, $25,000 per year plus $25 per $25,000 of insured value over $16,000,000
k. Springs
l. Consulting fee of $120,000 paid to efficiency specialists
m. Electricity costs of $0.13 per kilowatt-hour
n. Salesperson's salary, $80,000 plus 4% of the selling price of each sofa sold
o. Foam rubber for cushion fillings
p. Janitorial supplies, $2,500 per month
q. Employer's FICA taxes on controller's salary of $180,000
r. Salary of designers
s. Wages of sewing machine operators
t. Sewing supplies

Instructions

Classify the preceding costs as either fixed, variable, or mixed. Use the following tabular headings and place an X in the appropriate column. Identify each cost by letter in the cost column.

Cost	Fixed Cost	Variable Cost	Mixed Cost

PR 4-2B Break-even sales under present and proposed conditions

OBJ. 2, 3

✔ 3. 29,375 units

SHOW ME HOW

Howard Industries Inc., operating at full capacity, sold 64,000 units at a price of $45 per unit during the current year. Its income statement is as follows:

Sales		$2,880,000
Cost of goods sold		1,400,000
Gross profit		$1,480,000
Expenses:		
Selling expenses	$400,000	
Administrative expenses	387,500	
Total expenses		787,500
Income from operations		$ 692,500

The division of costs between variable and fixed is as follows:

	Variable	Fixed
Cost of goods sold	75%	25%
Selling expenses	60%	40%
Administrative expenses	80%	20%

Management is considering a plant expansion program for the following year that will permit an increase of $900,000 in yearly sales. The expansion will increase fixed costs by $212,500 but will not affect the relationship between sales and variable costs.

Instructions

1. Determine the total fixed costs and the total variable costs for the current year.
2. Determine (a) the unit variable cost and (b) the unit contribution margin for the current year.
3. Compute the break-even sales (units) for the current year.
4. Compute the break-even sales (units) under the proposed program for the following year.
5. Determine the amount of sales (units) that would be necessary under the proposed program to realize the $692,500 of income from operations that was earned in the current year.
6. Determine the maximum income from operations possible with the expanded plant.
7. If the proposal is accepted and sales remain at the current level, what will the income or loss from operations be for the following year?
8. Based on the data given, would you recommend accepting the proposal? Explain.

PR 4-3B Break-even sales and cost-volume-profit chart

OBJ. 3, 4

✔ 1. 20,000 units

For the coming year, Culpeper Products Inc. anticipates a unit selling price of $150, a unit variable cost of $110, and fixed costs of $800,000.

Instructions

1. Compute the anticipated break-even sales (units).
2. Compute the sales (units) required to realize income from operations of $300,000.
3. Construct a cost-volume-profit chart, assuming maximum sales of 40,000 units within the relevant range.
4. Determine the probable income (loss) from operations if sales total 32,000 units.

PR 4-4B Break-even sales and cost-volume-profit chart

OBJ. 3, 4

✔ 1. 3,000 units

Last year, Parr Co. had sales of $900,000, based on a unit selling price of $200. The variable cost per unit was $125, and fixed costs were $225,000. The maximum sales within Parr Co.'s relevant range are 7,500 units. Parr Co. is considering a proposal to spend an additional $112,500 on billboard advertising during the current year in an attempt to increase sales and utilize unused capacity.

Instructions

1. Construct a cost-volume-profit chart indicating the break-even sales for last year. Verify your answer, using the break-even equation.
2. Using the cost-volume-profit chart prepared in part (1), determine (a) the income from operations for last year and (b) the maximum income from operations that could have been realized during the year. Verify your answers arithmetically.
3. Construct a cost-volume-profit chart indicating the break-even sales for the current year, assuming that a noncancellable contract is signed for the additional billboard advertising. No changes are expected in the selling price or other costs. Verify your answer, using the break-even equation.
4. Using the cost-volume-profit chart prepared in part (3), determine (a) the income from operations if sales total 6,000 units and (b) the maximum income from operations that could be realized during the year. Verify your answers arithmetically.

PR 4-5B Sales mix and break-even sales

OBJ. 5

✔ 1. 4,500 units

Data related to the expected sales of two types of frozen pizzas for Norfolk Frozen Foods Inc. for the current year, which is typical of recent years, are as follows:

Products	Unit Selling Price	Unit Variable Cost	Sales Mix
12" Pizza	$12	$3	30%
16" Pizza	15	4	70%

(Continued)

The estimated fixed costs for the current year are $46,800.

Instructions

1. Determine the estimated units of sales of the overall (total) product, E, necessary to reach the break-even point for the current year.
2. Based on the break-even sales (units) in part (1), determine the unit sales of both the 12″ pizza and 16″ pizza for the current year.
3. Assume that the sales mix was 50% 12″ pizza and 50% 16″ pizza. Compare the break-even point with that in part (1). Why is it so different?

✔ 3. 8,000 units

PR 4-6B Contribution margin, break-even sales, cost-volume-profit chart, margin of safety, and operating leverage OBJ. 2, 3, 4, 5

Belmain Co. expects to maintain the same inventories at the end of 2016 as at the beginning of the year. The total of all production costs for the year is therefore assumed to be equal to the cost of goods sold. With this in mind, the various department heads were asked to submit estimates of the costs for their departments during the year. A summary report of these estimates is as follows:

	Estimated Fixed Cost	Estimated Variable Cost (per unit sold)
Production costs:		
Direct materials	—	$50.00
Direct labor	—	30.00
Factory overhead	$ 350,000	6.00
Selling expenses:		
Sales salaries and commissions	340,000	4.00
Advertising	116,000	—
Travel	4,000	—
Miscellaneous selling expense	2,300	1.00
Administrative expenses:		
Office and officers' salaries	325,000	—
Supplies	6,000	4.00
Miscellaneous administrative expense	8,700	1.00
Total	$1,152,000	$96.00

It is expected that 12,000 units will be sold at a price of $240 a unit. Maximum sales within the relevant range are 18,000 units.

Instructions

1. Prepare an estimated income statement for 2016.
2. What is the expected contribution margin ratio?
3. Determine the break-even sales in units and dollars.
4. Construct a cost-volume-profit chart indicating the break-even sales.
5. What is the expected margin of safety in dollars and as a percentage of sales?
6. Determine the operating leverage.

Cases & Projects

CP 4-1 Ethics and professional conduct in business

Edward Seymour is a financial consultant to Cornish Inc., a real estate syndicate. Cornish Inc. finances and develops commercial real estate (office buildings). The completed projects are then sold as limited partnership interests to individual investors. The syndicate makes a profit on the sale of these partnership interests. Edward provides financial information for the offering prospectus, which is a document that provides the financial and legal details of the limited partnership offerings. In one of the projects, the bank has financed the construction of a commercial office building at a rate of 10% for the first four years, after which time the rate jumps to 15% for the remaining 20 years of the mortgage. The interest costs are one of the major ongoing costs of a real estate project. Edward has reported prominently in the prospectus that the break-even occupancy for the first four years is 65%. This is the amount of office space that must be leased to cover the interest and general upkeep costs over the first four years. The 65% break-even is very low and thus communicates a low risk to potential investors. Edward uses the 65% break-even rate as a major marketing tool in selling the limited partnership interests. Buried in the fine print of the prospectus is additional information that would allow an astute investor to determine that the break-even occupancy will jump to 95% after the fourth year because of the contracted increase in the mortgage interest rate. Edward believes prospective investors are adequately informed as to the risk of the investment.

Comment on the ethical considerations of this situation.

CP 4-2 Break-even sales, contribution margin

"For a student, a grade of 65 percent is nothing to write home about. But for the airline . . . [industry], filling 65 percent of the seats . . . is the difference between profit and loss.

The [economy] might be just strong enough to sustain all the carriers on a cash basis, but not strong enough to bring any significant profitability to the industry. . . . For the airlines . . ., the emphasis will be on trying to consolidate routes and raise ticket prices. . . ."

Source: Edwin McDowell, "Empty Seats, Empty Beds, Empty Pockets," *The New York Times*, January 6, 1992, p. C3.

The airline industry is notorious for boom and bust cycles. Why is airline profitability very sensitive to these cycles? Do you think that during a down cycle the strategy to consolidate routes and raise ticket prices is reasonable? What would make this strategy succeed or fail? Why?

CP 4-3 Break-even analysis

Somerset Inc. has finished a new video game, *Snowboard Challenge*. Management is now considering its marketing strategies. The following information is available:

Anticipated sales price per unit	$80
Variable cost per unit*	$35
Anticipated volume	1,000,000 units
Production costs	$20,000,000
Anticipated advertising	$15,000,000

*The cost of the video game, packaging, and copying costs.

Two managers, James Hamilton and Thomas Seymour, had the following discussion of ways to increase the profitability of this new offering:

James: I think we need to think of some way to increase our profitability. Do you have any ideas?

Thomas: Well, I think the best strategy would be to become aggressive on price.

James: How aggressive?

Thomas: If we drop the price to $60 per unit and maintain our advertising budget at $15,000,000, I think we will generate total sales of 2,000,000 units.

James: I think that's the wrong way to go. You're giving too much up on price. Instead, I think we need to follow an aggressive advertising strategy.

Thomas: How aggressive?

James: If we increase our advertising to a total of $25,000,000, we should be able to increase sales volume to 1,400,000 units without any change in price.

Thomas: I don't think that's reasonable. We'll never cover the increased advertising costs.

Which strategy is best: Do nothing? Follow the advice of Thomas Seymour? Or follow James Hamilton's strategy?

CP 4-4 Variable costs and activity bases in decision making

The owner of Warwick Printing, a printing company, is planning direct labor needs for the upcoming year. The owner has provided you with the following information for next year's plans:

	One Color	Two Color	Three Color	Four Color	Total
Number of banners	212	274	616	698	1,800

Each color on the banner must be printed one at a time. Thus, for example, a four-color banner will need to be run through the printing operation four separate times. The total production volume last year was 800 banners, as follows:

	One Color	Two Color	Three Color	Total
Number of banners	180	240	380	800

As you can see, the four-color banner is a new product offering for the upcoming year. The owner believes that the expected 1,000-unit increase in volume from last year means that direct labor expenses should increase by 125% (1,000 ÷ 800). What do you think?

CP 4-5 Variable costs and activity bases in decision making

Sales volume has been dropping at Mumford Industries. During this time, however, the Shipping Department manager has been under severe financial constraints. The manager knows that most of the Shipping Department's effort is related to pulling inventory from the warehouse for each order and performing the paperwork. The paperwork involves preparing shipping documents for each order. Thus, the pulling and paperwork effort associated with each sales order is essentially the same, regardless of the size of the order. The Shipping Department manager has discussed the financial situation with senior management. Senior management has responded by pointing out that sales volume has been dropping, so that the amount of work in the Shipping Department should be dropping. Thus, senior management told the Shipping Department manager that costs should be decreasing in the department.

The Shipping Department manager prepared the following information:

Month	Sales Volume	Number of Customer Orders	Sales Volume per Order
January	$472,000	1,180	400
February	475,800	1,220	390
March	456,950	1,235	370
April	425,000	1,250	340
May	464,750	1,430	325
June	421,200	1,350	312
July	414,000	1,380	300
August	430,700	1,475	292

Given this information, how would you respond to senior management?

CP 4-6 Break-even analysis

Group Project

Break-even analysis is one of the most fundamental tools for managing any kind of business unit. Consider the management of your university or college. In a group, brainstorm some applications of break-even analysis at your university or college. Identify three areas where break-even analysis might be used. For each area, identify the revenues, variable costs, and fixed costs that would be used in the calculation.

Variable Costing for Management Analysis

Adobe Systems, Inc.

Assume that you have three different options for a summer job. How would you evaluate these options? Naturally there are many things to consider, including how much you could earn from each job.

Determining how much you could earn from each job may not be as simple as comparing the wage rate per hour. For example, a job as an office clerk at a local company pays $8 per hour. A job delivering pizza pays $10 per hour (including estimated tips), although you must use your own transportation. Another job working in a beach resort over 500 miles away from your home pays $8 per hour. All three jobs offer 40 hours per week for the whole summer. If these options were ranked according to their pay per hour, the pizza delivery job would be the most attractive. However, the costs associated with each job must also be evaluated. For example, the office job may require that you pay for downtown parking and purchase office clothes. The pizza delivery job will require you to pay for gas and maintenance for your car. The resort job will require you to move to the resort city and incur additional living costs. Only by considering the costs for each job will you be able to determine which job will provide you with the most income.

Just as you should evaluate the relative income of various choices, a business also evaluates the income earned from its choices. Important choices include the products offered and the geographical regions to be served.

A company will often evaluate the profitability of products and regions. For example, **Adobe Systems Inc.**, one of the largest software companies in the world, determines the income earned from its various product lines, such as Acrobat®, Photoshop®, Premier®, and Dreamweaver® software. Adobe uses this information to establish product line pricing, as well as sales, support, and development effort. Likewise, Adobe evaluates the income earned in the geographic regions it serves, such as the United States, Europe, and Asia. Again, such information aids management in managing revenue and expenses within the regions.

In this chapter, how businesses measure profitability using absorption costing and variable costing is discussed. After illustrating and comparing these concepts, how businesses use them for controlling costs, pricing products, planning production, analyzing market segments, and analyzing contribution margins is described and illustrated.

Learning Objectives

After studying this chapter, you should be able to:	*Example Exercises*
OBJ 1 Describe and illustrate reporting income from operations under absorption and variable costing.	
Income from Operations Under Absorption Costing and Variable Costing	
Absorption Costing	
Variable Costing	EE 5-1
Units Manufactured Equal Units Sold	
Units Manufactured Exceed Units Sold	EE 5-2
Units Manufactured Less Than Units Sold	EE 5-3
Effects on Income from Operations	
OBJ 2 Describe and illustrate the effects of absorption and variable costing on analyzing income from operations.	
Income Analysis Under Absorption and Variable Costing	EE 5-4
OBJ 3 Describe management's use of absorption and variable costing.	
Using Absorption and Variable Costing	
Controlling Costs	
Pricing Products	
Planning Production	
Analyzing Contribution Margins	
Analyzing Market Segments	
OBJ 4 Use variable costing for analyzing market segments, including product, territories, and salespersons segments.	
Analyzing Market Segments	
Sales Territory Profitability Analysis	
Product Profitability Analysis	
Salesperson Profitability Analysis	EE 5-5
OBJ 5 Use variable costing for analyzing and explaining changes in contribution margin as a result of quantity and price factors.	
Contribution Margin Analysis	EE 5-6
OBJ 6 Describe and illustrate the use of variable costing for service firms.	
Variable Costing for Service Firms	
Reporting Income from Operations Using Variable Costing for a Service Company	
Market Segment Analysis for Service Company	
Contribution Margin Analysis	

At a Glance 5 Page 203

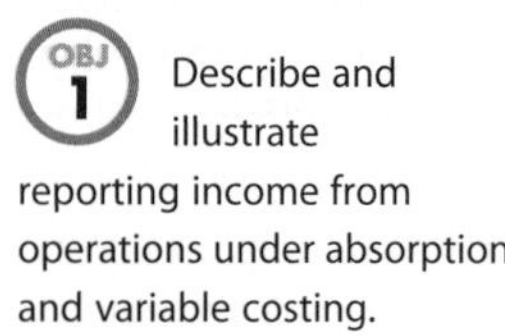
OBJ 1 Describe and illustrate reporting income from operations under absorption and variable costing.

Income from Operations Under Absorption Costing and Variable Costing

Income from operations is one of the most important items reported by a company. Depending on the decision-making needs of management, income from operations can be determined using absorption or variable costing.

Different regions of the world emphasize different approaches to reporting income. For example, Scandinavian companies have a strong variable costing tradition, while German cost accountants have developed some of the most advanced absorption costing practices in the world.

Absorption Costing

Absorption costing is required under generally accepted accounting principles for financial statements distributed to external users. Under absorption costing, the cost of goods manufactured includes direct materials, direct labor, and factory overhead costs. Both fixed and variable factory costs are included as part of factory overhead. In the financial statements, these costs are included in the cost of goods sold (income statement) and inventory (balance sheet).

The reporting of income from operations under absorption costing is as follows:

Sales	$XXX
Cost of goods sold	XXX
Gross profit	$XXX
Selling and administrative expenses	XXX
Income from operations	$XXX

The income statements illustrated in the preceding chapters of this text have used absorption costing.

Variable Costing

For internal use in decision making, managers often use variable costing. Under **variable costing**, sometimes called *direct costing*, the cost of goods manufactured includes only variable manufacturing costs. Thus, the cost of goods manufactured consists of the following:

- Direct materials
- Direct labor
- *Variable* factory overhead

Under variable costing, *fixed* factory overhead costs are not a part of the cost of goods manufactured. Instead, fixed factory overhead costs are treated as a period expense. Exhibit 1 illustrates the differences between absorption costing and variable costing.

EXHIBIT 1

Absorption Costing Versus Variable Costing

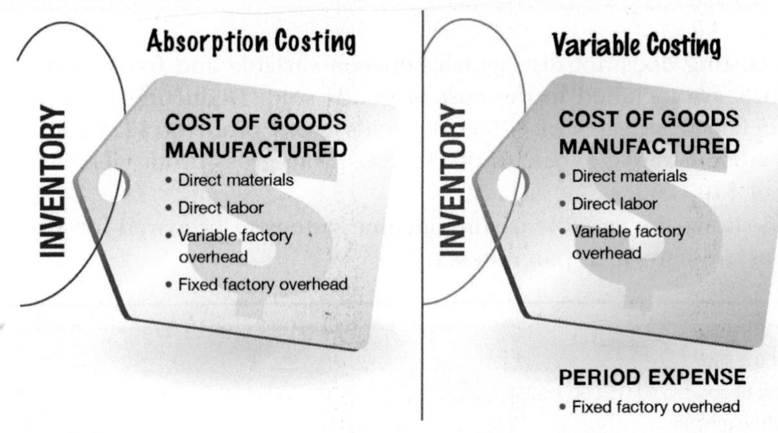

The reporting of income from operations under variable costing is as follows:

Sales		$XXX
Variable cost of goods sold		XXX
Manufacturing margin		$XXX
Variable selling and administrative expenses		XXX
Contribution margin		$XXX
Fixed costs:		
Fixed manufacturing costs	$XXX	
Fixed selling and administrative expenses	XXX	XXX
Income from operations		$XXX

Manufacturing margin is the excess of sales over variable cost of goods sold:

Manufacturing Margin = Sales – Variable Cost of Goods Sold

Variable cost of goods sold consists of direct materials, direct labor, and variable factory overhead for the units sold. **Contribution margin** is the excess of manufacturing margin over variable selling and administrative expenses:

Contribution Margin = Manufacturing Margin – Variable Selling and Administrative Expenses

Subtracting fixed costs from contribution margin yields *income from operations*:

Income from Operations = Contribution Margin – Fixed Costs

To illustrate variable costing and absorption costing, assume that Martinez Co. manufactures 15,000 units, which are sold at a price of $50. The related costs and expenses for Martinez are as follows:

	Total Cost	Number of Units	Unit Cost
Manufacturing costs:			
Variable	$375,000	15,000	$25
Fixed	150,000	15,000	10
Total	$525,000		$35
Selling and administrative expenses:			
Variable	$ 75,000	15,000	$ 5
Fixed	50,000		
Total	$125,000		

Exhibit 2 shows the absorption costing income statement prepared for Martinez. The computations are shown in parentheses.

EXHIBIT 2

Absorption Costing Income Statement

Sales (15,000 × $50)	$750,000
Cost of goods sold (15,000 × $35)	525,000
Gross profit	$225,000
Selling and administrative expenses ($75,000 + $50,000)	125,000
Income from operations	$100,000

Absorption costing does not distinguish between variable and fixed costs. All manufacturing costs are included in the cost of goods sold. Deducting the cost of goods sold of $525,000 from sales of $750,000 yields gross profit of $225,000. Deducting selling and administrative expenses of $125,000 from gross profit yields income from operations of $100,000.

Exhibit 3 shows the variable costing income statement prepared for Martinez. The computations are shown in parentheses.

EXHIBIT 3

Variable Costing Income Statement

Sales (15,000 × $50)		$750,000
Variable cost of goods sold (15,000 × $25)		375,000
Manufacturing margin		$375,000
Variable selling and administrative expenses (15,000 × $5)		75,000
Contribution margin		$300,000
Fixed costs:		
Fixed manufacturing costs	$150,000	
Fixed selling and administrative expenses	50,000	200,000
Income from operations		$100,000

Note:
The variable costing income statement includes only variable manufacturing costs in the cost of goods sold.

Variable costing income reports variable costs separately from fixed costs. Deducting the variable cost of goods sold of $375,000 from sales of $750,000 yields the manufacturing margin of $375,000. Deducting variable selling and administrative expenses of $75,000 from the manufacturing margin yields the contribution margin of $300,000. Deducting fixed costs of $200,000 from the contribution margin yields income from operations of $100,000.

The contribution margin reported in Exhibit 3 is the same as that used in Chapter 4. That is, the contribution margin is sales less variable costs and expenses. The only difference is that Exhibit 3 reports manufacturing margin before deducting variable selling and administrative expenses.

Example Exercise 5-1 Variable Costing

OBJ 1

Leone Company has the following information for March:

Sales	$450,000
Variable cost of goods sold	220,000
Fixed manufacturing costs	80,000
Variable selling and administrative expenses	50,000
Fixed selling and administrative expenses	35,000

Determine (a) the manufacturing margin, (b) the contribution margin, and (c) income from operations for Leone Company for the month of March.

Follow My Example 5-1

a. $230,000 ($450,000 – $220,000)
b. $180,000 ($230,000 – $50,000)
c. $65,000 ($180,000 – $80,000 – $35,000)

Practice Exercises: PE 5-1A, PE 5-1B

Units Manufactured Equal Units Sold

In Exhibits 2 and 3, Martinez manufactured and sold 15,000 units. Thus, the variable and absorption costing income statements reported the same income from operations of $100,000. When the number of units manufactured equals the number of units sold, income from operations will be the same under both methods.

Units Manufactured Exceed Units Sold

When units manufactured exceed the units sold, the variable costing income from operations will be *less* than it is for absorption costing. To illustrate, assume that only 12,000 units of the 15,000 units Martinez manufactured were sold.

Exhibit 4 shows the absorption and variable costing income statements when units manufactured exceed units sold.

EXHIBIT 4

Units Manufactured Exceed Units Sold

Variable Costing Income Statement		
Sales (12,000 × $50)		$600,000
Variable cost of goods sold:		
Variable cost of goods manufactured (15,000 × $25)	$375,000	
Less ending inventory (3,000 × $25)	75,000	
Variable cost of goods sold		300,000
Manufacturing margin		$300,000
Variable selling and administrative expenses (12,000 × $5)		60,000
Contribution margin		$240,000
Fixed costs:		
Fixed manufacturing costs	$150,000	
Fixed selling and administrative expenses	50,000	200,000
Income from operations		$ 40,000
Absorption Costing Income Statement		
Sales (12,000 × $50)		$600,000
Cost of goods sold:		
Cost of goods manufactured (15,000 × $35)	$525,000	
Less ending inventory (3,000 × $35)	105,000	
Cost of goods sold		420,000
Gross profit		$180,000
Selling and administrative expenses [(12,000 × $5) + $50,000]		110,000
Income from operations		$ 70,000

Exhibit 4 shows a $30,000 ($70,000 – $40,000) difference in income from operations. This difference is due to the fixed manufacturing costs. All of the $150,000 of fixed manufacturing costs is included as a period expense in the variable costing statement. However, the 3,000 units of ending inventory in the absorption costing statement includes $30,000 (3,000 units × $10) of fixed manufacturing costs. By being included in inventory, this $30,000 is thus excluded from the cost of goods sold. Thus, the absorption costing income from operations is $30,000 higher than the income from operations for variable costing.

Example Exercise 5-2 Variable Costing—Production Exceeds Sales

Fixed manufacturing costs are $40 per unit, and variable manufacturing costs are $120 per unit. Production was 125,000 units, while sales were 120,000 units. Determine (a) whether variable costing income from operations is less than or greater than absorption costing income from operations, and (b) the difference in variable costing and absorption costing income from operations.

Follow My Example 5-2

a. Variable costing income from operations is less than absorption costing income from operations.
b. $200,000 ($40 per unit × 5,000 units)

Practice Exercises: PE 5-2A, PE 5-2B

Units Manufactured Less Than Units Sold

When the units manufactured are less than the number of units sold, the variable costing income from operations will be *greater* than that of absorption costing. To illustrate, assume that beginning inventory, units manufactured, and units sold for Martinez were as follows:

Beginning inventory	5,000 units
Units manufactured during current period	10,000 units
Units sold during the current period at $50 per unit	15,000 units

Martinez's manufacturing costs and selling and administrative expenses are as follows:

	Total Cost	Number of Units	Unit Cost
Beginning inventory (5,000 units):			
Manufacturing costs:			
Variable	$125,000	5,000	$25
Fixed	50,000	5,000	10
Total	$175,000		$35
Current period (10,000 units):			
Manufacturing costs:			
Variable	$250,000	10,000	$25
Fixed	150,000	10,000	15
Total	$400,000		$40
Selling and administrative expenses:			
Variable	$ 75,000	15,000	$5
Fixed	50,000		
Total	$125,000		

Exhibit 5 shows the absorption and variable costing income statement for Martinez when units manufactured are less than units sold.

EXHIBIT 5

Units Manufactured Are Less Than Units Sold

Absorption Costing Income Statement		
Sales (15,000 × $50)		$750,000
Cost of goods sold:		
Beginning inventory (5,000 × $35)	$175,000	
Cost of goods manufactured (10,000 × $40)	400,000	
Cost of goods sold		575,000
Gross profit		$175,000
Selling and administrative expenses ($75,000 + $50,000)		125,000
Income from operations		$ 50,000
Variable Costing Income Statement		
Sales (15,000 × $50)		$750,000
Variable cost of goods sold:		
Beginning inventory (5,000 × $25)	$125,000	
Variable cost of goods manufactured (10,000 × $25)	250,000	
Variable cost of goods sold		375,000
Manufacturing margin		$375,000
Variable selling and administrative expenses (15,000 × $5)		75,000
Contribution margin		$300,000
Fixed costs:		
Fixed manufacturing costs	$150,000	
Fixed selling and administrative expenses	50,000	200,000
Income from operations		$100,000

Exhibit 5 shows a $50,000 ($100,000 – $50,000) difference in income from operations. This difference is due to the fixed manufacturing costs. The beginning inventory under absorption costing includes $50,000 (5,000 units × $10) of fixed manufacturing costs incurred in the preceding period. By being included in the beginning inventory, this $50,000 is included in the cost of goods sold for the current period. Under variable costing, this $50,000 was included as an expense in an income statement of a prior period. Thus, the variable costing income from operations is $50,000 higher than the income from operations for absorption costing.

Example Exercise 5-3 Variable Costing—Sales Exceed Production

The beginning inventory is 6,000 units. All of the units that were manufactured during the period and the 6,000 units of beginning inventory were sold. The beginning inventory fixed manufacturing costs are $60 per unit, and variable manufacturing costs are $300 per unit. Determine (a) whether variable costing income from operations is less than or greater than absorption costing income from operations, and (b) the difference in variable costing and absorption costing income from operations.

Follow My Example 5-3

a. Variable costing income from operations is greater than absorption costing income from operations.
b. $360,000 ($60 per unit × 6,000 units)

Practice Exercises: PE 5-3A, PE 5-3B

Effects on Income from Operations

The preceding examples illustrate the effects on income from operations of using absorption and variable costing. These effects are summarized in Exhibit 6.

EXHIBIT 6

Effects on Income from Operations under Absorption and Variable Costing

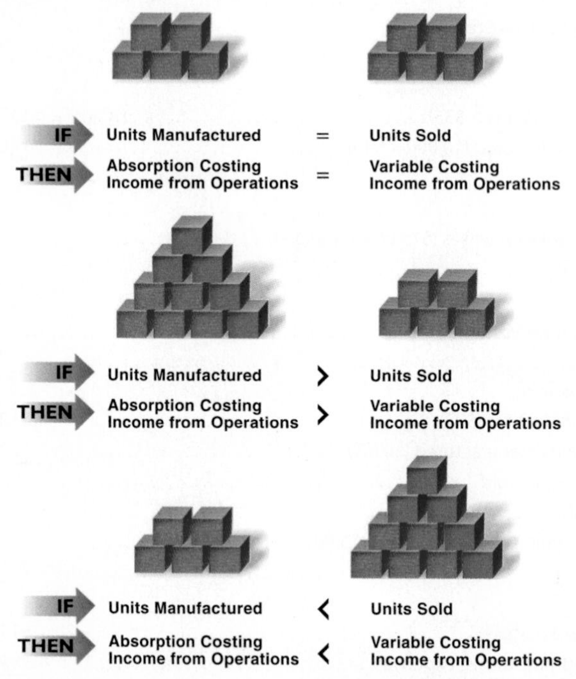

OBJ 2 Describe and illustrate the effects of absorption and variable costing on analyzing income from operations.

Income Analysis Under Absorption and Variable Costing

Whenever the units manufactured differ from the units sold, finished goods inventory is affected. When the units manufactured are greater than the units sold, finished goods inventory increases. Under absorption costing, a portion of this increase is related to the allocation of fixed manufacturing overhead to ending inventory. As a result, increases or decreases in income from operations can be due to changes in inventory levels. In analyzing income from operations, such increases and decreases could be misinterpreted as operating efficiencies or inefficiencies.

To illustrate, assume that Frand Manufacturing Company has no beginning inventory and sales are estimated to be 20,000 units at $75 per unit. Also, assume that sales will not change if more than 20,000 units are manufactured.

Frand's management is evaluating whether to manufacture 20,000 units (Proposal 1) or 25,000 units (Proposal 2). The costs and expenses related to each proposal follow.

Proposal 1: 20,000 Units to Be Manufactured and Sold

	Total Cost	Number of Units	Unit Cost
Manufacturing costs:			
Variable	$ 700,000	20,000	$35
Fixed	400,000	20,000	20*
Total	$1,100,000		$55
Selling and administrative expenses:			
Variable	$ 100,000	20,000	$ 5
Fixed	100,000		
Total	$ 200,000		

*$400,000 ÷ 20,000 units

Proposal 2: 25,000 Units to Be Manufactured and 20,000 Units to Be Sold

	Total Cost	Number of Units	Unit Cost
Manufacturing costs:			
Variable	$ 875,000	25,000	$35
Fixed	400,000	25,000	16*
Total	$1,275,000		$51
Selling and administrative expenses:			
Variable	$ 100,000	20,000	$ 5
Fixed	100,000		
Total	$ 200,000		

*$400,000 ÷ 25,000 units

The absorption costing income statements for each proposal are shown in Exhibit 7.

EXHIBIT 7

Absorption Costing Income Statements for Two Production Levels

Frand Manufacturing Company
Absorption Costing Income Statements

	Proposal 1 20,000 Units Manufactured	Proposal 2 25,000 Units Manufactured
Sales (20,000 units × $75)	$1,500,000	$1,500,000
Cost of goods sold:		
Cost of goods manufactured:		
(20,000 units × $55)	$1,100,000	
(25,000 units × $51)		$1,275,000
Less ending inventory:		
(5,000 units × $51)		255,000
Cost of goods sold	$1,100,000	$1,020,000
Gross profit	$ 400,000	$ 480,000
Selling and administrative expenses:		
($100,000 + $100,000)	200,000	200,000
Income from operations	$ 200,000	$ 280,000

Exhibit 7 shows that if Frand manufactures 25,000 units, sells 20,000 units, and adds the 5,000 units to finished goods inventory (Proposal 2), income from operations will be $280,000. In contrast, if Frand manufactures and sells 20,000 units (Proposal 1), income from operations will be $200,000. In other words, Frand can increase income from operations by $80,000 ($280,000 – $200,000) by simply increasing finished goods inventory by 5,000 units.

The $80,000 increase in income from operations under Proposal 2 is caused by the allocation of the fixed manufacturing costs of $400,000 over a greater number of units manufactured. Specifically, an increase in production from 20,000 units to 25,000 units means that the fixed manufacturing cost per unit decreases from $20 ($400,000 ÷ 20,000 units) to $16 ($400,000 ÷ 25,000 units). Thus, the cost of goods sold when 25,000 units are manufactured is $4 per unit less, or $80,000 less in total (20,000 units sold × $4). Since the cost of goods sold is less, income from operations is $80,000 more when 25,000 units rather than 20,000 units are manufactured.

Managers should be careful in analyzing income from operations under absorption costing when finished goods inventory changes. Increases in income from operations may be created by simply increasing finished goods inventory. Thus, managers could misinterpret such increases (or decreases) in income from operations as due to changes in sales volume, prices, or costs.

Under variable costing, income from operations is $200,000, regardless of whether 20,000 units or 25,000 units are manufactured. This is because no fixed manufacturing costs are allocated to the units manufactured. Instead, all fixed manufacturing costs are treated as a period expense.

To illustrate, Exhibit 8 shows the variable costing income statements for Frand for the production of 20,000 units, 25,000 units, and 30,000 units. In each case, the income from operations is $200,000.

EXHIBIT 8

Variable Costing Income Statements for Three Production Levels

Frand Manufacturing Company
Variable Costing Income Statements

	20,000 Units Manufactured	25,000 Units Manufactured	30,000 Units Manufactured
Sales (20,000 units × $75)	$1,500,000	$1,500,000	$1,500,000
Variable cost of goods sold:			
Variable cost of goods manufactured:			
(20,000 units × $35)	$ 700,000		
(25,000 units × $35)		$ 875,000	
(30,000 units × $35)			$1,050,000
Less ending inventory:			
(0 units × $35)	0		
(5,000 units × $35)		175,000	
(10,000 units × $35)			350,000
Variable cost of goods sold	$ 700,000	$ 700,000	$ 700,000
Manufacturing margin	$ 800,000	$ 800,000	$ 800,000
Variable selling and administrative expenses	100,000	100,000	100,000
Contribution margin	$ 700,000	$ 700,000	$ 700,000
Fixed costs:			
Fixed manufacturing costs	$ 400,000	$ 400,000	$ 400,000
Fixed selling and administrative expenses	100,000	100,000	100,000
Total fixed costs	$ 500,000	$ 500,000	$ 500,000
Income from operations	$ 200,000	$ 200,000	$ 200,000

Integrity, Objectivity, and Ethics in Business

TAKING AN "ABSORPTION HIT"

Aligning production to demand is a critical decision in business. Managers must not allow the temporary benefits of excess production through higher absorption of fixed costs to guide their decisions. Likewise, if demand falls, production should be dropped and inventory liquidated to match the new demand level, even though earnings will be penalized. The following interchange provides an example of an appropriate response to lowered demand for H.J. Heinz Company:

Analyst's question: *It seems.... that you're guiding to a little bit of a drop in performance between 3Q (third Quarter) and 4Q (fourth Quarter).... if so, maybe you could walk us through some of the drivers of that relative softness.*

Heinz executive's response: *No, I think, frankly, we're real pleased with the performance in the business.... We're also aggressively taking out inventory in the fourth quarter. And as you know, as you reduce inventory, you take an absorption hit. You're pulling basically fixed costs off the balance sheet into the P&L and there's a hit associated with that, but we think that's the right thing to do, to pull inventory out and to drive cash flow. So now, we feel very good about the business and feel very good about the fact that we're taking it to the middle of the range and taking up the bottom end of our guidance.*

Management operating with integrity will seek the tangible benefits of reducing inventory, even though there may be an adverse impact on published financial statements caused by absorption costing.

Source of question and response from http://seekingalpha.com/article/375151-h-j-heinz-management-discusses-q3-2012-results-earnings-call-transcript?page=6&p=qanda. Accessed February 2012.

As shown, absorption costing may encourage managers to produce inventory. This is because producing inventory absorbs fixed manufacturing costs, which increases income from operations. However, producing inventory leads to higher handling, storage, financing, and obsolescence costs. For this reason, many accountants believe that variable costing should be used by management for evaluating operating performance.

Example Exercise 5-4 Analyzing Income Under Absorption and Variable Costing

Variable manufacturing costs are $100 per unit, and fixed manufacturing costs are $50,000. Sales are estimated to be 4,000 units.

a. How much would absorption costing income from operations differ between a plan to produce 4,000 units and a plan to produce 5,000 units?
b. How much would variable costing income from operations differ between the two production plans?

Follow My Example 5-4

a. $10,000 greater in producing 5,000 units. 4,000 units × ($12.50[1] – $10.00[2]), or [1,000 units × ($50,000 ÷ 5,000 units)].
b. There would be no difference in variable costing income from operations between the two plans.

[1]$50,000 ÷ 4,000 units
[2]$50,000 ÷ 5,000 units

Practice Exercises: PE 5-4A, PE 5-4B

Using Absorption and Variable Costing

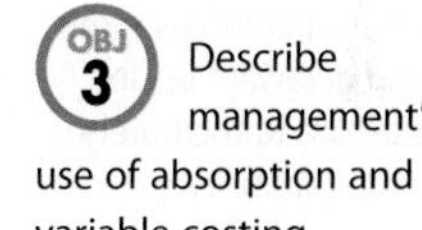

Describe management's use of absorption and variable costing.

Each decision-making situation should be carefully analyzed in deciding whether absorption or variable costing reporting would be more useful. As a basis for discussion, the use of absorption and variable costing in the following decision-making situations is described:

- Controlling costs
- Pricing products
- Planning production
- Analyzing contribution margins
- Analyzing market segments

The role of accounting reports in these decision-making situations is shown in Exhibit 9.

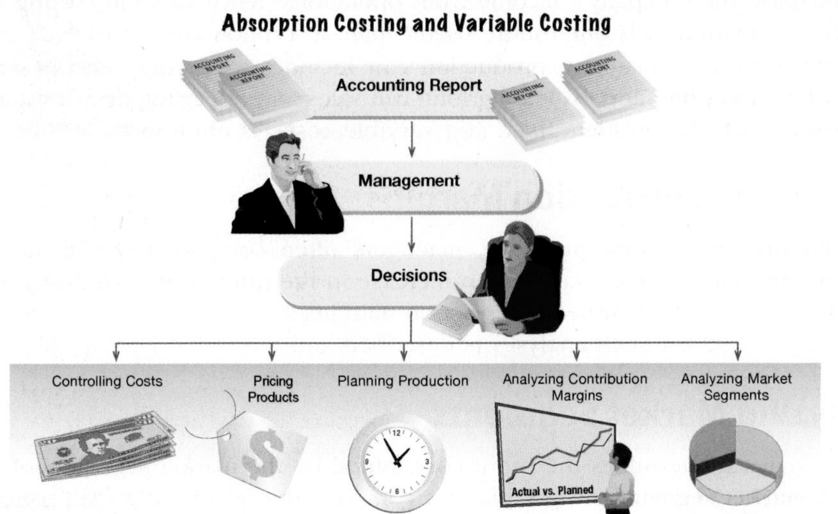

EXHIBIT 9

Accounting Reports and Management Decisions

Controlling Costs

All costs are controllable in the long run by someone within a business. However, not all costs are controllable at the same level of management. For example, plant supervisors control the use of direct materials in their departments. They have no control, though, over insurance costs related to the property, plant, and equipment.

For a level of management, **controllable costs** are costs that can be influenced (increased or decreased) by management at that level. **Noncontrollable costs** are costs that another level of management controls. This distinction is useful for reporting costs to those responsible for their control.

Variable manufacturing costs are controlled by operating management. In contrast, fixed manufacturing overhead costs such as the salaries of production supervisors are normally controlled at a higher level of management. Likewise, control of the variable and fixed operating expenses usually involves different levels of management. Since fixed costs and expenses are reported separately under variable costing, variable costing reports are normally more useful than absorption costing reports for controlling costs.

Pricing Products

Major hotel chains, such as **Marriott**, **Hilton**, and **Hyatt**, often provide "weekend getaway" packages, which provide discounts for weekend stays in their city hotels. As long as the weekend rates exceed the variable costs, the "weekend getaway" pricing will contribute to the hotel's short-run profitability.

Many factors enter into determining the selling price of a product. However, the cost of making the product is significant in all pricing decisions.

In the short run, fixed costs cannot be avoided. Thus, the selling price of a product should at least be equal to the variable costs of making and selling it. Any price above this minimum selling price contributes to covering fixed costs and generating income. Since variable costing reports variable and fixed costs and expenses separately, it is often more useful than absorption costing for setting short-run prices.

In the long run, a company must set its selling price high enough to cover all costs and expenses (variable and fixed) and generate income. Since absorption costing includes fixed and variable costs in the cost of manufacturing a product, absorption costing is often more useful than variable costing for setting long-term prices.

Planning Production

In the short run, planning production is limited to existing capacity. In many cases, operating decisions must be made quickly before opportunities are lost.

To illustrate, a company with seasonal demand for its products may have an opportunity to obtain an off-season order that will not interfere with its current production schedule. The relevant factors for such a short-run decision are the additional revenues and the additional variable costs associated with the order. If the revenues from the order exceed the related variable costs, the order will increase contribution margin and, thus, increase the company's income from operations. Since variable costing reports contribution margin, it is often more useful than absorption costing in such cases.

In the long run, planning production can include expanding existing capacity. Thus, when analyzing and evaluating long-run sales and operating decisions, absorption costing, which considers fixed and variable costs, is often more useful.

Analyzing Contribution Margins

For planning and control purposes, managers often compare planned and actual contribution margins. For example, an increase in the price of fuel could have a significant impact on the planned contribution margins of an airline. The use of variable costing as a basis for such analyses is described and illustrated later in this chapter.

Analyzing Market Segments

Market analysis determines the profit contributed by the market segments of a company. A **market segment** is a portion of a company that can be analyzed using sales,

Business  **Connection**

DIRECT MATERIALS COST

Apple has become one of the most financially successful companies of the past decade by using variable cost information to carefully price its iPod family of products. The cost of an iPod consists almost entirely of direct materials and other variable costs. For example, Apple's sixth generation iPod nano was reported to have a total cost of $45.10, of which $43.73 is direct materials. Thus, when designing a new iPod or iPhone, Apple has to carefully balance product features with the variable cost of direct materials. For the sixth generation iPod nano, Apple added touch screen technology and a more powerful battery, while removing the camera feature. This careful balancing of cost and functionality allowed Apple to offer a new generation of iPod nano at an enticing price, highlighting how Apple's awareness and understanding of variable cost information has been a key element of the company's financial success.

Source: A. Rassweiler, "ISuppli Estimates New iPod Nano Bill of Materials at $43.73," iSuppli, Applied Market Intelligence.

costs, and expenses to determine its profitability. Examples of market segments include sales territories, products, salespersons, and customers. Variable costing as an aid in decision making regarding market segments is discussed next.

Analyzing Market Segments

Use variable costing for analyzing market segments, including product, territories, and salespersons segments.

Companies can report income for internal decision making using either absorption or variable costing. Absorption costing is often used for long-term analysis of market segments. This type of analysis is illustrated in Chapter 11. Variable costing is often used for short-term analysis of market segments. In this section, segment profitability reporting using variable costing is described and illustrated.

Most companies prepare variable costing reports for each product. These reports are often used for product pricing and deciding whether to discontinue a product. In addition, variable costing reports may be prepared for geographic areas, customers, distribution channels, or salespersons. A *distribution channel* is the method for selling a product to a customer.

To illustrate analysis of market segments using variable costing, the following data for the month ending March 31 for Camelot Fragrance Company are used:

Camelot Fragrance Company
Sales and Production Data
For the Month Ended March 31

	Northern Territory	Southern Territory	Total
Sales:			
Gwenevere	$60,000	$30,000	$ 90,000
Lancelot	20,000	50,000	70,000
Total territory sales	$80,000	$80,000	$160,000
Variable production costs:			
Gwenevere (12% of sales)	$ 7,200	$ 3,600	$ 10,800
Lancelot (12% of sales)	2,400	6,000	8,400
Total variable production cost by territory	$ 9,600	$ 9,600	$ 19,200
Promotion costs:			
Gwenevere (variable at 30% of sales)	$18,000	$ 9,000	$ 27,000
Lancelot (variable at 20% of sales)	4,000	10,000	14,000
Total promotion cost by territory	$22,000	$19,000	$ 41,000
Sales commissions:			
Gwenevere (variable at 20% of sales)	$12,000	$ 6,000	$ 18,000
Lancelot (variable at 10% of sales)	2,000	5,000	7,000
Total sales commissions by territory	$14,000	$11,000	$ 25,000

Camelot Fragrance manufactures and sells the Gwenevere perfume for women and the Lancelot cologne for men. To simplify, no inventories are assumed to exist at the beginning or end of March.

Sales Territory Profitability Analysis

An income statement presenting the contribution margin by sales territories is often used in evaluating past performance and in directing future sales efforts. Sales territory profitability analysis may lead management to do the following:

- Reduce costs in lower-profit sales territories
- Increase sales efforts in higher-profit territories

To illustrate sales territory profitability analysis, Exhibit 10 shows the contribution margin for the Northern and Southern territories of Camelot Fragrance Company. As Exhibit 10 indicates, the Northern Territory is generating $34,400 of contribution margin, while the Southern Territory is generating $40,400 of contribution margin.

EXHIBIT 10

Contribution Margin by Sales Territory Report

Camelot Fragrance Company
Contribution Margin by Sales Territory
For the Month Ended March 31

	Northern Territory		Southern Territory	
Sales		$80,000		$80,000
Variable cost of goods sold		9,600		9,600
Manufacturing margin		$70,400		$70,400
Variable selling expenses:				
Promotion costs	$22,000		$19,000	
Sales commissions	14,000	36,000	11,000	30,000
Contribution margin		$34,400		$40,400
Contribution margin ratio		43%		50.5%

In addition to the contribution margin, the contribution margin ratio for each territory is shown in Exhibit 10. The contribution margin ratio is computed as follows:

$$\text{Contribution Margin Ratio} = \frac{\text{Contribution Margin}}{\text{Sales}}$$

Exhibit 10 indicates that the Northern Territory has a contribution margin ratio of 43% ($34,400 ÷ $80,000). In contrast, the Southern Territory has a contribution margin ratio of 50.5% ($40,400 ÷ $80,000).

The Coca-Cola Company earns over 75% of its total corporate profits outside of the United States. As a result, Coca-Cola management continues to expand operations and sales efforts around the world.

The difference in profit of the Northern and Southern territories is due to the difference in sales mix between the territories. **Sales mix**, sometimes referred to as *product mix*, is the relative amount of sales among the various products. The sales mix is computed by dividing the sales of each product by the total sales of each territory. Sales mix of the Northern and Southern territories is as follows:

	Northern Territory		Southern Territory	
Product	**Sales**	**Sales Mix**	**Sales**	**Sales Mix**
Gwenevere	$60,000	75%	$30,000	37.5%
Lancelot	20,000	25	50,000	62.5
Total	$80,000	100%	$80,000	100.0%

As shown, 62.5% of the Southern Territory's sales are sales of Lancelot. Since the Southern Territory's contribution margin ($40,400) is higher (as shown in Exhibit 10) than that of the Northern Territory ($34,400), Lancelot must be more profitable than Gwenevere. To verify this, product profitability analysis is performed.

Product Profitability Analysis

A company should focus its sales efforts on products that will provide the maximum total contribution margin. In doing so, product profitability analysis is often used by management in making decisions regarding product sales and promotional efforts.

To illustrate product profitability analysis, Exhibit 11 shows the contribution margin by product for Camelot Fragrance Company.

EXHIBIT 11

Contribution Margin by Product Line Report

Camelot Fragrance Company
Contribution Margin by Product Line
For the Month Ended March 31

	Gwenevere		Lancelot	
Sales		$90,000		$70,000
Variable cost of goods sold		10,800		8,400
Manufacturing margin		$79,200		$61,600
Variable selling expenses:				
Promotion costs	$27,000		$14,000	
Sales commissions	18,000	45,000	7,000	21,000
Contribution margin		$34,200		$40,600
Contribution margin ratio		38%		58%

Exhibit 11 indicates that Lancelot's contribution margin ratio (58%) is greater than Gwenevere's (38%). Lancelot's higher contribution margin ratio is a result of its lower promotion and sales commissions costs. Thus, management should consider the following:

- Emphasizing Lancelot in its marketing plans
- Reducing Gwenevere's promotion and sales commissions costs
- Increasing the price of Gwenevere

Salesperson Profitability Analysis

A salesperson profitability report is useful in evaluating sales performance. Such a report normally includes total sales, variable cost of goods sold, variable selling expenses, contribution margin, and contribution margin ratio for each salesperson.

Exhibit 12 illustrates such a salesperson profitability report for three salespersons in the Northern Territory of Camelot Fragrance Company. The exhibit indicates that Beth Williams produced the greatest contribution margin ($15,200), but had the lowest contribution margin ratio (38%). Beth sold $40,000 of product, which is twice as much product as the other two salespersons. However, Beth sold only Gwenevere, which has the lowest contribution margin ratio (from Exhibit 11). The other two salespersons sold equal amounts of Gwenevere and Lancelot. As a result, Inez Rodriguez and Deshawn Thomas had higher contribution margin ratios because they sold more Lancelot. The Northern Territory manager could use this report to encourage Inez and Deshawn to sell more total product, while encouraging Beth to sell more Lancelot.

EXHIBIT 12

Contribution Margin by Salesperson Report

Camelot Fragrance Company
Contribution Margin by Salesperson—Northern Territory
For the Month Ended March 31

	Inez Rodriguez	Deshawn Thomas	Beth Williams	Northern Territory—Total
Sales	$20,000	$20,000	$40,000	$80,000
Variable cost of goods sold	2,400	2,400	4,800	9,600
Manufacturing margin	$17,600	$17,600	$35,200	$70,400
Variable selling expenses:				
Promotion costs	$ 5,000	$ 5,000	$12,000	$22,000
Sales commissions	3,000	3,000	8,000	14,000
	$ 8,000	$ 8,000	$20,000	$36,000
Contribution margin	$ 9,600	$ 9,600	$15,200	$34,400
Contribution margin ratio	48%	48%	38%	43%
Sales mix (% Lancelot sales)	50%	50%	0	25%

Other factors should also be considered in evaluating salespersons' performance. For example, sales growth rates, years of experience, customer service, territory size, and actual performance compared to budgeted performance may also be important.

Example Exercise 5-5 Contribution Margin by Segment

OBJ 4

The following data are for Moss Creek Apparel:

	East	West
Sales volume (units):		
Shirts	6,000	5,000
Shorts	4,000	8,000
Sales price:		
Shirts	$12	$13
Shorts	$16	$18
Variable cost per unit:		
Shirts	$ 7	$ 7
Shorts	$10	$10

Determine the contribution margin for (a) Shorts and (b) the West Region.

Follow My Example 5-5

a. $88,000 [4,000 units × ($16 – $10)] + [8,000 units × ($18 – $10)]
b. $94,000 [5,000 units × ($13 – $7)] + [8,000 units × ($18 – $10)]

Practice Exercises: PE 5-5A, PE 5-5B

Service Focus

CHIPOTLE MEXICAN GRILL CONTRIBUTION MARGIN BY STORE

Chipotle Mexican Grill's annual report identifies revenues and costs for its company-owned restaurant operations. Assume that food, beverage, packaging, and labor are variable and that occupancy and other expenses are fixed. A contribution margin and income from operations can be constructed for the restaurants as follows for the year ended December 31, 2013 (in thousands):

Sales		$3,214,591
Variable restaurant expenses:		
Food, beverage, and packaging	$1,073,514	
Labor	739,800	
Total variable restaurant operating costs		1,813,314
Contribution margin		$1,401,277
Occupancy and other expenses		546,508
Income from operations		$ 854,769

The annual report also indicates that Chipotle Mexican Grill has 1,595 restaurants, all company-owned. Dividing the numbers above by 1,595 yields the contribution margin and income from operations per restaurant as follows (in thousands):

Sales	$2,015
Variable restaurant expenses	1,137
Contribution margin	$ 878
Occupancy and other expenses	343
Income from operations	$ 535

Chipotle Mexican Grill can use this information for pricing products; evaluating the sensitivity of store profitability to changes in sales volume, prices, and costs; and analyzing profitability by geographic segment.

Source: Chipotle Mexican Grill, Inc. Form 10-K. Annual Report pursuant to Section 13 or 15(d) of the Securities Exchange Act of 1934. For the fiscal year ended December 31, 2013. Securities and Exchange Commission, Washington D.C. 20549.

Contribution Margin Analysis

OBJ 5 Use variable costing for analyzing and explaining changes in contribution margin as a result of quantity and price factors.

Managers often use contribution margin in planning and controlling operations. In doing so, managers use contribution margin analysis. **Contribution margin analysis** focuses on explaining the differences between planned and actual contribution margins.

Contribution margin is defined as sales less variable costs. Thus, a difference between the planned and actual contribution margin may be caused by an increase or a decrease in:

- Sales
- Variable costs

An increase or a decrease in sales or variable costs may in turn be due to an increase or a decrease in the:

- Number of units sold
- Unit sales price or unit cost

The effects of the preceding factors on sales or variable costs may be stated as follows:

- **Quantity factor:** The effect of a difference in the number of units sold, assuming no change in unit sales price or unit cost. The *sales quantity factor* and the *variable cost quantity factor* are computed as follows:

Sales Quantity Factor = (Actual Units Sold − Planned Units of Sales) × Planned Sales Price

Variable Cost Quantity Factor = (Planned Units of Sales − Actual Units Sold) × Planned Unit Cost

The preceding factors are computed so that a positive amount increases contribution margin and a negative amount decreases contribution margin.

- **Unit price factor** or *unit cost factor*: The effect of a difference in unit sales price or unit cost on the number of units sold. The unit price factor and unit cost factor are computed as follows:

Unit Price Factor = (Actual Selling Price per Unit – Planned Selling Price per Unit) × Actual Units Sold

Unit Cost Factor = (Planned Cost per Unit – Actual Cost per Unit) × Actual Units Sold

The preceding factors are computed so that a positive amount increases contribution margin and a negative amount decreases contribution margin.

The effects of the preceding factors on contribution margin are summarized in Exhibit 13.

EXHIBIT 13

Contribution Margin Analysis

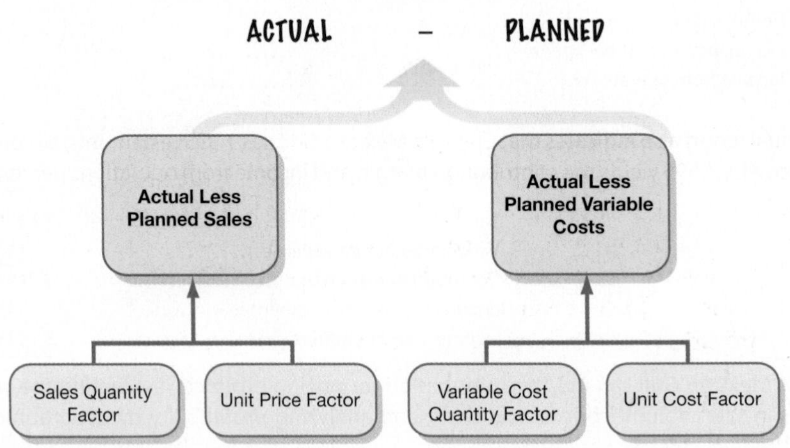

To illustrate, the following data for the year ended December 31, for Noble Inc., which sells a single product, are used:[1]

	Actual	Planned
Sales	$937,500	$800,000
Less: Variable cost of goods sold	$425,000	$350,000
Variable selling and administrative expenses	162,500	125,000
Total	$587,500	$475,000
Contribution margin	$350,000	$325,000
Number of units sold	125,000	100,000
Per unit:		
Sales price	$7.50	$8.00
Variable cost of goods sold	3.40	3.50
Variable selling and administrative expenses	1.30	1.25

Exhibit 14 shows the contribution margin analysis report for Noble Inc. for the year ended December 31. The exhibit indicates that the favorable difference of $25,000 ($350,000 – $325,000) between the actual and planned contribution margins was due in large part to an increase in the quantity sold (sales quantity factor) of $200,000. This $200,000 increase was partially offset by a decrease in the unit sales price (unit price factor) of $62,500 and an increase in the amount of variable costs of $112,500 ($75,000 + $37,500).

[1] To simplify, it is assumed that Noble Inc. sells a single product. The analysis would be more complex, but the principles would be the same, if more than one product were sold.

Noble Inc. Contribution Margin Analysis For the Year Ended December 31		
Planned contribution margin		$325,000
Effect of changes in sales:		
Sales quantity factor (125,000 units – 100,000 units) × $8.00	$200,000	
Unit price factor ($7.50 – $8.00) × 125,000 units	–62,500	
Total effect of changes in sales		137,500
Effect of changes in variable cost of goods sold:		
Variable cost quantity factor (100,000 units – 125,000 units) × $3.50	–$ 87,500	
Unit cost factor ($3.50 – $3.40) × 125,000 units	12,500	
Total effect of changes in variable cost of goods sold		–75,000
Effect of changes in selling and administrative expenses:		
Variable cost quantity factor (100,000 units – 125,000 units) × $1.25	–$ 31,250	
Unit cost factor ($1.25 – $1.30) × 125,000 units	–6,250	
Total effect of changes in selling and administrative expenses		–37,500
Actual contribution margin		$350,000

EXHIBIT 14

Contribution Margin Analysis Report

The contribution margin analysis reports are useful to management in evaluating past performance and in planning future operations. For example, the impact of the $0.50 reduction in the unit sales price by Noble Inc. on the number of units sold and on the total sales for the year is useful information in determining whether further price reductions might be desirable.

The contribution margin analysis report also highlights the impact of changes in unit variable costs and expenses. For example, the $0.05 increase in the unit variable selling and administrative expenses might be a result of increased advertising expenditures. If so, the increase in the number of units sold could be attributed to both the $0.50 price reduction and the increased advertising.

***Example Exercise 5-6* Contribution Margin Analysis**

The actual price for a product was $48 per unit, while the planned price was $40 per unit. The volume increased by 5,000 units to 60,000 actual total units. Determine (a) the quantity factor and (b) the price factor for sales.

Follow My Example 5-6

a. $200,000 increase in sales (5,000 units × $40 per unit)
b. $480,000 increase in sales [($48 – $40) × 60,000 units]

Practice Exercises: PE 5-6A, PE 5-6B

Variable Costing for Service Firms

OBJ 6 Describe and illustrate the use of variable costing for service firms.

Variable costing and the use of variable costing for manufacturing firms have been discussed earlier in this chapter. Service companies also use variable costing, contribution margin analysis, and segment analysis.

Reporting Income from Operations Using Variable Costing for a Service Company

Unlike a manufacturing company, a service company does not make or sell a product. Thus, service companies do not have inventory. Since service companies have no inventory, they do not use absorption costing to allocate fixed costs. In addition, variable costing reports of service companies do not report a manufacturing margin.

To illustrate variable costing for a service company, Blue Skies Airlines Inc., which operates as a small commercial airline, is used. The variable and fixed costs of Blue Skies are shown in Exhibit 15.

EXHIBIT 15

Costs of Blue Skies Airlines Inc.

Cost	Amount	Cost Behavior	Activity Base
Depreciation expense	$3,600,000	Fixed	
Food and beverage service expense	444,000	Variable	Number of passengers
Fuel expense	4,080,000	Variable	Number of miles flown
Rental expense	800,000	Fixed	
Selling expense	3,256,000	Variable	Number of passengers
Wages expense	6,120,000	Variable	Number of miles flown

As discussed in Chapter 4, a cost is classified as a fixed or variable cost according to how it changes relative to an activity base. A common activity for a manufacturing firm is the number of units produced. In contrast, most service companies use several activity bases.

To illustrate, Blue Skies uses the activity base *number of passengers* for food and beverage service and selling expenses. Blue Skies uses *number of miles flown* for fuel and wage expenses.

The variable costing income statement for Blue Skies, assuming revenue of $19,238,000, is shown in Exhibit 16.

EXHIBIT 16

Variable Costing Income Statement for a Service Company

Blue Skies Airlines Inc.
Variable Costing Income Statement
For the Month Ended April 30, 2016

Revenue		$19,238,000
Variable costs:		
Fuel expense	$4,080,000	
Wages expense	6,120,000	
Food and beverage service expense	444,000	
Selling expense	3,256,000	
Total variable costs		13,900,000
Contribution margin		$ 5,338,000
Fixed costs:		
Depreciation expense	$3,600,000	
Rental expense	800,000	
Total fixed costs		4,400,000
Income from operations		$ 938,000

Unlike a manufacturing company, Exhibit 16 does not report cost of goods sold, inventory, or manufacturing margin. However, as shown in Exhibit 16, contribution margin is reported separately from income from operations.

Market Segment Analysis for Service Company

A contribution margin report for service companies can be used to analyze and evaluate market segments. Typical segments for various service companies are shown in Exhibit 17.

Service Industry	Market Segments
Electric power	Regions, customer types (industrial, consumer)
Banking	Customer types (commercial, retail), products (loans, savings accounts)
Airlines	Products (passengers, cargo), routes
Railroads	Products (commodity type), routes
Hotels	Hotel properties
Telecommunications	Customer type (commercial, retail), service type (voice, data)
Health care	Procedure, payment type (Medicare, insured)

EXHIBIT 17

Service Industry Market Segments

To illustrate, a contribution margin report segmented by route is used for Blue Skies Airlines Inc. In preparing the report, the following data for April are used:

	Chicago/Atlanta	Atlanta/LA	LA/Chicago
Average ticket price per passenger	$400	$1,075	$805
Total passengers served	16,000	7,000	6,600
Total miles flown	56,000	88,000	60,000

The variable costs per unit are as follows:

Fuel	$ 20 per mile
Wages	30 per mile
Food and beverage service	15 per passenger
Selling	110 per passenger

A contribution margin report for Blue Skies is shown in Exhibit 18. The report is segmented by the routes (city pairs) flown.

Blue Skies Airlines Inc.
Contribution Margin by Route
For the Month Ended April 30

	Chicago/ Atlanta	Atlanta/ Los Angeles	Los Angeles/ Chicago	Total
Revenue				
(Ticket price × No. of passengers)	$ 6,400,000	$ 7,525,000	$ 5,313,000	$19,238,000
Aircraft fuel				
($20 × No. of miles flown)	(1,120,000)	(1,760,000)	(1,200,000)	(4,080,000)
Wages and benefits				
($30 × No. of miles flown)	(1,680,000)	(2,640,000)	(1,800,000)	(6,120,000)
Food and beverage service				
($15 × No. of passengers)	(240,000)	(105,000)	(99,000)	(444,000)
Selling expenses				
($110 × No. of passengers)	(1,760,000)	(770,000)	(726,000)	(3,256,000)
Contribution margin......................	$ 1,600,000	$ 2,250,000	$ 1,488,000	$ 5,338,000
Contribution margin ratio* (rounded)	25%	30%	28%	28%

*Contribution margin/revenue

EXHIBIT 18

Contribution Margin by Segment Report for a Service Company

Exhibit 18 indicates that the Chicago/Atlanta route has the lowest contribution margin ratio of 25%. In contrast, the Atlanta/Los Angeles route has the highest contribution margin ratio of 30%.

Contribution Margin Analysis

Blue Skies Airlines Inc. is also used to illustrate contribution margin analysis. Specifically, assume that Blue Skies decides to try to improve the contribution margin of its Chicago/Atlanta route during May by decreasing ticket prices. Thus, Blue Skies decreases the ticket price from $400 to $380 beginning May 1. As a result, the number of tickets sold (passengers) increased from 16,000 to 20,000. However, the cost per mile also increased during May from $20 to $22 due to increasing fuel prices.

The actual and planned results for the Chicago/Atlanta route during May follow. The planned amounts are based on the April results without considering the price change or cost per mile increase. The highlighted numbers indicate changes during May.

	Chicago/Atlanta Route	
	Actual, May	Planned, May
Revenue	$7,600,000	$6,400,000
Less variable expenses:		
Aircraft fuel	$1,232,000	$1,120,000
Wages and benefits	1,680,000	1,680,000
Food and beverage service	300,000	240,000
Selling expenses and commissions	2,200,000	1,760,000
Total	$5,412,000	$4,800,000
Contribution margin	$2,188,000	$1,600,000
Contribution margin ratio	29%	25%
Number of miles flown	56,000	56,000
Number of passengers flown	20,000	16,000
Per unit:		
Ticket price	$380	$400
Fuel expense	22	20
Wages expense	30	30
Food and beverage service expense	15	15
Selling expense	110	110

Using the preceding data, a contribution margin analysis report can be prepared for the Chicago/Atlanta route for May as shown in Exhibit 19. Since the planned and actual wages and benefits expense are the same ($1,680,000), its quantity and unit cost factors are not included in Exhibit 19.

EXHIBIT 19

Contribution Margin Analysis Report—Service Company

Blue Skies Airlines Inc.
Contribution Margin Analysis
Chicago/Atlanta Route
For the Month Ended May 31

Planned contribution margin		$1,600,000
Effect of changes in revenue:		
Revenue quantity factor (20,000 pass. – 16,000 pass.) × $400	$1,600,000	
Unit price factor ($380 – $400) × 20,000 passengers	(400,000)	
Total effect of changes in revenue		1,200,000
Effect of changes in fuel cost:		
Variable cost quantity factor (56,000 miles – 56,000 miles) × $20	$ 0	
Unit cost factor ($20 – $22) × 56,000 miles	(112,000)	
Total effect of changes in fuel costs		(112,000)
Effect of changes in food and beverage expenses:		
Variable cost quantity factor (16,000 pass. – 20,000 pass.) × $15	$ (60,000)	
Unit cost factor ($15 – $15) × 20,000 passengers	0	
Total effect of changes in food and beverage expenses		(60,000)
Effect of changes in selling and commission expenses:		
Variable cost quantity factor (16,000 pass. – 20,000 pass.) × $110	$ (440,000)	
Unit cost factor ($110 – $110) × 20,000 passengers	0	
Total effect of changes in selling and administrative expenses		(440,000)
Actual contribution margin		$2,188,000

Exhibit 19 indicates that the price decrease generated an additional $1,200,000 in revenue. This consists of $1,600,000 from an increased number of passengers (revenue quantity factor) and a $400,000 revenue reduction from the decrease in ticket price (unit price factor).

The increased fuel costs (by $2 per mile) reduced the contribution margin by $112,000 (unit cost factor). The increased number of passengers also increased the food and beverage service costs by $60,000 and the selling costs by $440,000 (variable cost quantity factors). The net increase in contribution margin is $588,000 ($2,188,000 – $1,600,000).

At a Glance 5

Describe and illustrate reporting income from operations under absorption and variable costing.

Key Points Under absorption costing, the cost of goods manufactured is comprised of all direct materials, direct labor, and factory overhead costs (both fixed and variable). Under variable costing, the cost of goods manufactured is composed of only variable costs: direct materials, direct labor, and variable factory overhead costs. Fixed factory overhead costs are considered a period expense.

The variable costing income statement is structured differently than a traditional absorption costing income statement. Sales less variable cost of goods sold is presented as manufacturing margin. Manufacturing margin less variable selling and administrative expenses is presented as contribution margin. Contribution margin less fixed costs is presented as income from operations.

Learning Outcomes	*Example Exercises*	*Practice Exercises*
• Describe the difference between absorption and variable costing.		
• Prepare a variable costing income statement for a manufacturer.	**EE5-1**	**PE5-1A, 5-1B**
• Evaluate the difference between the variable and absorption costing income statements when production exceeds sales.	**EE5-2**	**PE5-2A, 5-2B**
• Evaluate the difference between the variable and absorption costing income statements when sales exceed production.	**EE5-3**	**PE5-3A, 5-3B**

Describe and illustrate the effects of absorption and variable costing on analyzing income from operations.

Key Points Management should be aware of the effects of changes in inventory levels on income from operations reported under variable costing and absorption costing. If absorption costing is used, managers could misinterpret increases or decreases in income from operations due to changes in inventory levels to be the result of operating efficiencies or inefficiencies.

Learning Outcome	*Example Exercises*	*Practice Exercises*
• Determine absorption costing and variable costing income under different planned levels of production for a given sales level.	**EE5-4**	**PE5-4A, 5-4B**

Describe management's use of absorption and variable costing.

Key Points Variable costing is especially useful at the operating level of management because the amount of variable manufacturing costs are controllable at this level. The fixed factory overhead costs are ordinarily controllable by a higher level of management.

In the short run, variable costing may be useful in establishing the selling price of a product. This price should be at least equal to the variable costs of making and selling the product. In the long run, however, absorption costing is useful in establishing selling prices because all costs must be covered and a reasonable amount of operating income earned.

Learning Outcomes	Example Exercises	Practice Exercises
• Describe management's use of variable and absorption costing for controlling costs, pricing products, planning production, analyzing contribution margins, and analyzing market segments.		

Use variable costing for analyzing market segments, including product, territories, and salespersons segments.

Key Points Variable costing can support management decision making in analyzing and evaluating market segments, such as territories, products, salespersons, and customers. Contribution margin reports by segment can be used by managers to support price decisions, evaluate cost changes, and plan volume changes.

Learning Outcomes	Example Exercises	Practice Exercises
• Describe management's uses of contribution margin reports by segment.		
• Prepare a contribution margin report by sales territory.		
• Prepare a contribution margin report by product.		
• Prepare a contribution margin report by salesperson.	**EE5-5**	**PE5-5A, 5-5B**

Use variable costing for analyzing and explaining changes in contribution margin as a result of quantity and price factors.

Key Points Contribution margin analysis is the systematic examination of differences between planned and actual contribution margins. These differences can be caused by an increase/decrease in the amount of sales or variable costs, which can be caused by changes in the amount of units sold, unit sales price, or unit cost.

Learning Outcome	Example Exercises	Practice Exercises
• Prepare a contribution margin analysis identifying changes between actual and planned contribution margin by price/cost and quantity factors.	**EE5-6**	**PE5-6A, 5-6B**

Describe and illustrate the use of variable costing for service firms.

Key Points Service firms will not have inventories, manufacturing margin, or cost of goods sold. Service firms can prepare variable costing income statements and contribution margin reports for market segments. In addition, service firms can use contribution margin analysis to plan and control operations.

Learning Outcomes	Example Exercises	Practice Exercises
• Prepare a variable costing income statement for a service firm.		
• Prepare contribution margin reports by market segments for a service firm.		
• Prepare a contribution margin analysis for a service firm.		

Key Terms

absorption costing (182)
contribution margin (183)
contribution margin analysis (197)
controllable costs (192)
manufacturing margin (183)
market segment (192)
noncontrollable costs (192)
quantity factor (197)
sales mix (194)
unit price (cost) factor (198)
variable cost of goods sold (183)
variable costing (183)

Illustrative Problem

During the current period, McLaughlin Company sold 60,000 units of product at $30 per unit. At the beginning of the period, there were 10,000 units in inventory and McLaughlin Company manufactured 50,000 units during the period. The manufacturing costs and selling and administrative expenses were as follows:

	Total Cost	Number of Units	Unit Cost
Beginning inventory:			
Direct materials	$ 67,000	10,000	$ 6.70
Direct labor	155,000	10,000	15.50
Variable factory overhead	18,000	10,000	1.80
Fixed factory overhead	20,000	10,000	2.00
Total	$ 260,000		$26.00
Current period costs:			
Direct materials	$ 350,000	50,000	$ 7.00
Direct labor	810,000	50,000	16.20
Variable factory overhead	90,000	50,000	1.80
Fixed factory overhead	100,000	50,000	2.00
Total	$1,350,000		$27.00
Selling and administrative expenses:			
Variable	$ 65,000		
Fixed	45,000		
Total	$ 110,000		

Instructions

1. Prepare an income statement based on the absorption costing concept.
2. Prepare an income statement based on the variable costing concept.
3. Give the reason for the difference in the amount of income from operations in parts (1) and (2).

Solution

1.

Absorption Costing Income Statement

Sales (60,000 × $30)		$1,800,000
Cost of goods sold:		
Beginning inventory (10,000 × $26)	$ 260,000	
Cost of goods manufactured (50,000 × $27)	1,350,000	
Cost of goods sold		1,610,000
Gross profit		$ 190,000
Selling and administrative expenses ($65,000 + $45,000)		110,000
Income from operations		$ 80,000

2.

Variable Costing Income Statement		
Sales (60,000 × $30)		$1,800,000
Variable cost of goods sold:		
Beginning inventory (10,000 × $24)	$ 240,000	
Variable cost of goods manufactured (50,000 × $25)	1,250,000	
Variable cost of goods sold		1,490,000
Manufacturing margin		$ 310,000
Variable selling and administrative expenses		65,000
Contribution margin		$ 245,000
Fixed costs:		
Fixed manufacturing costs	$ 100,000	
Fixed selling and administrative expenses	45,000	145,000
Income from operations		$ 100,000

3. The difference of $20,000 ($100,000 – $80,000) in the amount of income from operations is attributable to the different treatment of the fixed manufacturing costs. The beginning inventory in the absorption costing income statement includes $20,000 (10,000 units × $2) of fixed manufacturing costs incurred in the preceding period. This $20,000 was included as an expense in a variable costing income statement of a prior period. Therefore, none of it is included as an expense in the current period variable costing income statement.

Discussion Questions

1. What types of costs are customarily included in the cost of manufactured products under (a) the absorption costing concept and (b) the variable costing concept?
2. Which type of manufacturing cost (direct materials, direct labor, variable factory overhead, fixed factory overhead) is included in the cost of goods manufactured under the absorption costing concept but is excluded from the cost of goods manufactured under the variable costing concept?
3. Which of the following costs would be included in the cost of a manufactured product according to the variable costing concept: (a) rent on factory building, (b) direct materials, (c) property taxes on factory building, (d) electricity purchased to operate factory equipment, (e) salary of factory supervisor, (f) depreciation on factory building, (g) direct labor?
4. In the variable costing income statement, how are the fixed manufacturing costs reported, and how are the fixed selling and administrative expenses reported?
5. Since all costs of operating a business are controllable, what is the significance of the term *noncontrollable cost*?
6. Discuss how financial data prepared on the basis of variable costing can assist management in the development of short-run pricing policies.
7. Why might management analyze product profitability?
8. Explain why rewarding sales personnel on the basis of total sales might not be in the best interests of a business whose goal is to maximize profits.
9. Discuss the two factors affecting both sales and variable costs to which a change in contribution margin can be attributed.
10. How is the quantity factor for an increase or a decrease in the amount of sales computed in using contribution margin analysis?
11. Explain why service companies use different activity bases than manufacturing companies to classify costs as fixed or variable.

Practice Exercises

SHOW ME HOW

EE 5-1 p. 185

PE 5-1A Variable costing **OBJ. 1**

Light Company has the following information for January:

Sales	$648,000
Variable cost of goods sold	233,200
Fixed manufacturing costs	155,500
Variable selling and administrative expenses	51,800
Fixed selling and administrative expenses	36,800

Determine (a) the manufacturing margin, (b) the contribution margin, and (c) income from operations for Light Company for the month of January.

SHOW ME HOW

EE 5-1 p. 185

PE 5-1B Variable costing **OBJ. 1**

Marley Company has the following information for March:

Sales	$912,000
Variable cost of goods sold	474,000
Fixed manufacturing costs	82,000
Variable selling and administrative expenses	238,100
Fixed selling and administrative expenses	54,700

Determine (a) the manufacturing margin, (b) the contribution margin, and (c) income from operations for Marley Company for the month of March.

SHOW ME HOW

EE 5-2 p. 186

PE 5-2A Variable costing—production exceeds sales **OBJ. 1**

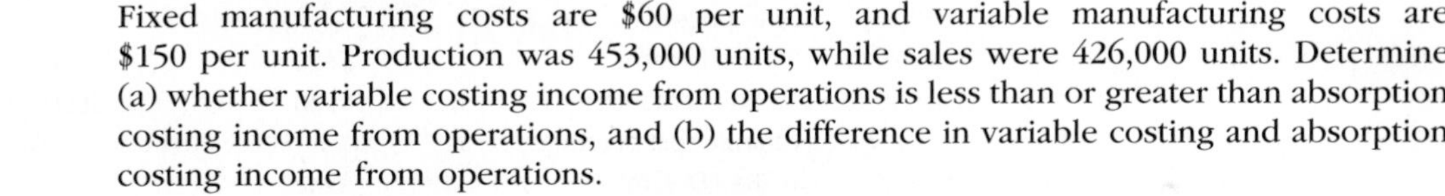

Fixed manufacturing costs are $60 per unit, and variable manufacturing costs are $150 per unit. Production was 453,000 units, while sales were 426,000 units. Determine (a) whether variable costing income from operations is less than or greater than absorption costing income from operations, and (b) the difference in variable costing and absorption costing income from operations.

SHOW ME HOW

EE 5-2 p. 186

PE 5-2B Variable costing—production exceeds sales **OBJ. 1**

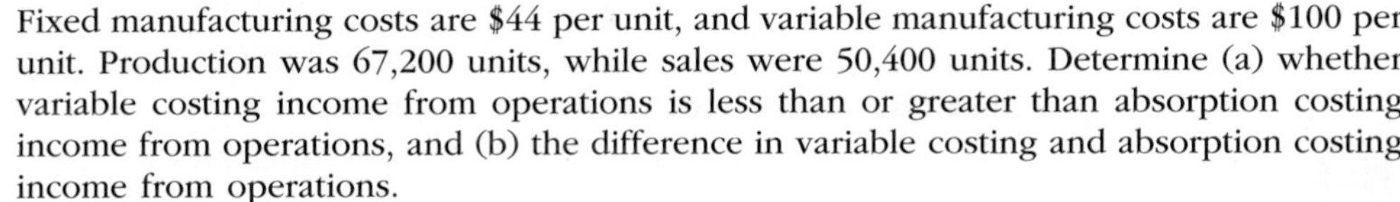

Fixed manufacturing costs are $44 per unit, and variable manufacturing costs are $100 per unit. Production was 67,200 units, while sales were 50,400 units. Determine (a) whether variable costing income from operations is less than or greater than absorption costing income from operations, and (b) the difference in variable costing and absorption costing income from operations.

SHOW ME HOW

EE 5-3 p. 187

PE 5-3A Variable costing—sales exceed production **OBJ. 1**

The beginning inventory is 11,600 units. All of the units that were manufactured during the period and 11,600 units of the beginning inventory were sold. The beginning inventory fixed manufacturing costs are $32 per unit, and variable manufacturing costs are $72 per unit. Determine (a) whether variable costing income from operations is less than or greater than absorption costing income from operations, and (b) the difference in variable costing and absorption costing income from operations.

SHOW ME HOW

EE 5-3 p. 187

PE 5-3B Variable costing—sales exceed production **OBJ. 1**

The beginning inventory is 52,800 units. All of the units that were manufactured during the period and 52,800 units of the beginning inventory were sold. The beginning inventory

(Continued)

fixed manufacturing costs are $14.70 per unit, and variable manufacturing costs are $30 per unit. Determine (a) whether variable costing income from operations is less than or greater than absorption costing income from operations, and (b) the difference in variable costing and absorption costing income from operations.

SHOW ME HOW

EE 5-4 *p. 191*

PE 5-4A Analyzing income under absorption and variable costing **OBJ. 2**

Variable manufacturing costs are $13 per unit, and fixed manufacturing costs are $75,000. Sales are estimated to be 12,000 units.

a. How much would absorption costing income from operations differ between a plan to produce 12,000 units and a plan to produce 15,000 units?

b. How much would variable costing income from operations differ between the two production plans?

SHOW ME HOW

EE 5-4 *p. 191*

PE 5-4B Analyzing income under absorption and variable costing **OBJ. 2**

Variable manufacturing costs are $126 per unit, and fixed manufacturing costs are $157,500. Sales are estimated to be 10,000 units.

a. How much would absorption costing income from operations differ between a plan to produce 10,000 units and a plan to produce 15,000 units?

b. How much would variable costing income from operations differ between the two production plans?

SHOW ME HOW

EE 5-5 *p. 196*

PE 5-5A Contribution margin by segment **OBJ. 4**

The following information is for Olivio Coaster Bikes Inc.:

	North	South
Sales volume (units):		
Red Dream	50,000	66,000
Blue Marauder	112,000	140,000
Sales price:		
Red Dream	$480	$500
Blue Marauder	$560	$600
Variable cost per unit:		
Red Dream	$248	$248
Blue Marauder	$260	$260

Determine the contribution margin for (a) Red Dream and (b) North Region.

SHOW ME HOW

EE 5-5 *p. 196*

PE 5-5B Contribution margin by segment **OBJ. 4**

The following information is for LaPlanche Industries Inc.:

	East	West
Sales volume (units):		
Product XX	45,000	38,000
Product YY	60,000	50,000
Sales price:		
Product XX	$700	$660
Product YY	$728	$720
Variable cost per unit:		
Product XX	$336	$336
Product YY	$360	$360

Determine the contribution margin for (a) Product YY and (b) West Region.

SHOW ME HOW

EE 5-6 *p. 199*

PE 5-6A Contribution margin analysis **OBJ. 5**

The actual price for a product was $28 per unit, while the planned price was $25 per unit. The volume decreased by 20,000 units to 410,000 actual total units. Determine (a) the sales quantity factor and (b) the unit price factor for sales.

SHOW ME HOW

EE 5-6 *p. 199*

PE 5-6B Contribution margin analysis **OBJ. 5**

The actual variable cost of goods sold for a product was $140 per unit, while the planned variable cost of goods sold was $136 per unit. The volume increased by 2,400 units to 14,000 actual total units. Determine (a) the variable cost quantity factor and (b) the unit cost factor for variable cost of goods sold.

Exercises

EX 5-1 Inventory valuation under absorption costing and variable costing **OBJ. 1**

✔ b. Inventory, $780,800

At the end of the first year of operations, 6,400 units remained in the finished goods inventory. The unit manufacturing costs during the year were as follows:

Direct materials	$75
Direct labor	35
Fixed factory overhead	15
Variable factory overhead	12

Determine the cost of the finished goods inventory reported on the balance sheet under (a) the absorption costing concept and (b) the variable costing concept.

EX 5-2 Income statements under absorption costing and variable costing **OBJ. 1**

✔ a. Income from operations, $750,000

SHOW ME HOW

Frigid Motors Inc. assembles and sells snowmobile engines. The company began operations on July 1, 2016, and operated at 100% of capacity during the first month. The following data summarize the results for July:

Sales (35,000 units)		$8,750,000
Production costs (42,500 units):		
Direct materials	$4,250,000	
Direct labor	2,125,000	
Variable factory overhead	1,062,500	
Fixed factory overhead	637,500	8,075,000
Selling and administrative expenses:		
Variable selling and administrative expenses	$1,150,000	
Fixed selling and administrative expenses	200,000	1,350,000

a. Prepare an income statement according to the absorption costing concept.

b. Prepare an income statement according to the variable costing concept.

c. What is the reason for the difference in the amount of income from operations reported in (a) and (b)?

EX 5-3 Income statements under absorption costing and variable costing **OBJ. 1**

✔ b. Income from operations, $1,842,000

SHOW ME HOW

Bionic Cotton Inc. manufactures and sells high-quality sporting goods equipment under its highly recognizable Cool Cat logo. The company began operations on January 1, 2016, and operated at 100% of capacity (90,000 units) during the first month, creating an ending inventory of 8,000 units. During February, the company produced 82,000 garments during the month but sold 90,000 units at $100 per unit. The February manufacturing costs and selling and administrative expenses were as follows:

(Continued)

	Number of Units	Unit Cost	Total Cost
Manufacturing costs in February beginning inventory:			
Variable	8,000	$50	$ 400,000
Fixed	8,000	10	80,000
Total		$60	$ 480,000
February manufacturing costs:			
Variable	82,000	$50	$4,100,000
Fixed	82,000	12	984,000
Total		$62	$5,084,000
Selling and administrative expenses:			
Variable			$1,350,000
Fixed			324,000
Total			$1,674,000

a. Prepare an income statement according to the absorption costing concept for February.

b. Prepare an income statement according to the variable costing concept for February.

c. What is the reason for the difference in the amount of income from operations reported in (a) and (b)?

EX 5-4 Cost of goods manufactured, using variable costing and absorption costing

OBJ. 1

✔ **b. Unit cost of goods manufactured, $275**

On December 31, the end of the first year of operations, Frankenreiter Inc. manufactured 25,600 units and sold 24,000 units. The following income statement was prepared, based on the variable costing concept:

Frankenreiter Inc.
Variable Costing Income Statement
For the Year Ended December 31, 2016

Sales		$9,600,000
Variable cost of goods sold:		
Variable cost of goods manufactured	$5,376,000	
Less inventory, June 30	336,000	
Variable cost of goods sold		5,040,000
Manufacturing margin		$4,560,000
Variable selling and administrative expenses		1,150,000
Contribution margin		$3,410,000
Fixed costs:		
Fixed manufacturing costs	$1,664,000	
Fixed selling and administrative expenses	890,000	2,554,000
Income from operations		$ 856,000

Determine the unit cost of goods manufactured, based on (a) the variable costing concept and (b) the absorption costing concept.

EX 5-5 Variable costing income statement

OBJ. 1

✔ **Income from operations, $203,000**

SHOW ME HOW

On June 30, the end of the first month of operations, Bastile Company prepared the following income statement, based on the absorption costing concept:

Bastile Company
Absorption Costing Income Statement
For the Month Ended June 30, 2016

Sales (20,000 units)		$2,000,000
Cost of goods sold:		
Cost of goods manufactured (24,000 units)	$1,920,000	
Less inventory, June 30 (4,000 units)	320,000	
Cost of goods sold		1,600,000
Gross profit		$ 400,000
Selling and administrative expenses		165,000
Income from operations		$ 235,000

If the fixed manufacturing costs were $192,000 and the variable selling and administrative expenses were $92,400 prepare an income statement according to the variable costing concept.

✔ **Income from operations, $1,187,500**

SHOW ME HOW

EX 5-6 Absorption costing income statement **OBJ. 1**

On July 31, the end of the first month of operations, Del Ray Equipment Company prepared the following income statement, based on the variable costing concept:

Del Ray Equipment Company
Variable Costing Income Statement
For the Month Ended July 31, 2016

Sales (50,000 units)		$6,250,000
Variable cost of goods sold:		
Variable cost of goods manufactured	$3,100,000	
Less inventory, July 31 (12,000 units)	600,000	
Variable cost of goods sold		2,500,000
Manufacturing margin		$3,750,000
Variable selling and administrative expenses		1,575,000
Contribution margin		$2,175,000
Fixed costs:		
Fixed manufacturing costs	$ 620,000	
Fixed selling and administrative expenses	487,500	1,107,500
Income from operations		$1,067,500

Prepare an income statement under absorption costing.

✔ **a. Income from operations, $11,402**

EX 5-7 Variable costing income statement **OBJ. 1**

The following data were adapted from a recent income statement of **Procter & Gamble Company**:

	(in millions)
Sales	$84,167
Operating costs:	
Cost of products sold	$42,428
Marketing, administrative, and other expenses	30,337
Total operating costs	$72,765
Income from operations	$11,402

Assume that the variable amount of each category of operating costs is as follows:

	(in millions)
Cost of products sold	$23,760
Marketing, administrative, and other expenses	12,135

a. Based on the data given, prepare a variable costing income statement for Procter & Gamble Company, assuming that the company maintained constant inventory levels during the period.

b. If Procter & Gamble reduced its inventories during the period, what impact would that have on the income from operations determined under absorption costing?

EX 5-8 Estimated income statements, using absorption and variable costing — OBJ. 1, 2

✔ a. 1. Income from operations, $136,700 (36,000 units)

SHOW ME HOW

Prior to the first month of operations ending July 31, 2016, Muzenski Industries Inc. estimated the following operating results:

Sales (28,800 × $75)	$2,160,000
Manufacturing costs (28,800 units):	
Direct materials	1,324,800
Direct labor	316,800
Variable factory overhead	144,000
Fixed factory overhead	216,000
Fixed selling and administrative expenses	29,400
Variable selling and administrative expenses	35,500

The company is evaluating a proposal to manufacture 36,000 units instead of 28,800 units, thus creating an ending inventory of 7,200 units. Manufacturing the additional units will not change sales, unit variable factory overhead costs, total fixed factory overhead cost, or total selling and administrative expenses.

a. Prepare an estimated income statement, comparing operating results if 28,800 and 36,000 units are manufactured in (1) the absorption costing format and (2) the variable costing format.

b. What is the reason for the difference in income from operations reported for the two levels of production by the absorption costing income statement?

EX 5-9 Variable and absorption costing — OBJ. 1

✔ a. Contribution margin, $6,263

Ansara Company had the following abbreviated income statement for the year ended December 31, 2016:

	(in millions)
Sales	$18,769
Cost of goods sold	$15,471
Selling, administrative, and other expenses	2,049
Total expenses	$17,520
Income from operations	$ 1,249

Assume that there were $3,860 million fixed manufacturing costs and $1,170 million fixed selling, administrative, and other costs for the year.

The finished goods inventories at the beginning and end of the year from the balance sheet were as follows:

January 1	$2,354 million
December 31	$2,408 million

Assume that 30% of the beginning and ending inventory consists of fixed costs. Assume work in process and materials inventory were unchanged during the period.

a. Prepare an income statement according to the variable costing concept for Ansara Company for 2016.

b. Explain the difference between the amount of income from operations reported under the absorption costing and variable costing concepts.

EX 5-10 Variable and absorption costing—three products — OBJ. 2, 3

Happy Feet Inc. manufactures and sells three types of shoes. The income statements prepared under the absorption costing method for the three shoes are as follows:

Happy Feet Inc.
Product Income Statements—Absorption Costing
For the Year Ended December 31, 2016

	Cross Training Shoes	Golf Shoes	Running Shoes
Revenues	$800,000	$690,000	$625,000
Cost of goods sold	416,000	338,100	418,750
Gross profit	$384,000	$351,900	$206,250
Selling and administrative expenses	336,000	248,400	350,000
Income from operations	$ 48,000	$103,500	$(143,750)

In addition, you have determined the following information with respect to allocated fixed costs:

	Cross Training Shoes	Golf Shoes	Running Shoes
Fixed costs:			
Cost of goods sold	$128,000	$89,700	$118,750
Selling and administrative expenses	96,000	82,800	118,750

These fixed costs are used to support all three product lines. In addition, you have determined that the inventory is negligible.

The management of the company has deemed the profit performance of the running shoe line as unacceptable. As a result, it has decided to eliminate the running shoe line. Management does not expect to be able to increase sales in the other two lines. However, as a result of eliminating the running shoe line, management expects the profits of the company to increase by $143,750.

a. Do you agree with management's decision and conclusions?

b. Prepare a variable costing income statement for the three products.

c. Use the report in (b) to determine the profit impact of eliminating the running shoe line, assuming no other changes.

EX 5-11 Change in sales mix and contribution margin — OBJ. 4

Head Pops Inc. manufactures two models of solar powered noise-canceling headphones: Sun Sound and Ear Bling models. The company is operating at less than full capacity. Market research indicates that 28,000 additional Sun Sound and 30,000 additional Ear Bling headphones could be sold. The income from operations by unit of product is as follows:

	Sun Sound Headphone	Ear Bling Headphone
Sales price	$140.00	$125.00
Variable cost of goods sold	78.40	70.00
Manufacturing margin	$ 61.60	$ 55.00
Variable selling and administrative expenses	28.00	25.00
Contribution margin	$ 33.60	$ 30.00
Fixed manufacturing costs	14.00	12.50
Income from operations	$ 19.60	$ 17.50

Prepare an analysis indicating the increase or decrease in total profitability if 28,000 additional Sun Sound and 30,000 additional Ear Bling headphones are produced and sold, assuming that there is sufficient capacity for the additional production.

EX 5-12 Product profitability analysis — OBJ. 4

✔ a. Desert Dragon contribution margin, $4,583,250

PowerTrain Sports Inc. manufactures and sells two styles of All Terrain Vehicles (ATVs), the Mountain Monster, and Desert Dragon from a single manufacturing facility. The manufacturing facility operates at 100% of capacity. The following per unit information is available for the two products:

(Continued)

	Mountain Monster	Desert Dragon
Sales price	$5,400	$5,250
Variable cost of goods sold	3,285	3,400
Manufacturing margin	$2,115	$1,850
Variable selling expenses	1,035	905
Contribution margin	$1,080	$ 945
Fixed expenses	485	310
Income from operations	$ 595	$ 635

In addition, the following sales unit volume information for the period is as follows:

	Mountain Monster	Desert Dragon
Sales unit volume	5,000	4,850

a. Prepare a contribution margin by product report. Calculate the contribution margin ratio for each product as a whole percent, rounded to two decimal places.

b. What advice would you give to the management of PowerTrain Sports Inc. regarding the relative profitability of the two products?

EX 5-13 Territory and product profitability analysis

OBJ. 4

✔ a. East contribution margin, $640,000

Coast to Coast Surfboards Inc. manufactures and sells two styles of surfboards, Atlantic Wave and Pacific Pounder. These surfboards are sold in two regions, East Coast and West Coast. Information about the two surfboards is as follows:

	Atlantic Waves	Pacific Pounder
Sales price	$200	$120
Variable cost of goods sold per unit	150	90
Manufacturing margin per unit	$ 50	$ 30
Variable selling expense per unit	34	16
Contribution margin per unit	$ 16	$ 14

The sales unit volume for the sales territories and products for the period is as follows:

	East Coast	West Coast
Atlantic Wave	40,000	25,000
Pacific Pounder	0	25,000

a. Prepare a contribution margin by sales territory report. Calculate the contribution margin ratio for each territory as a whole percent, rounded to two decimal places.

b. What advice would you give to the management of Coast to Coast Surfboards regarding the relative profitability of the two territories?

EX 5-14 Sales territory and salesperson profitability analysis

OBJ. 4

✔ a. Todd contribution margin, $887,040

SHOW ME HOW

Reyes Industries Inc. manufactures and sells a variety of commercial vehicles in the North east and South west regions. There are two salespersons assigned to each territory. Higher commission rates go to the most experienced salespersons. The following sales statistics are available for each salesperson:

	Northeast		Southwest	
	Cassy G.	Todd	Tim	Jeff
Average per unit:				
Sales price	$96,000	$84,000	$108,000	$78,000
Variable cost of goods sold	57,600	33,600	64,800	31,200
Commission rate	12%	16%	16%	12%
Units sold	28	24	24	38
Manufacturing margin ratio	40%	60%	40%	60%

a. 1. Prepare a contribution margin by salesperson report. Calculate the contribution margin ratio for each salesperson.

2. Interpret the report.

b. 1. Prepare a contribution margin by territory report. Calculate the contribution margin for each territory as a percent, rounded to one decimal place.

2. Interpret the report.

✔ a. Electric Power, $824.92

EX 5-15 Segment profitability analysis — OBJ. 4

The marketing segment sales for **Caterpillar, Inc.**, for a recent year follow:

Caterpillar, Inc.
Machinery and Engines Marketing Segment Sales
(in millions)

	Building Construction Products	Cat Japan	Core Components	Earth-moving	Electric Power	Excavation	Large Power Systems	Logistics	Marine & Petroleum Power	Mining	Turbines
Sales	$2,217	$1,225	$1,234	$5,045	$2,847	$4,562	$2,885	$659	$2,132	$3,975	$3,321

In addition, assume the following information:

	Building Construction Products	Cat Japan	Core Components	Earth-moving	Electric Power	Excavation	Large Power Systems	Logistics	Marine & Petroleum Power	Mining	Turbines
Variable cost of goods sold as a percent of sales	45%	55%	49%	51%	54%	52%	53%	50%	50%	52%	48%
Dealer commissions as a percent of sales	9%	11%	8%	8%	10%	6%	5%	10%	9%	7%	9%
Variable promotion expenses (in millions)	310	120	150	600	200	600	300	75	270	480	400

a. Use the sales information and the additional assumed information to prepare a contribution margin by segment report. Round to two decimal places. In addition, calculate the contribution margin ratio for each segment as a percentage, rounded to one decimal place.

b. Prepare a table showing the manufacturing margin, dealer commissions, and variable promotion expenses as a percent of sales for each segment. Round whole percents to one decimal place.

c. Use the information in (a) and (b) to interpret the segment performance.

✔ a. Filmed entertainment, 68%

EX 5-16 Segment contribution margin analysis — OBJ. 4, 6

The operating revenues of the three largest business segments for **Time Warner, Inc.**, for a recent year follow. Each segment includes a number of businesses, examples of which are indicated in parentheses.

Time Warner, Inc.
Segment Revenues
(in millions)

Filmed Entertainment (Warner Bros.)	$14,204
Networks (CNN, HBO, WB)	12,018
Publishing (*Time, People, Sports Illustrated*)	3,436

Assume that the variable costs as a percent of sales for each segment are as follows:

Filmed Entertainment	35%
Networks	32%
Publishing	72%

a. Determine the contribution margin (round to whole millions) and contribution margin ratio (round to whole percents) for each segment from the information given.

(Continued)

b. Why is the contribution margin ratio for the Publishing segment smaller than for the other segments?

c. Does your answer to (b) mean that the other segments are more profitable businesses than the Publishing segment?

EX 5-17 Contribution margin analysis—sales **OBJ. 5**

Buy Best Inc. sells electronic equipment. Management decided early in the year to reduce the price of the speakers in order to increase sales volume. As a result, for the year ended December 31, the sales increased by $31,875 from the planned level of $1,048,125. The following information is available from the accounting records for the year ended December 31.

	Actual	Planned	Increase or (Decrease)
Sales	$1,080,000	$1,048,125	$31,875
Number of units sold	36,000	32,250	3,750
Sales price	$30.00	$32.50	$(2.50)
Variable cost per unit	$10.00	$10.00	0

a. Prepare an analysis of the sales quantity and unit price factors.

b. Did the price decrease generate sufficient volume to result in a net increase in contribution margin if the actual variable cost per unit was $10, as planned?

EX 5-18 Contribution margin analysis—sales **OBJ. 5**

✔ Sales quantity factor, $(600,000)

The following data for Romero Products Inc. are available:

For the Year Ended December 31	Actual	Planned	Difference—Increase or (Decrease)
Sales	$8,360,000	$8,200,000	$160,000
Less:			
Variable cost of goods sold	$3,496,000	$3,280,000	$216,000
Variable selling and administrative expenses	760,000	902,000	(142,000)
Total variable costs	$4,256,000	$4,182,000	$ 74,000
Contribution margin	$4,104,000	$4,018,000	$ 86,000
Number of units sold	38,000	41,000	
Per unit:			
Sales price	$220	$200	
Variable cost of goods sold	92	80	
Variable selling and administrative expenses	20	22	

Prepare an analysis of the sales quantity and unit price factors.

EX 5-19 Contribution margin analysis—variable costs **OBJ. 5**

✔ Variable cost of goods sold quantity factor, $240,000

Based on the data in Exercise 5-18, prepare a contribution analysis of the variable costs for Romero Products Inc. for the year ended December 31.

EX 5-20 Variable costing income statement for a service company **OBJ. 4, 6**

East Coast Railroad Company transports commodities among three routes (city-pairs): Atlanta/Baltimore, Baltimore/Pittsburgh, and Pittsburgh/Atlanta. Significant costs, their cost behavior, and activity rates for April are as follows:

Cost	Amount	Cost Behavior	Activity Rate
Labor costs for loading and unloading railcars	$ 175,582	Variable	$46.00 per railcar
Fuel costs	460,226	Variable	12.40 per train-mile
Train crew labor costs	267,228	Variable	7.20 per train-mile
Switchyard labor costs	118,327	Variable	31.00 per railcar
Track and equipment depreciation	194,400	Fixed	
Maintenance	129,600	Fixed	
	$1,345,363		

Operating statistics from the management information system reveal the following for April:

	Atlanta/ Baltimore	Baltimore/ Pittsburgh	Pittsburgh/ Atlanta	Total
Number of train-miles	12,835	10,200	14,080	37,115
Number of railcars	425	2,160	1,232	3,817
Revenue per railcar	$600	$275	$440	

a. Prepare a contribution margin by route report for East Coast Railroad Company for the month of April. Calculate the contribution margin ratio in whole percents, rounded to one decimal place.

b. Evaluate the route performance of the railroad using the report in (a).

EX 5-21 Contribution margin reporting and analysis for a service company OBJ. 5, 6

The management of East Coast Railroad Company introduced in Exercise 5-20 improved the profitability of the Atlanta/Baltimore route in May by reducing the price of a railcar from $600 to $500. This price reduction increased the demand for rail services. Thus, the number of railcars increased by 275 railcars to a total of 700 railcars. This was accomplished by increasing the size of each train but not the number of trains. Thus, the number of train-miles was unchanged. All the activity rates remained unchanged.

a. Prepare a contribution margin report for the Atlanta/Baltimore route for May. Calculate the contribution margin ratio in percentage terms to one decimal place.

b. Prepare a contribution margin analysis to evaluate management's actions in May. Assume that the May planned quantity, price, and unit cost was the same as April.

EX 5-22 Variable costing income statement and contribution margin analysis for a service company OBJ. 5, 6

The actual and planned data for Underwater University for the Fall term 2016 were as follows:

	Actual	Planned
Enrollment	4,500	4,125
Tuition per credit hour	$120	$135
Credit hours	60,450	43,200
Registration, records, and marketing cost per enrolled student	$275	$275
Instructional costs per credit hour	$64	$60
Depreciation on classrooms and equipment	$825,600	$825,600

Registration, records, and marketing costs vary by the number of enrolled students, while instructional costs vary by the number of credit hours. Depreciation is a fixed cost.

a. Prepare a variable costing income statement showing the contribution margin and income from operations for the Fall 2016 term.

b. Prepare a contribution margin analysis report comparing planned with actual performance for the Fall 2016 term.

Problems: Series A

PR 5-1A Absorption and variable costing income statements — OBJ. 1, 2

✓ 2. Income from operations, $304,000

SHOW ME HOW

During the first month of operations ended May 31, 2016, Frost Point Fridge Company manufactured 40,000 mini refrigerators, of which 36,000 were sold. Operating data for the month are summarized as follows:

Sales		$6,480,000
Manufacturing costs:		
Direct materials	$3,200,000	
Direct labor	1,120,000	
Variable manufacturing cost	880,000	
Fixed manufacturing cost	560,000	5,760,000
Selling and administrative expenses:		
Variable	$ 648,000	
Fixed	288,000	936,000

Instructions

1. Prepare an income statement based on the absorption costing concept.
2. Prepare an income statement based on the variable costing concept.
3. Explain the reason for the difference in the amount of income from operations reported in (1) and (2).

PR 5-2A Income statements under absorption costing and variable costing — OBJ. 1, 2

✓ 2. Contribution margin, $92,800

The demand for solvent, one of numerous products manufactured by Mac n' Cheese Industries Inc., has dropped sharply because of recent competition from a similar product. The company's chemists are currently completing tests of various new formulas, and it is anticipated that the manufacture of a superior product can be started on June 1, one month in the future. No changes will be needed in the present production facilities to manufacture the new product because only the mixture of the various materials will be changed.

The controller has been asked by the president of the company for advice on whether to continue production during May or to suspend the manufacture of solvent until June 1. The controller has assembled the following pertinent data:

Mac n' Cheese Industries Inc.
Income Statement—Solvent
For the Month Ended April 30, 2016

Sales (4,000 units)	$500,000
Cost of goods sold	424,000
Gross profit	$ 76,000
Selling and administrative expenses	102,000
Loss from operations	$ (26,000)

The production costs and selling and administrative expenses, based on production of 4,000 units in April, are as follows:

Direct materials	$45 per unit
Direct labor	20 per unit
Variable manufacturing cost	16 per unit
Variable selling and administrative expenses	15 per unit
Fixed manufacturing cost	$100,000 for April
Fixed selling and administrative expenses	42,000 for April

Sales for May are expected to drop about 20% below those of the preceding month. No significant changes are anticipated in the fixed costs or variable costs per unit. No extra costs will be incurred in discontinuing operations in the portion of the plant associated with solvent. The inventory of solvent at the beginning and end of May is expected to be inconsequential.

Instructions

1. Prepare an estimated income statement in absorption costing form for May for solvent, assuming that production continues during the month. Round amounts to two decimals.
2. Prepare an estimated income statement in variable costing form for May for solvent, assuming that production continues during the month. Round amounts to two decimals.
3. What would be the estimated loss in income from operations if the solvent production were temporarily suspended for May?
4. What advice should the controller give to management?

PR 5-3A Absorption and variable costing income statements for two months and analysis

OBJ. 1, 2

✓ 1. b. Income from operations, $38,205

SHOW ME HOW

During the first month of operations ended March 31, 2016, Hip and Conscious Clothing Company produced 55,500 designer cowboy hats, of which 51,450 were sold. Operating data for the month are summarized as follows:

Sales		$771,750
Manufacturing costs:		
Direct materials	$471,750	
Direct labor	127,650	
Variable manufacturing cost	61,050	
Fixed manufacturing cost	55,500	715,950
Selling and administrative expenses:		
Variable	$ 36,015	
Fixed	25,725	61,740

During April, Hip and Conscious Clothing produced 47,400 designer cowboy hats and sold 51,450 cowboy hats. Operating data for April are summarized as follows:

Sales		$771,750
Manufacturing costs:		
Direct materials	$402,900	
Direct labor	109,020	
Variable manufacturing cost	52,140	
Fixed manufacturing cost	55,500	619,560
Selling and administrative expenses:		
Variable	$ 36,015	
Fixed	25,725	61,740

Instructions

1. Using the absorption costing concept, prepare income statements for (a) March and (b) April.
2. Using the variable costing concept, prepare income statements for (a) March and (b) April.
3. a. Explain the reason for the differences in the amount of income from operations in (1) and (2) for March.

   b. Explain the reason for the differences in the amount of income from operations in (1) and (2) for April.
4. Based on your answers to (1) and (2), did Hip and Conscious Clothing Company operate more profitably in March or in April? Explain.

PR 5-4A Salespersons' report and analysis

OBJ. 4

✔ 1. Dix contribution margin ratio, 44%

Walthman Industries Inc. employs seven salespersons to sell and distribute its product throughout the state. Data taken from reports received from the salespersons during the year ended December 31 are as follows:

Salesperson	Total Sales	Variable Cost of Goods Sold	Variable Selling Expenses
Case	$610,000	$268,400	$109,800
Dix	603,000	241,200	96,480
Johnson	588,000	305,760	105,840
LaFave	586,000	281,280	123,060
Orcas	616,000	221,760	86,240
Sussman	620,000	310,000	124,000
Willbond	592,000	272,320	88,800

Instructions

1. Prepare a table indicating contribution margin, variable cost of goods sold as a percent of sales, variable selling expenses as a percent of sales, and contribution margin ratio by salesperson. Round whole percents to a single digit.
2. Which salesperson generated the highest contribution margin ratio for the year and why?
3. Briefly list factors other than contribution margin that should be considered in evaluating the performance of salespersons.

PR 5-5A Segment variable costing income statement and effect on income of change in operations

OBJ. 4

✔ 1. Income from operations, $85,790

Valdespin Company manufactures three sizes of camping tents—small (S), medium (M), and large (L). The income statement has consistently indicated a net loss for the M size, and management is considering three proposals: (1) continue Size M, (2) discontinue Size M and reduce total output accordingly, or (3) discontinue Size M and conduct an advertising campaign to expand the sales of Size S so that the entire plant capacity can continue to be used.

If Proposal 2 is selected and Size M is discontinued and production curtailed, the annual fixed production costs and fixed operating expenses could be reduced by $46,080 and $32,240 respectively. If Proposal 3 is selected, it is anticipated that an additional annual expenditure of $34,560 for the rental of additional warehouse space would yield an additional 130% in Size S sales volume. It is also assumed that the increased production of Size S would utilize the plant facilities released by the discontinuance of Size M.

The sales and costs have been relatively stable over the past few years, and they are expected to remain so for the foreseeable future. The income statement for the past year ended June 30, 2016, is as follows:

	Size			
	S	M	L	Total
Sales	$668,000	$737,300	$ 956,160	$2,361,460
Cost of goods sold:				
Variable costs	$300,000	$357,120	$437,760	$1,094,880
Fixed costs	74,880	138,250	172,800	385,930
Total cost of goods sold	$374,880	$495,370	$ 610,560	$1,480,810
Gross profit	$293,120	$241,930	$ 345,600	$ 880,650
Less operating expenses:				
Variable expenses	$132,480	$155,500	$ 195,840	$ 483,820
Fixed expenses	92,160	103,680	115,200	311,040
Total operating expenses	$224,640	$ 259,180	$ 311,040	$ 794,860
Income from operations	$ 68,480	$ (17,250)	$ 34,560	$ 85,790

Instructions

1. Prepare an income statement for the past year in the variable costing format. Use the following headings:

Size			
S	M	L	Total

Data for each style should be reported through contribution margin. The fixed costs should be deducted from the total contribution margin, as reported in the "Total" column, to determine income from operations.

2. Based on the income statement prepared in (1) and the other data presented, determine the amount by which total annual income from operations would be reduced below its present level if Proposal 2 is accepted.
3. Prepare an income statement in the variable costing format, indicating the projected annual income from operations if Proposal 3 is accepted. Use the following headings:

Size		
S	L	Total

Data for each style should be reported through contribution margin. The fixed costs should be deducted from the total contribution margin as reported in the "Total" column. For purposes of this problem, the expenditure of $34,560 for the rental of additional warehouse space can be added to the fixed operating expenses.

4. By how much would total annual income increase above its present level if Proposal 3 is accepted? Explain.

PR 5-6A Contribution margin analysis

OBJ. 5

1. Sales quantity factor, $(343,750)

Dozier Industries Inc. manufactures only one product. For the year ended December 31, the contribution margin increased by $38,500 from the planned level of $1,386,000 The president of Dozier Industries Inc. has expressed some concern about such a small increase and has requested a follow-up report.

The following data have been gathered from the accounting records for the year ended December 31:

	Actual	Planned	Difference—Increase (Decrease)
Sales	$ 2,772,000	$ 2,750,000	$ 22,000
Less:			
Variable cost of goods sold	$ 1,058,750	$ 1,122,000	$(63,250)
Variable selling and administrative expenses	288,750	242,000	46,750
Total	$1,347,500	$1,364,000	$(16,500)
Contribution margin	$1,424,500	$1,386,000	$38,500
Number of units sold	19,250	22,000	
Per unit:			
Sales price	$144	$125	
Variable cost of goods sold	55	51	
Variable selling and administrative expenses	15	11	

Instructions

1. Prepare a contribution margin analysis report for the year ended December 31.
2. At a meeting of the board of directors on January 30, the president, after reviewing the contribution margin analysis report, made the following comment:

It looks as if the price increase of $19 had the effect of decreasing sales volume. However, this was a favorable tradeoff. The variable cost of goods sold was less than planned. Apparently, we are efficiently managing our variable cost of goods sold. However, the variable selling and administrative expenses appear out of control. Let's look into these expenses and get them under control! Also, let's consider increasing the sales price to $160 and continue this favorable tradeoff between higher price and lower volume.

Do you agree with the president's comment? Explain.

Problems: Series B

PR 5-1B Absorption and variable costing income statements — OBJ. 1, 2

✔ 2. Contribution margin, $666,000

SHOW ME HOW

During the first month of operations ended July 31, 2016, YoSan Inc. manufactured 2,400 flat panel televisions, of which 2,000 were sold. Operating data for the month are summarized as follows:

Sales		$2,150,000
Manufacturing costs:		
Direct materials	$960,000	
Direct labor	420,000	
Variable manufacturing cost	156,000	
Fixed manufacturing cost	288,000	1,824,000
Selling and administrative expenses:		
Variable	$204,000	
Fixed	96,000	300,000

Instructions

1. Prepare an income statement based on the absorption costing concept.
2. Prepare an income statement based on the variable costing concept.
3. Explain the reason for the difference in the amount of income from operations reported in (1) and (2).

PR 5-2B Income statements under absorption costing and variable costing — OBJ. 1, 2

✔ 2. Contribution margin, $960,000

The demand for aloe vera hand lotion, one of numerous products manufactured by Smooth Skin Care Products Inc., has dropped sharply because of recent competition from a similar product. The company's chemists are currently completing tests of various new formulas, and it is anticipated that the manufacture of a superior product can be started on December 1, one month in the future. No changes will be needed in the present production facilities to manufacture the new product because only the mixture of the various materials will be changed.

The controller has been asked by the president of the company for advice on whether to continue production during November or to suspend the manufacture of aloe vera hand lotion until December 1. The controller has assembled the following pertinent data:

Smooth Skin Care Products Inc.
Income Statement—Aloe Vera Hand Lotion
For the Month Ended October 31, 2016

Sales (400,000 units)	$32,000,000
Cost of goods sold	28,330,000
Gross profit	$ 3,670,000
Selling and administrative expenses	4,270,000
Loss from operations	$ (600,000)

The production costs and selling and administrative expenses, based on production of 400,000 units in October, are as follows:

Direct materials	$15 per unit
Direct labor	17 per unit
Variable manufacturing cost	35 per unit
Variable selling and administrative expenses	10 per unit
Fixed manufacturing cost	$1,530,000 for October
Fixed selling and administrative expenses	270,000 for October

Sales for November are expected to drop about 20% below those of the preceding month. No significant changes are anticipated in the fixed costs or variable costs per unit. No extra costs will be incurred in discontinuing operations in the portion of the plant associated with aloe vera hand lotion. The inventory of aloe vera hand lotion at the beginning and end of November is expected to be inconsequential.

Instructions

1. Prepare an estimated income statement in absorption costing form for November for aloe vera hand lotion, assuming that production continues during the month.

2. Prepare an estimated income statement in variable costing form for November for aloe vera hand lotion, assuming that production continues during the month.
3. What would be the estimated loss in income from operations if the aloe vera hand lotion production were temporarily suspended for November?
4. What advice should the controller give to management?

PR 5-3B Absorption and variable costing income statements for two months and analysis OBJ. 1, 2

✔ 2. a. Manufacturing margin, $37,440

SHOW ME HOW

During the first month of operations ended July 31, 2016, Head Gear Inc. manufactured 6,400 hats, of which 5,200 were sold. Operating data for the month are summarized as follows:

Sales		$104,000
Manufacturing costs:		
Direct materials	$47,360	
Direct labor	22,400	
Variable manufacturing cost	12,160	
Fixed manufacturing cost	15,360	97,280
Selling and administrative expenses:		
Variable	$10,920	
Fixed	5,200	16,120

During August Head Gear Inc. manufactured 4,000 hats and sold 5,200 hats. Operating data for August are summarized as follows:

Sales		$104,000
Manufacturing costs:		
Direct materials	$29,600	
Direct labor	14,000	
Variable manufacturing cost	7,600	
Fixed manufacturing cost	15,360	66,560
Selling and administrative expenses:		
Variable	$10,920	
Fixed	5,200	16,120

Instructions

1. Using the absorption costing concept, prepare income statements for (a) July and (b) August.
2. Using the variable costing concept, prepare income statements for (a) July and (b) August.
3. a. Explain the reason for the differences in the amount of income from operations in (1) and (2) for July.

   b. Explain the reason for the differences in the amount of income from operations in (1) and (2) for August.
4. Based on your answers to (1) and (2), did Head Gear Inc. operate more profitably in July or in August? Explain.

PR 5-4B Salespersons' report and analysis OBJ. 4

✔ 1. Crowell contribution margin ratio, 44%

Pachec Inc. employs seven salespersons to sell and distribute its product throughout the state. Data taken from reports received from the salespersons during the year ended June 30 are as follows:

Salesperson	Total Sales	Variable Cost of Goods Sold	Variable Selling Expenses
Asarenka	$437,500	$196,875	$ 83,125
Crowell	570,000	228,000	91,200
Dempster	675,000	310,500	141,750
MacLean	587,500	246,750	123,375
Ortiz	525,000	215,250	126,000
Sullivan	587,500	246,750	99,875
Williams	575,000	253,000	115,000

(Continued)

Instructions

1. Prepare a table indicating contribution margin, variable cost of goods sold as a percent of sales, variable selling expenses as a percent of sales, and contribution margin ratio by salesperson. (Round whole percent to one digit after decimal point.)
2. Which salesperson generated the highest contribution margin ratio for the year and why?
3. Briefly list factors other than contribution margin that should be considered in evaluating the performance of salespersons.

PR 5-5B Variable costing income statement and effect on income of change in operations

OBJ. 4

✔ **3. Income from operations, $106,820**

Kimbrell Inc. manufactures three sizes of utility tables—small (S), medium (M), and large (L). The income statement has consistently indicated a net loss for the M size, and management is considering three proposals: (1) continue Size M, (2) discontinue Size M and reduce total output accordingly, or (3) discontinue Size M and conduct an advertising campaign to expand the sales of Size S so that the entire plant capacity can continue to be used.

If Proposal 2 is selected and Size M is discontinued and production curtailed, the annual fixed production costs and fixed operating expenses could be reduced by $142,500 and $28,350, respectively. If Proposal 3 is selected, it is anticipated that an additional annual expenditure of $85,050 for the salary of an assistant brand manager (classified as a fixed operating expense) would yield an additional 130% in Size S sales volume. It is also assumed that the increased production of Size S would utilize the plant facilities released by the discontinuance of Size M.

The sales and costs have been relatively stable over the past few years, and they are expected to remain so for the foreseeable future. The income statement for the past year ended December 31, 2016, is as follows:

	Size			
	S	**M**	**L**	**Total**
Sales	$990,000	$1,087,500	$945,000	$3,022,500
Cost of goods sold:				
Variable costs	$538,500	$ 718,500	$567,000	$1,824,000
Fixed costs	241,000	288,000	250,000	779,000
Total cost of goods sold	$779,500	$1,006,500	$817,000	$2,603,000
Gross profit	$210,500	$ 81,000	$128,000	$ 419,500
Less operating expenses:				
Variable expenses	$118,100	$ 108,750	$ 85,050	$ 311,900
Fixed expenses	32,125	42,525	14,250	88,900
Total operating expenses	$150,225	$ 151,275	$ 99,300	$ 400,800
Income from operations	$ 60,275	$ (70,275)	$ 28,700	$ 18,700

Instructions

1. Prepare an income statement for the past year in the variable costing format. Use the following headings:

Size			
S	M	L	Total

Data for each style should be reported through contribution margin. The fixed costs should be deducted from the total contribution margin, as reported in the "Total" column, to determine income from operations.

2. Based on the income statement prepared in (1) and the other data presented above, determine the amount by which total annual income from operations would be reduced below its present level if Proposal 2 is accepted.
3. Prepare an income statement in the variable costing format, indicating the projected annual income from operations if Proposal 3 is accepted. Use the following headings:

Size		
S	L	Total

Data for each style should be reported through contribution margin. The fixed costs should be deducted from the total contribution margin as reported in the "Total" column. For purposes of this problem, the additional expenditure of $85,050 for the assistant brand manager's salary can be added to the fixed operating expenses.

4. By how much would total annual income increase above its present level if Proposal 3 is accepted? Explain.

PR 5-6B Contribution margin analysis **OBJ. 5**

✔ 1. Sales quantity factor, $310,500

Mathews Company manufactures only one product. For the year ended December 31, the contribution margin decreased by $126,000 from the planned level of $540,000. The president of Mathews Company has expressed some concern about this decrease and has requested a follow-up report.

The following data have been gathered from the accounting records for the year ended December 31:

	Actual	Planned	Difference—Increase or (Decrease)
Sales	$2,277,000	$2,070,000	$207,000
Less:			
Variable cost of goods sold	$1,035,000	$ 990,000	$ 45,000
Variable selling and administrative expenses	828,000	540,000	288,000
Total	$1,863,000	$1,530,000	$333,000
Contribution margin	$ 414,000	$ 540,000	$(126,000)
Number of units sold	34,500	30,000	
Per unit:			
Sales price	$66	$69	
Variable cost of goods sold	30	33	
Variable selling and administrative expenses	24	18	

Instructions

1. Prepare a contribution margin analysis report for the year ended December 31.
2. At a meeting of the board of directors on January 30, the president, after reviewing the contribution margin analysis report, made the following comment:

   It looks as if the price decrease of $3.00 had the effect of increasing sales. However, we lost control over the variable cost of goods sold and variable selling and administrative expenses. Let's look into these expenses and get them under control! Also, let's consider decreasing the sales price to $60 to increase sales further.

   Do you agree with the president's comment? Explain.

Cases & Projects

CP 5-1 Ethics and professional conduct in business

The Southwest Division of Texcaliber Inc. uses absorption costing for profit reporting. The general manager of the Southwest Division is concerned about meeting the income objectives of the division. At the beginning of the reporting period, the division had an adequate supply of inventory. The general manager has decided to increase production of goods in the plant in order to allocate fixed manufacturing cost over a greater number of units. Unfortunately, the increased production cannot be sold and will increase the inventory. However, the impact on earnings will be positive because the lower cost per unit will be matched against sales. The general manager has come to Aston Melon, the controller, to determine exactly how much additional production is required in order to increase net income enough to meet the division's profit objectives. Aston analyzes the data and determines that the inventory will need to be increased by 30% in order to absorb enough fixed costs and meet the income objective. Aston reports this information to the division manager.

Discuss whether Aston is acting in an ethical manner.

CP 5-2 Inventories under absorption costing

BendOR, Inc. manufactures control panels for the electronics industry and has just completed its first year of operations. The following discussion took place between the controller, Gordon Merrick, and the company president, Matt McCray:

Matt: I've been looking over our first year's performance by quarters. Our earnings have been increasing each quarter, even though our sales have been flat and our prices and costs have not changed. Why is this?

Gordon: Our actual sales have stayed even throughout the year, but we've been increasing the utilization of our factory every quarter. By keeping our factory utilization high, we will keep our costs down by allocating the fixed plant costs over a greater number of units. Naturally, this causes our cost per unit to be lower than it would be otherwise.

Matt: Yes, but what good is this if we have been unable to sell everything that we make? Our inventory is also increasing.

Gordon: This is true. However, our unit costs are lower because of the additional production. When these lower costs are matched against sales, it has a positive impact on our earnings.

Matt: Are you saying that we are able to create additional earnings merely by building inventory? Can this be true?

Gordon: Well, I've never thought about it quite that way . . . but I guess so.

Matt: And another thing. What will happen if we begin to reduce our production in order to liquidate the inventory? Don't tell me our earnings will go down even though our production effort drops!

Gordon: Well . . .

Matt: There must be a better way. I'd like our quarterly income statements to reflect what's really going on. I don't want our income reports to reward building inventory and penalize reducing inventory.

Gordon: I'm not sure what I can do—we have to follow generally accepted accounting principles.

1. Why does reporting income under generally accepted accounting principles "reward" building inventory and "penalize" reducing inventory?
2. What advice would you give to Gordon in responding to Matt's concern about the present method of profit reporting?

CP 5-3 Segmented contribution margin analysis

Bon Jager Inc. manufactures and sells devices used in cardiovascular surgery. The company has two salespersons, Dean and Martin.

A contribution margin by salesperson report was prepared as follows:

Bon Jager Inc.
Contribution Margin by Salesperson

	Dean	Martin
Sales	$400,000	$480,000
Variable cost of goods sold	184,000	264,000
Manufacturing margin	216,000	216,000
Variable promotion expenses	72,000	43,200
Variable sales commission expenses	56,000	67,200
	128,000	110,400
Contribution margin	88,000	105,600
Manufacturing margin as a percent of sales (manufacturing margin ratio)	54%	45%
Contribution margin ratio	22%	22%

Interpret the report, and provide recommendations to the two salespersons for improving profitability.

CP 5-4 Margin analysis

Jellnick Equipment Inc. manufactures and sells kitchen cooking products throughout the state. The company employs four salespersons. The following contribution margin by salesperson analysis was prepared:

Jellnick Equipment Inc.
Contribution Margin Analysis by Salesperson

	Danica	Kyle	Richard	Tom
Sales	$165,000	$187,000	$176,000	$132,000
Variable cost of goods sold	57,750	93,500	88,000	66,000
Manufacturing margin	$107,250	$ 93,500	$ 88,000	$ 66,000
Variable selling expenses:				
Commissions	$ 6,600	$ 7,480	$ 7,040	$ 5,280
Promotion expenses	47,850	44,880	42,240	31,680
Total variable selling expenses	$ 54,450	$ 52,360	$ 49,280	$ 36,960
Contribution margin	$ 52,800	$ 41,140	$ 38,720	$ 29,040

1. Calculate the manufacturing margin as a percent of sales and the contribution margin ratio for each salesperson.
2. Explain the results of the analysis.

CP 5-5 Contribution margin analysis

Trans Sport Company sells sporting goods to retailers in three different states—Florida, Georgia, and Tennessee. The following profit analysis by state was prepared by the company:

	Florida	Georgia	Tennessee
Revenue	$1,125,000	$1,000,000	$1,181,250
Cost of goods sold	562,500	535,000	562,500
Gross profit	$ 562,500	$ 465,000	$ 618,750
Selling expenses	365,600	337,500	420,000
Income from operations	$ 196,900	$ 127,500	$ 198,750

The following fixed costs have also been provided:

	Florida	Georgia	Tennessee
Fixed manufacturing costs	$112,500	$225,000	$126,500
Fixed selling expenses	84,375	135,000	113,625

In addition, assume that inventories have been negligible.

Management believes it could increase state sales by 20%, without increasing any of the fixed costs, by spending an additional $42,200 per state on advertising.

1. Prepare a contribution margin by state report for Trans Sport Company.
2. Determine how much state operating profit will be generated for an additional $42,200 per state on advertising.
3. Which state will provide the greatest profit return for a $42,200 increase in advertising? Why?

CP 5-6 Absorption costing

Group Project

Craig Company is a family-owned business in which you own 20% of the common stock and your brothers and sisters own the remaining shares. The employment contract of Craig's new president, Ajay Pinder, stipulates a base salary of $140,000 per year plus 10% of income from operations in excess of $670,000. Craig uses the absorption costing method of reporting income from operations, which has averaged approximately $670,000 for the past several years.

Sales for 2016, Pinder's first year as president of Craig Company, are estimated at 44,000 units at a selling price of $106 per unit. To maximize the use of Craig's productive capacity, Pinder has decided to manufacture 55,000 units, rather than the 44,000 units of estimated sales. The beginning inventory at January 1, 2016, is insignificant in amount, and the manufacturing costs and selling and administrative expenses for the production of 44,000 and 55,000 units are as follows:

(Continued)

44,000 Units to Be Manufactured

	Number of Units	Unit Cost	Total Cost
Manufacturing costs:			
Variable	44,000	$50.00	$2,200,000
Fixed	44,000	11.00	484,000
Total		$61.00	$2,684,000
Selling and administrative expenses:			
Variable	$ 1,050,000		
Fixed	330,000		
Total	$1,380,000		

55,000 Units to Be Manufactured

	Number of Units	Unit Cost	Total Cost
Manufacturing costs:			
Variable	55,000	$50.00	$2,750,000
Fixed	55,000	8.80	484,000
Total		$58.80	$3,234,000
Selling and administrative expenses:			
Variable	$1,050,000		
Fixed	330,000		
Total	$1,380,000		

1. In one group, prepare an absorption costing income statement for the year ending December 31, 2016, based on sales of 44,000 units and the manufacture of 44,000 units. In the other group, conduct the same analysis, assuming production of 55,000 units.
2. Explain the difference in the income from operations reported in (1).
3. Compute Pinder's total salary for the year 2016, based on sales of 44,000 units and the manufacture of 44,000 units (Group 1) and 55,000 units (Group 2). Compare your answers.
4. In addition to maximizing the use of Craig Company's productive capacity, why might Pinder wish to manufacture 55,000 units rather than 44,000 units?
5. Can you suggest an alternative way in which Pinder's salary could be determined, using a base salary of $140,000 and 10% of income from operations in excess of $670,000, so that the salary could not be increased by simply manufacturing more units?

Budgeting

Hendrick Motorsport

You may have financial goals for your life. To achieve these goals, it is necessary to plan for future expenses. For example, you may consider taking a part-time job to save money for school expenses for the coming school year. How much money would you need to earn and save in order to pay these expenses? One way to find an answer to this question would be to prepare a budget. A budget would show an estimate of your expenses associated with school, such as tuition, fees, and books. In addition, you would have expenses for day-to-day living, such as rent, food, and clothing. You might also have expenses for travel and entertainment. Once the school year begins, you can use the budget as a tool for guiding your spending priorities during the year.

The budget is used in businesses in much the same way it can be used in personal life. For example, **Hendrick Motorsport**, featuring drivers Dale Earnhardt, Jr., Jeff Gordon, and Jimmy Johnson, uses budget information to remain one of the most valuable racing teams in NASCAR. Hendrick uses budgets to keep revenues greater than expenses. For example, Hendrick plans revenues from car sponsorships and winnings. Primary and secondary sponsorships (car decals) can provide as much as 70% of the revenues for a typical race team. Costs include salaries, engines, tires, cars, travel, and research and development. In addition, star drivers such as Dale Earnhardt, Jr. can earn as much as $28 million in salary, winnings, and endorsements. Overall, Hendrick is estimated to earn $179 million in revenues and $16.6 million in operating income from their four race teams. The budget provides the company with a "game plan" for the year. In this chapter, you will see how budgets can be used for financial planning and control.

Source: Kurt Badenhausen, "Hendrick Motorsports Tops list of Nascar's Most Valuable Teams," *Forbes*, March 13, 2013. Bob Pockrass, "NASCAR's Highest Paid drivers make their money from a variety of sources," *Sporting News*, December 4, 2012. Ed Hilton, "Under the Hood at Hendrick Motorsports", *Chicago Tribune*, July 13, 2007.

Learning Objectives

After studying this chapter, you should be able to: *Example Exercises*

OBJ 1 **Describe budgeting, its objectives, and its impact on human behavior.**
Nature and Objectives of Budgeting
- Objectives of Budgeting
- Human Behavior and Budgeting

OBJ 2 **Describe the basic elements of the budget process, the two major types of budgeting, and the use of computers in budgeting.**
Budgeting Systems
- Static Budget
- Flexible Budget — EE 6-1
- Computerized Budgeting Systems

OBJ 3 **Describe the master budget for a manufacturing company.**
Master Budget

OBJ 4 **Prepare the basic operating budgets for a manufacturing company.**
Operating Budgets
- Sales Budget
- Production Budget — EE 6-2
- Direct Materials Purchases Budget — EE 6-3
- Direct Labor Cost Budget — EE 6-4
- Factory Overhead Cost Budget
- Cost of Goods Sold Budget — EE 6-5
- Selling and Administrative Expenses Budget
- Budgeted Income Statement

OBJ 5 **Prepare financial budgets for a manufacturing company.**
Financial Budgets
- Cash Budget — EE 6-6
- Capital Expenditures Budget
- Budgeted Balance Sheet

At a Glance 6 Page 250

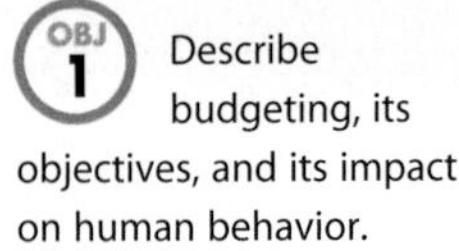
Describe budgeting, its objectives, and its impact on human behavior.

Nature and Objectives of Budgeting

Budgets play an important role for organizations of all sizes and forms. For example, budgets are used in managing the operations of government agencies, churches, hospitals, and other nonprofit organizations. Individuals and families also use budgeting in managing their financial affairs. This chapter describes and illustrates budgeting for a manufacturing company.

Objectives of Budgeting

Budgeting involves (1) establishing specific goals, (2) executing plans to achieve the goals, and (3) periodically comparing actual results with the goals. In doing so, budgeting affects the following managerial functions:

- Planning
- Directing
- Controlling

The relationships of these activities are illustrated in Exhibit 1.

Planning involves setting goals to guide decisions and help motivate employees. The planning process often identifies where operations can be improved.

Directing involves decisions and actions to achieve budgeted goals. A budgetary unit of a company is called a **responsibility center**. Each responsibility center is led by a manager who has the authority and responsibility for achieving the center's budgeted goals.

EXHIBIT 1 **Planning, Directing, and Controlling**

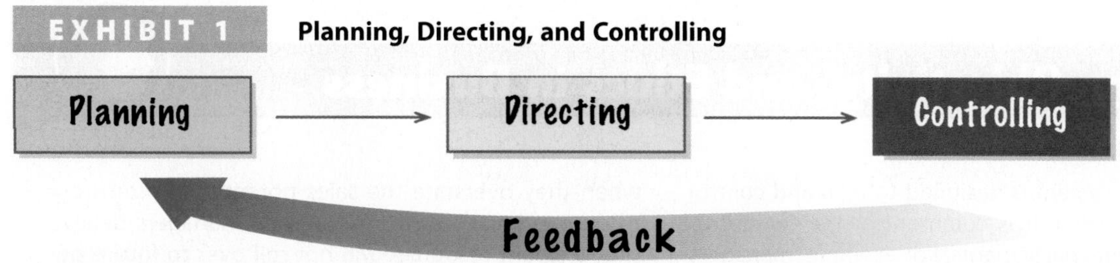

Controlling involves comparing actual performance against the budgeted goals. Such comparisons provide feedback to managers and employees about their performance. If necessary, responsibility centers can use such feedback to adjust their activities in the future.

Human Behavior and Budgeting

Human behavior problems can arise in the budgeting process in the following situations:

- Budgeted goals are set too tight, which are very hard or impossible to achieve.
- Budgeted goals are set too loose, which are very easy to achieve.
- Budgeted goals conflict with the objectives of the company and employees.

These behavior problems are illustrated in Exhibit 2.

EXHIBIT 2 **Human Behavior Problems in Budgeting**

Setting Budget Goals Too Tightly Employees and managers may become discouraged if budgeted goals are set too high. That is, if budgeted goals are viewed as unrealistic or unachievable, the budget may have a negative effect on the ability of the company to achieve its goals.

Reasonable, attainable goals are more likely to motivate employees and managers. For this reason, it is important for employees and managers to be involved in the budgeting process. Involving employees in the budgeting process provides them with a sense of control and, thus, more of a commitment in meeting budgeted goals.

Setting Budget Goals Too Loosely Although it is desirable to establish attainable goals, it is undesirable to plan budget goals that are too easy. Such budget "padding" is termed **budgetary slack**. Managers may plan slack in their budgets to provide a "cushion" for unexpected events. However, slack budgets may create inefficiency by reducing the budgetary incentive to trim spending.

Setting Conflicting Budget Goals **Goal conflict** occurs when the employees' or managers' self-interest differs from the company's objectives or goals. To illustrate, assume that the sales department manager is given an increased sales goal and as a result accepts customers who are poor credit risks. Thus, while the sales department might meet sales goals, the overall firm may suffer reduced profitability from bad debts.

Integrity, Objectivity, and Ethics in Business

BUDGET GAMES

The budgeting system is designed to plan and control a business. However, it is common for the budget to be "gamed" by its participants. For example, managers may pad their budgets with excess resources. In this way, the managers have additional resources for unexpected events during the period. If the budget is being used to establish the incentive plan, then sales managers have incentives to understate the sales potential of a territory to ensure hitting their quotas. Other times, managers engage in "land grabbing," which occurs when they overstate the sales potential of a territory to guarantee access to resources. If managers believe that unspent resources will not roll over to future periods, then they may be encouraged to "spend it or lose it," causing wasteful expenditures. These types of problems can be partially overcome by separating the budget into planning and incentive components. This is why many organizations have two budget processes, one for resource planning and another, more challenging budget, for motivating managers.

OBJ 2 Describe the basic elements of the budget process, the two major types of budgeting, and the use of computers in budgeting.

Budgeting Systems

Budgeting systems vary among companies and industries. For example, the budget system used by **Ford Motor Company** differs from that used by **Delta Air Lines**. However, the basic budgeting concepts discussed in this section apply to all types of businesses and organizations.

The budgetary period for operating activities normally includes the fiscal year of a company. A year is short enough that future operations can be estimated fairly accurately, yet long enough that the future can be viewed in a broad context. However, for control purposes, annual budgets are usually subdivided into shorter time periods, such as quarters of the year, months, or weeks.

A variation of fiscal-year budgeting, called **continuous budgeting**, maintains a 12-month projection into the future. The 12-month budget is continually revised by replacing the data for the month just ended with the budget data for the same month in the next year. A continuous budget is illustrated in Exhibit 3.

EXHIBIT 3 **Continuous Budgeting**

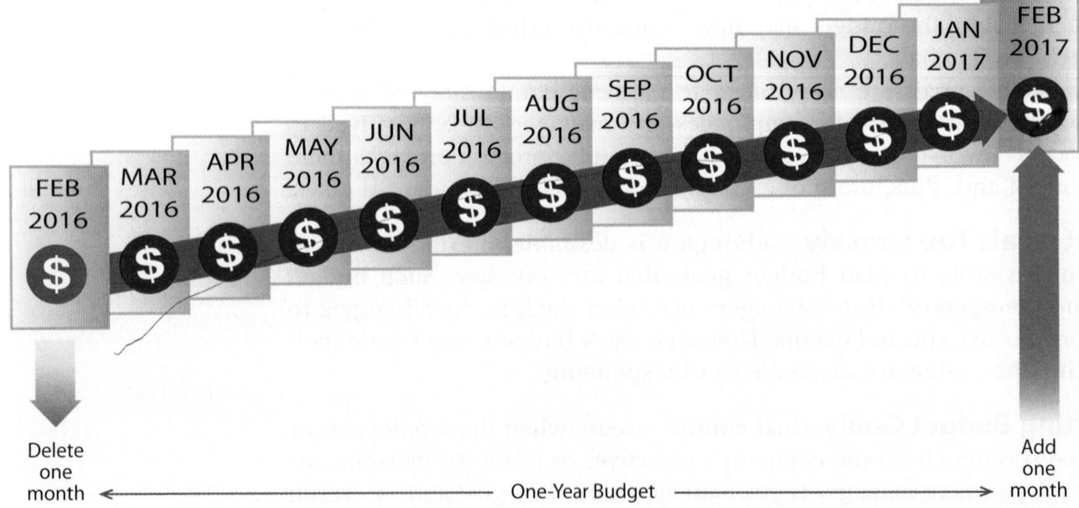

Developing an annual budget usually begins several months prior to the end of the current year. This responsibility is normally assigned to a budget committee. Such a committee often consists of the budget director, the controller, the treasurer, the production manager, and the sales manager. The budget process is monitored and summarized by the Accounting Department, which reports to the committee.

There are several methods of developing budget estimates. One method, called **zero-based budgeting**, requires managers to estimate sales, production, and other operating data as though operations are being started for the first time. This approach has the benefit of taking a fresh view of operations each year. A more common approach is to start with last year's budget and revise it for actual results and expected changes for the coming year. Two major budgets using this approach are the static budget and the flexible budget.

Static Budget

A **static budget** shows the expected results of a responsibility center for only one activity level. Once the budget has been determined, it is not changed, even if the activity changes. Static budgeting is used by many service companies, governmental entities, and for some functions of manufacturing companies, such as purchasing, engineering, and accounting.

To illustrate, the static budget for the Assembly Department of Colter Manufacturing Company is shown in Exhibit 4.

EXHIBIT 4

Static Budget

	A	B
1	Colter Manufacturing Company	
2	Assembly Department Budget	
3	For the Year Ending July 31, 2016	
4	Direct labor	$40,000
5	Electric power	5,000
6	Supervisor salaries	15,000
7	Total department costs	$60,000

A disadvantage of static budgets is that they do not adjust for changes in activity levels. For example, assume that the Assembly Department of Colter Manufacturing spent $70,800 for the year ended July 31, 2016. Thus, the Assembly Department spent $10,800 ($70,800 – $60,000), or 18% ($10,800 ÷ $60,000) more than budgeted. Is this good news or bad news?

The first reaction is that this is bad news and the Assembly Department was inefficient in spending more than budgeted. However, assume that the Assembly Department's budget was based on plans to assemble 8,000 units during the year. If 10,000 units were actually assembled, the additional $10,800 spent in excess of budget might be good news. That is, the Assembly Department assembled 25% (2,000 units ÷ 8,000 units) more than planned for only 18% more cost. In this case, a static budget may not be useful for controlling costs.

Service Focus

FILM BUDGETING

Service businesses, like film and entertainment, use budgets as a roadmap to control expenses. In film production, the budget is a valuable tool to manage the tension between creative expression and cost.

The film budget is a static budget that can be divided into three major categories:

- above the line
- below the line
- post-production costs

The *above the line* costs include costs attributed to creative talent, such as the lead cast's and director's salaries and script fees. The *below the line* costs include the remaining costs to create the film, including location, costume, and prop rentals; permits; and other production costs. The *post-production costs* include the costs to complete the film, including editing, sound, and special effects. Marketing has a separate budget.

The total cost of the film is influenced by many decisions, including the cost of story rights, location, star quality of creative talent, union representation in the production crew, music, and special effects. Even a low-budget Indie (independent) documentary could easily have a budget of more than $1 million. In contrast, a special effect-laden Hollywood film could have a budget in excess of $200 million.

Flexible Budget

Note:
Flexible budgets show expected results for several activity levels.

Unlike static budgets, **flexible budgets** show the expected results of a responsibility center for several activity levels. A flexible budget is, in effect, a series of static budgets for different levels of activity.

To illustrate, a flexible budget for the Assembly Department of Colter Manufacturing Company is shown in Exhibit 5.

EXHIBIT 5

Flexible Budget

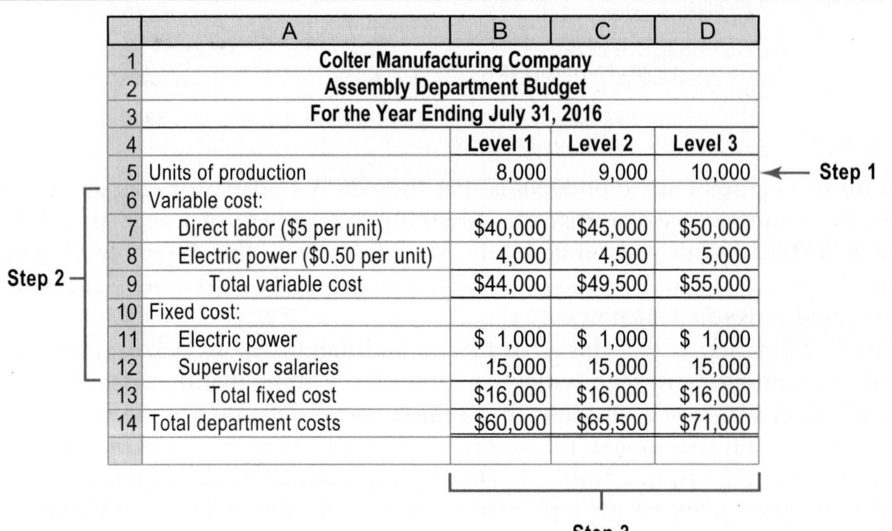

	A	B	C	D
1	Colter Manufacturing Company			
2	Assembly Department Budget			
3	For the Year Ending July 31, 2016			
4		Level 1	Level 2	Level 3
5	Units of production	8,000	9,000	10,000
6	Variable cost:			
7	Direct labor ($5 per unit)	$40,000	$45,000	$50,000
8	Electric power ($0.50 per unit)	4,000	4,500	5,000
9	Total variable cost	$44,000	$49,500	$55,000
10	Fixed cost:			
11	Electric power	$ 1,000	$ 1,000	$ 1,000
12	Supervisor salaries	15,000	15,000	15,000
13	Total fixed cost	$16,000	$16,000	$16,000
14	Total department costs	$60,000	$65,500	$71,000

A flexible budget is constructed as follows:

- Step 1. Identify the relevant activity levels. The relevant levels of activity could be expressed in units, machine hours, direct labor hours, or some other activity base. In Exhibit 5, the levels of activity are 8,000, 9,000, and 10,000 units of production.
- Step 2. Identify the fixed and variable cost components of the costs being budgeted. In Exhibit 5, the electric power cost is separated into its fixed cost ($1,000 per year) and variable cost ($0.50 per unit). The direct labor is a variable cost, and the supervisor salaries are all fixed costs.
- Step 3. Prepare the budget for each activity level by multiplying the variable cost per unit by the activity level and then adding the monthly fixed cost.

With a flexible budget, actual costs can be compared to the budgeted costs for actual activity. To illustrate, assume that the Assembly Department spent $70,800 to produce 10,000 units. Exhibit 5 indicates that the Assembly Department was *under* budget by $200 ($71,000 – $70,800).

Under the static budget in Exhibit 4, the Assembly Department was $10,800 *over* budget. This comparison is illustrated in Exhibit 6.

The flexible budget for the Assembly Department is much more accurate and useful than the static budget. This is because the flexible budget adjusts for changes in the level of activity. Flexible budgets can be used in service businesses when the variable costs can be associated to an activity. For example, hospital room expenses are related to number of patients, or transportation fuel costs are related to number of miles.

EXHIBIT 6 **Static and Flexible Budgets**

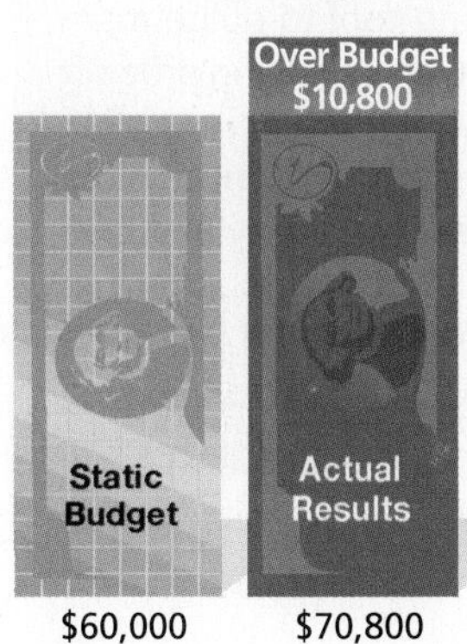

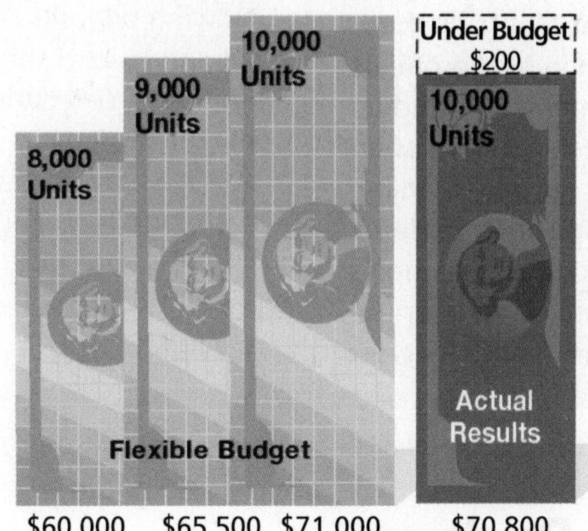

Example Exercise 6-1 Flexible Budgeting

OBJ 2

At the beginning of the period, the Assembly Department budgeted direct labor of $45,000 and supervisor salaries of $30,000 for 5,000 hours of production. The department actually completed 6,000 hours of production. Determine the budget for the department, assuming that it uses flexible budgeting.

Follow My Example 6-1

Variable cost:	
Direct labor (6,000 hours × $9* per hour)	$54,000
Fixed cost:	
Supervisor salaries	30,000
Total department costs	$84,000

*$45,000 ÷ 5,000 hours

Practice Exercises: PE 6-1A, PE 6-1B

Computerized Budgeting Systems

In developing budgets, companies use a variety of computerized approaches. Two of the most popular computerized approaches use:

- Spreadsheet software such as Microsoft Excel
- Integrated budget and planning (B&P) software systems

Spreadsheets ease budget preparation by summarizing budget information in linked spreadsheets across the organization. In addition, the impact of proposed changes in various assumptions or operating alternatives can be analyzed on a spreadsheet.

Fujitsu, a Japanese technology company, used B&P to reduce its budgeting process from 6–8 weeks down to 10–15 days.

B&P software systems use the Web (Intranet) to link thousands of employees together during the budget process. Employees can input budget data onto Web pages that are integrated and summarized throughout the company. In this way, a company can quickly and consistently integrate top-level strategies and goals to lower-level operational goals.

Business  Connection

BUILD VERSUS HARVEST

Budgeting systems are not "one size fits all" solutions but must adapt to the underlying business conditions. For example, a business can adopt either a build strategy or a harvest strategy. A *build* strategy is one where the business is designing, launching, and growing new products and markets. **Apple, Inc.**'s iPad® is an example of a product managed under a build strategy. A *harvest* strategy is often employed for business units with mature products enjoying high market share in low-growth industries. **H.J. Heinz Company**'s ketchup and **P&G**'s *Ivory* soap are examples of such products. A build strategy often has greater uncertainty, unpredictability, and change than a harvest strategy. The difference between these strategies implies different budgeting approaches.

The build strategy should employ a budget approach that is flexible to the uncertainty of the business. Thus, budgets should adapt to changing conditions by allowing periodic revisions and flexible targets. The budget serves as a short-term planning tool to guide management in executing an uncertain and evolving product market strategy.

In a harvest strategy, the business is often much more stable and is managed to maximize profitability and cash flow. Because cost control is much more important in this strategy, the budget is used to restrict the actions of managers.

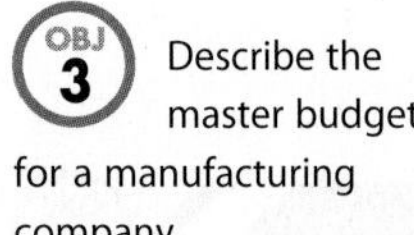
OBJ 3 Describe the master budget for a manufacturing company.

Master Budget

The **master budget** is an integrated set of operating and financial budgets for a period of time. Most companies prepare a master budget on a yearly basis. Exhibit 7 shows that the operating budgets can be used to prepare a budgeted income statement, while the financial budgets provide information for a budgeted balance sheet.

EXHIBIT 7

Master Budget for a Manufacturing Company

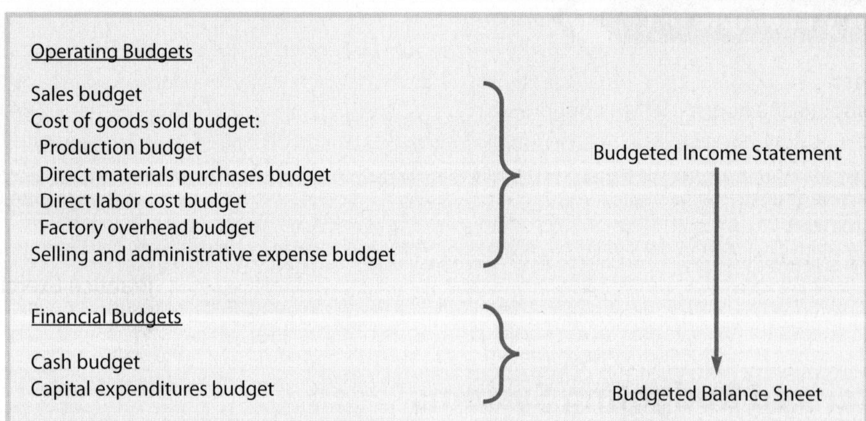

The master budget begins with preparing the operating budgets, which form the budgeted income statement. Exhibit 8 shows the relationships among the operating budgets leading to an income statement budget.

EXHIBIT 8

Operating Budgets

Sales Budget

Production Budget

Direct Materials Purchases Budget

Direct Labor Cost Budget

Factory Overhead Cost Budget

Selling & Admin. Expenses Budget

Cost of Goods Sold Budget

Budgeted Income Statement

Operating Budgets

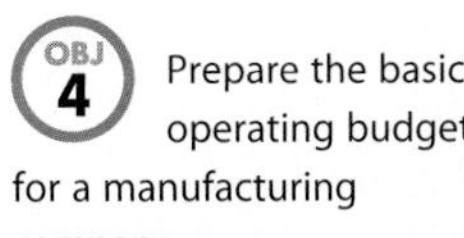

Prepare the basic operating budgets for a manufacturing company.

The integrated operating budgets that support the income statement budget are illustrated for **Elite Accessories Inc.**, a small manufacturing company of personal accessories.

Sales Budget

The **sales budget** begins by estimating the quantity of sales. The prior year's sales are often used as a starting point. These sales quantities are then revised for such factors as planned advertising and promotion, projected pricing changes, and expected industry and general economic conditions.

Once sales quantities are estimated, the budgeted sales revenue can be determined as follows:

Budgeted Revenue = Expected Sales Volume × Expected Unit Sales Price

To illustrate, **Elite Accessories Inc.** manufactures wallets and handbags that are sold in two regions, the East and West regions. Elite Accessories estimates the following sales volumes and prices for 2016:

	East Region Sales Volume	West Region Sales Volume	Unit Selling Price
Wallets	287,000	241,000	$12
Handbags	156,400	123,600	25

Exhibit 9 illustrates the sales budget for Elite Accessories based on the preceding data.

EXHIBIT 9

Sales Budget

	A	B	C	D
1	Elite Accessories Inc.			
2	Sales Budget			
3	For the Year Ending December 31, 2016			
4		Unit Sales	Unit Selling	
5	Product and Region	Volume	Price	Total Sales
6	Wallet:			
7	East	287,000	$12.00	$ 3,444,000
8	West	241,000	12.00	2,892,000
9	Total	528,000		$ 6,336,000
10				
11	Handbag:			
12	East	156,400	$25.00	$ 3,910,000
13	West	123,600	25.00	3,090,000
14	Total	280,000		$ 7,000,000
15				
16	Total revenue from sales			$13,336,000

Production Budget

The production budget should be integrated with the sales budget to ensure that production and sales are kept in balance during the year. The **production budget** estimates the number of units to be manufactured to meet budgeted sales and desired inventory levels.

The budgeted units to be produced are determined as follows:

Expected units to be sold	XXX units
Plus desired units in ending inventory	+ XXX
Less estimated units in beginning inventory	– XXX
Total units to be produced	XXX units

Elite Accessories Inc. expects the following inventories of wallets and handbags:

	Estimated Inventory, January 1, 2016	Desired Inventory, December 31, 2016
Wallets	88,000	80,000
Handbags	48,000	60,000

Exhibit 10 illustrates the production budget for Elite Accessories.

EXHIBIT 10

Production Budget

	A	B	C
1	Elite Accessories Inc.		
2	Production Budget		
3	For the Year Ending December 31, 2016		
4		Units	
5		Wallet	Handbag
6	Expected units to be sold (from Exhibit 9)	528,000	280,000
7	Plus desired ending inventory, December 31, 2016	80,000	60,000
8	Total	608,000	340,000
9	Less estimated beginning inventory, January 1, 2016	88,000	48,000
10	Total units to be produced	520,000	292,000

Example Exercise 6-2 Production Budget

Landon Awards Co. projected sales of 45,000 brass plaques for 2016. The estimated January 1, 2016, inventory is 3,000 units, and the desired December 31, 2016, inventory is 5,000 units. What is the budgeted production (in units) for 2016?

Follow My Example 6-2

Expected units to be sold	45,000
Plus desired ending inventory, December 31, 2016	5,000
Total	50,000
Less estimated beginning inventory, January 1, 2016	3,000
Total units to be produced	47,000

Practice Exercises: PE 6-2A, PE 6-2B

Direct Materials Purchases Budget

The direct materials purchases budget should be integrated with the production budget to ensure that production is not interrupted during the year. The **direct materials purchases budget** estimates the quantities of direct materials to be purchased to support budgeted production and desired inventory levels and can be developed in three steps.

Step 1 Determine the budgeted direct material required for production, which is computed as follows:

Budgeted Direct Material Required for Production = Budgeted Production Volume (from Exhibit 10) × Direct Material Quantity Expected per Unit

To illustrate, **Elite Accessories Inc.** uses leather and lining in producing wallets and handbags. The quantity of direct materials expected to be used for each unit of product is as follows:

Wallet	Handbag
Leather: 0.30 sq. yd. per unit	Leather: 1.25 sq. yds. per unit
Lining: 0.10 sq. yd. per unit	Lining: 0.50 sq. yd. per unit

For the wallet, the direct material required for production is computed as follows:

Leather: 520,000 units × 0.30 sq. yd. per unit = 156,000 sq. yds.
Lining: 520,000 units × 0.10 sq. yd. per unit = 52,000 sq. yds.

For the handbag, the direct material required for production is computed as follows:

Leather: 292,000 units × 1.25 sq. yd. per unit = 365,000 sq. yds.
Lining: 292,000 units × 0.50 sq. yd. per unit = 146,000 sq. yds.

Step 2 The budgeted material required for production is adjusted for beginning and ending inventories to determine the direct materials to be purchased for each material, as follows:

Materials required for production (Step 1)	XXX
Plus desired ending materials inventory	+XXX
Less estimated beginning materials inventory	–XXX
Direct material quantity to be purchased	XXX

Step 3 The budgeted direct materials to be purchased is computed as follows:

Budgeted Direct Material to be Purchased = Direct Material Quantity to be Purchased (Step 2) × Unit Price

Complete Direct Materials Purchases Budget The following inventory and unit price information for **Elite Accessories Inc.** is expected:

	Estimated Direct Materials Inventory, January 1, 2016	Desired Direct Materials Inventory, December 31, 2016
Leather	18,000 sq. yds.	20,000 sq. yds.
Lining	15,000 sq. yds.	12,000 sq. yds.

The estimated price per square yard of leather and lining during 2016 follows:

	Price per Square Yard
Leather	$4.50
Lining	1.20

Exhibit 11 illustrates the complete direct materials purchases budget for Elite Accessories by combining all three steps into a single schedule.

EXHIBIT 11

Direct Materials Purchases Budget

	A	B	C	D	E
1		Elite Accessories Inc.			
2		Direct Materials Purchases Budget			
3		For the Year Ending December 31, 2016			
4			Direct Materials		
5			Leather	Lining	Total
6	Square yards required for production:				
7 (Step 1.)	Wallet (Note A)		156,000	52,000	
8	Handbag (Note B)		365,000	146,000	
9 (Step 2.)	Plus desired inventory, December 31, 2016		20,000	12,000	
10	Total		541,000	210,000	
11	Less estimated inventory, January 1, 2016		18,000	15,000	
12	Total square yards to be purchased		523,000	195,000	
13 (Step 3.)	Unit price (per square yard)		× $4.50	× $1.20	
14	Total direct materials to be purchased		$2,353,500	$234,000	$2,587,500
15					
16	Note A:	Leather: 520,000 units × 0.30 sq. yd. per unit = 156,000 sq. yds.			
17		Lining: 520,000 units × 0.10 sq. yd. per unit = 52,000 sq. yds.			
18					
19	Note B:	Leather: 292,000 units × 1.25 sq. yds. per unit = 365,000 sq. yds.			
20		Lining: 292,000 units × 0.50 sq. yd. per unit = 146,000 sq. yds.			

The timing of the direct materials purchases should be coordinated between the purchasing and production departments so that production is not interrupted.

Example Exercise 6-3 Direct Materials Purchases Budget

Landon Awards Co. budgeted production of 47,000 brass plaques in 2016. Brass sheet is required to produce a brass plaque. Assume 96 square inches of brass sheet are required for each brass plaque. The estimated January 1, 2016, brass sheet inventory is 240,000 square inches. The desired December 31, 2016, brass sheet inventory is 200,000 square inches. If brass sheet costs $0.12 per square inch, determine the direct materials purchases budget for 2016.

Follow My Example 6-3

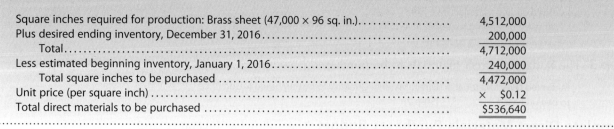

Square inches required for production: Brass sheet (47,000 × 96 sq. in.)	4,512,000
Plus desired ending inventory, December 31, 2016	200,000
Total	4,712,000
Less estimated beginning inventory, January 1, 2016	240,000
Total square inches to be purchased	4,472,000
Unit price (per square inch)	× $0.12
Total direct materials to be purchased	$536,640

Practice Exercises: PE 6-3A, PE 6-3B

Direct Labor Cost Budget

The **direct labor cost budget** estimates the direct labor hours and related cost needed to support budgeted production. Production managers study work methods to provide estimates used in preparing the direct labor cost budget.

The direct labor cost budget for each department is determined in two steps, as follows.

Step 1 Determine the budgeted direct labor hours required for production, which is computed as follows:

Budgeted Direct Labor Hours Required for Production = Budgeted Production Volume (from Exhibit 10) × Direct Labor Hours Expected per Unit

To illustrate, **Elite Accessories Inc.**'s production managers estimate the following direct labor hours are needed to produce a wallet and handbag:

Wallet	Handbag
Cutting Department: 0.10 hr. per unit	Cutting Department: 0.15 hr. per unit
Sewing Department: 0.25 hr. per unit	Sewing Department: 0.40 hr. per unit

Thus, for the wallet, the budgeted direct labor hours required for production is computed as follows:

Cutting: 520,000 units × 0.10 hr. per unit = 52,000 direct labor hours
Sewing: 520,000 units × 0.25 hr. per unit = 130,000 direct labor hours

For the handbag, the budgeted direct labor hours required for production is computed as follows:

Cutting: 292,000 units × 0.15 hr. per unit = 43,800 direct labor hours
Sewing: 292,000 units × 0.40 hr. per unit = 116,800 direct labor hours

Step 2 Determine the total direct labor cost as follows:

Direct Labor Cost = Direct Labor Required for Production (Step 1) × Hourly Rate

The estimated direct labor hourly rates for the Cutting and Sewing departments for **Elite Accessories, Inc.** during 2016 follow:

	Hourly Rate
Cutting Department	$12
Sewing Department	15

Complete Direct Labor Cost Budget Exhibit 12 illustrates the direct labor cost budget by combining both steps for **Elite Accessories Inc.**

EXHIBIT 12
Direct Labor Cost Budget

		A	B	C	D	E
	1	Elite Accessories Inc.				
	2	Direct Labor Cost Budget				
	3	For the Year Ending December 31, 2016				
	4			Cutting	Sewing	Total
	5	Hours required for production:				
Step 1.	6	Wallet (Note A)		52,000	130,000	
Step 1.	7	Handbag (Note B)		43,800	116,800	
Step 2.	8	Total		95,800	246,800	
Step 2.	9	Hourly rate		× $12.00	× $15.00	
Step 2.	10	Total direct labor cost		$1,149,600	$3,702,000	$4,851,600
	11					
	12	Note A:	Cutting Department: 520,000 units × 0.10 hr. per unit = 52,000 hrs.			
	13		Sewing Department: 520,000 units × 0.25 hr. per unit = 130,000 hrs.			
	14					
	15	Note B:	Cutting Department: 292,000 units × 0.15 hr. per unit = 43,800 hrs.			
	16		Sewing Department: 292,000 units × 0.40 hr. per unit = 116,800 hrs.			

The direct labor needs should be coordinated between the production and personnel departments so that there will be enough labor available for production.

Example Exercise 6-4 Direct Labor Cost Budget

OBJ 4

Landon Awards Co. budgeted production of 47,000 brass plaques in 2016. Each plaque requires engraving. Assume that 12 minutes are required to engrave each plaque. If engraving labor costs $11.00 per hour, determine the direct labor cost budget for 2016.

Follow My Example 6-4

Hours required for engraving:	
Brass plaque (47,000 × 12 min.)	564,000 min.
Convert minutes to hours	÷ 60 min.
Engraving hours	9,400 hrs.
Hourly rate	× $11.00
Total direct labor cost	$103,400

Practice Exercises: PE 6-4A, PE 6-4B

Factory Overhead Cost Budget

The **factory overhead cost budget** estimates the cost for each item of factory overhead needed to support budgeted production.

Exhibit 13 illustrates the factory overhead cost budget for **Elite Accessories Inc.**

EXHIBIT 13

Factory Overhead Cost Budget

	A	B
1	Elite Accessories Inc.	
2	Factory Overhead Cost Budget	
3	For the Year Ending December 31, 2016	
4	Indirect factory wages	$ 732,800
5	Supervisor salaries	360,000
6	Power and light	306,000
7	Depreciation of plant and equipment	288,000
8	Indirect materials	182,800
9	Maintenance	140,280
10	Insurance and property taxes	79,200
11	Total factory overhead cost	$2,089,080

The factory overhead cost budget shown in Exhibit 13 may be supported by departmental schedules. Such schedules normally separate factory overhead costs into fixed and variable costs to better enable department managers to monitor and evaluate costs during the year.

The factory overhead cost budget should be integrated with the production budget to ensure that production is not interrupted during the year.

Cost of Goods Sold Budget

The **cost of goods sold budget** is prepared by integrating the following budgets:

- Direct materials purchases budget (Exhibit 11)
- Direct labor cost budget (Exhibit 12)
- Factory overhead cost budget (Exhibit 13)

In addition, the estimated and desired inventories for direct materials, work in process, and finished goods must be integrated into the cost of goods sold budget.

Elite Accessories Inc. expects the following direct materials, work in process, and finished goods inventories:

	Estimated Inventory, January 1, 2016	Desired Inventory, December 31, 2016
Direct materials:		
Leather	$ 81,000 (18,000 sq. yds. × $4.50)	$ 90,000 (20,000 sq. yds. × $4.50)
Lining	18,000 (15,000 sq. yds. × $1.20)	14,400 (12,000 sq. yds. × $1.20)
Total direct materials	$ 99,000	$ 104,400
Work in process	$ 214,400	$ 220,000
Finished goods	$1,095,600	$1,565,000

The cost of goods sold budget for Elite Accessories in Exhibit 14 indicates that total manufacturing costs of $9,522,780 are budgeted to be incurred in 2016. Of this total, $2,582,100 is budgeted for direct materials, $4,851,600 is budgeted for direct labor, and $2,089,080 is budgeted for factory overhead. After considering work in process inventories, the total budgeted cost of goods manufactured and transferred to finished goods during 2016 is $9,517,180. Based on expected sales, the budgeted cost of goods sold is $9,047,780.

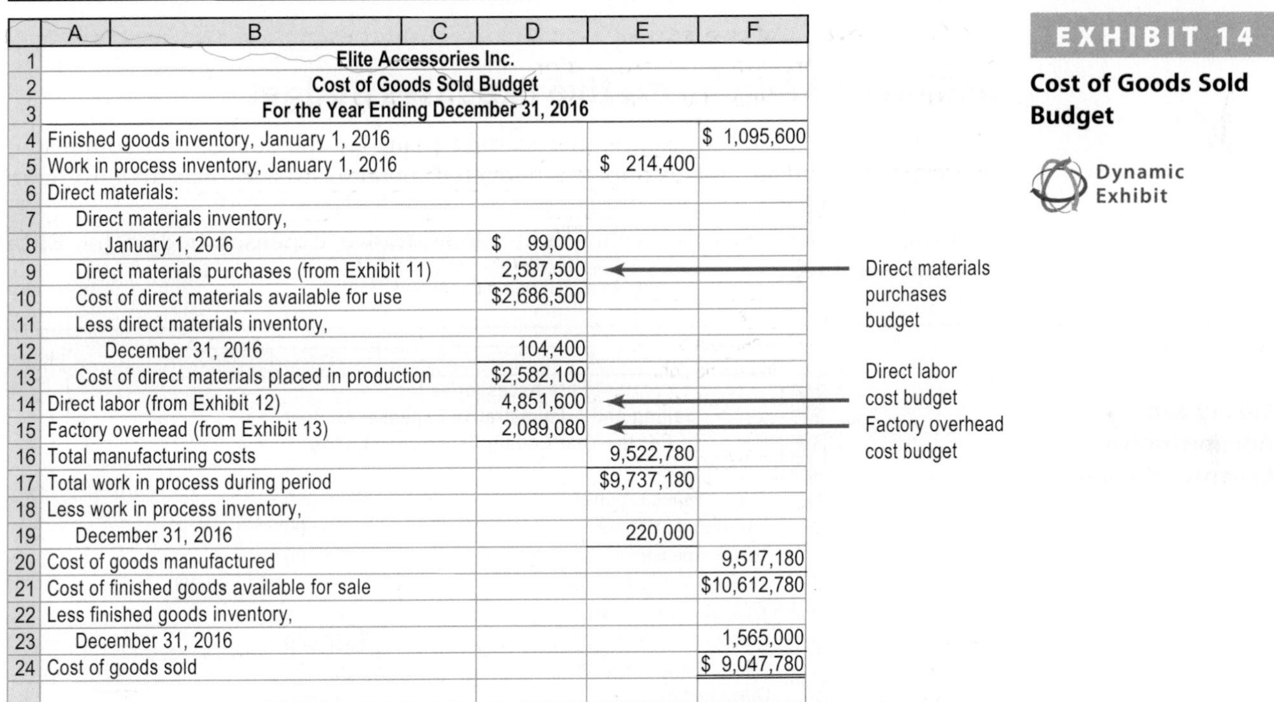

	A / B / C	D	E	F
1	Elite Accessories Inc.			
2	Cost of Goods Sold Budget			
3	For the Year Ending December 31, 2016			
4	Finished goods inventory, January 1, 2016			$ 1,095,600
5	Work in process inventory, January 1, 2016		$ 214,400	
6	Direct materials:			
7	Direct materials inventory,			
8	January 1, 2016	$ 99,000		
9	Direct materials purchases (from Exhibit 11)	2,587,500		
10	Cost of direct materials available for use	$2,686,500		
11	Less direct materials inventory,			
12	December 31, 2016	104,400		
13	Cost of direct materials placed in production	$2,582,100		
14	Direct labor (from Exhibit 12)	4,851,600		
15	Factory overhead (from Exhibit 13)	2,089,080		
16	Total manufacturing costs		9,522,780	
17	Total work in process during period		$9,737,180	
18	Less work in process inventory,			
19	December 31, 2016		220,000	
20	Cost of goods manufactured			9,517,180
21	Cost of finished goods available for sale			$10,612,780
22	Less finished goods inventory,			
23	December 31, 2016			1,565,000
24	Cost of goods sold			$ 9,047,780

EXHIBIT 14

Cost of Goods Sold Budget

Dynamic Exhibit

Example Exercise 6-5 Cost of Goods Sold Budget

OBJ 4

Prepare a cost of goods sold budget for Landon Awards Co. using the information in Example Exercises 6-3 and 6-4. Assume the estimated inventories on January 1, 2016, for finished goods and work in process were $54,000 and $47,000, respectively. Also assume the desired inventories on December 31, 2016, for finished goods and work in process were $50,000 and $49,000, respectively. Factory overhead was budgeted for $126,000.

(Continued)

Follow My Example 6-5

Finished goods inventory, January 1, 2016			$ 54,000
Work in process inventory, January 1, 2016		$ 47,000	
Direct materials:			
Direct materials inventory, January 1, 2014 (240,000 × $0.12, from EE 6-3)	$ 28,800		
Direct materials purchases (from EE 6-3)	536,640		
Cost of direct materials available for use	$565,440		
Less direct materials inventory, December 31, 2016 (200,000 × $0.12, from EE 6-3)	24,000		
Cost of direct materials placed in production	$541,440		
Direct labor (from EE 6-4)	103,400		
Factory overhead	126,000		
Total manufacturing costs		770,840	
Total work in process during period		$817,840	
Less work in process inventory, December 31, 2016		49,000	
Cost of goods manufactured			768,840
Cost of finished goods available for sale			$822,840
Less finished goods inventory, December 31, 2016			50,000
Cost of goods sold			$772,840

Practice Exercises: PE 6-5A, PE 6-5B

Selling and Administrative Expenses Budget

The sales budget is often used as the starting point for the selling and administrative expenses budget. For example, a budgeted increase in sales may require more advertising expenses.

Exhibit 15 illustrates the selling and administrative expenses budget for **Elite Accessories Inc.**

EXHIBIT 15

Selling and Administrative Expenses Budget

	A	B	C
1	**Elite Accessories Inc.**		
2	**Selling and Administrative Expenses Budget**		
3	**For the Year Ending December 31, 2016**		
4	Selling expenses:		
5	Sales salaries expense	$715,000	
6	Advertising expense	360,000	
7	Travel expense	115,000	
8	Total selling expenses		$1,190,000
9	Administrative expenses:		
10	Officers' salaries expense	$360,000	
11	Office salaries expense	258,000	
12	Office rent expense	34,500	
13	Office supplies expense	17,500	
14	Miscellaneous administrative expenses	25,000	
15	Total administrative expenses		695,000
16	Total selling and administrative expenses		$1,885,000

The selling and administrative expenses budget shown in Exhibit 15 is normally supported by departmental schedules. For example, an advertising expense schedule for the Marketing Department could include the advertising media to be used (newspaper, direct mail, television), quantities (column inches, number of pieces, minutes), and related costs per unit.

Budgeted Income Statement

The budgeted income statement for **Elite Accessories Inc.** in Exhibit 16 is prepared by integrating the following budgets:

- Sales budget (Exhibit 9)
- Cost of goods sold budget (Exhibit 14)
- Selling and administrative expenses budget (Exhibit 15)

In addition, estimates of other income, other expense, and income tax are also integrated into the budgeted income statement.

This budget summarizes the budgeted operating activities of the company. In doing so, the budgeted income statement allows management to assess the effects of estimated sales, costs, and expenses on profits for the year.

EXHIBIT 16 Budgeted Income Statement

	A	B	C	
1	Elite Accessories Inc.			
2	Budgeted Income Statement			
3	For the Year Ending December 31, 2016			
4	Revenue from sales (from Exhibit 9)		$13,336,000	← Sales budget
5	Cost of goods sold (from Exhibit 14)		9,047,780	← Cost of goods sold budget
6				
7	Gross profit		$ 4,288,220	
8	Selling and administrative expenses:			
9	Selling expenses (from Exhibit 15)	$1,190,000		Selling and administrative expenses budget
10	Administrative expenses (from Exhibit 15)	695,000		
11	Total selling and administrative expenses		1,885,000	
12	Income from operations		$ 2,403,220	
13	Other income:			
14	Interest revenue	$ 98,000		
15	Other expenses:			
16	Interest expense	90,000	8,000	
17	Income before income tax		$ 2,411,220	
18	Income tax		600,000	
19	Net income		$ 1,811,220	

Financial Budgets

OBJ 5 Prepare financial budgets for a manufacturing company.

While the operating budgets reflect the operating activities of the company, the financial budgets reflect the financing and investing activities. In this section, the following financial budgets are described and illustrated:

- Cash budget
- Capital expenditures budget

Cash Budget

The **cash budget** estimates the expected receipts (inflows) and payments (outflows) of cash for a period of time. The cash budget is integrated with the various operating budgets. In addition, the capital expenditures budget, dividends, and equity or long-term debt financing plans of the company affect the cash budget.

Note:
The cash budget presents the expected receipts and payments of cash for a period of time.

To illustrate, a monthly cash budget for January, February, and March 2016 for **Elite Accessories Inc.** is prepared. The preparation of the cash budget begins by estimating cash receipts.

Estimated Cash Receipts The primary source of estimated cash receipts is from cash sales and collections on account. In addition, cash receipts may be obtained from plans to issue equity or debt financing as well as other sources such as interest revenue.

To estimate cash receipts from cash sales and collections on account, a *schedule of collections from sales* is prepared. To illustrate, the following data for **Elite Accessories Inc.** are used:

	January	February	March
Sales:			
Budgeted sales	$1,080,000	$1,240,000	$970,000
Accounts Receivable:			
Accounts receivable January 1, 2016	$480,000		
Receipts from sales on account:			
From prior month's sales on account	40%		
From current month's sales on account	60		
	100%		

The budgeted cash collected for any month is the sum of the cash collected from previous month's sales and the cash collected from current month's sales. To illustrate, the cash collected in February is 40% of cash collected on sales in January ($1,080,000 × 40%) added to 60% of cash collected on sales in February ($1,240,000 × 60%), shown as follows:

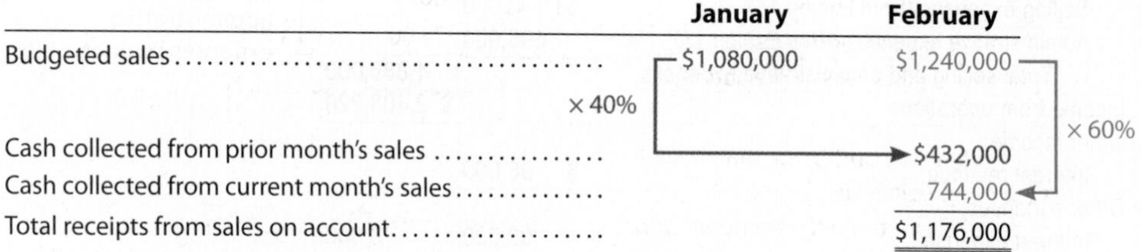

	January	February
Budgeted sales	$1,080,000	$1,240,000
	× 40%	× 60%
Cash collected from prior month's sales		$432,000
Cash collected from current month's sales		744,000
Total receipts from sales on account		$1,176,000

Using the preceding data, Exhibit 17 shows the schedule of collections from sales for Elite Accessories for all three months. To simplify, it is assumed that all accounts receivable are collected and there are no cash sales.

EXHIBIT 17

Schedule of Collections from Sales

	A	B	C	D	E
1	Elite Accessories Inc.				
2	Schedule of Collections from Sales				
3	For the Three Months Ending March 31, 2016				
4			January	February	March
5	Cash collected from prior month's sales—Note A		480,000	432,000	496,000
6	Cash collected from current month's sales—Note B		648,000	744,000	582,000
7	Total receipts from sales on account		$1,128,000	$1,176,000	$1,078,000
8					
9	Note A:	$480,000, given as January 1, 2016, Accounts Receivable balance			
10		$432,000 = $1,080,000 × 40%			
11		$496,000 = $1,240,000 × 40%			
12					
13	Note B:	$648,000 = $1,080,000 × 60%			
14		$744,000 = $1,240,000 × 60%			
15		$582,000 = $970,000 × 60%			

Estimated Cash Payments Estimated cash payments must be budgeted for operating costs and expenses such as manufacturing costs, selling expenses, and administrative expenses. In addition, estimated cash payments may be planned for capital expenditures, dividends, interest payments, or long-term debt payments.

To estimate cash payments for manufacturing costs, a *schedule of payments for manufacturing costs* is prepared. To illustrate, the following data for **Elite Accessories Inc.** are used:

	January	February	March
Manufacturing Costs:			
Budgeted manufacturing costs	$840,000	$780,000	$812,000
Depreciation on machines included in manufacturing costs	24,000	24,000	24,000
Accounts Payable:			
Accounts payable, January 1, 2016	$190,000		
Payments of manufacturing costs on account:			
From prior month's manufacturing costs	25%		
From current month's manufacturing costs	75		
	100%		

The budgeted cash payments for any month are the sum of the cash paid from previous month's manufacturing costs (less depreciation) and the cash paid from current month's manufacturing costs (less depreciation). To illustrate, the cash paid in February is 25% of manufacturing costs (less depreciation) in January [($840,000 – $24,000) × 25%] added to 75% of cash paid on manufacturing costs (less depreciation) in February [($780,000 – $24,000) × 75%], computed as follows:

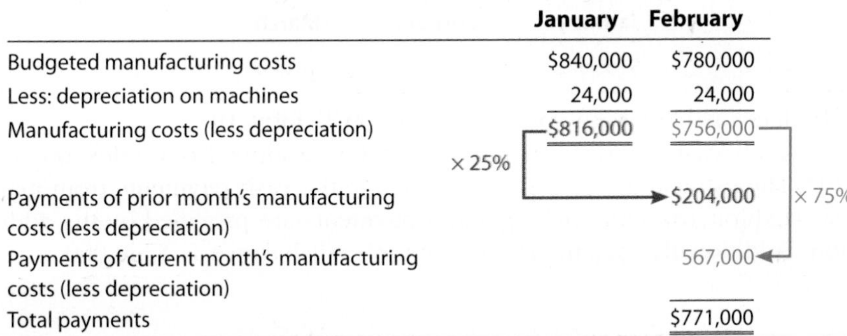

	January	February
Budgeted manufacturing costs	$840,000	$780,000
Less: depreciation on machines	24,000	24,000
Manufacturing costs (less depreciation)	$816,000	$756,000
Payments of prior month's manufacturing costs (less depreciation) (× 25%)		$204,000
Payments of current month's manufacturing costs (less depreciation) (× 75%)		567,000
Total payments		$771,000

Using the preceding data, Exhibit 18 shows the schedule of payments for manufacturing costs for Elite Accessories for all three months.

EXHIBIT 18

Schedule of Payments for Manufacturing Costs

	A	B	C	D	E
1	Elite Accessories Inc.				
2	Schedule of Payments for Manufacturing Costs				
3	For the Three Months Ending March 31, 2016				
4			January	February	March
5	Payments of prior month's manufacturing costs				
6	{[25% × previous month's manufacturing costs				
7	(less depreciation)]—Note A}		$190,000	$204,000	$189,000
8	Payments of current month's manufacturing costs				
9	{[75% × current month's manufacturing costs				
10	(less depreciation)]—Note B}		612,000	567,000	591,000
11	Total payments		$802,000	$771,000	$780,000
12					
13	Note A:	$190,000, given as January 1, 2016, Accounts Payable balance			
14		$204,000 = ($840,000 – $24,000) × 25%			
15		$189,000 = ($780,000 – $24,000) × 25%			
16					
17	Note B:	$612,000 = ($840,000 – $24,000) × 75%			
18		$567,000 = ($780,000 – $24,000) × 75%			
19		$591,000 = ($812,000 – $24,000) × 75%			

Completing the Cash Budget The cash budget is structured for a budget period as follows:

Budget Period:

Estimated cash receipts	
– Estimated cash payments	
Cash increase (decrease)	
+ Cash balance at the beginning of the month	
Cash balance at the end of the month	→ Becomes the beginning balance for the next period
– Minimum cash balance	
Excess (deficiency)	

The budgeted balance at the end of the period is determined by adding the net increase (decrease) for the period to the beginning cash balance. The ending balance is compared to a minimum cash balance to support operations as determined by management. Any difference between the ending balance and the minimum cash balance represents an excess or deficiency that may require management action.

To illustrate, assume the following additional data for **Elite Accessories Inc.**:

Cash balance on January 1, 2016	$225,000
Quarterly taxes paid on March 31, 2016	150,000
Quarterly interest expense paid on January 10, 2016	22,500
Quarterly interest revenue received on March 21, 2016	24,500
Sewing equipment purchased in February 2016	274,000
Selling and administrative expenses (paid in month incurred):	

January	February	March
$160,000	$165,000	$145,000

The cash budget for Elite Accessories is shown in Exhibit 19.

The estimated cash receipts include the total receipts from sales on account (Exhibit 17). The estimated cash payments include the cash payments from manufacturing costs (Exhibit 18). Other receipts and payments are provided by the additional information. Additionally, assume the minimum cash balance is $340,000.

EXHIBIT 19

Cash Budget

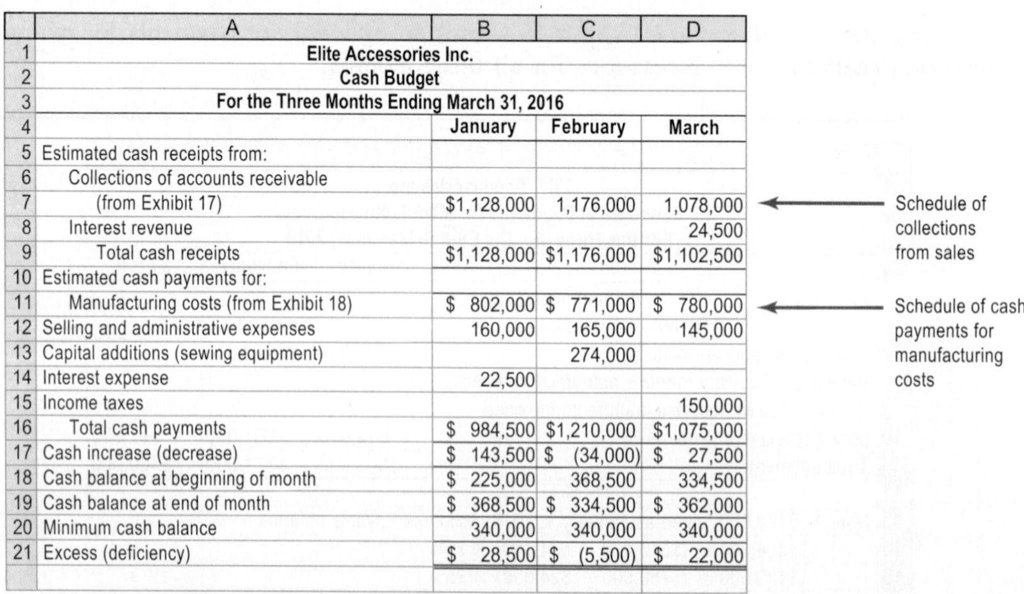

	A	B	C	D
1	Elite Accessories Inc.			
2	Cash Budget			
3	For the Three Months Ending March 31, 2016			
4		January	February	March
5	Estimated cash receipts from:			
6	Collections of accounts receivable			
7	(from Exhibit 17)	$1,128,000	1,176,000	1,078,000
8	Interest revenue			24,500
9	Total cash receipts	$1,128,000	$1,176,000	$1,102,500
10	Estimated cash payments for:			
11	Manufacturing costs (from Exhibit 18)	$ 802,000	$ 771,000	$ 780,000
12	Selling and administrative expenses	160,000	165,000	145,000
13	Capital additions (sewing equipment)		274,000	
14	Interest expense	22,500		
15	Income taxes			150,000
16	Total cash payments	$ 984,500	$1,210,000	$1,075,000
17	Cash increase (decrease)	$ 143,500	$ (34,000)	$ 27,500
18	Cash balance at beginning of month	$ 225,000	368,500	334,500
19	Cash balance at end of month	$ 368,500	$ 334,500	$ 362,000
20	Minimum cash balance	340,000	340,000	340,000
21	Excess (deficiency)	$ 28,500	$ (5,500)	$ 22,000

Exhibit 19 indicates that Elite Accessories expects a cash excess at the end of January of $28,500. This excess could be invested in temporary income-producing securities such as U.S. Treasury bills or notes. In contrast, the estimated cash deficiency at the end of February of $5,500 might require Elite Accessories to borrow cash from its bank.

Example Exercise 6-6 Cash Budget

OBJ 5

Landon Awards Co. collects 25% of its sales on account in the month of the sale and 75% in the month following the sale. If sales on account are budgeted to be $100,000 for March and $126,000 for April, what are the budgeted cash receipts from sales on account for April?

Follow My Example 6-6

	April
Collections from March sales (75% x $100,000)	$ 75,000
Collections from April sales (25% x $126,000)	31,500
Total receipts from sales on account	$106,500

Practice Exercises: PE 6-6A, PE 6-6B

Capital Expenditures Budget

The **capital expenditures budget** summarizes plans for acquiring fixed assets. Such expenditures are necessary as machinery and other fixed assets wear out or become obsolete. In addition, purchasing additional fixed assets may be necessary to meet increasing demand for the company's product.

To illustrate, a five-year capital expenditures budget for **Elite Accessories Inc.** is shown in Exhibit 20.

EXHIBIT 20

Capital Expenditures Budget

	A	B	C	D	E	F
1	Elite Accessories Inc.					
2	Capital Expenditures Budget					
3	For the Five Years Ending December 31, 2020					
4	Item	2016	2017	2018	2019	2020
5	Machinery—Cutting Department	$400,000			$280,000	$360,000
6	Machinery—Sewing Department	274,000	$260,000	$560,000	200,000	
7	Office equipment		90,000			60,000
8	Total	$674,000	$350,000	$560,000	$480,000	$420,000

As shown in Exhibit 20, capital expenditures budgets are often prepared for five to ten years into the future. This is necessary because fixed assets often must be ordered years in advance. Likewise, it could take years to construct new buildings or other production facilities.

The capital expenditures budget should be integrated with the operating and financing budgets. For example, depreciation of new manufacturing equipment affects the factory overhead cost budget. The plans for financing the capital expenditures also affect the cash budget.

Budgeted Balance Sheet

The budgeted balance sheet is prepared based on the operating and financial budgets of the master budget. The budgeted balance sheet is dated as of the end of the budget period and is similar to a normal balance sheet except that estimated amounts are used. For this reason, a budgeted balance sheet for Elite Accessories Inc. is not illustrated.

At a Glance 6

OBJ 1 Describe budgeting, its objectives, and its impact on human behavior.

Key Points Budgeting involves (1) establishing plans (planning), (2) directing operations (directing), and (3) evaluating performance (controlling). In addition, budgets should be established to avoid human behavior problems.

Learning Outcomes	Example Exercises	Practice Exercises
• Describe the planning, directing, controlling, and feedback elements of the budget process.		
• Describe the behavioral issues associated with tight goals, loose goals, and goal conflict.		

OBJ 2 Describe the basic elements of the budget process, the two major types of budgeting, and the use of computers in budgeting.

Key Points The budget estimates received by the budget committee should be carefully studied, analyzed, revised, and integrated. The static and flexible budgets are two major budgeting approaches. Computers can be used to make the budget process more efficient and organizationally integrated.

Learning Outcomes	Example Exercises	Practice Exercises
• Describe a static budget and explain when it might be used.		
• Describe and prepare a flexible budget and explain when it might be used.	EE6-1	PE6-1A, 6-1B
• Describe the role of computers in the budget process.		

OBJ 3 Describe the master budget for a manufacturing company.

Key Points The master budget consists of operating and financial budgets.

Learning Outcome	Example Exercises	Practice Exercises
• Illustrate the connection between the major operating and financial budgets.		

Prepare the basic operating budgets for a manufacturing company.

Key Points The basic operating budgets are the sales budget, production budget, direct materials purchases budget, direct labor cost budget, factory overhead cost budget, cost of goods sold budget, and selling and administrative expenses budget. These can then be combined to prepare an income statement budget.

Learning Outcomes	Example Exercises	Practice Exercises
• Prepare a sales budget.		
• Prepare a production budget.	EE6-2	PE6-2A, 6-2B
• Prepare a direct materials purchases budget.	EE6-3	PE6-3A, 6-3B
• Prepare a direct labor cost budget.	EE6-4	PE6-4A, 6-4B
• Prepare a factory overhead cost budget.		
• Prepare a cost of goods sold budget.	EE6-5	PE6-5A, 6-5B
• Prepare a selling and administrative expenses budget.		
• Prepare an income statement budget.		

Prepare financial budgets for a manufacturing company.

Key Points The cash budget and capital expenditures budget are financial budgets showing the investing and financing activities of the firm.

Learning Outcomes	Example Exercises	Practice Exercises
• Prepare cash receipts and cash payments schedules.	EE6-6	PE6-6A, 6-6B
• Prepare a cash budget.		
• Prepare a capital expenditures budget.		

Key Terms

budgets (230)
budgetary slack (231)
capital expenditures budget (249)
cash budget (245)
continuous budgeting (232)
cost of goods sold budget (242)
direct labor cost budget (240)
direct materials purchases budget (239)
factory overhead cost budget (242)
flexible budgets (234)
goal conflict (231)
master budget (236)
production budget (238)
responsibility center (230)
sales budget (237)
static budget (233)
zero-based budgeting (233)

Illustrative Problem

Selected information concerning sales and production for Cabot Co. for July 2016 are summarized as follows:

a. Estimated sales:

Product K:	40,000 units at $30 per unit
Product L:	20,000 units at $65 per unit

b. Estimated inventories, July 1, 2016:

Material A:	4,000 lbs.	Product K:	3,000 units at $17 per unit	$ 51,000
Material B:	3,500 lbs.	Product L:	2,700 units at $35 per unit	94,500
		Total		$145,500

There were no work in process inventories estimated for July 1, 2016.

c. Desired inventories at July 31, 2016:

Material A:	3,000 lbs.	Product K:	2,500 units at $17 per unit	$ 42,500
Material B:	2,500 lbs.	Product L:	2,000 units at $35 per unit	70,000
		Total		$112,500

There were no work in process inventories desired for July 31, 2016.

d. Direct materials used in production:

	Product K	Product L
Material A:	0.7 lb. per unit	3.5 lbs. per unit
Material B:	1.2 lbs. per unit	1.8 lbs. per unit

e. Unit costs for direct materials:

Material A:	$4.00 per lb.
Material B:	$2.00 per lb.

f. Direct labor requirements:

	Department 1	Department 2
Product K	0.4 hr. per unit	0.15 hr. per unit
Product L	0.6 hr. per unit	0.25 hr. per unit

g.

	Department 1	Department 2
Direct labor rate	$12.00 per hr.	$16.00 per hr.

h. Estimated factory overhead costs for July:

Indirect factory wages	$200,000
Depreciation of plant and equipment	40,000
Power and light	25,000
Indirect materials	34,000
Total	$299,000

Instructions

1. Prepare a sales budget for July.
2. Prepare a production budget for July.
3. Prepare a direct materials purchases budget for July.
4. Prepare a direct labor cost budget for July.
5. Prepare a cost of goods sold budget for July.

Solution

1.

	A	B	C	D
1	Cabot Co.			
2	Sales Budget			
3	For the Month Ending July 31, 2016			
4	Product	Unit Sales Volume	Unit Selling Price	Total Sales
5	Product K	40,000	$30.00	$1,200,000
6	Product L	20,000	65.00	1,300,000
7	Total revenue from sales			$2,500,000

2.

	A	B	C
1	Cabot Co.		
2	Production Budget		
3	For the Month Ending July 31, 2016		
4		Units	
5		Product K	Product L
6	Sales	40,000	20,000
7	Plus desired inventories at July 31, 2016	2,500	2,000
8	Total	42,500	22,000
9	Less estimated inventories, July 1, 2016	3,000	2,700
10	Total production	39,500	19,300

3.

	A	B	C	D	E	F	G
1	Cabot Co.						
2	Direct Materials Purchases Budget						
3	For the Month Ending July 31, 2016						
4			Direct Materials				
5			Material A		Material B		Total
6	Units required for production:						
7	Product K (39,500 × lbs. per unit)		27,650	lbs.*	47,400	lbs.*	
8	Product L (19,300 × lbs. per unit)		67,550	**	34,740	**	
9	Plus desired units of inventory,						
10	July 31, 2016		3,000		2,500		
11	Total		98,200	lbs.	84,640	lbs.	
12	Less estimated units of inventory,						
13	July 1, 2016		4,000		3,500		
14	Total units to be purchased		94,200	lbs.	81,140	lbs.	
15	Unit price		× $4.00		× $2.00		
16	Total direct materials purchases		$376,800		$162,280		$539,080
17							
18	*27,650 = 39,500 × 0.7	47,400 = 39,500 × 1.2					
19	**67,550 = 19,300 × 3.5	34,740 = 19,300 × 1.8					

4.

	A	B	C	D	E	F	G
1	Cabot Co.						
2	Direct Labor Cost Budget						
3	For the Month Ending July 31, 2016						
4			Department 1		Department 2		Total
5	Hours required for production:						
6	Product K (39,500 × hrs. per unit)		15,800	*	5,925	*	
7	Product L (19,300 × hrs. per unit)		11,580	**	4,825	**	
8	Total		27,380		10,750		
9	Hourly rate		×$12.00		×$16.00		
10	Total direct labor cost		$328,560		$172,000		$500,560
11							
12	*15,800 = 39,500 × 0.4	5,925 = 39,500 × 0.15					
13	**11,580 = 19,300 × 0.6	4,825 = 19,300 × 0.25					

5.

	A	B	C	D
1	Cabot Co.			
2	Cost of Goods Sold Budget			
3	For the Month Ending July 31, 2016			
4	Finished goods inventory, July 1, 2016			$ 145,500
5	Direct materials:			
6	Direct materials inventory, July 1, 2016 (Note A)		$ 23,000	
7	Direct materials purchases		539,080	
8	Cost of direct materials available for use		$562,080	
9	Less direct materials inventory, July 31, 2016 (Note B)		17,000	
10	Cost of direct materials placed in production		$545,080	
11	Direct labor		500,560	
12	Factory overhead		299,000	
13	Cost of goods manufactured			1,344,640
14	Cost of finished goods available for sale			$1,490,140
15	Less finished goods inventory, July 31, 2016			112,500
16	Cost of goods sold			$1,377,640
17				
18	Note A:			
19	Material A 4,000 lbs. at $4.00 per lb.	$16,000		
20	Material B 3,500 lbs. at $2.00 per lb.	7,000		
21	Direct materials inventory, July 1, 2016	$23,000		
22				
23	Note B:			
24	Material A 3,000 lbs. at $4.00 per lb.	$12,000		
25	Material B 2,500 lbs. at $2.00 per lb.	5,000		
26	Direct materials inventory, July 31, 2016	$17,000		

Discussion Questions

1. What are the three major objectives of budgeting?
2. Briefly describe the type of human behavior problems that might arise if budget goals are set too tightly.
3. What behavioral problems are associated with setting a budget too loosely?
4. What behavioral problems are associated with establishing conflicting goals within the budget?
5. Under what circumstances would a static budget be appropriate?
6. How do computerized budgeting systems aid firms in the budgeting process?

7. Why should the production requirements set forth in the production budget be carefully coordinated with the sales budget?
8. Why should the timing of direct materials purchases be closely coordinated with the production budget?
9. a. Discuss the purpose of the cash budget.
   b. If the cash for the first quarter of the fiscal year indicates excess cash at the end of each of the first two months, how might the excess cash be used?
10. Give an example of how the capital expenditures budget affects other operating budgets.

Practice Exercises

SHOW ME HOW

EE 6-1 *p. 235*

PE 6-1A Flexible budgeting — OBJ. 2

At the beginning of the period, the Assembly Department budgeted direct labor of $112,000 and property tax of $12,000 for 7,000 hours of production. The department actually completed 7,500 hours of production. Determine the budget for the department, assuming that it uses flexible budgeting.

SHOW ME HOW

EE 6-1 *p. 235*

PE 6-1B Flexible budgeting — OBJ. 2

At the beginning of the period, the Fabricating Department budgeted direct labor of $9,280 and equipment depreciation of $2,300 for 640 hours of production. The department actually completed 600 hours of production. Determine the budget for the department, assuming that it uses flexible budgeting.

SHOW ME HOW

EE 6-2 *p. 238*

PE 6-2A Production budget — OBJ. 4

MyLife Chronicles Inc. projected sales of 240,000 diaries for 2016. The estimated January 1, 2016, inventory is 19,900 units, and the desired December 31, 2016, inventory is 18,800 units. What is the budgeted production (in units) for 2016?

SHOW ME HOW

EE 6-2 *p. 238*

PE 6-2B Production budget — OBJ. 4

Magnolia Candle Inc. projected sales of 75,000 candles for 2016. The estimated January 1, 2016, inventory is 3,500 units, and the desired December 31, 2016, inventory is 2,700 units. What is the budgeted production (in units) for 2016?

SHOW ME HOW

EE 6-3 *p. 240*

PE 6-3A Direct materials purchases budget — OBJ. 4

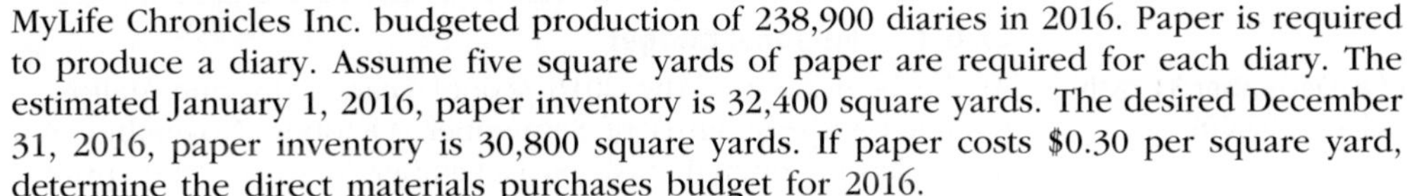
MyLife Chronicles Inc. budgeted production of 238,900 diaries in 2016. Paper is required to produce a diary. Assume five square yards of paper are required for each diary. The estimated January 1, 2016, paper inventory is 32,400 square yards. The desired December 31, 2016, paper inventory is 30,800 square yards. If paper costs $0.30 per square yard, determine the direct materials purchases budget for 2016.

SHOW ME HOW

EE 6-3 *p. 240*

PE 6-3B Direct materials purchases budget — OBJ. 4

Magnolia Candle Inc. budgeted production of 74,200 candles in 2016. Wax is required to produce a candle. Assume eight ounces (one-half of a pound) of wax is required for each candle. The estimated January 1, 2016, wax inventory is 2,500 pounds. The desired December 31, 2016, wax inventory is 2,100 pounds. If candle wax costs $4.10 per pound, determine the direct materials purchases budget for 2016.

SHOW ME HOW

EE 6-4 p. 242 **PE 6-4A Direct labor cost budget** OBJ. 4

MyLife Chronicles Inc. budgeted production of 238,900 diaries in 2016. Each diary requires assembly. Assume that six minutes are required to assemble each diary. If assembly labor costs $12.00 per hour, determine the direct labor cost budget for 2016.

SHOW ME HOW

EE 6-4 p. 242 **PE 6-4B Direct labor cost budget** OBJ. 4

Magnolia Candle Inc. budgeted production of 74,200 candles in 2016. Each candle requires molding. Assume that 12 minutes are required to mold each candle. If molding labor costs $14.00 per hour, determine the direct labor cost budget for 2016.

SHOW ME HOW

EE 6-5 p. 243 **PE 6-5A Cost of goods sold budget** OBJ. 4

Prepare a cost of goods sold budget for MyLife Chronicles Inc. using the information in Practice Exercises 6-3A and 6-4A. Assume the estimated inventories on January 1, 2016, for finished goods and work in process were $25,000 and $19,000, respectively. Also assume the desired inventories on December 31, 2016, for finished goods and work in process were $31,500 and $16,700, respectively. Factory overhead was budgeted at $197,100.

SHOW ME HOW

EE 6-5 p. 243 **PE 6-5B Cost of goods sold budget** OBJ. 4

Prepare a cost of goods sold budget for Magnolia Candle Inc. using the information in Practice Exercises 6-3B and 6-4B. Assume the estimated inventories on January 1, 2016, for finished goods and work in process were $9,800 and $3,600, respectively. Also assume the desired inventories on December 31, 2016, for finished goods and work in process were $12,900 and $3,500, respectively. Factory overhead was budgeted at $109,600.

SHOW ME HOW

EE 6-6 p. 249 **PE 6-6A Cash budget** OBJ. 5

MyLife Chronicles Inc. collects 30% of its sales on account in the month of the sale and 70% in the month following the sale. If sales on account are budgeted to be $170,000 for June and $200,000 for July, what are the budgeted cash receipts from sales on account for July?

SHOW ME HOW

EE 6-6 p. 249 **PE 6-6B Cash budget** OBJ. 5

Magnolia Candle Inc. pays 10% of its purchases on account in the month of the purchase and 90% in the month following the purchase. If purchases are budgeted to be $11,900 for March and $12,700 for April, what are the budgeted cash payments for purchases on account for April?

Exercises

EX 6-1 Personal budget OBJ. 2, 5

✔ a. December 31 cash balance, $3,000

SHOW ME HOW

At the beginning of the 2016 school year, Katherine Malloy decided to prepare a cash budget for the months of September, October, November, and December. The budget must plan for enough cash on December 31 to pay the spring semester tuition, which is the same as the fall tuition. The following information relates to the budget:

Cash balance, September 1 (from a summer job)	$5,750
Purchase season football tickets in September	210
Additional entertainment for each month	275
Pay fall semester tuition in September	3,700
Pay rent at the beginning of each month	600
Pay for food each month	235
Pay apartment deposit on September 2 (to be returned December 15)	500
Part-time job earnings each month (net of taxes)	1,400

a. Prepare a cash budget for September, October, November, and December.

b. Are the four monthly budgets that are presented prepared as static budgets or flexible budgets?

c. What are the budget implications for Katherine Malloy?

✔ **Total selling and administrative expenses at $400,000 sales, $332,500**

SHOW ME HOW

EX 6-2 Flexible budget for selling and administrative expenses for a service company

OBJ. 2, 4

Cloud Productivity Inc. uses flexible budgets that are based on the following data:

Sales commissions	14% of sales
Advertising expense	18% of sales
Miscellaneous administrative expense	$6,500 per month plus 12% of sales
Office salaries expense	$28,000 per month
Customer support expenses	$12,000 per month plus 20% of sales
Research and development expense	$30,000 per month

Prepare a flexible selling and administrative expenses budget for March 2016 for sales volumes of $400,000, $500,000, and $600,000.

✔ **b. Excess of actual over budget for March, $25,000**

SHOW ME HOW

EX 6-3 Static budget versus flexible budget

OBJ. 2, 4

The production supervisor of the Machining Department for Rodriguez Company agreed to the following monthly static budget for the upcoming year:

Rodriguez Company
Machining Department
Monthly Production Budget

Wages	$384,000
Utilities	36,000
Depreciation	60,000
Total	$480,000

The actual amount spent and the actual units produced in the first three months of 2016 in the Machining Department were as follows:

	Amount Spent	Units Produced
January	$400,000	90,000
February	440,000	100,000
March	470,000	110,000

The Machining Department supervisor has been very pleased with this performance because actual expenditures for January–March have been less than the monthly static budget of $480,000. However, the plant manager believes that the budget should not remain fixed for every month but should "flex" or adjust to the volume of work that is produced in the Machining Department. Additional budget information for the Machining Department is as follows:

Wages per hour	$16.00
Utility cost per direct labor hour	$1.50
Direct labor hours per unit	0.20
Planned monthly unit production	120,000

a. Prepare a flexible budget for the actual units produced for January, February, and March in the Machining Department. Assume depreciation is a fixed cost.

b. Compare the flexible budget with the actual expenditures for the first three months. What does this comparison suggest?

✔ Total department cost at 18,000 units, $253,700

SHOW ME HOW

EX 6-4 Flexible budget for Assembly Department **OBJ. 2**

Steelcase Inc. is one of the largest manufacturers of office furniture in the United States. In Grand Rapids, Michigan, it assembles filing cabinets in an Assembly Department. Assume the following information for the Assembly Department:

Direct labor per filing cabinet	12 minutes
Supervisor salaries	$150,000 per month
Depreciation	$24,500 per month
Direct labor rate	$22 per hour

Prepare a flexible budget for 18,000, 20,000, and 22,000 filing cabinets for the month of August 2016 in the Assembly Department, similar to Exhibit 5.

✔ Small scale budgeted production, 80,700 units

SHOW ME HOW

EX 6-5 Production budget **OBJ. 4**

True Tab Inc. produces a small and large version of its popular electronic scale. The anticipated unit sales for the scales by sales region are as follows:

	Small Scale	Large Scale
North Region unit sales	38,000	67,000
South Region unit sales	43,000	79,000
Total	81,000	146,000

The finished goods inventory estimated for July 1, 2017, for the small and large scale models is 1,800 and 2,200 units, respectively. The desired finished goods inventory for July 31, 2017, for the small and large scale models is 1,500 and 2,500 units, respectively.

Prepare a production budget for the small and large scales for the month ended July 31, 2017.

✔ b. Model DL total production, 4,830 units

SHOW ME HOW

EX 6-6 Sales and production budgets **OBJ. 4**

SoundLab Inc. manufactures two models of speakers, DL and XL. Based on the following production and sales data for September 2016, prepare (a) a sales budget and (b) a production budget:

	DL	XL
Estimated inventory (units), September 1	340	92
Desired inventory (units), September 30	300	101
Expected sales volume (units):		
East Region	2,560	1,080
West Region	2,310	930
Unit sales price	$190	$300

✔ Total professional fees earned, $10,270,000

EX 6-7 Professional fees earned budget for a service company **OBJ. 4**

Rollins and Cohen, CPAs, offer three types of services to clients: auditing, tax, and small business accounting. Based on experience and projected growth, the following billable hours have been estimated for the year ending December 31, 2016:

	Billable Hours
Audit Department:	
Staff	22,400
Partners	7,900
Tax Department:	
Staff	13,200
Partners	5,500
Small Business Accounting Department:	
Staff	3,000
Partners	600

The average billing rate for staff is $150 per hour, and the average billing rate for partners is $320 per hour. Prepare a professional fees earned budget for Rollins and Cohen, CPAs, for the year ending December 31, 2016, using the following column headings and showing the estimated professional fees by type of service rendered:

Billable Hours	Hourly Rate	Total Revenue

EX 6-8 Professional labor cost budget for a service company OBJ. 4

✔ Staff total labor cost, $1,737,000

Based on the data in Exercise 6-7 and assuming that the average compensation per hour for staff is $45 and for partners is $140, prepare a professional labor cost budget for each department for Rollins and Cohen, CPAs, for the year ending December 31, 2016. Use the following column headings:

Staff	Partners

EX 6-9 Direct materials purchases budget OBJ. 4

✔ Total cheese purchases, $35,448

SHOW ME HOW

Romano's Frozen Pizza Inc. has determined from its production budget the following estimated production volumes for 12" and 16" frozen pizzas for September 2016:

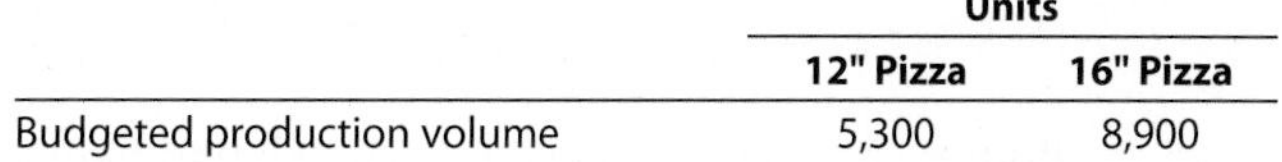

	Units	
	12" Pizza	16" Pizza
Budgeted production volume	5,300	8,900

There are three direct materials used in producing the two types of pizza. The quantities of direct materials expected to be used for each pizza are as follows:

	12" Pizza	16" Pizza
Direct materials:		
Dough	0.70 lb. per unit	1.50 lbs. per unit
Tomato	0.40	0.70
Cheese	0.60	1.30

In addition, Romano's has determined the following information about each material:

	Dough	Tomato	Cheese
Estimated inventory, September 1, 2016	520 lbs.	200 lbs.	295 lbs.
Desired inventory, September 30, 2016	580 lbs.	185 lbs.	315 lbs.
Price per pound	$0.80	$1.60	$2.40

Prepare September's direct materials purchases budget for Romano's Frozen Pizza Inc.

EX 6-10 Direct materials purchases budget OBJ. 4

✔ Concentrate budgeted purchases, $47,400

Coca-Cola Enterprises is the largest bottler of Coca-Cola® in Western Europe. The company purchases Coke® and Sprite® concentrate from **The Coca-Cola Company**, dilutes and mixes the concentrate with carbonated water, and then fills the blended beverage into cans or plastic two-liter bottles. Assume that the estimated production for Coke and Sprite two-liter bottles at the Wakefield, UK, bottling plant are as follows for the month of May:

Coke	153,000 two-liter bottles
Sprite	86,500 two-liter bottles

In addition, assume that the concentrate costs $75 per pound for both Coke and Sprite and is used at a rate of 0.15 pound per 100 liters of carbonated water in blending Coke and 0.10 pound per 100 liters of carbonated water in blending Sprite. Assume that two liters of carbonated water are used for each two-liter bottle of finished product. Assume further that two-liter bottles cost $0.08 per bottle and carbonated water costs $0.06 per liter.

Prepare a direct materials purchases budget for May 2016, assuming inventories are ignored, because there are no changes between beginning and ending inventories for concentrate, bottles, and carbonated water.

EX 6-11 Direct materials purchases budget

OBJ. 4

✔ Total steel belt purchases, $291,200

Anticipated sales for Safety Grip Company were 42,000 passenger car tires and 19,000 truck tires. Rubber and steel belts are used in producing passenger car and truck tires as follows:

	Passenger Car	Truck
Rubber	35 lbs. per unit	78 lbs. per unit
Steel belts	5 lbs. per unit	8 lbs. per unit

The purchase prices of rubber and steel are $1.20 and $0.80 per pound, respectively. The desired ending inventories of rubber and steel belts are 40,000 and 10,000 pounds, respectively. The estimated beginning inventories for rubber and steel belts are 46,000 and 8,000 pounds, respectively.

Prepare a direct materials purchases budget for Safety Grip Company for the year ended December 31, 2016.

EX 6-12 Direct labor cost budget

OBJ. 4

✔ Total direct labor cost, Assembly, $31,080

Ace Racket Company manufactures two types of tennis rackets, the Junior and Pro Striker models. The production budget for July for the two rackets is as follows:

	Junior	Pro Striker
Production budget	1,500 units	6,200 units

Both rackets are produced in two departments, Forming and Assembly. The direct labor hours required for each racket are estimated as follows:

	Forming Department	Assembly Department
Junior	0.16 hour per unit	0.24 hour per unit
Pro Striker	0.20 hour per unit	0.30 hour per unit

The direct labor rate for each department is as follows:

Forming Department	$18.00 per hour
Assembly Department	$14.00 per hour

Prepare the direct labor cost budget for July 2016.

EX 6-13 Direct labor budget for a service business

OBJ. 4

✔ Average weekday total, $2,640

Ambassador Suites Inc. operates a downtown hotel property that has 300 rooms. On average, 80% of Ambassador Suites' rooms are occupied on weekdays, and 40% are occupied during the weekend. The manager has asked you to develop a direct labor budget for the housekeeping and restaurant staff for weekdays and weekends. You have determined that the housekeeping staff requires 30 minutes to clean each occupied room. The housekeeping staff is paid $14 per hour. The housekeeping labor cost is fully variable to the number of occupied rooms. The restaurant has six full-time staff (eight-hour day) on duty, regardless of occupancy. However, for every 60 occupied rooms, an additional person is brought in to work in the restaurant for the eight-hour day. The restaurant staff is paid $12 per hour.

Determine the estimated housekeeping, restaurant, and total direct labor cost for an average weekday and average weekend day. Format the budget in two columns, labeled as weekday and weekend day.

EX 6-14 Production and direct labor cost budgets

OBJ. 4

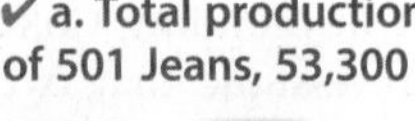

✔ a. Total production of 501 Jeans, 53,300

Levi Strauss & Co. manufactures slacks and jeans under a variety of brand names, such as Dockers® and 501 Jeans®. Slacks and jeans are assembled by a variety of different sewing operations. Assume that the sales budget for Dockers and 501 Jeans shows estimated sales of 23,600 and 53,100 pairs, respectively, for May 2016. The finished goods inventory is assumed as follows:

	Dockers	501 Jeans
May 1 estimated inventory	670	1,660
May 31 desired inventory	420	1,860

Assume the following direct labor data per 10 pairs of Dockers and 501 Jeans for four different sewing operations:

	Direct Labor per 10 Pairs	
	Dockers	**501 Jeans**
Inseam	18 minutes	9 minutes
Outerseam	20	14
Pockets	6	9
Zipper	12	6
Total	56 minutes	38 minutes

a. Prepare a production budget for May. Prepare the budget in two columns: Dockers® and 501 Jeans®.

b. Prepare the May direct labor cost budget for the four sewing operations, assuming a $13 wage per hour for the inseam and outerseam sewing operations and a $15 wage per hour for the pocket and zipper sewing operations. Prepare the direct labor cost budget in four columns: inseam, outerseam, pockets, and zipper.

EX 6-15 Factory overhead cost budget

OBJ. 4

✔ Total variable factory overhead costs, $268,000

Sweet Tooth Candy Company budgeted the following costs for anticipated production for August 2016:

Advertising expenses	$232,000	Production supervisor wages	$135,000
Manufacturing supplies	14,000	Production control wages	32,000
Power and light	48,000	Executive officer salaries	310,000
Sales commissions	298,000	Materials management wages	39,000
Factory insurance	30,000	Factory depreciation	22,000

Prepare a factory overhead cost budget, separating variable and fixed costs. Assume that factory insurance and depreciation are the only fixed factory costs.

EX 6-16 Cost of goods sold budget

OBJ. 4

✔ Cost of goods sold, $3,788,100

Delaware Chemical Company uses oil to produce two types of plastic products, P1 and P2. Delaware budgeted 35,000 barrels of oil for purchase in June for $90 per barrel. Direct labor budgeted in the chemical process was $240,000 for June. Factory overhead was budgeted $400,000 during June. The inventories on June 1 were estimated to be:

Oil	$15,200
P1	8,300
P2	8,600
Work in process	12,900

The desired inventories on June 30 were:

Oil	$16,100
P1	9,400
P2	7,900
Work in process	13,500

Use the preceding information to prepare a cost of goods sold budget for June 2017.

EX 6-17 Cost of goods sold budget

OBJ. 4

✔ Cost of goods sold, $488,360

The controller of MingWare Ceramics Inc. wishes to prepare a cost of goods sold budget for September. The controller assembled the following information for constructing the cost of goods sold budget:

Direct materials:	**Enamel**	**Paint**	**Porcelain**	**Total**
Total direct materials purchases budgeted for September	$36,780	$6,130	$145,500	$188,410
Estimated inventory, September 1, 2016	1,240	950	4,250	6,440
Desired inventory, September 30, 2016	1,890	1,070	5,870	8,830

Direct labor cost:	Kiln Department		Decorating Department	Total
Total direct labor cost budgeted for September	$47,900		$145,700	$193,600
Finished goods inventories:	**Dish**	**Bowl**	**Figurine**	**Total**
Estimated inventory, September 1, 2016	$5,780	$3,080	$2,640	$11,500
Desired inventory, September 30, 2016	3,710	2,670	3,290	9,670
Work in process inventories:				
Estimated inventory, September 1, 2016	$3,400			
Desired inventory, September 30, 2016	1,990			
Budgeted factory overhead costs for September:				
Indirect factory wages	$ 81,900			
Depreciation of plant and equipment	14,300			
Power and light	5,200			
Indirect materials	4,100			
Total	$105,500			

Use the preceding information to prepare a cost of goods sold budget for September 2016.

EX 6-18 Schedule of cash collections of accounts receivable — OBJ. 5

✔ Total cash collected in July, $163,050

SHOW ME HOW

Pet Place Supplies Inc., a pet wholesale supplier, was organized on May 1, 2016. Projected sales for each of the first three months of operations are as follows:

May	$134,000
June	155,000
July	169,000

All sales are on account. Sixty-five percent of sales are expected to be collected in the month of the sale, 30% in the month following the sale, and the remainder in the second month following the sale.

Prepare a schedule indicating cash collections from sales for May, June, and July.

EX 6-19 Schedule of cash collections of accounts receivable — OBJ. 5

✔ Total cash collected in October, $62,550

OfficeMart Inc. has "cash and carry" customers and credit customers. OfficeMart estimates that 25% of monthly sales are to cash customers, while the remaining sales are to credit customers. Of the credit customers, 30% pay their accounts in the month of sale, while the remaining 70% pay their accounts in the month following the month of sale. Projected sales for the next three months of 2016 are as follows:

October	$58,000
November	65,000
December	72,000

The Accounts Receivable balance on September 30, 2016, was $35,000.

Prepare a schedule of cash collections from sales for October, November, and December.

EX 6-20 Schedule of cash payments for a service company — OBJ. 5

✔ Total cash payments in May, $58,490

Horizon Financial Inc. was organized on February 28, 2016. Projected selling and administrative expenses for each of the first three months of operations are as follows:

March	$52,400
April	64,200
May	68,900

Depreciation, insurance, and property taxes represent $9,000 of the estimated monthly expenses. The annual insurance premium was paid on February 28, and property taxes for the year will be paid in June. Seventy percent of the remainder of the expenses are expected to be paid in the month in which they are incurred, with the balance to be paid in the following month.

Prepare a schedule indicating cash payments for selling and administrative expenses for March, April, and May.

EX 6-21 Schedule of cash payments for a service company OBJ. 5

✔ Total cash payments in March, $113,740

EastGate Physical Therapy Inc. is planning its cash payments for operations for the first quarter (January–March), 2017. The Accrued Expenses Payable balance on January 1 is $15,000. The budgeted expenses for the next three months are as follows:

	January	February	March
Salaries	$56,900	$ 68,100	$ 72,200
Utilities	2,400	2,600	2,500
Other operating expenses	32,300	41,500	44,700
Total	$91,600	$112,200	$119,400

Other operating expenses include $3,000 of monthly depreciation expense and $500 of monthly insurance expense that was prepaid for the year on May 1 of the previous year. Of the remaining expenses, 70% are paid in the month in which they are incurred, with the remainder paid in the following month. The Accrued Expenses Payable balance on January 1 relates to the expenses incurred in December.

Prepare a schedule of cash payments for operations for January, February, and March.

EX 6-22 Capital expenditures budget OBJ. 5

✔ Total capital expenditures in 2016, $4,000,000

On January 1, 2016, the controller of Omicron Inc. is planning capital expenditures for the years 2016–2019. The following interviews helped the controller collect the necessary information for the capital expenditures budget:

Director of Facilities: A construction contract was signed in late 2015 for the construction of a new factory building at a contract cost of $10,000,000. The construction is scheduled to begin in 2016 and be completed in 2017.

Vice President of Manufacturing: Once the new factory building is finished, we plan to purchase $1.5 million in equipment in late 2017. I expect that an additional $200,000 will be needed early in the following year (2018) to test and install the equipment before we can begin production. If sales continue to grow, I expect we'll need to invest another $1,000,000 in equipment in 2019.

Chief Operating Officer: We have really been growing lately. I wouldn't be surprised if we need to expand the size of our new factory building in 2019 by at least 35%. Fortunately, we expect inflation to have minimal impact on construction costs over the next four years. Additionally, I would expect the cost of the expansion to be proportional to the size of the expansion.

Director of Information Systems: We need to upgrade our information systems to wireless network technology. It doesn't make sense to do this until after the new factory building is completed and producing product. During 2018, once the factory is up and running, we should equip the whole facility with wireless technology. I think it would cost us $800,000 today to install the technology. However, prices have been dropping by 25% per year, so it should be less expensive at a later date.

Chief Financial Officer: I am excited about our long-term prospects. My only short-term concern is managing our cash flow while we expend the $4,000,000 of construction costs on the portion of the new factory building scheduled to be completed in 2016.

Use this interview information to prepare a capital expenditures budget for Omicron Inc. for the years 2016–2019.

Problems: Series A

PR 6-1A Forecast sales volume and sales budget OBJ. 4

✔ 3. Total revenue from sales, $878,403

For 2016, Raphael Frame Company prepared the sales budget that follows.

At the end of December 2016, the following unit sales data were reported for the year:

	Unit Sales	
	8" × 10" Frame	12" × 16" Frame
East	8,755	3,686
Central	6,510	3,090
West	12,348	5,616

Raphael Frame Company
Sales Budget
For the Year Ending December 31, 2016

Product and Area	Unit Sales Volume	Unit Selling Price	Total Sales
8" × 10" Frame:			
East	8,500	$16	$136,000
Central	6,200	16	99,200
West	12,600	16	201,600
Total	27,300		$436,800
12" × 16" Frame:			
East	3,800	$30	$114,000
Central	3,000	30	90,000
West	5,400	30	162,000
Total	12,200		$366,000
Total revenue from sales			$802,800

For the year ending December 31, 2017, unit sales are expected to follow the patterns established during the year ending December 31, 2016. The unit selling price for the 8" × 10" frame is expected to increase to $17 and the unit selling price for the 12" × 16" frame is expected to increase to $32, effective January 1, 2017.

Instructions

1. Compute the increase or decrease of actual unit sales for the year ended December 31, 2016, over budget. Place your answers in a columnar table with the following format:

	Unit Sales, Year Ended 2016		Increase (Decrease) Actual Over Budget	
	Budget	Actual Sales	Amount	Percent
8" × 10" Frame:				
East				
Central				
West				
12" × 16" Frame:				
East				
Central				
West				

2. Assuming that the increase or decrease in actual sales to budget indicated in part (1) is to continue in 2017, compute the unit sales volume to be used for preparing the sales budget for the year ending December 31, 2017. Place your answers in a columnar table similar to that in part (1) but with the following column heads. Round budgeted units to the nearest unit.

2016 Actual Units	Percentage Increase (Decrease)	2017 Budgeted Units (rounded)

3. Prepare a sales budget for the year ending December 31, 2017.

PR 6-2A Sales, production, direct materials purchases, and direct labor cost budgets OBJ. 4

✔ 3. Total direct materials purchases, $771,490

The budget director of Gourmet Grill Company requests estimates of sales, production, and other operating data from the various administrative units every month. Selected information concerning sales and production for July 2016 is summarized as follows:

a. Estimated sales for July by sales territory:

Maine:	
Backyard Chef	310 units at $700 per unit
Master Chef	150 units at $1,200 per unit
Vermont:	
Backyard Chef	240 units at $750 per unit
Master Chef	110 units at $1,300 per unit

New Hampshire:

Backyard Chef	360 units at $750 per unit
Master Chef	180 units at $1,400 per unit

b. Estimated inventories at July 1:

Direct materials:		Finished products:	
Grates	290 units	Backyard Chef	30 units
Stainless steel	1,500 lbs.	Master Chef	32 units
Burner subassemblies	170 units		
Shelves	340 units		

c. Desired inventories at July 31:

Direct materials:		Finished products:	
Grates	340 units	Backyard Chef	40 units
Stainless steel	1,800 lbs.	Master Chef	22 units
Burner subassemblies	155 units		
Shelves	315 units		

d. Direct materials used in production:

In manufacture of Backyard Chef:	
Grates	3 units per unit of product
Stainless steel	24 lbs. per unit of product
Burner subassemblies	2 units per unit of product
Shelves	4 units per unit of product
In manufacture of Master Chef:	
Grates	6 units per unit of product
Stainless steel	42 lbs. per unit of product
Burner subassemblies	4 units per unit of product
Shelves	5 units per unit of product

e. Anticipated purchase price for direct materials:

Grates	$15 per unit	Burner subassemblies	110 per unit
Stainless steel	$6 per lb.	Shelves	$10 per unit

f. Direct labor requirements:

Backyard Chef:	
Stamping Department	0.50 hr. at $17 per hr.
Forming Department	0.60 hr. at $15 per hr.
Assembly Department	1.0 hr. at $14 per hr.
Master Chef:	
Stamping Department	0.60 hr. at $17 per hr.
Forming Department	0.80 hr. at $15 per hr.
Assembly Department	1.50 hrs. at $14 per hr.

Instructions

1. Prepare a sales budget for July.
2. Prepare a production budget for July.
3. Prepare a direct materials purchases budget for July.
4. Prepare a direct labor cost budget for July.

PR 6-3A Budgeted income statement and supporting budgets **OBJ. 4**

✔ **4. Total direct labor cost in Fabrication Dept., $29,216**

The budget director of Feathered Friends Inc., with the assistance of the controller, treasurer, production manager, and sales manager, has gathered the following data for use in developing the budgeted income statement for December 2016:

a. Estimated sales for December:

Bird house	3,200 units at $50 per unit
Bird feeder	3,000 units at $70 per unit

b. Estimated inventories at December 1:

Direct materials:		Finished products:	
Wood	200 ft.	Bird house.......	320 units at $27 per unit
Plastic........	240 lbs.	Bird feeder.......	270 units at $40 per unit

c. Desired inventories at December 31:

Direct materials:		Finished products:	
Wood	220 ft.	Bird house.......	290 units at $27 per unit
Plastic........	200 lbs.	Bird feeder.......	250 units at $41 per unit

d. Direct materials used in production:

In manufacture of Bird House:		In manufacture of Bird Feeder:	
Wood	0.80 ft. per unit of product	Wood	1.20 ft. per unit of product
Plastic...........	0.50 lb. per unit of product	Plastic...........	0.75 lb. per unit of product

e. Anticipated cost of purchases and beginning and ending inventory of direct materials:

Wood	$7.00 per ft.	Plastic.................	$1.00 per lb.

f. Direct labor requirements:

Bird House:	
Fabrication Department	0.20 hr. at $16 per hr.
Assembly Department..	0.30 hr. at $12 per hr.
Bird Feeder:	
Fabrication Department	0.40 hr. at $16 per hr.
Assembly Department..	0.35 hr. at $12 per hr.

g. Estimated factory overhead costs for December:

Indirect factory wages	$75,000	Power and light	$6,000
Depreciation of plant and equipment	23,000	Insurance and property tax	5,000

h. Estimated operating expenses for December:

Sales salaries expense	$70,000
Advertising expense	18,000
Office salaries expense	21,000
Depreciation expense—office equipment	600
Telephone expense—selling	550
Telephone expense—administrative	250
Travel expense—selling	4,000
Office supplies expense	200
Miscellaneous administrative expense	400

i. Estimated other income and expense for December:

Interest revenue	$200
Interest expense	122

j. Estimated tax rate: 30%

Instructions

1. Prepare a sales budget for December.
2. Prepare a production budget for December.
3. Prepare a direct materials purchases budget for December.
4. Prepare a direct labor cost budget for December.
5. Prepare a factory overhead cost budget for December.
6. Prepare a cost of goods sold budget for December. Work in process at the beginning of December is estimated to be $29,000, and work in process at the end of December is estimated to be $35,400.
7. Prepare a selling and administrative expenses budget for December.
8. Prepare a budgeted income statement for December.

✔ 1. July deficiency, $2,200

SHOW ME HOW

PR 6-4A Cash budget OBJ. 5

The controller of Sonoma Housewares Inc. instructs you to prepare a monthly cash budget for the next three months. You are presented with the following budget information:

	May	June	July
Sales	$86,000	$90,000	$95,000
Manufacturing costs	34,000	39,000	44,000
Selling and administrative expenses	15,000	16,000	22,000
Capital expenditures			80,000

The company expects to sell about 10% of its merchandise for cash. Of sales on account, 70% are expected to be collected in the month following the sale and the remainder the following month (second month following sale). Depreciation, insurance, and property tax expense represent $3,500 of the estimated monthly manufacturing costs. The annual insurance premium is paid in September, and the annual property taxes are paid in November. Of the remainder of the manufacturing costs, 80% are expected to be paid in the month in which they are incurred and the balance in the following month.

Current assets as of May 1 include cash of $33,000, marketable securities of $40,000, and accounts receivable of $90,000 ($72,000 from April sales and $18,000 from March sales). Sales on account for March and April were $60,000 and $72,000, respectively. Current liabilities as of May 1 include $6,000 of accounts payable incurred in April for manufacturing costs. All selling and administrative expenses are paid in cash in the period they are incurred. An estimated income tax payment of $14,000 will be made in June. Sonoma's regular quarterly dividend of $5,000 is expected to be declared in June and paid in July. Management desires to maintain a minimum cash balance of $30,000.

Instructions

1. Prepare a monthly cash budget and supporting schedules for May, June, and July 2016.
2. On the basis of the cash budget prepared in part (1), what recommendation should be made to the controller?

✔ 1. Budgeted net income, $96,600

PR 6-5A Budgeted income statement and balance sheet OBJ. 4, 5

As a preliminary to requesting budget estimates of sales, costs, and expenses for the fiscal year beginning January 1, 2017, the following tentative trial balance as of December 31, 2016, is prepared by the Accounting Department of Regina Soap Co.:

Cash	$ 85,000	
Accounts Receivable	125,600	
Finished Goods	69,300	
Work in Process	32,500	
Materials	48,900	
Prepaid Expenses	2,600	
Plant and Equipment	325,000	
Accumulated Depreciation—Plant and Equipment		$156,200
Accounts Payable		62,000
Common Stock, $10 par		180,000
Retained Earnings		290,700
	$688,900	$688,900

Factory output and sales for 2017 are expected to total 200,000 units of product, which are to be sold at $5.00 per unit. The quantities and costs of the inventories at December 31, 2017, are expected to remain unchanged from the balances at the beginning of the year.

Budget estimates of manufacturing costs and operating expenses for the year are summarized as follows:

	Estimated Costs and Expenses	
	Fixed (Total for Year)	Variable (Per Unit Sold)
Cost of goods manufactured and sold:		
Direct materials	—	$1.10
Direct labor	—	0.65
Factory overhead:		
Depreciation of plant and equipment	$40,000	—
Other factory overhead	12,000	0.40
Selling expenses:		
Sales salaries and commissions	46,000	0.45
Advertising	64,000	—
Miscellaneous selling expense	6,000	0.25
Administrative expenses:		
Office and officers salaries	72,400	0.12
Supplies	5,000	0.10
Miscellaneous administrative expense	4,000	0.05

Balances of accounts receivable, prepaid expenses, and accounts payable at the end of the year are not expected to differ significantly from the beginning balances. Federal income tax of $30,000 on 2017 taxable income will be paid during 2017. Regular quarterly cash dividends of $0.15 per share are expected to be declared and paid in March, June, September, and December on 18,000 shares of common stock outstanding. It is anticipated that fixed assets will be purchased for $75,000 cash in May.

Instructions

1. Prepare a budgeted income statement for 2017.
2. Prepare a budgeted balance sheet as of December 31, 2017, with supporting calculations.

Problems: Series B

PR 6-1B Forecast sales volume and sales budget

OBJ. 4

✔ 3. Total revenue from sales, $2,148,950

Sentinel Systems Inc. prepared the following sales budget for 2016:

Sentinel Systems Inc.
Sales Budget
For the Year Ending December 31, 2016

Product and Area	Unit Sales Volume	Unit Selling Price	Total Sales
Home Alert System:			
United States	1,700	$200	$ 340,000
Europe	580	200	116,000
Asia	450	200	90,000
Total	2,730		$ 546,000
Business Alert System:			
United States	980	$750	$ 735,000
Europe	350	750	262,500
Asia	240	750	180,000
Total	1,570		$1,177,500
Total revenue from sales			$1,723,500

At the end of December 2016, the following unit sales data were reported for the year:

	Unit Sales	
	Home Alert System	**Business Alert System**
United States	1,734	1,078
Europe	609	329
Asia	432	252

For the year ending December 31, 2017, unit sales are expected to follow the patterns established during the year ending December 31, 2016. The unit selling price for the Home Alert System is expected to increase to $250, and the unit selling price for the Business Alert System is expected to be decreased to $820, effective January 1, 2017.

Instructions

1. Compute the increase or decrease of actual unit sales for the year ended December 31, 2016, over budget. Place your answers in a columnar table with the following format:

	Unit Sales, Year Ended 2016		Increase (Decrease) Actual Over Budget	
	Budget	**Actual Sales**	**Amount**	**Percent**
Home Alert System:				
United States				
Europe				
Asia				
Business Alert System:				
United States				
Europe				
Asia				

2. Assuming that the increase or decrease in actual sales to budget indicated in part (1) is to continue in 2017, compute the unit sales volume to be used for preparing the sales budget for the year ending December 31, 2017. Place your answers in a columnar table similar to that in part (1) but with the following column heads. Round budgeted units to the nearest unit.

2016 Actual Units	Percentage Increase (Decrease)	2017 Budgeted Units (rounded)

3. Prepare a sales budget for the year ending December 31, 2017.

PR 6-2B Sales, production, direct materials purchases, and direct labor cost budgets OBJ. 4

✔ 3. Total direct materials purchases, $987,478

The budget director of Royal Furniture Company requests estimates of sales, production, and other operating data from the various administrative units every month. Selected information concerning sales and production for February 2016 is summarized as follows:

a. Estimated sales of King and Prince chairs for February by sales territory:

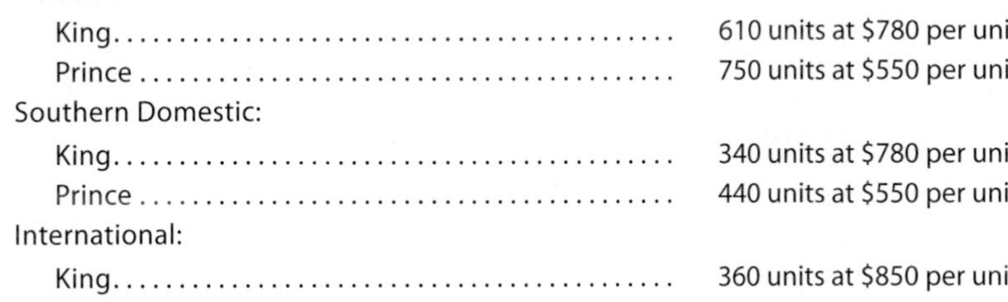

Northern Domestic:

King.	610 units at $780 per unit
Prince	750 units at $550 per unit

Southern Domestic:

King.	340 units at $780 per unit
Prince	440 units at $550 per unit

International:

King.	360 units at $850 per unit
Prince	290 units at $600 per unit

b. Estimated inventories at February 1:

Direct materials:		Finished products:	
Fabric	420 sq. yds.	King.	90 units
Wood	580 linear ft.	Prince	25 units
Filler	250 cu. ft.		
Springs.	660 units		

c. Desired inventories at February 28:

Direct materials:		Finished products:	
Fabric	390 sq. yds.	King	80 units
Wood	650 linear ft.	Prince	35 units
Filler	300 cu. ft.		
Springs	540 units		

d. Direct materials used in production:

In manufacture of King:	
Fabric	6.0 sq. yds. per unit of product
Wood	38 linear ft. per unit of product
Filler	4.2 cu. ft. per unit of product
Springs	16 units per unit of product
In manufacture of Prince:	
Fabric	4.0 sq. yds. per unit of product
Wood	26 linear ft. per unit of product
Filler	3.4 cu. ft. per unit of product
Springs	12 units per unit of product

e. Anticipated purchase price for direct materials:

Fabric	$12.00 per sq. yd.	Filler	$3.00 per cu. ft.
Wood	7.00 per linear ft.	Springs	4.50 per unit

f. Direct labor requirements:

King:	
Framing Department	1.2 hrs. at $12 per hr.
Cutting Department	0.5 hr. at $14 per hr.
Upholstery Department	0.8 hr. at $15 per hr.
Prince:	
Framing Department	1.0 hr. at $12 per hr.
Cutting Department	0.4 hr. at $14 per hr.
Upholstery Department	0.6 hr. at $15 per hr.

Instructions

1. Prepare a sales budget for February.
2. Prepare a production budget for February.
3. Prepare a direct materials purchases budget for February.
4. Prepare a direct labor cost budget for February.

PR 6-3B Budgeted income statement and supporting budgets **OBJ. 4**

✔ **4. Total direct labor cost in Assembly Dept., $171,766**

The budget director of Gold Medal Athletic Co., with the assistance of the controller, treasurer, production manager, and sales manager, has gathered the following data for use in developing the budgeted income statement for March 2016:

a. Estimated sales for March:

Batting helmet	1,200 units at $40 per unit
Football helmet	6,500 units at $160 per unit

b. Estimated inventories at March 1:

Direct materials:		Finished products:	
Plastic	90 lbs.	Batting helmet	40 units at $25 per unit
Foam lining	80 lbs.	Football helmet	240 units at $77 per unit

c. Desired inventories at March 31:

Direct materials:		Finished products:	
Plastic	50 lbs.	Batting helmet	50 units at $25 per unit
Foam lining	65 lbs.	Football helmet	220 units at $78 per unit

d. Direct materials used in production:

In manufacture of batting helmet:	
Plastic	1.20 lbs. per unit of product
Foam lining	0.50 lb. per unit of product
In manufacture of football helmet:	
Plastic	3.50 lbs. per unit of product
Foam lining	1.50 lbs. per unit of product

e. Anticipated cost of purchases and beginning and ending inventory of direct materials:

Plastic	$6.00 per lb.
Foam lining	$4.00 per lb.

f. Direct labor requirements:

Batting helmet:	
Molding Department	0.20 hr. at $20 per hr.
Assembly Department	0.50 hr. at $14 per hr.
Football helmet:	
Molding Department	0.50 hr. at $20 per hr.
Assembly Department	1.80 hrs. at $14 per hr.

g. Estimated factory overhead costs for March:

Indirect factory wages	$86,000	Power and light	$4,000
Depreciation of plant and equipment	12,000	Insurance and property tax	2,300

h. Estimated operating expenses for March:

Sales salaries expense	$184,300
Advertising expense	87,200
Office salaries expense	32,400
Depreciation expense—office equipment	3,800
Telephone expense—selling	5,800
Telephone expense—administrative	1,200
Travel expense—selling	9,000
Office supplies expense	1,100
Miscellaneous administrative expense	1,000

i. Estimated other income and expense for March:

Interest revenue	$940
Interest expense	872

j. Estimated tax rate: 30%

Instructions

1. Prepare a sales budget for March.
2. Prepare a production budget for March.
3. Prepare a direct materials purchases budget for March.
4. Prepare a direct labor cost budget for March.
5. Prepare a factory overhead cost budget for March.
6. Prepare a cost of goods sold budget for March. Work in process at the beginning of March is estimated to be $15,300, and work in process at the end of March is desired to be $14,800.
7. Prepare a selling and administrative expenses budget for March.
8. Prepare a budgeted income statement for March.

PR 6-4B Cash budget

OBJ. 5

✔ 1. August deficiency, $9,000

SHOW ME HOW

The controller of Mercury Shoes Inc. instructs you to prepare a monthly cash budget for the next three months. You are presented with the following budget information:

	June	July	August
Sales	$160,000	$185,000	$200,000
Manufacturing costs	66,000	82,000	105,000
Selling and administrative expenses	40,000	46,000	51,000
Capital expenditures	—	—	120,000

The company expects to sell about 10% of its merchandise for cash. Of sales on account, 60% are expected to be collected in the month following the sale and the remainder the following month (second month after sale). Depreciation, insurance, and property tax expense represent $12,000 of the estimated monthly manufacturing costs. The annual insurance premium is paid in February, and the annual property taxes are paid in November. Of the remainder of the manufacturing costs, 80% are expected to be paid in the month in which they are incurred and the balance in the following month.

Current assets as of June 1 include cash of $42,000, marketable securities of $25,000, and accounts receivable of $198,000 ($150,000 from May sales and $48,000 from April sales). Sales on account in April and May were $120,000 and $150,000, respectively. Current liabilities as of June 1 include $13,000 of accounts payable incurred in May for manufacturing costs. All selling and administrative expenses are paid in cash in the period they are incurred. An estimated income tax payment of $24,000 will be made in July. Mercury Shoes' regular quarterly dividend of $15,000 is expected to be declared in July and paid in August. Management desires to maintain a minimum cash balance of $40,000.

Instructions

1. Prepare a monthly cash budget and supporting schedules for June, July, and August 2016.
2. On the basis of the cash budget prepared in part (1), what recommendation should be made to the controller?

PR 6-5B Budgeted income statement and balance sheet

OBJ. 4, 5

✔ 1. Budgeted net income, $114,660

As a preliminary to requesting budget estimates of sales, costs, and expenses for the fiscal year beginning January 1, 2017, the following tentative trial balance as of December 31, 2016, is prepared by the Accounting Department of Mesa Publishing Co.:

Cash	$ 26,000	
Accounts Receivable	23,800	
Finished Goods	16,900	
Work in Process	4,200	
Materials	6,400	
Prepaid Expenses	600	
Plant and Equipment	82,000	
Accumulated Depreciation—Plant and Equipment		$ 32,000
Accounts Payable		14,800
Common Stock, $1.50 par		30,000
Retained Earnings		83,100
	$159,900	$159,900

Factory output and sales for 2017 are expected to total 3,800 units of product, which are to be sold at $120 per unit. The quantities and costs of the inventories at December 31, 2017, are expected to remain unchanged from the balances at the beginning of the year.

Budget estimates of manufacturing costs and operating expenses for the year are summarized as follows:

	Estimated Costs and Expenses	
	Fixed (Total for Year)	**Variable (Per Unit Sold)**
Cost of goods manufactured and sold:		
Direct materials	—	$30.00
Direct labor	—	8.40
Factory overhead:		
Depreciation of plant and equipment	$ 4,000	—
Other factory overhead	1,400	4.80
Selling expenses:		
Sales salaries and commissions	12,800	13.50
Advertising	13,200	—
Miscellaneous selling expense	1,000	2.50
Administrative expenses:		
Office and officers salaries	7,800	7.00
Supplies	500	1.20
Miscellaneous administrative expense	400	2.40

Balances of accounts receivable, prepaid expenses, and accounts payable at the end of the year are not expected to differ significantly from the beginning balances. Federal income tax of $35,000 on 2017 taxable income will be paid during 2017. Regular quarterly cash dividends of $0.20 per share are expected to be declared and paid in March, June, September, and December on 20,000 shares of common stock outstanding. It is anticipated that fixed assets will be purchased for $22,000 cash in May.

Instructions

1. Prepare a budgeted income statement for 2017.
2. Prepare a budgeted balance sheet as of December 31, 2017, with supporting calculations.

Cases & Projects

CP 6-1 Ethics and professional conduct in business

The director of marketing for Starr Computer Co., Megan Hewitt, had the following discussion with the company controller, Cam Morley, on July 26 of the current year:

Megan: Cam, it looks like I'm going to spend much less than indicated on my July budget.

Cam: I'm glad to hear it.

Megan: Well, I'm not so sure it's good news. I'm concerned that the president will see that I'm under budget and reduce my budget in the future. The only reason that I look good is that we've delayed an advertising campaign. Once the campaign hits in September, I'm sure my actual expenditures will go up. You see, we are also having our sales convention in September. Having the advertising campaign and the convention at the same time is going to kill my September numbers.

Cam: I don't think that's anything to worry about. We all expect some variation in actual spending month to month. What's really important is staying within the budgeted targets for the year. Does that look as if it's going to be a problem?

Megan: I don't think so, but just the same, I'd like to be on the safe side.

Cam: What do you mean?

Megan: Well, this is what I'd like to do. I want to pay the convention-related costs in advance this month. I'll pay the hotel for room and convention space and purchase the airline tickets in advance. In this way, I can charge all these expenditures to July's budget. This would cause my actual expenses to come close to budget for July. Moreover, when the big advertising campaign hits in September, I won't have to worry about expenditures for the convention on my September budget as well. The convention costs will already be paid. Thus, my September expenses should be pretty close to budget.

Cam: I can't tell you when to make your convention purchases, but I'm not too sure that it should be expensed on July's budget.

Megan: What's the problem? It looks like "no harm, no foul" to me. I can't see that there's anything wrong with this—it's just smart management.

How should Cam Morley respond to Megan Hewitt's request to expense the advanced payments for convention-related costs against July's budget?

CP 6-2 Evaluating budgeting systems in a service company

Children's Hospital of the King's Daughters Health System in Norfolk, Virginia, introduced a new budgeting method that allowed the hospital's annual plan to be updated for changes in operating plans. For example, if the budget was based on 400 patient-days (number of patients × number of days in the hospital) and the actual count rose to 450 patient-days, the variable costs of staffing, lab work, and medication costs could be adjusted to reflect this change. The budget manager stated, "I work with hospital directors to turn data into meaningful information and effect change before the month ends."

a. What budgeting methods are being used under the new approach?

b. Why are these methods superior to the former approaches?

CP 6-3 Static budget for a service company

A bank manager of City Savings Bank Inc. uses the managerial accounting system to track the costs of operating the various departments within the bank. The departments include Cash Management, Trust, Commercial Loans, Mortgage Loans, Operations, Credit Card, and Branch Services. The static budget and actual results for the Operations Department are as follows:

Resources	Budget	Actual
Salaries	$200,000	$200,000
Benefits	30,000	30,000
Supplies	45,000	42,000
Travel	20,000	30,000
Training	25,000	35,000
Overtime	25,000	20,000
Total	$345,000	$357,000
Excess of actual over budget		$ 12,000

a. What information is provided by the budget? Specifically, what questions can the bank manager ask of the Operations Department manager?

b. What information does the static budget fail to provide? Specifically, could the budget information be presented differently to provide even more insight for the bank manager?

CP 6-4 Objectives of the master budget

Domino's Pizza L.L.C. operates pizza delivery and carry-out restaurants. The annual report describes its business as follows:

We offer a focused menu of high-quality, value-priced pizza with three types of crust (Hand-Tossed, Thin Crust, and Deep Dish), along with buffalo wings, bread sticks, cheesy bread, CinnaStix®, and Coca-Cola® products. Our hand-tossed pizza is made from fresh dough produced in our regional distribution centers. We prepare every pizza using real cheese, pizza sauce made from fresh tomatoes, and a choice of high-quality meat and vegetable toppings in generous portions. Our focused menu and use of premium ingredients enable us to consistently and efficiently produce the highest-quality pizza.

Over the 41 years since our founding, we have developed a simple, cost-efficient model. We offer a limited menu, our stores are designed for delivery and carry-out, and we do not generally offer dine-in service. As a result, our stores require relatively small, lower-rent locations and limited capital expenditures.

How would a master budget support planning, directing, and control for Domino's?

CP 6-5 Integrity and evaluating budgeting systems

The city of Milton has an annual budget cycle that begins on July 1 and ends on June 30. At the beginning of each budget year, an annual budget is established for each department. The annual budget is divided by 12 months to provide a constant monthly static budget. On June 30, all unspent budgeted monies for the budget year from the various city departments must be "returned" to the General Fund. Thus, if department heads fail to use their budget by year-end, they will lose it. A budget analyst prepared a chart of the difference between the monthly actual and budgeted amounts for the recent fiscal year. The chart was as follows:

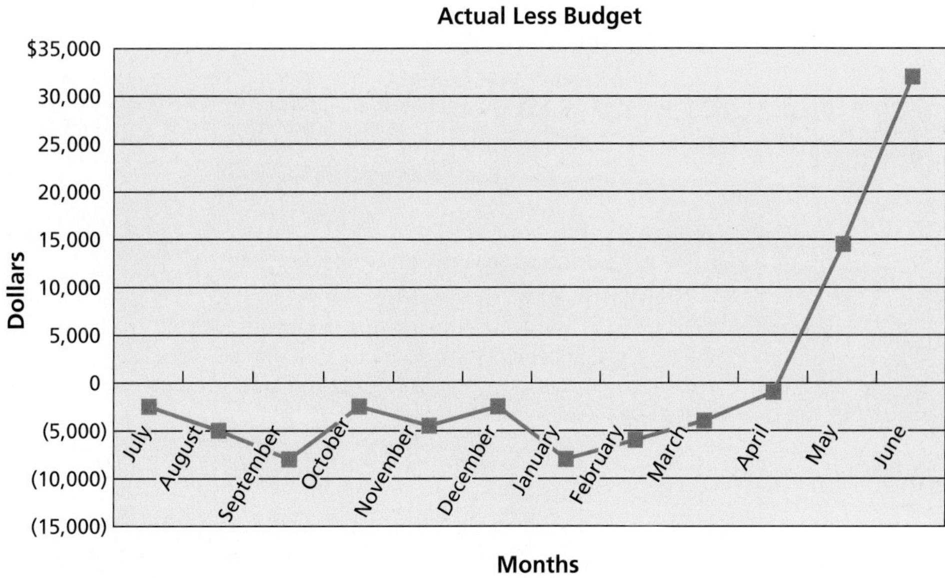

a. Interpret the chart.

b. Suggest an improvement in the budget system.

CP 6-6 Budget for a state government

Internet Project

Group Project

In a group, find the home page of the state in which you presently live. The home page will be of the form *www.statename.gov*. For example, the state of Tennessee would be found at www.tennessee.gov. At the home page site, search for annual budget information.

1. What are the budgeted sources of revenue and their percentage breakdown?
2. What are the major categories of budgeted expenditures (or appropriations) and their percentage breakdown?
3. Is the projected budget in balance?

CHAPTER 7

Performance Evaluation Using Variances from Standard Costs

BMW Group—Mini Cooper

When you play a sport, you are evaluated with respect to how well you perform compared to a standard or to a competitor. In bowling, for example, your score is compared to a perfect score of 300 or to the scores of your competitors. In this class, you are compared to performance standards. These standards are often described in terms of letter grades, which provide a measure of how well you achieved the class objectives. In your job, you are also evaluated according to performance standards.

Just as your class performance is evaluated, managers are evaluated according to goals and plans. For example, **BMW Group** uses manufacturing standards at its automobile assembly plants to guide performance. The Mini Cooper, a BMW Group car, is manufactured in a modern facility in Oxford, England. There are a number of performance targets used in this plant. For example, the bodyshell is welded by more than 250 robots so as to be two to three times stiffer than rival cars. In addition, the bodyshell dimensions are tested to the accuracy of the width of a human hair. Such performance standards are not surprising given the automotive racing background of John W. Cooper, the designer of the original Mini Cooper.

If you want to get a view of the BMW manufacturing process, go to the BMW Web site and search the phrase "How an automobile is born."

Performance is often measured as the difference between actual results and planned results. In this chapter, we will discuss and illustrate the ways in which business performance is evaluated.

Learning Objectives

After studying this chapter, you should be able to: *Example Exercises*

OBJ 1 Describe the types of standards and how they are established.
Standards
- Setting Standards
- Types of Standards
- Reviewing and Revising Standards
- Criticisms of Standard Costs

OBJ 2 Describe and illustrate how standards are used in budgeting.
Budgetary Performance Evaluation
- Budget Performance Report
- Manufacturing Cost Variances

OBJ 3 Compute and interpret direct materials and direct labor variances.
Direct Materials and Direct Labor Variances
- Direct Materials Variances — EE 7-1
- Direct Labor Variances — EE 7-2

OBJ 4 Compute and interpret factory overhead controllable and volume variances.
Factory Overhead Variances
- The Factory Overhead Flexible Budget
- Variable Factory Overhead Controllable Variance — EE 7-3
- Fixed Factory Overhead Volume Variance — EE 7-4
- Reporting Factory Overhead Variances
- Factory Overhead Account

OBJ 5 Journalize the entries for recording standards in the accounts and prepare an income statement that includes variances from standard.
Recording and Reporting Variances from Standards — EE 7-5, 7-6

OBJ 6 Describe and provide examples of nonfinancial performance measures.
Nonfinancial Performance Measures — EE 7-7

At a Glance 7 Page 300

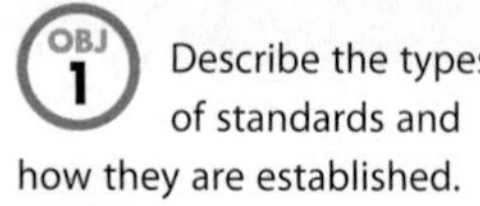
Describe the types of standards and how they are established.

Drivers for **United Parcel Service (UPS)** are expected to drive a standard distance per day. Salespersons for **The Limited** are expected to meet sales standards.

Standards

Standards are performance goals. Manufacturing companies normally use **standard cost** for each of the three following product costs:

- Direct materials
- Direct labor
- Factory overhead

Accounting systems that use standards for product costs are called **standard cost systems**. Standard cost systems enable management to determine the following:

- How much a product *should* cost (standard cost)
- How much it does cost (actual cost)

When actual costs are compared with standard costs, the exceptions or cost variances are reported. This reporting by the *principle of exceptions* allows management to focus on correcting the cost variances.

Setting Standards

The standard-setting process normally requires the joint efforts of accountants, engineers, and other management personnel. The accountant converts the results of judgments and process studies into dollars and cents. Engineers with the aid of operation managers identify the materials, labor, and machine requirements needed to produce the product. For example, engineers estimate direct materials by studying the product specifications and estimating normal spoilage. Time and motion studies may be used to determine the direct labor required for each manufacturing operation. Engineering studies may also be used to determine standards for factory overhead, such as the amount of power needed to operate machinery.

Types of Standards

Standards imply an acceptable level of production efficiency. One of the major objectives in setting standards is to motivate employees to achieve efficient operations.

Ideal standards, or *theoretical standards*, are standards that can be achieved only under perfect operating conditions, such as no idle time, no machine breakdowns, and no materials spoilage. Such standards may have a negative impact on performance because they may be viewed by employees as unrealistic.

Currently attainable standards, sometimes called *normal standards*, are standards that can be attained with reasonable effort. Such standards, which are used by most companies, allow for normal production difficulties and mistakes. When reasonable standards are used, employees focus more on cost and are more likely to put forth their best efforts.

An example from the game of golf illustrates the distinction between ideal and normal standards. In golf, *par* is an ideal standard for most players. Each player's USGA (United States Golf Association) handicap is the player's normal standard. The motivation of average players is to beat their handicaps because beating par is unrealistic for most players.

Reviewing and Revising Standards

Standard costs should be periodically reviewed to ensure that they reflect current operating conditions. Standards should not be revised, however, just because they differ from actual costs. For example, the direct labor standard would not be revised just because employees are unable to meet properly set standards. On the other hand, standards should be revised when prices, product designs, labor rates, or manufacturing methods change.

Integrity, Objectivity, and Ethics in Business

COMPANY REPUTATION: THE BEST OF THE BEST

Harris Interactive annually ranks American corporations in terms of reputation. The ranking is based on how respondents rate corporations on 20 attributes in six major areas. The six areas are emotional appeal, products and services, financial performance, workplace environment, social responsibility, and vision and leadership. What are the five highest ranked companies in its 2013 survey? The five highest (best) ranked companies were **Amazon.com**, **Apple Inc.**, **The Walt Disney Company**, **Google**, and **Johnson & Johnson**.

Source: Harris Interactive, February 2012.

Criticisms of Standard Costs

Some criticisms of using standard costs for performance evaluation include the following:

- Standards limit operating improvements by discouraging improvement beyond the standard.
- Standards are too difficult to maintain in a dynamic manufacturing environment, resulting in "stale standards."
- Standards can cause employees to lose sight of the larger objectives of the organization by focusing only on efficiency improvement.
- Standards can cause employees to unduly focus on their own operations to the possible harm of other operations that rely on them.

Regardless of these criticisms, standards are used widely. In addition, standard costs are only one part of the performance evaluation system used by most companies. As discussed in this chapter, other nonfinancial performance measures are often used to supplement standard costs, with the result that many of the preceding criticisms are overcome.

Business  **Connection**

STANDARD COSTING IN ACTION: EXPANDING BREWING OPERATIONS

In 2011, U.S. west coast craft brewers **Sierra Nevada** (CA) and **New Belgium** (CO) announced plans to expand their brewing operations to the Asheville, North Carolina, area. Both companies considered the standard cost of their product when making the decision to expand, and in selecting Asheville as their east coast location. The standard price of direct materials includes the cost of shipping direct materials to the manufacturers' place of business. The Asheville location was desirable when considering these costs.

In addition, New Belgium projected that their Fort Collins, Colorado, brewery would reach maximum capacity in three to five years. While operating at 100% capacity creates a favorable overhead volume variance, exceeding 100% of capacity makes it very difficult to meet customer demand. Thus, New Belgium felt adding a new brewery prior to reaching 100% capacity at Fort Collins was supported. In both cases, standard costing was used to support the expansion and location decisions.

Sources: H. Dornbusch, "The Case For Low Mileage Beer," Brewers Association.org; J. McCurry, "Hops City: Beer Culture Comes to a Head in the Asheville Region," *Site Selection*, July 2012; J. Shikes, "New Belgium, maker of Fat Tire, plans a second brewery on the East Coast," *Denver Westward*, May 19, 2011.

Describe and illustrate how standards are used in budgeting.

Budgetary Performance Evaluation

As discussed in Chapter 6, the master budget assists a company in planning, directing, and controlling performance. The control function, or budgetary performance evaluation, compares the actual performance against the budget.

To illustrate, **Western Rider Inc.**, a manufacturer of blue jeans, uses standard costs in its budgets. The standards for direct materials, direct labor, and factory overhead are separated into the following two components:

- Standard price
- Standard quantity

The standard cost per unit for direct materials, direct labor, and factory overhead is computed as follows:

$$\text{Standard Cost per Unit} = \text{Standard Price} \times \text{Standard Quantity}$$

Western Rider's standard costs per unit for its XL jeans are shown in Exhibit 1.

EXHIBIT 1

Standard Cost for XL Jeans

Manufacturing Costs	**Standard Price**	×	**Standard Quantity per Pair**	=	**Standard Cost per Pair of XL Jeans**
Direct materials	$5.00 per sq. yd.		1.5 sq. yds.		$ 7.50
Direct labor	$9.00 per hr.		0.80 hr. per pair		7.20
Factory overhead	$6.00 per hr.		0.80 hr. per pair		4.80
Total standard cost per pair					$19.50

As shown in Exhibit 1, the standard cost per pair of XL jeans is $19.50, which consists of $7.50 for direct materials, $7.20 for direct labor, and $4.80 for factory overhead.

The standard price and standard quantity are separated for each product cost. For example, Exhibit 1 indicates that for each pair of XL jeans, the standard price for direct materials is $5.00 per square yard and the standard quantity is 1.5 square yards. The standard price and quantity are separated because the department responsible for their control is normally different. For example, the direct materials price per square yard is controlled by the Purchasing Department, and the direct materials quantity per pair is controlled by the Production Department.

As illustrated in Chapter 21, the master budget is prepared based on planned sales and production. The budgeted costs for materials purchases, direct labor, and factory overhead are determined by multiplying their standard costs per unit by the planned level of production. Budgeted (standard) costs are then compared to actual costs during the year for control purposes.

Budget Performance Report

The differences between actual and standard costs are called **cost variances**. A **favorable cost variance** occurs when the actual cost is less than the standard cost. An **unfavorable cost variance** occurs when the actual cost exceeds the standard cost. These cost variances are illustrated in Exhibit 2.

EXHIBIT 2

Cost Variances

Favorable Cost Variance	**Unfavorable Cost Variance**
Actual cost < Standard cost at actual volumes	Actual cost > Standard cost at actual volumes

The report that summarizes actual costs, standard costs, and the differences for the units produced is called a **budget performance report**. To illustrate, assume that **Western Rider Inc.** produced the following pairs of jeans during June:

XL jeans produced and sold		5,000 pairs
Actual costs incurred in the june:		
Direct materials	$ 40,150	
Direct labor	38,500	
Factory overhead	22,400	
Total costs incurred	$101,050	

Exhibit 3 illustrates the budget performance report for June for Western Rider.

The budget performance report shown in Exhibit 3 is based on the actual units produced in June of 5,000 XL jeans. Even though 6,000 XL jeans might have been *planned* for production, the budget performance report is based on *actual* production.

EXHIBIT 3 **Budget Performance Report**

Western Rider Inc.
Budget Performance Report
For the Month Ended June 30, 2016

Manufacturing Costs	Actual Costs	Standard Cost at Actual Volume (5,000 pairs of XL Jeans)*	Cost Variance—(Favorable) Unfavorable
Direct materials	$ 40,150	$37,500	$ 2,650
Direct labor	38,500	36,000	2,500
Factory overhead	22,400	24,000	(1,600)
Total manufacturing costs	$101,050	$97,500	$ 3,550

*5,000 pairs × $7.50 per pair = $37,500
5,000 pairs × $7.20 per pair = $36,000
5,000 pairs × $4.80 per pair = $24,000

Manufacturing Cost Variances

The **total manufacturing cost variance** is the difference between total standard costs and total actual cost for the units produced. As shown in Exhibit 3, the total manufacturing cost unfavorable variance is $3,550, which consists of an unfavorable direct materials cost variance of $2,650, and unfavorable direct labor cost variance of $2,500, and a favorable factory overhead cost variance of $1,600.

For control purposes, each product cost variance is separated into two additional variances as shown in Exhibit 4.

EXHIBIT 4 **Manufacturing Cost Variances**

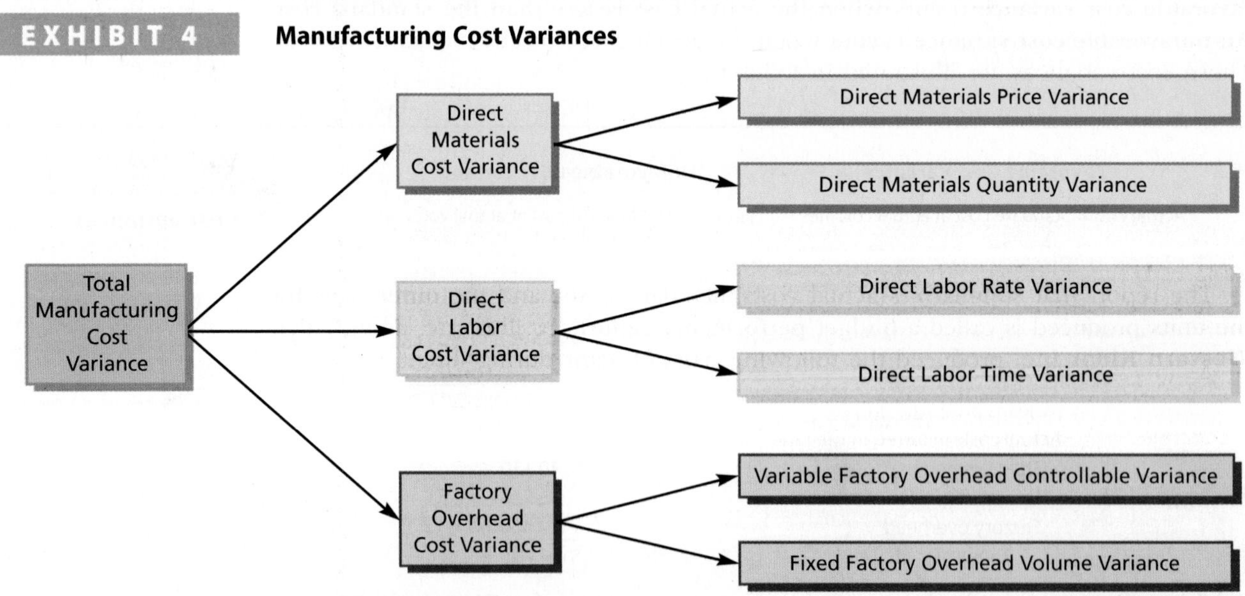

The total direct materials variance is separated into a *price* variance and a *quantity* variance. This is because standard and actual direct materials costs are computed as follows:

Actual Direct Materials Cost	=	Actual Price	×	Actual Quantity
Standard Direct Materials Cost	=	Standard Price	×	Standard Quantity
Direct Materials Cost Variance	=	Price Difference	+	Quantity Difference

Thus, the actual and standard direct materials costs may differ because of a price difference (variance), a quantity difference (variance), or both.

Likewise, the total direct labor variance is separated into a *rate* variance and a *time* variance. This is because standard and actual direct labor costs are computed as follows:

Actual Direct Labor Cost	=	Actual Rate	× Actual Time
Standard Direct Labor Cost	=	Standard Rate	× Standard Time
Direct Labor Cost Variance	=	Rate Difference	+ Time Difference

Therefore, the actual and standard direct labor costs may differ because of a rate difference (variance), a time difference (variance), or both.

The total factory overhead variance is separated into a *controllable* variance and a *volume* variance. Because factory overhead has fixed and variable cost elements, it uses different variances than direct materials and direct labor, which are variable costs.

In the next sections, the price and quantity variances for direct materials, the rate and time variances for direct labor, and the controllable and volume variances for factory overhead are further described and illustrated.

Direct Materials and Direct Labor Variances

OBJ 3 Compute and interpret direct materials and direct labor variances.

As indicated in the prior section, the total direct materials and direct labor variances are separated into the direct materials cost and direct labor cost variances for analysis and control purposes. These variances are illustrated in Exhibit 5.

EXHIBIT 5

Direct Materials and Direct Labor Cost Variances

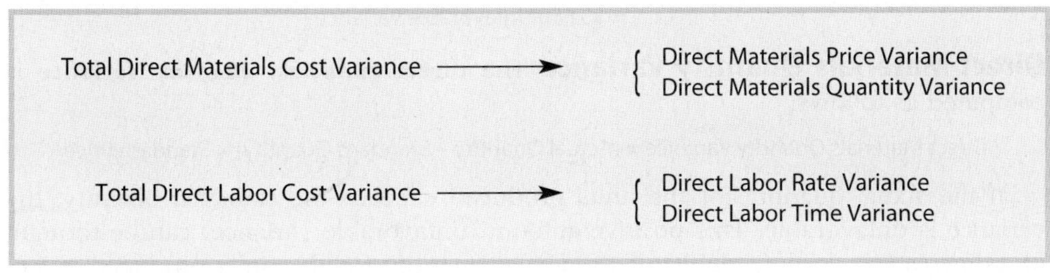

As a basis for illustration, the variances for Western Rider's June operations shown in Exhibit 3 are used.

Direct Materials Variances

During June, **Western Rider Inc.** reported an unfavorable total direct materials cost variance of $2,650 for the production of 5,000 XL style jeans, as shown in Exhibit 3. This variance was based on the following actual and standard costs:

Actual costs	$40,150
Standard costs	37,500
Total direct materials cost variance	$ 2,650

The actual costs incurred of $40,150 consist of the following:

Actual Direct Materials Cost = Actual Price × Actual Quantity
= ($5.50 per sq. yd.) × (7,300 sq. yds.)
= $40,150

The standard costs of $37,500 consist of the following:

Standard Direct Materials Cost = Standard Price × Standard Quantity
= $5.00 per sq. yd. × 7,500 sq. yds.
= $37,500

The standard price of $5.00 per square yard is taken from Exhibit 1. In addition, Exhibit 1 indicates that 1.5 square yards is the standard quantity of materials for producing one pair of XL jeans. Thus, 7,500 (5,000 × 1.5) square yards is the standard quantity of materials for producing 5,000 pairs of XL jeans.

Comparing the actual and standard cost computations indicates that the total direct materials unfavorable cost variance of $2,650 is caused by the following:

- A price per square yard of $0.50 ($5.50 – $5.00) more than standard
- A quantity usage of 200 square yards (7,300 sq. yds. – 7,500 sq. yds.) less than standard

The impact of these differences from standard is reported and analyzed as a direct materials *price* variance and direct materials *quantity* variance.

Direct Materials Price Variance The **direct materials price variance** is computed as follows:

Direct Materials Price Variance = (Actual Price – Standard Price) × Actual Quantity

If the actual price per unit exceeds the standard price per unit, the variance is unfavorable. This positive amount (unfavorable variance) can be thought of as increasing costs (a debit). If the actual price per unit is less than the standard price per unit, the variance is favorable. This negative amount (favorable variance) can be thought of as decreasing costs (a credit).

To illustrate, the direct materials price variance for **Western Rider Inc.** for June is $3,650 (unfavorable), computed as follows:[1]

Direct Materials Price Variance = (Actual Price – Standard Price) × Actual Quantity
= ($5.50 – $5.00) × 7,300 sq. yds.
= $3,650 Unfavorable Variance

Direct Materials Quantity Variance The **direct materials quantity variance** is computed as follows:

Direct Materials Quantity Variance = (Actual Quantity – Standard Quantity) × Standard Price

If the actual quantity for the units produced exceeds the standard quantity, the variance is unfavorable. This positive amount (unfavorable variance) can be thought of as increasing costs (a debit). If the actual quantity for the units produced is less than the standard quantity, the variance is favorable. This negative amount (favorable variance) can be thought of as decreasing costs (a credit).

To illustrate, the direct materials quantity variance for **Western Rider Inc.** for June is $1,000 (favorable), computed as follows:

Direct Materials Quantity Variance = (Actual Quantity – Standard Quantity) × Standard Price
= (7,300 sq. yds. – 7,500 sq. yds.) × $5.00
= –$1,000 Favorable Variance

Direct Materials Variance Relationships The relationship among the *total* direct materials cost variance, the direct materials *price* variance, and the direct materials *quantity* variance is shown in Exhibit 6.

Reporting Direct Materials Variances The direct materials quantity variances should be reported to the manager responsible for the variance. For example, an unfavorable quantity variance might be caused by either of the following:

- Equipment that has not been properly maintained
- Low-quality (inferior) direct materials

[1] To simplify, it is assumed that there is no change in the beginning and ending materials inventories. Thus, the amount of materials budgeted for production equals the amount purchased.

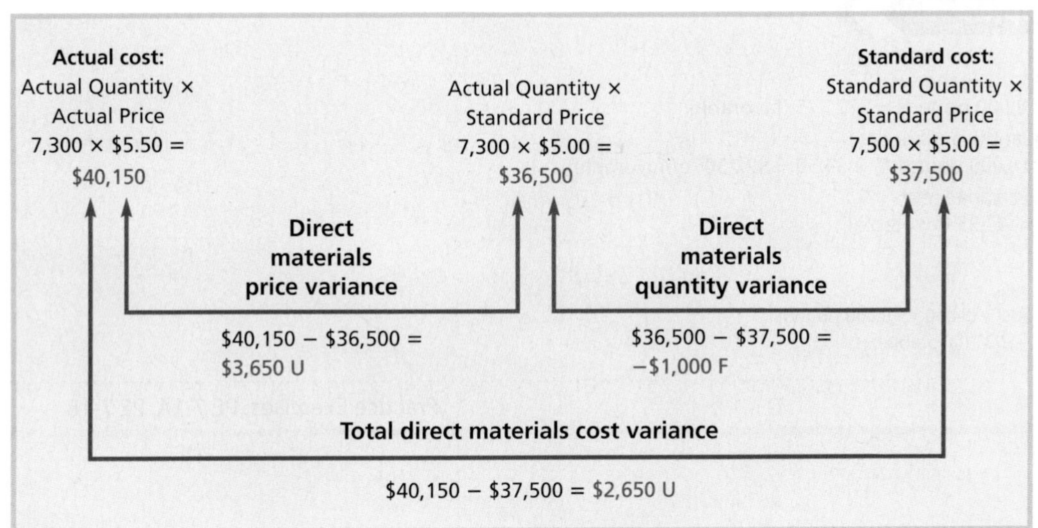

EXHIBIT 6

Direct Materials Variance Relationships

In the first case, the Operating Department responsible for maintaining the equipment should be held responsible for the variance. In the second case, the Purchasing Department should be held responsible.

Not all variances are controllable. For example, an unfavorable materials price variance might be due to market-wide price increases. In this case, there is nothing the Purchasing Department might have done to avoid the unfavorable variance. On the other hand, if materials of the same quality could have been purchased from another supplier at the standard price, the variance was controllable.

Service  Focus

STANDARD COSTING IN THE RESTAURANT INDUSTRY

Many restaurants use standard costs to manage their business. Food costs are typically the largest expense for a restaurant. As a result, many restaurants use food quantity standards to control food costs by establishing the amount of food that is served to a customer. For example, Red Lobster restaurants, a division of **Darden Restuarants, Inc.**, establishes food quantity standards for the number of shrimp, scallops, or clams on a seafood plate.

The second largest cost to most restaurants is labor cost. Many restaurants base their labor cost standards on the labor cost percentage, which is the ratio of total labor cost to total sales. This ratio helps the restaurants of Darden Restaurants, Inc., including the Olive Garden and Red Lobster, control and monitor labor costs. Focusing on this metric has paid off in recent years, as Darden's labor cost percentage dropped from 33.1% of sales in 2010, to 30.4% in the first quarter of 2013. This disciplined focus on food and labor cost standards has helped Darden increase earnings by 4% in the first quarter of 2013.

Source: N. Irwin, "What Olive Garden and Red Lobster tell us about the economy," *The Washington Post*, September 21, 2012.

Example Exercise 7-1 Direct Materials Variances

Tip Top Corp. produces a product that requires six standard pounds per unit. The standard price is $4.50 per pound. If 3,000 units required 18,500 pounds, which were purchased at $4.35 per pound, what is the direct materials (a) price variance, (b) quantity variance, and (c) cost variance?

(*Continued*)

Follow My Example 7-1

a. Direct materials price variance:
($4.35 – $4.50) × 18,500 pounds = –$2,775 (favorable)
b. Direct materials quantity variance:
(18,500 pounds – 18,000 pounds*) × $4.50 = $2,250 (unfavorable)
c. Direct materials cost variance:**
–$2,775 + $2,250 = –$525 (favorable)

* 3,000 units × 6 pounds
** Also computed as follows:
($4.35 × 18,500 pounds) – ($4.50 × 18,000 pounds)
$80,475 – $81,000 = –$525 (favorable)

Practice Exercises: PE 7-1A, PE 7-1B

Direct Labor Variances

The **Internal Revenue Service** publishes a time standard for completing a tax return. The average 1040EZ return is expected to require eight hours to prepare.

During June, **Western Rider Inc.** reported an unfavorable total direct labor cost variance of $2,500 for the production of 5,000 XL style jeans, as shown in Exhibit 3. This variance was based on the following actual and standard costs:

Actual costs	$38,500
Standard costs	36,000
Total direct labor cost variance	$ 2,500

The actual costs incurred of $38,500 consist of the following:

Actual Direct Labor Cost = Actual Rate per Hour × Actual Time
= $10.00 per hr. × 3,850 hrs.
= $38,500

The standard costs of $36,000 consist of the following:

Standard Direct Labor Cost = Standard Rate per Hour × Standard Time
= $9.00 per hr. × 4,000 hrs.
= $36,000

The standard rate of $9.00 per direct labor hour is taken from Exhibit 1. In addition, Exhibit 1 indicates that 0.80 hour is the standard time required for producing one pair of XL jeans. Thus, 4,000 (5,000 units × 0.80 hr.) direct labor hours is the standard for producing 5,000 pairs of XL jeans.

Comparing the actual and standard cost computations indicates that the total direct labor unfavorable cost variance of $2,500 is caused by the following:

- A rate of $1.00 per hour ($10.00 – $9.00) more than standard
- A quantity of 150 hours (4,000 hrs. – 3,850 hrs.) less than standard

The impact of these differences from standard is reported and analyzed as a direct labor *rate* variance and a direct labor *time* variance.

Direct Labor Rate Variance The **direct labor rate variance** is computed as follows:

Direct Labor Rate Variance = (Actual Rate per Hour – Standard Rate per Hour) × Actual Hours

If the actual rate per hour exceeds the standard rate per hour, the variance is unfavorable. This positive amount (unfavorable variance) can be thought of as increasing costs (a debit). If the actual rate per hour is less than the standard rate per hour, the variance is favorable. This negative amount (favorable variance) can be thought of as decreasing costs (a credit).

To illustrate, the direct labor rate variance for **Western Rider Inc.** in June is $3,850 (unfavorable), computed as follows:

Direct Labor Rate Variance = (Actual Rate per Hour − Standard Rate per Hour) × Actual Hours
= ($10.00 − $9.00) × 3,850 hours
= $3,850 Unfavorable Variance

Direct Labor Time Variance The **direct labor time variance** is computed as follows:

Direct Labor Time Variance = (Actual Direct Labor Hours − Standard Direct Labor Hours) × Standard Rate per Hour

If the actual direct labor hours for the units produced exceeds the standard direct labor hours, the variance is unfavorable. This positive amount (unfavorable variance) can be thought of as increasing costs (a debit). If the actual direct labor hours for the units produced is less than the standard direct labor hours, the variance is favorable. This negative amount (favorable variance) can be thought of as decreasing costs (a credit).

To illustrate, the direct labor time variance for **Western Rider Inc.** for June is $1,350 (favorable) computed as follows:

Direct Labor Time Variance = (Actual Direct Labor Hours − Standard Direct Labor Hours) × Standard Rate per Hour
= (3,850 hours − 4,000 direct labor hours) × $9.00
= − $1,350 Favorable Variance

Direct Labor Variance Relationships The relationships among the *total* direct labor cost variance, the direct labor *rate* variance, and the direct labor *time* variance is shown in Exhibit 7.

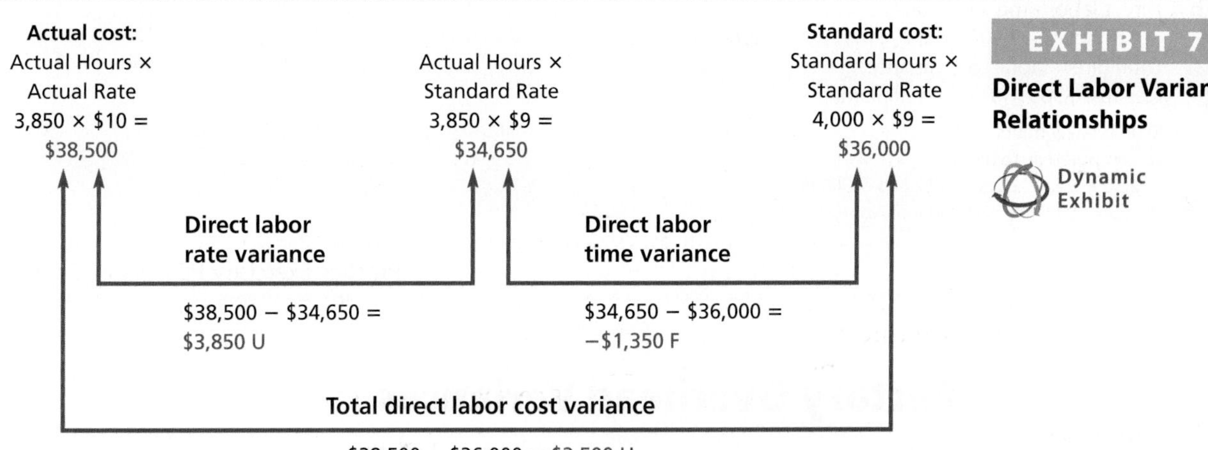

EXHIBIT 7

Direct Labor Variance Relationships

Dynamic Exhibit

Reporting Direct Labor Variances Production supervisors are normally responsible for controlling direct labor cost. For example, an investigation could reveal the following causes for unfavorable rate and time variances:

- An unfavorable rate variance may be caused by the improper scheduling and use of employees. In such cases, skilled, highly paid employees may be used in jobs that are normally performed by unskilled, lower-paid employees. In this case, the unfavorable rate variance should be reported to the managers who schedule work assignments.

- An unfavorable time variance may be caused by a shortage of skilled employees. In such cases, there may be an abnormally high turnover rate among skilled employees. In this case, production supervisors with high turnover rates should be questioned as to why their employees are quitting.

Direct Labor Standards for Nonmanufacturing Activities Direct labor time standards can also be developed for use in administrative, selling, and service activities. This is most appropriate when the activity involves a repetitive task that produces a common output. In these cases, the use of standards is similar to that for a manufactured product.

To illustrate, standards could be developed for customer service personnel who process sales orders. A standard time for processing a sales order (the output) could be developed and used to control sales order processing costs. Similar standards could be developed for computer help desk operators, nurses, and insurance application processors.

When labor-related activities are not repetitive, direct labor time standards are less commonly used. For example, the time spent by a senior executive or the work of a research and development scientist would not normally be controlled using time standards.

Example Exercise 7-2 Direct Labor Variances

Tip Top Corp. produces a product that requires 2.5 standard hours per unit at a standard hourly rate of $12 per hour. If 3,000 units required 7,420 hours at an hourly rate of $12.30 per hour, what is the (a) direct labor rate variance, (b) direct labor time variance, and (c) total direct labor cost variance?

Follow My Example 7-2

a. Direct labor rate variance:
($12.30 – $12.00) × 7,420 hours = $2,226 (unfavorable)

b. Direct labor time variance:
(7,420 hours – 7,500 hours*) × $12.00 = –$960 (favorable)

c. Total direct labor cost variance:**
$2,226 – $960 = $1,266 (unfavorable)

*3,000 units × 2.5 hours
** Also computed as follows:
($12.30 × 7,420 hours) – ($12.00 × 7,500 hours)
$91,266 – $90,000 = $1,266 (unfavorable)

Practice Exercises: PE 7-2A, PE 7-2B

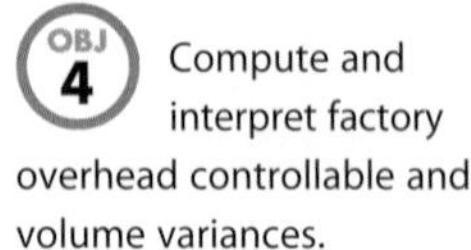

Compute and interpret factory overhead controllable and volume variances.

Factory Overhead Variances

Factory overhead costs are analyzed differently than direct labor and direct materials costs. This is because factory overhead costs have fixed and variable cost elements. For example, indirect materials and factory supplies normally behave as a variable cost as units produced changes. In contrast, straight-line plant depreciation on factory machinery is a fixed cost.

Factory overhead costs are budgeted and controlled by separating factory overhead into fixed and variable components. Doing so allows the preparation of flexible budgets and the analysis of factory overhead controllable and volume variances.

The Factory Overhead Flexible Budget

The preparation of a flexible budget was described and illustrated in Chapter 26. Exhibit 8 illustrates a flexible factory overhead budget for **Western Rider Inc.** for June 2016.

EXHIBIT 8

Factory Overhead Cost Budget Indicating Standard Factory Overhead Rate

	A	B	C	D	E
1	Western Rider Inc.				
2	Factory Overhead Cost Budget				
3	For the Month Ending June 30, 2016				
4	Percent of normal capacity	80%	90%	100%	110%
5	Units produced	5,000	5,625	6,250	6,875
6	Direct labor hours (0.80 hr. per unit)	4,000	4,500	5,000	5,500
7	Budgeted factory overhead:				
8	Variable costs:				
9	Indirect factory wages	$ 8,000	$ 9,000	$10,000	$11,000
10	Power and light	4,000	4,500	5,000	5,500
11	Indirect materials	2,400	2,700	3,000	3,300
12	Total variable cost	$14,400	$16,200	$18,000	$19,800
13	Fixed costs:				
14	Supervisory salaries	$ 5,500	$ 5,500	$ 5,500	$ 5,500
15	Depreciation of plant				
16	and equipment	4,500	4,500	4,500	4,500
17	Insurance and property taxes	2,000	2,000	2,000	2,000
18	Total fixed cost	$12,000	$12,000	$12,000	$12,000
19	Total factory overhead cost	$26,400	$28,200	$30,000	$31,800
20					
21	Factory overhead rate per direct labor hour, $30,000 ÷ 5,000 hours = $6.00				

Exhibit 8 indicates that the budgeted factory overhead rate for Western Rider is $6.00, computed as follows:

$$\text{Factory Overhead Rate} = \frac{\text{Budgeted Factory Overhead at Normal Capacity}}{\text{Normal Productive Capacity}}$$

$$= \frac{\$30{,}000}{5{,}000 \text{ direct labor hrs.}} = \$6.00 \text{ per direct labor hr.}$$

The normal productive capacity is expressed in terms of an activity base such as direct labor hours, direct labor cost, or machine hours. For Western Rider, 100% of normal capacity is 5,000 direct labor hours. The budgeted factory overhead cost at 100% of normal capacity is $30,000, which consists of variable overhead of $18,000 and fixed overhead of $12,000.

For analysis purposes, the budgeted factory overhead rate is subdivided into a variable factory overhead rate and a fixed factory overhead rate. For Western Rider, the variable overhead rate is $3.60 per direct labor hour, and the fixed overhead rate is $2.40 per direct labor hour, computed as follows:

$$\text{Variable Factory Overhead Rate} = \frac{\text{Budgeted Variable Overhead at Normal Capacity}}{\text{Normal Productive Capacity}}$$

$$= \frac{\$18{,}000}{5{,}000 \text{ direct labor hrs.}} = \$3.60 \text{ per direct labor hr.}$$

$$\text{Fixed Factory Overhead Rate} = \frac{\text{Budgeted Fixed Overhead at Normal Capacity}}{\text{Normal Productive Capacity}}$$

$$= \frac{\$12{,}000}{5{,}000 \text{ direct labor hrs.}} = \$2.40 \text{ per direct labor hr.}$$

To summarize, the budgeted factory overhead rates for Western Rider Inc. are as follows:

Variable factory overhead rate	$3.60
Fixed factory overhead rate	2.40
Total factory overhead rate	$6.00

As mentioned previously, factory overhead variances can be separated into a controllable variance and a volume variance as discussed in the next sections.

Variable Factory Overhead Controllable Variance

The variable factory overhead **controllable variance** is the difference between the actual variable overhead costs and the budgeted variable overhead for actual production. It is computed as follows:

$$\text{Variable Factory Overhead Controllable Variance} = \text{Actual Variable Factory Overhead} - \text{Budgeted Variable Factory Overhead}$$

If the actual variable overhead is less than the budgeted variable overhead, the variance is favorable. If the actual variable overhead exceeds the budgeted variable overhead, the variance is unfavorable.

The **budgeted variable factory overhead** is the standard variable overhead for the *actual* units produced. It is computed as follows:

$$\text{Budgeted Variable Factory Overhead} = \text{Standard Hours for Actual Units Produced} \times \text{Variable Factory Overhead Rate}$$

To illustrate, the budgeted variable overhead for **Western Rider Inc.** for June, when 5,000 units of XL jeans were produced, is $14,400, computed as follows:

$$\begin{aligned}\text{Budgeted Variable Factory Overhead} &= \text{Standard Hours for Actual Units Produced} \times \text{Variable Factory Overhead Rate}\\ &= 4{,}000 \text{ direct labor hrs.} \times \$3.60\\ &= \$14{,}400\end{aligned}$$

The preceding computation is based on the fact that Western Rider produced 5,000 XL jeans, which requires a standard of 4,000 (5,000 units × 0.8 hr.) direct labor hours. The variable factory overhead rate of $3.60 was computed earlier. Thus, the budgeted variable factory overhead is $14,400 (4,000 direct labor hrs. × $3.60).

During June, assume that Western Rider incurred the following actual factory overhead costs:

	Actual Costs in June
Variable factory overhead	$10,400
Fixed factory overhead	12,000
Total actual factory overhead	$22,400

Based on the actual variable factory overhead incurred in June, the variable factory overhead controllable variance is a $4,000 favorable variance, computed as follows:

$$\begin{aligned}\text{Variable Factory Overhead Controllable Variance} &= \text{Actual Variable Factory Overhead} - \text{Budgeted Variable Factory Overhead}\\ &= \$10{,}400 - \$14{,}400\\ &= -\$4{,}000 \text{ Favorable Variance}\end{aligned}$$

The variable factory overhead controllable variance indicates the ability to keep the factory overhead costs within the budget limits. Because variable factory overhead costs are normally controllable at the department level, responsibility for controlling this variance usually rests with department supervisors.

Example Exercise 7-3 Factory Overhead Controllable Variance

Tip Top Corp. produced 3,000 units of product that required 2.5 standard hours per unit. The standard variable overhead cost per unit is $2.20 per hour. The actual variable factory overhead was $16,850. Determine the variable factory overhead controllable variance.

Follow My Example 7-3

Variable Factory Overhead Controllable Variance = Actual Variable Factory Overhead − Budgeted Variable Factory Overhead
= $16,850 − [(3,000 units × 2.5 hrs.) × $2.20]
= $16,850 − $16,500
= $350 (unfavorable)

Practice Exercises: PE 7-3A, PE 7-3B

Fixed Factory Overhead Volume Variance

Western Rider's budgeted factory overhead is based on a 100% normal capacity of 5,000 direct labor hours, as shown in Exhibit 8. This is the expected capacity that management believes will be used under normal business conditions. Exhibit 8 indicates that the 5,000 direct labor hours is less than the total available capacity of 110%, which is 5,500 direct labor hours.

The fixed factory overhead **volume variance** is the difference between the budgeted fixed overhead at 100% of normal capacity and the standard fixed overhead for the actual units produced. It is computed as follows:

$$\text{Fixed Factory Overhead Volume Variance} = \left(\text{Standard Hours for 100\% of Normal Capacity} - \text{Standard Hours for Actual Units Produced}\right) \times \text{Fixed Factory Overhead Rate}$$

The volume variance measures the use of fixed overhead resources (plant and equipment). The interpretation of an unfavorable and a favorable fixed factory overhead volume variance is as follows:

- *Unfavorable* fixed factory overhead volume variance. The actual units produced is *less than* 100% of normal capacity; thus, the company used its fixed overhead resources (plant and equipment) less than would be expected under normal operating conditions.
- *Favorable* fixed factory overhead volume variance. The actual units produced is *more than* 100% of normal capacity; thus, the company used its fixed overhead resources (plant and equipment) more than would be expected under normal operating conditions.

To illustrate, the fixed factory overhead volume variance for **Western Rider Inc.** is a $2,400 unfavorable variance, computed as follows:

$$\text{Fixed Factory Overhead Volume Variance} = \left(\text{Standard Hours for 100\% of Normal Capacity} - \text{Standard Hours for Actual Units Produced}\right) \times \text{Fixed Factory Overhead Rate}$$

$$= \left(\text{5,000 direct labor hrs.} - \text{4,000 direct labor hrs.}\right) \times \$2.40$$

$$= \$2{,}400 \text{ Unfavorable Variance}$$

Because Western Rider produced 5,000 XL jeans during June, the standard for the actual units produced is 4,000 (5,000 units × 0.80) direct labor hours. This is 1,000 hours less than the 5,000 standard hours of normal capacity. The fixed overhead rate of $2.40 was computed earlier. Thus, the unfavorable fixed factory overhead volume variance is $2,400 (1,000 direct labor hrs. × $2.40).

Exhibit 9 illustrates graphically the fixed factory overhead volume variance for **Western Rider Inc.** The budgeted fixed overhead does not change and is $12,000 at all levels of production. At 100% of normal capacity (5,000 direct labor hours), the standard fixed overhead line intersects the budgeted fixed costs line. For production levels *more than* 100% of normal capacity (5,000 direct labor hours), the volume variance is *favorable*. For production levels *less than* 100% of normal capacity (5,000 direct labor hours), the volume variance is *unfavorable*.

EXHIBIT 9

Graph of Fixed Overhead Volume Variance

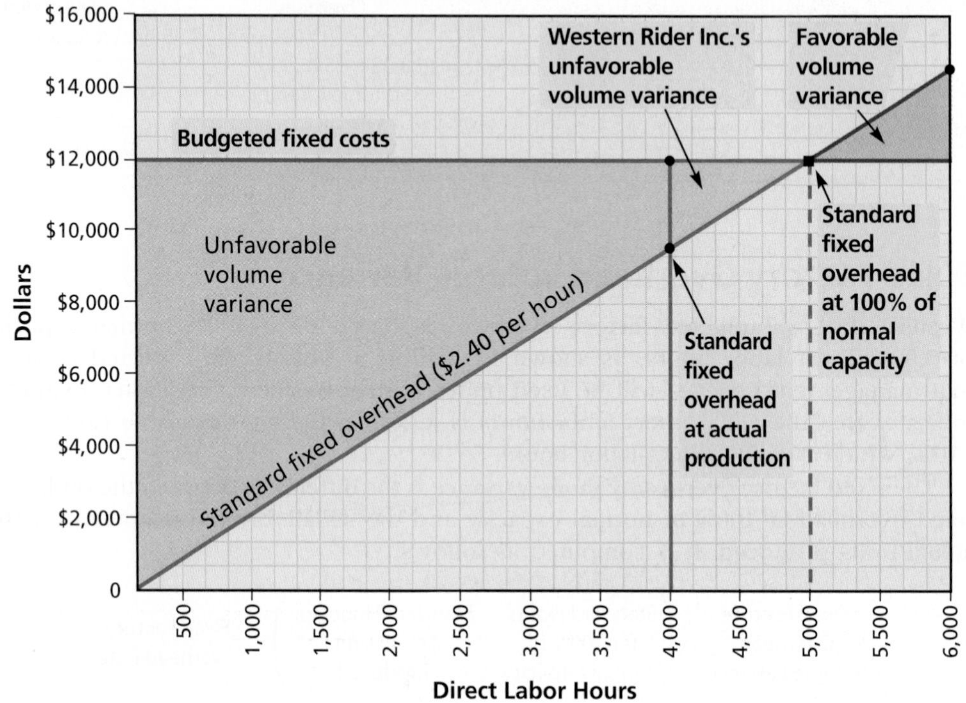

Exhibit 9 indicates that Western Rider's fixed factory overhead volume variance is unfavorable in June because the actual production is 4,000 direct labor hours, or 80% of normal volume. The unfavorable volume variance of $2,400 can be viewed as the cost of the unused capacity (1,000 direct labor hours).

An unfavorable volume variance may be due to factors such as the following:

- Failure to maintain an even flow of work
- Machine breakdowns
- Work stoppages caused by lack of materials or skilled labor
- Lack of enough sales orders to keep the factory operating at normal capacity

Management should determine the causes of the unfavorable variance and consider taking corrective action. For example, a volume variance caused by an uneven flow of work could be remedied by changing operating procedures. Lack of sales orders may be corrected through increased advertising.

Favorable volume variances may not always be desirable. For example, in an attempt to create a favorable volume variance, manufacturing managers might run the factory above the normal capacity. However, if the additional production cannot be sold, it must be stored as inventory, which would incur storage costs.

Example Exercise 7-4 Factory Overhead Volume Variance

Tip Top Corp. produced 3,000 units of product that required 2.5 standard hours per unit. The standard fixed overhead cost per unit is $0.90 per hour at 8,000 hours, which is 100% of normal capacity. Determine the fixed factory overhead volume variance.

Follow My Example 7-4

Fixed Factory Overhead Volume Variance = (Standard Hours for 100% of Normal Capacity – Standard Hours for Actual Units Produced) × Fixed Factory Overhead Rate
= [8,000 hrs. – (3,000 units × 2.5 hrs.)] × $0.90
= (8,000 hrs. – 7,500 hrs.) × $0.90
= $450 (unfavorable)

Practice Exercises: PE 7-4A, PE 7-4B

Reporting Factory Overhead Variances

The total factory overhead cost variance can also be determined as the sum of the variable factory overhead controllable and fixed factory overhead volume variances, computed as follows for **Western Rider Inc.**:

Variable factory overhead controllable variance	–$4,000	Favorable Variance
Fixed factory overhead volume variance	2,400	Unfavorable Variance
Total factory overhead cost variance	–$1,600	Favorable Variance

A **factory overhead cost variance report** is useful to management in controlling factory overhead costs. Budgeted and actual costs for variable and fixed factory overhead along with the related controllable and volume variances are reported by each cost element.

Exhibit 10 illustrates a factory overhead cost variance report for Western Rider Inc. for June.

EXHIBIT 10

Factory Overhead Cost Variance Report

	A	B	C	D	E
1	Western Rider Inc.				
2	Factory Overhead Cost Variance Report				
3	For the Month Ending June 30, 2016				
4	Productive capacity for the month (100% of normal)		5,000 hours		
5	Actual production for the month		4,000 hours		
6					
7		Budget			
8		(at Actual		Variances	
9		Production)	Actual	Favorable	Unfavorable
10	Variable factory overhead costs:				
11	Indirect factory wages	$ 8,000	$ 5,100	$2,900	
12	Power and light	4,000	4,200		$ 200
13	Indirect materials	2,400	1,100	1,300	
14	Total variable factory				
15	overhead cost	$14,400	$10,400		
16	Fixed factory overhead costs:				
17	Supervisory salaries	$ 5,500	$ 5,500		
18	Depreciation of plant and				
19	equipment	4,500	4,500		
20	Insurance and property taxes	2,000	2,000		
21	Total fixed factory				
22	overhead cost	$12,000	$12,000		
23	Total factory overhead cost	$26,400	$22,400		
24	Total controllable variances			$4,200	$ 200
25					
26					
27	Net controllable variance—favorable				$4,000
28	Volume variance—unfavorable:				
29	Capacity not used at the standard rate for fixed				
30	factory overhead—1,000 × $2.40				2,400
31	Total factory overhead cost variance—favorable				$1,600

Factory Overhead Account

To illustrate, the applied factory overhead for **Western Rider Inc.** for the 5,000 XL jeans produced in June is $24,000, computed as follows:

Applied Factory Overhead = Standard Hours for Actual Units Produced × Total Factory Overhead Rate
= (5,000 jeans × 0.80 direct labor hr. per pair of jeans) × $6.00
= 4,000 direct labor hrs. × $6.00 = $24,000

The total actual factory overhead for Western Rider, as shown in Exhibit 10, was $22,400. Thus, the total factory overhead cost variance for Western Rider for June is a $1,600 favorable variance, computed as follows:

Total Factory Overhead Cost Variance = Actual Factory Overhead – Applied Factory Overhead

= $22,400 – $24,000 = –$1,600 Favorable Variance

At the end of the period, the factory overhead account normally has a balance. A debit balance in Factory Overhead represents underapplied overhead. Underapplied overhead occurs when actual factory overhead costs exceed the applied factory overhead. A credit balance in Factory Overhead represents overapplied overhead. Overapplied overhead occurs when actual factory overhead costs are less than the applied factory overhead.

The difference between the actual factory overhead and the applied factory overhead is the total factory overhead cost variance. Thus, underapplied and overapplied factory overhead account balances represent the following total factory overhead cost variances:

- *Underapplied* Factory Overhead = *Unfavorable* Total Factory Overhead Cost Variance
- *Overapplied* Factory Overhead = *Favorable* Total Factory Overhead Cost Variance

The factory overhead account for **Western Rider Inc.** for the month ending June 30, 2016, is as follows:

Factory Overhead

Actual factory overhead ($10,400 + $12,000)	22,400		24,000 Applied factory overhead (4,000 hrs. × $6.00 per hr.)
		Bal., June 30	1,600 Overapplied factory overhead

The $1,600 overapplied factory overhead account balance and the favorable total factory overhead cost variance shown in Exhibit 10 are the same.

The variable factory overhead controllable variance and the volume variance can be computed by comparing the factory overhead account with the budgeted total overhead for the actual level produced, as shown in Exhibit 11.

The controllable and volume variances are determined as follows:

- The difference between the actual overhead incurred and the budgeted overhead is the *controllable* variance.
- The difference between the applied overhead and the budgeted overhead is the *volume* variance.

If the actual factory overhead exceeds (is less than) the budgeted factory overhead, the controllable variance is unfavorable (favorable). In contrast, if the applied factory overhead is less than (exceeds) the budgeted factory overhead, the volume variance is unfavorable (favorable).

EXHIBIT 11 **Factory Overhead Variances**

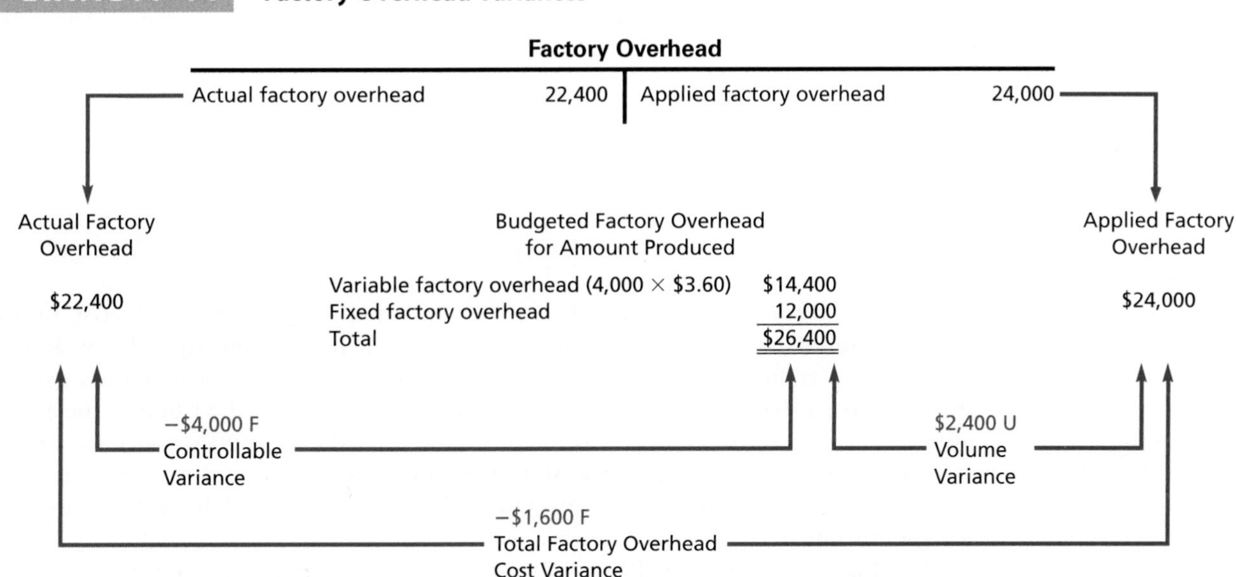

Recording and Reporting Variances from Standards

OBJ 5 Journalize the entries for recording standards in the accounts and prepare an income statement that includes variances from standard.

Standard costs may be used as a management tool to control costs separately from the accounts in the general ledger. However, many companies include standard costs in their accounts. One method for doing so records standard costs and variances at the same time the actual product costs are recorded.

To illustrate, assume that **Western Rider Inc.** purchased, on account, the 7,300 square yards of blue denim used at $5.50 per square yard. The standard price for direct materials is $5.00 per square yard. The entry to record the purchase and the unfavorable direct materials price variance is as follows:

				Debit	Credit
		Materials (7,300 sq. yds. x $5.00)		36,500	
		Direct Materials Price Variance		3,650	
		Accounts Payable (7,300 sq. yds. x $5.50)			40,150

The materials account is debited for the *actual quantity* purchased at the *standard price*, $36,500 (7,300 square yards x $5.00). Accounts Payable is credited for the $40,150 actual cost and the amount due the supplier. The difference of $3,650 is the unfavorable direct materials price variance [($5.50 – $5.00) x 7,300 sq. yds.]. It is recorded by debiting Direct Materials Price Variance. If the variance had been favorable, Direct Materials Price Variance would have been credited for the variance.

A debit balance in the direct materials price variance account represents an unfavorable variance. Likewise, a credit balance in the direct materials price variance account represents a favorable variance.

The direct materials quantity variance is recorded in a similar manner. For example, **Western Rider Inc.** used 7,300 square yards of blue denim to produce 5,000 pairs of XL jeans. The standard quantity of denim for the 5,000 jeans produced is 7,500 square yards. The entry to record the materials used is as follows:

	Work in Process (7,500 sq. yds. × $5.00)		37,500	
	Direct Materials Quantity Variance			1,000
	Materials (7,300 sq. yds. × $5.00)			36,500

Work in Process is debited for $37,500, which is the standard cost of the direct materials required to produce 5,000 XL jeans (7,500 sq. yds. × $5.00). Materials is credited for $36,500, which is the actual quantity of materials used at the standard price (7,300 sq. yds. × $5.00). The difference of $1,000 is the favorable direct materials quantity variance [(7,300 sq. yds. – 7,500 sq. yds.) × $5.00]. It is recorded by crediting Direct Materials Quantity Variance. If the variance had been unfavorable, Direct Materials Quantity Variance would have been debited for the variance.

A debit balance in the direct materials quantity variance account represents an unfavorable variance. Likewise, a credit balance in the direct materials quantity variance account represents a favorable variance.

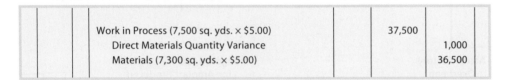

Example Exercise 7-5 Standard Cost Journal Entries

OBJ 5

Tip Top Corp. produced 3,000 units that require six standard pounds per unit at the $4.50 standard price per pound. The company actually used 18,500 pounds in production. Journalize the entry to record the standard direct materials used in production.

Follow My Example 7-5

Work in Process (18,000* pounds × $4.50)	81,000	
Direct Materials Quantity Variance [(18,500 pounds – 18,000 pounds) × $4.50]	2,250	
Materials (18,500 pounds × $4.50)		83,250

*3,000 units × 6 pounds per unit = 18,000 standard pounds for units produced

Practice Exercises: PE 7-5A, PE 7-5B

The journal entries to record the standard costs and variances for *direct labor* are similar to those for direct materials. These entries are summarized as follows:

- Work in Process is debited for the standard cost of direct labor.
- Wages Payable is credited for the actual direct labor cost incurred.
- Direct Labor Rate Variance is debited for an unfavorable variance and credited for a favorable variance.
- Direct Labor Time Variance is debited for an unfavorable variance and credited for a favorable variance.

As illustrated in the prior section, the factory overhead account already incorporates standard costs and variances into its journal entries. That is, Factory Overhead is debited for actual factory overhead and credited for applied (standard) factory overhead. The ending balance of factory overhead (overapplied or underapplied) is the total factory overhead cost variance. By comparing the actual factory overhead with the budgeted factory overhead, the controllable variance can be determined. By comparing the budgeted factory overhead with the applied factory overhead, the volume variance can be determined.

When goods are completed, Finished Goods is debited and Work in Process is credited for the standard cost of the product transferred.

At the end of the period, the balances of each of the variance accounts indicate the net favorable or unfavorable variance for the period. These variances may be reported in an income statement prepared for management's use.

Exhibit 12 is an example of an income statement for **Western Rider Inc.** that includes variances. In Exhibit 12, a sales price of $28 per pair of jeans, selling expenses of $14,500, and administrative expenses of $11,225 are assumed.

EXHIBIT 12

Variance from Standards in Income Statement

Western Rider Inc.
Income Statement
For the Month Ended June 30, 2016

Sales			$140,000[1]
Cost of goods sold—at standard			97,500[2]
Gross profit—at standard			$ 42,500
	Favorable	**Unfavorable**	
Less variances from standard cost:			
Direct materials price		$ 3,650	
Direct materials quantity	$1,000		
Direct labor rate		3,850	
Direct labor time	1,350		
Factory overhead controllable	4,000		
Factory overhead volume		2,400	3,550
Gross profit			$ 38,950
Operating expenses:			
Selling expenses		$14,500	
Administrative expenses		11,225	25,725
Income before income tax			$ 13,225

[1]5,000 × $28

[2]$37,500 + $36,000 + $24,000 (from Exhibit 3), or 5,000 × $19.50 (from Exhibit 1)

The income statement shown in Exhibit 12 is for internal use by management. That is, variances are not reported to external users. Thus, the variances shown in Exhibit 12 must be transferred to other accounts in preparing an income statement for external users.

In preparing an income statement for external users, the balances of the variance accounts are normally transferred to Cost of Goods Sold. However, if the variances are significant or if many of the products manufactured are still in inventory, the variances should be allocated to Work in Process, Finished Goods, and Cost of Goods Sold. Such an allocation, in effect, converts these account balances from standard cost to actual cost.

Example Exercise 7-6 Income Statement with Variances

Prepare an income statement for the year ended December 31, 2016, through gross profit for Tip Top Corp. using the variance data in Example Exercises 7-1 through 7-4. Assume Tip Top sold 3,000 units at $100 per unit.

(Continued)

Follow My Example 7-6

Tip Top Corp.
Income Statement through Gross Profit
For the Year Ended December 31, 2016

	Favorable	Unfavorable	
Sales (3,000 units × $100)			$300,000
Cost of goods sold—at standard			194,250*
Gross profit—at standard			$105,750
Less variances from standard cost:			
Direct materials price (EE7-1)	$2,775		
Direct materials quantity (EE7-1)		$2,250	
Direct labor rate (EE7-2)		2,226	
Direct labor time (EE7-2)	960		
Factory overhead controllable (EE7-3)		350	
Factory overhead volume (EE7-4)		450	1,541
Gross profit—actual			$104,209

*Direct materials (3,000 units × 6 lbs. × $4.50)	$ 81,000
Direct labor (3,000 units × 2.5 hrs. × $12.00)	90,000
Factory overhead [3,000 units × 2.5 hrs. × ($2.20 + $0.90)]	23,250
Cost of goods sold at standard	$194,250

Practice Exercises: PE 7-6A, PE 7-6B

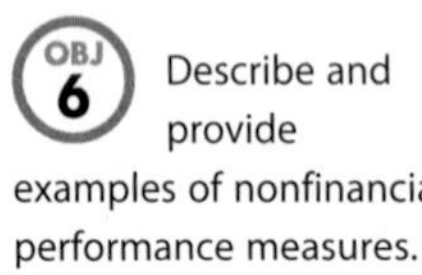
Describe and provide examples of nonfinancial performance measures.

Nonfinancial Performance Measures

Many companies supplement standard costs and variances from standards with nonfinancial performance measures. A **nonfinancial performance measure** expresses performance in a measure other than dollars. For example, airlines use on-time performance, percent of bags lost, and number of customer complaints as nonfinancial performance measures. Such measures are often used to evaluate the time, quality, or quantity of a business activity.

Using financial and nonfinancial performance measures aids managers and employees in considering multiple performance objectives. Such measures often bring additional perspectives, such as quality of work, to evaluating performance. Some examples of nonfinancial performance measures are shown in Exhibit 13.

EXHIBIT 13

Nonfinancial Performance Measures

- Inventory turnover
- Percent on-time delivery
- Elapsed time between a customer order and product delivery
- Customer preference rankings compared to competitors
- Response time to a service call
- Time to develop new products
- Employee satisfaction
- Number of customer complaints

Nonfinancial measures are often linked to either the inputs or outputs of an activity or process. A **process** is a sequence of activities for performing a task. The relationship between an activity or a process and its inputs and outputs is shown in Exhibit 14.

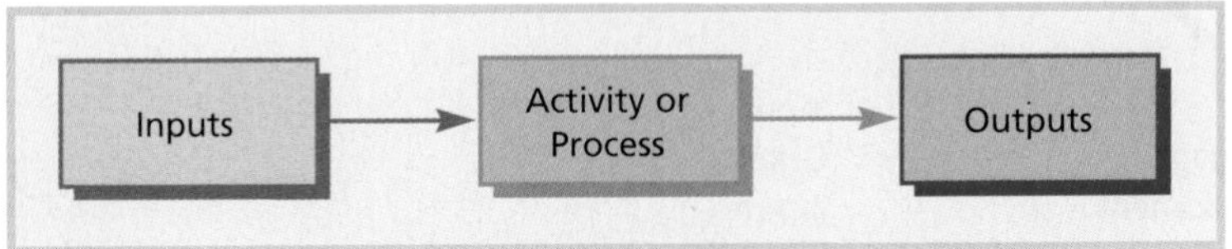

EXHIBIT 14

Relationship Between a Process and Its Inputs and Outputs

To illustrate, the counter service activity of a fast-food restaurant is used. The inputs/outputs for providing counter service at a fast-food restaurant are shown in Exhibit 15.

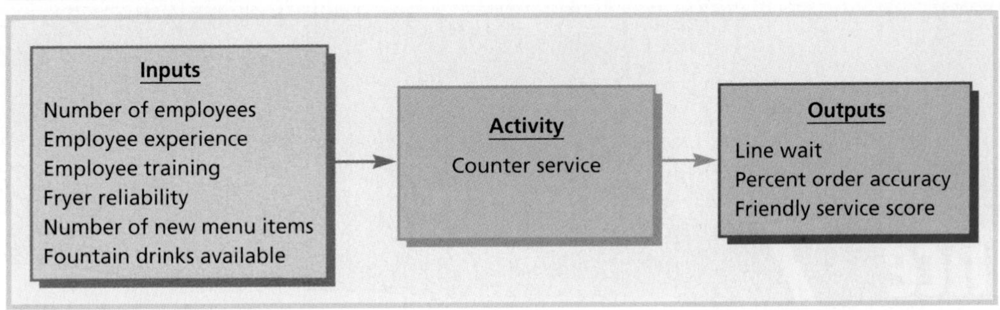

EXHIBIT 15

Inputs / Outputs for a Fast-Food Restaurant

The customer service outputs of the counter service activity include the following:

- Line wait for the customer
- Percent order accuracy in serving the customer
- Friendly service experience for the customer

Some of the inputs that impact the customer service outputs include the following:

- Number of employees
- Employee experience
- Employee training
- Fryer (and other cooking equipment) reliability
- Number of new menu items
- Fountain drink availability

A fast-food restaurant can develop a set of linked nonfinancial performance measures across inputs and outputs. The output measures tell management how the activity is performing, such as keeping the line wait to a minimum. The input measures are used to improve the output measures. For example, if the customer line wait is too long, then improving employee training or hiring more employees could improve the output (decrease customer line wait).

Example Exercise 7-7 Activity Inputs and Outputs

The following are inputs and outputs to the baggage claim process of an airline:

Baggage handler training
Time customers wait for returned baggage
Maintenance of baggage handling equipment
Number of baggage handlers
Number of damaged bags
On-time flight performance

Identify whether each is an input or output to the baggage claim process.

(Continued)

Follow My Example 7-7

Baggage handler training	Input
Time customers wait for returned baggage	Output
Maintenance of baggage handling equipment	Input
Number of baggage handlers	Input
Number of damaged bags	Output
On-time flight performance	Input

Practice Exercises: PE 7-7A, PE 7-7B

At a Glance 7

Describe the types of standards and how they are established.

Key Points Standards represent performance goals that can be compared to actual results in evaluating performance. Standards are established so that they are neither too high nor too low, but are attainable.

Learning Outcomes	Example Exercises	Practice Exercises
• Define *ideal* and *currently attainable standards* and explain how they are used in setting standards. • Describe some of the criticisms of the use of standards.		

Describe and illustrate how standards are used in budgeting.

Key Points Budgets are prepared by multiplying the standard cost per unit by the planned production. To measure performance, the standard cost per unit is multiplied by the actual number of units produced, and the actual results are compared with the standard cost at actual volumes (cost variance).

Learning Outcomes	Example Exercises	Practice Exercises
• Compute the standard cost per unit of production for materials, labor, and factory overhead. • Compute the direct materials, direct labor, and factory overhead cost variances. • Prepare a budget performance report.		

Compute and interpret direct materials and direct labor variances.

Key Points The direct materials cost variance can be separated into direct materials price and quantity variances. The direct labor cost variance can be separated into direct labor rate and time variances.

Learning Outcomes	Example Exercises	Practice Exercises
• Compute and interpret direct materials price and quantity variances.	**EE7-1**	**PE7-1A, 7-1B**
• Compute and interpret direct labor rate and time variances.	**EE7-2**	**PE7-2A, 7-2B**
• Describe and illustrate how time standards are used in nonmanufacturing settings.		

Compute and interpret factory overhead controllable and volume variances.

Key Points The factory overhead cost variance can be separated into a variable factory overhead controllable variance and a fixed factory overhead volume variance.

Learning Outcomes	Example Exercises	Practice Exercises
• Prepare a factory overhead flexible budget.		
• Compute and interpret the variable factory overhead controllable variance.	**EE7-3**	**PE7-3A, 7-3B**
• Compute and interpret the fixed factory overhead volume variance.	**EE7-4**	**PE7-4A, 7-4B**
• Prepare a factory overhead cost variance report.		
• Evaluate factory overhead variances, using a T account.		

Journalize the entries for recording standards in the accounts and prepare an income statement that includes variances from standard.

Key Points Standard costs and variances can be recorded in the accounts at the same time the manufacturing costs are recorded in the accounts. Work in Process is debited at standard. Under a standard cost system, the cost of goods sold will be reported at standard cost. Manufacturing variances can be disclosed on the income statement to adjust the gross profit at standard to the actual gross profit.

Learning Outcomes	Example Exercises	Practice Exercises
• Journalize the entries to record the purchase and use of direct materials at standard, recording favorable or unfavorable variances.	**EE7-5**	**PE7-5A, 7-5B**
• Prepare an income statement, disclosing favorable and unfavorable direct materials, direct labor, and factory overhead variances.	**EE7-6**	**PE7-6A, 7-6B**

Describe and provide examples of nonfinancial performance measures.

Key Points Many companies use a combination of financial and nonfinancial measures in order for multiple perspectives to be incorporated in evaluating performance. Nonfinancial measures are often used in conjunction with the inputs or outputs of a process or an activity.

Learning Outcomes	Example Exercises	Practice Exercises
• Define, provide the rationale for, and provide examples of nonfinancial performance measures.		
• Identify nonfinancial inputs and outputs of an activity.	EE7-7	PE7-7A, 7-7B

Key Terms

budget performance report (281)
budgeted variable factory overhead (290)
controllable variance (290)
cost variances (281)
currently attainable standards (279)
direct labor rate variance (286)
direct labor time variance (287)
direct materials price variance (284)
direct materials quantity variance (284)
factory overhead cost variance report (293)
favorable cost variance (281)
ideal standards (279)
nonfinancial performance measure (298)
process (298)
standard cost (278)
standard cost systems (278)
standards (278)
total manufacturing cost variance (282)
unfavorable cost variance (281)
volume variance (291)

Illustrative Problem

Hawley Inc. manufactures designer iPod cases for national distribution. The standard costs for the manufacture of Folk Art style baskets were as follows:

	Standard Costs	Actual Costs
Direct materials	1,500 lbs. at $35	1,600 lbs. at $32
Direct labor	4,800 hrs. at $11	4,500 hrs. at $11.80
Factory overhead	Rates per labor hour, based on 100% of normal capacity of 5,500 labor hrs.:	
	Variable cost, $2.40	$12,300 variable cost
	Fixed cost, $3.50	$19,250 fixed cost

Instructions

1. Determine the direct materials price variance, direct materials quantity variance, and total direct materials cost variance for the designer iPod cases.
2. Determine the direct labor rate variance, direct labor time variance, and total direct labor cost variance for the designer iPod cases.
3. Determine the variable factory overhead controllable variance, fixed factory overhead volume variance, and total factory overhead cost variance for the designer iPod cases.

Solution

1. **Direct Materials Cost Variance**

Price variance:

Direct Materials Price Variance = (Actual Price – Standard Price) × Actual Quantity
= ($32 per lb. – $35 per lb.) × 1,600 lbs.
= –$4,800 Favorable Variance

Quantity variance:

Direct Materials Quantity Variance = (Actual Quantity – Standard Quantity) × Standard Price
= (1,600 lbs. – 1,500 lbs.) × $35 per lb.
= $3,500 Unfavorable Variance

Total direct materials cost variance:

Direct Materials Cost Variance = Direct Materials Quantity Variance + Direct Materials Price Variance
= $3,500 + ($4,800)
= –$1,300 Favorable Variance

2. **Direct Labor Cost Variance**

Rate variance:

Direct Labor Rate Variance = (Actual Rate per Hour – Standard Rate per Hour) × Actual Hours
= ($11.80 – $11.00) × 4,500 hrs.
= $3,600 Unfavorable Variance

Time variance:

Direct Labor Time Variance = (Actual Direct Labor Hours – Standard Direct Labor Hours) × Standard Rate per Hour
= (4,500 hrs. – 4,800 hrs.) × $11.00 per hour
= –$3,300 Favorable Variance

Total direct labor cost variance:

Direct Labor Cost Variance = Direct Labor Time Variance + Direct Labor Rate Variance
= ($3,300) + $3,600
= $300 Unfavorable Variance

3. **Factory Overhead Cost Variance**

Variable factory overhead controllable variance:

Variable Factory Overhead Controllable Variance = Actual Variable Factory Overhead – Budgeted Variable Factory Overhead
= $12,300 – $11,520*
= $780 Unfavorable Variance

*4,800 hrs. × $2.40 per hour

Fixed factory overhead volume variance:

Fixed Factory Overhead Volume Variance = (Standard Hours for 100% of Normal Capacity – Standard Hours for Actual Units Produced) × Fixed Factory Overhead Rate
= (5,500 hrs. – 4,800 hrs.) × $3.50 per hr.
= $2,450 Unfavorable Variance

Total factory overhead cost variance:

Factory Overhead Cost Variance = Variable Factory Overhead Controllable Variance + Fixed Factory Overhead Volume Variance
= $780 + $2,450
= $3,230 Unfavorable Variance

Discussion Questions

1. What are the basic objectives in the use of standard costs?
2. What is meant by reporting by the "principle of exceptions," as the term is used in reference to cost control?
3. What are the two variances between the actual cost and the standard cost for direct materials?
4. The materials cost variance report for Nickols Inc. indicates a large favorable materials price variance and a significant unfavorable materials quantity variance. What might have caused these offsetting variances?
5. a. What are the two variances between the actual cost and the standard cost for direct labor?

   b. Who generally has control over the direct labor cost variances?
6. A new assistant controller recently was heard to remark: "All the assembly workers in this plant are covered by union contracts, so there should be no labor variances." Was the controller's remark correct? Discuss.
7. Would the use of standards be appropriate in a nonmanufacturing setting, such as a fast-food restaurant?
8. a. Describe the two variances between the actual costs and the standard costs for factory overhead.

   b. What is a factory overhead cost variance report?
9. If variances are recorded in the accounts at the time the manufacturing costs are incurred, what does a debit balance in Direct Materials Price Variance represent?
10. Briefly explain why firms might use nonfinancial performance measures.

Practice Exercises

EE 7-1 *p.285*

PE 7-1A Direct materials variances

OBJ. 3

Lo-bed Company produces a product that requires two standard gallons per unit. The standard price is $20.00 per gallon. If 4,000 units required 8,200 gallons, which were purchased at $19.75 per gallon, what is the direct materials (a) price variance, (b) quantity variance, and (c) cost variance?

EE 7-1 *p.285*

PE 7-1B Direct materials variances

OBJ. 3

Dvorak Company produces a product that requires five standard pounds per unit. The standard price is $2.50 per pound. If 1,000 units required 4,500 pounds, which were purchased at $3.00 per pound, what is the direct materials (a) price variance, (b) quantity variance, and (c) cost variance?

EE 7-2 *p.288*

PE 7-2A Direct labor variances

OBJ. 3

Lo-bed Company produces a product that requires four standard hours per unit at a standard hourly rate of $28.00 per hour. If 4,000 units required 16,750 hours at an hourly rate of $28.40 per hour, what is the direct labor (a) rate variance, (b) time variance, and (c) cost variance?

SHOW ME HOW

EE 7-2 *p.288* **PE 7-2B Direct labor variances** **OBJ. 3**

Dvorak Company produces a product that requires three standard hours per unit at a standard hourly rate of $17 per hour. If 1,000 units required 2,800 hours at an hourly rate of $16.50 per hour, what is the direct labor (a) rate variance, (b) time variance, and (c) cost variance?

SHOW ME HOW

EE 7-3 *p.291* **PE 7-3A Factory overhead controllable variance** **OBJ. 4**

Lo-bed Company produced 4,000 units of product that required four standard hours per unit. The standard variable overhead cost per unit is $3.00 per hour. The actual variable factory overhead was $51,240. Determine the variable factory overhead controllable variance.

SHOW ME HOW

EE 7-3 *p.291* **PE 7-3B Factory overhead controllable variance** **OBJ. 4**

Dvorak Company produced 1,000 units of product that required three standard hours per unit. The standard variable overhead cost per unit is $1.40 per hour. The actual variable factory overhead was $4,000. Determine the variable factory overhead controllable variance.

SHOW ME HOW

EE 7-4 *p.292* **PE 7-4A Factory overhead volume variance** **OBJ. 4**

Lo-bed Company produced 4,000 units of product that required four standard hours per unit. The standard fixed overhead cost per unit is $1.20 per hour at 16,400 hours, which is 100% of normal capacity. Determine the fixed factory overhead volume variance.

SHOW ME HOW

EE 7-4 *p.292* **PE 7-4B Factory overhead volume variance** **OBJ. 4**

Dvorak Company produced 1,000 units of product that required three standard hours per unit. The standard fixed overhead cost per unit is $0.60 per hour at 3,500 hours, which is 100% of normal capacity. Determine the fixed factory overhead volume variance.

SHOW ME HOW

EE 7-5 *p. 296* **PE 7-5A Standard cost journal entries** **OBJ. 5**

Lo-bed Company produced 4,000 units that require two standard gallons per unit at $20.00 standard price per gallon. The company actually used 8,200 gallons in production. Journalize the entry to record the standard direct materials used in production.

SHOW ME HOW

EE 7-5 *p. 296* **PE 7-5B Standard cost journal entries** **OBJ. 5**

Dvorak Company produced 1,000 units that require five standard pounds per unit at $2.50 standard price per pound. The company actually used 4,500 pounds in production. Journalize the entry to record the standard direct materials used in production.

SHOW ME HOW

EE 7-6 *p. 297* **PE 7-6A Income statement with variances** **OBJ. 5**

Prepare a 2016 income statement through gross profit for Lo-bed Company, using the variance data in Practice Exercises 7-1A, 7-2A, 7-3A, and 7-4A. Assume Lo-bed sold 4,000 units at $250 per unit.

SHOW ME HOW

EE 7-6 *p. 297* **PE 7-6B Income statement with variances** **OBJ. 5**

Prepare a 2016 income statement through gross profit for Dvorak Company, using the variance data in Practice Exercises 7-1B, 7-2B, 7-3B, and 7-4B. Assume Dvorak sold 1,000 units at $90 per unit.

EE 7-7 p. 299

SHOW ME HOW

PE 7-7A Activity inputs and outputs **OBJ. 6**

The following are inputs and outputs to the copying process of a copy shop:

Number of employee errors
Number of times paper supply runs out
Copy machine downtime (broken)
Number of pages copied per hour
Number of customer complaints
Percent jobs done on time

Identify whether each is an input or output to the copying process.

EE 7-7 p. 299

SHOW ME HOW

PE 7-7B Activity inputs and outputs **OBJ. 6**

The following are inputs and outputs to the cooking process of a restaurant:

Number of times ingredients are missing
Number of customer complaints
Number of hours kitchen equipment is down for repairs
Number of server order mistakes
Percent of meals prepared on time
Number of unexpected cook absences

Identify whether each is an input or output to the cooking process.

Exercises

SHOW ME HOW

EX 7-1 Standard direct materials cost per unit **OBJ. 2**

Choco La Ti-Da Company produces chocolate bars. The primary materials used in producing chocolate bars are cocoa, sugar, and milk. The standard costs for a batch of chocolate (4,500 bars) are as follows:

Ingredient	Quantity	Price
Cocoa	510 lbs.	$1.50 per lb.
Sugar	160 lbs.	$0.50 per lb.
Milk	100 gal.	$3.25 per gal.

Determine the standard direct materials cost per bar of chocolate.

SHOW ME HOW

EX 7-2 Standard product cost **OBJ. 2**

Wood You Lie To Me Furniture Company manufactures designer home furniture. Wood You Lie To Me uses a standard cost system. The direct labor, direct materials, and factory overhead standards for an unfinished dining room table are as follows:

Direct labor:	standard rate	$24.00 per hr.
	standard time per unit	4.0 hrs.
Direct materials (oak):	standard price	$22.00 per bd. ft.
	standard quantity	32 bd. ft.
Variable factory overhead:	standard rate	$3.00 per direct labor hr.
Fixed factory overhead:	standard rate	$2.00 per direct labor hr.

a. Determine the standard cost per dining room table.

b. Why would Wood You Lie To Me Furniture Company use a standard cost system?

EX 7-3 Budget performance report **OBJ. 2**

✔ b. Direct labor cost variance, $580 F

SHOW ME HOW

Genie in a Bottle Company (GBC) manufactures plastic two-liter bottles for the beverage industry. The cost standards per 100 two-liter bottles are as follows:

Cost Category	Standard Cost per 100 Two-Liter Bottles
Direct labor	$ 2.00
Direct materials	9.10
Factory overhead	0.55
Total	$11.65

At the beginning of July, GBC management planned to produce 400,000 bottles. The actual number of bottles produced for July was 406,000 bottles. The actual costs for July of the current year were as follows:

Cost Category	Actual Cost for the Month Ended July 31
Direct labor	$ 7,540
Direct materials	35,750
Factory overhead	2,680
Total	$45,970

a. Prepare the July manufacturing standard cost budget (direct labor, direct materials, and factory overhead) for GBC, assuming planned production.

b. Prepare a budget performance report for manufacturing costs, showing the total cost variances for direct materials, direct labor, and factory overhead for July.

c. Interpret the budget performance report.

EX 7-4 Direct materials variances **OBJ. 3**

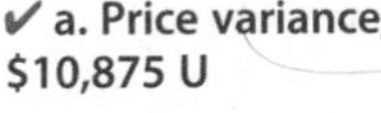

✔ a. Price variance, $10,875 U

SHOW ME HOW

The following data relate to the direct materials cost for the production of 4,000 automobile tires:

Actual:	72,500 lbs. at $3.30
Standard:	75,160 lbs. at $3.15

a. Determine the direct materials price variance, direct materials quantity variance, and total direct materials cost variance.

b. To whom should the variances be reported for analysis and control?

EX 7-5 Direct materials variances **OBJ. 3**

✔ Quantity variance, $300 U

SHOW ME HOW

The Silicone Engine Inc. produces wrist-worn tablet computers. The company uses Thin Film Crystal (TFC) LCD displays for its products. Each tablet uses one display. The company produced 580 tablets during December. However, due to LCD defects, the company actually used 600 LCD displays during December. Each display has a standard cost of $15.00. Six hundred LCD displays were purchased for December production at a cost of $8,550.

Determine the price variance, quantity variance, and total direct materials cost variance for December.

EX 7-6 Standard direct materials cost per unit from variance data **OBJ. 2, 3**

SHOW ME HOW

The following data relating to direct materials cost for October of the current year are taken from the records of Good Clean Fun Inc., a manufacturer of organic toys:

Quantity of direct materials used	3,000 lbs.
Actual unit price of direct materials	$5.50 per lb.
Units of finished product manufactured	1,400 units
Standard direct materials per unit of finished product	2 lbs.
Direct materials quantity variance—unfavorable	$1,000
Direct materials price variance—unfavorable	$1,500

Determine the standard direct materials cost per unit of finished product, assuming that there was no inventory of work in process at either the beginning or the end of the month.

SHOW ME HOW

EX 7-7 Standard product cost, direct materials variance **OBJ. 2, 3**

H.J. Heinz Company uses standards to control its materials costs. Assume that a batch of ketchup (3,128 pounds) has the following standards:

	Standard Quantity	Standard Price
Whole tomatoes	4,000 lbs.	$ 0.60 per lb.
Vinegar	260 gal.	2.25 per gal.
Corn syrup	25 gal.	28.00 per gal.
Salt	100 lbs.	2.25 per lb.

The actual materials in a batch may vary from the standard due to tomato characteristics. Assume that the actual quantities of materials for batch K-111 were as follows:

4,250 lbs. of tomatoes
275 gal. of vinegar
22 gal. of corn syrup
90 lbs. of salt

a. Determine the standard unit materials cost per pound for a standard batch.

b. Determine the direct materials quantity variance for batch K-111. Round your answer to the nearest cent.

✔ a. Rate variance, $4,225 F

SHOW ME HOW

EX 7-8 Direct labor variances **OBJ. 3**

The following data relate to labor cost for production of 20,000 cellular telephones:

Actual:	8,450 hrs. at $22.50
Standard:	8,400 hrs. at $23.00

a. Determine the direct labor rate variance, direct labor time variance, and total direct labor cost variance.

b. Discuss what might have caused these variances.

✔ a. Time variance, $525 U

SHOW ME HOW

EX 7-9 Direct labor variances **OBJ. 3, 5**

Reincarnation Bicycle Company manufactures commuter bicycles from recycled materials. The following data for April of the current year are available:

Quantity of direct labor used	1,530 hrs.
Actual rate for direct labor	$17.00 per hr.
Bicycles completed in April	500
Standard direct labor per bicycle	3 hrs.
Standard rate for direct labor	$17.50 per hr.

a. Determine the direct labor rate variance, time variance, and total direct labor cost variance.

b. How much direct labor should be debited to Work in Process?

✔ a. Cutting Department rate variance, $638 favorable

EX 7-10 Direct labor variances **OBJ. 3**

The Greeson Clothes Company produced 25,000 units during June of the current year. The Cutting Department used 6,380 direct labor hours at an actual rate of $10.90 per hour. The Sewing Department used 9,875 direct labor hours at an actual rate of $11.12 per hour. Assume there were no work in process inventories in either department at the beginning or end of the month. The standard labor rate is $11.00. The standard labor time for the Cutting and Sewing departments is 0.25 hour and 0.4 hour per unit, respectively.

a. Determine the direct labor rate, direct labor time, and total direct labor cost variance for the (1) Cutting Department and (2) Sewing Department.

b. Interpret your results.

EX 7-11 Direct labor standards for nonmanufacturing expenses OBJ. 3

✓ a. $2,400

Englert Hospital began using standards to evaluate its Admissions Department. The standard was broken into two types of admissions as follows:

Type of Admission	Standard Time to Complete Admission Record
Unscheduled admission	30 min.
Scheduled admission	15 min.

The unscheduled admission took longer because name, address, and insurance information needed to be determined and verified at the time of admission. Information was collected on scheduled admissions prior to the admissions, which was less time consuming.

The Admissions Department employs four full-time people (40 productive hours per week, with no overtime) at $15 per hour. For the most recent week, the department handled 140 unscheduled and 350 scheduled admissions.

a. How much was actually spent on labor for the week?

b. What are the standard hours for the actual volume for the week?

c. Calculate a time variance, and report how well the department performed for the week.

EX 7-12 Direct labor standards for a service company OBJ. 2, 3

One of the operations in the **United States Postal Service** is a mechanical mail sorting operation. In this operation, letter mail is sorted at a rate of 1.5 letters per second. The letter is mechanically sorted from a three-digit code input by an operator sitting at a keyboard. The manager of the mechanical sorting operation wishes to determine the number of temporary employees to hire for December. The manager estimates that there will be an additional 24,192,000 pieces of mail in December, due to the upcoming holiday season.

Assume that the sorting operators are temporary employees. The union contract requires that temporary employees be hired for one month at a time. Each temporary employee is hired to work 160 hours in the month.

a. How many temporary employees should the manager hire for December?

b. If each temporary employee earns a standard $16.40 per hour, what would be the labor time variance if the actual number of additional letters sorted in December was 23,895,000?

EX 7-13 Direct labor variances for a service company

SHOW ME HOW

Hit-n-Run Food Trucks, Inc. owns and operates food trucks (mobile kitchens) throughout the west coast. The company's employees have varying wage levels depending on their experience and length of time with the company. Employees work eight hour shifts and are assigned to a truck each day based on labor needs to support the daily menu. One of their trucks, Jose O'Brien's Mobile Fiesta, specializes in Irish-Mexican fusion cuisine. The truck offers a single menu item which changes daily. On November 11, the truck prepared 200 of its most popular item, the Irish Breakfast Enchiladas. The following data are available for that day:

Quantity of direct labor used	24 hrs.
(3 employees, working 8 hour shifts)	
Actual rate for direct labor	$15.00 per hr.
Standard direct labor per meal	0.1 hr.
Standard rate for direct labor	$15.50 per hr.

a. Determine the direct labor rate variance, direct labor time variance, and the total direct labor cost variance.

b. Discuss what might have caused these variances.

EX 7-14 Direct materials and direct labor variances — OBJ. 3

✔ Direct materials quantity variance, $1,100 U

SHOW ME HOW

At the beginning of June, Bezco Toy Company budgeted 5,000 toy action figures to be manufactured in June at standard direct materials and direct labor costs as follows:

Direct materials	$50,000
Direct labor	36,000
Total	$86,000

The standard materials price is $4.00 per pound. The standard direct labor rate is $18.00 per hour. At the end of June, the actual direct materials and direct labor costs were as follows:

Actual direct materials	$49,600
Actual direct labor	34,020
Total	$83,620

There were no direct materials price or direct labor rate variances for June. In addition, assume no changes in the direct materials inventory balances in June. Bezco Toy Company actually produced 4,850 units during June.

Determine the direct materials quantity and direct labor time variances.

EX 7-15 Flexible overhead budget — OBJ. 4

✔ Total factory overhead, 22,000 hrs., $443,600

Leno Manufacturing Company prepared the following factory overhead cost budget for the Press Department for October of the current year, during which it expected to require 20,000 hours of productive capacity in the department:

Variable overhead cost:		
Indirect factory labor	$180,000	
Power and light	12,000	
Indirect materials	64,000	
Total variable overhead cost		$256,000
Fixed overhead cost:		
Supervisory salaries	$ 80,000	
Depreciation of plant and equipment	50,000	
Insurance and property taxes	32,000	
Total fixed overhead cost		162,000
Total factory overhead cost		$418,000

Assuming that the estimated costs for November are the same as for October, prepare a flexible factory overhead cost budget for the Press Department for November for 18,000, 20,000, and 22,000 hours of production.

EX 7-16 Flexible overhead budget — OBJ. 4

Wiki Wiki Company has determined that the variable overhead rate is $4.50 per direct labor hour in the Fabrication Department. The normal production capacity for the Fabrication Department is 10,000 hours for the month. Fixed costs are budgeted at $60,000 for the month.

a. Prepare a monthly factory overhead flexible budget for 9,000, 10,000, and 11,000 hours of production.

b. How much overhead would be applied to production if 9,000 hours were used in the department during the month?

EX 7-17 Factory overhead cost variances **OBJ. 4**

✔ Volume variance, $6,000 U

The following data relate to factory overhead cost for the production of 10,000 computers:

Actual:	Variable factory overhead	$262,000
	Fixed factory overhead	90,000
Standard:	14,000 hrs. at $25	350,000

If productive capacity of 100% was 15,000 hours and the total factory overhead cost budgeted at the level of 14,000 standard hours was $356,000, determine the variable factory overhead controllable variance, fixed factory overhead volume variance, and total factory overhead cost variance. The fixed factory overhead rate was $6.00 per hour.

EX 7-18 Factory overhead cost variances **OBJ. 4**

✔ a. $13,000 F

Blumen Textiles Corporation began April with a budget for 90,000 hours of production in the Weaving Department. The department has a full capacity of 100,000 hours under normal business conditions. The budgeted overhead at the planned volumes at the beginning of April was as follows:

Variable overhead	$540,000
Fixed overhead	240,000
Total	$780,000

The actual factory overhead was $782,000 for April. The actual fixed factory overhead was as budgeted. During April, the Weaving Department had standard hours at actual production volume of 92,500 hours.

a. Determine the variable factory overhead controllable variance.

b. Determine the fixed factory overhead volume variance.

EX 7-19 Factory overhead variance corrections **OBJ. 4**

The data related to Shunda Enterprises Inc.'s factory overhead cost for the production of 100,000 units of product are as follows:

Actual:	Variable factory overhead	$458,000
	Fixed factory overhead	494,000
Standard:	132,000 hrs. at $7.30 ($3.50 for variable factory overhead)	963,600

Productive capacity at 100% of normal was 130,000 hours, and the factory overhead cost budgeted at the level of 132,000 standard hours was $956,000. Based on these data, the chief cost accountant prepared the following variance analysis:

Variable factory overhead controllable variance:		
Actual variable factory overhead cost incurred	$458,000	
Budgeted variable factory overhead for 132,000 hours	462,000	
Variance—favorable		–$ 4,000
Fixed factory overhead volume variance:		
Normal productive capacity at 100%	130,000 hrs.	
Standard for amount produced	132,000	
Productive capacity not used	2,000 hrs.	
Standard variable factory overhead rate	× $7.30	
Variance—unfavorable		14,600
Total factory overhead cost variance—unfavorable		$10,600

Identify the errors in the factory overhead cost variance analysis.

✔ Net controllable variance, $900 U

EX 7-20 Factory overhead cost variance report — OBJ. 4

Tannin Products Inc. prepared the following factory overhead cost budget for the Trim Department for July of the current year, during which it expected to use 20,000 hours for production:

Variable overhead cost:		
Indirect factory labor	$46,000	
Power and light	12,000	
Indirect materials	20,000	
Total variable overhead cost		$ 78,000
Fixed overhead cost:		
Supervisory salaries	$54,500	
Depreciation of plant and equipment	40,000	
Insurance and property taxes	35,500	
Total fixed overhead cost		130,000
Total factory overhead cost		$208,000

Tannin has available 25,000 hours of monthly productive capacity in the Trim Department under normal business conditions. During July, the Trim Department actually used 22,000 hours for production. The actual fixed costs were as budgeted. The actual variable overhead for July was as follows:

Actual variable factory overhead cost:	
Indirect factory labor	$49,700
Power and light	13,000
Indirect materials	24,000
Total variable cost	$86,700

Construct a factory overhead cost variance report for the Trim Department for July.

EX 7-21 Recording standards in accounts — OBJ. 5

Cioffi Manufacturing Company incorporates standards in its accounts and identifies variances at the time the manufacturing costs are incurred. Journalize the entries to record the following transactions:

a. Purchased 2,450 units of copper tubing on account at $52.00 per unit. The standard price is $48.50 per unit.

b. Used 1,900 units of copper tubing in the process of manufacturing 200 air conditioners. Ten units of copper tubing are required, at standard, to produce one air conditioner.

EX 7-22 Recording standards in accounts — OBJ. 5

The Assembly Department produced 5,000 units of product during March. Each unit required 2.20 standard direct labor hours. There were 11,500 actual hours used in the Assembly Department during March at an actual rate of $17.60 per hour. The standard direct labor rate is $18.00 per hour. Assuming direct labor for a month is paid on the fifth day of the following month, journalize the direct labor in the Assembly Department on March 31.

✔ Income before income tax, $85,900

EX 7-23 Income statement indicating standard cost variances — OBJ. 5

The following data were taken from the records of Griggs Company for December 2016:

Administrative expenses	$100,800
Cost of goods sold (at standard)	550,000
Direct materials price variance—unfavorable	1,680
Direct materials quantity variance—favorable	560
Direct labor rate variance—favorable	1,120
Direct labor time variance—unfavorable	490
Variable factory overhead controllable variance—favorable	210
Fixed factory overhead volume variance—unfavorable	3,080
Interest expense	2,940
Sales	868,000
Selling expenses	125,000

Prepare an income statement for presentation to management.

EX 7-24 Nonfinancial performance measures OBJ. 6

Diamond Inc. is an Internet retailer of woodworking equipment. Customers order woodworking equipment from the company, using an online catalog. The company processes these orders and delivers the requested product from its warehouse. The company wants to provide customers with an excellent purchase experience in order to expand the business through favorable word-of-mouth advertising and to drive repeat business. To help monitor performance, the company developed a set of performance measures for its order placement and delivery process:

Average computer response time to customer "clicks"
Dollar amount of returned goods
Elapsed time between customer order and product delivery
Maintenance dollars divided by hardware investment
Number of customer complaints divided by the number of orders
Number of misfilled orders divided by the number of orders
Number of orders per warehouse employee
Number of page faults or errors due to software programming errors
Number of software fixes per week
Server (computer) downtime
Training dollars per programmer

a. For each performance measure, identify it as either an input or output measure related to the "order placement and delivery" process.

b. Provide an explanation for each performance measure.

EX 7-25 Nonfinancial performance measures OBJ. 6

Alpha University wishes to monitor the efficiency and quality of its course registration process.

a. Identify three input and three output measures for this process.

b. Why would Alpha University use nonfinancial measures for monitoring this process?

Problems: Series A

PR 7-1A Direct materials and direct labor variance analysis OBJ. 2, 3

✔ c. Direct labor time variance, $1,260 U

SHOW ME HOW

Fancy Fixture Company manufactures faucets in a small manufacturing facility. The faucets are made from brass. Manufacturing has 100 employees. Each employee presently provides 40 hours of labor per week. Information about a production week is as follows:

Standard wage per hr.	$21.00
Standard labor time per faucet	20 min.
Standard number of lbs. of brass	5 lbs.
Standard price per lb. of brass	$2.80
Actual price per lb. of brass	$2.72
Actual lbs. of brass used during the week	59,875 lbs.
Number of faucets produced during the week	11,820
Actual wage per hr.	$21.40
Actual hrs. for the week	4,000 hrs.

Instructions

Determine (a) the standard cost per unit for direct materials and direct labor; (b) the direct materials price variance, direct materials quantity variance, and total direct materials cost variance; and (c) the direct labor rate variance, direct labor time variance, and total direct labor cost variance.

✔ 1. a. Direct materials quantity variance, $625 F

PR 7-2A Flexible budgeting and variance analysis **OBJ. 1, 2, 3**

I Love My Chocolate Company makes dark chocolate and light chocolate. Both products require cocoa and sugar. The following planning information has been made available:

	Standard Amount per Case		
	Dark Chocolate	**Light Chocolate**	**Standard Price per Pound**
Cocoa	12 lbs.	8 lbs.	$7.25
Sugar	10 lbs.	14 lbs.	1.40
Standard labor time	0.50 hr.	0.60 hr.	

	Dark Chocolate	**Light Chocolate**
Planned production	4,700 cases	11,000 cases
Standard labor rate	$15.50 per hr.	$15.50 per hr.

I Love My Chocolate Company does not expect there to be any beginning or ending inventories of cocoa or sugar. At the end of the budget year, I Love My Chocolate Company had the following actual results:

	Dark Chocolate	**Light Chocolate**
Actual production (cases)	5,000	10,000
	Actual Price per Pound	**Actual Pounds Purchased and Used**
Cocoa	$7.33	140,300
Sugar	1.35	188,000
	Actual Labor Rate	**Actual Labor Hours Used**
Dark chocolate	$15.25 per hr.	2,360
Light chocolate	15.80 per hr.	6,120

Instructions

1. Prepare the following variance analyses for both chocolates and the total, based on the actual results and production levels at the end of the budget year:
   a. Direct materials price, quantity, and total variance.
   b. Direct labor rate, time, and total variance.
2. Why are the standard amounts in part (1) based on the actual production for the year instead of the planned production for the year?

✔ c. Controllable variance, $180 U

PR 7-3A Direct materials, direct labor, and factory overhead cost variance analysis **OBJ. 3, 4**

Adamantane Inc. processes a base chemical into plastic. Standard costs and actual costs for direct materials, direct labor, and factory overhead incurred for the manufacture of 15,000 units of product were as follows:

	Standard Costs	**Actual Costs**
Direct materials	5,000 lbs. at $50.00	4,950 lbs. at $50.60
Direct labor	3,000 hrs. at $25.00	2,945 hrs. at $25.60
Factory overhead	Rates per direct labor hr., based on 100% of normal capacity of 3,200 direct labor hrs.:	
	Variable cost, $5.50	$16,680 variable cost
	Fixed cost, $4.00	$12,800 fixed cost

Each unit requires 0.2 hour of direct labor.

Instructions

Determine (a) the direct materials price variance, direct materials quantity variance, and total direct materials cost variance; (b) the direct labor rate variance, direct labor time variance, and total direct labor cost variance; and (c) the variable factory overhead controllable variance, fixed factory overhead volume variance, and total factory overhead cost variance.

✔ Controllable variance, $770 U

General Ledger

PR 7-4A Factory overhead cost variance report **OBJ. 4**

Tiger Equipment Inc., a manufacturer of construction equipment, prepared the following factory overhead cost budget for the Welding Department for May of the current year. The company expected to operate the department at 100% of normal capacity of 8,400 hours.

Variable costs:		
Indirect factory wages	$30,240	
Power and light	20,160	
Indirect materials	16,800	
Total variable cost		$ 67,200
Fixed costs:		
Supervisory salaries	$20,000	
Depreciation of plant and equipment	36,200	
Insurance and property taxes	15,200	
Total fixed cost		71,400
Total factory overhead cost		$138,600

During May, the department operated at 8,860 standard hours, and the factory overhead costs incurred were indirect factory wages, $32,400; power and light, $21,000; indirect materials, $18,250; supervisory salaries, $20,000; depreciation of plant and equipment, $36,200; and insurance and property taxes, $15,200.

Instructions

Prepare a factory overhead cost variance report for May. To be useful for cost control, the budgeted amounts should be based on 8,860 hours.

PR 7-5A Standards for nonmanufacturing expenses **OBJ. 3, 6**

✔ 3. $1,600 U

CodeHead Software Inc. does software development. One important activity in software development is writing software code. The manager of the WordPro Development Team determined that the average software programmer could write 25 lines of code in an hour. The plan for the first week in May called for 4,650 lines of code to be written on the WordPro product. The WordPro Team has five programmers. Each programmer is hired from an employment firm that requires temporary employees to be hired for a minimum of a 40-hour week. Programmers are paid $32.00 per hour. The manager offered a bonus if the team could generate more lines for the week, without overtime. Due to a project emergency, the programmers wrote more code in the first week of May than planned. The actual amount of code written in the first week of May was 5,650 lines, without overtime. As a result, the bonus caused the average programmer's hourly rate to increase to $40.00 per hour during the first week in May.

Instructions

1. If the team generated 4,650 lines of code according to the original plan, what would have been the labor time variance?
2. What was the actual labor time variance as a result of generating 5,650 lines of code?
3. What was the labor rate variance as a result of the bonus?
4. Are there any performance-related issues that the labor time and rate variances fail to consider? Explain.
5. The manager is trying to determine if a better decision would have been to hire a temporary programmer to meet the higher programming demand in the first week of May, rather than paying out the bonus. If another employee was hired from the employment firm, what would have been the labor time variance in the first week?
6. Which decision is better, paying the bonus or hiring another programmer?

Problems: Series B

PR 7-1B Direct materials and direct labor variance analysis OBJ. 2, 3

✔ c. Rate variance, $200 F

SHOW ME HOW

Lenni Clothing Co. manufactures clothing in a small manufacturing facility. Manufacturing has 25 employees. Each employee presently provides 40 hours of productive labor per week. Information about a production week is as follows:

Standard wage per hr.	$12.00
Standard labor time per unit	12 min.
Standard number of yds. of fabric per unit	5.0 yds.
Standard price per yd. of fabric	$5.00
Actual price per yd. of fabric	$5.10
Actual yds. of fabric used during the week	26,200 yds.
Number of units produced during the week	5,220
Actual wage per hr.	$11.80
Actual hrs. for the week	1,000 hrs.

Instructions

Determine (a) the standard cost per unit for direct materials and direct labor; (b) the price variance, quantity variance, and total direct materials cost variance; and (c) the rate variance, time variance, and total direct labor cost variance.

PR 7-2B Flexible budgeting and variance analysis OBJ. 1, 2, 3

✔ 1. a. Direct materials price variance, $12,220 U

I'm Really Cold Coat Company makes women's and men's coats. Both products require filler and lining material. The following planning information has been made available:

	Standard Amount per Unit		
	Women's Coats	Men's Coats	Standard Price per Unit
Filler	4.0 lbs.	5.20 lbs.	$2.00 per lb.
Liner	7.00 yds.	9.40 yds.	8.00 per yd.
Standard labor time	0.40 hr.	0.50 hr.	

	Women's Coats	Men's Coats
Planned production	5,000 units	6,200 units
Standard labor rate	$14.00 per hr.	$13.00 per hr.

I'm Really Cold Coat Company does not expect there to be any beginning or ending inventories of filler and lining material. At the end of the budget year, I'm Really Cold Coat Company experienced the following actual results:

	Women's Coats	Men's Coats
Actual production	4,400	5,800
	Actual Price per Unit	**Actual Quantity Purchased and Used**
Filler	$1.90 per lb.	48,000
Liner	8.20 per yd.	85,100
	Actual Labor Rate	**Actual Labor Hours Used**
Women's coats	$14.10 per hr.	1,825
Men's coats	13.30 per hr.	2,800

The expected beginning inventory and desired ending inventory were realized.

Instructions

1. Prepare the following variance analyses for both coats and the total, based on the actual results and production levels at the end of the budget year:
   a. Direct materials price, quantity, and total variance.
   b. Direct labor rate, time, and total variance.
2. Why are the standard amounts in part (1) based on the actual production at the end of the year instead of the planned production at the beginning of the year?

PR 7-3B Direct materials, direct labor, and factory overhead cost variance analysis

OBJ. 3, 4

✔ a. Direct materials price variance, $10,100 U

Road Gripper Tire Co. manufactures automobile tires. Standard costs and actual costs for direct materials, direct labor, and factory overhead incurred for the manufacture of 4,160 tires were as follows:

	Standard Costs	Actual Costs
Direct materials	100,000 lbs. at $6.40	101,000 lbs. at $6.50
Direct labor	2,080 hrs. at $15.75	2,000 hrs. at $15.40
Factory overhead	Rates per direct labor hr., based on 100% of normal capacity of 2,000 direct labor hrs.:	
	Variable cost, $4.00	$8,200 variable cost
	Fixed cost, $6.00	$12,000 fixed cost

Each tire requires 0.5 hour of direct labor.

Instructions

Determine (a) the direct materials price variance, direct materials quantity variance, and total direct materials cost variance; (b) the direct labor rate variance, direct labor time variance, and total direct labor cost variance; and (c) the variable factory overhead controllable variance, fixed factory overhead volume variance, and total factory overhead cost variance.

PR 7-4B Factory overhead cost variance report

OBJ. 4

✔ Controllable variance, $1,450 F

General Ledger

Feeling Better Medical Inc., a manufacturer of disposable medical supplies, prepared the following factory overhead cost budget for the Assembly Department for October of the current year. The company expected to operate the department at 100% of normal capacity of 30,000 hours.

Variable costs:		
Indirect factory wages	$247,500	
Power and light	189,000	
Indirect materials	52,500	
Total variable cost		$489,000
Fixed costs:		
Supervisory salaries	$126,000	
Depreciation of plant and equipment	70,000	
Insurance and property taxes	44,000	
Total fixed cost		240,000
Total factory overhead cost		$729,000

During October, the department operated at 28,500 hours, and the factory overhead costs incurred were indirect factory wages, $234,000; power and light, $178,500; indirect materials, $50,600; supervisory salaries, $126,000; depreciation of plant and equipment, $70,000; and insurance and property taxes, $44,000.

Instructions

Prepare a factory overhead cost variance report for October. To be useful for cost control, the budgeted amounts should be based on 28,500 hours.

PR 7-5B Standards for nonmanufacturing expenses for a service company

OBJ. 3, 6

✔ 2. $161 F

The Radiology Department provides imaging services for Emergency Medical Center. One important activity in the Radiology Department is transcribing digitally recorded analyses of images into a written report. The manager of the Radiology Department determined that the average transcriptionist could type 700 lines of a report in an hour. The plan for the first week in May called for 81,900 typed lines to be written. The Radiology Department has three transcriptionists. Each transcriptionist is hired from an employment firm that requires temporary employees to be hired for a minimum of a 40-hour week. Transcriptionists are

(Continued)

paid $23.00 per hour. The manager offered a bonus if the department could type more lines for the week, without overtime. Due to high service demands, the transcriptionists typed more lines in the first week of May than planned. The actual amount of lines typed in the first week of May was 88,900 lines, without overtime. As a result, the bonus caused the average transcriptionist hourly rate to increase to $30.00 per hour during the first week in May.

Instructions

1. If the department typed 81,900 lines according to the original plan, what would have been the labor time variance?
2. What was the labor time variance as a result of typing 88,900 lines?
3. What was the labor rate variance as a result of the bonus?
4. The manager is trying to determine if a better decision would have been to hire a temporary transcriptionist to meet the higher typing demands in the first week of May, rather than paying out the bonus. If another employee was hired from the employment firm, what would have been the labor time variance in the first week?
5. Which decision is better, paying the bonus or hiring another transcriptionist?
6. Are there any performance-related issues that the labor time and rate variances fail to consider? Explain.

Comprehensive Problem 5

Genuine Spice Inc. began operations on January 1, 2016. The company produces eight-ounce bottles of hand and body lotion called *Eternal Beauty*. The lotion is sold wholesale in 12-bottle cases for $100 per case. There is a selling commission of $20 per case. The January direct materials, direct labor, and factory overhead costs are as follows:

DIRECT MATERIALS

	Cost Behavior	Units per Case	Cost per Unit	Direct Materials Cost per Case
Cream base	Variable	100 ozs.	$0.02	$ 2.00
Natural oils	Variable	30 ozs.	0.30	9.00
Bottle (8-oz.)	Variable	12 bottles	0.50	6.00
				$17.00

DIRECT LABOR

Department	Cost Behavior	Time per Case	Labor Rate per Hour	Direct Labor Cost per Case
Mixing	Variable	20 min.	$18.00	$6.00
Filling	Variable	5	14.40	1.20
		25 min.		$7.20

FACTORY OVERHEAD

	Cost Behavior	Total Cost
Utilities	Mixed	$ 600
Facility lease	Fixed	14,000
Equipment depreciation	Fixed	4,300
Supplies	Fixed	660
		$19,560

Part A—Break-Even Analysis

The management of Genuine Spice Inc. wishes to determine the number of cases required to break even per month. The utilities cost, which is part of factory overhead, is a mixed cost. The following information was gathered from the first six months of operation regarding this cost:

2016	Case Production	Utility Total Cost
January	500	$600
February	800	660
March	1,200	740
April	1,100	720
May	950	690
June	1,025	705

Instructions

1. Determine the fixed and variable portion of the utility cost using the high-low method.
2. Determine the contribution margin per case.
3. Determine the fixed costs per month, including the utility fixed cost from part (1).
4. Determine the break-even number of cases per month.

✔ 2. $55.60

Part B—August Budgets

During July of the current year, the management of Genuine Spice Inc. asked the controller to prepare August manufacturing and income statement budgets. Demand was expected to be 1,500 cases at $100 per case for August. Inventory planning information is provided as follows:

Finished Goods Inventory:

	Cases	Cost
Estimated finished goods inventory, August 1, 2016	300	$12,000
Desired finished goods inventory, August 31, 2016	175	7,000

Materials Inventory:

	Cream Base (ozs.)	Oils (ozs.)	Bottles (bottles)
Estimated materials inventory, August 1, 2016	250	290	600
Desired materials inventory, August 31, 2016	1,000	360	240

There was negligible work in process inventory assumed for either the beginning or end of the month; thus, none was assumed. In addition, there was no change in the cost per unit or estimated units per case operating data from January.

Instructions

5. Prepare the August production budget.
6. Prepare the August direct materials purchases budget.
7. Prepare the August direct labor budget. Round the hours required for production to the nearest hour.
8. Prepare the August factory overhead budget.
9. Prepare the August budgeted income statement, including selling expenses.

✔ 6. Bottles purchased, $8,070

Part C—August Variance Analysis

During September of the current year, the controller was asked to perform variance analyses for August. The January operating data provided the standard prices, rates, times, and quantities per case. There were 1,500 actual cases produced during August, which was 250 more cases than planned at the beginning of the month. Actual data for August were as follows:

	Actual Direct Materials Price per Unit	Actual Direct Materials Quantity per Case
Cream base	$0.016 per oz.	102 ozs.
Natural oils	$0.32 per oz.	31 ozs.
Bottle (8-oz.)	$0.42 per bottle	12.5 bottles

	Actual Direct Labor Rate	Actual Direct Labor Time per Case
Mixing	$18.20	19.50 min.
Filling	14.00	5.60 min.

Actual variable overhead	$305.00
Normal volume	1,600 cases

The prices of the materials were different than standard due to fluctuations in market prices. The standard quantity of materials used per case was an ideal standard. The Mixing Department used a higher grade labor classification during the month, thus causing the actual labor rate to exceed standard. The Filling Department used a lower grade labor classification during the month, thus causing the actual labor rate to be less than standard.

Instructions

10. Determine and interpret the direct materials price and quantity variances for the three materials.
11. Determine and interpret the direct labor rate and time variances for the two departments. Round hours to the nearest hour.
12. Determine and interpret the factory overhead controllable variance.
13. Determine and interpret the factory overhead volume variance.
14. Why are the standard direct labor and direct materials costs in the calculations for parts (10) and (11) based on the actual 1,500-case production volume rather than the planned 1,250 cases of production used in the budgets for parts (6) and (7)?

✔ 11. Mixing time variance, $216 F

✔ 12. $5 U

Cases & Projects

CP 7-1 Ethics and professional conduct in business using nonmanufacturing standards

Dash Riprock is a cost analyst with Safe Insurance Company. Safe is applying standards to its claims payment operation. Claims payment is a repetitive operation that could be evaluated with standards. Dash used time and motion studies to identify an ideal standard of 36 claims processed per hour. The Claims Processing Department manager, Henry Tudor, has rejected this standard and has argued that the standard should be 30 claims processed per hour. Henry and Dash were unable to agree, so they decided to discuss this matter openly at a joint meeting with the vice president of operations, who would arbitrate a final decision. Prior to the meeting, Dash wrote the following memo to the VP:

To: Anne Boleyn, Vice President of Operations
From: Dash Riprock
Re: Standards in the Claims Processing Department

As you know, Henry and I are scheduled to meet with you to discuss our disagreement with respect to the appropriate standards for the Claims Processing Department. I have conducted time and motion studies and have determined that the ideal standard is 36 claims processed per hour. Henry argues that 30 claims processed per hour would be more appropriate. I believe he is trying to "pad" the budget with some slack. I'm not sure what he is trying to get away with, but I believe a tight standard will drive efficiency up in his area. I hope you will agree when we meet with you next week.

Discuss the ethical and professional issues in this situation.

CP 7-2 Nonfinancial performance measures

The senior management of Tungston Company has proposed the following three performance measures for the company:

1. Net income as a percent of stockholders' equity
2. Revenue growth
3. Employee satisfaction

Management believes these three measures combine both financial and nonfinancial measures and are thus superior to using just financial measures.

What advice would you give Tungston Company for improving its performance measurement system?

CP 7-3 Variance interpretation

You have been asked to investigate some cost problems in the Assembly Department of Ruthenium Electronics Co., a consumer electronics company. To begin your investigation, you have obtained the following budget performance report for the department for the last quarter:

Ruthenium Electronics Co.—Assembly Department
Quarterly Budget Performance Report

	Standard Quantity at Standard Rates	Actual Quantity at Standard Rates	Quantity Variances
Direct labor	$157,500	$227,500	$ 70,000 U
Direct materials	297,500	385,000	87,500 U
Total	$455,000	$612,500	$157,500 U

The following reports were also obtained:

Ruthenium Electronics Co.—Purchasing Department
Quarterly Budget Performance Report

	Actual Quantity at Standard Rates	Actual Quantity at Actual Rates	Price Variance
Direct materials	$437,500	$385,000	–$52,500 F

Ruthenium Electronics Co.—Fabrication Department
Quarterly Budget Performance Report

	Standard Quantity at Standard Rates	Actual Quantity at Standard Rates	Quantity Variances
Direct labor	$245,000	$203,000	–$42,000 F
Direct materials	140,000	140,000	0
Total	$385,000	$343,000	–$42,000 F

You also interviewed the Assembly Department supervisor. Excerpts from the interview follow:

Q: What explains the poor performance in your department?

A: Listen, you've got to understand what it's been like in this department recently. Lately, it seems no matter how hard we try, we can't seem to make the standards. I'm not sure what is going on, but we've been having a lot of problems lately.

Q: What kind of problems?

A: Well, for instance, all this quarter we've been requisitioning purchased parts from the material storeroom, and the parts just didn't fit together very well. I'm not sure what is going on, but during most of this quarter we've had to scrap and sort purchased parts—just to get our assemblies put together. Naturally, all this takes time and material. And that's not all.

Q: Go on.

A: All this quarter, the work that we've been receiving from the Fabrication Department has been shoddy. I mean, maybe around 20% of the stuff that comes in from Fabrication just can't be assembled. The fabrication is all wrong. As a result, we've had to scrap and rework a lot of the stuff. Naturally, this has just shot our quantity variances.

Interpret the variance reports in light of the comments by the Assembly Department supervisor.

CP 7-4 Variance interpretation

Vanadium Audio Inc. is a small manufacturer of electronic musical instruments. The plant manager received the following variable factory overhead report for the period:

	Actual	Budgeted Variable Factory Overhead at Actual Production	Controllable Variance
Supplies	$ 42,000	$ 39,780	$ 2,220 U
Power and light	52,500	50,900	1,600 U
Indirect factory wages	39,100	30,600	8,500 U
Total	$133,600	$121,280	$12,320 U

Actual units produced: 15,000 (90% of practical capacity)

The plant manager is not pleased with the $12,320 unfavorable variable factory overhead controllable variance and has come to discuss the matter with the controller. The following discussion occurred:

Plant Manager: I just received this factory report for the latest month of operation. I'm not very pleased with these figures. Before these numbers go to headquarters, you and I will need to reach an understanding.

Controller: Go ahead, what's the problem?

Plant Manager: What's the problem? Well, everything. Look at the variance. It's too large. If I understand the accounting approach being used here, you are assuming that my costs are variable to the units produced. Thus, as the production volume declines, so should these costs. Well, I don't believe that these costs are variable at all. I think they are fixed costs. As a result, when we operate below capacity, the costs really don't go down at all. I'm being penalized for costs I have no control over at all. I need this report to be redone to reflect this fact. If anything, the difference between actual and budget is essentially a volume variance. Listen, I know that you're a team player. You really need to reconsider your assumptions on this one.

If you were in the controller's position, how would you respond to the plant manager?

CP 7-5 Nonmanufacturing performance measures—government

Internet Project

Group Project

Municipal governments are discovering that you can control only what you measure. As a result, many municipal governments are introducing nonfinancial performance measures to help improve municipal services. In a group, use the Google search engine to perform a search for "municipal government performance measurement." Google will provide a list of Internet sites that outline various city efforts in using nonfinancial performance measures. As a group, report on the types of measures used by one of the cities from the search.

CHAPTER 8

Performance Evaluation for Decentralized Operations

Caterpillar, Inc.

Have you ever wondered why large retail stores like **Macy's**, **JC Penney**, and **Sears** are divided into departments? Organizing into departments allows retailers to provide products and expertise in specialized areas while offering a wide range of products. Departments also allow companies to assign responsibility for financial performance. This information can be used to make product decisions, evaluate operations, and guide company strategy. Strong departmental performance might be attributable to a good department manager, while weak departmental performance may be the result of a product mix that has low customer appeal. By tracking departmental performance, companies can identify and reward excellent performance and take corrective action in departments that are performing poorly.

Like retailers, most businesses organize into operational units, such as divisions and departments. For example, **Caterpillar, Inc.**, manufactures a variety of equipment and machinery and is organized into a number of different segments, including Construction Industries, Resource Industries, and Power Systems. The Construction Industries Segment manufactures construction equipment such as tractors, dump trucks, and loaders. The Resource Industries segment makes equipment for the mining industry, such as off-highway and mining trucks. The Power Systems segment manufactures equipment that is used to generate power, such as engines and turbines for power plants.

Managers at Caterpillar, Inc., are responsible for running their business segment. Each segment is evaluated on segment profit, which excludes certain expense items from the calculation of profit that are not within the control of the business segment. The company uses segment profit to determine how to allocate resources between business segments and to plan and control the company's operations.

In this chapter, the role of accounting in assisting managers in planning and controlling organizational units, such as departments, divisions, and stores, is described and illustrated.

Learning Objectives

After studying this chapter, you should be able to: | Example Exercises

OBJ	Objective	Example Exercises
1	**Describe the advantages and disadvantages of decentralized operations.** Centralized and Decentralized Operations Advantages of Decentralization Disadvantages of Decentralization Responsibility Accounting	
2	**Prepare a responsibility accounting report for a cost center.** Responsibility Accounting for Cost Centers	EE 8-1
3	**Prepare responsibility accounting reports for a profit center.** Responsibility Accounting for Profit Centers Service Department Charges Profit Center Reporting	 EE 8-2 EE 8-3
4	**Compute and interpret the rate of return on investment, the residual income, and the balanced scorecard for an investment center.** Responsibility Accounting for Investment Centers Rate of Return on Investment Residual Income The Balanced Scorecard	 EE 8-4 EE 8-5
5	**Describe and illustrate how the market price, negotiated price, and cost price approaches to transfer pricing may be used by decentralized segments of a business.** Transfer Pricing Market Price Approach Negotiated Price Approach Cost Price Approach	 EE 8-6

At a Glance 8 Page 342

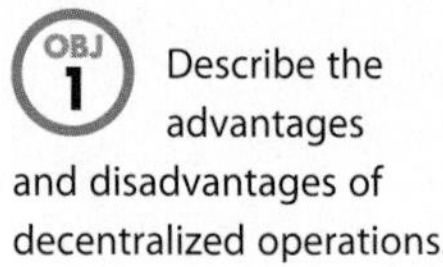

Describe the advantages and disadvantages of decentralized operations.

Centralized and Decentralized Operations

In a *centralized* company, all major planning and operating decisions are made by top management. For example, a one-person, owner-manager-operated company is centralized because all plans and decisions are made by one person. In a small owner-manager-operated business, centralization may be desirable. This is because the owner-manager's close supervision ensures that the business will be operated in the way the owner-manager wishes.

In a *decentralized* company, managers of separate divisions or units are delegated operating responsibility. The division (unit) managers are responsible for planning and controlling the operations of their divisions. Divisions are often structured around products, customers, or regions.

The proper amount of decentralization for a company depends on the company's unique circumstances. For example, in some companies, division managers have authority over all operations, including fixed asset purchases. In other companies, division managers have authority over profits but not fixed asset purchases.

Advantages of Decentralization

For large companies, it is difficult for top management to:

- Maintain daily contact with all operations, and
- Maintain operating expertise in all product lines and services

In such cases, delegating authority to managers closest to the operations usually results in better decisions. These managers often anticipate and react to operating data more quickly than could top management. These managers can also focus their attention on becoming "experts" in their area of operation.

Decentralized operations provide excellent training for managers. Delegating responsibility allows managers to develop managerial experience early in their careers. This helps a company retain managers, some of whom may be later promoted to top management positions.

Managers of decentralized operations often work closely with customers. As a result, they tend to identify with customers and, thus, are often more creative in suggesting operating and product improvements. This helps create good customer relations.

Disadvantages of Decentralization

A primary disadvantage of decentralized operations is that decisions made by one manager may negatively affect the profits of the company. For example, managers of divisions whose products compete with one another might start a price war that decreases the profits of both divisions and, thus, the overall company.

Another disadvantage of decentralized operations is that assets and expenses may be duplicated across divisions. For example, each manager of a product line might have a separate sales force and office support staff.

The advantages and disadvantages of decentralization are summarized in Exhibit 1.

EXHIBIT 1

Advantages and Disadvantages of Decentralized Operations

Advantages of Decentralization

- Allows managers closest to the operations to make decisions
- Provides excellent training for managers
- Allows managers to become experts in their area of operation
- Helps retain managers
- Improves creativity and customer relations

Disadvantages of Decentralization

- Decisions made by managers may negatively affect the profits of the company
- Duplicates assets and expenses

Business Connection

STEVE JOBS: CENTRALIZED OPERATIONS AT APPLE

Apple Inc.'s meteoric rise from a second-tier computer maker in the early 2000s to the standard for all things technology by the end of the decade was no accident. The company's success was the result of a centralized operation, where Apple CEO Steve Jobs had ultimate control over the company's strategic and operational decisions. As Andrew Keen noted in his interview of Job's biographer, Walter Isaacson, it was Jobs' "obsessive end-to-end control of products—from chip manufacture to the retail experience—that most defined Steve's remarkable tenure as Apple CEO." This centralized business model also drove Apple's success. Unfortunately, Steve Jobs died in October 2011, creating a void at the top of the company's centralized operation. Since Job's death, Apple has struggled with how to adapt its highly successful centralized business model to the loss of the person that controlled the company's decisions.

Source: A. Keen, "Keen On ... Walter Isaacson: Sometimes It's Nice to Be In The Hands of a Control Freak," *AOLTech.com*, December 19, 2011.

Responsibility Accounting

In a decentralized business, accounting assists managers in evaluating and controlling their areas of responsibility, called *responsibility centers*. **Responsibility accounting** is the process of measuring and reporting operating data by responsibility center.

Three types of responsibility centers are as follows:

- *Cost centers,* which have responsibility over costs
- *Profit centers,* which have responsibility over revenues and costs
- *Investment centers,* which have responsibility over revenues, costs, and investment in assets

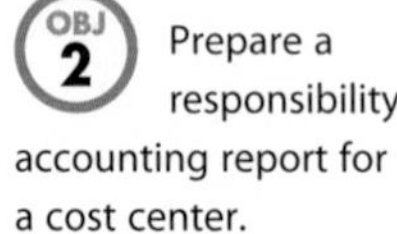

Prepare a responsibility accounting report for a cost center.

Responsibility Accounting for Cost Centers

A **cost center** manager has responsibility for controlling costs. For example, the supervisor of the Power Department has responsibility for the costs of providing power. A cost center manager does not make decisions concerning sales or the amount of fixed assets invested in the center.

Cost centers may vary in size from a small department to an entire manufacturing plant. In addition, cost centers may exist within other cost centers. For example, an entire university or college could be viewed as a cost center, and each college and department within the university could also be a cost center, as shown in Exhibit 2.

EXHIBIT 2 **Cost Centers in a University**

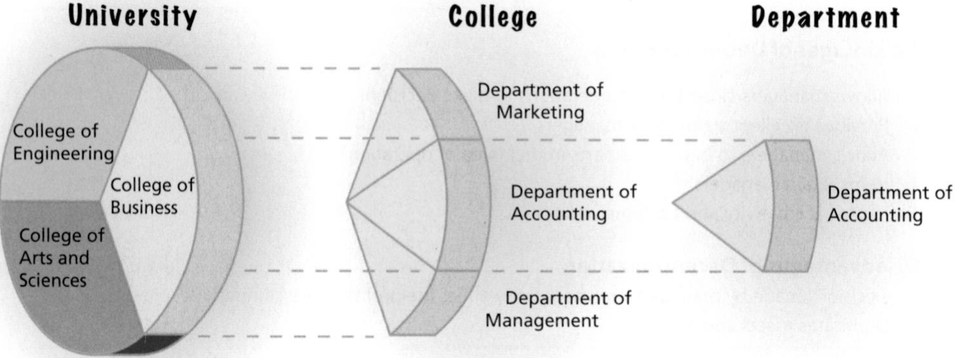

Responsibility accounting for cost centers focuses on the controlling and reporting of costs. Budget performance reports that report budgeted and actual costs are normally prepared for each cost center.

Exhibit 3 illustrates budget performance reports for the following cost centers:

- Vice President, Production
- Manager, Plant A
- Supervisor, Department 1—Plant A

Exhibit 3 shows how cost centers are often linked together within a company. For example, the budget performance report for Department 1—Plant A supports the report for Plant A, which supports the report for the vice president of production.

The reports in Exhibit 3 show the budgeted costs and actual costs along with the differences. Each difference is classified as either *over* budget or *under* budget. Such reports allow cost center managers to focus on areas of significant differences.

For example, the supervisor for Department 1 of Plant A can focus on why the materials cost was over budget. The supervisor might discover that excess materials were scrapped. This could be due to such factors as machine malfunctions, improperly trained employees, or low-quality materials.

As shown in Exhibit 3, responsibility accounting reports are usually more summarized for higher levels of management. For example, the budget performance report for the manager of Plant A shows only administration and departmental data. This report enables the plant manager to identify the departments responsible for major differences. Likewise, the report for the vice president of production summarizes the cost data for each plant.

EXHIBIT 3

Responsibility Accounting Reports for Cost Centers

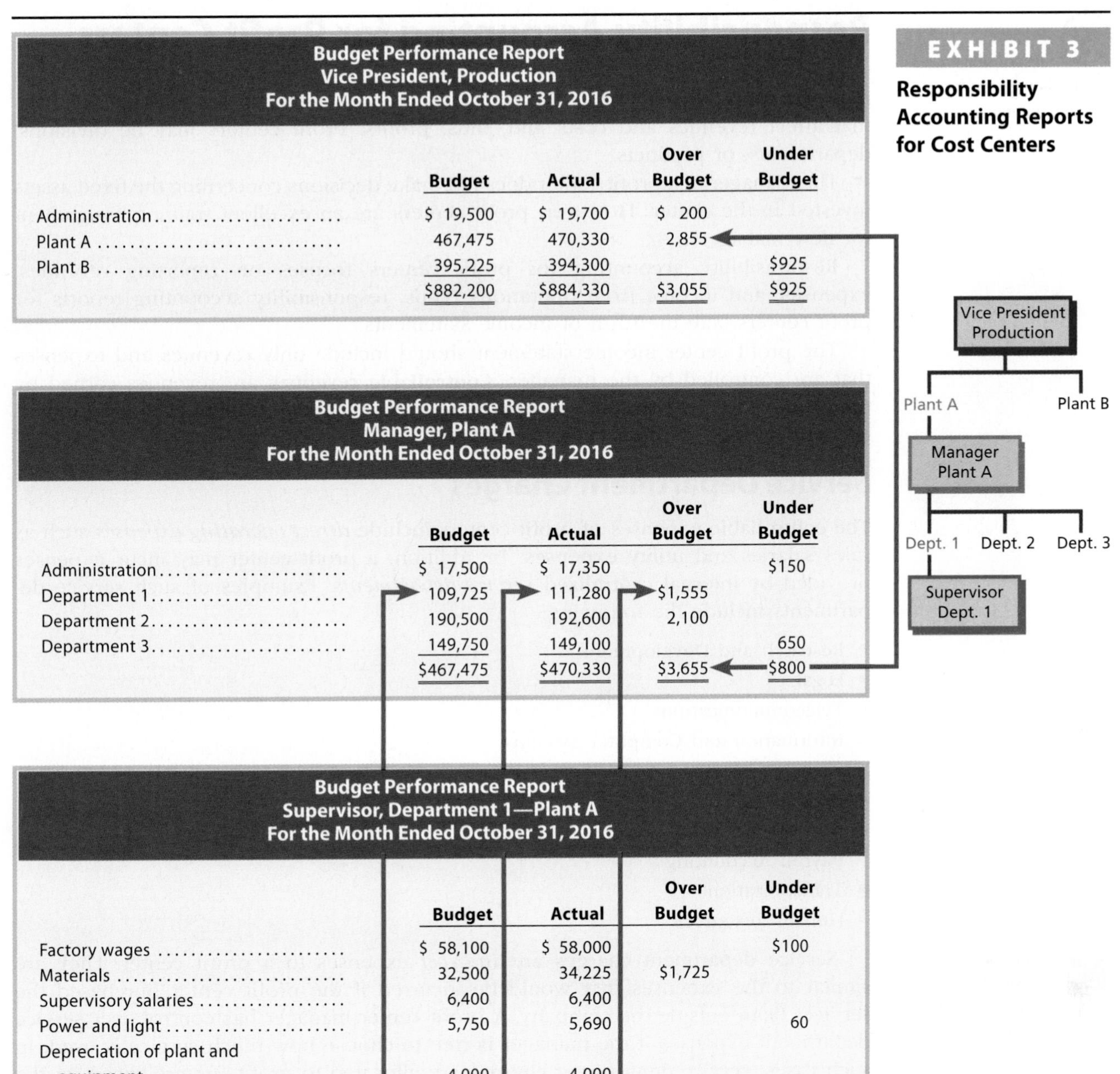

Budget Performance Report
Vice President, Production
For the Month Ended October 31, 2016

	Budget	Actual	Over Budget	Under Budget
Administration	$ 19,500	$ 19,700	$ 200	
Plant A	467,475	470,330	2,855	
Plant B	395,225	394,300		$925
	$882,200	$884,330	$3,055	$925

Budget Performance Report
Manager, Plant A
For the Month Ended October 31, 2016

	Budget	Actual	Over Budget	Under Budget
Administration	$ 17,500	$ 17,350		$150
Department 1	109,725	111,280	$1,555	
Department 2	190,500	192,600	2,100	
Department 3	149,750	149,100		650
	$467,475	$470,330	$3,655	$800

Budget Performance Report
Supervisor, Department 1—Plant A
For the Month Ended October 31, 2016

	Budget	Actual	Over Budget	Under Budget
Factory wages	$ 58,100	$ 58,000		$100
Materials	32,500	34,225	$1,725	
Supervisory salaries	6,400	6,400		
Power and light	5,750	5,690		60
Depreciation of plant and equipment	4,000	4,000		
Maintenance	2,000	1,990		10
Insurance and property taxes	975	975		
	$109,725	$111,280	$1,725	$170

Example Exercise 8-1 Budgetary Performance for Cost Center

OBJ 2

Nuclear Power Company's costs were over budget by $24,000. The company is divided into North and South regions. The North Region's costs were under budget by $2,000. Determine the amount that the South Region's costs were over or under budget.

Follow My Example 8-1

$26,000 over budget ($24,000 + $2,000)

Practice Exercises: PE 8-1A, PE 8-1B

Prepare responsibility accounting reports for a profit center.

Responsibility Accounting for Profit Centers

A **profit center** manager has the responsibility and authority for making decisions that affect revenues and costs and, thus, profits. Profit centers may be divisions, departments, or products.

The manager of a profit center does not make decisions concerning the fixed assets invested in the center. However, profit centers are an excellent training assignment for new managers.

Responsibility accounting for profit centers focuses on reporting revenues, expenses, and income from operations. Thus, responsibility accounting reports for profit centers take the form of income statements.

The profit center income statement should include only revenues and expenses that are controlled by the manager. **Controllable revenues** are revenues earned by the profit center. **Controllable expenses** are costs that can be influenced (controlled) by the decisions of profit center managers.

Service Department Charges

The controllable expenses of profit centers include *direct operating expenses* such as sales salaries and utility expenses. In addition, a profit center may incur expenses provided by internal centralized *service departments*. Examples of such service departments include the following:

- Research and Development
- Legal
- Telecommunications
- Information and Computer Systems
- Facilities Management
- Purchasing
- Advertising
- Payroll Accounting
- Transportation
- Human Resources

Employees of **IBM** speak of "green money" and "blue money." Green money comes from customers. Blue money comes from providing services to other IBM departments via service department charges. IBM employees note that blue money is easier to earn than green money; yet from the stockholders' perspective, green money is the only money that counts.

Service department charges are *indirect* expenses to a profit center. They are similar to the expenses that would be incurred if the profit center purchased the services from outside the company. A profit center manager has control over service department expenses if the manager is free to choose how much service is used. In such cases, **service department charges** are allocated to profit centers based on the usage of the service by each profit center.

To illustrate, Nova Entertainment Group (NEG), a diversified entertainment company, is used. NEG has the following two operating divisions organized as profit centers:

- Theme Park Division
- Movie Production Division

The revenues and direct operating expenses for the two divisions follow. The operating expenses consist of direct expenses, such as the wages and salaries of a division's employees.

	Theme Park Division	Movie Production Division
Revenues	$6,000,000	$2,500,000
Operating expenses	2,495,000	405,000

NEG's service departments and the expenses they incurred for the year ended December 31, 2016, are as follows:

Purchasing	$400,000
Payroll Accounting	255,000
Legal	250,000
Total	$905,000

An activity base for each service department is used to charge service department expenses to the Theme Park and Movie Production divisions. The activity base for each service department is a measure of the services performed. For NEG, the service department activity bases are as follows:

Department	Activity Base
Purchasing	Number of purchase requisitions
Payroll Accounting	Number of payroll checks
Legal	Number of billed hours

The use of services by the Theme Park and Movie Production divisions is as follows:

	Service Usage		
Division	**Purchasing**	**Payroll Accounting**	**Legal**
Theme Park	25,000 purchase requisitions	12,000 payroll checks	100 billed hrs.
Movie Production	15,000	3,000	900
Total	40,000 purchase requisitions	15,000 payroll checks	1,000 billed hrs.

The rates at which services are charged to each division are called *service department charge rates*. These rates are computed as follows:

$$\text{Service Department Charge Rate} = \frac{\text{Service Department Expense}}{\text{Total Service Department Usage}}$$

NEG's service department charge rates are computed as follows:

$$\text{Purchasing Charge Rate} = \frac{\$400{,}000}{40{,}000 \text{ purchase requisitions}} = \$10 \text{ per purchase requisition}$$

$$\text{Payroll Charge Rate} = \frac{\$255{,}000}{15{,}000 \text{ payroll checks}} = \$17 \text{ per payroll check}$$

$$\text{Legal Charge Rate} = \frac{\$250{,}000}{1{,}000 \text{ billed hrs.}} = \$250 \text{ per hr.}$$

The services used by each division are multiplied by the service department charge rates to determine the service charges for each division, computed as follows:

$$\text{Service Department Charge} = \text{Service Usage} \times \text{Service Department Charge Rate}$$

Exhibit 4 illustrates the service department charges and related computations for NEG's Theme Park and Movie Production divisions.

EXHIBIT 4

Service Department Charges to NEG Divisions

Nova Entertainment Group
Service Department Charges to NEG Divisions
For the Year Ended December 31, 2016

Service Department	Theme Park Division	Movie Production Division
Purchasing (Note A)	$250,000	$150,000
Payroll Accounting (Note B)	204,000	51,000
Legal (Note C)	25,000	225,000
Total service department charges	$479,000	$426,000

Note A:
25,000 purchase requisitions × $10 per purchase requisition = $250,000
15,000 purchase requisitions × $10 per purchase requisition = $150,000
Note B:
12,000 payroll checks × $17 per check = $204,000
3,000 payroll checks × $17 per check = $51,000
Note C:
100 hours × $250 per hour = $25,000
900 hours × $250 per hour = $225,000

The differences in the service department charges between the two divisions can be explained by the nature of their operations and, thus, usage of services. For example, the Theme Park Division employs many part-time employees who are paid weekly. As a result, the Theme Park Division requires 12,000 payroll checks and incurs a $204,000 payroll service department charge (12,000 × $17). In contrast, the Movie Production Division has more permanent employees who are paid monthly. Thus, the Movie Production Division requires only 3,000 payroll checks and incurs a payroll service department charge of $51,000 (3,000 × $17).

Example Exercise 8-2 Service Department Charges

OBJ 3

The centralized legal department of Johnson Company has expenses of $600,000. The department has provided a total of 2,000 hours of service for the period. The East Division has used 500 hours of legal service during the period, and the West Division has used 1,500 hours. How much should each division be charged for legal services?

Follow My Example 8-2

East Division Service Charge for Legal Department:
$150,000 = 500 billed hours × ($600,000 ÷ 2,000 hours)

West Division Service Charge for Legal Department:
$450,000 = 1,500 billed hours × ($600,000 ÷ 2,000 hours)

Practice Exercises: PE 8-2A, PE 8-2B

Profit Center Reporting

The divisional income statements for NEG are shown in Exhibit 5.

EXHIBIT 5

Divisional Income Statements—NEG

Nova Entertainment Group
Divisional Income Statements
For the Year Ended December 31, 2016

	Theme Park Division	Movie Production Division
Revenues*	$6,000,000	$2,500,000
Operating expenses	2,495,000	405,000
Income from operations before service department charges	$3,505,000	$2,095,000
Less service department charges:		
Purchasing	$ 250,000	$ 150,000
Payroll Accounting	204,000	51,000
Legal	25,000	225,000
Total service department charges	$ 479,000	$ 426,000
Income from operations	$3,026,000	$1,669,000

*For a profit center that sells products, the income statement would show: Sales – Cost of goods sold = Gross profit. The operating expenses would be deducted from the gross profit to get the income from operations before service department charges.

In evaluating the profit center manager, the income from operations should be compared over time to a budget. However, it should not be compared across profit centers because the profit centers are usually different in terms of size, products, and customers.

Example Exercise 8-3 Income from Operations for Profit Center

OBJ 3

Using the data for Johnson Company from Example Exercise 8-2 along with the following data, determine the divisional income from operations for the East and West divisions:

	East Division	West Division
Sales	$3,000,000	$8,000,000
Cost of goods sold	1,650,000	4,200,000
Selling expenses	850,000	1,850,000

Follow My Example 8-3

	East Division	West Division
Sales	$3,000,000	$8,000,000
Cost of goods sold	1,650,000	4,200,000
Gross profit	$1,350,000	$3,800,000
Selling expenses	850,000	1,850,000
Income from operations before service department charges	$ 500,000	$1,950,000
Service department charges	150,000	450,000
Income from operations	$ 350,000	$1,500,000

Practice Exercises: PE 8-3A, PE 8-3B

Responsibility Accounting for Investment Centers

OBJ 4 Compute and interpret the rate of return on investment, the residual income, and the balanced scorecard for an investment center.

An **investment center** manager has the responsibility and the authority to make decisions that affect not only costs and revenues but also the assets invested in the center. Investment centers are often used in diversified companies organized by divisions. In such cases, the divisional manager has authority similar to that of a chief operating officer or president of a company.

Because investment center managers have responsibility for revenues and expenses, *income from operations* is part of investment center reporting. In addition, because the manager has responsibility for the assets invested in the center, the following two additional measures of performance are used:

- Rate of return on investment
- Residual income

To illustrate, DataLink Inc., a cellular phone company with three regional divisions, is used. Condensed divisional income statements for the Northern, Central, and Southern divisions of DataLink are shown in Exhibit 6.

EXHIBIT 6

Divisional Income Statements—DataLink Inc.

DataLink Inc.
Divisional Income Statements
For the Year Ended December 31, 2016

	Northern Division	Central Division	Southern Division
Revenues	$560,000	$672,000	$750,000
Operating expenses	336,000	470,400	562,500
Income from operations before service department charges	$224,000	$201,600	$187,500
Service department charges	154,000	117,600	112,500
Income from operations	$ 70,000	$ 84,000	$ 75,000

Using only income from operations, the Central Division is the most profitable division. However, income from operations does not reflect the amount of assets invested in each center. For example, the Central Division could have twice as many assets as the Northern Division. For this reason, performance measures that consider the amount of invested assets, such as the rate of return on investment and residual income, are used.

Rate of Return on Investment

Because investment center managers control the amount of assets invested in their centers, they should be evaluated based on the use of these assets. One measure that considers the amount of assets invested is the **rate of return on investment (ROI)** or *rate of return on assets*. It is computed as follows:

$$\text{Rate of Return on Investment (ROI)} = \frac{\text{Income from Operations}}{\text{Invested Assets}}$$

The rate of return on investment is useful because the three factors subject to control by divisional managers (revenues, expenses, and invested assets) are considered. The higher the rate of return on investment, the better the division is using its assets to generate income. In effect, the rate of return on investment measures the income (return) on each dollar invested. As a result, the rate of return on investment can be used as a common basis for comparing divisions with each other.

To illustrate, the invested assets of DataLink's three divisions are as follows:

	Invested Assets
Northern Division	$350,000
Central Division	700,000
Southern Division	500,000

Using the income from operations for each division shown in Exhibit 6, the rate of return on investment for each division is computed as follows:

Northern Division:

$$\text{Rate of Return on Investment} = \frac{\text{Income from Operations}}{\text{Invested Assets}} = \frac{\$70{,}000}{\$350{,}000} = 20\%$$

Central Division:

$$\text{Rate of Return on Investment} = \frac{\text{Income from Operations}}{\text{Invested Assets}} = \frac{\$84{,}000}{\$700{,}000} = 12\%$$

Southern Division:

$$\text{Rate of Return on Investment} = \frac{\text{Income from Operations}}{\text{Invested Assets}} = \frac{\$75{,}000}{\$500{,}000} = 15\%$$

Although the Central Division generated the largest income from operations, its rate of return on investment (12%) is the lowest. Hence, relative to the assets invested, the Central Division is the least profitable division. In comparison, the rate of return on investment of the Northern Division is 20%, and the Southern Division is 15%.

To analyze differences in the rate of return on investment across divisions, the **DuPont formula** for the rate of return on investment is often used.[1] The DuPont formula views the rate of return on investment as the product of the following two factors:

- **Profit margin**, which is the ratio of income from operations to sales.
- **Investment turnover**, which is the ratio of sales to invested assets.

[1] The DuPont formula was created by a financial executive of **E. I. du Pont de Nemours and Company** in 1919.

Using the DuPont formula, the rate of return on investment is expressed as follows:

$$\text{Rate of Return on Investment} = \text{Profit Margin} \times \text{Investment Turnover}$$

$$\text{Rate of Return on Investment} = \frac{\text{Income from Operations}}{\text{Sales}} \times \frac{\text{Sales}}{\text{Invested Assets}}$$

The DuPont formula is useful in evaluating divisions. This is because the profit margin and the investment turnover reflect the following underlying operating relationships of each division:

- Profit margin indicates *operating profitability* by computing the rate of profit earned on each sales dollar.
- Investment turnover indicates *operating efficiency* by computing the number of sales dollars generated by each dollar of invested assets.

If a division's profit margin increases, and all other factors remain the same, the division's rate of return on investment will increase. For example, a division might add more profitable products to its sales mix and, thus, increase its operating profit, profit margin, and rate of return on investment.

If a division's investment turnover increases, and all other factors remain the same, the division's rate of return on investment will increase. For example, a division might attempt to increase sales through special sales promotions and thus increase operating efficiency, investment turnover, and rate of return on investment.

The rate of return on investment, profit margin, and investment turnover operate in relationship to one another. Specifically, more income can be earned by either increasing the investment turnover, increasing the profit margin, or both.

Using the DuPont formula yields the same rate of return on investment for each of DataLink's divisions, computed as follows:

$$\text{Rate of Return on Investment} = \frac{\text{Income from Operations}}{\text{Sales}} \times \frac{\text{Sales}}{\text{Invested Assets}}$$

Northern Division:

$$\text{Rate of Return on Investment} = \frac{\$70{,}000}{\$560{,}000} \times \frac{\$560{,}000}{\$350{,}000} = 12.5\% \times 1.6 = 20\%$$

Central Division:

$$\text{Rate of Return on Investment} = \frac{\$84{,}000}{\$672{,}000} \times \frac{\$672{,}000}{\$700{,}000} = 12.5\% \times 0.96 = 12\%$$

Southern Division:

$$\text{Rate of Return on Investment} = \frac{\$75{,}000}{\$750{,}000} \times \frac{\$750{,}000}{\$500{,}000} = 10\% \times 1.5 = 15\%$$

The Northern and Central divisions have the same profit margins of 12.5%. However, the Northern Division's investment turnover of 1.6 is larger than that of the Central Division's turnover of 0.96. By using its invested assets more efficiently, the Northern Division's rate of return on investment of 20% is 8 percentage points higher than the Central Division's rate of return of 12%.

The Southern Division's profit margin of 10% and investment turnover of 1.5 are lower than those of the Northern Division. The product of these factors results in a return on investment of 15% for the Southern Division, compared to 20% for the Northern Division.

Even though the Southern Division's profit margin is lower than the Central Division's, its higher turnover of 1.5 results in a rate of return of 15%, which is greater than the Central Division's rate of return of 12%.

To increase the rate of return on investment, the profit margin and investment turnover for a division may be analyzed. For example, assume that the Northern Division is in a highly competitive industry in which the profit margin cannot be easily increased. As a result, the division manager might focus on increasing the investment turnover.

To illustrate, assume that the revenues of the Northern Division could be increased by $56,000 through increasing operating expenses, such as advertising, to $385,000. The Northern Division's income from operations will increase from $70,000 to $77,000, computed as follows:

Revenues ($560,000 + $56,000)	$616,000
Operating expenses	385,000
Income from operations before service department charges	$231,000
Service department charges	154,000
Income from operations	$ 77,000

The rate of return on investment for the Northern Division, using the DuPont formula, is recomputed as follows:

$$\text{Rate of Return on Investment} = \frac{\$77{,}000}{\$616{,}000} \times \frac{\$616{,}000}{\$350{,}000} = 12.5\% \times 1.76 = 22\%$$

Although the Northern Division's profit margin remains the same (12.5%), the investment turnover has increased from 1.6 to 1.76, an increase of 10% (0.16 ÷ 1.6). The 10% increase in investment turnover increases the rate of return on investment by 10% (from 20% to 22%).

The rate of return on investment is also useful in deciding where to invest additional assets or expand operations. For example, DataLink should give priority to expanding operations in the Northern Division because it earns the highest rate of return on investment. In other words, an investment in the Northern Division will return 20 cents (20%) on each dollar invested. In contrast, investments in the Central and Southern divisions will earn only 12 cents and 15 cents, respectively, per dollar invested.

A disadvantage of the rate of return on investment as a performance measure is that it may lead divisional managers to reject new investments that could be profitable for the company as a whole. To illustrate, assume the following rates of return for the Northern Division of DataLink:

Current rate of return on investment	20%
Minimum acceptable rate of return on investment set by top management	10%
Expected rate of return on investment for new project	14%

If the manager of the Northern Division invests in the new project, the Northern Division's overall rate of return will decrease from 20% due to averaging. Thus, the division manager might decide to reject the project, even though the new project's expected rate of return of 14% exceeds DataLink's minimum acceptable rate of return of 10%.

Example Exercise 8-4 Profit Margin, Investment Turnover, and ROI

Campbell Company has income from operations of $35,000, invested assets of $140,000, and sales of $437,500. Use the DuPont formula to compute the rate of return on investment and show (a) the profit margin, (b) the investment turnover, and (c) the rate of return on investment.

Follow My Example 8-4

a. Profit Margin = $35,000 ÷ $437,500 = 8%

b. Investment Turnover = $437,500 ÷ $140,000 = 3.125

c. Rate of Return on Investment = 8% × 3.125 = 25%

Practice Exercises: PE 8-4A, PE 8-4B

Residual Income

Residual income is useful in overcoming some of the disadvantages of the rate of return on investment. **Residual income** is the excess of income from operations over a minimum acceptable income from operations, as shown in Exhibit 7.

EXHIBIT 7

Residual Income

Income from operations	\$XXX
Less minimum acceptable income from operations as a percent of invested assets	XXX
Residual income	\$XXX

The minimum acceptable income from operations is computed by multiplying the company minimum rate of return by the invested assets. The minimum rate is set by top management, based on such factors as the cost of financing.

To illustrate, assume that DataLink Inc. has established 10% as the minimum acceptable rate of return on divisional assets. The residual incomes for the three divisions are shown in Exhibit 8.

EXHIBIT 8

Residual Income—DataLink, Inc.

	Northern Division	Central Division	Southern Division
Income from operations	\$70,000	\$84,000	\$75,000
Less minimum acceptable income from operations as a percent of invested assets:			
\$350,000 × 10%	35,000		
\$700,000 × 10%		70,000	
\$500,000 × 10%			50,000
Residual income	\$35,000	\$14,000	\$25,000

As shown in Exhibit 8, the Northern Division has more residual income (\$35,000) than the other divisions, even though it has the least amount of income from operations (\$70,000). This is because the invested assets are less for the Northern Division than for the other divisions.

The major advantage of residual income as a performance measure is that it considers both the minimum acceptable rate of return, invested assets, and the income from operations for each division. In doing so, residual income encourages division managers to maximize income from operations in excess of the minimum. This provides an incentive to accept any project that is expected to have a rate of return in excess of the minimum.

To illustrate, assume the following rates of return for the Northern Division of DataLink:

Current rate of return on investment	20%
Minimum acceptable rate of return on investment set by top management	10%
Expected rate of return on investment for new project	14%

If the manager of the Northern Division is evaluated on new projects using only return on investment, the division manager might decide to reject the new project. This is because investing in the new project will decrease Northern's current rate of return of 20%. While this helps the division maintain its high ROI, it hurts the company as a whole because the expected rate of return of 14% exceeds DataLink's minimum acceptable rate of return of 10%.

In contrast, if the manager of the Northern Division is evaluated using residual income, the new project would probably be accepted because it will increase the Northern Division's residual income. In this way, residual income supports both divisional and overall company objectives.

Example Exercise 8-5 Residual Income (OBJ 4)

The Wholesale Division of PeanutCo has income from operations of $87,000 and assets of $240,000. The minimum acceptable rate of return on assets is 12%. What is the residual income for the division?

Follow My Example 8-5

Income from operations	$87,000
Minimum acceptable income from operations as a percent of assets ($240,000 × 12%)	28,800
Residual income	$58,200

Practice Exercises: PE 8-5A, PE 8-5B

The Balanced Scorecard[2]

The **balanced scorecard** is a set of multiple performance measures for a company. In addition to financial performance, a balanced scorecard normally includes performance measures for customer service, innovation and learning, and internal processes, as shown in Exhibit 9.

EXHIBIT 9

The Balanced Scorecard

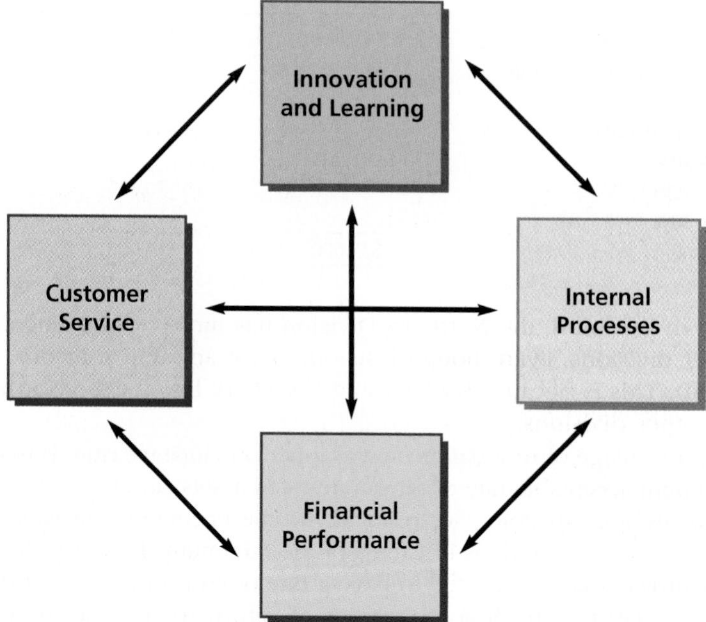

Performance measures for learning and innovation often revolve around a company's research and development efforts. For example, the number of new products developed during a year and the time it takes to bring new products to the market are performance measures for innovation. Performance measures for learning could include the number of employee training sessions and the number of employees who are cross-trained in several skills.

Performance measures for customer service include the number of customer complaints and the number of repeat customers. Customer surveys can also be used to gather measures of customer satisfaction with the company as compared to competitors.

Performance measures for internal processes include the length of time it takes to manufacture a product. The amount of scrap and waste is a measure of the efficiency

[2] The balanced scorecard was developed by R. S. Kaplan and D. P. Norton and explained in *The Balanced Scorecard: Translating Strategy into Action* (Cambridge: Harvard Business School Press, 1996).

of a company's manufacturing processes. The number of customer returns is a performance measure of both the manufacturing and sales ordering processes.

All companies will use financial performance measures. Some financial performance measures have been discussed earlier in this chapter and include income from operations, rate of return on investment, and residual income.

The balanced scorecard attempts to identify the underlying nonfinancial drivers, or causes, of financial performance related to innovation and learning, customer service, and internal processes. In this way, the financial performance may be improved. For example, customer satisfaction is often measured by the number of repeat customers. By increasing the number of repeat customers, sales and income from operations can be increased.

Hilton Hotels Corporation uses a balanced scorecard to measure employee satisfaction, customer loyalty, and financial performance.

Some common performance measures used in the balanced scorecard approach are shown in Exhibit 10.

EXHIBIT 10

Balanced Scorecard Performance Measures

Innovation and Learning
- Number of new products
- Number of new patents
- Number of cross-trained employees
- Number of training hours
- Number of ethics violations
- Employee turnover

Internal Processes
- Waste and scrap
- Time to manufacture products
- Number of defects
- Number of rejected sales orders
- Number of stockouts
- Labor utilization

Customer Service
- Number of repeat customers
- Customer brand recognition
- Delivery time to customer
- Customer satisfaction
- Number of sales returns
- Customer complaints

Financial
- Sales
- Income from operations
- Return on investment
- Profit margin and investment turnover
- Residual income
- Actual versus budgeted (standard) costs

Service  Focus

TURNING AROUND CHARLES SCHWAB

Customer service is a key component to any balanced scorecard, and it is a particularly critical component in service industries. Since 2003, **Bain & Company** consulting has helped companies improve customer service by focusing on a customer loyalty metric called the *Net Promoter Score*. This metric, when used as part of a balanced scorecard, evaluates customer service by assessing how likely a customer is to recommend the company to others.

The Charles Schwab Corporation is a full-service financial advisory firm that was founded in 1973. In 2004, the company was struggling. Although Schwab had been built on delivering exceptional customer service, the company had lost its way. When customers were surveyed, they gave Schwab a negative 35% Net Promoter Score, indicating that more customers wanted to see the company fail than would be willing to promote the company to others.

In response, Schwab enlisted Bain to help them improve the customer experience and customer loyalty. Bain helped Schwab develop and implement a Client Promoter System that focused on embedding the Client Promoter Score deep within the company's values and core strategy. As Schwab CEO Walt Bettinger describes, "If you serve clients in the way that you would like to be served, they are going to want to do more business with you." The results were significant. By 2008, the company's stock price had more than doubled, and in 2010, Schwab received a Net Promoter Score of 46%, the highest in its sector.

Source: "Schwab Earns Highest Customer Loyalty Ranking Among Brokerage & Investment Firms in Satmetrix Net Promoter's 2010 Industry Report," *BusinessWire*, March 25, 2010. "Seeing the world through the client's eyes," Bain & Co., http://www.netpromotersystem.com/videos/trailblazer-video/charles-schwab.aspx

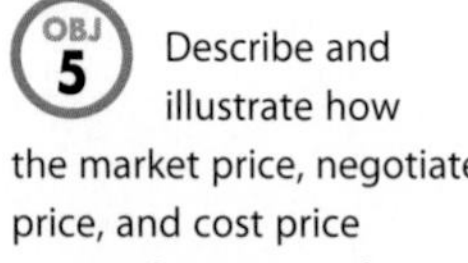

Describe and illustrate how the market price, negotiated price, and cost price approaches to transfer pricing may be used by decentralized segments of a business.

Transfer Pricing

When divisions transfer products or render services to each other, a **transfer price** is used to charge for the products or services.[3] Because transfer prices will affect a division's financial performance, setting a transfer price is a sensitive matter for the managers of both the selling and buying divisions.

Three common approaches to setting transfer prices are as follows:

- Market price approach
- Negotiated price approach
- Cost approach

Transfer prices may be used for cost, profit, or investment centers. The objective of setting a transfer price is to motivate managers to behave in a manner that will increase the overall company income. As will be illustrated, however, transfer prices may be misused in such a way that overall company income suffers.

Transfer prices can be set as low as the variable cost per unit or as high as the market price. Often, transfer prices are negotiated at some point between variable cost per unit and market price. Exhibit 11 shows the possible range of transfer prices.

EXHIBIT 11

Commonly Used Transfer Prices

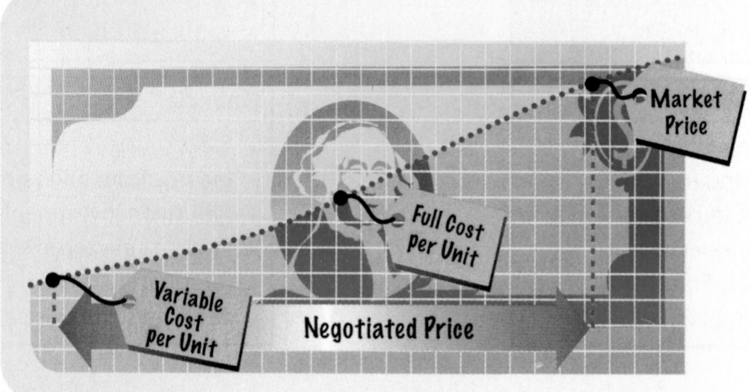

To illustrate, Wilson Company, a packaged snack food company with no service departments, is used. Wilson has two operating divisions (Eastern and Western) that are organized as investment centers. Condensed income statements for Wilson, assuming no transfers between divisions, are shown in Exhibit 12.

EXHIBIT 12

Income Statements—No Transfers Between Divisions

Wilson Company
Income Statements
For the Year Ended December 31, 2016

	Eastern Division	Western Division	Total Company
Sales:			
50,000 units × $20 per unit	$1,000,000		$1,000,000
20,000 units × $40 per unit		$800,000	800,000
			$1,800,000
Expenses:			
Variable:			
50,000 units × $10 per unit	$ 500,000		$ 500,000
20,000 units × $30* per unit		$600,000	600,000
Fixed	300,000	100,000	400,000
Total expenses	$ 800,000	$700,000	$1,500,000
Income from operations	$ 200,000	$100,000	$ 300,000

*$20 of the $30 per unit represents materials costs, and the remaining $10 per unit represents other variable conversion expenses incurred within the Western Division.

[3] The discussion in this chapter highlights the essential concepts of transfer pricing. In-depth discussion of transfer pricing can be found in advanced texts.

Market Price Approach

Using the **market price approach**, the transfer price is the price at which the product or service transferred could be sold to outside buyers. If an outside market exists for the product or service transferred, the current market price may be a proper transfer price.

Transfer Price = Market Price

To illustrate, assume that materials used by Wilson in producing snack food in the Western Division are currently purchased from an outside supplier at $20 per unit. The same materials are produced by the Eastern Division. The Eastern Division is operating at full capacity of 50,000 units and can sell all it produces to either the Western Division or to outside buyers.

A transfer price of $20 per unit (the market price) has no effect on the Eastern Division's income or total company income. The Eastern Division will earn revenues of $20 per unit on all its production and sales, regardless of who buys its product.

Likewise, the Western Division will pay $20 per unit for materials (the market price). Thus, the use of the market price as the transfer price has no effect on the Eastern Division's income or total company income.

In this situation, the use of the market price as the transfer price is proper. The condensed divisional income statements for Wilson would be the same as shown in Exhibit 12.

Negotiated Price Approach

If unused or excess capacity exists in the supplying division (the Eastern Division), and the transfer price is equal to the market price, total company profit may not be maximized. This is because the manager of the Western Division will be indifferent toward purchasing materials from the Eastern Division or from outside suppliers. That is, in both cases the Western Division manager pays $20 per unit (the market price). As a result, the Western Division may purchase the materials from outside suppliers.

If, however, the Western Division purchases the materials from the Eastern Division, the difference between the market price of $20 and the variable costs of the Eastern Division of $10 per unit (from Exhibit 12) can cover fixed costs and contribute to overall company profits. Thus, the Western Division manager should be encouraged to purchase the materials from the Eastern Division.

The **negotiated price approach** allows the managers to agree (negotiate) among themselves on a transfer price. The only constraint is that the transfer price be less than the market price but greater than the supplying division's variable costs per unit, as follows:

Variable Costs per Unit < Transfer Price < Market Price

To illustrate, assume that instead of a capacity of 50,000 units, the Eastern Division's capacity is 70,000 units. In addition, assume that the Eastern Division can continue to sell only 50,000 units to outside buyers.

A transfer price less than $20 would encourage the manager of the Western Division to purchase from the Eastern Division. This is because the Western Division is currently purchasing its materials from outside suppliers at a cost of $20 per unit. Thus, its materials cost would decrease, and its income from operations would increase.

At the same time, a transfer price above the Eastern Division's variable costs per unit of $10 would encourage the manager of the Eastern Division to supply materials to the Western Division. In doing so, the Eastern Division's income from operations would also increase.

Exhibit 13 illustrates the divisional and company income statements, assuming that the Eastern and Western division managers agree to a transfer price of $15.

The Eastern Division increases its sales by $300,000 (20,000 units × $15 per unit) to $1,300,000. As a result, the Eastern Division's income from operations increases by $100,000 ($300,000 sales – $200,000 variable costs) to $300,000, as shown in Exhibit 13.

EXHIBIT 13

Income Statements—Negotiated Transfer Price

Dynamic Exhibit

Wilson Company
Income Statements
For the Year Ended December 31, 2016

	Eastern Division	Western Division	Total Company
Sales:			
50,000 units × $20 per unit	$1,000,000		$1,000,000
20,000 units × $15 per unit	300,000		300,000
20,000 units × $40 per unit		$800,000	800,000
	$1,300,000	$800,000	$2,100,000
Expenses:			
Variable:			
70,000 units × $10 per unit	$ 700,000		$ 700,000
20,000 units × $25* per unit		$500,000	500,000
Fixed	300,000	100,000	400,000
Total expenses	$1,000,000	$600,000	$1,600,000
Income from operations	$ 300,000	$200,000	$ 500,000

*$10 of the $25 represents variable conversion expenses incurred solely within the Western Division, and $15 per unit represents the transfer price per unit from the Eastern Division.

The increase of $100,000 in the Eastern Division's income can also be computed as follows:

Increase in Eastern (Supplying) Division's Income from Operations = (Transfer Price – Variable Cost per Unit) × Units Transferred

= ($15 – $10) × 20,000 units = $100,000

The Western Division's materials cost decreases by $5 per unit ($20 – $15) for a total of $100,000 (20,000 units × $5 per unit). Thus, the Western Division's income from operations increases by $100,000 to $200,000, as shown in Exhibit 13.

The increase of $100,000 in the Western Division's income can also be computed as follows:

Increase in Western (Purchasing) Division's Income from Operations = (Market Price – Transfer Price) × Units Transferred

= ($20 – $15) × 20,000 units = $100,000

Comparing Exhibits 12 and 13 shows that Wilson's income from operations increased by $200,000, computed as follows:

	Income from Operations		
	No Units Transferred (Exhibit 12)	20,000 Units Transferred at $15 per Unit (Exhibit 13)	Increase (Decrease)
Eastern Division	$200,000	$300,000	$100,000
Western Division	100,000	200,000	100,000
Wilson Company	$300,000	$500,000	$200,000

In the preceding illustration, any negotiated transfer price between $10 and $20 is acceptable, as shown in the following formula:

Variable Costs per Unit < Transfer Price < Market Price
$10 < Transfer Price < $20

Any transfer price within this range will increase the overall income from operations for Wilson by $200,000. However, the increases in the Eastern and Western divisions' income from operations will vary depending on the transfer price.

To illustrate, a transfer price of $16 would increase the Eastern Division's income from operations by $120,000, computed as follows:

Increase in Eastern (Supplying) Division's Income from Operations = (Transfer Price – Variable Cost per Unit) × Units Transferred

= ($16 – $10) × 20,000 units = $120,000

A transfer price of $16 would increase the Western Division's income from operations by $80,000, computed as follows:

Increase in Western (Purchasing) Division's Income from Operations = (Market Price – Transfer Price) × Units Transferred

= ($20 – $16) × 20,000 units = $80,000

With a transfer price of $16, Wilson Company's income from operations still increases by $200,000, which consists of the Eastern Division's increase of $120,000 plus the Western Division's increase of $80,000.

As shown, a negotiated price provides each division manager with an incentive to negotiate the transfer of materials. At the same time, the overall company's income from operations will also increase. However, the negotiated approach only applies when the supplying division has excess capacity. In other words, the supplying division cannot sell all its production to outside buyers at the market price.

Example Exercise 8-6 Transfer Pricing

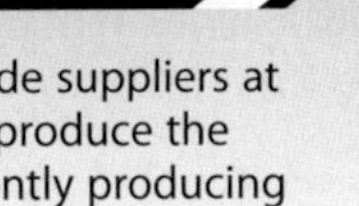

The materials used by the Winston-Salem Division of Fox Company are currently purchased from outside suppliers at $30 per unit. These same materials are produced by Fox's Flagstaff Division. The Flagstaff Division can produce the materials needed by the Winston-Salem Division at a variable cost of $15 per unit. The division is currently producing 70,000 units and has capacity of 100,000 units. The two divisions have recently negotiated a transfer price of $22 per unit for 30,000 units. By how much will each division's income increase as a result of this transfer?

Follow My Example 8-6

Increase in Flagstaff (Supplying) Division's Income from Operations = (Transfer Price – Variable Cost per Unit) × Units Transferred

= ($22 – $15) × 30,000 units = $210,000

Increase in Winston-Salem (Purchasing) Division's Income from Operations = (Market Price – Transfer Price) × Units Transferred

= ($30 – $22) × 30,000 units = $240,000

Practice Exercises: PE 8-6A, PE 8-6B

Cost Price Approach

Under the **cost price approach**, cost is used to set transfer prices. A variety of costs may be used in this approach, including the following:

- Total product cost per unit
- Variable product cost per unit

If total product cost per unit is used, direct materials, direct labor, and factory overhead are included in the transfer price. If variable product cost per unit is used, the fixed factory overhead cost is excluded from the transfer price.

Actual costs or standard (budgeted) costs may be used in applying the cost price approach. If actual costs are used, inefficiencies of the producing (supplying) division are transferred to the purchasing division. Thus, there is little incentive for the producing (supplying) division to control costs. For this reason, most companies use standard costs in the cost price approach. In this way, differences between actual and standard costs remain with the producing (supplying) division for cost control purposes.

The cost price approach is most often used when the responsibility centers are organized as cost centers. When the responsibility centers are organized as profit or investment centers, the cost price approach is normally not used.

For example, using the cost price approach when the supplying division is organized as a profit center ignores the supplying division manager's responsibility for earning profits. In this case, using the cost price approach prevents the supplying division from reporting any profit (revenues – costs) on the units transferred. As a result, the division manager has little incentive to transfer units to another division, even though it may be in the best interests of the company.

Integrity, Objectivity, and Ethics in Business

THE ETHICS OF TRANSFER PRICES

Transfer prices allow large multinational companies to minimize taxes by shifting taxable income from countries with high tax rates to countries with low taxes. For example, a British company will pay U.S. taxes on income from its U.S. division, and British taxes on income from its British division. Because this company can set its own transfer price, it can minimize its overall tax bill by setting a high transfer price when transferring goods to the United States This increases cost of goods sold for the highly taxed U.S division and increases sales for the lesser taxed British division. The overall result is a lower tax bill for the multinational company as a whole. In recent years, government tax authorities like the Internal Revenue Service (IRS) have become concerned with tax avoidance through transfer price manipulation. In response, many countries now have guidelines for setting transfer prices that assure that transfer prices are not subject to manipulation for tax purposes.

Source: L. Eden, and L. M. Smith, "The Ethics of Transfer Pricing," unpublished working paper, Texas A&M University, 2011.

At a Glance 8

OBJ 1 Describe the advantages and disadvantages of decentralized operations.

Key Points In a centralized business, all major planning and operating decisions are made by top management. In a decentralized business, these responsibilities are delegated to unit managers. Decentralization may be more effective because operational decisions are made by the managers closest to the operations.

Learning Outcomes	Example Exercises	Practice Exercises
• Describe the advantages of decentralization.		
• Describe the disadvantages of decentralization.		
• Describe the common types of responsibility centers and the role of responsibility accounting.		

Prepare a responsibility accounting report for a cost center.

Key Points Cost centers limit the responsibility and authority of managers to decisions related to the costs of their unit. The primary tools for planning and controlling are budgets and budget performance reports.

Learning Outcomes	Example Exercises	Practice Exercises
• Describe cost centers.		
• Describe the responsibility reporting for a cost center.		
• Compute the costs over (under) budget for a cost center.	EE8-1	PE8-1A, 8-1B

Prepare responsibility accounting reports for a profit center.

Key Points In a profit center, managers have the responsibility and authority to make decisions that affect both revenues and costs. Responsibility reports for a profit center usually show income from operations for the unit.

Learning Outcomes	Example Exercises	Practice Exercises
• Describe profit centers.		
• Determine how service department charges are allocated to profit centers.	EE8-2	PE8-2A, 8-2B
• Describe the responsibility reporting for a profit center.		
• Compute income from operations for a profit center.	EE8-3	PE8-3A, 8-3B

Compute and interpret the rate of return on investment, the residual income, and the balanced scorecard for an investment center.

Key Points In an investment center, the unit manager has the responsibility and authority to make decisions that affect the unit's revenues, expenses, and assets invested in the center. Three measures are commonly used to assess investment center performance: return on investment (ROI), residual income, and the balanced scorecard. These measures are often used to compare investment center performance.

Learning Outcomes	Example Exercises	Practice Exercises
• Describe investment centers.		
• Describe the responsibility reporting for an investment center.		
• Compute the profit margin, investment turnover, and rate of return on investment (ROI).	EE8-4	PE8-4A, 8-4B
• Compute residual income.	EE8-5	PE8-5A, 8-5B
• Describe the balanced scorecard approach.		

Describe and illustrate how the market price, negotiated price, and cost price approaches to transfer pricing may be used by decentralized segments of a business.

Key Points When divisions within a company transfer products or provide services to each other, a transfer price is used to charge for the products or services. Transfer prices should be set so that the overall company income is increased when goods are transferred between divisions. One of three approaches is typically used to establish transfer prices: market price, negotiated price, or cost price.

Learning Outcomes	Example Exercises	Practice Exercises
• Describe how companies determine the price used to transfer products or services between divisions.		
• Determine transfer prices using the market price approach.		
• Determine transfer prices using the negotiated price approach.	EE8-6	PE8-6A, 8-6B
• Describe the cost price approach to determining transfer price.		

Key Terms

balanced scorecard (336)
controllable expenses (328)
controllable revenues (328)
cost center (326)
cost price approach (341)
DuPont formula (332)
investment center (331)
investment turnover (332)
market price approach (339)
negotiated price approach (339)
profit center (328)
profit margin (332)
rate of return on investment (ROI) (332)
residual income (335)
responsibility accounting (325)
service department charges (328)
transfer price (338)

Illustrative Problem

Quinn Company has two divisions, Domestic and International. Invested assets and condensed income statement data for each division for the year ended December 31, 2016, are as follows:

	Domestic Division	International Division
Revenues	$675,000	$480,000
Operating expenses	450,000	372,400
Service department charges	90,000	50,000
Invested assets	600,000	384,000

Instructions

1. Prepare condensed income statements for the past year for each division.
2. Using the DuPont formula, determine the profit margin, investment turnover, and rate of return on investment for each division.
3. If management's minimum acceptable rate of return is 10%, determine the residual income for each division.

Solution

1.

Quinn Company
Divisional Income Statements
For the Year Ended December 31, 2016

	Domestic Division	International Division
Revenues	$675,000	$480,000
Operating expenses	450,000	372,400
Income from operations before service department charges	$225,000	$107,600
Service department charges	90,000	50,000
Income from operations	$135,000	$ 57,600

2. Rate of Return on Investment = Profit Margin × Investment Turnover

$$\text{Rate of Return on Investment} = \frac{\text{Income from Operations}}{\text{Sales}} \times \frac{\text{Sales}}{\text{Invested Assets}}$$

$$\text{Domestic Division: ROI} = \frac{\$135{,}000}{\$675{,}000} \times \frac{\$675{,}000}{\$600{,}000}$$

$$= 20\% \times 1.125$$

$$= 22.5\%$$

$$\text{International Division: ROI} = \frac{\$57{,}600}{\$480{,}000} \times \frac{\$480{,}000}{\$384{,}000}$$

$$= 12\% \times 1.25$$

$$= 15\%$$

3. Domestic Division: $75,000 [$135,000 – (10% × $600,000)]
International Division: $19,200 [$57,600 – (10% × $384,000)]

Discussion Questions

1. Differentiate between centralized and decentralized operations.
2. Differentiate between a profit center and an investment center.
3. **Weyerhaeuser** developed a system that assigns service department expenses to user divisions on the basis of actual services consumed by the division. Here are a number of Weyerhaeuser's activities in its central Financial Services Department:
   - Payroll
   - Accounts payable
   - Accounts receivable
   - Database administration—report preparation

   For each activity, identify an activity base that could be used to charge user divisions for service.
4. What is the major shortcoming of using income from operations as a performance measure for investment centers?
5. In a decentralized company in which the divisions are organized as investment centers, how could a division be considered the least profitable even though it earned the largest amount of income from operations?
6. How does using the rate of return on investment facilitate comparability between divisions of decentralized companies?
7. Why would a firm use a balanced scorecard in evaluating divisional performance?
8. What is the objective of transfer pricing?
9. When is the negotiated price approach preferred over the market price approach in setting transfer prices?
10. When using the negotiated price approach to transfer pricing, within what range should the transfer price be established?

Practice Exercises

SHOW ME HOW

EE 8-1 *p. 327*

PE 8-1A Budgetary performance for cost center **OBJ. 2**

Caroline Company's costs were over budget by $319,000. The company is divided into West and East regions. The East Region's costs were under budget by $47,500. Determine the amount that the West Region's costs were over or under budget.

SHOW ME HOW

EE 8-1 *p. 327*

PE 8-1B Budgetary performance for cost center **OBJ. 2**

Conley Company's costs were under budget by $198,000. The company is divided into North and South regions. The North Region's costs were over budget by $52,000. Determine the amount that the South Region's costs were over or under budget.

SHOW ME HOW

EE 8-2 *p. 330*

PE 8-2A Service department charges **OBJ. 3**

The centralized employee travel department of Camtro Company has expenses of $528,000. The department has serviced a total of 6,000 travel reservations for the period. The Southeast Division has made 2,400 reservations during the period, and the Pacific Northwest Division has made 3,600 reservations. How much should each division be charged for travel services?

SHOW ME HOW

EE 8-2 *p. 330*

PE 8-2B Service department charges **OBJ. 3**

The centralized computer technology department of Lee Company has expenses of $264,000. The department has provided a total of 2,500 hours of service for the period. The Retail Division has used 1,125 hours of computer technology service during the period, and the Commercial Division has used 1,375 hours of computer technology service. How much should each division be charged for computer technology department services?

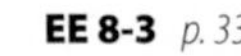

EE 8-3 *p. 331*

SHOW ME HOW

PE 8-3A Income from operations for profit center **OBJ. 3**

Using the data for Camtro Company from Practice Exercise 8-2A along with the following data, determine the divisional income from operations for the Northeast and Pacific divisions:

	Northeast Division	Pacific Division
Sales	$1,155,000	$1,204,000
Cost of goods sold	590,800	658,000
Selling expenses	231,000	252,000

SHOW ME HOW

EE 8-3 *p. 331*

PE 8-3B Income from operations for profit center **OBJ. 3**

Using the data for Lee Company from Practice Exercise 8-2B along with the following data, determine the divisional income from operations for the Division and the Commercial Division:

	Retail Division	Commercial Division
Sales	$945,000	$966,000
Cost of goods sold	504,000	559,300
Selling expenses	156,800	175,000

EE 8-4 *p. 334*

PE 8-4A Profit margin, investment turnover, and ROI — OBJ. 4

Cash Company has income from operations of $112,500, invested assets of $750,000, and sales of $1,875,000. Use the DuPont formula to compute the rate of return on investment and show (a) the profit margin, (b) the investment turnover, and (c) the rate of return on investment.

EE 8-4 *p. 334*

PE 8-4B Profit margin, investment turnover, and ROI — OBJ. 4

Briggs Company has income from operations of $36,000, invested assets of $180,000, and sales of $720,000. Use the DuPont formula to compute the rate of return on investment and show (a) the profit margin, (b) the investment turnover, and (c) the rate of return on investment.

EE 8-5 *p. 336*

PE 8-5A Residual income — OBJ. 4

The Consumer Division of Hernandez Company has income from operations of $90,000 and assets of $450,000. The minimum acceptable rate of return on assets is 10%. What is the residual income for the division?

EE 8-5 *p. 336*

PE 8-5B Residual income — OBJ. 4

The Commercial Division of Herring Company has income from operations of $420,000 and assets of $910,000. The minimum acceptable rate of return on assets is 8%. What is the residual income for the division?

EE 8-6 *p. 341*

PE 8-6A Transfer pricing — OBJ. 5

The materials used by the North Division of Horton Company are currently purchased from outside suppliers at $60 per unit. These same materials are produced by Horton's South Division. The South Division can produce the materials needed by the North Division at a variable cost of $42 per unit. The division is currently producing 200,000 units and has capacity of 250,000 units. The two divisions have recently negotiated a transfer price of $52 per unit for 30,000 units. By how much will each division's income increase as a result of this transfer?

EE 8-6 *p. 341*

PE 8-6B Transfer pricing — OBJ. 5

The materials used by the Multinomah Division of Isbister Company are currently purchased from outside suppliers at $90 per unit. These same materials are produced by the Pembroke Division. The Pembroke Division can produce the materials needed by the Multinomah Division at a variable cost of $75 per unit. The division is currently producing 120,000 units and has capacity of 150,000 units. The two divisions have recently negotiated a transfer price of $82 per unit for 15,000 units. By how much will each division's income increase as a result of this transfer?

Exercises

✔ a. (c) $3,540

EX 8-1 Budget performance reports for cost centers — OBJ. 2

Partially completed budget performance reports for Saskatoon Company, a manufacturer of light duty motors, follow:

Saskatoon Company
Budget Performance Report—Vice President, Production
For the Month Ended June 30, 2016

Plant	Budget	Actual	Over Budget	Under Budget
Eastern Region	$936,000	$933,750		$2,250
Central Region	669,600	666,000		3,600
Western Region	(g)	(h)	(i)	
	(j)	(k)	$ (l)	$5,850

(Continued)

Saskatoon Company
Budget Performance Report—Manager, Western Region Plant
For the Month Ended June 30, 2016

Department	Budget	Actual	Over Budget	Under Budget
Chip Fabrication	(a)	(b)	(c)	
Electronic Assembly	$191,250	$194,040	$ 2,520	
Final Assembly	308,250	307,440		$810
	(d)	(e)	$ (f)	$810

Saskatoon Company
Budget Performance Report—Supervisor, Chip Fabrication
For the Month Ended June 30, 2016

Cost	Budget	Actual	Over Budget	Under Budget
Factory wages	$ 59,940	$ 61,500	$1,560	
Materials	156,600	155,520		$1,080
Power and light	8,640	10,260	1,620	
Maintenance	15,120	16,560	1,440	
	$240,300	$243,840	$4,620	$1,080

a. Complete the budget performance reports by determining the correct amounts for the lettered spaces.

b. Compose a memo to Robin Mooney, vice president of production for Saskatoon Company, explaining the performance of the production division for May.

EX 8-2 Divisional income statements **OBJ. 3**

✔ Commercial Division income from operations, $179,890

The following data were summarized from the accounting records for Jersey Coast Construction Company for the year ended June 30, 2016:

Cost of goods sold:		Service department charges:	
Commercial Division	$912,250	Commercial Division	$112,560
Residential Division	423,675	Residential Division	67,830
Administrative expenses:		Sales:	
Commercial Division	$149,800	Commercial Division	$1,354,500
Residential Division	128,625	Residential Division	743,780

Prepare divisional income statements for Jersey Coast Construction Company.

EX 8-3 Service department charges and activity bases **OBJ. 3**

For each of the following service departments, identify an activity base that could be used for charging the expense to the profit center:

a. Legal
b. Duplication services
c. Electronic data processing
d. Central purchasing
e. Telecommunications
f. Accounts receivable

✔ c. 2

EX 8-4 Activity bases for service department charges OBJ. 3

For each of the following service departments, select the activity base listed that is most appropriate for charging service expenses to responsible units:

Service Department	Activity Base
a. Accounts Receivable	1. Number of conference attendees
b. Central Purchasing	2. Number of computers
c. Computer Support	3. Number of employees trained
d. Conferences	4. Number of cell phone minutes used
e. Employee Travel	5. Number of purchase requisitions
f. Payroll Accounting	6. Number of sales invoices
g. Telecommunications	7. Number of payroll checks
h. Training	8. Number of travel claims

✔ **b. Residential payroll, $33,400**

SHOW ME HOW

EX 8-5 Service department charges OBJ. 3

In divisional income statements prepared for LeFevre Company, the Payroll Department costs are charged back to user divisions on the basis of the number of payroll distributions, and the Purchasing Department costs are charged back on the basis of the number of purchase requisitions. The Payroll Department had expenses of $75,400, and the Purchasing Department had expenses of $42,000 for the year. The following annual data for Residential, Commercial, and Government Contract divisions were obtained from corporate records:

	Residential	Commercial	Government Contract
Sales	$1,000,000	$1,600,000	$3,200,000
Number of employees:			
Weekly payroll (52 weeks per year)	300	150	200
Monthly payroll	75	160	90
Number of purchase requisitions per year	4,000	3,500	3,000

a. Determine the total amount of payroll checks and purchase requisitions processed per year by the company and each division.

b. Using the activity base information in (a), determine the annual amount of payroll and purchasing costs charged back to the Residential, Commercial, and Government Contract divisions from payroll and purchasing services.

c. Why does the Residential Division have a larger service department charge than the other two divisions, even though its sales are lower?

✔ **b. Help desk, $93,600**

EX 8-6 Service department charges and activity bases OBJ. 3

Middler Corporation, a manufacturer of electronics and communications systems, uses a service department charge system to charge profit centers with Computing and Communications Services (CCS) service department costs. The following table identifies an abbreviated list of service categories and activity bases used by the CCS department. The table also includes some assumed cost and activity base quantity information for each service for October.

CCS Service Category	Activity Base	Budgeted Cost	Budgeted Activity Base Quantity
Help desk	Number of calls	$160,000	3,200
Network center	Number of devices monitored	735,000	9,800
Electronic mail	Number of user accounts	100,000	10,000
Smart phone support	Number of smart phones issued	124,600	8,900

One of the profit centers for Middler Corporation is the Communication Systems (COMM) sector. Assume the following information for the COMM sector:

- The sector has 5,200 employees, of whom 25% are office employees.
- All the office employees have been issued a smart phone, and 96% of them have a computer on the network.

(Continued)

- One hundred percent of the employees with a computer also have an e-mail account.
- The average number of help desk calls for October was 1.5 calls per individual with a computer.
- There are 600 additional printers, servers, and peripherals on the network beyond the personal computers.

a. Determine the service charge rate for the four CCS service categories for October.

b. Determine the charges to the COMM sector for the four CCS service categories for October.

EX 8-7 Divisional income statements with service department charges OBJ. 3

✔ Commercial income from operations, $1,261,260

SHOW ME HOW

Yozamba Technology has two divisions, Consumer and Commercial, and two corporate service departments, Tech Support and Purchasing. The corporate expenses for the year ended December 31, 2016, are as follows:

Tech Support Department	$ 516,000
Purchasing Department	89,600
Other corporate administrative expenses	560,000
Total corporate expense	$1,165,600

The other corporate administrative expenses include officers' salaries and other expenses required by the corporation. The Tech Support Department charges the divisions for services rendered, based on the number of computers in the department, and the Purchasing Department charges divisions for services, based on the number of purchase orders for each department. The usage of service by the two divisions is as follows:

	Tech Support	Purchasing
Consumer Division	375 computers	1,960 purchase orders
Commercial Division	225	3,640
Total	600 computers	5,600 purchase orders

The service department charges of the Tech Support Department and the Purchasing Department are considered controllable by the divisions. Corporate administrative expenses are not considered controllable by the divisions. The revenues, cost of goods sold, and operating expenses for the two divisions are as follows:

	Consumer	Commercial
Revenues	$7,430,000	$6,184,000
Cost of goods sold	4,123,000	3,125,000
Operating expenses	1,465,000	1,546,000

Prepare the divisional income statements for the two divisions.

EX 8-8 Corrections to service department charges for a service company OBJ. 3

✔ b. Income from operations, Cargo Division, $84,400

Wild Sun Airlines Inc. has two divisions organized as profit centers, the Passenger Division and the Cargo Division. The following divisional income statements were prepared:

Wild Sun Airlines Inc.
Divisional Income Statements
For the Year Ended December 31, 2016

	Passenger Division		Cargo Division	
Revenues		$3,025,000		$3,025,000
Operating expenses		2,450,000		2,736,000
Income from operations before service department charges		$ 575,000		$ 289,000
Less service department charges:				
Training	$125,000		$125,000	
Flight scheduling	108,000		108,000	
Reservations	151,200	384,200	151,200	384,200
Income from operations		$ 190,800		$ (95,200)

The service department charge rate for the service department costs was based on revenues. Because the revenues of the two divisions were the same, the service department charges to each division were also the same.

The following additional information is available:

	Passenger Division	Cargo Division	Total
Number of personnel trained	350	150	500
Number of flights	800	1,200	2,000
Number of reservations requested	20,000	0	20,000

a. Does the income from operations for the two divisions accurately measure performance? Explain.

b. Correct the divisional income statements, using the activity bases provided in revising the service department charges.

EX 8-9 Profit center responsibility reporting

OBJ. 3

✔ **Income from operations, Summer Sports Division, $1,499,400**

SHOW ME HOW

XSport Sporting Goods Co. operates two divisions—the Winter Sports Division and the Summer Sports Division. The following income and expense accounts were provided from the trial balance as of December 31, 2016, the end of the fiscal year, after all adjustments, including those for inventories, were recorded and posted:

Sales—Winter Sports Division	$10,500,000
Sales—Summer Sports Division	13,600,000
Cost of Goods Sold—Winter Sports Division	6,300,000
Cost of Goods Sold—Summer Sports Division	7,888,000
Sales Expense—Winter Sports Division	1,680,000
Sales Expense—Summer Sports Division	1,904,000
Administrative Expense—Winter Sports Division	1,050,000
Administrative Expense—Summer Sports Division	1,210,400
Advertising Expense	482,000
Transportation Expense	240,000
Accounts Receivable Collection Expense	120,500
Warehouse Expense	1,200,000

The bases to be used in allocating expenses, together with other essential information, are as follows:

a. Advertising expense—incurred at headquarters, charged back to divisions on the basis of usage: Winter Sports Division, $216,900; Summer Sports Division, $265,100.

b. Transportation expense—charged back to divisions at a charge rate of $8.00 per bill of lading: Winter Sports Division, 14,400 bills of lading; Summer Sports Division, 15,600 bills of lading.

c. Accounts receivable collection expense—incurred at headquarters, charged back to divisions at a charge rate of $5.00 per invoice: Winter Sports Division, 9,640 sales invoices; Summer Sports Division, 14,460 sales invoices.

d. Warehouse expense—charged back to divisions on the basis of floor space used in storing division products: Winter Sports Division, 94,000 square feet; Summer Sports Division, 106,000 square feet.

Prepare a divisional income statement with two column headings: Winter Sports Division and Summer Sports Division. Provide supporting calculations for service department charges.

EX 8-10 Rate of return on investment **OBJ. 4**

✔ a. Retail, 26%

The income from operations and the amount of invested assets in each division of Magentic Zero Industries are as follows:

	Income from Operations	Invested Assets
Retail Division	$343,200	$1,320,000
Commercial Division	320,000	1,600,000
Internet Division	176,000	800,000

a. Compute the rate of return on investment for each division.

b. Which division is the most profitable per dollar invested?

EX 8-11 Residual income **OBJ. 4**

✔ a. Retail Division, $211,200

SHOW
ME HOW

Based on the data in Exercise 8-10, assume that management has established a 10% minimum acceptable rate of return for invested assets.

a. Determine the residual income for each division.

b. Which division has the most residual income?

EX 8-12 Determining missing items in rate of return computation **OBJ. 4**

✔ d. 3.00

One item is omitted from each of the following computations of the rate of return on investment:

Rate of Return on Investment	=	Profit Margin	×	Investment Turnover
13.2%	=	6%	×	(a)
(b)	=	10%	×	1.80
10.5%	=	(c)	×	1.50
15%	=	5%	×	(d)
(e)	=	12%	×	1.10

Determine the missing items, identifying each by the appropriate letter.

EX 8-13 Profit margin, investment turnover, and rate of return on investment **OBJ. 4**

✔ a. ROI, 28%

The condensed income statement for the Consumer Products Division of Bantastic Industries Inc. is as follows (assuming no service department charges):

Sales	$16,000,000
Cost of goods sold	11,660,000
Gross profit	$ 4,340,000
Administrative expenses	2,100,000
Income from operations	$ 2,240,000

The manager of the Consumer Products Division is considering ways to increase the rate of return on investment.

a. Using the DuPont formula for rate of return on investment, determine the profit margin, investment turnover, and rate of return on investment of the Consumer Products Division, assuming that $8,000,000 of assets have been invested in the Consumer Products Division.

b. If expenses could be reduced by $320,000 without decreasing sales, what would be the impact on the profit margin, investment turnover, and rate of return on investment for the Consumer Products Division?

EX 8-14 Rate of return on investment **OBJ. 4**

✔ a. Media Networks ROI, 23.8%

The Walt Disney Company has four profitable business segments, described as follows:

- **Media Networks:** The ABC television and radio network, Disney channel, ESPN, A&E, E!, and Disney.com
- **Parks and Resorts:** Walt Disney World Resort, Disneyland, Disney Cruise Line, and other resort properties

- **Studio Entertainment:** Walt Disney Pictures, Touchstone Pictures, Hollywood Pictures, Miramax Films, and Buena Vista Theatrical Productions
- **Consumer Products:** Character merchandising, Disney stores, books, and magazines

Disney recently reported sector income from operations, revenue, and invested assets (in millions) as follows:

	Income from Operations	Revenue	Invested Assets
Media Networks	$6,818	$20,356	$28,627
Parks and Resorts	2,220	14,087	22,056
Studio Entertainment	661	5,979	14,750
Consumer Products	1,112	3,811	7,506

a. Use the DuPont formula to determine the rate of return on investment for the four Disney sectors. Round whole percents to one decimal place and investment turnover to two decimal places.

b. How do the four sectors differ in their profit margin, investment turnover, and return on investment?

EX 8-15 Determining missing items in rate of return and residual income computations — OBJ. 4

✔ c. $46,250

Data for Uberto Company are presented in the following table of rates of return on investment and residual incomes:

Invested Assets	Income from Operations	Rate of Return on Investment	Minimum Rate of Return	Minimum Acceptable Income from Operations	Residual Income
$925,000	$185,000	(a)	15%	(b)	(c)
$775,000	(d)	(e)	(f)	$93,000	$23,250
$450,000	(g)	18%	(h)	$58,500	(i)
$610,000	$97,600	(j)	12%	(k)	(l)

Determine the missing items, identifying each item by the appropriate letter.

EX 8-16 Determining missing items from computations — OBJ. 4

✔ a. (e) $300,000

Data for the North, South, East, and West divisions of Free Bird Company are as follows:

	Sales	Income from Operations	Invested Assets	Rate of Return on Investment	Profit Margin	Investment Turnover
North	$860,000	(a)	(b)	17.5%	7.0%	(c)
South	(d)	$51,300	(e)	(f)	4.5%	3.8
East	$1,020,000	(g)	$680,000	15.0%	(h)	(i)
West	$1,120,000	$89,600	$560,000	(j)	(k)	(l)

a. Determine the missing items, identifying each by the letters (a) through (l). Round percents and investment turnover to one decimal place.

b. Determine the residual income for each division, assuming that the minimum acceptable rate of return established by management is 12%.

c. Which division is the most profitable in terms of (1) return on investment and (2) residual income?

EX 8-17 Rate of return on investment, residual income for a service company — OBJ. 4

Starwood Hotels & Resorts Worldwide provides lodging services around the world. The company is separated into two major divisions.

- **Hotel Ownership:** Hotels owned and operated by Starwood.
- **Vacation Ownership:** Resort properties developed, owned, and operated for timeshare vacation owners.

(Continued)

Financial information for each division, from a recent annual report, is as follows (in millions):

	Hotel Ownership	Vacation Ownership
Revenues	$4,383	$ 688
Income from operations	571	105
Total assets	6,440	2,139

a. Use the DuPont formula to determine the return on investment for each of the Starwood business divisions. Round whole percents to one decimal place and investment turnover to two decimal places.

b. Determine the residual income for each division, assuming a minimum acceptable income of 5% of total assets. Round minimal acceptable return to the nearest million dollars.

c. Interpret your results.

EX 8-18 Balanced scorecard for a service company **OBJ. 4**

American Express Company is a major financial services company, noted for its American Express® card. Some of the performance measures used by the company in its balanced scorecard follow:

Average card member spending	Number of Internet features
Cards in force	Number of merchant signings
Earnings growth	Number of new card launches
Hours of credit consultant training	Return on equity
Investment in information technology	Revenue growth
Number of card choices	

For each measure, identify whether the measure best fits the innovation, customer, internal process, or financial dimension of the balanced scorecard.

EX 8-19 Building a balanced scorecard **OBJ. 4**

Hit-n-Run Inc. owns and operates 10 food trucks (mobile kitchens) throughout metropolitan Los Angeles. Each food truck has a different food theme, such as Irish-Mexican fusion, traditional Mexican street food, Ethiopian cuisine, and Lebanese-Italian fusion. The company was founded three years ago by Juanita O'Brien when she opened a single food truck with a unique menu. As her business has grown, she has become concerned about her ability to manage and control the business. O'Brien describes how the company was built, its key success factors, and its recent growth.

"I built the company from the ground up. In the beginning it was just me. I drove the truck, set the menu, bought the ingredients, prepared the meals, served the meals, cleaned the kitchen, and maintained the equipment. I made unique meals from quality ingredients, and didn't serve anything that wasn't perfect. I changed my location daily, and notified customers of my location via twitter.

As my customer base grew, I hired employees to help me in the truck. Then one day I realized that I had a formula that could be expanded to multiple trucks. Before I knew it, I had 10 trucks and was hiring people to do everything that I used to do by myself. Now, I work with my team to build the menu, set daily locations for the trucks, and manage the operations of the business.

My business model is based on providing the highest quality street food and charging more for it than other trucks. You won't get the cheapest meal at one of my trucks, but you will get the best. The superior quality allows me to price my meals a little bit higher than the other trucks. My employees are critical to my success. I pay them a better wage than they could make on other food trucks, and I expect more from them. I rely on them to maintain the quality that I established when I opened my first truck.

Things are going great, but I'm feeling overwhelmed. So far, the growth in sales has led to a growth in profitability—but I'm getting nervous. If quality starts to fall off, my brand value erodes, and that could affect the prices that I charge for my meals and the success of my business."

Create balanced scorecard measures for Hit-n-Run Food Trucks. Identify whether these measures best fit the innovation, customer, internal process, or financial dimension of the balanced scorecard.

EX 8-20 Decision on transfer pricing **OBJ. 5**

✔ a. $3,000,000

Materials used by the Instrument Division of XPort Industries are currently purchased from outside suppliers at a cost of $210 per unit. However, the same materials are available from the Components Division. The Components Division has unused capacity and can produce the materials needed by the Instrument Division at a variable cost of $160 per unit.

a. If a transfer price of $180 per unit is established and 60,000 units of materials are transferred, with no reduction in the Components Division's current sales, how much would XPort Industries' total income from operations increase?

b. How much would the Instrument Division's income from operations increase?

c. How much would the Components Division's income from operations increase?

EX 8-21 Decision on transfer pricing **OBJ. 5**

✔ b. $1,200,000

Based on XPort Industries' data in Exercise 8-20, assume that a transfer price of $190 has been established and that 60,000 units of materials are transferred, with no reduction in the Components Division's current sales.

a. How much would XPort Industries' total income from operations increase?

b. How much would the Instrument Division's income from operations increase?

c. How much would the Components Division's income from operations increase?

d. If the negotiated price approach is used, what would be the range of acceptable transfer prices and why?

Problems: Series A

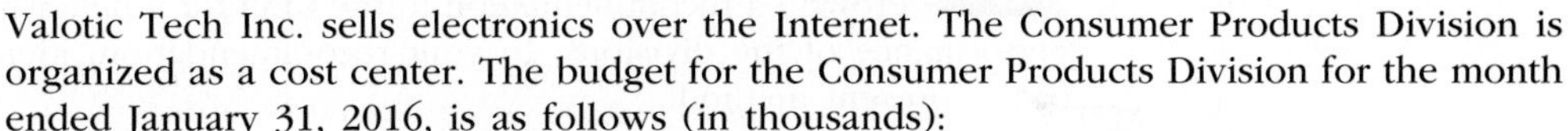

PR 8-1A Budget performance report for a cost center **OBJ. 2**

Valotic Tech Inc. sells electronics over the Internet. The Consumer Products Division is organized as a cost center. The budget for the Consumer Products Division for the month ended January 31, 2016, is as follows (in thousands):

Customer service salaries	$ 546,840
Insurance and property taxes	114,660
Distribution salaries	872,340
Marketing salaries	1,028,370
Engineer salaries	836,850
Warehouse wages	586,110
Equipment depreciation	183,792
Total	$4,168,962

During January, the costs incurred in the Consumer Products Division were as follows:

Customer service salaries	$ 602,350
Insurance and property taxes	110,240
Distribution salaries	861,200
Marketing salaries	1,085,230
Engineer salaries	820,008
Warehouse wages	562,632
Equipment depreciation	183,610
Total	$4,225,270

Instructions

1. Prepare a budget performance report for the director of the Consumer Products Division for the month of January.
2. For which costs might the director be expected to request supplemental reports?

PR 8-2A Profit center responsibility reporting for a service company **OBJ. 3**

✔ 1. Income from operations, Central Division, $430,560

SHOW ME HOW

Traxonia Railroad Inc. has three regional divisions organized as profit centers. The chief executive officer (CEO) evaluates divisional performance, using income from operations as a percent of revenues. The following quarterly income and expense accounts were provided from the trial balance as of December 31, 2016:

Revenues—East	$ 870,000
Revenues—West	1,032,000
Revenues—Central	1,872,000
Operating Expenses—East	563,300
Operating Expenses—West	618,240
Operating Expenses—Central	1,166,940
Corporate Expenses—Shareholder Relations	154,000
Corporate Expenses—Customer Support	400,000
Corporate Expenses—Legal	270,000
General Corporate Officers' Salaries	275,000

The company operates three service departments: Shareholder Relations, Customer Support, and Legal. The Shareholder Relations Department conducts a variety of services for shareholders of the company. The Customer Support Department is the company's point of contact for new service, complaints, and requests for repair. The department believes that the number of customer contacts is an activity base for this work. The Legal Department provides legal services for division management. The department believes that the number of hours billed is an activity base for this work. The following additional information has been gathered:

	East	West	Central
Number of customer contacts	5,000	6,000	9,000
Number of hours billed	1,350	2,160	1,890

Instructions

1. Prepare quarterly income statements showing income from operations for the three divisions. Use three column headings: East, West, and Central.
2. Identify the most successful division according to the profit margin.
3. Provide a recommendation to the CEO for a better method for evaluating the performance of the divisions. In your recommendation, identify the major weakness of the present method.

PR 8-3A Divisional income statements and rate of return on investment analysis **OBJ. 4**

✔ 2. Cereal Division ROI, 10.0%

The Crunchy Granola Company is a diversified food company that specializes in all natural foods. The company has three operating divisions organized as investment centers. Condensed data taken from the records of the three divisions for the year ended June 30, 2016, are as follows:

	Cereal Division	Snack Cake Division	Retail Bakeries Division
Sales	$25,000,000	$8,000,000	$9,750,000
Cost of goods sold	16,670,000	5,575,000	6,795,000
Operating expenses	7,330,000	1,945,000	2,272,500
Invested assets	10,000,000	4,000,000	6,500,000

The management of The Crunchy Granola Company is evaluating each division as a basis for planning a future expansion of operations.

Instructions

1. Prepare condensed divisional income statements for the three divisions, assuming that there were no service department charges.
2. Using the DuPont formula for rate of return on investment, compute the profit margin, investment turnover, and rate of return on investment for each division.
3. If available funds permit the expansion of operations of only one division, which of the divisions would you recommend for expansion, based on parts (1) and (2)? Explain.

✔ 1. ROI, 16.8%

PR 8-4A Effect of proposals on divisional performance OBJ. 4

A condensed income statement for the Commercial Division of Maxell Manufacturing Inc. for the year ended December 31, 2016, is as follows:

Sales	$3,500,000
Cost of goods sold	2,480,000
Gross profit	$1,020,000
Operating expenses	600,000
Income from operations	$ 420,000
Invested assets	$2,500,000

Assume that the Commercial Division received no charges from service departments. The president of Maxell Manufacturing has indicated that the division's rate of return on a $2,500,000 investment must be increased to at least 21% by the end of the next year if operations are to continue. The division manager is considering the following three proposals:

Proposal 1: Transfer equipment with a book value of $312,500 to other divisions at no gain or loss and lease similar equipment. The annual lease payments would exceed the amount of depreciation expense on the old equipment by $105,000. This increase in expense would be included as part of the cost of goods sold. Sales would remain unchanged.

Proposal 2: Purchase new and more efficient machining equipment and thereby reduce the cost of goods sold by $560,000 after considering the effects of depreciation expense on the new equipment. Sales would remain unchanged, and the old equipment, which has no remaining book value, would be scrapped at no gain or loss. The new equipment would increase invested assets by an additional $1,875,000 for the year.

Proposal 3: Reduce invested assets by discontinuing a product line. This action would eliminate sales of $595,000, reduce cost of goods sold by $406,700, and reduce operating expenses by $175,000. Assets of $1,338,000 would be transferred to other divisions at no gain or loss.

Instructions

1. Using the DuPont formula for rate of return on investment, determine the profit margin, investment turnover, and rate of return on investment for the Commercial Division for the past year.
2. Prepare condensed estimated income statements and compute the invested assets for each proposal.
3. Using the DuPont formula for rate of return on investment, determine the profit margin, investment turnover, and rate of return on investment for each proposal.
4. Which of the three proposals would meet the required 21% rate of return on investment?
5. If the Commercial Division were in an industry where the profit margin could not be increased, how much would the investment turnover have to increase to meet the president's required 21% rate of return on investment? Round to one decimal place.

✔ 2. Business Division ROI, 20.0%

PR 8-5A Divisional performance analysis and evaluation OBJ. 4

The vice president of operations of Pavone Company is evaluating the performance of two divisions organized as investment centers. Invested assets and condensed income statement data for the past year for each division are as follows:

	Business Division	Consumer Division
Sales	$2,500,000	$2,550,000
Cost of goods sold	1,320,000	1,350,000
Operating expenses	930,000	843,000
Invested assets	1,250,000	2,125,000

Instructions

1. Prepare condensed divisional income statements for the year ended December 31, 2016, assuming that there were no service department charges.
2. Using the DuPont formula for rate of return on investment, determine the profit margin, investment turnover, and rate of return on investment for each division.
3. If management desires a minimum acceptable rate of return of 17%, determine the residual income for each division.
4. Discuss the evaluation of the two divisions, using the performance measures determined in parts (1), (2), and (3).

PR 8-6A Transfer pricing **OBJ. 5**

✔ 3. Total income from operations, $1,759,680

Garcon Inc. manufactures electronic products, with two operating divisions, the Consumer and Commercial divisions. Condensed divisional income statements, which involve no intracompany transfers and which include a breakdown of expenses into variable and fixed components, are as follows:

Garcon Inc.
Divisional Income Statements
For the Year Ended December 31, 2016

	Consumer Division	Commercial Division	Total
Sales:			
14,400 units @ $144 per unit	$2,073,600		$2,073,600
21,600 units @ $275 per unit		$5,940,000	5,940,000
	$2,073,600	$5,940,000	$8,013,600
Expenses:			
Variable:			
14,400 units @ $104 per unit	$1,497,600		$1,497,600
21,600 units @ $193* per unit		$4,168,800	4,168,800
Fixed	200,000	520,000	720,000
Total expenses	$1,697,600	$4,688,800	$6,386,400
Income from operations	$ 376,000	$1,251,200	$1,627,200

*$150 of the $193 per unit represents materials costs, and the remaining $43 per unit represents other variable conversion expenses incurred within the Commercial Division.

The Consumer Division is presently producing 14,400 units out of a total capacity of 17,280 units. Materials used in producing the Commercial Division's product are currently purchased from outside suppliers at a price of $150 per unit. The Consumer Division is able to produce the materials used by the Commercial Division. Except for the possible transfer of materials between divisions, no changes are expected in sales and expenses.

Instructions

1. Would the market price of $150 per unit be an appropriate transfer price for Garcon Inc.? Explain.
2. If the Commercial Division purchases 2,880 units from the Consumer Division, rather than externally, at a negotiated transfer price of $115 per unit, how much would the income from operations of each division and the total company income from operations increase?
3. Prepare condensed divisional income statements for Garcon Inc. based on the data in part (2).
4. If a transfer price of $126 per unit is negotiated, how much would the income from operations of each division and the total company income from operations increase?
5. a. What is the range of possible negotiated transfer prices that would be acceptable for Garcon Inc.?

   b. Assuming that the managers of the two divisions cannot agree on a transfer price, what price would you suggest as the transfer price?

Problems: Series B

PR 8-1B Budget performance report for a cost center **OBJ. 2**

The Eastern District of Adelson Inc. is organized as a cost center. The budget for the Eastern District of Adelson Inc. for the month ended December 31, 2016, is as follows:

Sales salaries	$ 819,840
System administration salaries	448,152
Customer service salaries	152,600
Billing salaries	98,760
Maintenance	271,104
Depreciation of plant and equipment	92,232
Insurance and property taxes	41,280
Total	$1,923,968

During December, the costs incurred in the Eastern District were as follows:

Sales salaries	$ 818,880
System administration salaries	447,720
Customer service salaries	183,120
Billing salaries	98,100
Maintenance	273,000
Depreciation of plant and equipment	92,232
Insurance and property taxes	41,400
Total	$1,954,452

Instructions

1. Prepare a budget performance report for the manager of the Eastern District of Adelson for the month of December.
2. For which costs might the supervisor be expected to request supplemental reports?

PR 8-2B Profit center responsibility reporting for a service company **OBJ. 3**

✔ 1. Income from operations, West Region, $820,800

Thomas Railroad Company organizes its three divisions, the North (N), South (S), and West (W) regions, as profit centers. The chief executive officer (CEO) evaluates divisional performance, using income from operations as a percent of revenues. The following quarterly income and expense accounts were provided from the trial balance as of December 31, 2016:

Revenues—N Region	$3,780,000
Revenues—S Region	5,673,000
Revenues—W Region	5,130,000
Operating Expenses—N Region	2,678,500
Operating Expenses—S Region	4,494,890
Operating Expenses—W Region	3,770,050
Corporate Expenses—Dispatching	182,000
Corporate Expenses—Equipment Management	1,200,000
Corporate Expenses—Treasurer's	734,000
General Corporate Officers' Salaries	1,380,000

The company operates three service departments: the Dispatching Department, the Equipment Management Department, and the Treasurer's Department. The Dispatching Department manages the scheduling and releasing of completed trains. The Equipment Management Department manages the railroad cars inventories. It makes sure the right freight cars are at the right place at the right time. The Treasurer's Department conducts a variety of services for the company as a whole. The following additional information has been gathered:

	North	South	West
Number of scheduled trains	650	1,105	845
Number of railroad cars in inventory	6,000	8,400	9,600

Instructions

1. Prepare quarterly income statements showing income from operations for the three regions. Use three column headings: North, South, and West.
2. Identify the most successful region according to the profit margin.
3. Provide a recommendation to the CEO for a better method for evaluating the performance of the regions. In your recommendation, identify the major weakness of the present method.

PR 8-3B Divisional income statements and rate of return on investment analysis OBJ. 4

✔ 2. Mutual Fund Division, ROI, 22.4%

E.F. Lynch Company is a diversified investment company with three operating divisions organized as investment centers. Condensed data taken from the records of the three divisions for the year ended June 30, 2016, are as follows:

	Mutual Fund Division	Electronic Brokerage Division	Investment Banking Division
Fee revenue	$4,140,000	$3,360,000	$4,560,000
Operating expenses	2,980,800	3,091,200	3,739,200
Invested assets	5,175,000	1,120,000	3,800,000

The management of E.F. Lynch Company is evaluating each division as a basis for planning a future expansion of operations.

Instructions

1. Prepare condensed divisional income statements for the three divisions, assuming that there were no service department charges.
2. Using the DuPont formula for rate of return on investment, compute the profit margin, investment turnover, and rate of return on investment for each division.
3. If available funds permit the expansion of operations of only one division, which of the divisions would you recommend for expansion, based on parts (1) and (2)? Explain.

PR 8-4B Effect of proposals on divisional performance OBJ. 4

✔ 3. Proposal 3 ROI, 16.0%

A condensed income statement for the Electronics Division of Gihbli Industries Inc. for the year ended December 31, 2016, is as follows:

Sales	$1,575,000
Cost of goods sold	891,000
Gross profit	$ 684,000
Operating expenses	558,000
Income from operations	$ 126,000
Invested assets	$1,050,000

Assume that the Electronics Division received no charges from service departments.

The president of Gihbli Industries Inc. has indicated that the division's rate of return on a $1,050,000 investment must be increased to at least 20% by the end of the next year if operations are to continue. The division manager is considering the following three proposals:

Proposal 1: Transfer equipment with a book value of $300,000 to other divisions at no gain or loss and lease similar equipment. The annual lease payments would be less than the amount of depreciation expense on the old equipment by $31,400. This decrease in expense would be included as part of the cost of goods sold. Sales would remain unchanged.

Proposal 2: Reduce invested assets by discontinuing a product line. This action would eliminate sales of $180,000, reduce cost of goods sold by $119,550, and reduce operating expenses by $60,000. Assets of $112,500 would be transferred to other divisions at no gain or loss.

Proposal 3: Purchase new and more efficient machinery and thereby reduce the cost of goods sold by $189,000 after considering the effects of depreciation expense on the new equipment. Sales would remain unchanged, and the old machinery, which has no remaining book value, would be scrapped at no gain or loss. The new machinery would increase invested assets by $918,750 for the year.

Instructions

1. Using the DuPont formula for rate of return on investment, determine the profit margin, investment turnover, and rate of return on investment for the Electronics Division for the past year. Round investment turnover and the rate of return to one decimal place.
2. Prepare condensed estimated income statements and compute the invested assets for each proposal.

3. Using the DuPont formula for rate of return on investment, determine the profit margin, investment turnover, and rate of return on investment for each proposal. Round investment turnover and the rate of return to one decimal place.
4. Which of the three proposals would meet the required 20% rate of return on investment?
5. If the Electronics Division were in an industry where the profit margin could not be increased, how much would the investment turnover have to increase to meet the president's required 20% rate of return on investment? Round to one decimal place.

PR 8-5B Divisional performance analysis and evaluation OBJ. 4

✔ 2. Road Bike Division ROI, 12.0%

SHOW ME HOW

The vice president of operations of Free Ride Bike Company is evaluating the performance of two divisions organized as investment centers. Invested assets and condensed income statement data for the past year for each division are as follows:

	Road Bike Division	Mountain Bike Division
Sales	$1,728,000	$1,760,000
Cost of goods sold	1,380,000	1,400,000
Operating expenses	175,200	236,800
Invested assets	1,440,000	800,000

Instructions

1. Prepare condensed divisional income statements for the year ended December 31, 2016, assuming that there were no service department charges.
2. Using the DuPont formula for rate of return on investment, determine the profit margin, investment turnover, and rate of return on investment for each division.
3. If management's minimum acceptable rate of return is 10%, determine the residual income for each division.
4. Discuss the evaluation of the two divisions, using the performance measures determined in parts (1), (2), and (3).

PR 8-6B Transfer pricing OBJ. 5

✔ 3. Navigational Systems Division, $179,410

Exoplex Industries Inc. is a diversified aerospace company, including two operating divisions, Semiconductors and Navigational Systems divisions. Condensed divisional income statements, which involve no intracompany transfers and include a breakdown of expenses into variable and fixed components, are as follows:

Exoplex Industries Inc.
Divisional Income Statements
For the Year Ended December 31, 2016

	Semiconductors Division	Navigational Systems Division	Total
Sales:			
2,240 units @ $396 per unit	$887,040		$ 887,040
3,675 units @ $590 per unit		$2,168,250	2,168,250
	$887,040	$2,168,250	$3,055,290
Expenses:			
Variable:			
2,240 units @ $232 per unit	$519,680		$ 519,680
3,675 units @ $472* per unit		$1,734,600	1,734,600
Fixed	220,000	325,000	545,000
Total expenses	$739,680	$2,059,600	$2,799,280
Income from operations	$147,360	$ 108,650	$ 256,010

*$432 of the $472 per unit represents materials costs, and the remaining $40 per unit represents other variable conversion expenses incurred within the Navigational Systems Division.

The Semiconductors Division is presently producing 2,240 units out of a total capacity of 2,820 units. Materials used in producing the Navigational Systems Division's product are currently purchased from outside suppliers at a price of $432 per unit. The

(Continued)

Semiconductors Division is able to produce the components used by the Navigational Systems Division. Except for the possible transfer of materials between divisions, no changes are expected in sales and expenses.

Instructions

1. Would the market price of $432 per unit be an appropriate transfer price for Exoplex Industries Inc.? Explain.
2. If the Navigational Systems Division purchases 580 units from the Semiconductors Division, rather than externally, at a negotiated transfer price of $310 per unit, how much would the income from operations of each division and total company income from operations increase?
3. Prepare condensed divisional income statements for Exoplex Industries Inc. based on the data in part (2).
4. If a transfer price of $340 per unit is negotiated, how much would the income from operations of each division and total company income from operations increase?
5. a. What is the range of possible negotiated transfer prices that would be acceptable for Exoplex Industries Inc.?
   b. Assuming that the managers of the two divisions cannot agree on a transfer price, what price would you suggest as the transfer price?

Cases & Projects

CP 8-1 Ethics and professional conduct in business

Rambotix Company has two divisions, the Semiconductor Division and the X-ray Division. The X-ray Division may purchase semiconductors from the Semiconductor Division or from outside suppliers. The Semiconductor Division sells semiconductor products both internally and externally. The market price for semiconductors is $100 per 100 semiconductors. Dave Bryant is the controller of the X-ray Division, and Howard Hillman is the controller of the Semiconductor Division. The following conversation took place between Dave and Howard:

Dave: I hear you are having problems selling semiconductors out of your division. Maybe I can help.

Howard: You've got that right. We're producing and selling at about 90% of our capacity to outsiders. Last year we were selling 100% of capacity. Would it be possible for your division to pick up some of our excess capacity? After all, we are part of the same company.

Dave: What kind of price could you give me?

Howard: Well, you know as well as I that we are under strict profit responsibility in our divisions, so I would expect to get market price, $100 for 100 semiconductors.

Dave: I'm not so sure we can swing that. I was expecting a price break from a "sister" division.

Howard: Hey, I can only take this "sister" stuff so far. If I give you a price break, our profits will fall from last year's levels. I don't think I could explain that. I'm sorry, but I must remain firm—market price. After all, it's only fair—that's what you would have to pay from an external supplier.

Dave: Fair or not, I think we'll pass. Sorry we couldn't have helped.

Was Dave behaving ethically by trying to force the Semiconductor Division into a price break? Comment on Howard's reactions.

CP 8-2 Service department charges

The Customer Service Department of Door Industries Inc. asked the Publications Department to prepare a brochure for its training program. The Publications Department delivered the brochures and charged the Customer Service Department a rate that was 25% higher than could be obtained from an outside printing company. The policy of the company required the Customer Service Department to use the internal publications group for brochures. The Publications Department claimed that it had a drop in demand for its services during the fiscal year, so it had to charge higher prices in order to recover its payroll and fixed costs.

Should the cost of the brochure be transferred to the Customer Service Department in order to hold the Customer Service Department head accountable for the cost of the brochure? What changes in policy would you recommend?

CP 8-3 Evaluating divisional performance

The three divisions of Yummy Foods are Snack Goods, Cereal, and Frozen Foods. The divisions are structured as investment centers. The following responsibility reports were prepared for the three divisions for the prior year:

	Snack Goods	Cereal	Frozen Foods
Revenues	$2,200,000	$2,520,000	$2,100,000
Operating expenses	1,366,600	1,122,000	976,800
Income from operations before service department charges	$ 833,400	$1,398,000	$1,123,200
Service department charges:			
Promotion	$ 300,000	$ 600,000	$ 468,000
Legal	137,400	243,600	235,200
Total service department charges	$ 437,400	$ 843,600	$ 703,200
Income from operations	$ 396,000	$ 554,400	$ 420,000
Invested assets	$2,000,000	$1,680,000	$1,750,000

1. Which division is making the best use of invested assets and should be given priority for future capital investments?
2. Assuming that the minimum acceptable rate of return on new projects is 19%, would all investments that produce a return in excess of 19% be accepted by the divisions?
3. Can you identify opportunities for improving the company's financial performance?

CP 8-4 Evaluating division performance over time

The Norsk Division of Gridiron Concepts Inc. has been experiencing revenue and profit growth during the years 2014–2016. The divisional income statements follow:

Gridiron Concepts Inc.
Divisional Income Statements, Norsk Division
For the Years Ended December 31, 2014–2016

	2014	2015	2016
Sales	$1,470,000	$2,100,000	$2,450,000
Cost of goods sold	1,064,000	1,498,000	1,680,000
Gross profit	$ 406,000	$ 602,000	$ 770,000
Operating expenses	185,500	224,000	231,000
Income from operations	$ 220,500	$ 378,000	$ 539,000

Assume that there are no charges from service departments. The vice president of the division, Tom Yang, is proud of his division's performance over the last three years. The president of Gridiron Concepts Inc., Anna Evans, is discussing the division's performance with Tom, as follows:

Tom: As you can see, we've had a successful three years in the Norsk Division.

Anna: I'm not too sure.

Tom: What do you mean? Look at our results. Our income from operations has more than doubled, while our profit margins are improving.

Anna: I am looking at your results. However, your income statements fail to include one very important piece of information, namely, the invested assets. You have been investing a great deal of assets into the division. You had $735,000 in invested assets in 2014, $1,500,000 in 2015, and $3,500,000 in 2016.

Tom: You are right. I've needed the assets in order to upgrade our technologies and expand our operations. The additional assets are one reason we have been able to grow and improve our profit margins. I don't see that this is a problem.

Anna: The problem is that we must maintain a 15% rate of return on invested assets.

(Continued)

1. Determine the profit margins for the Norsk Division for 2014–2016.
2. Compute the investment turnover for the Norsk Division for 2014–2016. Round to two decimal places.
3. Compute the rate of return on investment for the Norsk Division for 2014–2016.
4. Evaluate the division's performance over the 2014–2016 time period. Why was Anna concerned about the performance?

CP 8-5 Evaluating division performance

Last Resort Industries Inc. is a privately held diversified company with five separate divisions organized as investment centers. A condensed income statement for the Specialty Products Division for the past year, assuming no service department charges, is as follows:

Last Resort Industries Inc.—Specialty Products Division
Income Statement
For the Year Ended December 31, 2015

Sales	$32,400,000
Cost of goods sold	24,300,000
Gross profit	$ 8,100,000
Operating expenses	3,240,000
Income from operations	$ 4,860,000
Invested assets	$27,000,000

The manager of the Specialty Products Division was recently presented with the opportunity to add an additional product line, which would require invested assets of $14,400,000. A projected income statement for the new product line is as follows:

New Product Line
Projected Income Statement
For the Year Ended December 31, 2016

Sales	$12,960,000
Cost of goods sold	7,500,000
Gross profit	$ 5,460,000
Operating expenses	3,127,200
Income from operations	$ 2,332,800

The Specialty Products Division currently has $27,000,000 in invested assets, and Last Resort Industries Inc.'s overall rate of return on investment, including all divisions, is 10%. Each division manager is evaluated on the basis of divisional rate of return on investment. A bonus is paid, in $8,000 increments, for each whole percentage point that the division's rate of return on investment exceeds the company average.

The president is concerned that the manager of the Specialty Products Division rejected the addition of the new product line, even though all estimates indicated that the product line would be profitable and would increase overall company income. You have been asked to analyze the possible reasons why the Specialty Products Division manager rejected the new product line.

1. Determine the rate of return on investment for the Specialty Products Division for the past year.
2. Determine the Specialty Products Division manager's bonus for the past year.
3. Determine the estimated rate of return on investment for the new product line. Round whole percents to one decimal place and investment turnover to two decimal places.
4. Why might the manager of the Specialty Products Division decide to reject the new product line? Support your answer by determining the projected rate of return on investment for 2016, assuming that the new product line was launched in the Specialty Products Division, and 2016 actual operating results were similar to those of 2015.
5. Can you suggest an alternative performance measure for motivating division managers to accept new investment opportunities that would increase the overall company income and rate of return on investment?

CHAPTER 9

Differential Analysis and Product Pricing

Facebook

Many of the decisions that you make depend on comparing the estimated costs of alternatives. The payoff from such comparisons is described in the following report from a University of Michigan study:

Richard Nisbett and two colleagues quizzed Michigan faculty members and university seniors on such questions as how often they walk out on a bad movie, refuse to finish a bad meal, start over on a weak term paper, or abandon a research project that no longer looks promising. They believe that people who cut their losses this way are following sound economic rules: calculating the net benefits of alternative courses of action, writing off past costs that can't be recovered, and weighing the opportunity to use future time and effort more profitably elsewhere.

Among students, those who have learned to use cost-benefit analysis frequently are apt to have far better grades than their Scholastic Aptitude Test scores would have predicted. Again, the more economics courses the students have, the more likely they are to apply cost-benefit analysis outside the classroom.

Dr. Nisbett concedes that for many Americans, cost-benefit rules often appear to conflict with such traditional principles as "never give up" and "waste not, want not."

Managers must also evaluate the costs and benefits of alternative actions. **Facebook**, the largest social networking site in the world, was cofounded by Mark Zuckerberg in 2004. Since then, it has grown to more than 1 billion users and made Zuckerberg a multibillionaire.

Facebook has plans to grow to well over 1 billion users worldwide. Such growth involves decisions about where to expand. For example, expanding the site to new languages and countries involves software programming, marketing, and computer hardware costs. The benefits include adding new users to Facebook.

Analysis of the benefits and costs might lead Facebook to expand in some languages before others. For example, such an analysis might lead Facebook to expand in Swedish before it expands in Tok Pisin (the language of Papua New Guinea).

In this chapter, differential analysis, which reports the effects of decisions on total revenues and costs, is discussed. Practical approaches to setting product prices are also described and illustrated. Finally, how production bottlenecks influence pricing and other decisions is also discussed.

Source: Alan L. Otten, "Economic Perspective Produces Steady Yields," from People Patterns, *The Wall Street Journal*, March 31,1992, p. B1.

Learning Objectives

After studying this chapter, you should be able to: *Example Exercises*

OBJ 1	**Prepare differential analysis reports for a variety of managerial decisions.**	
	Differential Analysis	
	Lease or Sell	EE 9-1
	Discontinue a Segment or Product	EE 9-2
	Make or Buy	EE 9-3
	Replace Equipment	EE 9-4
	Process or Sell	EE 9-5
	Accept Business at a Special Price	EE 9-6
OBJ 2	**Determine the selling price of a product, using the product cost concept.**	
	Setting Normal Product Selling Prices	
	Product Cost Concept	EE 9-7
	Target Costing	
OBJ 3	**Compute the relative profitability of products in bottleneck production processes.**	
	Production Bottlenecks	EE 9-8

At a Glance 9 Page 387

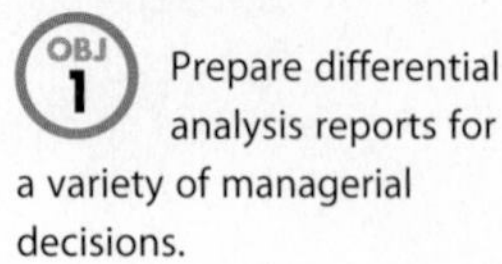
Prepare differential analysis reports for a variety of managerial decisions.

Differential Analysis

Managerial decision making involves choosing between alternative courses of action. Although the managerial decision-making process varies by the type of decision, it normally involves the following steps:

- Step 1. Identify the objective of the decision, which is normally maximizing income.
- Step 2. Identify alternative courses of action.
- Step 3. Gather information and perform a differential analysis.
- Step 4. Make a decision.
- Step 5. Review, analyze, and assess the results of the decision.

To illustrate, assume Bryant Restaurants Inc. is deciding whether to replace some of its customer seating (tables) with a salad bar. The differential analysis decision-making process is as follows.

Step 1 *Identify the objective of the decision.*
Bryant Restaurants' objective is to increase its income.

Step 2 *Identify alternative courses of action.*
The alternative courses of action are:

1. Use floor space for existing tables.
2. Replace the tables with a salad bar.

Step 3 *Gather information and perform a differential analysis.*
The following relevant data have been gathered:

	Tables (Alternative 1)	Salad Bar (Alternative 2)
Revenues	$100,000	$120,000
Costs	60,000	65,000
Income (loss)	$ 40,000	$ 55,000

The preceding information is used to perform differential analysis. **Differential analysis**, sometimes called *incremental analysis*, analyzes differential revenues and costs in order to determine the differential impact on income of two alternative courses of action.

Differential revenue is the amount of increase or decrease in revenue that is expected from a course of action compared to an alternative. **Differential cost** is the amount of increase or decrease in cost that is expected from a course of action as compared to an alternative. **Differential income (loss)** is the difference between the differential revenue and differential costs. Differential income indicates that a decision is expected to increase income, while a differential loss indicates the decision is expected to decrease income.

To illustrate, the differential analysis as of July 11 of the current year for Bryant Restaurants is shown in Exhibit 1.

EXHIBIT 1

Differential Analysis—Bryant Restaurants

Differential Analysis
Tables (Alternative 1) or Salad Bar (Alternative 2)
July 11

	Tables (Alternative 1)	Salad Bar (Alternative 2)	Differential Effect on Income (Alternative 2)
Revenues	$100,000	$120,000	$20,000
Costs	−60,000	−65,000	−5,000
Income (loss)	$ 40,000	$ 55,000	$15,000

The differential analysis is prepared in three columns, where positive amounts indicate the effect is to increase income and negative amounts indicate the effect is to decrease income. The first column is the revenues, costs, and income for maintaining floor space for tables (Alternative 1). The second column is the revenues, costs, and income for using that floor space for a salad bar (Alternative 2). The third column is the difference between the revenue, costs, and income of one alternative over the other.

In Exhibit 1, the salad bar is being considered over retaining the existing tables. Thus, Column 3 in Exhibit 1 is expressed in terms of Alternative 2 (salad bar) over Alternative 1 (tables).

In Exhibit 1, the differential revenue of a salad bar over tables is $20,000 ($120,000 – $100,000). Because the increased revenue would increase income, it is entered as a positive $20,000 in the Differential Effect on Income column. The differential cost of a salad bar over tables is $5,000 ($65,000 – $60,000). Because the increased costs will decrease income, it is entered as a negative $5,000 in the Differential Effect on Income column.

The differential income (loss) of a salad bar over tables of $15,000 is determined by subtracting the differential costs from the differential revenues in the Differential Effect on Income column. Thus, installing a salad bar increases income by $15,000.

The preceding differential revenue, costs, and income can also be determined using the following formulas:

Differential Revenue = Revenue (Alt. 2) – Revenue (Alt. 1)
= $120,000 – $100,000 = $20,000

Differential Costs = Costs (Alt. 2) – Costs (Alt. 1)
= –$65,000 – (–$60,000) = –$5,000

Differential Income (Loss) = Income (Alt. 2) – Income (Alt. 1)
= $55,000 – $40,000 = $15,000

Step 4 *Make a decision.*
Based upon the differential analysis report shown in Exhibit 1, Bryant Restaurants should decide to replace some of its tables with a salad bar. Doing so will increase its income by $15,000.

Step 5 *Review, analyze, and assess the results of the decision.*
Over time, Bryant Restaurants' decision should be reviewed based upon actual revenues and costs. If the actual revenues and costs differ significantly from those gathered in Step 3, another differential analysis might be necessary to verify that the correct decision was made.

In this chapter, differential analysis is illustrated for the following common decisions:

- Leasing or selling equipment
- Discontinuing an unprofitable segment
- Manufacturing or purchasing a needed part
- Replacing fixed assets
- Selling a product or processing further
- Accepting additional business at a special price

Lease or Sell

Management may lease or sell a piece of equipment that is no longer needed. This may occur when a company changes its manufacturing process and can no longer use the equipment in the manufacturing process. In making a decision, differential analysis can be used.

To illustrate, assume that on June 22 of the current year, Marcus Company is considering leasing or disposing of the following equipment:

Cost of equipment	$200,000
Less accumulated depreciation	120,000
Book value	$ 80,000
Lease (Alternative 1):	
Total revenue for five-year lease	$160,000
Total estimated repair, insurance, and property tax expenses during life of lease	35,000
Residual value at end of fifth year of lease	0
Sell (Alternative 2):	
Sales price	$100,000
Commission on sales	6%

Exhibit 2 shows the differential analysis of whether to lease (Alternative 1) or sell (Alternative 2) the equipment.

EXHIBIT 2

Differential Analysis—Lease or Sell Equipment

Differential Analysis
Lease Equipment (Alternative 1) or Sell Equipment (Alternative 2)
June 22

	Lease Equipment (Alternative 1)	Sell Equipment (Alternative 2)	Differential Effect on Income (Alternative 2)
Revenues	$160,000	$100,000	−$60,000
Costs	−35,000	−6,000	29,000
Income (loss)	$125,000	$ 94,000	−$31,000

If the equipment is sold, differential revenues will decrease by $60,000, differential costs will decrease by $29,000, and the differential effect on income is a decrease of $31,000. Thus, the decision should be to lease the equipment.

Exhibit 2 includes only the differential revenues and differential costs associated with the lease-or-sell decision. The $80,000 book value ($200,000 – $120,000) of the equipment is a *sunk cost* and is not considered in the differential analysis. **Sunk costs** are costs that have been incurred in the past, cannot be recouped, and are not relevant to future decisions. That is, the $80,000 is not affected regardless of which decision is made. For example, if the $80,000 were included in Exhibit 2, the costs for each alternative would both increase by $80,000, but the differential effect on income of –$31,000 would remain unchanged.

Have you ever walked out on a bad movie? The cost of the ticket is a sunk cost and, thus, irrelevant to the decision to walk out early.

To simplify, the following factors were not considered in Exhibit 2:

- Differential revenue from investing funds
- Differential income tax

Differential revenue, such as interest revenue, could arise from investing the cash created by the two alternatives. Differential income tax could also arise from differences in income. These factors are discussed in Chapter 10.

Example Exercise 9-1 Lease or Sell

Casper Company owns office space with a cost of $100,000 and accumulated depreciation of $30,000 that can be sold for $150,000, less a 6% broker commission. Alternatively, the office space can be leased by Casper Company for 10 years for a total of $170,000, at the end of which there is no residual value. In addition, repair, insurance, and property tax that would be incurred by Casper Company on the rented office space would total $24,000 over the 10 years. Prepare a differential analysis on May 30, as to whether Casper Company should lease (Alternative 1) or sell (Alternative 2) the office space.

Follow My Example 9-1

Differential Analysis
Lease Office Space (Alternative 1) or Sell Office Space (Alternative 2)
May 30

	Lease Office Space (Alternative 1)	Sell Office Space (Alternative 2)	Differential Effect on Income (Alternative 2)
Revenues	$170,000	$150,000	–$20,000
Costs	–24,000	–9,000*	15,000
Income (loss)	$146,000	$141,000	–$ 5,000

*$150,000 × 6%

Casper Company should lease the office space.

Practice Exercises: PE 9-1A, PE 9-1B

Discontinue a Segment or Product

A product, department, branch, territory, or other segment of a business may be generating losses. As a result, management may consider discontinuing (eliminating) the product or segment. In such cases, it may be erroneously assumed that the total company income will increase by eliminating the operating loss.

Discontinuing the product or segment usually eliminates all of the product's or segment's variable costs. Such costs include direct materials, direct labor, variable factory overhead, and sales commissions. However, fixed costs such as depreciation, insurance, and property taxes may not be eliminated. Thus, it is possible for total company income to decrease rather than increase if the unprofitable product or segment is discontinued.

To illustrate, the income statement for Battle Creek Cereal Co. is shown in Exhibit 3. As shown in Exhibit 3, Bran Flakes incurred an operating loss of $11,000. Because Bran Flakes has incurred annual losses for several years, management is considering discontinuing it.

EXHIBIT 3

Income (Loss) by Product

Battle Creek Cereal Co.
Condensed Income Statement
For the Year Ended August 31, 2016

	Corn Flakes	Toasted Oats	Bran Flakes	Total Company
Sales	$500,000	$400,000	$100,000	$1,000,000
Cost of goods sold:				
Variable costs	$220,000	$200,000	$ 60,000	$ 480,000
Fixed costs	120,000	80,000	20,000	220,000
Total cost of goods sold	$340,000	$280,000	$ 80,000	$ 700,000
Gross profit	$160,000	$120,000	$ 20,000	$ 300,000
Operating expenses:				
Variable expenses	$ 95,000	$ 60,000	$ 25,000	$ 180,000
Fixed expenses	25,000	20,000	6,000	51,000
Total operating expenses	$120,000	$ 80,000	$ 31,000	$ 231,000
Income (loss) from operations	$ 40,000	$ 40,000	$ (11,000)	$ 69,000

However, the differential analysis dated September 29, 2016, in Exhibit 4 indicates that discontinuing Bran Flakes (Alternative 2) actually decreases operating income by $15,000, even though it incurs a net loss of $11,000. This is because discontinuing Bran Flakes has no effect on fixed costs and expenses.

Exhibit 4 only considers the short-term (one-year) effects of discontinuing Bran Flakes. When discontinuing a product or segment, long-term effects should also be considered. For example, employee morale and productivity might suffer if employees have to be laid off or relocated.

EXHIBIT 4

Differential Analysis—Continue or Discontinue Bran Flakes

Differential Analysis
Continue Bran Flakes (Alternative 1) or Discontinue Bran Flakes (Alternative 2)
September 29, 2016

	Continue Bran Flakes (Alternative 1)	Discontinue Bran Flakes (Alternative 2)	Differential Effect on Income (Alternative 2)
Revenues	$100,000	$ 0	–$100,000
Costs:			
Variable	–$ 85,000	$ 0	$ 85,000
Fixed	–26,000	–26,000	0
Total costs	–$111,000	–$26,000	$ 85,000
Income (loss)	–$ 11,000	–$26,000	–$ 15,000

Example Exercise 9-2 Discontinue a Segment

Product K has revenue of $65,000, variable cost of goods sold of $50,000, variable selling expenses of $12,000, and fixed costs of $25,000, creating a loss from operations of $22,000. Prepare a differential analysis dated February 22 to determine if Product K should be continued (Alternative 1) or discontinued (Alternative 2), assuming fixed costs are unaffected by the decision.

Follow My Example 9-2

Differential Analysis
Continue K (Alternative 1) or Discontinue K (Alternative 2)
February 22

	Continue Product K (Alternative 1)	Discontinue Product K (Alternative 2)	Differential Effect on Income (Alternative 2)
Revenues	$65,000	$ 0	–$65,000
Costs:			
Variable	–$62,000*	$ 0	$62,000
Fixed	–25,000	–25,000	0
Total costs	–$87,000	–$25,000	$62,000
Income (loss)	–$22,000	–$25,000	–$ 3,000

*$50,000 + $12,000

Product K should be continued.

Practice Exercises: PE 9-2A, PE 9-2B

Make or Buy

Companies often manufacture products made up of components that are assembled into a final product. For example, an automobile manufacturer assembles tires, radios, motors, interior seats, transmissions, and other parts into a finished automobile. In such cases, the manufacturer must decide whether to make a part or purchase it from a supplier.

Differential analysis can be used to decide whether to make or buy a part. The analysis is similar whether management is considering making a part that is currently being purchased or purchasing a part that is currently being made.

To illustrate, assume that an automobile manufacturer has been purchasing instrument panels for $240 a unit. The factory is currently operating at 80% of capacity, and no major increase in production is expected in the near future. The cost per unit of manufacturing an instrument panel internally is estimated on February 15 as follows:

Direct materials	$ 80
Direct labor	80
Variable factory overhead	52
Fixed factory overhead	68
Total cost per unit	$280

If the make price of $280 is simply compared with the buy price of $240, the decision is to buy the instrument panel. However, if unused capacity could be used in manufacturing the part, only the variable factory overhead costs would increase.

The differential analysis for this make (Alternative 1) or buy (Alternative 2) decision is shown in Exhibit 5. The fixed factory overhead cannot be eliminated by purchasing the panels. Thus, both alternatives include the fixed factory overhead. The differential analysis indicates there is a loss of $28 per unit from buying the instrument panels. Thus, the instrument panels should be manufactured.

EXHIBIT 5

Differential Analysis—Make or Buy Instrument Panels

Differential Analysis Make Panels (Alternative 1) or Buy Panels (Alternative 2) February 15	Make Panels (Alternative 1)	Buy Panels (Alternative 2)	Differential Effect on Income (Alternative 2)
Unit costs:			
Purchase price	$ 0	-$240	-$240
Direct materials	-80	0	80
Direct labor	-80	0	80
Variable factory overhead	-52	0	52
Fixed factory overhead	-68	-68	0
Income (loss)	-$280	-$308	-$ 28

Other factors should also be considered in the analysis. For example, productive capacity used to make the instrument panel would not be available for other production. The decision may also affect the future business relationship with the instrument panel supplier. For example, if the supplier provides other parts, the company's decision to make instrument panels might jeopardize the timely delivery of other parts.

Example Exercise 9-3 Make or Buy

A company manufactures a subcomponent of an assembly for $80 per unit, including fixed costs of $25 per unit. A proposal is offered to purchase the subcomponent from an outside source for $60 per unit, plus $5 per unit freight. Prepare a differential analysis dated November 2, to determine whether the company should make (Alternative 1) or buy (Alternative 2) the subcomponent, assuming fixed costs are unaffected by the decision.

Follow My Example 9-3

Differential Analysis Make Subcomponent (Alternative 1) or Buy Subcomponent (Alternative 2) November 2	Make Subcomponent (Alternative 1)	Buy Subcomponent (Alternative 2)	Differential Effect on Income (Alternative 2)
Unit costs:			
Purchase price	$ 0	-$60	-$60
Freight	0	-5	-5
Variable costs ($80 – $25)	-55	0	55
Fixed factory overhead	-25	-25	0
Income (loss)	-$80	-$90	-$10

The company should make the subcomponent.

Practice Exercises: PE 9-3A, PE 9-3B

Replace Equipment

The usefulness of a fixed asset may decrease before it is worn out. For example, old equipment may no longer be as efficient as new equipment.

Differential analysis can be used for decisions to replace fixed assets such as equipment and machinery. The analysis normally focuses on the costs of continuing to use the old equipment versus replacing the equipment. The book value of the old equipment is a sunk cost and, thus, is irrelevant.

To illustrate, assume that on November 28 of the current year, a business is considering replacing an old machine with a new machine:

Old Machine	
Book value	$100,000
Estimated annual variable manufacturing costs	225,000
Estimated selling price	25,000
Estimated remaining useful life	5 years
New Machine	
Purchase price of new machine	$250,000
Estimated annual variable manufacturing costs	150,000
Estimated residual value	0
Estimated useful life	5 years

The differential analysis for whether to continue with the old machine (Alternative 1) or replace the old machine with a new machine (Alternative 2) is shown in Exhibit 6.

EXHIBIT 6

Differential Analysis—Continue with or Replace Old Equipment

Differential Analysis
Continue with Old Machine (Alternative 1) or Replace Old Machine (Alternative 2)
November 28

	Continue with Old Machine (Alternative 1)	Replace Old Machine (Alternative 2)	Differential Effect on Income (Alternative 2)
Revenues:			
Proceeds from sale of old machine	$ 0	$ 25,000	$ 25,000
Costs:			
Purchase price	$ 0	–$ 250,000	–$250,000
Variable manufacturing costs (5 years)	–1,125,000	–750,000	375,000
Total costs	–$1,125,000	–$1,000,000	$125,000
Income (loss)	–$1,125,000	–$ 975,000	$150,000

As shown in Exhibit 6, there is five-year differential effect on income of $150,000 (or $30,000 per year) from replacing the machine. Thus, the decision should be to purchase the new machine and sell the old machine.

Other factors are often important in equipment replacement decisions. For example, differences between the remaining useful life of the old equipment and the estimated life of the new equipment could exist. In addition, the new equipment might improve the overall quality of the product and, thus, increase sales.

The time value of money and other uses for the cash needed to purchase the new equipment could also affect the decision to replace equipment.[1] The revenue that is forgone from an alternative use of an asset, such as cash, is called an **opportunity cost**. Although the opportunity cost is not recorded in the accounting records, it is useful in analyzing alternative courses of action.

[1] The time value of money in purchasing equipment (capital assets) is discussed in Chapter 10.

Example Exercise 9-4 Replace Equipment

A machine with a book value of $32,000 has an estimated four-year life. A proposal is offered to sell the old machine for $10,000 and replace it with a new machine at a cost of $45,000. The new machine has a four-year life with no residual value. The new machine would reduce annual direct labor costs from $33,000 to $22,000. Prepare a differential analysis dated October 7 on whether to continue with the old machine (Alternative 1) or replace the old machine (Alternative 2).

Follow My Example 9-4

Differential Analysis
Continue with Old Machine (Alternative 1) or Replace Old Machine (Alternative 2)
October 7

	Continue with Old Machine (Alternative 1)	Replace Old Machine (Alternative 2)	Differential Effect on Income (Alternative 2)
Revenues:			
Proceeds from sale of old machine	$ 0	$ 10,000	$10,000
Costs:			
Purchase price	$ 0	-$ 45,000	-$45,000
Direct labor (4 years)	-132,000*	-88,000**	44,000
Total costs	-$132,000	-$133,000	-$ 1,000
Total income (loss)	-$132,000	-$123,000	$ 9,000

*$33,000 × 4 years
**$22,000 × 4 years

The old machine should be sold and replaced with the new machine.

Practice Exercises: PE 9-4A, PE 9-4B

Process or Sell

During manufacturing, a product normally progresses through various stages or processes. In some cases, a product can be sold at an intermediate stage of production, or it can be processed further and then sold.

Differential analysis can be used to decide whether to sell a product at an intermediate stage or to process it further. In doing so, the differential revenues and costs from further processing are compared. The costs of producing the intermediate product do not change, regardless of whether the intermediate product is sold or processed further.

To illustrate, assume that a business produces kerosene as an intermediate product as follows:

Kerosene:	
Batch size	4,000 gallons
Cost of producing kerosene	$2,400 per batch
Selling price	$2.50 per gallon

The kerosene can be processed further to yield gasoline as follows:

Gasoline:	
Input batch size	4,000 gallons
Less evaporation (20%)	800 (4,000 × 20%)
Output batch size	3,200 gallons
Cost of producing gasoline	$3,050 per batch
Selling price	$3.50 per gallon

Exhibit 7 shows the differential analysis dated October 1 for whether to sell kerosene (Alternative 1) or process it further into gasoline (Alternative 2).

As shown in Exhibit 7, there is additional income of $550 per batch from further processing the kerosene into gasoline. Therefore, the decision should be to process the kerosene further into gasoline.

EXHIBIT 7

Differential Analysis—Sell Kerosene or Process Further into Gasoline

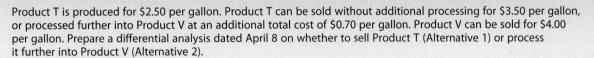

Differential Analysis
Sell Kerosene (Alternative 1) or Process Further into Gasoline (Alternative 2)
October 1

	Sell Kerosene (Alternative 1)	Process Further into Gasoline (Alternative 2)	Differential Effect on Income (Alternative 2)
Revenues	$10,000*	$11,200**	$1,200
Costs	–2,400	–3,050	–650
Income (loss)	$ 7,600	$ 8,150	$ 550

*4,000 gallons × $2.50
**(4,000 gallons – 800 gallons) × $3.50

Example Exercise 9-5 Process or Sell

Product T is produced for $2.50 per gallon. Product T can be sold without additional processing for $3.50 per gallon, or processed further into Product V at an additional total cost of $0.70 per gallon. Product V can be sold for $4.00 per gallon. Prepare a differential analysis dated April 8 on whether to sell Product T (Alternative 1) or process it further into Product V (Alternative 2).

Follow My Example 9-5

Differential Analysis
Sell Product T (Alternative 1) or Process Further into Product V (Alternative 2)
April 8

	Sell Product T (Alternative 1)	Process Further into Product V (Alternative 2)	Differential Effect on Income (Alternative 2)
Revenues, per unit	$3.50	$4.00	$0.50
Costs, per unit	–2.50	–3.20*	–0.70
Income (loss), per unit	$1.00	$0.80	–$0.20

*$2.50 + $0.70

The decision should be to sell Product T.

Practice Exercises: PE 9-5A, PE 9-5B

Accept Business at a Special Price

A company may be offered the opportunity to sell its products at prices other than normal prices. For example, an exporter may offer to sell a company's products overseas at special discount prices.

Differential analysis can be used to decide whether to accept additional business at a special price. The differential revenue from accepting the additional business is compared to the differential costs of producing and delivering the product to the customer.

The differential costs of accepting additional business depend on whether the company is operating at less than capacity. If the company is operating at less than full capacity, then the additional production does not increase fixed manufacturing costs. However, selling and administrative expenses may change because of the additional business.

To illustrate, assume that B-Ball Inc. manufactures basketballs as follows:

Monthly productive capacity	12,500 basketballs
Current monthly sales	10,000 basketballs
Normal (domestic) selling price	$30.00 per basketball
Manufacturing costs:	
Variable costs	$12.50 per basketball
Fixed costs	7.50
Total	$20.00 per basketball

On March 10 of the current year, B-Ball Inc. received an offer from an exporter for 5,000 basketballs at $18 each. Production can be spread over three months without interfering with normal production or incurring overtime costs. Pricing policies in the domestic market will not be affected.

As shown in Exhibit 8, a differential analysis on whether to reject the order (Alternative 1) or accept the order (Alternative 2) shows that the special order should be accepted. The special business is accepted even though the sales price of $18 per unit is less than the manufacturing cost of $20 per unit because the fixed costs are not affected by the decision and are, thus, omitted from the analysis.

EXHIBIT 8

Differential Analysis—Accept Business at a Special Price

Differential Analysis
Reject Order (Alternative 1) or Accept Order (Alternative 2)
March 10

	Reject Order (Alternative 1)	Accept Order (Alternative 2)	Differential Effect on Income (Alternative 2)
Revenues	$0	$90,000*	$90,000
Costs:			
Variable manufacturing costs	0	−62,500**	−62,500
Income (loss)	$0	$27,500	$27,500

*5,000 units × $18
**5,000 units × $12.50 variable cost per unit

Proposals to sell products at special prices often require additional considerations. For example, special prices in one geographic area may result in price reductions in other areas, with the result that total company sales revenues decrease. Manufacturers must also conform to the Robinson-Patman Act, which prohibits price discrimination within the United States unless price differences can be justified by different costs.

Business Connection

60% OFF!

Priceline.com Inc. was founded in the late 1990s and has become a successful survivor of the Internet revolution. Priceline offers deep discounts of up to 60% for travel services, such as hotels and travel. How does it work? For hotel services, Priceline has arrangements with hotels to provide deeply discounted rooms. These rooms are resold to customers on Priceline's Web site. Why do hotels provide rooms at such a large discount? If the hotel has unused rooms, the variable cost of an incremental guest is low relative to the fixed cost of the room. Thus, during low occupancy times, any price greater than the variable cost of providing the room can add to the profitability of the hotel. Thus, hotels view Priceline as an additional source of profit from filling unused rooms during low demand periods.

Example Exercise 9-6 Accept Business at Special Price

Product D is normally sold for $4.40 per unit. A special price of $3.60 is offered for the export market. The variable production cost is $3.00 per unit. An additional export tariff of 10% of revenue must be paid for all export products. Assume there is sufficient capacity for the special order. Prepare a differential analysis dated January 14 on whether to reject (Alternative 1) or accept (Alternative 2) the special order.

Follow My Example 9-6

Differential Analysis
Reject Order (Alternative 1) or Accept Order (Alternative 2)
January 14

	Reject Order (Alternative 1)	Accept Order (Alternative 2)	Differential Effect on Income (Alternative 2)
Per unit:			
Revenues	$0	$3.60	$3.60
Costs:			
Variable manufacturing costs	$0	–$3.00	–$3.00
Export tariff	0	–0.36*	–0.36
Total costs	$0	–$3.36	–$3.36
Income (loss)	$0	$0.24	$0.24

*$3.60 × 10%

The special order should be accepted.

Practice Exercises: PE 9-6A, PE 9-6B

Setting Normal Product Selling Prices

OBJ 2 Determine the selling price of a product, using the product cost concept.

The *normal* selling price is the target selling price to be achieved in the long term. The normal selling price must be set high enough to cover all costs and expenses (fixed and variable) and provide a reasonable profit. Otherwise, the business will not survive.

In contrast, in deciding whether to accept additional business at a special price, only differential costs are considered. Any price greater than the differential costs will increase profits in the short term. However, in the long term, products are sold at normal prices rather than special prices.

Managers can use one of two market methods to determine selling price:

- Demand-based concept
- Competition-based concept

The demand-based concept sets the price according to the demand for the product. If there is high demand for the product, then the price is set high. Likewise, if there is a low demand for the product, then the price is set low.

The competition-based concept sets the price according to the price offered by competitors. For example, if a competitor reduces the price, then management adjusts the price to meet the competition. The market-based pricing approaches are discussed in greater detail in marketing courses.

Managers can also use one of three cost-plus methods to determine the selling price:

- Product cost concept
- Total cost concept
- Variable cost concept

The product cost concept is illustrated in this section. The total cost and variable cost concepts are illustrated in the appendix to this chapter.

Service Focus

REVENUE MANAGEMENT

Did you know that it is common to sit next to a person on a flight who paid much more for that seat than you did for yours (or vice versa)? While this may not seem fair, this practice is consistent with a type of differential analysis called revenue management. Revenue management strives to yield the maximum amount of profit from a perishable good. Examples of perishable goods in service include a seat on a flight, a hotel room for a given night, a ticket for a given event, or a cruise ship berth for a given voyage. The service is perishable because, once the date passes, the "product" expires.

Consider **Delta Air Lines**. Delta maximizes the profitability on a given flight by taking into account different customer behaviors and preferences. For example, a business person may pay a very high price for an airline ticket booked one day in advance to attend an emergency meeting. Next to her may be a college student on the same flight who booked two month's in advance at a very low price. The difference in behavior yields a different price. The airline sells early bookings at very favorable prices to fill out the flight. However, late emergency business bookings are priced high because the inventory of seats have diminished and, thus, have become valuable. However, if too many seats remain unoccupied very close to the flight time, the airline may release them at deep discounts to standby passengers to fill the flight. Thus, the flight is filled with different priced seats for different customers, all in attempt to fill the flight as profitably as possible.

Product Cost Concept

Cost-plus methods determine the normal selling price by estimating a cost amount per unit and adding a markup, computed as follows:

Normal Selling Price = Cost Amount per Unit + Markup

Management determines the markup based on the desired profit for the product. The markup should be sufficient to earn the desired profit plus cover any costs and expenses that are not included in the cost amount.

As shown in Exhibit 9, under the **product cost concept**, only the costs of manufacturing the product, termed the *product costs*, are included in the cost amount per unit to which the markup is added. Estimated selling expenses, administrative expenses, and desired profit are included in the markup. The markup per unit is then computed and added to the product cost per unit to determine the normal selling price.

EXHIBIT 9

Product Cost Concept

DESIRED SELLING PRICE
$
MARKUP:
Administrative Expense
+
Selling Expense
+
Desired Profit
$
PRODUCT COST:
Manufacturing Cost

The product cost concept is applied using the following steps:

- Step 1. Estimate the total product costs as follows:

Product costs:	
Direct materials	$XXX
Direct labor	XXX
Factory overhead	XXX
Total product cost	$XXX

- Step 2. Estimate the total selling and administrative expenses.
- Step 3. Divide the total product cost by the number of units expected to be produced and sold to determine the total product cost per unit, computed as follows:

$$\text{Product Cost per Unit} = \frac{\text{Total Product Cost}}{\text{Estimated Units Produced and Sold}}$$

- Step 4. Compute the markup percentage as follows:

$$\text{Markup Percentage} = \frac{\text{Desired Profit} + \text{Total Selling and Administrative Expenses}}{\text{Total Product Cost}}$$

The numerator of the markup percentage is the desired profit plus the total selling and administrative expenses. These expenses must be included in the markup percentage because they are not included in the cost amount to which the markup is added.

The desired profit is normally computed based on a rate of return on assets as follows:

$$\text{Desired Profit} = \text{Desired Rate of Return} \times \text{Total Assets}$$

- Step 5. Determine the markup per unit by multiplying the markup percentage times the product cost per unit as follows:

$$\text{Markup per Unit} = \text{Markup Percentage} \times \text{Product Cost per Unit}$$

- Step 6. Determine the normal selling price by adding the markup per unit to the product cost per unit as follows:

Product cost per unit	$XXX
Markup per unit	XXX
Normal selling price per unit	$XXX

To illustrate, assume the following data for 100,000 calculators that Digital Solutions Inc. expects to produce and sell during the current year:

Manufacturing costs:	
Direct materials ($3.00 × 100,000)	$ 300,000
Direct labor ($10.00 × 100,000)	1,000,000
Factory overhead	200,000
Total manufacturing costs	$1,500,000
Selling and administrative expenses	170,000
Total cost	$1,670,000
Total assets	$800,000
Desired rate of return	20%

The normal selling price of $18.30 is determined under the product cost concept as follows:

- Step 1. Total product cost: $1,500,000
- Step 2. Total selling and administrative expenses: $170,000
- Step 3. Total product cost per unit: $15.00

$$\text{Total Cost per Unit} = \frac{\text{Total Product Cost}}{\text{Estimated Units Produced and Sold}} = \frac{\$1{,}500{,}000}{100{,}000 \text{ units}} = \$15.00 \text{ per unit}$$

- Step 4. Markup percentage: 22%

$$\text{Desired Profit} = \text{Desired Rate of Return} \times \text{Total Assets} = 20\% \times \$800{,}000 = \$160{,}000$$

$$\text{Markup Percentage} = \frac{\text{Desired Profit} + \text{Total Selling and Administrative Expenses}}{\text{Total Product Cost}}$$

$$= \frac{\$160{,}000 + \$170{,}000}{\$1{,}500{,}000} = \frac{\$330{,}000}{\$1{,}500{,}000} = 22\%$$

- Step 5. Markup per unit: $3.30

$$\text{Markup per Unit} = \text{Markup Percentage} \times \text{Product Cost per Unit}$$
$$= 22\% \times \$15.00 = \$3.30 \text{ per unit}$$

- Step 6. Normal selling price: $18.30

Total product cost per unit	$15.00
Markup per unit	3.30
Normal selling price per unit	$18.30

Product cost estimates, rather than actual costs, may be used in computing the markup. Management should be careful, however, when using estimated or standard costs in applying the cost-plus approach. Specifically, estimates should be based on normal (attainable) operating levels and not theoretical (ideal) levels of performance. In product pricing, the use of estimates based on ideal operating performance could lead to setting product prices too low.

Example Exercise 9-7 Product Cost Markup Percentage

Apex Corporation produces and sells Product Z at a total cost of $30 per unit, of which $20 is product cost and $10 is selling and administrative expenses. In addition, the total cost of $30 is made up of $18 variable cost and $12 fixed cost. The desired profit is $3 per unit. Determine the markup percentage on product cost.

Follow My Example 9-7

Markup percentage on product cost: $\frac{\$3 + \$10}{\$20} = 65\%$

Practice Exercises: PE 9-7A, PE 9-7B

Integrity, Objectivity, and Ethics in Business

PRICE FIXING

Federal law prevents companies competing in similar markets from sharing cost and price information, or what is commonly termed "price fixing." For example, the Federal Trade Commission (FTC) brought a suit against **U-Haul** for releasing company-wide memorandums to its managers telling them to encourage competitors to match U-Haul price increases. Commenting on the case, the chairman of the FTC stated, "It's a bedrock principle that you can't conspire with your competitors to fix prices, and shouldn't even try."

Source: Edward Wyatt, "U-Haul to Settle with Trade Agency in Case on Truck Rental Price-Fixing," *The New York Times*, June 10, 2010, p. B3.

Target Costing

Target costing is a method of setting prices that combines market-based pricing with a cost-reduction emphasis. Under target costing, a future selling price is anticipated, using the demand-based or the competition-based concepts. The target cost is then determined by subtracting a desired profit from the expected selling price, computed as follows:

$$\text{Target Cost} = \text{Expected Selling Price} - \text{Desired Profit}$$

Target costing tries to reduce costs as shown in Exhibit 10. The bar at the left in Exhibit 10 shows the actual cost and profit that can be earned during the current period. The bar at the right shows that the market price is expected to decline in the future. The target cost is estimated as the difference between the expected market price and the desired profit.

The target cost is normally less than the current cost. Thus, managers must try to reduce costs from the design and manufacture of the product. The planned cost reduction is sometimes referred to as the cost drift. Costs can be reduced in a variety of ways such as the following:

- Simplifying the design
- Reducing the cost of direct materials
- Reducing the direct labor costs
- Eliminating waste

Target costing is especially useful in highly competitive markets such as the market for personal computers. Such markets require continual product cost reductions to remain competitive.

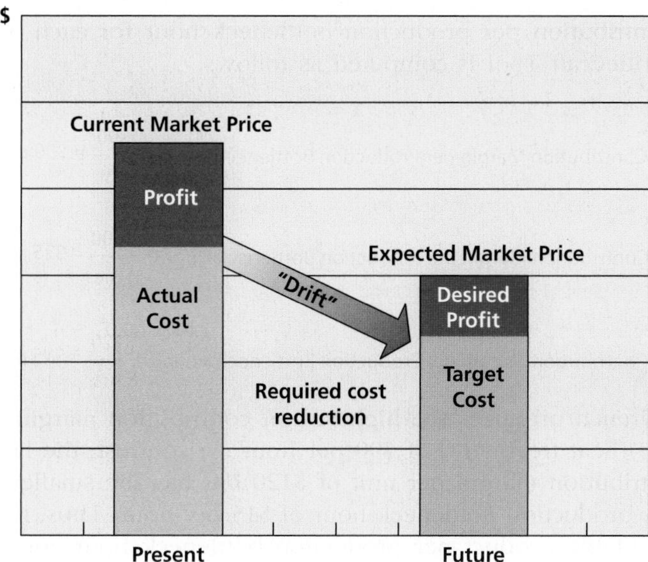

EXHIBIT 10

Target Cost Concept

Production Bottlenecks

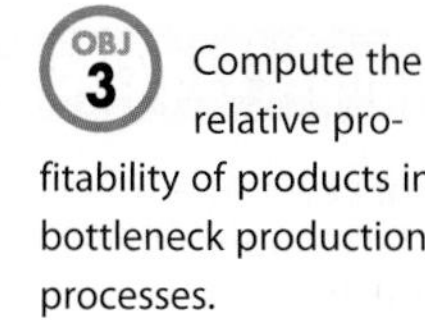

Compute the relative profitability of products in bottleneck production processes.

A **production bottleneck** (or *constraint*) is a point in the manufacturing process where the demand for the company's product exceeds the ability to produce the product. The **theory of constraints (TOC)** is a manufacturing strategy that focuses on reducing the influence of bottlenecks on production processes.

When a company has a production bottleneck in its production process, it should attempt to maximize its profits, subject to the production bottleneck. In doing so, the unit contribution margin of each product per production bottleneck constraint is used.

To illustrate, assume that PrideCraft Tool Company makes three types of wrenches: small, medium, and large. All three products are processed through a heat treatment operation, which hardens the steel tools. PrideCraft Tool's heat treatment process is operating at full capacity and is a production bottleneck. The product unit contribution margin and the number of hours of heat treatment used by each type of wrench are as follows:

	Small Wrench	Medium Wrench	Large Wrench
Unit selling price	$130	$140	$160
Unit variable cost	40	40	40
Unit contribution margin	$ 90	$100	$120
Heat treatment hours per unit	1 hr.	4 hrs.	8 hrs.

The large wrench appears to be the most profitable product because its unit contribution margin of $120 is the greatest. However, the unit contribution margin can be misleading in a production bottleneck operation.

In a production bottleneck operation, the best measure of profitability is the unit contribution margin per production bottleneck constraint. For PrideCraft Tool, the production bottleneck constraint is heat treatment process hours. Therefore, the unit contribution margin per bottleneck constraint is expressed as follows:

$$\text{Unit Contribution Margin per Production Bottleneck Hour} = \frac{\text{Unit Contribution Margin}}{\text{Heat Treatment Hours per Unit}}$$

The unit contribution per production bottleneck hour for each of the wrenches produced by PrideCraft Tool is computed as follows:

Small Wrenches

$$\text{Unit Contribution Margin per Production Bottleneck Hour} = \frac{\$90}{1 \text{ hr.}} = \$90 \text{ per hr.}$$

Medium Wrenches

$$\text{Unit Contribution Margin per Production Bottleneck Hour} = \frac{\$100}{4 \text{ hrs.}} = \$25 \text{ per hr.}$$

Large Wrenches

$$\text{Unit Contribution Margin per Production Bottleneck Hour} = \frac{\$120}{8 \text{ hrs.}} = \$15 \text{ per hr.}$$

The small wrench produces the highest unit contribution margin per production bottleneck hour (heat treatment) of $90 per hour. In contrast, the large wrench has the largest contribution margin per unit of $120 but has the smallest unit contribution margin per production bottleneck hour of $15 per hour. Thus, the small wrench is the most profitable product per production bottleneck hour and is the one that should be emphasized in the market.

Example Exercise 9-8 Bottleneck Profit

Product A has a unit contribution margin of $15. Product B has a unit contribution margin of $20. Product A requires three furnace hours, while Product B requires five furnace hours. Determine the most profitable product, assuming the furnace is a constraint.

Follow My Example 9-8

	Product A	Product B
Unit contribution margin	$15	$20
Furnace hours per unit	÷ 3	÷ 5
Unit contribution margin per production bottleneck hour	$ 5	$ 4

Product A is the most profitable in using bottleneck resources.

Practice Exercises: PE 9-8A, PE 9-8B

APPENDIX

Total and Variable Cost Concepts to Setting Normal Price

Recall from the chapter that cost-plus methods determine the normal selling price by estimating a cost amount per unit and adding a markup, as follows:

Normal Selling Price = Cost Amount per Unit + Markup

Management determines the markup based on the desired profit for the product. The markup should be sufficient to earn the desired profit plus cover any cost and expenses that are not included in the cost amount. The product cost concept was discussed in the chapter, and the total and variable cost concepts are discussed in this appendix.

Total Cost Concept

As shown in Exhibit 11, under the **total cost concept**, manufacturing cost plus the selling and administrative expenses are included in the total cost per unit. The markup per unit is then computed and added to the total cost per unit to determine the normal selling price.

EXHIBIT 11

Total Cost Concept

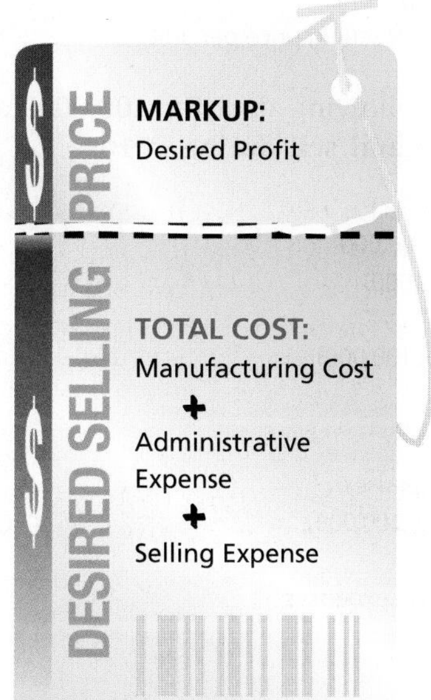

The total cost concept is applied using the following steps:

- Step 1. Estimate the total manufacturing cost as follows:

Manufacturing costs:	
Direct materials	$XXX
Direct labor	XXX
Factory overhead	XXX
Total manufacturing cost	$XXX

- Step 2. Estimate the total selling and administrative expenses.
- Step 3. Estimate the total cost as follows:

Total manufacturing costs	$XXX
Selling and administrative expenses	XXX
Total cost	$XXX

- Step 4. Divide the total cost by the number of units expected to be produced and sold to determine the total cost per unit, as follows:

$$\text{Total Cost per Unit} = \frac{\text{Total Cost}}{\text{Estimated Units Produced and Sold}}$$

- Step 5. Compute the markup percentage as follows:

$$\text{Markup Percentage} = \frac{\text{Desired Profit}}{\text{Total Cost}}$$

The desired profit is normally computed based on a rate of return on assets as follows:

$$\text{Desired Profit} = \text{Desired Rate of Return} \times \text{Total Assets}$$

- Step 6. Determine the markup per unit by multiplying the markup percentage times the total cost per unit as follows:

$$\text{Markup per Unit} = \text{Markup Percentage} \times \text{Total Cost per Unit}$$

- Step 7. Determine the normal selling price by adding the markup per unit to the total cost per unit as follows:

Total cost per unit	$XXX
Markup per unit	XXX
Normal selling price per unit	$XXX

To illustrate, assume the following data for 100,000 calculators that Digital Solutions Inc. expects to produce and sell during 2016:

Manufacturing costs:		
Direct materials ($3.00 × 100,000)		$ 300,000
Direct labor ($10.00 × 100,000)		1,000,000
Factory overhead:		
Variable costs ($1.50 × 100,000)	$150,000	
Fixed costs	50,000	200,000
Total manufacturing cost		$1,500,000
Selling and administrative expenses:		
Variable expenses ($1.50 × 100,000)	$150,000	
Fixed costs	20,000	
Total selling and administrative expenses		170,000
Total cost		$1,670,000
Desired rate of return		20%
Total assets		$ 800,000

Using the total cost concept, the normal selling price of $18.30 is determined as follows:

- Step 1. Total manufacturing cost: $1,500,000
- Step 2. Total selling and administrative expenses: $170,000
- Step 3. Total cost: $1,670,000
- Step 4. Total cost per unit: $16.70

$$\text{Total Cost per Unit} = \frac{\text{Total Cost}}{\text{Estimated Units Produced and Sold}} = \frac{\$1{,}670{,}000}{100{,}000 \text{ units}} = \$16.70 \text{ per unit}$$

- Step 5. Markup percentage: 9.6% (rounded)

$$\text{Desired Profit} = \text{Desired Rate of Return} \times \text{Total Assets} = 20\% \times \$800{,}000 = \$160{,}000$$

$$\text{Markup Percentage} = \frac{\text{Desired Profit}}{\text{Total Cost}} = \frac{\$160{,}000}{\$1{,}670{,}000} = 9.6\% \text{ (rounded)}$$

- Step 6. Markup per unit: $1.60

$$\text{Markup per Unit} = \text{Markup Percentage} \times \text{Total Cost per Unit}$$
$$= 9.6\% \times \$16.70 = \$1.60 \text{ per unit}$$

- Step 7. Normal selling price: $18.30

Total cost per unit	$16.70
Markup per unit	1.60
Normal selling price per unit	$18.30

The ability of the selling price of $18.30 to generate the desired profit of $160,000 is illustrated by the income statement that follows:

Digital Solutions Inc.
Income Statement
For the Year Ended December 31, 2016

Sales (100,000 units × $18.30)		$1,830,000
Expenses:		
Variable (100,000 units × $16.00)	$1,600,000	
Fixed ($50,000 + $20,000)	70,000	1,670,000
Income from operations		$ 160,000

The total cost concept is often used by contractors who sell products to government agencies. This is because in many cases government contractors are required by law to be reimbursed for their products on a total-cost-plus-profit basis.

Variable Cost Concept

As shown in Exhibit 12, under the **variable cost concept**, only variable costs are included in the cost amount per unit to which the markup is added. All variable

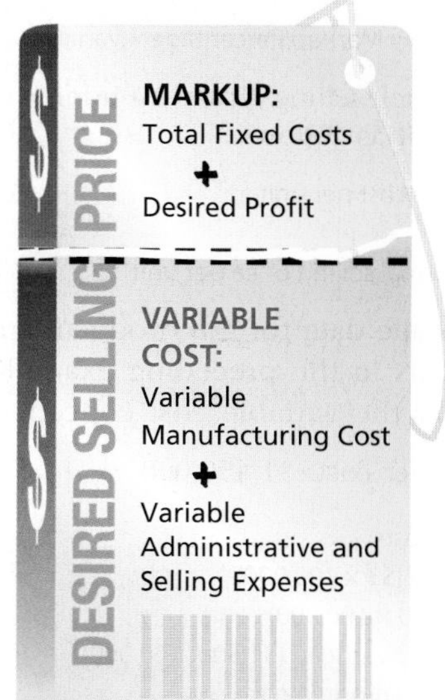

EXHIBIT 12
Variable Cost Concept

manufacturing costs, as well as variable selling and administrative expenses, are included in the cost amount. Fixed manufacturing costs, fixed selling and administrative expenses, and desired profit are included in the markup. The markup per unit is then added to the variable cost per unit to determine the normal selling price.

The variable cost concept is applied using the following steps:

- Step 1. Estimate the total variable product cost as follows:

Variable product costs:	
Direct materials	$XXX
Direct labor	XXX
Variable factory overhead	XXX
Total variable product cost	$XXX

- Step 2. Estimate the total variable selling and administrative expenses.
- Step 3. Determine the total variable cost as follows:

Total variable product cost	$XXX
Total variable selling and administrative expenses	XXX
Total variable cost	$XXX

- Step 4. Compute the variable cost per unit as follows:

$$\text{Variable Cost per Unit} = \frac{\text{Total Variable Cost}}{\text{Estimated Units Produced and Sold}}$$

- Step 5. Compute the markup percentage as follows:

$$\text{Markup Percentage} = \frac{\text{Desired Profit} + \text{Total Fixed Costs and Expenses}}{\text{Total Variable Cost}}$$

The numerator of the markup percentage is the desired profit plus the total fixed costs (fixed factory overhead) and expenses (selling and administrative). These fixed costs and expenses must be included in the markup percentage because they are not included in the cost amount to which the markup is added.

As illustrated for the total and product cost concepts, the desired profit is normally computed based on a rate of return on assets as follows:

$$\text{Desired Profit} = \text{Desired Rate of Return} \times \text{Total Assets}$$

- Step 6. Determine the markup per unit by multiplying the markup percentage times the variable cost per unit as follows:

$$\text{Markup per Unit} = \text{Markup Percentage} \times \text{Variable Cost per Unit}$$

- Step 7. Determine the normal selling price by adding the markup per unit to the variable cost per unit as follows:

Variable cost per unit	$XXX
Markup per unit	XXX
Normal selling price per unit	$XXX

To illustrate, assume the same data for the production and sale of 100,000 calculators by Digital Solutions Inc. as in the preceding example. The normal selling price of $18.30 is determined under the variable cost concept as follows:

- Step 1. Total variable product cost: $1,450,000

Variable product costs:	
Direct materials ($3 × 100,000)	$ 300,000
Direct labor ($10 × 100,000)	1,000,000
Variable factory overhead ($1.50 × 100,000)	150,000
Total variable product cost	$1,450,000

- Step 2. Total variable selling and administrative expenses: $150,000 ($1.50 × 100,000)
- Step 3. Total variable cost: $1,600,000 ($1,450,000 + $150,000)
- Step 4. Variable cost per unit: $16.00

$$\text{Variable Cost per Unit} = \frac{\text{Total Variable Cost}}{\text{Estimated Units Produced and Sold}} = \frac{\$1{,}600{,}000}{100{,}000 \text{ units}} = \$16 \text{ per unit}$$

- Step 5. Markup percentage: 14.4% (rounded)

$$\text{Desired Profit} = \text{Desired Rate of Return} \times \text{Total Assets} = 20\% \times \$800{,}000 = \$160{,}000$$

$$\text{Markup Percentage} = \frac{\text{Desired Profit} + \text{Total Fixed Costs and Expenses}}{\text{Total Variable Cost}}$$

$$= \frac{\$160{,}000 + \$50{,}000 + \$20{,}000}{\$1{,}600{,}000} = \frac{\$230{,}000}{\$1{,}600{,}000}$$

$$= 14.4\% \text{ (rounded)}$$

- Step 6. Markup per unit: $2.30

$$\text{Markup per Unit} = \text{Markup Percentage} \times \text{Variable Cost per Unit}$$
$$= 14.4\% \times \$16.00 = \$2.30 \text{ per unit}$$

- Step 7. Normal selling price: $18.30

Total variable cost per unit	$16.00
Markup per unit	2.30
Normal selling price per unit	$18.30

At a Glance 9

Prepare differential analysis reports for a variety of managerial decisions.

Key Points Differential analysis reports for various decisions are illustrated in the text. Each analysis focuses on the differential effects on income (loss) for alternative courses of action.

Learning Outcomes	Example Exercises	Practice Exercises
• Prepare a lease or sell differential analysis.	EE9-1	PE9-1A, 9-1B
• Prepare a discontinued segment differential analysis.	EE9-2	PE9-2A, 9-2B
• Prepare a make-or-buy differential analysis.	EE9-3	PE9-3A, 9-3B
• Prepare an equipment replacement differential analysis.	EE9-4	PE9-4A, 9-4B
• Prepare a process-or-sell differential analysis.	EE9-5	PE9-5A, 9-5B
• Prepare an accept business at a special price differential analysis.	EE9-6	PE9-6A, 9-6B

Determine the selling price of a product, using the product cost concept.

Key Points The three cost concepts commonly used in applying the cost-plus approach to product pricing are the product cost, total cost (appendix), and variable cost (appendix) concepts.

Target costing combines market-based methods with a cost-reduction emphasis.

Learning Outcomes	Example Exercises	Practice Exercises
• Compute the markup percentage, using the product cost concept.	EE9-7	PE9-7A, 9-7B
• Define and describe target costing.		

Compute the relative profitability of products in bottleneck production processes.

Key Points The relative profitability of a product in a bottleneck production environment is determined by dividing the unit contribution margin by the bottleneck hours per unit.

Learning Outcome	Example Exercises	Practice Exercises
• Compute the unit contribution margin per bottleneck hour.	EE9-8	PE9-8A, 9-8B

Key Terms

differential analysis (367)
differential cost (367)
differential income (loss) (367)
differential revenue (367)
opportunity cost (373)
product cost concept (378)
production bottleneck (381)
sunk cost (369)
target costing (380)
theory of constraints (TOC) (381)
total cost concept (383)
variable cost concept (385)

Illustrative Problem

Inez Company recently began production of a new product, a digital clock, which required the investment of $1,600,000 in assets. The costs of producing and selling 80,000 units of the digital clock are estimated as follows:

Variable costs:	
Direct materials	$10.00 per unit
Direct labor	6.00
Factory overhead	4.00
Selling and administrative expenses	5.00
Total	$25.00 per unit
Fixed costs:	
Factory overhead	$800,000
Selling and administrative expenses	400,000

Inez Company is currently considering establishing a selling price for the digital clock. The president of Inez Company has decided to use the cost-plus approach to product pricing and has indicated that the digital clock must earn a 10% rate of return on invested assets.

Instructions

1. Determine the amount of desired profit from the production and sale of the digital clock.
2. Assuming that the product cost concept is used, determine (a) the cost amount per unit, (b) the markup percentage, and (c) the selling price of the digital clock.
3. Under what conditions should Inez Company consider using activity-based costing rather than a single factory overhead allocation rate in allocating factory overhead to the digital clock?
4. Assume the market price for similar digital clocks was estimated at $38. Compute the reduction in manufacturing cost per unit needed to maintain the desired profit and existing selling and administrative expenses under target costing.
5. Assume that for the current year, the selling price of the digital clock was $42 per unit. To date, 60,000 units have been produced and sold, and analysis of the domestic market indicates that 15,000 additional units are expected to be sold during the remainder of the year. On August 7 Inez Company received an offer from Wong Inc. for 4,000 units of the digital clock at $28 each. Wong Inc. will market the units in Korea under its own brand name, and no selling and administrative expenses associated with the sale will be incurred by Inez Company. The additional business is not expected to affect the domestic sales of the digital clock, and the additional units could be produced during the current year, using existing capacity. Prepare a differential analysis dated August 7 to determine whether to reject (Alternative 1) or accept (Alternative 2) the special order from Wong.

Solution

1. $160,000 ($1,600,000 × 10%)
2. a. Total manufacturing costs:

Variable ($20 × 80,000 units)	$1,600,000
Fixed factory overhead	800,000
Total	$2,400,000

Cost amount per unit: $2,400,000 ÷ 80,000 units = $30.00

b. $$\text{Markup Percentage} = \frac{\text{Desired Profit} + \text{Total Selling and Administrative Expenses}}{\text{Total Product Cost}}$$

$$= \frac{\$160{,}000 + \$400{,}000 + (\$5 \times 80{,}000 \text{ units})}{\$2{,}400{,}000}$$

$$= \frac{\$160{,}000 + \$400{,}000 + \$400{,}000}{\$2{,}400{,}000}$$

$$= \frac{\$960{,}000}{\$2{,}400{,}000} = 40\%$$

c.

Cost amount per unit	$30.00
Markup ($30 × 40%)	12.00
Selling price	$42.00

3. Inez should consider using activity-based costing for factory overhead allocation when the product and manufacturing operations are complex. For example, if the digital clock was introduced as one among many different consumer digital products, then it is likely these products will consume factory activities in different ways. If this is combined with complex manufacturing and manufacturing support processes, then

it is likely a single overhead allocation rate will lead to distorted factory overhead allocation. Specifically, the digital clock is a new product. Thus, it is likely that it will consume more factory overhead than existing stable and mature products. In this case, a single rate would result in the digital clock being undercosted compared to results using activity-based rates for factory overhead allocation.

4.

Current selling price	$42
Expected selling price	−38
Required reduction in manufacturing cost to maintain same profit	$ 4

Revised revenue and cost figures:

	Current	Desired
Selling price	$42	$38
Costs:		
Variable selling and administrative expenses per unit	$ 5	$ 5
Fixed selling and administrative expenses per unit ($400,000 ÷ 80,000 units)	5	5
Existing manufacturing cost per unit [part (2)]	30	
Target manufacturing cost per unit ($30 – $4)		26
Total costs	$40	$36
Profit	$ 2	$ 2

5.

Differential Analysis—Wong Inc. Special Order
Reject Order (Alternative 1) or Accept Order (Alternative 2)
August 7

	Reject Order (Alternative 1)	Accept Order (Alternative 2)	Differential Effect on Income (Alternative 2)
Revenues	$0	$112,000*	$112,000
Costs:			
Variable manufacturing costs	0	−80,000**	−80,000
Income (loss)	$0	$ 32,000	$ 32,000

*4,000 units × $28 per unit
**4,000 units × $20 per unit

The proposal should be accepted.

Discussion Questions

1. Explain the meaning of (a) differential revenue, (b) differential cost, and (c) differential income.
2. A company could sell a building for $250,000 or lease it for $2,500 per month. What would need to be considered in determining if the lease option would be preferred?
3. A chemical company has a commodity-grade and premium-grade product. Why might the company elect to process the commodity-grade product further to the premium-grade product?
4. A company accepts incremental business at a special price that exceeds the variable cost. What other issues must the company consider in deciding whether to accept the business?
5. A company fabricates a component at a cost of $6.00. A supplier offers to supply the same component for $5.50. Under what circumstances is it reasonable to purchase from the supplier?
6. Many fast-food restaurant chains, such as McDonald's, will occasionally discontinue restaurants in their system. What are some financial considerations in deciding to eliminate a store?
7. In the long run, the normal selling price must be set high enough to cover what factors?

8. Although the cost-plus approach to product pricing may be used by management as a general guideline, what are some examples of other factors that managers should also consider in setting product prices?
9. How does the target cost concept differ from cost-plus approaches?
10. What is the appropriate measure of a product's value when a firm is operating under production bottlenecks?

Practice Exercises

EE 9-1 *p. 369*

PE 9-1A Lease or sell

OBJ. 1

SHOW ME HOW

Claxon Company owns a machine with a cost of $305,000 and accumulated depreciation of $65,000 that can be sold for $262,000, less a 5% sales commission. Alternatively, the machine can be leased by Claxon Company for three years for a total of $272,000, at the end of which there is no residual value. In addition, the repair, insurance, and property tax expense that would be incurred by Claxon Company on the machine would total $21,600 over the three years. Prepare a differential analysis on January 12 as to whether Claxon Company should lease (Alternative 1) or sell (Alternative 2) the machine.

EE 9-1 *p. 369*

PE 9-1B Lease or sell

OBJ. 1

SHOW ME HOW

Timberlake Company owns equipment with a cost of $165,000 and accumulated depreciation of $60,000 that can be sold for $82,000, less a 6% sales commission. Alternatively, the equipment can be leased by Timberlake Company for five years for a total of $84,600, at the end of which there is no residual value. In addition, the repair, insurance, and property tax expense that would be incurred by Timberlake Company on the equipment would total $7,950 over the five years. Prepare a differential analysis on March 23 as to whether Timberlake Company should lease (Alternative 1) or sell (Alternative 2) the equipment.

EE 9-2 *p. 371*

PE 9-2A Discontinue a segment

OBJ. 1

SHOW ME HOW

Product TS-20 has revenue of $102,000, variable cost of goods sold of $52,500, variable selling expenses of $21,500, and fixed costs of $35,000, creating a loss from operations of $7,000. Prepare a differential analysis as of September 12 to determine if Product TS-20 should be continued (Alternative 1) or discontinued (Alternative 2), assuming fixed costs are unaffected by the decision.

EE 9-2 *p. 371*

PE 9-2B Discontinue a segment

OBJ. 1

SHOW ME HOW

Product B has revenue of $39,500, variable cost of goods sold of $25,500, variable selling expenses of $16,500, and fixed costs of $15,000, creating a loss from operations of $17,500. Prepare a differential analysis as of May 9 to determine if Product B should be continued (Alternative 1) or discontinued (Alternative 2), assuming fixed costs are unaffected by the decision.

EE 9-3 *p. 372*

PE 9-3A Make or buy

OBJ. 1

SHOW ME HOW

A restaurant bakes its own bread for a cost of $165 per unit (100 loaves), including fixed costs of $43 per unit. A proposal is offered to purchase bread from an outside source for $110 per unit, plus $15 per unit for delivery. Prepare a differential analysis dated August 16 to determine whether the company should make (Alternative 1) or buy (Alternative 2) the bread, assuming fixed costs are unaffected by the decision.

EE 9-3 p. 372

PE 9-3B Make or buy

OBJ. 1

A company manufactures various sized plastic bottles for its medicinal product. The manufacturing cost for small bottles is $67 per unit (100 bottles), including fixed costs of $22 per unit. A proposal is offered to purchase small bottles from an outside source for $35 per unit, plus $5 per unit for freight. Prepare a differential analysis dated March 30 to determine whether the company should make (Alternative 1) or buy (Alternative 2) the bottles, assuming fixed costs are unaffected by the decision.

EE 9-4 p. 374

PE 9-4A Replace equipment

OBJ. 1

A machine with a book value of $126,000 has an estimated six-year life. A proposal is offered to sell the old machine for $84,000 and replace it with a new machine at a cost of $145,000. The new machine has a six-year life with no residual value. The new machine would reduce annual direct labor costs from $55,000 to $43,000. Prepare a differential analysis dated February 18 on whether to continue with the old machine (Alternative 1) or replace the old machine (Alternative 2).

EE 9-4 p. 374

PE 9-4B Replace equipment

OBJ. 1

A machine with a book value of $80,000 has an estimated five-year life. A proposal is offered to sell the old machine for $50,500 and replace it with a new machine at a cost of $75,000. The new machine has a five-year life with no residual value. The new machine would reduce annual direct labor costs from $11,200 to $7,400. Prepare a differential analysis dated April 11 on whether to continue with the old machine (Alternative 1) or replace the old machine (Alternative 2).

EE 9-5 p. 375

PE 9-5A Process or sell

OBJ. 1

Product T is produced for $5.90 per pound. Product T can be sold without additional processing for $7.10 per pound, or processed further into Product U at an additional cost of $0.74 per pound. Product U can be sold for $8.00 per pound. Prepare a differential analysis dated August 2 on whether to sell Product T (Alternative 1) or process further into Product U (Alternative 2).

EE 9-5 p. 375

PE 9-5B Process or sell

OBJ. 1

Product D is produced for $24 per gallon. Product D can be sold without additional processing for $36 per gallon, or processed further into Product E at an additional cost of $9 per gallon. Product E can be sold for $43 per gallon. Prepare a differential analysis dated February 26 on whether to sell Product D (Alternative 1) or process further into Product E (Alternative 2).

EE 9-6 p. 377

PE 9-6A Accept business at special price

OBJ. 1

Product R is normally sold for $52 per unit. A special price of $42 is offered for the export market. The variable production cost is $30 per unit. An additional export tariff of 30% of revenue must be paid for all export products. Assume there is sufficient capacity for the special order. Prepare a differential analysis dated October 23 on whether to reject (Alternative 1) or accept (Alternative 2) the special order.

EE 9-6 p. 377

PE 9-6B Accept business at special price

OBJ. 1

SHOW
ME HOW

Product A is normally sold for $9.60 per unit. A special price of $7.20 is offered for the export market. The variable production cost is $5.00 per unit. An additional export tariff of 15% of revenue must be paid for all export products. Assume there is sufficient capacity for the special order. Prepare a differential analysis dated March 16 on whether to reject (Alternative 1) or accept (Alternative 2) the special order.

EE 9-7 *p. 380*

SHOW ME HOW

PE 9-7A Product cost markup percentage **OBJ. 2**

Magna Lighting Inc. produces and sells lighting fixtures. An entry light has a total cost of $125 per unit, of which $80 is product cost and $45 is selling and administrative expenses. In addition, the total cost of $125 is made up of $90 variable cost and $35 fixed cost. The desired profit is $55 per unit. Determine the markup percentage on product cost.

EE 9-7 *p. 380*

SHOW ME HOW

PE 9-7B Product cost markup percentage **OBJ. 2**

Green Thumb Garden Tools Inc. produces and sells home and garden tools and equipment. A lawnmower has a total cost of $230 per unit, of which $160 is product cost and $70 is selling and administrative expenses. In addition, the total cost of $230 is made up of $120 variable cost and $110 fixed cost. The desired profit is $58 per unit. Determine the markup percentage on product cost.

EE 9-8 *p. 382*

SHOW ME HOW

PE 9-8A Bottleneck profit **OBJ. 3**

Product A has a unit contribution margin of $24. Product B has a unit contribution margin of $30. Product A requires four testing hours, while Product B requires six testing hours. Determine the most profitable product, assuming the testing is a bottleneck constraint.

EE 9-8 *p. 382*

SHOW ME HOW

PE 9-8B Bottleneck profit **OBJ. 3**

Product K has a unit contribution margin of $120. Product L has a unit contribution margin of $100. Product K requires five furnace hours, while Product L requires four furnace hours. Determine the most profitable product, assuming the furnace is a bottleneck constraint.

Exercises

✔ a. Differential revenue from selling, $5,000

SHOW ME HOW

EX 9-1 Differential analysis for a lease or sell decision **OBJ. 1**

Eclipse Construction Company is considering selling excess machinery with a book value of $280,000 (original cost of $400,000 less accumulated depreciation of $120,000) for $221,000, less a 5% brokerage commission. Alternatively, the machinery can be leased for a total of $216,000 for five years, after which it is expected to have no residual value. During the period of the lease, Eclipse Construction Company's costs of repairs, insurance, and property tax expenses are expected to be $14,200.

a. Prepare a differential analysis, dated April 16 to determine whether Eclipse should lease (Alternative 1) or sell (Alternative 2) the machinery.

b. On the basis of the data presented, would it be advisable to lease or sell the machinery? Explain.

SHOW ME HOW

EX 9-2 Differential analysis for a lease or buy decision **OBJ. 1**

Carr Corporation is considering new equipment. The equipment can be purchased from an overseas supplier for $3,900. The freight and installation costs for the equipment are $515. If purchased, annual repairs and maintenance are estimated to be $410 per year over the four-year useful life of the equipment. Alternatively, Carr can lease the equipment from a domestic supplier for $1,750 per year for four years, with no additional costs. Prepare a differential analysis dated August 4 to determine whether Carr should lease (Alternative 1) or purchase (Alternative 2) the equipment. *Hint:* This is a "lease or *buy*" decision, which must be analyzed from the perspective of the equipment user, as opposed to the equipment owner.

✔ a. Differential revenues, –$390,000

SHOW ME HOW

EX 9-3 Differential analysis for a discontinued product **OBJ. 1**

A condensed income statement by product line for Celestial Beverage Inc. indicated the following for Star Cola for the past year:

(Continued)

Sales	$390,000
Cost of goods sold	184,000
Gross profit	$206,000
Operating expenses	255,000
Loss from operations	$ (49,000)

It is estimated that 20% of the cost of goods sold represents fixed factory overhead costs and that 30% of the operating expenses are fixed. Because Star Cola is only one of many products, the fixed costs will not be materially affected if the product is discontinued.

a. Prepare a differential analysis, dated January 21 to determine whether Star Cola should be continued (Alternative 1) or discontinued (Alternative 2).

b. Should Star Cola be retained? Explain.

EX 9-4 Differential analysis for a discontinued product **OBJ. 1**

✔ a. Alternative 1 loss, $2,200

The condensed product-line income statement for Dish N' Dat Company for the month of March is as follows:

Dish N' Dat Company
Product-Line Income Statement
For the Month Ended March 31, 2016

	Bowls	Plates	Cups
Sales	$71,000	$105,700	$31,300
Cost of goods sold	32,600	42,300	16,800
Gross profit	$38,400	$ 63,400	$14,500
Selling and administrative expenses	27,400	42,800	16,700
Income from operations	$11,000	$ 20,600	$ (2,200)

Fixed costs are 15% of the cost of goods sold and 40% of the selling and administrative expenses. Dish N' Dat assumes that fixed costs would not be materially affected if the Cups line were discontinued.

a. Prepare a differential analysis dated March 31, 2016, to determine if Cups should be continued (Alternative 1) or discontinued (Alternative 2).

b. Should the Cups line be retained? Explain.

EX 9-5 Segment analysis for a service company **OBJ. 1**

Charles Schwab Corporation is one of the more innovative brokerage and financial service companies in the United States. The company recently provided information about its major business segments as follows (in millions):

	Investor Services	Institutional Services
Revenues	$3,228	$1,583
Income from operations	865	514
Depreciation	148	48

a. How does a brokerage company like Schwab define the "Investor Services" and "Institutional Services" segments? Use the Internet to develop your answer.

b. Provide a specific example of a variable and fixed cost in the "Investor Services" segment.

c. Estimate the contribution margin for each segment, assuming depreciation represents the majority of fixed costs.

d. If Schwab decided to sell its "Institutional Services" accounts to another company, estimate how much operating income would decline.

EX 9-6 Decision to discontinue a product OBJ. 1

On the basis of the following data, the general manager of Featherweight Shoes Inc. decided to discontinue Children's Shoes because it reduced income from operations by $17,000. What is the flaw in this decision, if it is assumed fixed costs would not be materially affected by the discontinuance?

Featherweight Shoes Inc.
Product-Line Income Statement
For the Year Ended April 30, 2016

	Children's Shoes	Men's Shoes	Women's Shoes	Total
Sales	$235,000	$300,000	$500,000	$1,035,000
Costs of goods sold:				
Variable costs	$130,000	$150,000	$220,000	$ 500,000
Fixed costs	41,000	60,000	120,000	221,000
Total cost of goods sold	$171,000	$210,000	$340,000	$ 721,000
Gross profit	$ 64,000	$ 90,000	$160,000	$ 314,000
Selling and adminstrative expenses:				
Variable selling and admin. expenses	$ 46,000	$ 45,000	$ 95,000	$ 186,000
Fixed selling and admin. expenses	35,000	20,000	25,000	80,000
Total selling and admin. expenses	$ 81,000	$ 65,000	$120,000	$ 266,000
Income (loss) from operations	$ (17,000)	$ 25,000	$ 40,000	$ 48,000

EX 9-7 Make-or-buy decision OBJ. 1

✔ a. Differential loss from buying, $2.00 per case

SHOW ME HOW

Jupiter Computer Company has been purchasing carrying cases for its portable computers at a purchase price of $70 per unit. The company, which is currently operating below full capacity, charges factory overhead to production at the rate of 40% of direct labor cost. The fully absorbed unit costs to produce comparable carrying cases are expected to be as follows:

Direct materials	$45
Direct labor	20
Factory overhead (40% of direct labor)	8
Total cost per unit	$73

If Jupiter Computer Company manufactures the carrying cases, fixed factory overhead costs will not increase and variable factory overhead costs associated with the cases are expected to be 15% of the direct labor costs.

a. Prepare a differential analysis, dated July 19 to determine whether the company should make (Alternative 1) or buy (Alternative 2) the carrying case.

b. On the basis of the data presented, would it be advisable to make the carrying cases or to continue buying them? Explain.

EX 9-8 Make-or-buy decision for a service company OBJ. 1

The Theater Arts Guild of Dallas (TAG-D) employs five people in its Publication Department. These people lay out pages for pamphlets, brochures, magazines, and other publications for the TAG-D productions. The pages are delivered to an outside company for printing. The company is considering an outside publication service for the layout work. The outside service is quoting a price of $13 per layout page. The budget for the Publication Department for the current year is as follows:

Salaries	$224,000
Benefits	36,000
Supplies	21,000
Office expenses	39,000
Office depreciation	28,000
Computer depreciation	24,000
Total	$372,000

(Continued)

The department expects to lay out 24,000 pages for the current year. The Publication Department office space and equipment would be used for future administrative needs, if the department's function were purchased from the outside.

a. Prepare a differential analysis dated February 22 to determine whether TAG-D should lay out pages internally (Alternative 1) or purchase layout services from the outside (Alternative 2).

b. On the basis of your analysis in part (a), should the page layout work be purchased from an outside company?

c. What additional considerations might factor into the decision making?

EX 9-9 Machine replacement decision — OBJ. 1

A company is considering replacing an old piece of machinery, which cost $600,000 and has $350,000 of accumulated depreciation to date, with a new machine that has a purchase price of $545,000. The old machine could be sold for $231,000. The annual variable production costs associated with the old machine are estimated to be $61,000 per year for eight years. The annual variable production costs for the new machine are estimated to be $19,000 per year for eight years.

a. Prepare a differential analysis dated September 13 to determine whether to continue with (Alternative 1) or replace (Alternative 2) the old machine.

b. What is the sunk cost in this situation?

EX 9-10 Differential analysis for machine replacement — OBJ. 1

✔ a. Differential loss, $2,500

Kim Kwon Digital Components Company assembles circuit boards by using a manually operated machine to insert electronic components. The original cost of the machine is $60,000, the accumulated depreciation is $24,000, its remaining useful life is five years, and its residual value is negligible. On May 4 of the current year, a proposal was made to replace the present manufacturing procedure with a fully automatic machine that has a purchase price of $180,000. The automatic machine has an estimated useful life of five years and no significant residual value. For use in evaluating the proposal, the accountant accumulated the following annual data on present and proposed operations:

	Present Operations	Proposed Operations
Sales	$205,000	$205,000
Direct materials	$ 72,000	$ 72,000
Direct labor	51,000	—
Power and maintenance	5,000	18,000
Taxes, insurance, etc.	1,500	4,000
Selling and administrative expenses	45,000	45,000
Total expenses	$174,500	$139,000

a. Prepare a differential analysis dated May 4 to determine whether to continue with the old machine (Alternative 1) or replace the old machine (Alternative 2). Prepare the analysis over the useful life of the new machine.

b. Based only on the data presented, should the proposal be accepted?

c. What are some of the other factors that should be considered before a final decision is made?

EX 9-11 Sell or process further — OBJ. 1

Portland Lumber Company incurs a cost of $452 per hundred board feet (hbf) in processing certain "rough-cut" lumber, which it sells for $611 per hbf. An alternative is to produce a "finished cut" at a total processing cost of $559 per hbf, which can be sold for $748 per hbf. Prepare a differential analysis dated June 14 on whether to sell rough-cut lumber (Alternative 1) or process further into finished-cut lumber (Alternative 2).

EX 9-12 Sell or process further **OBJ. 1**

Rise N' Shine Coffee Company produces Columbian coffee in batches of 6,000 pounds. The standard quantity of materials required in the process is 6,000 pounds, which cost $5.50 per pound. Columbian coffee can be sold without further processing for $9.22 per pound. Columbian coffee can also be processed further to yield Decaf Columbian, which can be sold for $11.88 per pound. The processing into Decaf Columbian requires additional processing costs of $10,230 per batch. The additional processing will also cause a 5% loss of product due to evaporation.

a. Prepare a differential analysis dated October 6 on whether to sell regular Columbian (Alternative 1) or process further into Decaf Columbian (Alternative 2).

b. Should Rise N' Shine sell Columbian coffee or process further and sell Decaf Columbian?

c. Determine the price of Decaf Columbian that would cause neither an advantage nor a disadvantage for processing further and selling Decaf Columbian.

EX 9-13 Decision on accepting additional business **OBJ. 1**

✔ **a. Differential income, $54,000**

Homestead Jeans Co. has an annual plant capacity of 65,000 units, and current production is 45,000 units. Monthly fixed costs are $54,000, and variable costs are $29 per unit. The present selling price is $42 per unit. On November 12 of the current year, the company received an offer from Dawkins Company for 18,000 units of the product at $32 each. Dawkins Company will market the units in a foreign country under its own brand name. The additional business is not expected to affect the domestic selling price or quantity of sales of Homestead Jeans Co.

a. Prepare a differential analysis dated November 12 on whether to reject (Alternative 1) or accept (Alternative 2) the Dawkins order.

b. Briefly explain the reason why accepting this additional business will increase operating income.

c. What is the minimum price per unit that would produce a positive contribution margin?

EX 9-14 Accepting business at a special price **OBJ. 1**

Portable Power Company expects to operate at 80% of productive capacity during July. The total manufacturing costs for July for the production of 25,000 batteries are budgeted as follows:

Direct materials	$162,500
Direct labor	70,000
Variable factory overhead	30,000
Fixed factory overhead	112,500
Total manufacturing costs	$375,000

The company has an opportunity to submit a bid for 2,500 batteries to be delivered by July 31 to a government agency. If the contract is obtained, it is anticipated that the additional activity will not interfere with normal production during July or increase the selling or administrative expenses. What is the unit cost below which Portable Power Company should not go in bidding on the government contract?

EX 9-15 Decision on accepting additional business **OBJ. 1**

✔ **a. Differential revenue, $2,320,000**

Brightstone Tire and Rubber Company has capacity to produce 170,000 tires. Brightstone presently produces and sells 130,000 tires for the North American market at a price of $175 per tire. Brightstone is evaluating a special order from a European automobile company, Euro Motors. Euro is offering to buy 20,000 tires for $116 per tire. Brightstone's accounting system indicates that the total cost per tire is as follows:

(Continued)

Direct materials	$ 56
Direct labor	22
Factory overhead (60% variable)	25
Selling and administrative expenses (45% variable)	26
Total	$129

Brightstone pays a selling commission equal to 5% of the selling price on North American orders, which is included in the variable portion of the selling and administrative expenses. However, this special order would not have a sales commission. If the order was accepted, the tires would be shipped overseas for an additional shipping cost of $7.50 per tire. In addition, Euro has made the order conditional on receiving European safety certification. Brightstone estimates that this certification would cost $165,000.

a. Prepare a differential analysis dated January 21 on whether to reject (Alternative 1) or accept (Alternative 2) the special order from Euro Motors.

b. What is the minimum price per unit that would be financially acceptable to Brightstone?

EX 9-16 Accepting business at a special price for a service company

Cityscape Hotels has 200 rooms available in a major metropolitan city. The hotel is able to attract business customers during the weekdays, and leisure customers during the weekend. However, the leisure customers on weekends occupy fewer rooms than do business customers on weekdays. Thus, Cityscape plans to provide special weekend pricing to attract additional leisure customers. A hotel room is priced at $180 per room night. The cost of a hotel room night includes the following:

	Cost Per Room Night (at normal occupancy)
Housekeeping service	$ 23
Utilities	7
Amenities	3
Hotel depreciation	55
Hotel staff (excluding housekeeping)	42
Total	$130

a. What is the contribution margin for a room night if only the hotel depreciation and hotel staff are assumed fixed for all occupancy levels?

b. What should be considered in setting a discount price for the weekends?

EX 9-17 Product cost concept of product pricing **OBJ. 2**

✔ b. $40

SHOW ME HOW

La Femme Accessories Inc. produces women's handbags. The cost of producing 800 handbags is as follows:

Direct materials	$18,000
Direct labor	8,500
Factory overhead	5,500
Total manufacturing cost	$32,000

The selling and administrative expenses are $17,000. The management desires a profit equal to 22% of invested assets of $250,000.

a. Determine the amount of desired profit from the production and sale of 800 handbags.

b. Determine the product cost per unit for the production of 800 handbags.

c. Determine the product cost markup percentage for handbags.

d. Determine the selling price of handbags.

✔ d. $325

EX 9-18 Product cost concept of product costing **OBJ. 2**

Smart Stream Inc. uses the product cost concept of applying the cost-plus approach to product pricing. The costs of producing and selling 10,000 cellular phones are as follows:

Variable costs per unit:		Fixed costs:	
Direct materials	$150	Factory overhead	$350,000
Direct labor	25	Selling and admin. exp.	140,000
Factory overhead	40		
Selling and administrative expenses	25		
Total	$240		

Smart Stream desires a profit equal to a 30% rate of return on invested assets of $1,200,000.

a. Determine the amount of desired profit from the production and sale of 10,000 cellular phones.

b. Determine the product cost and the cost amount per unit for the production of 10,000 cellular phones.

c. Determine the product cost markup percentage for cellular phones.

d. Determine the selling price of cellular phones.

EX 9-19 Target costing **OBJ. 2**

Toyota Motor Corporation uses target costing. Assume that Toyota marketing personnel estimate that the competitive selling price for the Camry in the upcoming model year will need to be $27,000. Assume further that the Camry's total unit cost for the upcoming model year is estimated to be $22,500 and that Toyota requires a 20% profit margin on selling price (which is equivalent to a 25% markup on total cost).

a. What price will Toyota establish for the Camry for the upcoming model year?

b. What impact will target costing have on Toyota, given the assumed information?

✔ b. $30

EX 9-20 Target costing **OBJ. 2**

Instant Image Inc. manufactures color laser printers. Model J20 presently sells for $460 and has a product cost of $230, as follows:

Direct materials	$175
Direct labor	40
Factory overhead	15
Total	$230

It is estimated that the competitive selling price for color laser printers of this type will drop to $400 next year. Instant Image has established a target cost to maintain its historical markup percentage on product cost. Engineers have provided the following cost reduction ideas:

1. Purchase a plastic printer cover with snap-on assembly, rather than with screws. This will reduce the amount of direct labor by 15 minutes per unit.
2. Add an inspection step that will add six minutes per unit of direct labor but reduce the materials cost by $20 per unit.
3. Decrease the cycle time of the injection molding machine from four minutes to three minutes per part. Forty percent of the direct labor and 48% of the factory overhead are related to running injection molding machines.

The direct labor rate is $30 per hour.

a. Determine the target cost for Model J20, assuming that the historical markup on product cost and selling price is maintained.

b. Determine the required cost reduction.

c. Evaluate the three engineering improvements together to determine if the required cost reduction (drift) can be achieved.

EX 9-21 Product decisions under bottlenecked operations **OBJ. 3**

Mill Metals Inc. has three grades of metal product, Type 5, Type 10, and Type 20. Financial data for the three grades are as follows:

	Type 5	Type 10	Type 20
Revenues	$43,000	$49,000	$56,500
Variable cost	$34,000	$28,000	$26,500
Fixed cost	8,000	8,000	8,000
Total cost	$42,000	$36,000	$34,500
Income from operations	$ 1,000	$13,000	$22,000
Number of units	÷ 5,000	÷ 5,000	÷ 5,000
Income from operations per unit	$ 0.20	$ 2.60	$ 4.40

Mill's operations require all three grades to be melted in a furnace before being formed. The furnace runs 24 hours a day, 7 days a week, and is a production bottleneck. The furnace hours required per unit of each product are as follows:

Type 5:	6 hours
Type 10:	6 hours
Type 20:	12 hours

The Marketing Department is considering a new marketing and sales campaign.

Which product should be emphasized in the marketing and sales campaign in order to maximize profitability?

EX 9-22 Product decisions under bottlenecked operations **OBJ. 3**

✔ a. Total income from operations, $269,000

Youngstown Glass Company manufactures three types of safety plate glass: large, medium, and small. All three products have high demand. Thus, Youngstown Glass is able to sell all the safety glass that it can make. The production process includes an autoclave operation, which is a pressurized heat treatment. The autoclave is a production bottleneck. Total fixed costs are $85,000 for the company as a whole. In addition, the following information is available about the three products:

	Large	Medium	Small
Unit selling price	$184	$160	$100
Unit variable cost	130	120	76
Unit contribution margin	$ 54	$ 40	$ 24
Autoclave hours per unit	3	2	1
Total process hours per unit	5	4	2
Budgeted units of production	3,000	3,000	3,000

a. Determine the contribution margin by glass type and the total company income from operations for the budgeted units of production.

b. Prepare an analysis showing which product is the most profitable per bottleneck hour.

Appendix
EX 9-23 Total cost concept of product pricing

✔ b. 12.46%

Based on the data presented in Exercise 9-18, assume that Smart Stream Inc. uses the total cost concept of applying the cost-plus approach to product pricing.

a. Determine the total costs and the total cost amount per unit for the production and sale of 10,000 cellular phones.

b. Determine the total cost markup percentage (rounded to two decimal places) for cellular phones.

c. Determine the selling price of cellular phones. Round to the nearest dollar.

Appendix
EX 9-24 Variable cost concept of product pricing

✔ b. 35.42%

Based on the data presented in Exercise 9-18, assume that Smart Stream Inc. uses the variable cost concept of applying the cost-plus approach to product pricing.

a. Determine the variable costs and the variable cost amount per unit for the production and sale of 10,000 cellular phones.

b. Determine the variable cost markup percentage (rounded to two decimal places) for cellular phones.

c. Determine the selling price of cellular phones. Round to the nearest dollar.

Problems: Series A

PR 9-1A Differential analysis involving opportunity costs — OBJ. 1

On October 1, White Way Stores Inc. is considering leasing a building and purchasing the necessary equipment to operate a retail store. Alternatively, the company could use the funds to invest in $180,000 of 6% U.S. Treasury bonds that mature in 16 years. The bonds could be purchased at face value. The following data have been assembled:

Cost of store equipment	$180,000
Life of store equipment	16 years
Estimated residual value of store equipment	$15,000
Yearly costs to operate the store, excluding depreciation of store equipment	$58,000
Yearly expected revenues—years 1–8	$85,000
Yearly expected revenues—years 9–16	$73,000

Instructions

1. Prepare a differential analysis as of October 1 presenting the proposed operation of the store for the 16 years (Alternative 1) as compared with investing in U.S. Treasury bonds (Alternative 2).
2. Based on the results disclosed by the differential analysis, should the proposal be accepted?
3. If the proposal is accepted, what would be the total estimated income from operations of the store for the 16 years?

PR 9-2A Differential analysis for machine replacement proposal — OBJ. 1

Lexigraphic Printing Company is considering replacing a machine that has been used in its factory for four years. Relevant data associated with the operations of the old machine and the new machine, neither of which has any estimated residual value, are as follows:

Old Machine	
Cost of machine, 10-year life	$89,000
Annual depreciation (straight-line)	8,900
Annual manufacturing costs, excluding depreciation	23,600
Annual nonmanufacturing operating expenses	6,100
Annual revenue	74,200
Current estimated selling price of machine	29,700

New Machine	
Purchase price of machine, six-year life	$119,700
Annual depreciation (straight-line)	19,950
Estimated annual manufacturing costs, excluding depreciation	6,900

Annual nonmanufacturing operating expenses and revenue are not expected to be affected by purchase of the new machine.

(Continued)

Instructions

1. Prepare a differential analysis as of April 30 comparing operations using the present machine (Alternative 1) with operations using the new machine (Alternative 2). The analysis should indicate the total differential income that would result over the six-year period if the new machine is acquired.
2. List other factors that should be considered before a final decision is reached.

✔ 1. Differential revenue, −$10,000

SHOW ME HOW

PR 9-3A Differential analysis for sales promotion proposal OBJ. 1

Parisian Cosmetics Company is planning a one-month campaign for September to promote sales of one of its two cosmetics products. A total of $140,000 has been budgeted for advertising, contests, redeemable coupons, and other promotional activities. The following data have been assembled for their possible usefulness in deciding which of the products to select for the campaign:

	Moisturizer	Perfume
Unit selling price	$55	$60
Unit production costs:		
Direct materials	$ 9	$14
Direct labor	3	5
Variable factory overhead	3	5
Fixed factory overhead	6	4
Total unit production costs	$21	$28
Unit variable selling expenses	16	15
Unit fixed selling expenses	12	6
Total unit costs	$49	$49
Operating income per unit	$ 6	$11

No increase in facilities would be necessary to produce and sell the increased output. It is anticipated that 22,000 additional units of moisturizer or 20,000 additional units of perfume could be sold from the campaign without changing the unit selling price of either product.

Instructions

1. Prepare a differential analysis as of August 21 to determine whether to promote moisturizer (Alternative 1) or perfume (Alternative 2).
2. The sales manager had tentatively decided to promote perfume, estimating that operating income would be increased by $80,000 ($11 operating income per unit for 20,000 units, less promotion expenses of $140,000). The manager also believed that the selection of moisturizer would reduce operating income by $8,000 ($6 operating income per unit for 22,000 units, less promotion expenses of $140,000). State briefly your reasons for supporting or opposing the tentative decision.

✔ 1. Raw sugar income, $23,800

PR 9-4A Differential analysis for further processing OBJ. 1

The management of Dominican Sugar Company is considering whether to process further raw sugar into refined sugar. Refined sugar can be sold for $2.20 per pound, and raw sugar can be sold without further processing for $1.40 per pound. Raw sugar is produced in batches of 42,000 pounds by processing 100,000 pounds of sugar cane, which costs $0.35 per pound of cane. Refined sugar will require additional processing costs of $0.50 per pound of raw sugar, and 1.25 pounds of raw sugar will produce 1 pound of refined sugar.

Instructions

1. Prepare a differential analysis as of March 24 to determine whether to sell raw sugar (Alternative 1) or process further into refined sugar (Alternative 2).
2. Briefly report your recommendations.

Appendix
PR 9-5A Product pricing using the cost-plus approach concepts; differential analysis for accepting additional business **OBJ. 1, 2**

✔ **2. b. Markup percentage, 44%**

Crystal Displays Inc. recently began production of a new product, flat panel displays, which required the investment of $1,500,000 in assets. The costs of producing and selling 5,000 units of flat panel displays are estimated as follows:

Variable costs per unit:		Fixed costs:	
Direct materials	$120	Factory overhead	$250,000
Direct labor	30	Selling and administrative expenses	150,000
Factory overhead	50		
Selling and administrative expenses	35		
Total	$235		

Crystal Displays Inc. is currently considering establishing a selling price for flat panel displays. The president of Crystal Displays has decided to use the cost-plus approach to product pricing and has indicated that the displays must earn a 15% rate of return on invested assets.

Instructions

1. Determine the amount of desired profit from the production and sale of flat panel displays.
2. Assuming that the product cost concept is used, determine (a) the cost amount per unit, (b) the markup percentage, and (c) the selling price of flat panel displays.
3. (*Appendix*) Assuming that the total cost concept is used, determine (a) the cost amount per unit, (b) the markup percentage (rounded to two decimal places), and (c) the selling price of flat panel displays (rounded to nearest whole dollar).
4. (*Appendix*) Assuming that the variable cost concept is used, determine (a) the cost amount per unit, (b) the markup percentage (rounded to two decimal places), and (c) the selling price of flat panel displays (rounded to nearest whole dollar).
5. Comment on any additional considerations that could influence establishing the selling price for flat panel displays.
6. Assume that as of August 1, 3,000 units of flat panel displays have been produced and sold during the current year. Analysis of the domestic market indicates that 2,000 additional units are expected to be sold during the remainder of the year at the normal product price determined under the product cost concept. On August 3, Crystal Displays Inc. received an offer from Maple Leaf Visual Inc. for 800 units of flat panel displays at $225 each. Maple Leaf Visual Inc. will market the units in Canada under its own brand name, and no variable selling and administrative expenses associated with the sale will be incurred by Crystal Displays Inc. The additional business is not expected to affect the domestic sales of flat panel displays, and the additional units could be produced using existing factory, selling, and administrative capacity.
   a. Prepare a differential analysis of the proposed sale to Maple Leaf Visual Inc.
   b. Based on the differential analysis in part (a), should the proposal be accepted?

PR 9-6A Product pricing and profit analysis with bottleneck operations **OBJ. 3**

✔ **1. High Grade, $10**

Hercules Steel Company produces three grades of steel: high, good, and regular grade. Each of these products (grades) has high demand in the market, and Hercules is able to sell as much as it can produce of all three. The furnace operation is a bottleneck in the process and is running at 100% of capacity. Hercules wants to improve steel operation profitability. The variable conversion cost is $15 per process hour. The fixed cost is $200,000. In addition, the cost analyst was able to determine the following information about the three products:

	High Grade	Good Grade	Regular Grade
Budgeted units produced	5,000	5,000	5,000
Total process hours per unit	12	11	10
Furnace hours per unit	4	3	2.5
Unit selling price	$280	$270	$250
Direct materials cost per unit	$90	$84	$80

(*Continued*)

The furnace operation is part of the total process for each of these three products. Thus, for example, 4.0 of the 12.0 hours required to process High Grade steel are associated with the furnace.

Instructions

1. Determine the unit contribution margin for each product.
2. Provide an analysis to determine the relative product profitability, assuming that the furnace is a bottleneck.

Problems: Series B

PR 9-1B Differential analysis involving opportunity costs OBJ. 1

On July 1, Coastal Distribution Company is considering leasing a building and buying the necessary equipment to operate a public warehouse. Alternatively, the company could use the funds to invest in $740,000 of 5% U.S. Treasury bonds that mature in 14 years. The bonds could be purchased at face value. The following data have been assembled:

Cost of equipment	$740,000
Life of equipment	14 years
Estimated residual value of equipment	$75,000
Yearly costs to operate the warehouse, excluding depreciation of equipment	$175,000
Yearly expected revenues—years 1–7	$280,000
Yearly expected revenues—years 8–14	$240,000

Instructions

1. Prepare a differential analysis as of July 1 presenting the proposed operation of the warehouse for the 14 years (Alternative 1) as compared with investing in U.S. Treasury bonds (Alternative 2).
2. Based on the results disclosed by the differential analysis, should the proposal be accepted?
3. If the proposal is accepted, what is the total estimated income from operations of the warehouse for the 14 years?

PR 9-2B Differential analysis for machine replacement proposal OBJ. 1

Flint Tooling Company is considering replacing a machine that has been used in its factory for two years. Relevant data associated with the operations of the old machine and the new machine, neither of which has any estimated residual value, are as follows:

Old Machine	
Cost of machine, eight-year life	$38,000
Annual depreciation (straight-line)	4,750
Annual manufacturing costs, excluding depreciation	12,400
Annual nonmanufacturing operating expenses	2,700
Annual revenue	32,400
Current estimated selling price of the machine	12,900

New Machine	
Cost of machine, six-year life	$57,000
Annual depreciation (straight-line)	9,500
Estimated annual manufacturing costs, exclusive of depreciation	3,400

Annual nonmanufacturing operating expenses and revenue are not expected to be affected by purchase of the new machine.

Instructions

1. Prepare a differential analysis as of November 8 comparing operations using the present machine (Alternative 1) with operations using the new machine (Alternative 2). The analysis should indicate the differential income that would result over the six-year period if the new machine is acquired.
2. List other factors that should be considered before a final decision is reached.

PR 9-3B Differential analysis for sales promotion proposal **OBJ. 1**

✔ 1. Differential revenue, $105,000

SHOW ME HOW

Sole Mates Inc. is planning a one-month campaign for July to promote sales of one of its two shoe products. A total of $100,000 has been budgeted for advertising, contests, redeemable coupons, and other promotional activities. The following data have been assembled for their possible usefulness in deciding which of the products to select for the campaign:

	Tennis Shoe	Walking Shoe
Unit selling price	$85	$100
Unit production costs:		
Direct materials	$19	$ 32
Direct labor	8	12
Variable factory overhead	7	5
Fixed factory overhead	16	11
Total unit production costs	$50	$ 60
Unit variable selling expenses	6	10
Unit fixed selling expenses	20	15
Total unit costs	$76	$ 85
Operating income per unit	$ 9	$ 15

No increase in facilities would be necessary to produce and sell the increased output. It is anticipated that 7,000 additional units of tennis shoes or 7,000 additional units of walking shoes could be sold without changing the unit selling price of either product.

Instructions

1. Prepare a differential analysis as of June 19 to determine whether to promote tennis shoes (Alternative 1) or walking shoes (Alternative 2).
2. The sales manager had tentatively decided to promote walking shoes, estimating that operating income would be increased by $5,000 ($15 operating income per unit for 7,000 units, less promotion expenses of $100,000). The manager also believed that the selection of tennis shoes would reduce operating income by $37,000 ($9 operating income per unit for 7,000 units, less promotion expenses of $100,000). State briefly your reasons for supporting or opposing the tentative decision.

PR 9-4B Differential analysis for further processing **OBJ. 1**

✔ 1. Ingot income, $35,500

The management of International Aluminum Co. is considering whether to process aluminum ingot further into rolled aluminum. Rolled aluminum can be sold for $2,200 per ton, and ingot can be sold without further processing for $1,100 per ton. Ingot is produced in batches of 80 tons by smelting 500 tons of bauxite, which costs $105 per ton of bauxite. Rolled aluminum will require additional processing costs of $620 per ton of ingot, and 1.25 tons of ingot will produce 1 ton of rolled aluminum (due to trim losses).

Instructions

1. Prepare a differential analysis as of February 5 to determine whether to sell aluminum ingot (Alternative 1) or process further into rolled aluminum (Alternative 2).
2. Briefly report your recommendations.

Appendix
PR 9-5B Product pricing using the cost-plus approach concepts; differential analysis for accepting additional business **OBJ. 1, 2**

✔ 2. b. Markup percentage, 30%

Night Glow Inc. recently began production of a new product, the halogen light, which required the investment of $600,000 in assets. The costs of producing and selling 10,000 halogen lights are estimated as follows:

Variable costs per unit:		Fixed costs:	
Direct materials	$32	Factory overhead	$180,000
Direct labor	12	Selling and administrative expenses	80,000
Factory overhead	8		
Selling and administrative expenses	7		
Total	$59		

Night Glow Inc. is currently considering establishing a selling price for the halogen light. The president of Night Glow Inc. has decided to use the cost-plus approach to product pricing and has indicated that the halogen light must earn a 10% rate of return on invested assets.

Instructions

1. Determine the amount of desired profit from the production and sale of the halogen light.
2. Assuming that the product cost concept is used, determine (a) the cost amount per unit, (b) the markup percentage, and (c) the selling price of the halogen light.
3. (*Appendix*) Assuming that the total cost concept is used, determine (a) the cost amount per unit, (b) the markup percentage (rounded to two decimal places), and (c) the selling price of the halogen light (rounded to the nearest whole dollar).
4. (*Appendix*) Assuming that the variable cost concept is used, determine (a) the cost amount per unit, (b) the markup percentage (rounded to two decimal places), and (c) the selling price of the halogen light (rounded to nearest whole dollar).
5. Comment on any additional considerations that could influence establishing the selling price for the halogen light.
6. Assume that as of September 1, 7,000 units of halogen light have been produced and sold during the current year. Analysis of the domestic market indicates that 3,000 additional units of the halogen light are expected to be sold during the remainder of the year at the normal product price determined under the product cost concept. On September 5, Night Glow Inc. received an offer from Tokyo Lighting Inc. for 1,600 units of the halogen light at $57 each. Tokyo Lighting Inc. will market the units in Japan under its own brand name, and no variable selling and administrative expenses associated with the sale will be incurred by Night Glow Inc. The additional business is not expected to affect the domestic sales of the halogen light, and the additional units could be produced using existing productive, selling, and administrative capacity.
   a. Prepare a differential analysis of the proposed sale to Tokyo Lighting Inc.
   b. Based on the differential analysis in part (a), should the proposal be accepted?

PR 9-6B Product pricing and profit analysis with bottleneck operations **OBJ. 3**

✔ 1. Ethylene, $15

Wilmington Chemical Company produces three products: ethylene, butane, and ester. Each of these products has high demand in the market, and Wilmington Chemical is able to sell as much as it can produce of all three. The reaction operation is a bottleneck in the process and is running at 100% of capacity. Wilmington wants to improve chemical operation profitability. The variable conversion cost is $10 per process hour. The fixed cost is $400,000. In addition, the cost analyst was able to determine the following information about the three products:

	Ethylene	Butane	Ester
Budgeted units produced	9,000	9,000	9,000
Total process hours per unit	4.0	4.0	3.0
Reactor hours per unit	1.5	1.0	0.5
Unit selling price	$170	$155	$130
Direct materials cost per unit	$115	$88	$85

The reaction operation is part of the total process for each of these three products. Thus, for example, 1.5 of the 4.0 hours required to process ethylene is associated with the reactor.

Instructions

1. Determine the unit contribution margin for each product.
2. Provide an analysis to determine the relative product profitabilities, assuming that the reactor is a bottleneck.

Cases & Projects

CP 9-1 Ethics and professional conduct in business

Aaron McKinney is a cost accountant for Majik Systems Inc. Martin Dodd, vice president of marketing, has asked Aaron to meet with representatives of Majik Systems' major competitor to discuss product cost data. Martin indicates that the sharing of these data will enable Majik Systems to determine a fair and equitable price for its products.

Would it be ethical for Aaron to attend the meeting and share the relevant cost data?

CP 9-2 Decision on accepting additional business

A manager of Varden Sporting Goods Company is considering accepting an order from an overseas customer. This customer has requested an order for 20,000 dozen golf balls at a price of $22 per dozen. The variable cost to manufacture a dozen golf balls is $18 per dozen. The full cost is $25 per dozen. Varden has a normal selling price of $35 per dozen. Varden's plant has just enough excess capacity on the second shift to make the overseas order.

What are some considerations in accepting or rejecting this order?

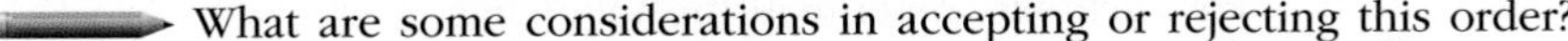

CP 9-3 Accept business at a special price for a service company

If you are not familiar with **Priceline.com Inc.**, go to its Web site. Assume that an individual "names a price" of $85 on Priceline.com for a room in Nashville, Tennessee, on August 22. Assume that August 22 is a Saturday, with low expected room demand in Nashville at a **Marriott International, Inc.**, hotel, so there is excess room capacity. The fully allocated cost per room per day is assumed from hotel records as follows:

Housekeeping labor cost*	$ 38
Hotel depreciation expense	43
Cost of room supplies (soap, paper, etc.)	8
Laundry labor and material cost*	10
Cost of desk staff	6
Utility cost (mostly air conditioning)	5
Total cost per room per day	$110

*Both housekeeping and laundry staff include many part-time workers, so that the workload is variable to demand.

Should Marriott accept the customer bid for a night in Nashville on August 22 at a price of $85?

CP 9-4 Cost-plus and target costing concepts

The following conversation took place between Juanita Jackson, vice president of marketing, and Les Miles, controller of Diamond Computer Company:

Juanita: I am really excited about our new computer coming out. I think it will be a real market success.

Les: I'm really glad you think so. I know that our success will be determined by our price. If our price is too high, our competitors will be the ones with the market success.

Juanita: Don't worry about it. We'll just mark our product cost up by 25%, and it will all work out. I know we'll make money at those markups. By the way, what does the estimated product cost look like?

Les: Well, there's the rub. The product cost looks as if it's going to come in at around $1,200. With a 25% markup, that will give us a selling price of $1,500.

Juanita: I see your concern. That's a little high. Our research indicates that computer prices are dropping and that this type of computer should be selling for around $1,250 when we release it to the market.

Les: I'm not sure what to do.

Juanita: Let me see if I can help. How much of the $1,200 is fixed cost?

Les: About $200.

Juanita: There you go. The fixed cost is sunk. We don't need to consider it in our pricing decision. If we reduce the product cost by $200, the new price with a 25% markup would be right at $1,250. Boy, I was really worried for a minute there. I knew something wasn't right.

a. If you were Les, how would you respond to Juanita's solution to the pricing problem?

b. How might target costing be used to help solve this pricing dilemma?

CP 9-5 Pricing decisions and markup on variable costs

Internet Project

Group Project

Many businesses are offering their products and services over the Internet. Some of these companies and their Internet addresses follow:

Company Name	Internet Address (URL)	Product
Delta Air Lines	www.delta.com	Airline tickets
Amazon.com	www.amazon.com	Books
Dell Inc.	www.dell.com	Personal computers

a. In groups of three, assign each person in your group to one of the Internet sites listed. For each site, determine the following:

1. A product (or service) description
2. A product price
3. A list of costs that are required sell the product selected in part (1) as listed in the annual report on SEC Form 10-K

J STOCK/STOCKSHOT/ALAMY

CHAPTER

10

Capital Investment Analysis

Vail Resorts, Inc.

Why are you paying tuition, studying this text, and spending time and money on a higher education? Most people believe that the money and time spent now will return them more earnings in the future. That is, the cost of higher education is an investment in your future earning ability. How would you know if this investment is worth it?

One method would be for you to compare the cost of a higher education against the estimated increase in your future earning power. The bigger the difference between your expected future earnings and the cost of your education, the better the investment. A business also evaluates its investments in fixed assets by comparing the initial cost of the investment to its future earnings and cash flows.

For example, **Vail Resorts, Inc.**, is one of the largest ski resort owner operators in the world. They are known for their Vail, Breckenridge, and Keystone ski resorts, among others. A ski resort requires significant investments in property and equipment. Thus, Vail routinely makes major investments in new or improved amenities, lodging, retail, lifts, snowmaking and grooming equipment, and technology infrastructure. These investments are evaluated by their ability to enhance cash flows.

In this chapter, the methods used to make investment decisions, which may involve thousands, millions, or even billions of dollars, are described and illustrated. The similarities and differences among the most commonly used methods of evaluating investment proposals, as well as the benefits of each method, are emphasized. Factors that can complicate the analysis are also discussed.

Learning Objectives

After studying this chapter, you should be able to: *Example Exercises*

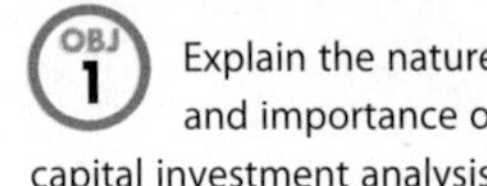
OBJ 1 Explain the nature and importance of capital investment analysis.

The Walt Disney Company and its partners will commit more than $4.4 billion to build Shanghai Disneyland, which is scheduled to open in 2016.

Nature of Capital Investment Analysis

Companies use capital investment analysis to evaluate long-term investments. **Capital investment analysis** (or *capital budgeting*) is the process by which management plans, evaluates, and controls investments in fixed assets. Capital investments use funds and affect operations for many years and must earn a reasonable rate of return. Thus, capital investment decisions are some of the most important decisions that management makes.

Capital investment evaluation methods can be grouped into the following categories:

Methods That Do Not Use Present Values

- Average rate of return method
- Cash payback method

Methods That Use Present Values

- Net present value method
- Internal rate of return method

The two methods that use present values consider the time value of money. The **time value of money concept** recognizes that a dollar today is worth more than a dollar tomorrow because today's dollar can earn interest.

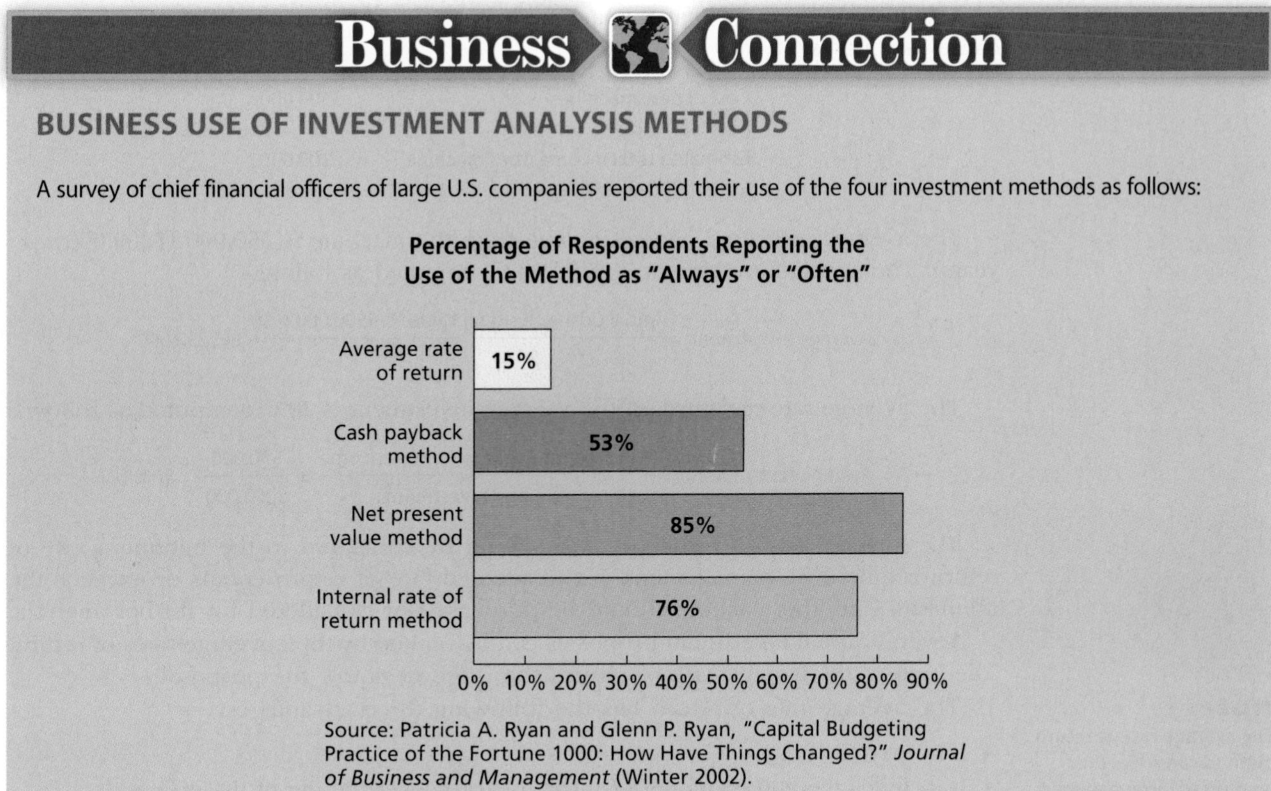

Business Connection
BUSINESS USE OF INVESTMENT ANALYSIS METHODS
A survey of chief financial officers of large U.S. companies reported their use of the four investment methods as follows:
Percentage of Respondents Reporting the Use of the Method as "Always" or "Often"
Average rate of return
15%
Cash payback method
53%
Net present value method
85%
Internal rate of return method
76%
0% 10% 20% 30% 40% 50% 60% 70% 80% 90%
Source: Patricia A. Ryan and Glenn P. Ryan, "Capital Budgeting Practice of the Fortune 1000: How Have Things Changed?" Journal of Business and Management (Winter 2002).

Methods Not Using Present Values

OBJ 2 Evaluate capital investment proposals, using the average rate of return and cash payback methods.

The methods not using present values are often useful in evaluating capital investment proposals that have relatively short useful lives. In such cases, the timing of the cash flows (the time value of money) is less important.

Because the methods not using present values are easy to use, they are often used to screen proposals. Minimum standards for accepting proposals are set, and proposals not meeting these standards are dropped. If a proposal meets the minimum standards, it may be subject to further analysis using the present value methods.

Average Rate of Return Method

The **average rate of return**, sometimes called the *accounting rate of return*, measures the average income as a percent of the average investment. The average rate of return is computed as follows:

$$\text{Average Rate of Return} = \frac{\text{Estimated Average Annual Income}}{\text{Average Investment}}$$

In the preceding equation, the numerator is the average of the annual income expected to be earned from the investment over its life, after deducting depreciation. The denominator is the average investment (book value) over the life of the investment. Assuming straight-line depreciation, the average investment is computed as follows:

$$\text{Average Investment} = \frac{\text{Initial Cost} + \text{Residual Value}}{2}$$

To illustrate, assume that management is evaluating the purchase of a new machine as follows:

Cost of new machine	$500,000
Residual value	0
Estimated total income from machine	200,000
Expected useful life	4 years

The average estimated annual income from the machine is $50,000 ($200,000 ÷ 4 years). The average investment is $250,000, computed as follows:

$$\text{Average Investment} = \frac{\text{Initial Cost} + \text{Residual Value}}{2} = \frac{\$500{,}000 + \$0}{2} = \$250{,}000$$

The average rate of return on the average investment is 20%, computed as follows:

$$\text{Average Rate of Return} = \frac{\text{Estimated Average Annual Income}}{\text{Average Investment}} = \frac{\$50{,}000}{\$250{,}000} = 20\%$$

The average rate of return of 20% should be compared to the minimum rate of return required by management. If the average rate of return equals or exceeds the minimum rate, the machine should be purchased or considered for further analysis.

Several capital investment proposals can be ranked by their average rates of return. The higher the average rate of return, the more desirable the proposal.

Note:
The average rate of return method considers the amount of income earned over the life of a proposal.

The average rate of return has the following three advantages:

- It is easy to compute.
- It includes the entire amount of income earned over the life of the proposal.
- It emphasizes accounting income, which is often used by investors and creditors in evaluating management performance.

The average rate of return has the following two disadvantages:

- It does not directly consider the expected cash flows from the proposal.
- It does not directly consider the timing of the expected cash flows.

Example Exercise 10-1 Average Rate of Return

OBJ 2

Determine the average rate of return for a project that is estimated to yield total income of $273,600 over three years, has a cost of $690,000, and has a $70,000 residual value.

Follow My Example 10-1

Estimated average annual income	$91,200 ($273,600 ÷ 3 years)
Average investment	$380,000 ($690,000 + $70,000) ÷ 2
Average rate of return	24% ($91,200 ÷ $380,000)

Practice Exercises: PE 10-1A, PE 10-1B

Cash Payback Method

A capital investment uses cash and must return cash in the future to be successful. The expected period of time between the date of an investment and the recovery in cash of the amount invested is the **cash payback period**.

When annual net cash inflows are equal, the cash payback period is computed as follows:

$$\text{Cash Payback Period} = \frac{\text{Initial Cost}}{\text{Annual Net Cash Inflow}}$$

To illustrate, assume that management is evaluating the purchase of the following new machine:

Cost of new machine	$200,000
Cash revenues from machine per year	50,000
Expenses of machine per year	30,000
Depreciation per year	20,000

To simplify, the revenues and expenses other than depreciation are assumed to be in cash. Hence, the net cash inflow per year from use of the machine is as follows:

Net cash inflow per year:		
Cash revenues from machine		$50,000
Less cash expenses of machine:		
Expenses of machine	$30,000	
Less depreciation	20,000	10,000
Net cash inflow per year		$40,000

The time required for the net cash flow to equal the cost of the new machine is the payback period. Thus, the estimated cash payback period for the investment is five years, computed as follows:

$$\text{Cash Payback Period} = \frac{\text{Initial Cost}}{\text{Annual Net Cash Inflow}} = \frac{\$200{,}000}{\$40{,}000} = 5 \text{ years}$$

In the preceding illustration, the annual net cash inflows are equal ($40,000 per year). When the annual net cash inflows are not equal, the cash payback period is determined by adding the annual net cash inflows until the cumulative total equals the initial cost of the proposed investment.

To illustrate, assume that a proposed investment has an initial cost of $400,000. The annual and cumulative net cash inflows over the proposal's six-year life are as follows:

Year	Net Cash Flow	Cumulative Net Cash Flow
1	$ 60,000	$ 60,000
2	80,000	140,000
3	105,000	245,000
4	155,000	400,000
5	100,000	500,000
6	90,000	590,000

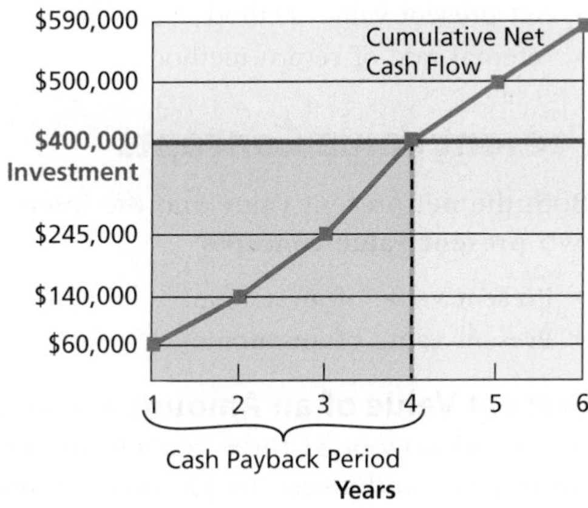

The cumulative net cash flow at the end of Year 4 equals the initial cost of the investment, $400,000. Thus, the payback period is four years.

If the initial cost of the proposed investment had been $450,000, the cash payback period would occur during Year 5. Because $100,000 of net cash flow is expected during Year 5, the additional $50,000 to increase the cumulative total to $450,000 occurs halfway through the year ($50,000 ÷ $100,000). Thus, the cash payback period would be 4½ years.[1]

A short cash payback period is desirable. This is because the sooner cash is recovered, the sooner it can be reinvested in other projects. In addition, there is less chance of losses from changing economic or business conditions. A short cash payback period is also desirable for quickly repaying any debt used to purchase the investment.

[1] Unless otherwise stated, net cash inflows are received uniformly throughout the year.

The cash payback method has the following two advantages:

- It is simple to use and understand.
- It analyzes cash flows.

The cash payback method has the following two disadvantages:

- It ignores cash flows occurring after the payback period.
- It does not use present value concepts in valuing cash flows occurring in different periods.

Example Exercise 10-2 Cash Payback Period OBJ 2

A project has estimated annual net cash flows of $30,000. It is estimated to cost $105,000. Determine the cash payback period.

Follow My Example 10-2

3.5 years ($105,000 ÷ $30,000)

Practice Exercises: PE 10-2A, PE 10-2B

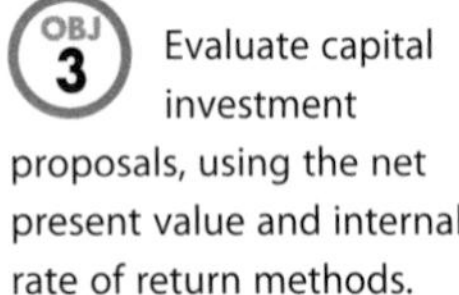

Evaluate capital investment proposals, using the net present value and internal rate of return methods.

Methods Using Present Values

An investment in fixed assets may be viewed as purchasing a series of net cash flows over a period of time. The timing of when the net cash flows will be received is important in determining the value of a proposed investment.

Present value methods use the amount and timing of the net cash flows in evaluating an investment. The two methods of evaluating capital investments using present values are as follows:

- Net present value method
- Internal rate of return method

Present Value Concepts

Both the net present value and the internal rate of return methods use the following two **present value concepts**:

- Present value of an amount
- Present value of an annuity

Present Value of an Amount If you were given the choice, would you prefer to receive $1 now or $1 three years from now? You should prefer to receive $1 now, because you could invest the $1 and earn interest for three years. As a result, the amount you would have after three years would be greater than $1.

To illustrate, assume that you have $1 to invest as follows:

Amount to be invested	$1
Period to be invested	3 years
Interest rate	12%

After one year, the $1 earns interest of $0.12 ($1 × 12%) and, thus, will grow to $1.12 ($1 × 1.12). In the second year, the $1.12 earns 12% interest of $0.134 ($1.12 × 12%) and, thus, will grow to $1.254 ($1.12 × 1.12) by the end of the second year. This process of interest earning interest is called *compounding*. By the end of the third year, your $1 investment will grow to $1.404 as shown in Exhibit 1.

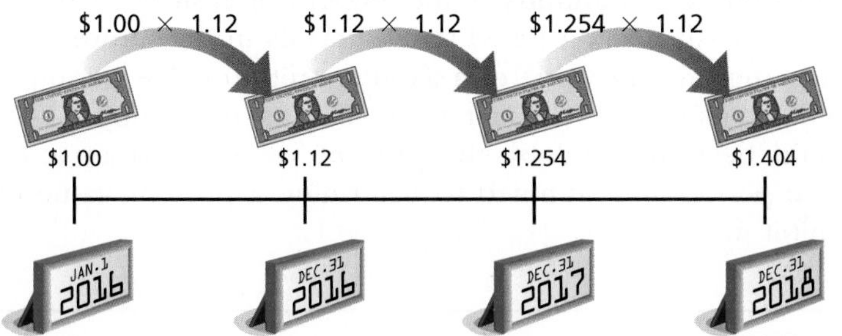

EXHIBIT 1

Compound Amount of $1 for Three Periods at 12%

On January 1, 2016, what is the present value of $1.404 to be received on December 31, 2018? This is a present value question. The answer can be determined with the aid of a present value of $1 table. For example, the partial table in Exhibit 2 indicates that the present value of $1 to be received in three years with earnings compounded at the rate of 12% per year is 0.712.[2]

EXHIBIT 2

Partial Present Value of $1 Table

Present Value of $1 at Compound Interest

Year	6%	10%	12%	15%	20%
1	0.943	0.909	0.893	0.870	0.833
2	0.890	0.826	0.797	0.756	0.694
3	0.840	0.751	0.712	0.658	0.579
4	0.792	0.683	0.636	0.572	0.482
5	0.747	0.621	0.567	0.497	0.402
6	0.705	0.564	0.507	0.432	0.335
7	0.665	0.513	0.452	0.376	0.279
8	0.627	0.467	0.404	0.327	0.233
9	0.592	0.424	0.361	0.284	0.194
10	0.558	0.386	0.322	0.247	0.162

Multiplying 0.712 by $1.404 yields $1 as follows:

Present Value		Amount to Be Received in 3 Years		Present Value of $1 to Be Received in 3 Years (from Exhibit 2)
$1	=	$1.404	×	0.712

That is, the present value of $1.404 to be received in three years using a compound interest rate of 12% is $1, as shown in Exhibit 3.

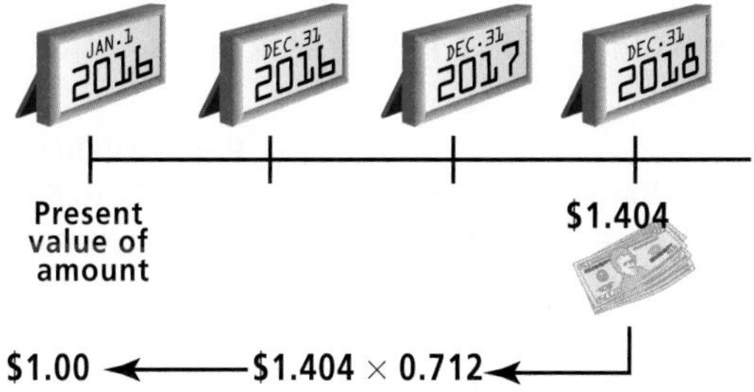

EXHIBIT 3

Present Value of an Amount of $1.404

Present Value of an Annuity An **annuity** is a series of equal net cash flows at fixed time intervals. Annuities are very common in business. Cash payments for monthly rent, salaries, and bond interest are all examples of annuities.

[2] The present value factors in the table are rounded to three decimal places. More complete tables of present values are in Appendix A.

The **present value of an annuity** is the amount of cash needed today to yield a series of equal net cash flows at fixed time intervals in the future.

To illustrate, the present value of a $100 annuity for five periods at 12% could be determined by using the present value factors in Exhibit 2. Each $100 net cash flow could be multiplied by the present value of $1 at a 12% factor for the appropriate period and summed to determine a present value of $360.50, as shown in Exhibit 4.

EXHIBIT 4

Present Value of a $100 Amount for Five Consecutive Periods

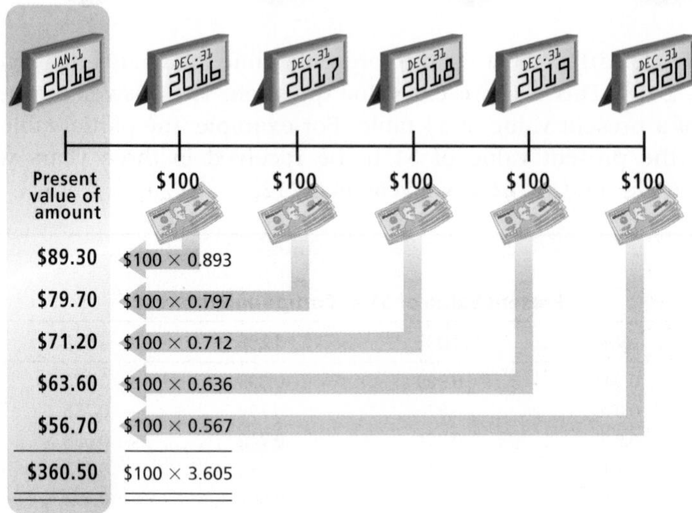

Using a present value of an annuity table is a simpler approach. Exhibit 5 is a partial table of present value annuity factors.[3]

The present value factors in the table shown in Exhibit 5 are the sum of the present value of $1 factors in Exhibit 2 for the number of annuity periods. Thus, 3.605 in the annuity table (Exhibit 5) is the sum of the five present value of $1 factors at 12% from Exhibit 2, computed as follows:

	Present Value of $1 (Exhibit 2)
Present value of $1 for 1 year @12%	0.893
Present value of $1 for 2 years @12%	0.797
Present value of $1 for 3 years @12%	0.712
Present value of $1 for 4 years @12%	0.636
Present value of $1 for 5 years @12%	0.567
Present value of an annuity of $1 for 5 years (from Exhibit 5)	3.605

Multiplying $100 by 3.605 yields $360.50 as follows:

Present Value		Amount to Be Received Annually for 5 Years		Present Value of an Annuity of $1 to Be Received for 5 Years (Exhibit 5)
$360.50	=	$100	×	3.605

Thus, $360.50 is the same amount that was determined in the preceding illustration by five successive multiplications.

[3] The present value factors in the table are rounded to three decimal places. More complete tables of present values are in Appendix A.

Present Value of an Annuity of $1 at Compound Interest					
Year	**6%**	**10%**	**12%**	**15%**	**20%**
1	0.943	0.909	0.893	0.870	0.833
2	1.833	1.736	1.690	1.626	1.528
3	2.673	2.487	2.402	2.283	2.106
4	3.465	3.170	3.037	2.855	2.589
5	4.212	3.791	3.605	3.353	2.991
6	4.917	4.355	4.111	3.785	3.326
7	5.582	4.868	4.564	4.160	3.605
8	6.210	5.335	4.968	4.487	3.837
9	6.802	5.759	5.328	4.772	4.031
10	7.360	6.145	5.650	5.019	4.192

EXHIBIT 5

Partial Present Value of an Annuity Table

Net Present Value Method and Index

The net present value method and present value index are often used in combination, as we illustrate in this section.

Net Present Value Method

The **net present value method** compares the amount to be invested with the present value of the net cash inflows. It is sometimes called the *discounted cash flow method.*

The interest rate (return) used in net present value analysis is the company's minimum desired rate of return. This rate, sometimes termed the *hurdle rate*, is based on such factors as the purpose of the investment and the cost of obtaining funds for the investment. If the present value of the cash inflows equals or exceeds the amount to be invested, the proposal is desirable.

To illustrate, assume the following data for a proposed investment in new equipment:

Note:
The net present value method compares an investment's initial cash outflow with the present value of its cash inflows.

Cost of new equipment	$200,000
Expected useful life	5 years
Minimum desired rate of return	10%
Expected cash flows to be received each year:	
Year 1	$ 70,000
Year 2	60,000
Year 3	50,000
Year 4	40,000
Year 5	40,000
Total expected cash flows	$260,000

The present value of the net cash flow for each year is computed by multiplying the net cash flow for the year by the present value factor of $1 for that year, as follows:

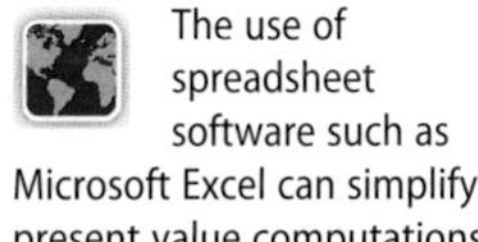
The use of spreadsheet software such as Microsoft Excel can simplify present value computations.

Year	Present Value of $1 at 10%	×	Net Cash Flow	=	Present Value of Net Cash Flow
1	0.909		$ 70,000		$ 63,630
2	0.826		60,000		49,560
3	0.751		50,000		37,550
4	0.683		40,000		27,320
5	0.621		40,000		24,840
Total			$260,000		$202,900
Less amount to be invested					200,000
Net present value					$ 2,900

The preceding computations are also graphically illustrated in Exhibit 6.

EXHIBIT 6

Present Value of Equipment Cash Flows

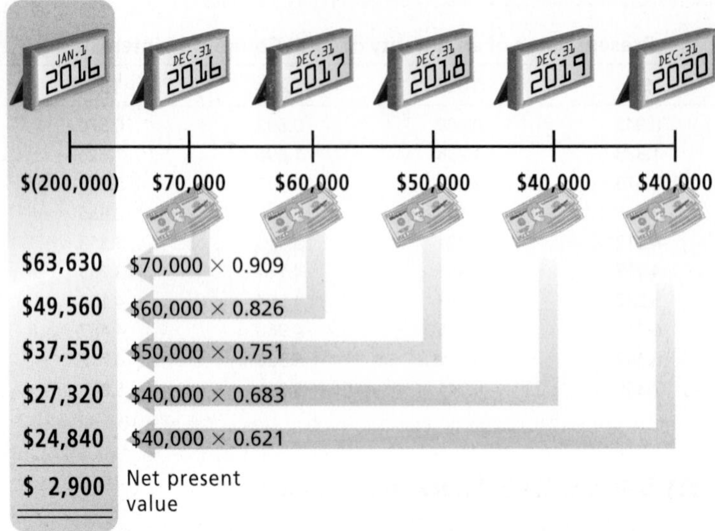

The net present value of $2,900 indicates that the purchase of the new equipment is expected to recover the investment and provide more than the minimum rate of return of 10%. Thus, the purchase of the new equipment is desirable.

The net present value method has the following three advantages:

- It considers the cash flows of the investment.
- It considers the time value of money.
- It can rank projects with equal lives, using the present value index.

The net present value method has the following two disadvantages:

- It has more complex computations than methods that don't use present value.
- It assumes the cash flows can be reinvested at the minimum desired rate of return, which may not be valid.

Present Value Index

When capital investment funds are limited and the proposals involve different investments, a ranking of the proposals can be prepared by using a present value index. The **present value index** is computed as follows:

$$\text{Present Value Index} = \frac{\text{Total Present Value of Net Cash Flow}}{\text{Amount to Be Invested}}$$

The present value index for the investment in the preceding illustration is 1.0145, computed as follows:

$$\text{Present Value Index} = \frac{\$202{,}900}{\$200{,}000} = 1.0145$$

Assume that a company is considering three proposals. The net present value and the present value index for each proposal are as follows:

	Proposal A	Proposal B	Proposal C
Total present value of net cash flow	$107,000	$86,400	$86,400
Less amount to be invested	100,000	80,000	90,000
Net present value	$ 7,000	$ 6,400	$ (3,600)
Present value index:			
Proposal A ($107,000 ÷ $100,000)	1.07		
Proposal B ($86,400 ÷ $80,000)		1.08	
Proposal C ($86,400 ÷ $90,000)			0.96

A project will have a present value index greater than 1 when the net present value is positive. This is the case for Proposals A and B. When the net present value is negative, the present value index will be less than 1, as is the case for Proposal C.

Although Proposal A has the largest net present value, the present value indices indicate that it is not as desirable as Proposal B. That is, Proposal B returns $1.08 present value per dollar invested, whereas Proposal A returns only $1.07. Proposal B requires an investment of $80,000, compared to an investment of $100,000 for Proposal A. The possible use of the $20,000 difference between Proposals A and B investments should also be considered before making a final decision.

Example Exercise 10-3 Net Present Value OBJ 3

A project has estimated annual net cash flows of $50,000 for seven years and is estimated to cost $240,000. Assume a minimum acceptable rate of return of 12%. Using Exhibit 5, determine (a) the net present value of the project and (b) the present value index, rounded to two decimal places.

Follow My Example 10-3

a. ($11,800) [($50,000 × 4.564) – $240,000]
b. 0.95 ($228,200 ÷ $240,000)

Practice Exercises: PE 10-3A, PE 10-3B

Internal Rate of Return Method

The **internal rate of return (IRR) method** uses present value concepts to compute the rate of return from a capital investment proposal based on its expected net cash flows. This method, sometimes called the *time-adjusted rate of return method*, starts with the proposal's net cash flows and works backward to estimate the proposal's expected rate of return.

To illustrate, assume that management is evaluating the following proposal to purchase new equipment:

Cost of new equipment	$33,530
Yearly expected cash flows to be received	$10,000
Expected life	5 years
Minimum desired rate of return	12%

The present value of the net cash flows, using the present value of an annuity table in Exhibit 5, is $2,520, as shown in Exhibit 7.

EXHIBIT 7

Net Present Value Analysis at 12%

Annual net cash flow (at the end of each of five years)	$10,000
Present value of an annuity of $1 at 12% for five years (Exhibit 5)	× 3.605
Present value of annual net cash flows	$36,050
Less amount to be invested	33,530
Net present value	$ 2,520

In Exhibit 7, the $36,050 present value of the cash inflows, based on a 12% rate of return, is greater than the $33,530 to be invested. Thus, the internal rate of return must be greater than 12%. Through trial and error, the rate of return equating the $33,530 cost of the investment with the present value of the net cash flows can be determined to be 15%, as shown in Exhibit 8.

EXHIBIT 8

Present Value of an Annuity at the Internal Rate of Return Rate

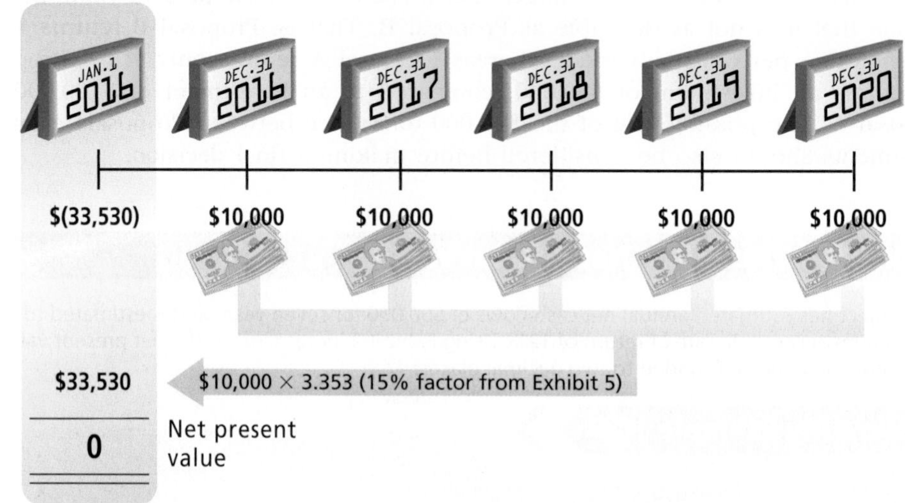

When equal annual net cash flows are expected from a proposal, as in the preceding example, the internal rate of return can be determined as follows:[4]

- Step 1. Determine a present value factor for an annuity of $1 as follows:

$$\text{Present Value Factor for an Annuity of \$1} = \frac{\text{Amount to Be Invested}}{\text{Equal Annual Net Cash Flows}}$$

- Step 2. Locate the present value factor determined in Step 1 in the present value of an annuity of $1 table (Exhibit 5) as follows:
  a. Locate the number of years of expected useful life of the investment in the Year column.
  b. Proceed horizontally across the table until you find the present value factor computed in Step 1.
- Step 3. Identify the internal rate of return by the heading of the column in which the present value factor in Step 2 is located.

To illustrate, assume that management is evaluating the following proposal to purchase new equipment:

Cost of new equipment	$97,360
Yearly expected cash flows to be received	$20,000
Expected useful life	7 years

[4] To simplify, equal annual net cash flows are assumed. If the net cash flows are not equal, spreadsheet software can be used to determine the rate of return.

The present value factor for an annuity of $1 is 4.868, computed as follows:

$$\text{Present Value Factor for an Annuity of \$1} = \frac{\text{Amount to Be Invested}}{\text{Equal Annual Net Cash Flows}}$$

$$= \frac{\$97{,}360}{\$20{,}000} = 4.868$$

Using the partial present value of an annuity of $1 table shown in Exhibit 9 and a period of seven years, the factor 4.868 is related to 10%. Thus, the internal rate of return for this proposal is 10%.

EXHIBIT 9 **Steps to Determine the Internal Rate of Return**

Present Value of an Annuity of $1 at Compound Interest

	Year	6%		Step 3 10%	12%
	1	0.943		0.909	0.893
	2	1.833		1.736	1.690
	3	2.673		2.487	2.402
	4	3.465		3.170	3.037
	5	4.212		3.791	3.605
	6	4.917	**Step 2(b)**	4.355	4.111
Step 2(a)	7	5.582	→	4.868	4.564
	8	6.210		5.335	4.968
	9	6.802		5.759	5.328
	10	7.360		6.145	5.650

Step 1: Determine present value factor for an annuity of $1 $= \frac{\$97{,}360}{\$20{,}000} = 4.868$

If the minimum acceptable rate of return is 10%, then the proposal is considered acceptable. Several proposals can be ranked by their internal rates of return. The proposal with the highest rate is the most desirable.

The internal rate of return method has the following three advantages:

- It considers the cash flows of the investment.
- It considers the time value of money.
- It ranks proposals based upon the cash flows over their complete useful life, even if the project lives are not the same.

The internal rate of return method has the following two disadvantages:

- It has complex computations, requiring a computer if the periodic cash flows are not equal.
- It assumes the cash received from a proposal can be reinvested at the internal rate of return, which may not be valid.

Example Exercise 10-4 Internal Rate of Return

A project is estimated to cost $208,175 and provide annual net cash flows of $55,000 for six years. Determine the internal rate of return for this project, using Exhibit 5.

Follow My Example 10-4

15% [($208,175 ÷ $55,000) = 3.785, the present value of an annuity factor for six periods at 15%, from Exhibit 5]

Practice Exercises: PE 10-4A, PE 10-4B

Business Connection

PANERA BREAD STORE RATE OF RETURN

Panera Bread owns, operates, and franchises bakery-cafes throughout the United States. A recent annual report to the Securities and Exchange Commission (SEC Form 10-K) allowed the following information to be determined about an average company-owned store:

Operating profit	$ 470,000
Depreciation	96,000
Investment book value	1,000,000

Assume that the operating profit and depreciation will remain unchanged for the next 15 years. Assume operating profit plus depreciation approximates annual net cash flows and that the investment residual value will be zero. Lastly, assume the investment book value approximates the current investment required to open a store. The average rate of return and internal rate of return can then be estimated. The average rate of return on a company-owned store is:

$$\frac{\$470{,}000}{\$1{,}000{,}000 \div 2} = 94\%$$

The internal rate of return is calculated by first determining the present value of an annuity of $1:

$$\text{Present Value of an Annuity of } \$1 = \frac{\$1{,}000{,}000}{\$470{,}000 + \$96{,}000} = 1.77$$

For a period of three years, this factor implies an internal rate of return of more than 20% (from Exhibit 5). However, if we more realistically assumed these cash flows for 15 years, Panera's company-owned stores generate an estimated internal rate of return of approximately 57% (from a spreadsheet calculation). Clearly, both investment evaluation methods indicate a highly successful business.

Source: Panera Bread, *Form 10-K for the Fiscal Year Ended December 25, 2012.*

List and describe factors that complicate capital investment analysis.

Factors That Complicate Capital Investment Analysis

Four widely used methods of evaluating capital investment proposals have been described and illustrated in this chapter. In practice, additional factors such as the following may impact capital investment decisions:

- Income tax
- Proposals with unequal lives
- Leasing versus purchasing
- Uncertainty
- Changes in price levels
- Qualitative factors

Income Tax

The impact of income taxes on capital investment decisions can be material. For example, in determining depreciation for federal income tax purposes, useful lives that are much shorter than the actual useful lives are often used. Also, depreciation for tax purposes often differs from depreciation for financial statement purposes. As a result, the timing of the cash flows for income taxes can have a significant impact on capital investment analysis.[5]

Unequal Proposal Lives

The prior capital investment illustrations assumed that the alternative proposals had the same useful lives. In practice, however, proposals often have different lives.

To illustrate, assume that a company is considering purchasing a new truck or a new computer network. The data for each proposal follows:

[5] The impact of taxes on capital investment analysis is covered in advanced accounting textbooks.

	Truck	Computer Network
Cost	$100,000	$100,000
Minimum desired rate of return	10%	10%
Expected useful life	8 years	5 years
Yearly expected cash flows to be received:		
Year 1	$ 30,000	$ 30,000
Year 2	30,000	30,000
Year 3	25,000	30,000
Year 4	20,000	30,000
Year 5	15,000	35,000
Year 6	15,000	0
Year 7	10,000	0
Year 8	10,000	0
Total	$155,000	$155,000

The expected cash flows and net present value for each proposal are shown in Exhibit 10. Because of the unequal useful lives, however, the net present values in Exhibit 10 are not comparable.

EXHIBIT 10 **Net Present Value Analysis—Unequal Lives of Proposals**

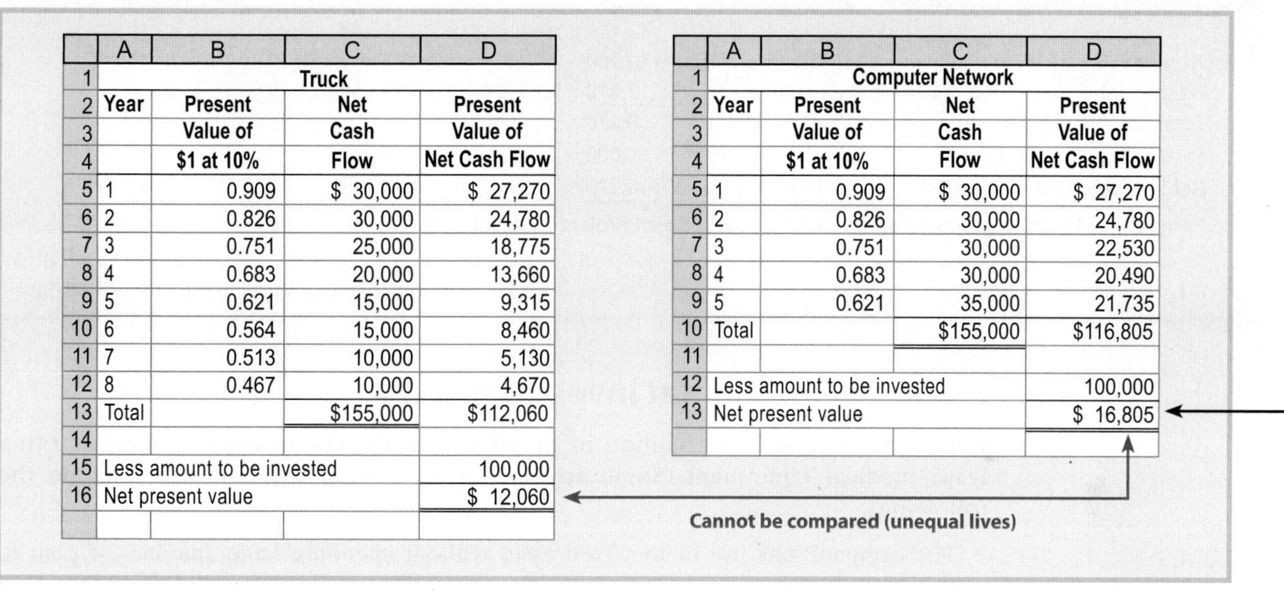

	A	B	C	D
1			Truck	
2	Year	Present	Net	Present
3		Value of	Cash	Value of
4		$1 at 10%	Flow	Net Cash Flow
5	1	0.909	$ 30,000	$ 27,270
6	2	0.826	30,000	24,780
7	3	0.751	25,000	18,775
8	4	0.683	20,000	13,660
9	5	0.621	15,000	9,315
10	6	0.564	15,000	8,460
11	7	0.513	10,000	5,130
12	8	0.467	10,000	4,670
13	Total		$155,000	$112,060
14				
15	Less amount to be invested			100,000
16	Net present value			$ 12,060

	A	B	C	D
1			Computer Network	
2	Year	Present	Net	Present
3		Value of	Cash	Value of
4		$1 at 10%	Flow	Net Cash Flow
5	1	0.909	$ 30,000	$ 27,270
6	2	0.826	30,000	24,780
7	3	0.751	30,000	22,530
8	4	0.683	30,000	20,490
9	5	0.621	35,000	21,735
10	Total		$155,000	$116,805
11				
12	Less amount to be invested			100,000
13	Net present value			$ 16,805

EXHIBIT 11

Net Present Value Analysis—Equalized Lives of Proposals

	A	B	C	D
1		Truck—Revised to 5-Year Life		
2	Year	Present	Net	Present
3		Value of	Cash	Value of
4		$1 at 10%	Flow	Net Cash Flow
5	1	0.909	$ 30,000	$ 27,270
6	2	0.826	30,000	24,780
7	3	0.751	25,000	18,775
8	4	0.683	20,000	13,660
9	5	0.621	15,000	9,315
10	5 (Residual			
11	value)	0.621	40,000	24,840
12	Total		$160,000	$118,640
13				
14	Less amount to be invested			100,000
15	Net present value			$ 18,640

Truck Net Present Value Greater than Computer Network Net Present Value by $1,835

Compared (equal lives)

To make the proposals comparable, the useful lives are adjusted to end at the same time. In this illustration, this is done by assuming that the truck will be sold at the end of five years. The selling price (residual value) of the truck at the end of five years is estimated and included in the cash inflows. Both proposals will then cover five years; thus, the net present value analyses will be comparable.

To illustrate, assume that the truck's estimated selling price (residual value) at the end of Year 5 is $40,000. Exhibit 11 shows the truck's revised present value analysis assuming a five-year life.

As shown in Exhibit 11, the net present value for the truck exceeds the net present value for the computer network by $1,835 ($18,640 – $16,805). Thus, the truck is the more attractive of the two proposals.

Example Exercise 10-5 Net Present Value—Unequal Lives

Project 1 requires an original investment of $50,000. The project will yield cash flows of $12,000 per year for seven years. Project 2 has a calculated net present value of $8,900 over a five-year life. Project 1 could be sold at the end of five years for a price of $30,000. (a) Determine the net present value of Project 1 over a five-year life, with residual value, assuming a minimum rate of return of 12%. (b) Which project provides the greatest net present value?

Follow My Example 10-5

a. Present value of $12,000 per year at 12% for 5 years	$43,260	[$12,000 × 3.605 (Exhibit 5, 12%, 5 years)]
Present value of $30,000 at 12% at the end of 5 years	17,010	[$30,000 × 0.567 (Exhibit 2, 12%, 5 years)]
Total present value of Project 1	$60,270	
Total cost of Project 1	50,000	
Net present value of Project 1	$10,270	

b. Project 1—$10,270 is greater than the net present value of Project 2, $8,900.

Practice Exercises: PE 10-5A, PE 10-5B

Lease Versus Capital Investment

Leasing fixed assets is common in many industries. For example, hospitals often lease medical equipment. Some advantages of leasing a fixed asset include the following:

- The company has use of the fixed asset without spending large amounts of cash to purchase the asset.
- The company eliminates the risk of owning an obsolete asset.
- The company may deduct the annual lease payments for income tax purposes.

A disadvantage of leasing a fixed asset is that it is normally more costly than purchasing the asset. This is because the lessor (owner of the asset) includes in the rental price not only the costs of owning the asset, but also a profit.

The methods of evaluating capital investment proposals illustrated in this chapter can also be used to decide whether to lease or purchase a fixed asset.

Uncertainty

All capital investment analyses rely on factors that are uncertain. For example, estimates of revenues, expenses, and cash flows are uncertain. This is especially true for long-term capital investments. Errors in one or more of the estimates could lead to incorrect decisions. Methods that consider the impact of uncertainty on capital investment analysis are discussed in advanced accounting and finance textbooks.

Service  Focus

IF YOU BUILD IT, THEY WILL COME

A business model describes how an organization delivers products or services to make a profit. Many service companies use what is termed a *network business model.* A network business model connects people and businesses with each other or to a centralized service. Examples of network service businesses include telecommunication, transportation, power and natural gas distribution, cable, satellite, and internet companies. Network businesses often require significant investment in physical assets in order to create the network. Often this is described as a *Field of Dreams strategy* (from the movie of that name) because the network can only generate revenue once it is largely built. For example, a cell phone company draws value from having many cell towers linking many callers together. A critical mass of cell towers must be pre-built in order to establish the business. This is risky. As a result, network business carefully evaluate capital investments prior to building networks.

Changes in Price Levels

Price levels normally change as the economy improves or deteriorates. General price levels often increase in a rapidly growing economy, which is called **inflation**. During such periods, the rate of return on an investment should exceed the rising price level. If this is not the case, the cash returned on the investment will be less than expected.

Price levels may also change for foreign investments. This occurs as currency exchange rates change. **Currency exchange rates** are the rates at which currency in another country can be exchanged for U.S. dollars.

If the amount of local dollars that can be exchanged for one U.S. dollar increases, then the local currency is said to be weakening to the dollar. When a company has an investment in another country where the local currency is weakening, the return on the investment, as expressed in U.S. dollars, is adversely impacted. This is because the expected amount of local currency returned on the investment would purchase fewer U.S. dollars.[6]

Qualitative Considerations

Some benefits of capital investments are qualitative in nature and cannot be estimated in dollar terms. However, if a company does not consider qualitative considerations, an acceptable investment proposal could be rejected.

Some examples of qualitative considerations that may influence capital investment analysis include the investment proposal's impact on the following:

- Product quality
- Manufacturing flexibility
- Employee morale
- Manufacturing productivity
- Market (strategic) opportunities

Many qualitative factors may be as important as, if not more important than, quantitative factors.

Integrity, Objectivity, and Ethics in Business

ASSUMPTION FUDGING

The results of any capital budgeting analysis depend on many subjective estimates, such as the cash flows, discount rate, time period, and total investment amount. The results of the analysis should be used to either support or reject a project. Capital budgeting should not be used to justify an assumed net present value. That is, the analyst should not work backwards, filling in assumed numbers that will produce the desired net present value. Such a reverse approach reduces the credibility of the entire process.

[6] Further discussion on accounting for foreign currency transactions is available on the companion Web site at www.cengagebrain.com.

Diagram the capital rationing process.

Capital Rationing

Capital rationing is the process by which management allocates funds among competing capital investment proposals. In this process, management often uses a combination of the methods described in this chapter.

Exhibit 12 illustrates the capital rationing decision process. Alternative proposals are initially screened by establishing minimum standards, using the cash payback and the average rate of return methods. The proposals that survive this screening are further analyzed, using the net present value and internal rate of return methods.

EXHIBIT 12 **Capital Rationing Decision Process**

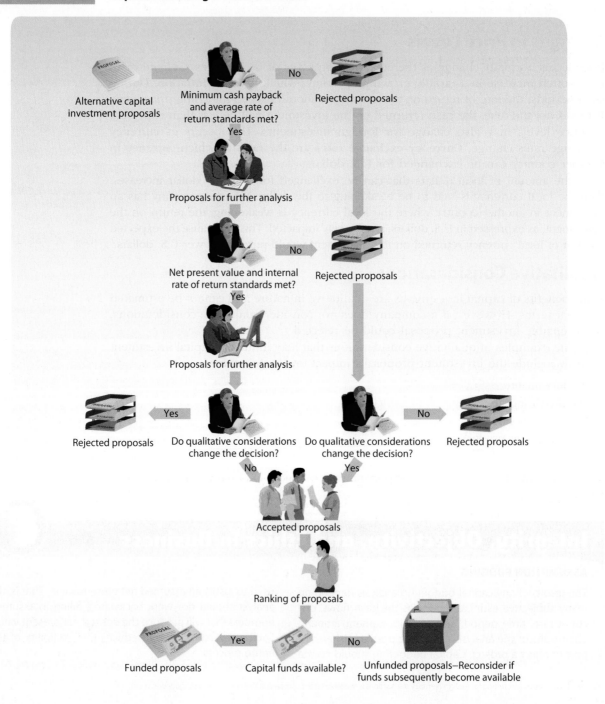

Alternative capital investment proposals

No

Minimum cash payback and average rate of return standards met?

Rejected proposals

Yes

Proposals for further analysis

No

Net present value and internal rate of return standards met?

Rejected proposals

Yes

Proposals for further analysis

Rejected proposals

Yes

Do qualitative considerations change the decision?

Do qualitative considerations change the decision?

No

Rejected proposals

No

Yes

Accepted proposals

Ranking of proposals

Funded proposals

Yes

Capital funds available?

No

Unfunded proposals–Reconsider if funds subsequently become available

Qualitative factors related to each proposal should also be considered throughout the capital rationing process. For example, new equipment might improve the quality of the product and, thus, increase consumer satisfaction and sales.

At the end of the capital rationing process, accepted proposals are ranked and compared with the funds available. Proposals that are selected for funding are included in the capital expenditures budget. Unfunded proposals may be reconsidered if funds later become available.

At a Glance 10

Explain the nature and importance of capital investment analysis.

Key Points Capital investment analysis is the process by which management plans, evaluates, and controls investments involving fixed assets. Capital investment analysis is important to a business because such investments affect profitability for a long period of time.

Learning Outcome	Example Exercises	Practice Exercises
• Describe the purpose of capital investment analysis.		

Evaluate capital investment proposals, using the average rate of return and cash payback methods.

Key Points The average rate of return method measures the expected profitability of an investment in fixed assets. The expected period of time that will pass between the date of an investment and the complete recovery in cash (or equivalent) of the amount invested is the cash payback period.

Learning Outcomes	Example Exercises	Practice Exercises
• Compute the average rate of return of a project.	EE10-1	PE10-1A, 10-1B
• Compute the cash payback period of a project.	EE10-2	PE10-2A, 10-2B

Evaluate capital investment proposals, using the net present value and internal rate of return methods.

Key Points The net present value method uses present values to compute the net present value of the cash flows expected from a proposal. The internal rate of return method uses present values to compute the rate of return from the net cash flows expected from capital investment proposals.

Learning Outcomes	Example Exercises	Practice Exercises
• Compute the net present value of a project.	EE10-3	PE10-3A, 10-3B
• Compute the internal rate of return of a project.	EE10-4	PE10-4A, 10-4B

List and describe factors that complicate capital investment analysis.

Key Points Factors that may complicate capital investment analysis include the impact of income tax, unequal lives of alternative proposals, leasing, uncertainty, changes in price levels, and qualitative considerations.

Learning Outcomes	Example Exercises	Practice Exercises
• Describe the impact of income taxes in capital investment analysis.		
• Evaluate projects with unequal lives.	**EE10-5**	**PE10-5A, 10-5B**
• Describe leasing versus capital investment.		
• Describe uncertainty, changes in price levels, and qualitative considerations in capital investment analysis.		

Diagram the capital rationing process.

Key Points Capital rationing refers to the process by which management allocates available investment funds among competing capital investment proposals. A diagram of the capital rationing process appears in Exhibit 12.

Learning Outcomes	Example Exercises	Practice Exercises
• Define *capital rationing*.		
• Diagram the capital rationing process.		

Key Terms

annuity (415)
average rate of return (411)
capital investment analysis (410)
capital rationing (426)
cash payback period (412)
currency exchange rate (425)
inflation (425)
internal rate of return (IRR) method (419)
net present value method (417)
present value concepts (414)
present value index (418)
present value of an annuity (416)
time value of money concept (410)

Illustrative Problem

The capital investment committee of Hopewell Company is currently considering two investments. The estimated income from operations and net cash flows expected from each investment are as follows:

	Truck		Equipment	
Year	**Income from Operations**	**Net Cash Flow**	**Income from Operations**	**Net Cash Flow**
1	$ 6,000	$ 22,000	$13,000	$ 29,000
2	9,000	25,000	10,000	26,000
3	10,000	26,000	8,000	24,000
4	8,000	24,000	8,000	24,000
5	11,000	27,000	3,000	19,000
	$44,000	$124,000	$42,000	$122,000

Each investment requires $80,000. Straight-line depreciation will be used, and no residual value is expected. The committee has selected a rate of 15% for purposes of the net present value analysis.

Instructions

1. Compute the following:
   a. The average rate of return for each investment.
   b. The net present value for each investment. Use the present value of $1 table appearing in this chapter (Exhibit 2).
2. Why is the net present value of the equipment greater than the truck, even though its average rate of return is less?
3. Prepare a summary for the capital investment committee, advising it on the relative merits of the two investments.

Solution

1. a. Average rate of return for the truck:

$$\frac{\$44{,}000 \div 5}{(\$80{,}000 + \$0) \div 2} = 22\%$$

Average rate of return for the equipment:

$$\frac{\$42{,}000 \div 5}{(\$80{,}000 + \$0) \div 2} = 21\%$$

b. Net present value analysis:

		Net Cash Flow		Present Value of Net Cash Flow	
Year	**Present Value of $1 at 15%**	**Truck**	**Equipment**	**Truck**	**Equipment**
1	0.870	$ 22,000	$ 29,000	$19,140	$25,230
2	0.756	25,000	26,000	18,900	19,656
3	0.658	26,000	24,000	17,108	15,792
4	0.572	24,000	24,000	13,728	13,728
5	0.497	27,000	19,000	13,419	9,443
Total		$124,000	$122,000	$82,295	$83,849
Less amount to be invested				80,000	80,000
Net present value				$ 2,295	$ 3,849

2. The equipment has a lower average rate of return than the truck because the equipment's total income from operations for the five years is $42,000, which is $2,000 less than the truck's. Even so, the net present value of the equipment is greater than that of the truck because the equipment has higher cash flows in the early years.

3. Both investments exceed the selected rate established for the net present value analysis. The truck has a higher average rate of return, but the equipment offers a larger net present value. Thus, if only one of the two investments can be accepted, the equipment would be the more attractive.

Discussion Questions

1. What are the principal objections to the use of the average rate of return method in evaluating capital investment proposals?
2. Discuss the principal limitations of the cash payback method for evaluating capital investment proposals.
3. Why would the average rate of return differ from the internal rate of return on the same project?
4. Your boss has suggested that a one-year payback period is the same as a 100% average rate of return. Do you agree?
5. Why would the cash payback method understate the attractiveness of a project with a large residual value?
6. Why would the use of the cash payback period for analyzing the financial performance of theatrical releases from a motion picture production studio be supported over the net present value method?
7. A net present value analysis used to evaluate a proposed equipment acquisition indicated a $7,900 net present value. What is the meaning of the $7,900 as it relates to the desirability of the proposal?
8. Two projects have an identical net present value of $9,000. Are both projects equal in desirability?
9. What are the major disadvantages of the use of the net present value method of analyzing capital investment proposals?
10. What are the major disadvantages of the use of the internal rate of return method of analyzing capital investment proposals?
11. What are the major advantages of leasing a fixed asset rather than purchasing it?
12. Give an example of a qualitative factor that should be considered in a capital investment analysis related to acquiring automated factory equipment.

Practice Exercises

EE 10-1 p.412

SHOW ME HOW

PE 10-1A Average rate of return **OBJ. 2**

Determine the average rate of return for a project that is estimated to yield total income of $170,000 over five years, has a cost of $320,000, and has a $20,000 residual value.

EE 10-1 p.412

SHOW ME HOW

PE 10-1B Average rate of return **OBJ. 2**

Determine the average rate of return for a project that is estimated to yield total income of $36,000 over three years, has a cost of $70,000, and has a $10,000 residual value.

EE 10-2 *p.414*

PE 10-2A Cash payback period — OBJ. 2

A project has estimated annual net cash flows of $118,600. It is estimated to cost $616,720. Determine the cash payback period. Round to one decimal place.

EE 10-2 *p.414*

PE 10-2B Cash payback period — OBJ. 2

A project has estimated annual net cash flows of $9,300. It is estimated to cost $41,850. Determine the cash payback period. Round to one decimal place.

EE 10-3 *p.419*

PE 10-3A Net present value — OBJ. 3

A project has estimated annual net cash flows of $6,800 for five years and is estimated to cost $23,125. Assume a minimum acceptable rate of return of 12%. Using Exhibit 5, determine (1) the net present value of the project and (2) the present value index, rounded to two decimal places.

EE 10-3 *p.419*

PE 10-3B Net present value — OBJ. 3

A project has estimated annual net cash flows of $96,200 for four years and is estimated to cost $315,500. Assume a minimum acceptable rate of return of 10%. Using Exhibit 5, determine (1) the net present value of the project and (2) the present value index, rounded to two decimal places.

EE 10-4 *p.421*

PE 10-4A Internal rate of return — OBJ. 3

A project is estimated to cost $104,328 and provide annual net cash flows of $21,000 for eight years. Determine the internal rate of return for this project, using Exhibit 5.

EE 10-4 *p.421*

PE 10-4B Internal rate of return — OBJ. 3

A project is estimated to cost $362,672 and provide annual net cash flows of $76,000 for nine years. Determine the internal rate of return for this project, using Exhibit 5.

EE 10-5 *p.424*

PE 10-5A Net present value—unequal lives — OBJ. 4

Project A requires an original investment of $32,600. The project will yield cash flows of $7,000 per year for nine years. Project B has a calculated net present value of $3,500 over a six-year life. Project A could be sold at the end of six years for a price of $15,000. (a) Determine the net present value of Project A over a six-year life, with residual value, assuming a minimum rate of return of 12%. (b) Which project provides the greatest net present value?

EE 10-5 *p.424*

PE 10-5B Net present value—unequal lives — OBJ. 4

Project 1 requires an original investment of $55,000. The project will yield cash flows of $15,000 per year for seven years. Project 2 has a calculated net present value of $5,000 over a four-year life. Project 1 could be sold at the end of four years for a price of $38,000. (a) Determine the net present value of Project 1 over a four-year life, with residual value, assuming a minimum rate of return of 20%. (b) Which project provides the greatest net present value?

Exercises

EX 10-1 Average rate of return — OBJ. 2

✔ Testing equipment, 7%

The following data are accumulated by ChemLab Inc. in evaluating two competing capital investment proposals:

	Testing Equipment	Vehicle
Amount of investment	$86,000	$30,000
Useful life	6 years	8 years
Estimated residual value	0	0
Estimated total income over the useful life	$18,060	$12,000

Determine the expected average rate of return for each proposal.

EX 10-2 Average rate of return—cost savings **OBJ. 2**

Midwest Fabricators Inc. is considering an investment in equipment that will replace direct labor. The equipment has a cost of $132,000 with a $16,000 residual value and a 10-year life. The equipment will replace one employee who has an average wage of $34,000 per year. In addition, the equipment will have operating and energy costs of $5,380 per year.

Determine the average rate of return on the equipment, giving effect to straight-line depreciation on the investment.

✔ Average annual income, $405,000

SHOW ME HOW

EX 10-3 Average rate of return—new product **OBJ. 2**

Galactic Inc. is considering an investment in new equipment that will be used to manufacture a smartphone. The phone is expected to generate additional annual sales of 6,000 units at $250 per unit. The equipment has a cost of $850,000, residual value of $50,000, and an eight-year life. The equipment can only be used to manufacture the phone. The cost to manufacture the phone follows:

Cost per unit:	
Direct labor	$ 15.00
Direct materials	134.00
Factory overhead (including depreciation)	33.50
Total cost per unit	$182.50

Determine the average rate of return on the equipment.

Year 1: $(168,500)

SHOW ME HOW

EX 10-4 Calculate cash flows **OBJ. 2**

Nature's Way Inc. is planning to invest in new manufacturing equipment to make a new garden tool. The new garden tool is expected to generate additional annual sales of 2,500 units at $60 each. The new manufacturing equipment will cost $227,000 and is expected to have a 10-year life and $17,000 residual value. Selling expenses related to the new product are expected to be 5% of sales revenue. The cost to manufacture the product includes the following on a per-unit basis:

Direct labor	$ 8.00
Direct materials	22.00
Fixed factory overhead—depreciation	8.40
Variable factory overhead	3.60
Total	$42.00

Determine the net cash flows for the first year of the project, Years 2–9, and for the last year of the project.

✔ Location 1: 5 years

SHOW ME HOW

EX 10-5 Cash payback period for a service company **OBJ. 2**

Fidelity Bancorp Inc. is evaluating two capital investment proposals for a drive-up ATM kiosk, each requiring an investment of $280,000 and each with an eight-year life and expected total net cash flows of $448,000. Location 1 is expected to provide equal annual net cash flows of $56,000, and Location 2 is expected to have the following unequal annual net cash flows:

Year 1	$90,000	Year 5	$42,000
Year 2	70,000	Year 6	42,000
Year 3	60,000	Year 7	42,000
Year 4	60,000	Year 8	42,000

Determine the cash payback period for both location proposals.

EX 10-6 Cash payback method **OBJ. 2**

Lily Products Company is considering an investment in one of two new product lines. The investment required for either product line is $540,000. The net cash flows associated with each product are as follows:

Year	Liquid Soap	Body Lotion
1	$170,000	$ 90,000
2	150,000	90,000
3	120,000	90,000
4	100,000	90,000
5	70,000	90,000
6	40,000	90,000
7	40,000	90,000
8	30,000	90,000
Total	$720,000	$720,000

a. Recommend a product offering to Lily Products Company, based on the cash payback period for each product line.

b. Why is one product line preferred over the other, even though they both have the same total net cash flows through eight periods?

EX 10-7 Net present value method **OBJ. 3**

✔ a. NPV, $4,238

SHOW ME HOW

The following data are accumulated by Dillon Company in evaluating the purchase of $39,600 of equipment, having a four-year useful life:

	Net Income	Net Cash Flow
Year 1	$ 4,100	$14,000
Year 2	8,100	18,000
Year 3	7,100	17,000
Year 4	2,100	12,000

a. Assuming that the desired rate of return is 15%, determine the net present value for the proposal. Use the table of the present value of $1 appearing in Exhibit 2 of this chapter.

b. Would management be likely to look with favor on the proposal? Explain.

EX 10-8 Net present value method for a service company **OBJ. 3**

✔ a. 2016, $13,000

AM Express Inc. is considering the purchase of an additional delivery vehicle for $55,000 on January 1, 2016. The truck is expected to have a five-year life with an expected residual value of $15,000 at the end of five years. The expected additional revenues from the added delivery capacity are anticipated to be $58,000 per year for each of the next five years. A driver will cost $42,000 in 2016, with an expected annual salary increase of $1,000 for each year thereafter. The annual operating costs for the truck are estimated to be $3,000 per year.

a. Determine the expected annual net cash flows from the delivery truck investment for 2016–2020.

b. Calculate the net present value of the investment, assuming that the minimum desired rate of return is 12%. Use the present value of $1 table appearing in Exhibit 2 of this chapter.

c. Is the additional truck a good investment based on your analysis? Explain.

EX 10-9 Net present value method—annuity for a service company **OBJ. 3**

✔ a. $22 million

Winter Lake Hotels is considering the construction of a new hotel for $150 million. The expected life of the hotel is 30 years, with no residual value. The hotel is expected to earn revenues of $55 million per year. Total expenses, including depreciation, are expected to be $38 million per year. Winter Lake management has set a minimum acceptable rate of return of 14%.

(Continued)

a. Determine the equal annual net cash flows from operating the hotel.

b. Calculate the net present value of the new hotel, using the present value of an annuity of $1 table found in Appendix A. Round to the nearest million dollars.

c. Does your analysis support construction of the new hotel? Explain.

EX 10-10 Net present value method—annuity

OBJ. 3

✔ a. $46,000

Briggs Excavation Company is planning an investment of $132,000 for a bulldozer. The bulldozer is expected to operate for 1,500 hours per year for five years. Customers will be charged $110 per hour for bulldozer work. The bulldozer operator costs $28 per hour in wages and benefits. The bulldozer is expected to require annual maintenance costing $8,000. The bulldozer uses fuel that is expected to cost $46 per hour of bulldozer operation.

a. Determine the equal annual net cash flows from operating the bulldozer.

b. Determine the net present value of the investment, assuming that the desired rate of return is 10%. Use the present value of an annuity of $1 table in the chapter (Exhibit 5). Round to the nearest dollar.

c. Should Briggs invest in the bulldozer, based on this analysis? Explain.

d. Determine the number of operating hours such that the present value of cash flows equals the amount to be invested.

EX 10-11 Net present value method for a service company

OBJ. 3

✔ a. $157,600,000

Carnival Corporation has recently placed into service some of the largest cruise ships in the world. One of these ships, the *Carnival Breeze*, can hold up to 3,600 passengers, and it can cost $750 million to build. Assume the following additional information:

- There will be 330 cruise days per year operated at a full capacity of 3,600 passengers.
- The variable expenses per passenger are estimated to be $140 per cruise day.
- The revenue per passenger is expected to be $340 per cruise day.
- The fixed expenses for running the ship, other than depreciation, are estimated to be $80,000,000 per year.
- The ship has a service life of 10 years, with a residual value of $140,000,000 at the end of 10 years.

a. Determine the annual net cash flow from operating the cruise ship.

b. Determine the net present value of this investment, assuming a 12% minimum rate of return. Use the present value tables provided in the chapter in determining your answer.

EX 10-12 Present value index

OBJ. 3

✔ Ft. Collins, 0.98

Dip N' Dunk Doughnuts has computed the net present value for capital expenditure at two locations. Relevant data related to the computation are as follows:

	Ft. Collins	Boulder
Total present value of net cash flow	$607,600	$624,000
Less amount to be invested	620,000	600,000
Net present value	$(12,400)	$ 24,000

a. Determine the present value index for each proposal.

b. Which location does your analysis support? Explain.

EX 10-13 Net present value method and present value index **OBJ. 3**

✔ b. Packing machine, 1.55

Diamond & Turf Inc. is considering an investment in one of two machines. The sewing machine will increase productivity from sewing 150 baseballs per hour to sewing 290 per hour. The contribution margin per unit is $0.32 per baseball. Assume that any increased production of baseballs can be sold. The second machine is an automatic packing machine for the golf ball line. The packing machine will reduce packing labor cost. The labor cost saved is equivalent to $21 per hour. The sewing machine will cost $260,000, have an eight-year life, and will operate for 1,800 hours per year. The packing machine will cost $85,000, have an eight-year life, and will operate for 1,400 hours per year. Diamond & Turf seeks a minimum rate of return of 15% on its investments.

a. Determine the net present value for the two machines. Use the present value of an annuity of $1 table in the chapter (Exhibit 5). Round to the nearest dollar.

b. Determine the present value index for the two machines. Round to two decimal places.

c. If Diamond & Turf has sufficient funds for only one of the machines and qualitative factors are equal between the two machines, in which machine should it invest? Explain.

EX 10-14 Average rate of return, cash payback period, net present value method for a service company **OBJ. 2, 3**

✔ b. 5 years

SHOW ME HOW

Bi-Coastal Railroad Inc. is considering acquiring equipment at a cost of $520,000. The equipment has an estimated life of eight years and no residual value. It is expected to provide yearly net cash flows of $104,000. The company's minimum desired rate of return for net present value analysis is 10%.

Compute the following:

a. The average rate of return, giving effect to straight-line depreciation on the investment.

b. The cash payback period.

c. The net present value. Use the present value of an annuity of $1 table appearing in this chapter (Exhibit 5). Round to the nearest dollar.

EX 10-15 Cash payback period, net present value analysis, and qualitative considerations **OBJ. 2, 3, 4**

✔ a. 4 years

The plant manager of Shenzhen Electronics Company is considering the purchase of new automated assembly equipment. The new equipment will cost $1,400,000. The manager believes that the new investment will result in direct labor savings of $350,000 per year for 10 years.

a. What is the payback period on this project?

b. What is the net present value, assuming a 10% rate of return? Use the present value of an annuity of $1 table in Exhibit 5.

c. What else should the manager consider in the analysis?

EX 10-16 Internal rate of return method **OBJ. 3**

✔ a. 3.785

SHOW ME HOW

The internal rate of return method is used by Testerman Construction Co. in analyzing a capital expenditure proposal that involves an investment of $113,550 and annual net cash flows of $30,000 for each of the six years of its useful life.

a. Determine a present value factor for an annuity of $1, which can be used in determining the internal rate of return.

b. Using the factor determined in part (a) and the present value of an annuity of $1 table appearing in this chapter (Exhibit 5), determine the internal rate of return for the proposal.

EX 10-17 Internal rate of return method for a service company OBJ. 3, 4

The Canyons Resort, a Utah ski resort, recently announced a $415 million expansion of lodging properties, lifts, and terrain. Assume that this investment is estimated to produce $99 million in equal annual cash flows for each of the first 10 years of the project life.

a. Determine the expected internal rate of return of this project for 10 years, using the present value of an annuity of $1 table found in Exhibit 5.

b. What are some uncertainties that could reduce the internal rate of return of this project?

EX 10-18 Internal rate of return method—two projects OBJ. 3

✔ a. Delivery truck, 15%

Munch N' Crunch Snack Company is considering two possible investments: a delivery truck or a bagging machine. The delivery truck would cost $43,056 and could be used to deliver an additional 95,000 bags of pretzels per year. Each bag of pretzels can be sold for a contribution margin of $0.45. The delivery truck operating expenses, excluding depreciation, are $1.35 per mile for 24,000 miles per year. The bagging machine would replace an old bagging machine, and its net investment cost would be $61,614. The new machine would require three fewer hours of direct labor per day. Direct labor is $18 per hour. There are 250 operating days in the year. Both the truck and the bagging machine are estimated to have seven-year lives. The minimum rate of return is 13%. However, Munch N' Crunch has funds to invest in only one of the projects.

a. Compute the internal rate of return for each investment. Use the present value of an annuity of $1 table appearing in this chapter (Exhibit 5).

b. Provide a memo to management, with a recommendation.

EX 10-19 Net present value method and internal rate of return method for a service company OBJ. 3

✔ a. ($12,845)

Buckeye Healthcare Corp. is proposing to spend $186,725 on an eight-year project that has estimated net cash flows of $35,000 for each of the eight years.

a. Compute the net present value, using a rate of return of 12%. Use the present value of an annuity of $1 table in the chapter (Exhibit 5).

b. Based on the analysis prepared in part (a), is the rate of return (1) more than 12%, (2) 12%, or (3) less than 12%? Explain.

c. Determine the internal rate of return by computing a present value factor for an annuity of $1 and using the present value of an annuity of $1 table presented in the text (Exhibit 5).

EX 10-20 Identify error in capital investment analysis calculations OBJ. 3

Artscape Inc. is considering the purchase of automated machinery that is expected to have a useful life of five years and no residual value. The average rate of return on the average investment has been computed to be 20%, and the cash payback period was computed to be 5.5 years.

Do you see any reason to question the validity of the data presented? Explain.

EX 10-21 Net present value—unequal lives OBJ. 3, 4

✔ Net present value, Processing mill, $196,220

Bunker Hill Mining Company has two competing proposals: a processing mill and an electric shovel. Both pieces of equipment have an initial investment of $750,000. The net cash flows estimated for the two proposals are as follows:

	Net Cash Flow	
Year	Processing Mill	Electric Shovel
1	$310,000	$330,000
2	260,000	325,000
3	260,000	325,000
4	260,000	320,000
5	180,000	
6	130,000	
7	120,000	
8	120,000	

The estimated residual value of the processing mill at the end of Year 4 is $280,000.

Determine which equipment should be favored, comparing the net present values of the two proposals and assuming a minimum rate of return of 15%. Use the present value tables presented in this chapter (Exhibits 2 and 5).

EX 10-22 Net present value—unequal lives

OBJ. 3, 4

Daisy's Creamery Inc. is considering one of two investment options. Option 1 is a $75,000 investment in new blending equipment that is expected to produce equal annual cash flows of $19,000 for each of seven years. Option 2 is a $90,000 investment in a new computer system that is expected to produce equal annual cash flows of $27,000 for each of five years. The residual value of the blending equipment at the end of the fifth year is estimated to be $15,000. The computer system has no expected residual value at the end of the fifth year.

Assume there is sufficient capital to fund only one of the projects. Determine which project should be selected, comparing the (a) net present values and (b) present value indices of the two projects. Assume a minimum rate of return of 10%. Round the present value index to two decimal places. Use the present value tables presented in this chapter (Exhibits 2 and 5).

Problems: Series A

PR 10-1A Average rate of return method, net present value method, and analysis for a service company

OBJ. 2, 3

✔ 1. a. 34%

SHOW ME HOW

The capital investment committee of Touch of Eden Landscaping Company is considering two capital investments. The estimated income from operations and net cash flows from each investment are as follows:

	Front-End Loader		Greenhouse Fixtures	
Year	**Income from Operations**	**Net Cash Flow**	**Income from Operations**	**Net Cash Flow**
1	$23,000	$ 35,000	$10,200	$ 22,200
2	20,000	32,000	10,200	22,200
3	12,000	24,000	10,200	22,200
4	(2,000)	10,000	10,200	22,200
5	(2,000)	10,000	10,200	22,200
	$51,000	$111,000	$51,000	$111,000

Each project requires an investment of $60,000. Straight-line depreciation will be used, and no residual value is expected. The committee has selected a rate of 12% for purposes of the net present value analysis.

Instructions

1. Compute the following:
   a. The average rate of return for each investment. Round to one decimal place.
   b. The net present value for each investment. Use the present value of $1 table appearing in this chapter (Exhibit 2). Round present values to the nearest dollar.
2. Prepare a brief report for the capital investment committee, advising it on the relative merits of the two investments.

PR 10-2A Cash payback period, net present value method, and analysis — OBJ. 2, 3

✔ 1. b. Plant expansion, $305,040

Elite Apparel Inc. is considering two investment projects. The estimated net cash flows from each project are as follows:

Year	Plant Expansion	Retail Store Expansion
1	$ 450,000	$ 500,000
2	450,000	400,000
3	340,000	350,000
4	280,000	250,000
5	180,000	200,000
Total	$1,700,000	$1,700,000

Each project requires an investment of $900,000. A rate of 15% has been selected for the net present value analysis.

Instructions

1. Compute the following for each product:
   a. Cash payback period.
   b. The net present value. Use the present value of $1 table appearing in this chapter (Exhibit 2).
2. Prepare a brief report advising management on the relative merits of each project.

PR 10-3A Net present value method, present value index, and analysis for a service company — OBJ. 3

✔ 2. Computer Network, 1.20

Continental Railroad Company is evaluating three capital investment proposals by using the net present value method. Relevant data related to the proposals are summarized as follows:

	Maintenance Equipment	Ramp Facilities	Computer Network
Amount to be invested	$8,000,000	$20,000,000	$9,000,000
Annual net cash flows:			
Year 1	4,000,000	12,000,000	6,000,000
Year 2	3,500,000	10,000,000	5,000,000
Year 3	2,500,000	9,000,000	4,000,000

Instructions

1. Assuming that the desired rate of return is 20%, prepare a net present value analysis for each proposal. Use the present value of $1 table appearing in this chapter (Exhibit 2).
2. Determine a present value index for each proposal. Round to two decimal places.
3. Which proposal offers the largest amount of present value per dollar of investment? Explain.

PR 10-4A Net present value method, internal rate of return method, and analysis for a service company — OBJ. 3

✔ 1. a. Wind turbines, $82,600

The management of Advanced Alternative Power Inc. is considering two capital investment projects. The estimated net cash flows from each project are as follows:

Year	Wind Turbines	Biofuel Equipment
1	$280,000	$300,000
2	280,000	300,000
3	280,000	300,000
4	280,000	300,000

The wind turbines require an investment of $887,600, while the biofuel equipment requires an investment of $911,100. No residual value is expected from either project.

Instructions

1. Compute the following for each project:
   a. The net present value. Use a rate of 6% and the present value of an annuity of $1 table appearing in this chapter (Exhibit 5).
   b. A present value index. Round to two decimal places.
2. Determine the internal rate of return for each project by (a) computing a present value factor for an annuity of $1 and (b) using the present value of an annuity of $1 table appearing in this chapter (Exhibit 5).
3. What advantage does the internal rate of return method have over the net present value method in comparing projects?

PR 10-5A Alternative capital investments — OBJ. 3, 4

✔ 1. Servers, $11,105

The investment committee of Sentry Insurance Co. is evaluating two projects, office expansion and upgrade to computer servers. The projects have different useful lives, but each requires an investment of $490,000. The estimated net cash flows from each project are as follows:

	Net Cash Flows	
Year	**Office Expansion**	**Servers**
1	$125,000	$165,000
2	125,000	165,000
3	125,000	165,000
4	125,000	165,000
5	125,000	
6	125,000	

The committee has selected a rate of 12% for purposes of net present value analysis. It also estimates that the residual value at the end of each project's useful life is $0, but at the end of the fourth year, the office expansion's residual value would be $180,000.

Instructions

1. For each project, compute the net present value. Use the present value of an annuity of $1 table appearing in this chapter (Exhibit 5). (Ignore the unequal lives of the projects.)
2. For each project, compute the net present value, assuming that the office expansion is adjusted to a four-year life for purposes of analysis. Use the present value of $1 table appearing in this chapter (Exhibit 2).
3. Prepare a report to the investment committee, providing your advice on the relative merits of the two projects.

PR 10-6A Capital rationing decision for a service company involving four proposals — OBJ. 2, 3, 5

✔ 5. Proposal C, 1.57

Renaissance Capital Group is considering allocating a limited amount of capital investment funds among four proposals. The amount of proposed investment, estimated income from operations, and net cash flow for each proposal are as follows:

	Investment	Year	Income from Operations	Net Cash Flow
Proposal A:	$680,000	1	$ 64,000	$200,000
		2	64,000	200,000
		3	64,000	200,000
		4	24,000	160,000
		5	24,000	160,000
			$240,000	$920,000
Proposal B:	$320,000	1	$ 26,000	$ 90,000
		2	26,000	90,000
		3	6,000	70,000
		4	6,000	70,000
		5	(44,000)	20,000
			$ 20,000	$340,000

(Continued)

Proposal C:	$108,000	1	$ 33,400	$ 55,000
		2	31,400	53,000
		3	28,400	50,000
		4	25,400	47,000
		5	23,400	45,000
			$142,000	$ 250,000
Proposal D:	$400,000	1	$100,000	$ 180,000
		2	100,000	180,000
		3	80,000	160,000
		4	20,000	100,000
		5	0	80,000
			$300,000	$700,000

The company's capital rationing policy requires a maximum cash payback period of three years. In addition, a minimum average rate of return of 12% is required on all projects. If the preceding standards are met, the net present value method and present value indexes are used to rank the remaining proposals.

Instructions

1. Compute the cash payback period for each of the four proposals.
2. Giving effect to straight-line depreciation on the investments and assuming no estimated residual value, compute the average rate of return for each of the four proposals. Round to one decimal place.
3. Using the following format, summarize the results of your computations in parts (1) and (2). By placing the calculated amounts in the first two columns on the left and by placing a check mark in the appropriate column to the right, indicate which proposals should be accepted for further analysis and which should be rejected.

Proposal	Cash Payback Period	Average Rate of Return	Accept for Further Analysis	Reject
A				
B				
C				
D				

4. For the proposals accepted for further analysis in part (3), compute the net present value. Use a rate of 15% and the present value of $1 table appearing in this chapter (Exhibit 2).
5. Compute the present value index for each of the proposals in part (4). Round to two decimal places.
6. Rank the proposals from most attractive to least attractive, based on the present values of net cash flows computed in part (4).
7. Rank the proposals from most attractive to least attractive, based on the present value indexes computed in part (5).
8. Based on the analyses, comment on the relative attractiveness of the proposals ranked in parts (6) and (7).

Problems: Series B

✔ 1. a. 18.7%

SHOW ME HOW

PR 10-1B Average rate of return method, net present value method, and analysis for a service company **OBJ. 2, 3**

The capital investment committee of Ellis Transport and Storage Inc. is considering two investment projects. The estimated income from operations and net cash flows from each investment are as follows:

Year	Warehouse: Income from Operations	Warehouse: Net Cash Flow	Tracking Technology: Income from Operations	Tracking Technology: Net Cash Flow
1	$ 61,400	$135,000	$ 34,400	$108,000
2	51,400	125,000	34,400	108,000
3	36,400	110,000	34,400	108,000
4	26,400	100,000	34,400	108,000
5	(3,600)	70,000	34,400	108,000
Total	$172,000	$540,000	$172,000	$540,000

Each project requires an investment of $368,000. Straight-line depreciation will be used, and no residual value is expected. The committee has selected a rate of 15% for purposes of the net present value analysis.

Instructions

1. Compute the following:
   a. The average rate of return for each investment. Round to one decimal place.
   b. The net present value for each investment. Use the present value of $1 table appearing in this chapter (Exhibit 2). Round present values to the nearest dollar.
2. Prepare a brief report for the capital investment committee, advising it on the relative merits of the two projects.

PR 10-2B Cash payback period, net present value method, and analysis for a service company

OBJ. 2, 3

✔ 1. b. *Pro Gamer,* $49,465

Social Circle Publications Inc. is considering two new magazine products. The estimated net cash flows from each product are as follows:

Year	*Sound Cellar*	*Pro Gamer*
1	$ 65,000	$ 70,000
2	60,000	55,000
3	25,000	35,000
4	25,000	30,000
5	45,000	30,000
Total	$220,000	$220,000

Each product requires an investment of $125,000. A rate of 10% has been selected for the net present value analysis.

Instructions

1. Compute the following for each product:
   a. Cash payback period.
   b. The net present value. Use the present value of $1 table appearing in this chapter (Exhibit 2).
2. Prepare a brief report advising management on the relative merits of each of the two products.

PR 10-3B Net present value method, present value index, and analysis for a service company

OBJ. 3

✔ 2. Branch office expansion, 0.95

First United Bank Inc. is evaluating three capital investment projects by using the net present value method. Relevant data related to the projects are summarized as follows:

	Branch Office Expansion	Computer System Upgrade	ATM Kiosk Expansion
Amount to be invested	$420,000	$350,000	$520,000
Annual net cash flows:			
Year 1	200,000	190,000	275,000
Year 2	160,000	180,000	250,000
Year 3	160,000	170,000	250,000

(Continued)

Instructions

1. Assuming that the desired rate of return is 15%, prepare a net present value analysis for each project. Use the present value of $1 table appearing in this chapter (Exhibit 2).
2. Determine a present value index for each project. Round to two decimal places.
3. Which project offers the largest amount of present value per dollar of investment? Explain.

PR 10-4B Net present value method, internal rate of return method, and analysis for a service company OBJ. 3

✔ 1. a. *After Hours* $100,800

The management of Style Networks Inc. is considering two TV show projects. The estimated net cash flows from each project are as follows:

Year	*After Hours*	*Sun Fun*
1	$320,000	$290,000
2	320,000	290,000
3	320,000	290,000
4	320,000	290,000

After Hours requires an investment of $913,600, while *Sun Fun* requires an investment of $880,730. No residual value is expected from either project.

Instructions

1. Compute the following for each project:
   a. The net present value. Use a rate of 10% and the present value of an annuity of $1 table appearing in this chapter (Exhibit 5).
   b. A present value index. Round to two decimal places.
2. Determine the internal rate of return for each project by (a) computing a present value factor for an annuity of $1 and (b) using the present value of an annuity of $1 table appearing in this chapter (Exhibit 5).
3. What advantage does the internal rate of return method have over the net present value method in comparing projects?

PR 10-5B Alternative capital investments OBJ. 3, 4

✔ 1. Topeka, $135,600

The investment committee of Auntie M's Restaurants Inc. is evaluating two restaurant sites. The sites have different useful lives, but each requires an investment of $900,000. The estimated net cash flows from each site are as follows:

	Net Cash Flows	
Year	Wichita	Topeka
1	$310,000	$400,000
2	310,000	400,000
3	310,000	400,000
4	310,000	400,000
5	310,000	
6	310,000	

The committee has selected a rate of 20% for purposes of net present value analysis. It also estimates that the residual value at the end of each restaurant's useful life is $0, but at the end of the fourth year, Wichita's residual value would be $500,000.

Instructions

1. For each site, compute the net present value. Use the present value of an annuity of $1 table appearing in this chapter (Exhibit 5). (Ignore the unequal lives of the projects.)
2. For each site, compute the net present value, assuming that Wichita is adjusted to a four-year life for purposes of analysis. Use the present value of $1 table appearing in this chapter (Exhibit 2).
3. Prepare a report to the investment committee, providing your advice on the relative merits of the two sites.

PR 10-6B Capital rationing decision for a service company involving four proposals

OBJ. 2, 3, 5

✔ 5. Proposal B, 1.13

Clearcast Communications Inc. is considering allocating a limited amount of capital investment funds among four proposals. The amount of proposed investment, estimated income from operations, and net cash flow for each proposal are as follows:

	Investment	Year	Income from Operations	Net Cash Flow
Proposal A:	$450,000	1	$ 30,000	$120,000
		2	30,000	120,000
		3	20,000	110,000
		4	10,000	100,000
		5	(30,000)	60,000
			$ 60,000	$510,000
Proposal B:	$200,000	1	$ 60,000	$100,000
		2	40,000	80,000
		3	20,000	60,000
		4	(10,000)	30,000
		5	(20,000)	20,000
			$ 90,000	$290,000
Proposal C:	$320,000	1	$ 36,000	$100,000
		2	26,000	90,000
		3	26,000	90,000
		4	16,000	80,000
		5	16,000	80,000
			$120,000	$440,000
Proposal D:	$540,000	1	$ 92,000	$200,000
		2	72,000	180,000
		3	52,000	160,000
		4	12,000	120,000
		5	(8,000)	100,000
			$220,000	$760,000

The company's capital rationing policy requires a maximum cash payback period of three years. In addition, a minimum average rate of return of 12% is required on all projects. If the preceding standards are met, the net present value method and present value indexes are used to rank the remaining proposals.

Instructions

1. Compute the cash payback period for each of the four proposals.
2. Giving effect to straight-line depreciation on the investments and assuming no estimated residual value, compute the average rate of return for each of the four proposals. Round to one decimal place.
3. Using the following format, summarize the results of your computations in parts (1) and (2). By placing the calculated amounts in the first two columns on the left and by placing a check mark in the appropriate column to the right, indicate which proposals should be accepted for further analysis and which should be rejected.

Proposal	Cash Payback Period	Average Rate of Return	Accept for Further Analysis	Reject
A				
B				
C				
D				

4. For the proposals accepted for further analysis in part (3), compute the net present value. Use a rate of 12% and the present value of $1 table appearing in this chapter (Exhibit 2).
5. Compute the present value index for each of the proposals in part (4). Round to two decimal places.

(Continued)

6. Rank the proposals from most attractive to least attractive, based on the present values of net cash flows computed in part (4).
7. Rank the proposals from most attractive to least attractive, based on the present value indexes computed in part (5). Round to two decimal places.
8. Based on the analyses, comment on the relative attractiveness of the proposals ranked in parts (6) and (7).

Cases & Projects

CP 10-1 Ethics and professional conduct in business

Danielle Hastings was recently hired as a cost analyst by CareNet Medical Supplies Inc. One of Danielle's first assignments was to perform a net present value analysis for a new warehouse. Danielle performed the analysis and calculated a present value index of 0.75. The plant manager, Jerrod Moore, is very intent on purchasing the warehouse because he believes that more storage space is needed. Jerrod asks Danielle into his office and the following conversation takes place:

Jerrod: Danielle, you're new here, aren't you?

Danielle: Yes, I am.

Jerrod: Well, Danielle, I'm not at all pleased with the capital investment analysis that you performed on this new warehouse. I need that warehouse for my production. If I don't get it, where am I going to place our output?

Danielle: Well, we need to get product into our customers' hands.

Jerrod: I agree, and we need a warehouse to do that.

Danielle: My analysis does not support constructing a new warehouse. The numbers don't lie; the warehouse does not meet our investment return targets. In fact, it seems to me that purchasing a warehouse does not add much value to the business. We need to be producing product to satisfy customer orders, not to fill a warehouse.

Jerrod: The headquarters people will not allow me to build the warehouse if the numbers don't add up. You know as well as I that many assumptions go into your net present value analysis. Why don't you relax some of your assumptions so that the financial savings will offset the cost?

Danielle: I'm willing to discuss my assumptions with you. Maybe I overlooked something.

Jerrod: Good. Here's what I want you to do. I see in your analysis that you don't project greater sales as a result of the warehouse. It seems to me that if we can store more goods, then we will have more to sell. Thus, logically, a larger warehouse translates into more sales. If you incorporate this into your analysis, I think you'll see that the numbers will work out. Why don't you work it through and come back with a new analysis. I'm really counting on you on this one. Let's get off to a good start together and see if we can get this project accepted.

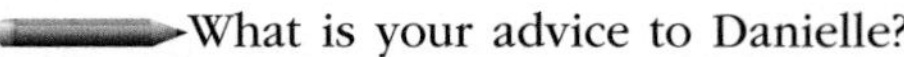What is your advice to Danielle?

CP 10-2 Personal investment analysis for a service company

A Masters of Accountancy degree at Central University costs $12,000 for an additional fifth year of education beyond the bachelor's degree. Assume that all tuition is paid at the beginning of the year. A student considering this investment must evaluate the present value of cash flows from possessing a graduate degree versus holding only the undergraduate degree. Assume that the average student with an undergraduate degree is expected to earn an annual salary of $50,000 per year (assumed to be paid at the end of the year) for 10 years. Assume that the average student with a graduate Masters of Accountancy degree is expected to earn an annual salary of $66,000 per year (assumed to be paid at the end of the year) for nine years after graduation. Assume a minimum rate of return of 10%.

1. Determine the net present value of cash flows from an undergraduate degree. Use the present value table provided in this chapter in Exhibit 5.
2. Determine the net present value of cash flows from a Masters of Accountancy degree, assuming no salary is earned during the graduate year of schooling.
3. What is the net advantage or disadvantage of pursuing a graduate degree under these assumptions?

CP 10-3 Changing prices

Global Electronics Inc. invested $1,000,000 to build a plant in a foreign country. The labor and materials used in production are purchased locally. The plant expansion was estimated to produce an internal rate of return of 20% in U.S. dollar terms. Due to a currency crisis, the currency exchange rate between the local currency and the U.S. dollar doubled from two local units per U.S. dollar to four local units per U.S. dollar.

a. Assume that the plant produced and sold product in the local economy. Explain what impact this change in the currency exchange rate would have on the project's internal rate of return.

b. Assume that the plant produced product in the local economy but exported the product back to the United States for sale. Explain what impact the change in the currency exchange rate would have on the project's internal rate of return under this assumption.

CP 10-4 Qualitative issues in investment analysis

The following are some selected quotes from senior executives:

CEO, **Worthington Industries** *(a high-technology steel company): "We try to find the best technology, stay ahead of the competition, and serve the customer. . . . We'll make any investment that will pay back quickly . . . but if it is something that we really see as a must down the road, payback is not going to be that important."*

Chairman of **Amgen Inc.** *(a biotech company): "You cannot really run the numbers, do net present value calculations, because the uncertainties are really gigantic. . . . You decide on a project you want to run, and then you run the numbers [as a reality check on your assumptions]. Success in a business like this is much more dependent on tracking rather than on predicting, much more dependent on seeing results over time, tracking and adjusting and readjusting, much more dynamic, much more flexible."*

Chief Financial Officer of **Merck & Co., Inc.** *(a pharmaceutical company): ". . . at the individual product level—the development of a successful new product requires on the order of $230 million in R&D, spread over more than a decade—discounted cash flow style analysis does not become a factor until development is near the point of manufacturing scale-up effort. Prior to that point, given the uncertainties associated with new product development, it would be lunacy in our business to decide that we know exactly what's going to happen to a product once it gets out."*

Explain the role of capital investment analysis for these companies.

CP 10-5 Net present value method for a service company

Metro-Goldwyn-Mayer Studios Inc. (MGM) is a major producer and distributor of theatrical and television filmed entertainment. Regarding theatrical films, MGM states, "Our feature films are exploited through a series of sequential domestic and international distribution channels, typically beginning with theatrical exhibition. Thereafter, feature films are first made available for home video (online downloads) generally six months after theatrical release; for pay television, one year after theatrical release; and for syndication, approximately three to five years after theatrical release."

Assume that MGM produces a film during early 2016 at a cost of $340 million and releases it halfway through the year. During the last half of 2016, the film earns revenues of $420 million at the box office. The film requires $90 million of advertising during the release. One year later, by the end of 2017, the film is expected to earn MGM net cash flows from online downloads of $60 million. By the end of 2018, the film is expected to earn MGM $20 million from pay TV; and by the end of 2019, the film is expected to earn $10 million from syndication.

a. Determine the net present value of the film as of the beginning of 2016 if the desired rate of return is 20%. To simplify present value calculations, assume all annual net cash flows occur at the end of each year. Use the table of the present value of $1 appearing in Exhibit 2 of this chapter. Round to the nearest whole million dollars.

b. Under the assumptions provided here, is the film expected to be financially successful?

CP 10-6 Capital investment analysis

Internet Project

Group Project

In one group, find a local business, such as a copy shop, that rents time on desktop computers for an hourly rate. Determine the hourly rate. In the other group, determine the price of a mid-range desktop computer at www.dell.com. Combine this information from the two groups and perform a capital budgeting analysis. Assume that one student will use the computer for 40 hours per semester for the next three years. Also assume that the minimum rate of return is 10%. Use the interest tables in Appendix A in performing your analysis. [*Hint:* Use the appropriate present value of an annuity of $1 factor for 5% compounded for six semiannual periods (periods = 6).]

Does your analysis support the student purchasing the computer?

AP IMAGES/THE DAILY TIMES/LINDSAY PIERCE

CHAPTER 11

Cost Allocation and Activity-Based Costing

Cold Stone Creamery

Have you ever had to request service repairs on an appliance at your home? The repair person may arrive and take five minutes to replace a part. Yet, the bill may indicate a minimum charge for more than five minutes of work.

Why might there be a minimum charge for a service call? The answer is that the service person must charge for the time and expense of coming to your house. In a sense, the bill reflects two elements of service: (1) the cost of coming to your house and (2) the cost of the repair. The first portion of the bill reflects the time required to "set up" the job. The second part of the bill reflects the cost of performing the repair. The setup charge will be the same, whether the repairs take five minutes or five hours. In contrast, the actual repair charge will vary with the time on the job.

Like the repair person, companies must be careful that the cost of their products and services accurately reflect the different activities involved in producing the product or service. Otherwise, the cost of products and services may be distorted and lead to improper management decisions.

To illustrate, **Cold Stone Creamery**, a chain of super premium ice cream shops, uses activity-based costing to determine the cost of its ice cream products, such as cones, mixings, cakes, frozen yogurt, smoothies, and sorbets. The costs of activities, such as scooping and mixing, are added to the cost of the ingredients to determine the total cost of each product. As stated by Cold Stone's president:

". . . it only makes sense to have the price you pay for the product be reflective of the activities involved in making it for you."*

In this chapter, three different methods of allocating factory overhead to products are described and illustrated. In addition, product cost distortions resulting from improper factory overhead allocations are discussed. The chapter concludes by describing activity-based costing for selling and administrative expenses and its use in service businesses.

*Quote from "Experiencing Accounting Videos," Activity-Based Costing. © Cengage Learning, 2008.

Learning Objectives

After studying this chapter, you should be able to: | *Example Exercises*

Objective	Example Exercises
OBJ 1 **Identify three methods used for allocating factory overhead costs to products.**	
Product Costing Allocation Methods	
OBJ 2 **Use a single plantwide factory overhead rate for product costing.**	
Single Plantwide Factory Overhead Rate Method	EE 11-1
OBJ 3 **Use multiple production department factory overhead rates for product costing.**	
Multiple Production Department Factory Overhead Rate Method	
Department Overhead Rates and Allocation	EE 11-2
Distortion of Product Costs	EE 11-2
OBJ 4 **Use activity-based costing for product costing.**	
Activity-Based Costing Method	
Activity Rates and Allocation	EE 11-3
Distortion in Product Costs	EE 11-3
Dangers of Product Cost Distortion	EE 11-3
OBJ 5 **Use activity-based costing to allocate selling and administrative expenses to products.**	
Activity-Based Costing for Selling and Administrative Expenses	EE 11-4
OBJ 6 **Use activity-based costing in a service business.**	
Activity-Based Costing in Service Businesses	EE 11-5

At a Glance 11 Page 466

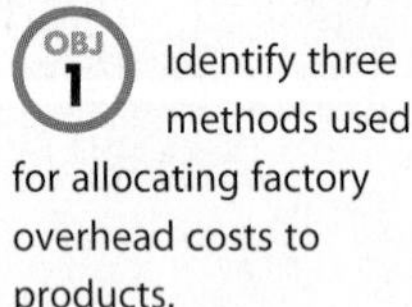

Identify three methods used for allocating factory overhead costs to products.

Product Costing Allocation Methods

Determining the cost of a product is termed **product costing**. Product costs consist of direct materials, direct labor, and factory overhead. The direct materials and direct labor are direct costs that can be traced to the product. However, factory overhead includes indirect costs that must be allocated to the product as shown in Exhibit 1.

EXHIBIT 1

Allocation of Factory Overhead Costs

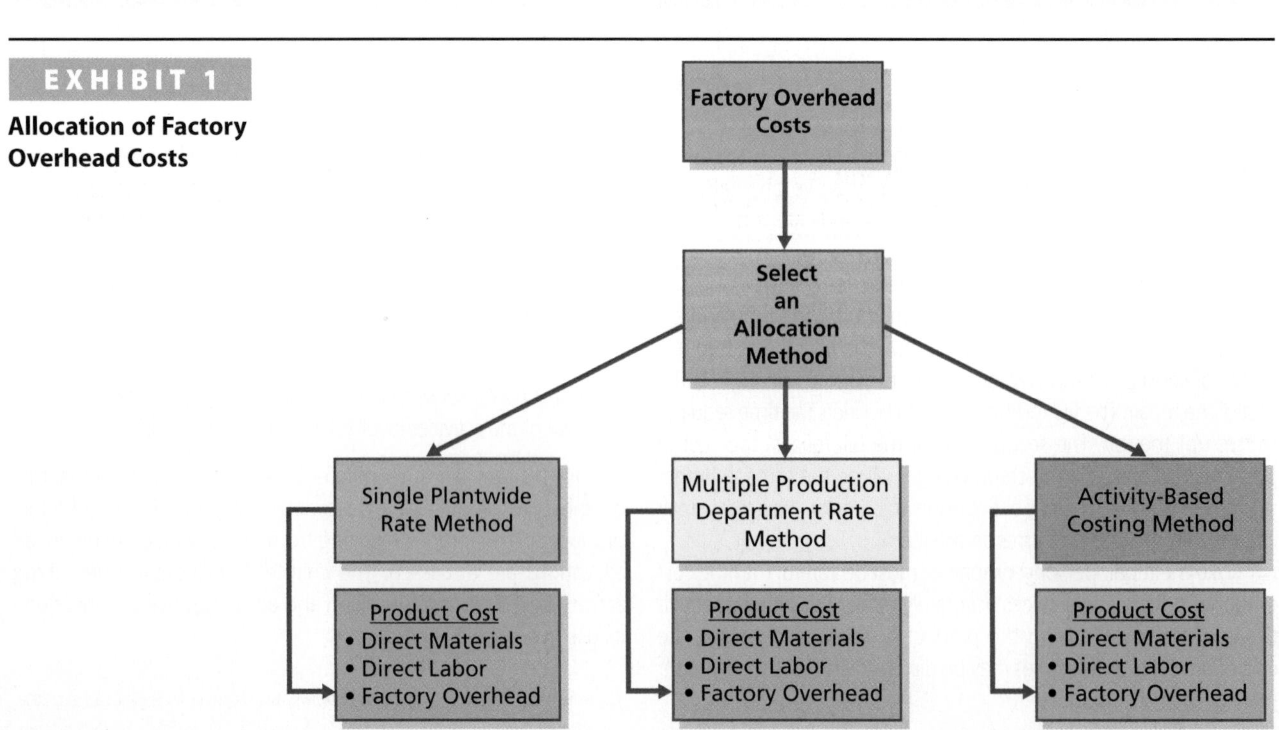

In Chapter 2, the allocation of factory overhead using a predetermined factory overhead rate was illustrated. The most common methods of allocating factory overhead using predetermined factory overhead rates are:

- Single plantwide factory overhead rate method
- Multiple production department factory overhead rate method
- Activity-based costing method

The choice of allocation method is important to managers because the allocation affects the product cost, as shown in Exhibit 1. Managers are concerned about the accuracy of product costs, which are used for decisions such as determining product mix, establishing product price, and determining whether to discontinue a product line.

Single Plantwide Factory Overhead Rate Method

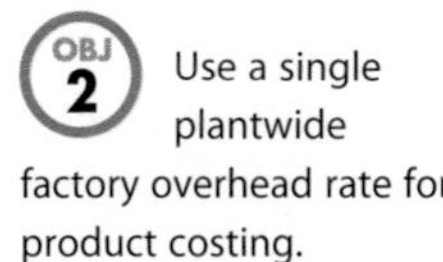
Use a single plantwide factory overhead rate for product costing.

A company may use a predetermined factory overhead rate to allocate factory overhead costs to products. Under the **single plantwide factory overhead rate method**, factory overhead costs are allocated to products using only one rate.

To illustrate, assume the following data for **Ruiz Company**, which manufactures snowmobiles and riding mowers in a single factory:

Total budgeted factory overhead costs for the year	$1,600,000
Total budgeted direct labor hours (computed as follows)...................	20,000 hours

The total budgeted direct labor hours are computed as follows:

	Snowmobiles	Riding Mowers	Total
Planned production for the year...........	1,000 units	1,000 units	
Direct labor hours per unit	× 10 hours	× 10 hours	
Budgeted direct labor hours	10,000 hours	10,000 hours	20,000 hours

Under the single plantwide factory overhead rate method, the $1,600,000 budgeted factory overhead is applied to all products by using one rate. This rate is computed as follows:

$$\text{Single Plantwide Factory Overhead Rate} = \frac{\text{Total Budgeted Factory Overhead}}{\text{Total Budgeted Plantwide Allocation Base}}$$

The budgeted allocation base is a measure of operating activity in the factory. Common allocation bases would include direct labor hours, direct labor dollars, and machine hours. Ruiz allocates factory overhead using budgeted direct labor hours as the plantwide allocation base. Thus, Ruiz's single plantwide factory overhead rate is $80 per direct labor hour, computed as follows:

$$\text{Single Plantwide Factory Overhead Rate} = \frac{\$1{,}600{,}000}{20{,}000 \text{ direct labor hours}}$$

$$= \$80 \text{ per direct labor hour}$$

Ruiz uses the plantwide rate of $80 per direct labor hour to allocate factory overhead to snowmobiles and riding mowers, computed as follows:

	Single Plantwide Factory Overhead Rate	×	Direct Labor Hours per Unit	=	Factory Overhead Cost per Unit
Snowmobile	$80 per direct labor hour	×	10 direct labor hours	=	$800
Riding mower	$80 per direct labor hour	×	10 direct labor hours	=	$800

The factory overhead allocated to each product is $800. This is because each product uses the same number of direct labor hours.

The effects of Ruiz Company using the single plantwide factory overhead rate method are summarized in Exhibit 2.

EXHIBIT 2

Single Plantwide Factory Overhead Rate Method—Ruiz Company

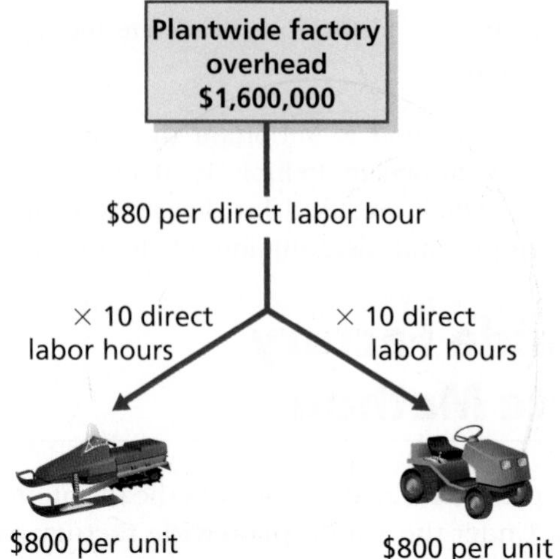

Many military contractors use a single plantwide rate for allocating factory overhead costs to products, such as jet fighters.

The primary advantage of using the single plantwide overhead rate method is that it is simple and inexpensive to use. However, the single plantwide rate assumes that the factory overhead costs are consumed in the same way by all products. For example, in the preceding illustration Ruiz assumes that factory overhead costs are consumed as each direct labor hour is incurred.

The preceding assumption may be valid for companies that manufacture one or a few products. However, if a company manufactures products that consume factory overhead costs in different ways, a single plantwide rate may not accurately allocate factory overhead costs to the products.

Example Exercise 11-1 Single Plantwide Factory Overhead Rate

The total factory overhead for Morris Company is budgeted for the year at $650,000. Morris manufactures two office furniture products: a credenza and desk. The credenza and desk each require four direct labor hours (dlh) to manufacture. Each product is budgeted for 5,000 units of production for the year. Determine (a) the total number of budgeted direct labor hours for the year, (b) the single plantwide factory overhead rate, and (c) the factory overhead allocated per unit for each product using the single plantwide factory overhead rate.

Follow My Example 11-1

a. Credenza: 5,000 units × 4 direct labor hours = 20,000 direct labor hours
   Desk: 5,000 units × 4 direct labor hours = 20,000
   40,000 direct labor hours

b. Single plantwide factory overhead rate: $650,000 ÷ 40,000 dlh = $16.25 per dlh

c. Credenza: $16.25 per direct labor hour × 4 dlh per unit = $65 per unit
   Desk: $16.25 per direct labor hour × 4 dlh per unit = $65 per unit

Practice Exercises: PE 11-1A, PE 11-1B

Integrity, Objectivity, and Ethics in Business

FRAUD AGAINST YOU AND ME

The U.S. government makes a wide variety of purchases. Two of the largest are health care purchases under Medicare and military equipment. The purchase price for these and other items is often determined by the cost plus some profit. The cost is often the sum of direct costs plus allocated overhead. Due to the complexity of determining cost, government agencies review the amount charged for products and services. In the event of disagreement between the contractor and the government, the U.S. government may sue the contractor under the False Claims Act, which provides for three times the government's damages plus civil penalties. In 2013, the U.S. Department of Justice recovered $3.8 billion from false claims acts. Of this amount, $2.6 billion involved health care frauds. Most of the cases were the result of allegations by private citizens under the act's whistleblower provision.

Source: *Top 20 Cases*, The False Claims Act Legal Center of the TAF Education Fund, www.taf.org.

Multiple Production Department Factory Overhead Rate Method

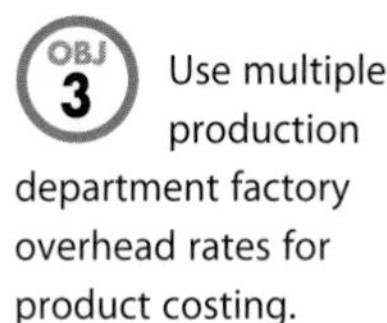

OBJ 3 Use multiple production department factory overhead rates for product costing.

When production departments *differ significantly* in their manufacturing processes, factory overhead costs are normally incurred differently in each department. In such cases, factory overhead costs may be more accurately allocated using multiple production department factory overhead rates.

The **multiple production department factory overhead rate method** uses different rates for each production department to allocate factory overhead costs to products. In contrast, the single plantwide rate method uses only one rate to allocate factory overhead costs. Exhibit 3 illustrates how these two methods differ.

EXHIBIT 3

Comparison of Single Plantwide Rate and Multiple Production Department Rate Methods

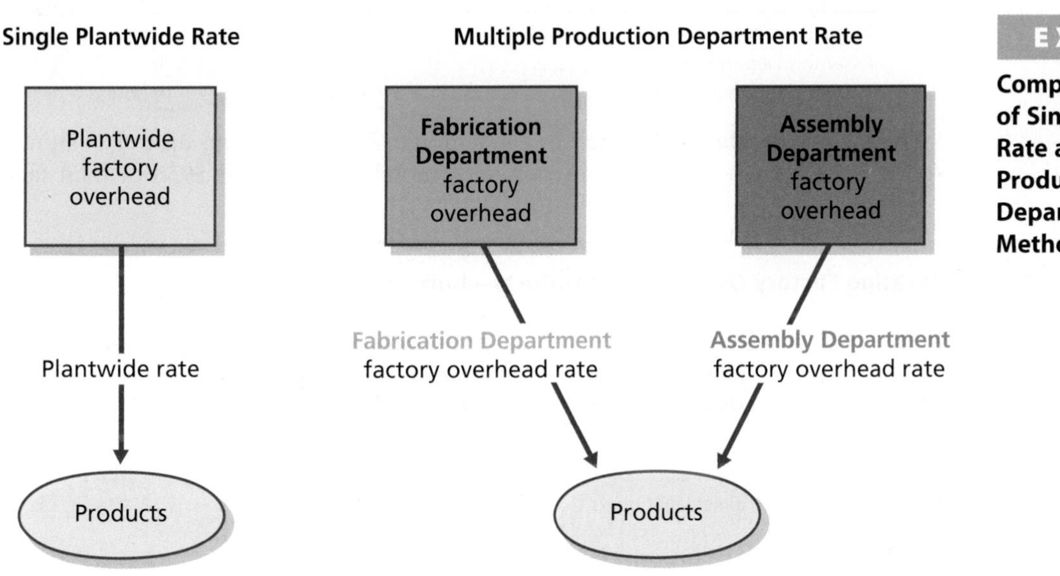

To illustrate the multiple production department factory overhead rate method, the prior illustration for **Ruiz Company** is used. In doing so, assume that Ruiz uses the following two production departments in the manufacture of snowmobiles and riding mowers:

- Fabrication Department, which cuts metal to the shape of the product.
- Assembly Department, which manually assembles machined pieces into a final product.

The total budgeted factory overhead for Ruiz is $1,600,000 divided into the Fabrication and Assembly departments as follows:[1]

[1] Factory overhead costs are assigned to production departments using methods discussed in advanced cost accounting textbooks.

	Budgeted Factory Overhead Costs
Fabrication Department	$1,030,000
Assembly Department	570,000
Total budgeted factory overhead costs	$1,600,000

As illustrated, the Fabrication Department incurs nearly twice the factory overhead of the Assembly Department. This is because the Fabrication Department has more machinery and equipment that uses more power, incurs more equipment depreciation, and uses more factory supplies.

Department Overhead Rates and Allocation

Each **production department factory overhead rate** is computed as follows:

$$\text{Production Department Factory Overhead Rate} = \frac{\text{Budgeted Department Factory Overhead}}{\text{Budgeted Department Allocation Base}}$$

To illustrate, assume that **Ruiz Company** uses direct labor hours as the allocation base for the Fabrication and Assembly departments.[2] Each department uses 10,000 direct labor hours. Thus, the factory overhead rates are as follows:

$$\text{Fabrication Department Factory Overhead Rate} = \frac{\$1{,}030{,}000}{10{,}000 \text{ direct labor hours}} = \$103 \text{ direct labor hours}$$

$$\text{Assembly Department Factory Overhead Rate} = \frac{\$570{,}000}{10{,}000 \text{ direct labor hours}} = \$57 \text{ direct labor hours}$$

Ten direct labor hours are required for the manufacture of each snowmobile and riding mower. These 10 hours are consumed in the Fabrication and Assembly departments as follows:

	Snowmobile	Riding Mower
Fabrication Department	8 hours	2 hours
Assembly Department	2	8
Direct labor hours per unit	10 hours	10 hours

The factory overhead allocated to each snowmobile and riding mower is shown in Exhibit 4. As shown in Exhibit 4, each snowmobile is allocated $938 of total factory

EXHIBIT 4 **Allocating Factory Overhead to Products—Ruiz Company**

	Allocation Base Usage per Unit	×	Production Department Factory Overhead Rate	=	Allocated Factory Overhead per Unit of Product
Snowmobile					
Fabrication Department	8 direct labor hours	×	$103 per dlh	=	$824
Assembly Department	2 direct labor hours	×	$ 57 per dlh	=	114
Total factory overhead cost per snowmobile					$938
Riding mower					
Fabrication Department	2 direct labor hours	×	$103 per dlh	=	$206
Assembly Department	8 direct labor hours	×	$ 57 per dlh	=	456
Total factory overhead cost per riding mower					$662

[2] Departments need not use the same allocation base. The allocation base should be associated with the operating activity of the department.

overhead costs. In contrast, each riding mower is allocated $662 of factory overhead costs.

Exhibit 5 summarizes the multiple production department rate allocation method for Ruiz. Exhibit 5 indicates that the Fabrication Department factory overhead rate is $103 per direct labor hour, while the Assembly Department rate is $57 per direct labor hour. Since the snowmobile uses more Fabrication Department direct labor hours than does the riding mower, the total overhead allocated to each snowmobile is $276 greater ($938 – $662) than the amount allocated to each riding mower.

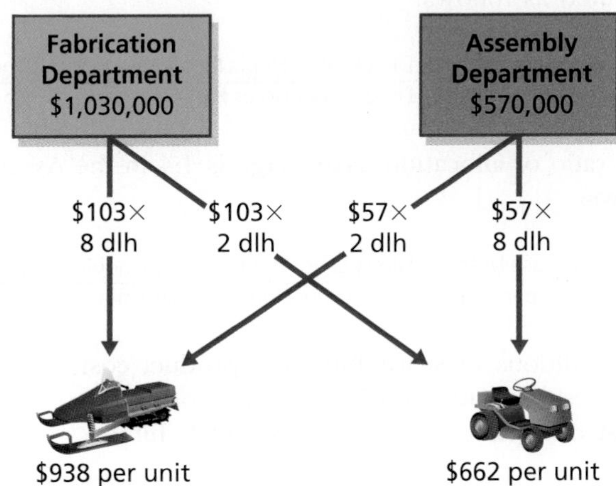

EXHIBIT 5

Multiple Production Department Rate Method—Ruiz Company

Distortion of Product Costs

The differences in **Ruiz Company**'s factory overhead for each snowmobile and riding mower using the single plantwide and the multiple production department factory overhead rate methods are as follows:

	Factory Overhead Cost per Unit		
	Single Plantwide Method	**Multiple Production Department Method**	**Difference**
Snowmobile...............	$800	$938	$(138)
Riding mower.............	800	662	138

The single plantwide factory overhead rate distorts the product cost of both the snowmobile and riding mower. That is, the snowmobile is not allocated enough cost and, thus, is undercosted by $138. In contrast, the riding mower is allocated too much cost and is overcosted by $138 ($800 – $662).

Note:
The single plantwide factory overhead rate distorts product cost by averaging high and low factory overhead costs.

The preceding cost distortions are caused by averaging the differences between the high factory overhead costs in the Fabrication Department and the low factory overhead costs in the Assembly Department. Using the single plantwide rate, it is assumed that all factory overhead is directly related to a single allocation base for the entire plant. This assumption is not realistic for Ruiz. Thus, using a single plantwide rate distorted the product costs of snowmobiles and riding mowers.

The following conditions indicate that a single plantwide factory overhead rate may cause product cost distortions:

- **Condition 1**: *Differences in production department factory overhead rates.* Some departments have high rates, whereas others have low rates.
- **Condition 2**: *Differences among products in the ratios of allocation base usage within a department and across departments.* Some products have a

high ratio of allocation base usage within departments, whereas other products have a low ratio of allocation base usage within the same departments.

To illustrate, Condition 1 exists for Ruiz because the factory overhead rate for the Fabrication Department is $103 per direct labor hour, whereas the rate for the Assembly Department is only $57 per direct labor hour. However, this condition by itself will not cause product cost distortions.

Condition 2 also exists for Ruiz. The snowmobile consumes eight direct labor hours in the Fabrication Department, whereas the riding mower consumes only two direct labor hours. Thus, the ratio of allocation base usage is 4:1 in the Fabrication Department, computed as follows:[3]

$$\frac{\text{Ratio of Allocation Base Usage}}{\text{in the Fabrication Department}} = \frac{\text{Direct Labor Hours for snowmobiles}}{\text{Direct Labor Hours for riding mowers}} = \frac{8 \text{ hours}}{2 \text{ hours}} = 4{:}1$$

In contrast, the ratio of allocation base usage is 1:4 in the Assembly Department, computed as follows:

$$\frac{\text{Ratio of Allocation Base Usage}}{\text{in the Fabrication Department}} = \frac{\text{Direct Labor Hours for snowmobiles}}{\text{Direct Labor Hours for riding mowers}} = \frac{2 \text{ hours}}{8 \text{ hours}} = 1{:}4$$

Because both conditions exist for Ruiz, the product costs from using the single plantwide factory overhead rate are distorted. The preceding conditions and the resulting product cost distortions are summarized in Exhibit 6.

EXHIBIT 6 **Conditions for Product Cost Distortion—Ruiz Company**

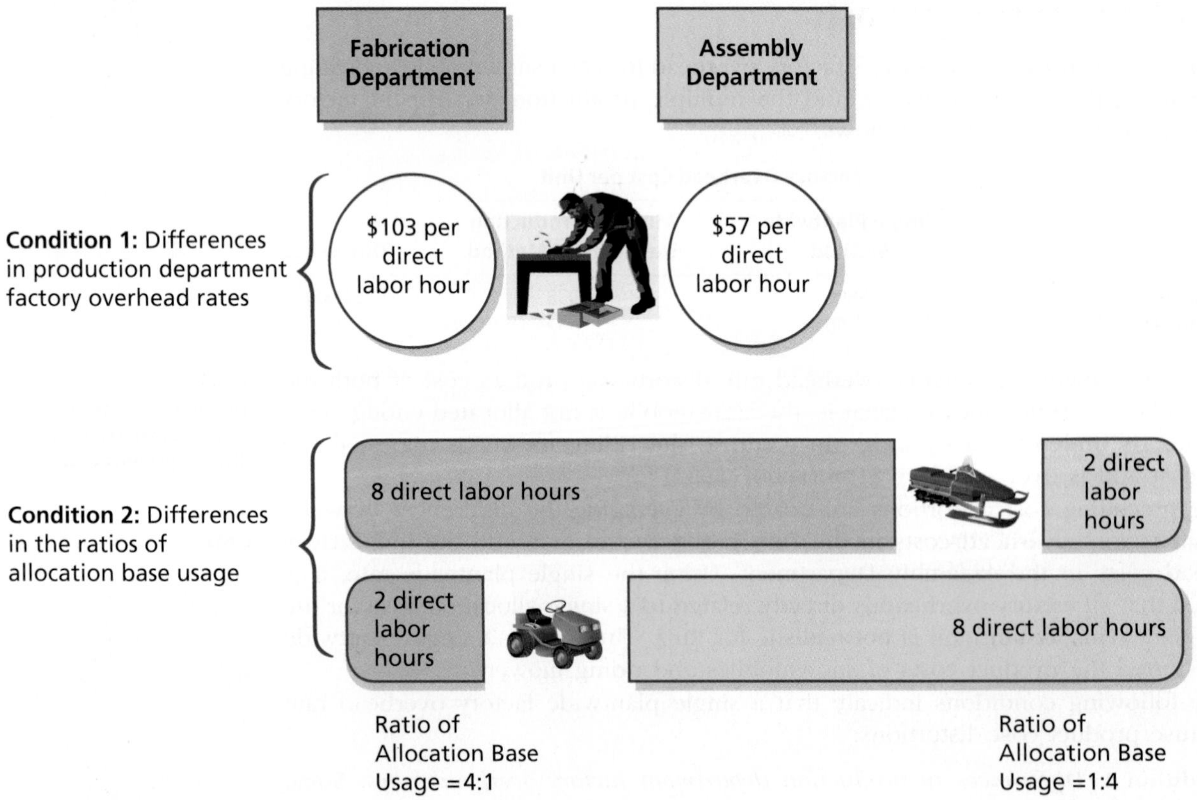

Fabrication Department

Assembly Department

Condition 1: Differences in production department factory overhead rates

$103 per direct labor hour

$57 per direct labor hour

Condition 2: Differences in the ratios of allocation base usage

8 direct labor hours

2 direct labor hours

2 direct labor hours

8 direct labor hours

Ratio of Allocation Base Usage = 4:1

Ratio of Allocation Base Usage = 1:4

[3] The numerator and denominator could be switched as long as the ratio is computed the same for each department. This is because the objective is to compare whether differences exist in the ratio of allocation base usage across products and departments.

Example Exercise 11-2 Multiple Production Department Factory Overhead Rates

The total factory overhead for Morris Company is budgeted for the year at $600,000 and divided into two departments: Fabrication, $420,000 and Assembly, $180,000. Morris manufactures two office furniture products: credenzas and desks. Each credenza requires one direct labor hour (dlh) in Fabrication and three direct labor hours in Assembly. Each desk requires three direct labor hours in Fabrication and one direct labor hour in Assembly. Each product is budgeted for 5,000 units of production for the year. Determine (a) the total number of budgeted direct labor hours for the year in each department, (b) the departmental factory overhead rates for both departments, and (c) the factory overhead allocated per unit for each product, using the department factory overhead allocation rates.

Follow My Example 11-2

a. Fabrication: (5,000 credenzas × 1 dlh) + (5,000 desks × 3 dlh) = 20,000 direct labor hours
   Assembly: (5,000 credenzas × 3 dlh) + (5,000 desks × 1 dlh) = 20,000 direct labor hours

b. Fabrication Department rate: $420,000 ÷ 20,000 direct labor hours = $21.00 per dlh
   Assembly Department rate: $180,000 ÷ 20,000 direct labor hours = $9.00 per dlh

c. Credenza:

Fabrication Department	1 dlh × $21.00 =	$21.00
Assembly Department	3 dlh × $ 9.00 =	27.00
Total factory overhead per credenza		$48.00

Desk:

Fabrication Department	3 dlh × $21.00 =	$63.00
Assembly Department	1 dlh × $ 9.00 =	9.00
Total factory overhead per desk		$72.00

Practice Exercises: PE 11-2A, PE 11-2B

Activity-Based Costing Method

Use activity-based costing for product costing.

As illustrated in the preceding section, product costs may be distorted when a single plantwide factory overhead rate is used. However, product costs may also be distorted when multiple production department factory overhead rates are used. Activity-based costing further reduces the possibility of product cost distortions.

The **activity-based costing (ABC) method** provides an alternative approach for allocating factory overhead that uses multiple factory overhead rates based on different activities. **Activities** are the types of work, or actions, involved in a manufacturing or service process. For example, the assembly, inspection, and engineering design functions are activities that might be used to allocate overhead.

Under activity-based costing, factory overhead costs are initially budgeted for activities, sometimes called *activity cost pools*, such as machine usage, inspections, moving, production setups, and engineering activities.[4] In contrast, when multiple production department factory overhead rates are used, factory overhead costs are first accounted for in production departments.

Exhibit 7 illustrates how activity-based costing differs from the multiple production department method.

[4] The activity rate is based on budgeted activity costs. Activity-based budgeting and the reconciliation of budgeted activity costs to actual costs are topics covered in advanced texts.

EXHIBIT 7 **Multiple Production Department Factory Overhead Rate Method vs. Activity-Based Costing**

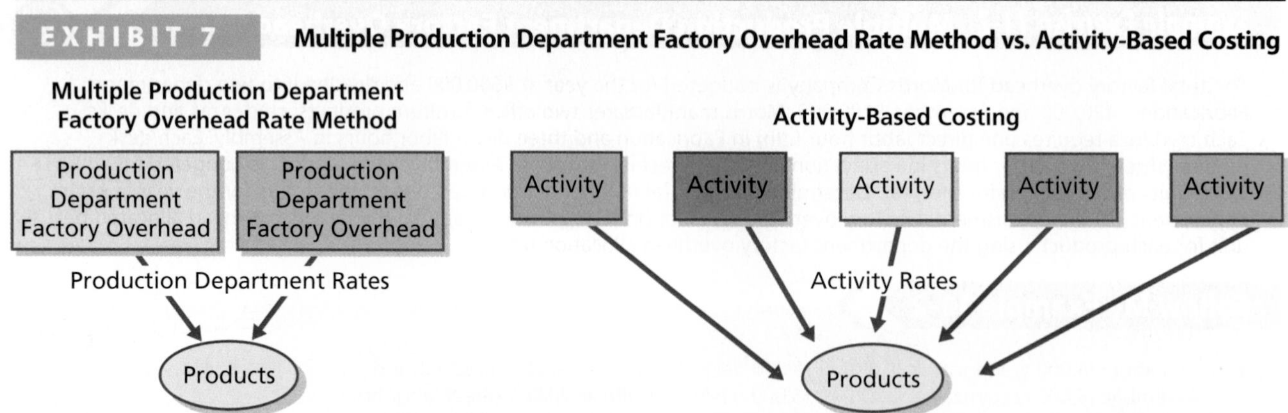

To illustrate the activity-based costing method, the prior illustration for **Ruiz Company** is used. Assume that the following activities have been identified for producing snowmobiles and riding mowers:

- *Fabrication*, which consists of cutting metal to shape the product. This activity is machine-intensive.
- *Assembly*, which consists of manually assembling machined pieces into a final product. This activity is labor-intensive.
- *Setup*, which consists of changing tooling in machines in preparation for making a new product. Each production run requires a **setup**.
- *Quality-control inspections*, which consist of inspecting the product for conformance to specifications. Inspection requires product tear down and reassembly.
- *Engineering changes*, which consist of processing changes in design or process specifications for a product. The document that initiates changing a product or process is called an **engineering change order (ECO)**.

Fabrication and assembly are now identified as *activities* rather than *departments*. As a result, the setup, quality-control inspections, and engineering change functions that were previously allocated to the Fabrication and Assembly departments are now classified as separate activities.

The budgeted cost for each activity is as follows:

Activity	Budgeted Activity Cost
Fabrication	$ 530,000
Assembly	70,000
Setup	480,000
Quality-control inspections	312,000
Engineering changes	208,000
Total budgeted activity costs	$1,600,000

The costs for the fabrication and assembly activities are less than the costs shown in the preceding section where these activities were identified as production departments. This is because the costs of setup, quality-control inspections, and engineering changes, which total $1,000,000 ($480,000 + $312,000 + $208,000), have now been separated into their own activity cost pools.

Activity Rates and Allocation

The budgeted activity costs are assigned to products using factory overhead rates for each activity. These rates are called **activity rates** because they are related to activities. Activity rates are computed as follows:

$$\text{Activity Rate} = \frac{\text{Budgeted Activity Cost}}{\text{Total Activity-Base Usage}}$$

The term **activity base**, rather than *allocation base*, is used because the base is related to an activity.

Note: Activity rates are computed by dividing the budgeted activity cost pool by the total estimated activity-base usage.

To illustrate, assume that snowmobiles are a new product for **Ruiz Company**, and engineers are still making minor design changes. Ruiz has produced riding mowers for many years. Activity-base usage for the two products are as follows:

	Snowmobile	Riding Mower
Estimated units of total production	1,000 units	1,000 units
Estimated setups	100 setups	20 setups
Quality-control inspections	100 inspections (10%)	4 inspections (0.4%)
Estimated engineering change orders	12 change orders	4 change orders

The number of direct labor hours used by each product is 10,000 hours, computed as follows:

	Direct Labor Hours per Unit	Number of Units of Production	Total Direct Labor Hours
Snowmobile:			
Fabrication Department	8 hours	1,000 units	8,000 hours
Assembly Department	2 hours	1,000 units	2,000 hours
Total			10,000 hours
Riding Mower:			
Fabrication Department	2 hours	1,000 units	2,000 hours
Assembly Department	8 hours	1,000 units	8,000 hours
Total			10,000 hours

Exhibit 8 summarizes the activity-base usage quantities for each product.

EXHIBIT 8 **Activity Bases—Ruiz Company**

	Activity-Base Usage				
Products	**Fabrication**	**Assembly**	**Setup**	**Quality-Control Inspections**	**Engineering Changes**
Snowmobile	8,000 dlh	2,000 dlh	100 setups	100 inspections	12 ECOs
Riding mower	2,000	8,000	20	4	4
Total activity-base usage	10,000 dlh	10,000 dlh	120 setups	104 inspections	16 ECOs

The activity rates for Ruiz are shown in Exhibit 9.

EXHIBIT 9 **Activity Rates—Ruiz Company**

Activity	**Budgeted Activity Cost**	÷	**Total Activity-Base Usage**	=	**Activity Rate**
Fabrication	$530,000	÷	10,000 direct labor hours	=	$53 per direct labor hour
Assembly	$ 70,000	÷	10,000 direct labor hours	=	$7 per direct labor hour
Setup	$480,000	÷	120 setups	=	$4,000 per setup
Quality-control inspections	$312,000	÷	104 inspections	=	$3,000 per inspection
Engineering changes	$208,000	÷	16 engineering changes	=	$13,000 per engineering change order

The factory overhead cost per unit is computed as follows:

$$\frac{\text{Activity-Base Usage} \times \text{Activity Rate}}{\text{Total Units of Estimated Production}}$$

or

$$\frac{\text{Total Factory Overhead Cost}}{\text{Total Units of Estimated Production}}$$

These computations for Ruiz's snowmobile and riding mower are shown in Exhibit 10.

EXHIBIT 10 **Activity-Based Product Cost Calculations**

	A	B	C	D	E	F	G	H	I	J	K	L
1				Snowmobile						Riding Mower		
2		Activity-Base		Activity		Activity		Activity-Base		Activity		Activity
3	Activity	Usage	×	Rate	=	Cost		Usage	×	Rate	=	Cost
4												
5	Fabrication	8,000 dlh		$53/dlh		$ 424,000		2,000 dlh		$53/dlh		$106,000
6	Assembly	2,000 dlh		$7/dlh		14,000		8,000 dlh		$7/dlh		56,000
7	Setup	100 setups		$4,000/setup		400,000		20 setups		$4,000/setup		80,000
8	Quality-control											
9	inspections	100 inspections		$3,000/insp.		300,000		4 inspections		$3,000/insp.		12,000
10	Engineering											
11	changes	12 ECOs		$13,000/ECO		156,000		4 ECOs		$13,000/ECO		52,000
12	Total factory											
13	overhead cost					$1,294,000						$306,000
14	Budgeted units											
15	of production					1,000						1,000
16	Factory overhead											
17	cost per unit					$ 1,294						$ 306

The activity-based costing method for Ruiz is summarized in Exhibit 11.

EXHIBIT 11 **Activity Bases—Ruiz Company**

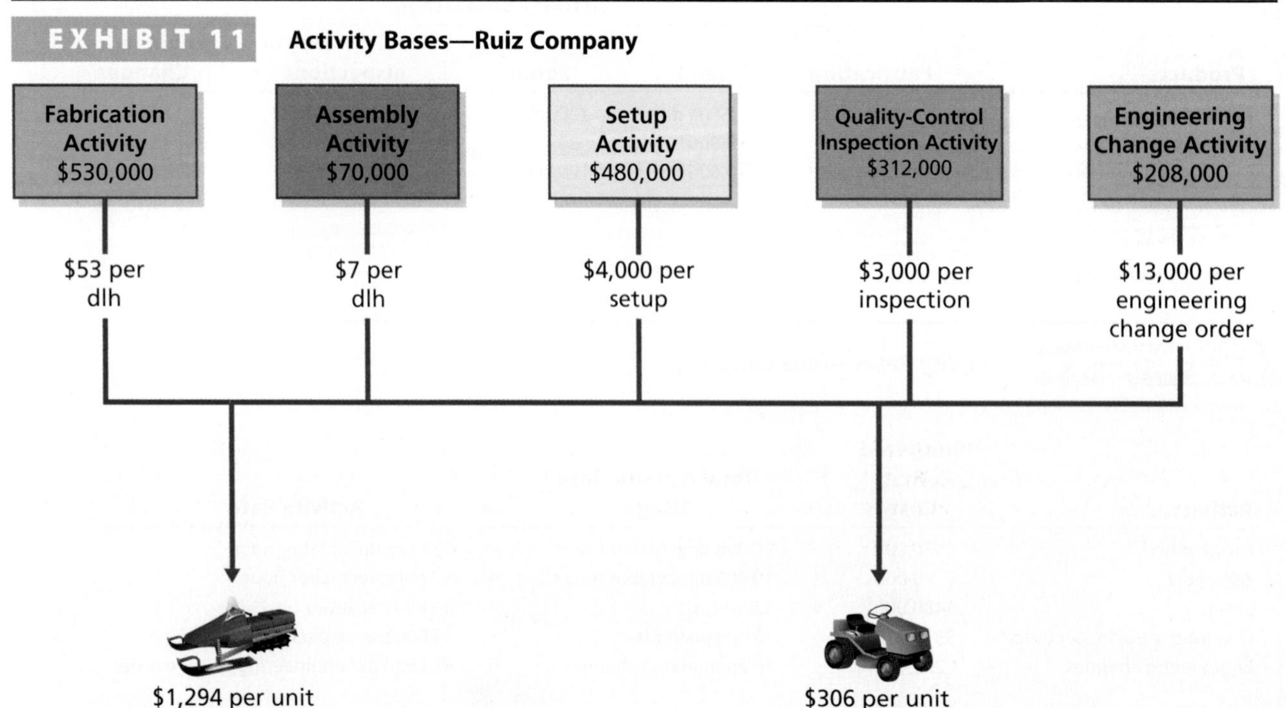

Distortion in Product Costs

The factory overhead costs per unit for **Ruiz Company** using the three allocation methods are shown in Exhibit 12.

EXHIBIT 12 **Overhead Cost Allocation Methods: Ruiz Company**

	Factory Overhead Cost per Unit—Three Cost Allocation Methods		
	Single Plantwide Rate	**Multiple Production Department Rates**	**Activity-Based Costing**
Snowmobile	$800	$938	$1,294
Riding mower	800	662	306

The activity-based costing method produces different factory overhead costs per unit (product costs) than the multiple department factory overhead rate method. This difference is caused by how the $1,000,000 of setup, quality control, and engineering change activities are allocated.

Under the multiple production department factory overhead rate method, setup, quality control, and engineering change costs were allocated using departmental rates based on direct labor hours. However, snowmobiles and riding mowers did *not* consume these *activities* in proportion to direct labor hours. That is, each snowmobile consumed a larger portion of the setup, quality-control inspection, and engineering change activities. This was true even though each product consumed 10,000 direct labor hours. As a result, activity-based costing allocated more of the cost of these activities to the snowmobile. Only under the activity-based approach were these differences reflected in the factory overhead cost allocations and thus in the product costs.

Dangers of Product Cost Distortion

If **Ruiz Company** used the $800 factory overhead cost allocation (single plantwide rate) instead of activity-based costing for pricing snowmobiles and riding mowers, the following would likely result:

- The snowmobile would be *underpriced* because its factory overhead cost would be understated by $494 ($1,294 – $800).
- The riding mower would be *overpriced* because its factory overhead cost would be overstated by $494 ($800 – $306).

As a result, Ruiz would likely lose sales of riding mowers because they are overpriced. In contrast, sale of snowmobiles would increase because they are underpriced. Due to these pricing errors, Ruiz might incorrectly decide to expand production of snowmobiles and discontinue making riding mowers.

If Ruiz uses the activity-based costing method, its product costs would be more accurate. Thus, Ruiz would have a better starting point for making proper pricing decisions. Although the product cost distortions are not as great, similar results would occur if Ruiz had used the multiple production department rate method.

ArvinMeritor, Inc., discovered that incorrect factory overhead cost allocations had "overcosted" some of its products by roughly 20%. As a result, these products were overpriced and began losing market share.

Example Exercise 11-3 Activity-Based Costing: Factory Overhead Costs

OBJ 4

The total factory overhead for Morris Company is budgeted for the year at $600,000, divided into four activities: fabrication, $300,000; assembly, $120,000; setup, $100,000; and materials handling, $80,000. Morris manufactures two office furniture products: a credenza and desk. The activity-base usage quantities for each product by each activity are estimated as follows:

	Fabrication	Assembly	Setup	Materials Handling
Credenza	5,000 dlh	15,000 dlh	30 setups	50 moves
Desk	15,000	5,000	220	350
Total activity-base usage	20,000 dlh	20,000 dlh	250 setups	400 moves

Each product is budgeted for 5,000 units of production for the year. Determine (a) the activity rates for each activity and (b) the activity-based factory overhead per unit for each product.

Follow My Example 11-3

a. Fabrication: $300,000 ÷ 20,000 direct labor hours = $15 per dlh
Assembly: $120,000 ÷ 20,000 direct labor hours = $6 per dlh
Setup: $100,000 ÷ 250 setups = $400 per setup
Materials handling: $80,000 ÷ 400 moves = $200 per move

	A	B	C	D	E	F	G	H	I	J	K	L
1				Credenza						Desk		
2		Activity-Base		Activity		Activity		Activity-Base		Activity		Activity
3	Activity	Usage	×	Rate	=	Cost		Usage	×	Rate	=	Cost
4												
5	Fabrication	5,000 dlh		$15 per dlh		$ 75,000		15,000 dlh		$15 per dlh		$225,000
6	Assembly	15,000 dlh		$6 per dlh		90,000		5,000 dlh		$6 per dlh		30,000
7	Setup	30 setups		$400/setup		12,000		220 setups		$400/setup		88,000
8	Materials handling	50 moves		$200/move		10,000		350 moves		$200/move		70,000
9	Total					$187,000						$413,000
10	Budgeted units					÷ 5,000						÷ 5,000
11	Factory overhead											
12	per unit					$ 37.40						$ 82.60

Practice Exercises: PE 11-3A, PE 11-3B

OBJ 5 Use activity-based costing to allocate selling and administrative expenses to products.

Activity-Based Costing for Selling and Administrative Expenses

Generally accepted accounting principles (GAAP) require that selling and administrative expenses be reported as period expenses on the income statement. However, selling and administrative expenses may be allocated to products for managerial decision making. For example, selling and administrative expenses may be allocated for analyzing product profitability.

One method of allocating selling and administrative expenses to the products is based on sales volumes. However, products may consume activities in ways that are unrelated to their sales volumes. When this occurs, activity-based costing may be a more accurate method of allocation.

To illustrate, assume that Abacus Company has two products, Ipso and Facto. Both products have the same total sales volume. However, Ipso and Facto consume selling and administrative activities differently, as shown in Exhibit 13.

If Abacus's selling and administrative expenses are allocated on the basis of sales volumes, the same amount of expense would be allocated to Ipso and Facto. This is

Selling and Administrative Activities	Ipso	Facto
Post-sale technical support	Product is easy to use by the customer.	Product requires specialized training in order to be used by the customer.
Order writing	Product requires no technical informationfrom the customer.	Product requires detailed technical information from the customer.
Promotional support	Product requires no promotional effort.	Product requires extensive promotional effort.
Order entry	Product is purchased in large volumes per order.	Product is purchased in small volumes per order.
Customer return processing	Product has few customer returns.	Product has many customer returns.
Shipping document preparation	Product is shipped domestically.	Product is shipped internationally, requiring customs and export documents.
Shipping and handling	Product is not hazardous.	Product is hazardous, requiring specialized shipping and handling.
Field service	Product has few warranty claims.	Product has many warranty claims.

EXHIBIT 13

Selling and Administrative Activity Product Differences

because Ipso and Facto have the same sales volume. However, as Exhibit 13 implies, such an allocation would be misleading.

The activity-based costing method can be used to allocate the selling and administrative activities to Ipso and Facto. Activity-based costing allocates selling and administrative expenses based on how each product consumes activities.

To illustrate, assume that Abacus's field warranty service activity has a budgeted cost of $150,000. Additionally, assume that 100 warranty claims are estimated for the period. Using warranty claims as an activity base, the warranty claim activity rate is $1,500, computed as follows:

$$\text{Activity Rate} = \frac{\text{Budgeted Activity Cost}}{\text{Total Activity-Base Usage}}$$

$$\text{Warranty Claim Activity Rate} = \frac{\text{Budgeted Warranty Claim Expenses}}{\text{Total Estimated Warranty Claim}}$$

$$= \frac{\$150{,}000}{100 \text{ claims}} = \$1{,}500 \text{ per warranty claim}$$

Assuming that Ipso had 10 warranty claims and Facto had 90 warranty claims, the field service activity expenses would be allocated to each product as follows:

Ipso: 10 warranty claims × $1,500 per warranty claim = $ 15,000
Facto: 90 warranty claims × $1,500 per warranty claim = $135,000

The remaining selling and administrative activities could be allocated to Ipso and Facto in a similar manner.

ExxonMobil Corporation allocated selling and administrative activities, such as engineering calls, order taking, market research, and advertising, to its lubricant products.

In some cases, selling and administrative expenses may be more related to *customer* behaviors than to differences in products. That is, some customers may demand more service and selling activities than other customers. In such cases, activity-based costing would allocate selling and administrative expenses to customers.

Example Exercise 11-4 Activity-Based Costing: Selling and Administrative Expenses

Converse Company manufactures and sells LCD display products. Converse uses activity-based costing to determine the cost of the customer return processing and the shipping activity. The customer return processing activity has an activity rate of $90 per return, and the shipping activity has an activity rate of $15 per shipment. Converse shipped 4,000 units of LCD Model A1 in 2,200 shipments (some shipments are more than one unit). There were 200 returns. Determine the (a) total and (b) per-unit customer return processing and shipping activity cost for Model A1.

Follow My Example 11-4

a. Return activity: 200 returns × $90 per return = $18,000
   Shipping activity: 2,200 shipments × $15 per shipment = 33,000
   Total activity cost $51,000

b. $12.75 per unit ($51,000 ÷ 4,000 units)

Practice Exercises: PE 11-4A, PE 11-4B

Use activity-based costing in a service business.

Activity-Based Costing in Service Businesses

Service companies need to determine the cost of their services so that they can make pricing, promoting, and other decisions. The use of single and multiple department overhead rate methods may lead to distortions similar to those of manufacturing firms. Thus, many service companies use activity-based costing for determining the cost of services.

To illustrate, assume that Hopewell Hospital uses activity-based costing to allocate hospital overhead to patients. Hopewell applies activity-based costing as follows:

- Step 1. Identifying activities.
- Step 2. Determining activity rates for each activity.
- Step 3. Allocating overhead costs to patients based upon activity-base usage.

Hopewell has identified the following activities:

- Admission
- Radiological testing
- Operating room
- Pathological testing
- Dietary and laundry

Each activity has an estimated patient activity-base usage. Based on the budgeted costs for each activity and related estimated activity-base usage, the activity rates shown in Exhibit 14 were developed.

To illustrate, assume the following data for radiological testing:

Budgeted costs	$960,000
Total estimated activity-base usage	3,000 images

The activity rate of $320 per radiological image is computed as follows:

$$\text{Activity Rate} = \frac{\text{Budgeted Activity Cost}}{\text{Total Activity-Base Usage}}$$

$$\text{Radiological Testing Activity Rate} = \frac{\text{Budgeted Radiological Testing}}{\text{Total Estimated Images}}$$

$$= \frac{\$960{,}000}{3{,}000 \text{ images}} = \$320 \text{ per image}$$

EXHIBIT 14 **Activity-Based Costing Method—Hopewell Hospital**

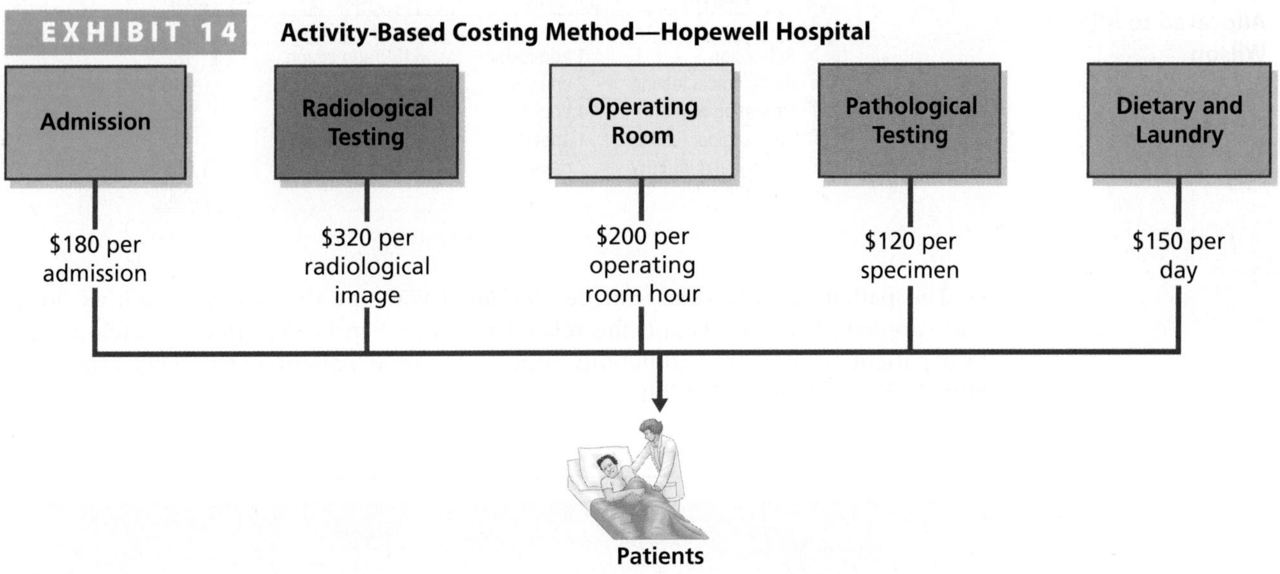

The activity rates for the other activities are determined in a similar manner. These activity rates along with the patient activity-base usage are used to allocate costs to patients as follows:

$$\text{Activity Cost Allocated to Patient} = \text{Patient Activity-Base Usage} \times \text{Activity Rate}$$

To illustrate, assume that Mia Wilson was a patient of the hospital. The hospital overhead services (activities) performed for Mia Wilson were as follows:

	Patient (Mia Wilson) Activity-Base Usage
Admission	1 admission
Radiological testing	2 images
Operating room	4 hours
Pathological testing	1 specimen
Dietary and laundry	7 days

Service  Focus

UNIVERSITY AND COMMUNITY PARTNERSHIP—LEARNING YOUR ABC'S

Students at Harvard's **Kennedy School of Government** joined with the city of Somerville, Massachusetts, in building an activity-based cost system for the city. The students volunteered several hours a week in four-person teams, interviewing city officials within 18 departments. The students were able to determine activity costs, such as the cost to fill a pothole, processing a building permit, or responding to a four-alarm fire. Their study was used by the city in forming the city budget. As stated by some of the students participating on this project: "It makes sense to use the resources of the university for community building. . . . Real-world experience is a tremendous thing to have in your back pocket. We learned from the mayor and the fire chief, who are seasoned professionals in their own right."

Source: *Kennedy School Bulletin*, Spring 2005, "Easy as A-B-C: Students Take on the Somerville Budget Overhaul."

Based on the preceding services (activities), the Hopewell Hospital overhead costs allocated to Mia Wilson total $2,790, as computed in Exhibit 15.

EXHIBIT 15

Hopewell Hospital Overhead Costs Allocated to Mia Wilson

	A	B	C	D	E	F
1		Patient Name: Mia Wilson				
2		Activity-Base		Activity		Activity
3	Activity	Usage	×	Rate	=	Cost
4						
5	Admission	1 admission		$180/admission		$ 180
6	Radiological testing	2 images		$320/image		640
7	Operating room	4 hours		$200/hour		800
8	Pathological testing	1 specimen		$120/specimen		120
9	Dietary and laundry	7 days		$150/day		1,050
10	Total					$2,790

The patient activity costs can be combined with the direct costs, such as drugs and supplies. These costs and the related revenues can be reported for each patient in a patient (customer) profitability report. A partial patient profitability report for Hopewell is shown in Exhibit 16.

EXHIBIT 16

Customer Profitability Report—Hopewell Hospital

Hopewell Hospital
Patient (Customer) Profitability Report
For the Period Ending December 31

	Adcock, Aesha	Birini, Sergey	Diaz, Mateo	Wilson, Mia
Revenues	$9,500	$21,400	$5,050	$3,300
Less patient costs:				
Drugs and supplies	$ 400	$ 1,000	$ 300	$ 200
Admission	180	180	180	180
Radiological testing	1,280	2,560	1,280	640
Operating room	2,400	6,400	1,600	800
Pathological testing	240	600	120	120
Dietary and laundry	4,200	14,700	1,050	1,050
Total patient costs	$8,700	$25,440	$4,530	$2,990
Income from operations	$ 800	$ (4,040)	$ 520	$ 310

Exhibit 16 can be used by hospital administrators for decisions on pricing or services. For example, there was a large loss on services provided to Sergey Birini. Investigation might reveal that some of the services provided to Birini were not reimbursed by insurance. As a result, Hopewell might lobby the insurance company to reimburse these services or request higher insurance reimbursement on other services.

Example Exercise 11-5 Activity-Based Costing for a Service Business

The Metro Radiology Clinic uses activity-based costing to determine the cost of servicing patients. There are three activities: patient administration, imaging, and diagnostic services. The activity rates associated with each activity are $45 per patient visit, $320 per X-ray image, and $450 per diagnosis. Filipa Valdez went to the clinic and had two X-rays, each of which was read and interpreted by a doctor. Determine the total activity-based cost of Valdez's visit.

Follow My Example 11-5

Patient administration	45	(1 visit × $45)
Imaging	$ 640	(2 images × $320)
Diagnosis	900	(2 diagnoses × $450)
Total activity cost	$1,585	

Practice Exercises: PE 11-5A, PE 11-5B

Business  Connection

FINDING THE RIGHT NICHE

Businesses often attempt to divide a market into its unique characteristics, called *market segmentation*. Once a market segment is identified, product, price, promotion, and location strategies are tailored to fit that market. This is a better approach for many products and services than following a "one size fits all" strategy. Activity-based costing can be used to help tailor organizational effort toward different segments. For example, **Fidelity Investments** uses activity-based costing to tailor its sales and marketing strategies to different wealth segments. Thus, a higher wealth segment could rely on personal sales activities, while less wealthy segments would rely on less costly sales activities, such as mass mail. Popular forms of segmentation and their common characteristics follow:

Form of Segmentation	Characteristics
Demographic	Age, education, gender, income, race
Geographic	Region, city, country
Psychographic	Lifestyle, values, attitudes
Benefit	Benefits provided
Volume	Light vs. heavy use

Examples for each of these forms of segmentation are as follows:

- *Demographic:* Fidelity Investments tailors sales and marketing strategies to different wealth segments.
- *Geographic:* Pro sports teams offer merchandise in their home cities.
- *Psychographic:* **The Body Shop** markets all-natural beauty products to consumers who value cosmetic products that have not been animal-tested.
- *Benefit:* **Cold Stone Creamery** sells a premium ice cream product with customized toppings.
- *Volume:* **Delta Air Lines** provides additional benefits, such as class upgrades, free air travel, and boarding priority, to its frequent fliers.

At a Glance 11

Identify three methods used for allocating factory costs to products.

Key Points Three cost allocation methods used for determining product costs are the (1) single plantwide factory overhead rate method, (2) multiple production department rate method, and (3) activity-based costing method.

Learning Outcome	Example Exercises	Practice Exercises
• List the three methods for allocating factory overhead costs to products.		

Use a single plantwide factory overhead rate for product costing.

Key Points A single plantwide factory overhead rate can be used to allocate all plant overhead to all products. The single plantwide factory overhead rate is simple to apply, but can lead to product cost distortions.

Learning Outcomes	Example Exercises	Practice Exercises
• Compute the single plantwide factory overhead rate and use it to allocate factory overhead costs to products. • Identify the conditions that favor the use of a single plantwide factory overhead rate for allocating factory overhead costs to products.	**EE11-1**	**PE11-1A, 11-1B**

Use multiple production department factory overhead rates for product costing.

Key Points Product costing using multiple production department factory overhead rates requires identifying the factory overhead by each production department. Using these rates can result in greater accuracy than using single plantwide factory overhead rates when:
1. There are significant differences in the factory overhead rates across different production departments.
2. The products require different ratios of allocation-base usage in each production department.

Learning Outcomes	Example Exercises	Practice Exercises
• Compute multiple production department overhead rates and use these rates to allocate factory overhead costs to products. • Identify and describe the two conditions that favor the use of multiple production department factory overhead rates for allocating factory overhead costs to products as compared to the single plantwide factory overhead rate method.	**EE11-2**	**PE11-2A, 11-2B**

Use activity-based costing for product costing.

Key Points Activity-based costing requires factory overhead to be budgeted to activities. The budgeted activity costs are allocated to products by multiplying activity rates by the activity-base quantity consumed for each product. Activity-based costing is more accurate when products consume activities in proportions unrelated to plantwide or departmental allocation bases.

Learning Outcomes	Example Exercises	Practice Exercises
• Compute activity rates and use these rates to allocate factory overhead costs to products. • Identify the conditions that favor the use of activity-based rates for allocating factory overhead costs to products, as compared to the other two methods of cost allocation. • Compare the three factory overhead allocation methods and describe the causes of cost allocation distortion.	EE11-3	PE11-3A, 11-3B

Use activity-based costing to allocate selling and administrative expenses to products.

Key Points Selling and administrative expenses can be allocated to products for management profit reporting, using activity-based costing. Activity-based costing would be preferred when the products use selling and administrative activities in ratios that are unrelated to their sales volumes.

Learning Outcomes	Example Exercises	Practice Exercises
• Compute selling and administrative activity rates and use these rates to allocate selling and administrative expenses to either a product or customer. • Identify the conditions that would favor the use of activity-based costing for allocating selling and administrative expenses.	EE11-4	PE11-4A, 11-4B

Use activity-based costing in a service business.

Key Points Activity-based costing may be applied in service settings to determine the cost of individual service offerings. Service costs are determined by multiplying activity rates by the amount of activity-base quantities consumed by the customer using the service offering.

Learning Outcomes	Example Exercises	Practice Exercises
• Compute activity rates for service offerings and use these rates to allocate indirect costs to either a service product line or a customer. • Prepare a customer profitability report using the cost of activities. • Describe how activity-based cost information can be used in a service business for improved decision making.	EE11-5	PE11-5A, 11-5B

Key Terms

activities (455)
activity base (457)
activity rates (456)
activity-based costing (ABC) method (455)
engineering change order (ECO) (456)
multiple production department factory overhead rate method (451)
product costing (448)
production department factory overhead rate (452)
setup (456)
single plantwide factory overhead rate method (449)

Illustrative Problem

Hammer Company plans to use activity-based costing to determine its product costs. It presently uses a single plantwide factory overhead rate for allocating factory overhead to products, based on direct labor hours. The total factory overhead cost is as follows:

Department	Factory Overhead
Production Support	$1,225,000
Production (factory overhead only)	175,000
Total cost	$1,400,000

The company determined that it performed four major activities in the Production Support Department. These activities, along with their budgeted activity costs, are as follows:

Production Support Activities	Budgeted Activity Cost
Setup	$ 428,750
Production control	245,000
Quality control	183,750
Materials management	367,500
Total	$1,225,000

Hammer estimated the following activity-base usage and units produced for each of its three products:

Products	Number of Units	Direct Labor Hrs.	Setups	Production Orders	Inspections	Material Requisitions
LCD TV	10,000	25,000	80	80	35	320
Tablet	2,000	10,000	40	40	40	400
Smart phone	50,000	140,000	5	5	0	30
Total cost	62,000	175,000	125	125	75	750

Instructions

1. Determine the factory overhead cost per unit for the LCD TV, tablet, and smart phone under the single plantwide factory overhead rate method. Use direct labor hours as the activity base.
2. Determine the factory overhead cost per unit for the LCD TV, tablet, and smart phone under activity-based costing. Round to two decimal places.
3. Which method provides more accurate product costing? Why?

Solution

1. Single Plantwide Factory Overhead Rate = $\frac{\$1,400,000}{175,000 \text{ direct labor hours}}$

= \$8 per direct labor hour

Factory overhead cost per unit:

	LCD TV	Tablet	Smart Phone
Number of direct labor hours	25,000	10,000	140,000
Single plantwide factory overhead rate	× \$8/dlh	× \$8/dlh	× \$8/dlh
Total factory overhead	\$200,000	\$ 80,000	\$ 1,120,000
Number of units	÷ 10,000	÷ 2,000	÷ 50,000
Factory overhead cost per unit	\$ 20.00	\$ 40.00	\$ 22.40

2. Under activity-based costing, an activity rate must be determined for each activity pool:

Activity	Budgeted Activity Cost	÷	Total Activity-Base Usage	=	Activity Rate
Setup	\$428,750	÷	125 setups	=	\$3,430 per setup
Production control	\$245,000	÷	125 production orders	=	\$1,960 per production order
Quality control	\$183,750	÷	75 inspections	=	\$2,450 per inspection
Materials management	\$367,500	÷	750 requisitions	=	\$490 per requisition
Production	\$175,000	÷	175,000 direct labor hours	=	\$1 per direct labor hour

These activity rates can be used to determine the activity-based factory overhead cost per unit as follows:

LCD TV

Activity	Activity-Base Usage	×	Activity Rate	=	Activity Cost
Setup	80 setups	×	\$3,430	=	\$274,400
Production control	80 production orders	×	\$1,960	=	156,800
Quality control	35 inspections	×	\$2,450	=	85,750
Materials management	320 requisitions	×	\$490	=	156,800
Production	25,000 direct labor hrs.	×	\$1	=	25,000
Total factory overhead					\$698,750
Unit volume					÷ 10,000
Factory overhead cost per unit					\$ 69.88

Tablet

Activity	Activity-Base Usage	×	Activity Rate	=	Activity Cost
Setup	40 setups	×	\$3,430	=	\$137,200
Production control	40 production orders	×	\$1,960	=	78,400
Quality control	40 inspections	×	\$2,450	=	98,000
Materials management	400 requisitions	×	\$490	=	196,000
Production	10,000 direct labor hrs.	×	\$1	=	10,000
Total factory overhead					\$519,600
Unit volume					÷ 2,000
Factory overhead cost per unit					\$ 259.80

Smart phone

Activity	Activity-Base Usage	×	Activity Rate	=	Activity Cost
Setup	5 setups	×	$3,430	=	$ 17,150
Production control	5 production orders	×	$1,960	=	9,800
Quality control	0 inspections	×	$2,450	=	0
Materials management	30 requisitions	×	$490	=	14,700
Production	140,000 direct labor hrs.	×	$1	=	140,000
Total factory overhead					$181,650
Unit volume					÷ 50,000
Factory overhead cost per unit					$ 3.63

3 Activity-based costing is more accurate, compared to the single plantwide factory overhead rate method. Activity-based costing properly shows that the smart phone is actually less expensive to make, while the other two products are more expensive to make. The reason is that the single plantwide factory overhead rate method fails to account for activity costs correctly. The setup, production control, quality-control, and materials management activities are all performed on products in amounts that are proportionately different than their volumes. For example, the tablet requires many of these activities relative to its actual unit volume. The tablet requires 40 setups over a volume of 2,000 units (average production run size = 50 units), while the smart phone has only 5 setups over 50,000 units (average production run size = 10,000 units). Thus, the tablet requires greater support costs relative to the smart phone.

The smart phone requires minimum activity support because it is scheduled in large batches and requires no inspections (has high quality) and few requisitions. The other two products exhibit the opposite characteristics.

Discussion Questions

1. Why would management be concerned about the accuracy of product costs?
2. Why would a manufacturing company with multiple production departments still prefer to use a single plantwide overhead rate?
3. How do the multiple production department and the single plantwide factory overhead rate methods differ?
4. Under what two conditions would the multiple production department factory overhead rate method provide more accurate product costs than the single plantwide factory overhead rate method?
5. How does activity-based costing differ from the multiple production department factory overhead rate method?
6. Shipping, selling, marketing, sales order processing, return processing, and advertising activities can be related to products by using activity-based costing. Would allocating these activities to products for financial statement reporting be acceptable according to GAAP?
7. What would happen to net income if the activities noted in Discussion Question 6 were allocated to products for financial statement reporting and the inventory increased?
8. Under what circumstances might the activity-based costing method provide more accurate product costs than the multiple production department factory overhead rate method?
9. When might activity-based costing be preferred over using a relative amount of product sales in allocating selling and administrative expenses to products?
10.  How can activity-based costing be used in service companies?

Practice Exercises

SHOW ME HOW

EE 11-1 *p. 450*

PE 11-1A Single plantwide factory overhead rate **OBJ. 2**

The total factory overhead for Diva-nation Inc. is budgeted for the year at $180,000. Diva-nation manufactures two types of men's pants: jeans and khakis. The jeans and khakis each require 0.10 direct labor hour for manufacture. Each product is budgeted for 20,000 units of production for the year. Determine (a) the total number of budgeted direct labor hours for the year, (b) the single plantwide factory overhead rate, and (c) the factory overhead allocated per unit for each product using the single plantwide factory overhead rate.

SHOW ME HOW

EE 11-1 *p. 450*

PE 11-1B Single plantwide factory overhead rate **OBJ. 2**

The total factory overhead for Bardot Marine Company is budgeted for the year at $600,000. Bardot Marine manufactures two types of boats: speedboats and bass boats. The speedboat and bass boat each require 12 direct labor hours for manufacture. Each product is budgeted for 250 units of production for the year. Determine (a) the total number of budgeted direct labor hours for the year, (b) the single plantwide factory overhead rate, and (c) the factory overhead allocated per unit for each product using the single plantwide factory overhead rate.

SHOW ME HOW

EE 11-2 *p. 455*

PE 11-2A Multiple production department factory overhead rates **OBJ. 3**

The total factory overhead for Diva-nation is budgeted for the year at $180,000, divided into two departments: Cutting, $60,000, and Sewing, $120,000. Diva-nation manufactures two types of men's pants: jeans and khakis. The jeans require 0.04 direct labor hour in Cutting and 0.06 direct labor hour in Sewing. The khakis require 0.06 direct labor hour in Cutting and 0.04 direct labor hour in Sewing. Each product is budgeted for 20,000 units of production for the year. Determine (a) the total number of budgeted direct labor hours for the year in each department, (b) the departmental factory overhead rates for both departments, and (c) the factory overhead allocated per unit for each product using the department factory overhead allocation rates.

SHOW ME HOW

EE 11-2 *p. 455*

PE 11-2B Multiple production department factory overhead rates **OBJ. 3**

The total factory overhead for Bardot Marine Company is budgeted for the year at $600,000 divided into two departments: Fabrication, $420,000, and Assembly, $180,000. Bardot Marine manufactures two types of boats: speedboats and bass boats. The speedboats require 8 direct labor hours in Fabrication and 4 direct labor hours in Assembly. The bass boats require 4 direct labor hours in Fabrication and 8 direct labor hours in Assembly. Each product is budgeted for 250 units of production for the year. Determine (a) the total number of budgeted direct labor hours for the year in each department, (b) the departmental factory overhead rates for both departments, and (c) the factory overhead allocated per unit for each product using the department factory overhead allocation rates.

SHOW ME HOW

EE 11-3 *p. 460*

PE 11-3A Activity-based costing: factory overhead costs **OBJ. 4**

The total factory overhead for Diva-nation is budgeted for the year at $180,000, divided into four activities: cutting, $18,000; sewing, $36,000; setup, $96,000; and inspection, $30,000. Diva-nation manufactures two types of men's pants: jeans and khakis. The activity-base usage quantities for each product by each activity are as follows:

	Cutting	Sewing	Setup	Inspection
Jeans	800 dlh	1,200 dlh	1,400 setups	3,000 inspections
Khakis	1,200	800	1,000	2,000
	2,000 dlh	2,000 dlh	2,400 setups	5,000 inspections

Each product is budgeted for 20,000 units of production for the year. Determine (a) the activity rates for each activity and (b) the activity-based factory overhead per unit for each product.

EE 11-3 p. 460

SHOW ME HOW

PE 11-3B Activity-based costing: factory overhead costs — OBJ. 4

The total factory overhead for Bardot Marine Company is budgeted for the year at $600,000, divided into four activities: fabrication, $204,000; assembly, $105,000; setup, $156,000; and inspection, $135,000. Bardot Marine manufactures two types of boats: speedboats and bass boats. The activity-base usage quantities for each product by each activity are as follows:

	Fabrication	Assembly	Setup	Inspection
Speedboat	2,000 dlh	1,000 dlh	300 setups	1,100 inspections
Bass boat	1,000	2,000	100	400
	3,000 dlh	3,000 dlh	400 setups	1,500 inspections

Each product is budgeted for 250 units of production for the year. Determine (a) the activity rates for each activity and (b) the activity-based factory overhead per unit for each product.

EE 11-4 p. 462

SHOW ME HOW

PE 11-4A Activity-based costing: selling and administrative expenses — OBJ. 5

Fancy Feet Company manufactures and sells shoes. Fancy Feet uses activity-based costing to determine the cost of the sales order processing and the shipping activity. The sales order processing activity has an activity rate of $12 per sales order, and the shipping activity has an activity rate of $20 per shipment. Fancy Feet sold 27,500 units of walking shoes, which consisted of 5,000 orders and 1,400 shipments. Determine (a) the total and (b) the per-unit sales order processing and shipping activity cost for walking shoes.

EE 11-4 p. 462

SHOW ME HOW

PE 11-4B Activity-based costing: selling and administrative expenses — OBJ. 5

Jungle Junior Company manufactures and sells outdoor play equipment. Jungle Junior uses activity-based costing to determine the cost of the sales order processing and the customer return activity. The sales order processing activity has an activity rate of $20 per sales order, and the customer return activity has an activity rate of $100 per return. Jungle Junior sold 2,500 swing sets, which consisted of 750 orders and 80 returns. Determine (a) the total and (b) the per-unit sales order processing and customer return activity cost for swing sets.

EE 11-5 p. 464

SHOW ME HOW

PE 11-5A Activity-based costing for a service business — OBJ. 6

Draper Bank uses activity-based costing to determine the cost of servicing customers. There are three activity pools: teller transaction processing, check processing, and ATM transaction processing. The activity rates associated with each activity pool are $3.50 per teller transaction, $0.12 per canceled check, and $0.10 per ATM transaction. Corner Cleaners Inc. had 12 teller transactions, 100 canceled checks, and 20 ATM transactions during the month. Determine the total monthly activity-based cost for Corner Cleaners Inc. during the month.

EE 11-5 p. 464

SHOW ME HOW

PE 11-5B Activity-based costing for a service business — OBJ. 6

Sterling Hotel uses activity-based costing to determine the cost of servicing customers. There are three activity pools: guest check-in, room cleaning, and meal service. The activity rates associated with each activity pool are $8.00 per guest check-in, $25.00 per room cleaning, and $4.00 per served meal (not including food). Ginny Campbell visited the hotel for a 3-night stay. Campbell had three meals in the hotel during her visit. Determine the total activity-based cost for Campbell's visit.

Exercises

EX 11-1 Single plantwide factory overhead rate

OBJ. 2

Nixon Machine Parts Inc.'s Fabrication Department incurred $560,000 of factory overhead cost in producing gears and sprockets. The two products consumed a total of 8,000 direct machine hours. Of that amount, sprockets consumed 5,150 direct machine hours.

Determine the total amount of factory overhead that should be allocated to sprockets using machine hours as the allocation base.

EX 11-2 Single plantwide factory overhead rate

OBJ. 2

✔ a. $40 per direct labor hour

Matt's Music Inc. makes three musical instruments: trumpets, tubas, and trombones. The budgeted factory overhead cost is $188,000. Factory overhead is allocated to the three products on the basis of direct labor hours. The products have the following budgeted production volume and direct labor hours per unit:

	Budgeted Production Volume	Direct Labor Hours per Unit
Trumpets	2,100 units	0.8
Tubas	750	1.6
Trombones	1,300	1.4

a. Determine the single plantwide factory overhead rate.
b. Use the factory overhead rate in (a) to determine the amount of total and per-unit factory overhead allocated to each of the three products.

EX 11-3 Single plantwide factory overhead rate

OBJ. 2

✔ a. $60 per processing hour

Salty Sensations Snacks Company manufactures three types of snack foods: tortilla chips, potato chips, and pretzels. The company has budgeted the following costs for the upcoming period:

Factory depreciation	$ 31,360
Indirect labor	78,400
Factory electricity	7,840
Indirect materials	35,400
Selling expenses	25,000
Administrative expenses	18,000
Total costs	$196,000

Factory overhead is allocated to the three products on the basis of processing hours. The products had the following production budget and processing hours per case:

	Budgeted Volume (Cases)	Processing Hours per Case
Tortilla chips	4,000	0.20
Potato chips	5,000	0.15
Pretzels	2,500	0.40
Total	11,500	

a. Determine the single plantwide factory overhead rate.
b. Use the factory overhead rate in (a) to determine the amount of total and per-case factory overhead allocated to each of the three products under generally accepted accounting principles.

EX 11-4 Product costs and product profitability reports, using a single plantwide factory overhead rate OBJ. 2

✔ c. Pistons gross profit, $108,000

SHOW ME HOW

Orange County Engine Parts Inc. (OCEP) produces three products—pistons, valves, and cams—for the heavy equipment industry. OCEP has a very simple production process and product line and uses a single plantwide factory overhead rate to allocate overhead to the three products. The factory overhead rate is based on direct labor hours. Information about the three products for 2016 is as follows:

	Budgeted Volume (Units)	Direct Labor Hours per Unit	Price per Unit	Direct Materials per Unit
Pistons	7,200	0.20	$50	$25
Valves	28,800	0.15	10	4
Cams	1,200	0.32	70	29

The estimated direct labor rate is $20 per direct labor hour. Beginning and ending inventories are negligible and are, thus, assumed to be zero. The budgeted factory overhead for OCEP is $184,320.

a. Determine the plantwide factory overhead rate.
b. Determine the factory overhead and direct labor cost per unit for each product.
c. Use the information provided to construct a budgeted gross profit report by product line for the year ended December 31, 2016. Include the gross profit as a percent of sales in the last line of your report, rounded to one decimal place.
d. What does the report in (c) indicate to you?

EX 11-5 Multiple production department factory overhead rate method OBJ. 3

✔ b. Small glove, $25.00 per unit

SHOW ME HOW

Hand Armour, Inc. produces three types of high performance sports gloves: small, medium, and large. A glove pattern is first stenciled onto leather in the Pattern Department. The stenciled patterns are then sent to the Cut and Sew Department, where the glove is cut and sewed together. Sports Glove uses the multiple production department factory overhead rate method of allocating factory overhead costs. Its factory overhead costs were budgeted as follows:

Pattern Department overhead	$288,000
Cut and Sew Department overhead	412,500
Total	$700,500

The direct labor estimated for each production department was as follows:

Pattern Department	2,880 direct labor hours
Cut and Sew Department	3,300
Total	6,180 direct labor hours

Direct labor hours are used to allocate the production department overhead to the products. The direct labor hours per unit for each product for each production department were obtained from the engineering records as follows:

Production Departments	Small Glove	Medium Glove	Large Glove
Pattern Department	0.10	0.12	0.14
Cut and Sew Department	0.12	0.14	0.16
Direct labor hours per unit	0.22	0.26	0.30

a. Determine the two production department factory overhead rates.
b. Use the two production department factory overhead rates to determine the factory overhead per unit for each product.

EX 11-6 Single plantwide and multiple production department factory overhead rate methods and product cost distortion **OBJ. 2, 3**

✔ b. Residential motor, $330 per unit

Pineapple Motor Company manufactures two types of specialty electric motors, a commercial motor and a residential motor, through two production departments, Assembly and Testing. Presently, the company uses a single plantwide factory overhead rate for allocating factory overhead to the two products. However, management is considering using the multiple production department factory overhead rate method. The following factory overhead was budgeted for Pineapple:

Assembly Department	$240,000
Testing Department	750,000
Total	$990,000

Direct machine hours were estimated as follows:

Assembly Department	3,000 hours
Testing Department	6,000
Total	9,000 hours

In addition, the direct machine hours (dmh) used to produce a unit of each product in each department were determined from engineering records, as follows:

	Commercial	Residential
Assembly Department	1.5 dmh	1.0 dmh
Testing Department	3.0	2.0
Total machine hours per unit	4.5 dmh	3.0 dmh

a. Determine the per-unit factory overhead allocated to the commercial and residential motors under the single plantwide factory overhead rate method, using direct machine hours as the allocation base.

b. Determine the per-unit factory overhead allocated to the commercial and residential motors under the multiple production department factory overhead rate method, using direct machine hours as the allocation base for each department.

c. Recommend to management a product costing approach, based on your analyses in (a) and (b). Support your recommendation.

EX 11-7 Single plantwide and multiple production department factory overhead rate methods and product cost distortion **OBJ. 2, 3**

✔ b. Diesel engine, $370 per unit

The management of Firebolt Industries Inc. manufactures gasoline and diesel engines through two production departments, Fabrication and Assembly. Management needs accurate product cost information in order to guide product strategy. Presently, the company uses a single plantwide factory overhead rate for allocating factory overhead to the two products. However, management is considering the multiple production department factory overhead rate method. The following factory overhead was budgeted for Firebolt:

Fabrication Department factory overhead	$550,000
Assembly Department factory overhead	250,000
Total	$800,000

Direct labor hours were estimated as follows:

Fabrication Department	5,000 hours
Assembly Department	5,000
Total	10,000 hours

In addition, the direct labor hours (dlh) used to produce a unit of each product in each department were determined from engineering records, as follows:

Production Departments	Gasoline Engine	Diesel Engine
Fabrication Department	3.0 dlh	2.0 dlh
Assembly Department	2.0	3.0
Direct labor hours per unit	5.0 dlh	5.0 dlh

a. Determine the per-unit factory overhead allocated to the gasoline and diesel engines under the single plantwide factory overhead rate method, using direct labor hours as the activity base.

b. Determine the per-unit factory overhead allocated to the gasoline and diesel engines under the multiple production department factory overhead rate method, using direct labor hours as the activity base for each department.

c. Recommend to management a product costing approach, based on your analyses in (a) and (b). Support your recommendation.

EX 11-8 Identifying activity bases in an activity-based cost system — OBJ. 4

Select Foods Inc. uses activity-based costing to determine product costs. For each activity listed in the left column, match an appropriate activity base from the right column. You may use items in the activity-base list more than once or not at all.

Activity	Activity Base
Accounting reports	Engineering change orders
Customer return processing	Kilowatt hours used
Electric power	Number of accounting reports
Human resources	Number of customers
Inventory control	Number of customer orders
Invoice and collecting	Number of customer returns
Machine depreciation	Number of employees
Materials handling	Number of inspections
Order shipping	Number of inventory transactions
Payroll	Number of machine hours
Production control	Number of material moves
Production setup	Number of payroll checks processed
Purchasing	Number of production orders
Quality control	Number of purchase orders
Sales order processing	Number of sales orders
	Number of setups

EX 11-9 Product costs using activity rates — OBJ. 4

✔ b. $405,000

Nozama.com Inc. sells consumer electronics over the Internet. For the next period, the budgeted cost of the sales order processing activity is $540,000 and 60,000 sales orders are estimated to be processed.

a. Determine the activity rate of the sales order processing activity.

b. Determine the amount of sales order processing cost that Nozama.com would receive if it had 45,000 sales orders.

EX 11-10 Product costs using activity rates — OBJ. 4

✔ Treadmill activity cost per unit, $135

Endurance Enterprises Inc. manufactures elliptical exercise machines and treadmills. The products are produced in its Fabrication and Assembly production departments. In addition to production activities, several other activities are required to produce the two products. These activities and their associated activity rates are as follows:

Activity	Activity Rate
Fabrication	$30 per machine hour
Assembly	$15 per direct labor hour
Setup	$50 per setup
Inspecting	$25 per inspection
Production scheduling	$15 per production order
Purchasing	$10 per purchase order

The activity-base usage quantities and units produced for each product were as follows:

Activity Base	Elliptical Machines	Treadmill
Machine hours	800	500
Direct labor hours	210	90
Setups	24	10
Inspections	140	160
Production orders	20	10
Purchase orders	85	60
Units produced	300	160

Use the activity rate and usage information to calculate the total activity cost and activity cost per unit for each product.

EX 11-11 Activity rates and product costs using activity-based costing OBJ. 4

✔ b. Dining room lighting fixtures, $50 per unit

Lightsquare Inc. manufactures entry and dining room lighting fixtures. Five activities are used in manufacturing the fixtures. These activities and their associated budgeted activity costs and activity bases are as follows:

Activity	Budgeted Activity Cost	Activity Base
Casting	$127,750	Machine hours
Assembly	63,200	Direct labor hours
Inspecting	21,330	Number of inspections
Setup	28,750	Number of setups
Materials handling	31,600	Number of loads

Corporate records were obtained to estimate the amount of activity to be used by the two products. The estimated activity-base usage quantities and units produced follow:

Activity Base	Entry	Dining	Total
Machine hours	2500	1,150	3,650
Direct labor hours	960	2,200	3,160
Number of inspections	860	325	1,185
Number of setups	170	60	230
Number of loads	570	220	790
Units produced	5,541	2,128	7,669

a. Determine the activity rate for each activity.
b. Use the activity rates in (a) to determine the total and per-unit activity costs associated with each product.

EX 11-12 Activity cost pools, activity rates, and product costs using activity-based costing OBJ. 4

✔ b. Ovens, $75 per unit

Hipster Home Appliances Inc. is estimating the activity cost associated with producing ovens and refrigerators. The indirect labor can be traced into four separate activity pools, based on time records provided by the employees. The budgeted activity cost and activity-base information are provided as follows:

Activity	Activity Pool Cost	Activity Base
Procurement	$66,000	Number of purchase orders
Scheduling	4,120	Number of production orders
Materials handling	13,280	Number of moves
Product development	8,100	Number of engineering changes
Total cost	$91,500	

The estimated activity-base usage and unit information for two product lines was determined from corporate records as follows:

	Number of Purchase Orders	Number of Production Orders	Number of Moves	Number of Engineering Changes	Units
Ovens	400	136	240	68	740
Refrigerators	260	70	175	40	600
Totals	660	206	415	108	1,340

a. Determine the activity rate for each activity cost pool.
b. Determine the activity-based cost per unit of each product.

EX 11-13 Activity-based costing and product cost distortion — OBJ. 2, 4

✔ c. Cell phones, $1.68 per unit

Digital Storage Concept Inc. is considering a change to activity-based product costing. The company produces two products, cell phones and tablet PCs, in a single production department. The production department is estimated to require 3,750 direct labor hours. The total indirect labor is budgeted to be $375,000.

Time records from indirect labor employees revealed that they spent 40% of their time setting up production runs and 60% of their time supporting actual production.

The following information about cell phones and tablet PCs was determined from the corporate records:

	Number of Setups	Direct Labor Hours	Units
Cell phones	600	1,875	93,750
Tablet PCs	1,400	1,875	93,750
Total	2,000	3,750	187,500

a. Determine the indirect labor cost per unit allocated to cell phones and tablet PCs under a single plantwide factory overhead rate system using the direct labor hours as the allocation base.
b. Determine the budgeted activity costs and activity rates for the indirect labor under activity-based costing. Assume two activities—one for setup and the other for production support.
c. Determine the activity cost per unit for indirect labor allocated to each product under activity-based costing.
d. Why are the per-unit allocated costs in (a) different from the per-unit activity cost assigned to the products in (c)?

EX 11-14 Multiple production department factory overhead rate method — OBJ. 3

✔ b. Blender, $18.20 per unit

Four Finger Appliance Company manufactures small kitchen appliances. The product line consists of blenders and toaster ovens. Four Finger Appliance presently uses the multiple production department factory overhead rate method. The factory overhead is as follows:

Assembly Department	$186,000
Test and Pack Department	120,000
Total	$306,000

The direct labor information for the production of 7,500 units of each product is as follows:

	Assembly Department	Test and Pack Department
Blender	750 dlh	2,250 dlh
Toaster oven	2,250	750
Total	3,000 dlh	3,000 dlh

Four Finger Appliance used direct labor hours to allocate production department factory overhead to products.

a. Determine the two production department factory overhead rates.
b. Determine the total factory overhead and the factory overhead per unit allocated to each product.

EX 11-15 Activity-based costing and product cost distortion — OBJ. 4

✔ b. Blender, $23.60 per unit

The management of Four Finger Appliance Company in Exercise 11-14 has asked you to use activity-based costing to allocate factory overhead costs to the two products. You have determined that $81,000 of factory overhead from each of the production departments can be associated with setup activity ($162,000 in total). Company records indicate that blenders required 135 setups, while the toaster ovens required only 45 setups. Each product has a production volume of 7,500 units.

a. Determine the three activity rates (assembly, test and pack, and setup).
b. Determine the total factory overhead and factory overhead per unit allocated to each product using the activity rates in (a).

EX 11-16 Single plantwide rate and activity-based costing — OBJ. 2, 4

✔ a. Low, Col. C, 93.5%

Whirlpool Corporation conducted an activity-based costing study of its Evansville, Indiana, plant in order to identify its most profitable products. Assume that we select three representative refrigerators (out of 333): one low-, one medium-, and one high-volume refrigerator. Additionally, we assume the following activity-base information for each of the three refrigerators:

Three Representative Refrigerators	Number of Machine Hours	Number of Setups	Number of Sales Orders	Number of Units
Refrigerator—Low Volume	24	14	38	160
Refrigerator—Medium Volume	225	13	88	1,500
Refrigerator—High Volume	900	9	120	6,000

Prior to conducting the study, the factory overhead allocation was based on a single machine hour rate. The machine hour rate was $200 per hour. After conducting the activity-based costing study, assume that three activities were used to allocate the factory overhead. The new activity rate information is assumed to be as follows:

	Machining Activity	Setup Activity	Sales Order Processing Activity
Activity rate	$160	$240	$55

a. Complete the following table, using the single machine hour rate to determine the per-unit factory overhead for each refrigerator (Column A) and the three activity-based rates to determine the activity-based factory overhead per unit (Column B). Finally, compute the percent change in per-unit allocation from the single to activity-based rate methods (Column C). Round per-unit overhead to two decimal places and percents to one decimal place.

Product Volume Class	Column A Single Rate Overhead Allocation per Unit	Column B ABC Overhead Allocation per Unit	Column C Percent Change in Allocation (Col. B – Col. A)/Col. A
Low			
Medium			
High			

b. Why is the traditional overhead rate per machine hour greater under the single rate method than under the activity-based method?
c. Interpret Column C in your table from part (a).

EX 11-17 Evaluating selling and administrative cost allocations **OBJ. 5**

Gordon Gecco Furniture Company has two major product lines with the following characteristics:

- Commercial office furniture: Few large orders, little advertising support, shipments in full truckloads, and low handling complexity
- Home office furniture: Many small orders, large advertising support, shipments in partial truckloads, and high handling complexity

The company produced the following profitability report for management:

Gordon Gecco Furniture Company
Product Profitability Report
For the Year Ended December 31

	Commercial Office Furniture	Home Office Furniture	Total
Revenue	$5,600,000	$2,800,000	$8,400,000
Cost of goods sold	2,100,000	980,000	3,080,000
Gross profit	$3,500,000	$1,820,000	$5,320,000
Selling and administrative expenses	1,680,000	840,000	2,520,000
Income from operations	$1,820,000	$ 980,000	$2,800,000

The selling and administrative expenses are allocated to the products on the basis of relative sales dollars.

Evaluate the accuracy of this report and recommend an alternative approach.

EX 11-18 Construct and interpret a product profitability report, allocating selling and administrative expenses **OBJ. 5**

✔ **b. Generators operating profit-to-sales, 23.83%**

SHOW ME HOW

Volt-Gear Inc. manufactures power equipment. Volt-Gear has two primary products—generators and air compressors. The following report was prepared by the controller for Volt-Gear senior marketing management for the year ended December 31:

	Generators	Air Compressors	Total
Revenue	$2,000,000	$1,400,000	$3,400,000
Cost of goods sold	1,400,000	980,000	2,380,000
Gross profit	$ 600,000	$ 420,000	$1,020,000
Selling and administrative expenses			353,000
Income from operations			$ 667,000

The marketing management team was concerned that the selling and administrative expenses were not traced to the products. Marketing management believed that some products consumed larger amounts of selling and administrative expense than did other products. To verify this, the controller was asked to prepare a complete product profitability report, using activity-based costing.

The controller determined that selling and administrative expenses consisted of two activities: sales order processing and post-sale customer service. The controller was able to determine the activity base and activity rate for each activity, as follows:

Activity	Activity Base	Activity Rate
Sales order processing	Sales orders	$ 80 per sales order
Post-sale customer service	Service requests	$300 per customer service request

The controller determined the following activity-base usage information about each product:

	Generators	Air Compressors
Number of sales orders	980	1,160
Number of service requests	150	456

a. Determine the activity cost of each product for sales order processing and post-sale customer service activities.
b. Use the information in (a) to prepare a complete product profitability report dated for the year ended December 31. Calculate the gross profit to sales and the income from operations to sales percentages for each product.
c. Interpret the product profitability report. How should management respond to the report?

✔ a. Customer 1, Income from operations after customer service activities, $9,854

SHOW ME HOW

EX 11-19 Activity-based costing and customer profitability OBJ. 5

Schneider Electric manufactures power distribution equipment for commercial customers, such as hospitals and manufacturers. Activity-based costing was used to determine customer profitability. Customer service activities were assigned to individual customers, using the following assumed customer service activities, activity base, and activity rate:

Customer Service Activity	Activity Base	Activity Rate
Bid preparation	Number of bid requests	$200/request
Shipment	Number of shipments	$16/shipment
Support standard items	Number of standard items ordered	$20/std. item
Support nonstandard items	Number of nonstandard items ordered	$75/nonstd. item

Assume that the company had the following gross profit information for three representative customers:

	Customer 1	Customer 2	Customer 3
Revenue	$39,000	$26,000	$31,200
Cost of goods sold	24,180	13,520	15,600
Gross profit	$14,820	$12,480	$15,600
Gross profit as a percent of sales	38%	48%	50%

The administrative records indicated that the activity-base usage quantities for each customer were as follows:

Activity Base	Customer 1	Customer 2	Customer 3
Number of bid requests	12	8	25
Number of shipments	16	24	45
Number of standard items ordered	48	38	56
Number of nonstandard items ordered	18	30	54

a. Prepare a customer profitability report dated for the year ended December 31, 2016, showing (1) the income from operations after customer service activities, (2) the gross profit as a percent of sales, and (3) the income from operations after customer service activities as a percent of sales. Prepare the report with a column for each customer. Round percentages to the nearest whole percent.
b. Interpret the report in part (a).

EX 11-20 Activity-based costing for a service company OBJ. 6

✔ a. Patient Umit, $6,025

Crosswinds Hospital plans to use activity-based costing to assign hospital indirect costs to the care of patients. The hospital has identified the following activities and activity rates for the hospital indirect costs:

Activity	Activity Rate
Room and meals	$240 per day
Radiology	$215 per image
Pharmacy	$ 50 per physician order
Chemistry lab	$ 80 per test
Operating room	$1,000 per operating room hour

The activity usage information associated with the two patients is as follows:

	Patient Putin	Patient Umit
Number of days	6 days	4 days
Number of images	4 images	3 images
Number of physician orders	6 orders	2 orders
Number of tests	5 tests	4 tests
Number of operating room hours	8 hours	4 hours

a. Determine the activity cost associated with each patient.
b. Why is the total activity cost different for the two patients?

✔ a. Auto, Income from operations, $820,380

SHOW ME HOW

EX 11-21 Activity-based costing for a service company **OBJ. 5, 6**

Safety First Insurance Company carries three major lines of insurance: auto, workers' compensation, and homeowners. The company has prepared the following report:

Safety First Insurance Company
Product Profitability Report
For the Year Ended December 31

	Auto	Workers' Compensation	Homeowners
Premium revenue	$5,750,000	$6,240,000	$8,160,000
Less estimated claims	4,312,500	4,680,000	6,120,000
Underwriting income	$1,437,500	$1,560,000	$2,040,000
Underwriting income as a percent of premium revenue	25%	25%	25%

Management is concerned that the administrative expenses may make some of the insurance lines unprofitable. However, the administrative expenses have not been allocated to the insurance lines. The controller has suggested that the administrative expenses could be assigned to the insurance lines using activity-based costing. The administrative expenses are comprised of five activities. The activities and their rates are as follows:

	Activity Rates
New policy processing	$120 per new policy
Cancellation processing	$175 per cancellation
Claim audits	$320 per claim audit
Claim disbursements processing	$104 per disbursement
Premium collection processing	$24 per premium collected

Activity-base usage data for each line of insurance was retrieved from the corporate records and follows:

	Auto	Workers' Compensation	Homeowners
Number of new policies	1,320	1,500	4,080
Number of canceled policies	480	240	2,160
Number of audited claims	385	120	960
Number of claim disbursements	480	216	840
Number of premiums collected	8,400	1,800	15,000

a. Complete the product profitability report through the administrative activities. Determine the income from operations as a percent of premium revenue, rounded to the nearest whole percent.
b. Interpret the report.

Problems Series A

PR 11-1A Single plantwide factory overhead rate **OBJ. 2**

✔ 1. b. $48 per machine hour

Orange County Chrome Company manufactures three chrome-plated products—automobile bumpers, valve covers, and wheels. These products are manufactured in two production departments (Stamping and Plating). The factory overhead for Orange County Chrome is $220,800.

The three products consume both machine hours and direct labor hours in the two production departments as follows:

	Direct Labor Hours	Machine Hours
Stamping Department		
Automobile bumpers	560	800
Valve covers	300	560
Wheels	340	600
	1,200	1,960
Plating Department		
Automobile bumpers	170	1,170
Valve covers	180	710
Wheels	175	760
	525	2,640
Total	1,725	4,600

Instructions

1. Determine the single plantwide factory overhead rate, using each of the following allocation bases: (a) direct labor hours and (b) machine hours.
2. Determine the product factory overhead costs, using (a) the direct labor hour plantwide factory overhead rate and (b) the machine hour plantwide factory overhead rate.

PR 11-2A Multiple production department factor overhead rates **OBJ. 3**

✔ 2. Wheels, $63,040

The management of Orange County Chrome Company, described in Problem 11-1A, now plans to use the multiple production department factory overhead rate method. The total factory overhead associated with each department is as follows:

Stamping Department	$115,200
Plating Department	105,600
Total	$220,800

Instructions

1. Determine the multiple production department factory overhead rates, using direct labor hours for the Stamping Department and machine hours for the Plating Department.
2. Determine the product factory overhead costs, using the multiple production department rates in (1).

PR 11-3A Activity-based and department rate product costing and product cost distortions **OBJ. 3, 4**

✔ 2. Snowboards, $390,000 and $65

Black and Blue Sports Inc. manufactures two products: snowboards and skis. The factory overhead incurred is as follows:

Indirect labor	$507,000
Cutting Department	156,000
Finishing Department	192,000
Total	$855,000

The activity base associated with the two production departments is direct labor hours. The indirect labor can be assigned to two different activities as follows:

Activity	Budgeted Activity Cost	Activity Base
Production control	$237,000	Number of production runs
Materials handling	270,000	Number of moves
Total	$507,000	

The activity-base usage quantities and units produced for the two products follow:

	Number of Production Runs	Number of Moves	Direct Labor Hours—Cutting	Direct Labor Hours—Finishing	Units Produced
Snowboards	430	5,000	4,000	2,000	6,000
Skis	70	2,500	2,000	4,000	6,000
Total	500	7,500	6,000	6,000	12,000

Instructions

1. Determine the factory overhead rates under the multiple production department rate method. Assume that indirect labor is associated with the production departments, so that the total factory overhead is $315,000 and $540,000 for the Cutting and Finishing departments, respectively.
2. Determine the total and per-unit factory overhead costs allocated to each product, using the multiple production department overhead rates in (1).
3. Determine the activity rates, assuming that the indirect labor is associated with activities rather than with the production departments.
4. Determine the total and per-unit cost assigned to each product under activity-based costing.
5. Explain the difference in the per-unit overhead allocated to each product under the multiple production department factory overhead rate and activity-based costing methods.

PR 11-4A Activity-based product costing

OBJ. 4

✓ 2. Z4 total activity cost, $195,300

Teldar Manufacturing Company is a diversified manufacturer that manufactures three products (M5, Z4, and I8) in a continuous production process. Senior management has asked the controller to conduct an activity-based costing study. The controller identified the amount of factory overhead required by the critical activities of the organization as follows:

Activity	Activity Cost Pool
Production	$264,000
Setup	96,000
Material handling	9,600
Inspection	50,000
Product engineering	150,000
Total	$569,600

The activity bases identified for each activity are as follows:

Activity	Activity Base
Production	Machine hours
Setup	Number of setups
Material handling	Number of parts
Inspection	Number of inspection hours
Product engineering	Number of engineering hours

The activity-base usage quantities and units produced for the three products were determined from corporate records and are as follows:

	Machine Hours	Number of Setups	Number of Parts	Number of Inspection Hours	Number of Engineering Hours	Units
M5	1,000	60	80	450	125	1,250
Z4	800	120	150	300	175	1,000
I8	400	220	250	250	200	500
Total	2,200	400	480	1,000	500	2,750

Each product requires 0.8 machine hour per unit.

Instructions

1. Determine the activity rate for each activity.
2. Determine the total and per-unit activity cost for all three products.
3. Why aren't the activity unit costs equal across all three products since they require the same machine time per unit?

PR 11-5A Allocating selling and administrative expenses using activity-based costing OBJ. 5

✔ 3. Break-a-Leg Hospital loss from operations, ($50,900)

SHOW ME HOW

Cold Zone Mechancial Inc. manufactures cooling units for commercial buildings. The price and cost of goods sold for each unit are as follows:

Price	$75,000 per unit
Cost of goods sold	60,000
Gross profit	$15,000 per unit

In addition, the company incurs selling and administrative expenses of $231,880. The company wishes to assign these costs to its three major customers, Good Knowledge University, Hot Shotz Arena, and Break-a-Leg Hospital. These expenses are related to three major nonmanufacturing activities: customer service, project bidding, and engineering support. The engineering support is in the form of engineering changes that are placed by the customer to change the design of a product. The budgeted activity costs and activity bases associated with these activities are:

Activity	Budgeted Activity Cost	Activity Base
Customer service	$ 83,720	Number of service requests
Project bidding	61,360	Number of bids
Engineering support	86,800	Number of customer design changes
Total costs	$231,880	

Activity-base usage and unit volume information for the three customers is as follows:

	Good Knowledge University	Hot Shotz Arena	Break-a-Leg Hospital	Total
Number of service requests	60	52	210	322
Number of bids	36	18	50	104
Number of customer design changes	45	30	142	217
Unit volume	22	14	6	42

Instructions

1. Determine the activity rates for each of the three nonmanufacturing activity pools.
2. Determine the activity costs allocated to the three customers, using the activity rates in (1).

(Continued)

3. Construct customer profitability reports for the three customers, dated for the year ended December 31, using the activity costs in (2). The reports should disclose the gross profit and income from operations associated with each customer.
4. Provide recommendations to management, based on the profitability reports in (3).

PR 11-6A Product costing and decision analysis for a service company

OBJ. 6

✔ 3. Procedure B excess, $597,700

Pleasant Stay Medical Inc. wishes to determine its product costs. Pleasant Stay offers a variety of medical procedures (operations) that are considered its "products." The overhead has been separated into three major activities. The annual estimated activity costs and activity bases follow:

Activity	Budgeted Activity Cost	Activity Base
Scheduling and admitting	$ 432,000	Number of patients
Housekeeping	4,212,000	Number of patient days
Nursing	5,376,000	Weighted care unit
Total costs	$10,020,000	

Total "patient days" are determined by multiplying the number of patients by the average length of stay in the hospital. A weighted care unit (wcu) is a measure of nursing effort used to care for patients. There were 192,000 weighted care units estimated for the year. In addition, Pleasant Stay estimated 6,000 patients and 27,000 patient days for the year. (The average patient is expected to have a a little more than a four-day stay in the hospital.)

During a portion of the year, Pleasant Stay collected patient information for three selected procedures, as follows:

	Activity-Base Usage
Procedure A	
Number of patients	280
Average length of stay	× 6 days
Patient days	1,680
Weighted care units	19,200
Procedure B	
Number of patients	650
Average length of stay	× 5 days
Patient days	3,250
Weighted care units	6,000
Procedure C	
Number of patients	1,200
Average length of stay	× 4 days
Patient days	4,800
Weighted care units	24,000

Private insurance reimburses the hospital for these activities at a fixed daily rate of $406 per patient day for all three procedures.

Instructions

1. Determine the activity rates.
2. Determine the activity cost for each procedure.
3. Determine the excess or deficiency of reimbursements to activity cost.
4. Interpret your results.

Problems Series B

PR 11-1B Single plantwide factory overhead rate **OBJ. 2**

✔ 1. b. $111 per machine hour

Spotted Cow Dairy Company manufactures three products—whole milk, skim milk, and cream—in two production departments, Blending and Packing. The factory overhead for Spotted Cow Dairy is $299,700.

The three products consume both machine hours and direct labor hours in the two production departments as follows:

	Direct Labor Hours	Machine Hours
Blending Department		
Whole milk	260	650
Skim milk	245	710
Cream	215	260
	720	1,620
Packing Department		
Whole milk	470	500
Skim milk	300	415
Cream	130	165
	900	1,080
Total	1,620	2,700

Instructions

1. Determine the single plantwide factory overhead rate, using each of the following allocation bases: (a) direct labor hours and (b) machine hours.
2. Determine the product factory overhead costs, using (a) the direct labor hour plantwide factory overhead rate and (b) the machine hour plantwide factory overhead rate.

PR 11-2B Multiple production department factory overhead rates **OBJ. 3**

✔ 2. Cream, $46,150

The management of Spotted Cow Dairy Company, described in Problem 11-1B, now plans to use the multiple production department factory overhead rate method. The total factory overhead associated with each department is as follows:

Blending Department	$178,200
Packing Department	121,500
Total	$299,700

Instructions

1. Determine the multiple production department factory overhead rates, using machine hours for the Blending Department and direct labor hours for the Packing Department.
2. Determine the product factory overhead costs, using the multiple production department rates in (1).

PR 11-3B Activity-based department rate product costing and product cost distortions **OBJ. 3, 4**

✔ 4. Loudspeakers, $465,430 and $66.49

Big Sound Inc. manufactures two products: receivers and loudspeakers. The factory overhead incurred is as follows:

Indirect labor	$400,400
Subassembly Department	198,800
Final Assembly Department	114,800
Total	$714,000

(Continued)

The activity base associated with the two production departments is direct labor hours. The indirect labor can be assigned to two different activities as follows:

Activity	Budgeted Activity Cost	Activity Base
Setup	$138,600	Number of setups
Quality control	261,800	Number of inspections
Total	$400,400	

The activity-base usage quantities and units produced for the two products follow:

	Number of Setups	Number of Inspections	Direct Labor Hours—Subassembly	Direct Labor Hours—Final Assembly	Units Produced
Receivers	80	450	875	525	7,000
Loudspeakers	320	1,750	525	875	7,000
Total	400	2,200	1,400	1,400	14,000

Instructions

1. Determine the factory overhead rates under the multiple production department rate method. Assume that indirect labor is associated with the production departments, so that the total factory overhead is $420,000 and $294,000 for the Subassembly and Final Assembly departments, respectively.
2. Determine the total and per-unit factory overhead costs allocated to each product, using the multiple production department overhead rates in (1).
3. Determine the activity rates, assuming that the indirect labor is associated with activities rather than with the production departments.
4. Determine the total and per-unit cost assigned to each product under activity-based costing.
5. Explain the difference in the per-unit overhead allocated to each product under the multiple production department factory overhead rate and activity-based costing methods.

PR 11-4B Activity-based product costing

OBJ. 4

✔ **2. Brown sugar total activity cost, $293,600**

Sweet Sugar Company manufactures three products (white sugar, brown sugar, and powdered sugar) in a continuous production process. Senior management has asked the controller to conduct an activity-based costing study. The controller identified the amount of factory overhead required by the critical activities of the organization as follows:

Activity	Budgeted Activity Cost
Production	$500,000
Setup	144,000
Inspection	44,000
Shipping	115,000
Customer service	84,000
Total	$887,000

The activity bases identified for each activity are as follows:

Activity	Activity Base
Production	Machine hours
Setup	Number of setups
Inspection	Number of inspections
Shipping	Number of customer orders
Customer service	Number of customer service requests

The activity-base usage quantities and units produced for the three products were determined from corporate records and are as follows:

	Machine Hours	Number of Setups	Number of Inspections	Number of Customer Orders	Customer Service Requests	Units
White sugar	5,000	85	220	1,150	60	10,000
Brown sugar	2,500	170	330	2,600	350	5,000
Powdered sugar	2,500	195	550	2,000	190	5,000
Total	10,000	450	1,100	5,750	600	20,000

Each product requires 0.5 machine hour per unit.

Instructions

1. Determine the activity rate for each activity.
2. Determine the total and per-unit activity cost for all three products. Round to two decimal places.
3. Why aren't the activity unit costs equal across all three products since they require the same machine time per unit?

PR 11-5B Allocating selling and administrative expenses using activity-based costing — OBJ. 5

✔ 3. Supply Universe, income from operations, $283,820

SHOW ME HOW

Shrute Inc. manufactures office copiers, which are sold to retailers. The price and cost of goods sold for each copier are as follows:

Price	$1,110 per unit
Cost of goods sold	682
Gross profit	$ 428 per unit

In addition, the company incurs selling and administrative expenses of $414,030. The company wishes to assign these costs to its three major retail customers, The Warehouse, Kosmo Co., and Supply Universe. These expenses are related to its three major nonmanufacturing activities: customer service, sales order processing, and advertising support. The advertising support is in the form of advertisements that are placed by Shrute Inc. to support the retailer's sale of Shrute copiers to consumers. The budgeted activity costs and activity bases associated with these activities are:

Activity	Budgeted Activity Cost	Activity Base
Customer service	$ 76,860	Number of service requests
Sales order processing	25,920	Number of sales orders
Advertising support	311,250	Number of ads placed
Total activity cost	$414,030	

Activity-base usage and unit volume information for the three customers is as follows:

	The Warehouse	Kosmo Co.	Supply Universe	Total
Number of service requests	62	340	25	427
Number of sales orders	300	640	140	1,080
Number of ads placed	25	180	44	249
Unit volume	810	810	810	2,430

Instructions

1. Determine the activity rates for each of the three nonmanufacturing activities.
2. Determine the activity costs allocated to the three customers, using the activity rates in (1).
3. Construct customer profitability reports for the three customers, dated for the year ended December 31, using the activity costs in (2). The reports should disclose the gross profit and income from operations associated with each customer.
4. Provide recommendations to management, based on the profitability reports in (3).

✔ 3. Flight 102 income from operations, $4,415

PR 11-6B Product costing and decision analysis for a service company

OBJ. 6

Blue Star Airline provides passenger airline service, using small jets. The airline connects four major cities: Charlotte, Pittsburgh, Detroit, and San Francisco. The company expects to fly 170,000 miles during a month. The following costs are budgeted for a month:

Fuel	$2,120,000
Ground personnel	788,500
Crew salaries	850,000
Depreciation	430,000
Total costs	$4,188,500

Blue Star management wishes to assign these costs to individual flights in order to gauge the profitability of its service offerings. The following activity bases were identified with the budgeted costs:

Airline Cost	Activity Base
Fuel, crew, and depreciation costs	Number of miles flown
Ground personnel	Number of arrivals and departures at an airport

The size of the company's ground operation in each city is determined by the size of the workforce. The following monthly data are available from corporate records for each terminal operation:

Terminal City	Ground Personnel Cost	Number of Arrivals/Departures
Charlotte	$256,000	320
Pittsburgh	97,500	130
Detroit	129,000	150
San Francisco	306,000	340
Total	$788,500	940

Three recent representative flights have been selected for the profitability study. Their characteristics are as follows:

	Description	Miles Flown	Number of Passengers	Ticket Price per Passenger
Flight 101	Charlotte to San Francisco	2,000	80	$695.00
Flight 102	Detroit to Charlotte	800	50	441.50
Flight 103	Charlotte to Pittsburgh	400	20	382.00

Instructions

1. Determine the fuel, crew, and depreciation cost per mile flown.
2. Determine the cost per arrival or departure by terminal city.
3. Use the information in (1) and (2) to construct a profitability report for the three flights. Each flight has a single arrival and departure to its origin and destination city pairs.
4. Evaluate flight profitability by determining the break-even number of passengers required for each flight assuming all the costs of a flight are fixed. Round to the nearest whole number.

Cases & Projects

CP 11-1 Ethics and professional conduct in business

The controller of Tri Con Global Systems Inc. devised a new costing system based on tracing the cost of activities to products. The controller was able to measure post-manufacturing activities, such as selling, promotional, and distribution activities, and allocate these activities to products in order to have a more complete view of the company's product costs. This effort produced better strategic information about the relative profitability of product lines. In addition, the controller used the same product cost information for inventory valuation on the financial statements. Surprisingly, the controller discovered that the company's reported net income was larger under this scheme than under the traditional costing approach.

Why was the net income larger, and how would you react to the controller's action?

CP 11-2 Identifying product cost distortion

Beachside Beverages Company manufactures soft drinks. Information about two products is as follows:

	Volume	Sales Price per Case	Gross Profit per Case
Storm Soda	800,000 cases	$30	$12
Fizz Wiz	10,000 cases	30	12

It is known that both products have the same direct materials and direct labor costs per case. Beachside Beverages allocates factory overhead to products by using a single plantwide factory overhead rate, based on direct labor cost. Additional information about the two products is as follows:

Storm Soda: Requires minor process preparation and sterilization prior to processing. The ingredients are acquired locally. The formulation is simple, and it is easy to maintain quality. Lastly, the product is sold in large bulk (full truckload) orders.

Fizz Wiz: Requires extensive process preparation and sterilization prior to processing. The ingredients are from Jamaica, requiring complex import controls. The formulation is complex, and it is thus difficult to maintain quality. Lastly, the product is sold in small (less than full truckload) orders.

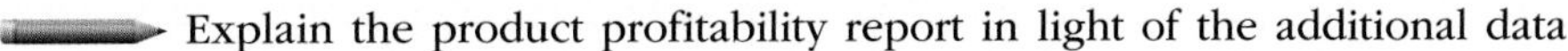

Explain the product profitability report in light of the additional data.

CP 11-3 Activity-based costing for a service company

Wells Fargo Insurance Services (WFIS) is an insurance brokerage company that classified insurance products as either "easy" or "difficult." Easy and difficult products were defined as follows:

Easy: Electronic claims, few inquiries, mature product

Difficult: Paper claims, complex claims to process, many inquiries, a new product with complex options

The company originally allocated processing and service expenses on the basis of revenue. Under this traditional allocation approach, the product profitability report revealed the following:

	Easy Product	Difficult Product	Total
Revenue	$600	$400	$1,000
Processing and service expenses	420	280	700
Income from operations	$180	$120	$ 300
Operating income margin	30%	30%	30%

WFIS decided to use activity-based costing to allocate the processing and service expenses. The following activity-based costing analysis of the same data illustrates a much different profit picture for the two types of products:

	Easy Product	Difficult Product	Total
Revenue	$600	$ 400	$1,000
Processing and service expenses	183	517	700
Income from operations	$417	$(117)	$ 300
Operating income margin	70%	(29%)	30%

Explain why the activity-based profitability report reveals different information from the traditional sales allocation report.

Source: Dan Patras and Kevin Clancy, "ABC in the Service Industry: Product Line Profitability at Acordia, Inc." *As Easy as ABC Newsletter*, Issue 12, Spring 1993.

CP 11-4 Using a product profitability report to guide strategic decisions

The controller of Boom Box Sounds Inc. prepared the following product profitability report for management, using activity-based costing methods for allocating both the factory overhead and the marketing expenses. As such, the controller has confidence in the accuracy of this report. In addition, the controller interviewed the vice president of marketing, who indicated that the floor loudspeakers were an older product that was highly recognized in the marketplace. The ribbon loudspeakers were a new product that was recently launched. The ribbon loudspeakers are a new technology that have no competition in the marketplace, and it is hoped that they will become an important future addition to the company's product portfolio. Initial indications are that the product is well received by customers. The controller believes that the manufacturing costs for all three products are in line with expectations.

	Floor Loudspeakers	Bookshelf Loudspeakers	Ribbon Loudspeakers	Totals
Sales	$1,500,000	$1,200,000	$900,000	$3,600,000
Less cost of goods sold	1,050,000	720,000	810,000	2,580,000
Gross profit	$ 450,000	$ 480,000	$ 90,000	$1,020,000
Less marketing expenses	600,000	120,000	72,000	792,000
Income from operations	$ (150,000)	$ 360,000	$ 18,000	$ 228,000

1. Calculate the gross profit and income from operations to sales ratios for each product.
2. Write a memo using the product profitability report and the calculations in (1) to make recommendations to management with respect to strategies for the three products.

CP 11-5 Product cost distortion

Aldin Aster, president of Teldar Tech Inc., was reviewing the product profitability reports with the controller, Francie Newburn. The following conversation took place:

Aldin: I've been reviewing the product profitability reports. Our high-volume calculator, the T-100, appears to be unprofitable, while some of our lower-volume specialty calculators in the T-900 series appear to be very profitable. These results do not make sense to me. How are the product profits determined?

Francie: First, we identify the revenues associated with each product line. This information comes directly from our sales order system and is very accurate. Next, we identify the direct materials and direct labor associated with making each of the calculators. Again, this information is very accurate. The final cost that must be considered is the factory overhead. Factory overhead is allocated to the products, based on the direct labor hours used to assemble the calculator.

Aldin: What about distribution, promotion, and other post-manufacturing costs that can be associated with the product?

Francie: According to generally accepted accounting principles, we expense them in the period that they are incurred and do not treat them as product costs.

Aldin: Another thing, you say that you allocate factory overhead according to direct labor hours. Yet I know that the T-900 series specialty products have very low volumes but require extensive engineering, testing, and materials management effort. They are our newer, more complex products. It seems that these sources of factory overhead will end up being allocated to the T-100 line because it is the high-volume and therefore high direct labor hour product. Yet the T-100 line is easy to make and requires very little support from our engineering, testing, and materials management personnel.

Francie: I'm not too sure. I do know that our product costing approach is similar to that used by many different types of companies. I don't think we could all be wrong.

Is Aldin Aster's concern valid, and how might Francie Newburn redesign the cost allocation system to address Aldin's concern?

CP 11-6 Allocating administrative costs for a service company

Banks have a variety of products, such as savings accounts, checking accounts, certificates of deposit (CDs), and loans. Assume that you were assigned the task of determining the administrative costs of "checking and savings accounts" as a complete product line. What are some of the activities associated with checking and savings accounts? In answering this question, consider the activities that you might perform with your checking and savings accounts. For each activity, what would be an activity base that could be used to allocate the activity cost to the checking and savings accounts product line?

© BANANA STOCK/FIRST LIGHT

Lean Principles, Lean Accounting, and Activity Analysis

Precor

When you order the salad bar at the local restaurant, you are able to serve yourself at your own pace. There is no waiting for the waitress to take the order or for the cook to prepare the meal. You are able to move directly to the salad bar and select from various offerings. You might wish to have salad with lettuce, cole slaw, bacon bits, croutons, and salad dressing. The offerings are arranged in a row so that you can build your salad as you move down the salad bar.

Many manufacturers are producing products in much the same way that the salad bar is designed to satisfy each customer's needs. Like customers at the salad bar, products move through a production process as they are built for each customer. Such a process eliminates many sources of waste, which is why it is called *lean*.

Using lean practices can improve performance. For example, when **Precor**, a manufacturer of fitness equipment, used lean principles, it improved its manufacturing operations and achieved the following results:

- Increased on-time shipments from near 40% to above 90%.
- Decreased direct labor costs by 30%.
- Reduced the number of suppliers from 3,000 to under 250.
- Reduced inventory by 40%.
- Reduced warranty claims by almost 60%.

In this chapter, lean practices are described and illustrated. The chapter concludes by describing and illustrating the accounting for quality costs and activity analysis.

Learning Objectives

After studying this chapter, you should be able to:

		Example Exercises
OBJ 1	**Describe lean manufacturing practices.**	
	Lean Principles	
	Reducing Inventory	
	Reducing Lead Times	
	Reducing Setup Time	EE 12-1
	Emphasizing Product-Oriented Layout	EE 12-2
	Emphasizing Employee Involvement	EE 12-2
	Emphasizing Pull Manufacturing	EE 12-2
	Emphasizing Zero Defects	EE 12-2
	Emphasizing Supply Chain Management	EE 12-2
OBJ 2	**Describe the implications of lean manufacturing on the accounting system.**	
	Lean Accounting	
	Fewer Transactions	EE 12-3
	Combined Accounts	EE 12-3
	Nonfinancial Performance Measures	
	Direct Tracing of Overhead	
OBJ 3	**Describe and illustrate activity analysis for improving operations.**	
	Activity Analysis	
	Costs of Quality	
	Quality Activity Analysis	EE 12-4
	Value-Added Activity Analysis	
	Process Activity Analysis	EE 12-5

At a Glance 12 Page 511

OBJ 1 Describe lean manufacturing practices.

Lean Principles

Lean enterprise A business that produces products or services with high quality, low cost, fast response, and immediate availability using lean principles.

The **lean enterprise** is a business that produces products or services with high quality, low cost, fast response, and immediate availability. **Lean manufacturing**, sometimes called *just-in-time processing (JIT)*, accomplishes these objectives in a manufacturing setting. Both manufacturing and nonmanufacturing businesses use **lean principles** to accomplish these service and cost objectives. However, these principles will be discussed within the context of lean manufacturing. Lean manufacturing principles are listed and contrasted with traditional manufacturing principles in Exhibit 1.

EXHIBIT 1 Lean versus Traditional Manufacturing Principles

Issue	Lean Manufacturing	Traditional Manufacturing
Inventory	Reduces inventory.	Increases inventory to protect against process problems.
Lead time	Reduces lead time.	Increases lead time to protect against uncertainty.
Setup time	Reduces setup time.	Disregards setup time as an improvement priority.
Production layout	Emphasizes product-oriented layout.	Emphasizes process-oriented layout.
Role of the employee	Emphasizes team-oriented employee involvement.	Emphasizes work of individuals, following manager instructions.
Production scheduling policy	Emphasizes pull manufacturing.	Emphasizes push manufacturing.
Quality	Emphasizes zero defects.	Tolerates defects.
Suppliers and customers	Emphasizes supply chain management.	Treats suppliers and customers as "arm's-length," independent entities.

Reducing Inventory

Lean manufacturing views inventory as wasteful and unnecessary, and thus emphasizes reducing or eliminating inventory.

Under traditional manufacturing, inventory often hides underlying production problems. For example, if machine breakdowns occur, work in process inventories can be used to keep production running in other departments while the machines are being repaired. Likewise, inventories can be used to hide problems caused by a shortage of trained employees, unreliable suppliers, or poor product quality.

In contrast, lean manufacturing solves and removes production problems. In this way, raw materials, work in process, and finished goods inventories are reduced or eliminated.

The role of inventory in manufacturing can be illustrated using a river, as shown in Exhibit 2. Inventory is the water in a river. The rocks at the bottom of the river are production problems. When the water level (inventory) is high, the rocks (production problems) at the bottom of the river are hidden. As the water level (inventory) drops, the rocks (production problems) become visible, one by one. Lean manufacturing reduces the water level (inventory), exposes the rocks (production problems), and removes the rocks so that the river can flow smoothly.

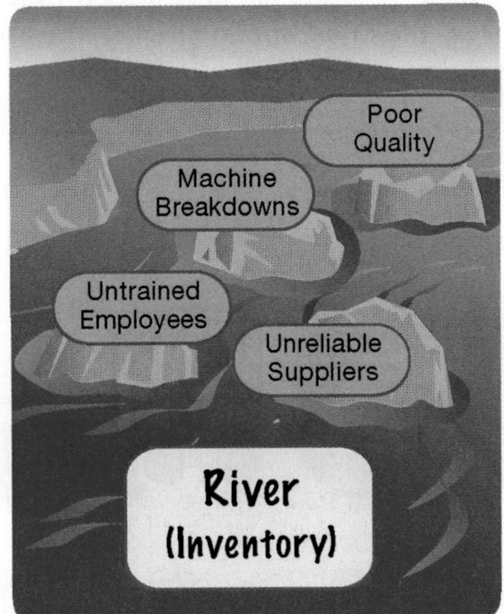

EXHIBIT 2

Inventory's Role in Manufacturing

Integrity, Objectivity, and Ethics in Business

THE INVENTORY SHIFT

Some managers take a shortcut to reducing inventory by shifting inventory to their suppliers. With this tactic, the hard work of improving processes is avoided. Enlightened managers realize that such tactics often have short-lived savings. Suppliers will eventually increase their prices to compensate for the additional inventory holding costs, thus resulting in no savings. Therefore, shifting a problem doesn't eliminate a problem.

Reducing Lead Times

Lead time, sometimes called *throughput time*, measures the time interval between a product entering production (is started) and when it is completed (finished). That is, lead time measures how long it takes to manufacture a product. To illustrate, in Exhibit 3, if a product enters production at 1:00 P.M. and is completed at 5:00 P.M., the lead time is four hours.

EXHIBIT 3

Lead Time

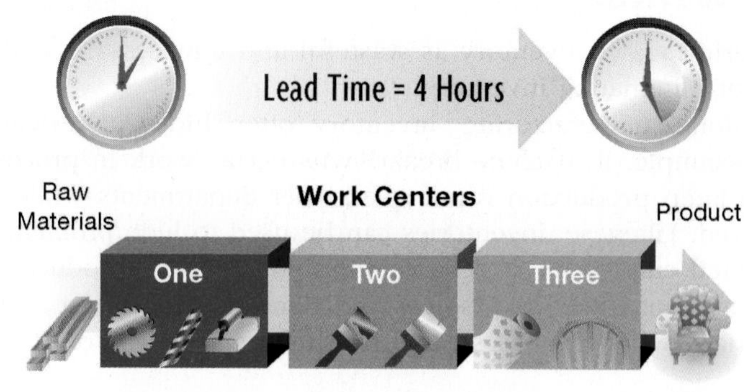

The lead time can be classified as one of the following:

- **Value-added lead time**, which is the time spent in converting raw materials into a finished unit of product
- **Non-value-added lead time**, which is the time spent while the unit of product is waiting to enter the next production process or is moved from one process to another

Exhibit 4 illustrates value-added and non-value-added lead time. The time spent drilling and packing the unit of product is value-added time. The time spent waiting to enter the next process or the time spent moving the unit of product from one process to another is non-value-added time.

EXHIBIT 4 **Components of Lead Time**

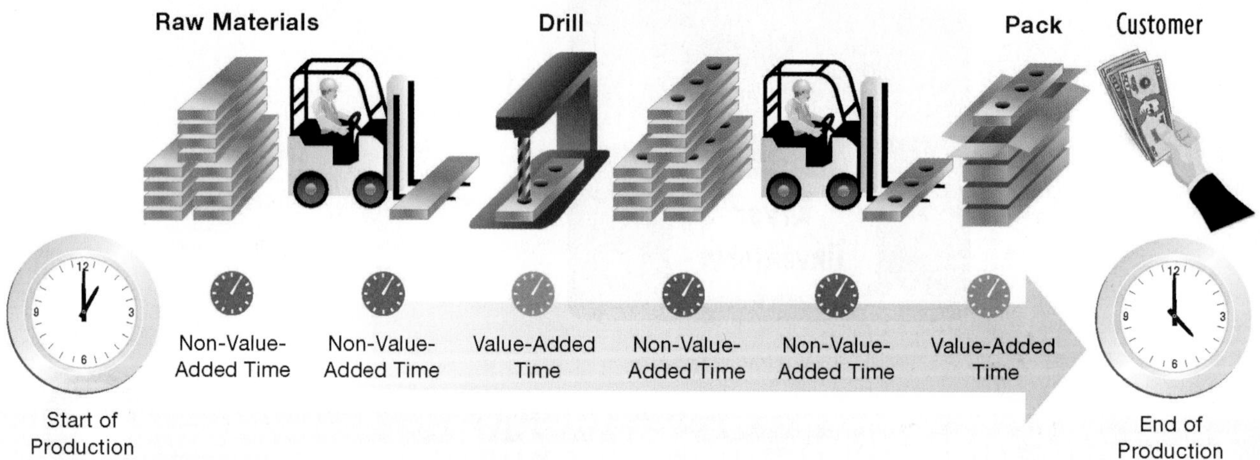

The **value-added ratio** is computed as follows:

$$\text{Value-Added Ratio} = \frac{\text{Value-Added Lead Time}}{\text{Total Lead Time}}$$

To illustrate, assume that the lead time to manufacture a unit of product is as follows (value-added times are highlighted):

Move raw materials to machining	5 minutes
Machining	35
Move time to assembly	10
Assembly	20
Move time to packing	15
Wait time for packing	30
Packing	10
Total lead time	125 minutes

The value-added ratio for the preceding product is 52%, computed as follows:

$$\text{Value-Added Ratio} = \frac{\text{Value-Added Lead Time}}{\text{Total Lead Time}}$$

$$= \frac{(35 + 20 + 10)\text{ minutes}}{125\text{ minutes}} = \frac{65\text{ minutes}}{125\text{ minutes}} = 52\%$$

A low value-added ratio indicates a poor manufacturing process. A good manufacturing process will reduce non-value-added lead time to a minimum and thus have a high value-added ratio.

Lean manufacturing reduces or eliminates non-value-added time. In contrast, traditional manufacturing processes may have a value-added ratio as small as 5%.

Crown Audio reduced the lead time between receiving and delivering a customer order from 30 days to 12 hours by using lean principles.

Reducing Setup Time

A *setup* is the effort spent preparing an operation or process for production. A **batch size** is the amount of production in units of product that is produced after a setup. If setups are long and costly, the batch size for the related production run is normally large. Large batch sizes allow setup costs to be spread over more units and, thus, reduce the cost per unit. However, large batch sizes increase inventory and lead time.

Exhibit 5 shows the relationship between setup times and lead time.

EXHIBIT 5 **Relationship between Setup Times and Lead Time**

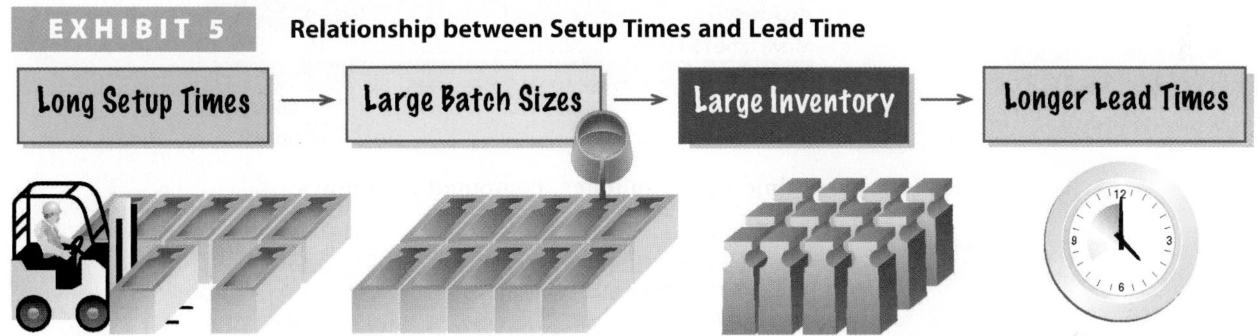

To help understand the relationship of batch sizes to lead-time, consider a group of 10 friends purchasing a ticket at a single-window ticket counter as shown in Exhibit 6.

EXHIBIT 6

Batch Size and Lead Time

The friends are traveling together, so they are like a "batch" of production. If each friend takes one minute to purchase a ticket, the other nine friends are either waiting in line, or waiting for the remaining friends to finish. Thus, it takes 10 minutes for all of the friends to receive tickets as a group, but it took only one minute for any one friend to actually buy a ticket.

The amount of time each friend is waiting is called within-batch wait time. The total within-batch wait time is computed as follows:

$$\text{Total Within-Batch Wait Time} = (\text{Value-Added Time}) \times (\text{Batch Size} - 1)$$

In this example, the value-added time is the 1 minute to purchase a ticket. So the total within-batch wait time is 9 minutes, computed as follows:

$$\text{Total Within-Batch Wait Time} = 1\text{ minute} \times (10 - 1) = 9\text{ minutes}$$

The value added ratio is 10%, computed as follows:

$$\text{Value-Added Ratio} = \frac{\text{Value-Added Lead Time}}{\text{Total Lead Time}}$$

$$= \frac{1 \text{ minute}}{10 \text{ minutes}} = 10\%$$

Now consider someone buying a ticket without a group of friends present. A single person would only take one minute to buy the ticket, with no waiting for friends. In this case, the lead-time drops down to one minute, or simply the time to purchase the ticket, and the value-added ratio is 100%.

Lean manufacturing emphasizes decreasing setup times in order to reduce the batch size, whereas traditional manufacturing does not treat setup improvement as an important priority. By reducing batch sizes, work in process inventory and within-batch wait time decrease, thus reducing total lead-time and increasing the value-added ratio.

To illustrate in a manufacturing setting, assume that Automotive Components Inc. manufactures engine starters as follows (value-added times are highlighted):

	Processing Time per Unit
Move raw materials to Machining	5 minutes
Machining	7
Move time to Assembly	10
Assembly	9
Move time to Testing	10
Testing	8
Total	49 minutes
Batch size	40 units

The total lead time is 985 minutes, computed as follows:

Value-added time (7 + 9 + 8)	24 minutes
Move time (5 + 10 + 10)	25
Total within-batch wait time	936*
Total time	985 minutes

*Total Within-Batch Wait Time = (Value-Added Time) × (Batch Size – 1)
= (7 + 9 + 8) minutes × (40 – 1) = 24 minutes × 39
= 936 minutes

Tech Industries improved an injection machine setup so that the number of process steps was reduced from 84 to 19 and the setup time was reduced from five hours to one hour.

Of the total lead time of 985 minutes, 24 minutes is value-added time and 961 minutes (985 – 24) is non-value-added time. The total non-value-added time of 961 minutes can also be determined as the sum of the total within-batch time of 936 minutes plus the move time of 25 minutes.

Based on the preceding data, the value-added ratio is approximately 2.4%, computed as follows:

$$\text{Value-Added Ratio} = \frac{\text{Value-Added Lead Time}}{\text{Total Lead Time}}$$

$$= \frac{(7+9+8) \text{ minutes}}{985 \text{ minutes}} = \frac{24 \text{ minutes}}{985 \text{ minutes}} = 2.4\% \text{ (rounded)}$$

Thus, the non-value-added time for Automotive Components Inc. is approximately 97.6% (100% – 2.4%).

Automotive Components can increase its value-added ratio by reducing setups so that the batch size is one unit, called *one-piece flow*. Automotive Components could also move the Machining, Assembly, and Testing activities closer to each other so that the move time could be reduced. With these changes, Automotive Components' value-added ratio would increase.

Business  Connection

P&G'S "PIT STOPS"

What do Procter & Gamble and Formula One racing have in common? The answer begins with P&G's Packing Department, which is where detergents and other products are filled on a "pack line." Containers move down the pack line and are filled with products from a packing machine. When it was time to change from a 36-oz. to a 54-oz. *Tide* box, for example, the changeover involved stopping the line, adjusting guide rails, retrieving items from the tool room, placing items back in the tool room, changing and cleaning the pack heads, and performing routine maintenance. Changing the pack line could be a very difficult process and typically took up to several hours.

Management realized that it was important to reduce this time significantly in order to become more flexible and cost efficient in packing products. Where could they learn how to do setups faster? They turned to Formula One racing, reasoning that a pit stop was much like a setup. As a result, P&G videotaped actual Formula One pit stops. These videos were used to form the following principles for conducting a fast setup:

- Position the tools near their point of use on the line prior to stopping the line, to reduce time going back and forth to the tool room.
- Arrange the tools in the exact order of work, so that no time is wasted looking for a tool.
- Have each employee perform a very specific task during the setup.
- Design the workflow so that employees don't interfere with each other.
- Have each employee in position at the moment the line is stopped.
- Train each employee, and practice, practice, practice.
- Put a stop watch on the setup process.
- Plot improvements over time on a visible chart.

As a result of these changes, P&G was able to reduce pack-line setup time from several hours to 20 minutes. This decrease allowed the company to reduce lead time and to improve the cost performance of the Packing Department.

Example Exercise 12-1 Lead Time

OBJ 1

The Helping Hands glove company manufactures gloves in the cutting and assembly process. Gloves are manufactured in 50-glove batch sizes. The cutting time is 4 minutes per glove. The assembly time is 6 minutes per glove. It takes 12 minutes to move a batch of gloves from cutting to assembly.

a. Compute the value-added, non-value-added, and total lead time of this process.
b. Compute the value-added ratio. Round to one decimal place.

Follow My Example 12-1

a. Value-added lead time:	10 min.	= (4 min. + 6 min.)
Non-value-added lead time:		
Total within-batch wait time	490	= (4 + 6) minutes × (50 – 1)
Move time	12	
Total lead time	512 min.	

b. Value-added ratio: $\frac{10 \text{ min.}}{512 \text{ min.}}$ = 2.0% (rounded)

Practice Exercises: PE 12-1A, PE 12-1B

Emphasizing Product-Oriented Layout

Manufacturing processes can be organized around a product, which is called a **product-oriented layout** (or *product cells*). Alternatively, manufacturing processes can be organized around a process, which is called a **process-oriented layout**.

Lean manufacturing normally organizes manufacturing around products rather than processes. Organizing work around products reduces:

- Moving materials and products between processes
- Work in process inventory
- Lead time
- Production costs

In addition, a product-oriented layout improves coordination among the various work activities, or operations, of the facility.

Emphasizing Employee Involvement

Traditional manufacturing often values direct labor employees only for their manual labor, whereas lean manufacturing values labor for contributions beyond labor tasks, using employee involvement. **Employee involvement** is a management approach that grants employees the responsibility and authority to make decisions about operations. Employee involvement is often applied in lean manufacturing by organizing employees into *product cells*. Within each product cell, employees are organized as teams where the employees are cross-trained to perform any operation within the product cell.

To illustrate, employees learn how to operate several different machines within their product cell. In addition, team members are trained to perform functions traditionally performed by centralized service departments. For example, product cell employees may perform their own equipment maintenance, quality control, housekeeping, and improvement studies.

Emphasizing Pull Manufacturing

Pull manufacturing (or *make to order*) is an important lean practice. In pull manufacturing, products are manufactured only as they are needed by the customer. Products can be thought of as being pulled through the manufacturing process. In other words, the status of the next operation determines when products are moved or produced. If the next operation is busy, production stops so that work in process does not pile up in front of the busy operation. When the next operation is ready, the product is moved to that operation.

A system used in pull manufacturing is *kanban*, which is Japanese for "cards." Electronic cards or containers signal production quantities to be filled by the preceding operation. The cards link the customer's order for a product back through each stage of production. In other words, when a consumer orders a product, a kanban card triggers the manufacture of the product.

In contrast, the traditional approach to manufacturing is based on estimated customer demand. This principle is called **push manufacturing** (or make to stock). In push manufacturing, products are manufactured according to a production schedule that is based upon estimated sales. The schedule "pushes" product into inventory before customer orders are received. As a result, push manufacturers normally have more inventory than pull manufacturers.

Emphasizing Zero Defects

Lean manufacturing attempts to eliminate poor quality. Poor quality creates:

- Scrap
- Rework, which is fixing product made wrong the first time
- Disruption in the production process
- Dissatisfied customers
- Warranty costs and expenses

One way to improve product quality and manufacturing processes is Six Sigma. **Six Sigma** was developed by **Motorola Corporation** and consists of five steps: define, measure, analyze, improve, and control (DMAIC).[1] Since its development, Six Sigma has been adopted by thousands of organizations worldwide.

Emphasizing Supply Chain Management

Supply chain management coordinates and controls the flow of materials, services, information, and finances with suppliers, manufacturers, and customers. Supply chain management partners with suppliers using long-term agreements. These agreements ensure that products are delivered with the right quality, at the right cost, at the right time.

[1] The term "six sigma" refers to a statistical property where a process has less than 3.4 defects per one million items.

To enhance the interchange of information between suppliers and customers, supply chain management often uses:

- **Electronic data interchange (EDI)**, which uses computers to electronically communicate orders, relay information, and make or receive payments from one organization to another
- **Radio frequency identification devices (RFID)**, which are electronic tags (chips) placed on or embedded within products that can be read by radio waves that allow instant monitoring of product location
- **Enterprise resource planning (ERP)** systems, which are used to plan and control internal and supply chain operations

Business  Connection

LEAN MANUFACTURING IN ACTION

- Yamaha manufactures musical instruments such as trumpets, horns, saxophones, clarinets, and flutes using **product-oriented layouts**.
- Sony uses **employee involvement** to organize employees into small four-person teams to completely assemble a camcorder, doing everything from soldering to testing. This team-based approach reduces assembly time from 70 minutes to 15 minutes per camcorder.
- Kenney Manufacturing Company, a manufacturer of window shades, estimated that 50% of its window shade process was non-value-added. By using **pull manufacturing** and changing the line layout, it was able to reduce inventory by 82% and lead time by 84%.
- Motorola has claimed over $17 billion in savings from **Six Sigma**.
- Hyundia/Kia Motors Group will use 20 million RFID tags annually to track automotive parts from its suppliers, providing greater **supply chain** transparency and flexibility.

Lean Principles for Nonmanufacturing Processes

All of the lean principles discussed for a manufacturer can be adapted to service businesses or administrative processes. Examples of service businesses that use lean principles include hospitals, banks, insurance companies, and hotels. Examples of administrative processes that use lean principles include processing of insurance applications, product designs, and sales orders. In the case of a service business, the "product" is normally the customer or patient. In the case of administrative processes, the "product" is normally information.

For example, a traditional accounting department delivers month-end financial statements using a sequential, process-oriented layout. Using lean principles, the lead time for producing financial statements can be reduced significantly by employing a product-oriented layout. In this case, the "products" are the individual inputs to financial statement consolidation from the payroll, accounts payable, and accounts receivable functions. A product layout may allow these inputs to be processed in parallel, rather than sequentially, thus reducing non-value-added lead time.

Service  Focus

LEAN HEALTHCARE

Lean principles can be used in many health care settings, from the patient admissions process to design of the operating room procedures. Lean principles applied to healthcare include reducing patient lead-time, enhancing employee involvement through patient care teams, improving quality, reducing medical supply inventory, and designing the hospital around a product-oriented layout. For example, a product-oriented layout can be employed by designing health care delivery around a particular patient class. Thus, X-Ray equipment can be placed near a patient class, such as emergency room (ER) patients, rather than inefficiently transporting ER patients to a centralized X-Ray department. A further example involves patient lead-time. An operating room (OR) can use lean principles to reduce the turn-around time (TAT). TAT is the amount of time consumed between finishing one patient and starting a second patient in the OR. It is similar to setup time in manufacturing. Hospital Corporation of America organized OR supplies in wheeled carts, "pulled" supplies into the OR, and improved team communication to reduce TAT, supply inventory, and OR space utilization.

Source: Glover, Wiljeana J., Van Aken, Eileen M., and Creehan, Kevin, "Case Study on Using Lean Principles to Improve Turnaround Time and First Case Starts in an Operating Room," *Proceedings of the 2009 Society for Health Systems Conference and Expo.*

Example Exercise 12-2 Lean Features OBJ 1

Which of the following are features of a lean manufacturing system?

a. Reduced space
b. Larger inventory
c. Longer lead times
d. Reduced setups

Follow My Example 12-2

a. Reduced space
d. Reduced setups

Practice Exercises: PE 12-2A, PE 12-2B

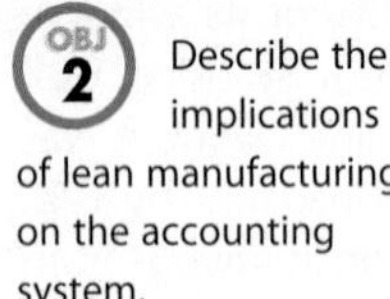

Describe the implications of lean manufacturing on the accounting system.

Lean Accounting

In lean manufacturing, the accounting system reflects the lean philosophy. Such systems are called **lean accounting**, and have the following characteristics:

- *Fewer transactions.* There are fewer transactions to record, thus simplifying the accounting system.
- *Combined accounts.* All in-process work is combined with raw materials to form a new account, **Raw and In Process (RIP) Inventory**. Direct labor is also combined with other costs to form a new account titled **Conversion Costs**.
- *Nonfinancial performance measures.* Nonfinancial performance measures are emphasized.
- *Direct tracing of overhead.* Indirect labor is directly assigned to product cells; thus, less factory overhead is allocated to products.

Fewer Transactions

The traditional process cost accounting system accumulates product costs by department. These costs are transferred from department to department as the product is manufactured. Thus, materials are recorded into and out of work in process inventories as the product moves through the factory.

The recording of product costs by departments facilitates the control of costs. However, this requires that many transactions and costs be recorded and reported. This adds cost and complexity to the cost accounting system.

In lean manufacturing, there is less need for cost control. This is because lower inventory levels make problems more visible. That is, managers don't need accounting reports to indicate problems because any problems become immediately known.

The lean accounting system uses **backflush accounting**. Backflush accounting simplifies the accounting system by eliminating the accumulation and transfer of product costs by departments, but instead, pulls material and conversion costs directly to finished goods. Thus, efficiency is gained by not transferring costs through intermediate departmental work in process accounts.

Combined Accounts

Materials are received directly by the product cells and enter immediately into production. Thus, there is no central materials inventory location (warehouse) or a materials account. Instead, lean accounting debits all materials and conversion costs to an account titled *Raw and In Process Inventory*. Doing so combines materials and work in process costs into one account.

Lean manufacturing often does not use a separate direct labor cost classification. This is because the employees in product cells perform many tasks. Some of these tasks could be classified as direct, such as performing operations, and some as indirect, such as performing repairs. Thus, labor cost (direct and indirect) is combined with other product cell overhead costs and recorded in an account titled *Conversion Costs*.

To illustrate, assume the following data for Anderson Metal Fabricators, a manufacturer of metal covers for electronic test equipment:

Budgeted conversion cost	$2,400,000
Planned hours of production...............	1,920 hours

The cell conversion cost rate is determined as follows:

$$\text{Cell Conversion Cost Rate} = \frac{\text{Budgeted Conversion Cost}}{\text{Planned Hours of Production}}$$

$$= \frac{\$2{,}400{,}000}{1{,}920 \text{ hours}} = \$1{,}250 \text{ per hour}$$

The cell conversion rate is similar to a predetermined factory overhead rate, except that it includes all conversion costs in the numerator.

Assume that Anderson Metal's cover product cell is expected to require 0.02 hour of manufacturing time per unit. Thus, the conversion cost for the cover is $25 per unit, computed as follows:

$$\text{Conversion Cost for Cover} = \text{Manufacturing Time} \times \text{Cell Conversion Cost Rate}$$

$$= 0.02 \text{ hour} \times \$1{,}250 = \$25 \text{ per unit}$$

The recording of selected lean accounting transactions for Anderson Metal Fabricators for April is illustrated in Exhibit 7.

EXHIBIT 7 **Transactions Using Lean Accounting—Anderson Metal Fabricators**

Transaction	Journal Entry			Comment	
Steel coil is purchased for producing 8,000 covers. The purchase cost was $120,000, or $15 per unit.	Raw and In Process Inventory........ Accounts Payable .... To record materials purchases.	120,000	 120,000	Note that the materials purchased are debited to the combined account, Raw and In Process Inventory. A separate materials account is not used, because materials are received directly in the product cells, rather than in an inventory location.	
Conversion costs are applied to 8,000 covers at a rate of $25 per cover.	Raw and In Process Inventory........ Conversion Costs................. To record applied conversion costs of the medium-cover line.	200,000	 200,000	The raw and in process inventory account is used to accumulate the applied cell conversion costs during the period. The credit to Conversion Costs is similar to the treatment of applied factory overhead.	
All 8,000 covers were completed in the cell. The raw and in process inventory account is reduced by the $15 per unit materials cost and the $25 per unit conversion cost.	Finished Goods Inventory........... Raw and In Process Inventory .... To transfer the cost of completed units to finished goods.	320,000	 320,000	Materials ($15 × 8,000 units) .... Conversion ($25 × 8,000 units) .... Total .... After the cost of the completed units is transferred from the raw and in process inventory account, the account's balance is zero. There are no units left in process within the cell.[2] This is a backflush transaction.	$120,000 200,000 $320,000
Of the 8,000 units completed, 7,800 were sold and shipped to customers at $70 per unit, leaving 200 finished units in stock. Thus, the finished goods inventory account has a balance of $8,000 (200 × $40).	Accounts Receivable................. Sales............................. To record sales. Cost of Goods Sold .... Finished Goods .... To record cost of goods sold.	546,000 312,000	 546,000 312,000	Units sold .... Conversion and materials cost per unit .... Transferred to Cost of Goods Sold	7,800 × $40 $312,000

[2] The actual conversion cost per unit may be different from the budgeted conversion cost per unit due to cell inefficiency, improvements in processing methods, or excess scrap. These deviations from the budgeted cost can be accounted for as cost variances, as illustrated in more advanced texts.

Example Exercise 12-3 Lean Accounting

The budgeted conversion costs for a lean cell are $142,500 for 1,900 production hours. Each unit produced by the cell requires 10 minutes of cell process time. During the month, 1,050 units are manufactured in the cell. The estimated materials cost is $46 per unit. Provide the following journal entries:

a. Materials are purchased to produce 1,100 units.
b. Conversion costs are applied to 1,050 units of production.
c. 1,030 units are completed and placed into finished goods.

Follow My Example 12-3

a.	Raw and In Process Inventory	50,600*	
	Accounts Payable		50,600
	*$46 per unit × 1,100 units		
b.	Raw and In Process Inventory	13,125*	
	Conversion Costs		13,125
	*[($142,500 ÷ 1,900 hours) × (10 min. ÷ 60 min.)] = $12.50 per unit; $12.50 × 1,050 units = $13,125		
c.	Finished Goods Inventory	60,255*	
	Raw and In Process Inventory		60,255
	*($46.00 + $12.50) × 1,030 units		

Practice Exercises: PE 12-3A, PE 12-3B

Nonfinancial Performance Measures

Lean manufacturing normally uses nonfinancial measures to help guide short-term operating performance. A **nonfinancial measure** is operating information not stated in dollar terms. Examples of nonfinancial measures of performance include:

- Lead time
- Value-added ratio
- Setup time
- Number of production line stops
- Number of units scrapped
- Deviations from scheduled production
- Number of failed inspections

Most companies use a combination of financial and nonfinancial operating measures, which are often referred to as *key performance indicators* (or *KPIs*). Nonfinancial measures are often available more quickly than financial measures. Thus, nonfinancial measures are often used for day-to-day operating decisions that require quick feedback. In contrast, traditional financial accounting measures are often used for longer-term operating decisions.

Direct Tracing of Overhead

In lean manufacturing, many indirect tasks are assigned to a product cell. For example, maintenance department personnel may be assigned to a product cell and cross-trained to perform other operations. Thus, the salary of maintenance personnel can be traced directly to the product cell, and thus, to the product.

In traditional manufacturing, maintenance personnel are part of the maintenance department. The cost of the maintenance department is then allocated to products based on predetermined factory overhead rates. Such allocations are not necessary when maintenance personnel are assigned directly to a product cell.

Activity Analysis

OBJ 3 Describe and illustrate activity analysis for improving operations.

In Chapter 26, we discussed activity-based costing for product costing. Activities can also be used to support operational improvement in the lean enterprise using activity analysis. **Activity analysis** determines the cost of activities for the purpose of determining the cost of the following:

- Quality
- Value-added activities
- Processes

Costs of Quality

Competition encourages businesses to emphasize high-quality products, services, and processes. In doing so, businesses incur **costs of quality**, as illustrated in Exhibit 8. These costs of quality can be classified as follows:

- **Prevention costs**, which are costs of preventing defects before or during the manufacture of the product or delivery of services
  Examples: Costs of engineering good product design, controlling vendor quality, training equipment operators, maintaining equipment
- **Appraisal costs**, which are costs of activities that detect, measure, evaluate, and inspect products and processes to ensure that they meet customer needs
  Examples: Costs of inspecting and testing products
- **Internal failure costs**, which are costs associated with defects discovered before the product is delivered to the consumer
  Examples: Cost of scrap and rework
- **External failure costs**, which are costs incurred after defective products have been delivered to consumers
  Examples: Cost of recalls and warranty work

EXHIBIT 8 **Costs of Quality**

Costs of Controlling Quality

Costs of Failing to Control Quality

Prevention Costs

Appraisal Costs

Internal Failure Costs

External Failure Costs

Prevention and appraisal costs can be thought of as costs of controlling quality *before* any products are known to be defective. Internal and external failure costs can be thought of as the cost of controlling quality *after* products have become defective. Internal and external failure costs also can be thought of as the costs of "failing to control quality" through prevention and appraisal efforts.

Prevention and appraisal costs are incurred *before* the product is manufactured or delivered to the customer. Prevention costs are incurred in an attempt to permanently improve product quality. In contrast, appraisal costs are incurred in an attempt to limit the amount of defective products that "slip out the door."

Internal and external failure costs are incurred *after* the defective products have been discovered. In addition to costs of scrap and rework, internal failure costs may be incurred for lost equipment time because of rework and the costs of carrying additional inventory used for reworking. In addition to costs of recall and warranty work, external failure costs include the loss of customer goodwill. Although the loss of customer goodwill is difficult to measure, it may be the largest and most important quality control cost.

The relationship between the costs of quality is shown in Exhibit 9. The graph in Exhibit 9 indicates that as prevention and appraisal costs (blue line) increase, the percent of good units increases. In contrast, as internal and external failure costs (green line) decrease, the percent of good units increases. Total quality cost (red line) is the sum of the prevention/appraisal costs and internal/external failure costs.

EXHIBIT 9 **The Relationship between the Costs of Quality**

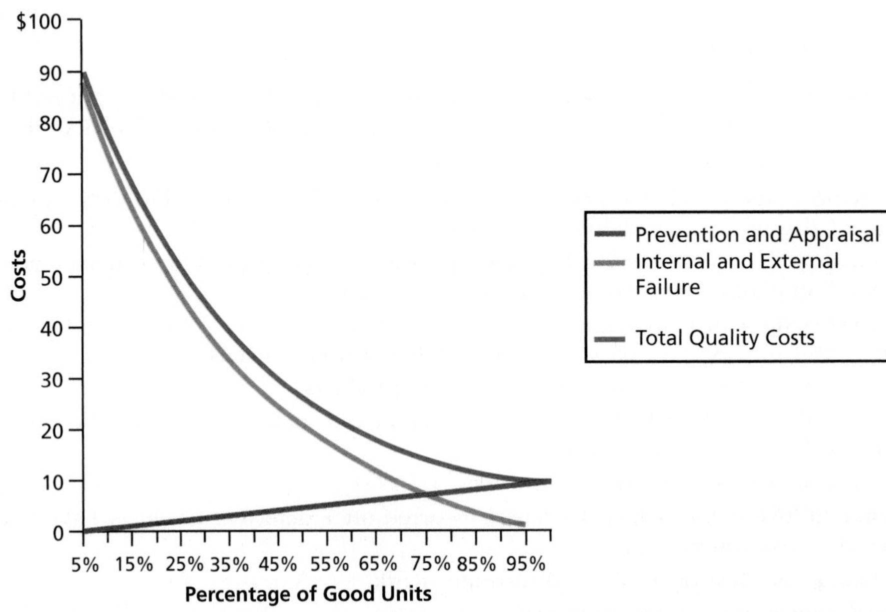

The optimal level of quality (percent of good units) is the one that minimizes the total quality costs. At this point, prevention and appraisal costs are balanced against internal and external failure costs. Exhibit 9 indicates that the optimal level of quality occurs at (or near) 100% quality. This is because prevention and appraisal costs grow moderately as quality increases. However, the costs of internal and external failure drop dramatically as quality increases.

Quality Activity Analysis

An activity analysis of quality quantifies the costs of quality in dollar terms. To illustrate, the quality control activities, activity costs, and quality cost classifications for Gifford Company, a consumer electronics company, are shown in Exhibit 10.

EXHIBIT 10

Quality Control Activity Analysis—Gifford Company

Quality Control Activities	Activity Cost	Quality Cost Classification
Design engineering	$ 55,000	Prevention
Disposing of rejected materials	160,000	Internal Failure
Finished goods inspection	140,000	Appraisal
Materials inspection	70,000	Appraisal
Preventive maintenance	80,000	Prevention
Processing returned materials	150,000	External Failure
Disposing of scrap	195,000	Internal Failure
Assessing vendor quality	45,000	Prevention
Rework	380,000	Internal Failure
Warranty work	225,000	External Failure
Total activity cost	$1,500,000	

Pareto Chart of Quality Costs One method of reporting quality cost information is using a Pareto chart. A **Pareto chart** is a bar chart that shows the totals of an attribute for a number of categories. The categories are ranked and shown left to right, so that the largest total attribute is on the left and the smallest total is on the right.

To illustrate, Exhibit 11 is a Pareto chart for the quality control activities in Exhibit 10.

EXHIBIT 11

Pareto Chart of Quality Costs

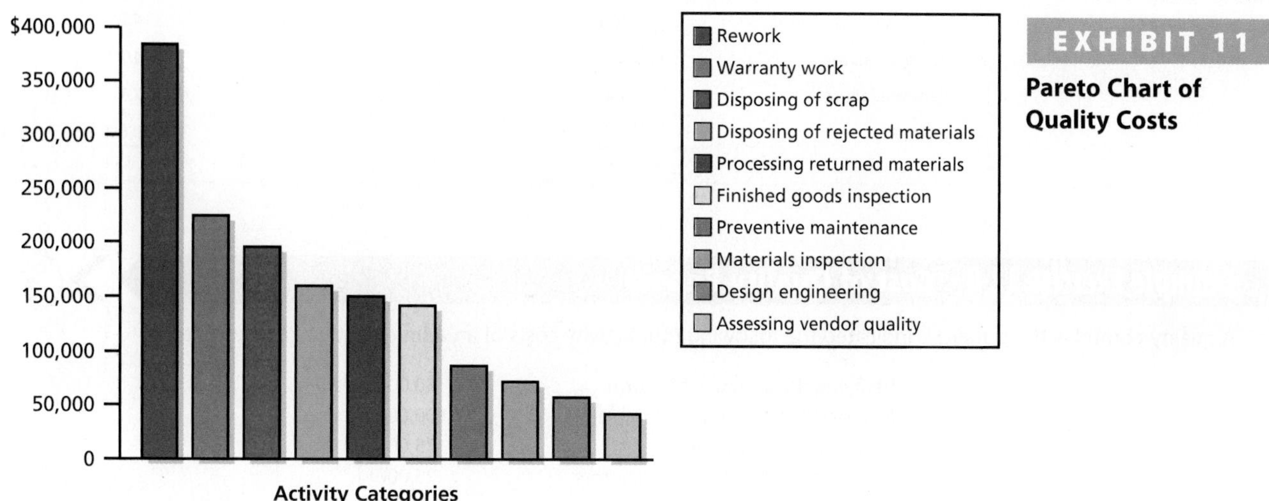

In Exhibit 11, the vertical axis is dollars, which represents quality control costs. The horizontal axis represents activity categories, which are the ten quality control cost activities. The ten quality control cost categories are ranked from the one with the largest total on the left to the one with the smallest total on the right. Thus, the largest bar on the left is rework costs ($380,000), the second bar is warranty work ($225,000), and so on.

The Pareto chart gives managers a quick visual tool for identifying the most important quality control cost categories. Exhibit 11 indicates that Gifford Company should focus efforts on reducing rework and warranty costs.

Cost of Quality Report The costs of quality also can be summarized in a cost of quality report. A **cost of quality report** normally reports the following:

- Total activity cost for each quality cost classification
- Percent of total quality costs associated with each classification
- Percent of each quality cost classification to sales

Exhibit 12 is a cost of quality report for Gifford Company, based on assumed sales of $5,000,000. Exhibit 12 indicates that only 12% of the total quality cost is the cost of preventing quality problems, while 14% is the cost of appraisal activities. Thus, prevention and appraisal costs make up only 26% of the total quality control costs. In contrast, 74% (49% + 25%) of the quality control costs are incurred for internal (49%) and external failure (25%) costs. In addition, internal and external failure costs are 22.2% (14.7% + 7.5%) of sales.

Exhibit 12 implies that Gifford Company is not spending enough on prevention and appraisal activities. By spending more on prevention and appraisal, internal and external failure costs will decrease, as was shown in Exhibit 9.

EXHIBIT 12

Cost of Quality Report—Gifford Company

Gifford Company
Cost of Quality Report

Quality Cost Classification	Quality Cost	Percent of Total Quality Cost	Percent of Total Sales
Prevention	$ 180,000	12%	3.6%
Appraisal	210,000	14	4.2
Internal failure	735,000	49	14.7
External failure	375,000	25	7.5
Total	$1,500,000	100%	30.0%

Example Exercise 12-4 Cost of Quality Report

OBJ 3

A quality control activity analysis indicated the following four activity costs of an administrative department:

Verifying the accuracy of a form	$ 50,000
Responding to customer complaints	100,000
Correcting errors in forms	75,000
Redesigning forms to reduce errors	25,000
Total	$250,000

Sales are $2,000,000. Prepare a cost of quality report.

Follow My Example 12-4

Cost of Quality Report

Quality Cost Classification	Quality Cost	Percent of Total Quality Cost	Percent of Total Sales
Prevention	$ 25,000	10%	1.25%
Appraisal	50,000	20	2.50
Internal failure	75,000	30	3.75
External failure	100,000	40	5.00
Total	$250,000	100%	12.50%

Practice Exercises: PE 12-4A, PE 12-4B

Value-Added Activity Analysis

In the preceding section, the quality control activities of Gifford Company were classified as prevention, appraisal, internal failure, and external failure activities. Activities also may be classified as follows:

- Value-added
- Non-value-added

A **value-added activity** is one that is necessary to meet customer requirements. A **non-value-added activity** is *not* required by the customer but occurs because of mistakes, errors, omissions, and process failures.

To illustrate, Exhibit 13 shows the value-added and non-value-added classification for the quality control activities for Gifford Company.[3] This exhibit also reveals

[3] We use the quality control activities for illustrating the value-added and non-value-added activities in this section. However, a value-added/non-value-added activity analysis can be done for any activity in a business, not just quality control activities.

EXHIBIT 13

Value-Added/ Non-Value-Added Quality Control Activities

Quality Control Activities	Activity Cost	Classification
Design engineering	$ 55,000	Value-added
Disposing of rejected materials	160,000	Non-value-added
Finished goods inspection	140,000	Value-added
Materials inspection	70,000	Value-added
Preventive maintenance	80,000	Value-added
Processing returned materials	150,000	Non-value-added
Disposing of scrap	195,000	Non-value-added
Assessing vendor quality	45,000	Value-added
Rework	380,000	Non-value-added
Warranty work	225,000	Non-value-added
Total activity cost	$1,500,000	

that internal and external failure costs are classified as non-value-added. In contrast, prevention and appraisal costs are classified as value-added.[4]

A summary of the value-added and non-value-added activities follows. The summary expresses value-added and non-value-added costs as a percent of total costs.

Classification	Amount	Percent
Value-added	$ 390,000	26%
Non-value-added	1,110,000	74
Total	$1,500,000	100%

The preceding summary indicates that 74% of Gifford Company's quality control activities are non-value-added. This should motivate Gifford Company to make improvements to reduce non-value-added activities.

Process Activity Analysis

Activity analysis can be used to evaluate business processes. A **process** is a series of activities that converts an input into an output. In other words, a process is a set of activities linked together by inputs and outputs. Common business processes include the following:

- Procurement
- Product development
- Manufacturing
- Distribution
- Sales order fulfillment

Exhibit 14 shows a sales order fulfillment process for Masters Company. This process converts a customer order (the input) into a product received by the customer (the output).

EXHIBIT 14 **Sales Order Fulfillment Process**

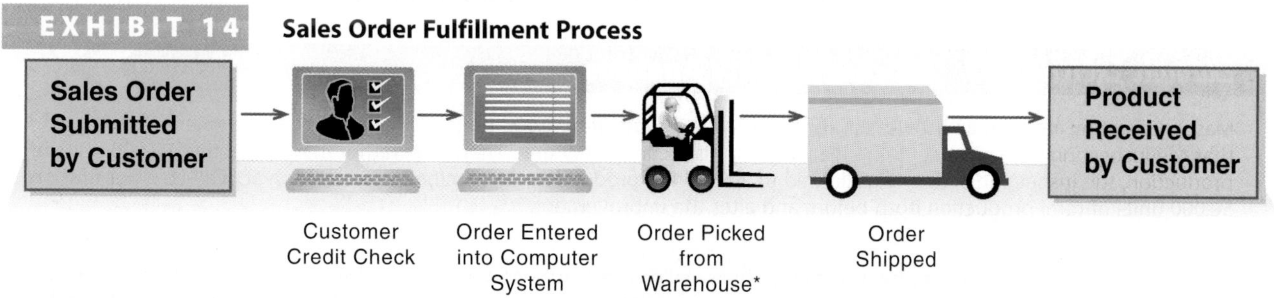

*Operators driving forklifts receive a list of orders, drive to stacking locations within the warehouse, pick the orders, and then transport them back to an area to prepare for shipment.

[4] Some believe that appraisal costs are non-value-added. They argue that if the product had been made correctly, then no inspection would be required. We take a less strict view and assume that appraisal costs are value-added.

Exhibit 14 indicates that Masters Company's sales order fulfillment process has the following four activities:

- Customer credit check
- Order entered into computer system
- Order picked from warehouse
- Order shipped

A process activity analysis can be used to determine the cost of the preceding activities. To illustrate, assume that a process activity analysis determines that the cost of the four activities is as follows:

Sales Order Fulfillment Activities	Activity Cost	Percent of Total Process Cost
Customer credit check	$14,400	18%
Order entered into computer system	9,600	12
Order picked from warehouse	36,000	45
Order shipped	20,000	25
Total sales order fulfillment process cost	$80,000	100%

If 10,000 sales orders are filled during the current period, the per-unit process cost is $8 per order ($80,000 ÷ 10,000 orders).

Management can use process activity analysis to improve a process. To illustrate, assume that Masters Company sets a cost improvement target of $6 per order. A $2 reduction per order ($8 – $6) requires improving efficiency or eliminating unnecessary activities.

Masters Company determines that only *new* customers need to have a credit check. If this change is made, it is estimated that only 25% of sales orders would require credit checks. In addition, by revising the warehouse product layout, it is estimated that the cost of picking orders can be reduced by 35%.

Assuming that 10,000 orders will be filled, the cost savings from these two improvements are as follows:

Sales Order Fulfillment Activities	Activity Cost Prior to Improvement	Activity Cost After Improvement	Activity Cost Savings
Customer credit check	$14,400	$ 3,600*	$10,800
Order entered in computer system	9,600	9,600	0
Order picked from warehouse	36,000	23,400**	12,600
Order shipped	20,000	20,000	0
Total sales order fulfillment process cost	$80,000	$56,600	$23,400
Cost per order (total cost divided by 10,000 orders)	$8.00	$5.66	

*$14,400 × 25%

**$36,000 – ($36,000 × 35%)

As illustrated, the activity changes generate a savings of $23,400.[5] In addition, the cost per order is reduced to $5.66, which is less than the $6.00 per order targeted cost.[6]

Example Exercise 12-5 Process Activity Analysis

Mason Company incurred an activity cost of $120,000 for inspecting 50,000 units of production. Management determined that the inspecting objectives could be met without inspecting every unit. Therefore, rather than inspecting 50,000 units of production, the inspection activity was limited to 20% of the production. Determine the inspection activity cost per unit on 50,000 units of total production both before and after the improvement.

(Continued)

[5] This analysis assumes that the activity costs are variable to the inputs and outputs of the process. While this is likely true for processes primarily using labor, such as a sales order fulfillment process, other types of processes may have significant fixed costs that would not change with changes of inputs and outputs.

[6] Process activity analysis also can be integrated into a company's budgeting system using flexible budgets. Process activity analysis used in this way is discussed in advanced texts.

Follow My Example 12-5

Inspection activity before improvement: $120,000 ÷ 50,000 units = $2.40 per unit
Inspection activity after improvement:

Revised inspection cost	(20% × 50,000 units) × $2.40 per unit = $24,000
Revised inspection cost per unit	$24,000 ÷ 50,000 units = $0.48 per unit

Practice Exercises: PE 12-5A, PE 12-5B

At a Glance 12

Describe Lean manufacturing principles.

Key Points Lean manufacturing emphasizes reduced lead time, a product-oriented production layout, a team-oriented work environment, setup time reduction, pull manufacturing, high quality, and supplier and customer partnering in order to improve the supply chain.

Learning Outcomes	Example Exercises	Practice Exercises
• Describe the relationships among setup time, batch size, inventory, and lead time.		
• Compute lead time and the value-added ratio.	**EE12-1**	**PE12-1A, 12-1B**
• Identify the characteristics of a lean manufacturing environment and compare it to traditional approaches.	**EE12-2**	**PE12-2A, 12-2B**

Describe the implications of lean manufacturing on the accounting system.

Key Points Under lean manufacturing, the lean accounting system will have fewer transactions, will combine the materials and work in process accounts, and will account for direct labor as a part of cell conversion cost. Lean accounting will use nonfinancial reporting measures and result in more direct tracing of factory overhead to product cells.

Learning Outcomes	Example Exercises	Practice Exercises
• Identify the implications of the lean philosophy for lean accounting.		
• Prepare lean accounting journal entries for material purchases, application of cell conversion cost, and transfer of cell costs to finished goods.	**EE12-3**	**PE12-3A, 12-3B**
• Describe nonfinancial performance measures.		

Describe and illustrate activity analysis for improving operations.

Key Points Companies use activity analysis to identify the costs of quality, which include prevention, appraisal, internal failure, and external failure costs. The quality cost activities may be reported on a Pareto chart or quality cost report. An alternative method for categorizing activities is by value-added and non-value-added classifications. An activity analysis also can be used to improve the cost of processes.

Learning Outcomes	Example Exercises	Practice Exercises
• Define the costs of quality.		
• Define and prepare a Pareto chart.		
• Prepare a cost of quality report.	EE12-4	PE12-4A, 12-4B
• Identify value-added and non-value-added activity costs.		
• Use process activity analysis to measure process improvement.	EE12-5	PE12-5A, 12-5B

Key Terms

activity analysis (505)
appraisal costs (505)
backflush accounting (502)
batch size (497)
conversion costs (502)
cost of quality report (507)
costs of quality (505)
electronic data interchange (EDI) (501)
employee involvement (500)
enterprise resource planning (ERP) (501)
external failure costs (505)
internal failure costs (505)
lead time (495)
lean accounting (502)
lean enterprise (494)
lean manufacturing (494)
lean principles (494)
nonfinancial measure (504)
non-value-added activity (508)
non-value-added lead time (495)
Pareto chart (507)
prevention costs (505)
process (509)
process-oriented layout (499)
product-oriented layout (499)
pull manufacturing (500)
push manufacturing (500)
radio frequency identification devices (RFID) (501)
Raw and In Process (RIP) Inventory (502)
Six Sigma (500)
supply chain management (501)
value-added activity (508)
value-added lead time (495)
value-added ratio (496)

Illustrative Problem

Krisco Company operates under the lean philosophy. As such, it has a production cell for its microwave ovens. The conversion cost for 2,400 hours of production is budgeted for the year at $4,800,000.

During January, 2,000 microwave ovens were started and completed. Each oven requires six minutes of cell processing time. The materials cost for each oven is $100.

Instructions

Use lean accounting to:

1. Determine the budgeted cell conversion cost per hour.
2. Determine the manufacturing cost per unit.
3. Journalize the entry to record the costs charged to the production cell in January.
4. Journalize the entry to record the costs transferred to finished goods.

Solution

1. Budgeted Cell Conversion Cost Rate = $\frac{\$4,800,000}{2,400 \text{ hours}}$ = $2,000 per cell hour

2.
Materials	$100 per unit
Conversion cost [($2,000 per hour ÷ 60 min.) × 6 min.]	200
Total	$300 per unit

3.	Raw and In Process Inventory	200,000	
	Accounts Payable		200,000
	To record materials costs.		
	(2,000 units × $100 per unit)		
	Raw and In Process Inventory	400,000	
	Conversion Costs		400,000
	To record conversion costs.		
	(2,000 units × $200 per unit)		
4.	Finished Goods (2,000 × $300 per unit)	600,000	
	Raw and In Process Inventory		600,000
	To record finished production.		

Discussion Questions

1. What is the benefit of the lean philosophy?
2. What are some examples of non-value-added lead time?
3. Why is a product-oriented layout preferred by lean manufacturers over a process-oriented layout?
4. How is setup time related to lead time?
5. Why do lean manufacturers favor pull or "make to order" manufacturing?
6. Why would a lean manufacturer strive to produce zero defects?
7. How is supply chain management different from traditional supplier and customer relationships?
8. Why does lean accounting result in fewer transactions?
9. Why do lean manufacturers use a "raw and in process inventory" account, rather than separately reporting materials and work in process?
10. Why is the direct labor cost category eliminated in many lean manufacturing environments?
11. How does a Pareto chart assist management?
12. What is the benefit of identifying non-value-added activities?
13. What ways can the cost of a process be improved?

Practice Exercises

EE 12-1 *p. 499*

PE 12-1A Lead time

OBJ. 1

The Swift Mountain Ski Company manufactures skis in the finishing and assembly process. Skis are manufactured in 30-ski batch sizes. The finishing time is 14 minutes per ski. The assembly time is 10 minutes per ski. It takes 8 minutes to move a batch of skis from finishing to assembly.

a. Compute the value-added, non-value-added, and total lead time of this process.
b. Compute the value-added ratio. Round to one decimal place.

EE 12-1 *p. 499*

PE 12-1B Lead time

OBJ. 1

The Texas Jean Company manufactures jeans in the cutting and sewing process. Jeans are manufactured in 100-jean batch sizes. The cutting time is 11 minutes per jean. The sewing time is 8 minutes per jean. It takes 15 minutes to move a batch of jeans from cutting to sewing.

a. Compute the value-added, non-value-added, and total lead time of this process.
b. Compute the value-added ratio. Round to one decimal place.

SHOW ME HOW

EE 12-2 *p. 501*

PE 12-2A Lean features **OBJ. 1**

Which of the following are features of a lean manufacturing system?

a. Production pace matches demand
b. Centralized work in process inventory locations
c. Push scheduling
d. Receive raw materials directly to manufacturing cells

SHOW ME HOW

EE 12-2 *p. 501*

PE 12-2B Lean features **OBJ. 1**

Which of the following are features of a lean manufacturing system?

a. Centralized maintenance areas
b. Smaller batch sizes
c. Employee involvement
d. Less wasted movement of material and people

SHOW ME HOW

EE 12-3 *p. 504*

PE 12-3A Lean accounting **OBJ. 2**

The annual budgeted conversion costs for a lean cell are $663,000 for 1,950 production hours. Each unit produced by the cell requires 15 minutes of cell process time. During the month, 665 units are manufactured in the cell. The estimated materials costs are $160 per unit. Provide the following journal entries:

a. Materials are purchased to produce 700 units.
b. Conversion costs are applied to 665 units of production.
c. 650 units are completed and placed into finished goods.

SHOW ME HOW

EE 12-3 *p. 504*

PE 12-3B Lean accounting **OBJ. 2**

The annual budgeted conversion costs for a lean cell are $144,000 for 1,800 production hours. Each unit produced by the cell requires 9 minutes of cell process time. During the month, 1,000 units are manufactured in the cell. The estimated materials costs are $65 per unit. Provide the following journal entries:

a. Materials are purchased to produce 1,050 units.
b. Conversion costs are applied to 1,000 units of production.
c. 980 units are completed and placed into finished goods.

SHOW ME HOW

EE 12-4 *p. 508*

PE 12-4A Cost of quality report **OBJ. 3**

A quality control activity analysis indicated the following four activity costs of a manufacturing department:

Rework	$ 39,000
Inspecting incoming raw materials	51,000
Warranty work	27,000
Process improvement effort	183,000
Total	$300,000

Sales are $1,000,000. Prepare a cost of quality report. Round percents to one decimal place.

SHOW ME HOW

EE 12-4 *p. 508*

PE 12-4B Cost of quality report **OBJ. 3**

A quality control activity analysis indicated the following four activity costs of a hotel:

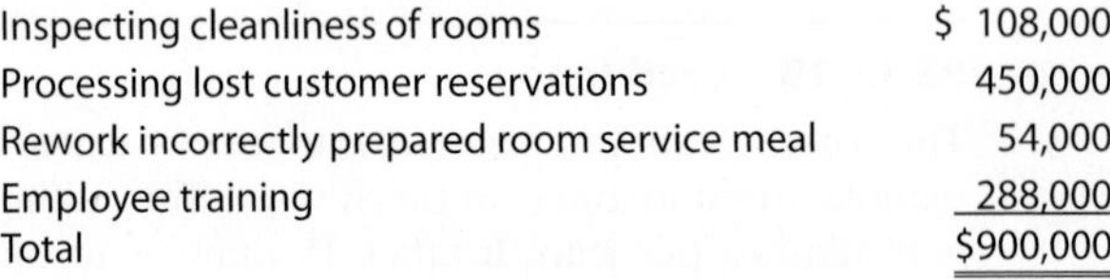

Inspecting cleanliness of rooms	$ 108,000
Processing lost customer reservations	450,000
Rework incorrectly prepared room service meal	54,000
Employee training	288,000
Total	$900,000

Sales are $3,000,000. Prepare a cost of quality report.

SHOW ME HOW

EE 12-5 *p. 510*

PE 12-5A Process activity analysis — OBJ. 3

Lexter Company incurred an activity cost of $180,000 for inspecting 25,000 units of production. Management determined that the inspecting objectives could be met without inspecting every unit. Therefore, rather than inspecting 25,000 units of production, the inspection activity was limited to 40% of the production. Determine the inspection activity cost per unit on 25,000 units of total production both before and after the improvement.

SHOW ME HOW

EE 12-5 *p. 510*

PE 12-5B Process activity analysis — OBJ. 3

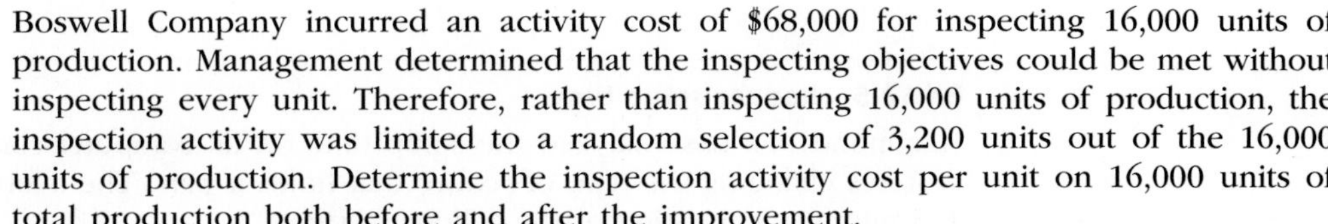

Boswell Company incurred an activity cost of $68,000 for inspecting 16,000 units of production. Management determined that the inspecting objectives could be met without inspecting every unit. Therefore, rather than inspecting 16,000 units of production, the inspection activity was limited to a random selection of 3,200 units out of the 16,000 units of production. Determine the inspection activity cost per unit on 16,000 units of total production both before and after the improvement.

Exercises

EX 12-1 Lean principles — OBJ. 1

The chief executive officer (CEO) of Platnum Inc. has just returned from a management seminar describing the benefits of the lean philosophy. The CEO issued the following statement after returning from the conference:

This company will become a lean manufacturing company. Presently, we have too much inventory. To become lean, we need to eliminate the excess inventory. Therefore, I want all employees to begin reducing inventories until we make products "just-in-time." Thank you for your cooperation.

How would you respond to the CEO's statement?

EX 12-2 Lean as a strategy — OBJ. 1

The American textile industry has moved much of its operations offshore in the pursuit of lower labor costs. Textile imports have risen from 2% of all textile production in 1962 to over 70% in 2012. Offshore manufacturers make long runs of standard mass-market apparel items. These are then brought to the United States in container ships, requiring significant time between original order and delivery. As a result, retail customers must accurately forecast market demands for imported apparel items.

Assuming that you work for a U.S.-based textile company, how would you recommend responding to the low-cost imports?

EX 12-3 Lean principles — OBJ. 1

Active Apparel Company manufactures various styles of men's casual wear. Shirts are cut and assembled by a workforce that is paid by piece rate. This means that they are paid according to the amount of work completed during a period of time. To illustrate, if the piece rate is $0.15 per sleeve assembled, and the worker assembles 700 sleeves during the day, then the worker would be paid $105 (700 × $0.15) for the day's work.

The company is considering adopting a lean manufacturing philosophy by organizing work cells around various types of products and employing pull manufacturing. However, no change is expected in the compensation policy. On this point, the manufacturing manager stated the following:

"Piecework compensation provides an incentive to work fast. Without it, the workers will just goof off and expect a full day's pay. We can't pay straight hourly wages—at least not in this industry."

How would you respond to the manufacturing manager's comments?

EX 12-4 Lead time analysis

OBJ. 1

Palm Pals Inc. manufactures toy stuffed animals. The direct labor time required to cut, sew, and stuff a toy is 12 minutes per unit. The company makes two types of stuffed toys—a lion and a bear. The lion is assembled in lot sizes of 40 units per batch, while the bear is assembled in lot sizes of 5 units per batch. Since each product has direct labor time of 12 minutes per unit, management has determined that the lead time for each product is 12 minutes.

Is management correct? What are the lead times for each product?

EX 12-5 Reduce setup time

OBJ. 1

Hammond Inc. has analyzed the setup time on its computer-controlled lathe. The setup requires changing the type of fixture that holds a part. The average setup time has been 135 minutes, consisting of the following steps:

Turn off machine and remove fixture from lathe	10 minutes
Go to tool room with fixture	15
Record replacement of fixture to tool room	18
Return to lathe	20
Clean lathe	15
Return to tool room	20
Record withdrawal of new fixture from tool room	12
Return to lathe	15
Install new fixture and turn on machine	10
Total setup time	135 minutes

a. Why should management be concerned about improving setup time?

b. What do you recommend to Hammond Inc. for improving setup time?

c. How much time would be required for a setup, using your suggestion in (b)?

EX 12-6 Calculate lead time

OBJ. 1

Flint Fabricators Inc. machines metal parts for the automotive industry. Under the traditional manufacturing approach, the parts are machined through two processes: milling and finishing. Parts are produced in batch sizes of 30 parts. A part requires 5 minutes in milling and 7 minutes in finishing. The move time between the two operations for a complete batch is 5 minutes.

Under the lean philosophy, the part is produced in a cell that includes both the milling and finishing operations. The operating time is unchanged; however, the batch size is reduced to 4 parts and the move time is eliminated.

Determine the value-added, non-value-added, and total lead times, and the value-added ratio under the traditional and lean manufacturing methods. Round percentages to one decimal place.

EX 12-7 Calculate lead time

OBJ. 1

Williams Optical Inc. is considering a new lean product cell. The present manufacturing approach produces a product in four separate steps. The production batch sizes are 45 units. The process time for each step is as follows:

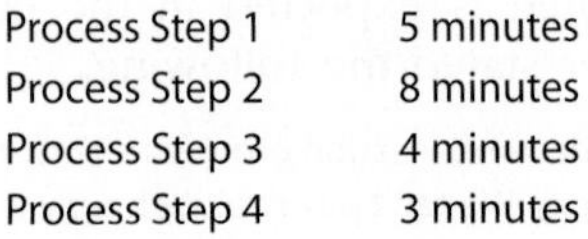

Process Step 1	5 minutes
Process Step 2	8 minutes
Process Step 3	4 minutes
Process Step 4	3 minutes

✔ b. Non-value-added, 50 minutes

The time required to move each batch between steps is 5 minutes. In addition, the time to move raw materials to Process Step 1 is also 5 minutes, and the time to move completed units from Process Step 4 to finished goods inventory is 5 minutes.

The new lean layout will allow the company to reduce the batch sizes from 45 units to 3 units. The time required to move each batch between steps and the inventory locations will be reduced to 2 minutes. The processing time in each step will stay the same.

Determine the value-added, non-value-added, and total lead times, and the value-added ratio under the (a) present and (b) proposed production approaches. Round percentages to one decimal place.

EX 12-8 Lead time calculation for a service company **OBJ. 1**

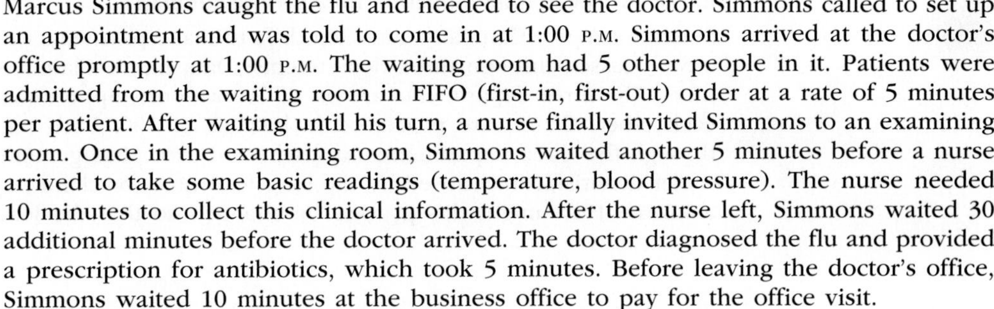

Marcus Simmons caught the flu and needed to see the doctor. Simmons called to set up an appointment and was told to come in at 1:00 P.M. Simmons arrived at the doctor's office promptly at 1:00 P.M. The waiting room had 5 other people in it. Patients were admitted from the waiting room in FIFO (first-in, first-out) order at a rate of 5 minutes per patient. After waiting until his turn, a nurse finally invited Simmons to an examining room. Once in the examining room, Simmons waited another 5 minutes before a nurse arrived to take some basic readings (temperature, blood pressure). The nurse needed 10 minutes to collect this clinical information. After the nurse left, Simmons waited 30 additional minutes before the doctor arrived. The doctor diagnosed the flu and provided a prescription for antibiotics, which took 5 minutes. Before leaving the doctor's office, Simmons waited 10 minutes at the business office to pay for the office visit.

Simmons spent 5 minutes walking next door to fill the prescription at the pharmacy. There were four people in front of Simmons, each person requiring 5 minutes to fill and purchase a prescription. Simmons arrived home 15 minutes after paying for his prescription.

a. What time does Simmons arrive home?

b. How much of the total elapsed time from 1:00 P.M. until when Simmons arrived home was non-value-added time?

c. What is the value-added ratio?

d. Why does the doctor require patients to wait so long for service?

EX 12-9 Suppy chain management **OBJ. 1**

The following is an excerpt from a recent article discussing supplier relationships with the Big Three North American automakers.

"The Big Three select suppliers on the basis of lowest price and annual price reductions," said Neil De Koker, president of the Original Equipment Suppliers Association. "They look globally for the lowest parts prices from the lowest cost countries," De Koker said. "There is little trust and respect. Collaboration is missing." Japanese auto makers want long-term supplier relationships. They select suppliers as a person would a mate. The Big Three are quick to beat down prices with methods such as electronic auctions or rebidding work to a competitor. The Japanese are equally tough on price but are committed to maintaining supplier continuity. "They work with you to arrive at a competitive price, and they are willing to pay because they want long-term partnering," said Carl Code, a vice president at Ernie Green Industries. "They [**Honda** and **Toyota**] want suppliers to make enough money to stay in business, grow, and bring them innovation." The Big Three's supply chain model is not much different from the one set by Henry Ford. In 1913, he set up the system of independent supplier firms operating at arm's length on short-term contracts. One consequence of the Big Three's low-price-at-all-costs mentality is that suppliers are reluctant to offer them their cutting-edge technology out of fear the contract will be resourced before the research and development costs are recouped.

Source: Robert Sherefkin and Amy Wilson, "Suppliers Prefer Japanese Business Model," *Rubber & Plastics News*, March 17, 2003, Vol. 24, No. 11.

a. Contrast the Japanese supply chain model with that of the Big Three.

b. Why might a supplier prefer the Japanese model?

c. What benefits might accrue to the Big Three by adopting the Japanese supply chain practices?

EX 12-10 Employee involvement OBJ. 1

Quickie Designs Inc. uses teams in the manufacture of lightweight wheelchairs. Two features of its team approach are team hiring and peer reviews. Under team hiring, the team recruits, interviews, and hires new team members from within the organization. Using peer reviews, the team evaluates each member of the team with regard to quality, knowledge, teamwork, goal performance, attendance, and safety. These reviews provide feedback to the team member for improvement.

How do these two team approaches differ from using managers to hire and evaluate employees?

EX 12-11 Lead time reduction for a service company OBJ. 1

Shield Insurance Company takes ten days to make payments on insurance claims. Claims are processed through three departments: Data Input, Claims Audit, and Claims Adjustment. The three departments are on different floors, approximately one hour apart from each other. Claims are processed in batches of 100. Each batch of 100 claims moves through the three departments on a wheeled cart. Management is concerned about customer dissatisfaction caused by the long lead time for claim payments.

How might this process be changed so that the lead time could be reduced significantly?

EX 12-12 Lean principles for a service company OBJ. 1

The management of Grill Rite Burger fast-food franchise wants to provide hamburgers quickly to customers. It has been using a process by which precooked hamburgers are prepared and placed under hot lamps. These hamburgers are then sold to customers. In this process, every customer receives the same type of hamburger and dressing (ketchup, onions, mustard). If a customer wants something different, then a "special order" must be cooked to the customer's requirements. This requires the customer to wait several minutes, which often slows down the service line. Grill Rite has been receiving more and more special orders from customers, which has been slowing service down considerably.

a. Is the Grill Rite service delivery system best described as a push or pull system? Explain.

b. How might you use lean principles to provide customers quick service, yet still allow them to custom order their burgers?

EX 12-13 Accounting issues in a lean environment OBJ. 2

Pinnacle Technologies has recently implemented a lean manufacturing approach. A production manager has approached the controller with the following comments:

I am very upset with our accounting system now that we have implemented our new lean manufacturing methods. It seems as if all I'm doing is paperwork. Our product is moving so fast through the manufacturing process that the paperwork can hardly keep up. For example, it just doesn't make sense to me to fill out daily labor reports. The employees are assigned to complete cells, performing many different tasks. I can't keep up with direct labor reports on each individual task. I thought we were trying to eliminate waste. Yet the information requirements of the accounting system are slowing us down and adding to overall lead time. Moreover, I'm still getting my monthly variance reports. I don't think that these are necessary. I have nonfinancial performance measures that are more timely than these reports. Besides, the employees don't really understand accounting variances. How about giving some information that I can really use?

What accounting system changes would you suggest in light of the production department manager's criticisms?

EX 12-14 Lean accounting

OBJ. 2

✔ b. $31.50

SHOW ME HOW

Right Now Video Inc. uses a lean manufacturing strategy to manufacture DVR (digital video recorder) players. The company manufactures DVR players through a single product cell. The budgeted conversion cost for the year is $420,000 for 2,000 production hours. Each unit requires 9 minutes of cell process time. During July, 1,100 DVR players are manufactured in the cell. The materials cost per unit is $135. The following summary transactions took place during July:

1. Materials are purchased for July production.
2. Conversion costs were applied to production.
3. 1,100 DVR players are assembled and placed in finished goods.
4. 1,060 DVR players are sold for $335 per unit.

a. Determine the budgeted cell conversion cost per hour.
b. Determine the budgeted cell conversion cost per unit.
c. Journalize the summary transactions (1)–(4) for July.

EX 12-15 Lean accounting

OBJ. 2

✔ a. $92

SHOW ME HOW

Ever-Brite Lighting Inc. manufactures lighting fixtures, using lean manufacturing methods. Style BB-01 has a materials cost per unit of $45. The budgeted conversion cost for the year is $193,200 for 2,100 production hours. A unit of Style BB-01 requires 15 minutes of cell production time. The following transactions took place during December:

1. Materials were acquired to assemble 700 Style BB-01 units for December.
2. Conversion costs were applied to 700 Style BB-01 units of production.
3. 685 units of Style BB-01 were completed in December.
4. 670 units of Style BB-01 were sold in December for $128 per unit.

a. Determine the budgeted cell conversion cost per hour.
b. Determine the budgeted cell conversion cost per unit.
c. Journalize the summary transactions (1)–(4) for December.

EX 12-16 Lean accounting

OBJ. 2

✔ b. Finished goods, $2,490

SHOW ME HOW

Audio Escape Inc. manufactures audio speakers. Each speaker requires $145 per unit of direct materials. The speaker manufacturing assembly cell includes the following estimated costs for the period:

Speaker assembly cell, estimated costs:	
Labor	$ 6,300
Depreciation	2,800
Supplies	2,400
Power	1,100
Total cell costs for the period	$12,600

The operating plan calls for 180 operating hours for the period. Each speaker requires 18 minutes of cell process time. The unit selling price for each speaker is $360. During the period, the following transactions occurred:

1. Purchased materials to produce 625 speaker units.
2. Applied conversion costs to production of 600 speaker units.
3. Completed and transferred 585 speaker units to finished goods.
4. Sold 570 speaker units.

There were no inventories at the beginning of the period.

a. Journalize the summary transactions (1)–(4) for the period.
b. Determine the ending balance for raw and in process inventory and finished goods inventory.

EX 12-17 Pareto chart **OBJ. 3**

Silicon Solutions Inc. manufactures RAM memory chips for personal computers. An activity analysis was conducted, and the following activity costs were identified with the manufacture and sale of memory chips:

Activities	Activity Cost
Correct shipment errors	$ 144,000
Disposing of scrap	90,000
Emergency equipment maintenance	99,000
Employee training	36,000
Final inspection	81,000
Inspecting incoming materials	54,000
Preventive equipment maintenance	27,000
Processing customer returns	90,000
Scrap reporting	36,000
Supplier development	9,000
Warranty claims	234,000
Total	$900,000

Prepare a Pareto chart of these activities.

✔ **a. Appraisal, 15% of total quality cost**

SHOW ME HOW

EX 12-18 Cost of quality report **OBJ. 3**

a. Using the information in Exercise 12-17, identify the cost of quality classification for each activity.

b. Prepare of cost of quality report. Assume sales for the period were $3,000,000. Round percents to one decimal place.

c. Interpret the cost of quality report.

EX 12-19 Pareto chart for a service company **OBJ. 1, 3**

Digital River Inc. provides cable TV and Internet service to the local community. The activities and activity costs of Digital Light are identified as follows:

Activities	Activity Cost
Billing error correction	$ 36,000
Cable signal testing	96,000
Reinstalling service (installed incorrectly the first time)	30,000
Repairing satellite equipment	36,000
Repairing underground cable connections to the customer	18,000
Replacing old technology cable with higher quality cable	168,000
Replacing old technology signal switches with higher quality switches	126,000
Responding to customer home repair requests	24,000
Training employees	66,000
Total	$600,000

Prepare a Pareto chart of these activities.

✔ **a. External failure, 18% of total cost**

SHOW ME HOW

EX 12-20 Cost of quality and value-added/non-value-added reports for a service company **OBJ. 1, 3**

a. Using the information in Exercise 12-19, identify the cost of quality classification for each activity and whether the activity is value-added or non value-added.

b. Prepare a cost of quality report. Assume that sales are $2,000,000. Round percentages to one decimal place.

c. Prepare a value-added/non-value-added analysis.

d. Interpret the information in (b) and (c).

✔ **a. $0.08 per can**

EX 12-21 Process activity analysis **OBJ. 3**

The Brite Beverage Company bottles soft drinks into aluminum cans. The manufacturing process consists of three activities:

1. **Mixing:** water, sugar, and beverage concentrate are mixed.
2. **Filling:** mixed beverage is filled into 12-oz. cans.
3. **Packaging:** properly filled cans are boxed into cardboard "fridge packs."

The activity costs associated with these activities for the period are as follows:

Mixing	$216,000
Filling	168,000
Packaging	96,000
Total	$480,000

The activity costs do not include materials costs, which are ignored for this analysis. Each can is expected to contain 12 ounces of beverage. Thus, after being filled, each can is automatically weighed. If a can is too light, it is rejected, or "kicked," from the filling line prior to being packaged. The primary cause of kicks is heat expansion. With heat expansion, the beverage overflows during filling, resulting in underweight cans.

This process begins by mixing and filling 6,300,000 cans during the period, of which only 6,000,000 cans are actually packaged. Three hundred thousand cans are rejected due to underweight kicks.

A process improvement team has determined that cooling the cans prior to filling them will reduce the amount of overflows due to expansion. After this improvement, the number of kicks is expected to decline from 300,000 cans to 63,000 cans, thus increasing the number of filled cans to 6,237,000 [6,000,000 + (300,000 − 63,000)].

a. Determine the total activity cost per packaged can under present operations.

b. Determine the amount of increased packaging activity costs from the expected improvements.

c. Determine the expected total activity cost per packaged can after improvements. Round to two decimal places.

EX 12-22 Process activity analysis for a service company **OBJ. 1, 3**

✔ b. $100 per claim payment

SHOW ME HOW

Continental Insurance Company has a process for making payments on insurance claims as follows:

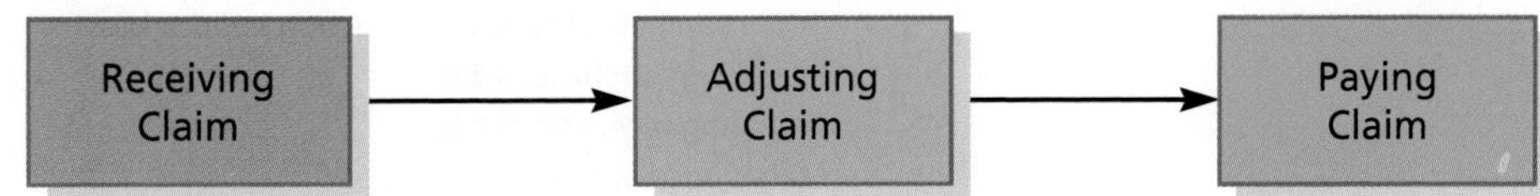

An activity analysis revealed that the cost of these activities was as follows:

Receiving claim	$ 80,000
Adjusting claim	240,000
Paying claim	80,000
Total	$400,000

This process includes only the cost of processing the claim payments, not the actual amount of the claim payments. The adjusting activity involves verifying and estimating the amount of the claim and is variable to the number of claims adjusted.

The process received, adjusted, and paid 4,000 claims during the period. All claims were treated identically in this process.

To improve the cost of this process, management has determined that claims should be segregated into two categories. Claims under $1,000 and claims greater than $1,000: claims under $1,000 would not be adjusted but would be accepted upon the insured's evidence of claim. Claims above $1,000 would be adjusted. It is estimated that 70% of the claims are under $1,000 and would thus be paid without adjustment. It is also estimated that the additional effort to segregate claims would add 15% to the "receiving claim" activity cost.

a. Develop a table showing the percent of individual activity cost to the total process cost.

b. Determine the average total process cost per claim payment, assuming 4,000 total claims.

(Continued)

c. Prepare a table showing the changes in the activity costs as a result of the changes proposed by management. Show columns of activity cost prior to improvement, after improvement, and savings.

d. Estimate the average cost per claim payment, assuming that the changes proposed by management are enacted for 4,000 total claims.

EX 12-23 Process activity analysis

OBJ. 1, 3

✔ b. $20 per payment

The procurement process for Omni Wholesale Company includes a series of activities that transforms a materials requisition into a vendor check. The process begins with a request for materials. The requesting department prepares and sends a materials request form to the Purchasing Department. The Purchasing Department then places a request for a quote to vendors. Vendors prepare bids in response to the request for a quote. A vendor is selected based on the lowest bid. A purchase order to the low-bid vendor is prepared. The vendor delivers the materials to the company, whereupon a receiving ticket is prepared. Payment to the vendor is authorized if the materials request form, receiving ticket, and vendor invoice are in agreement. These three documents fail to agree 40% of the time, initiating effort to reconcile the differences. Once the three documents agree, a check is issued. The process can be diagrammed as follows:

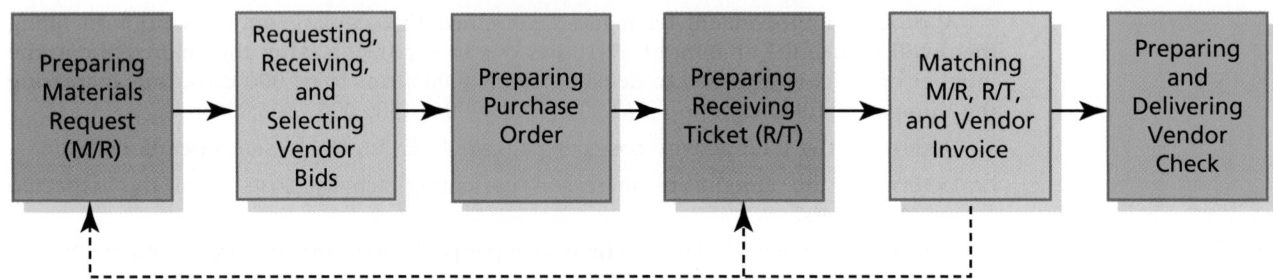

Correcting Reconciliation Differences

An activity analysis indicated the following activity costs with this process:

Activity	Cost
Preparing materials request	$ 36,000
Requesting, receiving, and selecting vendor bids	100,000
Preparing purchase order	20,000
Preparing receiving ticket	24,000
Matching M/R, R/T, and invoice	48,000
Correcting reconciliation differences	140,000
Preparing and delivering vendor payment	32,000
Total process activity cost	$400,000

On average, the process handles 20,000 individual requests for materials that result in 20,000 individual payments to vendors.

Management proposes to improve this process in two ways. First, the Purchasing Department will develop a preapproved vendor list for which orders can be placed without a request for quote. It is expected that this will reduce the cost of requesting and receiving vendor bids by 75%. Second, additional training and standardization will be provided to reduce errors introduced into the materials requisition form and receiving tickets. It is expected that this will reduce the number of reconciliation differences from 40% to 10%, over an average of 20,000 payments.

a. Develop a table showing the percent of individual activity cost to the total process cost.

b. Determine the average total process cost per vendor payment, assuming 20,000 payments.

c. Prepare a table showing the improvements in the activity costs as a result of the changes proposed by management. Show columns of activity cost prior to improvement, after improvement, and savings.

d. Estimate the average cost per vendor payment, assuming that the changes proposed by management are enacted for 20,000 total payments. Round to the nearest cent.

Problems Series A

PR 12-1A Lean principles — OBJ. 1

Soft Glow, Inc. manufactures light bulbs. Their purchasing policy requires that the purchasing agents place each quarter's purchasing requirements out for bid. This is because the Purchasing Department is evaluated solely by its ability to get the lowest purchase prices. The lowest bidder receives the order for the next quarter (90 working days).

To make its bulb products, Soft Glow requires 45,000 pounds of glass per quarter. Soft Glow received two glass bids for the third quarter, as follows:

- *Mid-States Glass Company:* \$28.00 per pound of glass. Delivery schedule: 45,000 (500 lbs. × 90 days) pounds at the beginning of July to last for 3 months.
- *Cleveland Glass Company:* \$28.20 per pound of glass. Delivery schedule: 500 pounds per working day (90 days in the quarter).-

Soft Glow accepted Mid-States Glass Company's bid because it was the low-cost bid.

Instructions

1. Comment on Soft Glow's purchasing policy.
2. What are the additional (hidden) costs, beyond price, of Mid-States Glass Company's bid? Why weren't these costs considered?
3. Considering just inventory financing costs, what is the additional cost per pound of Mid-States Glass Company's bid if the annual cost of money is 10%? (*Hint:* Determine the average value of glass inventory held for the quarter and multiply by the quarterly interest charge, then divide by the number of pounds.)

PR 12-2A Lead time — OBJ. 1

✔ 1. Total wait time, 1,741 minutes

Sound Tek Inc. manufactures electronic stereo equipment. The manufacturing process includes printed circuit (PC) board assembly, final assembly, testing, and shipping. In the PC board assembly operation, a number of individuals are responsible for assembling electronic components into printed circuit boards. Each operator is responsible for soldering components according to a given set of instructions. Operators work on batches of 45 printed circuit boards. Each board requires 5 minutes of board assembly time. After each batch is completed, the operator moves the assembled boards to the final assembly area. This move takes 10 minutes to complete.

The final assembly for each stereo unit requires 15 minutes and is also done in batches of 45 units. A batch of 45 stereos is moved into the test building, which is across the street. The move takes 20 minutes. Before conducting the test, the test equipment must be set up for the particular stereo model. The test setup requires 25 minutes. The units wait while the setup is performed. In the final test, the 45-unit batch is tested one at a time. Each test requires 9 minutes. The completed batch, after all testing, is sent to shipping for packaging and final shipment to customers. A complete batch of 45 units is sent from testing to shipping. The Shipping Department is located next to testing. Thus, there is no move time between these two operations. Packaging and labeling requires 10 minutes per unit.

Instructions

1. Determine the amount of value-added and non-value-added lead time and the value-added ratio in this process for an average stereo unit in a batch of 45 units. Round percentages to one decimal place. Categorize the non-value-added time into wait and move time.
2. How could this process be improved so as to reduce the amount of waste in the process?

✔ 4. Raw and In Process Inventory, \$74,250

PR 12-3A Lean accounting — OBJ. 2

Formula One Displays Inc. manufactures and assembles automobile instrument panels for both Yokohama Motors and Detroit Motors. The process consists of a lean product cell for each customer's instrument assembly. The data that follow concern only the Yokohama lean cell.

(Continued)

For the year, Grand Prix Displays Inc. budgeted the following costs for the Yokohama production cell:

Conversion Cost Categories	Budget
Labor	$585,000
Supplies	45,000
Utilities	30,000
Total	$660,000

Grand Prix Displays Inc. plans 2,200 hours of production for the Yokohama cell for the year. The materials cost is $180 per instrument assembly. Each assembly requires 15 minutes of cell assembly time. There was no November 1 inventory for either Raw and In Process Inventory or Finished Goods Inventory.

The following summary events took place in the Yokohama cell during November:

a. Electronic parts and wiring were purchased to produce 9,000 instrument assemblies in November.

b. Conversion costs were applied for the production of 8,800 units in November.

c. 8,650 units were started, completed, and transferred to finished goods in November.

d. 8,600 units were shipped to customers at a price of $400 per unit.

Instructions

1. Determine the budgeted cell conversion cost per hour.
2. Determine the budgeted cell conversion cost per unit.
3. Journalize the summary transactions (a) through (d).
4. Determine the ending balance in Raw and In Process Inventory and Finished Goods Inventory.
5. How does the accounting in a lean environment differ from traditional accounting?

PR 12-4A Pareto chart and cost of quality report for a service company — OBJ. 1, 3

✔ 3. Non-value-added, 61%

The administrator of Hope Hospital has been asked to perform an activity analysis of the emergency room (ER). The ER activities include cost of quality and other patient care activities. The lab tests and transportation are hospital services external to the ER for determining external failure costs. The result of the activity analysis is summarized as follows:

Activities	Activity Cost
Patient registration	$ 6,400
Verifying patient information	9,600
Assigning patients	12,800
Searching/waiting for doctor	8,000
Doctor exam	4,800
Waiting for transport	17,600
Transporting patients	16,000
Verifying lab orders	14,400
Searching for equipment	8,000
Incorrect labs	12,800
Lab tests	17,600
Counting supplies	19,200
Looking for supplies	8,000
Staff training	4,800
Total	$160,000

Instructions

1. Prepare a Pareto chart of the ER activities.
2. Classify the activities into prevention, appraisal, internal failure, external failure, and other patient care activities. Classify the activities into value-added and non-value added activities.
3. Use the activity cost information to determine the percentages of total ER costs that are prevention, appraisal, internal failure, external failure, and other patient care activities.
4. Determine the percentages of the total ER costs that are value- and non-value-added.
5. Interpret the information.

Problems Series B

PR 12-1B Lean principles

OBJ. 1

HD Hogg Motorcycle Company manufactures a variety of motorcycles. Hogg's purchasing policy requires that the purchasing agents place each quarter's purchasing requirements out for bid. This is because the Purchasing Department is evaluated solely by its ability to get the lowest purchase prices. The lowest cost bidder receives the order for the next quarter (90 days). To make its motorcycles, Hogg requires 4,500 frames per quarter. Hogg received two frame bids for the third quarter, as follows:

- *Famous Frames, Inc.:* $301 per frame. Delivery schedule: 50 frames per working day (90 days in the quarter).
- *Iron Horse Frames Inc.:* $300 per frame. Delivery schedule: 4,500 (50 frames × 90 days) frames at the beginning of July to last for three months.

Hogg accepted Iron Horse Frames Inc.'s bid because it was the low-cost bid.

Instructions

1. Comment on Hogg's purchasing policy.
2. What are the additional (hidden) costs, beyond price, of Iron Horse Frames Inc.'s bid? Why weren't these costs considered?
3. Considering just inventory financing costs, what is the additional cost per frame of Iron Horse Frames Inc.'s bid if the annual cost of money is 12%? (*Hint:* Determine the average value of frame inventory held for the quarter and multiply by the quarterly interest charge, then divide by the number of frames.)

PR 12-2B Lead time

OBJ. 1

✓ 1. Total wait time, 2,010 minutes

Master Chef Appliance Company manufactures home kitchen appliances. The manufacturing process includes stamping, final assembly, testing, and shipping. In the stamping operation, a number of individuals are responsible for stamping the steel outer surface of the appliance. The stamping operation is set up prior to each run. A run of 40 stampings is completed after each setup. A setup requires 60 minutes. The parts wait for the setup to be completed before stamping begins. Each stamping requires 5 minutes of operating time. After each batch is completed, the operator moves the stamped covers to the final assembly area. This move takes 10 minutes to complete.

The final assembly for each appliance unit requires 22 minutes and is also done in batches of 40 appliance units. The batch of 40 appliance units is moved into the test building, which is across the street. The move takes 25 minutes. In the final test, the 40-unit batch is tested one at a time. Each test requires 8 minutes. The completed units are sent to shipping for packaging and final shipment to customers. A complete batch of 40 units is sent from testing to shipping. The Shipping Department is located next to testing. Thus, there is no move time between these two operations. Packaging and shipment labeling requires 15 minutes per unit.

Instructions

1. Determine the amount of value-added and non-value-added lead time and the value-added ratio in this process for an average kitchen appliance in a batch of 40 units. Round percentages to one decimal place. Categorize the non-value-added time into wait and move time.
2. How could this process be improved so as to reduce the amount of waste in the process?

PR 12-3B Lean accounting

OBJ. 2

✓ 4. Raw and In Process Inventory, $97,900

Com-Tel Inc. manufactures and assembles two models of smart phones—the Tiger Model and the Lion Model. The process consists of a lean cell for each product. The data that follow concern only the Lion Model lean cell.

(Continued)

For the year, Com-Tel Inc. budgeted these costs for the Lion Model production cell:

Conversion Cost Categories	Budget
Labor	$122,000
Supplies	49,000
Utilities	18,000
Total	$189,000

Com-Tel plans 2,100 hours of production for the Lion Model cell for the year. The materials cost is $185 per unit. Each assembly requires 12 minutes of cell assembly time. There was no May 1 inventory for either Raw and In Process Inventory or Finished Goods Inventory.

The following summary events took place in the Lion Model cell during May:

a. Electronic parts were purchased to produce 10,700 Lion Model assemblies in May.

b. Conversion costs were applied for 10,500 units of production in May.

c. 10,200 units were completed and transferred to finished goods in May.

d. 10,000 units were shipped to customers at a price of $500 per unit.

Instructions

1. Determine the budgeted cell conversion cost per hour.
2. Determine the budgeted cell conversion cost per unit.
3. Journalize the summary transactions (a) through (d).
4. Determine the ending balance in Raw and In Process Inventory and Finished Goods Inventory.
5. How does the accounting in a lean environment differ from traditional accounting?

PR 12-4B Pareto chart and cost of quality report for a manufacturing company **OBJ. 3**

✔ 3. Non-value-added, 35%

The president of Mission Inc. has been concerned about the growth in costs over the last several years. The president asked the controller to perform an activity analysis to gain a better insight into these costs. The activity analysis revealed the following:

Activities	Activity Cost
Correcting invoice errors	$ 7,500
Disposing of incoming materials with poor quality	15,000
Disposing of scrap	27,500
Expediting late production	22,500
Final inspection	20,000
Inspecting incoming materials	5,000
Inspecting work in process	25,000
Preventive machine maintenance	15,000
Producing product	97,500
Responding to customer quality complaints	15,000
Total	$250,000

The production process is complicated by quality problems, requiring the production manager to expedite production and dispose of scrap.

Instructions

1. Prepare a Pareto chart of the company activities.
2. Classify the activities into prevention, appraisal, internal failure, external failure, and not costs of quality (producing product). Classify the activities into value-added and non-value added activities.
3. Use the activity cost information to determine the percentages of total costs that are prevention, appraisal, internal failure, external failure, and not costs of quality.
4. Determine the percentages of total costs that are value- and non-value-added.
5. Interpret the information.

Cases & Projects

CP 12-1 Ethics and professional conduct in business

In August, Lannister Company introduced a new performance measurement system in manufacturing operations. One of the new performance measures was lead time. The lead time was determined by tagging a random sample of items with a log sheet throughout the month. This log sheet recorded the time that the item started and the time that it ended production, as well as all steps in between. The controller collected the log sheets and calculated the average lead time of the tagged products. This number was reported to central management and was used to evaluate the performance of the plant manager. The plant was under extreme pressure to reduce lead time because of poor lead time results reported in September.

The following memo was intercepted by the controller.

Date: October 1
To: Hourly Employees
From: Plant Manager

During last month, you noticed that some of the products were tagged with a log sheet. This sheet records the time that a product enters production and the time that it leaves production. The difference between these two times is termed the "lead time." Our plant is evaluated on improving lead time. From now on, I ask all of you to keep an eye out for the tagged items. When you receive a tagged item, it is to receive special attention. Work on that item first, and then immediately move it to the next operation. Under no circumstances should tagged items wait on any other work that you have. Naturally, report accurate information. I insist that you record the correct times on the log sheet as the product goes through your operations.

 How should the controller respond to this discovery?

CP 12-2 Lean principles

Reliant Products Inc. manufactures electric space heaters. While the CEO, Lynn Jennings, is visiting the production facility, the following conversation takes place with the plant manager, Aaron Clark:

Lynn: As I walk around the facility, I can't help noticing all the materials inventories. What's going on?

Aaron: I have found our suppliers to be very unreliable in meeting their delivery commitments. Thus, I keep a lot of materials on hand so as to not risk running out and shutting down production.

Lynn: Not only do I see a lot of materials inventory, but there also seems to be a lot of finished goods inventory on hand. Why is this?

Aaron: As you know, I am evaluated on maintaining a low cost per unit. The one way that I am able to reduce my unit costs is by producing as many space heaters as possible. This allows me to spread my fixed costs over a larger base. When orders are down, the excess production builds up as inventory, as we are seeing now. But don't worry—I'm really keeping our unit costs down this way.

Lynn: I'm not so sure. It seems that this inventory must cost us something.

Aaron: Not really. I'll eventually use the materials and we'll eventually sell the finished goods. By keeping the plant busy, I'm using our plant assets wisely. This is reflected in the low unit costs that I'm able to maintain.

If you were Lynn Jennings, how would you respond to Aaron Clark? What recommendations would you provide Aaron Clark?

CP 12-3 Lean principles

Maxxim Inc. prepared the following performance graphs for the prior year:

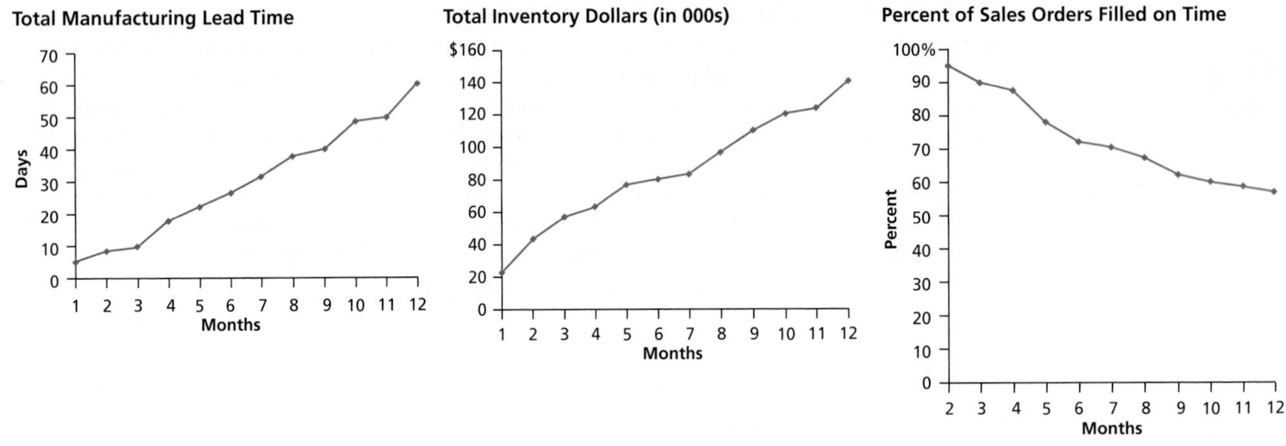

What do these appear to indicate?

CP 12-4 Value-added and non-value-added activity costs

Pryor Company prepared the following factory overhead report from its general ledger:

Indirect labor	$250,000
Fringe benefits	30,000
Supplies	70,000
Depreciation	50,000
Total	$400,000

The management of Pryor Company was dissatisfied with this report and asked the controller to prepare an activity analysis of the same information. This activity analysis was as follows:

Processing sales orders	$ 68,000	17%
Disposing of scrap	96,000	24
Expediting work orders	80,000	20
Producing parts	44,000	11
Resolving supplier quality problems	56,000	14
Reissuing corrected purchase orders	40,000	10
Expediting customer orders	16,000	4
Total	$400,000	100%

Interpret the activity analysis by identifying value-added and non-value-added activity costs. How does the activity cost report differ from the general ledger report?

CP 12-5 Lead time

Group Project

In groups of two to four people, visit a sit-down restaurant and do a lead time study. If more than one group chooses to visit the same restaurant, choose different times for your visits. Note the time when you walk in the door of the restaurant and the time when you walk out the door after you have eaten. The difference between these two times is the total lead time of your restaurant experience. While in the restaurant, determine the time spent on non-value-added time, such as wait time, and the time spent on value-added eating time. Note the various activities and the time required to perform each activity during your visit to the restaurant. Compare your analyses, identifying possible reasons for differences in the times recorded by groups that visited the same restaurant.

Statement of Cash Flows

National Beverage Co.

Suppose you were to receive $100 from an event. Would it make a difference what the event was? Yes, it would! If you received $100 for your birthday, then it's a gift. If you received $100 as a result of working part time for a week, then it's the result of your effort. If you received $100 as a loan, then it's money that you will have to pay back in the future. If you received $100 as a result of selling your iPod, then it's the result of selling an asset. Thus, $100 received can be associated with different types of events, and these events have different meanings to you, and different implications for your future. You would much rather receive a $100 gift than take out a $100 loan. Likewise, company stakeholders view inflows and outflows of cash differently, depending on their source.

Companies are required to report information about the events causing a change in cash over a period of time. This information is reported in the statement of cash flows. One such company is **National Beverage**, which is an alternative beverage company, known for its innovative soft drinks, enhanced juices and waters, and fortified powders and supplements. You have probably seen the company's **Shasta** and **Faygo** soft drinks, or **LaCroix**, **Everfresh**, and **Crystal Bay** drinks at your local grocery or convenience store. As with any company, cash is important to National Beverage. Without cash, National Beverage would be unable to expand its brands, distribute its product, support extreme sports, or provide a return for its owners. Thus, its managers are concerned about the sources and uses of cash.

In previous chapters, we have used the income statement, balance sheet, statement of retained earnings, and other information to analyze the effects of management decisions on a business's financial position and operating performance. In this chapter, we focus on the events causing a change in cash by presenting the preparation and use of the statement of cash flows.

Learning Objectives

After studying this chapter, you should be able to: | *Example Exercises*

OBJ 1 **Describe the cash flow activities reported in the statement of cash flows.**
Reporting Cash Flows
- Cash Flows from Operating Activities
- Cash Flows from Investing Activities
- Cash Flows from Financing Activities — EE 13-1
- Noncash Investing and Financing Activities
- No Cash Flow per Share
- Format of the Statement of Cash Flows

OBJ 2 **Prepare a statement of cash flows, using the indirect method.**
Preparing the Statement of Cash Flows—The Indirect Method
- Retained Earnings
- Adjustments to Net Income — EE 13-2, 3, 4
- Dividends
- Common Stock
- Bonds Payable
- Building
- Land — EE 13-5
- Preparing the Statement of Cash Flows

OBJ 3 **Prepare a statement of cash flows, using the direct method.**
Preparing the Statement of Cash Flows—The Direct Method
- Cash Received from Customers — EE 13-6
- Cash Payments for Merchandise — EE 13-7
- Cash Payments for Operating Expenses
- Gain on Sale of Land
- Interest Expense
- Cash Payments for Income Taxes
- Reporting Cash Flows from Operating Activities—Direct Method

OBJ 4 **Describe and illustrate the use of free cash flow in evaluating a company's cash flow.**
Financial Analysis and Interpretation: Free Cash Flow — EE 13-8

At a Glance 13 Page 556

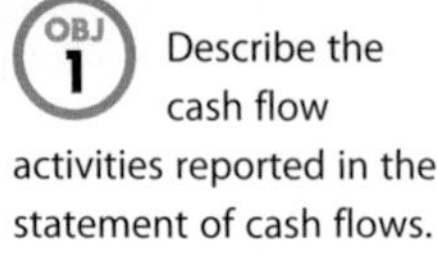
Describe the cash flow activities reported in the statement of cash flows.

Reporting Cash Flows

The **statement of cash flows** reports a company's cash inflows and outflows for a period.[1] The statement of cash flows provides useful information about a company's ability to do the following:

- Generate cash from operations
- Maintain and expand its operating capacity
- Meet its financial obligations
- Pay dividends

The statement of cash flows is used by managers in evaluating past operations and in planning future investing and financing activities. It is also used by external users such as investors and creditors to assess a company's profit potential and ability to pay its debt and pay dividends.

Note:
The statement of cash flows reports cash flows from operating, investing, and financing activities.

The statement of cash flows reports three types of cash flow activities, as follows:

1. **Cash flows from operating activities** are the cash flows from transactions that affect the net income of the company.

   Example: Purchase and sale of merchandise by a retailer.

2. **Cash flows from investing activities** are the cash flows from transactions that affect investments in the noncurrent assets of the company.

   Example: Purchase and sale of fixed assets, such as equipment and buildings.

[1] As used in this chapter, *cash* refers to cash and cash equivalents. Examples of cash equivalents include short-term, highly liquid investments, such as money market accounts, bank certificates of deposit, and U.S. Treasury bills.

3. **Cash flows from financing activities** are the cash flows from transactions that affect the debt and equity of the company.

   Example: Issuing or retiring equity and debt securities.

The cash flows are reported in the statement of cash flows as follows:

Cash flows from operating activities	$XXX
Cash flows from investing activities	XXX
Cash flows from financing activities	XXX
Net increase or decrease in cash for the period	$XXX
Cash at the beginning of the period	XXX
Cash at the end of the period	$XXX

The ending cash on the statement of cash flows equals the cash reported on the company's balance sheet at the end of the year.

Exhibit 1 illustrates the sources (increases) and uses (decreases) of cash by each of the three cash flow activities. A *source* of cash causes the cash flow to increase and is called a *cash inflow*. A *use* of cash causes cash flow to decrease and is called *cash outflow*.

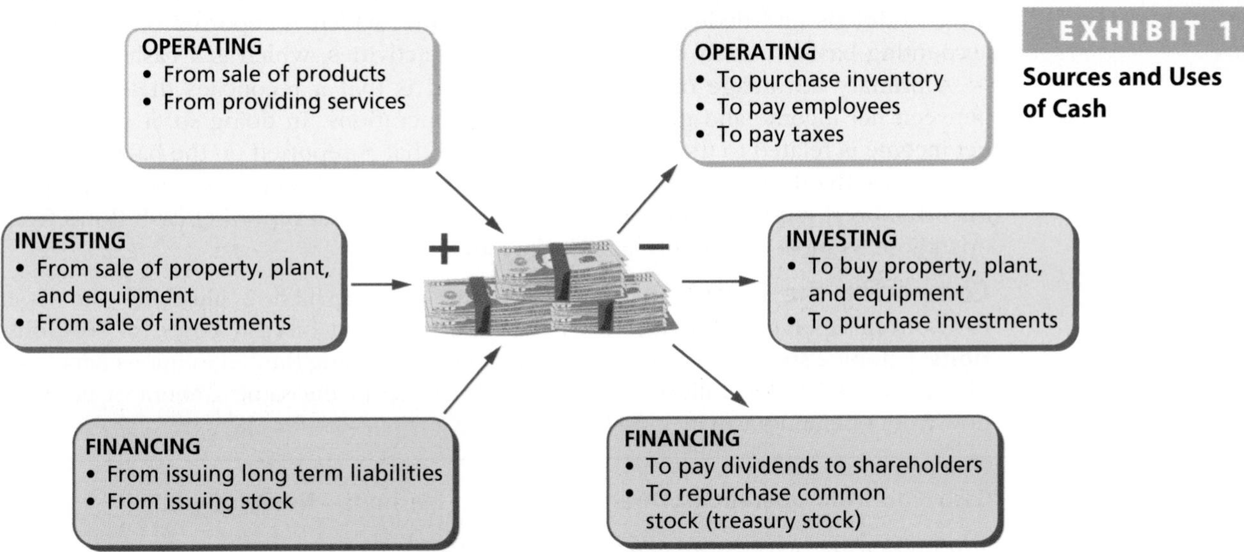

EXHIBIT 1

Sources and Uses of Cash

Cash Flows from Operating Activities

Cash flows from operating activities reports the cash inflows and outflows from a company's day-to-day operations. Companies may select one of two alternative methods for reporting cash flows from operating activities in the statement of cash flows:

- The direct method
- The indirect method

Both methods result in the same amount of cash flows from operating activities. They differ in the way they report cash flows from operating activities.

In fiscal 2012, **Google Inc.** generated $16.6 billion in net cash flow from operating activities.

The Direct Method The **direct method** reports operating cash inflows (receipts) and cash outflows (payments) as follows:

Cash flows from operating activities:		
Cash received from customers		$XXX
Less: Cash payments for merchandise	$XXX	
Cash payments for operating expenses	XXX	
Cash payments for interest	XXX	
Cash payments for income taxes	XXX	XXX
Net cash flow from operating activities		$XXX

The primary operating cash inflow is cash received from customers. The primary operating cash outflows are cash payments for merchandise, operating expenses, interest, and income tax payments. The cash received from operating activities less the cash payments for operating activities is the net cash flow from operating activities.

The primary advantage of the direct method is that it *directly* reports cash receipts and cash payments in the statement of cash flows. Its primary disadvantage is that these data may not be readily available in the accounting records. Thus, the direct method is normally more costly to prepare and, as a result, is used infrequently in practice.

The Indirect Method The **indirect method** reports cash flows from operating activities by beginning with net income and adjusting it for revenues and expenses that do not involve the receipt or payment of cash, as follows:

Cash flows from operating activities:		
Net income	$XXX	
Adjustments to reconcile net income to net cash flow from operating activities	XXX	
Net cash flow from operating activities		$XXX

The adjustments to reconcile net income to net cash flow from operating activities include such items as depreciation and gains or losses on fixed assets. Changes in current operating assets and liabilities such as accounts receivable or accounts payable are also added or deducted, depending on their effect on cash flows. In effect, these additions and deductions adjust net income, which is reported on an accrual accounting basis, to cash flows from operating activities, which is a cash basis.

A primary advantage of the indirect method is that it reconciles the differences between net income and net cash flows from operations. In doing so, it shows how net income is related to the ending cash balance that is reported on the balance sheet.

Because the data are readily available, the indirect method is less costly to prepare than the direct method. As a result, the indirect method of reporting cash flows from operations is most commonly used in practice.

Comparing the Direct and Indirect Methods Exhibit 2 illustrates the Cash Flows from Operating Activities section of the statement of cash flows for **NetSolutions**. Exhibit 2 shows the direct and indirect methods using the NetSolutions data from Chapter 1. As Exhibit 2 illustrates, both methods report the same amount of net cash flow from operating activities, $2,900.

EXHIBIT 2 **Cash Flow from Operations: Direct and Indirect Methods—NetSolutions**

Direct Method

Cash flows from operating activities:	
Cash received from customers	$7,500
Deduct cash payments for expenses and payments to creditors	4,600
Net cash flow from operating activities	$2,900

Indirect Method

Cash flows from operating activities:	
Net income	$3,050
Add increase in accounts payable	400
	$3,450
Deduct increase in supplies	550
Net cash flow from operating activities	$2,900

the same

Business  Connection

CASH CRUNCH!

In late 2011, **American Airlines**' deteriorating cash flow situation forced the company to file for bankruptcy. At the time, the airline had generated $235 million in net cash flow from operating activities for the nine-month period ending September 31, 2011, while spending $1.1 billion on additional property, plant, and equipment. The property, plant, and equipment purchases were paid for by issuing additional debt. By Thanksgiving 2011, it became clear that the company's weak net cash flow from operating activities would not be sufficient to pay off the airline's massive debt. On November 29, 2011, the airline filed for bankruptcy. In February 2013, American and **U.S. Airways** announced plans to merge, creating the largest airline in the world.

Source: M. Curriden and N. Posgate, "American Airlines bankruptcy, merger deals were complex, expensive," *Dallas Morning News*, February 17, 2013.

Cash Flows from Investing Activities

Cash flows from investing activities show the cash inflows and outflows related to changes in a company's long-term assets. Cash flows from investing activities are reported on the statement of cash flows as follows:

Cash flows from investing activities:		
Cash inflows from investing activities	$XXX	
Less cash used for investing activities	XXX	
Net cash flows from investing activities		$XXX

Cash inflows from investing activities normally arise from selling fixed assets, investments, and intangible assets. Cash outflows normally include payments to purchase fixed assets, investments, and intangible assets.

Cash Flows from Financing Activities

Cash flows from financing activities show the cash inflows and outflows related to changes in a company's long-term liabilities and stockholders' equity. Cash flows from financing activities are reported on the statement of cash flows as follows:

In March 2013, U.S. companies in the S&P 500 index were expected to pay $300 billion in dividends to investors during 2013.

Cash flows from financing activities:		
Cash inflows from financing activities	$XXX	
Less cash used for financing activities	XXX	
Net cash flow from financing activities		$XXX

Cash inflows from financing activities normally arise from issuing long-term debt or equity securities. For example, issuing bonds, notes payable, preferred stock, and common stock creates cash inflows from financing activities. Cash outflows from financing activities include paying cash dividends, repaying long-term debt, and acquiring treasury stock.

Noncash Investing and Financing Activities

A company may enter into transactions involving investing and financing activities that do not *directly* affect cash. For example, a company may issue common stock to retire long-term debt. Although this transaction does not directly affect cash, it does eliminate future cash payments for interest and for paying the bonds when they mature. Because such transactions *indirectly* affect cash flows, they are reported in a separate section of the statement of cash flows. This section usually appears at the bottom of the statement of cash flows.

Format of the Statement of Cash Flows

The statement of cash flows presents the cash flows generated by, or used for, the three activities previously discussed: operating, investing, and financing. These three activities are always reported in the same order, following the format illustrated in Exhibit 3.

EXHIBIT 3

Format of the Statement of Cash Flows

COMPANY NAME
Statement of Cash Flows
For the Year Ended xxxx

Cash flows from operating activities		
(List of individual items, as illustrated in Exhibit 1)	XXX	
Net cash flows from operating activities		$XXX
Cash flows from investing activities		
(List of individual items, as illustrated in Exhibit 1)	XXX	
Net cash flows from (used for) investing activities		XXX
Cash flows from financing activities		
(List of individual items, as illustrated in Exhibit 1)	XXX	
Net cash flows from (used for) financing activities		XXX
Increase (decrease) in cash		$XXX
Cash at the beginning of the period		XXX
Cash at the end of the period		$XXX
Noncash investing and financing activites		$XXX

Example Exercise 13-1 Classifying Cash Flows

Identify whether each of the following would be reported as an operating, investing, or financing activity in the statement of cash flows:

a. Purchase of patent
b. Payment of cash dividend
c. Disposal of equipment
d. Cash sales
e. Purchase of treasury stock
f. Payment of wages expense

Follow My Example 13-1

a. Investing
b. Financing
c. Investing
d. Operating
e. Financing
f. Operating

Practice Exercises: PE 13-1A, PE 13-1B

No Cash Flow per Share

Cash flow per share is sometimes reported in the financial press. As reported, cash flow per share is normally computed as *cash flow from operations divided by the number of common shares outstanding.* However, such reporting may be misleading because of the following:

- Users may misinterpret cash flow per share as the per-share amount available for dividends. This would not be the case if the cash generated by operations is required for repaying loans or for reinvesting in the business.
- Users may misinterpret cash flow per share as equivalent to (or better than) earnings per share.

For these reasons, the financial statements, including the statement of cash flows, should not report cash flow per share.

OBJ 2 Prepare a statement of cash flows, using the indirect method.

Preparing the Statement of Cash Flows—The Indirect Method

The indirect method of reporting cash flows from operating activities uses the logic that a change in any balance sheet account (including cash) can be analyzed in terms of changes in the other balance sheet accounts. Thus, by analyzing changes in noncash balance sheet accounts, any change in the cash account can be *indirectly* determined.

To illustrate, the accounting equation can be solved for cash as follows:

$$\text{Assets} = \text{Liabilities} + \text{Stockholders' Equity}$$
$$\text{Cash} + \text{Noncash Assets} = \text{Liabilities} + \text{Stockholders' Equity}$$
$$\text{Cash} = \text{Liabilities} + \text{Stockholders' Equity} - \text{Noncash Assets}$$

Therefore, any change in the cash account can be determined by analyzing changes in the liability, stockholders' equity, and noncash asset accounts as follows:

$$\textit{Change} \text{ in Cash} = \textit{Change} \text{ in Liabilities} + \textit{Change} \text{ in Stockholders' Equity} - \textit{Change} \text{ in Noncash Assets}$$

Under the indirect method, there is no order in which the balance sheet accounts must be analyzed. However, net income (or net loss) is the first amount reported on the statement of cash flows. Because net income (or net loss) is a component of any change in Retained Earnings, the first account normally analyzed is Retained Earnings.

To illustrate the indirect method, the income statement and comparative balance sheets for **Rundell Inc.**, shown in Exhibit 4, are used. Ledger accounts and other data supporting the income statement and balance sheet are presented as needed.[2]

EXHIBIT 4

Income Statement and Comparative Balance Sheet

Rundell Inc.
Income Statement
For the Year Ended December 31, 2016

Sales		$1,180,000
Cost of merchandise sold		790,000
Gross profit		$ 390,000
Operating expenses:		
Depreciation expense	$ 7,000	
Other operating expenses	196,000	
Total operating expenses		203,000
Income from operations		$ 187,000
Other income:		
Gain on sale of land	$ 12,000	
Other expense:		
Interest expense	8,000	4,000
Income before income tax		$ 191,000
Income tax expense		83,000
Net income		$ 108,000

Rundell Inc.
Comparative Balance Sheet
December 31, 2016 and 2015

	2016	2015	Increase Decrease*
Assets			
Cash	$ 97,500	$ 26,000	$ 71,500
Accounts receivable (net)	74,000	65,000	9,000
Inventories	172,000	180,000	8,000*
Land	80,000	125,000	45,000*
Building	260,000	200,000	60,000
Accumulated depreciation—building	(65,300)	(58,300)	7,000**
Total assets	$618,200	$537,700	$ 80,500
Liabilities			
Accounts payable (merchandise creditors)	$ 43,500	$ 46,700	$ 3,200*
Accrued expenses payable (operating expenses)	26,500	24,300	2,200
Income taxes payable	7,900	8,400	500*
Dividends payable	14,000	10,000	4,000
Bonds payable	100,000	150,000	50,000*
Total liabilities	$191,900	$239,400	$ 47,500*
Stockholders' Equity			
Common stock ($2 par)	$ 24,000	$ 16,000	$ 8,000
Paid-in capital in excess of par	120,000	80,000	40,000
Retained earnings	282,300	202,300	80,000
Total stockholders' equity	$426,300	$298,300	$128,000
Total liabilities and stockholders' equity	$618,200	$537,700	$ 80,500

**There is a $7,000 increase to Accumulated Depreciation—Building, which is a contra asset account. As a result, the $7,000 increase in this account must be subtracted in summing to the increase in Total assets of $80,500.

[2] An appendix that discusses using a spreadsheet (work sheet) as an aid in assembling data for the statement of cash flows is presented at the end of this chapter. This appendix illustrates the use of this spreadsheet in reporting cash flows from operating activities using the indirect method.

Retained Earnings

The comparative balance sheet for **Rundell Inc.** shows that retained earnings increased $80,000 during the year. The retained earnings account that follows indicates how this change occurred:

Account *Retained Earnings* — Account No.

Date		Item	Debit	Credit	Balance Debit	Balance Credit
2016 Jan.	1	Balance				202,300
Dec.	31	Net income		108,000		310,300
	31	Cash dividends	28,000			282,300

The retained earnings account indicates that the $80,000 ($108,000 − $28,000) change resulted from net income of $108,000 and cash dividends of $28,000. The net income of $108,000 is the first amount reported in the Cash Flows from Operating Activities section.

Adjustments to Net Income

The net income of $108,000 reported by **Rundell Inc.** does not equal the cash flows from operating activities for the period. This is because net income is determined using the accrual method of accounting.

Under the accrual method of accounting, revenues and expenses are recorded at different times from when cash is received or paid. For example, merchandise may be sold on account and the cash received at a later date. Likewise, insurance premiums may be paid in the current period but expensed in a following period.

Thus, under the indirect method, adjustments to net income must be made to determine cash flows from operating activities. The typical adjustments to net income are shown in Exhibit 5.[3]

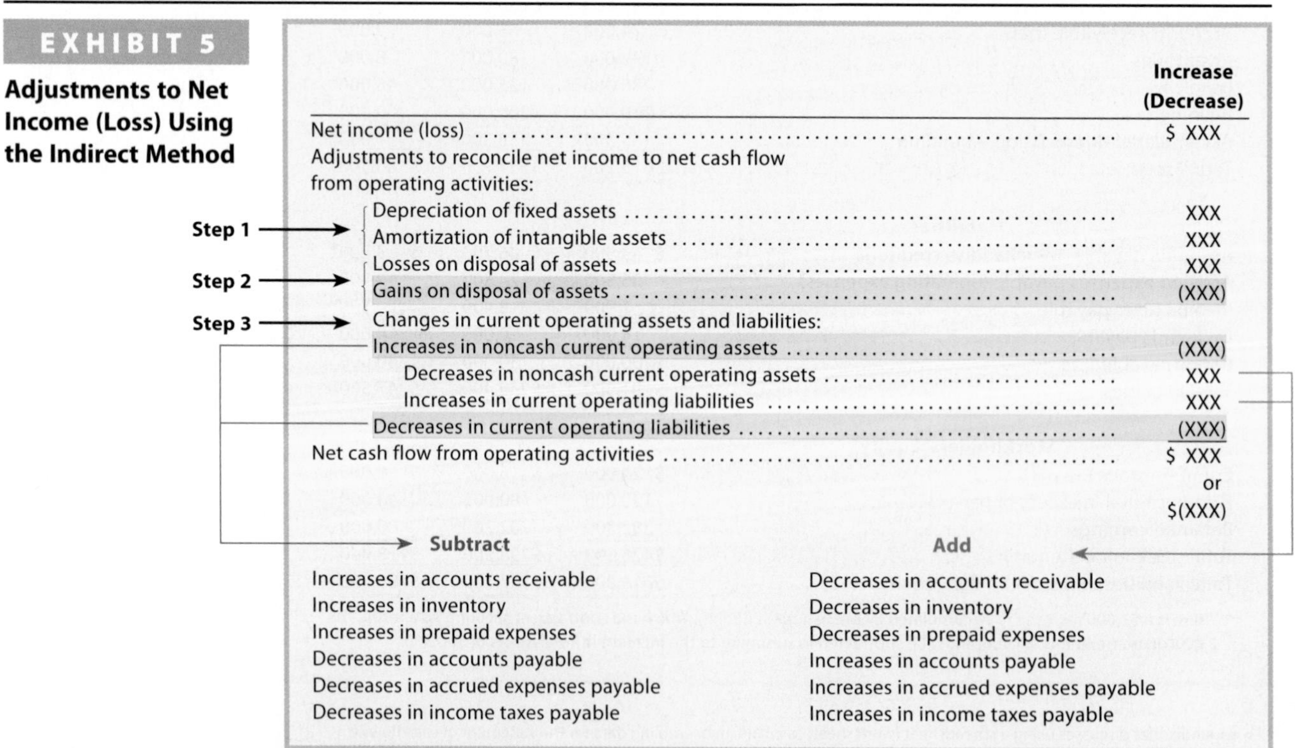

EXHIBIT 5

Adjustments to Net Income (Loss) Using the Indirect Method

		Increase (Decrease)
	Net income (loss)	$ XXX
	Adjustments to reconcile net income to net cash flow from operating activities:	
Step 1	Depreciation of fixed assets	XXX
	Amortization of intangible assets	XXX
Step 2	Losses on disposal of assets	XXX
	Gains on disposal of assets	(XXX)
Step 3	Changes in current operating assets and liabilities:	
	Increases in noncash current operating assets	(XXX)
	Decreases in noncash current operating assets	XXX
	Increases in current operating liabilities	XXX
	Decreases in current operating liabilities	(XXX)
	Net cash flow from operating activities	$ XXX or $(XXX)

Subtract	Add
Increases in accounts receivable	Decreases in accounts receivable
Increases in inventory	Decreases in inventory
Increases in prepaid expenses	Decreases in prepaid expenses
Decreases in accounts payable	Increases in accounts payable
Decreases in accrued expenses payable	Increases in accrued expenses payable
Decreases in income taxes payable	Increases in income taxes payable

[3] Other items that also require adjustments to net income to obtain cash flows from operating activities include amortization of bonds payable discounts (add), losses on debt retirement (add), amortization of bonds payable premiums (deduct), and gains on retirement of debt (deduct).

Net income is normally adjusted to cash flows from operating activities, using the following steps:

- Step 1. Expenses that do not affect cash are added. Such expenses decrease net income but do not involve cash payments and, thus, are added to net income.

  Example: Depreciation of fixed assets and amortization of intangible assets are added to net income.
- Step 2. Losses on the disposal of assets are added and gains on the disposal of assets are deducted. The disposal (sale) of assets is an investing activity rather than an operating activity. However, such losses and gains are reported as part of net income. As a result, any *losses* on disposal of assets are *added* back to net income. Likewise, any *gains* on disposal of assets are *deducted* from net income.

  Example: Land costing $100,000 is sold for $90,000. The loss of $10,000 is added back to net income.
- Step 3. Changes in current operating assets and liabilities are added or deducted as follows:
  - Increases in noncash current operating assets are deducted.
  - Decreases in noncash current operating assets are added.
  - Increases in current operating liabilities are added.
  - Decreases in current operating liabilities are deducted.

  Example: A sale of $10,000 on account increases sales, accounts receivable, and net income by $10,000. However, cash is not affected. Thus, the $10,000 increase in accounts receivable is deducted. Similar adjustments are required for the changes in the other current asset and liability accounts, such as inventory, prepaid expenses, accounts payable, accrued expenses payable, and income taxes payable, as shown in Exhibit 5.

Example Exercise 13-2 Adjustments to Net Income—Indirect Method

Omni Corporation's accumulated depreciation increased by $12,000, while $3,400 of patent amortization was recognized between balance sheet dates. There were no purchases or sales of depreciable or intangible assets during the year. In addition, the income statement showed a gain of $4,100 from the sale of land. Reconcile Omni's net income of $50,000 to net cash flow from operating activities.

Follow My Example 13-2

Net income	$50,000
Adjustments to reconcile net income to net cash flow from operating activities:	
Depreciation	12,000
Amortization of patents	3,400
Gain from sale of land	(4,100)
Net cash flow from operating activities	$61,300

Practice Exercises: PE 13-2A, PE 13-2B

The Cash Flows from Operating Activities section of **Rundell Inc.'s** statement of cash flows is shown in Exhibit 6.

Rundell's net income of $108,000 is converted to cash flows from operating activities of $100,500 as follows:

Step 1. Add depreciation of $7,000.

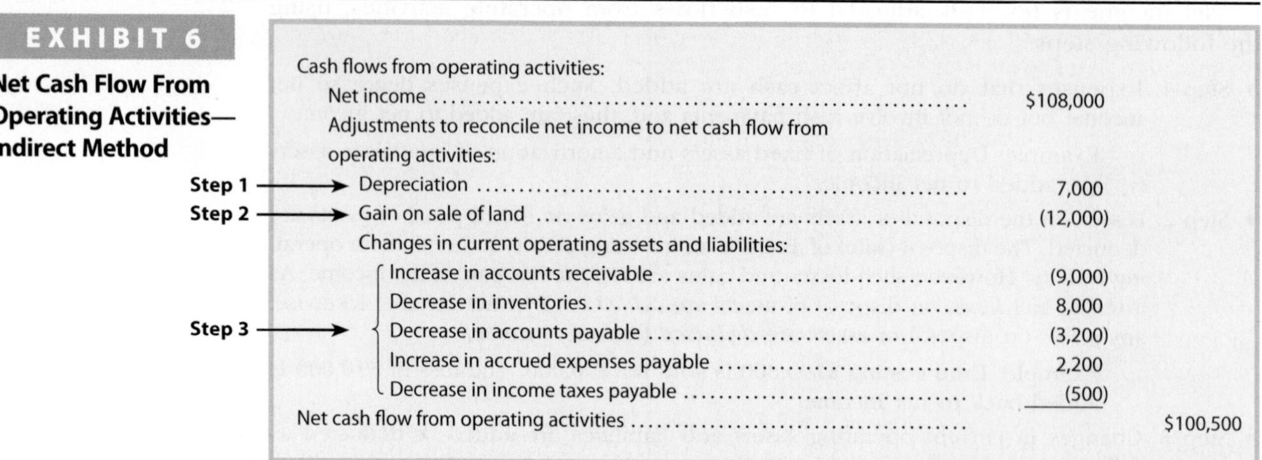

EXHIBIT 6

Net Cash Flow From Operating Activities—Indirect Method

Cash flows from operating activities:			
Net income			$108,000
Adjustments to reconcile net income to net cash flow from operating activities:			
Step 1 →	Depreciation	7,000	
Step 2 →	Gain on sale of land	(12,000)	
	Changes in current operating assets and liabilities:		
Step 3 →	Increase in accounts receivable	(9,000)	
Step 3 →	Decrease in inventories	8,000	
Step 3 →	Decrease in accounts payable	(3,200)	
Step 3 →	Increase in accrued expenses payable	2,200	
Step 3 →	Decrease in income taxes payable	(500)	
Net cash flow from operating activities			$100,500

Analysis: The comparative balance sheet in Exhibit 4 indicates that Accumulated Depreciation—Building increased by $7,000. The following account indicates that depreciation for the year was $7,000 for the building:

Account *Accumulated Depreciation—Building* — Account No.

Date		Item	Debit	Credit	Balance Debit	Balance Credit
2016 Jan.	1	Balance				58,300
Dec.	31	Depreciation for year		7,000		65,300

Step 2. Deduct the gain on the sale of land of $12,000.
Analysis: The income statement in Exhibit 4 reports a gain of $12,000 from the sale of land. The proceeds, which include the gain, are reported in the Investing section of the statement of cash flows.[4] Thus, the gain of $12,000 is deducted from net income in determining cash flows from operating activities.

Step 3. Add and deduct changes in current operating assets and liabilities excluding cash.
Analysis: The increases and decreases in the current operating asset and current liability accounts excluding cash are as follows:

Accounts	December 31, 2016	December 31, 2015	Increase Decrease*
Accounts Receivable (net)	$ 74,000	$ 65,000	$9,000
Inventories	172,000	180,000	8,000*
Accounts Payable (merchandise creditors)	43,500	46,700	3,200*
Accrued Expenses Payable (operating expenses)	26,500	24,300	2,200
Income Taxes Payable	7,900	8,400	500*

Accounts receivable (net): The $9,000 increase is deducted from net income. This is because the $9,000 increase in accounts receivable indicates that sales on account were $9,000 more than the cash received from customers. Thus, sales (and net income) includes $9,000 that was not received in cash during the year.

Inventories: The $8,000 decrease is added to net income. This is because the $8,000 decrease in inventories indicates that the cost of merchandise *sold* exceeds the cost of the merchandise *purchased* during the year by $8,000. In other words, the cost of merchandise sold includes $8,000 of goods from inventory that were not purchased (used cash) during the year.

Accounts payable (merchandise creditors): The $3,200 decrease is deducted from net income. This is because a decrease in accounts payable indicates that the cash

[4] The reporting of the proceeds (cash flows) from the sale of land as part of investing activities is discussed later in this chapter.

payments to merchandise creditors exceed the merchandise *purchased on account* by $3,200. Therefore, the cost of merchandise sold is $3,200 less than the cash paid to merchandise creditors during the year.

Accrued expenses payable (operating expenses): The $2,200 increase is added to net income. This is because an increase in accrued expenses payable indicates that operating expenses exceed the cash payments for operating expenses by $2,200. In other words, operating expenses reported on the income statement include $2,200 that did not require a cash outflow during the year.

Income taxes payable: The $500 decrease is deducted from net income. This is because a decrease in income taxes payable indicates that taxes paid exceed the amount of taxes incurred during the year by $500. In other words, the amount reported on the income statement for income tax expense is less than the amount paid by $500.

Example Exercise 13-3 Changes in Current Operating Assets and Liabilities—Indirect Method

Victor Corporation's current operating assets and liabilities from the company's comparative balance sheet were as follows:

	Dec. 31, 2016	Dec. 31, 2015
Accounts receivable	$ 6,500	$ 4,900
Inventory	12,300	15,000
Accounts payable	4,800	5,200
Dividends payable	5,000	4,000

Adjust Victor's net income of $70,000 for changes in operating assets and liabilities to arrive at cash flows from operating activities.

Follow My Example 13-3

Net income	$70,000
Adjustments to reconcile net income to net cash flow from operating activities:	
Changes in current operating assets and liabilities:	
Increase in accounts receivable	(1,600)
Decrease in inventory	2,700
Decrease in accounts payable	(400)
Net cash flow from operating activities	$70,700

Note: The change in dividends payable impacts the cash paid for dividends, which is disclosed under financing activities.

Practice Exercises: PE 13-3A, PE 13-3B

Using the preceding analyses, Rundell's net income of $108,000 is converted to cash flows from operating activities of $100,500 as shown in Exhibit 6.

Integrity, Objectivity, and Ethics in Business

CREDIT POLICY AND CASH FLOW

Investors frequently use net cash flow from operating activities to assess a company's financial health. If a company is financially healthy, net cash flow from operating activities should be roughly consistent with accrual basis net income. Questions arise, however, when a company's net cash flow from operating activities significantly lags net income. There are two scenarios which can cause this to happen:

- Sales on account are never collected in cash.
- Large cash purchases for inventory are never sold, or sell at a very slow pace.

Both of these scenarios increase net income, without a corresponding increase in net cash flow from operating activities. Prudent investors are often skeptical when they observe these scenarios and tend to avoid these types of investments until the cash flows become clear.

Source: Argersinger, M., "How Companies Fake It (With Cash Flow)," *Daily Finance Investor Center*, July 17, 2011.

Example Exercise 13-4 Cash Flows from Operating Activities—Indirect Method

OBJ 2

Omicron Inc. reported the following data:

Net income	$120,000
Depreciation expense	12,000
Loss on disposal of equipment	15,000
Increase in accounts receivable	5,000
Decrease in accounts payable	2,000

Prepare the Cash Flows from Operating Activities section of the statement of cash flows, using the indirect method.

Follow My Example 13-4

Cash flows from operating activities:		
Net income	$120,000	
Adjustments to reconcile net income to net cash flow from operating activities:		
Depreciation expense	12,000	
Loss on disposal of equipment	15,000	
Changes in current operating assets and liabilities:		
Increase in accounts receivable	(5,000)	
Decrease in accounts payable	(2,000)	
Net cash flow from operating activities		$140,000

Practice Exercises: PE 13-4A, PE 13-4B

Dividends

The retained earnings account of **Rundell Inc.** indicates cash dividends of $28,000 were declared during the year. However, the following dividends payable account indicates that only $24,000 of dividends were paid during the year:

Account *Dividends Payable* Account No.

Date		Item	Debit	Credit	Balance Debit	Balance Credit
2016 Jan.	1	Balance				10,000
	10	Cash paid	10,000		—	—
June	20	Dividends declared		14,000		14,000
July	10	Cash paid	14,000		—	—
Dec.	20	Dividends declared		14,000		14,000

Because dividend payments are a financing activity, the dividend payment of $24,000 is reported in the Financing Activities section of the statement of cash flows, as follows:

Cash flows from financing activities:	
Cash paid for dividends	$24,000

Common Stock

The common stock account of **Rundell Inc.** increased by $8,000, and the paid-in capital in excess of par—common stock account increased by $40,000, as follows:

Account *Common Stock*						Account No.
					Balance	
Date		Item	Debit	Credit	Debit	Credit
2016 Jan.	1	Balance				16,000
Nov.	1	4,000 shares issued for cash		8,000		24,000

Account *Paid-In Capital in Excess of Par—Common Stock*						Account No.
					Balance	
Date		Item	Debit	Credit	Debit	Credit
2016 Jan.	1	Balance				80,000
Nov.	1	4,000 shares issued for cash		40,000		120,000

These increases were from issuing 4,000 shares of common stock for $12 per share. This cash inflow is reported in the Financing Activities section as follows:

Cash flows from financing activities:	
Cash received from sale of common stock	$48,000

Bonds Payable

The bonds payable account of **Rundell Inc.** decreased by $50,000, as follows:

Account *Bonds Payable*						Account No.
					Balance	
Date		Item	Debit	Credit	Debit	Credit
2016 Jan.	1	Balance				150,000
June	1	Retired by payment of cash at face amount	50,000			100,000

This decrease is from retiring the bonds by a cash payment for their face amount. This cash outflow is reported in the Financing Activities section as follows:

Cash flows from financing activities:	
Cash paid to retire bonds payable	$50,000

Building

The building account of **Rundell Inc.** increased by $60,000, and the accumulated depreciation—building account increased by $7,000, as follows:

Account *Building*						Account No.
					Balance	
Date		**Item**	**Debit**	**Credit**	**Debit**	**Credit**
2016 Jan.	1	Balance			200,000	
Dec.	27	Purchased for cash	60,000		260,000	

Account *Accumulated Depreciation—Building*						Account No.
					Balance	
Date		**Item**	**Debit**	**Credit**	**Debit**	**Credit**
2016 Jan.	1	Balance				58,300
Dec.	31	Depreciation for the year		7,000		65,300

The purchase of a building for cash of $60,000 is reported as an outflow of cash in the Investing Activities section as follows:

Cash flows from investing activities:	
Cash paid for purchase of building	$60,000

The credit in the accumulated depreciation—building account represents depreciation expense for the year. This depreciation expense of $7,000 on the building was added to net income in determining cash flows from operating activities, as reported in Exhibit 6.

Land

The $45,000 decline in the land account of **Rundell Inc.** was from two transactions, as follows:

Account *Land*						Account No.
					Balance	
Date		**Item**	**Debit**	**Credit**	**Debit**	**Credit**
2016 Jan.	1	Balance			125,000	
June	8	Sold for $72,000 cash		60,000	65,000	
Oct.	12	Purchased for $15,000 cash	15,000		80,000	

The June 8 transaction is the sale of land with a cost of $60,000 for $72,000 in cash. The $72,000 proceeds from the sale are reported in the Investing Activities section as follows:

Cash flows from investing activities:	
Cash received from sale of land	$72,000

The proceeds of $72,000 include the $12,000 gain on the sale of land and the $60,000 cost (book value) of the land. As shown in Exhibit 6, the $12,000 gain is deducted from net income in the Cash Flows from Operating Activities section. This is so that the $12,000 cash inflow related to the gain is not included twice as a cash inflow.

The October 12 transaction is the purchase of land for cash of $15,000. This transaction is reported as an outflow of cash in the Investing Activities section as follows:

Cash flows from investing activities:	
Cash paid for purchase of land	$15,000

Example Exercise 13-5 Land Transactions on the Statement of Cash Flows

OBJ 2

Alpha Corporation purchased land for $125,000. Later in the year, the company sold a different piece of land with a book value of $165,000 for $200,000. How are the effects of these transactions reported on the statement of cash flows?

Follow My Example 13-5

The gain on the sale of the land is deducted from net income, as follows:

Gain on sale of land	$ (35,000)

The purchase and sale of land is reported as part of cash flows from investing activities, as follows:

Cash received from sale of land	$200,000
Cash paid for purchase of land	(125,000)

Practice Exercises: PE 13-5A, PE 13-5B

Preparing the Statement of Cash Flows

The statement of cash flows for **Rundell Inc.**, using the indirect method, is shown in Exhibit 7. The statement of cash flows indicates that cash increased by $71,500 during the year. The most significant increase in net cash flows ($100,500) was from operating activities. The most significant use of cash ($26,000) was for financing activities. The ending balance of cash on December 31, 2016, is $97,500. This ending cash balance is also reported on the December 31, 2016, balance sheet shown in Exhibit 4.

EXHIBIT 7

Statement of Cash Flows—Indirect Method

Rundell Inc.
Statement of Cash Flows
For the Year Ended December 31, 2016

Cash flows from operating activities:			
Net income		$108,000	
Adjustments to reconcile net income to net cash flow from operating activities:			
Depreciation		7,000	
Gain on sale of land		(12,000)	
Changes in current operating assets and liabilities:			
Increase in accounts receivable		(9,000)	
Decrease in inventories		8,000	
Decrease in accounts payable		(3,200)	
Increase in accrued expenses payable		2,200	
Decrease in income taxes payable		(500)	
Net cash flow from operating activities			$100,500
Cash flows from investing activities:			
Cash received from sale of land		$ 72,000	
Less: Cash paid for purchase of land	$15,000		
Cash paid for purchase of building	60,000	75,000	
Net cash flow used for investing activities			(3,000)
Cash flows from financing activities:			
Cash received from sale of common stock		$ 48,000	
Less: Cash paid to retire bonds payable	$50,000		
Cash paid for dividends	24,000	74,000	
Net cash flow used for financing activities			(26,000)
Increase in cash			$ 71,500
Cash at the beginning of the year			26,000
Cash at the end of the year			$ 97,500

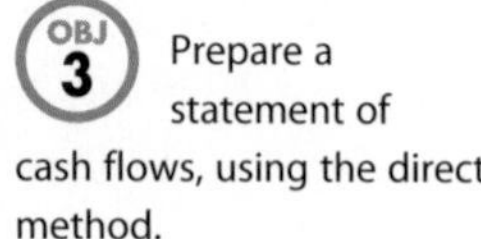

Prepare a statement of cash flows, using the direct method.

Preparing the Statement of Cash Flows—The Direct Method

The direct method reports cash flows from operating activities as follows:

Cash flows from operating activities:		
Cash received from customers		$ XXX
Less: Cash payments for merchandise	$ XXX	
Cash payments for operating expenses	XXX	
Cash payments for interest	XXX	
Cash payments for income taxes	XXX	XXX
Net cash flow from operating activities		$ XXX

The Cash Flows from Investing and Financing Activities sections of the statement of cash flows are exactly the same under both the direct and indirect methods. The amount of net cash flow from operating activities is also the same, but the manner in which it is reported is different.

Under the direct method, the income statement is adjusted to cash flows from operating activities as shown in Exhibit 8.

EXHIBIT 8

Converting Income Statement to Cash Flows from Operating Activities using the Direct Method

Income Statement	Adjusted to	Cash Flows from Operating Activities
Sales	→	Cash received from customers
Cost of merchandise sold	→	Cash payments for merchandise
Operating expenses:		
Depreciation expense	N/A	N/A
Other operating expenses	→	Cash payments for operating expenses
Gain on sale of land	N/A	N/A
Interest expense	→	Cash payments for interest
Income tax expense	→	Cash payments for income taxes
Net income	→	Net cash flow from operating activities

N/A—Not applicable

As shown in Exhibit 8, depreciation expense is not adjusted or reported as part of cash flows from operating activities. This is because deprecation expense does not involve a cash outflow. The gain on the sale of the land is also not adjusted and is not reported as part of cash flows from operating activities. This is because the cash flow from operating activities is determined directly, rather than by reconciling net income. The cash proceeds from the sale of the land are reported as an investing activity.

To illustrate the direct method, the income statement and comparative balance sheet for Rundell Inc., shown in Exhibit 4, are used.

Cash Received from Customers

The income statement (shown in Exhibit 4) of **Rundell Inc.** reports sales of $1,180,000. To determine the cash received from customers, the $1,180,000 is adjusted for any increase or decrease in accounts receivable. The adjustment is summarized in Exhibit 9.

EXHIBIT 9

Determining the Cash Received from Customers

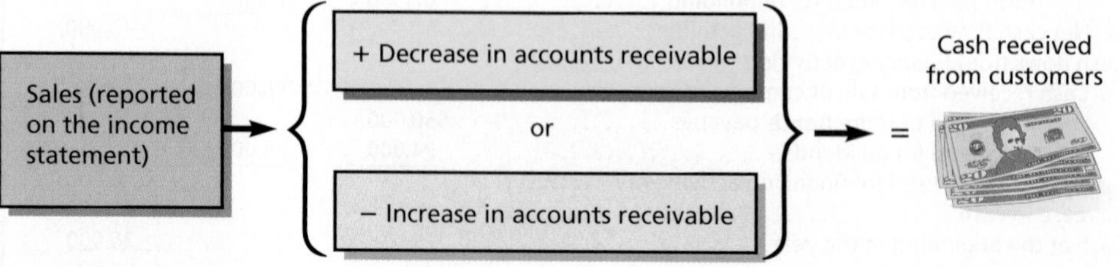

The cash received from customers is $1,171,000, computed as follows:

Sales	$1,180,000
Less increase in accounts receivable	9,000
Cash received from customers	$1,171,000

The increase of $9,000 in accounts receivable (shown in Exhibit 4) during 2016 indicates that sales on account exceeded cash received from customers by $9,000. In other words, sales include $9,000 that did not result in a cash inflow during the year. Thus, $9,000 is deducted from sales to determine the cash received from customers.

Example Exercise 13-6 Cash Received from Customers—Direct Method

Sales reported on the income statement were $350,000. The accounts receivable balance declined $8,000 over the year. Determine the amount of cash received from customers.

Follow My Example 13-6

Sales	$350,000
Add decrease in accounts receivable	8,000
Cash received from customers	$358,000

Practice Exercises: PE 13-6A, PE 13-6B

Cash Payments for Merchandise

The income statement (shown in Exhibit 4) for **Rundell Inc.** reports cost of merchandise sold of $790,000. To determine the cash payments for merchandise, the $790,000 is adjusted for any increases or decreases in inventories and accounts payable. Assuming the accounts payable are owed to merchandise suppliers, the adjustment is summarized in Exhibit 10.

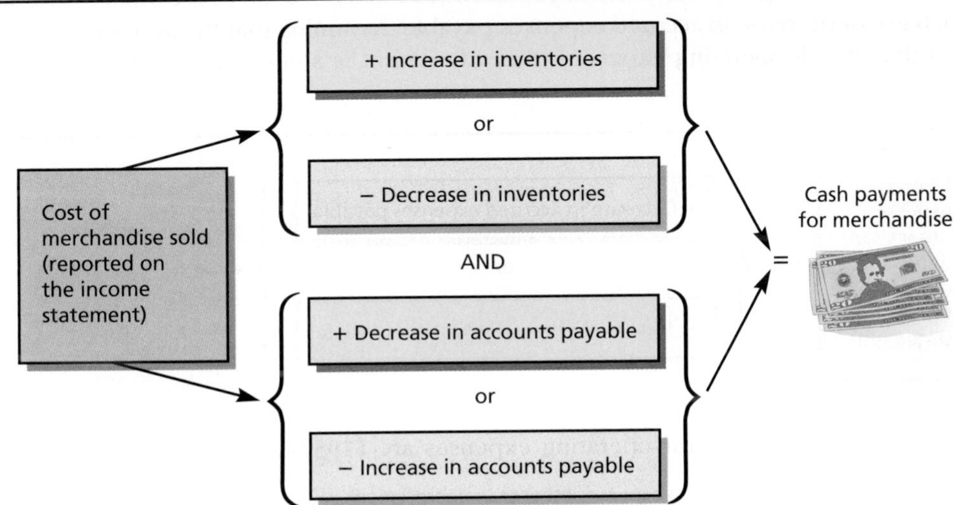

EXHIBIT 10

Determining the Cash Payments for Merchandise

The cash payments for merchandise are $785,200, computed as follows:

Cost of merchandise sold	$790,000
Deduct decrease in inventories	(8,000)
Add decrease in accounts payable	3,200
Cash payments for merchandise	$785,200

The $8,000 decrease in inventories (from Exhibit 4) indicates that the merchandise sold exceeded the cost of the merchandise purchased by $8,000. In other words, the cost of merchandise sold includes $8,000 of goods sold from inventory that did not require a cash outflow during the year. Thus, $8,000 is deducted from the cost of merchandise sold in determining the cash payments for merchandise.

The $3,200 decrease in accounts payable (from Exhibit 4) indicates that cash payments for merchandise were $3,200 more than the purchases on account during 2016. Therefore, $3,200 is added to the cost of merchandise sold in determining the cash payments for merchandise.

Example Exercise 13-7 Cash Payments for Merchandise—Direct Method

The cost of merchandise sold reported on the income statement was $145,000. The accounts payable balance increased by $4,000, and the inventory balance increased by $9,000 over the year. Determine the amount of cash paid for merchandise.

Follow My Example 13-7

Cost of merchandise sold	$145,000
Add increase in inventories	9,000
Deduct increase in accounts payable	(4,000)
Cash paid for merchandise	$150,000

Practice Exercises: PE 13-7A, PE 13-7B

Cash Payments for Operating Expenses

The income statement for **Rundell Inc.** (from Exhibit 4) reports total operating expenses of $203,000, which includes depreciation expense of $7,000. Because depreciation expense does not require a cash outflow, it is omitted from cash payments for operating expenses.

To determine the cash payments for operating expenses, the other operating expenses (excluding depreciation) of $196,000 ($203,000 − $7,000) are adjusted for any increase or decrease in accrued expenses payable. Assuming that the accrued expenses payable are all operating expenses, this adjustment is summarized in Exhibit 11.

EXHIBIT 11

Determining the Cash Payments for Operating Expenses

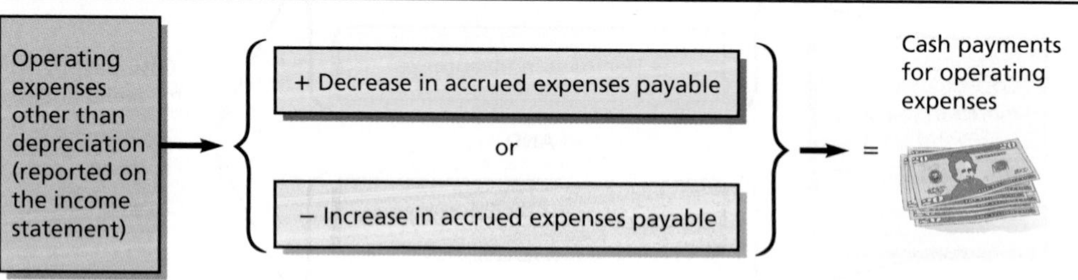

The cash payments for operating expenses are $193,800, computed as follows:

Operating expenses other than depreciation	$196,000
Deduct increase in accrued expenses payable	(2,200)
Cash payments for operating expenses	$193,800

The increase in accrued expenses payable (from Exhibit 4) indicates that the cash payments for operating expenses were $2,200 less than the amount reported for operating expenses during the year. Thus, $2,200 is deducted from the operating expenses in determining the cash payments for operating expenses.

Gain on Sale of Land

The income statement for **Rundell Inc.** (from Exhibit 4) reports a gain of $12,000 on the sale of land. The sale of land is an investing activity. Thus, the proceeds from the sale, which include the gain, are reported as part of the cash flows from investing activities.

Interest Expense

The income statement for **Rundell Inc.** (from Exhibit 4) reports interest expense of $8,000. To determine the cash payments for interest, the $8,000 is adjusted for any increases or decreases in interest payable. The adjustment is summarized in Exhibit 12.

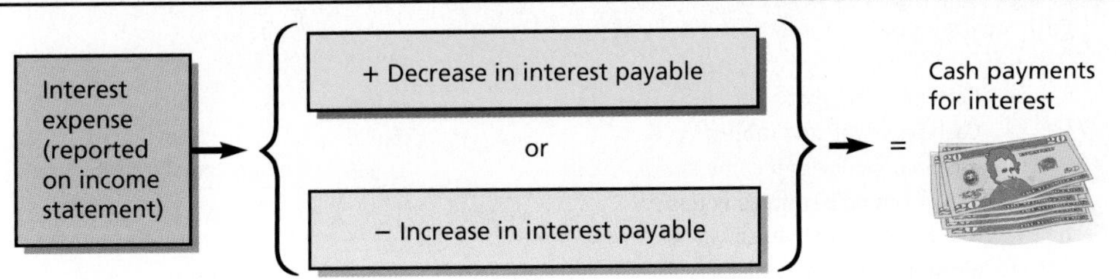

EXHIBIT 12

Determining the Cash Payments for Interest

The comparative balance sheet of Rundell in Exhibit 4 indicates no interest payable. This is because the interest expense on the bonds payable is paid on June 1 and December 31. Because there is no interest payable, no adjustment of the interest expense of $8,000 is necessary.

Cash Payments for Income Taxes

The income statement for **Rundell Inc.** (from Exhibit 3) reports income tax expense of $83,000. To determine the cash payments for income taxes, the $83,000 is adjusted for any increases or decreases in income taxes payable. The adjustment is summarized in Exhibit 13.

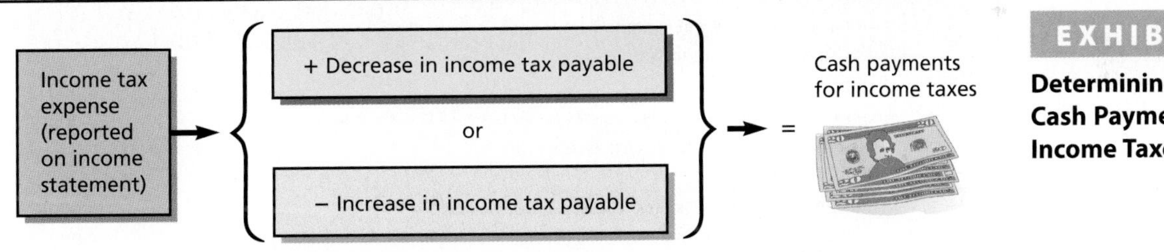

EXHIBIT 13

Determining the Cash Payments for Income Taxes

The cash payments for income taxes are $83,500, computed as follows:

Income tax expense	$83,000
Add decrease in income taxes payable	500
Cash payments for income taxes	$83,500

The $500 decrease in income taxes payable (from Exhibit 4) indicates that the cash payments for income taxes were $500 more than the amount reported for income tax expense during 2016. Thus, $500 is added to the income tax expense in determining the cash payments for income taxes.

Reporting Cash Flows from Operating Activities—Direct Method

The statement of cash flows for **Rundell Inc.**, using the direct method for reporting cash flows from operating activities, is shown in Exhibit 14. The portions of the statement that differ from those prepared under the indirect method are highlighted.

EXHIBIT 14

Statement of Cash Flows—Direct Method

Rundell Inc.
Statement of Cash Flows
For the Year Ended December 31, 2016

Cash flows from operating activities:			
Cash received from customers		$1,171,000	
Deduct: Cash payments for merchandise	$785,200		
Cash payments for operating expenses	193,800		
Cash payments for interest	8,000		
Cash payments for income taxes	83,500	1,070,500	
Net cash flow from operating activities			$100,500
Cash flows from investing activities:			
Cash received from sale of land		$ 72,000	
Less: Cash paid for purchase of land	$ 15,000		
Cash paid for purchase of building	60,000	75,000	
Net cash flow used for investing activities			(3,000)
Cash flows from financing activities:			
Cash received from sale of common stock		$ 48,000	
Less: Cash paid to retire bonds payable	$ 50,000		
Cash paid for dividends	24,000	74,000	
Net cash flow used for financing activities			(26,000)
Increase in cash			$ 71,500
Cash at the beginning of the year			26,000
Cash at the end of the year			$ 97,500
Schedule Reconciling Net Income with Cash Flows from Operating Activities:			
Cash flows from operating activities:			
Net income			$108,000
Adjustments to reconcile net income to net cash flow from operating activities:			
Depreciation			7,000
Gain on sale of land			(12,000)
Changes in current operating assets and liabilities:			
Increase in accounts receivable			(9,000)
Decrease in inventory			8,000
Decrease in accounts payable			(3,200)
Increase in accrued expenses payable			2,200
Decrease in income taxes payable			(500)
Net cash flow from operating activities			$100,500

Exhibit 14 also includes the separate schedule reconciling net income and net cash flow from operating activities. This schedule is included in the statement of cash flows when the direct method is used. This schedule is similar to the Cash Flows from Operating Activities section prepared under the indirect method.

International  Connection

IFRS FOR STATEMENT OF CASH FLOWS

The statement of cash flows is required under International Financial Reporting Standards (IFRS). The statement of cash flows under IFRS is similar to that reported under U.S. GAAP in that the statement has separate sections for operating, investing, and financing activities. Like U.S. GAAP, IFRS also allow the use of either the indirect or direct method of reporting cash flows from operating activities. IFRS differ from U.S. GAAP in some minor areas, including:

- Interest paid can be reported as either an operating or a financing activity, while interest received can be reported as either an operating or an investing activity. In contrast, U.S. GAAP reports interest paid or received as an operating activity.
- Dividends paid can be reported as either an operating or a financing activity, while dividends received can be reported as either an operating or an investing activity. In contrast, U.S. GAAP reports dividends paid as a financing activity and dividends received as an operating activity.
- Cash flows to pay taxes are reported as a separate line in the operating activities, in contrast to U.S. GAAP, which does not require a separate line disclosure.

* IFRS are further discussed and illustrated in this chapter.

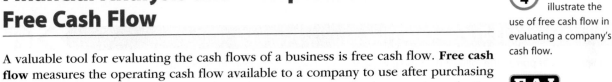

Financial Analysis and Interpretation: Free Cash Flow

Describe and illustrate the use of free cash flow in evaluating a company's cash flow.

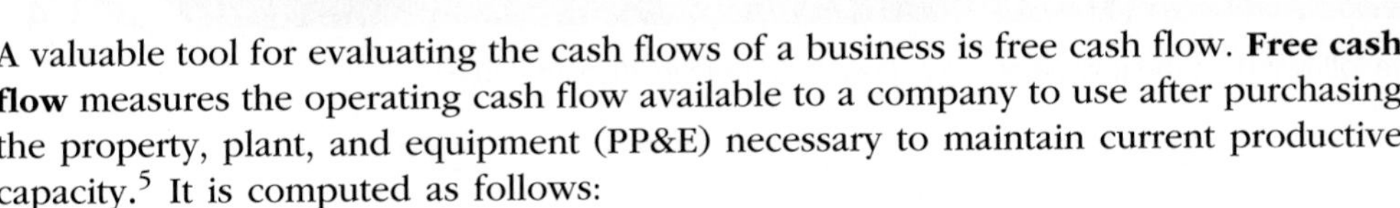

A valuable tool for evaluating the cash flows of a business is free cash flow. **Free cash flow** measures the operating cash flow available to a company to use after purchasing the property, plant, and equipment (PP&E) necessary to maintain current productive capacity.[5] It is computed as follows:

Cash flow from operating activities	$XXX
Less: Investments in PP&E needed to maintain current production	XXX
Free cash flow	$XXX

Analysts often use free cash flow, rather than cash flows from operating activities, to measure the financial strength of a business. Industries such as airlines, railroads, and telecommunications companies must invest heavily in new equipment to remain competitive. Such investments can significantly reduce free cash flow. For example, **Verizon Communications Inc.**'s free cash flow is approximately 51% of the cash flow from operating activities. In contrast, **Apple Inc.**'s free cash flow is approximately 89% of the cash flow from operating activities.

To illustrate, the cash flow from operating activities for **Research in Motion, Inc.**, maker of BlackBerry® smartphones, was $2,912 million in a recent fiscal year. The statement of cash flows indicated that the cash invested in property, plant, and equipment was $902 million. Assuming that the amount invested in property, plant, and equipment is necessary to maintain productive capacity, free cash flow would be computed as follows (in millions):

Cash flow from operating activities	$2,912
Less: Investments in PP&E needed to maintain current production	902
Free cash flow	$2,010

Research in Motion's free cash flow was 69% of cash flow from operations and more than 10% of sales. Compare this to the calculation of free cash flows for Apple Inc.

[5] Productive capacity is the number of goods the company is currently producing and selling.

(a computer company), **The Coca-Cola Company** (a beverage company), and Verizon Communications, Inc. (a telecommunications company), that follows (in millions):

	Apple Inc.	The Coca-Cola Company	Verizon Communications, Inc.
Sales	$156,508	$48,017	$115,846
Cash flow from operating activities	50,856	10,645	31,486
Less: Investments in PP&E needed to maintain current production	8,295	2,870	16,175
Free cash flow	$ 42,561	$ 7,775	$ 15,311
Free cash flow as a percentage of cash flow from operations	84%	73%	49%
Free cash flow as a percentage of sales	27%	16%	13%

Positive free cash flow is considered favorable. A company that has free cash flow is able to fund internal growth, retire debt, pay dividends, and benefit from financial flexibility. A company with no free cash flow is unable to maintain current productive capacity. Lack of free cash flow can be an early indicator of liquidity problems. As one analyst notes, "Free cash flow gives the company firepower to reduce debt and ultimately generate consistent, actual income."[6]

Example Exercise 13-8 Free Cash Flow

Omnicron Inc. reported the following on the company's cash flow statement in 2016 and 2015:

	2016	2015
Net cash flow from operating activities	$140,000	$120,000
Net cash flow used for investing activities	(120,000)	(80,000)
Net cash flow used for financing activities	(20,000)	(32,000)

Seventy-five percent of the net cash flow used for investing activities was used to replace existing capacity.

a. Determine Omnicron's free cash flow.

b. Has Omnicron's free cash flow improved or declined from 2015 to 2016?

Follow My Example 13-8

a.

	2016	2015
Net cash flow from operating activities	$140,000	$120,000
Less: Investments in fixed assets to maintain current production	90,000[1]	60,000[2]
Free cash flow	$ 50,000	$ 60,000

[1] $120,000 × 75%
[2] $80,000 × 75%

b. The change from $60,000 to $50,000 indicates an unfavorable trend.

Practice Exercises: PE 13-8A, PE 13-8B

[6] Jill Krutick, *Fortune*, March 30, 1998, p. 106.

APPENDIX

Spreadsheet (Work Sheet) for Statement of Cash Flows—The Indirect Method

A spreadsheet (work sheet) may be used in preparing the statement of cash flows. However, whether or not a spreadsheet (work sheet) is used, the concepts presented in this chapter are not affected.

The data for **Rundell Inc.**, presented in Exhibit 4 are used as a basis for illustrating the spreadsheet (work sheet) for the indirect method. The steps in preparing this spreadsheet (work sheet), shown in Exhibit 15, are as follows:

- Step 1. List the title of each balance sheet account in the Accounts column.
- Step 2. For each balance sheet account, enter its balance as of December 31, 2015, in the first column and its balance as of December 31, 2016, in the last column. Place the credit balances in parentheses.
- Step 3. Add the December 31, 2015 and 2016 column totals, which should total to zero.
- Step 4. Analyze the change during the year in each noncash account to determine its net increase (decrease) and classify the change as affecting cash flows from operating activities, investing activities, financing activities, or noncash investing and financing activities.
- Step 5. Indicate the effect of the change on cash flows by making entries in the Transactions columns.
- Step 6. After all noncash accounts have been analyzed, enter the net increase (decrease) in cash during the period.
- Step 7. Add the Debit and Credit Transactions columns. The totals should be equal.

Analyzing Accounts

In analyzing the noncash accounts (Step 4), try to determine the type of cash flow activity (operating, investing, or financing) that led to the change in the account. As each noncash account is analyzed, an entry (Step 5) is made on the spreadsheet (work sheet) for the type of cash flow activity that caused the change. After all noncash accounts have been analyzed, an entry (Step 6) is made for the increase (decrease) in cash during the period.

The entries made on the spreadsheet are not posted to the ledger. They are only used in preparing and summarizing the data on the spreadsheet.

The order in which the accounts are analyzed is not important. However, it is more efficient to begin with Retained Earnings and proceed upward in the account listing.

Retained Earnings

The spreadsheet (work sheet) shows a Retained Earnings balance of $202,300 at December 31, 2015, and $282,300 at December 31, 2016. Thus, Retained Earnings increased $80,000 during the year. This increase is from the following:

- Net income of $108,000
- Declaring cash dividends of $28,000

To identify the cash flows from these activities, two entries are made on the spreadsheet.

EXHIBIT 15 **End-of-Period Spreadsheet (Work Sheet) for Statement of Cash Flows—Indirect Method**

Step 2

	A	B	C	D	E	F	G
1	Rundell Inc.						
2	End-of-Period Spreadsheet (Work Sheet) for Statement of Cash Flows						
3	For the Year Ended December 31, 2016						
4	Accounts	Balance,	Transactions				Balance,
5		Dec. 31, 2015		Debit		Credit	Dec. 31, 2016
6	Cash	26,000	(o)	71,500			97,500
7	Accounts receivable (net)	65,000	(n)	9,000			74,000
8	Inventories	180,000			(m)	8,000	172,000
9	Land	125,000	(k)	15,000	(l)	60,000	80,000
10	Building	200,000	(j)	60,000			260,000
11	Accumulated depreciation—building	(58,300)			(i)	7,000	(65,300)
12	Accounts payable (merchandise creditors)	(46,700)	(h)	3,200			(43,500)
13	Accrued expenses payable (operating expenses)	(24,300)			(g)	2,200	(26,500)
14	Income taxes payable	(8,400)	(f)	500			(7,900)
15	Dividends payable	(10,000)			(e)	4,000	(14,000)
16	Bonds payable	(150,000)	(d)	50,000			(100,000)
17	Common stock	(16,000)			(c)	8,000	(24,000)
18	Paid-in capital in excess of par	(80,000)			(c)	40,000	(120,000)
19	Retained earnings	(202,300)	(b)	28,000	(a)	108,000	(282,300)
20	Totals Step 3 →	0		237,200		237,200	0 ← Step 3
21	Operating activities:						
22	Net income		(a)	108,000			
23	Depreciation of building		(i)	7,000			
24	Gain on sale of land				(l)	12,000	
25	Increase in accounts receivable				(n)	9,000	
26	Decrease in inventories		(m)	8,000			
27	Decrease in accounts payable				(h)	3,200	
28	Increase in accrued expenses payable		(g)	2,200			
29	Decrease in income taxes payable				(f)	500	
30	Investing activities:						
31	Sale of land		(l)	72,000			
32	Purchase of land				(k)	15,000	
33	Purchase of building				(j)	60,000	
34	Financing activities:						
35	Issued common stock		(c)	48,000			
36	Retired bonds payable				(d)	50,000	
37	Declared cash dividends				(b)	28,000	
38	Increase in dividends payable		(e)	4,000			
39	Net increase in cash				(o)	71,500	
40	Totals			249,200		249,200	

Step 1 (rows 6–20)

Steps 4–7

The $108,000 is reported on the statement of cash flows as part of cash flows from operating activities. Thus, an entry is made in the Transactions columns on the spreadsheet, as follows:

(a) Operating Activities—Net Income	108,000	
Retained Earnings		108,000

The preceding entry accounts for the net income portion of the change to Retained Earnings. It also identifies the cash flow in the bottom portion of the spreadsheet as related to operating activities.

The $28,000 of dividends is reported as a financing activity on the statement of cash flows. Thus, an entry is made in the Transactions columns on the spreadsheet, as follows:

		Debit	Credit
(b)	Retained Earnings	28,000	
	Financing Activities—Declared Cash Dividends		28,000

The preceding entry accounts for the dividends portion of the change to Retained Earnings. It also identifies the cash flow in the bottom portion of the spreadsheet as related to financing activities. The $28,000 of declared dividends will be adjusted later for the actual amount of cash dividends paid during the year.

Other Accounts

The entries for the other noncash accounts are made in the spreadsheet in a manner similar to entries (a) and (b). A summary of these entries follows:

		Debit	Credit
(c)	Financing Activities—Issued Common Stock	48,000	
	Common Stock		8,000
	Paid-In Capital in Excess of Par—Common Stock		40,000
(d)	Bonds Payable	50,000	
	Financing Activities—Retired Bonds Payable		50,000
(e)	Financing Activities—Increase in Dividends Payable	4,000	
	Dividends Payable		4,000
(f)	Income Taxes Payable	500	
	Operating Activities—Decrease in Income Taxes Payable		500
(g)	Operating Activities—Increase in Accrued Expenses Payable	2,200	
	Accrued Expenses Payable		2,200
(h)	Accounts Payable	3,200	
	Operating Activities—Decrease in Accounts Payable		3,200
(i)	Operating Activities—Depreciation of Building	7,000	
	Accumulated Depreciation—Building		7,000
(j)	Building	60,000	
	Investing Activities—Purchase of Building		60,000
(k)	Land	15,000	
	Investing Activities—Purchase of Land		15,000
(l)	Investing Activities—Sale of Land	72,000	
	Operating Activities—Gain on Sale of Land		12,000
	Land		60,000
(m)	Operating Activities—Decrease in Inventories	8,000	
	Inventories		8,000
(n)	Accounts Receivable	9,000	
	Operating Activities—Increase in Accounts Receivable		9,000
(o)	Cash	71,500	
	Net Increase in Cash		71,500

After all the balance sheet accounts are analyzed and the entries made on the spreadsheet (work sheet), all the operating, investing, and financing activities are identified in the bottom portion of the spreadsheet. The accuracy of the entries is verified by totaling the Debit and Credit Transactions columns. The totals of the columns should be equal.

Preparing the Statement of Cash Flows

The statement of cash flows prepared from the spreadsheet is identical to the statement in Exhibit 7. The data for the three sections of the statement are obtained from the bottom portion of the spreadsheet.

At a Glance 13

Describe the cash flow activities reported in the statement of cash flows.

Key Points The statement of cash flows reports cash receipts and cash payments by three types of activities: operating activities, investing activities, and financing activities. Cash flows from operating activities reports the cash inflows and outflows from a company's day-to-day operations. Cash flows from investing activities reports the cash inflows and outflows related to changes in a company's long-term assets. Cash flows from financing activities reports the cash inflows and outflows related to changes in a company's long-term liabilities and stockholders' equity. Investing and financing for a business may be affected by transactions that do not involve cash. The effect of such transactions should be reported in a separate schedule accompanying the statement of cash flows.

Learning Outcome	*Example Exercises*	*Practice Exercises*
• Classify transactions that either provide or use cash into either operating, investing, or financing activities.	**EE13-1**	**PE13-1A, 13-1B**

Prepare a statement of cash flows, using the indirect method.

Key Points The indirect method reports cash flows from operating activities by adjusting net income for revenues and expenses that do not involve the receipt or payment of cash. Noncash expenses such as depreciation are added back to net income. Gains and losses on the disposal of assets are added to or deducted from net income. Changes in current operating assets and liabilities are added to or subtracted from net income, depending on their effect on cash. Cash flows from investing activities and cash flows from financing activities are reported below cash flows from operating activities in the statement of cash flows.

Learning Outcomes	*Example Exercises*	*Practice Exercises*
• Determine cash flows from operating activities under the indirect method by adjusting net income for noncash expenses and gains and losses from asset disposals.	**EE13-2**	**PE13-2A, 13-2B**
• Determine cash flows from operating activities under the indirect method by adjusting net income for changes in current operating assets and liabilities.	**EE13-3**	**PE13-3A, 13-3B**
• Prepare the Cash Flows from Operating Activities section of the statement of cash flows, using the indirect method.	**EE13-4**	**PE13-4A, 13-4B**
• Prepare the Cash Flows from Investing Activities and Cash Flows from Financing Activities sections of the statement of cash flows.	**EE13-5**	**PE13-5A, 13-5B**

Prepare a statement of cash flows, using the direct method.

Key Points The amount of cash flows from operating activities is the same under both the direct and indirect methods, but the manner in which cash flows operating activities is reported is different. The direct method reports cash flows from operating activities by major classes of operating cash receipts and cash payments. The difference between the major classes of total operating cash receipts and total operating cash payments is the net cash flow from operating activities. The Cash Flows from Investing and Financing Activities sections of the statement are the same under both the direct and indirect methods.

Learning Outcome	Example Exercises	Practice Exercises
• Prepare the cash flows from operating activities section of the statement of cash flows under the direct method.	**EE13-6** **EE13-7**	**PE13-6A, 13-6B** **PE13-7A, 13-7B**

Describe and illustrate the use of free cash flow in evaluating a company's cash flow.

Key Points Free cash flow measures the operating cash flow available for company use after purchasing the fixed assets that are necessary to maintain current productive capacity. It is calculated by subtracting these fixed asset purchases from net cash flow from operating activities. A company with strong free cash flow is able to fund internal growth, retire debt, pay dividends, and enjoy financial flexibility. A company with weak free cash flow has much less financial flexibility.

Learning Outcomes	Example Exercises	Practice Exercises
• Describe free cash flow.		
• Calculate and evaluate free cash flow.	**EE13-8**	**PE13-8A, 13-8B**

Key Terms

cash flow per share (534)
cash flows from financing activities (531)
cash flows from investing activities (530)
cash flows from operating activities (530)
direct method (531)
free cash flow (549)
indirect method (532)
statement of cash flows (530)

Illustrative Problem

The comparative balance sheet of Dowling Company for December 31, 2016 and 2015, is as follows:

Dowling Company
Comparative Balance Sheet
December 31, 2016 and 2015

	2016	2015
Assets		
Cash	$ 140,350	$ 95,900
Accounts receivable (net)	95,300	102,300
Inventories	165,200	157,900
Prepaid expenses	6,240	5,860
Investments (long-term)	35,700	84,700
Land	75,000	90,000
Buildings	375,000	260,000
Accumulated depreciation—buildings	(71,300)	(58,300)
Machinery and equipment	428,300	428,300
Accumulated depreciation—machinery and equipment	(148,500)	(138,000)
Patents	58,000	65,000
Total assets	$1,159,290	$1,093,660
Liabilities and Stockholders' Equity		
Accounts payable (merchandise creditors)	$ 43,500	$ 46,700
Accrued expenses payable (operating expenses)	14,000	12,500
Income taxes payable	7,900	8,400
Dividends payable	14,000	10,000
Mortgage note payable, due 2023	40,000	0
Bonds payable	150,000	250,000
Common stock, $30 par	450,000	375,000
Excess of issue price over par—common stock	66,250	41,250
Retained earnings	373,640	349,810
Total liabilities and stockholders' equity	$1,159,290	$1,093,660

The income statement for Dowling Company follows:

Dowling Company
Income Statement
For the Year Ended December 31, 2016

Sales		$1,100,000
Cost of merchandise sold		710,000
Gross profit		$ 390,000
Operating expenses:		
Depreciation expense	$ 23,500	
Patent amortization	7,000	
Other operating expenses	196,000	
Total operating expenses		226,500
Income from operations		$ 163,500
Other income:		
Gain on sale of investments	$ 11,000	
Other expense:		
Interest expense	26,000	(15,000)
Income before income tax		$ 148,500
Income tax expense		50,000
Net income		$ 98,500

An examination of the accounting records revealed the following additional information applicable to 2016:

a. Land costing $15,000 was sold for $15,000.

b. A mortgage note was issued for $40,000.

c. A building costing $115,000 was constructed.

d. 2,500 shares of common stock were issued at $40 in exchange for the bonds payable.

e. Cash dividends declared were $74,670.

Instructions

1. Prepare a statement of cash flows, using the indirect method of reporting cash flows from operating activities.
2. Prepare a statement of cash flows, using the direct method of reporting cash flows from operating activities.

Solution

1.

Dowling Company **Statement of Cash Flows—Indirect Method** **For the Year Ended December 31, 2016**			
Cash flows from operating activities:			
Net income		$ 98,500	
Adjustments to reconcile net income to net cash flow from operating activities:			
Depreciation		23,500	
Amortization of patents		7,000	
Gain on sale of investments		(11,000)	
Changes in current operating assets and liabilities:			
Decrease in accounts receivable		7,000	
Increase in inventories		(7,300)	
Increase in prepaid expenses		(380)	
Decrease in accounts payable		(3,200)	
Increase in accrued expenses payable		1,500	
Decrease in income taxes payable		(500)	
Net cash flow from operating activities			$115,120
Cash flows from investing activities:			
Cash received from sale of:			
Investments	$60,000[1]		
Land	15,000	$ 75,000	
Less: Cash paid for construction of building		115,000	
Net cash flow used for investing activities			(40,000)
Cash flows from financing activities:			
Cash received from issuing mortgage note payable		$ 40,000	
Less: Cash paid for dividends		70,670[2]	
Net cash flow used for financing activities			(30,670)
Increase in cash			$ 44,450
Cash at the beginning of the year			95,900
Cash at the end of the year			$140,350
Schedule of Noncash Investing and Financing Activities:			
Issued common stock to retire bonds payable			$100,000

[1] $60,000 = $11,000 gain + $49,000 (decrease in investments)

[2] $70,670 = $74,670 – $4,000 (increase in dividends)

2.

Dowling Company
Statement of Cash Flows—Direct Method
For the Year Ended December 31, 2016

Cash flows from operating activities:			
Cash received from customers[1]		$1,107,000	
Deduct: Cash paid for merchandise[2]	$720,500		
Cash paid for operating expenses[3]	194,880		
Cash paid for interest expense	26,000		
Cash paid for income tax[4]	50,500	991,880	
Net cash flow from operating activities			$115,120
Cash flows from investing activities:			
Cash received from sale of:			
Investments	$ 60,000[5]		
Land	15,000	$ 75,000	
Less: Cash paid for construction of building		115,000	
Net cash flow used for investing activities			(40,000)
Cash flows from financing activities:			
Cash received from issuing mortgage note payable		$ 40,000	
Less: Cash paid for dividends[6]		70,670	
Net cash flow used for financing activities			(30,670)
Increase in cash			$ 44,450
Cash at the beginning of the year			95,900
Cash at the end of the year			$140,350
Schedule of Noncash Investing and Financing Activities:			
Issued common stock to retire bonds payable			$100,000
Schedule Reconciling Net Income with Cash Flows from Operating Activities[7]			

Computations:

[1]$1,100,000 + $7,000 = $1,107,000
[2]$710,000 + $3,200 + $7,300 = $720,500
[3]$196,000 + $380 − $1,500 = $194,880
[4]$50,000 + $500 = $50,500
[5]$60,000 = $11,000 gain + $49,000 (decrease in investments)
[6]$74,670 + $10,000 − $14,000 = $70,670
[7]The content of this schedule is the same as the Operating Activities section of part (1) of this solution and is not reproduced here for the sake of brevity.

Discussion Questions

1. What is the principal disadvantage of the direct method of reporting cash flows from operating activities?
2. What are the major advantages of the indirect method of reporting cash flows from operating activities?
3. A corporation issued $2,000,000 of common stock in exchange for $2,000,000 of fixed assets. Where would this transaction be reported on the statement of cash flows?
4. A retail business, using the accrual method of accounting, owed merchandise creditors (accounts payable) $320,000 at the beginning of the year and $350,000 at the end of the year. How would the $30,000 increase be used to adjust net income in determining the amount of cash flows from operating activities by the indirect method? Explain.

5. If salaries payable was $100,000 at the beginning of the year and $75,000 at the end of the year, should $25,000 decrease be added to or deducted from income to determine the amount of cash flows from operating activities by the indirect method? Explain.

6. A long-term investment in bonds with a cost of $500,000 was sold for $600,000 cash. (a) What was the gain or loss on the sale? (b) What was the effect of the transaction on cash flows? (c) How should the transaction be reported on the statement of cash flows if cash flows from operating activities are reported by the indirect method?

7. A corporation issued $2,000,000 of 20-year bonds for cash at 98. How would the transaction be reported on the statement of cash flows?

8. Fully depreciated equipment costing $50,000 was discarded. What was the effect of the transaction on cash flows if (a) $15,000 cash is received for the equipment, (b) no cash is received for the equipment?

9. For the current year, Packers Company decided to switch from the indirect method to the direct method for reporting cash flows from operating activities on the statement of cash flows. Will the change cause the amount of net cash flow from operating activities to be larger, smaller, or the same as if the indirect method had been used? Explain.

10. Name five common major classes of operating cash receipts or operating cash payments presented on the statement of cash flows when the cash flows from operating activities are reported by the direct method.

Practice Exercises

EE 13-1 *p. 534*

SHOW ME HOW

PE 13-1A Classifying cash flows

OBJ. 1

Identify whether each of the following would be reported as an operating, investing, or financing activity on the statement of cash flows:

a. Repurchase of common stock
b. Cash received from customers
c. Payment of accounts payable
d. Retirement of bonds payable
e. Purchase of equipment
f. Purchase of inventory for cash

EE 13-1 *p. 534*

SHOW ME HOW

PE 13-1B Classifying cash flows

OBJ. 1

Identify whether each of the following would be reported as an operating, investing, or financing activity on the statement of cash flows:

a. Purchase of investments
b. Disposal of equipment
c. Payment for selling expenses
d. Collection of accounts receivable
e. Cash sales
f. Issuance of bonds payable

EE 13-2 *p. 537*

SHOW ME HOW

PE 13-2A Adjustments to net income—indirect method

OBJ. 2

Pearl Corporation's accumulated depreciation—furniture account increased by $8,400, while $3,080 of patent amortization was recognized between balance sheet dates. There were no purchases or sales of depreciable or intangible assets during the year. In addition, the income statement showed a loss of $4,480 from the sale of land. Reconcile a net income of $120,400 to net cash flow from operating activities.

EE 13-2 *p. 537*

SHOW ME HOW

PE 13-2B Adjustments to net income—indirect method

OBJ. 2

Ya Wen Corporation's accumulated depreciation—equipment account increased by $8,750, while $3,250 of patent amortization was recognized between balance sheet dates. There were no purchases or sales of depreciable or intangible assets during the year. In addition, the income statement showed a gain of $18,750 from the sale of investments. Reconcile a net income of $175,000 to net cash flow from operating activities.

EE 13-3 p. 539

SHOW ME HOW

PE 13-3A Changes in current operating assets and liabilities—indirect method **OBJ. 2**

Alpenrose Corporation's comparative balance sheet for current assets and liabilities was as follows:

	Dec. 31, 2016	Dec. 31, 2015
Accounts receivable	$27,000	$32,400
Inventory	18,000	15,480
Accounts payable	16,200	14,220
Dividends payable	49,500	53,100

Adjust net income of $207,000 for changes in operating assets and liabilities to arrive at net cash flow from operating activities.

EE 13-3 p. 539

SHOW ME HOW

PE 13-3B Changes in current operating assets and liabilities—indirect method **OBJ. 2**

Huluduey Corporation's comparative balance sheet for current assets and liabilities was as follows:

	Dec. 31, 2016	Dec. 31, 2015
Accounts receivable	$18,000	$14,400
Inventory	34,800	29,700
Accounts payable	27,600	20,700
Dividends payable	8,400	10,800

Adjust net income of $160,000 for changes in operating assets and liabilities to arrive at net cash flow from operating activities.

EE 13-4 p. 540

SHOW ME HOW

PE 13-4A Cash flows from operating activities—indirect method **OBJ. 2**

Pettygrove Inc. reported the following data:

Net income	$405,000
Depreciation expense	45,000
Gain on disposal of equipment	36,900
Decrease in accounts receivable	25,200
Decrease in accounts payable	6,480

Prepare the Cash Flows from Operating Activities section of the statement of cash flows, using the indirect method.

EE 13-4 p. 540

SHOW ME HOW

PE 13-4B Cash flows from operating activities—indirect method **OBJ. 2**

Staley Inc. reported the following data:

Net income	$280,000
Depreciation expense	48,000
Loss on disposal of equipment	19,520
Increase in accounts receivable	17,280
Increase in accounts payable	8,960

Prepare the Cash Flows from Operating Activities section of the statement of cash flows, using the indirect method.

EE 13-5 p. 543

SHOW ME HOW

PE 13-5A Land transactions on the statement of cash flows **OBJ. 2**

Milo Corporation purchased land for $540,000. Later in the year, the company sold a different piece of land with a book value of $270,000 for $180,000. How are the effects of these transactions reported on the statement of cash flows?

EE 13-5 *p. 543*

PE 13-5B Land transactions on the statement of cash flows **OBJ. 2**

IZ Corporation purchased land for $400,000. Later in the year, the company sold a different piece of land with a book value of $200,000 for $240,000. How are the effects of these transactions reported on the statement of cash flows?

EE 13-6 *p. 545*

PE 13-6A Cash received from customers—direct method **OBJ. 3**

Sales reported on the income statement were $480,000. The accounts receivable balance increased $54,000 over the year. Determine the amount of cash received from customers.

EE 13-6 *p. 545*

PE 13-6B Cash received from customers—direct method **OBJ. 3**

Sales reported on the income statement were $112,000. The accounts receivable balance decreased $10,500 over the year. Determine the amount of cash received from customers.

EE 13-7 *p. 546*

PE 13-7A Cash payments for merchandise—direct method **OBJ. 3**

The cost of merchandise sold reported on the income statement was $770,000. The accounts payable balance decreased $44,000, and the inventory balance decreased by $66,000 over the year. Determine the amount of cash paid for merchandise.

EE 13-7 *p. 546*

PE 13-7B Cash payments for merchandise—direct method **OBJ. 3**

The cost of merchandise sold reported on the income statement was $240,000. The accounts payable balance increased $12,000, and the inventory balance increased by $19,200 over the year. Determine the amount of cash paid for merchandise.

EE 13-8 *p. 550*

F·A·I

PE 13-8A Free cash flow **OBJ. 4**

McMahon Inc. reported the following on the company's statement of cash flows in 2016 and 2015:

	2016	2015
Net cash flow from operating activities	$ 294,000	$ 280,000
Net cash flow used for investing activities	(224,000)	(252,000)
Net cash flow used for financing activities	(63,000)	(42,000)

Seventy percent of the net cash flow used for investing activities was used to replace existing capacity.

a. Determine McMahon's free cash flow for both years.

b. Has McMahon's free cash flow improved or declined from 2015 to 2016?

EE 13-8 *p. 550*

F·A·I

PE 13-8B Free cash flow **OBJ. 4**

Dillin Inc. reported the following on the company's statement of cash flows in 2016 and 2015:

	2016	2015
Net cash flow from operating activities	$476,000	$455,000
Net cash flow used for investing activities	(427,000)	(378,000)
Net cash flow used for financing activities	(42,000)	(58,800)

Eighty percent of the net cash flow used for investing activities was used to replace existing capacity.

a. Determine Dillin's free cash flow for both years.

b. Has Dillin's free cash flow improved or declined from 2015 to 2016?

Exercises

EX 13-1 Cash flows from operating activities—net loss **OBJ. 1**

On its income statement for a recent year, **United Continental Holdings, Inc.**, the parent company of United Airlines, reported a net *loss* of $723 million from operations. On its statement of cash flows, it reported $935 million of cash flows from operating activities.

Explain this apparent contradiction between the loss and the positive cash flows.

EX 13-2 Effect of transactions on cash flows **OBJ. 1**

✔ a. Cash payment, $525,000

State the effect (cash receipt or payment and amount) of each of the following transactions, considered individually, on cash flows:

a. Retired $500,000 of bonds, on which there was $5,000 of unamortized discount, for $525,000.
b. Sold 6,000 shares of $20 par common stock for $30 per share.
c. Sold equipment with a book value of $98,200 for $117,500.
d. Purchased land for $322,000 cash.
e. Purchased a building by paying $75,000 cash and issuing a $62,500 mortgage note payable.
f. Sold a new issue of $300,000 of bonds at 101.
g. Purchased 2,500 shares of $40 par common stock as treasury stock at $50 per share.
h. Paid dividends of $2.00 per share. There were 50,000 shares issued and 10,000 shares of treasury stock.

EX 13-3 Classifying cash flows **OBJ. 1**

Identify the type of cash flow activity for each of the following events (operating, investing, or financing):

a. Net income
b. Paid cash dividends
c. Issued common stock
d. Issued bonds
e. Redeemed bonds
f. Sold long-term investments
g. Purchased treasury stock
h. Sold equipment
i. Issued preferred stock
j. Purchased buildings
k. Purchased patents

EX 13-4 Cash flows from operating activities—indirect method **OBJ. 2**

Indicate whether each of the following would be added to or deducted from net income in determining net cash flow from operating activities by the indirect method:

a. Decrease in merchandise inventory
b. Increase in accounts receivable
c. Increase in accounts payable
d. Loss on retirement of long-term debt
e. Depreciation of fixed assets
f. Decrease in notes receivable due in 60 days from customers
g. Increase in salaries payable
h. Decrease in prepaid expenses
i. Amortization of patent
j. Increase in notes payable due in 120 days to vendors
k. Gain on disposal of fixed assets

EX 13-5 Cash flows from operating activities—indirect method

OBJ. 1, 2

✔ Net cash flow from operating activities, $417,600

The net income reported on the income statement for the current year was $400,000. Depreciation recorded on store equipment for the year amounted to $16,000. Balances of the current asset and current liability accounts at the beginning and end of the year are as follows:

	End of Year	Beginning of Year
Cash	$41,600	$38,400
Accounts receivable (net)	30,400	28,000
Merchandise inventory	40,000	44,000
Prepaid expenses	4,800	3,600
Accounts payable (merchandise creditors)	40,000	36,000
Wages payable	21,200	24,000

a. Prepare the Cash Flows from Operating Activities section of the statement of cash flows, using the indirect method.

b. Briefly explain why net cash flow from operating activities is different than net income.

EX 13-6 Cash flows from operating activities—indirect method

OBJ. 1, 2

✔ Net cash flow from operating activities, $394,400

The net income reported on the income statement for the current year was $320,000. Depreciation recorded on equipment and a building amounted to $96,000 for the year. Balances of the current asset and current liability accounts at the beginning and end of the year are as follows:

	End of Year	Beginning of Year
Cash	$ 89,600	$ 96,000
Accounts receivable (net)	112,000	118,400
Inventories	224,000	200,000
Prepaid expenses	12,800	14,400
Accounts payable (merchandise creditors)	96,000	104,000
Salaries payable	16,000	13,600

a. Prepare the Cash Flows from Operating Activities section of the statement of cash flows, using the indirect method.

b. If the direct method had been used, would the net cash flow from operating activities have been the same? Explain.

EX 13-7 Cash flows from operating activities—indirect method

OBJ. 1, 2

✔ Net cash flow from operating activities, $525,410

The income statement disclosed the following items for 2016:

Depreciation expense	$ 57,600
Gain on disposal of equipment	33,600
Net income	508,000

Balances of the current assets and current liability accounts changed between December 31, 2015, and December 31, 2016, as follows:

	Increase (Decrease)
Accounts receivable	$8,960
Inventory	(5,120)
Prepaid insurance	(1,920)
Accounts payable	(6,080)
Income taxes payable	1,410
Dividends payable	2,200

a. Prepare the Cash Flows from Operating Activities section of the statement of cash flows, using the indirect method.

b. Briefly explain why net cash flows from operating activities is different than net income.

EX 13-8 Determining cash payments to stockholders **OBJ. 2**

The board of directors declared cash dividends totaling $585,000 during the current year. The comparative balance sheet indicates dividends payable of $167,625 at the beginning of the year and $146,250 at the end of the year. What was the amount of cash payments to stockholders during the year?

EX 13-9 Reporting changes in equipment on statement of cash flows **OBJ. 2**

An analysis of the general ledger accounts indicates that office equipment, which cost $202,500 and on which accumulated depreciation totaled $84,375 on the date of sale, was sold for $101,250 during the year. Using this information, indicate the items to be reported on the statement of cash flows.

EX 13-10 Reporting changes in equipment on statement of cash flows **OBJ. 2**

An analysis of the general ledger accounts indicates that delivery equipment, which cost $80,000 and on which accumulated depreciation totaled $36,000 on the date of sale, was sold for $37,200 during the year. Using this information, indicate the items to be reported on the statement of cash flows.

EX 13-11 Reporting land transactions on statement of cash flows **OBJ. 2**

On the basis of the details of the following fixed asset account, indicate the items to be reported on the statement of cash flows:

ACCOUNT *Land* ACCOUNT NO.

Date		Item	Debit	Credit	Balance	
					Debit	Credit
2016						
Jan.	1	Balance			868,000	
Mar.	12	Purchased for cash	104,300		972,300	
Oct.	4	Sold for $95,550		63,840	908,460	

EX 13-12 Reporting stockholders' equity items on statement of cash flows **OBJ. 2**

On the basis of the following stockholders' equity accounts, indicate the items, exclusive of net income, to be reported on the statement of cash flows. There were no unpaid dividends at either the beginning or the end of the year.

ACCOUNT *Common Stock, $40 par* ACCOUNT NO.

Date		Item	Debit	Credit	Balance	
					Debit	Credit
2016						
Jan.	1	Balance, 120,000 shares				4,800,000
Apr.	2	30,000 shares issued for cash		1,200,000		6,000,000
June	30	4,400-share stock dividend		176,000		6,176,000

ACCOUNT *Paid-In Capital in Excess of Par—Common Stock* ACCOUNT NO.

Date		Item	Debit	Credit	Balance	
					Debit	Credit
2016						
Jan.	1	Balance				360,000
Apr.	2	30,000 shares issued for cash		720,000		1,080,000
June	30	Stock dividend		114,400		1,194,400

ACCOUNT ***Retained Earnings*** **ACCOUNT NO.**

Date		Item	Debit	Credit	Balance Debit	Balance Credit
2016						
Jan.	1	Balance				2,000,000
June	30	Stock dividend	290,440			1,709,560
Dec.	30	Cash dividend	463,200			1,246,360
	31	Net income		1,440,000		2,686,360

EX 13-13 Reporting land acquisition for cash and mortgage note on statement of cash flows OBJ. 2

On the basis of the details of the following fixed asset account, indicate the items to be reported on the statement of cash flows:

ACCOUNT ***Land*** **ACCOUNT NO.**

Date		Item	Debit	Credit	Balance Debit	Balance Credit
2016						
Jan.	1	Balance			156,000	
Feb.	10	Purchased for cash	246,000		402,000	
Nov.	20	Purchased with long-term mortgage note	324,000		726,000	

EX 13-14 Reporting issuance and retirement of long-term debt OBJ. 2

On the basis of the details of the following bonds payable and related discount accounts, indicate the items to be reported in the Financing Activities section of the statement of cash flows, assuming no gain or loss on retiring the bonds:

ACCOUNT ***Bonds Payable*** **ACCOUNT NO.**

Date		Item	Debit	Credit	Balance Debit	Balance Credit
2016						
Jan.	1	Balance				750,000
	2	Retire bonds	150,000			600,000
June	30	Issue bonds		450,000		1,050,000

ACCOUNT ***Discount on Bonds Payable*** **ACCOUNT NO.**

Date		Item	Debit	Credit	Balance Debit	Balance Credit
2016						
Jan.	1	Balance			33,750	
	2	Retire bonds		12,000	21,750	
June	30	Issue bonds	30,000		51,750	
Dec.	31	Amortize discount		2,625	49,125	

EX 13-15 Determining net income from net cash flow from operating activities OBJ. 2

✔ Net income, $341,770

SHOW ME HOW

Curwen Inc. reported net cash flow from operating activities of $357,500 on its statement of cash flows for the year ended December 31, 2016. The following information was reported in the Cash Flows from Operating Activities section of the statement of cash flows, using the indirect method:

Decrease in income taxes payable	$ 7,700
Decrease in inventories	19,140
Depreciation	29,480
Gain on sale of investments	13,200
Increase in accounts payable	5,280
Increase in prepaid expenses	2,970
Increase in accounts receivable	14,300

a. Determine the net income reported by Curwen Inc. for the year ended December 31, 2016.

b. Briefly explain why Curwen's net income is different than net cash flow from operating activities.

EX 13-16 Cash flows from operating activities—indirect method OBJ. 2

✔ Net cash flow from operating activities, $42,174

Selected data derived from the income statement and balance sheet of **National Beverage Co.** for a recent year are as follows:

Income statement data (in thousands):	
Net earnings (loss)	$43,993
Losses on inventory write-down and fixed assets	7
Depreciation expense	10,174
Stock-based compensation expense (noncash)	290
Balance sheet data (in thousands):	
Increase in accounts receivable	5,679
Increase in inventory	7,509
Decrease in prepaid expenses	2,239
Decrease in accounts payable and other current liabilities	1,341

a. Prepare the Cash Flows from Operating Activities section of the statement of cash flows, using the indirect method for National Beverage Co.

b. Interpret your results in part (a).

EX 13-17 Statement of cash flows—indirect method OBJ. 2

✔ Net cash flow from operating activities, $150

SHOW ME HOW

The comparative balance sheet of Pelican Joe Industries Inc. for December 31, 2016 and 2015, is as follows:

	Dec. 31, 2016	Dec. 31, 2015
Assets		
Cash	$ 490	$ 160
Accounts receivable (net)	280	200
Inventories	175	110
Land	400	450
Equipment	225	175
Accumulated depreciation—equipment	(60)	(30)
Total assets	$1,510	$1,065
Liabilities and Stockholders' Equity		
Accounts payable (merchandise creditors)	$ 175	$ 160
Dividends payable	30	—
Common stock, $10 par	100	50
Paid-in capital: Excess of issue price over par—common stock	250	125
Retained earnings	955	730
Total liabilities and stockholders' equity	$1,510	$1,065

The following additional information is taken from the records:

1. Land was sold for $125.
2. Equipment was acquired for cash.
3. There were no disposals of equipment during the year.
4. The common stock was issued for cash.
5. There was a $325 credit to Retained Earnings for net income.
6. There was an $100 debit to Retained Earnings for cash dividends declared.

a. Prepare a statement of cash flows, using the indirect method of presenting cash flows from operating activities.

b. Was Pelican Joe Industries Inc. net cash flow from operations more or less than net income? What is the source of this difference?

EX 13-18 Statement of cash flows—indirect method **OBJ. 2**

List the errors you find in the following statement of cash flows. The cash balance at the beginning of the year was $240,000. All other amounts are correct, except the cash balance at the end of the year.

Shasta Inc.
Statement of Cash Flows
For the Year Ended December 31, 2016

Cash flows from operating activities:			
Net income		$360,000	
Adjustments to reconcile net income to net cash flow from operating activities:			
Depreciation		100,800	
Gain on sale of investments		17,280	
Changes in current operating assets and liabilities:			
Increase in accounts receivable		27,360	
Increase in inventories		(36,000)	
Increase in accounts payable		(3,600)	
Decrease in accrued expenses payable		(2,400)	
Net cash flow from operating activities			$ 463,440
Cash flows from investing activities:			
Cash received from sale of investments		$240,000	
Less: Cash paid for purchase of land	$259,200		
Cash paid for purchase of equipment	432,000	691,200	
Net cash flow used for investing activities			(415,200)
Cash flows from financing activities:			
Cash received from sale of common stock		$312,000	
Cash paid for dividends		132,000	
Net cash flow from financing activities			180,000
Increase in cash			$ 47,760
Cash at the end of the year			192,240
Cash at the beginning of the year			$ 240,000

EX 13-19 Cash flows from operating activities—direct method **OBJ. 3**

✔ a. $801,900

The cash flows from operating activities are reported by the direct method on the statement of cash flows. Determine the following:

a. If sales for the current year were $753,500 and accounts receivable decreased by $48,400 during the year, what was the amount of cash received from customers?

b. If income tax expense for the current year was $50,600 and income tax payable decreased by $5,500 during the year, what was the amount of cash payments for income taxes?

c. Briefly explain why the cash received from customers in (a) is different than sales.

EX 13-20 Cash paid for merchandise purchases **OBJ. 3**

The cost of merchandise sold for **Kohl's Corporation** for a recent year was $11,625 million. The balance sheet showed the following current account balances (in millions):

	Balance, End of Year	Balance, Beginning of Year
Merchandise inventories	$3,199	$3,036
Accounts payable	1,233	1,138

Determine the amount of cash payments for merchandise.

EX 13-21 Determining selected amounts for cash flows from operating activities—direct method **OBJ. 3**

✔ a. $1,025,800

Selected data taken from the accounting records of Ginis Inc. for the current year ended December 31 are as follows:

	Balance, December 31	Balance, January 1
Accrued expenses payable (operating expenses)	$ 12,650	$ 14,030
Accounts payable (merchandise creditors)	96,140	105,800
Inventories	178,020	193,430
Prepaid expenses	7,360	8,970

During the current year, the cost of merchandise sold was $1,031,550, and the operating expenses other than depreciation were $179,400. The direct method is used for presenting the cash flows from operating activities on the statement of cash flows.

Determine the amount reported on the statement of cash flows for (a) cash payments for merchandise and (b) cash payments for operating expenses.

EX 13-22 Cash flows from operating activities—direct method **OBJ. 3**

✔ Net cash flow from operating activities, $96,040

The income statement of Booker T Industries Inc. for the current year ended June 30 is as follows:

Sales		$511,000
Cost of merchandise sold		290,500
Gross profit		$220,500
Operating expenses:		
Depreciation expense	$ 39,200	
Other operating expenses	105,000	
Total operating expenses		144,200
Income before income tax		$ 76,300
Income tax expense		21,700
Net income		$ 54,600

Changes in the balances of selected accounts from the beginning to the end of the current year are as follows:

	Increase (Decrease)
Accounts receivable (net)	($11,760)
Inventories	3,920
Prepaid expenses	(3,780)
Accounts payable (merchandise creditors)	(7,980)
Accrued expenses payable (operating expenses)	1,260
Income tax payable	(2,660)

a. Prepare the Cash Flows from Operating Activities section of the statement of cash flows, using the direct method.

b. What does the direct method show about a company's cash flows from operating activities that is not shown using the indirect method?

EX 13-23 Cash flows from operating activities—direct method **OBJ. 3**

✔ **Net cash flow from operating activities, $123,860**

The income statement for Rhino Company for the current year ended June 30 and balances of selected accounts at the beginning and the end of the year are as follows:

Sales		$445,500
Cost of merchandise sold		154,000
Gross profit		$291,500
Operating expenses:		
Depreciation expense	$ 38,500	
Other operating expenses	115,280	
Total operating expenses		153,780
Income before income tax		$137,720
Income tax expense		39,600
Net income		$ 98,120

	End of Year	Beginning of Year
Accounts receivable (net)	$36,300	$31,240
Inventories	92,400	80,300
Prepaid expenses	14,520	15,840
Accounts payable (merchandise creditors)	67,540	62,700
Accrued expenses payable (operating expenses)	19,140	20,900
Income tax payable	4,400	4,400

Prepare the Cash Flows from Operating Activities section of the statement of cash flows, using the direct method.

EX 13-24 Free cash flow **OBJ. 4**

F·A·I

SHOW ME HOW

Sweeter Enterprises Inc. has cash flows from operating activities of $539,000. Cash flows used for investments in property, plant, and equipment totaled $210,000, of which 75% of this investment was used to replace existing capacity.

a. Determine the free cash flow for Sweeter Enterprises Inc.

b. How might a lender use free cash flow to determine whether or not to give Sweeter Enterprises Inc. a loan?

EX 13-25 Free cash flow **OBJ. 4**

The financial statements for **Nike, Inc.**, are provided in Appendix B at the end of the text.

a. Determine the free cash flow for the most recent fiscal year. Assume that 90% of the additions to property, plant, and equipment were used to maintain productive capacity. Round to the nearest thousand dollars.

b. How might a lender use free cash flow to determine whether or not to give Nike, Inc., a loan?

c. Would you feel comfortable giving Nike a loan, based on the free cash flow calculated in (a)?

EX 13-26 Free cash flow **OBJ. 4**

F·A·I

Lovato Motors Inc. has cash flows from operating activities of $720,000. Cash flows used for investments in property, plant, and equipment totaled $440,000, of which 85% of this investment was used to replace existing capacity.

Determine the free cash flow for Lovato Motors Inc.

Problems: Series A

PR 13-1A Statement of cash flows—indirect method

OBJ. 2

✔ Net cash flow from operating activities, $143,540

SHOW ME HOW

The comparative balance sheet of Cromme Inc. for December 31, 2016 and 2015, is shown as follows:

	Dec. 31, 2016	Dec. 31, 2015
Assets		
Cash	$ 625,760	$ 585,920
Accounts receivable (net)	227,840	208,960
Inventories	641,760	617,120
Investments	0	240,000
Land	328,000	0
Equipment	705,120	553,120
Accumulated depreciation—equipment	(166,400)	(148,000)
Total assets	$2,362,080	$2,057,120
Liabilities and Stockholders' Equity		
Accounts payable (merchandise creditors)	$ 424,480	$ 404,960
Accrued expenses payable (operating expenses)	42,240	52,640
Dividends payable	24,000	19,200
Common stock, $4 par	150,000	100,000
Paid-in capital: Excess of issue price over par—common stock	417,500	280,000
Retained earnings	1,303,860	1,200,320
Total liabilities and stockholders' equity	$2,362,080	$2,057,120

Additional data obtained from an examination of the accounts in the ledger for 2016 are as follows:

a. The investments were sold for $280,000 cash.
b. Equipment and land were acquired for cash.
c. There were no disposals of equipment during the year.
d. The common stock was issued for cash.
e. There was a $199,540 credit to Retained Earnings for net income.
f. There was a $96,000 debit to Retained Earnings for cash dividends declared.

Instructions

Prepare a statement of cash flows, using the indirect method of presenting cash flows from operating activities.

PR 13-2A Statement of cash flows—indirect method

OBJ. 2

✔ Net cash flow from operating activities, $419,200

SHOW ME HOW

The comparative balance sheet of Del Ray Enterprises Inc. at December 31, 2016 and 2015, is as follows:

	Dec. 31, 2016	Dec. 31, 2015
Assets		
Cash	$ 146,600	$ 179,800
Accounts receivable (net)	224,600	242,000
Merchandise inventory	321,600	299,200
Prepaid expenses	13,400	9,600
Equipment	655,000	537,000
Accumulated depreciation—equipment	(170,800)	(132,200)
Total assets	$1,190,400	$1,135,400
Liabilities and Stockholders' Equity		
Accounts payable (merchandise creditors)	$ 250,200	$ 237,600
Mortgage note payable	0	336,000
Common stock, $10 par	74,000	24,000
Paid-in capital: Excess of issue price over par—common stock	470,000	320,000
Retained earnings	396,200	217,800
Total liabilities and stockholders' equity	$1,190,400	$1,135,400

Additional data obtained from the income statement and from an examination of the accounts in the ledger for 2016 are as follows:

a. Net income, $332,000

b. Depreciation reported on the income statement, $83,400

c. Equipment was purchased at a cost of $162,800 and fully depreciated equipment costing $44,800 was discarded, with no salvage realized.

d. The mortgage note payable was not due until 2018 but the terms permitted earlier payment without penalty.

e. 10,000 shares of common stock were issued at $20 for cash.

f. Cash dividends declared and paid, $153,600

Instructions

Prepare a statement of cash flows, using the indirect method of presenting cash flows from operating activities.

PR 13-3A Statement of cash flows—indirect method

OBJ. 2

✔ Net cash flow from operating activities, $(169,600)

The comparative balance sheet of Whitman Co. at December 31, 2016 and 2015, is as follows:

	Dec. 31, 2016	Dec. 31, 2015
Assets		
Cash	$ 918,000	$ 964,800
Accounts receivable (net)	828,900	761,940
Inventories	1,268,460	1,162,980
Prepaid expenses	29,340	35,100
Land	315,900	479,700
Buildings	1,462,500	900,900
Accumulated depreciation—buildings	(408,600)	(382,320)
Equipment	512,280	454,680
Accumulated depreciation—equipment	(141,300)	(158,760)
Total assets	$4,785,480	$4,219,020
Liabilities and Stockholders' Equity		
Accounts payable (merchandise creditors)	$ 922,500	$ 958,320
Bonds payable	270,000	0
Common stock, $25 par	317,000	117,000
Paid-in capital: Excess of issue price over par—common stock	758,000	558,000
Retained earnings	2,517,980	2,585,700
Total liabilities and stockholders' equity	$4,785,480	$4,219,020

The noncurrent asset, noncurrent liability, and stockholders' equity accounts for 2016 are as follows:

ACCOUNT *Land* ACCOUNT NO.

Date		Item	Debit	Credit	Balance Debit	Balance Credit
2016						
Jan.	1	Balance			479,700	
Apr.	20	Realized $151,200 cash from sale		163,800	315,900	

ACCOUNT *Buildings* ACCOUNT NO.

Date		Item	Debit	Credit	Balance Debit	Balance Credit
2016						
Jan.	1	Balance			900,900	
Apr.	20	Acquired for cash	561,600		1,462,500	

(Continued)

ACCOUNT *Accumulated Depreciation—Buildings* ACCOUNT NO.

Date		Item	Debit	Credit	Balance Debit	Balance Credit
2016						
Jan.	1	Balance				382,320
Dec.	31	Depreciation for year		26,280		408,600

ACCOUNT *Equipment* ACCOUNT NO.

Date		Item	Debit	Credit	Balance Debit	Balance Credit
2016						
Jan.	1	Balance			454,680	
	26	Discarded, no salvage		46,800	407,880	
Aug.	11	Purchased for cash	104,400		512,280	

ACCOUNT *Accumulated Depreciation—Equipment* ACCOUNT NO.

Date		Item	Debit	Credit	Balance Debit	Balance Credit
2016						
Jan.	1	Balance				158,760
	26	Equipment discarded	46,800			111,960
Dec.	31	Depreciation for year		29,340		141,300

ACCOUNT *Bonds Payable* ACCOUNT NO.

Date		Item	Debit	Credit	Balance Debit	Balance Credit
2016						
May	1	Issued 20-year bonds		270,000		270,000

ACCOUNT *Common Stock, $25 par* ACCOUNT NO.

Date		Item	Debit	Credit	Balance Debit	Balance Credit
2016						
Jan.	1	Balance				117,000
Dec.	7	Issued 8,000 shares of common stock for $50 per share		200,000		317,000

ACCOUNT *Paid-In Capital in Excess of Par—Common Stock* ACCOUNT NO.

Date		Item	Debit	Credit	Balance Debit	Balance Credit
2016						
Jan.	1	Balance				558,000
Dec.	7	Issued 8,000 shares of common stock for $50 per share		200,000		758,000

ACCOUNT *Retained Earnings*					ACCOUNT NO.	
					Balance	
Date		Item	Debit	Credit	Debit	Credit
2016						
Jan.	1	Balance				2,585,700
Dec.	31	Net loss	35,320			2,550,380
	31	Cash dividends	32,400			2,517,980

Instructions

Prepare a statement of cash flows, using the indirect method of presenting cash flows from operating activities.

PR 13-4A Statement of cash flows—direct method **OBJ. 3**

✔ Net cash flow from operating activities, $293,600

General Ledger

SHOW ME HOW

The comparative balance sheet of Canace Products Inc. for December 31, 2016 and 2015, is as follows:

	Dec. 31, 2016	Dec. 31, 2015
Assets		
Cash	$ 643,400	$ 679,400
Accounts receivable (net)	566,800	547,400
Inventories	1,011,000	982,800
Investments	0	240,000
Land	520,000	0
Equipment	880,000	680,000
Accumulated depreciation	(244,400)	(200,400)
Total assets	$3,376,800	$2,929,200
Liabilities and Stockholders' Equity		
Accounts payable (merchandise creditors)	$ 771,800	$ 748,400
Accrued expenses payable (operating expenses)	63,400	70,800
Dividends payable	8,800	6,400
Common stock, $2 par	56,000	32,000
Paid-in capital: Excess of issue price over par—common stock	408,000	192,000
Retained earnings	2,068,800	1,879,600
Total liabilities and stockholders' equity	$3,376,800	$2,929,200

The income statement for the year ended December 31, 2016, is as follows:

Sales		$5,980,000
Cost of merchandise sold		2,452,000
Gross profit		$3,528,000
Operating expenses:		
Depreciation expense	$ 44,000	
Other operating expenses	3,100,000	
Total operating expenses		3,144,000
Operating income		$ 384,000
Other expense:		
Loss on sale of investments		(64,000)
Income before income tax		$ 320,000
Income tax expense		102,800
Net income		$ 217,200

Additional data obtained from an examination of the accounts in the ledger for 2016 are as follows:

a. Equipment and land were acquired for cash.

b. There were no disposals of equipment during the year.

(Continued)

c. The investments were sold for $176,000 cash.

d. The common stock was issued for cash.

e. There was a $28,000 debit to Retained Earnings for cash dividends declared.

Instructions

Prepare a statement of cash flows, using the direct method of presenting cash flows from operating activities.

✔ Net cash flow from operating activities, $143,540

PR 13-5A Statement of cash flows—direct method applied to PR 13-1A **OBJ. 3**

The comparative balance sheet of Cromme Inc. for December 31, 2016 and 2015, is as follows:

	Dec. 31, 2016	Dec. 31, 2015
Assets		
Cash	$ 625,760	$ 585,920
Accounts receivable (net)	227,840	208,960
Inventories	641,760	617,120
Investments	0	240,000
Land	328,000	0
Equipment	705,120	553,120
Accumulated depreciation—equipment	(166,400)	(148,000)
Total assets	$2,362,080	$2,057,120
Liabilities and Stockholders' Equity		
Accounts payable (merchandise creditors)	$ 424,480	$ 404,960
Accrued expenses payable (operating expenses)	42,240	52,640
Dividends payable	24,000	19,200
Common stock, $2 par	150,000	100,000
Paid-in capital: Excess of issue price over par—common stock	417,500	280,000
Retained earnings	1,303,860	1,200,320
Total liabilities and stockholders' equity	$2,362,080	$2,057,120

The income statement for the year ended December 31, 2016, is as follows:

Sales		$5,372,559
Cost of merchandise sold		3,306,190
Gross profit		$2,066,369
Operating expenses:		
Depreciation expense	$ 18,400	
Other operating expenses	1,755,402	
Total operating expenses		1,773,802
Operating income		$ 292,567
Other income:		
Gain on sale of investments		40,000
Income before income tax		$ 332,567
Income tax expense		133,027
Net income		$ 199,540

Additional data obtained from an examination of the accounts in the ledger for 2016 are as follows:

a. The investments were sold for $280,000 cash.

b. Equipment and land were acquired for cash.

c. There were no disposals of equipment during the year.

d. The common stock was issued for cash.

e. There was a $96,000 debit to Retained Earnings for cash dividends declared.

Instructions

Prepare a statement of cash flows, using the direct method of presenting cash flows from operating activities.

Problems: Series B

PR 13-1B Statement of cash flows—indirect method

OBJ. 2

✔ Net cash flow from operating activities, $154,260

SHOW ME HOW

The comparative balance sheet of Merrick Equipment Co. for December 31, 2016 and 2015, is as follows:

	Dec. 31, 2016	Dec. 31, 2015
Assets		
Cash	$ 70,720	$ 47,940
Accounts receivable (net)	207,230	188,190
Inventories	298,520	289,850
Investments	0	102,000
Land	295,800	0
Equipment	438,600	358,020
Accumulated depreciation—equipment	(99,110)	(84,320)
Total assets	$1,211,760	$901,680
Liabilities and Stockholders' Equity		
Accounts payable (merchandise creditors)	$ 205,700	$194,140
Accrued expenses payable (operating expenses)	30,600	26,860
Dividends payable	25,500	20,400
Common stock, $1 par	202,000	102,000
Paid-in capital: Excess of issue price over par—common stock	354,000	204,000
Retained earnings	393,960	354,280
Total liabilities and stockholders' equity	$1,211,760	$901,680

Additional data obtained from an examination of the accounts in the ledger for 2016 are as follows:

a. Equipment and land were acquired for cash.

b. There were no disposals of equipment during the year.

c. The investments were sold for $91,800 cash.

d. The common stock was issued for cash.

e. There was a $141,680 credit to Retained Earnings for net income.

f. There was a $102,000 debit to Retained Earnings for cash dividends declared.

Instructions

Prepare a statement of cash flows, using the indirect method of presenting cash flows from operating activities.

PR 13-2B Statement of cash flows—indirect method

OBJ. 2

✔ Net cash flow from operating activities, $561,400

SHOW ME HOW

The comparative balance sheet of Harris Industries Inc. at December 31, 2016 and 2015, is as follows:

	Dec. 31, 2016	Dec. 31, 2015
Assets		
Cash	$ 443,240	$ 360,920
Accounts receivable (net)	665,280	592,200
Inventories	887,880	1,022,560
Prepaid expenses	31,640	25,200
Land	302,400	302,400
Buildings	1,713,600	1,134,000
Accumulated depreciation—buildings	(466,200)	(414,540)
Machinery and equipment	781,200	781,200
Accumulated depreciation—machinery and equipment	(214,200)	(191,520)
Patents	106,960	112,000
Total assets	$4,251,800	$3,724,420

(Continued)

Liabilities and Stockholders' Equity		
Accounts payable (merchandise creditors)	$ 837,480	$ 927,080
Dividends payable	32,760	25,200
Salaries payable	78,960	87,080
Mortgage note payable, due 2017	224,000	0
Bonds payable	0	390,000
Common stock, $5 par	200,400	50,400
Paid-in capital: Excess of issue price over par—common stock	366,000	126,000
Retained earnings	2,512,200	2,118,660
Total liabilities and stockholders' equity	$4,251,800	$3,724,420

An examination of the income statement and the accounting records revealed the following additional information applicable to 2016:

a. Net income, $524,580.

b. Depreciation expense reported on the income statement: buildings, $51,660; machinery and equipment, $22,680.

c. Patent amortization reported on the income statement, $5,040.

d. A building was constructed for $579,600.

e. A mortgage note for $224,000 was issued for cash.

f. 30,000 shares of common stock were issued at $13 in exchange for the bonds payable.

g. Cash dividends declared, $131,040.

Instructions

Prepare a statement of cash flows, using the indirect method of presenting cash flows from operating activities.

PR 13-3B Statement of cash flows—indirect method

OBJ. 2

✔ Net cash flow from operating activities, $162,800

The comparative balance sheet of Coulson, Inc. at December 31, 2016 and 2015, is as follows:

	Dec. 31, 2016	Dec. 31, 2015
Assets		
Cash	$ 300,600	$ 337,800
Accounts receivable (net)	704,400	609,600
Inventories	918,600	865,800
Prepaid expenses	18,600	26,400
Land	990,000	1,386,000
Buildings	1,980,000	990,000
Accumulated depreciation—buildings	(397,200)	(366,000)
Equipment	660,600	529,800
Accumulated depreciation—equipment	(133,200)	(162,000)
Total assets	$5,042,400	$4,217,400
Liabilities and Stockholders' Equity		
Accounts payable (merchandise creditors)	$ 594,000	$ 631,200
Income taxes payable	26,400	21,600
Bonds payable	330,000	0
Common stock, $20 par	320,000	180,000
Paid-in capital: Excess of issue price over par—common stock	950,000	810,000
Retained earnings	2,822,000	2,574,600
Total liabilities and stockholders' equity	$5,042,400	$4,217,400

The noncurrent asset, noncurrent liability, and stockholders' equity accounts for 2016 are as follows:

ACCOUNT *Land* ACCOUNT NO.

Date		Item	Debit	Credit	Balance	
					Debit	**Credit**
2016						
Jan.	1	Balance			1,386,000	
Apr.	20	Realized $456,000 cash from sale		396,000	990,000	

ACCOUNT *Buildings* ACCOUNT NO.

Date		Item	Debit	Credit	Balance	
					Debit	**Credit**
2016						
Jan.	1	Balance			990,000	
Apr.	20	Acquired for cash	990,000		1,980,000	

ACCOUNT *Accumulated Depreciation—Buildings* ACCOUNT NO.

Date		Item	Debit	Credit	Balance	
					Debit	**Credit**
2016						
Jan.	1	Balance				366,000
Dec.	31	Depreciation for year		31,200		397,200

ACCOUNT *Equipment* ACCOUNT NO.

Date		Item	Debit	Credit	Balance	
					Debit	**Credit**
2016						
Jan.	1	Balance			529,800	
	26	Discarded, no salvage		66,000	463,800	
Aug.	11	Purchased for cash	196,800		660,600	

ACCOUNT *Accumulated Depreciation—Equipment* ACCOUNT NO.

Date		Item	Debit	Credit	Balance	
					Debit	**Credit**
2016						
Jan.	1	Balance				162,000
	26	Equipment discarded	66,000			96,000
Dec.	31	Depreciation for year		37,200		133,200

ACCOUNT *Bonds Payable* ACCOUNT NO.

Date		Item	Debit	Credit	Balance	
					Debit	**Credit**
2016						
May	1	Issued 20-year bonds		330,000		330,000

(Continued)

ACCOUNT *Common Stock, $20 par* ACCOUNT NO.

Date		Item	Debit	Credit	Balance Debit	Balance Credit
2016						
Jan.	1	Balance				180,000
Dec.	7	Issued 7,000 shares of common stock for $40 per share		140,000		320,000

ACCOUNT *Paid-In Capital in Excess of Par—Common Stock* ACCOUNT NO.

Date		Item	Debit	Credit	Balance Debit	Balance Credit
2016						
Jan.	1	Balance				810,000
Dec.	7	Issued 7,000 shares of common stock for $40 per share		140,000		950,000

ACCOUNT *Retained Earnings* ACCOUNT NO.

Date		Item	Debit	Credit	Balance Debit	Balance Credit
2016						
Jan.	1	Balance				2,574,600
Dec.	31	Net income		326,600		2,901,200
	31	Cash dividends	79,200			2,822,000

Instructions

Prepare a statement of cash flows, using the indirect method of presenting cash flows from operating activities.

PR 13-4B Statement of cash flows—direct method OBJ. 3

✔ **Net cash flow from operating activities, $509,220**

General Ledger

SHOW ME HOW

The comparative balance sheet of Martinez Inc. for December 31, 2016 and 2015, is as follows:

	Dec. 31, 2016	Dec. 31, 2015
Assets		
Cash	$ 661,920	$ 683,100
Accounts receivable (net)	992,640	914,400
Inventories	1,394,400	1,363,800
Investments	0	432,000
Land	960,000	0
Equipment	1,224,000	984,000
Accumulated depreciation—equipment	(481,500)	(368,400)
Total assets	$4,751,460	$4,008,900
Liabilities and Stockholders' Equity		
Accounts payable (merchandise creditors)	$1,080,000	$ 966,600
Accrued expenses payable (operating expenses)	67,800	79,200
Dividends payable	100,800	91,200
Common stock, $5 par	130,000	30,000
Paid-in capital: Excess of issue price over par—common stock	950,000	450,000
Retained earnings	2,422,860	2,391,900
Total liabilities and stockholders' equity	$4,751,460	$4,008,900

The income statement for the year ended December 31, 2016, is as follows:

Sales		$4,512,000
Cost of merchandise sold		2,352,000
Gross profit		$2,160,000
Operating expenses:		
Depreciation expense	$ 113,100	
Other operating expenses	1,344,840	
Total operating expenses		1,457,940
Operating income		$ 702,060
Other income:		
Gain on sale of investments		156,000
Income before income tax		$ 858,060
Income tax expense		299,100
Net income		$ 558,960

Additional data obtained from an examination of the accounts in the ledger for 2016 are as follows:

a. Equipment and land were acquired for cash.

b. There were no disposals of equipment during the year.

c. The investments were sold for $588,000 cash.

d. The common stock was issued for cash.

e. There was a $528,000 debit to Retained Earnings for cash dividends declared.

Instructions

Prepare a statement of cash flows, using the direct method of presenting cash flows from operating activities.

PR 13-5B Statement of cash flows—direct method applied to PR 13-1B OBJ. 3

✔ Net cash flow from operating activities, $154,260

The comparative balance sheet of Merrick Equipment Co. for Dec. 31, 2016 and 2015, is:

	Dec. 31, 2016	Dec. 31, 2015
Assets		
Cash	$ 70,720	$ 47,940
Accounts receivable (net)	207,230	188,190
Inventories	298,520	289,850
Investments	0	102,000
Land	295,800	0
Equipment	438,600	358,020
Accumulated depreciation—equipment	(99,110)	(84,320)
Total assets	$1,211,760	$ 901,680
Liabilities and Stockholders' Equity		
Accounts payable (merchandise creditors)	$ 205,700	$ 194,140
Accrued expenses payable (operating expenses)	30,600	26,860
Dividends payable	25,500	20,400
Common stock, $1 par	202,000	102,000
Paid-in capital: Excess of issue price over par—common stock	354,000	204,000
Retained earnings	393,960	354,280
Total liabilities and stockholders' equity	$1,211,760	$ 901,680

(Continued)

The income statement for the year ended December 31, 2016, is as follows:

Sales		$2,023,898
Cost of merchandise sold		1,245,476
Gross profit		$ 778,422
Operating expenses:		
Depreciation expense	$ 14,790	
Other operating expenses	517,299	
Total operating expenses		532,089
Operating income		$ 246,333
Other expenses:		
Loss on sale of investments		(10,200)
Income before income tax		$ 236,133
Income tax expense		94,453
Net income		$ 141,680

Additional data obtained from an examination of the accounts in the ledger for 2016 are as follows:

a. Equipment and land were acquired for cash.
b. There were no disposals of equipment during the year.
c. The investments were sold for $91,800 cash.
d. The common stock was issued for cash.
e. There was a $102,000 debit to Retained Earnings for cash dividends declared.

Instructions

Prepare a statement of cash flows, using the direct method of presenting cash flows from operating activities.

Cases & Projects

CP 13-1 Ethics and professional conduct in business

Lucas Hunter, president of Simmons Industries Inc., believes that reporting operating cash flow per share on the income statement would be a useful addition to the company's just completed financial statements. The following discussion took place between Lucas Hunter and Simmons' controller, John Jameson, in January, after the close of the fiscal year:

Lucas: I've been reviewing our financial statements for the last year. I am disappointed that our net income per share has dropped by 10% from last year. This won't look good to our shareholders. Is there anything we can do about this?

John: What do you mean? The past is the past, and the numbers are in. There isn't much that can be done about it. Our financial statements were prepared according to generally accepted accounting principles, and I don't see much leeway for significant change at this point.

Lucas: No, no. I'm not suggesting that we "cook the books." But look at the cash flow from operating activities on the statement of cash flows. The cash flow from operating activities has increased by 20%. This is very good news—and, I might add, useful information. The higher cash flow from operating activities will give our creditors comfort.

John: Well, the cash flow from operating activities is on the statement of cash flows, so I guess users will be able to see the improved cash flow figures there.

Lucas: This is true, but somehow I feel that this information should be given a much higher profile. I don't like this information being "buried" in the statement of cash flows. You know as well as I do that many users will focus on the income statement. Therefore, I think we ought to include an operating cash flow per share number on the face of the income statement—someplace under the earnings per share number. In this way, users will get the complete picture of our operating performance. Yes, our earnings per share dropped this year, but our cash flow from operating activities improved! And all the information is in one place where users can see and compare the figures. What do you think?

John: I've never really thought about it like that before. I guess we could put the operating cash flow per share on the income statement, under the earnings per share. Users would really benefit from this disclosure. Thanks for the idea—I'll start working on it.

Lucas: Glad to be of service.

How would you interpret this situation? Is John behaving in an ethical and professional manner?

CP 13-2 Using the statement of cash flows

You are considering an investment in a new start-up company, Giraffe Inc., an Internet service provider. A review of the company's financial statements reveals a negative retained earnings. In addition, it appears as though the company has been running a negative cash flow from operating activities since the company's inception.

How is the company staying in business under these circumstances? Could this be a good investment?

CP 13-3 Analysis of statement of cash flows

Dillip Lachgar is the president and majority shareholder of Argon Inc., a small retail store chain. Recently, Dillip submitted a loan application for Argon Inc. to Compound Bank. It called for a $600,000, 9%, 10-year loan to help finance the construction of a building and the purchase of store equipment, costing a total of $750,000. This will enable Argon Inc. to open a store in the town of Compound. Land for this purpose was acquired last year. The bank's loan officer requested a statement of cash flows in addition to the most recent income statement, balance sheet, and retained earnings statement that Dillip had submitted with the loan application.

As a close family friend, Dillip asked you to prepare a statement of cash flows. From the records provided, you prepared the following statement:

Argon Inc.
Statement of Cash Flows
For the Year Ended December 31, 2016

Cash flows from operating activities:		
Net income	$ 300,000	
Adjustments to reconcile net income to net cash flow from operating activities:		
Depreciation	84,000	
Gain on sale of investments	(30,000)	
Changes in current operating assets and liabilities:		
Decrease in accounts receivable	21,000	
Increase in inventories	(42,000)	
Increase in accounts payable	30,000	
Decrease in accrued expenses payable	(6,000)	
Net cash flow from operating activities		$ 357,000
Cash flows from investing activities:		
Cash received from investments sold	$ 180,000	
Less: Cash paid for purchase of store equipment	(120,000)	
Net cash flow from investing activities		60,000
Cash flows from financing activities:		
Cash paid for dividends	$ (126,000)	
Net cash flow used for financing activities		(126,000)
Increase in cash		$ 291,000
Cash at the beginning of the year		108,000
Cash at the end of the year		$ 399,000

Schedule of Noncash Financing and Investing Activities:

Issued common stock for land	$ 240,000

(Continued)

After reviewing the statement, Dillip telephoned you and commented, "Are you sure this statement is right?" Dillip then raised the following questions:

1. "How can depreciation be a cash flow?"
2. "Issuing common stock for the land is listed in a separate schedule. This transaction has nothing to do with cash! Shouldn't this transaction be eliminated from the statement?"
3. "How can the gain on the sale of investments be a deduction from net income in determining the cash flow from operating activities?"
4. "Why does the bank need this statement anyway? They can compute the increase in cash from the balance sheets for the last two years."

After jotting down Dillip's questions, you assured him that this statement was "right." But to alleviate Dillip's concern, you arranged a meeting for the following day.

a. How would you respond to each of Dillip's questions?

b. Do you think that the statement of cash flows enhances the chances of Argon Inc. receiving the loan? Discuss.

CP 13-4 Analysis of cash flow from operations

The Commercial Division of Tidewater Inc. provided the following information on its cash flow from operations:

Net income	$ 945,000
Increase in accounts receivable	(1,134,000)
Increase in inventory	(1,260,000)
Decrease in accounts payable	(189,000)
Depreciation	210,000
Cash flow from operating activities	$(1,428,000)

The manager of the Commercial Division provided the accompanying memo with this report:

From: Senior Vice President, Commercial Division

I am pleased to report that we had earnings of $945,000 over the last period. This resulted in a return on invested capital of 8%, which is near our targets for this division. I have been aggressive in building the revenue volume in the division. As a result, I am happy to report that we have increased the number of new credit card customers as a result of an aggressive marketing campaign. In addition, we have found some excellent merchandise opportunities. Some of our suppliers have made some of their apparel merchandise available at a deep discount. We have purchased as much of these goods as possible in order to improve profitability. I'm also happy to report that our vendor payment problems have improved. We are nearly caught up on our overdue payables balances.

Comment on the senior vice president's memo in light of the cash flow information.

CP 13-5 Statement of cash flows

Internet Project

Group Project

This activity will require two teams to retrieve cash flow statement information from the Internet. One team is to obtain the most recent year's statement of cash flows for **Johnson & Johnson**, and the other team the most recent year's statement of cash flows for **JetBlue Airways Corp.**

The statement of cash flows is included as part of the annual report information that is a required disclosure to the Securities and Exchange Commission (SEC). SEC documents can be retrieved using the EdgarScan™ service at www.sec.gov/edgar/searchedgar/companysearch.html.

To obtain annual report information, key in a company name in the appropriate space. EdgarScan will list the reports available to you for the company you've selected. Select the most recent annual report filing, identified as a 10-K or 10-K405. EdgarScan provides an outline of the report, including the separate financial statements. You can double-click the income statement and balance sheet for the selected company into an Excel™ spreadsheet for further analysis.

As a group, compare the two statements of cash flows.

a. How are Johnson & Johnson and JetBlue Airways Corp. similar or different regarding cash flows?

b. Compute and compare the free cash flow for each company, assuming additions to property, plant, and equipment replace current capacity.

CHAPTER 14

Financial Statement Analysis

Nike, Inc.

"Just do it." These three words identify one of the most recognizable brands in the world, **Nike**. While this phrase inspires athletes to "compete and achieve their potential," it also defines the company.

Nike began in 1964 as a partnership between University of Oregon track coach Bill Bowerman and one of his former student-athletes, Phil Knight. The two began by selling shoes imported from Japan out of the back of Knight's car to athletes at track and field events. As sales grew, the company opened retail outlets, calling itself **Blue Ribbon Sports**. The company also began to develop its own shoes. In 1971, the company commissioned a graphic design student at Portland State University to develop the swoosh logo for a fee of $35. In 1978, the company changed its name to Nike, and in 1980, it sold its first shares of stock to the public.

Nike would have been a great company to invest in at the time. If you had invested in Nike's common stock back in 1990, you would have paid $5.00 per share. As of April 2011, Nike's stock was worth $109.23 per share. Unfortunately, you can't invest using hindsight.

How can you select companies in which to invest? Like any significant purchase, you should do some research to guide your investment decision. If you were buying a car, for example, you might go to **Edmunds.com** to obtain reviews, ratings, prices, specifications, options, and fuel economies to evaluate different vehicles. In selecting companies to invest in, you can use financial analysis to gain insight into a company's past performance and future prospects. This chapter describes and illustrates common financial data that can be analyzed to assist you in making investment decisions such as whether or not to invest in Nike's stock.

Source: www.nikebiz.com/.

Learning Objectives

After studying this chapter, you should be able to: *Example Exercises*

		Example Exercises
OBJ 1	**Describe basic financial statement analytical methods.**	
	Basic Analytical Methods	
	Horizontal Analysis	EE 14-1
	Vertical Analysis	EE 14-2
	Common-Sized Statements	
	Other Analytical Measures	
OBJ 2	**Use financial statement analysis to assess the solvency of a business.**	
	Liquidity and Solvency Analysis	
	Current Position Analysis	EE 14-3
	Accounts Receivable Analysis	EE 14-4
	Inventory Analysis	EE 14-5
	Ratio of Fixed Assets to Long-Term Liabilities	
	Ratio of Liabilities to Stockholders' Equity	EE 14-6
	Number of Times Interest Charges Are Earned	EE 14-7
OBJ 3	**Use financial statement analysis to assess the profitability of a business.**	
	Profitability Analysis	
	Ratio of Sales to Assets	EE 14-8
	Rate Earned on Total Assets	EE 14-9
	Rate Earned on Stockholders' Equity	
	Rate Earned on Common Stockholders' Equity	EE 14-10
	Earnings per Share on Common Stock	
	Price-Earnings Ratio	EE 14-11
	Divdends per Share	
	Divdend Yield	
	Summary of Analytical Measures	
OBJ 4	**Describe the contents of corporate annual reports.**	
	Corporate Annual Reports	
	Management Discussion and Analysis	
	Report on Internal Control	
	Report on Fairness of the Financial Statements	

At a Glance 14 Page 611

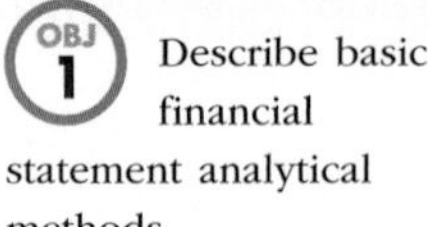
Describe basic financial statement analytical methods.

Basic Analytical Methods

Users analyze a company's financial statements using a variety of analytical methods. Three such methods are:

- Horizontal analysis
- Vertical analysis
- Common-sized statements

Horizontal Analysis

The analysis of increases and decreases in the amount and percentage of comparative financial statement items is called **horizontal analysis**. Each item on the most recent statement is compared with the same item on one or more earlier statements in terms of the following:

- *Amount* of increase or decrease
- *Percent* of increase or decrease

When comparing statements, the earlier statement is normally used as the base year for computing increases and decreases.

Exhibit 1 illustrates horizontal analysis for the December 31, 2016 and 2015, balance sheets of **Lincoln Company**. In Exhibit 1, the December 31, 2015, balance sheet (the earliest year presented) is used as the base year.

Exhibit 1 indicates that total assets decreased by $91,000 (7.4%), liabilities decreased by $133,000 (30.0%), and stockholders' equity increased by $42,000 (5.3%). Since the long-term investments account decreased by $82,500, it appears that most of the decrease in long-term liabilities of $100,000 was achieved through the sale of long-term investments.

EXHIBIT 1

Comparative Balance Sheet—Horizontal Analysis

Lincoln Company
Comparative Balance Sheet
December 31, 2016 and 2015

	Dec. 31, 2016	Dec. 31, 2015	Increase (Decrease) Amount	Increase (Decrease) Percent
Assets				
Current assets	$ 550,000	$ 533,000	$ 17,000	3.2%
Long-term investments	95,000	177,500	(82,500)	(46.5%)
Property, plant, and equipment (net)	444,500	470,000	(25,500)	(5.4%)
Intangible assets	50,000	50,000	—	—
Total assets	$1,139,500	$1,230,500	$ (91,000)	(7.4%)
Liabilities				
Current liabilities	$ 210,000	$ 243,000	$ (33,000)	(13.6%)
Long-term liabilities	100,000	200,000	(100,000)	(50.0%)
Total liabilities	$ 310,000	$ 443,000	$(133,000)	(30.0%)
Stockholders' Equity				
Preferred 6% stock, $100 par	$ 150,000	$ 150,000	—	—
Common stock, $10 par	500,000	500,000	—	—
Retained earnings	179,500	137,500	$ 42,000	30.5%
Total stockholders' equity	$ 829,500	$ 787,500	$ 42,000	5.3%
Total liabilities and stockholders' equity	$1,139,500	$1,230,500	$ (91,000)	(7.4%)

The balance sheets in Exhibit 1 may be expanded or supported by a separate schedule that includes the individual asset and liability accounts. For example, Exhibit 2 is a supporting schedule of **Lincoln Company**'s current asset accounts.

EXHIBIT 2

Comparative Schedule of Current Assets—Horizontal Analysis

Lincoln Company
Comparative Schedule of Current Assets
December 31, 2016 and 2015

	Dec. 31, 2016	Dec. 31, 2015	Increase (Decrease) Amount	Increase (Decrease) Percent
Cash	$ 90,500	$ 64,700	$ 25,800	39.9%
Temporary investments	75,000	60,000	15,000	25.0%
Accounts receivable (net)	115,000	120,000	(5,000)	(4.2%)
Inventories	264,000	283,000	(19,000)	(6.7%)
Prepaid expenses	5,500	5,300	200	3.8%
Total current assets	$550,000	$533,000	$ 17,000	3.2%

Exhibit 2 indicates that while cash and temporary investments increased, accounts receivable and inventories decreased. The decrease in accounts receivable could be caused by improved collection policies, which would increase cash. The decrease in inventories could be caused by increased sales.

Exhibit 3 illustrates horizontal analysis for the 2016 and 2015 income statements of **Lincoln Company**. Exhibit 3 indicates an increase in sales of $296,500, or 24.0%. However, the percentage increase in sales of 24.0% was accompanied by an even greater percentage increase in the cost of goods (merchandise) sold of 27.2%.[1] Thus, gross profit increased by only 19.7% rather than by the 24.0% increase in sales.

EXHIBIT 3

Comparative Income Statement—Horizontal Analysis

Lincoln Company
Comparative Income Statement
For the Years Ended December 31, 2016 and 2015

	2016	2015	Increase (Decrease) Amount	Increase (Decrease) Percent
Sales	$1,498,000	$1,200,000	$298,000	24.8%
Cost of goods sold	1,043,000	820,000	223,000	27.2%
Gross profit	$ 455,000	$ 380,000	$ 75,000	19.7%
Selling expenses	$ 191,000	$ 147,000	$ 44,000	29.9%
Administrative expenses	104,000	97,400	6,600	6.8%
Total operating expenses	$ 295,000	$ 244,400	$ 50,600	20.7%
Income from operations	$ 160,000	$ 135,600	$ 24,400	18.0%
Other income	8,500	11,000	(2,500)	(22.7%)
	$ 168,500	$ 146,600	$ 21,900	14.9%
Other expense (interest)	6,000	12,000	(6,000)	(50.0%)
Income before income tax	$ 162,500	$ 134,600	$ 27,900	20.7%
Income tax expense	71,500	58,100	13,400	23.1%
Net income	$ 91,000	$ 76,500	$ 14,500	19.0%

Exhibit 3 also indicates that selling expenses increased by 29.9%. Thus, the 24.0% increases in sales could have been caused by an advertising campaign, which increased selling expenses. Administrative expenses increased by only 6.8%, total operating expenses increased by 20.7%, and income from operations increased by 18.0%. Interest expense decreased by 50.0%. This decrease was probably caused by the 50.0% decrease in long-term liabilities (Exhibit 1). Overall, net income increased by 19.0%, a favorable result.

Exhibit 4 illustrates horizontal analysis for the 2016 and 2015 retained earnings statements of **Lincoln Company**. Exhibit 4 indicates that retained earnings increased by 30.5% for the year. The increase is due to net income of $91,000 for the year, less dividends of $49,000.

EXHIBIT 4

Comparative Retained Earnings Statement—Horizontal Analysis

Lincoln Company
Comparative Retained Earnings Statement
For the Years Ended December 31, 2016 and 2015

	2016	2015	Increase (Decrease) Amount	Increase (Decrease) Percent
Retained earnings, January 1	$137,500	$100,000	$37,500	37.5%
Net income for the year	91,000	76,500	14,500	19.0%
Total	$228,500	$176,500	$52,000	29.5%
Dividends:				
On preferred stock	$ 9,000	$ 9,000	—	—
On common stock	40,000	30,000	$10,000	33.3%
Total	$ 49,000	$ 39,000	$10,000	25.6%
Retained earnings, December 31	$179,500	$137,500	$42,000	30.5%

[1] The term *cost of goods sold* is often used in practice in place of *cost of merchandise sold*. Such usage is followed in this chapter.

Example Exercise 14-1 Horizontal Analysis

OBJ 1

The comparative cash and accounts receivable balances for a company follow:

	Dec. 31, 2016	Dec. 31, 2015
Cash	$62,500	$50,000
Accounts receivable (net)	74,400	80,000

Based on this information, what is the amount and percentage of increase or decrease that would be shown on a balance sheet with horizontal analysis?

Follow My Example 14-1

Cash $12,500 increase ($62,500 – $50,000), or 25%
Accounts receivable $5,600 decrease ($74,400 – $80,000), or (7%)

Practice Exercises: PE 14-1A, PE 14-1B

Vertical Analysis

The percentage analysis of the relationship of each component in a financial statement to a total within the statement is called **vertical analysis**. Although vertical analysis is applied to a single statement, it may be applied on the same statement over time. This enhances the analysis by showing how the percentages of each item have changed over time.

In vertical analysis of the balance sheet, the percentages are computed as follows:

- Each asset item is stated as a percent of the total assets.
- Each liability and stockholders' equity item is stated as a percent of the total liabilities and stockholders' equity.

Exhibit 5 illustrates the vertical analysis of the December 31, 2016 and 2015, balance sheets of **Lincoln Company**. Exhibit 5 indicates that current assets have increased from 43.3% to 48.3% of total assets. Long-term investments decreased from 14.4% to 8.3% of total assets. Stockholders' equity increased from 64.0% to 72.8%, with a comparable decrease in liabilities.

EXHIBIT 5

Comparative Balance Sheet—Vertical Analysis

Lincoln Company
Comparative Balance Sheet
December 31, 2016 and 2015

	Dec. 31, 2016		Dec. 31, 2015	
	Amount	**Percent**	**Amount**	**Percent**
Assets				
Current assets	$ 550,000	48.3%	$ 533,000	43.3%
Long-term investments	95,000	8.3	177,500	14.4
Property, plant, and equipment (net)	444,500	39.0	470,000	38.2
Intangible assets	50,000	4.4	50,000	4.1
Total assets	$1,139,500	100.0%	$1,230,500	100.0%
Liabilities				
Current liabilities	$ 210,000	18.4%	$ 243,000	19.7%
Long-term liabilities	100,000	8.8	200,000	16.3
Total liabilities	$ 310,000	27.2%	$ 443,000	36.0%
Stockholders' Equity				
Preferred 6% stock, $100 par	$ 150,000	13.2%	$ 150,000	12.2%
Common stock, $10 par	500,000	43.9	500,000	40.6
Retained earnings	179,500	15.7	137,500	11.2
Total stockholders' equity	$ 829,500	72.8%	$ 787,500	64.0%
Total liabilities and stockholders' equity	$1,139,500	100.0%	$1,230,500	100.0%

In a vertical analysis of the income statement, each item is stated as a percent of sales. Exhibit 6 illustrates the vertical analysis of the 2016 and 2015 income statements of **Lincoln Company**.

EXHIBIT 6

Comparative Income Statement—Vertical Analysis

Lincoln Company
Comparative Income Statement
For the Years Ended December 31, 2016 and 2015

	2016		2015	
	Amount	**Percent**	**Amount**	**Percent**
Sales	$1,498,000	100.0%	$1,200,000	100.0%
Cost of goods sold	1,043,000	69.6	820,000	68.3
Gross profit	$ 455,000	30.4%	$ 380,000	31.7%
Selling expenses	$ 191,000	12.8%	$ 147,000	12.3%
Administrative expenses	104,000	6.9	97,400	8.1
Total operating expenses	$ 295,000	19.7%	$ 244,400	20.4%
Income from operations	$ 160,000	10.7%	$ 135,600	11.3%
Other income	8,500	0.6	11,000	0.9
	$ 168,500	11.3%	$ 146,600	12.2%
Other expense (interest)	6,000	0.4	12,000	1.0
Income before income tax	$ 162,500	10.9%	$ 134,600	11.2%
Income tax expense	71,500	4.8	58,100	4.8
Net income	$ 91,000	6.1%	$ 76,500	6.4%

Exhibit 6 indicates a decrease in the gross profit rate from 31.7% in 2015 to 30.4% in 2016. Although this is only a 1.3 percentage point (31.7% – 30.4%) decrease, in dollars of potential gross profit, it represents a decrease of $19,474 (1.3% × $1,498,000) based on 2016 sales. Thus, a small percentage decrease can have a large dollar effect.

Example Exercise 14-2 Vertical Analysis

Income statement information for Lee Corporation follows:

Sales	$100,000
Cost of goods sold	65,000
Gross profit	$ 35,000

Prepare a vertical analysis of the income statement for Lee Corporation.

Follow My Example 14-2

	Amount	Percentage	
Sales	$100,000	100%	($100,000 ÷ $100,000)
Cost of goods sold	65,000	65	($65,000 ÷ $100,000)
Gross profit	$ 35,000	35%	($35,000 ÷ $100,000)

Practice Exercises: PE 14-2A, PE 14-2B

Common-Sized Statements

In a **common-sized statement**, all items are expressed as percentages, with no dollar amounts shown. Common-sized statements are often useful for comparing one company with another or for comparing a company with industry averages.

Exhibit 7 illustrates common-sized income statements for **Lincoln Company** and Madison Corporation. Exhibit 7 indicates that Lincoln has a slightly higher rate of gross profit (30.4%) than Madison (30.0%). However, Lincoln has a higher percentage of selling expenses (12.8%) and administrative expenses (6.9%) than does Madison (11.5% and 4.1%). As a result, the income from operations of Lincoln (10.7%) is less than that of Madison (14.4%).

EXHIBIT 7

Common-Sized Income Statements

	Lincoln Company	Madison Corporation
Sales	100.0%	100.0%
Cost of goods sold	69.6	70.0
Gross profit	30.4%	30.0%
Selling expenses	12.8%	11.5%
Administrative expenses	6.9	4.1
Total operating expenses	19.7%	15.6%
Income from operations	10.7%	14.4%
Other income	0.6	0.6
	11.3%	15.0%
Other expense (interest)	0.4	0.5
Income before income tax	10.9%	14.5%
Income tax expense	4.8	5.5
Net income	6.1%	9.0%

The unfavorable difference of 3.7 (14.4% – 10.7%) percentage points in income from operations would concern the managers and other stakeholders of Lincoln. The underlying causes of the difference should be investigated and possibly corrected. For example, Lincoln may decide to outsource some of its administrative duties so that its administrative expenses are more comparative to that of Madison.

Other Analytical Measures

Other relationships may be expressed in ratios and percentages. Often, these relationships are compared within the same statement and, thus, are a type of vertical analysis. Comparing these items with items from earlier periods is a type of horizontal analysis.

Analytical measures are not a definitive conclusion. They are only guides in evaluating financial and operating data. Many other factors, such as trends in the industry and general economic conditions, should also be considered when analyzing a company.

Liquidity and Solvency Analysis

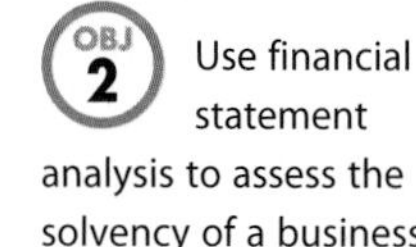

Use financial statement analysis to assess the solvency of a business.

All users of financial statements are interested in the ability of a company to do the following:

- Maintain liquidity and solvency
- Earn income, called **profitability**

The ability of a company to convert assets into cash is called **liquidity**, while the ability of a company to pay its debts is called **solvency**. Liquidity, solvency, and profitability are interrelated. For example, a company that cannot convert assets into cash may have difficulty taking advantage of profitable courses of action requiring immediate cash outlays. Likewise, a company that cannot pay its debts will have difficulty obtaining credit. A lack of credit will, in turn, limit the company's ability to purchase merchandise or expand operations, which decreases its profitability.

Liquidity and solvency are normally assessed using the following:

- Current position analysis
    - Working capital
    - Current ratio
    - Quick ratio
- Accounts receivable analysis
    - Accounts receivable turnover
    - Number of days' sales in receivables
- Inventory analysis
    - Inventory turnover
    - Number of days' sales in inventory
- The ratio of fixed assets to long-term liabilities
- The ratio of liabilities to stockholders' equity
- The number of times interest charges are earned

One popular printed source for industry ratios is *Annual Statement Studies* from Risk Management Association. Online analysis is available from Zacks Investment Research site at www.zacks.com.

The Lincoln Company financial statements presented earlier are used to illustrate the preceding analyses.

Current Position Analysis

A company's ability to pay its current liabilities is called **current position analysis**. It is a solvency measure of special interest to short-term creditors and includes the computation and analysis of the following:

- Working capital
- Current ratio
- Quick ratio

Working Capital A company's **working capital** is computed as follows:

Working Capital = Current Assets – Current Liabilities

To illustrate, the working capital for **Lincoln Company** for 2016 and 2015 is computed as follows:

	2016	2015
Current assets	$550,000	$533,000
Less current liabilities	210,000	243,000
Working capital	$340,000	$290,000

The working capital is used to evaluate a company's ability to pay current liabilities. A company's working capital is often monitored monthly, quarterly, or yearly by creditors and other debtors. However, it is difficult to use working capital to compare companies of different sizes. For example, working capital of $250,000 may be adequate for a local hardware store, but it would be inadequate for **The Home Depot**.

Current Ratio The **current ratio**, sometimes called the *working capital ratio*, is computed as follows:

$$\text{Current Ratio} = \frac{\text{Current Assets}}{\text{Current Liabilities}}$$

To illustrate, the current ratio for **Lincoln Company** is computed as follows:

	2016	2015
Current assets	$550,000	$533,000
Current liabilities	$210,000	$243,000
Current ratio	2.6 ($550,000 ÷ $210,000)	2.2 ($533,000 ÷ $243,000)

The current ratio is a more reliable indicator of a company's ability to pay its current liabilities than is working capital, and it is much easier to compare across companies. To illustrate, assume that as of December 31, 2016, the working capital of a competitor is much greater than $340,000, but its current ratio is only 1.3. Considering these facts alone, Lincoln, with its current ratio of 2.6, is in a more favorable position to obtain short-term credit than the competitor, which has the greater amount of working capital.

Quick Ratio One limitation of working capital and the current ratio is that they do not consider the types of current assets a company has and how easily they can be turned in to cash. Because of this, two companies may have the same working capital and current ratios but differ significantly in their ability to pay their current liabilities.

To illustrate, the current assets and liabilities for **Lincoln Company** and Jefferson Corporation as of December 31, 2016, are as follows:

	Lincoln Company	Jefferson Corporation
Current assets:		
Cash	$ 90,500	$ 45,500
Temporary investments	75,000	25,000
Accounts receivable (net)	115,000	90,000
Inventories	264,000	380,000
Prepaid expenses	5,500	9,500
Total current assets	$550,000	$550,000
Total current assets	$550,000	$550,000
Less current liabilities	210,000	210,000
Working capital	$340,000	$340,000
Current ratio ($550,000 ÷ $210,000)	2.6	2.6

Lincoln and Jefferson both have a working capital of $340,000 and current ratios of 2.6. Jefferson, however, has more of its current assets in inventories. These inventories must be sold and the receivables collected before all the current liabilities can be paid. This takes time. In addition, if the market for its product declines, Jefferson may have difficulty selling its inventory. This, in turn, could impair its ability to pay its current liabilities.

In contrast, Lincoln's current assets contain more cash, temporary investments, and accounts receivable, which can easily be converted to cash. Thus, Lincoln is in a stronger current position than Jefferson to pay its current liabilities.

A ratio that measures the "instant" debt-paying ability of a company is the **quick ratio**, sometimes called the *acid-test ratio*. The quick ratio is computed as follows:

$$\text{Quick Ratio} = \frac{\text{Quick Assets}}{\text{Current Liabilities}}$$

Quick assets are cash and other current assets that can be easily converted to cash. Quick assets normally include cash, temporary investments, and receivables but exclude inventories and prepaid assets.

To illustrate, the quick ratio for **Lincoln Company** is computed as follows:

	2016	2015
Quick assets:		
Cash	$ 90,500	$ 64,700
Temporary investments	75,000	60,000
Accounts receivable (net)	115,000	120,000
Total quick assets	$280,500	$244,700
Current liabilities	$210,000	$243,000
Quick ratio	1.3 ($280,500 ÷ $210,000)	1.0 ($244,700 ÷ $243,000)

Example Exercise 14-3 Current Position Analysis OBJ 2

The following items are reported on a company's balance sheet:

Cash	$300,000
Temporary investments	100,000
Accounts receivable (net)	200,000
Inventory	200,000
Accounts payable	400,000

Determine (a) the current ratio and (b) the quick ratio.

Follow My Example 14-3

a. Current Ratio = Current Assets ÷ Current Liabilities
= ($300,000 + $100,000 + $200,000 + $200,000) ÷ $400,000
= 2.0

b. Quick Ratio = Quick Assets ÷ Current Liabilities
= ($300,000 + $100,000 + $200,000) ÷ $400,000
= 1.5

Practice Exercises: PE 14-3A, PE 14-3B

Accounts Receivable Analysis

A company's ability to collect its accounts receivable is called **accounts receivable analysis.** It includes the computation and analysis of the following:

- Accounts receivable turnover
- Number of days' sales in receivables

Collecting accounts receivable as quickly as possible improves a company's liquidity. In addition, the cash collected from receivables may be used to improve or expand operations. Quick collection of receivables also reduces the risk of uncollectible accounts.

Accounts Receivable Turnover The **accounts receivable turnover** is computed as follows:

$$\text{Accounts Receivable Turnover} = \frac{\text{Sales}^2}{\text{Average Accounts Receivable}}$$

To illustrate, the accounts receivable turnover for **Lincoln Company** for 2016 and 2015 is computed as follows. Lincoln's accounts receivable balance at the beginning of 2015 is $140,000.

	2016	2015
Sales	$1,498,000	$1,200,000
Accounts receivable (net):		
Beginning of year	$ 120,000	$ 140,000
End of year	115,000	120,000
Total	$ 235,000	$ 260,000
Average accounts receivable	$117,500 ($235,000 ÷ 2)	$130,000 ($260,000 ÷ 2)
Accounts receivable turnover	12.7 ($1,498,000 ÷ $117,500)	9.2 ($1,200,000 ÷ $130,000)

The increase in Lincoln's accounts receivable turnover from 9.2 to 12.7 indicates that the collection of receivables has improved during 2016. This may be due to a change in how credit is granted, collection practices, or both.

[2] If known, *credit* sales should be used in the numerator. Because credit sales are not normally known by external users, we use sales in the numerator.

For Lincoln, the average accounts receivable was computed using the accounts receivable balance at the beginning and the end of the year. When sales are seasonal and, thus, vary throughout the year, monthly balances of receivables are often used. Also, if sales on account include notes receivable as well as accounts receivable, notes and accounts receivable are normally combined for analysis.

Number of Days' Sales in Receivables The **number of days' sales in receivables** is computed as follows:

$$\text{Number of Days' Sales in Receivables} = \frac{\text{Average Accounts Receivable}}{\text{Average Daily Sales}}$$

where

$$\text{Average Daily Sales} = \frac{\text{Sales}}{\text{365 days}}$$

To illustrate, the number of days' sales in receivables for **Lincoln Company** is computed as follows:

	2016	2015
Average accounts receivable	\$117,500 (\$235,000 ÷ 2)	\$130,000 (\$260,000 ÷ 2)
Average daily sales	\$4,104 (\$1,498,000 ÷ 365)	\$3,288 (\$1,200,000 ÷ 365)
Number of days' sales in receivables	28.6 (\$117,500 ÷ \$4,104)	39.5 (\$130,000 ÷ \$3,288)

The number of days' sales in receivables is an estimate of the time (in days) that the accounts receivable have been outstanding. The number of days' sales in receivables is often compared with a company's credit terms to evaluate the efficiency of the collection of receivables.

To illustrate, if Lincoln's credit terms are 2/10, n/30, then Lincoln was very *inefficient* in collecting receivables in 2015. In other words, receivables should have been collected in 30 days or less but were being collected in 39.5 days. Although collections improved during 2016 to 28.6 days, there is probably still room for improvement. On the other hand, if Lincoln's credit terms are n/45, then there is probably little room for improving collections.

Example Exercise 14-4 Accounts Receivable Analysis

OBJ 2

A company reports the following:

Sales	\$960,000
Average accounts receivable (net)	48,000

Determine (a) the accounts receivable turnover and (b) the number of days' sales in receivables. Round to one decimal place.

Follow My Example 14-4

a. Accounts Receivable Turnover = Sales ÷ Average Accounts Receivable
= \$960,000 ÷ \$48,000
= 20.0

b. Number of Days' Sales in Receivables = Average Accounts Receivable ÷ Average Daily Sales
= \$48,000 ÷ (\$960,000 ÷ 365) = \$48,000 ÷ \$2,630
= 18.3 days

Practice Exercises: PE 14-4A, PE 14-4B

Inventory Analysis

A company's ability to manage its inventory effectively is evaluated using **inventory analysis**. It includes the computation and analysis of the following:

- Inventory turnover
- Number of days' sales in inventory

Excess inventory decreases liquidity by tying up funds (cash) in inventory. In addition, excess inventory increases insurance expense, property taxes, storage costs, and other related expenses. These expenses further reduce funds that could be used elsewhere to improve or expand operations.

Excess inventory also increases the risk of losses because of price declines or obsolescence of the inventory. On the other hand, a company should keep enough inventory in stock so that it doesn't lose sales because of lack of inventory.

Inventory Turnover The **inventory turnover** is computed as follows:

$$\text{Inventory Turnover} = \frac{\text{Cost of Goods Sold}}{\text{Average Inventory}}$$

To illustrate, the inventory turnover for **Lincoln Company** for 2016 and 2015 is computed as follows. Lincoln's inventory balance at the beginning of 2015 is $311,000.

	2016	2015
Cost of goods sold	$1,043,000	$820,000
Inventories:		
Beginning of year	$ 283,000	$311,000
End of year	264,000	283,000
Total	$ 547,000	$594,000
Average inventory	$273,500 ($547,000 ÷ 2)	$297,000 ($594,000 ÷ 2)
Inventory turnover	3.8 ($1,043,000 ÷ $273,500)	2.8 ($820,000 ÷ $297,000)

The increase in Lincoln's inventory turnover from 2.8 to 3.8 indicates that the management of inventory has improved in 2016. The inventory turnover improved because of an increase in the cost of goods sold, which indicates more sales and a decrease in the average inventories.

What is considered a good inventory turnover varies by type of inventory, companies, and industries. For example, grocery stores have a higher inventory turnover than jewelers or furniture stores. Likewise, within a grocery store, perishable foods have a higher turnover than the soaps and cleansers.

Number of Days' Sales in Inventory The **number of days' sales in inventory** is computed as follows:

$$\text{Number of Days' Sales in Inventory} = \frac{\text{Average Inventory}}{\text{Average Daily Cost of Goods Sold}}$$

where

$$\text{Average Daily Cost of Goods Sold} = \frac{\text{Cost of Goods Sold}}{\text{365 days}}$$

To illustrate, the number of days' sales in inventory for **Lincoln Company** is computed as follows:

	2016	2015
Average inventory	$273,500 ($547,000 ÷ 2)	$297,000 ($594,000 ÷ 2)
Average daily cost of goods sold	$2,858 ($1,043,000 ÷ 365)	$2,247 ($820,000 ÷ 365)
Number of days' sales in inventory	95.7 ($273,500 ÷ $2,858)	132.2 ($297,000 ÷ $2,247)

The number of days' sales in inventory is a rough measure of the length of time it takes to purchase, sell, and replace the inventory. Lincoln's number of days' sales in inventory improved from 132.2 days to 95.7 days during 2016. This is a major improvement in managing inventory.

Example Exercise 14-5 Inventory Analysis OBJ 2

A company reports the following:

Cost of goods sold	$560,000
Average inventory	112,000

Determine (a) the inventory turnover and (b) the number of days' sales in inventory. Round to one decimal place.

Follow My Example 14-5

a. Inventory Turnover = Cost of Goods Sold ÷ Average Inventory
= $560,000 ÷ $112,000
= 5.0

b. Number of Days' Sales in Inventory = Average Inventory ÷ Average Daily Cost of Goods Sold
= $112,000 ÷ ($560,000 ÷ 365) = $112,000 ÷ $1,534
= 73.0 days

Practice Exercises: PE 14-5A, PE 14-5B

Ratio of Fixed Assets to Long-Term Liabilities

The **ratio of fixed assets to long-term liabilities** provides a measure of whether noteholders or bondholders will be paid. Because fixed assets are often pledged as security for long-term notes and bonds, it is computed as follows:

$$\text{Ratio of Fixed Assets to Long-Term Liabilities} = \frac{\text{Fixed Assets (net)}}{\text{Long-Term Liabilities}}$$

To illustrate, the ratio of fixed assets to long-term liabilities for **Lincoln Company** is computed as follows:

	2016	2015
Fixed assets (net)	$444,500	$470,000
Long-term liabilities	$100,000	$200,000
Ratio of fixed assets to long-term liabilities	4.4 ($444,500 ÷ $100,000)	2.4 ($470,000 ÷ $200,000)

During 2016, Lincoln's ratio of fixed assets to long-term liabilities increased from 2.4 to 4.4. This increase was due primarily to Lincoln paying off one-half of its long-term liabilities in 2016.

Ratio of Liabilities to Stockholders' Equity

The **ratio of liabilities to stockholders' equity** measures how much of the company is financed by debt and equity. It is computed as follows:

$$\text{Ratio of Liabilities to Stockholders' Equity} = \frac{\text{Total Liabilities}}{\text{Total Stockholders' Equity}}$$

To illustrate, the ratio of liabilities to stockholders' equity for **Lincoln Company** is computed as follows:

	2016	2015
Total liabilities	$310,000	$443,000
Total stockholders' equity	$829,500	$787,500
Ratio of liabilities to stockholders' equity	0.4 ($310,000 ÷ $829,500)	0.6 ($443,000 ÷ $787,500)

Lincoln's ratio of liabilities to stockholders' equity decreased from 0.6 to 0.4 during 2016. This is an improvement and indicates that Lincoln's creditors have an adequate margin of safety.

Example Exercise 14-6 Long-Term Solvency Analysis

OBJ 2

The following information was taken from Acme Company's balance sheet:

Fixed assets (net)	$1,400,000
Long-term liabilities	400,000
Total liabilities	560,000
Total stockholders' equity	1,400,000

Determine the company's (a) ratio of fixed assets to long-term liabilities and (b) ratio of liabilities to total stockholders' equity.

Follow My Example 14-6

a. Ratio of Fixed Assets to Long-Term Liabilities = Fixed Assets ÷ Long-Term Liabilities
= $1,400,000 ÷ $400,000
= 3.5

b. Ratio of Liabilities to Total Stockholders' Equity = Total Liabilities ÷ Total Stockholders' Equity
= $560,000 ÷ $1,400,000
= 0.4

Practice Exercises: PE 14-6A, PE 14-6B

Number of Times Interest Charges Are Earned

The **number of times interest charges are earned**, sometimes called the *fixed charge coverage ratio*, measures the risk that interest payments will not be made if earnings decrease. It is computed as follows:

$$\text{Number of Times Interest Charges Are Earned} = \frac{\text{Income Before Income Tax} + \text{Interest Expense}}{\text{Interest Expense}}$$

Interest expense is paid before income taxes. In other words, interest expense is deducted in determining taxable income and, thus, income tax. For this reason, income *before taxes* is used in computing the number of times interest charges are earned.

The *higher* the ratio the more likely interest payments will be paid if earnings decrease. To illustrate, the number of times interest charges are earned for **Lincoln Company** is computed as follows:

	2016	2015
Income before income tax	$162,500	$134,600
Add interest expense	6,000	12,000
Amount available to pay interest	$168,500	$146,600
Number of times interest charges are earned	28.1 ($168,500 ÷ $6,000)	12.2 ($146,600 ÷ $12,000)

The number of times interest charges are earned improved from 12.2 to 28.1 during 2016. This indicates that Lincoln has sufficient earnings to pay interest expense.

The number of times interest charges are earned can be adapted for use with dividends on preferred stock. In this case, the *number of times preferred dividends are earned* is computed as follows:

$$\text{Number of Times Preferred Dividends Are Earned} = \frac{\text{Net Income}}{\text{Preferred Dividends}}$$

Since dividends are paid after taxes, net income is used in computing the number of times preferred dividends are earned. The *higher* the ratio, the more likely preferred dividend payments will be paid if earnings decrease.

Example Exercise 14-7 Times Interest Charges Are Earned OBJ 2

A company reports the following:

Income before income tax	$250,000
Interest expense	100,000

Determine the number of times interest charges are earned.

Follow My Example 14-7

Number of Times Interest Charges Are Earned = (Income Before Income Tax + Interest Expense) ÷ Interest Expense
= ($250,000 + $100,000) ÷ $100,000
= 3.5

Practice Exercises: PE 14-7A, PE 14-7B

Profitability Analysis

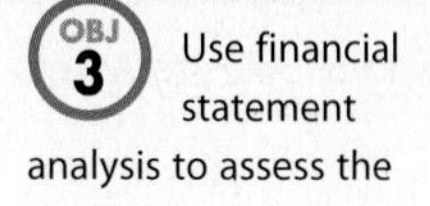

Use financial statement analysis to assess the profitability of a business.

Profitability analysis focuses on the ability of a company to earn profits. This ability is reflected in the company's operating results, as reported in its income statement. The ability to earn profits also depends on the assets the company has available for use in its operations, as reported in its balance sheet. Thus, income statement and balance sheet relationships are often used in evaluating profitability.

Note:
Profitability analysis focuses on the relationship between operating results and the resources available to a business.

Common profitability analyses include the following:

- Ratio of sales to assets
- Rate earned on total assets
- Rate earned on stockholders' equity
- Rate earned on common stockholders' equity
- Earnings per share on common stock
- Price-earnings ratio
- Dividends per share
- Dividend yield

Ratio of Sales to Assets

The **ratio of sales to assets** measures how effectively a company uses its assets. It is computed as follows:

$$\text{Ratio of Sales to Assets} = \frac{\text{Sales}}{\text{Average Total Assets (excluding long-term investments)}}$$

Note that any long-term investments are excluded in computing the ratio of sales to assets. This is because long-term investments are unrelated to normal operations and sales.

To illustrate, the ratio of sales to assets for **Lincoln Company** is computed as follows. Total assets (excluding long-term investments) are $1,010,000 at the beginning of 2015.

	2016	2015
Sales	$1,498,000	$1,200,000
Total assets (excluding long-term investments):		
Beginning of year	$1,053,000*	$1,010,000
End of year	1,044,500**	1,053,000*
Total	$2,097,500	$2,063,000
Average total assets	$1,048,750 ($2,097,500 ÷ 2)	$1,031,500 ($2,063,000 ÷ 2)
Ratio of sales to assets	1.4 ($1,498,000 ÷ $1,048,750)	1.2 ($1,200,000 ÷ $1,031,500)

*($1,230,500 – $177,500)
**($1,139,500 – $95,000)

For Lincoln, the average total assets was computed using total assets (excluding long-term investments) at the beginning and end of the year. The average total assets could also be based on monthly or quarterly averages.

The ratio of sales to assets indicates that Lincoln's use of its operating assets has improved in 2016. This was primarily due to the increase in sales in 2016.

Example Exercise 14-8 Sales to Assets

OBJ 3

A company reports the following:

Sales	$2,250,000
Average total assets	1,500,000

Determine the ratio of sales to assets.

Follow My Example 14-8

Ratio of Sales to Assets = Sales ÷ Average Total Assets
= $2,250,000 ÷ $1,500,000
= 1.5

Practice Exercises: PE 14-8A, PE 14-8B

Rate Earned on Total Assets

The **rate earned on total assets** measures the profitability of total assets, without considering how the assets are financed. In other words, this rate is not affected by the portion of assets financed by creditors or stockholders. It is computed as follows:

$$\text{Rate Earned on Total Assets} = \frac{\text{Income} + \text{Interest Expense}}{\text{Average Total Assets}}$$

The rate earned on total assets is computed by adding interest expense to net income. By adding interest expense to net income, the effect of whether the assets are financed by creditors (debt) or stockholders (equity) is eliminated. Because net income includes any income earned from long-term investments, the average total assets includes long-term investments as well as the net operating assets.

To illustrate, the rate earned on total assets by **Lincoln Company** is computed as follows. Total assets are $1,187,500 at the beginning of 2015.

	2016	2015
Net income	$ 91,000	$ 76,500
Plus interest expense	6,000	12,000
Total	$ 97,000	$ 88,500
Total assets:		
Beginning of year	$1,230,500	$1,187,500
End of year	1,139,500	1,230,500
Total	$2,370,000	$2,418,000
Average total assets	$1,185,000 ($2,370,000 ÷ 2)	$1,209,000 ($2,418,000 ÷ 2)
Rate earned on total assets	8.2% ($97,000 ÷ $1,185,000)	7.3% ($88,500 ÷ $1,209,000)

The rate earned on total assets improved from 7.3% to 8.2% during 2016.

The *rate earned on operating assets* is sometimes computed when there are large amounts of nonoperating income and expense. It is computed as follows:

$$\text{Rate Earned on Operating Assets} = \frac{\text{Income from Operations}}{\text{Average Operating Assets}}$$

Because Lincoln Company does not have a significant amount of nonoperating income and expense, the rate earned on operating assets is not illustrated.

Example Exercise 14-9 Rate Earned on Total Assets

OBJ 3

A company reports the following income statement and balance sheet information for the current year:

Net income	$ 125,000
Interest expense	25,000
Average total assets	2,000,000

Determine the rate earned on total assets.

Follow My Example 14-9

Rate Earned on Total Assets = (Net Income + Interest Expense) ÷ Average Total Assets
= ($125,000 + $25,000) ÷ $2,000,000
= $150,000 ÷ $2,000,000
= 7.5%

Practice Exercises: PE 14-9A, PE 14-9B

Rate Earned on Stockholders' Equity

The **rate earned on stockholders' equity** measures the rate of income earned on the amount invested by the stockholders. It is computed as follows:

$$\text{Rate Earned on Stockholders' Equity} = \frac{\text{Net Income}}{\text{Average Total Stockholders' Equity}}$$

To illustrate, the rate earned on stockholders' equity for **Lincoln Company** is computed as follows. Total stockholders' equity is $750,000 at the beginning of 2015.

	2016	2015
Net income	$ 91,000	$ 76,500
Stockholders' equity:		
Beginning of year	$ 787,500	$ 750,000
End of year	829,500	787,500
Total	$1,617,000	$1,537,500
Average stockholders' equity	$808,500 ($1,617,000 ÷ 2)	$768,750 ($1,537,500 ÷ 2)
Rate earned on stockholders' equity	11.3% ($91,000 ÷ $808,500)	10.0% ($76,500 ÷ $768,750)

The rate earned on stockholders' equity improved from 10.0% to 11.3% during 2016.

Leverage involves using debt to increase the return on an investment. The rate earned on stockholders' equity is normally higher than the rate earned on total assets. This is because of the effect of leverage.

For **Lincoln Company**, the effect of leverage for 2016 is 3.1% and for 2015 is 2.7% computed as follows:

	2016	2015
Rate earned on stockholders' equity	11.3%	10.0%
Less rate earned on total assets	8.2	7.3
Effect of leverage	3.1%	2.7%

Exhibit 8 shows the 2016 and 2015 effects of leverage for Lincoln.

Rate Earned on Common Stockholders' Equity

The **rate earned on common stockholders' equity** measures the rate of profits earned on the amount invested by the common stockholders. It is computed as follows:

$$\text{Rate Earned on Common Stockholders' Equity} = \frac{\text{Net Income} - \text{Preferred Dividends}}{\text{Average Common Stockholders' Equity}}$$

EXHIBIT 8

Effect of Leverage

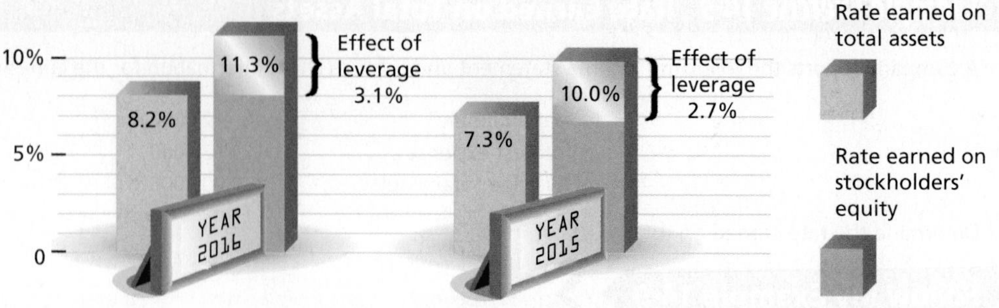

Because preferred stockholders rank ahead of the common stockholders in their claim on earnings, any preferred dividends are subtracted from net income in computing the rate earned on common stockholders' equity.

Lincoln Company had $150,000 of 6% preferred stock outstanding on December 31, 2016 and 2015. Thus, preferred dividends of $9,000 ($150,000 × 6%) are deducted from net income. Lincoln's common stockholders' equity is determined as follows:

	December 31		
	2016	**2015**	**2014**
Common stock, $10 par	$500,000	$500,000	$500,000
Retained earnings	179,500	137,500	100,000
Common stockholders' equity	$679,500	$637,500	$600,000

The retained earnings on December 31, 2014, of $100,000 is the same as the retained earnings on January 1, 2015, as shown in Lincoln's retained earnings statement in Exhibit 4.

Using this information, the rate earned on common stockholders' equity for Lincoln is computed as follows:

	2016	**2015**
Net income	$ 91,000	$ 76,500
Less preferred dividends	9,000	9,000
Total	$ 82,000	$ 67,500
Common stockholders' equity:		
Beginning of year	$ 637,500	$ 600,000
End of year	679,500*	637,500**
Total	$1,317,000	$1,237,500
Average common stockholders' equity	$658,500 ($1,317,000 ÷ 2)	$618,750 ($1,237,500 ÷ 2)
Rate earned on common stockholders' equity	12.5% ($82,000 ÷ $658,500)	10.9% ($67,500 ÷ $618,750)

*($829,500 – $150,000)
**($787,500 – $150,000)

Lincoln's rate earned on common stockholders' equity improved from 10.9% to 12.5% in 2016. This rate differs from the rates earned by Lincoln on total assets and stockholders' equity, which follow:

	2016	**2015**
Rate earned on total assets	8.2%	7.3%
Rate earned on stockholders' equity	11.3%	10.0%
Rate earned on common stockholders' equity	12.5%	10.9%

These rates differ because of leverage, as discussed in the preceding section.

Example Exercise 14-10 Common Stockholders' Profitability Analysis

OBJ 3

A company reports the following:

Net income	$ 125,000
Preferred dividends	5,000
Average stockholders' equity	1,000,000
Average common stockholders' equity	800,000

Determine (a) the rate earned on stockholders' equity and (b) the rate earned on common stockholders' equity.

Follow My Example 14-10

a. Rate Earned on Stockholders' Equity = Net Income ÷ Average Stockholders' Equity
= $125,000 ÷ $1,000,000
= 12.5%

b. Rate Earned on Common Stockholders' Equity = (Net Income – Preferred Dividends) ÷ Average Common Stockholders' Equity
= ($125,000 – $5,000) ÷ $800,000
= 15%

Practice Exercises: PE 14-10A, PE 14-10B

Earnings per Share on Common Stock

Earnings per share (EPS) on common stock measures the share of profits that are earned by a share of common stock. Earnings per share must be reported in the income statement. As a result, earnings per share (EPS) is often reported in the financial press. It is computed as follows:

$$\text{Earnings per Share (EPS) on Common Stock} = \frac{\text{Net Income} - \text{Preferred Dividends}}{\text{Shares of Common Stock Outstanding}}$$

When preferred and common stock are outstanding, preferred dividends are subtracted from net income to determine the income related to the common shares.

To illustrate, the earnings per share (EPS) of common stock for **Lincoln Company** is computed as follows:

	2016	2015
Net income	$91,000	$76,500
Preferred dividends	9,000	9,000
Total	$82,000	$67,500
Shares of common stock outstanding	50,000	50,000
Earnings per share on common stock	$1.64 ($82,000 ÷ 50,000)	$1.35 ($67,500 ÷ 50,000)

Lincoln had $150,000 of 6% preferred stock outstanding on December 31, 2016 and 2015. Thus, preferred dividends of $9,000 ($150,000 × 6%) are deducted from net income in computing earnings per share on common stock.

Lincoln did not issue any additional shares of common stock in 2016. If Lincoln had issued additional shares in 2016, a weighted average of common shares outstanding during the year would have been used.

Lincoln's earnings per share (EPS) on common stock improved from $1.35 to $1.64 during 2016.

Lincoln Company has a simple capital structure with only common stock and preferred stock outstanding. Many corporations, however, have complex capital structures with various types of equity securities outstanding, such as convertible preferred stock,

stock options, and stock warrants. In such cases, the possible effects of such securities on the shares of common stock outstanding are considered in reporting earnings per share. These possible effects are reported separately as *earnings per common share assuming dilution* or *diluted earnings per share*. This topic is described and illustrated in advanced accounting courses and textbooks.

Price-Earnings Ratio

The **price-earnings (P/E) ratio** on common stock measures a company's future earnings prospects. It is often quoted in the financial press and is computed as follows:

$$\text{Price-Earnings (P/E) Ratio} = \frac{\text{Market Price per Share of Common Stock}}{\text{Earnings per Share on Common Stock}}$$

To illustrate, the price-earnings (P/E) ratio for **Lincoln Company** is computed as follows:

	2016	2015
Market price per share of common stock	$41.00	$27.00
Earnings per share on common stock	$1.64	$1.35
Price-earnings ratio on common stock	25 ($41 ÷ $1.64)	20 ($27 ÷ $1.35)

The price-earnings ratio improved from 20 to 25 during 2016. In other words, a share of common stock of Lincoln was selling for 20 times earnings per share at the end of 2015. At the end of 2016, the common stock was selling for 25 times earnings per share. This indicates that the market expects Lincoln to experience favorable earnings in the future.

Example Exercise 14-11 Earnings per Share and Price-Earnings Ratio

A company reports the following:

Net income	$250,000
Preferred dividends	$15,000
Shares of common stock outstanding	20,000
Market price per share of common stock	$35.25

a. Determine the company's earnings per share on common stock.

b. Determine the company's price-earnings ratio. Round to one decimal place.

Follow My Example 14-11

a. Earnings per Share on Common Stock = (Net Income – Preferred Dividends) ÷ Shares of Common Stock Outstanding
= ($250,000 – $15,000) ÷ 20,000
= $11.75

b. Price-Earnings Ratio = Market Price per Share of Common Stock ÷ Earnings per Share on Common Stock
= $35.25 ÷ $11.75
= 3.0

Practice Exercises: PE 14-11A, PE 14-11B

Dividends per Share

Dividends per share measures the extent to which earnings are being distributed to common shareholders. It is computed as follows:

$$\text{Dividends per Share} = \frac{\text{Dividends on Common Stock}}{\text{Shares of Common Stock Outstanding}}$$

To illustrate, the dividends per share for **Lincoln Company** are computed as follows:

	2016	2015
Dividends on common stock	\$40,000	\$30,000
Shares of common stock outstanding	50,000	50,000
Dividends per share of common stock	\$0.80 (\$40,000 ÷ 50,000)	\$0.60 (\$30,000 ÷ 50,000)

The dividends per share of common stock increased from \$0.60 to \$0.80 during 2016.

Dividends per share are often reported with earnings per share. Comparing the two per-share amounts indicates the extent to which earnings are being retained for use in operations. To illustrate, the dividends and earnings per share for **Lincoln Company** are shown in Exhibit 9.

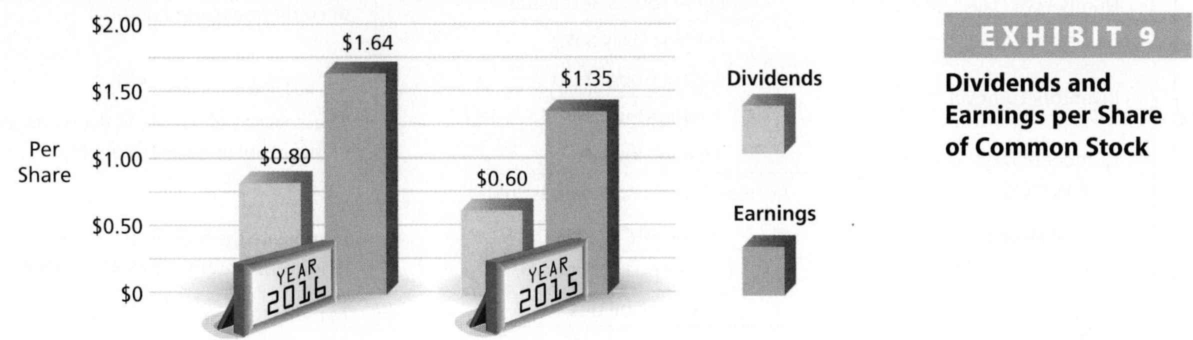

EXHIBIT 9

Dividends and Earnings per Share of Common Stock

Dividend Yield

The **dividend yield** on common stock measures the rate of return to common stockholders from cash dividends. It is of special interest to investors whose objective is to earn revenue (dividends) from their investment. It is computed as follows:

The dividends per share, dividend yield, and P/E ratio of a common stock are normally quoted on the daily listing of stock prices in *The Wall Street Journal* and on **Yahoo!**'s finance Web site.

$$\text{Dividend Yield} = \frac{\text{Dividends per Share of Common Stock}}{\text{Market Price per Share of Common Stock}}$$

To illustrate, the dividend yield for **Lincoln Company** is computed as follows:

	2016	2015
Dividends per share of common stock	\$0.80	\$0.60
Market price per share of common stock	\$41.00	\$27.00
Dividend yield on common stock	2.0% (\$0.80 ÷ \$41)	2.2% (\$0.60 ÷ \$27)

The dividend yield declined slightly from 2.2% to 2.0% in 2016. This decline was primarily due to the increase in the market price of Lincoln's common stock.

Summary of Analytical Measures

Exhibit 10 shows a summary of the solvency and profitability measures discussed in this chapter. The type of industry and the company's operations usually affect which measures are used. In many cases, additional measures are used for a specific industry. For example, airlines use *revenue per passenger mile* and *cost per available seat* as profitability measures. Likewise, hotels use *occupancy rates* as a profitability measure.

The analytical measures shown in Exhibit 10 are a useful starting point for analyzing a company's solvency and profitability. However, they are not a substitute for sound judgment. For example, the general economic and business environment should always be considered in analyzing a company's future prospects. In addition, any trends and interrelationships among the measures should be carefully studied.

EXHIBIT 10 Summary of Analytical Measures

		Method of Computation	Use
Liquidity and Solvency Measures	Working Capital	Current Assets – Current Liabilities	To indicate the ability to meet currently maturing obligations (measures solvency)
	Current Ratio	Current Assets / Current Liabilities	
	Quick Ratio	Quick Assets / Current Liabilities	To indicate instant debt-paying ability (measures solvency)
	Accounts Receivable Turnover	Sales / Average Accounts Receivable	To assess the efficiency in collecting receivables and in the management of credit (measures liquidity)
	Numbers of Days' Sales in Receivables	Average Accounts Receivable / Average Daily Sales	
	Inventory Turnover	Cost of Goods Sold / Average Inventory	To assess the efficiency in the management of inventory (measures liquidity)
	Number of Days' Sales in Inventory	Average Inventory / Average Daily Cost of Goods Sold	
	Ratio of Fixed Assets to Long-Term Liabilities	Fixed Assets (net) / Long-Term Liabilities	To indicate the margin of safety to long-term creditors (measures solvency)
	Ratio of Liabilities to Stockholders' Equity	Total Liabilities / Total Stockholders' Equity	To indicate the margin of safety to creditors (measures solvency)
	Number of Times Interest Charges Are Earned	Income Before Income Tax + Interest Expense / Interest Expense	To assess the risk to debtholders in terms of number of times interest charges were earned (measures solvency)
	Number of Times Preferred Dividends Are Earned	Net Income / Preferred Dividends	To assess the risk to preferred stockholders in terms of the number of times preferred dividends were earned (measures solvency)
Profitability Measures	Ratio of Sales to Assets	Sales / Average Total Assets (excluding long-term investments)	To assess the effectiveness in the use of assets
	Rate Earned on Total Assets	Net Income + Interest Expense / Average Total Assets	To assess the profitability of the assets
	Rate Earned on Stockholders' Equity	Net Income / Average Total Stockholders' Equity	To assess the profitability of the investment by stockholders
	Rate Earned on Common Stockholders' Equity	Net Income – Preferred Dividends / Average Common Stockholders' Equity	To assess the profitability of the investment by common stockholders
	Earnings per Share (EPS) on Common Stock	Net Income – Preferred Dividends / Shares of Common Stock Outstanding	
	Price-Earnings (P/E) Ratio	Market Price per Share of Common Stock / Earnings per Share on Common Stock	To indicate future earnings prospects, based on the relationship between market value of common stock and earnings
	Dividends per Share	Dividends on Common Stock / Shares of Common Stock Outstanding	To indicate the extent to which earnings are being distributed to common stockholders
	Dividend Yield	Dividends per Share of Common Stock / Market Price per Share of Common Stock	To indicate the rate of return to common stockholders in terms of dividends

Integrity, Objectivity, and Ethics in Business

CHARACTERISTICS OF FINANCIAL STATEMENT FRAUD

Each year the Association of Certified Fraud Examiners conducts a worldwide survey examining the characteristics of corporate fraud. The most recent study found that:

- 43.3% of frauds were detected by a tip from an employee or someone close to the company;
- Frauds committed by owners and executives tended to be much larger than those caused by employees;
- Most people who are caught committing fraud are first time offenders with clean employment histories; and
- In 81% of the cases, the person committing the fraud displayed one or more behavioral red flags such as living beyond their means, financial difficulties, and excessive control issues.

Fraud examiners can use these trends to help them narrow their focus when searching for fraud.

Source: 2012 Report to the Nations, Association of Certified Fraud Examiners, 2012.

Corporate Annual Reports

OBJ 4 Describe the contents of corporate annual reports.

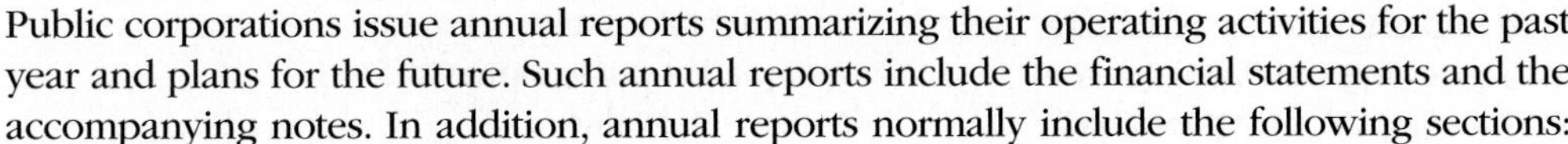

Public corporations issue annual reports summarizing their operating activities for the past year and plans for the future. Such annual reports include the financial statements and the accompanying notes. In addition, annual reports normally include the following sections:

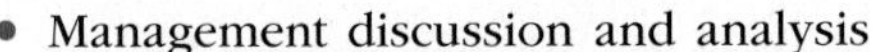

- Management discussion and analysis
- Report on internal control
- Report on fairness of the financial statements

Management Discussion and Analysis

Management's Discussion and Analysis (MD&A) is required in annual reports filed with the Securities and Exchange Commission. It includes management's analysis of current operations and its plans for the future. Typical items included in the MD&A are as follows:

- Management's analysis and explanations of any significant changes between the current and prior years' financial statements.
- Important accounting principles or policies that could affect interpretation of the financial statements, including the effect of changes in accounting principles or the adoption of new accounting principles.
- Management's assessment of the company's liquidity and the availability of capital to the company.
- Significant risk exposures that might affect the company.
- Any "off-balance-sheet" arrangements such as leases not included directly in the financial statements. Such arrangements are discussed in advanced accounting courses and textbooks.

Report on Internal Control

The Sarbanes-Oxley Act of 2002 requires a report on internal control by management. The report states management's responsibility for establishing and maintaining internal control. In addition, management's assessment of the effectiveness of internal controls over financial reporting is included in the report.

Sarbanes-Oxley also requires a public accounting firm to verify management's conclusions on internal control. Thus, two reports on internal control, one by management and one by a public accounting firm, are included in the annual report. In some situations, these may be combined into a single report on internal control.

Report on Fairness of the Financial Statements

All publicly held corporations are required to have an independent audit (examination) of their financial statements. The Certified Public Accounting (CPA) firm that conducts the audit renders an opinion, called the *Report of Independent Registered Public Accounting Firm*, on the fairness of the statements.

An opinion stating that the financial statements present fairly the financial position, results of operations, and cash flows of the company is said to be an *unqualified opinion*, sometimes called a *clean opinion*. Any report other than an unqualified opinion raises a "red flag" for financial statement users and requires further investigation as to its cause.

The annual report of **Nike Inc.** is shown in Appendix B. The Nike report includes the financial statements as well as the MD&A Report on Internal Control and the Report on Fairness of the Financial Statements.

Integrity, Objectivity, and Ethics in Business

BUY LOW, SELL HIGH

Research analysts work for banks, brokerages, or other financial institutions. Their job is to estimate the value of a company's common stock by reviewing and evaluating the company's business model, strategic plan, and financial performance. Based on this analysis, the analyst develops an estimate of a stock's value, which is called its *fundamental value*. Analysts then advise their clients to "buy" or "sell" a company's stock based on the following guidelines:

Current market price is greater than fundamental value	Sell
Current market price is lower than fundamental value	Buy

If analysts are doing their job well, their clients will enjoy large returns by buying stocks at low prices and selling them at high prices.

APPENDIX

Unusual Items on the Income Statement

Generally accepted accounting principles require that unusual items be reported separately on the income statement. This is because such items do not occur frequently and are typically unrelated to current operations. Without separate reporting of these items, users of the financial statements might be misled about current and future operations.

Unusual items on the income statement are classified as one of the following:

- Affecting the *current period* income statement
- Affecting a *prior period* income statement

Unusual Items Affecting the Current Period's Income Statement

Unusual items affecting the current period's income statement include the following:

- Discontinued operations
- Extraordinary items

These items are reported separately on the income statement for any period in which they occur.

Discontinued Operations A company may discontinue a component of its operations by selling or abandoning the component's operations. For example, a retailer might decide to sell its product only online and, thus, discontinue selling its merchandise at its retail outlets (stores).

If the discontinued component is (1) the result of a strategic shift and (2) has a major effect on the entity's operations and financial results, any gain or loss on discontinued operations is reported on the income statement as a *Gain (or loss) from discontinued operations*. It is reported immediately following *Income from continuing operations*.

To illustrate, assume that Jones Corporation produces and sells electrical products, hardware supplies, and lawn equipment. Because of a lack of profits, Jones discontinues its electrical products operation and sells the remaining inventory and other assets at a loss of $100,000. Exhibit 11 illustrates the reporting of the loss on discontinued operations.[3]

EXHIBIT 11

Unusual Items in the Income Statement

Jones Corporation Income Statement For the Year Ended December 31, 2016	
Sales	$12,350,000
Cost of merchandise sold	5,800,000
Gross profit	$ 6,550,000
Selling and administrative expenses	5,240,000
Income from continuing operations before income tax	$ 1,310,000
Income tax expense	620,000
Income from continuing operations	$ 690,000
Loss on discontinued operations	100,000
Income before extraordinary items	$ 590,000
Extraordinary items:	
Gain on condemnation of land	150,000
Net income	$ 740,000

In addition, a note to the financial statements should describe the operations sold, including the date operations were discontinued, and details about the assets, liabilities, income, and expenses of the discontinued component.

Extraordinary Items An **extraordinary item** is defined as an event or a transaction that has both of the following characteristics:

- Unusual in nature
- Infrequent in occurrence

Gains and losses from natural disasters such as floods, earthquakes, and fires are normally reported as extraordinary items, provided that they occur infrequently. Gains or losses from land or buildings taken (condemned) for public use are also reported as extraordinary items.

Any gain or loss from extraordinary items is reported on the income statement as *Gain (or loss) from extraordinary item*. It is reported immediately following *Income from continuing operations* and any *Gain (or loss) on discontinued operations*.

To illustrate, assume that land owned by Jones Corporation was taken for public use (condemned) by the local government. The condemnation of the land resulted in a gain of $150,000. Exhibit 11 illustrates the reporting of the extraordinary gain.[4,5]

[3] The gain or loss on discontinued operations is reported net of any tax effects. To simplify, the tax effects are not specifically identified in Exhibit 11.

[4] The gain or loss on extraordinary operations is reported net of any tax effects.

[5] At the time of this writing, the Financial Accounting Standards Board had released an exposure draft, which proposes eliminating extraordinary items as a separate line item on the income statement. The outcome of this proposal was uncertain at the time of this writing.

Reporting Earnings per Share Earnings per common share should be reported separately for discontinued operations and extraordinary items. To illustrate, a partial income statement for Jones Corporation is shown in Exhibit 12. The company has 200,000 shares of common stock outstanding.

Exhibit 12 reports earnings per common share for income from continuing operations, discontinued operations, and extraordinary items. However, only earnings per share for income from continuing operations and net income are required by generally accepted accounting principles. The other per-share amounts may be presented in the notes to the financial statements.

EXHIBIT 12

Income Statement with Earnings per Share

Jones Corporation Income Statement For the Year Ended December 31, 2016	
Earnings per common share:	
Income from continuing operations	$3.45
Loss on discontinued operations	0.50
Income before extraordinary items	$2.95
Extraordinary items:	
Gain on condemnation of land	0.75
Net income	$3.70

Unusual Items Affecting the Prior Period's Income Statement

An unusual item may occur that affects a prior period's income statement. Two such items are as follows:

- Errors in applying generally accepted accounting principles
- Changes from one generally accepted accounting principle to another

If an error is discovered in a prior period's financial statement, the prior-period statement and all following statements are restated and thus corrected.

A company may change from one generally accepted accounting principle to another. In this case, the prior-period financial statements are restated as if the new accounting principle had always been used.[6]

For both of the preceding items, the current-period earnings are not affected. That is, only the earnings reported in prior periods are restated. However, because the prior earnings are restated, the beginning balance of Retained Earnings may also have to be restated. This, in turn, may cause the restatement of other balance sheet accounts. Illustrations of these types of adjustments and restatements are provided in advanced accounting courses.

[6] Changes from one acceptable depreciation method to another acceptable depreciation method are an exception to this general rule and are to be treated prospectively as a change in estimate.

At a Glance 14

Describe basic financial statement analytical methods.

Key Points The basic financial statements provide much of the information users need to make economic decisions. Analytical procedures are used to compare items on a current financial statement with related items on earlier statements, or to examine relationships within a financial statement.

Learning Outcomes	Example Exercises	Practice Exercises
• Prepare a vertical analysis from a company's financial statements.	EE14-1	PE14-1A, 14-1B
• Prepare a horizontal analysis from a company's financial statements.	EE14-2	PE14-2A, 14-2B
• Prepare common-sized financial statements.		

Use financial statement analysis to assess the solvency of a business.

Key Points All users of financial statements are interested in the ability of a business to convert assets into cash (liquidity), pay its debts (solvency), and earn income (profitability). Liquidity, solvency, and profitability are interrelated. Liquidity and solvency are normally assessed by examining the following: current position analysis, accounts receivable analysis, inventory analysis, the ratio of fixed assets to long-term liabilities, the ratio of liabilities to stockholders' equity, and the number of times interest charges are earned.

Learning Outcomes	Example Exercises	Practice Exercises
• Determine working capital.		
• Compute and interpret the current ratio.	EE14-3	PE14-3A, 14-3B
• Compute and interpret the quick ratio.	EE14-3	PE14-3A, 14-3B
• Compute and interpret accounts receivable turnover.	EE14-4	PE14-4A, 14-4B
• Compute and interpret the number of days' sales in receivables.	EE14-4	PE14-4A, 14-4B
• Compute and interpret inventory turnover.	EE14-5	PE14-5A, 14-5B
• Compute and interpret the number of days' sales in inventory.	EE14-5	PE14-5A, 14-5B
• Compute and interpret the ratio of fixed assets to long-term liabilities.	EE14-6	PE14-6A, 14-6B
• Compute and interpret the ratio of liabilities to stockholders' equity.	EE14-6	PE14-6A, 14-6B
• Compute and interpret the number of times interest charges are earned.	EE14-7	PE14-7A, 14-7B

Use financial statement analysis to assess the profitability of a business.

Key Points Profitability analysis focuses on the ability of a company to earn profits. This ability is reflected in the company's operating results as reported on the income statement and resources available as reported on the balance sheet. Major analyses include the ratio of sales to assets, the rate earned on total assets, the rate earned on stockholders' equity, the rate earned on common stockholders' equity, earnings per share on common stock, the price-earnings ratio, dividends per share, and dividend yield.

Learning Outcomes	Example Exercises	Practice Exercises
• Compute and interpret the ratio of sales to assets.	EE14-8	PE14-8A, 14-8B
• Compute and interpret the rate earned on total assets.	EE14-9	PE14-9A, 14-9B
• Compute and interpret the rate earned on stockholders' equity.	EE14-10	PE14-10A, 14-10B
• Compute and interpret the rate earned on common stockholders' equity.	EE14-10	PE14-10A, 14-10B
• Compute and interpret the earnings per share on common stock.	EE14-11	PE14-11A, 14-11B
• Compute and interpret the price-earnings ratio.	EE14-11	PE14-11A, 14-11B
• Compute and interpret the dividends per share and dividend yield.		
• Describe the uses and limitations of analytical measures.		

Describe the contents of corporate annual reports.

Key Points Corporations normally issue annual reports to their stockholders and other interested parties. Such reports summarize the corporation's operating activities for the past year and plans for the future.

Learning Outcome	Example Exercises	Practice Exercises
• Describe the elements of a corporate annual report.		

Key Terms

accounts receivable analysis (594)
accounts receivable turnover (594)
common-sized statement (590)
current position analysis (592)
current ratio (592)
dividend yield (605)
dividends per share (604)
earnings per share (EPS) on common stock (603)
extraordinary item (609)
horizontal analysis (586)
inventory analysis (596)
inventory turnover (596)
leverage (601)
liquidity (591)
Management's Discussion and Analysis (MD&A) (607)
number of days' sales in inventory (596)
number of days' sales in receivables (595)
number of times interest charges are earned (598)
price-earnings (P/E) ratio (604)
profitability (591)
quick assets (593)
quick ratio (593)
rate earned on common stockholders' equity (601)
rate earned on stockholders' equity (601)
rate earned on total assets (600)
ratio of fixed assets to long-term liabilities (597)
ratio of liabilities to stockholders' equity (597)
ratio of sales to assets (599)
solvency (591)
vertical analysis (589)
working capital (592)

Illustrative Problem

Rainbow Paint Co.'s comparative financial statements for the years ending December 31, 2016 and 2015, are as follows. The market price of Rainbow Paint Co.'s common stock was $25 on December 31, 2016, and $30 on December 31, 2015.

Rainbow Paint Co.
Comparative Income Statement
For the Years Ended December 31, 2016 and 2015

	2016	2015
Sales	$5,000,000	$3,200,000
Cost of goods sold	3,400,000	2,080,000
Gross profit	$1,600,000	$1,120,000
Selling expenses	$ 650,000	$ 464,000
Administrative expenses	325,000	224,000
Total operating expenses	$ 975,000	$ 688,000
Income from operations	$ 625,000	$ 432,000
Other income	25,000	19,200
	$ 650,000	$ 451,200
Other expense (interest)	105,000	64,000
Income before income tax	$ 545,000	$ 387,200
Income tax expense	300,000	176,000
Net income	$ 245,000	$ 211,200

Rainbow Paint Co.
Comparative Retained Earnings Statement
For the Years Ended December 31, 2016 and 2015

	2016	2015
Retained earnings, January 1	$723,000	$581,800
Add net income for year	245,000	211,200
Total	$968,000	$793,000
Deduct dividends:		
On preferred stock	$ 40,000	$ 40,000
On common stock	45,000	30,000
Total	$ 85,000	$ 70,000
Retained earnings, December 31	$883,000	$723,000

Rainbow Paint Co.
Comparative Balance Sheet
December 31, 2016 and 2015

	Dec. 31, 2016	Dec. 31, 2015
Assets		
Current assets:		
Cash	$ 175,000	$ 125,000
Temporary investments	150,000	50,000
Accounts receivable (net)	425,000	325,000
Inventories	720,000	480,000
Prepaid expenses	30,000	20,000
Total current assets	$1,500,000	$1,000,000
Long-term investments	250,000	225,000
Property, plant, and equipment (net)	2,093,000	1,948,000
Total assets	$3,843,000	$3,173,000
Liabilities		
Current liabilities	$ 750,000	$ 650,000
Long-term liabilities:		
Mortgage note payable, 10%, due 2017	$ 410,000	—
Bonds payable, 8%, due 2020	800,000	$ 800,000
Total long-term liabilities	$1,210,000	$ 800,000
Total liabilities	$1,960,000	$1,450,000
Stockholders' Equity		
Preferred 8% stock, $100 par	$ 500,000	$ 500,000
Common stock, $10 par	500,000	500,000
Retained earnings	883,000	723,000
Total stockholders' equity	$1,883,000	$1,723,000
Total liabilities and stockholders' equity	$3,843,000	$3,173,000

Instructions

Determine the following measures for 2016:

1. Working capital
2. Current ratio
3. Quick ratio
4. Accounts receivable turnover
5. Number of days' sales in receivables
6. Inventory turnover
7. Number of days' sales in inventory
8. Ratio of fixed assets to long-term liabilities
9. Ratio of liabilities to stockholders' equity
10. Number of times interest charges are earned
11. Number of times preferred dividends are earned
12. Ratio of sales to assets
13. Rate earned on total assets
14. Rate earned on stockholders' equity

15. Rate earned on common stockholders' equity
16. Earnings per share on common stock
17. Price-earnings ratio
18. Dividends per share
19. Dividend yield

Solution

(Ratios are rounded to the nearest single digit after the decimal point.)

1. Working capital: $750,000
   $1,500,000 – $750,000
2. Current ratio: 2.0
   $1,500,000 ÷ $750,000
3. Quick ratio: 1.0
   $750,000 ÷ $750,000
4. Accounts receivable turnover: 13.3
   $5,000,000 ÷ [($425,000 + $325,000) ÷ 2]
5. Number of days' sales in receivables: 27.4 days
   $5,000,000 ÷ 365 days = $13,699
   $375,000 ÷ $13,699
6. Inventory turnover: 5.7
   $3,400,000 ÷ [($720,000 + $480,000) ÷ 2]
7. Number of days' sales in inventory: 64.4 days
   $3,400,000 ÷ 365 days = $9,315
   $600,000 ÷ $9,315
8. Ratio of fixed assets to long-term liabilities: 1.7
   $2,093,000 ÷ $1,210,000
9. Ratio of liabilities to stockholders' equity: 1.0
   $1,960,000 ÷ $1,883,000
10. Number of times interest charges are earned: 6.2
    ($545,000 + $105,000) ÷ $105,000
11. Number of times preferred dividends are earned: 6.1
    $245,000 ÷ $40,000
12. Ratio of sales to assets: 1.5
    $5,000,000 ÷ [($3,593,000 + $2,948,000) ÷ 2]
13. Rate earned on total assets: 10.0%
    ($245,000 + $105,000) ÷ [($3,843,000 + $3,173,000) ÷ 2]
14. Rate earned on stockholders' equity: 13.6%
    $245,000 ÷ [($1,883,000 + $1,723,000) ÷ 2]
15. Rate earned on common stockholders' equity: 15.7%
    ($245,000 – $40,000) ÷ [($1,383,000 + $1,223,000) ÷ 2]
16. Earnings per share on common stock: $4.10
    ($245,000 – $40,000) ÷ 50,000 shares
17. Price-earnings ratio: 6.1
    $25 ÷ $4.10
18. Dividends per share: $0.90
    $45,000 ÷ 50,000 shares
19. Dividend yield: 3.6%
    $0.90 ÷ $25

Discussion Questions

1. What is the difference between horizontal and vertical analysis of financial statements?
2. What is the advantage of using comparative statements for financial analysis rather than statements for a single date or period?
3. The current year's amount of net income (after income tax) is 25% larger than that of the preceding year. Does this indicate an improved operating performance? Discuss.
4. How would the current and quick ratios of a service business compare?
5. a. Why is it advantageous to have a high inventory turnover?
   b. Is it possible to have a high inventory turnover and a high number of days' sales in inventory? Discuss.
6. What do the following data taken from a comparative balance sheet indicate about the company's ability to borrow additional funds on a long-term basis in the current year as compared to the preceding year?

	Current Year	Preceding Year
Fixed assets (net)	$1,260,000	$1,360,000
Total long-term liabilities	300,000	400,000

7. a. How does the rate earned on total assets differ from the rate earned on stockholders' equity?
   b. Which ratio is normally higher? Explain.
8. **Kroger**, a grocery store, recently had a price-earnings ratio of 13.7, while the average price-earnings ratio in the grocery store industry was 22.5. What might explain this difference?
9. The dividend yield of **Suburban Propane** was 7.7% in a recent year, and the dividend yield of **Google** was 0% in the same year. What might explain the difference between these ratios?
10. Describe two reports provided by independent auditors in the annual report to shareholders.

Practice Exercises

EE 14-1 *p. 589*

PE 14-1A Horizontal analysis

OBJ. 1

SHOW ME HOW

The comparative temporary investments and inventory balances of a company follow.

	Current Year	Previous Year
Temporary investments	$59,280	$52,000
Inventory	70,680	76,000

Based on this information, what is the amount and percentage of increase or decrease that would be shown in a balance sheet with horizontal analysis?

EE 14-1 *p. 589*

PE 14-1B Horizontal analysis

OBJ. 1

SHOW ME HOW

The comparative accounts payable and long-term debt balances for a company follow.

	Current Year	Previous Year
Accounts payable	$111,000	$100,000
Long-term debt	132,680	124,000

Based on this information, what is the amount and percentage of increase or decrease that would be shown in a balance sheet with horizontal analysis?

EE 14-2 *p. 590* **PE 14-2A Vertical analysis** **OBJ. 1**

SHOW ME HOW

Income statement information for Axiom Corporation follows:

Sales	$725,000
Cost of goods sold	391,500
Gross profit	333,500

Prepare a vertical analysis of the income statement for Axiom Corporation.

EE 14-2 *p. 590* **PE 14-2B Vertical analysis** **OBJ. 1**

SHOW ME HOW

Income statement information for Einsworth Corporation follows:

Sales	$1,200,000
Cost of goods sold	780,000
Gross profit	420,000

Prepare a vertical analysis of the income statement for Einsworth Corporation.

EE 14-3 *p. 594* **PE 14-3A Current position analysis** **OBJ. 2**

SHOW ME HOW

The following items are reported on a company's balance sheet:

Cash	$160,000
Marketable securities	75,000
Accounts receivable (net)	65,000
Inventory	140,000
Accounts payable	200,000

Determine (a) the current ratio and (b) the quick ratio. Round to one decimal place.

EE 14-3 *p. 594* **PE 14-3B Current position analysis** **OBJ. 2**

SHOW ME HOW

The following items are reported on a company's balance sheet:

Cash	$210,000
Marketable securities	120,000
Accounts receivable (net)	110,000
Inventory	160,000
Accounts payable	200,000

Determine (a) the current ratio and (b) the quick ratio. Round to one decimal place.

EE 14-4 *p. 595* **PE 14-4A Accounts receivable analysis** **OBJ. 2**

SHOW ME HOW

A company reports the following:

Sales	$832,000
Average accounts receivable (net)	80,000

Determine (a) the accounts receivable turnover and (b) the number of days' sales in receivables. Round to one decimal place.

EE 14-4 *p. 595* **PE 14-4B Accounts receivable analysis** **OBJ. 2**

SHOW ME HOW

A company reports the following:

Sales	$3,150,000
Average accounts receivable (net)	210,000

Determine (a) the accounts receivable turnover and (b) the number of days' sales in receivables. Round to one decimal place.

EE 14-5 *p. 597*

PE 14-5A Inventory analysis

OBJ. 2

SHOW ME HOW

A company reports the following:

Cost of goods sold	$630,000
Average inventory	90,000

Determine (a) the inventory turnover and (b) the number of days' sales in inventory. Round to one decimal place.

EE 14-5 *p. 597*

PE 14-5B Inventory analysis

OBJ. 2

SHOW ME HOW

A company reports the following:

Cost of goods sold	$435,000
Average inventory	72,500

Determine (a) the inventory turnover and (b) the number of days' sales in inventory. Round to one decimal place.

EE 14-6 *p. 598*

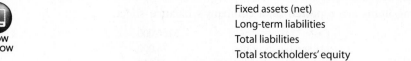

PE 14-6A Long-term solvency analysis

OBJ. 2

SHOW ME HOW

The following information was taken from Kellman Company's balance sheet:

Fixed assets (net)	$2,000,000
Long-term liabilities	800,000
Total liabilities	1,000,000
Total stockholders' equity	625,000

Determine the company's (a) ratio of fixed assets to long-term liabilities and (b) ratio of liabilities to stockholders' equity.

EE 14-6 *p. 598*

PE 14-6B Long-term solvency analysis

OBJ. 2

SHOW ME HOW

The following information was taken from Charu Company's balance sheet:

Fixed assets (net)	$860,000
Long-term liabilities	200,000
Total liabilities	600,000
Total stockholders' equity	250,000

Determine the company's (a) ratio of fixed assets to long-term liabilities and (b) ratio of liabilities to stockholders' equity.

EE 14-7 *p. 599*

PE 14-7A Times interest charges are earned

OBJ. 2

SHOW ME HOW

A company reports the following:

Income before income tax	$4,000,000
Interest expense	400,000

Determine the number of times interest charges are earned.

EE14-7 *p. 599*

PE 14-7B Times interest charges are earned

OBJ. 2

SHOW ME HOW

A company reports the following:

Income before income tax	$8,000,000
Interest expense	500,000

Determine the number of times interest charges are earned.

EE 14-8 *p. 600*

PE 14-8A Sales to assets

OBJ. 3

SHOW ME HOW

A company reports the following:

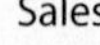

Sales	$1,800,000
Average total assets (excluding long-term investments)	1,125,000

Determine the ratio of sales to assets.

EE 14-8 *p. 600*

PE 14-8B Sales to assets

OBJ. 3

A company reports the following:

SHOW ME HOW

Sales	$4,400,000
Average total assets (excluding long-term investments)	2,000,000

Determine the ratio of sales to assets.

EE 14-9 *p. 601*

PE 14-9A Rate earned on total assets

OBJ. 3

A company reports the following income statement and balance sheet information for the current year:

SHOW ME HOW

Net income	$ 250,000
Interest expense	100,000
Average total assets	2,500,000

Determine the rate earned on total assets.

EE 14-9 *p. 601*

PE 14-9B Rate earned on total assets

OBJ. 3

A company reports the following income statement and balance sheet information for the current year:

SHOW ME HOW

Net income	$ 410,000
Interest expense	90,000
Average total assets	5,000,000

Determine the rate earned on total assets.

EE 14-10 *p. 603*

PE 14-10A Common stockholders' profitability analysis

OBJ. 3

A company reports the following:

SHOW ME HOW

Net income	$ 375,000
Preferred dividends	75,000
Average stockholders' equity	2,500,000
Average common stockholders' equity	1,875,000

Determine (a) the rate earned on stockholders' equity and (b) the rate earned on common stockholders' equity. Round to one decimal place.

EE 14-10 *p. 603*

PE 14-10B Common stockholders' profitability analysis

OBJ. 3

A company reports the following:

SHOW ME HOW

Net income	$1,000,000
Preferred dividends	50,000
Average stockholders' equity	6,250,000
Average common stockholders' equity	3,800,000

Determine (a) the rate earned on stockholders' equity and (b) the rate earned on common stockholders' equity. Round to one decimal place.

EE 14-11 *p. 604*

PE 14-11A Earnings per share and price-earnings ratio

OBJ. 3

A company reports the following:

SHOW ME HOW

Net income	$185,000
Preferred dividends	$25,000
Shares of common stock outstanding	100,000
Market price per share of common stock	$20

a. Determine the company's earnings per share on common stock.

b. Determine the company's price-earnings ratio.

EE 14-11 p. 604

PE 14-11B Earnings per share and price-earnings ratio OBJ. 3

A company reports the following:

Net income	$410,000
Preferred dividends	$60,000
Shares of common stock outstanding	50,000
Market price per share of common stock	$84

a. Determine the company's earnings per share on common stock.

b. Determine the company's price-earnings ratio.

Exercises

EX 14-1 Vertical analysis of income statement OBJ. 1

✔ a. Current year net income: $175,000; 7.0% of sales

Revenue and expense data for Gresham Inc. for two recent years are as follows:

	Current Year	Previous Year
Sales	$2,500,000	$2,350,000
Cost of goods sold	1,500,000	1,292,500
Selling expenses	300,000	376,000
Administrative expenses	375,000	305,500
Income tax expense	150,000	141,000

a. Prepare an income statement in comparative form, stating each item for both years as a percent of sales. Round to one decimal place.

b. Comment on the significant changes disclosed by the comparative income statement.

EX 14-2 Vertical analysis of income statement OBJ. 1

✔ a. Current fiscal year income from continuing operations, 13.0% of revenues

The following comparative income statement (in thousands of dollars) for the two recent fiscal years was adapted from the annual report of **Speedway Motorsports, Inc.**, owner and operator of several major motor speedways, such as the Atlanta, Texas, and Las Vegas Motor Speedways.

	Current Year	Previous Year
Revenues:		
Admissions	$116,034	$130,239
Event-related revenue	151,562	163,621
NASCAR broadcasting revenue	192,662	185,394
Other operating revenue	29,902	26,951
Total revenue	$490,160	$506,205
Expenses and other:		
Direct expense of events	$101,402	$106,204
NASCAR purse and sanction fees	122,950	120,146
Other direct expenses	18,908	20,352
General and administrative	183,215	241,223
Total expenses and other	$426,475	$487,925
Income from continuing operations	$ 63,685	$ 18,280

a. Prepare a comparative income statement for these two years in vertical form, stating each item as a percent of revenues. Round to one decimal place.

b. Comment on the significant changes.

EX 14-3 Common-sized income statement OBJ. 1

✔ a. Tannenhill net income: $120,000; 3.0% of sales

Revenue and expense data for the current calendar year for Tannenhill Company and for the electronics industry are as follows. The Tannenhill Company data are expressed in dollars. The electronics industry averages are expressed in percentages.

	Tannenhill Company	Electronics Industry Average
Sales	$4,000,000	100.0%
Cost of goods sold	2,120,000	60.0
Gross profit	$1,880,000	40.0%
Selling expenses	$1,080,000	24.0%
Administrative expenses	640,000	14.0
Total operating expenses	$1,720,000	38.0%
Operating income	$ 160,000	2.0%
Other income	120,000	3.0
	$ 280,000	5.0%
Other expense	80,000	2.0
Income before income tax	$ 200,000	3.0%
Income tax expense	80,000	2.0
Net income	$ 120,000	1.0%

a. Prepare a common-sized income statement comparing the results of operations for Tannenhill Company with the industry average. Round to one decimal place.

b. As far as the data permit, comment on significant relationships revealed by the comparisons.

EX 14-4 Vertical analysis of balance sheet

OBJ. 1

✔ Retained earnings, Current year, 40.0%

Balance sheet data for Novak Company on December 31, the end of two recent fiscal years, follows:

	Current Year	Previous Year
Current assets	$1,300,000	$ 945,000
Property, plant, and equipment	3,000,000	3,150,000
Intangible assets	700,000	405,000
Current liabilities	1,000,000	720,000
Long-term liabilities	1,500,000	1,575,000
Common stock	500,000	495,000
Retained earnings	2,000,000	1,710,000

Prepare a comparative balance sheet for both years, stating each asset as a percent of total assets and each liability and stockholders' equity item as a percent of the total liabilities and stockholders' equity. Round to one decimal place.

EX 14-5 Horizontal analysis of the income statement

OBJ. 1

✔ a. Net income increase, 80.0%

Income statement data for Moreno Company for two recent years ended December 31, are as follows:

	Current Year	Previous Year
Sales	$1,120,000	$1,000,000
Cost of goods sold	971,250	875,000
Gross profit	$ 148,750	$ 125,000
Selling expenses	$ 71,250	$ 62,500
Administrative expenses	56,000	50,000
Total operating expenses	$ 127,250	$ 112,500
Income before income tax	$ 21,500	$ 12,500
Income tax expense	8,000	5,000
Net income	$ 13,500	$ 7,500

a. Prepare a comparative income statement with horizontal analysis, indicating the increase (decrease) for the current year when compared with the previous year. Round to one decimal place.

b. What conclusions can be drawn from the horizontal analysis?

✔ **a. Current year working capital, $1,600,000**

SHOW ME HOW

EX 14-6 Current position analysis — OBJ. 2

The following data were taken from the balance sheet of Gostkowski Company at the end of two recent fiscal years:

	Current Year	Previous Year
Cash	$ 480,000	$ 392,000
Marketable securities	576,000	411,600
Accounts and notes receivable (net)	384,000	316,400
Inventories	408,000	333,200
Prepaid expenses	552,000	506,800
Total current assets	$2,400,000	$1,960,000
Accounts and notes payable (short-term)	$ 600,000	$ 525,000
Accrued liabilities	200,000	175,000
Total current liabilities	$ 800,000	$ 700,000

a. Determine for each year (1) the working capital, (2) the current ratio, and (3) the quick ratio. Round ratios to one decimal place.

b. What conclusions can be drawn from these data as to the company's ability to meet its currently maturing debts?

✔ **a. (1) Current year's current ratio, 1.1**

EX 14-7 Current position analysis — OBJ. 2

PepsiCo, Inc., the parent company of Frito-Lay snack foods and Pepsi beverages, had the following current assets and current liabilities at the end of two recent years:

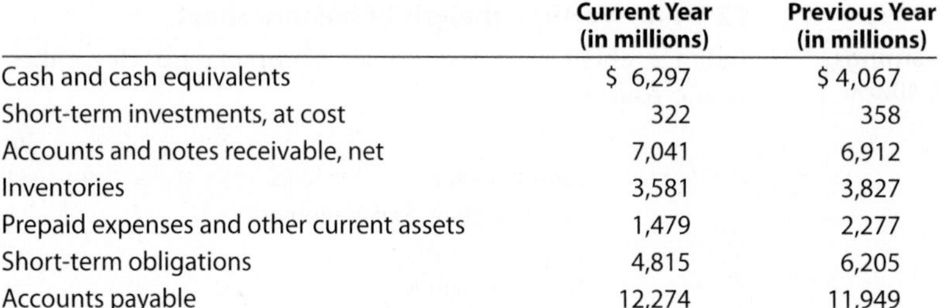

	Current Year (in millions)	Previous Year (in millions)
Cash and cash equivalents	$ 6,297	$ 4,067
Short-term investments, at cost	322	358
Accounts and notes receivable, net	7,041	6,912
Inventories	3,581	3,827
Prepaid expenses and other current assets	1,479	2,277
Short-term obligations	4,815	6,205
Accounts payable	12,274	11,949

a. Determine the (1) current ratio and (2) quick ratio for both years. Round to one decimal place.

b. What conclusions can you draw from these data?

EX 14-8 Current position analysis — OBJ. 2

The bond indenture for the 10-year, 9% debenture bonds issued January 2, 2015, required working capital of $100,000, a current ratio of 1.5, and a quick ratio of 1.0 at the end of each calendar year until the bonds mature. At December 31, 2016, the three measures were computed as follows:

1. Current assets:			
Cash	$102,000		
Temporary investments	48,000		
Accounts and notes receivable (net)	120,000		
Inventories	36,000		
Prepaid expenses	24,000		
Intangible assets	124,800		
Property, plant, and equipment	55,200		
Total current assets (net)		$510,000	
Current liabilities:			
Accounts and short-term notes payable	$ 96,000		
Accrued liabilities	204,000		
Total current liabilities		300,000	
Working capital		$210,000	
2. Current ratio	1.7	$510,000 ÷ $300,000	
3. Quick ratio	1.2	$115,200 ÷ $ 96,000	

a. List the errors in the determination of the three measures of current position analysis.

b. Is the company satisfying the terms of the bond indenture?

EX 14-9 Accounts receivable analysis **OBJ. 2**

✔ a. Accounts receivable turnover, 2016, 7.0

SHOW ME HOW

The following data are taken from the financial statements of Krawcheck Inc. Terms of all sales are 2/10, n/55.

	2016	2015	2014
Accounts receivable, end of year	$ 500,000	$ 475,000	$440,000
Sales on account	3,412,500	2,836,500	

a. For 2015 and 2016, determine (1) the accounts receivable turnover and (2) the number of days' sales in receivables. Round to the nearest dollar and one decimal place.

b. What conclusions can be drawn from these data concerning accounts receivable and credit policies?

EX 14-10 Accounts receivable analysis **OBJ. 2**

Xavier Stores Company and Lestrade Stores Inc. are large retail department stores. Both companies offer credit to their customers through their own credit card operations. Information from the financial statements for both companies for two recent years is as follows (all numbers are in millions):

	Xavier	Lestrade
Merchandise sales	$8,500,000	$4,585,000
Credit card receivables—beginning	820,000	600,000
Credit card receviables—ending	880,000	710,000

a. Determine the (1) accounts receivable turnover and (2) the number of days' sales in receivables for both companies. Round to one decimal place.

b. Compare the two companies with regard to their credit card policies.

EX 14-11 Inventory analysis **OBJ. 2**

✔ a. Inventory turnover, current year, 7.5

SHOW ME HOW

The following data were extracted from the income statement of Saleh Inc.:

	Current Year	Previous Year
Sales	$12,750,000	$13,284,000
Beginning inventories	840,000	800,000
Cost of goods sold	6,375,000	7,380,000
Ending inventories	860,000	840,000

a. Determine for each year (1) the inventory turnover and (2) the number of days' sales in inventory. Round to the nearest dollar and one decimal place.

b. What conclusions can be drawn from these data concerning the inventories?

EX 14-12 Inventory analysis **OBJ. 2**

✔ a. Dell inventory turnover, 32.1

Dell Inc. and **Hewlett-Packard Company (HP)** compete with each other in the personal computer market. Dell's primary strategy is to assemble computers to customer orders, rather than for inventory. Thus, for example, Dell will build and deliver a computer within four days of a customer entering an order on a Web page. Hewlett-Packard, on the other hand, builds some computers prior to receiving an order, then sells from this inventory once an order is received. Selected financial information for both companies from a recent year's financial statements follows (in millions):

	Dell Inc.	Hewlett-Packard Company
Sales	$56,940	$120,357
Cost of goods sold	44,754	92,385
Inventory, beginning of period	1,382	6,317
Inventory, end of period	1,404	7,490

(Continued)

a. Determine for both companies (1) the inventory turnover and (2) the number of days' sales in inventory. Round to one decimal place.

b. Interpret the inventory ratios by considering Dell's and Hewlett-Packard's operating strategies.

EX 14-13 Ratio of liabilities to stockholders' equity and number of times interest charges are earned OBJ. 2

✔ a. Ratio of liabilities to stockholders' equity, current year, 0.9

The following data were taken from the financial statements of Hunter Inc. for December 31 of two recent years:

	Current Year	Previous Year
Accounts payable	$ 924,000	$ 800,000
Current maturities of serial bonds payable	200,000	200,000
Serial bonds payable, 10%, issued 2009, due 2019	1,000,000	1,200,000
Common stock, $10 par value	250,000	250,000
Paid-in capital in excess of par	1,250,000	1,250,000
Retained earnings	860,000	500,000

The income before income tax was $480,000 and $420,000 for the current and previous years, respectively.

a. Determine the ratio of liabilities to stockholders' equity at the end of each year. Round to one decimal place.

b. Determine the number of times the bond interest charges are earned during the year for both years. Round to one decimal place.

c. What conclusions can be drawn from these data as to the company's ability to meet its currently maturing debts?

EX 14-14 Ratio of liabilities to stockholders' equity and number of times interest charges are earned OBJ. 2

✔ a. Hasbro, 1.9

Hasbro and **Mattel, Inc.**, are the two largest toy companies in North America. Condensed liabilities and stockholders' equity from a recent balance sheet are shown for each company as follows (in thousands):

	Hasbro	Mattel
Current liabilities	$ 960,435	$ 1,716,012
Long-term debt	1,396,421	1,100,000
Deferred liabilities	461,152	643,729
Total liabilities	$ 2,818,008	$ 3,459,741
Shareholders' equity:		
Common stock	$ 104,847	$ 441,369
Additional paid in capital	655,943	1,727,682
Retained earnings	3,354,545	3,515,181
Accumulated other comprehensive loss and other equity items	(72,307)	(464,486)
Treasury stock, at cost	(2,535,649)	(2,152,702)
Total stockholders' equity	$ 1,507,379	$ 3,067,044
Total liabilities and stockholders' equity	$ 4,325,387	$ 6,526,785

The income from operations and interest expense from the income statement for each company were as follows (in thousands):

	Hasbro	Mattel
Income from operations (before income tax)	$453,402	$945,045
Interest expense	117,403	88,835

a. Determine the ratio of liabilities to stockholders' equity for both companies. Round to one decimal place.

b. Determine the number of times interest charges are earned for both companies. Round to one decimal place.

c. Interpret the ratio differences between the two companies.

EX 14-15 Ratio of liabilities to stockholders' equity and ratio of fixed assets to long-term liabilities

OBJ. 2

✔ a. Mondelez International, Inc., 1.3

Recent balance sheet information for two companies in the food industry, **Mondelez International, Inc.**, and **The Hershey Company**, is as follows (in thousands of dollars):

	Mondelez	Hershey
Net property, plant, and equipment	$10,010,000	$1,674,071
Current liabilities	14,873,000	1,471,110
Long-term debt	15,574,000	1,530,967
Other long-term liabilities	12,816,000	716,013
Stockholders' equity	32,215,000	1,036,749

a. Determine the ratio of liabilities to stockholders' equity for both companies. Round to one decimal place.

b. Determine the ratio of fixed assets to long-term liabilities for both companies. Round to one decimal place.

c. Interpret the ratio differences between the two companies.

EX 14-16 Ratio of sales to assets

OBJ. 3

✔ a. YRC Worldwide, 1.5

Three major segments of the transportation industry are motor carriers, such as **YRC Worldwide**; railroads, such as **Union Pacific**; and transportation arrangement services, such as **C.H. Robinson Worldwide Inc.** Recent financial statement information for these three companies is shown as follows (in thousands of dollars):

	YRC Worldwide	Union Pacific	C.H. Robinson Worldwide Inc.
Sales	$4,334,640	$16,965,000	$9,274,305
Average total assets	2,812,504	42,636,000	1,914,974

a. Determine the ratio of sales to assets for all three companies. Round to one decimal place.

b. Assume that the ratio of sales to assets for each company represents their respective industry segment. Interpret the differences in the ratio of sales to assets in terms of the operating characteristics of each of the respective segments.

EX 14-17 Profitability ratios

OBJ. 3

✔ a. Rate earned on total assets, 2016, 12.0%

SHOW ME HOW

The following selected data were taken from the financial statements of Robinson Inc. for December 31, 2016, 2015 and 2014:

	December 31		
	2016	2015	2014
Total assets	$4,800,000	$4,400,000	$4,000,000
Notes payable (8% interest)	2,250,000	2,250,000	2,250,000
Common stock	250,000	250,000	250,000
Preferred 4% stock, $100 par (no change during year)	500,000	500,000	500,000
Retained earnings	1,574,000	1,222,000	750,000

The 2016 net income was $372,000, and the 2015 net income was $492,000. No dividends on common stock were declared between 2014 and 2016.

a. Determine the rate earned on total assets, the rate earned on stockholders' equity, and the rate earned on common stockholders' equity for the years 2015 and 2016. Round to one decimal place.

b. What conclusions can be drawn from these data as to the company's profitability?

EX 14-18 Profitability ratios

OBJ. 3

✔a. Year 3 rate earned on total assets, 12.2%

Ralph Lauren Corp. sells men's apparel through company-owned retail stores. Recent financial information for Ralph Lauren follows (all numbers in thousands):

	Fiscal Year 3	Fiscal Year 2	
Net income	$567,600	$479,500	
Interest expense	18,300	22,200	
	Fiscal Year 3	**Fiscal Year 2**	**Fiscal Year 1**
Total assets (at end of fiscal year)	$4,981,100	$4,648,900	$4,356,500
Total stockholders' equity (at end of fiscal year)	3,304,700	3,116,600	2,735,100

Assume the apparel industry average rate earned on total assets is 8.0%, and the average rate earned on stockholders' equity is 10.0% for the year ended April 2, Year 3.

a. Determine the rate earned on total assets for Ralph Lauren for fiscal Years 2 and 3. Round to one digit after the decimal place.

b. Determine the rate earned on stockholders' equity for Ralph Lauren for fiscal Years 2 and 3. Round to one decimal place.

c. Evaluate the two-year trend for the profitability ratios determined in (a) and (b).

d. Evaluate Ralph Lauren's profit performance relative to the industry.

EX 14-19 Six measures of solvency or profitability

OBJ. 2, 3

✔ c. Ratio of sales to assets, 4.2

The following data were taken from the financial statements of Gates Inc. for the current fiscal year. Assuming that long-term investments totaled $3,000,000 throughout the year and that total assets were $7,000,000 at the beginning of the current fiscal year, determine the following: (a) ratio of fixed assets to long-term liabilities, (b) ratio of liabilities to stockholders' equity, (c) ratio of sales to assets, (d) rate earned on total assets, (e) rate earned on stockholders' equity, and (f) rate earned on common stockholders' equity. Round to one decimal place.

Property, plant, and equipment (net)			$ 3,200,000
Liabilities:			
Current liabilities		$1,000,000	
Mortgage note payable, 6%, issued 2005, due 2021		2,000,000	
Total liabilities			$ 3,000,000
Stockholders' equity:			
Preferred $10 stock, $100 par (no change during year)			$ 1,000,000
Common stock, $10 par (no change during year)			2,000,000
Retained earnings:			
Balance, beginning of year	$1,570,000		
Net income	930,000	$2,500,000	
Preferred dividends	$ 100,000		
Common dividends	400,000	500,000	
Balance, end of year			2,000,000
Total stockholders' equity			$ 5,000,000
Sales			$18,900,000
Interest expense			$ 120,000

EX 14-20 Six measures of solvency or profitability

OBJ. 2, 3

✔ d. Price-earnings ratio, 10.0

The balance sheet for Garcon Inc. at the end of the current fiscal year indicated the following:

Bonds payable, 8% (issued in 2006, due in 2026)	$5,000,000
Preferred $4 stock, $50 par	2,500,000
Common stock, $10 par	5,000,000

Income before income tax was $3,000,000, and income taxes were $1,200,000 for the current year. Cash dividends paid on common stock during the current year totaled $1,200,000. The common stock was selling for $32 per share at the end of the year. Determine each of the following: (a) number of times bond interest charges are earned, (b) number of times preferred dividends are earned, (c) earnings per share on common stock, (d) price-earnings ratio, (e) dividends per share of common stock, and (f) dividend yield. Round to one decimal place, except earnings per share, which should be rounded to two decimal places.

EX 14-21 Earnings per share, price-earnings ratio, dividend yield **OBJ. 3**

✔ b. Price-earnings ratio, 15.0

SHOW ME HOW

The following information was taken from the financial statements of Tolbert Inc. for December 31 of the current fiscal year:

Common stock, $20 par (no change during the year)	$10,000,000
Preferred $4 stock, $40 par (no change during the year)	2,500,000

The net income was $1,750,000 and the declared dividends on the common stock were $1,125,000 for the current year. The market price of the common stock is $45 per share.

For the common stock, determine (a) the earnings per share, (b) the price-earnings ratio, (c) the dividends per share, and (d) the dividend yield. Round to one decimal place, except earnings per share, which should be rounded to two decimal places.

EX 14-22 Price-earnings ratio; dividend yield **OBJ. 3**

The table that follows shows the stock price, earnings per share, and dividends per share for three companies for a recent year:

	Price	Earnings per Share	Dividends per Share
Deere & Co.	$ 86.20	$ 8.71	$2.04
Google	873.32	36.75	0.00
The Coca-Cola Company	39.79	1.97	1.02

a. Determine the price-earnings ratio and dividend yield for the three companies. Round to one decimal place.

b. Explain the differences in these ratios across the three companies.

Appendix

EX 14-23 Earnings per share, extraordinary item

✔ b. Earnings per share on common stock, $7.60

The net income reported on the income statement of Cutler Co. was $4,000,000. There were 500,000 shares of $10 par common stock and 100,000 shares of $2 preferred stock outstanding throughout the current year. The income statement included two extraordinary items: an $800,000 gain from condemnation of land and a $400,000 loss arising from flood damage, both after applicable income tax. Determine the per-share figures for common stock for (a) income before extraordinary items and (b) net income.

Appendix

EX 14-24 Extraordinary item

Assume that the amount of each of the following items is material to the financial statements. Classify each item as either normally recurring (NR) or extraordinary (E).

a. Loss on the disposal of equipment considered to be obsolete because of the development of new technology.

b. Uninsured loss on building due to hurricane damage. The building was purchased by the company in 1910 and had not previously incurred hurricane damage.

c. Gain on sale of land condemned by the local government for a public works project.

d. Uninsured flood loss. (Flood insurance is unavailable because of periodic flooding in the area.)

e. Interest revenue on notes receivable.

f. Uncollectible accounts expense.

g. Loss on sale of investments in stocks and bonds.

Appendix

EX 14-25 Income statement and earnings per share for extraordinary items and discontinued operations

Apex Inc. reports the following for a recent year:

Income from continuing operations before income tax	$1,000,000
Extraordinary property loss from hurricane	$140,000*
Loss from discontinued operations	$240,000*
Weighted average number of shares outstanding	20,000
Applicable tax rate	40%

*Net of any tax effect.

a. Prepare a partial income statement for Apex Inc., beginning with income from continuing operations before income tax.

b. Calculate the earnings per common share for Apex Inc., including per-share amounts for unusual items.

Appendix

EX 14-26 Unusual items

Discuss whether Colston Company correctly reported the following items in the financial statements:

a. In a recent year, the company discovered a clerical error in the prior year's accounting records. As a result, the reported net income for the previous year was overstated by $45,000. The company corrected this error by restating the prior-year financial statements.

b. In a recent year, the company voluntarily changed its method of accounting for long-term construction contracts from the percentage of completion method to the completed contract method. Both methods are acceptable under generally accepted accounting principles. The cumulative effect of this change was reported as a separate component of income in the current period income statement.

Problems: Series A

PR 14-1A Horizontal analysis of income statement **OBJ. 1**

✔ 1. Sales, 12.5% increase

General Ledger

SHOW ME HOW

For 2016, Clapton Company reported a decline in net income. At the end of the year, S. Hand, the president, is presented with the following condensed comparative income statement:

Clapton Company
Comparative Income Statement
For the Years Ended December 31, 2016 and 2015

	2016	2015
Sales	$6,750,000	$6,000,000
Cost of goods sold	2,480,000	2,000,000
Gross profit	$4,270,000	$4,000,000
Selling expenses	$1,260,000	$1,000,000
Administrative expenses	625,000	500,000
Total operating expenses	$1,885,000	$1,500,000
Income from operations	$2,385,000	$2,500,000
Other income	110,000	100,000
Income before income tax	$2,495,000	$2,600,000
Income tax expense	60,000	50,000
Net income	$2,435,000	$2,550,000

Instructions

1. Prepare a comparative income statement with horizontal analysis for the two-year period, using 2015 as the base year. Round to one decimal place.
2. To the extent the data permit, comment on the significant relationships revealed by the horizontal analysis prepared in (1).

PR 14-2A Vertical analysis of income statement

OBJ. 1

✔ 1. Net income, 2016, 13.0%

General Ledger

For 2016, Indigo Company initiated a sales promotion campaign that included the expenditure of an additional $39,000 for advertising. At the end of the year, Lumi Neer, the president, is presented with the following condensed comparative income statement:

Indigo Company
Comparative Income Statement
For the Years Ended December 31, 2016 and 2015

	2016	2015
Sales	$820,000	$600,000
Cost of goods sold	311,600	240,000
Gross profit	$508,400	$360,000
Selling expenses	$164,000	$108,000
Administrative expenses	57,400	54,000
Total operating expenses	$221,400	$162,000
Income from operations	$287,000	$198,000
Other income	65,600	48,000
Income before income tax	$352,600	$246,000
Income tax expense	246,000	180,000
Net income	$106,600	$ 66,000

Instructions

1. Prepare a comparative income statement for the two-year period, presenting an analysis of each item in relationship to sales for each of the years. Round to one decimal place.
2. To the extent the data permit, comment on the significant relationships revealed by the vertical analysis prepared in (1).

PR 14-3A Effect of transactions on current position analysis

OBJ. 2

✔ 2. c. Current ratio, 2.0

Data pertaining to the current position of Forte Company are as follows:

Cash	$412,500
Marketable securities	187,500
Accounts and notes receivable (net)	300,000
Inventories	700,000
Prepaid expenses	50,000
Accounts payable	200,000
Notes payable (short-term)	250,000
Accrued expenses	300,000

Instructions

1. Compute (a) the working capital, (b) the current ratio, and (c) the quick ratio. Round to one decimal place.

(Continued)

2. List the following captions on a sheet of paper:

Transaction	Working Capital	Current Ratio	Quick Ratio

Compute the working capital, the current ratio, and the quick ratio after each of the following transactions, and record the results in the appropriate columns. *Consider each transaction separately* and assume that only that transaction affects the data given. Round to one decimal place.

a. Sold marketable securities at no gain or loss, $70,000.
b. Paid accounts payable, $125,000.
c. Purchased goods on account, $110,000.
d. Paid notes payable, $100,000.
e. Declared a cash dividend, $150,000.
f. Declared a common stock dividend on common stock, $50,000.
g. Borrowed cash from bank on a long-term note, $225,000.
h. Received cash on account, $125,000.
i. Issued additional shares of stock for cash, $600,000.
j. Paid cash for prepaid expenses, $10,000.

PR 14-4A Nineteen measures of solvency and profitability

OBJ. 2, 3

✔ 5. Number of days' sales in receivables, 36.5

The comparative financial statements of Bettancort Inc. are as follows. The market price of Bettancort Inc. common stock was $71.25 on December 31, 2016.

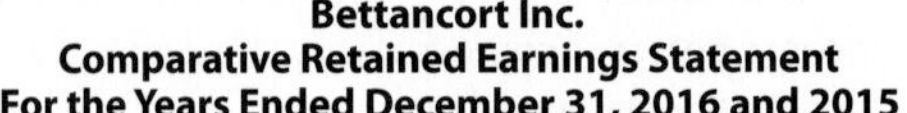

Bettancort Inc.
Comparative Retained Earnings Statement
For the Years Ended December 31, 2016 and 2015

	2016	2015
Retained earnings, January 1	$2,655,000	$2,400,000
Add net income for year	300,000	280,000
Total	$2,955,000	$2,680,000
Deduct dividends:		
On preferred stock	$ 15,000	$ 15,000
On common stock	10,000	10,000
Total	$ 25,000	$ 25,000
Retained earnings, December 31	$2,930,000	$2,655,000

Bettancort Inc.
Comparative Income Statement
For the Years Ended December 31, 2016 and 2015

	2016	2015
Sales	$1,200,000	$1,000,000
Cost of goods sold	500,000	475,000
Gross profit	$ 700,000	$ 525,000
Selling expenses	$ 240,000	$ 200,000
Administrative expenses	180,000	150,000
Total operating expenses	$ 420,000	$ 350,000
Income from operations	$ 280,000	$ 175,000
Other income	166,000	225,000
	$ 446,000	$ 400,000
Other expense (interest)	66,000	60,000
Income before income tax	$ 380,000	$ 340,000
Income tax expense	80,000	60,000
Net income	$ 300,000	$ 280,000

Bettancort Inc.
Comparative Balance Sheet
December 31, 2016 and 2015

	Dec. 31, 2016	Dec. 31, 2015
Assets		
Current assets:		
Cash	$ 450,000	$ 400,000
Marketable securities	300,000	260,000
Accounts receivable (net)	130,000	110,000
Inventories	67,000	58,000
Prepaid expenses	153,000	139,000
Total current assets	$1,100,000	$ 967,000
Long-term investments	2,350,000	2,200,000
Property, plant, and equipment (net)	1,320,000	1,188,000
Total assets	$4,770,000	$4,355,000
Liabilities		
Current liabilities	$ 440,000	$ 400,000
Long-term liabilities:		
Mortgage note payable, 8%, due 2021	$ 100,000	$ 0
Bonds payable, 5%, due 2017	1,000,000	1,000,000
Total long-term liabilities	$1,100,000	$1,000,000
Total liabilities	$1,540,000	$1,400,000
Stockholders' Equity		
Preferred $0.75 stock, $10 par	$ 200,000	$ 200,000
Common stock, $10 par	100,000	100,000
Retained earnings	2,930,000	2,655,000
Total stockholders' equity	$3,230,000	$2,955,000
Total liabilities and stockholders' equity	$4,770,000	$4,355,000

Instructions

Determine the following measures for 2016, rounding to one decimal place:

1. Working capital
2. Current ratio
3. Quick ratio
4. Accounts receivable turnover
5. Number of days' sales in receivables
6. Inventory turnover
7. Number of days' sales in inventory
8. Ratio of fixed assets to long-term liabilities
9. Ratio of liabilities to stockholders' equity
10. Number of times interest charges are earned
11. Number of times preferred dividends are earned
12. Ratio of sales to assets
13. Rate earned on total assets
14. Rate earned on stockholders' equity
15. Rate earned on common stockholders' equity
16. Earnings per share on common stock
17. Price-earnings ratio
18. Dividends per share of common stock
19. Dividend yield

PR 14-5A Solvency and profitability trend analysis

OBJ. 2, 3

Addai Company has provided the following comparative information:

	2016	2015	2014	2013	2012
Net income	$ 273,406	$ 367,976	$ 631,176	$ 884,000	$ 800,000
Interest expense	616,047	572,003	528,165	495,000	440,000
Income tax expense	31,749	53,560	106,720	160,000	200,000
Total assets (ending balance)	4,417,178	4,124,350	3,732,443	3,338,500	2,750,000
Total stockholders' equity (ending balance)	3,706,557	3,433,152	3,065,176	2,434,000	1,550,000
Average total assets	4,270,764	3,928,396	3,535,472	3,044,250	2,475,000
Average total stockholders' equity	3,569,855	3,249,164	2,749,588	1,992,000	1,150,000

You have been asked to evaluate the historical performance of the company over the last five years.

Selected industry ratios have remained relatively steady at the following levels for the last five years:

	2012–2016
Rate earned on total assets	28%
Rate earned on stockholders' equity	18%
Number of times interest charges are earned	2.7
Ratio of liabilities to stockholders' equity	0.4

Instructions

1. Prepare four line graphs with the ratio on the vertical axis and the years on the horizontal axis for the following four ratios (rounded to one decimal place):
   a. Rate earned on total assets
   b. Rate earned on stockholders' equity
   c. Number of times interest charges are earned
   d. Ratio of liabilities to stockholders' equity

   Display both the company ratio and the industry benchmark on each graph. That is, each graph should have two lines.
2. Prepare an analysis of the graphs in (1).

Problems: Series B

PR 14-1B Horizontal analysis of income statement

OBJ. 1

✔ 1. Sales, 30.0% increase

General Ledger

SHOW ME HOW

For 2016, Macklin Inc. reported a significant increase in net income. At the end of the year, John Mayer, the president, is presented with the following condensed comparative income statement:

Macklin Inc.
Comparative Income Statement
For the Years Ended December 31, 2016 and 2015

	2016	2015
Sales	$910,000	$700,000
Cost of goods sold	441,000	350,000
Gross profit	$469,000	$350,000
Selling expenses	$ 139,150	$115,000
Administrative expenses	99,450	85,000
Total operating expenses	$238,600	$200,000
Income from operations	$230,400	$150,000
Other income	65,000	50,000
Income before income tax	$295,400	$200,000
Income tax expense	65,000	50,000
Net income	$230,400	$150,000

Instructions

1. Prepare a comparative income statement with horizontal analysis for the two-year period, using 2015 as the base year. Round to one decimal place.
2. To the extent the data permit, comment on the significant relationships revealed by the horizontal analysis prepared in (1).

PR 14-2B Vertical analysis of income statement

OBJ. 1

✔ 1. Net income, 2015, 14.0%

General Ledger

For 2016, Fielder Industries Inc. initiated a sales promotion campaign that included the expenditure of an additional $40,000 for advertising. At the end of the year, Leif Grando, the president, is presented with the following condensed comparative income statement:

Fielder Industries Inc.
Comparative Income Statement
For the Years Ended December 31, 2016 and 2015

	2016	2015
Sales	$1,300,000	$1,180,000
Cost of goods sold	682,500	613,600
Gross profit	$ 617,500	$ 566,400
Selling expenses	$ 260,000	$ 188,800
Adminstrative expenses	169,000	177,000
Total operating expenses	$ 429,000	$ 365,800
Income from operations	$ 188,500	$ 200,600
Other income	78,000	70,800
Income before income tax	$ 266,500	$ 271,400
Income tax expense	117,000	106,200
Net income	$ 149,500	$ 165,200

Instructions

1. Prepare a comparative income statement for the two-year period, presenting an analysis of each item in relationship to sales for each of the years. Round to one decimal place.
2. To the extent the data permit, comment on the significant relationships revealed by the vertical analysis prepared in (1).

PR 14-3B Effect of transactions on current position analysis

OBJ. 2

✔ 2. g. Quick ratio, 1.6

Data pertaining to the current position of Lucroy Industries Inc. are as follows:

Cash	$ 800,000
Marketable securities	550,000
Accounts and notes receivable (net)	850,000
Inventories	700,000
Prepaid expenses	300,000
Accounts payable	1,200,000
Notes payable (short-term)	700,000
Accrued expenses	100,000

Instructions

1. Compute (a) the working capital, (b) the current ratio, and (c) the quick ratio. Round to one decimal place.
2. List the following captions on a sheet of paper:

Transaction	Working Capital	Current Ratio	Quick Ratio

Compute the working capital, the current ratio, and the quick ratio after each of the following transactions, and record the results in the appropriate columns. *Consider each transaction separately* and assume that only that transaction affects the data given. Round to one decimal place.

(Continued)

a. Sold marketable securities at no gain or loss, $500,000.
b. Paid accounts payable, $287,500.
c. Purchased goods on account, $400,000.
d. Paid notes payable, $125,000.
e. Declared a cash dividend, $325,000.
f. Declared a common stock dividend on common stock, $150,000.
g. Borrowed cash from bank on a long-term note, $1,000,000.
h. Received cash on account, $75,000.
i. Issued additional shares of stock for cash, $2,000,000.
j. Paid cash for prepaid expenses, $200,000.

PR 14-4B Nineteen measures of solvency and profitability

OBJ. 2, 3

✔ 9. Ratio of liabilities to stockholders' equity, 0.4

The comparative financial statements of Stargel Inc. are as follows. The market price of Stargel Inc. common stock was $119.70 on December 31, 2016.

Stargel Inc.
Comparative Retained Earnings Statement
For the Years Ended December 31, 2016 and 2015

	2016	2015
Retained earnings, January 1	$5,375,000	$4,545,000
Add net income for year	900,000	925,000
Total	$6,275,000	$5,470,000
Deduct dividends:		
On preferred stock	$ 45,000	$ 45,000
On common stock	50,000	50,000
Total	$ 95,000	$ 95,000
Retained earnings, December 31	$6,180,000	$5,375,000

Stargel Inc.
Comparative Income Statement
For the Years Ended December 31, 2016 and 2015

	2016	2015
Sales	$10,000,000	$9,400,000
Cost of goods sold	5,350,000	4,950,000
Gross profit	$ 4,650,000	$4,450,000
Selling expenses	$ 2,000,000	$1,880,000
Administrative expenses	1,500,000	1,410,000
Total operating expenses	$ 3,500,000	$3,290,000
Income from operations	$ 1,150,000	$1,160,000
Other income	150,000	140,000
	$ 1,300,000	$1,300,000
Other expense (interest)	170,000	150,000
Income before income tax	$ 1,130,000	$1,150,000
Income tax expense	230,000	225,000
Net income	$ 900,000	$ 925,000

Stargel Inc.
Comparative Balance Sheet
December 31, 2016 and 2015

	Dec. 31, 2016	Dec. 31, 2015
Assets		
Current assets:		
Cash	$ 500,000	$ 400,000
Marketable securities	1,010,000	1,000,000
Accounts receivable (net)	740,000	510,000
Inventories	1,190,000	950,000
Prepaid expenses	250,000	229,000
Total current assets	$3,690,000	$3,089,000
Long-term investments	2,350,000	2,300,000
Property, plant, and equipment (net)	3,740,000	3,366,000
Total assets	$9,780,000	$8,755,000
Liabilities		
Current liabilities	$ 900,000	$ 880,000
Long-term liabilities:		
Mortgage note payable, 8.8%, due 2021	$ 200,000	$ 0
Bonds payable, 9%, due 2017	1,500,000	1,500,000
Total long-term liabilities	$1,700,000	$1,500,000
Total liabilities	$2,600,000	$2,380,000
Stockholders' Equity		
Preferred $0.90 stock, $10 par	$ 500,000	$ 500,000
Common stock, $5 par	500,000	500,000
Retained earnings	6,180,000	5,375,000
Total stockholders' equity	$7,180,000	$6,375,000
Total liabilities and stockholders' equity	$9,780,000	$8,755,000

Instructions

Determine the following measures for 2016, rounding to one decimal place, except per-share amounts, which should be rounded to the nearest penny:

1. Working capital
2. Current ratio
3. Quick ratio
4. Accounts receivable turnover
5. Number of days' sales in receivables
6. Inventory turnover
7. Number of days' sales in inventory
8. Ratio of fixed assets to long-term liabilities
9. Ratio of liabilities to stockholders' equity
10. Number of times interest charges are earned
11. Number of times preferred dividends are earned
12. Ratio of sales to assets
13. Rate earned on total assets
14. Rate earned on stockholders' equity
15. Rate earned on common stockholders' equity
16. Earnings per share on common stock
17. Price-earnings ratio
18. Dividends per share of common stock
19. Dividend yield

PR 14-5B Solvency and profitability trend analysis OBJ. 2, 3

Crosby Company has provided the following comparative information:

	2016	2015	2014	2013	2012
Net income	$ 5,571,720	$ 3,714,480	$ 2,772,000	$ 1,848,000	$ 1,400,000
Interest expense	1,052,060	891,576	768,600	610,000	500,000
Income tax expense	1,225,572	845,222	640,320	441,600	320,000
Total assets (ending balance)	29,378,491	22,598,839	17,120,333	12,588,480	10,152,000
Total stockholders' equity (ending balance)	18,706,200	13,134,480	9,420,000	6,648,000	4,800,000
Average total assets	25,988,665	19,859,586	14,854,406	11,370,240	8,676,000
Average total stockholders' equity	15,920,340	11,277,240	8,034,000	5,724,000	4,100,000

You have been asked to evaluate the historical performance of the company over the last five years.

Selected industry ratios have remained relatively steady at the following levels for the last five years:

	2012–2016
Rate earned on total assets	19%
Rate earned on stockholders' equity	26%
Number of times interest charges are earned	3.4
Ratio of liabilities to stockholders' equity	1.4

Instructions

1. Prepare four line graphs with the ratio on the vertical axis and the years on the horizontal axis for the following four ratios (rounded to one decimal place):
   a. Rate earned on total assets
   b. Rate earned on stockholders' equity
   c. Number of times interest charges are earned
   d. Ratio of liabilities to stockholders' equity

   Display both the company ratio and the industry benchmark on each graph. That is, each graph should have two lines.
2. Prepare an analysis of the graphs in (1).

Nike, Inc., Problem

Financial Statement Analysis

The financial statements for **Nike, Inc.**, are presented in Appendix B at the end of the text. The following additional information (in thousands) is available:

Accounts receivable at May 31, 2010	$ 3,138
Inventories at May 31, 2010	2,715
Total assets at May 31, 2010	14,998
Stockholders' equity at May 31, 2010	9,843

Instructions

1. Determine the following measures for the fiscal years ended May 31, 2013 (fiscal 2012), and May 31, 2012 (fiscal 2011), rounding to one decimal place.
   a. Working capital
   b. Current ratio
   c. Quick ratio
   d. Accounts receivable turnover

e. Number of days' sales in receivables
f. Inventory turnover
g. Number of days' sales in inventory
h. Ratio of liabilities to stockholders' equity
i. Ratio of sales to assets
j. Rate earned on total assets, assuming interest expense is $23 million for the year ending May 31, 2013, and $31 million for the year ending May 31, 2012
k. Rate earned on common stockholders' equity
l. Price-earnings ratio, assuming that the market price was $61.66 per share on May 31, 2013, and $53.10 per share on May 31, 2012
m. Percentage relationship of net income to sales

2. What conclusions can be drawn from these analyses?

Cases & Projects

CP 14-1 Analysis of financing corporate growth

Assume that the president of Freeman Industries Inc. made the following statement in the Annual Report to Shareholders:

"The founding family and majority shareholders of the company do not believe in using debt to finance future growth. The founding family learned from hard experience during Prohibition and the Great Depression that debt can cause loss of flexibility and eventual loss of corporate control. The company will not place itself at such risk. As such, all future growth will be financed either by stock sales to the public or by internally generated resources."

As a public shareholder of this company, how would you respond to this policy?

CP 14-2 Receivables and inventory turnover

Rodgers Industries Inc. has completed its fiscal year on December 31. The auditor, Josh McCoy, has approached the CFO, Aaron Mathews, regarding the year-end receivables and inventory levels of Rodgers Industries. The following conversation takes place:

Josh: We are beginning our audit of Rodgers Industries and have prepared ratio analyses to determine if there have been significant changes in operations or financial position. This helps us guide the audit process. This analysis indicates that the inventory turnover has decreased from 5.1 to 2.7, while the accounts receivable turnover has decreased from 11 to 7. Could you explain this change in operations?

Aaron: There is little need for concern. The inventory represents computers that we were unable to sell during the holiday buying season. We are confident, however, that we will be able to sell these computers as we move into the next fiscal year.

Josh: What gives you this confidence?

Aaron: We will increase our advertising and provide some very attractive price concessions to move these machines. We have no choice. Newer technology is already out there, and we have to unload this inventory.

Josh: ... and the receivables?

Aaron: As you may be aware, the company is under tremendous pressure to expand sales and profits. As a result, we lowered our credit standards to our commercial customers so that we would be able to sell products to a broader customer base. As a result of this policy change, we have been able to expand sales by 35%.

Josh: Your responses have not been reassuring to me.

Aaron: I'm a little confused. Assets are good, right? Why don't you look at our current ratio? It has improved, hasn't it? I would think that you would view that very favorably.

Why is Josh concerned about the inventory and accounts receivable turnover ratios and Aaron's responses to them? What action may Josh need to take? How would you respond to Aaron's last comment?

CP 14-3 Vertical analysis

The condensed income statements through income from operations for Dell Inc. and Apple Inc. for recent fiscal years follow (numbers in millions of dollars):

	Dell Inc.	Apple Inc.
Sales	$56,940	$156,508
Cost of sales	44,754	87,846
Gross profit	$12,186	$68,662
Selling, general, and administrative expenses	$ 8,102	$10,040
Research and development	1,072	3,381
Operating expenses	$ 9,174	$13,421
Income from operations	$ 3,012	$55,241

Prepare comparative common-sized statements, rounding percents to one decimal place. Interpret the analyses.

CP 14-4 Profitability and stockholder ratios

Deere & Co. manufactures and distributes farm and construction machinery that it sells around the world. In addition to its manufacturing operations, Deere & Co.'s credit division loans money to customers to finance the purchase of their farm and construction equipment.

The following information is available for three recent years (in millions except per-share amounts):

	Year 3	Year 2	Year 1
Net income (loss)	$3,064.7	$2,799.9	$1,865.0
Preferred dividends	$0.00	$0.00	$0.00
Interest expense	$782.8	$759.4	$811.4
Shares outstanding for computing earnings per share	397	417	424
Cash dividend per share	$1.79	$1.52	$1.16
Average total assets	$52,237	$45,737	$42,200
Average stockholders' equity	$6,821	$6,545	$5,555
Average stock price per share	$79.27	$80.48	$61.18

1. Calculate the following ratios for each year (Round percentages to one decimal place):
   a. Rate earned on total assets
   b. Rate earned on stockholders' equity
   c. Earnings per share
   d. Dividend yield
   e. Price-earnings ratio
2. What is the ratio of average liabilities to average stockholders' equity for Year 3?
3. Based on these data, evaluate Deere & Co.'s performance.

CP 14-5 Comprehensive profitability and solvency analysis

Marriott International, Inc., and Hyatt Hotels Corporation are two major owners and managers of lodging and resort properties in the United States. Abstracted income statement information for the two companies is as follows for a recent year:

	Marriott (in millions)	Hyatt (in millions)
Operating profit before other expenses and interest	$ 677	$ 39
Other income (expenses)	54	118
Interest expense	(180)	(54)
Income before income taxes	$ 551	$103
Income tax expense	93	37
Net income	$ 458	$ 66

Balance sheet information is as follows:

	Marriott (in millions)	Hyatt (in millions)
Total liabilities	$7,398	$2,125
Total stockholders' equity	1,585	5,118
Total liabilities and stockholders' equity	$8,983	$7,243

The average liabilities, average stockholders' equity, and average total assets were as follows:

	Marriott (in millions)	Hyatt (in millions)
Average total liabilities	$7,095	$2,132
Average total stockholders' equity	1,364	5,067
Average total assets	8,458	7,199

1. Determine the following ratios for both companies (round to one decimal place after the whole percent):
   a. Rate earned on total assets
   b. Rate earned on stockholders' equity
   c. Number of times interest charges are earned
   d. Ratio of liabilities to stockholders' equity
2. Analyze and compare the two companies, using the information in (1).

Appendices

A Interest Tables

B Nike Inc., Form 10-K For the Fiscal Year Ended May 31, 2013

Appendix A

Interest Tables

Present Value of $1 at Compound Interest Due in *n* Periods

Periods	4.0%	4.5%	5%	5.5%	6%	6.5%	7%
1	0.96154	0.95694	0.95238	0.94787	0.94340	0.93897	0.93458
2	0.92456	0.91573	0.90703	0.89845	0.89000	0.88166	0.87344
3	0.88900	0.87630	0.86384	0.85161	0.83962	0.82785	0.81630
4	0.85480	0.83856	0.82270	0.80722	0.79209	0.77732	0.76290
5	0.82193	0.80245	0.78353	0.76513	0.74726	0.72988	0.71299
6	0.79031	0.76790	0.74622	0.72525	0.70496	0.68533	0.66634
7	0.75992	0.73483	0.71068	0.68744	0.66506	0.64351	0.62275
8	0.73069	0.70319	0.67684	0.65160	0.62741	0.60423	0.58201
9	0.70259	0.67290	0.64461	0.61763	0.59190	0.56735	0.54393
10	0.67556	0.64393	0.61391	0.58543	0.55839	0.53273	0.50835
11	0.64958	0.61620	0.58468	0.55491	0.52679	0.50021	0.47509
12	0.62460	0.58966	0.55684	0.52598	0.49697	0.46968	0.44401
13	0.60057	0.56427	0.53032	0.49856	0.46884	0.44102	0.41496
14	0.57748	0.53997	0.50507	0.47257	0.44230	0.41410	0.38782
15	0.55526	0.51672	0.48102	0.44793	0.41727	0.38883	0.36245
16	0.53391	0.49447	0.45811	0.42458	0.39365	0.36510	0.33873
17	0.51337	0.47318	0.43630	0.40245	0.37136	0.34281	0.31657
18	0.49363	0.45280	0.41552	0.38147	0.35034	0.32189	0.29586
19	0.47464	0.43330	0.39573	0.36158	0.33051	0.30224	0.27651
20	0.45639	0.41464	0.37689	0.34273	0.31180	0.28380	0.25842
21	0.43883	0.39679	0.35894	0.32486	0.29416	0.26648	0.24151
22	0.42196	0.37970	0.34185	0.30793	0.27751	0.25021	0.22571
23	0.40573	0.36335	0.32557	0.29187	0.26180	0.23494	0.21095
24	0.39012	0.34770	0.31007	0.27666	0.24698	0.22060	0.19715
25	0.37512	0.33273	0.29530	0.26223	0.23300	0.20714	0.18425
26	0.36069	0.31840	0.28124	0.24856	0.21981	0.19450	0.17220
27	0.34682	0.30469	0.26785	0.23560	0.20737	0.18263	0.16093
28	0.33348	0.29157	0.25509	0.22332	0.19563	0.17148	0.15040
29	0.32065	0.27902	0.24295	0.21168	0.18456	0.16101	0.14056
30	0.30832	0.26700	0.23138	0.20064	0.17411	0.15119	0.13137
31	0.29646	0.25550	0.22036	0.19018	0.16425	0.14196	0.12277
32	0.28506	0.24450	0.20987	0.18027	0.15496	0.13329	0.11474
33	0.27409	0.23397	0.19987	0.17087	0.14619	0.12516	0.10723
34	0.26355	0.22390	0.19035	0.16196	0.13791	0.11752	0.10022
35	0.25342	0.21425	0.18129	0.15352	0.13011	0.11035	0.09366
40	0.20829	0.17193	0.14205	0.11746	0.09722	0.08054	0.06678
45	0.17120	0.13796	0.11130	0.08988	0.07265	0.05879	0.04761
50	0.14071	0.11071	0.08720	0.06877	0.05429	0.04291	0.03395

Present Value of $1 at Compound Interest Due in *n* Periods

Periods	8%	9%	10%	11%	12%	13%	14%
1	0.92593	0.91743	0.90909	0.90090	0.89286	0.88496	0.87719
2	0.85734	0.84168	0.82645	0.81162	0.79719	0.78315	0.76947
3	0.79383	0.77218	0.75131	0.73119	0.71178	0.69305	0.67497
4	0.73503	0.70843	0.68301	0.65873	0.63552	0.61332	0.59208
5	0.68058	0.64993	0.62092	0.59345	0.56743	0.54276	0.51937
6	0.63017	0.59627	0.56447	0.53464	0.50663	0.48032	0.45559
7	0.58349	0.54703	0.51316	0.48166	0.45235	0.42506	0.39964
8	0.54027	0.50187	0.46651	0.43393	0.40388	0.37616	0.35056
9	0.50025	0.46043	0.42410	0.39092	0.36061	0.33288	0.30751
10	0.46319	0.42241	0.38554	0.35218	0.32197	0.29459	0.26974
11	0.42888	0.38753	0.35049	0.31728	0.28748	0.26070	0.23662
12	0.39711	0.35553	0.31863	0.28584	0.25668	0.23071	0.20756
13	0.36770	0.32618	0.28966	0.25751	0.22917	0.20416	0.18207
14	0.34046	0.29925	0.26333	0.23199	0.20462	0.18068	0.15971
15	0.31524	0.27454	0.23939	0.20900	0.18270	0.15989	0.14010
16	0.29189	0.25187	0.21763	0.18829	0.16312	0.14150	0.12289
17	0.27027	0.23107	0.19784	0.16963	0.14564	0.12522	0.10780
18	0.25025	0.21199	0.17986	0.15282	0.13004	0.11081	0.09456
19	0.23171	0.19449	0.16351	0.13768	0.11611	0.09806	0.08295
20	0.21455	0.17843	0.14864	0.12403	0.10367	0.08678	0.07276
21	0.19866	0.16370	0.13513	0.11174	0.09256	0.07680	0.06383
22	0.18394	0.15018	0.12285	0.10067	0.08264	0.06796	0.05599
23	0.17032	0.13778	0.11168	0.09069	0.07379	0.06014	0.04911
24	0.15770	0.12640	0.10153	0.08170	0.06588	0.05323	0.04308
25	0.14602	0.11597	0.09230	0.07361	0.05882	0.04710	0.03779
26	0.13520	0.10639	0.08391	0.06631	0.05252	0.04168	0.03315
27	0.12519	0.09761	0.07628	0.05974	0.04689	0.03689	0.02908
28	0.11591	0.08955	0.06934	0.05382	0.04187	0.03264	0.02551
29	0.10733	0.08215	0.06304	0.04849	0.03738	0.02889	0.02237
30	0.09938	0.07537	0.05731	0.04368	0.03338	0.02557	0.01963
31	0.09202	0.06915	0.05210	0.03935	0.02980	0.02262	0.01722
32	0.08520	0.06344	0.04736	0.03545	0.02661	0.02002	0.01510
33	0.07889	0.05820	0.04306	0.03194	0.02376	0.01772	0.01325
34	0.07305	0.05339	0.03914	0.02878	0.02121	0.01568	0.01162
35	0.06763	0.04899	0.03558	0.02592	0.01894	0.01388	0.01019
40	0.04603	0.03184	0.02209	0.01538	0.01075	0.00753	0.00529
45	0.03133	0.02069	0.01372	0.00913	0.00610	0.00409	0.00275
50	0.02132	0.01345	0.00852	0.00542	0.00346	0.00222	0.00143

Present Value of Ordinary Annuity of $1 per Period

Periods	4.0%	4.5%	5%	5.5%	6%	6.5%	7%
1	0.96154	0.95694	0.95238	0.94787	0.94340	0.93897	0.93458
2	1.88609	1.87267	1.85941	1.84632	1.83339	1.82063	1.80802
3	2.77509	2.74896	2.72325	2.69793	2.67301	2.64848	2.62432
4	3.62990	3.58753	3.54595	3.50515	3.46511	3.42580	3.38721
5	4.45182	4.38998	4.32948	4.27028	4.21236	4.15568	4.10020
6	5.24214	5.15787	5.07569	4.99553	4.91732	4.84101	4.76654
7	6.00205	5.89270	5.78637	5.68297	5.58238	5.48452	5.38929
8	6.73274	6.59589	6.46321	6.33457	6.20979	6.08875	5.97130
9	7.43533	7.26879	7.10782	6.95220	6.80169	6.65610	6.51523
10	8.11090	7.91272	7.72173	7.53763	7.36009	7.18883	7.02358
11	8.76048	8.52892	8.30641	8.09254	7.88687	7.68904	7.49867
12	9.38507	9.11858	8.86325	8.61852	8.38384	8.15873	7.94269
13	9.98565	9.68285	9.39357	9.11708	8.85268	8.59974	8.35765
14	10.56312	10.22283	9.89864	9.58965	9.29498	9.01384	8.74547
15	11.11839	10.73955	10.37966	10.03758	9.71225	9.40267	9.10791
16	11.65230	11.23402	10.83777	10.46216	10.10590	9.76776	9.44665
17	12.16567	11.70719	11.27407	10.86461	10.47726	10.11058	9.76322
18	12.65930	12.15999	11.68959	11.24607	10.82760	10.43247	10.05909
19	13.13394	12.59329	12.08532	11.60765	11.15812	10.73471	10.33560
20	13.59033	13.00794	12.46221	11.95038	11.46992	11.01851	10.59401
21	14.02916	13.40472	12.82115	12.27524	11.76408	11.28498	10.83553
22	14.45112	13.78442	13.16300	12.58317	12.04158	11.53520	11.06124
23	14.85684	14.14777	13.48857	12.87504	12.30338	11.77014	11.27219
24	15.24696	14.49548	13.79864	13.15170	12.55036	11.99074	11.46933
25	15.62208	14.82821	14.09394	13.41393	12.78336	12.19788	11.65358
26	15.98277	15.14661	14.37519	13.66250	13.00317	12.39237	11.82578
27	16.32959	15.45130	14.64303	13.89810	13.21053	12.57500	11.98671
28	16.66306	15.74287	14.89813	14.12142	13.40616	12.74648	12.13711
29	16.98371	16.02189	15.14107	14.33310	13.59072	12.90749	12.27767
30	17.29203	16.28889	15.37245	14.53375	13.76483	13.05868	12.40904
31	17.58849	16.54439	15.59281	14.72393	13.92909	13.20063	12.53181
32	17.87355	16.78889	15.80268	14.90420	14.08404	13.33393	12.64656
33	18.14765	17.02286	16.00255	15.07507	14.23023	13.45909	12.75379
34	18.41120	17.24676	16.19290	15.23703	14.36814	13.57661	12.85401
35	18.66461	17.46101	16.37419	15.39055	14.49825	13.68696	12.94767
40	19.79277	18.40158	17.15909	16.04612	15.04630	14.14553	13.33171
45	20.72004	19.15635	17.77407	16.54773	15.45583	14.48023	13.60552
50	21.48218	19.76201	18.25593	16.93152	15.76186	14.72452	13.80075

Present Value of Ordinary Annuity of $1 per Period

Periods	8%	9%	10%	11%	12%	13%	14%
1	0.92593	0.91743	0.90909	0.90090	0.89286	0.88496	0.87719
2	1.78326	1.75911	1.73554	1.71252	1.69005	1.66810	1.64666
3	2.57710	2.53129	2.48685	2.44371	2.40183	2.36115	2.32163
4	3.31213	3.23972	3.16987	3.10245	3.03735	2.97447	2.91371
5	3.99271	3.88965	3.79079	3.69590	3.60478	3.51723	3.43308
6	4.62288	4.48592	4.35526	4.23054	4.11141	3.99755	3.88867
7	5.20637	5.03295	4.86842	4.71220	4.56376	4.42261	4.28830
8	5.74664	5.53482	5.33493	5.14612	4.96764	4.79677	4.63886
9	6.24689	5.99525	5.75902	5.53705	5.32825	5.13166	4.94637
10	6.71008	6.41766	6.14457	5.88923	5.65022	5.42624	5.21612
11	7.13896	6.80519	6.49506	6.20652	5.93770	5.68694	5.45273
12	7.53608	7.16073	6.81369	6.49236	6.19437	5.91765	5.66029
13	7.90378	7.48690	7.10336	6.74987	6.42355	6.12181	5.84236
14	8.22424	7.78615	7.36669	6.96187	6.62817	6.30249	6.00207
15	8.55948	8.06069	7.60608	7.19087	6.81086	6.46238	6.14217
16	8.85137	8.31256	7.82371	7.37916	6.97399	6.60388	6.26506
17	9.12164	8.54363	8.02155	7.54879	7.11963	6.72909	6.37286
18	9.37189	8.75563	8.20141	7.70162	7.24967	6.83991	6.46742
19	9.60360	8.95011	8.36492	7.83929	7.36578	6.93797	6.55037
20	9.81815	9.12855	8.51356	7.96333	7.46944	7.02475	6.62313
21	10.01680	9.29224	8.64869	8.07507	7.56200	7.10155	6.68696
22	10.20074	9.44243	8.77154	8.17574	7.64465	7.16951	6.74294
23	10.37106	9.58021	8.88322	8.26643	7.71843	7.22966	6.79206
24	10.52876	9.70661	8.98474	8.34814	7.78432	7.28288	6.83514
25	10.67478	9.82258	9.07704	8.42174	7.84314	7.32998	6.87293
26	10.80998	9.92897	9.16095	8.48806	7.89566	7.37167	6.90608
27	10.93516	10.02658	9.23722	8.54780	7.94255	7.40856	6.93515
28	11.05108	10.11613	9.30657	8.60162	7.98442	7.44120	6.96066
29	11.15841	10.19828	9.36961	8.65011	8.02181	7.47009	6.98304
30	11.25778	10.27365	9.42691	8.69379	8.05518	7.49565	7.00266
31	11.34980	10.34280	9.47901	8.73315	8.08499	7.51828	7.01988
32	11.43500	10.40624	9.52638	8.76860	8.11159	7.53830	7.03498
33	11.51389	10.46444	9.56943	8.80054	8.13535	7.55602	7.04823
34	11.58693	10.51784	9.60857	8.82932	8.15656	7.57170	7.05985
35	11.65457	10.56682	9.64416	8.85524	8.17550	7.58557	7.07005
40	11.92461	10.75736	9.77905	8.95105	8.24378	7.63438	7.10504
45	12.10840	10.88120	9.86281	9.00791	8.28252	7.66086	7.12322
50	12.23348	10.96168	9.91481	9.04165	8.30450	7.67524	7.13266

Appendix B

Nike Inc., Form 10-K
For the Fiscal Year Ended May 31, 2013

NIKE INC

FORM 10-K
(Annual Report)

Filed 07/23/13 for the Period Ending 05/31/13

Address	ONE BOWERMAN DR
	BEAVERTON, OR 97005-6453
Telephone	5036713173
CIK	0000320187
Symbol	NKE
SIC Code	3021 - Rubber and Plastics Footwear
Industry	Footwear
Sector	Consumer Cyclical
Fiscal Year	05/31

Source: Nike Inc, *Form 10-K For the Fiscal Year Ended May 31, 2013.*

Management's Annual Report on Internal Control Over Financial Reporting

Management is responsible for establishing and maintaining adequate internal control over financial reporting, as such term is defined in Rule 13a-15(f) and Rule 15d-15(f) of the Securities Exchange Act of 1934, as amended. Internal control over financial reporting is a process designed to provide reasonable assurance regarding the reliability of financial reporting and the preparation of the financial statements for external purposes in accordance with generally accepted accounting principles in the United States of America. Internal control over financial reporting includes those policies and procedures that: (i) pertain to the maintenance of records that, in reasonable detail, accurately and fairly reflect the transactions and dispositions of assets of the Company; (ii) provide reasonable assurance that transactions are recorded as necessary to permit preparation of financial statements in accordance with generally accepted accounting principles, and that receipts and expenditures of the Company are being made only in accordance with authorizations of our management and directors; and (iii) provide reasonable assurance regarding prevention or timely detection of unauthorized acquisition, use or disposition of assets of the Company that could have a material effect on the financial statements.

While "reasonable assurance" is a high level of assurance, it does not mean absolute assurance. Because of its inherent limitations, internal control over financial reporting may not prevent or detect every misstatement and instance

of fraud. Controls are susceptible to manipulation, especially in instances of fraud caused by the collusion of two or more people, including our senior management. Also, projections of any evaluation of effectiveness to future periods are subject to the risk that controls may become inadequate because of changes in conditions, or that the degree of compliance with the policies or procedures may deteriorate.

Under the supervision and with the participation of our Chief Executive Officer and Chief Financial Officer, our management conducted an evaluation of the effectiveness of our internal control over financial reporting based upon the framework in *Internal Control — Integrated Framework* issued by the Committee of Sponsoring Organizations of the Treadway Commission (COSO). Based on the results of our evaluation, our management concluded that our internal control over financial reporting was effective as of May 31, 2013.

PricewaterhouseCoopers LLP, an independent registered public accounting firm, has audited (1) the consolidated financial statements and (2) the effectiveness of our internal control over financial reporting as of May 31, 2013, as stated in their report herein.

Mark G. Parker
President and Chief Executive Officer

Donald W. Blair
Chief Financial Officer

Report of Independent Registered Public Accounting Firm

To the Board of Directors and Shareholders of NIKE, Inc.:

In our opinion, the consolidated financial statements listed in the index appearing under Item 15(a)(1) present fairly, in all material respects, the financial position of NIKE, Inc. and its subsidiaries at May 31, 2013 and 2012, and the results of their operations and their cash flows for each of the three years in the period ended May 31, 2013 in conformity with accounting principles generally accepted in the United States of America. In addition, in our opinion, the financial statement schedule listed in the appendix appearing under Item 15(a)(2) presents fairly, in all material respects, the information set forth therein when read in conjunction with the related consolidated financial statements. Also in our opinion, the Company maintained, in all material respects, effective internal control over financial reporting as of May 31, 2013, based on criteria established in *Internal Control — Integrated Framework* issued by the Committee of Sponsoring Organizations of the Treadway Commission (COSO). The Company's management is responsible for these financial statements and financial statement schedule, for maintaining effective internal control over financial reporting and for its assessment of the effectiveness of internal control over financial reporting, included in Management's Annual Report on Internal Control Over Financial Reporting appearing under Item 8. Our responsibility is to express opinions on these financial statements, on the financial statement schedule, and on the Company's internal control over financial reporting based on our integrated audits. We conducted our audits in accordance with the standards of the Public Company Accounting Oversight Board (United States). Those standards require that we plan and perform the audits to obtain reasonable assurance about whether the financial statements are free of material misstatement and whether effective internal control over financial reporting was maintained in all material respects. Our audits of the financial statements included examining, on a test basis, evidence supporting the amounts and disclosures in the financial statements, assessing the accounting principles used and significant estimates made by management, and evaluating the overall financial statement presentation. Our audit of internal control over financial reporting included obtaining an understanding of internal control over financial reporting, assessing the risk that a material weakness exists, and testing and evaluating the design and operating effectiveness of internal control based on the assessed risk. Our audits also included performing such other procedures as we considered necessary in the circumstances. We believe that our audits provide a reasonable basis for our opinions.

A company's internal control over financial reporting is a process designed to provide reasonable assurance regarding the reliability of financial reporting and the preparation of financial statements for external purposes in accordance with generally accepted accounting principles. A company's internal control over financial reporting includes those policies and procedures that (i) pertain to the maintenance of records that, in reasonable detail, accurately and fairly reflect the transactions and dispositions of the assets of the company; (ii) provide reasonable assurance that transactions are recorded as necessary to permit preparation of financial statements in accordance with generally accepted accounting principles, and that receipts and expenditures of the company are being made only in accordance with authorizations of management and directors of the company; and (iii) provide reasonable assurance regarding prevention or timely detection of unauthorized acquisition, use, or disposition of the company's assets that could have a material effect on the financial statements.

Because of its inherent limitations, internal control over financial reporting may not prevent or detect misstatements. Also, projections of any evaluation of effectiveness to future periods are subject to the risk that controls may become inadequate because of changes in conditions, or that the degree of compliance with the policies or procedures may deteriorate.

/S/ PRICEWATERHOUSECOOPERS LLP

Portland, Oregon July 23, 2013

NIKE, Inc. Consolidated Statements Of Income

(In millions, except per share data)	Year Ended May 31, 2013	2012	2011
Income from continuing operations:			
Revenues	$ 25,313	$ 23,331	$ 20,117
Cost of sales	14,279	13,183	10,915
Gross profit	11,034	10,148	9,202
Demand creation expense	2,745	2,607	2,344
Operating overhead expense	5,035	4,458	4,017
Total selling and administrative expense	7,780	7,065	6,361
Interest (income) expense, net (Notes 6, 7 and 8)	(3)	4	4
Other (income) expense, net (Note 17)	(15)	54	(25)
Income before income taxes	3,272	3,025	2,862
Income tax expense (Note 9)	808	756	690
NET INCOME FROM CONTINUING OPERATIONS	**2,464**	**2,269**	**2,172**
NET INCOME (LOSS) FROM DISCONTINUED OPERATIONS	**21**	**(46)**	**(39)**
NET INCOME	**$ 2,485**	**$ 2,223**	**$ 2,133**
Earnings per share from continuing operations:			
Basic earnings per common share (Notes 1 and 12)	$ 2.75	$ 2.47	$ 2.28
Diluted earnings per common share (Notes 1 and 12)	$ 2.69	$ 2.42	$ 2.24
Earnings per share from discontinued operations:			
Basic earnings per common share (Notes 1 and 12)	$ 0.02	$ (0.05)	$ (0.04)
Diluted earnings per common share (Notes 1 and 12)	$ 0.02	$ (0.05)	$ (0.04)
Dividends declared per common share	$ 0.81	$ 0.70	$ 0.60

The accompanying notes to consolidated financial statements are an integral part of this statement.

NIKE, Inc. Consolidated Statements of Comprehensive Income

	Year Ended May 31,		
(In millions)	**2013**	**2012**	**2011**
Net income	$ 2,485	$ 2,223	$ 2,133
Other comprehensive income (loss), net of tax:			
Foreign currency translation and other[(1)]	30	(295)	263
Net gain (loss) on cash flow hedges[(2)]	117	255	(242)
Net gain (loss) on net investment hedges[(3)]	—	45	(57)
Reclassification to net income of previously deferred (gains) losses related to hedge derivative instruments[(4)]	(105)	49	(84)
Release of cumulative translation loss related to Umbro[(5)] (Notes 14 and 15)	83	—	—
Total other comprehensive income, net of tax	125	54	(120)
TOTAL COMPREHENSIVE INCOME	**$ 2,610**	**$ 2,277**	**$ 2,013**

(1) Net of tax (expense) benefit of $(12) million, $0 million, and $(121) million, respectively.

(2) Net of tax (expense) benefit of $(22) million, $(8) million, and $66 million, respectively.

(3) Net of tax benefit of $0 million, $0 million, and $28 million, respectively.

(4) Net of tax (benefit) expense of $0 million, $(14) million, and $24 million, respectively.

(5) Net of tax (benefit) of $(47) million, $0 million, and $0 million, respectively.

The accompanying notes to consolidated financial statements are an integral part of this statement.

NIKE, Inc. Consolidated Balance Sheets

	May 31,	
(In millions)	**2013**	**2012**
ASSETS		
Current assets:	$ 3,337	
Cash and equivalents		$ 2,317
Short-term investments (Note 6)	2,628	1,440
Accounts receivable, net (Note 1)	3,117	3,132
Inventories (Notes 1 and 2)	3,434	3,222
Deferred income taxes (Note 9)	308	262
Prepaid expenses and other current assets (Notes 6 and 17)	802	857
Assets of discontinued operations (Note 15)	—	615
Total current assets	13,626	11,845
Property, plant and equipment, net (Note 3)	2,452	2,209
Identifiable intangible assets, net (Note 4)	382	370
Goodwill (Note 4)	131	131
Deferred income taxes and other assets (Notes 6, 9 and 17)	993	910
TOTAL ASSETS	**$ 17,584**	**$ 15,465**
LIABILITIES AND SHAREHOLDERS' EQUITY		
Current liabilities:		
Current portion of long-term debt (Note 8)	$ 57	$ 49
Notes payable (Note 7)	121	108
Accounts payable (Note 7)	1,646	1,549
Accrued liabilities (Notes 5, 6 and 17)	1,986	1,941
Income taxes payable (Note 9)	98	65
Liabilities of discontinued operations (Note 15)	18	170
Total current liabilities	3,926	3,882
Long-term debt (Note 8)	1,210	228
Deferred income taxes and other liabilities (Notes 6, 9 and 17)	1,292	974
Commitments and contingencies (Note 16)	—	—
Redeemable Preferred Stock (Note 10)	—	—
Shareholders' equity:		
Common stock at stated value (Note 11):		
Class A convertible — 178 and 180 shares outstanding	—	—
Class B — 716 and 736 shares outstanding	3	3
Capital in excess of stated value	5,184	4,641
Accumulated other comprehensive income (Note 14)	274	149
Retained earnings	5,695	5,588
Total shareholders' equity	11,156	10,381
TOTAL LIABILITIES AND SHAREHOLDERS' EQUITY	**$ 17,584**	**$ 15,465**

The accompanying notes to consolidated financial statements are an integral part of this statement.

NIKE, Inc. Consolidated Statements of Cash Flows

	Year Ended May 31,		
(In millions)	**2013**	**2012**	**2011**
Cash provided by operations:			
Net income	$ 2,485	$ 2,223	$ 2,133
Income charges (credits) not affecting cash:			
Depreciation	438	373	335
Deferred income taxes	21	(60)	(76)
Stock-based compensation (Note 11)	174	130	105
Amortization and other	75	32	23
Net gain on divestitures	(124)	—	—
Changes in certain working capital components and other assets and liabilities:			
Decrease (increase) in accounts receivable	142	(323)	(273)
(Increase) in inventories	(197)	(805)	(551)
(Increase) in prepaid expenses and other current assets	(28)	(141)	(35)
Increase in accounts payable, accrued liabilities and income taxes payable	41	470	151
Cash provided by operations	3,027	1,899	1,812
Cash (used) provided by investing activities:			
Purchases of short-term investments	(3,702)	(2,705)	(7,616)
Maturities of short-term investments	1,501	2,585	4,313
Sales of short-term investments	998	1,244	2,766
Additions to property, plant and equipment	(636)	(597)	(432)
Disposals of property, plant and equipment	14	2	1
Proceeds from divestitures	786	—	—
Increase in other assets, net of other liabilities	(28)	(37)	(30)
Settlement of net investment hedges	—	22	(23)
Cash (used) provided by investing activities	(1,067)	514	(1,021)
Cash used by financing activities:			
Net proceeds from long-term debt issuance	986	—	—
Long-term debt payments, including current portion	(49)	(203)	(8)
Increase (decrease) in notes payable	15	(65)	41
Proceeds from exercise of stock options and other stock issuances	313	468	345
Excess tax benefits from share-based payment arrangements	72	115	64
Repurchase of common stock	(1,674)	(1,814)	(1,859)
Dividends — common and preferred	(703)	(619)	(555)
Cash used by financing activities	(1,040)	(2,118)	(1,972)
Effect of exchange rate changes	100	67	57
Net increase (decrease) in cash and equivalents	1,020	362	(1,124)
Cash and equivalents, beginning of year	2,317	1,955	3,079
CASH AND EQUIVALENTS, END OF YEAR	**$ 3,337**	**$ 2,317**	**$ 1,955**
Supplemental disclosure of cash flow information:			
Cash paid during the year for:			
Interest, net of capitalized interest	$ 20	$ 29	$ 32
Income taxes	702	638	736
Dividends declared and not paid	188	165	145

The accompanying notes to consolidated financial statements are an integral part of this statement.

NIKE, Inc. Consolidated Statements of Shareholders' Equity

	Common Stock				Capital in Excess of Stated Value	Accumulated Other Comprehensive Income	Retained Earnings	Total
	Class A		Class B					
(In millions, except per share data)	Shares	Amount	Shares	Amount				
Balance at May 31, 2010	**180**	**$ —**	**788**	**$ 3**	**$ 3,441**	**$ 215**	**$ 6,095**	**$ 9,754**
Stock options exercised			14		368			368
Repurchase of Class B Common Stock			(48)		(14)		(1,857)	(1,871)
Dividends on Common stock ($0.60 per share)							(569)	(569)
Issuance of shares to employees			2		49			49
Stock-based compensation (Note 11)					105			105
Forfeiture of shares from employees			—		(5)		(1)	(6)
Net income							2,133	2,133
Other Comprehensive Income						(120)		(120)
Balance at May 31, 2011	**180**	**$ —**	**756**	**$ 3**	**$ 3,944**	**$ 95**	**$ 5,801**	**$ 9,843**
Stock options exercised			18		528			528
Repurchase of Class B Common Stock			(40)		(12)		(1,793)	(1,805)
Dividends on Common stock ($0.70 per share)							(639)	(639)
Issuance of shares to employees			2		57			57
Stock-based compensation (Note 11)					130			130
Forfeiture of shares from employees			—		(6)		(4)	(10)
Net income							2,223	2,223
Other comprehensive income						54		54
Balance at May 31, 2012	**180**	**$ —**	**736**	**$ 3**	**$ 4,641**	**$ 149**	**$ 5,588**	**$ 10,381**
Stock options exercised			10		322			322
Conversion to Class B Common Stock	(2)		2					—
Repurchase of Class B Common Stock			(34)		(10)		(1,647)	(1,657)
Dividends on Common stock ($0.81 per share)							(727)	(727)
Issuance of shares to employees			2		65			65
Stock-based compensation (Note 11)					174			174
Forfeiture of shares from employees			—		(8)		(4)	(12)
Net income							2,485	2,485
Other comprehensive income						125		125
Balance at May 31, 2013	**178**	**$ —**	**716**	**$ 3**	**$ 5,184**	**$ 274**	**$ 5,695**	**$ 11,156**

The accompanying notes to consolidated financial statements are an integral part of this statement.

NOTE 1 — Summary of Significant Accounting Policies

Description of Business

NIKE, Inc. is a worldwide leader in the design, development and worldwide marketing and selling of athletic footwear, apparel, equipment, accessories and services. Wholly-owned NIKE, Inc. subsidiaries include Converse Inc., which designs, markets and distributes casual footwear, apparel and accessories and Hurley International LLC, which designs, markets and distributes action sports and youth lifestyle footwear, apparel and accessories.

Basis of Consolidation

The consolidated financial statements include the accounts of NIKE, Inc. and its subsidiaries (the "Company"). All significant intercompany transactions and balances have been eliminated.

The Company completed the sale of Cole Haan during the third quarter ended February 28, 2013 and completed the sale of Umbro during the second quarter ended November 30, 2012. As a result, the Company reports the operating results of Cole Haan and Umbro in the net income (loss) from discontinued operations line in the consolidated statements of income for all periods presented. In addition, the assets and liabilities associated with these businesses are reported as assets of discontinued operations and liabilities of discontinued operations, as appropriate, in the consolidated balance sheets (refer to Note 15 — Discontinued Operations). Unless otherwise indicated, the disclosures accompanying the consolidated financial statements reflect the Company's continuing operations.

On November 15, 2012, the Company announced a two-for-one split of both NIKE Class A and Class B Common shares. The stock split was a 100 percent stock dividend payable on December 24, 2012 to shareholders of record at the close of business December 10, 2012. Common stock began trading at the split-adjusted price on December 26, 2012. All share numbers and per share amounts presented reflect the stock split.

Recognition of Revenues

Wholesale revenues are recognized when title and the risks and rewards of ownership have passed to the customer, based on the terms of sale. This occurs upon shipment or upon receipt by the customer depending on the country of the sale and the agreement with the customer. Retail store revenues are recorded at the time of sale. Provisions for post-invoice sales discounts, returns and miscellaneous claims from customers are estimated and recorded as a reduction to revenue at the time of sale. Post-invoice sales discounts consist of contractual programs with certain customers or discretionary discounts that are expected to be granted to certain customers at a later date. Estimates of discretionary discounts, returns and claims are based on historical rates, specific identification of outstanding claims and outstanding returns not yet received from customers, and estimated discounts, returns and claims expected but not yet finalized with customers. As of May 31, 2013 and 2012, the Company's reserve balances for post-invoice sales discounts, returns and miscellaneous claims were $531 million and $455 million, respectively.

Cost of Sales

Cost of sales consists primarily of inventory costs, as well as warehousing costs (including the cost of warehouse labor), third party royalties, certain foreign currency hedge gains and losses, and research, design and development costs.

Shipping and Handling Costs

Shipping and handling costs are expensed as incurred and included in cost of sales.

Operating Overhead Expense

Operating overhead expense consists primarily of payroll and benefit related costs, rent, depreciation and amortization, professional services, and meetings and travel.

Demand Creation Expense

Demand creation expense consists of advertising and promotion costs, including costs of endorsement contracts, television, digital and print advertising, brand events, and retail brand presentation. Advertising production costs are expensed the first time an advertisement is run. Advertising placement costs are expensed in the month the advertising appears, while costs related to brand events are expensed when the event occurs. Costs related to retail brand presentation are expensed when the presentation is completed and delivered.

A significant amount of the Company's promotional expenses result from payments under endorsement contracts. Accounting for endorsement payments is based upon specific contract provisions. Generally, endorsement payments are expensed on a straight-line basis over the term of the contract after giving recognition to periodic performance compliance provisions of the contracts. Prepayments made under contracts are included in prepaid expenses or other assets depending on the period to which the prepayment applies.

Some of the contracts provide for contingent payments to endorsers based upon specific achievements in their sports (e.g., winning a championship). The Company records selling and administrative expense for these amounts when the endorser achieves the specific goal.

Some of the contracts provide for payments based upon endorsers maintaining a level of performance in their sport over an extended period of time (e.g., maintaining a top ranking in a sport for a year). These amounts are recorded in selling and administrative expense when the Company determines that it is probable that the specified level of performance will be maintained throughout the period. In these instances, to the extent that actual payments to the endorser differ from our estimate due to changes in the endorser's athletic performance, increased or decreased selling and administrative expense may be recorded in a future period.

Some of the contracts provide for royalty payments to endorsers based upon a predetermined percentage of sales of particular products. The Company expenses these payments in cost of sales as the related sales occur. In certain contracts, the Company offers minimum guaranteed royalty payments. For contractual obligations for which the Company estimates it will not meet the minimum guaranteed amount of royalty fees through sales of product, the Company records the amount of the guaranteed payment in excess of that earned through sales of product in selling and administrative expense uniformly over the remaining guarantee period.

Through cooperative advertising programs, the Company reimburses retail customers for certain costs of advertising the Company's products. The Company records these costs in selling and administrative expense at the point in time when it is obligated to its customers for the costs, which is when the related revenues are recognized. This obligation may arise prior to the related advertisement being run.

Total advertising and promotion expenses were $2,745 million, $2,607 million, and $2,344 million for the years ended May 31, 2013, 2012 and 2011, respectively. Prepaid advertising and promotion expenses recorded in prepaid expenses and other current assets totaled $386 million and $281 million at May 31, 2013 and 2012, respectively.

Cash and Equivalents

Cash and equivalents represent cash and short-term, highly liquid investments, including commercial paper, U.S. treasury, U.S. agency, and corporate debt securities with maturities of three months or less at date of purchase.

Short-Term Investments

Short-term investments consist of highly liquid investments, including commercial paper, U.S. treasury, U.S. agency, and corporate debt securities, with maturities over three months from the date of purchase. Debt securities that the Company has the ability and positive intent to hold to maturity are carried at amortized cost. At May 31, 2013 and 2012, the Company did not hold any short-term investments that were classified as trading or held-to- maturity.

At May 31, 2013 and 2012, short-term investments consisted of available- for-sale securities. Available-for-sale securities are recorded at fair value with unrealized gains and losses reported, net of tax, in other comprehensive income, unless unrealized losses are determined to be other than temporary. Realized gains and losses on the sale of securities are determined by specific identification. The Company considers all available-for-sale securities, including those with maturity dates beyond 12 months, as available to support current operational liquidity needs and therefore classifies all securities with maturity dates beyond three months at the date of purchase as current assets within short-term investments on the consolidated balance sheets.

Refer to Note 6 — Fair Value Measurements for more information on the Company's short-term investments.

Allowance for Uncollectible Accounts Receivable

Accounts receivable consists primarily of amounts receivable from customers. The Company makes ongoing estimates relating to the collectability of its accounts receivable and maintains an allowance for estimated losses resulting from the inability of its customers to make required payments. In determining the amount of the allowance, the Company considers historical levels of credit losses and makes judgments about the creditworthiness of significant customers based on ongoing credit evaluations. Accounts receivable with anticipated collection dates greater than 12 months from the balance sheet date and related allowances are considered non-current and recorded in other assets. The allowance for uncollectible accounts receivable was $104 million and $91 million at May 31, 2013 and 2012, respectively, of which $54 million and $45 million, respectively, was classified as long-term and recorded in other assets.

Inventory Valuation

Inventories are stated at lower of cost or market and valued primarily on an average cost basis. Inventory costs primarily consist of product cost from our suppliers, as well as freight, import duties, taxes, insurance and logistics and other handling fees.

Property, Plant and Equipment and Depreciation

Property, plant and equipment are recorded at cost. Depreciation for financial reporting purposes is determined on a straight-line basis for buildings and leasehold improvements over 2 to 40 years and for machinery and equipment over 2 to 15 years.

Depreciation and amortization of assets used in manufacturing, warehousing and product distribution are recorded in cost of sales. Depreciation and amortization of other assets are recorded in selling and administrative expense.

Software Development Costs

Internal Use Software. Expenditures for major software purchases and software developed for internal use are capitalized and amortized over a 2 to 10 year period on a straight-line basis. The Company's policy provides for the capitalization of external direct costs of materials and services associated with developing or obtaining internal use computer software. In addition, the Company also capitalizes certain payroll and payroll-related costs for employees who are directly associated with internal use computer software projects. The amount of capitalizable payroll costs with respect to these employees is limited to the time directly spent on such projects. Costs associated with preliminary project stage activities, training, maintenance and all other post-implementation stage activities are expensed as incurred.

Computer Software to be Sold, Leased or Otherwise Marketed. Development costs of computer software to be sold, leased, or otherwise marketed as an integral part of a product are subject to capitalization beginning when a product's technological feasibility has been established and ending when a product is available for general release to customers. In most instances, the Company's products are released soon after technological feasibility has been established. Therefore, costs incurred subsequent to achievement of technological feasibility are usually not significant, and generally most software development costs have been expensed as incurred.

Impairment of Long-Lived Assets

The Company reviews the carrying value of long-lived assets or asset groups to be used in operations whenever events or changes in circumstances indicate that the carrying amount of the assets might not be recoverable. Factors that would necessitate an impairment assessment include a significant adverse change in the extent or manner in which an asset is used, a significant adverse change in legal factors or the business climate that could affect the value of the asset, or a significant decline in the observable market value of an asset, among others. If such facts indicate a potential impairment, the Company would assess the recoverability of an asset group by determining if the carrying value of the asset group exceeds the sum of the projected undiscounted cash flows expected to result from the use and eventual disposition of the assets over the remaining economic life of the primary asset in the asset group. If the recoverability test indicates that the carrying value of the asset group is not recoverable, the Company will estimate the fair value of the asset group using appropriate valuation methodologies, which would typically include an estimate of discounted cash flows. Any impairment would be measured as the difference between the asset group's carrying amount and its estimated fair value.

Identifiable Intangible Assets and Goodwill

The Company performs annual impairment tests on goodwill and intangible assets with indefinite lives in the fourth quarter of each fiscal year, or when events occur or circumstances change that would, more likely than not, reduce the fair value of a reporting unit or an intangible asset with an indefinite life below its carrying value. Events or changes in circumstances that may trigger interim impairment reviews include significant changes in business climate, operating results, planned investments in the reporting unit, planned divestitures or an expectation that the carrying amount may not be recoverable, among other factors. The Company may first assess qualitative factors to determine whether it is more likely than not that the fair value of a reporting unit is less than its carrying amount. If, after assessing the totality of events and circumstances, the Company determines that it is more likely than not that the fair value of the reporting unit is greater than its carrying amount, the two-step impairment test is unnecessary. The two-step impairment test first requires the Company to estimate the fair value of its reporting units. If the carrying value of a reporting unit exceeds its fair value, the goodwill of that reporting unit is potentially impaired and the Company proceeds to step two of the impairment analysis. In step two of the analysis, the Company measures and records an impairment loss equal to the excess of the carrying value of the reporting unit's goodwill over its implied fair value, if any.

The Company generally bases its measurement of the fair value of a reporting unit on a blended analysis of the present value of future discounted cash flows and the market valuation approach. The discounted cash flows model indicates the fair value of the reporting unit based on the present value of the cash flows that the Company expects the reporting unit to generate in the future. The Company's significant estimates in the discounted cash flows model include: its weighted average cost of capital; long-term rate of growth and profitability of the reporting unit's business; and working capital effects. The market valuation approach indicates the fair value of the business based on a comparison of the reporting unit to comparable publicly traded companies in similar lines of business. Significant estimates in the market valuation approach model include identifying similar companies with comparable business factors such as size, growth, profitability, risk and return on investment, and assessing comparable revenue and operating income multiples in estimating the fair value of the reporting unit.

Indefinite-lived intangible assets primarily consist of acquired trade names and trademarks. The Company may first perform a qualitative assessment to determine whether it is more likely than not that an indefinite-lived intangible asset is impaired. If, after assessing the totality of events and circumstances, the Company determines that it is more likely than not that the indefinite-lived intangible asset is not impaired, no quantitative fair value measurement is necessary. If a quantitative fair value measurement calculation is required for these intangible assets, the Company utilizes the relief-from-royalty method. This method assumes that trade names and trademarks have value to the extent that their owner is relieved of the obligation to pay royalties for the benefits received from them. This method requires the Company to estimate the future revenue for the related brands, the appropriate royalty rate and the weighted average cost of capital.

Operating Leases

The Company leases retail store space, certain distribution and warehouse facilities, office space, and other non-real estate assets under operating leases. Operating lease agreements may contain rent escalation clauses, rent holidays or certain landlord incentives, including tenant improvement allowances. Rent expense for non-cancelable operating leases with scheduled rent increases or landlord incentives are recognized on a straight- line basis over the lease term, beginning with the effective lease commencement date, which is generally the date in which the Company takes possession of or controls the physical use of the property. Certain leases also provide for contingent rents, which are determined as a percentage of sales in excess of specified levels. A contingent rent liability is recognized together with the corresponding rent expense when specified levels have been achieved or when the Company determines that achieving the specified levels during the period is probable.

Fair Value Measurements

The Company measures certain financial assets and liabilities at fair value on a recurring basis, including derivatives and available-for-sale securities. Fair value is the price the Company would receive to sell an asset or pay to transfer a liability in an orderly transaction with a market participant at the measurement date. The Company uses a three-level hierarchy established by the Financial Accounting Standards Board ("FASB") that prioritizes fair value measurements based on the types of inputs used for the various valuation techniques (market approach, income approach, and cost approach).

The levels of hierarchy are described below:

- Level 1: Observable inputs such as quoted prices in active markets for identical assets or liabilities.
- Level 2: Inputs other than quoted prices that are observable for the asset or liability, either directly or indirectly; these include quoted prices for similar assets or liabilities in active markets and quoted prices for identical or similar assets or liabilities in markets that are not active.
- Level 3: Unobservable inputs for which there is little or no market data available, which require the reporting entity to develop its own assumptions.

The Company's assessment of the significance of a particular input to the fair value measurement in its entirety requires judgment and considers factors specific to the asset or liability. Financial assets and liabilities are classified in their entirety based on the most conservative level of input that is significant to the fair value measurement.

Pricing vendors are utilized for certain Level 1 and Level 2 investments. These vendors either provide a quoted market price in an active market or use observable inputs without applying significant adjustments in their pricing. Observable inputs include broker quotes, interest rates and yield curves observable at commonly quoted intervals, volatilities and credit risks. The Company's fair value processes include controls that are designed to ensure appropriate fair values are recorded. These controls include an analysis of period-over-period fluctuations and comparison to another independent pricing vendor.

Refer to Note 6 — Fair Value Measurements for additional information.

Foreign Currency Translation and Foreign Currency Transactions

Adjustments resulting from translating foreign functional currency financial statements into U.S. Dollars are included in the foreign currency translation adjustment, a component of accumulated other comprehensive income in shareholders' equity.

The Company's global subsidiaries have various assets and liabilities, primarily receivables and payables, which are denominated in currencies other than their functional currency. These balance sheet items are subject to remeasurement, the impact of which is recorded in other (income) expense, net, within the consolidated statements of income.

Accounting for Derivatives and Hedging Activities

The Company uses derivative financial instruments to reduce its exposure to changes in foreign currency exchange rates and interest rates. All derivatives are recorded at fair value on the balance sheet and changes in the fair value of derivative financial instruments are either recognized in other comprehensive income (a component of shareholders' equity), debt or net income depending on the nature of the underlying exposure, whether the derivative is formally designated as a hedge, and, if designated, the extent to which the hedge is effective. The Company classifies the cash flows at settlement from derivatives in the same category as the cash flows from the related hedged items. For undesignated hedges and designated cash flow hedges, this is within the cash provided by operations component of the consolidated statements of cash flows. For designated net investment hedges, this is generally within the cash provided or used by investing activities component of the cash flow statement. As our fair value hedges are receive-fixed, pay- variable interest rate swaps, the cash flows associated with these derivative instruments are periodic interest payments while the swaps are outstanding. These cash flows are reflected within the cash provided by operations component of the cash flow statement.

Refer to Note 17 — Risk Management and Derivatives for more information on the Company's risk management program and derivatives.

Stock-Based Compensation

The Company estimates the fair value of options and stock appreciation rights granted under the NIKE, Inc. 1990 Stock Incentive Plan (the "1990 Plan") and employees' purchase rights under the Employee Stock Purchase Plans ("ESPPs") using the Black-Scholes option pricing model. The Company recognizes this fair value, net of estimated forfeitures, as selling and administrative expense in the consolidated statements of income over the vesting period using the straight-line method.

Refer to Note 11 — Common Stock and Stock-Based Compensation for more information on the Company's stock programs.

Income Taxes

The Company accounts for income taxes using the asset and liability method. This approach requires the recognition of deferred tax assets and liabilities for the expected future tax consequences of temporary differences between the carrying amounts and the tax basis of assets and liabilities. The Company records a valuation allowance to reduce deferred tax assets to the amount management believes is more likely than not to be realized. United States income taxes are provided currently on financial statement earnings of non-U.S. subsidiaries that are expected to be repatriated. The Company determines annually the amount of undistributed non-U.S. earnings to invest indefinitely in its non-U.S. operations.

The Company recognizes a tax benefit from uncertain tax positions in the financial statements only when it is more likely than not that the position will be sustained upon examination by relevant tax authorities. The Company recognizes interest and penalties related to income tax matters in income tax expense.

Refer to Note 9 — Income Taxes for further discussion.

Earnings Per Share

Basic earnings per common share is calculated by dividing net income by the weighted average number of common shares outstanding during the year. Diluted earnings per common share is calculated by adjusting weighted average outstanding shares, assuming conversion of all potentially dilutive stock options and awards.

Refer to Note 12 — Earnings Per Share for further discussion.

Management Estimates

The preparation of financial statements in conformity with generally accepted accounting principles requires management to make estimates, including estimates relating to assumptions that affect the reported amounts of assets and liabilities and disclosure of contingent assets and liabilities at the date of financial statements and the reported amounts of revenues and expenses during the reporting period. Actual results could differ from these estimates.

Recently Adopted Accounting Standards

In July 2012, the FASB issued an accounting standards update intended to simplify how an entity tests indefinite-lived intangible assets other than goodwill for impairment by providing entities with an option to perform a qualitative assessment to determine whether further impairment testing is necessary. This accounting standard update will be effective for the Company beginning June 1, 2013, and early adoption is permitted. The Company early adopted this standard and the adoption did not have a material impact on its consolidated financial position or results of operations.

In September 2011, the FASB issued updated guidance on the periodic testing of goodwill for impairment. This guidance will allow companies to assess qualitative factors to determine if it is more-likely-than-not that goodwill might be impaired and whether it is necessary to perform the two-step goodwill impairment test required under current accounting standards. This new guidance was effective for the Company beginning June 1, 2012 and the adoption did not have a material effect on its consolidated financial position or results of operations.

In June 2011, the FASB issued guidance on the presentation of comprehensive income. This new guidance eliminates the current option to report other comprehensive income and its components in the statement of shareholders' equity. Companies are now required to present the components of net income and other comprehensive income in either one continuous statement, referred to as the statement of comprehensive income, or in two separate, but consecutive statements. This requirement was effective for the Company beginning June 1, 2012. As this guidance only amended the presentation of the components of comprehensive income, the adoption did not have an impact on the Company's consolidated financial position or results of operations. Further, this guidance required companies to present reclassification adjustments out of accumulated other comprehensive income by component in both the statement in which net income is presented and the statement in which other comprehensive income is presented. This requirement will be effective for the Company beginning June 1, 2013. As this guidance only amends the presentation of the components of comprehensive income, the Company does not anticipate the adoption will have an impact on the Company's consolidated financial position or results of operations.

Recently Issued Accounting Standards

In December 2011, the FASB issued guidance enhancing disclosure requirements surrounding the nature of an entity's right to offset and related arrangements associated with its financial instruments and derivative instruments. This new guidance requires companies to disclose both gross and net information about instruments and transactions eligible for offset in the statement of financial position and instruments and transactions subject to master netting arrangements. This new guidance is effective for the Company beginning June 1, 2013. As this guidance only requires expanded disclosures, the Company does not anticipate the adoption will have an impact on its consolidated financial position or results of operations.

NOTE 2 — Inventories

Inventory balances of $3,434 million and $3,222 million at May 31, 2013 and 2012, respectively, were substantially all finished goods.

NOTE 3 — Property, Plant and Equipment

Property, plant and equipment included the following:

(In millions)	As of May 31, 2013	2012
Land	$ 268	$ 252
Buildings	1,174	1,158
Machinery, equipment and internal-use software	2,985	2,654
Leasehold improvements	945	883
Construction in process	128	110
Total property, plant and equipment, gross	5,500	5,057
Less accumulated depreciation	3,048	2,848
TOTAL PROPERTY, PLANT AND EQUIPMENT, NET	**$ 2,452**	**$ 2,209**

Capitalized interest was not material for the years ended May 31, 2013, 2012, and 2011. The Company had $81 million in capital lease obligations as of May 31, 2013 included in machinery, equipment, and internal-use software; there were no capital lease obligations as of May 31, 2012.

NOTE 4 — Identifiable Intangible Assets and Goodwill

The following table summarizes the Company's identifiable intangible asset balances as of May 31, 2013 and 2012:

	As of May 31, 2013			As of May 31, 2012		
(In millions)	Gross Carrying Amount	Accumulated Amortization	Net Carrying Amount	Gross Carrying Amount	Accumulated Amortization	Net Carrying Amount
Amortized intangible assets:						
Patents	$ 119	$ (35)	$ 84	$ 99	$ (29)	$ 70
Trademarks	43	(32)	11	40	(26)	14
Other	20	(16)	4	19	(16)	3
TOTAL	**$ 182**	**$ (83)**	**$ 99**	**$ 158**	**$ (71)**	**$ 87**
Unamortized intangible assets — Trademarks			283			283
IDENTIFIABLE INTANGIBLE ASSETS, NET			**$ 382**			**$ 370**

Amortization expense, which is included in selling and administrative expense, was $14 million, $14 million, and $13 million for the years ended May 31, 2013, 2012, and 2011, respectively. The estimated amortization expense for intangible assets subject to amortization for each of the years ending May 31, 2014 through May 31, 2018 are as follows: 2014: $13 million; 2015: $9 million; 2016: $9 million; 2017: $7 million; 2018: $6 million.

Goodwill was $131 million at May 31, 2013 and May 31, 2012, respectively, and is included in the Company's "Other" category for segment reporting purposes. There were no accumulated impairment balances for goodwill as of either period end.

NOTE 5 — Accrued Liabilities

Accrued liabilities included the following:

(In millions)	As of May 31, 2013	As of May 31, 2012
Compensation and benefits, excluding taxes	$ 713	$ 691
Endorsement compensation	264	288
Taxes other than income taxes	192	169
Dividends payable	188	165
Import and logistics costs	111	133
Advertising and marketing	77	94
Fair value of derivatives	34	55
Other[(1)]	407	346
TOTAL ACCRUED LIABILITIES	**$ 1,986**	**$ 1,941**

(1) Other consists of various accrued expenses with no individual item accounting for more than 5% of the balance at May 31, 2013 and 2012.

NOTE 6 — Fair Value Measurements

The following table presents information about the Company's financial assets and liabilities measured at fair value on a recurring basis as of May 31, 2013 and 2012, and indicates the fair value hierarchy of the valuation techniques utilized by the Company to determine such fair value. Refer to Note 1 – Summary of Significant Accounting Policies for additional detail regarding the Company's fair value measurement methodology.

	As of May 31, 2013				
	Fair Value Measurements Using				
(In millions)	Level 1	Level 2	Level 3	Assets/Liabilities at Fair Value	Balance Sheet Classification
ASSETS					
Derivatives:					
Foreign exchange forwards and options	$ —	$ 278	$ —	$ 278	Other current assets and other long-term assets
Interest rate swap contracts	—	11	—	11	Other current assets and other long-term assets
Total derivatives	—	289	—	289	
Available-for-sale securities:					
U.S. Treasury securities	425	—	—	425	Cash and equivalents
U.S. Agency securities	—	20	—	20	Cash and equivalents
Commercial paper and bonds	—	1,035	—	1,035	Cash and equivalents
Money market funds	—	836	—	836	Cash and equivalents
U.S. Treasury securities	1,583	—	—	1,583	Short-term investments
U.S. Agency securities	—	401	—	401	Short-term investments
Commercial paper and bonds	—	644	—	644	Short-term investments
Non-marketable preferred stock	—	—	5	5	Other long-term assets
Total available-for-sale securities	2,008	2,936	5	4,949	
TOTAL ASSETS	**$ 2,008**	**$ 3,225**	**$ 5**	**$ 5,238**	
LIABILITIES					
Derivatives:					
Foreign exchange forwards and options	$ —	$ 34	$ —	$ 34	Accrued liabilities and other long-term liabilities
TOTAL LIABILITIES	**$ —**	**$ 34**	**$ —**	**$ 34**	

	As of May 31, 2012				
	Fair Value Measurements Using			Assets / Liabilities at	
(In millions)	Level 1	Level 2	Level 3	Fair Value	Balance Sheet Classification
ASSETS					
Derivatives:					
Foreign exchange forwards and options	$ —	$ 265	$ —	$ 265	Other current assets and other long-term assets
Embedded derivatives	—	1	—	1	Other current assets
Interest rate swap contracts	—	15	—	15	Other current assets and other long-term assets
Total derivatives	—	281	—	281	
Available-for-sale securities:					
U.S. Treasury securities	226	—	—	226	Cash and equivalents
U.S. Agency securities	—	254	—	254	Cash and equivalents
Commercial paper and bonds	—	159	—	159	Cash and equivalents
Money market funds	—	770	—	770	Cash and equivalents
U.S. Treasury securities	927	—	—	927	Short-term investments
U.S. Agency securities	—	230	—	230	Short-term investments
Commercial paper and bonds	—	283	—	283	Short-term investments
Non-marketable preferred stock	—	—	3	3	Other long-term assets
Total available-for-sale securities	1,153	1,696	3	2,852	
TOTAL ASSETS	**$ 1,153**	**$ 1,977**	**$ 3**	**$ 3,133**	
LIABILITIES					
Derivatives:					
Foreign exchange forwards and options	$ —	$ 55	$ —	$ 55	Accrued liabilities and other long-term liabilities
TOTAL LIABILITIES	**$ —**	**$ 55**	**$ —**	**$ 55**	

Derivative financial instruments include foreign exchange forwards and options, embedded derivatives and interest rate swap contracts. The fair value of derivative contracts is determined using observable market inputs such as the daily market foreign currency rates, forward pricing curves, currency volatilities, currency correlations and interest rates, and considers nonperformance risk of the Company and that of its counterparties. Adjustments relating to these nonperformance risks were not material at May 31, 2013 or 2012. Refer to Note 17 — Risk Management and Derivatives for additional detail.

Available-for-sale securities comprise investments in U.S. Treasury and Agency securities, money market funds, corporate commercial paper and bonds. These securities are valued using market prices on both active markets (Level 1) and less active markets (Level 2). Pricing vendors are utilized for certain Level 1 or Level 2 investments. These vendors either provide a quoted market price in an active market or use observable inputs without applying significant adjustments in their pricing. Observable inputs include broker quotes, interest rates and yield curves observable at commonly quoted intervals, volatilities and credit risks. The carrying amounts reflected in the consolidated balance sheets for short-term investments and cash and equivalents approximate fair value.

The Company's Level 3 assets comprise investments in certain non- marketable preferred stock. These investments are valued using internally developed models with unobservable inputs. These Level 3 investments are an immaterial portion of our portfolio. Changes in Level 3 investment assets were immaterial during the years ended May 31, 2013 and 2012.

No transfers among the levels within the fair value hierarchy occurred during the years ended May 31, 2013 or 2012.

As of May 31, 2013 and 2012, the Company had no assets or liabilities that were required to be measured at fair value on a non-recurring basis.

Short-Term Investments

As of May 31, 2013 and 2012, short-term investments consisted of available- for-sale securities. As of May 31, 2013, the Company held $2,229 million of available-for-sale securities with maturity dates within one year from the purchase date and $399 million with maturity dates over one year and less than five years from the purchase date within short-term investments. As of May 31, 2012, the Company held $1,129 million of available-for-sale securities with maturity dates within one year from purchase date and $311 million with maturity dates over one year and less than five years from purchase date within short-term investments.

Short-term investments classified as available-for-sale consist of the following at fair value:

(In millions)	As of May 31, 2013	2012
Available-for-sale investments:		
U.S. treasury and agencies	$ 1,984	$ 1,157
Commercial paper and bonds	644	283
TOTAL ACCRUED LIABILITIES	**$ 2,628**	**$ 1,440**

Included in interest (income) expense, net was interest income related to cash and equivalents and short-term investments of $26 million, $27 million, and $28 million for the years ended May 31, 2013, 2012, and 2011, respectively.

For fair value information regarding notes payable and long-term debt, refer to Note 7 — Short-Term Borrowings and Credit Lines and Note 8 — Long-Term Debt.

NOTE 7 — Short-Term Borrowings and Credit Lines

Notes payable and interest-bearing accounts payable to Sojitz Corporation of America ("Sojitz America") as of May 31, 2013 and 2012, are summarized below:

	As of May 31,			
	2013		2012	
(In millions)	Borrowings	Interest Rate	Borrowings	Interest Rate
Notes payable:				
U.S. operations	$ 20	0.00%[(1)]	$ 30	5.50%[(1)]
Non-U.S. operations	101	4.77%[(1)]	78	9.46%[(1)]
TOTAL NOTES PAYABLE	**$ 121**		**$ 108**	
Interest-Bearing Accounts Payable:				
Sojitz America	$ 55	0.99%	$ 75	1.10%

(1) Weighted average interest rate includes non-interest bearing overdrafts.

The carrying amounts reflected in the consolidated balance sheets for notes payable approximate fair value.

The Company purchases through Sojitz America certain athletic footwear, apparel and equipment it acquires from non-U.S. suppliers. These purchases are for the Company's operations outside of the United States, Europe and Japan. Accounts payable to Sojitz America are generally due up to 60 days after shipment of goods from the foreign port. The interest rate on such accounts payable is the 60-day London Interbank Offered Rate ("LIBOR") as of the beginning of the month of the invoice date, plus 0.75%.

As of May 31, 2013 and 2012, the Company had no amounts outstanding under its commercial paper program.

In November 2011, the Company entered into a committed credit facility agreement with a syndicate of banks which provides for up to $1 billion of borrowings pursuant to a revolving credit facility with the option to increase borrowings to $1.5 billion with lender approval. The facility matures on November 1, 2016, with a one-year extension option prior to both the second and third anniversary of the closing date, provided that extensions shall not extend beyond November 1, 2018. Based on the Company's current long- term senior unsecured debt ratings of A+ and A1 from Standard and Poor's Corporation and Moody's Investor Services, respectively, the interest rate charged on any outstanding borrowings would be the prevailing LIBOR plus 0.56%. The facility fee is 0.065% of the total commitment. Under this committed credit facility, the Company must maintain, among other things, certain minimum specified financial ratios with which the Company was in compliance at May 31, 2013. No amounts were outstanding under this facility as of May 31, 2013 or 2012.

NOTE 8 — Long-Term Debt

Long-term debt, net of unamortized premiums and discounts and swap fair value adjustments, comprises the following:

					Book Value Outstanding As of May 31,	
Scheduled Maturity (Dollars in millions)	Original Principal		Interest Rate	Interest Payments	2013	2012
Corporate Bond Payables:[4]						
July 23, 2012[1]	$	25	5.66%	Semi-Annually	$ —	$ 25
August 7, 2012[1]	$	15	5.40%	Semi-Annually	—	15
October 1, 2013	$	50	4.70%	Semi-Annually	50	50
October 15, 2015[1]	$	100	5.15%	Semi-Annually	111	115
May 1, 2023[5]	$	500	2.25%	Semi-Annually	499	—
May 1, 2043[5]	$	500	3.63%	Semi-Annually	499	—
Promissory Notes:[2]						
April 1, 2017	$	40	6.20%	Monthly	40	—
January 1, 2018	$	19	6.79%	Monthly	19	—
Japanese Yen Notes:					34	
August 20, 2001 through November 20, 2020[3]	¥	9,000	2.60%	Quarterly		50
August 20, 2001 through November 20, 2020[3]	¥	4,000	2.00%	Quarterly	15	22
Total					1,267	277
Less current maturities					57	49
TOTAL LONG-TERM DEBT					**$ 1,210**	**$ 228**

(1) The Company has entered into interest rate swap agreements whereby the Company receives fixed interest payments at the same rate as the note and pays variable interest payments based on the six-month LIBOR plus a spread. The swaps have the same notional amount and maturity date as the corresponding note. At May 31, 2013, the interest rates payable on these swap agreements ranged from approximately 0.3% to 0.4%.

(2) The Company assumed a total of $59 million in bonds payable on May 30, 2013 as part of its agreement to purchase certain Corporate properties, which was treated as a non-cash financing transaction. The property serves as collateral for the debt. The purchase of these properties was accounted for as a business combination where the total consideration of $85 million was allocated to the land and buildings acquired; no other tangible or intangible assets or liabilities resulted from the purchase. The bonds mature in 2017 and 2018 and the Company does not have the ability to re-negotiate the terms of the debt agreements and would incur significant financial penalties if the notes are paid off prior to maturity.

(3) NIKE Logistics YK assumed a total of ¥13.0 billion in loans as part of its agreement to purchase a distribution center in Japan, which serves as collateral for the loans. These loans mature in equal quarterly installments during the period August 20, 2001 through November 20, 2020.

(4) Senior unsecured obligations rank equally with our other unsecured and unsubordinated indebtedness.

(5) The bonds carry a make whole call provision and are redeemable at any time prior to maturity. The bonds also feature a par call provision payable 3 months and 6 months prior to the scheduled maturity date for the bonds maturing on May 1, 2023 and May 1, 2043, respectively.

The scheduled maturity of long-term debt in each of the years ending May 31, 2014 through 2018 are $57 million, $7 million, $108 million, $45 million and $25 million, respectively, at face value.

The fair value of the Company's long-term debt, including the current portion, was approximately $1,219 million at May 31, 2013 and $283 million at May 31, 2012. The fair value of long-term debt is estimated based upon quoted prices of similar instruments (level 2).

NOTE 9 — Income Taxes

Income before income taxes is as follows:

	Year Ended May 31,		
(In millions)	2013	2012	2011
Income before income taxes:			
United States	$ 1,240	$ 804	$ 1,040
Foreign	2,032	2,221	1,822
TOTAL INCOME BEFORE INCOME TAXES	$ 3,272	$ 3,025	$ 2,862

The provision for income taxes is as follows:

	Year Ended May 31,		
(In millions)	**2013**	**2012**	**2011**
Current:			
United States			
Federal	$ 434	$ 289	$ 298
State	69	51	57
Foreign	398	488	435
Total	901	828	790
Deferred:			
United States			
Federal	1	(48)	(62)
State	(4)	5	—
Foreign	(90)	(29)	(38)
Total	(93)	(72)	(100)
TOTAL INCOME TAX EXPENSE	**$ 808**	**$ 756**	**$ 690**

A reconciliation from the U.S. statutory federal income tax rate to the effective income tax rate is as follows:

	Year Ended May 31,		
	2013	**2012**	**2011**
Federal income tax rate	35.0%	35.0%	35.0%
State taxes, net of federal benefit	1.4%	1.3%	1.3%
Foreign earnings	-11.8%	-11.9%	-11.4%
Other, net	0.1%	0.6%	-0.8%
EFFECTIVE INCOME TAX RATE	**24.7%**	**25.0%**	**24.1%**

The effective tax rate from continuing operations for the year ended May 31, 2013 was 30 basis points lower than the effective tax rate from continuing operations for the year ended May 31, 2012 primarily due to tax benefits received from the intercompany sale of intellectual property rights outside of the U.S., the retroactive reinstatement of the research and development credit and the intra-period allocation of tax expense between continuing operations, discontinued operations, and other comprehensive income. The decrease in the effective tax rate was partially offset by a higher effective tax rate on operations as a result of an increase in earnings in higher tax jurisdictions. The effective tax rate from continuing operations for the year ended May 31, 2012 was 90 basis points higher than the effective tax rate from continuing operations for the year ended May 31, 2011 primarily due to the changes in uncertain tax positions partially offset by a reduction in the effective rate related to a decrease in earnings in higher tax jurisdictions.

Deferred tax assets and (liabilities) comprise the following:

	As of May 31,	
(In millions)	**2013**	**2012**
Deferred tax assets:		
Allowance for doubtful accounts	$ 20	$ 17
Inventories	40	37
Sales return reserves	101	84
Deferred compensation	197	186
Stock-based compensation	140	126
Reserves and accrued liabilities	66	66
Foreign loss carry-forwards	19	35
Foreign tax credit carry-forwards	106	216
Undistributed earnings of foreign subsidiaries	162	82
Other	47	62
Total deferred tax assets	898	911
Valuation allowance	(5)	(27)
Total deferred tax assets after valuation allowance	893	884
Deferred tax liabilities:		
Property, plant and equipment	(241)	(191)
Intangibles	(96)	(98)
Other	(20)	(22)
Total deferred tax liability	(357)	(311)
NET DEFERRED TAX ASSET	**$ 536**	**$ 573**

The following is a reconciliation of the changes in the gross balance of unrecognized tax benefits:

	As of May 31,		
(In millions)	**2013**	**2012**	**2011**
Unrecognized tax benefits, as of the beginning of the period	$ 285	$ 212	$ 282
Gross increases related to prior period tax positions	77	48	13
Gross decreases related to prior period tax positions	(3)	(25)	(98)
Gross increases related to current period tax positions	130	91	59
Gross decreases related to current period tax positions	(9)	(1)	(6)
Settlements	—	(20)	(43)
Lapse of statute of limitations	(21)	(9)	(8)
Changes due to currency translation	(12)	(11)	13
UNRECOGNIZED TAX BENEFITS, AS OF THE END OF THE PERIOD	**$ 447**	**$ 285**	**$ 212**

As of May 31, 2013, the total gross unrecognized tax benefits, excluding related interest and penalties, were $447 million, $281 million of which would affect the Company's effective tax rate if recognized in future periods.

The Company recognizes interest and penalties related to income tax matters in income tax expense. The liability for payment of interest and penalties increased $4 million, $17 million, and $10 million during the years ended May 31, 2013, 2012, and 2011, respectively. As of May 31, 2013 and 2012, accrued interest and penalties related to uncertain tax positions was $112 million and $108 million, respectively (excluding federal benefit).

The Company is subject to taxation primarily in the U.S., China, the Netherlands, and Brazil, as well as various state and other foreign jurisdictions. The Company has concluded substantially all U.S. federal income tax matters through fiscal 2010. The Company is currently under audit by the Internal Revenue Service for the 2011 through 2013 tax years. Many issues are at an advanced stage in the examination process, the most significant of which includes the negotiation of a U.S. Unilateral Advanced Pricing Agreement that covers intercompany transfer pricing issues for fiscal years May 31, 2011 through May 31, 2015. In addition, the Company is in appeals regarding the validation of foreign tax credits taken. The Company's major foreign jurisdictions, China, the Netherlands and Brazil, have concluded substantially all income tax matters through calendar 2005, fiscal 2007 and calendar 2006, respectively. Although the timing of resolution of audits is not certain, the Company evaluates all domestic and foreign audit issues in the aggregate, along with the expiration of applicable statutes of limitations, and estimates that it is reasonably possible the total gross unrecognized tax benefits could decrease by up to $86 million within the next 12 months.

We provide for United States income taxes on the undistributed earnings of foreign subsidiaries unless they are considered indefinitely reinvested outside the United States. At May 31, 2013, the indefinitely reinvested earnings in foreign subsidiaries upon which United States income taxes have not been provided was approximately $6.7 billion. If these undistributed earnings were repatriated to the United States, or if the shares of the relevant foreign subsidiaries were sold or otherwise transferred, they would generate foreign tax credits that would reduce the federal tax liability associated with the foreign dividend or the otherwise taxable transaction. Assuming a full utilization of the foreign tax credits, the potential net deferred tax liability associated with these temporary differences of undistributed earnings would be approximately $2.2 billion at May 31, 2013.

A portion of the Company's foreign operations are benefiting from a tax holiday, which will phase out in 2019. This tax holiday may be extended when certain conditions are met or may be terminated early if certain conditions are not met. The impact of this tax holiday decreased foreign taxes by $108 million, $117 million, and $36 million for the fiscal years ended May 31, 2013, 2012, and 2011, respectively. The benefit of the tax holiday on net income per share (diluted) was $0.12, $0.12, and $0.04 for the fiscal years ended May 31, 2013, 2012, and 2011, respectively.

Deferred tax assets at May 31, 2013 and 2012 were reduced by a valuation allowance relating to tax benefits of certain subsidiaries with operating losses. The net change in the valuation allowance was a decrease of $22 million, an increase of $23 million, and a decrease of $1 million for the years ended May 31, 2013, 2012, and 2011, respectively.

The Company does not anticipate that any foreign tax credit carry-forwards will expire unutilized.

The Company has available domestic and foreign loss carry-forwards of $58 million at May 31, 2013. Such losses will expire as follows:

	Year Ending May 31,						
(In millions)	**2014**	**2015**	**2016**	**2017**	**2018-2032**	**Indefinite**	**Total**
Net Operating Losses	$ —	—	2	—	52	4	$ 58

During the years ended May 31, 2013, 2012, and 2011, income tax benefits attributable to employee stock-based compensation transactions of $76 million, $120 million, and $68 million, respectively, were allocated to shareholders' equity.

NOTE 10 — Redeemable Preferred Stock

Sojitz America is the sole owner of the Company's authorized Redeemable Preferred Stock, $1 par value, which is redeemable at the option of Sojitz America or the Company at par value aggregating $0.3 million. A cumulative dividend of $0.10 per share is payable annually on May 31 and no dividends may be declared or paid on the common stock of the Company unless dividends on the Redeemable Preferred Stock have been declared and paid in full. There have been no changes in the Redeemable Preferred Stock in the three years ended May 31, 2013, 2012, and 2011. As the holder of the Redeemable Preferred Stock, Sojitz America does not have general voting rights but does have the right to vote as a separate class on the sale of all or substantially all of the assets of the Company and its subsidiaries, on merger, consolidation, liquidation or dissolution of the Company or on the sale or assignment of the NIKE trademark for athletic footwear sold in the United States. The Redeemable Preferred Stock has been fully issued to Sojitz America and is not blank check preferred stock. The Company's articles of incorporation do not permit the issuance of additional preferred stock.

NOTE 11 — Common Stock and Stock-Based Compensation

The authorized number of shares of Class A Common Stock, no par value, and Class B Common Stock, no par value, are 200 million and 1,200 million, respectively. Each share of Class A Common Stock is convertible into one share of Class B Common Stock. Voting rights of Class B Common Stock are limited in certain circumstances with respect to the election of directors. There are no differences in the dividend and liquidation preferences or participation rights of the Class A and Class B common shareholders.

In 1990, the Board of Directors adopted, and the shareholders approved, the NIKE, Inc. 1990 Stock Incentive Plan (the "1990 Plan"). The 1990 Plan provides for the issuance of up to 326 million previously unissued shares of Class B Common Stock in connection with stock options and other awards granted under the plan. The 1990 Plan authorizes the grant of non-statutory stock options, incentive stock options, stock appreciation rights, restricted stock, restricted stock units, and performance-based awards. The exercise price for stock options and stock appreciation rights may not be less than the fair market value of the underlying shares on the date of grant. A committee of the Board of Directors administers the 1990 Plan. The committee has the authority to determine the employees to whom awards will be made, the amount of the awards, and the other terms and conditions of the awards. Substantially all stock option grants outstanding under the 1990 Plan were granted in the first quarter of each fiscal year, vest ratably over four years, and expire 10 years from the date of grant.

The following table summarizes the Company's total stock-based compensation expense recognized in selling and administrative expense:

	Year Ended May 31,		
(In millions)	**2013**	**2012**	**2011**
Stock options(1)	$ 123	$ 96	$ 77
ESPPs	19	16	14
Restricted stock	32	18	14
TOTAL STOCK-BASED COMPENSATION EXPENSE	**$ 174**	**$ 130**	**$ 105**

(1) Expense for stock options includes the expense associated with stock appreciation rights. Accelerated stock option expense is recorded for employees eligible for accelerated stock option vesting upon retirement. Accelerated stock option expense for years ended May 31, 2013, 2012, and 2011 was $22 million, $17 million, and $12 million, respectively.

As of May 31, 2013, the Company had $199 million of unrecognized compensation costs from stock options, net of estimated forfeitures, to be recognized as selling and administrative expense over a weighted average period of 2.3 years.

The weighted average fair value per share of the options granted during the years ended May 31, 2013, 2012, and 2011, as computed using the Black-Scholes pricing model, was $12.71, $11.08, and $8.84, respectively. The weighted average assumptions used to estimate these fair values are as follows:

	Year Ended May 31,		
	2013	2012	2011
Dividend yield	1.5%	1.4%	1.6%
Expected volatility	35.0%	29.5%	31.5%
Weighted average expected life (in years)	5.3	5.0	5.0
Risk-free interest rate	0.6%	1.4%	1.7%

The Company estimates the expected volatility based on the implied volatility in market traded options on the Company's common stock with a term greater than one year, along with other factors. The weighted average expected life of options is based on an analysis of historical and expected future exercise patterns. The interest rate is based on the U.S. Treasury (constant maturity) risk-free rate in effect at the date of grant for periods corresponding with the expected term of the options.

The following summarizes the stock option transactions under the plan discussed above:

	Shares[(1)]	Weighted Average Option Price
	(In millions)	
Options outstanding May 31, 2010	72.2	$ 23.30
Exercised	(14.0)	21.35
Forfeited	(1.3)	29.03
Granted	12.7	34.60
Options outstanding May 31, 2011	69.6	$ 25.65
Exercised	(18.0)	22.81
Forfeited	(1.0)	35.61
Granted	13.7	45.87
Options outstanding May 31, 2012	64.3	$ 30.59
Exercised	(9.9)	24.70
Forfeited	(1.3)	40.14
Granted	14.6	46.55
Options outstanding May 31, 2013	67.7	$ 34.72
Options exercisable at May 31,		
2011	40.1	$ 22.03
2012	33.9	24.38
2013	35.9	27.70

(1) *Includes stock appreciation rights transactions.*

The weighted average contractual life remaining for options outstanding and options exercisable at May 31, 2013 was 6.3 years and 4.7 years, respectively. The aggregate intrinsic value for options outstanding and exercisable at May 31, 2013 was $1,823 million and $1,218 million, respectively. The aggregate intrinsic value was the amount by which the market value of the underlying stock exceeded the exercise price of the options. The total intrinsic value of the options exercised during the years ended May 31, 2013, 2012, and 2011 was $293 million, $453 million, and $267 million, respectively.

In addition to the 1990 Plan, the Company gives employees the right to purchase shares at a discount to the market price under employee stock purchase plans ("ESPPs"). Employees are eligible to participate through payroll deductions of up to 10% of their compensation. At the end of each six- month offering period, shares are purchased by the participants at 85% of the lower of the fair market value at the beginning or the end of the offering period. Employees purchased 1.6 million, 1.7 million, and 1.6 million shares during each of the three years ended May 31, 2013, 2012 and 2011, respectively.

From time to time, the Company grants restricted stock units and restricted stock to key employees under the 1990 Plan. The number of shares underlying such awards granted to employees during the years ended May 31, 2013, 2012, and 2011 were 1.6 million, 0.7 million, and 0.4 million with weighted average values per share of $46.86, $49.49, and $35.11, respectively. Recipients of restricted stock are entitled to cash dividends and to vote their respective shares throughout the period of restriction. Recipients of restricted stock units are entitled to dividend equivalent cash payments upon vesting. The value of all grants of restricted stock and restricted stock units was established by the market price on the date of grant. During the years ended May 31, 2013, 2012, and 2011, the aggregate fair value of restricted stock and restricted stock units vested was $25 million, $22 million, and $15 million, respectively, determined as of the date of vesting.

NOTE 12 — Earnings Per Share

The following is a reconciliation from basic earnings per share to diluted earnings per share. Options to purchase an additional 0.1 million, 0.2 million, and 0.3 million shares of common stock were outstanding at May 31, 2013, 2012, and 2011 respectively, but were not included in the computation of diluted earnings per share because the options were anti-dilutive.

(In millions, except per share data)	Year Ended May 31, 2013	2012	2011
Determination of shares:			
Weighted average common shares outstanding	897.3	920.0	951.1
Assumed conversion of dilutive stock options and awards	19.1	19.6	20.2
DILUTED WEIGHTED AVERAGE COMMON SHARES OUTSTANDING	**916.4**	**939.6**	**971.3**
Earnings per share from continuing operations:			
Basic earnings per common share	$ 2.75	$ 2.47	$ 2.28
Diluted earnings per common share	$ 2.69	$ 2.42	$ 2.24
Earnings per share from discontinued operations:			
Basic earnings per common share	$ 0.02	$ (0.05)	$ (0.04)
Diluted earnings per common share	$ 0.02	$ (0.05)	$ (0.04)
Basic earnings per common share for NIKE, Inc.	$ 2.77	$ 2.42	$ 2.24
Diluted earnings per common share for NIKE, Inc.	$ 2.71	$ 2.37	$ 2.20

NOTE 13 — Benefit Plans

The Company has a profit sharing plan available to most U.S.-based employees. The terms of the plan call for annual contributions by the Company as determined by the Board of Directors. A subsidiary of the Company also had a profit sharing plan available to its U.S.-based employees prior to fiscal 2012. The terms of the plan called for annual contributions as determined by the subsidiary's executive management. Contributions of $47 million, $40 million, and $39 million were made to the plans and are included in selling and administrative expense for the years ended May 31, 2013, 2012, and 2011, respectively. The Company has various 401(k) employee savings plans available to U.S.-based employees. The Company matches a portion of employee contributions. Company contributions to the savings plans were $46 million, $42 million, and $38 million for the years ended May 31, 2013, 2012, and 2011, respectively, and are included in selling and administrative expense.

The Company also has a Long-Term Incentive Plan ("LTIP") that was adopted by the Board of Directors and approved by shareholders in September 1997 and later amended in fiscal 2007. The Company recognized $50 million, $51 million, and $31 million of selling and administrative expense related to cash awards under the LTIP during the years ended May 31, 2013, 2012, and 2011, respectively.

The Company has pension plans in various countries worldwide. The pension plans are only available to local employees and are generally government mandated. The liability related to the unfunded pension liabilities of the plans was $104 million and $113 million at May 31, 2013 and May 31, 2012, respectively, which was primarily classified as long-term in other liabilities.

NOTE 14 — Accumulated Other Comprehensive Income

The components of accumulated other comprehensive income, net of tax, are as follows:

(In millions)	May 31 2013	2012
Cumulative translation adjustment and other	$ (14)	$ (127)
Net deferred gain on cash flow hedge derivatives	193	181
Net deferred gain on net investment hedge derivatives	95	95
ACCUMULATED OTHER COMPREHENSIVE INCOME	**$ 274**	**$ 149**

Refer to Note 17 — Risk Management and Derivatives for more information on the Company's risk management program and derivatives.

NOTE 15 — Discontinued Operations

The Company continually evaluates its existing portfolio of businesses to ensure resources are invested in those businesses that are accretive to the NIKE Brand and represent the largest growth potential and highest returns. During the year, the Company divested of Umbro and Cole Haan, allowing it to focus its resources on driving growth in the NIKE, Jordan, Converse and Hurley brands.

On February 1, 2013, the Company completed the sale of Cole Haan to Apax Partners for an agreed upon purchase price of $570 million and received at closing $561 million, net of $9 million of purchase price adjustments. The transaction resulted in a gain on sale of $231 million, net of $137 million in tax expense; this gain is included in the net income (loss) from discontinued operations line item on the consolidated statements of income. There were no adjustments to these recorded amounts as of May 31, 2013. Beginning November 30, 2012, the Company classified the Cole Haan disposal group as held-for-sale and presented the results of Cole Haan's operations in the net income (loss) from discontinued operations line item on the consolidated statements of income. From this date until the sale, the assets and liabilities of Cole Haan were recorded in the assets of discontinued operations and liabilities of discontinued operations line items on the consolidated balance sheets, respectively. Previously, these amounts were reported in the Company's segment presentation as "Other Businesses."

Under the sale agreement, the Company agreed to provide certain transition services to Cole Haan for an expected period of 3 to 9 months from the date of sale. The Company will also license NIKE proprietary Air and Lunar technologies to Cole Haan for a transition period. The continuing cash flows related to these items are not expected to be significant to Cole Haan and the Company will have no significant continuing involvement with Cole Haan beyond the transition services. Additionally, preexisting guarantees of certain Cole Haan lease payments remain in place after the sale; the maximum exposure under the guarantees is $44 million at May 31, 2013. The fair value of the guarantees is not material.

On November 30, 2012, the Company completed the sale of certain assets of Umbro to Iconix Brand Group ("Iconix") for $225 million. The Umbro disposal group was classified as held-for-sale as of November 30, 2012 and the results of Umbro's operations are presented in the net income (loss) from discontinued operations line item on the consolidated statements of income. The remaining liabilities of Umbro are recorded in the liabilities of discontinued operations line items on the consolidated balance sheets. Previously, these amounts were reported in the Company's segment presentation as "Other Businesses." Upon meeting the held-for-sale criteria, the Company recorded a loss of $107 million, net of tax, on the sale of Umbro and the loss is included in the net income (loss) from discontinued operations line item on the consolidated statements of income. The loss on sale was calculated as the net sales price less Umbro assets of $248 million, including intangibles, goodwill, and fixed assets, other miscellaneous charges of $22 million, and the release of the associated cumulative translation adjustment of $129 million. The tax benefit on the loss was $67 million. There were no adjustments to these recorded amounts as of May 31, 2013.

Under the sale agreement, the Company provided transition services to Iconix while certain markets were transitioned to Iconix-designated licensees. These transition services are complete and the Company has wound down the remaining operations of Umbro.

For the year ended May 31, 2013, net income (loss) from discontinued operations included, for both businesses, the net gain or loss on sale, net operating losses, tax expenses, and approximately $20 million in wind down costs.

Summarized results of the Company's discontinued operations are as follows:

	Year Ended May 31,		
(In millions)	2013	2012	2011
Revenues	$ 523	$ 796	$ 746
Income (loss) before income taxes	108	(43)	(18)
Income tax expense (benefit)	87	3	21
Net income (loss) from discontinued operations	**$ 21**	**$ (46)**	**$ (39)**

As of May 31, 2013 and 2012, the aggregate components of assets and liabilities classified as discontinued operations and included in current assets and current liabilities consisted of the following:

	As of May 31,	
(In millions)	2013	2012
Accounts Receivable, net	$ —	$ 148
Inventories	—	128
Deferred income taxes and other assets	—	35
Property, plant and equipment, net	—	70
Identifiable intangible assets, net	—	234
TOTAL ASSETS	**$ —**	**$ 615**
Accounts payable	$ 1	$ 42
Accrued liabilities	17	112
Deferred income taxes and other liabilities	—	16
TOTAL LIABILITIES	**$ 18**	**$ 170**

NOTE 16 — Commitments and Contingencies

The Company leases space for certain of its offices, warehouses and retail stores under leases expiring from 1 to 21 years after May 31, 2013. Rent expense was $482 million, $431 million, and $386 million for the years ended May 31, 2013, 2012 and 2011, respectively. Amounts of minimum future annual rental commitments under non-cancelable operating leases in each of the five years ending May 31, 2014 through 2018 are $403 million, $340 million, $304 million, $272 million, $225 million, respectively, and $816 million in later years. Amounts of minimum future annual commitments under non- cancelable capital leases in each of the four years ending May 31, 2014 through 2017 are $23 million, $28 million, $21 million, and $9 million, respectively; the Company has no capital lease obligations beyond the year ending May 31, 2017.

As of May 31, 2013 and 2012, the Company had letters of credit outstanding totaling $149 million and $137 million, respectively. These letters of credit were generally issued for the purchase of inventory and guarantees of the Company's performance under certain self-insurance and other programs.

In connection with various contracts and agreements, the Company provides routine indemnifications relating to the enforceability of intellectual property rights, coverage for legal issues that arise and other items where the Company is acting as the guarantor. Currently, the Company has several such agreements in place. However, based on the Company's historical experience and the estimated probability of future loss, the Company has determined that the fair value of such indemnifications is not material to the Company's financial position or results of operations.

In the ordinary course of its business, the Company is involved in various legal proceedings involving contractual and employment relationships, product liability claims, trademark rights, and a variety of other matters. While the Company cannot predict the outcome of its pending legal matters with certainty, the Company does not believe any currently identified claim, proceeding or litigation, either individually or in aggregate, will have a material impact on the Company's results of operations, financial position or cash flows.

NOTE 17 — Risk Management and Derivatives

The Company is exposed to global market risks, including the effect of changes in foreign currency exchange rates and interest rates, and uses derivatives to manage financial exposures that occur in the normal course of business. The Company does not hold or issue derivatives for trading or speculative purposes.

The Company may elect to designate certain derivatives as hedging instruments under the accounting standards for derivatives and hedging. The Company formally documents all relationships between designated hedging instruments and hedged items as well as its risk management objective and strategy for undertaking hedge transactions. This process includes linking all derivatives designated as hedges to either recognized assets or liabilities or forecasted transactions.

The majority of derivatives outstanding as of May 31, 2013 are designated as cash flow or fair value hedges. All derivatives are recognized on the balance sheet at fair value and classified based on the instrument's maturity date. The total notional amount of outstanding derivatives as of May 31, 2013 was approximately $9 billion, which primarily comprises cash flow hedges for Euro/U.S. Dollar, British Pound/Euro, and Japanese Yen/U.S. Dollar currency pairs. As of May 31, 2013, there were outstanding currency forward contracts with maturities up to 24 months.

The following table presents the fair values of derivative instruments included within the consolidated balance sheets as of May 31, 2013 and 2012:

	Asset Derivatives			Liability Derivatives		
(In millions)	**Balance Sheet Location**	**2013**	**2012**	**Balance Sheet Location**	**2013**	**2012**
Derivatives formally designated as hedging instruments:						
Foreign exchange forwards and options	Prepaid expenses and other current assets	$ 141	$ 203	Accrued liabilities	$ 12	$ 35
Foreign exchange forwards and options	Deferred income taxes and other long-term assets	79	7	Deferred income taxes and other long-term liabilities	—	—
Interest rate swap contracts	Deferred income taxes and other long-term assets	11	15	Deferred income taxes and other long-term liabilities	—	—
Total derivatives formally designated as hedging instruments		$ 231	$ 225		$ 12	$ 35
Derivatives not designated as hedging instruments:						
Foreign exchange forwards and options	Prepaid expenses and other current assets	$ 58	$ 55	Accrued liabilities	$ 22	$ 20
Embedded derivatives	Prepaid expenses and other current assets	—	1	Accrued liabilities	—	—
Total derivatives not designated as hedging instruments		58	56		22	20
TOTAL DERIVATIVES		**$ 289**	**$ 281**		**$ 34**	**$ 55**

The following tables present the amounts affecting the consolidated statements of income for years ended May 31, 2013, 2012 and 2011:

	Amount of Gain (Loss) Recognized in Other Comprehensive Income on Derivatives(1)			Amount of Gain (Loss) Reclassified From Accumulated Other Comprehensive Income into Income(1)			
	Year Ended May 31,			Location of Gain (Loss) Reclassified From Accumulated Other Comprehensive Income Into Income (1)	Year Ended May 31,		
(In millions)	**2013**	**2012**	**2013**		**2013**	**2012**	**2013**
Derivatives designated as cash flow hedges:							
Foreign exchange forwards and options	$ 42	$ (29)	$ (87)	Revenue	$ (19)	$ 5	$ (30)
Foreign exchange forwards and options	67	253	(152)	Cost of sales	113	(57)	103
Foreign exchange forwards and options	(3)	3	(4)	Selling and administrative expense	2	(2)	1
Foreign exchange forwards and options	33	36	(65)	Other (income) expense, net	9	(9)	34
Total designated cash flow hedges	$ 139	$ 263	$ (308)		$ 105	$ (63)	$ 108
Derivatives designated as net investment hedges:							
Foreign exchange forwards and options	$ —	$ 45	$ (85)	Other (income) expense, net	$ —	$ —	$ —

(1) *For the years ended May 31, 2013, 2012, and 2011, the amounts recorded in other (income) expense, net as a result of hedge ineffectiveness and the discontinuance of cash flow hedges because the forecasted transactions were no longer probable of occurring were immaterial.*

(In millions)	Amount of Gain (Loss) Recognized in Income on Derivatives — Year Ended May 31, 2013	2012	2011	Location of Gain (Loss) Recognized in Income on Derivatives
Derivatives designated as fair value hedges:				
Interest rate swaps[(1)]	$ 5	$ 6	$ 6	Interest (income) expense, net
Derivatives not designated as hedging instruments:				
Foreign exchange forwards and options	51	64	(30)	Other (income) expense, net
Embedded derivatives	$ (4)	$ 1	$ —	Other (income) expense, net

(1) *All interest rate swap agreements meet the shortcut method requirements under the accounting standards for derivatives and hedging. Accordingly, changes in the fair values of the interest rate swap agreements are considered to exactly offset changes in the fair value of the underlying long-term debt. Refer to "Fair Value Hedges" in this note for additional detail.*

Refer to Note 5 — Accrued Liabilities for derivative instruments recorded in accrued liabilities, Note 6 — Fair Value Measurements for a description of how the above financial instruments are valued, Note 14 — Accumulated Other Comprehensive Income and the consolidated statements of shareholders' equity for additional information on changes in other comprehensive income for the years ended May 31, 2013, 2012 and 2011.

Cash Flow Hedges

The purpose of the Company's foreign currency hedging activities is to protect the Company from the risk that the eventual cash flows resulting from transactions in foreign currencies will be adversely affected by changes in exchange rates. Foreign currency exposures that the Company may elect to hedge in this manner include product cost exposures, non-functional currency denominated external and intercompany revenues, selling and administrative expenses, investments in U.S. Dollar-denominated available- for-sale debt securities and certain other intercompany transactions.

Product cost exposures are primarily generated through non-functional currency denominated product purchases and the foreign currency adjustment program described below. NIKE entities primarily purchase products in two ways: (1) Certain NIKE entities purchase product from the NIKE Trading Company ("NTC"), a wholly-owned sourcing hub that buys NIKE branded products from third party factories, predominantly in U.S. Dollars. The NTC, whose functional currency is the U.S. Dollar, then sells the products to NIKE entities in their respective functional currencies. When the NTC sells to a NIKE entity with a different functional currency, the result is a foreign currency exposure for the NTC; (2) Other NIKE entities purchase product directly from third party factories in U.S. Dollars. These purchases generate a foreign currency exposure for those NIKE entities with a functional currency other than the U.S. Dollar.

In January 2012, the Company implemented a foreign currency adjustment program with certain factories. The program is designed to more effectively manage foreign currency risk by assuming certain of the factories' foreign currency exposures, some of which are natural offsets to our existing foreign currency exposures. Under this program, the Company's payments to these factories are adjusted for rate fluctuations in the basket of currencies ("factory currency exposure index") in which the labor, materials and overhead costs incurred by the factories in the production of NIKE branded products ("factory input costs") are denominated. For the portion of the indices denominated in the local or functional currency of the factory, the Company may elect to place formally designated cash flow hedges. For all currencies within the indices, excluding the U.S. Dollar and the local or functional currency of the factory, an embedded derivative contract is created upon the factory's acceptance of NIKE's purchase order. Embedded derivative contracts are separated from the related purchase order and their accounting treatment is described further below.

The Company's policy permits the utilization of derivatives to reduce its foreign currency exposures where internal netting or other strategies cannot be effectively employed. Hedged transactions are denominated primarily in Euros, British Pounds and Japanese Yen. The Company may enter into hedge contracts typically starting up to 12 to 18 months in advance of the forecasted transaction and may place incremental hedges for up to 100% of the exposure by the time the forecasted transaction occurs.

All changes in fair value of derivatives designated as cash flow hedges, excluding any ineffective portion, are recorded in other comprehensive income until net income is affected by the variability of cash flows of the hedged transaction. In most cases, amounts recorded in other comprehensive income will be released to net income some time after the maturity of the related derivative. Effective hedge results are classified within the consolidated statements of income in the same manner as the underlying exposure, with the results of hedges of non-functional currency denominated revenues and product cost exposures, excluding embedded derivatives as described below, recorded in revenues or cost of sales, when the underlying hedged transaction affects consolidated net income. Results of hedges of selling and administrative expense are recorded together with those costs when the related expense is recorded. Results of hedges of anticipated purchases and sales of U.S. Dollar-denominated available-for-sale securities are recorded in other (income) expense, net when the securities are sold. Results of hedges of certain anticipated intercompany transactions are recorded in other (income) expense, net when the transaction occurs. The Company classifies the cash flows at settlement from these designated cash flow hedge derivatives in the same category as the cash flows from the related hedged items, generally within the cash provided by operations component of the cash flow statement.

Premiums paid on options are initially recorded as deferred charges. The Company assesses the effectiveness of options based on the total cash flows method and records total changes in the options' fair value to other comprehensive income to the degree they are effective.

The Company formally assesses, both at a hedge's inception and on an ongoing basis, whether the derivatives that are used in the hedging transaction have been highly effective in offsetting changes in the cash flows of hedged items and whether those derivatives may be expected to remain highly effective in future periods. Effectiveness for cash flow hedges is assessed based on forward rates. Ineffectiveness was not material for the years ended May 31, 2013, 2012 and 2011.

The Company discontinues hedge accounting prospectively when (1) it determines that the derivative is no longer highly effective in offsetting changes in the cash flows of a hedged item (including hedged items such as firm commitments or forecasted transactions); (2) the derivative expires or is sold, terminated, or exercised; (3) it is no longer probable that the forecasted transaction will occur; or (4) management determines that designating the derivative as a hedging instrument is no longer appropriate.

When the Company discontinues hedge accounting because it is no longer probable that the forecasted transaction will occur in the originally expected period, but is expected to occur within an additional two-month period of time thereafter, the gain or loss on the derivative remains in accumulated other comprehensive income and is reclassified to net income when the forecasted transaction affects consolidated net income. However, if it is probable that a forecasted transaction will not occur by the end of the originally specified time period or within an additional two-month period of time thereafter, the gains and losses that were accumulated in other comprehensive income will be recognized immediately in other (income) expense, net. In all situations in which hedge accounting is discontinued and the derivative remains outstanding, the Company will carry the derivative at its fair value on the balance sheet, recognizing future changes in the fair value in other (income) expense, net. For the years ended May 31, 2013, 2012 and 2011, the amounts recorded in other (income) expense, net as a result of the discontinuance of cash flow hedging because the forecasted transaction was no longer probable of occurring were immaterial.

As of May 31, 2013, $132 million of deferred net gains (net of tax) on both outstanding and matured derivatives accumulated in other comprehensive income are expected to be reclassified to net income during the next 12 months concurrent with the underlying hedged transactions also being recorded in net income. Actual amounts ultimately reclassified to net income are dependent on the exchange rates in effect when derivative contracts that are currently outstanding mature. As of May 31, 2013, the maximum term over which the Company is hedging exposures to the variability of cash flows for its forecasted transactions is 24 months.

Fair Value Hedges

The Company is also exposed to the risk of changes in the fair value of certain fixed-rate debt attributable to changes in interest rates. Derivatives currently used by the Company to hedge this risk are receive-fixed, pay-variable interest rate swaps. As of May 31, 2013, all interest rate swap agreements are designated as fair value hedges of the related long-term debt and meet the shortcut method requirements under the accounting standards for derivatives and hedging. Accordingly, changes in the fair values of the interest rate swap agreements are considered to exactly offset changes in the fair value of the underlying long-term debt. The cash flows associated with the Company's fair value hedges are periodic interest payments while the swaps are outstanding, which are reflected within the cash provided by operations component of the cash flow statement. The Company recorded no ineffectiveness from its interest rate swaps designated as fair value hedges for the years ended May 31, 2013, 2012, or 2011.

Net Investment Hedges

The Company has hedged and may, in the future, hedge the risk of variability in foreign-currency-denominated net investments in wholly-owned international operations. All changes in fair value of the derivatives designated as net investment hedges, except ineffective portions, are reported in the cumulative translation adjustment component of other comprehensive income along with the foreign currency translation adjustments on those investments. The Company classifies the cash flows at settlement of its net investment hedges within the cash provided or used by investing component of the cash flow statement. The Company assesses hedge effectiveness based on changes in forward rates. The Company recorded no ineffectiveness from its net investment hedges for the years ended May 31, 2013, 2012, or 2011.

Embedded Derivatives

As part of the foreign currency adjustment program described above, currencies within the factory currency exposure indices that are neither the Dollar nor the local or functional currency of the factory, an embedded derivative contract is created upon the factory's acceptance of NIKE's purchase order. Embedded derivative contracts are treated as foreign currency forward contracts that are bifurcated from the related purchase order and recorded at fair value as a derivative asset or liability on the balance sheet with their corresponding change in fair value recognized in other (income) expense, net from the date a purchase order is accepted by a factory through the date the purchase price is no longer subject to foreign currency fluctuations. At May 31, 2013, the notional amount of embedded derivatives was approximately $136 million.

Undesignated Derivative Instruments

The Company may elect to enter into foreign exchange forwards to mitigate the change in fair value of specific assets and liabilities on the balance sheet and/or the embedded derivative contracts explained above. These forwards are not designated as hedging instruments under the accounting standards for derivatives and hedging. Accordingly, these undesignated instruments are recorded at fair value as a derivative asset or liability on the balance sheet with their corresponding change in fair value recognized in other (income) expense, net, together with the re-measurement gain or loss from the hedged balance sheet position or embedded derivative contract. The Company classifies the cash flows at settlement from undesignated instruments in the same category as the cash flows from the related hedged items, generally within the cash provided by operations component of the cash flow statement.

Credit Risk

The Company is exposed to credit-related losses in the event of non- performance by counterparties to hedging instruments. The counterparties to all derivative transactions are major financial institutions with investment grade credit ratings. However, this does not eliminate the Company's exposure to credit risk with these institutions. This credit risk is limited to the unrealized gains in such contracts should any of these counterparties fail to perform as contracted. To manage this risk, the Company has established strict counterparty credit guidelines that are continually monitored.

The Company's derivative contracts contain credit risk related contingent features designed to protect against significant deterioration in counterparties' creditworthiness and their ultimate ability to settle outstanding derivative contracts in the normal course of business. The Company's bilateral credit related contingent features generally require the owing entity, either the Company or the derivative counterparty, to post collateral for the portion of the fair value in excess of $50 million should the fair value of outstanding derivatives per counterparty be greater than $50 million. Additionally, a certain level of decline in credit rating of either the Company or the counterparty could also trigger collateral requirements. As of May 31, 2013, the Company was in compliance with all credit risk related contingent features and the fair value of its derivative instruments with credit risk related contingent features in a net liability position was insignificant. Accordingly, the Company was not required to post any collateral as a result of these contingent features. Further, as of May 31, 2013 those counterparties which were required to post collateral complied with such requirements. Given the considerations described above, the Company considers the impact of the risk of counterparty default to be immaterial.

NOTE 18 — Operating Segments and Related Information

Operating Segments. The Company's operating segments are evidence of the structure of the Company's internal organization. The major segments are defined by geographic regions for operations participating in NIKE Brand sales activity excluding NIKE Golf. Each NIKE Brand geographic segment operates predominantly in one industry: the design, development, marketing and selling of athletic footwear, apparel, and equipment. The Company's reportable operating segments for the NIKE Brand are: North America, Western Europe, Central & Eastern Europe, Greater China, Japan, and Emerging Markets. The Company's NIKE Brand Direct to Consumer operations are managed within each geographic segment.

The Company's "Other" category is broken into two components for presentation purposes to align with the way management views the Company. The "Global Brand Divisions" category primarily represents NIKE Brand licensing businesses that are not part of a geographic operating segment, demand creation and operating overhead expenses that are centrally managed for the NIKE Brand, and costs associated with product development and supply chain operations. The "Other Businesses" category consists of the activities of Converse Inc., Hurley International LLC, and NIKE Golf. Activities represented in the "Other" category are considered immaterial for individual disclosure.

Corporate consists largely of unallocated general and administrative expenses, including expenses associated with centrally managed departments, depreciation and amortization related to the Company's headquarters, unallocated insurance and benefit programs, including stock- based compensation, certain foreign currency gains and losses, including certain hedge gains and losses, certain corporate eliminations and other items.

The primary financial measure used by the Company to evaluate performance of individual operating segments is earnings before interest and taxes (commonly referred to as "EBIT"), which represents net income before interest (income) expense, net and income taxes in the consolidated statements of income. Reconciling items for EBIT represent corporate expense items that are not allocated to the operating segments for management reporting.

As part of our centrally managed foreign exchange risk management program, standard foreign currency rates are assigned twice per year to each NIKE Brand entity in our geographic operating segments and certain Other Businesses. These rates are set approximately nine months in advance of the future selling season based on average market spot rates in the calendar month preceding the date they are established. Inventories and cost of sales for geographic operating segments and certain Other Businesses reflect use of these standard rates to record non-functional currency product purchases in the entity's functional currency. Differences between assigned standard foreign currency rates and actual market rates are included in Corporate, together with foreign currency hedge gains and losses generated from our centrally managed foreign exchange risk management program and other conversion gains and losses.

Accounts receivable, inventories and property, plant and equipment for operating segments are regularly reviewed by management and are therefore provided below. Additions to long-lived assets as presented in the following table represent capital expenditures.

Certain prior year amounts have been reclassified to conform to fiscal 2013 presentation.

(In millions)	Year Ended May 31,		
	2013	2012	2011
REVENUE			
North America	$ 10,387	$ 8,839	$ 7,579
Western Europe	4,128	4,144	3,868
Central & Eastern Europe	1,287	1,200	1,040
Greater China	2,453	2,539	2,060
Japan	791	835	773
Emerging Markets	3,718	3,411	2,737
Global Brand Divisions	117	111	96
Total NIKE Brand	22,881	21,079	18,153
Other Businesses	2,500	2,298	2,041
Corporate	(68)	(46)	(77)
TOTAL NIKE CONSOLIDATED REVENUES	**$ 25,313**	**$ 23,331**	**$ 20,117**
EARNINGS BEFORE INTEREST AND TAXES			
North America	$ 2,534	$ 2,030	$ 1,736
Western Europe	640	597	730
Central & Eastern Europe	259	234	244
Greater China	809	911	777
Japan	133	136	114
Emerging Markets	1,011	853	688
Global Brand Divisions	(1,396)	(1,200)	(971)
Total NIKE Brand	3,990	3,561	3,318
Other Businesses	456	385	353
Corporate	(1,177)	(917)	(805)
Total NIKE Consolidated Earnings Before Interest and Taxes	3,269	3,029	2,866
Interest (income) expense, net	(3)	4	4
TOTAL NIKE CONSOLIDATED EARNINGS BEFORE TAXES	**$ 3,272**	**$ 3,025**	**$ 2,862**
ADDITIONS TO LONG-LIVED ASSETS			
North America	$ 201	$ 131	$ 79
Western Europe	74	93	75
Central & Eastern Europe	22	20	5
Greater China	52	38	43
Japan	6	14	9
Emerging Markets	49	27	21
Global Brand Divisions	216	131	44
Total NIKE Brand	620	454	276
Other Businesses	29	24	27
Corporate	131	109	118
TOTAL ADDITIONS TO LONG-LIVED ASSETS	**$ 780**	**$ 587**	**$ 421**
DEPRECIATION			
North America	$ 85	$ 78	$ 70
Western Europe	68	62	52
Central & Eastern Europe	9	6	4
Greater China	34	25	19
Japan	21	23	22
Emerging Markets	20	15	14
Global Brand Divisions	83	53	39
Total NIKE Brand	320	262	220
Other Businesses	24	25	24
Corporate	74	66	71
TOTAL DEPRECIATION	**$ 418**	**$ 353**	**$ 315**

(In millions)	As of May 31, 2013	2012
ACCOUNTS RECEIVABLE, NET		
North America	$ 1,214	$ 1,149
Western Europe	356	420
Central & Eastern Europe	301	261
Greater China	52	221
Japan	133	152
Emerging Markets	546	476
Global Brand Divisions	28	30
Total NIKE Brand	2,630	2,709
Other Businesses	436	401
Corporate	51	22
TOTAL ACCOUNTS RECEIVABLE, NET	**$ 3,117**	**$ 3,132**
INVENTORIES		
North America	$ 1,435	$ 1,272
Western Europe	539	488
Central & Eastern Europe	207	180
Greater China	204	217
Japan	60	83
Emerging Markets	555	521
Global Brand Divisions	32	35
Total NIKE Brand	3,032	2,796
Other Businesses	400	384
Corporate	2	42
TOTAL INVENTORIES	**$ 3,434**	**$ 3,222**
PROPERTY, PLANT AND EQUIPMENT, NET		
North America	$ 406	$ 378
Western Europe	326	314
Central & Eastern Europe	44	30
Greater China	213	191
Japan	269	359
Emerging Markets	89	59
Global Brand Divisions	353	205
Total NIKE Brand	1,700	1,536
Other Businesses	77	76
Corporate	675	597
TOTAL PROPERTY, PLANT AND EQUIPMENT, NET	**$ 2,452**	**$ 2,209**

Revenues by Major Product Lines. Revenues to external customers for NIKE Brand products are attributable to sales of footwear, apparel and equipment. Other revenues to external customers primarily include external sales by Converse, Hurley, and NIKE Golf.

(In millions)	Year Ended May 31, 2013	2012	2011
Footwear	$ 14,539	$ 13,428	$ 11,519
Apparel	6,820	6,336	5,516
Equipment	1,405	1,204	1,022
Other	2,549	2,363	2,060
TOTAL NIKE CONSOLIDATED REVENUES	**$ 25,313**	**$ 23,331**	**$ 20,117**

Glossary

A

absorption costing The reporting of the costs of manufactured products, normally direct materials, direct labor, and factory overhead, as product costs. (Chs. 4, 5)

accounts receivable analysis A company's ability to collect its accounts receivable. (Ch. 14)

accounts receivable turnover The relationship between net sales and accounts receivable, computed by dividing the net sales by the average net accounts receivable; measures how frequently during the year the accounts receivable are being converted to cash. (Ch. 14)

activity analysis The study of employee effort and other business records to determine the cost of activities. (Ch. 12)

activities The types of work, or actions, involved in a manufacturing process or service activity. (Ch. 11)

activity base (driver) A measure of activity that is related to changes in cost. Used in analyzing and classifying cost behavior. Activity bases are also used in the denominator in calculating the predetermined factory overhead rate to assign overhead costs to cost objects. (Chs. 2, 4, 11)

activity rate The estimated activity cost divided by estimated activity-base usage. (Ch. 11)

activity-based costing (ABC) A cost allocation method that identifies activities causing the incurrence of costs and allocates these costs to products (or other cost objects), based on activity drivers (bases). (Chs. 2, 11)

adjusting entries The journal entries that bring the accounts up to date at the end of the accounting period. (Ch. 3)

annuity A series of equal cash flows at fixed intervals. (Ch. 10)

appraisal costs Costs to detect, measure, evaluate, and audit products and process to ensure that they conform to customer requirements and performance standards. (Ch. 12)

average rate of return A method of evaluating capital investment proposals that focuses on the expected profitability of the investment. (Ch. 10)

B

backflush accounting Simplification of the accounting system by eliminating accumulation and transfer of costs as products move through production. (Ch. 12)

balanced scorecard A performance evaluation approach that incorporates multiple performance dimensions by combining financial and nonfinancial measures. (Ch. 8)

batch size The amount of production in units of product that is produced after a setup. (Ch. 12)

break-even point The level of business operations at which revenues and expired costs are equal. (Ch. 4)

budget An accounting device used to plan and control resources of operational departments and divisions. (Ch. 6)

budgetary slack Excess resources set within a budget to provide for uncertain events. (Ch. 6)

budgeted variable factory overhead The standard variable overhead for the actual units produced. (Ch. 7)

C

capital expenditures budget The budget summarizing future plans for acquiring plant facilities and equipment. (Ch. 6)

capital investment analysis The process by which management plans, evaluates, and controls long-term capital investments involving property, plant, and equipment. (Ch. 10)

capital rationing The process by which management plans, evaluates, and controls long-term capital investments involving fixed assets. (Ch. 10)

cash budget A budget of estimated cash receipts and payments. (Ch. 6)

cash flow per share Normally computed as cash flow from operations per share. (Ch. 13)

cash flows from financing activities The section of the statement of cash flows that reports cash flows from transactions affecting the equity and debt of the business. (Ch. 13)

cash flows from investing activities The section of the statement of cash flows that reports cash flows from transactions affecting investments in noncurrent assets. (Ch. 13)

cash flows from operating activities The section of the statement of cash flows that reports the cash transactions affecting the determination of net income. (Ch. 13)

cash payback period The expected period of time that will elapse between the date of a capital expenditure and the complete recovery in cash (or equivalent) of the amount invested. (Ch. 10)

common-sized statement A financial statement in which all items are expressed only in relative terms. (Ch. 14)

continuous budgeting A method of budgeting that provides for maintaining a 12-month projection into the future. (Ch. 6)

continuous process improvement A management approach that is part of the overall total quality management philosophy. The approach requires all employees to constantly improve processes of which they are a part or for which they have managerial responsibility. (Ch. 1)

contribution margin Sales less variable costs and variable selling and administrative expenses. (Chs. 4, 5)

contribution margin analysis The systematic examination of the differences between planned and actual contribution margins. (Ch. 5)

contribution margin ratio The percentage of each sales dollar that is available to cover the fixed costs and provide an operating income. (Ch. 4)

controllable costs Costs that can be influenced (increased, decreased, or eliminated) by someone such as a manager or factory worker. (Ch. 5)

controllable expenses Costs that can be influenced by the decisions of a manager. (Ch. 8)

controllable revenues Revenues earned by the profit center. (Ch. 8)

controllable variance The difference between the actual amount of variable factory overhead cost incurred and the amount of variable factory overhead budgeted for the standard product. (Ch. 7)

controller The chief management accountant of a division or other segment of a business. (Ch. 1)

controlling A phase in the management process that consists of monitoring the operating results of implemented plans and comparing the actual results with the expected results. (Ch. 1)

conversion costs The combination of direct labor and factory overhead costs. (Chs. 1, 12)

cost A payment of cash (or a commitment to pay cash in the future) for the purpose of generating revenues. (Ch. 1)

cost accounting systems Systems that measure, record, and report product costs. (Ch. 2)

cost allocation The process of assigning indirect cost to a cost object, such as a job. (Ch. 2)

cost behavior The manner in which a cost changes in relation to its activity base (driver). (Ch. 4)

cost center A decentralized unit in which the department or division manager has responsibility for the control of costs incurred and the authority to make decisions that affect these costs. (Ch. 8)

cost object The object or segment of operations to which costs are related for management's use, such as a product or department. (Ch. 1)

cost of finished goods available for sale The beginning finished goods inventory added to the cost of goods manufactured during the period. (Ch. 1)

cost of goods manufactured The total cost of making and finishing a product. (Ch. 1)

cost of goods sold The cost of finished goods available for sale minus the ending finished goods inventory. (Ch. 1)

cost of goods sold budget A budget of the estimated direct materials, direct labor, and factory overhead consumed by sold products. (Ch. 6)

cost of merchandise sold The cost that is reported as an expense when merchandise is sold. (Ch. 1)

cost of production report A report prepared periodically by a processing department, summarizing (1) the units for which the department is accountable and the disposition of those units and (2) the costs incurred by the department and the allocation of those costs between completed and incomplete production. (Ch. 3)

cost of quality report A report summarizing the costs, percent of total, and percent of sales by appraisal, prevention, internal failure, and external failure cost of quality categories. (Ch. 12)

cost per equivalent unit The rate used to allocate costs between completed and partially completed production. (Ch. 3)

cost price approach An approach to transfer pricing that uses cost as the basis for setting the transfer price. (Ch. 8)

cost variance The difference between actual cost and the flexible budget at actual volumes. (Ch. 7)

costs of quality The cost associated with controlling quality (prevention and appraisal) and failing to control quality (internal and external failure). (Ch. 12)

cost-volume-profit analysis The systematic examination of the relationships among selling prices, volume of sales and production, costs, expenses, and profits. (Ch. 4)

cost-volume-profit chart A chart used to assist management in understanding the relationships among costs, expenses, sales, and operating profit or loss. (Ch. 4)

currency exchange rate The rate at which currency in another country can be exchanged for local currency. (Ch. 10)

current position analysis A company's ability to pay its current liabilities. (Ch. 14)

current ratio A financial ratio that is computed by dividing current assets by current liabilities. (Ch. 14)

currently attainable standards Standards that represent levels of operation that can be attained with reasonable effort. (Ch. 7)

D

decision making A component inherent in the other management processes of planning, directing, controlling, and improving. (Ch. 1)

differential analysis The area of accounting concerned with the effect of alternative courses of action on revenues and costs. (Ch. 9)

differential cost The amount of increase or decrease in cost expected from a particular course of action compared with an alternative. (Ch. 9)

differential income (loss) The difference between the differential revenue and the differential costs. (Ch. 9)

differential revenue The amount of increase or decrease in revenue expected from a particular course of action as compared with an alternative. (Ch. 9)

direct costs Costs that can be traced directly to a cost object. (Ch. 1)

direct labor cost The wages of factory workers who are directly involved in converting materials into a finished product. (Ch. 1)

direct labor cost budget Budget that estimates direct labor hours and related costs needed to support budgeted production. (Ch. 6)

direct labor rate variance The cost associated with the difference between the standard rate and the actual rate paid for direct labor used in producing a commodity. (Ch. 7)

direct labor time variance The cost associated with the difference between the standard hours and the actual hours of direct labor spent producing a commodity. (Ch. 7)

direct materials cost The cost of materials that are an integral part of the finished product. (Ch. 1)

direct materials price variance The cost associated with the difference between the standard price and the actual price of direct materials used in producing a commodity. (Ch. 7)

direct materials purchases budget A budget that uses the production budget as a starting point to budget materials purchases. (Ch. 6)

direct materials quantity variance The cost associated with the difference between the standard quantity and the actual quantity of direct materials used in producing a commodity. (Ch. 7)

direct method A method of reporting the cash flows from operating activities as the difference between the operating cash receipts and the operating cash payments. (Ch. 13)

directing The process by which managers, given their assigned level of responsibilities, run day-to-day operations. (Ch. 1)

dividend yield A ratio, computed by dividing the annual dividends paid per share of common stock by the market price per share at a specific date, that indicates the rate of return to stockholders in terms of cash dividend distributions. (Ch. 14)

dividends per share Measures the extent to which earnings are being distributed to common shareholders. (Ch. 14)

DuPont formula An expanded expression of return on investment determined by multiplying the profit margin by the investment turnover. (Ch. 8)

E

earnings per share (EPS) on common stock The profitability ratio of net income available to common shareholders to the number of common shares outstanding. (Ch. 14)

electronic data interchange (EDI) An information technology that allows different business organizations to use computers to communicate orders, relay information, and make or receive payments. (Ch. 12)

employee involvement A philosophy that grants employees the responsibility and authority to make their own decisions about their operations. (Ch. 12)

engineering change order (ECO) The document that initiates changing a product or process. (Ch. 11)

enterprise resource planning (ERP) An integrated business and information system used by companies to plan and control both internal and supply chain operations. (Ch. 12)

equivalent units of production The number of production units that could have been completed within a given accounting period, given the resources consumed. (Ch. 3)

external failure costs The costs incurred after defective units or services have been delivered to consumers. (Ch. 12)

extraordinary item An event or a transaction that is both (1) unusual in nature and (2) infrequent in occurrence. (Ch. 14)

F

factory burden Another term for manufacturing overhead or factory overhead. (Ch. 1)

factory overhead cost All of the costs of producing a product except for direct materials and direct labor. (Ch. 1)

factory overhead cost budget Budget that estimates the cost for each item of factory overhead needed to support budgeted production. (Ch. 6)

factory overhead cost variance report Reports budgeted and actual costs for variable and fixed factory overhead along with the related controllable and volume variances. (Ch. 7)

favorable cost variance A variance that occurs when the actual cost is less than standard cost. (Ch. 7)

feedback Measures provided to operational employees or managers on the performance of subunits of the organization. These measures are used by employees to adjust a process or a behavior to achieve goals. See management by exception. (Ch. 1)

financial accounting The branch of accounting that is concerned with recording transactions using generally accepted accounting principles (GAAP) for a business or other economic unit and with a periodic preparation of various statements from such records. (Ch. 1)

finished goods inventory The direct materials costs, direct labor costs, and factory overhead costs of finished products that have not been sold. (Ch. 1)

finished goods ledger The subsidiary ledger that contains the individual accounts for each kind of commodity or product produced. (Ch. 2)

first-in, first-out (FIFO) inventory cost flow method The method of inventory costing based on the assumption that the costs of merchandise sold should be charged against revenue in the order in which the costs were incurred. (Ch. 3)

fixed costs Costs that tend to remain the same in amount, regardless of variations in the level of activity. (Ch. 4)

flexible budget A budget that adjusts for varying rates of activity. (Ch. 6)

free cash flow The amount of operating cash flow remaining after replacing current productive capacity and maintaining current dividends. (Ch. 13)

G

goal conflict A condition that occurs when individual objectives conflict with organizational objectives. (Ch. 6)

H

high-low method A technique that uses the highest and lowest total costs as a basis for estimating the variable cost per unit and the fixed cost component of a mixed cost. (Ch. 4)

horizontal analysis Financial analysis that compares an item in a current statement with the same item in prior statements. (Ch. 14)

I

ideal standards Standards that can be achieved only under perfect operating conditions, such as no idle time, no machine breakdowns, and no materials spoilage; also called theoretical standards. (Ch. 7)

indirect costs Costs that cannot be traced directly to a cost object. (Ch. 1)

indirect method A method of reporting the cash flows from operating activities as the net income from operations adjusted for all deferrals of past cash receipts and payments and all accruals of expected future cash receipts and payments. (Ch. 13)

inflation A period when prices in general are rising and the purchasing power of money is declining. (Ch. 10)

internal failure costs The costs associated with defects that are discovered by the organization before the product or service is delivered to the consumer. (Ch. 12)

internal rate of return (IRR) method A method of analysis of proposed capital investments that uses present value concepts to compute the rate of return from the net cash flows expected from the investment. (Ch. 10)

inventory analysis A company's ability to manage its inventory effectively. (Ch. 14)

inventory turnover The relationship between the volume of goods sold and inventory, computed by dividing the cost of goods sold by the average inventory. (Ch. 14)

investment center A decentralized unit in which the manager has the responsibility and authority to make decisions that affect not only costs and revenues but also the fixed assets available to the center. (Ch. 8)

investment turnover A component of the rate of return on investment, computed as the ratio of sales to invested assets. (Ch. 8)

J

job cost sheet An account in the work in process subsidiary ledger in which the costs charged to a particular job order are recorded. (Ch. 2)

job order cost system A type of cost accounting system that provides for a separate record of the cost of each particular quantity of product that passes through the factory. (Ch. 2)

L

lead time The elapsed time between starting a unit of product into the beginning of a process and its completion. (Ch. 12)

lean accounting An accounting system characterized by fewer transactions, combined accounts, nonfinancial performance measures, and direct tracing of overhead. (Ch. 12)

lean enterprise A business that produces products or services with high quality, low cost, fast response, and immediate availability using lean principles. (Ch. 12)

lean manufacturing (or just-in-time manufacturing) A manufacturing enterprise that uses lean principles. (Chs. 3, 12)

lean principles Principles associated with the lean enterprise that include reducing inventory, reducing lead time, reducing setup time, product/customer oriented layouts, employee involvement, pull scheduling, zero defects, and supply chain management. (Ch. 12)

leverage Using debt to increase the return on an investment. (Ch. 14)

line department A unit that is directly involved in the basic objectives of an organization. (Ch. 1)

liquidity The ability to convert assets into cash. (Ch. 14)

M

management (or managerial) accounting The branch of accounting that uses both historical and estimated data in providing information that management uses in conducting daily operations, in planning future operations, and in developing overall business strategies. (Ch. 1)

management by exception The philosophy of managing which involves monitoring the operating results of implemented plans and comparing the expected results with the actual results. This feedback allows management to isolate significant variations for further investigation and possible remedial action. (Ch. 1)

management process The five basic management functions of (1) planning, (2) directing, (3) controlling, (4) improving, and (5) decision making. (Ch. 1)

Management's Discussion and Analysis (MD&A) An annual report disclosure that provides management's analysis of the results of operations and financial condition. (Ch. 14)

manufacturing cells A grouping of processes where employees are cross-trained to perform more than one function. (Ch. 3)

manufacturing margin The variable cost of goods sold deducted from sales. (Ch. 5)

manufacturing overhead Costs, other than direct materials and direct labor costs, that are incurred in the manufacturing process. (Ch. 1)

margin of safety Indicates the possible decrease in sales that may occur before an operating loss results. (Ch. 4)

market price approach An approach to transfer pricing that uses the price at which the product or service transferred could be sold to outside buyers as the transfer price. (Ch. 8)

market segment A portion of business that can be assigned to a manager for profit responsibility. (Ch. 5)

master budget The comprehensive budget plan linking all the individual budgets related to sales, cost of goods sold, operating expenses, projects, capital expenditures, and cash. (Ch. 6)

materials inventory The cost of materials that have not yet entered into the manufacturing process. (Ch. 1)

materials ledger The subsidiary ledger containing the individual accounts for each type of material. (Ch. 2)

materials requisition The form or electronic transmission used by a manufacturing department to authorize materials issuances from the storeroom. (Ch. 2)

merchandise available for sale The cost of merchandise available for sale to customers calculated by adding the beginning merchandise inventory to net purchases. (Ch. 1)

mixed costs Costs with both variable and fixed characteristics, sometimes called semivariable or semifixed costs. (Ch. 4)

multiple production department factory overhead rate method A method that allocated factory overhead to product by using factory overhead rates for each production department. (Ch. 11)

N

negotiated price approach An approach to transfer pricing that allows managers of decentralized units to agree (negotiate) among themselves as to the transfer price. (Ch. 8)

net present value method A method of analysis of proposed capital investments that focuses on the present value of the cash flows expected from the investments. (Ch. 10)

noncontrollable cost Cost that cannot be influenced (increased, decreased, or eliminated) by someone such as a manager or factory worker. (Ch. 5)

nonfinancial measure A performance measure that has not been stated in dollar terms. (Ch. 12)

nonfinancial performance measure A performance measure expressed in units rather than dollars. (Ch. 7)

non-value-added activity The cost of activities that are perceived as unnecessary from the customer's perspective and are thus candidates for elimination. (Ch. 12)

non-value-added lead time The time that units wait in inventories, move unnecessarily, and wait during machine breakdowns. (Ch. 12)

number of days' sales in inventory The relationship between the volume of sales and inventory, computed by dividing the inventory at the end of the year by the average daily cost of goods sold. (Ch. 14)

number of days' sales in receivables The relationship between sales and accounts receivable, computed by dividing the net accounts receivable at the end of the year by the average daily sales. (Ch. 14)

number of times interest charges are earned A ratio that measures creditor margin of safety for interest payments, calculated as income before interest and taxes divided by interest expense. (Ch. 14)

O

objectives (goals) Developed in the planning stage, these reflect the direction and desired outcomes of certain courses of action. (Ch. 1)

operating leverage A measure of the relative mix of a business's variable costs and fixed costs, computed as contribution margin divided by operating income. (Ch. 4)

operational planning The development of short-term plans to achieve goals identified in a business's strategic plan. Sometimes called tactical planning. (Ch. 1)

opportunity cost The amount of income forgone from an alternative to a proposed use of cash or its equivalent. (Ch. 9)

overapplied factory overhead The amount of factory overhead applied in excess of the actual factory overhead costs incurred for production during a period. (Ch. 2)

P

Pareto chart A bar chart that shows the totals of a particular attribute for a number of categories, ranked left to right from the largest to smallest totals. (Ch. 12)

period costs Those costs that are used up in generating revenue during the current period and that are not involved in manufacturing a product, such as selling, general, and administrative expenses. (Ch. 1)

planning A phase of the management process whereby objectives are outlined and courses of action determined. (Ch. 1)

predetermined factory overhead rate The rate used to apply factory overhead costs to the goods manufactured. The rate is determined by dividing the budgeted overhead cost by the estimated activity usage at the beginning of the fiscal period. (Ch. 2)

present value concept Cash to be received (or paid) in the future is not the equivalent of the same amount of money received at an earlier date. (Ch. 10)

present value index An index computed by dividing the total present value of the net cash flow to be received from a proposed capital investment by the amount to be invested. (Ch. 10)

present value of an annuity The sum of the present values of a series of equal cash flows to be received at fixed intervals. (Ch. 10)

prevention costs Costs incurred to prevent defects from occurring during the design and delivery of products or services. (Ch. 12)

price-earnings (P/E) ratio The ratio of the market price per share of common stock, at a specific date, to the annual earnings per share. (Ch. 14)

prime costs The combination of direct materials and direct labor costs. (Ch. 1)

process A sequence of activities linked together for performing a particular task. (Chs. 7, 12)

process cost system A type of cost system that accumulates costs for each of the various departments within a manufacturing facility. (Chs. 2, 3)

process manufacturer A manufacturer that uses large machines to process a continuous flow of raw materials through various stages of completion into a finished state. (Ch. 3)

process-oriented layout Organizing work in a plant or administrative function around processes (tasks). (Ch. 12)

product cost concept A concept used in applying the cost-plus approach to product pricing in which only the costs of manufacturing the product, termed the product cost, are included in the cost amount to which the markup is added. (Ch. 9)

product costing Determining the cost of a product. (Ch. 11)

product costs The three components of manufacturing cost: direct materials, direct labor, and factory overhead costs. (Ch. 1)

production bottleneck A condition that occurs when product demand exceeds production capacity. (Ch. 9)

production budget A budget of estimated unit production. (Ch. 6)

production department factory overhead rates Rates determined by dividing the budgeted production department factory overhead by the budgeted allocation base for each department. (Ch. 11)

product-oriented layout Organizing work in a plant or administrative function around products; sometimes referred to as product cells. (Ch. 12)

profit center A decentralized unit in which the manager has the responsibility and the authority to make decisions that affect both costs and revenues (and thus profits). (Ch. 8)

profit margin A component of the rate of return on investment, computed as the ratio of income from operations to sales. (Ch. 8)

profit-volume chart A chart used to assist management in understanding the relationship between profit and volume. (Ch. 4)

profitability The ability of a firm to earn income. (Ch. 14)

pull manufacturing A just-in-time method wherein customer orders trigger the release of finished goods, which triggers production, which triggers release of materials from suppliers. (Ch. 12)

push manufacturing Materials are released into production and work in process is released into finished goods in anticipation of future sales. (Ch. 12)

Q

quantity factor The effect of a difference in the number of units sold, assuming no change in unit sales price or unit cost. (Ch. 5)

quick assets Cash and other current assets that can be quickly converted to cash, such as marketable securities and receivables. (Ch. 14)

quick ratio A financial ratio that measures the ability to pay current liabilities with quick assets (cash, marketable securities, accounts receivable). (Ch. 14)

R

radio frequency identification devices (RFID) Electronic tags (chips) placed on or embedded within products that can be read by radio waves that allow instant monitoring or production location. (Ch. 12)

rate earned on common stockholders' equity A measure of profitability computed by dividing net income, reduced by preferred dividend requirements, by common stockholders' equity. (Ch. 14)

rate earned on stockholders' equity A measure of profitability computed by dividing net income by total stockholders' equity. (Ch. 14)

rate earned on total assets A measure of the profitability of assets, without regard to the equity of creditors and stockholders in the assets. (Ch. 14)

rate of return on investment (ROI) A measure of managerial efficiency in the use of investments in assets, computed as income from operations divided by invested assets. (Ch. 8)

ratio of fixed assets to long-term liabilities A leverage ratio that measures the margin of safety of long-term creditors, calculated as the net fixed assets divided by the long-term liabilities. (Ch. 14)

ratio of liabilities to stockholders' equity A comprehensive leverage ratio that measures the relationship of the claims of creditors to stockholders' equity. (Ch. 14)

ratio of sales to assets Ratio that measures how effectively a company uses its assets, computed as net sales divided by average total assets. (Ch. 14)

Raw and In Process (RIP) Inventory The capitalized cost of direct materials purchases, labor, and overhead charged to the production cell. (Ch. 12)

receiving report The form or electronic transmission used by the receiving personnel to indicate that materials have been received and inspected. (Ch. 2)

relevant range The range of activity over which changes in cost are of interest to management. (Ch. 4)

residual income The excess of divisional income from operations over a "minimum" acceptable income from operations. (Ch. 8)

responsibility accounting The process of measuring and reporting operating data by areas of responsibility. (Ch. 8)

responsibility center An organizational unit for which a manager is assigned responsibility over costs, revenues, or assets. (Ch. 6)

S

sales budget One of the major elements of the income statement budget that indicates the quantity of estimated sales and the expected unit selling price. (Ch. 7)

sales discounts From the seller's perspective, discounts that a seller may offer the buyer for early payment. (Ch. 6)

sales mix The relative distribution of sales among the various products available for sale. (Chs. 4, 5)

service department charges The costs of services provided by an internal service department and transferred to a responsibility center. (Ch. 8)

setup An overhead activity that consists of changing tooling in machines in preparation for making a new product. (Ch. 11)

single plantwide factory overhead rate method A method that allocates all factory overhead to products by using a single factory overhead rate. (Ch. 11)

Six Sigma A quality improvement process developed by Motorola Corporation consisting of five steps: define, measure, analyze, improve, and control (DMAIC). (Ch. 12)

solvency The ability of a firm to pay its debts as they come due. (Ch. 14)

staff department A unit that provides services, assistance, and advice to the departments with line or other staff responsibilities. (Ch. 1)

standard cost A detailed estimate of what a product should cost. (Ch. 7)

standard cost systems Accounting systems that use standards for each element of manufacturing cost entering into the finished product. (Ch. 7)

standards Performance goals, often relating to how much a product should cost. (Ch. 7)

statement of cash flows A summary of the cash receipts and cash payments for a specific period of time, such as a month or a year. (Ch. 13)

statement of cost of goods manufactured The income statement of manufacturing companies. (Ch. 1)

static budget A budget that does not adjust to changes in activity levels. (Ch. 6)

strategic planning The development of a long-range course of action to achieve business goals. (Ch. 1)

strategies The means by which business goals and objectives will be achieved. (Ch. 1)

sunk cost A cost that is not affected by subsequent decisions. (Ch. 9)

supply chain management The coordination and control of materials, services, information, and finances as they move in a process from supplier, through the manufacturer, wholesaler, and retailer to the consumer. (Ch. 12)

T

target costing The target cost is determined by subtracting a desired profit from a market method determined price. The resulting target cost is used to motivate cost improvements in design and manufacture. (Ch. 9)

theory of constraints (TOC) A manufacturing strategy that attempts to remove the influence of bottlenecks (constraints) on a process. (Ch. 9)

time tickets The form on which the amount of time spent by each employee and the labor cost incurred for each individual job, or for factory overhead, are recorded. (Ch. 2)

time value of money concept The concept that an amount of money invested today will earn income. (Ch. 10)

total cost concept A concept used in applying the cost-plus approach to product pricing in which all the costs of manufacturing the product plus the selling and administrative expenses are included in the cost amount to which the markup is added. (Ch. 9)

total manufacturing cost variance The difference between total standard costs and total actual costs for units produced. (Ch. 7)

transfer price The price charged one decentralized unit by another for the goods or services provided. (Ch. 8)

U

underapplied factory overhead The amount of actual factory overhead in excess of the factory overhead applied to production during a period. (Ch. 2)

unfavorable cost variance A variance that occurs when the actual cost exceeds the standard cost. (Ch. 7)

unit contribution margin The dollars available from each unit of sales to cover fixed costs and provide operating profits. (Ch. 4)

unit price (cost) factor The effect of a difference in unit sales price or unit cost on the number of units sold. (Ch. 5)

V

value-added activity The cost of activities that are needed to meet customer requirements. (Ch. 12)

value-added lead time The time required to manufacture a unit of product or other output. (Ch. 12)

value-added ratio The ratio of the value-added lead time to the total lead time. (Ch. 12)

variable cost concept A concept used in applying the cost-plus approach to product pricing in which only the variable costs are included in the cost amount to which the markup is added. (Ch. 9)

variable cost of goods sold Consists of direct materials, direct labor, and variable factory overhead for the units sold. (Ch. 5)

variable costing The concept that considers the cost of products manufactured to be composed only of those manufacturing costs that increase or decrease as the volume of production rises or falls (direct materials, direct labor, and variable factory overhead). (Chs. 4, 5)

variable costs Costs that vary in total dollar amount as the level of activity changes. (Ch. 4)

vertical analysis An analysis that compares each item in a current statement with a total amount within the same statement. (Ch. 14)

volume variance The difference between the budgeted fixed overhead at 100% of normal capacity and the standard fixed overhead for the actual production achieved during the period. (Ch. 7)

W

whole units The number of units in production during a period, whether completed or not. (Ch. 3)

work in process inventory The direct materials costs, the direct labor costs, and the applied factory overhead costs that have entered into the manufacturing process but are associated with products that have not been finished. (Ch. 1)

working capital The excess of the current assets of a business over its current liabilities. (Ch. 14)

Y

yield A measure of materials usage efficiency. (Ch. 3)

Z

zero-based budgeting A concept of budgeting that requires all levels of management to start from zero and estimate budget data as if there had been no previous activities in their units. (Ch. 6)

Index

A

B

C

D

E

F

T

U

The Basics

Accounting Equation:

Assets = Liabilities + Stockholders' Equity

T Account:

Account Title	
Left side	Right side
debit	credit

Rules of Debit and Credit:

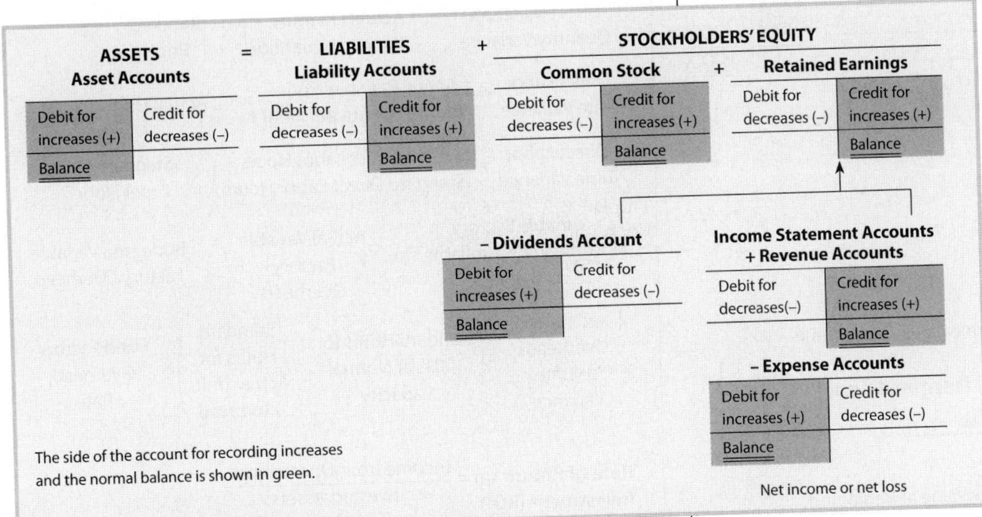

Analyzing and Journalizing Transactions

1. Carefully read the description of the transaction to determine whether an asset, liability, capital stock, retained earnings, revenue, expense, or dividends account is affected.
2. For each account affected by the transaction, determine whether the account increases or decreases.
3. Determine whether each increase or decrease should be recorded as a debit or a credit, following the rules of debit and credit.
4. Record the transaction using a journal entry.
5. Periodically post journal entries to the accounts in the ledger.
6. Prepare an unadjusted trial balance at the end of the period.

Financial Statements:

- **Income statement:** A summary of the revenue and expenses of a business entity for a specific period of time, such as a month or a year.
- **Retained Earnings Statement:** A summary of the changes in the retained earnings of a business entity that have occurred during a specific period of time, such as a month or a year.
- **Balance sheet:** A list of the assets, liabilities, and stockholders' equity of a business entity as of a specific date, usually at the close of the last day of a month or a year.
- **Statement of Cash Flows:** A summary of the cash receipts and cash payments of a business entity for a specific period of time, such as a month or a year.

Accounting Cycle:

1. Transactions are analyzed and recorded in the journal.
2. Transactions are posted to the ledger.
3. An unadjusted trial balance is prepared.
4. Adjustment data are assembled and analyzed.
5. An optional end-of-period spreadsheet is prepared.
6. Adjusting entries are journalized and posted to the ledger.
7. An adjusted trial balance is prepared.
8. Financial statements are prepared.
9. Closing entries are journalized and posted to the ledger.
10. A post-closing trial balance is prepared.

Types of Adjusting Entries:

- Prepaid expense (deferred expense)
- Unearned revenue (deferred revenue)
- Accrued revenue (accrued asset)
- Accrued expense (accrued liability)
- Depreciation expense

Each entry will always affect both a balance sheet account and an income statement account.

Closing Entries:

1. Revenue account balances are transferred to an account called Income Summary.
2. Expense account balances are transferred to an account called Income Summary.
3. The balance of Income Summary (net income or net loss) is transferred to Retained Earnings.
4. The balance of the owner's drawing account is transferred to Retained Earnings.

Shipping Terms:

	FOB Shipping Point	FOB Destination
Ownership (title) passes to buyer when merchandise is	delivered to freight carrier	delivered to buyer
Freight costs are paid by..........................	buyer	seller

Format for Bank Reconciliation:

Cash balance according to bank statement		\$XXX
Add: Additions by company not on bank statement	\$XXX	
Bank errors	XXX	XXX
		\$XXX
Deduct: Deductions by company not on bank statement	\$XXX	
Bank errors	XXX	XXX
Adjusted balance		\$XXX
Cash balance according to company's records		\$XXX
Add: Additions by bank not recorded by company	\$XXX	
Company errors	XXX	XXX
		\$XXX
Deduct: Deductions by bank not recorded by company	\$XXX	
Company errors	XXX	XXX
Adjusted balance		\$XXX

Inventory Costing Methods:

- First-in, First-out (FIFO)
- Last-in, First-out (LIFO)
- Average Cost

Interest Computations:

Interest = Face Amount (or Principal) × Rate × Time

Methods of Determining Annual Depreciation:

Straight-Line: $\frac{\text{Cost} - \text{Estimated Residual Value}}{\text{Estimated Life}}$

Double-Declining-Balance: Rate* × Book Value at Beginning of Period

*Rate is commonly twice the straight-line rate (1 ÷ Estimated Life).

Adjustments to Net Income (Loss) Using the Indirect Method:

	Increase (Decrease)
Net income (loss)	\$ XXX
Adjustments to reconcile net income to net cash flow from operating activities:	
Depreciation of fixed assets	XXX
Amortization of intangible assets	XXX
Losses on disposal of assets	XXX
Gains on disposal of assets	(XXX)
Changes in current operating assets and liabilities:	
Increases in noncash current operating assets	(XXX)
Decreases in noncash current operating assets	XXX
Increases in current operating liabilities	XXX
Decreases in current operating liabilities	(XXX)
Net cash flow from operating activities	\$ XXX or \$(XXX)

Contribution Margin Ratio = $\frac{\text{Sales} - \text{Variable Costs}}{\text{Sales}}$

Break-Even Sales (Units) = $\frac{\text{Fixed Costs}}{\text{Unit Contribution Margin}}$

Sales (Units) = $\frac{\text{Fixed Costs} + \text{Target Profit}}{\text{Unit Contribution Margin}}$

Margin of Safety = $\frac{\text{Sales} - \text{Sales at Break-Even Point}}{\text{Sales}}$

Operating Leverage = $\frac{\text{Contribution Margin}}{\text{Income from Operations}}$

Variances:

Direct Materials Price Variance = (Actual Price − Standard Price) × Actual Quantity

Direct Materials Quantity Variance = (Actual Quantity − Standard Quantity) × Standard Price

Direct Labor Rate Variance = (Actual Rate per Hour − Standard Rate per Hour) × Actual Hours

Direct Labor Time Variance = (Actual Direct Labor Hours − Standard Direct Labor Hours) × Standard Rate per Hour

Variable Factory Overhead Controllable Variance = Actual Variable Factory Overhead − Budgeted Variable Factory Overhead

Fixed Factory Overhead Volume Variance = (Standard Hours for 100% of Normal Capacity − Standard Hours for Actual Units Produced) × Fixed Factory Overhead Rate

Rate of Return on Investment (ROI) = $\frac{\text{Income from Operations}}{\text{Invested Assets}}$

Alternative ROI Computation:

$$\text{ROI} = \frac{\text{Income from Operations}}{\text{Sales}} \times \frac{\text{Sales}}{\text{Invested Assets}}$$

Capital Investment Analysis Methods:

Methods That Ignore Present Values:

- Average Rate of Return Method
- Cash Payback Method

Methods That Use Present Values:

- Net Present Value Method
- Internal Rate of Return Method

Average Rate of Return = $\frac{\text{Estimated Average Annual Income}}{\text{Average Investment}}$

Present Value Index = $\frac{\text{Total Present Value of Net Cash Flow}}{\text{Amount to Be Invested}}$

Present Value Factor for an Annuity of \$1 = $\frac{\text{Amount to Be Invested}}{\text{Equal Annual Net Cash Flows}}$

Abbreviations and Acronyms Commonly Used in Business and Accounting

AAA	American Accounting Association
ABC	Activity-based costing
AICPA	American Institute of Certified Public Accountants
B2B	Business-to-business
B2C	Business-to-consumer
CFO	Chief Financial Officer
CMA	Certified Management Accountant
COGM	Cost of goods manufactured
COGS	Cost of goods sold
CPA	Certified Public Accountant
Cr.	Credit
CVP	Cost-volume-profit
Dr.	Debit
EFT	Electronic funds transfer
EPS	Earnings per share
ERP	Enterprise resource planning
FASB	Financial Accounting Standards Board
FICA tax	Federal Insurance Contributions Act tax
FIFO	First-in, first-out
FOB	Free on board
FUTA	Federal unemployment compensation tax
GAAP	Generally accepted accounting principles
IASB	International Accounting Standards Board
IFRS	International Financial Reporting Standards
IMA	Institute of Management Accountants
IRC	Internal Revenue Code
IRR	Internal rate of return
IRS	Internal Revenue Service
JIT	Just-in-time
LIFO	Last-in, first-out
LCM	Lower of cost or market
MACRS	Modified Accelerated Cost Recovery System
MD&A	Management's Discussion and Analysis
n/30	Net 30
n/eom	Net, end-of-month
NPV	Net present value
NSF	Not sufficient funds
P/E Ratio	Price-earnings ratio
POS	Point of sale
ROI	Return on investment
R&D	Research and development
SCM	Supply chain management
SEC	Securities and Exchange Commission
SOX	Sarbanes-Oxley Act
TQC	Total quality control
W-4	Employee's Withholding Allowance Certificate
WIP	Work in process

Classification of Accounts

Account Title	*Account Classification*	*Normal Balance*	*Financial Statement*
Accounts Payable	Current liability	Credit	Balance sheet
Accounts Receivable	Current asset	Debit	Balance sheet
Accumulated Depletion	Contra fixed asset	Credit	Balance sheet
Accumulated Depreciation	Contra fixed asset	Credit	Balance sheet
Advertising Expense	Operating expense	Debit	Income statement
Allowance for Doubtful Accounts	Contra current asset	Credit	Balance sheet
Amortization Expense	Operating expense	Debit	Income statement
Bonds Payable	Long-term liability	Credit	Balance sheet
Building	Fixed asset	Debit	Balance sheet
Cash	Current asset	Debit	Balance sheet
Cash Dividends	Stockholders' equity	Debit	Retained earnings statement
Cash Dividends Payable	Current liability	Credit	Balance sheet
Common Stock	Stockholders' equity	Credit	Balance sheet
Cost of Merchandise (Goods) Sold	Cost of merchandise (goods) sold	Debit	Income statement
Customer Refunds Payable	Current liability	Credit	Balance sheet
Delivery Expense	Operating expense	Debit	Income statement
Depletion Expense	Operating expense	Debit	Income statement
Discount on Bonds Payable	Long-term liability	Debit	Balance sheet
Dividend Revenue	Other income	Credit	Income statement
Dividends	Stockholders' equity	Debit	Retained earnings statement
Employees Federal Income Tax Payable	Current liability	Credit	Balance sheet
Equipment	Fixed asset	Debit	Balance sheet
Estimated Returns Inventory	Current asset	Debit	Balance sheet
Factory Overhead (Overapplied)	Deferred credit	Credit	Balance sheet (interim)
Factory Overhead (Underapplied)	Deferred debit	Debit	Balance sheet (interim)
Federal Income Tax Payable	Current liability	Credit	Balance sheet
Federal Unemployment Tax Payable	Current liability	Credit	Balance sheet
Finished Goods	Current asset	Debit	Balance sheet
Freight In	Cost of merchandise sold	Debit	Income statement
Freight Out	Operating expense	Debit	Income statement
Gain on Disposal of Fixed Assets	Other income	Credit	Income statement
Gain on Redemption of Bonds	Other income	Credit	Income statement
Gain on Sale of Investments	Other income	Credit	Income statement
Goodwill	Intangible asset	Debit	Balance sheet
Income Tax Expense	Income tax	Debit	Income statement
Income Tax Payable	Current liability	Credit	Balance sheet
Insurance Expense	Operating expense	Debit	Income statement
Interest Expense	Other expense	Debit	Income statement
Interest Receivable	Current asset	Debit	Balance sheet
Interest Revenue	Other income	Credit	Income statement
Investment in Bonds	Investment	Debit	Balance sheet
Investment in Stocks	Investment	Debit	Balance sheet
Investment in Subsidiary	Investment	Debit	Balance sheet
Land	Fixed asset	Debit	Balance sheet
Loss on Disposal of Fixed Assets	Other expense	Debit	Income statement
Loss on Redemption of Bonds	Other expense	Debit	Income statement

Account Title	*Account Classification*	*Normal Balance*	*Financial Statement*
Loss on Sale of Investments	Other expense	Debit	Income statement
Marketable Securities	Current asset	Debit	Balance sheet
Materials	Current asset	Debit	Balance sheet
Medicare Tax Payable	Current liability	Credit	Balance sheet
Merchandise Inventory	Current asset/Cost of merchandise sold	Debit	Balance sheet/Income statement
Notes Payable	Current liability/Long-term liability	Credit	Balance sheet
Notes Receivable	Current asset/Investment	Debit	Balance sheet
Patents	Intangible asset	Debit	Balance sheet
Paid-In Capital from Sale of Treasury Stock	Stockholders' equity	Credit	Balance sheet
Paid-In Capital in Excess of Par (Stated Value)	Stockholders' equity	Credit	Balance sheet
Payroll Tax Expense	Operating expense	Debit	Income statement
Pension Expense	Operating expense	Debit	Income statement
Petty Cash	Current asset	Debit	Balance sheet
Preferred Stock	Stockholders' equity	Credit	Balance sheet
Premium on Bonds Payable	Long-term liability	Credit	Balance sheet
Prepaid Insurance	Current asset	Debit	Balance sheet
Prepaid Rent	Current asset	Debit	Balance sheet
Purchases	Cost of merchandise sold	Debit	Income statement
Purchases Discounts	Cost of merchandise sold	Credit	Income statement
Purchases Returns and Allowances	Cost of merchandise sold	Credit	Income statement
Rent Expense	Operating expense	Debit	Income statement
Rent Revenue	Other income	Credit	Income statement
Retained Earnings	Stockholders' equity	Credit	Balance sheet/Retained earnings statement
Salaries Expense	Operating expense	Debit	Income statement
Salaries Payable	Current liability	Credit	Balance sheet
Sales Tax Payable	Current liability	Credit	Balance sheet
Social Security Tax Payable	Current liability	Credit	Balance sheet
State Unemployment Tax Payable	Current liability	Credit	Balance sheet
Stock Dividends	Stockholders' equity	Debit	Retained earnings statement
Stock Dividends Distributable	Stockholders' equity	Credit	Balance sheet
Supplies	Current asset	Debit	Balance sheet
Supplies Expense	Operating expense	Debit	Income statement
Treasury Stock	Stockholders' equity	Debit	Balance sheet
Uncollectible Accounts Expense	Operating expense	Debit	Income statement
Unearned Rent	Current liability	Credit	Balance sheet
Utilities Expense	Operating expense	Debit	Income statement
Vacation Pay Expense	Operating expense	Debit	Income statement
Vacation Pay Payable	Current liability/Long-term liability	Credit	Balance sheet
Work in Process	Current asset	Debit	Balance sheet

STUDY TIPS

What Successful Students Are Saying

In a recent survey of students who took financial and managerial accounting courses, students stated that, in order to be successful in these courses, students should (in order of importance):

- Complete assigned homework
- Attend class and pay attention during the lecture
- Study
- Ask for help or get a tutor
- Complete ungraded practice assignments or review exercises

- ❑ Did you read the chapter from the required textbook prior to attending class?
- ❑ Did you attend class?
- ❑ Did you take notes during class?
- ❑ Did you ask questions of the professor either during or after class when you did not understand a concept being taught?
- ❑ Did you complete all assigned homework?
- ❑ Did you complete ungraded practice assignments or review exercises to better learn and understand accounting concepts?
- ❑ Did you obtain an explanation from the professor for incorrect answers?
- ❑ Did you utilize additional resources provided such as demonstration videos & tutorials?

Successful students spent an average of 4 hours per week outside of class time studying, including completing assigned homework.

You just need to put in the effort. If you work through the homework problems and show up to class, you will do well.

—Brandy J. Gibson, Business Administration Major Ivy Tech Community College

Do not put off homework – it is more important than you know – and when in need – ASK FOR HELP!!

—Sally Cross, Accounting Major Ivy Tech Community College

You need to attend every class and pay attention. Take good notes and do all the homework.

—Melinda Lallier, Accounting Major Community College of Rhode Island

Come to class every day – if you miss a class, you miss a lot of notes and example problems. Homework is vital and so is studying for tests – you need to learn the different formulas and equations.

—Shannon Green, General Business Major Community College of Rhode Island

Anyone can succeed at learning & understanding accounting concepts!

How? Preparation, time management, & practice!

Abbreviations and Acronyms Commonly Used in Business and Accounting

AAA	American Accounting Association
ABC	Activity-based costing
AICPA	American Institute of Certified Public Accountants
B2B	Business-to-business
B2C	Business-to-consumer
CFO	Chief Financial Officer
CMA	Certified Management Accountant
COGM	Cost of goods manufactured
COGS	Cost of goods sold
CPA	Certified Public Accountant
Cr.	Credit
CVP	Cost-volume-profit
Dr.	Debit
EFT	Electronic funds transfer
EPS	Earnings per share
ERP	Enterprise resource planning
FASB	Financial Accounting Standards Board
FICA tax	Federal Insurance Contributions Act tax
FIFO	First-in, first-out
FOB	Free on board
FUTA	Federal unemployment compensation tax
GAAP	Generally accepted accounting principles
IASB	International Accounting Standards Board
IFRS	International Financial Reporting Standards
IMA	Institute of Management Accountants
IRC	Internal Revenue Code
IRR	Internal rate of return
IRS	Internal Revenue Service
JIT	Just-in-time
LIFO	Last-in, first-out
LCM	Lower of cost or market
MACRS	Modified Accelerated Cost Recovery System
MD&A	Management's Discussion and Analysis
n/30	Net 30
n/eom	Net, end-of-month
NPV	Net present value
NSF	Not sufficient funds
P/E Ratio	Price-earnings ratio
POS	Point of sale
ROI	Return on investment
R&D	Research and development
SCM	Supply chain management
SEC	Securities and Exchange Commission
SOX	Sarbanes-Oxley Act
TQC	Total quality control
W-4	Employee's Withholding Allowance Certificate
WIP	Work in process

Classification of Accounts

Account Title	*Account Classification*	*Normal Balance*	*Financial Statement*
Accounts Payable	Current liability	Credit	Balance sheet
Accounts Receivable	Current asset	Debit	Balance sheet
Accumulated Depletion	Contra fixed asset	Credit	Balance sheet
Accumulated Depreciation	Contra fixed asset	Credit	Balance sheet
Advertising Expense	Operating expense	Debit	Income statement
Allowance for Doubtful Accounts	Contra current asset	Credit	Balance sheet
Amortization Expense	Operating expense	Debit	Income statement
Bonds Payable	Long-term liability	Credit	Balance sheet
Building	Fixed asset	Debit	Balance sheet
Cash	Current asset	Debit	Balance sheet
Cash Dividends	Stockholders' equity	Debit	Retained earnings statement
Cash Dividends Payable	Current liability	Credit	Balance sheet
Common Stock	Stockholders' equity	Credit	Balance sheet
Cost of Merchandise (Goods) Sold	Cost of merchandise (goods) sold	Debit	Income statement
Customer Refunds Payable	Current liability	Credit	Balance sheet
Delivery Expense	Operating expense	Debit	Income statement
Depletion Expense	Operating expense	Debit	Income statement
Discount on Bonds Payable	Long-term liability	Debit	Balance sheet
Dividend Revenue	Other income	Credit	Income statement
Dividends	Stockholders' equity	Debit	Retained earnings statement
Employees Federal Income Tax Payable	Current liability	Credit	Balance sheet
Equipment	Fixed asset	Debit	Balance sheet
Estimated Returns Inventory	Current asset	Debit	Balance sheet
Factory Overhead (Overapplied)	Deferred credit	Credit	Balance sheet (interim)
Factory Overhead (Underapplied)	Deferred debit	Debit	Balance sheet (interim)
Federal Income Tax Payable	Current liability	Credit	Balance sheet
Federal Unemployment Tax Payable	Current liability	Credit	Balance sheet
Finished Goods	Current asset	Debit	Balance sheet
Freight In	Cost of merchandise sold	Debit	Income statement
Freight Out	Operating expense	Debit	Income statement
Gain on Disposal of Fixed Assets	Other income	Credit	Income statement
Gain on Redemption of Bonds	Other income	Credit	Income statement
Gain on Sale of Investments	Other income	Credit	Income statement
Goodwill	Intangible asset	Debit	Balance sheet
Income Tax Expense	Income tax	Debit	Income statement
Income Tax Payable	Current liability	Credit	Balance sheet
Insurance Expense	Operating expense	Debit	Income statement
Interest Expense	Other expense	Debit	Income statement
Interest Receivable	Current asset	Debit	Balance sheet
Interest Revenue	Other income	Credit	Income statement
Investment in Bonds	Investment	Debit	Balance sheet
Investment in Stocks	Investment	Debit	Balance sheet
Investment in Subsidiary	Investment	Debit	Balance sheet
Land	Fixed asset	Debit	Balance sheet
Loss on Disposal of Fixed Assets	Other expense	Debit	Income statement
Loss on Redemption of Bonds	Other expense	Debit	Income statement